KFO
94
.S69
2002
v.2
c.2

D1537376

OHIO NORTHERN
UNIVERSITY

DEC 3 0 2002

TAGGART LAW LIBRARY

BALDWIN'S
OHIO PRACTICE

SOWALD MORGANSTERN
DOMESTIC RELATIONS LAW

2

Chs. 22-End
Appendix
Tables
Index

FOURTH EDITION

By
Beatrice K. Sowald
and
Stanley Morganstern
General Editors

For Customer Assistance Call 1-800-328-4880

Mat #40106628

American Law Reports; Corpus Juris Secundum; Federal Reporter; Federal Rules Decisions; Federal Supplement; Ohio Jurisprudence; Ohio Reports; United States Code Annotated; USCA; Westlaw; West's; West's Supreme Court Reporter; WIN; and *Wright & Miller, Federal Practice & Procedure* are registered trademarks used herein under license. Registered in the U.S. Patent and Trademark Office.

Baldwin's; Baldwin's Ohio Administrative Code, Approved Edition; Baldwin's Ohio Legislative Service Annotated; Baldwin's Ohio Monthly Record; Baldwin's Ohio Practice Series; Code News; KeyCite; Merrick-Rippner; Ohio Unreported Appellate Decisions; and *Westlaw Is Natural* are trademarks used herein under license.

West Group has created this publication to provide you with accurate and authoritative information concerning the subject matter covered. However, this publication was not necessarily prepared by persons licensed to practice law in a particular jurisdiction. West Group is not engaged in rendering legal or other professional advice, and this publication is not a substitute for the advice of an attorney. If you require legal or other expert advice, you should seek the services of a competent attorney or other professional.

©2002 by West Group. All rights reserved. This publication contains the results of proprietary research. No part of this book may be reproduced or transmitted in any form or by any means, electronic or mechanical, including photocopying, recording, or by any information storage and retrieval system, without prior permission in writing from the publisher.

ISBN # 0-8322-0907-4

For information, please call or write:
West Group
Cleveland Office
6111 Oak Tree Boulevard
P.O. Box 318063
Cleveland, Ohio 44131
        800/362-4500

The paper used in this publication meets the minimum requirements of American National Standard for Information Sciences—Permanence of Paper for Printed Library Materials, ANSI Z92.48-1984.

Table of Abbreviations

A.2d	Atlantic Reporter, Second Series
Abs.	Ohio Law Abstracts
A.D.2d	Appellate Division Reports, Second Series
Ala. Crim. App.	Alabama Court of Criminal Appeals
Ala.	Alabama
A.L.R. Fed.	American Law Reports, Federal Series
Am.	Amended; America; American
Amend.	Amendment
Amer.	America
Am. J. Pub. Health	American Journal of Public Health
Am. Psychol.	American Psychologist
Ann.	Annotated
App.	Appellate Court
Ariz.	Arizona Reports
Ariz. Rev. Stat. Ann.	Arizona Revised Statutes Annotated
Ark.	Arkansas
Art.	Article
ASPO	Anti-stalking protection order
Ass'n	Association
B.C. L. Rev.	Boston College Law Review
BYU J. Pub. L.	BYU Journal of Public Law
BYU L. Rev.	Brigham Young University Law Review
Cal. App.3d	California Appellate Reports, Third Series
Cal. App.4th	California Appellate Reports, Fourth Series
Cal. Evid. Code	West's Annotated California Code, Evidence
Cal. Fam. Code	West's Annotated California Code, Family
Cal. Rptr.	West's California Reporter
Cal. Rptr.2d	West's California Reporter, Second Series
Case W. Res. L. Rev.	Case Western Reserve Law Review
cert. denied	certiorari denied
Ch.	Chapter
Civ. R.	Ohio Rules of Civil Procedure
Co.	Company
Colo.	Colorado
Cong.	Congress
Conn.	Connecticut
Corp.	Corporation
C.P.	Common Pleas Court
CPO	Civil protection order
Crim. R.	Ohio Rules of Criminal Procedure
Ct.	Court
Ctr.	Center
Cuy.	Cuyahoga County

D.C. Intrafamily R.	District of Columbia Superior Court Rules of the Family Division, Intrafamily Proceedings
Del.	Delaware
Dist. Ct. App.	District Court of Appeals
Div.	Division
D.R.	Disciplinary Rules, Code of Professional Responsibility
D.R. R.	Domestic Relations Court Rule
DSM	Diagnostic and Statistical Manual
ed.	edition; editor
eff.	effective
Evid. R.	Ohio Rules of Evidence
F.2d	Federal Reporter, Second Series
F.3d	Federal Reporter, Third Series
Fam.	Family
Fam. Advoc.	Family Advocate
Fam. L. Q.	Family Law Quarterly
FBI	Federal Bureau of Investigation
Fed.	Federal Reporter
Fla.	Florida
Fla. B. J.	Florida Bar Journal
Fla. Stat. Ann.	Florida Statutes Annotated
F.Supp.	Federal Supplement
FVPSA	Family Violence Prevention and Services Act
Geo. L. J.	Georgetown Law Journal
Ham.	Hamilton County
Haw.	Hawaii Reports
H.B.	House Bill
H. Con. Res.	U.S. House of Representatives Congressional Resolution
Idaho	Idaho Reports
Ill. App.3d	Illinois Appellate Court Reports, Third Series
Inc.	Incorporated
Ind. L. J.	Indiana Law Journal
Int'l J. Health Servs.	International Journal of Health Services
J.	Journal
JAMA	Journal of the American Medical Association
J. Clin. Psychol.	Journal of Clinical Psychology
Judges' J.	The Judges' Journal
Just.	Justice
Juv.	Juvenile
Juv. & Fam. Ct. J.	Juvenile and Family Court Journal
Kan.	Kansas
Kan. App.2d	Kansas Court of Appeals Reports, Second Series
Ky.	Kentucky
L.	Law
La.	Louisiana
LEADS	Law Enforcement Automation Data System
L.Ed.	United States Supreme Court Reports, Lawyers' Edition

Pa.	Pennsylvania State Reports
Pa. D. & C.4th	Pennsylvania District and County Reports, Fourth Series
Pa. Stat. Ann.	Purdon's Pennsylvania Statutes Annotated
Pa. Super.	Pennsylvania Superior Court Reports
Phila.	Philadelphia County Reporter
PKPA	Parental Kidnapping Prevention Act
Pub.	Public
Q.	Quarterly
RC	Revised Code of Ohio
Rev.	Review; Revised
Rptr.	Reporter
Rts.	Rights
S.B.	Senate Bill
S. Cal. Rev. L. & Women's Stud.	Southern California Review of Law & Women's Studies
S.C. L. Rev.	South Carolina Law Review
S.Ct.	United States Supreme Court Reporter
S.D.	South Dakota Reports
S.E.2d	South Eastern Reporter, Second Series
Servs.	Services
So.2d	Southern Reporter, Second Series
Soc. Work	Social Work
Soc. Work Res. & Abstracts	Social Work Research and Abstracts
SSN	Social security number
Stat.	Statutes
Sub.	Substitute
Summ.	Summit County
Supp.	Supplement
Sup. R.	Rules of Superintendence for the Courts of Ohio
S.W.2d	South Western Reporter, Second Series
Temp. L. Q.	Temple University Law Quarterly
Tex. Fam. Code Ann.	Vernon's Texas Codes Annotated, Family
tit.	Title
TPO	Temporary protection order
TRO	Temporary restraining order
U.	University
UCCJA	Uniform Child Custody Jurisdiction Act
U.C. Davis L. Rev.	University of California at Davis Law Review
U. Cin. L. Rev.	University of Cincinnati Law Review
U.S.	United States Supreme Court Reports
U.S.C.A.	United States Code, Annotated
U.S. Const.	United States Constitution
v.	versus
Va.	Virginia
Vand. L. Rev.	Vanderbilt Law Review
VAWA	Violence Against Women Act of 1994

Westlaw® Electronic Research Guide

Coordinating Legal Research with Westlaw

Baldwin's Ohio Practice Series, Domestic Relations Law is an essential aid to legal research. Westlaw provides a vast, online library of over 10,000 collections of documents and services that can supplement research begun in this publication, encompassing:

- Federal and state primary law (statutes, regulations, rules, and case law), including West's editorial enhancements, such as headnotes, Key Number classifications, annotations

- Secondary law resources (texts and treatises published by West and by other publishers, as well as law reviews)

- Legal news

- Directories of attorneys and experts

- Court records and filings

- KeyCite™

Specialized topical subsets of these resources have been created for more than thirty areas of practice.

In addition to legal information, there are general news and reference databases and a broad array of specialized materials frequently useful in connection with legal matters, covering accounting, business, environment, ethics, finance, medicine, social and physical sciences.

This guide will focus on a few aspects of Westlaw use to supplement research begun in this publication, and will direct you to additional sources of assistance.

Databases

A database is a collection of documents with some features in common. It may contain statutes, court decisions, administrative materials, commentaries, news or other information. Each database has a unique identifier, used in many Westlaw commands to select a database of interest. For example, the database containing Ohio cases has the indentifier OH-CS.

The Westlaw Directory is a comprehensive list of databases with information about each database, including the types of documents each contains. The first page of a standard or customized Westlaw Directory is displayed upon signing on to Westlaw, except when prior, saved research is resumed.

A special subdirectory, accessible from the main Westlaw Directory, lists databases applicable to Family Law research.

Databases of potential interest in connection with your research include:

OHFL-CS	Ohio Family Law Cases
FFL-CS	Federal Cases—Family Law
FFL-USCA	U.S. Code Sections—Family Law
FL-TP	Law Reviews, Texts & Journals—Family Law
WLD-FAM	West's Legal Dictionary—Family
WLD-OH	West's Legal Dictionary—Ohio
CANJFL	Canadian Journal of Family Law
FAMADVO	Family Advocate (ABA)
FAMLQ	Family Law Quarterly (ABA)
FAMLV-LH	Family and Medical Leave Act—Legislative History (Arnold & Porter)
INPADOC	INPADOC / Family & Legal Status (DIALOG)
OTP-INPADOC	ONTAP INPADOC / Family & Legal Status (DIALOG)
ULVLJFL	University of Louisville Journal of Family Law (Univ. of Louisville)

For information as to currentness and search tips regarding any Westlaw database, enter the SCOPE feature. It is not necessary to include the identifier to obtain scope information about the currently selected database.

Westlaw Highlights

Use of this publication may be supplemented through the Westlaw Bulletin (WLB), the Westlaw Ohio State Bulletin (WSB-OH) and various Topical Highlights, including Family Law Highlights (WTH-LB). Highlights databases contain summaries of significant judicial, legislative and administrative developments and are updated daily; they are searchable both from an automatic list of recent documents and using general Westlaw search methods for documents accumulated over time. The full text of any judicial decision may be retrieved by using the FIND feature.

Consult the Westlaw Directory for a complete, current listing of highlights databases.

Retrieving Cases Citing This Publication

To retrieve cases citing this publication, sign on to a case law database and enter a query in the following form:

Sowald /10 "Domestic Relations"

Retrieving a Specific Case

The FIND command can be used to quickly retrieve a case whose citation is known. For example:

FI 580 N.E.2d 335

Updating Case Law Research

KeyCite™ is an enhanced citator service that integrates all the case law on Westlaw. KeyCite provides direct and negative indirect history for any case within the scope of its coverage, citations to other decisions and secondary materials on Westlaw that have mentioned or discussed the cited case, and a complete integration with West's Key Number System so that you can track a legal issue explored in a case. KeyCite is as current as Westlaw and includes all cases on Westlaw, including unpublished opinions.

Retrieving Statutes, Court Rules and Regulations

Annotated and unannotated versions of the Ohio statutes are searchable on Westlaw (identifiers OH-ST-ANN and OH-ST), as are Ohio court rules (OH-RULES) and Ohio Administrative Code (OH-ADC).

The United States Code and United States Code Annotated are searchable databases on Westlaw (identifiers USC and USCA, respectively), as are federal court rules (US-RULES) and regulations (CFR).

In addition, the FIND command may be used to retrieve specific provisions by citation, obviating the need for database selection or search.

Updating Research in re Statutes,
Rules and Regulations

When viewing a statute, rule, or regulation on Westlaw after a search or FIND command, it is easy to update your research. A yellow or red flag symbol or other notation will appear on the screen if relevant amendments, repeals, or other new material is available. Clicking on the flag or notation will display the material.

Documents used to update Ohio statutes are also searchable in Ohio Legislative Service (OH-LEGIS). Those used to update rules are searchable in Ohio Orders (OH-ORDERS).

Documents used to update federal statutes, rules, and regulations are searchable in the United States Public Laws (US-PL), Federal Orders (US-ORDERS) and Federal Register (FR) databases, respectively.

Using Westlaw as a Citator

For research beyond the coverage of any citator service, go directly to the databases (cases, for example) containing citing documents and use standard Westlaw search techniques to retrieve documents citing specific constitutional provisions, statutes, standard jury instructions or other authorities.

Fortunately, the specific portion of a citation is often reasonably distinctive, such as 22:636.1, 301.65, 401(k), 12-21-5, 12052. When it is, a search on that specific portion alone may retrieve applicable documents without any substantial number of inapplicable ones (unless the number happens to be coincidentally popular in another context). Ohio statutes fall into this category.

Similarly, if the citation involves more than one number, such as 42 U.S.C.A. § 1201, a search containing both numbers (e.g., 42 +5 1201) is likely to produce mostly desired information, even though the component numbers are common.

If necessary, the search may be limited in several ways:

A. Switch from a general database to one containing mostly cases within the subject area of the cite being researched;

B. Use a connector (&, /S, /P, etc.) to narrow the search to documents including terms which are highly likely to accompany the correct citation in the context of the issue being researched;

C. Include other citation information in the query. Because of the variety of citation formats used in documents, this option should be used primarily where other options prove insufficient. Below are illustrative queries for any database containing Ohio cases.

Civ.Rule Civ Civil O.R.C.P. R.C.P. /7 56

will retrieve cases citing Civil Procedure Rule 56; and

(appellate /2 procedure rule) App.Proc! App.Rule R.A.P. /7 33

will retrieve cases citing Appellate Procedure Rule 33.

Alternative Retrieval Methods

WIN® (Westlaw Is Natural™) allows you to frame your issue in plain English to retrieve documents:

Does parent have right to counsel in contempt proceeding for failure to make child support payment?

Alternatively, retrieval may be focused by use of the Terms and Connectors method:

DI(CONTEMPT /P CHILD! /P SUPPORT! PAY! PAID
/P ATTORNEY LAWYER COUNSEL)

In databases with Key Numbers, either of the above examples will identify Constitutional Law ☞ Divorce ☞ and Parent and Child ☞ as Key Numbers collecting headnotes relevant to this issue if there are pertinent cases.

As the Key Numbers are affixed to points of law by trained specialists based on conceptual understanding of the case, relevant cases that were not retrieved by either of the language-dependent methods will often be found at a Key Number.

Similarly, citations in retrieved documents (to cases, statutes, rules, etc.) may suggest additional, fruitful research using other Westlaw databases (e.g., annotated statutes, rules) or services (e.g., KeyCite™).

Key Number Search

Frequently, case law research rapidly converges on a few topics, headings and Key Numbers within West's Key Number System that are likely to contain relevant cases. These may be discovered from known, relevant reported cases from any jurisdiction; Library References in West publications; browsing in a digest; or browsing the Key Number System on Westlaw using the JUMP feature or the KEY command.

Once discovered, topics, subheadings or Key Numbers are useful as search terms (in databases containing reported cases) alone or with other search terms, to focus the search within a narrow range of potentially relevant material.

For example, to retrieve cases with at least one headnote classified to Parent and Child ⌀2.5, sign on to a case law database and enter

285k2.5 [use with other search terms, if desired]

The topic name (Parent and Child) is replaced by its numerical equivalent (285) and the ⌀ by the letter k. A list of topics and their numerical equivalents is in the Westlaw Reference Manual and is displayed in Westlaw when the KEY command is entered.

Other topics of special interest include: Abortion and Birth Control (4), Adoption (17), Children Out-of-Wedlock (76H), Husband and Wife (205), Incest (207), Infants (211), and Marriage (253).

Using JUMP

Westlaw's JUMP feature allows you to move from one document to another or from one part of a document to another, then easily return to your original place, without losing your original result. Opportunities to move in this manner are marked in the text with either blue, underlined text or a JUMP symbol (▶). Whenever you see the JUMP symbol, you may move to the place designated by the adjacent reference by using the Tab or arrow keys, or mouse click to position the cursor on the JUMP symbol, then pressing Enter or clicking again with the mouse.

Within the text of a court opinion, JUMP arrows are adjacent to case cites and federal statute cites, and adjacent to parenthesized numbers marking discussions corresponding to headnotes.

On a screen containing the text of a headnote, the JUMP arrows allow movement to the corresponding discussion in the text of the opinion,

▶ (3)

and allow browsing West's Key Number System beginning at various heading levels:

▶ 76E CHILD SUPPORT
▶ 76Ek440 ENFORCEMENT - In general
▶ 76Ek26 Equality of duty of mother and father
▶ 76Ek650 ABANDONMENT OR NEGLECT TO SUPPORT - In general

General Information

The information provided above illustrates some of the ways Westlaw can complement research using this publication. However, this brief overview illustrates only some of the power of Westlaw. The full range of Westlaw search techniques is available to support your research.

Please consult the Westlaw Reference Manual for additional information or assistance or call West's Reference Attorneys at 1-800-REF-ATTY (1-800-733-2889).

For information about subscribing to Westlaw, please call 1-800-328-9352.

Related West Products

OHIO DATABASES ON WESTLAW

Cases, General & Topical

Statutes & Court Rules

Legislative Service, Bills & Bill Tracking

Administrative & Executive Materials

Public Information, Records & Filings

Baldwin's Ohio Practice Series

Ohio Jurisprudence 3d

Ohio Forms, Legal & Business

Law Reviews, Bar Journals & Legal Periodicals

Newspapers & Periodicals

Miscellany

CD-ROM

Baldwin's Ohio Revised Code Annotated with Ohio Administrative
Code, and SERB Official Reporter

Ohio Reports

Ohio Unreported Appellate Decisions

Baldwin's Ohio Practice Library

West's Ohio Digest

Ohio Jurisprudence 3d

United States Code Annotated

West's Sixth Circuit Reporter

West's Federal District Court Reporter -- Sixth Circuit

West's Supreme Court Reporter

Federal Reporter, 1st, 2d, and 3d Series

Federal Supplement

Federal Rules Decisions

Wright & Miller, Federal Practice and Procedure

Topical CD-ROM Libraries

Ohio Jurisprudence Pleading and Practice Forms

Ohio Criminal Defense Motions

CIVIL PRACTICE AND PROCEDURE

Baldwin's Ohio Practice, Civil Practice, Klein, Darling, and Terez

Baldwin's Ohio Practice, Civil Practice Laws & Rules Annotated

Ohio Personal Injury Practice

Trial Handbook for Ohio Lawyers, Markus

CRIMINAL LAW AND PRACTICE

Baldwin's Ohio Practice, Criminal Law, Katz, Giannelli, Blair, and Pyle

Ohio Arrest, Search and Seizure

Baldwin's Ohio Practice, Ohio Criminal Justice, Katz and Giannelli (Eds.) (published in cooperation with the Case Western Reserve University School of Law)

Ohio Domestic Violence Law

Ohio Driving Under the Influence Law

Ohio Felony Sentencing Law

Trial Handbook for Ohio Lawyers, Markus

TRIAL AND APPELLATE PRACTICE

Baldwin's Ohio Practice, Evidence, Giannelli and Snyder

Baldwin's Ohio Practice, Rules of Evidence Handbook, Giannelli and Snyder

Ohio Appellate Practice

Trial Handbook for Ohio Lawyers, Markus

DOMESTIC RELATIONS AND FAMILY LAW

Baldwin's Ohio Practice, Domestic Relations Law, Sowald and Morganstern

Baldwin's Ohio Practice, Domestic Relations Laws and Rules Annotated

Ohio Domestic Violence Law

Domestic Relations Journal of Ohio

PROBATE AND JUVENILE LAW

Baldwin's Ohio Practice, Merrick-Rippner Probate Law, Carlin

Ohio Probate Code Annotated

Probate Law Journal of Ohio

Ohio Juvenile Law

REAL ESTATE

Ohio Landlord Tenant Law

Ohio Real Estate Law and Practice

BUSINESS AND LEGAL

Baldwin's Ohio Practice, Business Organizations, Blackford

Baldwin's Ohio Practice, Business Organizations Laws & Rules, Ekonomon and Allan (Eds.)

Ohio Consumer Law

LEGAL FORMS

Ohio Forms, Legal and Business

Ohio Forms and Transactions

Ohio Jurisprudence Pleading and Practice Forms

West's Legal Forms, 2d

TAX LAW

Baldwin's Ohio Tax Law and Rules

LABOR LAW

Ohio Civil Service & Collective Bargaining Laws & Rules Annotated

Ohio Employment Practices Law

Ohio Workers' Compensation Law Practice Guide

Workers' Compensation Journal of Ohio

GOVERNMENT

Baldwin's Ohio Township Law

Gotherman and Babbit, Ohio Municipal Law

Marburger & Hunt's Ohio Municipal Service

Ohio Election Laws Annotated

Ohio Planning and Zoning Law

SCHOOL LAW

Baldwin's Ohio School Law

Baldwin's Ohio School Law Journal

Ohio School Law Handbook

United States School Laws and Rules

BUILDING CONSTRUCTION AND CODE ENFORCEMENT

Ohio Accessibility Guidelines: Access to and Use of Buildings &
Facilities by Persons with Disabilities

Ohio Building Code and Related Codes

Know Your Code: A Guide to the OBC

Code News

NEED RESEARCH HELP?
If you have research questions concerning Westlaw or West
Publications, call West Reference Attorneys at
1-800-733-2889.

West*fax*
**Call 1-800-340-9378 to order full-text cases by fax. Mail
and overnight delivery also available. Cases include
current case history (reversed, overruled, etc.). Available
only in U.S.A. Order subject to approval of vendor.**

DO YOU RECYCLE POCKET PARTS?

West pockets parts are printed on recyclable paper and can be
collected and recycled with newspapers. Staples do not have to
be removed because recycling companies use magnets to extract
staples during the recycling process.

Summary of Contents

Detailed Volume
Table of Contents

Chapter 22

Child Support Enforcement Agencies

Chapter 23

Interstate and Foreign Support
Practice

Chapter 24

Relief from Judgment

Chapter 25
Pleading and Practice

Chapter 26

Discovery

Chapter 27

Jurisdiction and Venue

Chapter 28

Tax Considerations

Chapter 29

Government Retirement Benefits

Chapter 30

Dividing Private Retirement Benefits in Divorce

Chapter 31

Magistrates

Chapter 32

Appeals

Chapter 33

Bankruptcy

Chapter 34

Role of Attorney: Ethics

Chapter 35

Catholic Declaration of Nullity

Chapter 36

Jewish Divorce

Chapter 37

Mental Health Experts

Appendices

Chapter 22

Child Support Enforcement Agencies

By David W. Robertson and Robert J. Frankart, Esq.

◆ **Editor's Note:** Am. S.B. 180, effective 3-22-01, amended, enacted, and repealed various sections of the Revised Code that concern child support enforcement agency roles in establishing, enforcing, and modifying child support. The Appendix includes a Correlation Table to assist in identifying and locating the new sections.

KeyCite®: Cases and other legal materials listed in KeyCite Scope can be researched through West Group's KeyCite service on Westlaw®. Use KeyCite to check citations for form, parallel references, prior and later history, and comprehensive citator information, including citations to other decisions and secondary materials.

---

§ 22:1 History, mission, and organization

The county child support enforcement agencies have their origin in state legislation first enacted in 1967 to create a bureau of support in each common pleas court in the state.[1] The mission of each bureau was to "be responsible for the enforcement of orders for support and alimony."[2] By 1975, Congress recognized the need to enhance support enforcement on a nationwide basis and enacted Title IV-D of the Social Security Act to provide funding for state efforts in this regard.[3] In turn, in yet a further effort to "provide more efficient enforcement of court-ordered support," the General Assembly in 1978 enacted amended Senate Bill 87. The bill required most support payments to be made through bureaus of support, required the bureaus to monitor payments, and gave the court authority to withhold payments from wages if necessary.

In the ensuing decade, however, overall child support enforcement responsibility at the county level became increasingly fragmented among the bureau of support, the prosecuting attorney, and the county department of human services. The department of human services was responsible for implementing the major requirements of Title IV-D, which was designed to recoup the costs of public assistance and prevent more families from resorting to such assistance. On the other hand, this mission could be accomplished only through close cooperation with the bureau of support and the prosecuting attorney.

As a result, in 1987 the General Assembly dissolved the bureaus of support and consolidated all local support enforcement activities in the newly created child support enforcement agencies. As the name implies, the general mission of a child support enforcement agency (CSEA) is to provide various services to any child with an absent parent, for the purpose of locating the parent, establishing a support obligation in regard to the child, and collecting the support on a reliable basis.[4] To this end, each CSEA must develop and maintain a handbook of internal procedures documenting such items as agency organization, and the various forms and processes used in parent location, paternity establishment, and support establishment, enforcement, and distribution.[5]

The CSEA is an agency of county government, designated by resolution of the board of county commissioners to reside in one of four entities:

(1) The county department of human services;

[Section 22:1]

[1]132 H.B. 757.

[2]Former RC 2301.34(A).

[3]88 Stat. 2351, codified at 42 U.S.C.A. §§ 651 et seq.

[4]RC 3125.11; OAC 5101:1-29-01.

[5]OAC 5101:1-29-01.

(2) The office of the prosecuting attorney;

(3) A bureau within the court of common pleas; or

(4) A separate agency under the direct control of the board and administered by an official appointed by the board.[6]

This designation by the board may be changed at any time by further resolution. At least sixty days before the change takes effect, a notice must be sent to the state Department of Job and Family Services and such notice must be published in a local newspaper. As of August 31, 2001, sixty counties have lodged CSEAs in their departments of job and family services, nineteen in separate agencies, three in courts, and six with the prosecuting attorneys.

After designation of a CSEA, the board of county commissioners must enter into a contract to specify the services the CSEA is to provide and its operating procedures.[7] In turn, the CSEA must enter into written cooperative agreements with various other public entities to the extent necessary to accomplish its mission.[8] Funding of the overall CSEA operation is derived from a complex combination of sources, including interest and a 2% surcharge on all support collections, federal reimbursement under Title IV-D of the Social Security Act, state funds appropriated by the General Assembly, and county funds appropriated by the board of county commissioners.[9]

As with other offices of county government, the prosecuting attorney is the statutory legal advisor of the CSEA.[10] However, the CSEA may also employ its own staff attorneys to advise, assist, and represent it in the performance of its functions pertaining to the enforcement of support orders.[11] The agency also has extensive authority to contract with other public agencies or private vendors to assist in accomplishing its mission, and, with the obligee's permission, may even refer a case to a collection agent operating on a contingency fee arrangement.[12]

The CSEA is administered locally, but is under the supervision of the state department of job and family services.[13] The state department of job and family services has the responsibility to establish a statewide child support enforcement program that meets the requirements of Title IV-D of the Social Security Act.[14] To this end, the state department of job and family services must promulgate rules under RC Chapter 119

---

[6]RC 3125.10, RC 3125.12.

[7]RC 3125.12.

[8]RC 329.04, RC 3125.14.

[9]RC 2301.35(H); OAC 5101:1-31-01, OAC 5101:1-31-02, OAC 5101:1-31-30, OAC 5101:1-31-70.

[10]RC 309.09.

[11]RC 2301.354.

[12]RC 2301.35(C), RC 2301.42.

[13]RC 2301.35(C).

[14]RC 5101.31.

governing the operation of support enforcement by CSEAs.[15] The department must further ensure that all CSEAs comply with all state and federal standards for program operation and impose fiscal sanctions on those that do not.[16] This duty is accomplished by an extensive yearly review that must show compliance with specific criteria in at least 75% of the cases reviewed in order for the CSEA to avoid a financial sanction or the need to develop a corrective action plan.[17]

Despite the introduction of SETS (Support Enforcement Tracking System) and CSPC (Child Support Payment Central), with the resulting centralization of payment processing and much of the case record keeping of child support cases, the local CSEA is still the agency responsible for administering and enforcing child support orders within its county.[18]

§ 22:2   CSEA service delivery

To maximize federal reimbursement for CSEA activities, each child support case that is eligible for federal reimbursement must be made a "IV-D case" by the CSEA.[1] A IV-D case is simply one pursued on behalf of a recipient of various federally funded public assistance programs (Temporary Assistance to Needy Families (TANF) under Title IV-A of the Social Security Act,[2] foster care maintenance assistance under Title IV-E of the Act, or Medicaid under Title XIX of the Act), or pursuant to an application for IV-D services filed by any other person.[3] The distinction between a IV-D and non-IV-D case has additional significance given that a number of child support services offered by the CSEA are not available to non-IV-D cases:

(1) Access to the state and federal parent locator services;

(2) Withholding of support arrears from a payor's state and federal income tax refund or unemployment compensation benefit;

(3) Access to the assistance of the Internal Revenue Service for parent location information or support collection assistance; and

(4) Certification of a case to a federal district court for enforcement, when another state has failed to act on an Ohio support order.[4]

Any court that issues or modifies a child support order must require

---

[15]RC 2301.35(D)(1).

[16]RC 2301.35(E)(1).

[17]OAC 5101:1-29-04 to OAC 5101:1-29-042.

[18]RC 3125.11.

[Section 22:2]

[1]RC 3125.36; OAC 5101:1-29-05.

[2]RC Ch. 5107 designates the TANF program in Ohio as "Ohio Works First" (OWF).

[3]OAC 5101:1-29-05. See also ODHS Form 7076 "Application for child support services."

[4]OAC 5101:1-29-06.

the obligee to file a IV-D application.[5] Similarly, the CSEA must make a IV-D application available to all persons requesting the agency to issue an administrative order for parentage or child support.[6] Any out-of-state payee on a child support order issued within Ohio who does not receive TANF or Title IV-E benefits may choose to apply for IV-D services in Ohio rather than the other state.[7] The CSEA may charge an applicant who does not receive TANF or Title IV-E benefits a one-time fee of one dollar to cover all subsequent services including court filing fees.[8] Within twenty days of filing an application, the CSEA must notify the applicant whether the application has been accepted, and may refuse to accept it for only the following reasons:

(1) The person for whom support is sought (unless arrearages remain to be collected) is emancipated;

(2) The applicant seeks payment for medical costs, unrelated to an order for support or the maintenance of health insurance coverage; and

(3) The requested service is not related to the establishment of parentage or enforcement of support.[9]

Recipients of child support services from the CSEA are entitled to the due process protection of the administrative hearing system maintained by the state department of job and family services.[10] This system includes a record hearing at the CSEA, a written decision, and the right to appellate review by an attorney-hearing examiner in the state department of job and family services.[11] The CSEA must provide the recipient with a notice of the right to an administrative hearing upon the filing of an application for services, when the application is either accepted or denied, when any support order is being terminated, and when the case is being closed.[12] In addition, a hearing may be requested at any time the recipient alleges that the CSEA has failed to provide a required service, has acted erroneously in the case, or has failed to take action with reasonable promptness.[13] In limited circumstances, the noncustodial parent may make a hearing request.[14]

The CSEA provides an administrative hearing to aggrieved claimants in other circumstances, such as after an investigation of a support default, the issuance of an administrative order of parentage or support,

---

[5]RC 3125.36. Between October 1987, and July 1990, former RC 2301.35(C) provided that any beneficiary of a support order administered by a CSEA was deemed by operation of law to have applied for IV-D services. See 1987 H.B. 231.

[6]RC 3125.36.

[7]OAC 5101:1-30-56.

[8]OAC 5101:1-29-12, OAC 5101:1-31-23.

[9]OAC 5101:1-29-13.

[10]RC 2301.35(D)(1); OAC 5101:1-29-01, OAC 5101:6-1-01.

[11]OAC 5101:6-6-01, OAC 5101:6-7-01, OAC 5101:6-8-01.

[12]OAC 5101:6-2-07.

[13]OAC 5101:6-3-01.

[14]OAC 5101:6-3-01.

or on the modification of a support order.[15] Decisions issued as a result of these hearings are reviewed by the juvenile court, either by direct appeal or through a party bringing an original action.[16]

Occasionally, counsel for the obligor challenges the authority of the CSEA attorney to represent the obligee, especially if ancillary domestic relations issues are drawn into the proceeding. The judicial response to this challenge has generally been to uphold such representation on the theory that, assuming the obligee consents to the representation, only the Supreme Court may question the fitness of an attorney to practice law and that the representation does not prejudice the obligor.[17]

§ 22:3 Parent location

On receiving a request for child support services, the CSEA must first locate any absent parents. Within seventy-five days of a request for service, the CSEA must access all appropriate location sources.[1] This process begins with the obvious local sources of information and continues, if necessary, with referral of the case to the Ohio parent locator service (OPLS) and the federal parent locator service (FPLS).[2] The OPLS includes information links among various state agencies within Ohio, as well as their counterparts in a network of other states.[3]

Similarly, the FPLS has traditionally been a clearinghouse for location information from various federal agencies.[4] In 1996, however, Congress took several steps to enhance the effectiveness of the FPLS as part of a historic overhaul of various federal public assistance programs.[5] The FPLS now also includes a national case registry composed of case-specific information from all of the state automated child support tracking systems.[6] All states must enact a directory of new hires designed to require all employers, including those hiring independent contractors, to report to the state, within 20 days of hire, a person's name, address, and social security number.[7] In turn, the state must report this information

---

[15]RC 3111.49, RC 3111.50, RC 3119.64.

[16]RC 3111.49, RC 3111.50, RC 3119.64.

[17]See Henderson v. Henderson, 1989 WL 64047 (Ohio Ct. App. 5th Dist. Richland County 1989); State ex rel. Furniss v. Furniss, 1989 WL 140180 (Ohio Ct. App. 11th Dist. Trumbull County 1989); Hanni v. Hanni, 1990 WL 97591 (Ohio Ct. App. 7th Dist. Mahoning County 1990); Hucke v. Hucke, 1990 WL 125700 (Ohio Ct. App. 2d Dist. Montgomery County 1990).

[Section 22:3]
[1]OAC 5101:1-30-01.

[2]OAC 5101:1-30-01; see also § 23:10, Locating obligors and their assets—Federal resources.

[3]OAC 5101:1-30-11.

[4]OAC 5101:1-30-111.

[5]Personal Responsibility and Work Opportunity Reconciliation Act of 1996, Pub. L. No. 104-193, August 22, 1996; See also, "The Coming Revolution in Child Support Policy: Implications of the 1996 Welfare Act", ABA Family Law Quarterly, Fall 1996.

[6]42 U.S.C.A. § 653.

[7]RC 3121.89 through 3121.8910, RC 3121.09, and RC 3121.091.

to a national new hire directory, which also receives reports from federal employers.[8] The FPLS must match data between the new hire directory and the case registry every two days and promptly report matches to the OPLS.

At any rate, after submitting a case to OPLS, the CSEA must continue its local efforts and resubmit the case to OPLS on receipt of new information or on a quarterly basis.[9] Submission to OPLS automatically prompts a referral to FPLS, and cases remain in OPLS for up to three years, after which they may be considered for case closure if location has not been accomplished.[10] Parent location services are also available for the purposes of establishing or enforcing a child custody determination as against a parent or nonparent.[11] Any such request by a person to the CSEA must be supported by either a court order supporting the request, or a written request from any law enforcement agency official with a missing child report.[12]

§ 22:4   Establishing parentage

The CSEA must provide parentage establishment services for any IV-D case in which parentage has not been determined.[1] In all such cases, service of legal process necessary to establish parentage must be made within ninety days of locating the parent, unless diligent efforts have failed to produce successful service.[2]

Although parentage can be established in various civil and criminal proceedings, the two most common methods have historically been a parentage action under RC Chapter 3111 and consensual probate court legitimation under RC 2105.18. In recent years, however, in response to statutory changes in Title IV-D of the Social Security Act, the General Assembly has reshaped the paternity determination process to be one dominated by administrative rather than judicial processes. Former RC 2105.18 permitted a legitimation proceeding in probate court, which created a rebuttable presumption of parentage, putting it on the same legal plane as marriage to the child's mother or signing of the birth certificate.[3] Commencing January 1, 1998, acknowledgements are to be filed with the division of child support in the department of job and family services.[4]

A person is prohibited in most instances even from filing an original parentage action in juvenile court before having requested an adminis-

---

[8]42 U.S.C.A. § 653.

[9]OAC 5101:1-30-01, OAC 5101:1-30-08.

[10]OAC 5101:1-30-08, OAC 5101:1-30-11, OAC 5101:1-30-111.

[11]OAC 5101:1-30-04.

[12]OAC 5101:1-30-04.

[Section 22:4]

[1]OAC 5101:1-30-23.

[2]OAC 5101:1-30-25.

[3]Former RC 3111.03, prior to 1-1-98.

[4]RC 5101.314, as enacted by 1997 H.B. 352, eff. 1-1-98.

trative parentage determination from the CSEA.[5] The request for the administrative parentage determination must be made with the CSEA of the county in which the child resides. Further, once the request is made, the CSEA administrative officer must immediately issue an order for a genetic test.[6] The parties can agree to execute an acknowledgment of paternity. Senate Bill 180, which became effective March 22, 2001, provided that the filing of the paternity acknowledgment with the Office of Child Support within the Ohio Department of Job and Family Services (ODJFS), creates a presumption of paternity which becomes a final and enforceable determination of paternity, unless rescinded under the court rescission procedure, once the acknowledgment becomes final or overturned pursuant to RC 3119.96 to RC 3119.967.[7]

Where one of the parties declines to participate, or where the administrative parentage procedure otherwise is unsuccessful in establishing the existence or nonexistence of the parent-child relationship, a party may proceed to file an action in court under RC 3111.01 to RC 3111.19. On the other hand, RC 3111.84 specifies that an administrative parentage order is final if neither party brings an action in court within 30 days of the determination. Thus, where an alleged father did not object to the determination within that period, he could not later bring a court complaint to determine[8] whether he was the father, because the administrative order was res judicata. However, see RC 3119.96 to RC 3119.967

Whether in the administrative or court context, genetic blood testing is the key piece of evidence in resolving disputed cases. The tests have evolved beyond merely excluding putative fathers; for those not excluded, the testing in most cases results in a numerical "probability of paternity" in the 95% to 99% range. Because of such reliability and increased federal reimbursement for the costs of genetic testing, the CSEA must have a contractual relationship with a competent testing facility and must order such testing in any disputed parentage case.[9] Moreover, the CSEA must be made a party to any parentage action involving a IV-D case, and should genetic testing become necessary, then the CSEA not only schedules the test but pays for it, subject to later reimbursement by any party assessed costs by the court.[10] In an administrative proceeding at the CSEA, the finding of a 99% or greater probability of paternity requires the administrative officer to issue an order establishing a

---

[5]RC 3111.22. But see In re Ruff, 1999 WL 399230 (Ohio Ct. App. 2d Dist. Montgomery County 1999) (appellate court did not find that RC 3111.22(A)(1) is jurisdictional, thus juvenile court's jurisdiction over paternity actions was not curtailed by statute).

[6]RC 3111.38.

[7]RC 3111.03 and RC 3111.25.

[8]Richards v. Kazleman, 1994 WL 249826 (Ohio Ct. App. 5th Dist. Stark County 1994).

[9]RC 3111.41; RC 3111.43.

[10]RC 3111.07, RC 3111.09.

parent-child relationship.[11]

The state department of job and family services monitors the overall efficiency of each CSEA in processing cases where parentage is being established, and failure to perform adequately can result in the CSEA being required to formulate a paternity compliance plan or even having to pay financial sanctions.[12]

Finally, new procedures will be developed because Public Law No. 104-193[13] has mandated significant changes in the parentage determination process that must be implemented in the state by 1998. The Ohio General Assembly enacted 1997 House Bill 352, most sections of which take effect either October 1, 1997 or January 1, 1998, in response to the federal mandates.

The federal requirements, as set forth in the Personal Responsibility and Work Opportunity Reconciliation Act of 1996, are broad. Before unmarried parents can execute an acknowledgment form, they must be given oral and written notice "of the alternatives to, the legal consequences of, and the rights (including, if 1 parent is a minor, any rights afforded due to minority status) and responsibilities that arise from, signing the acknowledgment."[14] In fact, executing an acknowledgment will become the sole method for unmarried parents to get the father's name recorded on the child's birth certificate as the father, short of a court or administrative parentage order. Further, once signed, the acknowledgment results in 11a legal finding of paternity . . . (which further) judicial or administrative proceedings are not required or permitted to ratify"[15] unless either of the following occur:

(1) A party rescinds the acknowledgment within the earlier of 60 days or the date of any administrative or judicial proceeding relating to the child in which the party is involved as a legal party; or

(2) A party subsequently is successful in challenging the acknowledgment in court, but "only on the basis of fraud, duress, or material mistake of fact, with the burden of proof upon the challenger."[16]

Finally, the state must accord full faith and credit to an acknowledgment signed in any other state "according to its procedures."

In addition, the state is encouraged to consider making genetic test results the basis of a conclusive presumption of paternity. More radical still is the new ban on allowing jury trials in contested parentage cases.

2000 S.B. 180 also eliminates two prior paternity presumptions:[17]

(1) A man and the child's mother married or attempted to marry

---

[11]RC 3111.46.

[12]RC 2301.35(E)(2), RC 2301.357(A), RC 5101.324; OAC 5101:1-30-24, OAC 5101:1-30-242, OAC 5101:1-30-25.

[13]Personal Responsibility and Work Opportunity Reconciliation Act of 1996, Pub. L. No. 104-193, August 22, 1996.

[14]42 U.S.C.A. § 666(a)(5)(C)(i).

[15]42 U.S.C.A. § 666(a)(5)(E).

[16]42 U.S.C.A. § 666(a)(5)(D)(iii).

[17]RC 3111.03.

each other after the child's birth and the man has acknowledged paternity of the child in a writing sworn to before a notary public or the man is required to support the child by a written voluntary promise or by a court order.

(2) Genetic testing indicates a 99% or greater probability that a man is the biological father of the child.

2000 S.B. 180, by repealing former RC 3111.19, also eliminates the ability of parties, after a parentage action is brought, but before judgment, subject to approval of the court, to compromise the action by agreement in which parentage was not determined but a specific economic obligation was undertaken.

The bill also eliminates the requirement that the court direct the father to pay all of the birthing expenses. Now the expenses may be imposed against the appropriate party if to do so is not in violation of federal child support law.[18]

§ 22:5 Establishing parentage—Timely rescission

2000 S.B. 180 changes the administrative rescission procedure by requiring the following in RC 3111.27:

(1) Not later than sixty days after the date of the latest signature on the acknowledgment, one of the persons who signed it must request an administrative determination of whether there is a parent and child relationship between the man who signed the acknowledgment and the child who is the subject of the acknowledgment, instead of requesting an administrative determination of the existence or nonexistence of a parent and child relationship with respect to that child;

(2) An administrative determination must actually be issued determining that no parent and child relationship exists in order to rescind the acknowledgment;

(3) The Office of Child Support must verify that an administrative determination request has been made not later than the end of business day following the business day on which the office received the notice that the administrative determination request was made, instead of the same day;

(4) If the office verifies that an administrative determination was requested and the notice of the request was timely sent, the office must note the date the notice was received in its records and that the acknowledgment is subject to rescission, instead of rescinding the notice;

(5) If the office verifies that an administrative determination was requested and the notice of the request was timely sent, the office must direct the CSEA making the administrative determination to notify the office when it issues a determination;

(6) If the office cannot verify that an administrative determination was requested, the office must note the date the notice was received and that it was not verified.

---

[18]RC 3111.13.

§ 22:6   Establishing parentage—Rescission after final acknowledgment

House Bill 242, effective October 27, 2000, and incorporated into the codified provisions of S.B. 180, provides a new court rescission procedure for acknowledgments. There are two ways to rescind a final acknowledgment of paternity:[1]

(1) An action for rescission brought within a year after the acknowledgment becomes final because of fraud, duress, or material mistake of fact; or

(2) By a motion for relief from judgment pursuant to the newly enacted procedures of H.B. 242 and contained in RC 3119.96 to RC 3119.967, which require that the motion be filed in the juvenile court of the county in which the original judgment, court order, or administrative determination or order or child support order was made, or other court with jurisdiction and that the movant possesses a genetic test performed no more than six months prior to the date of filing the motion that finds zero percent probability that the movant is the father. The movant must not have adopted the child and the child must not have been conceived as the result of artificial insemination for the motion to be successful. Further, the court cannot grant relief if it finds a preponderance of evidence that the person knew he was not the natural father of the child when he signed the acknowledgment.

§ 22:7   Establishing support order

Within ninety days of locating the absent parent or establishing parentage, the CSEA must serve process necessary to begin an action to establish a support order or at least document that it has made a diligent effort to accomplish service.[1] As with parentage establishment, there are a number of distinct court actions that can be invoked to obtain a child support order.[2] Nevertheless, the General Assembly has acted to authorize an administrative officer at the CSEA to establish an enforceable administrative support order in a broad range of circumstances. For example, in any case in which the CSEA had made an administrative paternity determination, it is required to also make an administrative support order.[3] Moreover, in any instance in which a presumption of parentage arises under RC 3111.03, the CSEA is required to issue an administrative support order at the request of an interested person or

---

[Section 22:6]

[1]RC 2151.23, RC 3111.31, RC 3119.961, RC 3119.962.

[Section 22:7]

[1]OAC 5101:1-30-402.

[2]See RC 2151.231 (juvenile court original action), RC 3109.05 (domestic relations proceedings), RC 2151.36 (support of child subject to juvenile court commitment), RC 3113.31 (domestic violence proceedings), RC 3115.31 (UIFSA).

[3]RC 3111.81.

the CSEA itself.[4] Given the fact that RC 3111.03 includes the presumption created by a birth occurring during marriage, it is arguable that the CSEA is now authorized to make a support order in the situation in which the parties are married.

Regardless of the legal context of its creation, any administrative support order automatically becomes final and enforceable by a court unless a party files an original juvenile court support action within 30 days of the issuance of the administrative order.[5]

In establishing an administrative support order, the CSEA must compute the support amount by using the child support guidelines and worksheet prescribed in RC 3119.021, including the authority to determine potential income using imputed income that a parent would have earned if fully employed, based on various factors, and imputed income derived from applying passbook savings rates or other court-determined appropriate rates to non-income-producing assets of a parent.[6] In addition, when the CSEA issues an administrative support order, it is also required to issue an administrative order for the withholding of support from the income or assets of the payor. The range of possible withholding orders parallels the court's withholding requirements under RC 3121.02, which is applicable to all support orders.

If combined parental income is over $150,000, the CSEA must compute an obligation that is no less than what would be computed for a combined income of $150,000 unless it is not in the best interests of the children, obligee, the obligor or is unjust.[7]

Under 2000 S.B. 180, if a court or CSEA requires a parent to pay an amount for that parent's failure to support a child for a period of time prior to the date the court modifies or issues a child support order, or a CSEA modifies or issues an administrative order for the current support of the child, the court or CSEA must use the child support schedule in effect, and the income of the parents, for that period of time.[8]

If, due to unemployment or insufficient income of the absent parent, no support order is issued, then the CSEA must continue to review the case in its parent location function in order to keep abreast of any changes in the income or assets of the absent parent.[9]

The CSEA that computes child support is not permitted to determine that a parent receiving means tested public assistance is voluntarily unemployed or underemployed or to impute income unless not doing so would be unjust, inappropriate, or not in the child's best interests.[10]

§ 22:8 Support order enforcement—Wage and asset withholding

Ohio law provides for various enforcement mechanisms to assure that

---

[4]RC 3111.78; OAC 5101:1-32-02, OAC 5101:1-32-03.

[5]RC 3111.84.

[6]RC 3119.01.

[7]RC 3119.021 and RC 3119.04.

[8]RC 3119.05.

[9]OAC 5101:1-30-402. See also Enforcement of Spousal and Child Support Ch 19.

[10]RC 3119.05.

ordered support is paid on a regular basis.[1] The CSEA is involved in many of these enforcement procedures. The basic means to enforce support is requiring that each child support order be accompanied by an order withholding regular support payments by the obligor's employer, or other source of the obligor's income or assets, at the time a support order is issued by the court or CSEA.[2] The process of issuing withholding orders has also evolved into a largely administrative system in which the CSEA has supplanted the role that was once the exclusive domain of the court. In fact, RC 3121.02 now makes it clear that support withholding provisions are no longer even part of the underlying child support order, except for a general reference to the fact that the order will be withheld from wages or assets of the obligor in accordance with RC 3121.27. The specifics of withholding in an individual case will be determined by a new support withholding notice issued by the CSEA that will supplant the need for any separate withholding order to be issued by the court. Any initial support order made by a court must be accompanied by a support withholding notice, to be issued by the court or the CSEA. Subsequent withholding notices will all be issued by the CSEA. Neither the statutes nor administrative rules require actual certified mail delivery of the various notices involved with the withholding of support from wages or assets.[3]

Regardless of the source, withholding notices are final and enforceable by the court. The state department of human services is required to adopt standard forms for support withholding, which all courts and CSEAs are required to use.[4]

2000 S.B.180 permits an action to be maintained on an obligee's behalf against the state, to withhold support from payments owed or to be owed to an officer or employee of the state or an individual who is under contract with the state or is owed or to be owed money from the state, including an individual who is the sole shareholder of a corporation or the sole member of a limited liability company.[5]

Again, the forced march toward a largely administrative process throughout the child support enforcement arena is expanded upon by several additional provisions of Public Law No. 104-193.[6] By 1998, the CSEA must be given the authority under state law, "without the necessity of obtaining an order from any other judicial or administrative tribunal" to do all of the following in regard to "establishment, modifica-

---

[Section 22:8]

[1]See also Enforcement of Spousal and Child Support Ch 20.

[2]RC 3121.07, RC 3121.27, RC 3121.033, RC 5101.36; OAC 5101:1-30-411, OAC 5101:1-30-413.

[3]RC 3121.23.

[4]RC 3121.0311. See ODHS forms 4047, 4048, 4049.

[5]RC 3121.09 and RC 3121.091.

[6]Personal Responsibility and Work Opportunity Reconciliation Act of 1996, Pub. L. No. 104-193, August 22, 1996.

tion, or enforcement of support orders":[7]

(1) Order genetic testing;

(2) Issue and enforce subpoenas;

(3) Order any public or private entity to provide wage and benefit information regarding any employee or contractor, and also sanction any failure to respond to the order;

(4) Gain access to virtually any record maintained by any state or local government, or any public utility, cable company, or financial institution;

(5) Satisfy support arrearages by seizing payments from any state or local agency or any judgment, settlement, or lottery; attaching assets held in financial institutions and public and private retirement accounts; and imposing liens and forcing sales on available property.[8]

In response to these federal mandates, the Ohio General Assembly enacted 1997 House Bill 352, most sections of which took effect either October 1, 1997 or January 1, 1998. The department of job and family services adopted regulations to implement these changes and convert support orders to the new requirements.

RC 3123.21 provides that a withholding or deduction notice or an order to collect current support due under a support order and any arrearages owed pertaining to the same child or spouse must require the arrearage amount collected with each payment of current support to equal at least 20% of the current support payment unless, for good cause shown, a lesser arrearage amount is required to be collected.

§ 22:9 Support order enforcement—Lump-sum payments

A variation on the theme of regular support withholding is the requirement of ad hoc withholding from any lump-sum payments due an obligor from any payment source.[1] A notice of withholding issued to an employer must contain a notice that if the employer will be distributing to the obligor a lump-sum payment in excess of $150.00, then the employer must notify the CSEA at least forty-five days before payment is to be made or, if the obligor's right to the lump sum is determined less than forty-five days prior to the date of distribution, on the date of determination.[2] In this event, the employer must hold the funds for thirty days after due for payment. Meanwhile, the CSEA must determine

---

[7]42 U.S.C.A. § 666(c)(1).

[8]42 U.S.C.A. § 666. It should be noted that the statute indicates that all such actions are "subject to due process safeguards, including (as appropriate) requirements for notice, opportunity to contest the action, and opportunity for an appeal on the record to an independent administrative or judicial tribunal." 42 U.S.C.A. § 666(c)(1)(H).

[Section 22:9]

[1]RC 3121.037.

[2]RC 3121.037(A)(10), RC 3121.11, RC 3121.12 (formerly amount was $500, reduced by 1997 H.B. 352, eff. 1-1-98).

if the obligor is in default, and if so, request the court to order the employer to forward the lump sum or a designated amount to the CSEA.[3] If, on the other hand, the obligor is not in default, the court must notify the employer to distribute the funds to the obligor.[4]

Courts have been presented with the issue of how to define "default" for purposes of the lump-sum withholding provisions. In *Hartzell v. Albright*,[5] the obligor had an arrearage created by a retroactive parentage support order that accrued from the date of birth to the date of the order. The order required the obligor to satisfy the arrearage of $10,800 by paying $50 per month. The CSEA sought to intercept and apply a lump sum payable to the obligor. The appellate court affirmed the trial court's refusal to intercept the payment, since the record demonstrated the obligor was in full compliance with the support order and the repayment schedule. Similarly, in *Gladysz v. King*,[6] the court refused to allow attachment of an obligor's federal tax refund to satisfy a paternity "birthing cost" order of $2,000, where the obligor was in compliance with another part of the order that required additional payments of $5 per week to liquidate the arrearage.

2000 S.B. 180, through RC 3123.22, provides that if an obligor is paying off an arrearage through a withholding notice the CSEA may still take other enforcement efforts to collect the arrearage unless the parties agree in writing to limit other enforcement to tax intercepts.Another limitation of the application of the lump-sum recovery provision is in regard to a lump-sum payment made to the CSEA by the Bureau of Workers' Compensation pursuant to RC 3121.037. The Ohio Supreme Court has held that the child support recovery is subordinate to an attorney's lien arising out of a contingency fee contract between the attorney and obligor claimant.[7] The rationale for allowing the lien includes the argument that a contrary holding would discourage attorneys from representing claimants with outstanding child support obligations as well as the reality that the claimant would have no incentive to pursue such an award if, in addition to having to deduct all arrearages, the claimant had to pay his attorney.

On the other hand, where an employer had received withholding orders which contained instructions in the event there would be a lump-sum distribution to the employee-obligor, that employer could be held in

---

[3]RC 3121.12.

[4]RC 3121.12.

[5]Hartzell v. Albright, 1993 WL 405439 (Ohio Ct. App. 5th Dist. Stark County 1993); Geauga County Child Support Enforcement Agency v. Miller, 1999 WL 420646 (Ohio Ct. App. 11th Dist. Geauga County 1999).

[6]Gladysz v. King, 103 Ohio App. 3d 1, 658 N.E.2d 309 (2d Dist. Clark County 1995). RC 3123.22 (eff. 3-22-01) prospectively permits the CSEA to use additional enforcement measures to collect arrearages of new orders even though payment is being made on the arrearage pursuant to a court order.

[7]Rowan v. Rowan, 1993 WL 548553 (Ohio Ct. App. 11th Dist. Lake County 1993), judgment aff'd, 1995 -Ohio- 110, 72 Ohio St. 3d 486, 650 N.E.2d 1360 (1995).

contempt for not complying with the procedures.[8] It was not excused just because the benefit was to come from a retirement benefit department located out of state. Further, a lump-sum payment paid into the CSEA which is less than the total arrearage must be distributed to the obligee and cannot be split between the obligor and obligee.[9]

§ 22:10 Support order enforcement—Payment monitoring and default determination

The CSEA is responsible for monitoring whether payments under a support order are received, and must initiate an investigation if payment is in default.[1] The investigation must first determine whether the default is due to a failure of the employer or other entity to comply with the order. In this case, the CSEA can take action ranging from writing a letter to filing a court action for a fine or contempt citation.[2] 2000 S.B. 180 repeals a provision providing that if a payor or financial institution fails to comply with a withholding or deduction notice to enforce an administrative order, the CSEA that issued the notice must ask the court to find the payor or financial institution in contempt. Former RC 3111.23 and 3111.28 required the CSEA to take this action. Under Chapter 2705, the CSEA may still request the court to find the payor in contempt.

If the employer or other entity is not at fault, the CSEA investigation shifts to seeking other employment or assets of the obligor that could form the basis of a new withholding order.[3] The investigation findings, along with a recommendation of any revised withholding order, must be filed with the court and sent to the parties to the support order.[4] If the support payor feels that the CSEA made a mistake of fact in its proposed withholding action, the payor must request a CSEA administrative "mistake of fact" hearing within seven days of issuance of the advance notice, lest the action become automatically final and enforceable by the court.[5] If a hearing is requested, the CSEA must schedule it within five days and conduct it no more than five days later. Further, if the payor disagrees with the administrative hearing decision, it can be appealed to

---

[8]Sells v. Sells, 1995 WL 66369 (Ohio Ct. App. 9th Dist. Summit County 1995).

[9]Tardona v. Bell, 105 Ohio App. 3d 44, 663 N.E.2d 679 (12th Dist. Butler County 1995).

[Section 22:10]

[1]RC 3123.02, RC 3123.04.

[2]RC 2705.05, RC 3121.380, RC 3121.381; OAC 5101:1-30-416. See Burrs v. Burrs, 66 Ohio App. 3d 628, 585 N.E.2d 918 (2d Dist. Montgomery County 1991) (corporate employer paid a lump-sum payment of $8,032.18 to support obligor held in contempt for failure to notify CSEA of payment and required to pay support and alimony arrearages owed by obligor on the date of payment).

[3]OAC 5101:1-30-422.

[4]RC 3123.04. See Salter v. Salter, 1991 WL 1321512 (Ohio Ct. App. 6th Dist. Wood County 1991) (procedural requirements must be satisfied before court could direct county jail to withhold funds from defendant's inmate account for temporary support order).

[5]RC 3123.04.

the court within seven days; if so, it likewise is scheduled within five days and heard within five additional days.[6]

In conducting any investigation or hearings necessary to the performance of its duties, the CSEA may issue subpoenas, including duces tecum, administer oaths, and compel testimony from witnesses.[7] The CSEA is not required to pay attendance or travel fees to witnesses for hearings, and may apply to the court of common pleas to enforce compliance with any subpoena through a contempt citation.

2000 S.B. 180 repeals provisions providing that if the obligee under a child support order in default receives notice from the CSEA of the default and inability to enforce the order, the obligee may request the CSEA to maintain an action on the obligee's behalf to obtain judgment and execution of judgment through any available procedure. RC 2301.38 and RC 2301.40 were repealed in part.

§ 22:11   Support order enforcement—Payment monitoring— Record keeping

Authentication of a CSEA payment history record does not require a custodian of records to testify.[1] Pursuant to Evid. R. 902(4), extrinsic evidence of authenticity as a condition precedent to admissibility is not required for a copy of an official record or report that is certified as correct by the custodian. CSEA payment history records are official records or reports.

Since the advent in 2000 of both SETS (Support Enforcement Tracking System), which is the statewide federally mandated child support computer system, and CSPC (Child Support Payment Central), which processes payments in a central location in Columbus, Ohio, the payment records for child support cases are no longer maintained by the CSEAs but are maintained in a centralized database. These records nevertheless continue to be admissible by the CSEAs in child support cases under the same theory as former CSEA records since the Director of ODJFS is the custodian of these records and has appointed the CSEAs to certify them as correct pursuant to Evidence Rule 902(4).

§ 22:12   Support order enforcement—Miscellaneous remedies

If it does not locate an appropriate target for a withholding order, the CSEA can take further court action to require the obligor to disclose any fixed assets and proceed with any of the traditional collection procedures against such assets.[1] Other enforcement remedies include the following:

---

[6]RC 3123.05.

[7]RC 5101.37; OAC 5101:1-30-18.

[Section 22:11]

[1]Yarnevic v. Yarnevic, 1999 WL 125951 (Ohio Ct. App. 8th Dist. Cuyahoga County 1999).

[Section 22:12]

[1]RC 3123.14; OAC 5101:1-30-87, OAC 5101:1-30-871.

(1) Reporting the support default by the obligor to a consumer reporting agency;[2]

(2) Filing a contempt of court action against the obligor;[3]

(3) Collecting support arrearage from any state or federal income tax refund due the obligor;[4] Under S.B. 180, the state tax offset program can now be used to collect overpayment of child support to the obligee if the amount overpaid is not less than $150.[5]

(4) Withholding support from any veterans or military pay due the obligor;[6]

(5) Filing an action against an out-of-state obligor under the Uniform Interstate Family Support Act (UIFSA);[7]

(6) Sending a direct request for interstate income withholding under an existing withholding order to the central registry of the state where an out-of-state obligor is employed;[8]

(7) Referring case to Internal Revenue Service (IRS) for collection of support arrearage;[9]

(8) Filing a request in the U.S. District Court for enforcement of child support in the district in which the out-of-state obligor resides, where the state courts have failed to act;[10]

(9) Obtaining a court order for obligor to post cash bond;[11]

(10) Obtaining a court order for obligor to seek work in order to pay support;[12]

---

[2]RC 3123.92; OAC 5101:1-29-341, OAC 5101:1-29-342.

[3]RC 2705.031, RC 2705.05.

[4]RC 3123.81, RC 3123.821; OAC 5101:1-30-77 to OAC 5101:1-30-777, OAC 5101:1-30-89 to OAC 5101:1-30-892; Davis v. Davis, 1998 WL 258449 (Ohio Ct. App. 1st Dist. Hamilton County 1998) (CSEA has legal right to intercept tax refund and trial court has no right to allocate federal tax refund when a valid arrearage exists).

[5]RC 3123.82, RC 3123.821, RC 3123.822, RC 3123.823.

[6]OAC 5101:1-30-43 to OAC 5101:1-30-438.

[7]RC Ch. 3115; OAC 5101:1-30-51, OAC 5101:1-30-55. See Interstate and Foreign Support Practice Ch 23.

[8]OAC 5101:1-30-582

[9]OAC 5101:1-30-73. But see Gladysz v. King, 103 Ohio App. 3d 1, 658 N.E.2d 309 (2d Dist. Clark County 1995) (CSEA may be enjoined from referring case to IRS where obligor is complying with an order to liquidate arrearage with periodic payments). RC 3123.22 (eff. 3-22-01) prospectively permits the CSEA to use additional enforcement measures to collect arrearages of new orders even though payment is being made on the arrearage pursuant to a court order.

[10]OAC 5101:1-30-75

[11]RC 3123.03.

[12]RC 3123.03. Note also: Pub. L. No. 104-193 (Personal Responsibility and Work Opportunity Reconciliation Act of 1996, Pub. L. No. 104-193, August 22, 1996) adds a variation on this theme, requiring the state to order appropriate obligors to participate in the various "workfare" activities traditionally required only of public assistance recipients (42 U.S.C.A. § 666(a)). See also OAC 5101:1-30-405, which has authorized a similar program in Ohio on a pilot basis for several years. 1997 H.B. 352 amended RC 3113.21(D)(4), eff. 1-1-98, to implement this requirement.

(11) Submitting the obligor's name and photo for inclusion in county and state delinquent payor public poster program;[13] or

(12) Withholding support payments from unemployment compensation benefits due the obligor.[14]

(13) The CSEA may avoid fraudulent transfers[15]

(14) The CSEA may file liens against personal and real property of the obligor through the county recorder via RC 3123.66 and RC 3123.78.

The newest of this list of nontraditional support enforcement techniques is the suspension of the delinquent obligor's license to engage in a regulated occupation or profession.[16] The premise underlying the administration of the license suspension remedy is that the obligor who is in default has already been accorded elementary procedural due process through the RC 3123.03 notice and "mistake of fact" hearing regarding the issue of whether the obligor is in default of the child support order. Accordingly, the only further process given the obligor of the licensure suspension remedy is a copy of a "notice to suspend professional license" (ODJFS form 4041) sent to the appropriate licensure authority.[17] The notice contains the obligor's name, social security number, and the determination that the obligor is in default of a support order. Upon receipt of the notice, the licensure authority need only determine "that the individual is the individual named in the notice" in order to cause it to suspend any license currently held or applied for by the individual.[18] The statute specifically forbids the licensure authority from holding any hearing in regard to such a suspension.

Moreover, the state department of job and family services has been given authority to include commercial and individual drivers licenses within the ambit of the suspension remedy, upon implementation of an automated statewide support enforcement tracking system.[19] Effective January 1998, but also subject to implementation of the enforcement tracking system, hunting and fishing licenses held by an obligor in default may also be suspended.[20]

In recognition of the constitutional role of the Ohio Supreme Court in governing the bench and bar of the state, the statute specifically excludes the Court from its definition of regulated authorities. However, in response to legislative entreaty, the Court amended the Rules for Government of the Bar to include a final determination of default under a child support order by a court or CSEA as grounds for an ex parte interim

---

[13]RC 3123.962.

[14]RC 3121.07, RC 4141.282, OAC 5101:1-30-79.

[15]RC 1336.07 and RC 1336.08.

[16]RC 3123.41 through 3123.50.

[17]OAC 5101:1-30-88.

[18]RC 3123.47.

[19]RC 3123.61.

[20]RC 3123.62, enacted by 1997 H.B. 352.

license suspension.[21]

In any event, a suspended license cannot be reinstated until the CSEA has sent a "notice to reinstate/reissue professional license" (ODJFS form 4042), in the event that the obligor either has paid any outstanding arrearage or is complying with an existing or new order for current support and liquidation of the arrearage. Reinstatement must occur within seven days of receipt of such notice, if the obligor is otherwise eligible for licensure and pays any required reinstatement fee, up to a maximum of fifty dollars.[22]

The latest enforcement method is the Financial Institution Data Match (FIDM) program. The states are authorized by federal law,[23] to enter into agreements with financial institutions, which are exempt from any liability for participation in the program, in order to compare lists of delinquent obligors with records of account holders with those institutions.

If the CSEA identifies a delinquent obligor who is an account holder it can send an "access restriction" form to the financial institution which requires the financial institution to freeze access to the account. Any person with interest in the funds other than or in addition to the obligor is entitled to an administrative hearing and then a court hearing if desired, to show why they should not have their funds released to them. Any remaining amount owed the obligor is released to the CSEA.

The CSEA is required to provide the obligor with notices of the actions taken and afford the obligor a hearing as well before any funds of the obligor are seized.[24]

§ 22:13 Support collection and distribution

Not surprisingly, the extensive duties of the CSEA in the support establishment and enforcement process requires it to maintain a case record for each case, which traces the case activity chronologically and includes or incorporates by reference other relevant documentation, including the date of any support order, the names and addresses of the parties affected by it, and a record of payments, disbursements, and arrearages thereunder.[1] The record may be maintained on paper, and a record of payments and disbursements is maintained in SETS.[2] Access to the case record is guaranteed to the parties to the case, except for portions made confidential by various provisions of state and federal law.[3] Conversely, any unauthorized disclosure of child support case in-

---

[21]Amendment to Gov. Bar R. V § 5, eff.4-21-97.

[22]RC 3123.45.

[23]42 U.S.C.A. § 666a(17).

[24]RC 3123.24 to RC 3123.38 and RC 3121.74 to RC 3121.78.

[Section 22:13]

[1]RC 3125.15; OAC 5101:1-29-05.

[2]RC 3125.07; OAC 5101:1-29-05.

[3]RC 149.43, RC 1347.08, RC 3125.16; OAC 5101:1-29-071.

formation is a misdemeanor under state law.[4]

Any payment of money intended to satisfy an order for child support issued in this state must be made to Child Support Payment Central (CSPC) in the Office of Child Support (OCS) in the Ohio Department of Job and Family Services as trustee for remittance to the person entitled to receive payment.[5] The only exceptions to this provision are payments made in person at the CSEA which is still permitted to accept 'walk-in' payments. Any payment of money by an obligor directly to a custodial parent is presumed to be a gift and does not reduce the amount of child support owed. The obligor has the burden of rebutting the presumption.[6]

In cases where the original support order predated the enactment of this provision on December 1, 1986, and the direct payments to the obligee were in the same amount as the child support order, courts have either found that the presumption was rebutted or that there was no abuse of discretion in giving the obligor credit as a support payment.[7] Similarly, a lengthy period of acceptance of payments and inaction suggests an obligee's awareness that the payments are for support, as well as a waiver by the obligee of payment through the agency.[8] In order to facilitate the CSEA's role in distributing support payments, all parties to a support order have a continuing obligation to inform the CSEA of any change of name, address, or other conditions that may affect the administration of the order.[9] For its part, the CSEA must maintain an accurate and timely record for each support order that includes the following information:

(1) The date the order was entered;

(2) The current record of payments and disbursements;

(3) The amount of any accumulated arrearage;

(4) The date on which payments are required to be made; and

(5) The names and addresses of parties affected by the order.[10]

The CSEA payment record may be introduced at a hearing (see § 22:11, Support order enforcement—Payment monitoring—Record keeping). It is not the proper subject of judicial notice by the hearing authority since it is not included in Evid. R. 201 or Civ. R. 44.1.[11]

For each payment received, the CSEA must designate the date of col-

---

[4]RC 5101.31, RC 5101.99.

[5]RC 3121.44.

[6]RC 3121.45.

[7]Jacobs v. England, 1993 WL 414258 (Ohio Ct. App. 12th Dist. Warren County 1993).

[8]Gillis v. Gillis, 1993 WL 402773 (Ohio Ct. App. 2d Dist. Montgomery County 1993); York v. York, 1994 WL 313745 (Ohio Ct. App. 5th Dist. Richland County 1994) (department of human services, as assignee under Aid to Dependent Children, stands in the shoes of assignor; thus, defense of payment evidenced by prior judgment entry and notarized statement barred an arrearage finding).

[9]RC 3121.24.

[10]RC 3125.15.

[11]Maloney v. Maloney, 34 Ohio App. 3d 9, 516 N.E.2d 251 (11th Dist. Lake County 1986); Fellows v. Fellows, 1988 WL 63012 (Ohio Ct. App. 2d Dist. Montgomery County

lection as the date on which the payment is received at the initial collection point.[12] For payments made directly to the CSEA by the obligor, this date is the date of receipt by the CSEA. In instances of income withholding by an employer or some other financial entity, the date of collection is the date of the withholding, regardless of when the payment is subsequently received by the CSEA.

The CSEA is entitled to collect from the obligor an administrative collection fee of two percent of the support payment but not less than one dollar per month.[13] The obligor is required to pay this fee, formerly called poundage, with every payment of current support or arrearages. If the two percent processing charge is not paid, the CSEA must maintain a separate arrearage account of that amount and may not deduct the unpaid processing charge from any support payment due to the obligee under the support order.[14]

Any support payment due to an individual must be "disbursed" by the OCS/CSPC within two business days of receipt.[15] By contrast, "distribution" is the process used by the CSEA to allocate support collections in cases wherein OWF or Title IV-E foster care maintenance has been paid on behalf of the child.[16] The goal of distribution is to reimburse the state for such assistance within the guidelines of federal law governing the underlying programs, while paying any remainder to the child's caretaker.[17] If the CSEA/OCS receives a payment and is unable to locate the person entitled to it, the CSEA/OCS must act in accordance with applicable administrative rules.

On a quarterly basis, the department of job and family services must send child support payees who are current OWF recipients, or former recipients who still have a support assignment in effect, a notice detailing the amounts of support received and distributed on their behalf. 2000 S.B. 180 repeals the requirement that CSEAs report yearly to the Board of County Commissioners regarding the number of support orders, the number of defaults, and the disposition of cases relating to enforcement of support orders.[18]

The enactment of Public Law No. 104-93, Personal Responsibility and Work Opportunity Reconciliation Act of 1996, Pub. L. No. 104, August 22, 1996, affects the support distribution process. Although it extends from 1996 to 1997, a previous requirement for the state to have a statewide automated case tracking system, it also mandates a number of new requirements for the system thereafter, including transmission of withholding orders to employers, monitoring case default and imposing

---

1988). But see Armstrong v. Armstrong, 1993 WL 76940 (Ohio Ct. App. 2d Dist. Clark County 1993); but see RC 3115.27(C) for use in UIFSA proceedings.

[12]OAC 5101:1-30-10.1.

[13]RC 3119.27.

[14]RC 3121.58.

[15]OAC 5101:1-29-41(B)(1)(a), OAC 5101:1-29-31.

[16]OAC 5101:1-29-31.

[17]OAC 5101:1-29-31.

[18]RC 2301.41 was repealed.

automatic enforcement procedures, and implementation of a central case registry to interface with the federal case registry. This system, known as the Support Enforcement Tracking System (SETS), became fully operational in 2000. The automated unit to collect and disburse support payments, known as Child Support Payment Central (CSPC), became active in 2000. All payments are to be made through this system with the exception of walk-in payments at the CSEA. Employers are required to forward withheld wages to the CSPC within seven business days after they would have been paid to the employee.

2000 S.B. 180, effective March 22, 2001, clarifies that administrative orders are the same as court orders in that support payments must be sent to CSPC except in certain instances, which include payments made at the CSEA by the obligor. The bill also requires that CSEAs, with respect to orders that require payment of support to commence on a day other than the first day of a month, to compute the pro rata amount due under order for the first month.[19] The bill also permits each CSEA to develop a system and procedure for organized safekeeping and retrieval of administrative child support orders. The bill requires the CSEA administrative officer to register administrative orders with the CSEA system or with the clerk of court in its county.[20]

§ 22:14 Support modification—Overview

Just as the CSEA has been increasingly allowed to make administrative determinations of parentage and child support, so has it also been given extensive authority to review and modify support orders.[1] Court orders for child support traditionally have been subject to modification upon a significant change of circumstances by invoking the court's continuing jurisdiction pursuant to Civil Rule 75. The codification of formal child support guidelines, first by the Supreme Court in 1987 and incorporated into RC 3113.215 in 1990, quantified the amount of change needed to justify a support order modification.[2] Also in 1990, the General Assembly codified in RC 3113.216 an administrative procedure for modification of court support orders through the CSEA, subject to court review. Finally, in 1992 the CSEA was given similar authority in RC 3111.27 to review and modify administrative support orders. The child support guidelines are now contained in RC 3119.021.

A parent may request the CSEA to review that parent's current support obligation.[3] Since the agency must use the child support guidelines, if they cannot set the proper amount without deviating from the guidelines, the agency is to bring an action on behalf of the parent who

---

[19]RC 3121.54.

[20]RC 3111.83, RC 3111.831, RC 3111.832.

[Section 22:14]

[1]See Child Support Ch 19.

[2]RC 3119.79.

[3]OAC 5101:1-30-403(B).

requested the administrative review.[4]

The CSEA is thus now responsible for reviewing every three years most child support orders for obligees who have received public assistance that has not been fully reimbursed, even if neither party to the support order has made a request.[5] In all other cases, the review is initiated at the request of a party but can be done no more frequently than once every three years except in the following circumstances:

(1) The minimum amount of support is ordered based on the child support guidelines schedule at the time the order is entered due to the unemployment or underemployment of the obligor, and information becomes available that the obligor is no longer unemployed or has obtained more gainful employment;

(2) Either party has experienced a loss of employment for a period of at least six months that is beyond the party's control, and that can reasonably be expected to continue for an extended period of time;

(3) Either party becomes permanently disabled, thereby reducing the party's earning ability; three years have not passed since the last review; and the disability can be medically verified by the receipt of social security disability benefits or a physician's complete diagnosis and determination;

(4) Either party cannot pay support for the duration of the child's minority because of institutionalization or incarceration with no chance of parole, and no income or assets are available to the obligor which could be levied or attached for support;

(5) Either party to the support order has experienced a thirty percent change in gross income or income-producing assets;

(6) A child covered in the order has been deleted from the order because of emancipation;

(7) Health insurance inclusion or increased coverage has become available for a child covered in the support order; or

(8) The support order was based upon a guideline deviation which was supported by a set of circumstances that have now changed.[6]

The statutes set forth a detailed procedure to be followed by the CSEA in conducting such reviews. It must first send sixty days' advance written notice to the parties of the date for the review, along with a request that each party provide the CSEA, no later than the review date, the following information:

(1) The federal income tax return from the previous year;

(2) All pay stubs for the preceding six months;

(3) All other records evidencing the receipt of any other salary, wages, or compensation within the preceding six months; and

---

[4]OAC 5101:1-30-403(C); Matter of Stewart, 1998 WL 275560 (Ohio Ct. App. 3d Dist. Union County 1998).

[5]OAC 5101:1-30-403.

[6]OAC 5101:1-30-403.

(4) Any other information necessary to properly review the support order.

2000 S.B. 180 changes the criteria for determining when review of a child support order is not required in cases where the obligee has assigned the right to receive child support. The agency must determine that good cause for not cooperating in modifying the child support order exists with respect to the children who are subject of the child support order. Also, if the obligor and obligee live outside Ohio, this is a factor in determining if the review is required.[7]

The notice also advises the parties that a willful failure to provide the requested information constitutes contempt of court. Such failure requires the CSEA to notify the court; however, the CSEA then has the option of either requesting the court to issue a contempt citation or "take any action necessary to obtain the information or make any reasonable assumptions necessary with respect to the information the person in contempt of court did not provide to ensure a fair and equitable review of the child support order."

On the date established for the review, the CSEA calculates a revised child support order and sends the parties notice of that determination. In making its determination, the CSEA must take into consideration the child support guidelines set forth in RC 3119.021 and the cost of health insurance which the parties have been ordered to obtain for the children.

§ 22:15 Support modification—Review of court support orders

At this point in the administrative support modification process, there is a divergence of procedures depending upon whether the CSEA is reviewing a court support order or an administrative support order. RC 3119.63 provides that in regard to court support orders, the CSEA's modification decision forms the basis for a revised court support order unless a party requests a CSEA administrative hearing within thirty days of receiving the decision. If an administrative hearing is requested by a party, it is conducted in accordance with OAC 5101:1-30-404. The parties are given at least ten days' advance notice of the hearing date, which must be scheduled for a date no later than fifteen days after the CSEA receives the request. The hearing must be conducted by a licensed attorney or other qualified person designated by the CSEA with significant training or experience in conducting hearings which are subject to court review. The hearing officer must not have been involved in the original modification recommendation being appealed.

At the hearing either party may be represented by an attorney or other authorized representative and must be given an opportunity to offer testimony and other evidence. The hearing is relatively narrow in scope, addressing only whether the CSEA correctly evaluated the parties' income, or made reasonable assumptions regarding any party who failed to document the party's income, and whether the revised child support awarded was correctly computed. The administrative modifica-

---

[7]RC 3119.75.

tion hearing decision must be issued within ten days of the hearing and include findings of fact based on the evidence presented at the hearing, relevant citations of law, a conclusion regarding the correctness of the administrative modification recommendation, and a recommendation regarding the amount of child support to be ordered.

The hearing decision, including all exhibits, constitutes the administrative modification hearing record and is sent to both parties along with a notice that it will be submitted to the court for inclusion in a court support order unless a party files a written request with the CSEA for a court hearing within fifteen days of the issuance of the hearing decision. In that event, within fifteen days of the hearing request, the CSEA submits the request and the hearing record to the court, which must conduct a "mistake of fact" hearing in accordance with RC 3119.66. At any such hearing the CSEA does not represent either party.

RC 3119.70 prescribes the actions of the court in the administrative support modification process. If neither party requests court review of a CSEA hearing decision in this regard, the court must issue a revised child support order in the amount calculated by the CSEA. On the other hand, if court review is requested, the court must send the parties thirty days' notice of a hearing and order them to provide, if they have not already done so, the income documentation previously requested by the CSEA. At the hearing, the court must determine whether the revised amount of child support calculated by the CSEA is the appropriate amount. If so, the court must order that amount; if not, the court must determine the appropriate amount and incorporate it into an order. The trial court is not permitted to remand the matter back to the CSEA.[1]

On the other hand, a child support order which results from the CSEA conducting an administrative modification review of a court support order is a final order if there is no request for administrative hearing or appeal.[2] Therefore, in hearing a later motion to modify, the court is required to calculate any ten percent change by comparing a present calculation to the prior administrative order, and not an earlier decree or agreement.[3] However, a court errs in modifying or suspending child support where the CSEA does not follow the procedures mandated by statute and fails to provide notice and an opportunity for hearing.[4] The notice sent by the CSEA of its recommended revision of the child support amount must include reference to statute or rule, and the necessity to appeal to obtain a court hearing. It is not sufficient due process when the notice only stated that a party could request a mistake of fact

---

[Section 22:15]

[1]Valentine v. Valentine, 1993 WL 370656 (Ohio Ct. App. 5th Dist. Muskingum County 1993).

[2]Brady v. Brady, 1995 WL 628025 (Ohio Ct. App. 2d Dist. Montgomery County 1995), dismissed, appeal not allowed, 75 Ohio St. 3d 1422, 662 N.E.2d 25 (1996).

[3]Saunders v. Saunders, 1995 WL 98956 (Ohio Ct. App. 9th Dist. Lorain County 1995).

[4]Burley v. Johnston, 1996 WL 290947 (Ohio Ct. App. 7th Dist. Jefferson County 1996).

hearing.[5]

§ 22:16 Support modification—Review of administrative support orders

RC 3119.60 to RC 3119.71, as enacted by 2000 S.B. 180, with respect to administrative support orders, establishes a procedure for modifying orders if a CSEA can determine the appropriate amount of child support without deviating from the basic child support guidelines.

(1) The CSEA must give the obligor and obligee notice of the revised amount of child support to be paid under the administrative child support order, of their right to request an administrative hearing regarding the revised amount, of the procedures and deadlines for requesting the hearing, and that the CSEA will modify the order to include the revised support amount unless the obligor or obligee requests an administrative hearing on the revised amount of child support no later than thirty days after receipt of the notice.

(2) If no timely hearing request is received, the CSEA must modify the administrative child support order to include the revised amount of child support.

(3) If a timely hearing request is received, the CSEA must schedule a hearing; give the obligor and obligee notice of the date, time, and location of the hearing; conduct the hearing; redetermine at the hearing a revised amount of child support to be paid under the order; and modify the order to include the revised amount.

If the agency modifies an existing support order, the agency shall provide the obligee and obligor with notice of the change and shall include in the notice a statement that the obligor or obligee may object to the modified administrative support order by initiating an action under RC 2151.231.

§ 22:17 Support modification—Effective date of revised order

A revised amount of child support, determined by the CSEA and filed with the court pursuant to RC 3119.61, relates back to the first day of the month following the date certain on which the review began. In addition, if a party requests a court hearing on the revised amount, the trial court, if it modifies the order, shall have the order relate back to when the review began.

§ 22:18 Support modification—Administrative termination of support orders

A variation of an administrative modification procedure remains in RC 3119.87. It requires the support payee, and allows the support payor, to report to the CSEA any reason an existing support order should

---

[5]Duffy v. Duffy, 1995 WL 695002 (Ohio Ct. App. 12th Dist. Madison County 1995).

terminate. Such reasons include occurrences such as death, marriage, emancipation, enlistment in the armed services, deportation, or change of legal or physical custody of the child in question. On receipt of such a report, the CSEA must immediately conduct an investigation to determine if any reason exists for which the support order should terminate and, if so, notify the court that issued the order. The court then orders the impoundment of further support payments under the order and sets the case for a hearing for a determination of whether the support order should be terminated or modified or whether the court should take any other appropriate action.

RC 3119.87 to RC 3119.94:

(1) Eliminates change of physical custody as a reason for which a child support order should terminate.[1]

(2) Adds a provision permitting a CSEA, on its own initiative, to conduct an investigation if it has reason to believe there may be reason for which the child support order should terminate, which investigation must be done within twenty days from receipt of the information which gives rise to the belief.[2]

(3) Also requires the CSEA to make certain determinations pursuant to the termination investigation in addition to whether reasons to terminate exist including (a) There are other children subject to the child support order; (b) Whether the obligor owes any arrearages under the child support order; (c) Whether the CSEA believes it is necessary to continue withholding or deduction for other children or for arrearages.[3]

(4) If the CSEA determines that other children are subject to the order and it is necessary to continue withholding or deduction for other children, the CSEA must divide the child support due annually and per/month under the order by the number of children who are subject of the order and subtract the amount due for the child for whom the order should be terminated from the total child support amount due annually and per month. This investigation is not permitted to include a review of any other children who are subject to the child support order.[4]

(5) With respect to a court child support order, if the CSEA determines that the order should terminate, it immediately must notify the court that issued the order of the results of its investigation and submit to the court an order impounding any child support received under the order. The CSEA, with respect to an administrative order, must issue an administrative order impounding any child support received.[5]

(6) If the obligor or obligee timely requests an administrative hearing on the termination investigation conclusion, the CSEA must schedule a hearing on the issue, give the parties notice of the date, time, and loca-

---

[Section 22:18]
[1]RC 3119.88.
[2]RC 3119.89.
[3]RC 3119.89.
[4]RC 3119.89.
[5]RC 3119.90.

tion of the hearing, and conduct the hearing.[6]

§ 22:19 Spousal and medical support enforcement

The CSEA must also collect spousal support for any case subject to federal reimbursement for which there is a related child support order, although spousal support orders are not sought by the CSEA in such cases.[1] Because this is the only instance that federal funding is available for spousal support enforcement, the state department of job and family services does not require CSEAs to provide additional spousal support services.[2] On the other hand, because RC 3119.01 includes spousal support in its definition of "support order," it is clear that the CSEA has a key role in the enforcement and distribution of spousal support.[3] However, the trial court in *Sullivan v. Sullivan,*[4] declined to find the CSEA in contempt for failing to provide services to a spousal support obligee. The court accepted the CSEA's defense of impossibility due to a lack of funds to provide the services. Pursuant to RC 3121.441, the court may permit the obligor to make spousal support payments directly to the obligee.

In addition, in any case in which a court or CSEA issues or modifies a child support order, the court or CSEA must determine whether either or both of the parties have satisfactory health insurance coverage for the child, other than Medicaid.[5] If no such coverage exists, the court or CSEA must order one or both of the parties to obtain such coverage or be responsible for the child's health care costs. The CSEA is further responsible for notifying the court of any default in medical support orders and assisting parties in enforcing them.

RC 3119.46 requires ODJFS to adopt standard forms for the notice the CSEA is required to send requiring new employers to enroll the obligor or obligee, whichever is required to obtain the insurance by court order, in any insurance which would cover the children in question.

§ 22:20 Role of CSEA attorneys and party status of CSEA

The evolution of the CSEA from being a child support advocate, primarily for the obligee, into an adjudicative entity available to both obligee and obligor has sharpened the longstanding debate regarding the representational role of the CSEA attorney. Although there are no explicit state or federal statutory provisions discussing the issue, it is clear that the federal Office of Child Support Enforcement does require the CSEA to have attorneys on staff, to the extent that they are required

---

[6]RC 3119.91.

[Section 22:19]

[1]OAC 5101:1-29-05.

[2]RC 3125.05.

[3]See also RC 3119.01 et seq., which includes spousal support in the wage and asset withholding procedures overseen by the CSEA.

[4]Sullivan v. Sullivan, 76 Ohio Misc. 2d 1, 663 N.E.2d 751 (C.P. 1996).

[5]RC 3119.34, RC 3119.43; OAC 5101:1-32-05.

to attain and enforce paternity and child support orders.[1] On the other hand, the federal office does not express an opinion regarding the extent to which such attorneys have a fiduciary relationship with the parties to a child support proceeding.[2] Instead, it defers to state law on the question.

In 1990, the Supreme Court of Ohio's Board of Commissioners on Grievances and Discipline issued an advisory opinion[3] which remains the definitive statement in state law:

> The client of a Child Support Enforcement Agency (CSEA) is the state. The state, on behalf of the public, has a direct pecuniary interest in the CSEA work. This is true when the custodial parent receives Aid to Families with Dependent Children and when the parent does not receive AFDC. The custodial parent must be aware at the outset that the CSEA attorney only represents the interests of the state.

In turn, the state department of job and family services has informally advised CSEAs of this opinion, and included the following statement in its form application for child support services:

> In providing IV-D services, the CSEA and any of its contracted agents (e.g. prosecutors, attorneys, hearing officers, etc.) represent the best interest of the children of the State of Ohio, and do not represent any IV-D recipient or the recipient's personal interest.[4]

Although in most instances this distinction has little or no practical impact, it is clear that it can in some situations. For example, in *Dorsett v. Wheeler*,[4] where an action was filed by the CSEA attorney on behalf of a mother and her children, the appellate court found that the trial court had an affirmative duty to inquire as to status of plaintiff's legal representation, and its failure to do so had a material adverse effect on the proceeding and prejudiced the plaintiffs by not protecting the plaintiffs' rights to retroactive support and to defend against a request for change of name of the children. On the other hand, where the CSEA is essentially representing the state in collecting arrearages for support accruing while an obligee was receiving public assistance, the court in *Campbell v. Campbell*[5] held that neither the defense of laches nor principles of estoppel apply against the state, its agencies, or its agents, when exercising governmental functions. The obligor also could not argue the defense of implied waiver since the public interest in collect-

---

[Section 22:20]

[1]45 C.F.R. § 303.20.

[2]Office of Child Support Enforcement Transmittal No. IM-93-03 issued December 1993.

[3]Opinion No. 90-10 (June 15, 1990) Ohio Supreme Court Board of Commissioners on Grievances and Discipline.

[4]Ohio Department of Job and Family Services, Child Support Enforcement Information and Instructional Memorandum No. 11, September 2, 1994.

[4]Dorsett v. Wheeler, 101 Ohio App. 3d 716, 656 N.E.2d 698 (3d Dist. Paulding County 1995).

[5]Campbell v. Campbell, 87 Ohio App. 3d 48, 621 N.E.2d 853 (9th Dist. Wayne County 1993).

ing such an arrearage assigned to the state may not be waived by the county's default.

By contrast, state statutes have been amended over time in response to litigation, to clarify situations in which the CSEA has standing to assert its status as a party.[6] Nevertheless, myriad cases have arisen in this area, suggesting that it will continue to be an active topic of litigation whenever a party discovers an interest in trying to exclude participation of the CSEA in a particular case. The question of the CSEA's standing as a party in a trial court case and its right to appeal has been extensively litigated.[7]

In *Gladysz v. King*[8] the Clark County juvenile court had issued an order enjoining the CSEA from submitting a claim to the Internal Revenue Service under the Federal Tax Referral Offset Program to withhold monies from the obligor's refund to pay arrearages. While the CSEA was not a plaintiff or defendant in the action, it appeared on behalf of plaintiff with respect to child support issues. The agency was made subject to the injunctive relief ordered by the court. As such, it was found to be an interested party that could seek appellate review by filing a timely notice of appeal.

The danger inherent in CSEA counsel preparing the pleadings and filing Juvenile court petitions for the allocation of parental rights was recited in the concurring judge's opinion in *Brooks v. King*[9] The judge called into question whose interests the CSEA counsel represented and noted that a future change of custody would place the CSEA counsel in a direct conflict of interest. If the present obligor parent obtained custody and sought a support order, CSEA would be obligated to seek the maximum support order under the guidelines against the appellee who

---

[6]See RC 3111.07, CSEA as necessary party to court parentage action if a party is receiving public assistance on behalf of the child; RC 2151.231, CSEA of child's residence may bring juvenile court action for child support.

[7]In Matter of Hill, 1995 WL 527407 (Ohio Ct. App. 8th Dist. Cuyahoga County 1995) (CSEA has standing when its own support determination is at issue); Cuyahoga County Support Enforcement Agency v. Lovelace, 1995 WL 723315 (Ohio Ct. App. 8th Dist. Cuyahoga County 1995); State v. Sherrill, 1995 WL 739654 (Ohio Ct. App. 8th Dist. Cuyahoga County 1995) (standing to object to referee's orders); Starr v. Starr, 109 Ohio App. 3d 116, 671 N.E.2d 1097 (8th Dist. Cuyahoga County 1996) (CSEA can intervene in divorce action but cannot seek to void or vacate decree, nor is it necessary party to divorce; CSEA has standing to enforce in-kind payments of child support); State, Cuyahoga Support Enforcement Agency, ex rel. Rosello v. Perrin, 1996 WL 65835 (Ohio Ct. App. 8th Dist. Cuyahoga County 1996) (CSEA appealed trial court's failure to order full maternity expenses and failure to include separate order for health insurance); Benzinger v. Benzinger, 1996 WL 47203 (Ohio Ct. App. 1st Dist. Hamilton County 1996) (general assembly intended that the CSEA agencies be parties to all actions for the collection of child support); Matter of Calhoun-Comack, 1997 WL 711222 (Ohio Ct. App. 8th Dist. Cuyahoga County 1997) (CSEA without capacity to appeal a case where it was not a party to proceedings and never attempted to intervene); Collins v. Collins, 127 Ohio App. 3d 281, 712 N.E.2d 800 (12th Dist. Fayette County 1998) (CSEA is proper party to bring action to hold husband in contempt, despite CSEA's failure to file motion to intervene).

[8]Gladysz v. King, 103 Ohio App. 3d 1, 658 N.E.2d 309 (2d Dist. Clark County 1995).

[9]Brooks v. King, 2000 WL 862854 (Ohio Ct. App. 4th Dist. Lawrence County 2000).

was apparently being represented by the CSEA in the trial court and on appeal.

§ 22:21   Role of CSEA attorneys and party status of CSEA— Immunity

RC Chapter 2744 provides for immunity for political subdivisions when exercising governmental functions. RC 2744.03 declares the defenses or immunities that can be asserted to establish nonliability. According to the Ninth District Court of Appeals, the affirmative defense of sovereign immunity cannot be raised in a motion to dismiss pursuant to Civ. R. 12(B)(6).[1]

The CSEA is not immune from being sanctioned for frivolous conduct in pursuing litigation against an obligor who had fully paid his support obligation, especially since it did so on the basis of inconsistent and unreliable evidence. In *Campbell v. Center*,[2] the appellate court found that the CSEA was "obdurately pursuing harassing and frivolous litigation" against the obligor. The imposition of attorney fees against the agency is proper even though the trial court does not specifically reference RC 2323.51, the frivolous conduct statute.[3]

§ 22:22   Effect of 1997 House Bill 352—In general

On August 28, 1997, the governor signed 1997 House Bill 352, passed by the 122nd General Assembly. The bill was designed to implement many of the changes dictated by Congress in the Personal Responsibility and Work Opportunity Reconciliation Act of 1996, sometimes called the "Welfare Reform Act of 1996."[1]

The act also included a complete revamping of interstate enforcement by the adoption of the Uniform Interstate Family Support Act (UIFSA) and the statutory replacement of all provisions formerly known as Uniform Reciprocal Enforcement of Support Act (URESA).[2]

2000 S.B. 180, effective March 22, 2001, makes numerous technical changes to UIFSA, including changing the definition of a child support order to include: (1) An order concerning a child who has attained the age of majority under the issuing state's law if amounts for current support are required to be paid, or arrearages are owed, under the order;[3] (2) An order concerning a child who has attained the age of majority

---

[Section 22:21]

[1]Thomas v. O'Connor, 2000 WL 296080 (Ohio Ct. App. 9th Dist. Summit County 2000).

[2]Campbell v. Center, 2000 WL 270028 (Ohio Ct. App. 12th Dist. Butler County 2000).

[3]Hollon v. Hollon, 117 Ohio App. 3d 344, 690 N.E.2d 893 (4th Dist. Athens County 1996).

[Section 22:22]

[1]Pub. L. No. 104-193, August 22, 1996.

[2]See Ch 23 for discussion.

[3]RC 3115.01.

under the laws of this state but has not attained the age of majority under the laws of the issuing state if amounts for current support are required to be paid, or arrearages are owed, under the order. The bill also changes "employer" to "payor." The bill also provides that a payor subject to an income withholding order or multiple income withholding orders must comply with the law of the state of the obligor's principal place of employment, if the payor is the obligor's employer, or the payor's principal place of business, in all other cases.[4] The bill also permits a person to request the Office of Child Support to investigate whether the person is subject to a support order or has a duty of support. If the OCS determines the person is subject to a support order, the person may file a declaratory judgment action in the court of common pleas in which is located the employer's principal place of business.[5]

§ 22:23 Effect of 1997 House Bill 352—Parent location

House Bill 352 repeals prior law requiring the Ohio department of job and family services to maintain an index of pertinent information regarding all support orders, and substitutes the requirement that JFS establish a case registry of all support orders. The registry will tie into the centralized automated support tracking system being developed by the department.[1] Also linked to this system is the Directory of New Hires, created under prior law, but now applicable even to employers with fewer than twenty-five employees.[2] The bill also requires JFS to maintain a new Birth Registry that will be linked to the automated system. The department is thus able to compare the information on the support order registry with the new hire directory at regular intervals.[3]

The bill also expands access by JFS to personal information maintained by all levels of state government and to records maintained by public utilities.[4] Each party to a support order now is also required to update the CSEA regarding any changes to the party's residence phone number and driver's license number.[5]

§ 22:24 Effect of 1997 House Bill 352—Establishing parentage

The department of job and family services is required to revise its standard form for acknowledgment of paternity, to be in the form of an affidavit of acknowledgment, that advises the parties that they have the right to rescind the acknowledgment, but that they are waiving the

---

[4]RC 3115.33, RC 3115.34.
[5]RC 3115.37.

[Section 22:23]
[1]See RC 3125.07, RC 3125.81-3125.86.
[2]RC 3125.89-3125.8911.
[3]RC 3125.84, RC 3111.64-3111.67.
[4]RC 3125.41.
[5]RC 3125.41.

right to bring a separate paternity action.[1] The affidavit must be available through CSEAs, hospitals, and local registrars of vital statistics, but after January 1, 1998, will be filed with JFS's Birth Registry, rather than in local probate courts as under former RC 2105.18. Both parents must sign the affidavit, though the signatures need not occur simultaneously. No person may notarize the signature, however, if the person knows that another man is already presumed under law to be the father of the child.

2000 S.B. 180 provides that a presumption arises when the acknowledgment is filed with the ODJFS Office of Child Support and once the acknowledgment becomes final there is no longer a basis for a presumption. Instead, the final acknowledgment becomes a final and enforceable determination of paternity, unless it is rescinded under the court rescission procedure or is overturned by an action under RC 3119.96 to RC 3119.967.

In situations in which no finalized acknowledgment exists, parties must still participate in the administrative parentage adjudication process prior to filing a court action. The bill streamlines that process by eliminating the requirement that parties agree to genetic testing, and allowing the hearing officer to recommend that the juvenile court find a party in contempt for failure to comply with an administrative genetic testing order.[2] It also increases from 95% to 99% the "probability of paternity" percentage needed to support a parentage finding, in addition to eliminating the right to a jury trial in juvenile court.[3] .

Once a CSEA administrative officer is assigned to handle a request for the determination of parentage, he or she must issue a genetic testing order. At the conference the administrative officer may provide the mother and alleged father the opportunity to sign an acknowledgment of paternity only if no other man is presumed to be the father of the child. If they sign an acknowledgment, the administrative officer must cancel the genetic testing order. If no acknowledgment is filed, the parties must still submit to genetic testing.[4]

[Section 22:24]

[1]RC 3111.26, RC 3111.27, RC 3111.28, RC 3111.31.

[2]RC 2705.02, RC 3109.19, RC 3111.06, RC 3111.41, RC 3111.42.

[3]RC 3111.03, RC 3111.09, RC 3111.12, RC 3111.46.

[4]RC 3111.41 and RC 3111.44.

§ 22:26 Acknowledgment of paternity—Form
(Official form, JFS 07038, rev. 3-01)

STATE OF OHIO
Ohio Department of Job and Family Services

Acknowledgment of Paternity Affidavit
Ohio Revised Code Section 3111.31

Notice of Rights and Responsibilities and Due Process Safeguards

Completion of the Acknowledgment of Paternity Affidavit is voluntary.

- If an alleged father acknowledges a parent and child relationship, he is responsible for the support of the child.

- Either parent may rescind this acknowledgment no later than 60 days after the date of the latest signature by doing the following:

    1. Requesting an administrative parentage determination from the county child support enforcement agency in which the child or guardian or legal custodian of the child resides, and

    2. Delivering a written notice to the Ohio Department of Job and Family Services, Office of Child Support, Central Paternity Registry that includes the name of the child, the name of the county child support enforcement agency, and the date the administrative parentage request was made to the county agency.

    3. An order must be issued by the child support enforcement agency determining whether there is a parent and child relationship between the man and the child.

- Both persons who sign this affidavit waive any right to bring a court or administrative action to determine the parentage of this child, other than for purposes of rescinding this acknowledgment.

- After the 60 day period, the only way for either parent to rescind this acknowledgment is to bring a court action to rescind within one year after it has become final (the court action would need to be in compliance with ORC Sections 2151.232, 3111.28 or 3119.961).

- Unless a court order is issued, the mother is the sole residential parent and the legal custodian of the child. However, the natural father has the right to petition a court for an order granting him reasonable visitation and to petition the court for custody of the child. The mother and father will stand equal before the court for these determinations.

- The affidavit cannot be used if another man is legally presumed to be the father other than the man who is signing the affidavit. Legal presumptions of fatherhood include the following: 1) The man and the child's mother were married at the time of the child's birth; 2) The man and the child's mother were married and divorced no more than 300 days before the child's birth; 3) The man has already signed an Acknowledgment of Paternity Affidavit which has been filed with the Ohio Department of Job and Family Services, Office of Child Support and has not become final.

- **Do not erase, cross out, white out, or write over information. If an error is made, the parents should start over on a blank affidavit. All spaces in the child's, mother's and father's sections should be filled out. Type or print legibly in dark ink.**

- Both the natural father and mother of the child are required to sign this affidavit. The affidavit may be signed by both parents at the same time or at different times; however, each parent's signature must be notarized at the time of their signing.

- This affidavit must be sent not later than 10 calendar days after it has been completed, signed and notarized to the Ohio Department of Job and Family Services:

- If a new birth record is required, attach any evidence necessary to complete the new birth record such as the HEA 3029 (Determination of Paternity).

Central Paternity Registry
131 North High Street, Suite 320
Columbus, Ohio 43215
(614) 224-8909 or Toll Free at 1-888-810-6446

JFS 07038 (Rev. 3/2001)
(Formerly DHS 7038)

Please type or print in dark ink

CHILD'S INFORMATION

Name: _____   Sex: ☐ Male   ☐ Female
     (First)   (Middle)   (Last)

Date of Birth: _____ Place of Birth: _____
    (MO/DAY/YR)   (State)   (City)   (County)

Current Residence: _____
    (Full Street Address)   (City)   (State)   (Zip)

If a birth certificate for the child has already been filed, do you now wish to change the child's name? ☐ YES ☐ NO

If "YES", give the child's new name: _____
    (First)   (Middle)   (Last)

MOTHER'S AFFIRMATION *(Name at the time of child's birth)*

Name: _____   Maiden Name: _____
    (First)   (Middle)   (Last)

Address: _____ Phone: (___) _____
    (Full Street Address)   (City)   (County)   (State)   (Zip)   (Area Code) (Number)

Date of Birth: _____ State/Country of Birth: _____ Social Security Number: _____
    (MO/DAY/YR)

SIGNATURE AND NOTARIZATION

State of _____, County of _____, ss. I state under oath or by affirmation, that I have read, or had read to me, all information on both sides of this form; that the information I have supplied for this form is true to the best of my knowledge and belief; that I have received information regarding my legal rights and responsibilites; and that I am the natural mother of the child named on this form and will assume the parental duty of support for the child.

_____
Signature of Mother

Before me appeared the above-named person and signed this affidavit,
under oath or by affirmation, on this _____ day of _____,
in the year _____ .

_____   _____
Signature of Notary Public   (Expiration of Commission)

FATHER'S AFFIRMATION

Name: _____   Race/Ethnic Origin: _____
    (First)   (Middle)   (Last)

Address: _____ Phone: _____
    (Full Street Address)   (City)   (County)   (State)   (Zip)   (Area Code) (Number)

Date of Birth: _____ State/Country of Birth: _____ Social Security Number: _____
    (MO/DAY/YR)

Occupation: _____ Employer : _____ Education: *(Specify highest level 0-12/college 1-4,5+)* _____

SIGNATURE AND NOTARIZATION

State of _____, County of _____, ss. I state under oath or by affirmation, that I have read, or had read to me, all information on both sides of this form; that the information I have supplied for this form is true to the best of my knowledge and belief; that I have received information regarding my legal rights and responsibilities; that I consent to the jurisdiction of the courts of this state; and that I am the natural father of the child named on this form and will assume the parental duty of support for this child.

_____
Signature of Father

Before me appeared the above-named person and signed this affidavit,
under oath or by affirmation, on this _____ day of _____,
in the year _____ .

_____   _____
Signature of Notary Public   (Expiration of Commission)

EBC #	CSEA #	Registrar#	CPR#	ODH File#

Page 2 of 2

§ 22:27 Application for CSEA services, non-public assistance—Form

(Official form, ODJFS 07076, rev. 5-01)

APPLICATION FOR CHILD SUPPORT SERVICES
NON-PUBLIC ASSISTANCE APPLICANT

IMPORTANT: If you are receiving ADC or Medicaid, do **not** complete this application, because you became eligible for child support services when you became eligible to receive ADC or Medicaid.

I the undersigned, _____ request Child Support Services from the _____ County Child Support Enforcement Agency. I understand and agree to the following conditions:

A.   I am a resident of the County in which services are requested.

B.   Recipients of child support services shall cooperate to the best of their ability with the CSEA. *(See attached rights and responsibility information).*

The Child Support Enforcement Agency can assist you in providing the following services:

1.   **Location of Absent Parents.**

     The agency can assist in finding where an absent parent is currently living, in what city, town or state. The applicant can request **"Location Services Only"**, if the sole need is to find the whereabouts of the absent parent.

2.   **Establishment or Modification of Child Support and Medical Support.**

     The CSEA can assist you to obtain an order for support if you are separated, have been deserted or need to establish paternity *(fatherhood)*. The CSEA can also assist you in changing the amount of support orders *(modification)*, and to establish a medical support order.

3.   **Enforcement of Existing Orders.**

     The CSEA can help you collect current and back child support.

4.   **Federal and State Income Tax Refund Offset Submittals for the Collection of Child Support Arrearages.**

     The agency can assist in collecting back support *(arrearages)* by intercepting a non-payor's federal and state income tax refunds on some cases.

5.   **Withholding of Wages and Unearned Income for the Payment of Court Ordered Support.**

     The agency can help you get payroll deductions for current and back child support and can intercept unemployment compensation to collect child support.

6.   **Establishment of Paternity.**

     The agency can obtain an order for the establishment of paternity *(fatherhood)*, if you were not married to the father of the child. An absent parent may request paternity services.

7.   **Collection and Disbursement of Payments.**

     The CSEA can collect the child support for you, and send you a check for the amount of the payments received. Back support collected will be paid to you until all of the back support you are owed is paid.

     If you received ADC in the past and support was assigned to the state, back support collected will be paid to the state after you receive back support owed to you.

8.   **Interstate Collection of Child Support.**

     The agency can assist you in collecting support if the payor is living in another state or in some foreign countries.

C.   The only fee you can be charged for services is a one dollar application fee. Some counties pay this fee for the applicants.

D.   In providing IV-D services, the CSEA and any of its contracted agents (e.g., prosecutors, attorneys, hearing officers, etc.) represent the best interest of the children of the state of Ohio and do not represent any IV-D recipient or the IV-D recipient's personal interest.

APPLICANT INFORMATION *(INFORMATION ABOUT YOU)*	
Name	Date of Birth
Social Security Number (SSN)	Current Marital Status (Check One) ☐ Single ☐ Married ☑ Divorced ☑ Separated ☐ Deserted ☐ Widowed

Type(s) of Service(s) Requested: All services listed _____ Location of absent parent only _____
Other *(please explain)* _____

I understand that the Child Support Agency - within 20 days of receiving this application will contact me by a written notice to inform me if my case has been accepted for child support services (IV-D Services).

Signature of Applicant	Date

JFS 07076 (Rev. 5/2001)
(Formerly DHS 7076)

Applicants Name (Last, First, Middle)			Telephone Number (Home)
Address (Street/Route, P.O. Box)			(Work)
City, State, Zip Code			

INFORMATION ON CHILDREN

	Child 1	Child 2	Child 3	Child 4
a. Name				
b. Sex				
c. SSN				
d. Date of Birth (DOB)				
e. Name(s) of Absent Parent				
f. Has Paternity (Fatherhood) Been Established?				
g. Is There An Order For Support ☐ Yes ☐ No				

ABSENT PARENT INFORMATION OR PARENT ORDERED TO PAY CHILD SUPPORT

	Absent Parent #1	Absent Parent #2	Absent Parent #3
Name			
Address (City, State, Zip Code)			
SSN			
Date of Birth (DOB)			
Name of Employer			
Address of Employer (City, State, Zip Code)			
Amount of Support Ordered (Wk, Bi-Wk, Mo)			
Case Number on Support Order			
Date of Support Order			
Location Where Order Was Issued (City, County, State)			
Military Service Give Date and Branch Entered			
Arrest Record: Give Date and Place of Arrest			
If the absent parent has been on Public Assistance: Give Date and Place			
Give Name and Address of Current Spouse of Absent Parent			

● Have you ever been on public assistance? ☐ Yes ☐ No

When (Date)	Where (City and State)	County

FOR AGENCY USE ONLY

Case Name	Date Requested	Date Mailed or Provided
Case Number	Date Returned or File Date	

§ 22:28 Notice to withhold obligor income/assets—Form

(Official form, JFS 04047, rev. 11-01)

APPENDIX 3-1

ORDER/NOTICE TO WITHHOLD INCOME FOR CHILD AND SPOUSAL SUPPORT
(Ohio Revised Code 3121.037)

State __OHIO__

County _____

Date of Issuance _____

Order Number _____

FIPS Code _____

- Original Order/Notice
- Amended Order/Notice
- Terminate Order/Notice

RE: _____

Employer/Withholder's Federal EIN Number

Employee/Obligor's Name (Last, First, M I)

Employer/Withholder's Name

Employee/Obligor's Social Security Number

Employer/Withholder's Address

Employee/Obligor's Case Number

Worker's Compensation Claim Number

Employee/Obligor's Date of Birth

Financial Institution Account Number
Checking   •   Savings

Custodial Parent's Name (Last, First, MI)

Child(ren)'s Name(s):   DOB

Child(ren)'s Name(s):   DOB

ORDER INFORMATION: This is an Order/Notice to Withhold Income for Support based upon an order from _____. By law, you are required to deduct these amounts from the above-named employee's/obligor's income until further notice

❑ If checked, you are required to enroll the child(ren) identified above in any health insurance coverage available through the employee's/obligor's employment and to inform the child support enforcement agency of any lapses in coverage.

$_____ per _____ in current support

$_____ per _____ in past-due support   Arrears 12 weeks or greater? ❑ yes ❑ no

$_____ per _____ in medical support

$_____ per _____ Subtotal (for Ohio Bureau of Employment Services Withholding)

$_____ per _____ in other (specify)_____

for a Total of $_____ per _____ to be forwarded to the payee below.

You do not have to vary your pay cycle to be in compliance with the support order. If your pay cycle does not match the ordered support payment cycle, use the following to determine how much to withhold:

1. If pay cycle is weekly, multiply the monthly amount by 12 and divide by 52.
2. If pay cycle is every other week, multiply monthly amount by 12 and divide by 26.
3. If pay cycle is twice monthly, multiply monthly amount by 12 and divide by 24.

REMITTANCE INFORMATION:

An employer must begin withholding no later than the first pay period occurring __14__ business days after the date of this Order/Notice. Send payment immediately or within __7__ business days of the paydate/date of withholding. Ohio Law: Financial institutions are required to send the amount deducted no later than fourteen business days following the date this notice was mailed and are required to continue the deduction thereafter IMMEDIATELY, but not later than seven (7) business days after the payment or deduction is made. You are entitled to deduct a fee to defray the cost of withholding. Refer to the laws governing the work state of the employee for the allowable amount. Ohio Law: A withholder may deduct a fee of $2.00 or 1% of amount to be withheld, whichever is greater (including an employer paying worker's compensation). A financial institution may deduct a fee of $5.00 or a fee not to exceed the lowest rate, if any, charged for a similar debt transaction, whichever is less of the amount specified to be withheld.

The total withheld amount, including your fee, cannot exceed 65% of the employee's/obligor's aggregate disposable weekly earnings. For the purpose of the limitation on withholding, the following information is needed (see #9 on back for more information).

JFS 04047 (Rev. 11/2001)

When remitting payment, provide the Paydate/Date of Withholding, Obligor Name, Social Security Number, Case Number and the Order number. When remitting for more than one obligor, include the amount of payment for each person.

If you choose to remit by EFT/EDI, contact Ohio Child Support Payment Central to obtain bank file format. (See Page 4 of this document)

Make it payable to: Ohio Child Support Payment Central (CSPC)

Send check to: PO Box 182394

                              Columbus, OH 43218

Authorized by: (Ohio does not require a hand written signature)

If you or your employee/obligor have questions about the provisions of the notice or other communication, contact:_____of _____County Child Support Enforcement Agency by mail at _____:_____, by telephone at _____ or by FAX at _____or by internet at _____.

ADDITIONAL INFORMATION TO EMPLOYERS AND OTHER WITHHOLDERS

❏   If checked you are required to provide a copy of this form to your employee.

1.   Priority: Withholding under this Order/Notice has priority over any other legal process under State law against the same income. Federal tax levies in effect before receipt of this order have priority. If there are Federal tax levies in effect please contact the requesting agency listed below.

2.   Combining Payments: You can combine withheld amounts from more than one employee/obligor's income in a single payment to each agency requesting withholding. You must, however, separately identify the portion of the single payment that is attributable to each employee/obligor.

3.*   Reporting the Paydate/Date of Withholding: You must report the paydate/date of withholding when sending the payment. The paydate/date of withholding is the date on which amount was withheld from the employee's wages. You must comply with the law of the state of employee's/obligor's principal place of employment with respect to the time periods within which you must implement the withholding order and forward the child support payments.

4.*   Employee/Obligor with Multiple Support Withholdings: If there is more than one Order/Notice to Withhold Income for Child Support against this employee/obligor and you are unable to honor all support Order/Notices due to Federal or State withholding limits, you must follow the law of the state of employee's/obligor's principal place of employment. You must honor all Order/Notices to the greatest extent possible. (See #9 below)

Ohio Law: Payors shall prorate the amount due when two or more support orders are received for this obligor, which when combined exceed the limits of the Consumer Credit Protection Act. Multiply current support by a fraction with a numerator that represents the available amount of income and a denominator that represents the total amount designated for payment in the notices.

Payors shall allocate to each notice an amount for current support equal to the amount designated in that notice as current support multiplied by a fraction in which the numerator is the amount of personal earnings, payments, pensions, annuities, allowances, benefits, other sources of income, or savings available for withholding and the denominator is the total amount designated in all of the notices as current support.

If the total of the amounts designated in the notices as current support does not exceed the amount available for withholding under the Consumer Credit Protection Act, the payor shall pay all of the amounts designated as current support in the notices and shall allocate to each notice an amount for past-due support equal to the amount designated in that notice as past-due support multiplied by a fraction in which the numerator is the amount of income remaining available for withholding after the payment of current support and the denominator is the total amount designated in all of the notices as past-due support.

5. Termination Notification: You must promptly notify the payee when the employee/obligor is no longer working for you. Please provide the information requested and return a copy of this order/notice to the agency identified on page 2 of this form.

EMPLOYEE'S/OBLIGOR'S NAME: _____ SSN: _____

EMPLOYEE'S CASE IDENTIFIER: _____ DATE OF SEPARATION: _____

LAST KNOWN HOME ADDRESS: _____

NEW EMPLOYER'S ADDRESS: _____

Ohio Law: Payors shall notify this county child support enforcement agency in writing within ten business days after the date of any situation that occurs in which the payor ceases to pay sufficient income to satisfy the ordered support, including termination of employment, layoff of the obligor from employment, any leave of absence of the obligor without pay, termination of workers' compensation or benefits, or termination of any pension, annuity, allowance, or retirement benefit.

Payors shall notify this county child support enforcement agency in writing of any benefits other than personal earnings due this obligor due to: termination of employment, worker's compensation benefits, annuity, allowance other benefit, income, an account from which a deduction is made; the receipt of unemployment compensation, receipt of workers' compensation, severance pay, sick leave, lump sum payment of retirement benefits or contributions, bonus, profit sharing, or distributions; the opening of any new account at this or another known institution. In addition to the above required information, include the new employer's name, the social security number, date of birth and telephone number of the obligor.

Financial institutions must promptly notify this county child support enforcement agency, in writing, within ten days after the date of any termination of the account from which the deduction is being made and notify the agency, in writing, of the opening of a new account at that financial institution, the account number of the new account, the name of any other known financial institutions in which the obligor has any accounts and the numbers of those accounts. The financial institution must include in all notices the obligor's last known mailing address, last known residence address, and social security number.

6. Lump Sum Payments: You may be required to report and withhold from lump sum payments such as bonuses, commissions, or severance pay. If you have any questions about lump sum payments, contact the person or authority below.
Ohio Law: No later than the earlier of 45 days before the lump sum payment is to be made, or the date on which that determination is made, (if the obligor's right to the payment is determined less than 45 days before it is to be made), the payor shall notify the county Child Support Enforcement Agency of any lump sum payment of any kind of $150 or more that is to be paid to the obligor, hold each lump sum payment of $150 or more for 30 days after the date on which it would otherwise be paid to the obligor, and on order of the court or CSEA, pay all or a specified amount of the lump sum to the Office of Child Support.

7. Liability: If you fail to withhold income as the Order/Notice directs, you are liable for both the accumulated amount you should have withheld from the employee/obligor's income and any other penalties set by State law.
Ohio Law: If the payor fails to comply with this notice, the county child support enforcement agency will bring an action requesting the court to issue an order requiring the compliance pursuant to Ohio Revised Code section 3121.37 or 3121.371. The payor may be found guilty of contempt of court.

8. Anti-discrimination: You are subject to a fine determined under State law for discharging an employee/obligor from employment, refusing to employ, or taking disciplinary action against any employee/obligor because of a child support withholding.

9.   Withholding Limits: You may not withhold more than the lesser of: 1) the amounts allowed by the Federal Consumer Credit Protection Act (15 U.S.C. § 1673(b)); or 2) the amounts allowed by the State of the employee's obligor's principal place of employment. The Federal limit applies to the aggregate disposable weekly earnings (ADWE). ADWE is the net income left after making mandatory deductions such as: State, Federal, Local taxes; Social Security taxes; and Medicare taxes.

According to the federal Consumer Credit Protection Act (CCPA), the amount withheld is not allowed to exceed:

- 50 % of the noncustodial parent's disposable earnings if he/she is supporting a spouse, dependent child or both, other than a party in the support order.
- 60% of the noncustodial parent's disposable earnings if he/she is not supporting someone else.
- The Act also allows an additional 5% to be withheld above the maximum amount permitted if the noncustodial parent is twelve (12) or more weeks in arrearage.

Ohio Law: Financial institutions and unemployment compensation benefits are not subject to the CCPA. No more than 50% of the noncustodial parent's weekly unemployment benefit amount may be deducted.

*Note: If you or your agent are served with a copy of this order in the state that issued the order, you are to follow the law of the state that issued this order with respect to these items. This notice is final and enforceable by the court.

Child Support Payment Central

Ohio now offers a centralized source for making child support payments on behalf of your employees. You can make one payment to one central source.

With Ohio Child Support Payment Central (CSPC), you can use CSPC-Direct (electronic data interchange), or CSPC-Through Your Financial Institution (electronic funds transfer).

Call 1-888-965-2676 for your free Employer Kit.

§ 22:29 Addendum withholding notice to parties to a support order—Form

(Official form, JFS 04048, rev. 11-01)

Appendix 3-2
**ADDENDUM WITHHOLDING NOTICE
TO PARTIES TO A SUPPORT ORDER**

Obligee Name	Court or Administrative Order Number
Social Security Number	Case Number
Obligor Name	County
Social Security Number	Date

WHY YOU WERE GIVEN THIS NOTICE

This addendum notice is provided to the parties to the child/spousal support/withholding order in accordance with Ohio Revised Code sections 3121.036 and 3121.99.

DUTIES OF SUPPORT OBLIGOR BEFORE SUPPORT WITHHOLDING STARTS

As obligor, you are responsible for payment of support between the effective date of the support order and the date income withholding is initiated. Upon commencement of employment, the obligor may request the CSEA cancel any previous notices, if applicable, and to issue a notice requiring the withholding of an amount from his personal earnings for support.

WHEN THE SUPPORT OBLIGOR MUST NOTIFY THE CHILD SUPPORT ENFORCEMENT AGENCY

The notification must be in writing -- please use the back of this form if you want.

1. Of any change in the obligor's income source, and if the availability of any other sources of income or assets that can be the subject of any withholding or deduction.

2. A description of the nature of any new employment or income source, the name and business address and telephone number of the employer.

3. Of any change in the status of the account from which the amount of support is being deducted or the opening of a new account with any financial institution, of his commencement of employment, including self employment, or the availablity of any other sources of income that can be the subject of any withholding or deduction requirement.

4. The nature of any new employment or income source and the name, business address, and telephone number of the new employer or income source.

5. Any other information reasonably required by the court or agency.

WHEN THE TIME COMES FOR THE SUPPORT ORDER OR WITHHOLDING TO STOP

Ohio Revised Code sections 3119.94 and 3119.87 require the obligee to notify the child support enforcement agency of any reason for which support and withholding should terminate. The obligor is permitted to make this notification.

The reverse side of this form can be used to provide the required notices. Section A contains information that the obligor must provide. Section B contains information that the obligee must provide.

JFS 04048 (Rev. 11/2001)

Appendix 3-2

The Obligor shall check the appropriate boxes in Section A and fill in the needed information when any of these events occur. Section B may also be completed at Obligor's discretion. The custodial parent is obligated to complete Section B. Documents are to be mailed to:_____
COUNTY CHILD SUPPORT ENFORCEMENT AGENCY,_____. A willful failure by either party to notify is contempt of court. Contempt can be accompanied by a fine of not more than fifty dollars for a first offense, not more than one hundred dollars for a second offense, and not more than five hundred dollars for each subsequent offense.

NOTIFICATION

TO: _____ CSEA   DATE:_____

SECTION A - OBLIGOR NOTIFICATION

[ ]   I have terminated my employment effective _____, 20__. [ ] I will receive unemployment benefits of _____ per ____

[ ]   I will be employed as a _____ ,at (Name of new employer and Payroll Address and telephone number) _____
My new rate of pay will be $_____per_____. I am scheduled to receive [ ] 12 [ ] 24 [ ] 26 [ ] 52 pay checks per year.

[ ]   I will become self-employed effective _____,20__. The nature of said business is _____.
Said business shall have its business account at (Financial
Institution)_____ , (Address)_____
(City, State, Zip)_____ in the name of _____.
Account Number_____

[ ]   I am drawing [ ] sick leave [ ] disability benefits in the amount of $_____per _____starting on _____ from (Institution)
_____ (Address) _____(City, State, Zip)_____

[ ]   My Workers' Compensation will [ ] commence [ ] terminate [ ] increase [ ] decrease effective _____, 20__ to
$_____per _____ Claim No. _____

[ ]   I have opened a new Financial Institution Account in the name of:_____ Account
Number _____at (Name of Institution) _____ (Address)
_____ (City, State, Zip)_____.

[ ]   I am retiring effective _____, 20___ and will receive $_____ per _____ from
(Source) _____.
(Address)_____.

[ ]   I have acquired or expect to receive one or more of the following:

[ ]   Lump sum payment in excess of $150 as a result of:_____
from_____ whose address is _____.

[ ]   Real Property Located at:
_____

[ ]   Other property with a value in excess of $1000 described as
follows:_____
_____

[ ]   Other income or assets not otherwise included on this form such as lottery proceeds, inheritances, insurance settlements, tax refunds, etc. described as follows:_____.

OBLIGOR'S SIGNATURE_____

SECTION B - OBLIGEE NOTIFICATION

[ ]   Child Support for _____ born, _____, 20___; should stop because this child:

[ ]   graduated from high school on _____, 20____ [ ] no longer resides with me as of _____, 20__

[ ]   married on _____, 20___ [ ] enlisted in the Armed Forces on _____, 20__

[ ]   any other reason that child support should not be paid: Please describe:
_____
as of_____, 20__

[ ]   Alimony should stop on_____, 20__, Due to: [ ] Remarriage [ ] Death [ ] Full Time Employment [ ] Other, please
describe_____
_____

OBLIGEE'S SIGNATURE _____

§ 22:30   Advance notice to obligor of default and potential action—Form

(Official form, JFS 04049, rev. 10-01)

**ADVANCE NOTICE TO OBLIGOR
OF DEFAULT AND POTENTIAL ACTION**
(Revised Code 3123.03 through 3123.062)

Obligor Name: Court or Administrative Number:

Social Security Number: Case Number:

Mailing Date: County/Court or CSEA Official:
                                   Telephone:

PURPOSE OF THIS NOTICE

As determined by the court or child support enforcement agency (CSEA) of xxxxxxx County, you are determined to be in default of a support order. According to Section 3123.01 of the Ohio Revised Code, default is failure to pay an amount equal to or greater than one month's support. As of xxxxxxxxxxxxx, the amount of arrears you owe is xxxxxxxxxxxx. Subject to hearing rights described in this notice, a payment of xxxxxxx per month may be initiated to satisfy the arrears. This amount is in addition to the current support of xxxxxx per month.

An income withholding or deduction requirement may be initiated or increased (by at least 20% of current support) in order to satisfy an arrearage, as well as current support. Withholding may be imposed against income, including but not limited to, personal earnings, workers' compensation benefits, unemployment benefits, pensions, government benefits, insurance proceeds, lottery prize awards, lump sum payments and any other payments in money. A withholding or deduction notice will apply to all current and subsequent payors and financial institutions and will not be discontinued solely because the obligor pays any arrearage.

- Withholding may be imposed on funds on deposit in a financial institution.

- A lien may be imposed on your real and personal property.

- Your arrearage will be reported to a credit reporting agency. This may affect your credit rating.

- Your support case may be referred to a collection agency.

- An access restriction and a withdrawal directive may be placed on any account held by you at any financial institution.

- Any professional license you hold may be proposed for suspension upon exhaustion of all rights to contest the advance notice. This enforcement method may also be used if you fail to comply with a warrant or subpoena issued by the court or CSEA with respect to a proceeding to enforce a child support order.

- Your driver's license may be suspended or not renewed by the Bureau of Motor Vehicles upon exhaustion of all rights to contest the advance notice. This enforcement method may also be used if you fail to comply with a warrant or subpoena issued by the court or CSEA with respect to a proceeding to enforce a child support order.

- You may be refused a recreational license (e.g., hunting, fishing, trapping, etc.) or any recreational license you hold may be suspended upon exhaustion of all rights to contest the advance notice. This enforcement method may also be used if you fail to comply with a warrant or subpoena issued by the court or CSEA with respect to a proceeding to enforce a child support order.

YOUR RIGHT TO AN ADMINISTRATIVE HEARING

You are entitled to request an administrative hearing no later than 7 days after the date of this notice to determine if a mistake of fact was made in the notice. "Mistake of Fact" means an error in the amount of current or overdue support or in the identity of the alleged absent parent. The last page of this form is used to request an administrative hearing.

Upon exhaustion of all rights to contest withholding or deduction on the basis of a mistake of fact and no later than the expiration of 45 days after the issuance of this advance notice, the court or CSEA will issue one or more notices requiring withholding or deduction of wages or assets of the obligor, or the court shall issue one or more court orders imposing other appropriate requirements. The notice and court orders issued under Chapter 3121 of the Ohio Revised Code are final and are enforceable by the court.

ADMINISTRATIVE HEARING

If you request a hearing regarding this notice, the child support enforcement agency (CSEA) shall conduct an administrative hearing no later than 10 days after the date on which you file the request for the hearing. The agency will send you and the obligee written notice of the date, time, place, and purpose of the hearing at least 5 days before it is conducted. The notice to the obligor and obligee also will indicate that the obligor may present testimony and evidence at the hearing only in regard to the issue of whether a mistake of fact was made in the advance notice.

At the hearing, the CSEA shall determine whether a mistake of fact was made in the advance notice. If it determines that a mistake of fact was made, the CSEA shall determine the provisions that should be changed and included in a corrected notice and shall correct the advance notice accordingly. The CSEA shall send its determination to the obligor.

COURT HEARING

If you detect a mistake of fact in the corrected advance notice, you are entitled to file a written motion for a court hearing to determine whether a mistake of fact still exists no later than 7 days after the date of the CSEA determination.

To determine if a mistake of fact still exists in the advance notice or the corrected advance notice, the court will hold a hearing on the request as soon as possible, but no later than 10 days after the request is filed. If you request a court hearing, no later than 5 days before the date on which the court hearing is to be held, the court will send you and the obligee written notice by ordinary mail of the date, time, place, and purpose of the court hearing. The hearing will be limited to a determination of whether there is a mistake of fact in the advance notice or the corrected advance notice.

If, at a hearing conducted, the court detects a mistake of fact in the advance notice or the corrected advance notice, it will immediately correct the notice.

Request for an Administrative Mistake of Fact Hearing

•   I am requesting that the CSEA conduct an Administrative Mistake of Fact Hearing.

Your Name	Order Number
Street Address	Name of Obligor
City, State and Zip Code	CSEA Case Number
Your Signature	Date Mailed

This document must be received by the CSEA within 7 days of the mailing date on the first page.

Return this document to:
xxxxxxxxxxxxxxx County CSEA
xxxxxxxxxxxxxxxxxxxxxxxxxxx
xxxxxxxxxxxxxxxxxxxxxxxxxxx

JFS 04049
(Rev. 10/2001)

Chapter 23

Interstate and Foreign Support Practice

by Professor Joanne C. Brant and Professor James Leonard[*]

KeyCite®: Cases and other legal materials listed in KeyCite Scope can be researched through West Group's KeyCite service on Westlaw®. Use KeyCite to check citations for form, parallel references, prior and later history, and comprehensive citator information, including citations to other decisions and secondary materials.

---

[*]The authors would like to thank Kim Kislig for research assistance.

§ 23:1　Interstate support practice—In general

Interstate cases constitute a substantial portion of all support cases in the United States. A report by the U.S. Commission on Interstate Child Support indicated that interstate cases account for 30% of all child support cases nationwide.[1] Payment experience in interstate child support cases has been abysmal; in spite of making up one third of the total caseload, interstate cases account for only 10% of total payments. Even children with support orders in place fare poorly. While the percentage of mothers with support orders is approximately the same for intrastate and interstate cases, the father's state of residence has a significant effect on collection rates. The Commission's research indicated that mothers who know where the father lives in another state collect 60% of expected payments. Mothers who do not know the whereabouts of the father receive only 37%. These figures contrast with the 70% collection rate for intrastate cases with support orders.[2] A study by the University of Michigan indicated that 12% of separated parents live in different states within one year of divorce, 25% after three years, and 40% after eight years.[3] Interstate cases, therefore, have become a significant and challenging part of domestic relations practice.

Successful prosecution or defense of an interstate support case in one sense is not different from an intrastate case. Resolution will turn on three issues: (1) establishing parentage when necessary; (2) obtaining an award; and (3) enforcement. Attorneys handling interstate cases, however, face unique difficulties of both a practical and legal nature. Among the practical problems are the difficulty of locating an absent spouse or parent and the expense of litigating in a distant forum. On a legal plane, the most significant difficulties are acquiring personal jurisdiction over a non-resident obligor and securing support awards that are entitled to full faith and credit in other jurisdictions. Since the 1950s, both federal and state governments have enacted a series of laws attempting to lighten the practical and legal burdens of interstate support litigation. The most important are the original and revised versions of the Uniform Reciprocal Enforcement of Support Act (URESA and RURESA), the Uniform Interstate Family Support Act (UIFSA), the Full Faith and Credit for Child Support Orders Act, and several provisions of Title IV-D of the Social Security Act. These measures have been partially successful in easing the difficulties of interstate support litigation.

§ 23:2 Impediments to interstate support actions—Personal jurisdiction—In general

Counsel must be certain that any proceeding against an out-of-state obligor meets constitutional due process requirements as well as the provisions of the Ohio Civil Rules. Personal jurisdiction is, of course, a necessary component of any civil action: any judgment not supported by

---

[Section 23:1]

[1]U.S. Commission on Interstate Child Support, Supporting Our Children: A Blueprint for Reform, at 3 (1992) (hereinafter cited as Blueprint for Reform).

[2]For a detailed discussion of the shortcomings of interstate support actions, see Blueprint for Reform 1-30.

[3]Child Support Reference Manual (Child Support Project, Center on Children and the Law, American Bar Association) at II-2 (1990).

jurisdiction over the defendant is void and may be challenged later.[1] It is difficult, however, to overstate the importance of meeting personal jurisdiction requirements in any support action with an interstate dimension. Interstate support practice consists in large measure of enforcing a judgment entered by a court of the obligee's state of residence in another forum, usually the obligor's home state. Since judgments entered without personal jurisdiction are not entitled to full faith and credit in sister states,[2] counsel must anticipate such challenges by careful attention to jurisdictional requirements at every step.

§ 23:3   Impediments to interstate support actions—Personal jurisdiction—Constitutional requirements

The United States Supreme Court has applied federal constitutional standards to family law matters in a way that often makes it difficult to secure personal jurisdiction over an absent party or to enforce a valid order in other states. It is a bedrock requirement of the Due Process Clause of the Fourteenth Amendment that a court may not impose a personal obligation, including a support order,[1] unless it has personal jurisdiction over the defendant.[2] Historically, plaintiffs have achieved personal jurisdiction on the basis of personal service on the defendant within the forum,[3] the consent of a defendant by entering a general appearance or otherwise failing to raise an objection,[4] or the defendant's domicile[5] in the forum, in spite of his or her current absence. After the U.S. Supreme Court's decision in *International Shoe*,[6] courts were permitted to exercise personal jurisdiction over non-resident defendants so long as the latter had "certain minimum contacts" with the forum such that requiring a defense in that forum does not offend "traditional notions of fair play and substantial justice."[7]

Subsequent decisions by the Court have attempted to flesh out the

---

[Section 23:2]

[1]See § 23:3, Impediments to interstate support actions—Personal jurisdiction—Constitutional requirements; see generally Jurisdiction and Venue Ch 27.

[2]See § 23:8, Impediments to interstate support actions—Full faith and credit.

[Section 23:3]

[1]Kulko v. Superior Court of California In and For City and County of San Francisco, 436 U.S. 84, 98 S. Ct. 1690, 56 L. Ed. 2d 132 (1978).

[2]Pennoyer v. Neff, 95 U.S. 714, 24 L. Ed. 565 (1877).

[3]Burnham v. Superior Court of California, County of Marin, 495 U.S. 604, 110 S. Ct. 2105, 109 L. Ed. 2d 631 (1990).

[4]See, e.g., Civ. R. 12(H); Kennecorp Mtge. Brokers, Inc. v. Country Club Convalescent Hosp., Inc., 66 Ohio St. 3d 173, 1993-Ohio-203, 610 N.E.2d 987 (1993) (forum selection clause).

[5]Milliken v. Meyer, 311 U.S. 457, 61 S. Ct. 339, 85 L. Ed. 278, 132 A.L.R. 1357 (1940).

[6]International Shoe Co. v. State of Wash., Office of Unemployment Compensation and Placement, 326 U.S. 310, 66 S. Ct. 154, 90 L. Ed. 95, 161 A.L.R. 1057 (1945).

[7]International Shoe Co. v. State of Wash., Office of Unemployment Compensation and Placement, 326 U.S. 310, 316, 66 S. Ct. 154, 90 L. Ed. 95, 161 A.L.R. 1057 (1945); see also Depaulitte v. Depaulitte, 138 Ohio App. 3d 780, 742 N.E.2d 659 (2d Dist.

minimum contacts standard of *International Shoe*. While these cases cannot be reduced to a formula, certain general guidelines have emerged. First, the minimum contacts standard is a defendant-oriented scheme. Analysis is focused on whether it is fair to force the defendant to appear and defend; the fact that the forum is a more convenient place to litigate an action will not of itself confer personal jurisdiction.[8] Second, unilateral activity by a plaintiff cannot create personal jurisdiction. Rather, the defendant must initiate contact with the forum, personally avail himself or herself of the privileges of conducting activities in the state, and invoke the benefits and protections of the forum's laws.[9] Foreseeability is a factor in minimum contacts jurisprudence. However, the Court has held that personal jurisdiction is "foreseeable" when the defendant's contacts with the forum are such that he or she should reasonably anticipate being haled into court there.[10] Third, although purposeful contact by the defendant is necessary, it is not alone sufficient. Once over the purposeful contact hurdle, a court must then consider other factors which bear on the fairness of requiring defendant to appear in the forum.[11] Among these factors are the burden on the defendant, the forum's interest in the claim, the plaintiff's interest in convenient and effective relief, the interstate judicial system's interest in efficient resolution of controversies, and the shared interest of the states in furthering social policies.[12]

In *Kulko v. Superior Court*,[13] the Supreme Court considered the issue of personal jurisdiction in an interstate support claim. Husband and wife had been married in California but remained there only three days. During the marriage, the couple was domiciled in New York. After the Kulkos separated, the wife moved to California while the two children remained in New York. One year later, the husband consented to the daughter's relocation to California. The son followed three years later, apparently without the father's consent. The Court held that California did not have personal jurisdiction over the father in an action to modify child support. The Court reasoned that California had not met the *International Shoe* standard of sufficient minimal contact to justify asserting personal jurisdiction over a non-resident. It held that the father's

---

Montgomery County 2000), appeal allowed, 89 Ohio St. 3d 1429, 729 N.E.2d 1199 (2000) and appeal dismissed as improvidently allowed, 91 Ohio St. 3d 1201, 2001-Ohio-229, 740 N.E.2d 1103 (2001) (*International Shoe* applies in domestic relations contexts).

[8]Kulko v. Superior Court of California In and For City and County of San Francisco, 436 U.S. 84, 98 S. Ct. 1690, 56 L. Ed. 2d 132 (1978).

[9]Hanson v. Denckla, 357 U.S. 235, 78 S. Ct. 1228, 2 L. Ed. 2d 1283 (1958); Burger King Corp. v. Rudzewicz, 471 U.S. 462, 105 S. Ct. 2174, 85 L. Ed. 2d 528 (1985).

[10]World-Wide Volkswagen Corp. v. Woodson, 444 U.S. 286, 100 S. Ct. 559, 62 L. Ed. 2d 490 (1980).

[11]Burger King Corp. v. Rudzewicz, 471 U.S. 462, 105 S. Ct. 2174, 85 L. Ed. 2d 528 (1985).

[12]Burger King Corp. v. Rudzewicz, 471 U.S. 462, 105 S. Ct. 2174, 85 L. Ed. 2d 528 (1985).

[13]Kulko v. Superior Court of California In and For City and County of San Francisco, 436 U.S. 84, 94, 98 S. Ct. 1690, 56 L. Ed. 2d 132 (1978).

contacts with the forum were brief and unrelated to child support, and that by permitting a child to relocate to another forum, the father had not "purposefully availed" himself of the benefits of California. The Court was also influenced by the availability to the mother of a URESA proceeding.

Kulko has been difficult to apply in practice.[14] At a minimum, it means that the mere presence of a spouse or a child in the forum does not confer personal jurisdiction over a non-resident. Lower courts have reached inconsistent results on what additional contacts by the defendant are constitutionally necessary to confer personal jurisdiction. Most decisions agree that maintaining a marital domicile in the forum is sufficient contact even if the defendant has departed;[15] however, the mere fact that parties were married in a state will not confer personal jurisdiction.[16] There is disagreement in this situation: the parties have a marital domicile in the forum, then move away, and later one party moves back.[17] Likewise, courts have reacted differently to the argument that the failure of a non-resident defendant to support a resident is a tortious act with a sufficient effect within the forum to constitute sufficient minimum contacts.[18] Some courts hold that an act of intercourse which may have resulted in the conception of a child within the forum creates sufficient contacts to justify personal jurisdiction over a child support action.[19]

§ 23:4   Impediments to interstate support actions—Personal jurisdiction—Ohio Civil Rules—Transient service

In addition to meeting federal constitutional standards, actions against out-of-state obligors must meet the standards set by the Ohio Civil Rules. Personal service within Ohio under Civ. R. 4.1(B) is sufficient to confer personal jurisdiction over an out-of-state obligor even if

---

[14]For a more detailed discussion of constitutional personal jurisdiction requirements, see Jurisdiction and Venue Ch 27.

[15]See, e.g., Fraiberg v. Cuyahoga Cty. Court of Common Pleas, Domestic Relations Div., 76 Ohio St. 3d 374, 1996-Ohio-384, 667 N.E.2d 1189 (1996); Taylor v. Head, 323 Md. 546, 594 A.2d 115 (1991); In re the Marriage of Lontos, 89 Cal. App. 3d 61, 152 Cal. Rptr. 271 (4th Dist. 1979); Civ. R. 4.3(A)(8).

[16]Kulko v. Superior Court of California In and For City and County of San Francisco, 436 U.S. 84, 98 S. Ct. 1690, 56 L. Ed. 2d 132 (1978).

[17]Compare McGlothen v. Superior Court, 121 Cal. App. 3d 106, 175 Cal. Rptr. 129 (1st Dist. 1981) (effects and benefits of non-support constitute minimum contact with former marital domicile) with Hoerler v. Superior Court, 85 Cal. App. 3d 533, 149 Cal. Rptr. 569 (1st Dist. 1978) (insufficient contacts with former marital domicile).

[18]Compare In re the Marriage of Lontos, 89 Cal. App. 3d 61, 152 Cal. Rptr. 271 (4th Dist. 1979) (effect of non-support sufficient contact) with Matter of Marriage of Peck, 82 Wash. App. 809, 920 P.2d 236 (Div. 2 1996) (failure to support insufficient contact); State ex rel. Stone v. Court of Common Pleas of Cuyahoga County, Juvenile Div., 14 Ohio St. 3d 32, 470 N.E.2d 899 (1984) (failure to support is insufficient conduct or contact where non-resident defendant has never been in Ohio).

[19]RC 3111.06(B); see, e.g., Lake v. Butcher, 37 Wash. App. 228, 679 P.2d 409 (Div. 1 1984); County of Humboldt v. Harris, 206 Cal. App. 3d 857, 254 Cal. Rptr. 49 (1st Dist. 1988).

the defendant does not meet the minimum contact standards of *International Shoe*.[1] In *Lonigro v. Lonigro*,[2] the Second District concluded that transient service failed to meet the fairness standard of *International Shoe*. Subsequently, however, the U.S. Supreme Court's decision in *Burnham v. Superior Court*[3] found that transient service did not violate due process. In *Burnham*, the Court validated personal jurisdiction by service within the territory of the forum. Husband was a New Jersey resident while wife and children were residents of California. Husband was served in California while he was there both on business and to visit the children. The Court unanimously approved of transient service on these facts although the Court was divided on the rationale for the result. One group of four Justices felt that territorial sovereignty permitted transient service[4] while another four Justices contended that under *International Shoe* a defendant should normally expect to be served while present in the forum.[5] Counsel representing out-of-state obligors should be aware that a client may expose himself or herself to personal jurisdiction if present in the forum for any reason, including visitation with children.

§ 23:5 Impediments to interstate support actions—Personal jurisdiction—Ohio Civil Rules—Long-arm provisions

Plaintiffs may also find a jurisdictional basis under the long-arm provisions of Civ. R. 4.3. Certain provisions of Civ. R. 4.3 are pertinent to support actions with interstate dimensions:

(1) "Transacting any business in this state."[1]

(2) "Causing tortious injury by an act or omission in this state, including, but not limited to, actions arising out of the ownership, operation, or use of a motor vehicle or aircraft in this state."[2]

(3) "Causing tortious injury in this state to any person by an act outside this state committed with the purpose of injuring persons, when [the defendant] might reasonably have expected

---

[Section 23:4]

[1]See § 23:3, Impediments to interstate support actions—Personal jurisdiction—Constitutional requirements.

[2]Lonigro v. Lonigro, 1988 WL 79315 (Ohio Ct. App. 2d Dist. Montgomery County 1988).

[3]Burnham v. Superior Court of California, County of Marin, 495 U.S. 604, 110 S. Ct. 2105, 109 L. Ed. 2d 631 (1990).

[4]Burnham v. Superior Court of California, County of Marin, 495 U.S. 604, 110 S. Ct. 2105, 109 L. Ed. 2d 631 (1990) (opinion of Scalia, J.).

[5]Burnham v. Superior Court of California, County of Marin, 495 U.S. 604, 110 S. Ct. 2105, 109 L. Ed. 2d 631 (1990) (opinion of Brennan, J.).

[Section 23:5]

[1]Civ. R. 4.3(A)(1); see also RC 2307.382(A)(1).

[2]Civ. R. 4.3(A)(3); see also RC 2307.382(A)(3).

that some person would be injured by the act in this state."[3]

(4) "Living in the marital relationship within this state notwith-standing subsequent departure from this state, as to all obliga-tions arising for spousal support, custody, child support, or property settlement, if the other party to the marital relation-ship continues to reside in this state."[4]

Support actions involving married couples are likely to meet the rather accommodating standard of Civ. R. 4.3(A)(8) so long as the parties lived as man and wife in Ohio at some point and one is now present in the state. In *Fraiberg v. Cuyahoga County Court of Common Pleas*,[5] the Ohio Supreme Court considered the case of a couple who had been mar-ried in Ohio and lived there for 30 years but then became Florida domiciliaries. The couple later returned to Ohio for brief stays followed by the husband's return to Florida. Rejecting the husband's argument that Civ. R. 4.3(A)(8) required both parties to be domiciled in Ohio at the time of the divorce, the *Fraiberg* Court held that the couple's brief stays in Ohio constituted "living in the marital relationship in Ohio" and that it was not necessary for the parties to establish a marital domi-cile to meet the requirements of the Rule. The Court reasoned that the couple's birth, marriage, raising a family, long period of residence plus ownership of a business in Ohio met this standard.

Fraiberg represents a sound policy of preventing parties from defeat-ing jurisdiction under Civ. R. 4.3(A)(8) by relocating to another state before an action is commenced. The decision, however, offers no guid-ance beyond the facts of the case as to what constitutes living in a mar-ital relationship. In *Depaulitte v. Depaulitte*,[6] the Second District declined to extend the *Fraiberg* rule to a husband whose contacts with the forum were limited to visiting Ohio with his wife to search for a new residence and communication with his wife's Ohio attorney. Common sense indicates that such limited contacts do not amount to living in a marital relation in Ohio. A more generous interpretation of Civ. R. 4.3(A)(8), moreover, might have clashed with the minimum contacts requirement of *International Shoe*.

Finding a jurisdictional basis becomes more difficult if the parties have never lived in a marital relationship in Ohio. Counsel for the obligee must attempt to characterize the obligor's conduct as "transact-ing . . . business" or "[c]ausing tortious injury" to fit the other relevant subsections of Civ. R. 4.3. Lower courts have reached inconsistent conclu-sions when plaintiffs have proceeded on these theories. They are divided on the proposition that contact with a child or other person in Ohio is

---

[3]Civ. R. 4.3(A)(9); see also RC 2307.382(A)(6).

[4]Civ. R. 4.3(A)(8).

[5]Fraiberg v. Cuyahoga Cty. Court of Common Pleas, Domestic Relations Div., 76 Ohio St. 3d 374, 378, 1996-Ohio-384, 667 N.E.2d 1189 (1996).

[6]Depaulitte v. Depaulitte, 138 Ohio App. 3d 780, 742 N.E.2d 659 (2d Dist. Montgomery County 2000), appeal allowed, 89 Ohio St. 3d 1429, 729 N.E.2d 1199 (2000) and appeal dismissed as improvidently allowed, 91 Ohio St. 3d 1201, 2001-Ohio-229, 740 N.E.2d 1103 (2001).

"transacting business" under Civ. R. 4.3(A)(1).[7] Some, but not all, courts are also willing to treat the failure of an out-of-state obligor to support an Ohio obligee as a tortious act or omission causing an effect in Ohio under Civ. R. 4.3(A)(3) or Civ. R. 4.3(A)(9).[8]

Counsel for obligors should exercise caution when deciding to contest personal jurisdiction in an Ohio court. If the obligor makes an appearance that might be construed as more than a "special appearance," such as answering a complaint, then the obligor may be deemed to have waived any jurisdictional objections. Similarly, counsel should be wary of bringing a motion to set aside a default judgment under Civ. R. 60(B)[9] or seeking a writ of prohibition[10] based on lack of personal jurisdiction. Should the motion fail or writ be denied, courts of other states under principles of res judicata would be bound to give full faith and credit to the jurisdictional determination as well as any resulting support award.[11] Counsel for obligees should also remember that a default judgment does not cure defects in personal jurisdiction. In an enforcement proceeding in another forum, the obligor would be free to challenge the application of the long-arm provisions of the Civil Rules and raise the more general argument that, Civil Rules notwithstanding, the defendants lacked a sufficient nexus with Ohio to meet the minimum contacts standard of *International Shoe*.

---

[7]Compare Lella v. Lella, 1997 WL 778996 (Ohio Ct. App. 12th Dist. Butler County 1997) (finding jurisdiction); Yarnick v. Stegkamper, 1985 WL 6574 (Ohio Ct. App. 4th Dist. Lawrence County 1985) (same); with Massey-Norton v. Trammel, 61 Ohio App. 3d 394, 572 N.E.2d 821 (10th Dist. Franklin County 1989), dismissed, 44 Ohio St. 3d 714, 542 N.E.2d 1110 (1989) (no jurisdiction in paternity action); Hudgins v. Hudgins, 80 Ohio App. 3d 707, 610 N.E.2d 582 (3d Dist. Henry County 1992) (no jurisdiction in support action); Baker v. Baker, 1989 WL 3753 (Ohio Ct. App. 10th Dist. Franklin County 1989), dismissed, 44 Ohio St. 3d 714, 542 N.E.2d 1110 (1989) (same).

[8]Compare Upole by Burkey v. Caldwell, 1984 WL 14372 (Ohio Ct. App. 6th Dist. Wood County 1984) (jurisdiction under Civ. R. 4.3(A)(3)); Wayne Cty. Bur. of Support v. Wolfe, 71 Ohio App. 3d 765, 595 N.E.2d 421 (9th Dist. Wayne County 1991) (same); Holbert v. Holbert, 1997 WL 566191 (10th Dist. Ct. App., Franklin 9-11-97) (same); Hostetler v. Kennedy, 69 Ohio App. 3d 299, 590 N.E.2d 793 (9th Dist. Wayne County 1990) (jurisdiction under Civ. R. 4.3(A)(9)); with Massey-Norton v. Trammel, 61 Ohio App. 3d 394, 572 N.E.2d 821 (10th Dist. Franklin County 1989), dismissed, 44 Ohio St. 3d 714, 542 N.E.2d 1110 (1989) (no jurisdiction in paternity action under Civ. R. 4.3(A)(3)); Baker v. Baker, 1989 WL 3753 (Ohio Ct. App. 10th Dist. Franklin County 1989), dismissed, 44 Ohio St. 3d 714, 542 N.E.2d 1110 (1989) (same); Hudgins v. Hudgins, 80 Ohio App. 3d 707, 610 N.E.2d 582 (3d Dist. Henry County 1992) (no jurisdiction under Civ. R. 4.3(A)(9)); State ex rel. Wayne Cty. Child Support Enforcement Agency v. Tanner, 146 Ohio App. 3d 765, 2001-Ohio-1722, 768 N.E.2d 679 (9th Dist. Wayne County 2001) (same).

[9]See, e.g., Depaulitte v. Depaulitte, 138 Ohio App. 3d 780, 742 N.E.2d 659 (2d Dist. Montgomery County 2000), appeal allowed, 89 Ohio St. 3d 1429, 729 N.E.2d 1199 (2000) and appeal dismissed as improvidently allowed, 91 Ohio St. 3d 1201, 2001-Ohio-229, 740 N.E.2d 1103 (2001) (motion to set aside decree for want of personal jurisdiction).

[10]See, e.g., Fraiberg v. Cuyahoga Cty. Court of Common Pleas, Domestic Relations Div., 76 Ohio St. 3d 374, 378, 1996-Ohio-384, 667 N.E.2d 1189 (1996) (petition for writ of prohibition).

[11]Emig v. Massau, 140 Ohio App. 3d 119, 746 N.E.2d 707 (10th Dist. Franklin County 2000); see generally 63 Ohio Jur. 3d, Judgements § 348 et seq.

§ 23:6 Impediments to interstate support actions—Personal jurisdiction—Ohio Civil Rules—UIFSA's long-arm provisions

Plaintiffs may also utilize the long-arm provisions of UIFSA to establish personal jurisdiction over an out-of-state party. UIFSA's provisions, codified at RC 3115.03, are similar to those of the Ohio Civil Rules, but are tailored to domestic relations situations.[1]

§ 23:7 Impediments to interstate support actions—Personal jurisdiction—Ohio Civil Rules—Parentage determinations

Interstate support actions requiring a determination of parentage present special jurisdictional problems. Personal service within Ohio under Civ. R. 4.1(B) should be sufficient to confer personal jurisdiction in a parentage proceeding over an out-of-state defendant. RC 3111.06(B) confers personal jurisdiction in parentage actions over anyone who had sexual intercourse in Ohio and may thereby have conceived a child. A lack of consent to intercourse will not defeat jurisdiction.[1] However, obligees who cannot achieve transient jurisdiction or meet the test of RC 3111.06(B) may be hard pressed to acquire jurisdiction over an out-of-state obligor. Applications of Civ. R. 4.3(A)(3) or Civ. R. 4.3(A)(9) based on causing tortious injury within the state are not available in parentage cases. The Ohio Supreme Court has held that a failure to support a child is not such a tortious act. The Court, in *State ex rel. Stone v. Court of Common Pleas of Cuyahoga County, Juvenile Division,*[2] reasoned that support was ancillary to the issue of parentage and could not confer personal jurisdiction when neither the birth of the child nor its conception occurred in Ohio. Applying *Kulko*, the Court found that it would be unfair to require the defendant to conduct a defense in Ohio.[3]

The effect of *Stone* is to deny personal jurisdiction in interstate support cases involving parentage issues when some courts would grant it in a support-only action. In contrast, the Fourth District, in *Yarnick v. Stegkamper,*[4] showed great creativity in permitting jurisdiction in a parentage action on the basis that visiting a child in Ohio, sending support to the mother, and sending a birthday card constitutes "transacting business" within the state under Civ. R. 4.3(A)(1). The court made no

---

[Section 23:6]

[1]See § 23:28, UIFSA—Long-arm provisions.

[Section 23:7]

[1]Van Pham v. Redle, 29 Ohio App. 3d 213, 504 N.E.2d 1147 (9th Dist. Summit County 1985).

[2]State ex rel. Stone v. Court of Common Pleas of Cuyahoga County, Juvenile Div., 14 Ohio St. 3d 32, 470 N.E.2d 899 (1984).

[3]See also State ex rel. Wayne Cty. Child Support Enforcement Agency v. Tanner, 146 Ohio App. 3d 765, 2001-Ohio-1722, 768 N.E.2d 679 (9th Dist. Wayne County 2001) (denying personal jurisdiction in paternity action).

[4]Yarnick v. Stegkamper, 1985 WL 6574 (Ohio Ct. App. 4th Dist. Lawrence County 1985).

reference to *Stone*. Counsel would be unwise, however, to depend upon any lower court's willingness to side-step the rather harsh rule of *Stone*. Likewise, although default judgments are permitted in parentage actions,[5] such decisions are challengeable for want of personal jurisdiction when enforced in another forum. Thus, when deciding to pursue an in-state parentage action, counsel must weigh the benefits of proceeding in a local forum against the possibility that a determination may be challenged elsewhere for lack of jurisdiction.

§ 23:8 Impediments to interstate support actions—Full faith and credit

Article IV, § 1 of the United States Constitution commands the courts of one state to give full faith and credit to the judgments of sister states; i.e., they must recognize and enforce out-of-state judgments. Collateral attacks are permitted only on the basis of lack of personal or subject matter jurisdiction, or fraud.[1] Traditionally, the full faith and credit requirement has applied only to final, non-modifiable judgments.[2] To the extent that an unsatisfied support obligation has been reduced to a final judgment or has otherwise become final, it is owed recognition by all American jurisdictions.[3]

Problems arise with prospective obligations. Since child support orders are universally modifiable on a showing of changed circumstances, and spousal support orders are sometimes modifiable, the Full Faith and Credit Clause historically has raised no *constitutional* barrier when a court of one state chooses to ignore a support order of a sister state by modifying it. Here again, the complication of interstate support practice is significant. If a subsequent forum can relitigate or modify a custody order, then any support order against a non-resident is unreliable. Most full faith and credit problems have been corrected by amendments to the federal statute implementing the Full Faith and Credit Clause[4] and through program requirements under Title IV-D of the Social Security Act.[5]

§ 23:9 Locating obligors and their assets—In general

Perhaps the most frustrating aspect of an interstate support case is the attempt to locate an absent obligor, whether for purposes of establishing paternity, obtaining a support order, or enforcing it. There is an infinite variety of tracking resources, ranging from phone

---

[5]RC 3111.08(B).

[Section 23:8]

[1]Morris v. Jones, 329 U.S. 545, 67 S. Ct. 451, 91 L. Ed. 488, 168 A.L.R. 656 (1947).

[2]Sistare v. Sistare, 218 U.S. 1, 30 S. Ct. 682, 54 L. Ed. 905 (1910).

[3]Sistare v. Sistare, 218 U.S. 1, 30 S. Ct. 682, 54 L. Ed. 905 (1910).

[4]28 U.S.C.A. § 1738B; see § 23:21, Full Faith and Credit for Child Support Orders Act—In general.

[5]See § 23:15, In-state remedies—Determination of parentage; § 23.18, In-state remedies—Enforcement of support orders—Direct interstate income withholding.

directories to sophisticated on-line databases. As a general matter, the ability to trace a missing obligor will be determined by the practitioner's knowledge of information sources, his or her creativity in tapping unusual resources, and, most importantly, the client's ability to bear the costs. Some of the more frequently utilized resources in interstate situations are summarized below.

§ 23:10   Locating obligors and their assets—Federal resources

Title IV-D of the Social Security Act requires that the Secretary of the Department of Health and Human Services (HHS) maintain a Federal Parent Locator Service (FPLS).[1] The FPLS is operated by the Office of Child Support Enforcement and serves as a clearinghouse for access to useful databases maintained by several federal agencies including the Social Security Administration, the Internal Revenue Service, the Federal Bureau of Investigation, the Department of Defense, and the Veterans Administration.[2] Access to the FPLS is limited to "authorized persons" who include state IV-D agencies, courts with jurisdiction over custody and support, and, notably, parents and private attorneys.[3] FPLS services are not confined to Title IV-D (i.e., publicly enforced) support cases, but requests for searches by private attorneys must be funneled through a state IV-D agency.[4] The key bits of information in using the FPLS are a full name and a social security number, if known.[5] A successful FPLS search will yield a social security number (if previously unknown), an obligor's most recent address, plus the identity, address, and employer identification number of an employer.[6] FPLS services can be useful when an obligor is avoiding service or concealing an address or employment information.

Two provisions in the Personal Responsibility and Work Opportunity Reconciliation Act of 1996[7] (a.k.a. "Welfare Reform Act") have enhanced the utility of the FPLS considerably. Each state is required to have in place an automated State Directory of New Hires.[8] Employers are required to report the names, addresses, and social security numbers of new hires.[9] State directory information in turn will be transmitted to the National Directory of New Hires to be maintained by the FPLS.[10] States are also required to maintain a State Case Registry which

---

[Section 23:10]

[1]42 U.S.C.A. § 653(a); see also § 22:3, Parent location.

[2]42 U.S.C.A. § 653(E) (authorizing Secretary of HHS to utilize files and records of federal departments and agencies).

[3]42 U.S.C.A. § 653(c).

[4]45 C.F.R. § 302.35(c)(3); see § 23.12, Locating obligors and their assets—Ohio resources.

[5]45 C.F.R. § 303.70(c)(1-2).

[6]42 U.S.C.A. § 653(a)(2)(A).

[7]Pub. L. No. 104-192, 110 Stat. 2105 (1996).

[8]42 U.S.C.A. § 653a(a)(1).

[9]42 U.S.C.A. § 653a(b)(1)(A).

[10]42 U.S.C.A. § 653(i).

contains abstracts of each support case for which title IV-D services are being provided and of each support order established or modified in the state on or after October 1, 1998.[11] The registry includes such information as the names and social security numbers of parties to a support order.[12] These records must also be transmitted to the new Federal Case Registry of Child Support Orders.[13] The Welfare Reform Act instructs the Secretary of Health and Human Services to run computerized comparisons of these two registries and other components of the FPLS and report any match to the state agency responsible for the case.[14]

Still, the FPLS remains an imperfect resource. First, use of the service is expressly limited to cases involving establishing paternity or enforcing child support obligations,[15] and to cases involving child custody.[16] A party with a spousal support claim may, however, benefit indirectly when the FPLS is used on behalf of his or her children with their own claims against the obligor. Second, when the obligor's social security number is unknown, a time-consuming search request must be directed to the SSA or the IRS. Third, much FPLS data tends to be old. Fourth, requests may take weeks to process. Finally, FPLS is not useful where an obligor has assumed a false identity.

§ 23:11 Locating obligors and their assets—Worldwide military locator services

Each military service maintains a Worldwide Locator Service which is available to private attorneys as well as Title IV-D agencies. Use of this Locator Service requires a Service member's full name and social security number. A successful search will reveal the current duty station of the service member. Locator Service listings can lag 60 to 90 days behind reassignment. However, copies of re-assignment orders often are left at the prior duty station.[1]

§ 23:12 Locating obligors and their assets—Ohio resources

For the Ohio practitioner, the county Child Support Enforcement Agency (CSEA) is the most important resource for locating absent parents. Each CSEA is deemed the Title IV-D agency for the county and charged with carrying out the state's obligations under the federal law.[1] CSEAs provide location services by relying on the Support Enforcement

---

[11]42 U.S.C.A. § 654a(e)(1).

[12]42 U.S.C.A. § 653(h)(2).

[13]42 U.S.C.A. § 653(h)(1), 42 U.S.C.A. § 654a(f)(1).

[14]42 U.S.C.A. § 653(j)(2).

[15]42 U.S.C.A. § 653(a).

[16]42 U.S.C.A. § 663(a).

[Section 23:11]

[1]Useful suggestions for locating active-duty service personnel are found at OAC 5101:1-30-431.

[Section 23:12]

[1]RC 3125.11.

Tracking System (SETS), a composite database that includes information from the FPLS, the Bureau of Motor Vehicles, the State Employment Security Administration plus records from numerous state, federal and private sources.[2]

Requests for location services should be directed to the local Child Support Enforcement Agency. The requestor must file an application for Title IV-D services and, in some cases, pay a nominal fee.[3] Non-IV-D benefits recipients who have not secured a child support order may apply for "absent-parent-location-only service."[4] As with the FPLS, the Ohio Parent Locator Service (OPLS) is a useful but imperfect source; processing can be slow and the information is no better than the quality of the individual databases in the network.

For the private practitioner there are two significant limitations. First, information generated through the SETS may be used only for the purpose of locating the absent parent, custodial parent, or child to establish paternity, to secure child or medical support orders, and to resolve cases involving parental kidnapping and child custody determination.[5] Hence, OPLS is not available in spousal support cases but may be available indirectly when an obligee spouse is also pursuing claims on behalf of children. Second, persons who apply for "locate only" services, i.e., the same persons most likely to be represented by private counsel, are only entitled to receive the current address of an absent parent.[6] While an obligor's current address is an important step toward securing and enforcing an award, the practitioner must take additional, independent steps to identify an employer or assets.

§ 23:13   Locating obligors and their assets—Private resources

There are numerous private resources which may be useful in locating out-of-state residents. On-line, commercially operated databases may provide information that will locate an absent obligor. Companies such as Prentice Hall, Information America, Dun & Bradstreet, and Dialog offer extensive public record databases including bankruptcy filings, incorporation and partnership filings, judgments, liens, UCC filings, deeds and property transfers, and tax assessor files. Many of these services are carried by Westlaw® (and other electronic research services) and can be queried with familiar Westlaw search commands. While not locator services in the strict sense, commercial public records databases may supply a current address for an individual or information leading to a current address.

Commercial services are open to anyone willing and able to pay the user charges. Often the cost will make them unavailable to private clients of modest means. For those who can afford to utilize these ser-

---

[2]OAC 5101:1-30-01(D) and (E).

[3]OAC 5101:1-29-13(A) and (B).

[4]OAC 5101:1-29-13(C), OAC 5101:1-30-01(H).

[5]OAC 5101:1-30-01(B).

[6]OAC 5101:1-29-13(C)(4).

vices there are two principal advantages: First, there is no restriction on use of search results. Information may be used in spousal support actions to locate attachable assets. Second, these services can be accessed directly and immediately by private counsel. Users will not experience the frustrating delays that characterize public agency services. Since online services tend to be organized by jurisdiction, e.g., property transfers in individual states, they are most effectively used when the attorney has information that the absent obligor is present in a particular state or region; a search can then be confined to databases which are likely to yield information. Conversely, commercial services tend to be inefficient when the obligor's whereabouts are completely unknown.

Finally, there are a few Internet services to find persons and businesses. Since many are accessible free of charge, they offer an affordable though inferior alternative to commercial databases. Information is usually limited to address and phone number. A good example is Whitepages.com (http://whitepages.com). World Wide Web search engines such as Google or AltaVista might even prove useful. It is not inconceivable near the turn of the 21st century that a runaway parent would have a homepage with clues about his or her location.

§ 23:14 In-state remedies—In general

Although there are statutory mechanisms such as UIFSA which are designed specifically to pursue interstate support claims, actions against out-of-state obligors may also be brought under purely local procedures. By its terms, UIFSA is not an exclusive means for relief.[1] For example, counsel may choose to bring a support action against a non-resident father directly under RC 2151.231 rather than initiating a claim in another forum for later enforcement in Ohio under UIFSA. The decision to proceed locally involves several factors. Domestic relations practitioners tend to be more familiar, and therefore more comfortable, with local actions. Ohio law may be more favorable to a client; for example, Ohio child support guidelines may yield a higher award. There may also be a tactical advantage in bringing a claim in a particular venue. Actions brought by private counsel are also likely to be resolved more quickly than UIFSA cases prosecuted by public officials. On the other hand, success in a local action depends foremost on obtaining personal jurisdiction over the non-resident. Here it is sufficient to note that many types of local actions are available, and that there are often interstate implications to proceeding locally.[2]

§ 23:15 In-state remedies—Determination of parentage

It is advisable to resolve any issues of parentage as quickly as possible. The simplest method of establishing paternity against a non-resident is

---

[Section 23:14]

[1]RC 3115.02 (UIFSA remedies are in addition to other remedies).

[2]See Child Support Ch 19, Enforcement of Spousal and Child Support Ch 20, and Child Support Enforcement Agencies Ch 22.

a voluntary acknowledgment under RC 3111.23. If cooperation among the parties is not possible, then parentage may be established under RC Chapter 3111. In most cases, persons alleging parentage must request an administrative·determination by the county Child Support Enforcement Agency (CSEA).[1] CSEA must then order parties to submit to genetic testing.[2] If testing indicates a 99% or better probability of paternity, then CSEA must enter an administrative order establishing a parent-child relationship.[3] Such an order is final and enforceable unless challenged within 30 days by a judicial action pursuant to RC 3111.01 through RC 3111.18.

There are distinct advantages in an interstate case to securing parentage determinations either under RC 3111.23 or the administrative mechanism of Chapter 3111. These procedures are theoretically fast, cheap, and effective. (In practice, agency performance varies by location.) More importantly, unchallenged administrative determinations, as well as voluntary acknowledgments under RC 3111.23, are owed full faith and credit in other states: Title IV-D rules require that states have in effect legislation or rules recognizing all paternity determinations of other jurisdictions.[4] Much like voluntary acknowledgment under RC 3111.23, the administrative process works only if an out-of-state obligor cooperates. If any party fails to submit to genetic testing, the agency, at best, may enter an order that parentage is inconclusive.[5] A party must then bring an action in juvenile court or another court having jurisdiction.[6]

§ 23:16 In-state remedies—Determination of support

Child Support Enforcement Agencies are authorized to enter administrative support orders against any man presumed to be the father of a child under RC 3111.03.[1] Disputes over parentage are resolved as explained in the preceding section (§ 23:15, In-state remedies—Determination of parentage). Administrative support orders become final and enforceable within 30 days of issuance unless the obligor challenges the order by bringing an action under RC 2151.231 in juvenile or another court having jurisdiction.[2] Administrative support orders, like judicial determinations, are owed full faith and credit in other jurisdictions.[3] In the alternative, a party, without regard to marital status, may seek a child support order in juvenile court under RC 2151.231, except where

---

[Section 23:15]
  [1]RC 3111.38.
  [2]RC 3111.41.
  [3]RC 3111.46(A).
  [4]42 U.S.C.A. § 666(a)(11). See, e.g., RC 3111.02(B).
  [5]RC 3111.47.
  [6]RC 3111.381. For a detailed treatment of parentage actions, see Parentage Ch 3.

[Section 23:16]
  [1]RC 3111.78(A), RC 3111.81.
  [2]RC 3111.84.
  [3]42 U.S.C.A. § 666(a)(9)(B).

the presumption of paternity is based on voluntary acknowledgment.[4] Child support orders may also be established in actions for divorce, dissolution, or legal separation.[5] Spousal support orders are available in divorce and legal separation proceedings under RC 3105.18.[6]

§ 23:17 In-state remedies—Enforcement of support orders—In general

A variety of collection and enforcement provisions exist for Ohio support awards. The most important are the collection mechanisms set out in RC Chapter 3121, including automatic wage withholding, attachment of assets or benefits, and bond posting, plus the contempt power under RC Chapter 2705.[1] As a practical matter such enforcement mechanisms are of little use against a non-resident who is not employed or does not own property in Ohio.

§ 23:18 In-state remedies—Enforcement of support orders— Direct interstate income withholding

Amendments to Title IV-D of the federal Social Security Act have resulted in certain state law remedies which are useful in the interstate context. Perhaps the most important is the Title IV-D requirement for interstate income withholding. The Child Support Enforcement Amendments of 1984 required that states make their income withholding mechanisms available for support orders from other states.[1] The purpose of this amendment was to ensure that an obligee would have the benefit of automatic income withholding in spite of the obligor's current place of residence. Thus, an obligee in one state was permitted to enforce a support order in another state through the latter state's withholding system.

Until 1998, the federal mandate was carried out by former RC 3113.214. That statute established a cumbersome system by which the Department of Human Services received requests for interstate income withholding from IV-D agencies of other states, evaluated supporting documentation, and in a proper case forwarded copies of its findings, orders, and supporting documents to the Child Support Enforcement Agency in the appropriate county. The process of interstate withholding has been simplified under UIFSA. All states were required under the 1996 amendments to Title IV-D to adopt UIFSA by January 1, 1998. The Ohio General Assembly enacted 1997 House Bill 352, effective January 1, 1998, to implement these mandates. UIFSA, in pertinent part,

---

[4]RC 3111.78(A).

[5]RC 3105.21(A), RC 3109.05(A)(1). A detailed explanation may be found in Child Support Ch 19.

[6]A detailed explanation may be found in Spousal Support Ch 13.

[Section 23:17]

[1]A detailed explanation of support enforcement techniques is found in Enforcement of Spousal and Child Support Ch 20.

[Section 23:18]

[1]42 U.S.C.A. § 666(b)(9).

establishes the more efficient method of direct interstate withholding and registration by the obligee.[2]

§ 23:19   In-state remedies—Enforcement of support orders— Income tax refund intercept

There are limited opportunities to intercept an obligor's income tax refunds. Title IV-D provides for diversion of federal income tax refunds to satisfy unpaid support obligations.[1] RC 3123.81 implements this program. Tax refund offsets under this program are limited to Title IV-D cases;[2] hence, obligees must apply to the local Child Support Enforcement Agency (CSEA) for services. Tax offsets are carried out by a computerized comparison of support arrearages listed in the Support Enforcement Tracking System (SETS) with federally maintained databases of income tax refunds. Questions about the procedures and eligibility requirements for the program should be directed to local CSEA officials since the program description in the Ohio Administrative Code is, in many parts, unintelligible.[3] CSEAs may also seek to offset past due child support obligations against Ohio income tax refunds.[4] This remedy obviously has limited usefulness against a non-resident obligor.

§ 23:20   Enforcement of out-of-state support orders —In general

Enforcement of sister state support decrees is governed principally by two statutes: the federal Full Faith and Credit for Child Support Orders Act (FFCCSOA)[1] and the Uniform Interstate Family Support Act (UIFSA).[2] The former was enacted by the United States Congress in 1994 while the latter was adopted by Ohio, effective 1998, as a condition of continued funding under Title IV-D of the Social Security Act. Together these statutes have succeeded in eliminating the multiple order approach of the prior RURESA system, which was universally acknowledged to be ineffective, if not chaotic. Although the federal FFCCSOA would take precedence over the UIFSA under normal rules of preemption, the two statutes are usually compatible. In most cases, one can safely regard UIFSA as a proper elaboration of a state's full faith and credit obligations under the FFCCSOA. RURESA, however, has not passed from the legal scene yet. Ohio courts have continued to apply RURESA, as affected by the FFCCSOA, to cases pending when UIFSA

---

[2]See § 23:36, UIFSA—Direct enforcement of orders without registration; § 23:37, UIFSA—Registration of foreign orders for enforcement—Procedures for registration.

[Section 23:19]

[1]42 U.S.C.A. § 664(a)(1).

[2]OAC 5101:1-30-77(F)(1)(a).

[3]OAC 5101:1-30-77.

[4]OAC 5101:1-30-78(A).

[Section 23:20]

[1]Pub. L. No. 103-383, 108 Stat. 4063, codified at 28 U.S.C.A. § 1738B.

[2]Uniform Interstate Family Support Act (1992), reprinted in 9 Uniform Laws Annotated (1997 Cum. Supp.) at 316-390.

became effective. Hence, counsel will need to maintain familiarity with all three statutes for next few years.

§ 23:21 Full Faith and Credit for Child Support Orders Act—In general

In 1994, Congress enacted the Full Faith and Credit for Child Support Orders Act (FFCCSOA).[1] Passage of the Act marked perhaps the most significant change in interstate support practice since the promulgation of URESA in 1950. Following the recommendation of the United States Commission on Interstate Child Support,[2] Congress amended 28 U.S.C.A. § 1738, the federal statute which implements the Full Faith and Credit Clause of the Constitution,[3] to require states to recognize ongoing child support obligations as well as final, non-modifiable judgments. In the "findings" section of the FFCCSOA, Congress indicated that it was acting to protect children from a number of flaws in the present system including inconsistencies in the support laws of the states, the failure of states to give full faith and credit to sister state support orders, the existence of multiple orders for the same obligation, the burden on custodial parents of interstate enforcement, unnecessary relitigation of support matters, and a tendency of noncustodial parents to avoid payment of obligations by relocation.[4] FFCCSOA was amended in 1996 to bring its provisions into conformity with the Uniform Interstate Family Support Act.[5] The effect of the FFCCSOA was to eliminate a serious impediment to interstate support actions and to override the multiple order system permitted under URESA and RURESA.

The FFCCSOA employs a number of broad definitions which tend to maximize the effect of full faith and credit for support orders. "Child support" refers to payments of money, continuing support, arrearages, or benefits such as health insurance or child care.[6] "[C]hild support orders" are defined as judgments, decrees, or orders of a court requiring periodic or lump-sum payments, and include temporary as well as permanent orders, and modifications as well as initial orders.[7] "Court" under the FFCCSOA covers both judicial and administrative tribunals which are authorized by state law to enter or modify child support orders. Instead of the term "party," the Act prefers "contestant," which it defines as anyone who claims a right to receive child support, is a party to a proceeding which may result in a support order, or is under a child support order.[8] The state and its subdivisions are contestants if

---

[Section 23:21]

[1] 28 U.S.C.A. § 1738B.

[2] Blueprint for Reform at 91.

[3] U.S. Const. art. 4 § 1.

[4] Pub. L. No. 103-383, 108 Stat. 4063.

[5] See § 23:30, UIFSA—Reconciliation of orders of other states.

[6] 28 U.S.C.A. § 1738B(b).

[7] 28 U.S.C.A. § 1738B(b).

[8] 28 U.S.C.A. § 1738B(b).

they have been assigned child support rights.[9]

The crux of FFCCSOA is a requirement that the courts or tribunals of one state must "enforce according to its terms a child support order made consistently with [28 U.S.C.A. § 1738B] by a court of another State,"[10] and may not modify that order unless the issuing court loses its exclusive jurisdiction under the Act.[11] A court has acted consistently with the Act if, under state law: (1) it has subject matter jurisdiction over the support claim; (2) it has personal jurisdiction over the contestants; and (3) reasonable notice and an opportunity to be heard have been provided.[12] Once these requirements are met, the issuing court has "continuing, exclusive jurisdiction" over the order.[13] All other jurisdictions must enforce and refrain from modifying the order until another court meets the restrictive tests for modification.[14] Specifically, the jurisdiction of the decreeing state continues so long as the child or any one contestant resides in that state, or until the parties file written consent with the decreeing court permitting another state to assume continuing, exclusive jurisdiction.[15]

The prohibitory effects of a prior support order from another jurisdiction are illustrated by two recent decisions. In *Walker v. Amos*,[16] the mother of a child attempted to enforce an Indiana support order against an Ohio resident only to have the trial court suspend the defendant's support obligations. The First District properly reversed, among other reasons, on the straightforward grounds that Indiana retained continuing exclusive jurisdiction as the mother and child still resided in Indiana.

Emig v. Massau[17] illustrates both the simplicity of the rule and jurisdictional pitfalls in applying it. In 1978, the parties entered a stipulation agreement under a Missouri dissolution decree imposing a child support obligation on the father. A consent order for modification was entered in the Missouri court in 1990, although by that time the child and both parents no longer resided in the state. The father opposed a subsequent motion for modification in the Missouri court in 1994 on grounds that the court no longer had personal or subject matter jurisdiction over the claim. He initially entered a limited appearance to contest jurisdiction, but remained to litigate the modification once the court resolved the jurisdictional issues in the mother's favor. When the mother

---

[9]28 U.S.C.A. § 1738B(b).

[10]28 U.S.C.A. § 1738B(a)(1).

[11]28 U.S.C.A. § 1738B(a)(2).

[12]28 U.S.C.A. § 1738B(c).

[13]28 U.S.C.A. § 1738B(d).

[14]See Stansbury v. Stansbury, 1999 WL 668742 (Ohio Ct. App. 5th Dist. Licking County 1999), dismissed, appeal not allowed, 87 Ohio St. 3d 1458, 720 N.E.2d 541 (1999) (FFCCSOA precludes modification of foreign orders where issuing state has continuing, exclusive jurisdiction).

[15]28 U.S.C.A. § 1738(d).

[16]Walker v. Amos, 140 Ohio App. 3d 32, 746 N.E.2d 642 (1st Dist. Hamilton County 2000).

[17]Emig v. Massau, 140 Ohio App. 3d 119, 746 N.E.2d 707 (10th Dist. Franklin County 2000).

registered the modified Missouri decree for enforcement in Ohio, the father attempted to defeat the registration on grounds the Missouri court had lost jurisdiction of the parties. The father's defense was entirely jurisdictional. He made no attempt to modify the Missouri order.

It is likely that the father would have prevailed had he litigated the issues differently. Missouri had obviously lost continuing, exclusive jurisdiction under the terms of the FFCCSOA since all parties had moved out of Missouri. Even though the Missouri trial court's ruling was erroneous, the Tenth District correctly held that the father had litigated the issue and was not permitted under principles of res judicata to relitigate the issues in the Ohio court.[18] The father's only recourse was an appeal in Missouri. Secondly, his decision to litigate the modification motion after losing on the jurisdictional issues should be considered a general appearance that waived his objections to a lack of personal jurisdiction. The lesson of *Emig* is that counsel should carefully consider the tactical disadvantage of arguing to a court its lack of jurisdiction when the same arguments could be raised later in a neutral forum.

§ 23:22 Full Faith and Credit for Child Support Orders Act— Retroactivity

FFCCSOA became effective on October 20, 1994, but is silent as to retroactive application, as is the legislative history. The issue is most likely to arise when multiple orders for the same support obligation were issued under the old URESA system, and at least one order was entered before the effective date of the FFCCSOA. Ohio courts have taken different approaches to this matter.[1]

Sherman v. Fritz[2] illustrates the consequences of construing the FFCCSOA as non-retroactive. In 1985, an Ohio court issued a child support order against the father incident to a divorce. All parties and the children then relocated out-of-state. In a subsequent 1988 URESA proceeding in Florida, the father was ordered to pay obligations under the Ohio order, without modification, as well as arrearages. In 1990, the mother obtained an upward modification of child support from an Ohio court. In 1998, after the effective date of the FFCCSOA, the mother commenced another URESA proceeding in Florida which resulted in an order for the father to pay support under the modified Ohio order. Finally, in 2000, the father filed a motion in the Ohio court seeking relief, in pertinent part, from the 1990 Ohio modification order.

---

[18]See Sherrer v. Sherrer, 334 U.S. 343, 68 S. Ct. 1087, 92 L. Ed. 1429, 1 A.L.R.2d 1355 (1948).

[Section 23:22]

[1]Compare Dunn v. Dunn, 137 Ohio App. 3d 117, 738 N.E.2d 81 (12th Dist. Warren County 2000) (FFCCSOA applies retroactively to existing orders) with C. Elaine Sherman Appellee v. Robbin L. Fritz Appellant, 2001 WL 876973 (Ohio Ct. App. 6th Dist. 2001) (FFCCSOA does not apply retroactively to void judgments); In re Keighley, 1999-Ohio-947, 1999 WL 1084269 (Ohio Ct. App. 3d Dist. Union County 1999) (same).

[2]C. Elaine Sherman Appellee v. Robbin L. Fritz Appellant, 2001 WL 876973 (Ohio Ct. App. 6th Dist. 2001).

To the extent that the FFCCSOA applied, the father had a cogent argument. By the time of the 1990 modification, Ohio had lost continuing, exclusive jurisdiction under the terms of the Act due to the departure of the children and parties from the state. Florida, moreover, qualified for continuing, exclusive jurisdiction under the provisions of 42 U.S.C.A. § 1738B(c) and (d). The father argued that the FFCCSOA applied retroactively to deprive the Ohio court of subject matter jurisdiction to order a modification once all parties left the state in 1988. The Sixth District rejected the argument, reasoning that the FFCCSOA lacked any statement of an express intent that it apply retroactively.[3] A contrary decision in *Sherman* might have been a Pyrrhic victory for the father. He then would have been subject to a 1998 Florida order in the same amount enforceable in all states. The mother, however, would have been burdened by having to litigate future modifications in Florida.

Retroactive application will make a significant difference in situations where competing orders specify different levels of support. In *Dunn v. Dunn*,[4] a couple divorced in Ohio in 1988 but soon moved out-of-state. Subsequent URESA proceedings in California in 1992 resulted in an order to pay support at a reduced rate. The father complied with the terms of the California order. In 1998, however, the mother filed a motion in an Ohio court seeking a lump sum judgment against the father for arrearages under the more onerous Ohio order. The mother argued that the FFCCSOA's rules for prioritizing competing orders[5] should not be applied retroactively to halt the accumulation of arrearages under the Ohio order. The Twelfth District rejected this argument, reasoning that retroactivity was essential to the FFCCSOA's remedial purpose of eliminating competing orders for the same support obligation. The result from a practical point of view is attractive. A contrary decision would have left the father subject to inconsistent obligations contrary to the goals of the Act. The reasoning in *Dunn*, however, is amiss. The court goes to great lengths to justify the FFCCSOA as a procedural device that does not run afoul of the Ohio Constitution's ban on retroactive substantive legislation.[6] Retroactivity of the FFCCSOA, however, is an issue of federal and not state law. Federal law is binding on Ohio courts through the Supremacy Clause of the U.S. Constitution, the Ohio Constitution notwithstanding.

Dunn represents the better approach in dealing with orders issued before October 20, 1994. It is difficult not to have sympathy for obligees such as the mothers in *Dunn* and *Sherman* who risk reductions in child support levels. The holding in *Sherman* undoubtedly reflects a fear that countless pre-FFCCSOA decrees will be voided even though perfectly

---

[3]C. Elaine Sherman Appellee v. Robbin L. Fritz Appellant, 2001 WL 876973 (Ohio Ct. App. 6th Dist. 2001) (citing I.N.S. v. St. Cyr, 533 U.S. 289, 121 S. Ct. 2271, 2288, 150 L. Ed. 2d 347 (2001)).

[4]Dunn v. Dunn, 137 Ohio App. 3d 117, 738 N.E.2d 81 (12th Dist. Warren County 2000).

[5]See § 23:25, Full Faith and Credit for Child Support Orders Act—Reconciliation of orders.

[6]Ohio Const. Art. II, § 28.

valid when entered. Nevertheless, the FFCCSOA's goal of identifying a single, nationally enforceable support order would be severely compromised by an exception for competing orders existing on the effective date of the Act. It is also possible to avoid the retroactivity trap altogether. One can just as easily characterize the reconciliation rules of the Act as a system for determining the present effects of previously valid competing orders.

§ 23:23 Full Faith and Credit for Child Support Orders Act— Choice of law

FFCCSOA contains a general choice of law provision that a state should apply its own law when establishing, enforcing, or modifying a child support decree;[1] however, 28 U.S.C.A. § 1738B(h)(2) requires that a court apply the law of the issuing state when "interpreting a child support order including the duration of current payments and other obligations of support." The effect of § 1738B(h)(2) is to prevent a state court—which has either gained modification jurisdiction or is simply enforcing an out-of-state decree—from curtailing the duration of the obligations; it also serves to prevent forum shopping by obligees when more than one state might gain authority to modify an order under the FFCCSOA. Additionally, § 1738B(h)(3) directs courts enforcing arrearages under a child support order to apply the statute of limitations of the forum state or the state issuing the order, whichever is longer.

So far, only one Ohio court has applied the choice of law rule of 28 U.S.C.A. § 1738B(h)(2). In *State ex rel. Scioto County CSEA v. Adams*,[2] the husband and wife had divorced in New York. The wife later attempted to enforce the New York order through a RURESA proceeding in an Ohio court. Under New York law, the obligation to pay child support continued until age 21 in contrast to RC 3109.01 which sets 18 as the age of majority. Relying on the language of § 1738B(h)(2), the Second District properly rejected the husband's attempt to curtail his support obligation when his daughter had turned 18, reasoning that the FFCCSOA required the use of New York's age of majority as it affected the "duration" of the order.[3]

Much about § 1738B(h) remains hazy. The language of § 1738B(h)(2) gives no guidance as to what constitutes "interpreting" a child support order beyond the reference to the duration of orders; the legislative his-

---

[Section 23:23]

[1]28 U.S.C.A. § 1738B(h)(1).

[2]State ex rel. Scioto County Child Support Enforcement Agency v. Adams, 1999 WL 597257 (Ohio Ct. App. 4th Dist. Scioto County 1999).

[3]Compare Marriage of Lurie, 33 Cal. App.4th 658, 39 Cal. Rptr.2d 835 (1995) (applying California law to terminate New York decree under former 28 U.S.C.A. § 1738(g)(2)). Compare also Margaret Campbell Haynes, Federal Full Faith and Credit For Child Support Orders Act, 14 Del. L. 26, 28 n. 14 (1996) (arguing that *Lurie* was wrongly decided); State ex rel. Scioto County Child Support Enforcement Agency v. Adams, 1999 WL 597257 (Ohio Ct. App. 4th Dist. Scioto County 1999) (Harsha, J.) (distinguishing *Lurie* as a California order due to registration).

tory, moreover, does little more than restate the statute.[4] A sensible construction of § 1738B(h)(2) would require a court that has gained modification jurisdiction to apply the substantive law of the issuing state whenever a modification is sought. Congress specifically noted in the Findings section of the FFCCSOA the ill effects arising from the application of different state laws to the same support obligation, including forum shopping, a lack of finality in support orders, and excessive relitigation of cases.[5] Using the legal standard for a change of circumstances, for example, of the issuing state would tend to achieve Congress's stated goals.[6] In contrast, UIFSA permits a state that has gained modification jurisdiction to apply its own standard for change of circumstance (except for portions of the original decree that were unmodifiable under the original forum's law[7]). Given that Congress amended the FFCCSOA in 1996 to achieve consistency with UIFSA,[8] one can make an equally plausible argument that Congress intended the former statute to be compatible with the latter on the issue of choice of law for changed circumstances. The matter is far from clear.[9]

Also unclear is the range of § 1738B(h)(3)'s command to use the longer statute of limitations when enforcing an order. Does this provision affect the equitable defense of laches? There may be significant differences between the law of Ohio and an issuing state regarding a defense of laches. Ohio's willingness to entertain laches arguments[10] may not be permitted under the law of another state. While the Act requires choice of the longer of two statutes of limitations,[11] it is silent as to equitable defenses. It is simply unclear at this point whether a laches defense should be treated as a matter of enforcement governed by the law of the enforcing state or a matter of the duration or nature of an obligation governed by the law of the issuing state. So far, no Ohio court has addressed this precise issue. One court has assumed the availability of a laches defense under a comparable provision of UIFSA while holding

---

[4]S. Rep. No. 103-361, 103rd Cong., 2d Sess. (5 USCCAN 1994 3259, 3264).

[5]Pub. L. No. 103-383 § 2, 108 Stat. 4063, 4064; see also Paton v. Brill, 104 Ohio App. 3d 826, 663 N.E.2d 421 (10th Dist. Franklin County 1995) (discussing Congressional intent under FFCCSOA).

[6]See, e.g., Woodward v. Berkery, 714 So. 2d 1027 (Fla. Dist. Ct. App. 4th Dist. 1998) (applying 28 U.S.C.A. § 1738B(h)(2) to reverse grant of interim fees in action to modify New York decree unmodifiable under New York law).

[7]RC 3115.48(B); see, e.g., Cook v. Cook, 143 Ohio App. 3d 687, 758 N.E.2d 1158 (9th Dist. Lorain County 2001) (applying former RC 3113.215(B)(4) to modify a Georgia support order); see generally § 23:40, UIFSA—Registration of foreign orders for modification—Calculation factors.

[8]Pub. L. No. 104-193 § 322, 110 Stat. 2221; see also H. Conf. Rep. No. 104-725 (5 USCCAN 1996 2649, 2740-41).

[9]Compare LeTellier v. LeTellier, 40 S.W.3d 490, 90 A.L.R.5th 707 (Tenn. 2001) (holding that Congress intended for the FFCCSOA to be consistent with UIFSA; hence the former did not preempt the latter) with Tepper v. Hoch, 140 N.C. App. 354, 536 S.E.2d 654 (2000) (FFCCSOA preempts UIFSA when inconsistent).

[10]See § 23:47, RURESA—Defenses.

[11]28 U.S.C.A. § 1738B(h)(3).

that the defense failed because no prejudice had been shown.[12] A North Carolina court, however, has applied the Illinois law of laches to deny enforcement of arrearages under an Illinois support decree registered for enforcement.[13]

§ 23:24 Full Faith and Credit for Child Support Orders Act—Modification of orders

Modification is permitted only after the issuing forum has lost continuing, exclusive jurisdiction because the child and the individual contestants no longer reside there; alternatively, each individual may file a written consent with the issuing court agreeing to the assumption of continuing, exclusive jurisdiction and modification of the order by a second forum.[1] Jurisdiction is lost, however, when the child and *individual* contestants have moved out. Thus, jurisdiction may be lost even if support rights have been assigned to the local IV-D agency. The modifying jurisdiction must, of course, obtain jurisdiction over the contestants in its own right.[2] Once the new forum has issued an order in conformity with the FFCCSOA, it takes continuing, exclusive jurisdiction; that order is now controlling. The state issuing the original order must now enforce and not modify the order from the modifying state. The initial forum is, however, specifically permitted to enforce non-modifiable or accrued obligations under the original order.[3]

The mechanics of the FFCCSOA are illustrated nicely by the Tenth District's decision in *Paton v. Brill*.[4] There, husband and wife were divorced in Maryland; husband was ordered to pay $130 per week in support for the couple's two daughters. Husband then moved to Ohio. Wife initiated a RURESA action in Franklin County which resulted in a support order conforming to the Maryland award. In response to wife's contempt motion following non-payment, husband moved for a reduction in the support amount. Husband argued that the RURESA order was an Ohio rather than a Maryland order, and hence was modifiable. Rejecting this argument, the court of appeals held that Maryland had continuing, exclusive jurisdiction under the FFCCSOA, and no divesting event had occurred: the mother and children still resided there, and there was no evidence of written consent to jurisdiction in Ohio. Hence, Ohio courts

---

[12]Genessee County v. Christenson, 1999 WL 1071564 (Ohio Ct. App. 5th Dist. Delaware County 1999). See § 23:31, UIFSA—Civil provisions of general application—Standing and choice of law.

[13]Tepper v. Hoch, 140 N.C. App. 354, 536 S.E.2d 654 (2000) (applying Illinois law under 28 U.S.C.A. § 1738B(h)(2)).

[Section 23:24]

[1]28 U.S.C.A. § 1738B(e)(2).

[2]28 U.S.C.A. § 1738B(e)(1); 28 U.S.C.A. § 1738B(i).

[3]28 U.S.C.A. § 1738B(g).

[4]Paton v. Brill, 104 Ohio App. 3d 826, 663 N.E.2d 421 (10th Dist. Franklin County 1995); see also State ex rel. Scioto County Child Support Enforcement Agency v. Adams, 1999 WL 597257 (Ohio Ct. App. 4th Dist. Scioto County 1999), for an analysis of the Act by an appellate court.

were obliged to enforce the Maryland decree according to its own terms.

§ 23:25   Full Faith and Credit for Child Support Orders Act—
Reconciliation of orders

The versions of the Uniform Reciprocal Enforcement of Support Act in effect since the 1950s have permitted states to issue different support orders for the same child support obligation.[1] Consequently, there were a significant number of multiple order situations when the FFCCSOA was enacted.[2] The 1996 amendments to the FFCCSOA set up a priority system to determine which competing order is entitled to full faith and credit. The state which receives priority under the following rules becomes the state with continuing, exclusive jurisdiction over the support obligation.[3] The rules are as follows:

(1) If there is only one prior order, then that order must be recognized.[4]

(2) If two or more courts have issued child support orders for the same obligation, but only one court would have continuing, exclusive jurisdiction under the FFCCSOA, then that order must be recognized.[5]

(3) If two or more courts have issued child support orders for the same obligation, and more than one court would have continuing, exclusive jurisdiction under the FFCCSOA, then the order issued by the child's current home state must be recognized.[6] "[C]hild's home State" is defined as the state where the child has lived with a parent or person acting as a parent for six consecutive months disregarding temporary absences.[7] In the case of a child younger than six months old, it is the state where he or she has lived since birth.[8] If the child's home state has not issued an order, then the most recent order prevails.

(4) If two or more courts have issued child support orders for the same obligation but no court now has continuing, exclusive jurisdiction under the FFCCSOA, then any court meeting the jurisdictional requirements of the Act may issue an order which will be entitled to recognition.[9]

[Section 23:25]

[1]See § 23:46, RURESA—Modifications—Other states.

[2]S. Rep. No. 103-361, 103rd Cong., 2d Sess. at 6 (5 USCCAN 1994 3259, 3262); see also UIFSA 207 (Comment); Blueprint for Reform at 231.

[3]28 U.S.C.A. § 1738B(f)(5); Dunn v. Dunn, 137 Ohio App. 3d 117, 738 N.E.2d 81 (12th Dist. Warren County 2000).

[4]28 U.S.C.A. § 1738B(f)(1).

[5]28 U.S.C.A. § 1738B(f)(2).

[6]28 U.S.C.A. § 1738B(f)(3).

[7]28 U.S.C.A. § 1738B(b).

[8]28 U.S.C.A. § 1738B(b).

[9]28 U.S.C.A. § 1738B(f)(4).

§ 23:26 Full Faith and Credit for Child Support Orders Act— Reconciliation of orders—Examples

The following examples illustrate the application of the FFCCSOA reconciliation rules on multiple orders issued under the former RURESA system. Please note that interstate enforcement actions would now be brought under UIFSA.[1]

EXAMPLE 1.

FACTS: Harry and Sally are divorced in State A in 1991. Harry is ordered to pay $100 per week to support his two daughters. After Harry moves to State B in 1992, Sally goes on public assistance and assigns her support rights to the IV-D agency. The agency brings a RURESA petition in State A which results in a RURESA action in State B. The State B court then orders Harry to pay $50 per week for his two daughters. Sally and the children move to State C in 1993.

ANALYSIS: The State B order is entitled to recognition. Although both decrees conformed to 28 U.S.C.A. § 1738B(c) when issued, State A has lost continuing, exclusive jurisdiction since all of the individual contestants have moved out. State A as well as State C would be required to recognize the State B order.

EXAMPLE 2.

FACTS: John and Abigail are divorced in State A in 1991. John is ordered to pay $100 per week to support his two children. After John moves to State B in 1992, Abigail goes on public assistance and assigns her support rights to the IV-D agency. The agency brings a RURESA petition in State A which results in a RURESA action in State B. The State B court then orders John to pay $50 per week for his two daughters. Abigail and the children remain in State A.

ANALYSIS: Here the State A order is entitled to full faith and credit. Although both states still meet the requirements for continuing, exclusive jurisdiction of 28 U.S.C.A. § 1738B(c), State A is the children's home state. State B would be obliged to recognize the State A decree.

EXAMPLE 3.

FACTS: Adam and Eve are divorced in State A in 1991. Adam is ordered to pay $100 per week to support his two sons. After Adam moves to State B in 1992, Eve brings a RURESA petition in State A resulting in a RURESA action in State B. The State B court then orders Adam to pay $50 per week for his two sons. In 1993, Eve and the boys move to State C while Adam moves to State D. Eve now brings a RURESA petition in State C resulting in a RURESA proceeding in State D. The State D court then orders Adam to pay $150 per week for his two sons.

ANALYSIS: The State D order would prevail in all states. State A and State B have lost continuing, exclusive jurisdiction because all individual contestants have moved out.

§ 23:27 UIFSA—In general

In 1992, the National Conference of Commissioners on Uniform State Laws approved and recommended the enactment of the Uniform Inter-

---

[Section 23:26]

[1]See § 23:27, UIFSA—In general.

state Family Support Act (UIFSA).[1] Approval by the American Bar Association followed in 1993. The 1992 version of UIFSA reflected four years of deliberations by the Conference's Drafting Committee working in conjunction with the United States Commission on Interstate Child Support. A revised version of UIFSA was promulgated by the National Conference of Commissioners in 1996.[2] The Act was intended to replace URESA and RURESA. UIFSA was also different from other uniform acts, in that Congress required that states adopt the Act as part of their Title IV-D programs to remain eligible for federal funding. The Personal Responsibility and Work Opportunity Reconciliation Act of 1996 amended Title IV-D of the Social Security Act to require that all states adopt UIFSA by January 1, 1998,[3] in the form approved by the American Bar Association on February 9, 1993, along with any subsequent revisions made by the National Conference of Commissioners on Uniform State Laws before January 1, 1998.[4]

All states have adopted UIFSA, although some have made changes in the Act. Ohio repealed RURESA and adopted UIFSA, effective January 1, 1998, as part of 1997 H.B. 352. The Ohio version contains some variations from the official text of UIFSA. However, the General Assembly states in section 3 of the bill that any dissimilarity in the text reflects only technical changes, or the intent of the Commissioners as set out in the Comments to UIFSA.

Although not an abject failure, results under RURESA were disappointing. Since orders entered by responding or registering states did not supersede prior orders from other states, RURESA created a confusing system of multiple, often contradictory, orders for the same obligation.[5] Being a product of the 1950s-60s, RURESA also failed to reflect the pervasive effect of Title IV-D on support law. Perhaps the worst problems were the delays and failures in processing two-state petitions. Studies indicated delays of several months in establishing paternity or support orders.[6] UIFSA addressed these failures through expansion of personal jurisdiction (to permit litigation in the obligee's state of residence whenever possible), evidentiary and discovery reforms, simplified choice of law rules, a streamlined two-state transmission process, direct enforcement procedures, and severe limitations on modification of support orders.

Definitions under UIFSA are quite similar to RURESA. The Act

[Section 23:27]

[1]Uniform Interstate Family Support Act (1992), reprinted at 9 Uniform Laws Annotated (1997 Cum. Supp.) at 316-390.

[2]Uniform Interstate Family Support Act (1996), reprinted at 9 Uniform Laws Annotated (1997 Cum. Supp.) at 272-315 [hereinafter cited as UIFSA].

[3]Pub. L. No. 104-193 § 321, 110 Stat. 2221 (1996).

[4]42 U.S.C.A. § 666(f).

[5]See § 23:46, RURESA—Modifications—Other states.

[6]Blueprint for Reform at 229 (collecting studies).

retains familiar terms where possible such as "initiating"[7] and "responding"[8] state. In other respects, the definition section reflects significant
changes in the law made by UIFSA and other laws. For example, the
term "tribunal" means a court, administrative agency, or quasi-judicial
entity which may issue, enforce, or modify a support order, or establish
parentage,[9] thus reflecting the shift of support functions from judicial to
administrative bodies. The concept of reciprocity is effectively scrapped
under the definitions of initiating and responding states. These are now
defined as states sending or receiving petitions under UIFSA, URESA,
RURESA, or any substantially similar law.[10] "Support enforcement
agency" is defined to reflect the responsibilities of a Title IV-D enforcement agency.[11] The term "support order" specifically includes spousal as
well as child support.[12] "Child support order" is defined to include
monetary support, arrearages, health care or reimbursement, related
costs and fees, interest, income withholding requirements, and attorney
fees.[13] Ohio's version of UIFSA specifically provides that a child support
order includes orders under which the child has attained majority under
the law of the state issuing an order but arrearages are still owed,[14] and
cases where the child has attained majority in Ohio but not under the
law of the issuing state and obligations are still owed.[15] "Spousal support order" is defined broadly to include health care orders and
reimbursement as well as monetary support, income withholding
requirements, and attorney fees.[16]

Ohio's version of UIFSA also contains certain provisions which are not
part of the uniform act as promulgated by the National Conference of
Commissioners on Uniform State Laws. These supplementary sections
are intended to clarify how UIFSA relates to Ohio procedures. RC
3115.55(A) establishes that UIFSA actions are governed by the Civil
Rules unless otherwise specified. RC 3115.55(B) provides that the following are considered original actions subject to the service of process
requirements of the Civil Rules:

(1) Actions to establish support under RC 3115.31.
(2) Contests to direct withholding orders under RC 3115.37.
(3) Proceedings under RC 3115.43 and 3115.44 to contest the
    enforcement of an order registered for enforcement.
(4) Proceedings to register an order for modification under RC
    3115.46.

---

[7]RC 3115.01(G).
[8]RC 3115.01(Q).
[9]RC 3115.01(X).
[10]RC 3115.01(G), (Q).
[11]RC 3115.01(V).
[12]RC 3115.01(W).
[13]RC 3115.01(B).
[14]RC 3115.01(B)(1).
[15]RC 3115.01(B)(2).
[16]RC 3115.01(T).

(5) Parentage proceedings under RC 3115.52.

Similarly, RC 3115.55(C) requires that any attempt to invoke the continuing jurisdiction of a tribunal to enforce or modify a support order requires service under the Civil Rules. Finally, if the manner of notice is not specified either by UIFSA or the Civil Rules, then RC 3115.55(D) requires service by first class mail.

Ohio's version of the act also contains Ohio-specific venue provisions that do not appear in the uniform act. UIFSA itself is generally venue-neutral, and provides little guidance as to which court should entertain proceedings under RC Chapter 3115. When enacting 1997 H.B. 352, the General Assembly added RC 3115.56, providing that original actions under RC Chapter 3115 should be filed with the appropriate tribunal pursuant to RC 2151.23 and RC 2301.03. In effect, original actions will be brought in the juvenile court for the county unless otherwise assigned by RC 2301.03.[17] RC 3115.56 does not define an "original action." Presumably, the meaning is the same as in RC 3115.55(B).

§ 23:28   UIFSA—Long-arm provisions

UIFSA attempts to avoid the ills of multistate support actions by encouraging litigation in the obligee's state of residence. The primary device for achieving this goal is the expansion of each state's long-arm statute to the maximum extent permitted by the Due Process Clause of the 14th Amendment. RC 3115.03 sets out the following bases for personal jurisdiction over a non-resident:

(1) The individual is personally served within the state (RC 3115.03(A)).

(2) The individual submits to the jurisdiction of the state by consent, by entering a general appearance, or by filing a responsive document having the effect of waiving objections to personal jurisdiction (RC 3115.03(B)).

(3) The individual resided in the state with the child (RC 3115.03(C)).

(4) The individual resided in the state and provided prenatal expenses or support for the child (RC 3115.03(D)).

(5) The child resides in the state as a result of the acts or directives of the individual (RC 3115.03(E)).

(6) The individual engaged in sexual intercourse in the state and the child may have been conceived by that act of intercourse (RC 3115.03(F)).

(7) The individual asserted parentage in the putative father registry maintained pursuant to RC 3107.062 (RC 3115.03(G)).

(8) Any other basis for the exercise of personal jurisdiction (RC 3115.03(H)).

For the most part, RC 3115.03 is constitutionally untroublesome. RC

---

[17]RC 3115.56(B).

3115.03(A) codifies the U.S. Supreme Court's holding in *Burnham v. Superior Court*,[1] approving of personal jurisdiction by service within the territory of the forum.[2] Other provisions appear to fall within the established boundaries of due process. RC 3115.03(B) reflects the universally accepted rule that want of personal jurisdiction is a waivable defense. The requirements of RC 3115.03(C) and (D) that the defendant either reside with the child or provide prenatal assistance or support to the child while living in the state should survive minimum contacts analysis in most cases. Defendants falling into these categories normally meet the criterion of purposeful activity in the forum which invokes the benefits of the forum's law; moreover, it is reasonable for such persons to anticipate being required to defend a claim in the forum.[3] The same can be said of RC 3115.03(G)'s use of registration in the putative father registry. RC 3115.03(F) reflects the established rule that conception within the forum is a sufficient minimum contact (perhaps in a literal way). In a few instances, a defendant's nexus to the forum may be so slight that, in spite of meeting the tests of RC 3115.03(C), (D), (F), or (G), jurisdiction could be challenged as a constitutional matter under the *International Shoe* test. For example, all parties may have left the forum many years before a claim is brought there. RC 3115.03(H) is a catch-all provision simply permitting any assertion of jurisdiction consistent with the Due Process Clause.

One obviously problematic provision is RC 3115.03(E), permitting jurisdiction where a child resides in a state due to the acts or directives of a party. This formulation seems to include the facts of *Kulko*, which disapproved of jurisdiction under such circumstances. This subsection may simply reflect a decision by the Commissioners that *Kulko* needs to be relitigated under a new guise.

UIFSA's long-arm provisions work some significant changes in Ohio law. RC 3115.03 provides a long-arm statute that is tailored to family support actions. Many of the previous awkward attempts at fitting nonsupport under the rubric of a tortious omission or transacting business may now be abandoned in favor of more relevant provisions. Expansion of bases for jurisdiction in conjunction with the specificity and plain language in the Act will likely result in more frequent assertions of personal jurisdiction. Decisions among the lower courts are also likely to be more uniform thanks to the clearer language in the Act. Undoubtedly, there will continue to be litigation over the limits of jurisdiction under the Due Process Clause.[4] Although RC 3115.03 does not specifically mention spousal support, it was intended by the drafters to reach

---

[Section 23:28]

[1]Burnham v. Superior Court of California, County of Marin, 495 U.S. 604, 110 S. Ct. 2105, 109 L. Ed. 2d 631 (1990).

[2]See § 23:4, Impediments to interstate support actions—Personal jurisdiction—Ohio Civil Rules—Transient service.

[3]See § 23:3, Impediments to interstate support actions—Personal jurisdiction—Constitutional requirements.

[4]See, e.g., Fraiberg v. Cuyahoga Cty. Court of Common Pleas, Domestic Relations Div., 76 Ohio St. 3d 374, 1996-Ohio-384, 667 N.E.2d 1189 (1996).

such cases.[5] Expansion of personal jurisdiction in divorce actions will have the beneficial effect of consolidating support with other divorce issues in a single forum.

Once a plaintiff establishes a jurisdictional basis under RC 3115.03, there are two options. He or she may invoke the two-state process available under UIFSA.[6] Alternatively, the plaintiff may simply pursue an appropriate claim under Ohio law. In the latter case, other UIFSA provisions do not apply; the court would apply the substantive and procedural law of Ohio.[7] Two exceptions are that RC 3115.27, Special rules of evidence and procedure, and RC 3115.29, Assistance with discovery, are available in intrastate actions.[8]

§ 23:29   UIFSA—Subject matter jurisdiction

UIFSA also establishes rules for jurisdiction over the subject matter of support orders. RC 3115.05 authorizes a tribunal in the state to act either as an initiating or as a responding tribunal. This provision corresponds to the traditional RURESA function. The exception is that there now may be a responding tribunal without an initiating one due to the availability of direct filing under RC 3115.32.[1]

RC 3115.06 determines priority when there are simultaneous proceedings in more than one forum. RC 3115.06(A) permits an Ohio court to assume jurisdiction when a prior claim has been filed in another forum only when the following conditions are met: (1) the Ohio pleading was filed before the deadline in the other forum for filing a responsive pleading challenging jurisdiction; (2) the contesting party has actually raised a timely challenge in the other forum; and (3) if relevant, that Ohio is the home state of the child. Conversely, RC 3115.06(B) prohibits jurisdiction in Ohio when a subsequent action is filed elsewhere and these three criteria are met: (1) a petition is filed in the other forum within the time allowed for filing a responsive pleading challenging jurisdiction in Ohio; (2) an actual challenge has been timely raised in Ohio; and (3) if relevant, the other forum is the child's home state. The reference to the child's home state reflects the priority given to a support order issued by the child's home state under certain circumstances by RC 3115.09.[2]

Implicit in RC 3115.06 is the desirability of avoiding multiple orders from the outset. In spite of UIFSA's "one controlling order" philosophy, there is still a risk that two courts may establish competing support obligations. Unlike RURESA, obligors as well as obligees may seek to

---

[5]UIFSA 201 (Comment).

[6]See § 23:37, UIFSA—Registration of foreign orders for enforcement—Procedures for registration.

[7]UIFSA 201 (Comment); UIFSA 202 (Comment).

[8]RC 3115.04.

[Section 23:29]

[1]See § 23:36, UIFSA—Direct enforcement of orders without registration.

[2]See § 23:30, UIFSA—Reconciliation of orders of other states.

establish parentage or support orders. This situation is most likely when there is no prior order and each party sees a tactical advantage in litigating in the other's state. UIFSA attempts to resolve jurisdictional conflicts quickly through the requirement that any competing pleadings be filed within the deadline for raising jurisdictional challenges in the other forum. The provisions track comparable rules in Section 6 of the Uniform Child Custody Jurisdiction Act (UCCJA). Neither the text of RC 3115.06 nor the Commentary to Section 204 of UIFSA provides a rule of priority in the event that both jurisdictions opt to enter orders. Commentary following the section envisions communication and cooperation among all tribunals as under the UCCJA. In the event that cooperation fails, RC 3115.09's rules for prioritizing multiple orders presumably would apply as would the priority rules of FFCCSOA.[3]

RC 3115.07's rule of "continuing, exclusive jurisdiction" is the pivotal provision of UIFSA. This section provides that once an Ohio tribunal has assumed jurisdiction over a child support claim, it maintains exclusive jurisdiction over modification until one of two very restrictive criteria is met.[4] (Temporary orders issued pending resolution of jurisdictional conflicts do not create continuing, exclusive jurisdiction.[5]) All other jurisdictions which have enacted UIFSA are obligated to respect the continuing, exclusive jurisdiction of the Ohio forum.[6] The principal effect of this provision is to eliminate the multiple order system of RURESA. As long as it maintains jurisdiction, only the issuing forum may make modifications to the order.[7] Moreover, when other jurisdictions are called on to act as responding jurisdictions for purposes of enforcement, they are deemed to be enforcing the order of the original forum, not their own.[8]

An Ohio tribunal loses continuing, exclusive jurisdiction when the obligor, the individual obligee, and the child for whose benefit the support order is issued *all* no longer reside in Ohio. Alternatively, jurisdiction is lost when each individual party has filed a written consent with the Ohio tribunal agreeing that a tribunal of another state assume continuing, exclusive jurisdiction. Once either of these conditions is met, the Ohio tribunal must accept any modification of the support order of a tribunal of another forum acting pursuant to UIFSA or a similar law.[9] The Ohio tribunal retains authority to enforce its own order only to the extent of obligations accrued under the old order, non-modifiable aspects of the order, and relief for violations of the order occurring before

---

[3]See § 23:25, Full Faith and Credit for Child Support Orders Act—Reconciliation of orders; § 23:30, UIFSA—Reconciliation of orders of other states.

[4]RC 3115.07(A).

[5]RC 3115.07(E).

[6]UIFSA 205(d); UIFSA 206(c) (tribunal without continuing, exclusive jurisdiction may not modify); cf. RC 3115.07(D) (Ohio court to recognize orders of other states).

[7]UIFSA 205(e); cf. RC 3115.07(F) (continuing, exclusive jurisdiction of Ohio courts).

[8]UIFSA 601 (Comment).

[9]RC 3115.07(B).

modification.[10] RC 3115.07 does not explicitly define the status of an order between the time the issuing forum loses jurisdiction and another forum meets the requirements of the Act for modification jurisdiction. Commentary to Section 205 of the uniform act, however, indicates that the order remains valid and enforceable in the issuing state and any other state where it has been or may be registered for enforcement under UIFSA Sections 601 through 604.

UIFSA takes the noteworthy step in spousal support cases of limiting modification jurisdiction to the issuing forum throughout the existence of the order.[11] This provision is a significant departure from RURESA, which drew no distinctions between spousal and child support orders. The purpose of this rule is to avoid the serious choice of law problems that occur when spousal support orders are modified by a second jurisdiction. Commentary to Section 205 notes that there is wide variation in state law on the effect of remarriage or cohabitation on spousal support obligations.[12]

RC 3115.08 spells out the authority of tribunals in an interstate context when there are requests for enforcement or modification. The rules are simply correlatives of the jurisdiction rules in RC 3115.07. A tribunal which lacks continuing, exclusive jurisdiction over an order may still serve as an initiating tribunal to forward requests to a responding tribunal.[13] Conversely, a tribunal which has continuing, exclusive jurisdiction may serve as a responding tribunal to enforce or modify an order.[14] If the obligor has moved out of the issuing state, then the tribunal may apply RC 3115.27, Special rules of evidence and procedure, and RC 3115.29, Assistance with discovery, to obtain discovery in another forum.[15]

§ 23:30 UIFSA—Reconciliation of orders of other states

UIFSA makes careful provisions for reconciling child support orders from different jurisdictions. RC 3115.09 gives a detailed scheme for assigning priority to orders from different jurisdictions. These rules are intended primarily to accommodate multiple orders for the same obligation which arose under RURESA. To a lesser extent, the priority rules help to sort out contradictory orders which emerge under UIFSA in spite of RC 3115.06's provisions for simultaneous proceedings. Except for insignificant differences in terminology, the priority rules of Section 207 are identical to the priority rules under the Full Faith and Credit for Child Support Orders Act. Hence, RC 3115.09 simply codifies as

---

[10]RC 3115.07(C).

[11]RC 3115.07(F).

[12]UIFSA 205 (Comment).

[13]RC 3115.08(A).

[14]RC 3115.08(B).

[15]RC 3115.08(B).

state law the existing requirements of 28 U.S.C.A. § 1738B.[1]

In the event of uncertainty over which prior order should control under UIFSA, RC 3115.09(C) permits an individual party to request that an Ohio tribunal determine which order is controlling under the provisions of RC 3115.09(B). The requesting party must provide the tribunal with a certified copy of each prior order that is still in effect, and give notice to any other party who may be affected. If an Ohio tribunal enters an order identifying a controlling order, RC 3115.09(E) requires that it state the basis for its decision in the same order. The tribunal that issues the controlling order under RC 3115.09 gains "continuing, exclusive jurisdiction."[2] The party obtaining a determination under RC 3115.09 must file a certified copy with every tribunal that has issued or registered a prior support order.[3] A failure to do so, however, does not affect the validity or enforceability of the determination.[4]

RC 3115.10 deals with obligors who are subject to different child support orders for different obligees. UIFSA provides that if an Ohio tribunal is faced with registrations or petitions for enforcement of orders and at least one of the orders was issued by an out-of-state tribunal, then the Ohio tribunal must treat the multiple orders as if all had been issued in Ohio. The purpose of this seemingly cryptic formulation is to assure that all foreign support orders are treated on a par with domestic orders.[5] Given the Title IV-D provisions[6] subjecting wage withholding to limits under 15 U.S.C.A. § 1673(b), it is likely that collection efforts against many obligors will be insufficient to meet all support obligations.[7]

Finally, RC 3115.11 provides that any amounts paid under a support order of another state must be credited against an order for the same obligation issued by an Ohio tribunal. Specifically, the out-of-state order must cover the same time period, parties, and duty of support. This section carries over the rule of RURESA section 31 and former RC 3115.28 awarding pro tanto credit for payments actually made. Although UIFSA envisions a single support order, the drafters wisely included a credit rule foreseeing that it would take time before the UIFSA system was in place.[8]

[Section 23:30]

[1]See §§ 23.25-23.26, Full Faith and Credit for Child Support Orders Act—Reconciliation of orders, for a detailed explanation of the priority rules under 28 U.S.C.A. § 1738B.

[2]RC 3115.09(D); see, e.g., Hill v. Hill, 2002-Ohio-525, 2002 WL 191997 (Ohio Ct. App. 1st Dist. Hamilton County 2002) (using RC 3115.09 to determine which order is controlling where two states have continuing, exclusive jurisdiction).

[3]RC 3115.09(F).

[4]RC 3115.09(F).

[5]UIFSA 208 (Comment).

[6]42 U.S.C.A. § 666(b)(1).

[7]UIFSA 208 (Comment).

[8]UIFSA 209 (Comment).

§ 23:31 UIFSA—Civil provisions of general application— Standing and choice of law

RC 3115.12 through RC 3115.30 set out a number of provisions or procedures that are available under any UIFSA action unless otherwise provided. RC 3115.12 is an introductory provision. It reminds the reader, perhaps needlessly, that an individual or a support enforcement agency may commence a proceeding either by filing a complaint with an initiating tribunal in Ohio, or by direct filing in another state.

RC 3115.13 establishes liberal standing requirements for bringing an UIFSA action. It specifies that a minor parent as well as a guardian or other legal representative may bring an action on behalf of the minor's child. This provision carries over the rule of former RC 3115.11, which permitted a RURESA petition without appointment of a guardian ad litem.

Choice of law is controlled by RC 3115.14. This section departs significantly from RURESA's reliance on the law of the obligor's residence. Now the forum is to use its own procedural and substantive law applicable to similar support actions, including choice of law rules and remedies. The Ohio tribunal is specifically instructed to determine the duty of support and support levels under RC Chapters 3119, 3121, 3123, and 3125.[1] While this rule does not create uniformity among state laws, it does ensure that the same law will be applied in interstate and intrastate cases tried in the same forum. The drafters felt that efficient processing of cases required that decision-makers work with a single set of rules.[2] RC 3115.14, notably, parallels the main choice of law rule under the FFCCSOA, which calls for a state to apply its own law in proceedings to "establish, modify, or enforce a child support order."[3]

RC 3115.41 contains two critical exceptions: that the law of the issuing forum should govern the interpretation of the nature and duration of the award, and that the longest available statute of limitations should apply.[4] Again, this provision mimics the FFCCSOA's requirements that courts apply the law of the issuing state when construing the duration of an obligation and prefer the longest statute of limitations.[5] Like the FFCCSOA, these rules are somewhat ambiguous. It is not clear what constitutes interpreting the nature of an award or whether the instruction to apply the longest statute of limitations should be construed to include a defense of laches. In *Genessee County v. Christenson*,[6] a mother registered an out-of-state order for enforcement in Ohio under UIFSA

[Section 23:31]

[1]RC 3115.14.

[2]UIFSA 303 (Comment).

[3]28 U.S.C.A. § 1738B(h)(1). See § 23:23, Full Faith and Credit for Child Support Orders Act—Choice of law.

[4]See also § 23:37, UIFSA—Registration of foreign orders for enforcement—Procedures for registration.

[5]28 U.S.C.A. § 1738b(h)(2-3).

[6]Genessee County v. Christenson, 1999 WL 1071564 (Ohio Ct. App. 5th Dist. Delaware County 1999).

and sought a lump sum judgment for arrearages. The father raised a laches defense against a claim for arrearages based on the fact that the mother had hidden their minor daughter for nine years. The Fifth District sustained the trial court's denial of the laches defense as not being an abuse of discretion. The disposition of the father's motion assumed that Ohio law governed, and neither party argued otherwise. Counsel for obligors should be alert for situations where the application of another forum's law of laches might produce a different result, and argue accordingly.

§ 23:32 UIFSA—Civil provisions of general application—Duties of tribunals and agencies

UIFSA contains several sections defining the duties and powers of certain constituents of the support system. Some are simply mechanical improvements over RURESA. RC 3115.15 instructs an initiating tribunal, upon the filing of a petition, to forward three copies of the petition and any accompanying documents to an appropriate tribunal or support enforcement agency in a responding state or to a state information agency if the proper tribunal or agency is unknown. RC 3115.15(B) makes provision for responding states that have not yet adopted UIFSA. In such cases, an initiating Ohio tribunal is authorized to issue certificates or documents, or make findings as required by the law of the responding state. If the non-UIFSA responding state is a foreign nation, the Ohio tribunal may specify the amount of support sought as well as provide any documentation necessary to satisfy that nation's laws.

Noticeably absent is the RURESA requirement that the initiating tribunal make an initial determination that the obligor may owe a duty of support and that the responding state may obtain jurisdiction.[1] This process at best was perfunctory, and has been improved by making the initiating tribunal's functions strictly ministerial. RC 3115.16(A), in turn, requires responding tribunals to cause the petition to be filed and notify the petitioner.[2] Any orders entered by the responding court must be served on the petitioner, the respondent, and the initiating tribunal, if any.[3] In the event that a tribunal receives a petition that was erroneously filed or is otherwise inappropriate, that tribunal must forward the petition to the appropriate place and notify the petitioner.[4] This rule applies whether the tribunal is acting as an initiating or responding tribunal.[5]

Remedial powers are set out rather explicitly. RC 3115.16(B) gives an extensive list of remedial powers that a tribunal may exercise, including issuing or enforcing support orders, income withholding, contempt sanc-

---

[Section 23:32]

[1]See § 23:43, RURESA—Ohio as an initiating state.

[2]RC 3115.16(A).

[3]RC 3115.16(E).

[4]RC 3115.17.

[5]UIFSA 306 (Comment).

tions, imposition of liens, and so forth. Counsel should take note that these powers must be "consistent with the applicable sections of Chapters 3105, 3109, 3111, 3113, 3119, 3121, and 3125 of the Revised Code."[6] Thus, UIFSA does not create remedies that did not exist prior to enactment. The purpose of this limiting reference to existing state law is to permit courts and administrative agencies to operate within their ambits without disrupting existing structures.[7] In general, however, RC 3115.16(B) marks an improvement over the less specific provisions of former RC 3115.22 and RC 3115.23. RC 3115.16(C) requires that support orders under UIFSA or accompanying documents must include calculation sheets. The purpose of this rule is to ensure that interstate cases are subject to the federal requirement[8] that deviations from child support guidelines must be explained.[9] Finally, responding tribunals are forbidden to condition payment of UIFSA support orders on compliance with visitation orders.[10] This provision should not change the general practice in Ohio, embodied in *In re Byard*,[11] of keeping support and parenting issues separate.[12]

RC 3115.18 concerns the duties of a support enforcement agency under UIFSA, and implicitly acknowledges the shift of support enforcement activities to administrative agencies that has occurred since RURESA was drafted. The Act obligates the agency to provide services on request to petitioners in UIFSA proceedings[13] and sets forth a number of required services including taking all steps to enable a tribunal to take jurisdiction, set a hearing date, undertake an investigation, and notify a petitioner if jurisdiction cannot be obtained over a respondent.[14] These provisions are not significantly different from procedures required of a prosecutor under RURESA,[15] or the current operating procedures of a child support enforcement agency.

Certain aspects of RC 3115.18, however, are very different. Unlike RURESA,[16] this provision refers to the support enforcement agency instead of the prosecutor. While the prosecutor's office may fit within UIFSA's definition of a "support enforcement agency" as the official or

---

[6]RC 3115.16(B).

[7]UIFSA 305 (Comment).

[8]42 U.S.C.A. § 667.

[9]UIFSA 305 (Comment).

[10]RC 3115.16(D).

[11]In re Byard, 74 Ohio St. 3d 294, 1996-Ohio-163, 658 N.E.2d 735 (1996).

[12]In re Byard, 74 Ohio St. 3d 294, 1996-Ohio-163, 658 N.E.2d 735 (1996); Shanyfelt v. Shanyfelt, 118 Ohio App. 3d 243, 692 N.E.2d 642 (3d Dist. Crawford County 1997). See § 23:47, RURESA—Defenses.

[13]RC 3115.18(A).

[14]RC 3115.18(B).

[15]See, e.g., former RC 3115.10 (prosecutor to represent obligee in initiating state); former RC 3115.16(B) (prosecutor in responding state shall prosecute diligently); former RC 3115.17(A) (prosecutor to search for obligor or property); former RC 3113.21(B)(1)(b) (child support agency to conduct investigation).

[16]See, e.g., former RC 3115.10.

agency in charge of establishing and enforcing support orders,[17] the practice of assigning enforcement to the prosecutor is no longer prevalent. RC 3115.18 also sets up performance standards for communication with petitioners. The agency has two working days to send copies of written notices from tribunals[18] and copies of communications from respondents or their attorneys[19] to the petitioner. Perhaps the greatest difference in RC 3115.18 is the requirement that agency services be provided to any petitioner. Obligors as well as obligees may bring actions under UIFSA. This innovation will represent a significant change in practice for support agencies and has obvious funding implications. In the event that a support enforcement agency fails to perform its obligations under the Act, RC 3115.19 gives the Attorney General discretionary power to order the agency to comply or to provide services directly. Finally, RC 3115.20 explicitly permits private counsel in UIFSA proceedings instead of a support agency. RURESA was unclear on this point, although one Ohio case permitted private representation.[20]

UIFSA also sets out the responsibilities of the state information agency. RC 3115.21 designates the Department of Job and Family Services as Ohio's state information agency and makes it responsible for: (1) compiling lists of tribunals and enforcement agencies in the state with jurisdiction over support matters; (2) keeping a register of similar lists received from other states; (3) forwarding all documents received from an initiating court to a tribunal or state information agency in a place where jurisdiction exists over a party or the party's property; and (4) conducting a diligent search for an obligor and his or her property. This section makes no significant changes to former RC 3115.15.

§ 23:33 UIFSA—Civil provisions of general application— Procedural and evidentiary rules

RC 3115.22 is similar to former RC 3115.09(A). The petition must be verified and include the following information if known: the name, residential address, and social security numbers of the obligor and the obligee. In child support cases, the petition must also bear the name, sex, residential address, social security number, and date of birth of the child. The drafters also anticipated domestic violence situations. In the event that disclosure of identifying information would unreasonably endanger a child, or if an existing order so provides, RC 3115.23 authorizes a tribunal to enter an ex parte order limiting disclosure. A certified copy of every support order in effect must be submitted. As under RURESA,[1] the petitioner is at liberty to include any other relevant information. RC 3115.22 has two significant innovations. First, the

---

[17]RC 3115.01(V); see also RC 2301.35(A) (county commissioners may designate prosecuting attorney as child support enforcement agency).

[18]RC 3115.18(B)(4).

[19]RC 3115.18(B)(5).

[20]Lambright v. Pullen, 1988 WL 57506 (Ohio Ct. App. 6th Dist. Lucas County 1988).

[Section 23:33]

[1]Former RC 3115.09(A).

petition must specify the relief sought.[2] Second, the petition must conform substantially to the requirements of the federally mandated forms used by support enforcement agencies.[3] The latter innovation is designed to promote efficiency through standardization of forms.[4]

UIFSA continues the RURESA practice of not requiring a filing fee. Under RC 3115.24(A), a petitioner may not be assessed a filing fee. In practice, this formulation departs from the corresponding rule in former RC 3115.13 by waiving fees for both obligor and obligee. (Counsel should remember that UIFSA actions are not limited to obligees and public agencies.) Cost provisions, however, are similar to RURESA. Under former RC 3115.13, only an obligor (or the county) can be assessed costs. RC 3115.24(B) continues this practice by forbidding awards against obligees or support enforcement agencies unless state law provides otherwise. Costs include filing fees, attorney fees, necessary travel, and other expenses incurred by the obligee and his or her witnesses.[5] However, the award is now explicitly limited to a *prevailing* obligee.[6] As under RURESA, cost awards do not have priority over support awards. Finally, UIFSA permits assessment of costs and attorney fees if a tribunal finds that an action was undertaken primarily for delay.[7]

Of particular interest to attorneys is the provision of RC 3115.24(B) specifically permitting attorney fees to be awarded and enforced in the attorney's name. Granting fees directly to an attorney breaks with current practice. Ohio law presently views awards of attorney fees as spousal or child support. For example, in *Hamilton v. Hamilton*,[8] the Tenth District held that attorney fees awarded to an obligee in a contempt proceeding for non-support constituted "child support" under then RC 3113.21(O)(6) and (O)(7);[9] hence, they were subject to automatic wage withholding under then RC 3113.21(D)(1)(a). Similarly, courts have held that an award of attorney fees to a divorcing spouse is a form of support payable to the party and not the attorney.[10] Still, the break with past practice is not absolute. RC 3115.24(B) permits, but does not require, direct fee awards. Presumably, courts in UIFSA actions may continue to award attorney fees to the parties when there is a good rea-

---

[2]RC 3115.22(B).

[3]RC 3115.22(B).

[4]UIFSA 311 (Comment).

[5]RC 3115.24(B).

[6]RC 3115.24(B).

[7]RC 3115.24(C).

[8]Hamilton v. Hamilton, 40 Ohio App. 3d 190, 532 N.E.2d 213 (10th Dist. Franklin County 1988); see also Bratton v. Frederick, 109 Ohio App. 3d 13, 671 N.E.2d 1030 (3d Dist. Defiance County 1996) (attorney fees non-dischargeable support obligation in Chapter 7 bankruptcy).

[9]Comparable provisions now appear at RC 3119.01(A) and RC 3121.01(A).

[10]See, e.g., Reynolds v. Reynolds, 22 Ohio Op. 2d 162, 87 Ohio L. Abs. 250, 179 N.E.2d 160 (Ct. App. 4th Dist. Ross County 1961); Stout v. Stout, 3 Ohio App. 3d 279, 445 N.E.2d 253 (1st Dist. Hamilton County 1982); Gullia v. Gullia, 93 Ohio App. 3d 653, 639 N.E.2d 822 (8th Dist. Cuyahoga County 1994), cause dismissed, 70 Ohio St. 3d 1409, 637 N.E.2d 6 (1994).

son for doing so. For example, the obligee may already have paid his or her attorney fees, or it may be more effective in a particular case to rely on automatic wage withholding to secure payment.

RC 3115.25 concerns immunity for a petitioner and significantly expands on the RURESA rule in former RC 3115.29. Under RC 3115.25(A), direct or indirect participation (e.g., appearance through counsel or support agency services) does not confer personal jurisdiction in another proceeding. The possibility of jurisdiction by transient service is also eliminated by RC 3115.25(B)'s rule that the petitioner is not subject to service of process while physically present in the forum to participate in an UIFSA proceeding.[11] These immunities, however, do not apply to actions that arise from the petitioner's conduct in the forum that is unrelated to the UIFSA claim.[12] For example, the petitioner would be subject to litigation arising from a traffic accident occurring on the way to the courthouse. The immunity rules of RC 3115.25 do not apply if the tribunal is exercising long-arm jurisdiction over the respondent.[13]

Defenses of non-parentage may be raised only if the issue has not been determined beforehand.[14] At one level, this provision simply confirms the RURESA rule of res judicata in former RC 3115.24(A): parentage determinations are not subject to collateral attack elsewhere except where the prior proceeding was defective for want of jurisdiction or a denial of due process. However, RC 3115.26 is more embracing and refers to parentage issues "previously determined pursuant to law." This language establishes that parentage is determined by the law of the state issuing an order and implicitly acknowledges that state law varies greatly as to presumptions, defenses, and standing rules both before and after a formal determination of parentage. RC 3115.26 is intended to preempt litigation of parentage issues after registration for enforcement under RC 3115.39.[15] Commentary to Section 315 of the Uniform Act indicates that such issues of state law should be resolved outside of UIFSA through collateral actions in the issuing forum or the forum with continuing, exclusive jurisdiction.[16] RC 3115.26 does not apply when there is no prior determination of parentage or where the initiating tribunal lacked jurisdiction to determine parentage.[17] Given the variety of state laws on this matter, it may be difficult to know when parentage has been determined in the issuing state.

UIFSA sets out a number of special procedural rules designed to facil-

---

[11]RC 3115.24(B).

[12]RC 3115.24(C).

[13]RC 3115.04.

[14]RC 3115.26.

[15]See John J. Sampson, *UIFSA: An Interstate Support Act for the 21st Century*, 27 Fam. L. Q. 85, 139-40, n. 102-103 (1994).

[16]UIFSA 315 (Comment).

[17]See, e.g., Beam v. Beam, 2002-Ohio-2910, 2002 WL 1331989 (Ohio Ct. App. 2d Dist. Darke County 2002) (holding that UIFSA authorized husband to attack foreign state's jurisdiction to determine paternity).

itate interstate proceedings. RC 3115.27 combines certain RURESA rules with new provisions. As a general matter, the rules are designed to relieve the petitioner of the burdens of interstate litigation by taking advantage of new communications technologies and by avoiding hearsay problems.[18] These provisions are available under long-arm actions as well as in two-state UIFSA proceedings. The specific rules are:

(1) Physical presence of the petitioner before a responding tribunal is not necessary to establish, enforce, or modify a support order (RC 3115.27(A)). This rule expands on former RC 3115.18 which gave a court the discretion to continue a hearing and take evidence by deposition when an obligee was not present.

(2) Verified petitions, affidavits, documents substantially complying with federally mandated forms, and documents incorporated by reference are not excluded as hearsay if given under oath by a witness or party who resides out of state, and would otherwise have been admissible if given in person (RC 3115.27(B)). Former RC 3115.21(A) provided for admission of a certified copy of a support order as evidence of a duty to support. The UIFSA provision is obviously broader.

(3) Copies of child support payment records certified by the custodian are admissible to establish whether payments have been made (RC 3115.27(C)). This section has no direct counterpart in RURESA.

(4) Copies of bills for parentage testing and prenatal and postnatal care furnished to an adverse party at least ten days before trial are admissible to show the amount and reasonableness of such expenses (RC 3115.27(D)). This provision has no counterpart under RURESA.

(5) Documentary evidence may be transmitted from another state to a local tribunal by telephonic, telecopier, or other means which do not produce an original writing and may not be excluded based on the form of transmission (RC 3115.27(E)). This provision has no counterpart under RURESA. The effect is to relax the "best evidence" rule.

(6) Tribunals may permit a party or witness residing in another state to be deposed or give testimony by telephone, audiovisual, or electronic means at a designated tribunal in the other state. Tribunals of different states are required to cooperate in designating locations for deposition or testimony (RC 3115.27(F)). This provision has no counterpart in RURESA.

(7) An adverse inference may be drawn when a party refuses to testify on grounds of self-incrimination (RC 3115.27(G)). There is no direct counterpart of this rule under RURESA (although former RC 3115.19 did permit grants of use immunity). The UIFSA provision codifies a rule in effect in many states that adverse inferences may be drawn from a party's silence in a

---

[18]UIFSA 316 (Comment).

civil matter.[19]

(8) Privileges against disclosure of communications between spouses do not apply in UIFSA proceedings (RC 3115.27(H)). This section carries over the rule of former RC 3115.20 intact.

(9) A defense of spousal immunity is unavailable in UIFSA proceedings (RC 3115.27(I)). This provision carries over the rule of former RC 3115.08(A).

§ 23:34 UIFSA—Civil provisions of general application— Cooperation between tribunals

UIFSA breaks new ground with its provisions for cooperation between tribunals in the establishment and enforcement of support orders. RC 3115.28 permits an Ohio tribunal to communicate with a tribunal in another state and is modeled on Section 7(d) of the Uniform Child Custody Jurisdiction Act rather than any RURESA rule. RC 3115.29 authorizes tribunals to request the assistance of an out-of-state tribunal in obtaining discovery and, conversely, to compel a person within its own jurisdiction to comply with discovery orders from out-of-state. Under former RC 3115.18, a court in a responding state may designate a judge in an initiating state as a "person before whom a deposition may be taken." The UIFSA provision is broader and requires the cooperation of all jurisdictions involved in a support matter.

Finally, RC 3115.30 requires the support enforcement agency or the tribunal to disburse collections promptly. The same section requires agencies or tribunals to provide, on request of a party or an out-of-state support enforcement agency, a certified statement as to amounts collected and dates received. RC 3115.30 essentially carries over the requirements of former RC 3115.25.

§ 23:35 UIFSA—Establishment of support orders

RC 3115.31 concerns petitions for a responding tribunal to establish a support order in the first instance. RC 3115.31(A) authorizes a responding tribunal to enter an initial support order if no other state has taken continuing, exclusive jurisdiction over the matter and issued an order which is entitled to recognition. Of course, the tribunal must have personal jurisdiction over the respondent. It is important to remember that a tribunal acting under RC 3115.31 functions as a responding tribunal and may enter support orders only when the individual petitioner resides in another state or the support enforcement agency is located out-of-state. In-state residents would simply bring an action under state law as supplemented by the long-arm provisions of RC 3115.03 and the evidentiary and discovery rules in RC 3115.27 and RC

---

[19]UIFSA 316 (Comment).

3115.29.[1]

RC 3115.31(B) insists that parentage issues be resolved before the entry of a temporary order and provides three methods of proof: (1) a verified acknowledgment signed by the respondent; (2) a determination of parentage "by or pursuant to law"; or (3) presentation of clear and convincing evidence that the respondent is the parent. Neither the text of RC 3115.31(B) nor the commentary to Section 401 of the Uniform Act addresses determination of parentage "by or pursuant to law." Presumably the phrase has the same meaning as "by law" in RC 3115.26 where it includes presumptions of paternity such as signing a birth certificate as informant.[2] Unless there has been a prior determination, parentage will be tried under the law of the forum.[3]

Once a responding tribunal finds that an obligor indeed owes a duty of support, it must enter a support order plus other orders as appropriate under RC 3115.16. A copy of the order must then be transmitted to the initiating tribunal.[4] Payments under orders made pursuant to UIFSA must be made payable to the Office of Child Support in the Department of Job and Family Services.[5] Finally, RC 3115.31 provides instructions that a tribunal, making or modifying an order under that section or the former RC 3115.22 (i.e., under RURESA) on or after April 12, 1990, must comply with RC Chapters 3119, 3121, 3123, and 3125. The essence of this rule is a requirement that the tribunal modernize older awards by using the now standard techniques of child support schedules, automatic income withholding and enforcement following a default.

§ 23:36   UIFSA—Direct enforcement of orders without registration

UIFSA creates a direct enforcement mechanism against an obligor who is employed out-of-state. RC 3115.32 through RC 3115.37 permit direct transmission of an income withholding order to any person or entity outside of Ohio that meets the definition of payor under RC 3121.01.[1] In that section, a "payor" is defined broadly as any person or entity that pays or distributes income to an obligor.[2] A payor would include the obligor, if self-employed, an employer, and various governmental entities that distribute income substitutes such as the State Teachers Retirement Board or the Bureau of Workers' Compensation. It is unnecessary to commence an action or register the

---

[Section 23:35]

    [1]See § 23:28, UIFSA—Long-arm provisions; § 23:33, UIFSA—Civil provisions of general application—Procedural and evidentiary rules.

    [2]See § 23:33, UIFSA—Civil provisions of general application—Procedural and evidentiary rules.

    [3]UIFSA 315 (Comment).

    [4]RC 3115.31(C)(2).

    [5]RC 3115.31(C)(1).

[Section 23:36]

    [1]See RC 3115.01(N) (defining "payor" by reference to RC 3121.01).

    [2]RC 3121.01.

order in the other state.

RC 3115.33 establishes a payor's obligation to respect directly transmitted orders. So long as the order is "regular on its face," the payor must treat the order as if it had been issued in that state[3] and immediately provide a copy of the order to the obligor. The Act does not define the term "regular on its face" although the drafters' commentary optimistically calls for a liberal construction.[4] The goal of UIFSA's direct transmission mechanism is to permit enforcement of support orders outside of the more cumbersome registration process, when possible.[5]

Payors must withhold and distribute funds as directed by any order that meets the "test" of superficial regularity.[6] RC 3115.33(C) provides a measure of guidance to employers by requiring them to comply with withholding orders (or parts of orders) only if they specify the following:

(1) The amount and duration of periodic payments, stated as a sum certain (RC 3115.33(C)(1)).

(2) The person or agency to which payments are to be sent and an address (RC 3115.33(C)(2)).

(3) Medical support, either in the form of cash payments stated as a sum certain or as an order to provide employment-based health coverage (RC 3115.33(C)(3)).

(4) A sum certain representing fees and costs for a support enforcement agency, an issuing tribunal, or the obligee's attorney (RC 3115.33(C)(4)).

(5) A sum certain representing arrearages and interest (RC 3115.33(C)(5)).

Matters concerning a payor's processing fee for income withholding, limits set on maximum withholding levels, and time limits for initiating withholding are governed by the law of the obligor's principal place of employment.[7]

UIFSA anticipates situations in which payors will be faced with competing direct withholding requests and thus the need to prioritize withholding for multiple obligees. In the event of multiple income withholding orders for the same obligor, the payor is instructed to comply with the law of the obligor's principal place of employment, if the obligor is the payor's employee, and in all other cases with the law of the payor's principal place of business.[8] Compliance with UIFSA's direct withholding rules, moreover, confers immunity on the payor against civil liability

---

[3]RC 3115.33(B).

[4]UIFSA 501 (Comment).

[5]See § 23:37, UIFSA—Registration of foreign orders for enforcement—Procedures for registration.

[6]RC 3115.33(C).

[7]RC 3115.33(D).

[8]RC 3115.34.

to any individual or agency.[9] However, a payor who willfully fails to comply with a withholding order is subject to the same penalties as imposed for noncompliance with an intrastate order.[10]

Persons may contest the validity or enforcement of an order directly transmitted to an Ohio payor under RC 3115.37. "Obligors" who believe that they are not subject to such an order or otherwise have no duty of support, may request that the Office of Child Support (OCS) in the Department of Job and Family Services investigate. OCS in turn has 15 days to investigate and notify the requesting person of its determination. If OCS decides that the order is proper, the obligor may then bring an action for declaratory judgment under RC Chapter 2721.[11] Notice of the action must be given to any support agency providing services to the obligee, each payor who has received an income withholding order directly, and the person or agency designated to receive payment, or the obligee, if there is no such designation.[12]

Venue lies in the common pleas court of the county where the employer's principal place of business is located.[13] There are special rules for obligors who are not residents of Ohio. RC 3115.56(C), which has no counterpart in the Uniform Act, provides that out-of-state obligors must bring declaratory judgment actions against a payor in the county where the employer is "located."[14] The term "located" is not defined but presumably has the same meaning as the employer's "principal place of business" in RC 3115.37(A). Actions against financial institutions must be brought in the county where an account to be attached is located.[15] If venue cannot be determined by the previous rules, then the action lies in a county which borders the obligor's county of residence or in Franklin County.[16]

Choice of law issues in direct transmission contests may have been needlessly complicated by 1997 H.B. 352. Section 506 of the Uniform Act provides that the choice of law rules of Section 604 apply when directly transmitted orders are contested.[17] The latter section, in turn, provides that the nature and extent of a support obligation is to be judged under the law of the issuing state.[18] Curiously, the General Assembly omitted this choice of law instruction from Section 506's counterpart, RC 3115.37, even though the rule of UIFSA Section 604 has been enacted as RC 3115.41. It would be a mistake, however, to infer that the General Assembly intended a different choice of law rule without specifying one.

---

[9]RC 3115.35.

[10]RC 3115.36.

[11]RC 3115.37(A).

[12]RC 3115.37(B).

[13]RC 3115.37(A).

[14]RC 3115.56(C)(1).

[15]RC 3115.56(C)(2).

[16]RC 3115.56(C).

[17]UIFSA 506.

[18]UIFSA 604. See § 23:37, UIFSA—Registration of foreign orders for enforcement—Procedures for registration.

The omission is also inconsequential. As a practical matter, the obligor will be limited to two defenses under any state's law. Title IV-D rules limit defenses in intrastate withholding challenges to "mistake of fact" situations such as errors in calculation or mistaken identity.[19] State laws, including Ohio's,[20] have conformed to this requirement.[21] Obligors may also raise constitutional challenges to the order, such as lack of subject matter or personal jurisdiction. If at issue, the longer of two states' statutes of limitation would control.[22] Any other challenges to direct enforcement must be raised in the issuing forum.

UIFSA also permits transmission of income withholding orders directly to an Ohio support enforcement agency.[23] RC 3115.38 requires that the support enforcement agency undertake any relief available under administrative processes without registering the order under RC 3115.39.[24] If the obligor does not contest, administrative enforcement may proceed without registration. If the obligor does contest, then the support enforcement agency must register the order.[25]

§ 23:37 UIFSA—Registration of foreign orders for enforcement—Procedures for registration

UIFSA relies on registration of a foreign support order as the primary enforcement device for interstate cases.[1] RURESA included registration as an option for interstate enforcement.[2] Registration under UIFSA is conceptually distinct. Under both the two-state RURESA process as well as registration under RURESA, the resulting order in the responding state was generally viewed as a new order which co-existed with the order in the initiating state. Thus, the registering state was free to apply its own rules for vacating or modifying the registered order,[3] and often did. Under the "one order" philosophy of UIFSA, multiple orders will cease to exist. Responding states will be enforcing the order of another state, not their own.

Registration under UIFSA is a relatively simple process. Any interested person, including the obligor, the obligee, or a support enforce-

---

[19]42 U.S.C.A. § 666(b)(4)(A)(ii).

[20]See, e.g., RC 3123.04 (limiting challenges to mistake of fact).

[21]UIFSA 501 (Comment).

[22]UIFSA 604(b); RC 3115.41.

[23]RC 3115.38.

[24]RC 3115.38.

[25]RC 3115.38.

[Section 23:37]

[1]UIFSA 601 (Comment).

[2]Former RC 3115.32.

[3]UIFSA 603 (Comment); see, e.g., Lewis v. Lewis, 1997 WL 128566 (Ohio Ct. App. 10th Dist. Franklin County 1997) (modification of foreign order registered under RC 3115.32(G) permitted); Hudgins v. Hudgins, 80 Ohio App. 3d 707, 610 N.E.2d 582 (3d Dist. Henry County 1992) (same); Storey v. Storey, 1990 WL 119262 (Ohio Ct. App. 2d Dist. Greene County 1990) (same); but see Colston v. Colston, 1990 WL 127045 (Ohio Ct. App. 4th Dist. Ross County 1990) (registered order not modifiable).

ment agency, may send the following to the appropriate tribunal in the registering state:[4]

(1) A letter of transmittal requesting registration.

(2) Two copies (only one of which must be certified) of all orders to be registered, including modifications.

(3) A sworn statement by the person seeking registration or a custodian of pertinent records showing the amount of arrearages, if any.

(4) The name of the obligor and, if known, the obligor's address and social security number, the name and address of the obligor's employer and any other source of income, and a description and location of any non-exempt property of the obligor in the state.

(5) The name and address of the obligee and, if relevant, the agency or person to whom payments should be directed.

Upon receipt of this information, the registering tribunal must cause the support order to be filed along with all accompanying documents, regardless of form.[5] If the registering party seeks relief that requires a specific request or affirmative pleading under Ohio law, then an appropriate pleading may be filed at the same time as the request for registration or at a later date.[6] The effect is to put parties to an interstate case on a par with local litigants.[7]

Registration is perfected once an order is filed in an Ohio tribunal.[8] On registration, the order is enforceable under the same provisions and procedures as an order issued by an Ohio tribunal.[9] Tribunals in Ohio must recognize and enforce the issuing state's order but may not modify it except as permitted under the restrictive rules RC 3115.46 through RC 3115.51.[10]

Choice of law rules are set out in RC 3115.41. This section establishes two exceptions to the general UIFSA rule that the forum should apply its own procedural and substantive law.[11] First, the registering forum is required to apply the law of the issuing state when there are issues regarding the "nature, extent, amount, and duration" of the current obligation and the payment of arrearages. Inasmuch as the registering tribunal is enforcing the order of another state, it would make little sense for the enforcing forum to apply its own law. Arrearages are handled differently. RC 3115.41 provides that any difference in the statutes of limitations between the issuing and enforcing state must be

---

[4]RC 3115.39(A).

[5]RC 3115.39(B).

[6]RC 3115.39(C).

[7]UIFSA 602 (Comment).

[8]RC 3115.40.

[9]RC 3115.40.

[10]See § 23:39, UIFSA—Registration of foreign orders for modification.

[11]RC 3115.14.

resolved in favor of the longer period. UIFSA's drafters noted that accumulation of arrearages in the typical interstate case might be significant and that the obligor should not have the benefit of a forum with a shorter limitations period.[12]

§ 23:38 UIFSA—Registration of foreign orders for enforcement—Procedures for contesting a registered order

RC 3115.42 through RC 3115.45 govern procedures by which a party may challenge a registration. RC 3115.42 requires that, on registration of a foreign support order, the registering tribunal must give notice to all non-registering parties.[1] The notice must include a copy of the registered order plus any documents or other relevant material attached to the order.[2] Also, the notice must inform the non-registering party of the following:[3]

(1) The registered order is enforceable as of the date of registration in the same manner as an order issued by the registering tribunal;

(2) A hearing to contest validity must be requested within 20 days of the mailing or personal service of the notice;

(3) A failure to contest the order in a timely fashion will result in the confirmation and enforcement of the order and any arrearages, and that any future contest is precluded regarding any matter which could have been asserted; and

(4) The amount of any arrearages.

If the registered support order requires income withholding, the tribunal must issue a withholding notice to the obligor's employer under RC Chapter 3121.[4]

RC 3115.43 gives the non-registering party 20 days to request a hearing on the registration by filing a motion in the registering tribunal.[5] If a timely request is made, the tribunal must set a hearing and notify all parties by first class mail of the time and place.[6] At the hearing, the non-registering party may attempt to vacate the registration, to assert defenses to allegations of noncompliance, or to contest the remedies be-

---

[12]UIFSA 604 (Comment).

[Section 23:38]
[1]RC 3115.42(A).

[2]Genessee County v. Christenson, 1999 WL 1071564 (Ohio Ct. App. 5th Dist. Delaware County 1999) (court may rely on documents submitted with registration as evidence of arrearages).

[3]RC 3115.42(B).

[4]RC 3115.42(C).

[5]RC 3115.43(A).

[6]RC 3115.43(C).

ing sought or the amount of arrearages pursuant to RC 3115.44.[7] Failure to contest the order in a timely manner results in the confirmation of the registration by operation of law.[8]

Grounds for contesting registration are set out in RC 3115.44. As a general matter, they are quite limited and permit the contesting party only to demonstrate that the registered order is defective or has become inoperative, or that the obligor has complied with the order. One court has held that registration itself is not subject to minimum contacts analysis, reasoning the registration process is ex parte and that RC 3115.39 creates subject matter jurisdiction.[9] An obligor may, however, challenge the underlying order for want of personal jurisdiction under RC 3115.44(A)(1). Objections based on the content of an order are not permitted. Such arguments would run afoul of the rule limiting modifications to the forum with continuing, exclusive jurisdiction.[10] The contesting party has the burden of proving any of the following defenses:

(1) The issuing tribunal lacked personal jurisdiction over the contesting party (RC 3115.44(A)(1)).

(2) The order was obtained by fraud (RC 3115.44(A)(2)).

(3) The order has been vacated, suspended, or modified by a later order (RC 3115.44(A)(3)).

(4) The issuing tribunal has stayed the order pending appeal (RC 3115.44(A)(4)).

(5) There is a defense under the law of the registering state to the remedy sought (RC 3115.44(A)(5)).

(6) The contesting party has made full or partial payment (RC 3115.44(A)(6)).

(7) The statute of limitations as determined by RC 3115.41 precludes enforcement of arrearages (RC 3115.44(A)(7)).

Although the Act does not address this point, it seems obvious that principles of res judicata would prevent a challenging party from relying on any objection under RC 3115.44(A) which has been litigated in another forum. Enforcement of arrearages should be beyond challenge in most cases due to the Title IV-D requirement that accrued obligations be treated as final, non-modifiable judgments.[11]

Finally, RC 3115.44(C) provides that once an order is confirmed by operation of law (i.e., by failure to request a hearing on time) or after notice and hearing, it is final. No party may challenge any aspect of the order that could have been determined at the time of registration. Counsel should of course take careful note of UIFSA's narrow time frame for challenging registrations and act promptly when a contest is

---

[7]RC 3115.43(A).

[8]RC 3115.43(B).

[9]Compton v. Compton, 1999 WL 375578 (Ohio Ct. App. 2d Dist. Greene County 1999).

[10]RC 3115.07, RC 3115.40.

[11]42 U.S.C.A. § 666(a)(10); see also UIFSA 607 (Comment).

advisable. A failure to object to registration, however, does not negate the power to seek relief in the forum with continuing, exclusive jurisdiction.

§ 23:39 UIFSA—Registration of foreign orders for modification

Under URESA, Ohio was in the minority of jurisdictions which did not permit modification of a support order of another state when Ohio was the respondent state.[1] The provisions of the FFCCSOA and UIFSA basically adopted the prohibition of modification, allowing modification only in special limited situations. For instance, the state of Florida had permitted Florida's responding court to determine the extent to which an obligor's duty of support in the initiating URESA state would be enforced by a Florida responding court.[2] After the FFCCSOA the court concluded that the act preempted Florida law.[3]

RC 3115.46 through RC 3115.51 govern attempts to modify support orders. Under RC 3115.46, a party or support enforcement agency seeking to modify, or modify and enforce, a child support order of another state must register the order if it has not already been registered. Procedures for registration are the same as those found in RC 3115.39 (registration for enforcement). The petitioner may file a petition for modification at the time of registration or later. The petition must specify the grounds for modification. RC 3115.47 permits enforcement of an order registered for modification as if issued by a tribunal of the registering state; proposed modifications, however, must meet the strict requirements of RC 3115.48. The effect of RC 3115.47 is to permit interim enforcement of an existing order pending modification proceedings.

RC 3115.48 is the counterpart of RC 3115.07 ("continuing, exclusive jurisdiction") and determines when a registering Ohio tribunal gains jurisdiction to modify an order. A tribunal of a registering state may modify a support order only if it finds, after notice and hearing, that one of two conditions exist. The first condition is met when all of the following apply: (1) the child, the individual obligee, and the obligor no longer reside in the issuing state; (2) the petitioner seeking a modification is not a resident of the registering state; and (3) the respondent is subject to the personal jurisdiction of the registering state.[4] The second condition is met when both of the following apply: (1) an individual party or the child is subject to the personal jurisdiction of the registering state; and (2) all individual parties have filed a written consent in the issuing forum agreeing that the registering state may assume continuing,

---

[Section 23:39]
[1]State ex rel. Scioto County Child Support Enforcement Agency v. Adams, 1999 WL 597257 (Ohio Ct. App. 4th Dist. Scioto County 1999).

[2]Koon v. Boulder County, Dept. of Social Services, 494 So. 2d 1126 (Fla. 1986).

[3]State, Dept. of Revenue By and on Behalf of Jorda v. Fleet, 679 So. 2d 326 (Fla. Dist. Ct. App. 1st Dist. 1996).

[4]RC 3115.48(A)(1).

exclusive jurisdiction and may modify the support order.[5]

It is easier to understand the second condition. If the parties agree to transfer jurisdiction to another forum, the issuing state has little reason to second-guess their wisdom. Counsel should note that the agreement need only involve the "individual" parties. Thus, the wishes of a support agency to whom support rights have been assigned are irrelevant. The requirement that the registering state have personal jurisdiction over an individual party is easily met: the mere fact of bringing an action would confer personal jurisdiction over a petitioner.

A special rule for modification jurisdiction by consent applies when a child support order is issued by a tribunal of a foreign nation that has not enacted UIFSA or a comparable law. UIFSA's drafters feared situations where a foreign court would require the parties to appear personally before a modification would be ordered. If the individual obligees continue to reside in the foreign forum, then obligors under such orders who were also residents of American states could effectively veto modifications by refusing to appear before the issuing foreign tribunal and refusing consent to modification in a state tribunal.[6] RC 3115.48(A)(2) avoids this quandary by dispensing with the need for such an obligor who resides in Ohio to consent to modification jurisdiction. Thus, an Ohio tribunal would be permitted to modify a foreign child support order with the consent of the obligee alone and to assume continuing, exclusive jurisdiction over the order.

Policies underlying the first condition are less obvious. Under RC 3115.48(A)(1), the registering state may assume modification jurisdiction when the child and all individual parties have moved away from the issuing forum and the new forum has personal jurisdiction over the respondent. Certainly there is no reason to preserve jurisdiction in a forum that no longer has a direct connection to the child or the parties, especially when another forum has jurisdiction to act. However, RC 3115.48(A)(1) imposes the additional requirement that the party seeking the modification *not* be a resident of the registering state. The purpose of this unusual provision is to avoid the effects of "hometowning" which have plagued interstate support as well as custody cases.[7]

Drafters of the Act believed that the party seeking the modification should not have the advantage of litigating at home against a nonresident.[8] Commentary to Section 611 of the Uniform Act gives the example of the obligor who is served with notice of a modification hearing while visiting children in the obligee's home state. Although such service would comport with the minimal jurisdictional requirements of

---

[5]RC 3115.48(A)(2).

[6]UIFSA 611 (Comment).

[7]Compton v. Compton, 1999 WL 375578 (Ohio Ct. App. 2d Dist. Greene County 1999).

[8]UIFSA 611 (Comment).

Burnham[9] for transient service,[10] the motion would not meet the requirement that the movant be a non-resident. The obligee would have to bring a modification action elsewhere, most likely in the obligor's place of residence, to meet the requirements of Section 611. The burden is not completely one-sided. An obligor would be prevented from bringing a support modification "counterclaim" if the obligee initiates a custody action in the obligor's home state. UIFSA's requirement of non-resident status undoubtedly places a substantial burden on custodial parents who wish to modify support orders. An optimistic view is that the burden will be eased by the Act's easy registration procedures and special evidentiary rules.[11]

Interestingly, the FFCCSOA lacks UIFSA's requirement that the party seeking modification be a non-resident of the registering forum. Instead, 28 U.S.C.A. § 1738B(i) simply directs that persons seeking modification once jurisdiction has been lost by the issuing state should register the order "in a State with jurisdiction over the nonmovant for the purpose of modification." There is a plausible argument that the more permissive approach of the federal FFCCSOA preempts the state law non-resident rule of UIFSA. The argument, however, has been rejected by one court[12] and, as noted above, the preemptive effects of the FFCCSOA on UIFSA are unclear.[13]

Registration provisions of UIFSA are to facilitate enforcement of a support order of one state when the obligor has moved to another state. When an obligor moves from State A where the order originated, the order may be registered and enforced in the obligor's new state of residence. It does not contemplate a situation where the obligee has moved from State A and seeks to enforce or modify the support orders in the obligee's new state of residence.[14]

A special situation arises when all of the individual parties to a child support order have relocated to the same state. RC 3115.50 permits an Ohio tribunal to modify an order so long as none of the parties resides in the issuing state any longer, and all currently reside in Ohio. The child also must no longer reside in the issuing forum, but RC 3115.50 does not require that the child reside in Ohio. UIFSA provisions are applied selectively in proceedings under RC 3115.50. The general, jurisdictional, and other reconciliation rules found in RC 3115.01 through RC 3115.11 apply, as do the rules for registration, enforcement, and modification in

---

[9]Burnham v. Superior Court of California, County of Marin, 495 U.S. 604, 110 S. Ct. 2105, 109 L. Ed. 2d 631 (1990).

[10]See § 23:4, Impediments to interstate support actions—Personal jurisdiction—Ohio Civil Rules—Transient service.

[11]RC 3115.27, RC 3115.28, RC 3115.29.

[12]LeTellier v. LeTellier, 40 S.W.3d 490, 90 A.L.R.5th 707 (Tenn. 2001) (holding that Congress intended for the FFCCSOA to be consistent with UIFSA; hence the former did not preempt the latter).

[13]See § 23:23, Full Faith and Credit for Child Support Orders Act—Choice of law.

[14]RC 3115.48(A)(1); Lyles v. Lyles, 2001 WL 62539 (Ohio Ct. App. 2d Dist. Montgomery County 2001); Compton v. Compton, 1999 WL 375578 (Ohio Ct. App. 2d Dist. Greene County 1999).

RC 3115.39 through RC 3115.51. Ohio tribunals are also instructed to apply the "procedural and substantive laws of this state." Other UIFSA provisions are not applicable.

RC 3115.50 deviates from the corresponding section of the Uniform Act as promulgated by the National Conference of Commissioners on Uniform State Laws. Section 613 of UIFSA requires that the new forum apply only the jurisdictional and reconciliation rules of the Act (equivalent to RC 3115.01 through RC 3115.11). The drafters of the Uniform Act, however, intended to treat modification contests between parties who now reside in the same state as an intrastate matter to be governed by state law with slight enhancements from UIFSA.[15] It is not apparent, at least from the statutory language, what purpose the General Assembly had in mind when it added the highly "interstate" provisions of RC 3115.39 through RC 3115.51 regarding the enforcement and modification of other states' orders.

If an Ohio tribunal is authorized to modify an order under RC 3115.48, it will apply the "same requirements, procedures, and defenses that apply to the modifications of an order issued by a tribunal of . . . [Ohio]."[16] In other words, Ohio will apply its own standards for change of circumstances and its own child support guidelines. However, the Ohio tribunal may not alter nonmodifiable aspects of the prior order.[17] For example, if the issuing state recognizes a duty of support through age 21, the Ohio tribunal cannot apply a local rule terminating support at age 18.[18] If competing support orders have been issued for the same child and obligor, then the order that controls under RC 3115.09 determines which obligations are nonmodifiable.[19]

Once an Ohio tribunal has issued a modification consistent with RC 3115.48, that tribunal acquires continuing, exclusive jurisdiction over the support matter.[20] That order is entitled to recognition and enforcement by all other states upon registration. The petitioner must file a certified copy of the order with the prior issuing tribunal and with any tribunal where, to the petitioner's knowledge, the prior order had been registered.[21] RC 3115.49 and UIFSA obligate the state that issued the prior order to enforce the modified order upon registration.[22] Filing a certified copy of the modified order in the issuing tribunal under RC 3115.51 would not appear to meet RC 3115.39's requirements for registration. The original issuing forum is permitted to enforce the prior order as to arrearages accruing before modification, nonmodifiable provi-

---

[15]UIFSA 613 (Comment).
[16]RC 3115.48(B).
[17]RC 3115.48(C).
[18]UIFSA 611 (Comment).
[19]RC 3115.48(C).
[20]RC 3115.48(D).
[21]RC 3115.51.
[22]RC 3115.49; UIFSA 612.

sions of the order, and violations occurring before the modification.[23] Presumably, this provision is intended to allow the prior forum to enforce parts of an order that will survive any modification without the burden of commencing a new claim. Commentary to Section 612 of the Uniform Act gives the example of a contractual promise to establish a child's college education trust fund. If unmodifiable, the original forum would be empowered to enforce this provision regardless of the law of the modifying jurisdiction and without registration for enforcement. If the provision were genuinely unmodifiable, however, the modifying forum would not be able to alter it under RC 3115.48(C).[24]

§ 23:40 UIFSA—Registration of foreign orders for modification—Calculation factors

Once an Ohio court has gained jurisdiction to modify an order, it may apply Ohio law in determining whether a change of circumstances has occurred that would warrant a modification in a support orders. Specifically, an Ohio court may apply the Ohio rule that a 10% change in a child support amount, as calculated under this state's child support guidelines, constitutes a change in circumstances justifying a modification.[1] The exception is that an Ohio court may not modify portions of a prior decree which are unmodifiable.[2]

§ 23:41 UIFSA—Determination of parentage

UIFSA permits petitioners to bring direct parentage actions. Under RURESA, provisions for establishing paternity are limited. Former RC 3115.24(B) permitted an obligor to raise a *defense* of non-parentage so long as the matter has not been previously litigated. No explicit provision is made for direct parentage actions outside of support claims. UIFSA, however, permits "pure" parentage actions that are not joined with support claims. RC 3115.52(A) authorizes Ohio tribunals to serve as initiating or responding tribunals for the purpose of determining whether a petitioner or respondent is the parent of a child. Petitioners are free, of course, to join the parentage claim to a support action under RC 3115.31. Responding tribunals will apply their own law, including presumptions of parentage and choice of law rules.[1] Counsel should not make the decision to direct parentage actions to another forum lightly. There still exists a variety of presumptions under state law regarding

---

[23]RC 3115.49.

[24]Cook v. Cook, 143 Ohio App. 3d 687, 758 N.E.2d 1158 (9th Dist. Lorain County 2001).

[Section 23:40]

[1]RC 3119.79(A); see, e.g., Cook v. Cook, 143 Ohio App. 3d 687, 758 N.E.2d 1158 (9th Dist. Lorain County 2001) (applying former RC 3113.215(B)(4) to modify a Georgia support order).

[2]RC 3115.48(C); see, e.g., Cook v. Cook, 143 Ohio App. 3d 687, 758 N.E.2d 1158 (9th Dist. Lorain County 2001).

[Section 23:41]

[1]RC 3115.52(B).

parentage, and an equally broad array of rules for re-opening an initial determination. Any decision reached by a responding tribunal under RC 3115.52 or comparable statutes will be binding on the parties in other jurisdictions.[2] Such determinations, however, may be challenged for want of personal jurisdiction.[3]

§ 23:42 RURESA—In general

In 1950, the National Conference of Commissioners on Uniform State Laws promulgated the Uniform Reciprocal Enforcement of Support Act (URESA). The Act was followed by amendments in 1952 and 1958. Significant amendments in 1968 resulted in the retitled Revised Uniform Reciprocal Enforcement of Support Act (RURESA). At one time, some version of the Act was in effect in all American jurisdictions. The majority of states, including Ohio, adopted RURESA, although a significant number of states retained URESA or a similar version. Hence, URESA is hardly a uniform act in the strictest sense. As of mid-1997, about 35 states had repealed their versions of RURESA or URESA in favor of UIFSA. RURESA was in effect in Ohio until January 1, 1998.

It is critical that domestic relations practitioners understand that RURESA has ceased to be the law for new cases arising after January 1, 1998. The Personal Responsibility and Work Opportunity Reconciliation Act of 1996[1] amended Title IV-D of the Social Security Act to require that all states adopt UIFSA by January 1, 1998, as part of their Title IV-D plans, at the risk of losing federal funding. Ohio complied with the federal mandate by enacting 1997 H.B. 352, which repealed RURESA and adopted UIFSA, effective January 1, 1998. Since UIFSA does not by its terms provide for retroactive application to *pending* actions, RURESA should still apply to any actions that were on-going on January 1, 1998, UIFSA's effective date.[2] Ohio's version of UIFSA does provide that any orders already *issued* under RURESA remain in effect as issued, but may be modified or terminated under UIFSA.[3] UIFSA may not be used, however, to revive an action that had been barred under former RC 3115.06.[4] Decisions under RURESA, however, may be an important source for interpretation of similar provisions under UIFSA.

RURESA is essentially a procedural device to prosecute support

---

[2]RC 3115.26.

[3]RC 3115.44(A)(1); see Beam v. Beam, 2002-Ohio-2910, 2002 WL 1331989 (Ohio Ct. App. 2d Dist. Darke County 2002).

[Section 23:42]

[1]Pub. L. No. 104-193 § 321, 110 Stat. 2221 (1996).

[2]RC 1.48, RC 1.58; Nease v. Medical College Hosp., 64 Ohio St. 3d 396, 1992-Ohio-97, 596 N.E.2d 432 (1992) (statutes prospective unless General Assembly clearly indicates retrospective effect); see, e.g., State ex rel. Scioto County Child Support Enforcement Agency v. Adams, 1999 WL 597257 (Ohio Ct. App. 4th Dist. Scioto County 1999) (URESA applies to pending actions); Chamberlin v. Chamberlin, 1998 WL 274823 (Ohio Ct. App. 4th Dist. Washington County 1998) (same).

[3]RC 3115.57.

[4]RC 3115.57.

obligations against non-residents. It does not create independent support obligations; rather, it is available to enforce any "duty of support," which the Act defines as a "duty of support imposed or *imposable* by the law, or by order, decree, or judgment of any court."[5] "Law" in turn means "both common and statute law."[6] Thus, RURESA is available to enforce existing orders and, contrary to widely held misbeliefs, may be used to establish initial awards.[7] RURESA may also be used to make an initial paternity determination when non-paternity is raised as a defense in a RURESA proceeding.[8] The Act treats support obligations broadly, specifically including arrearages[9] and reimbursement of public agencies which have provided support to individual obligees.[10] Unlike UIFSA,[11] RURESA does not distinguish between spousal and child support. Resort to RURESA will not affect any other available rights, as remedies under RC Chapter 3115 are "in addition to, not in substitution for, any other remedies."[12]

RURESA neatly divides jurisdictions into two categories. The initiating state is the forum where "a proceeding pursuant to [RURESA] is commenced"[13] while the responding state is the forum where "any proceeding pursuant to the proceeding in the initiating state is or may be commenced."[14] In simpler English, petitions are filed in the initiating state for transmission to a responding state where the obligor is subject to process. In addition, RURESA permitted direct registration of foreign support orders by obligees.[15] Under former RC 3115.32, registered orders were then treated as orders of Ohio courts for purposes of enforcement and modification.[16]

Choice of law under RURESA depends, oddly enough, on the obligor's state of residence. Former RC 3115.06 provides that duties of support under RURESA "are those imposed under the laws of any state where the obligor was present for the period during which support is sought." In *Little v. Little*,[17] husband and wife were divorced in Florida. The Florida judgment incorporated a settlement which provided that husband

[5]Former RC 3115.01(B)(6) (emphasis added).

[6]Former RC 3115.01(B)(5).

[7]Swayne v. Newman, 131 Ohio App. 3d 793, 723 N.E.2d 1117 (4th Dist. Scioto County 1998) (where a decree is silent as to support, URESA confers subject matter jurisdiction to establish support where obligor is a resident).

[8]Former RC 3115.24(B).

[9]Former RC 3115.08(A).

[10]Former RC 3115.07.

[11]See § 23:29, UIFSA—Subject matter jurisdiction.

[12]Former RC 3115.02.

[13]Former RC 3115.01(B)(2).

[14]Former RC 3115.01(B)(3).

[15]Former RC 3115.32.

[16]Hudgins v. Hudgins, 80 Ohio App. 3d 707, 610 N.E.2d 582 (3d Dist. Henry County 1992).

[17]Little v. Little, 1991 WL 70723 (Ohio Ct. App. 2d Dist. Greene County 1991); see also State of N.Y. ex rel. Krytus v. Krytus, 1986 WL 3256 (Ohio Ct. App. 6th Dist. Wood County 1986).

would pay child support until the child reached the age of majority and that the agreement was to be governed by Florida law. Wife and child subsequently moved to Oklahoma where wife brought a RURESA petition against husband who had relocated to Ohio. The Second District held that an Ohio court, acting as a responding court under RURESA, should apply Ohio law since Ohio was the obligor's place of residence. Thus, the husband was obliged by RC 3103.03 to continue support past majority as long as the child continuously attended high school. Counsel should note, however, that *Little* was decided before the enactment of the Full Faith and Credit for Child Support Orders Act. Under the FFCCSOA, Ohio would have qualified for continuing, exclusive jurisdiction since all parties had left Florida, but would have been obliged to apply Florida law in determining the duration of support.[18]

Counsel should also take note that RURESA orders entered in a RURESA proceeding in a responding state do not necessarily supersede prior orders issued by the initiating state.[19] Registration of foreign orders under former RC 3115.32, which effectively converted a foreign into an Ohio support order, exacerbated this problem. Thus, obligors were subject to multiple and inconsistent orders for the same support obligation.[20] However, the multiple order system, as far as child support orders are involved, has been overridden by the enactment of the federal Full Faith and Credit for Child Support Orders Act, which generally requires states to enforce, and not modify, support decrees from sister states.[21] UIFSA imposes a similar requirement for both child support and spousal support orders.[22] The effect is to preempt those sections of RURESA, such as former RC 3115.06 and RC 3115.28,[23] which permit simultaneous orders in different jurisdictions.

§ 23:43   RURESA—Ohio as an initiating state

A RURESA action is initiated by the filing of a complaint[1] by the obligee or by any state or political subdivision which furnishes support to the obligee.[2] This gives the child support enforcement agency, for example, the right to file for reimbursement as well as for ongoing support. Standing rules for individual obligees are flexible. Former RC

---

[18]See § 23:23, Full Faith and Credit for Child Support Orders Act—Choice of law.

[19]Former RC 3115.28; In re Keighley, 1999-Ohio-947, 1999 WL 1084269 (Ohio Ct. App. 3d Dist. Union County 1999) (Florida's orders as responding state do not supersede child support order as issued by court in Ohio; jurisdiction remained in Ohio); Bobbs v. Cline, 116 Ohio App. 3d 46, 686 N.E.2d 556 (7th Dist. Jefferson County 1997) (same).

[20]See § 23:46, RURESA—Modifications—Other states.

[21]See § 23:21, Full Faith and Credit for Child Support Orders Act—In general.

[22]See § 23:29, UIFSA—Subject matter jurisdiction, § 23:39, UIFSA—Registration of foreign orders for modification.

[23]Paton v. Brill, 104 Ohio App. 3d 826, 663 N.E.2d 421 (10th Dist. Franklin County 1995).

[Section 23:43]
[1]Former RC 3115.09.
[2]Former RC 3115.07.

3115.11 permits anyone having legal custody of a minor to bring an action without the appointment of a guardian ad litem. This rule permits minor obligees to proceed without going through the cumbersome process of seeking appointment of a guardian ad litem. One court has read former RC 3115.11 broadly to permit a grandmother who had assumed the care of a child to initiate a RURESA action as the child's de facto guardian.[3] The complaining party may file pro se, through a private attorney, or through a Title IV-D agency. Jurisdiction over RURESA actions lies with "any trial court of record."[4]

RURESA requires that the complaint be verified and state the name, address, and circumstances of the obligor, and all other information pertinent to the case.[5] It is not necessary to allege specifically that the obligor is the father of the child.[6] The complaint presents an opportunity for obligee's counsel to include information favorable to the obligee. Thus, counsel should normally attach a certified copy of the previous support order, an affidavit signed by the obligee or an official of the child support enforcement agency setting forth the arrearage that exists, and a copy of the payment record to verify arrearages. Once the complaint is prepared, the original and three copies should be filed with the court.

The complaint must be reviewed by the initiating court to certify that it alleges sufficient facts to determine that the obligor may owe a duty of support and that a court of the responding jurisdiction may obtain jurisdiction over the obligor or his or her property.[7] This review is usually a cursory event. Upon certification, the court will forward three certified copies of the complaint, the certificate, and an authenticated copy of RC Chapter 3115, prior to its amendment by 1997 H.B. 352, to the responding court.[8] Former RC Chapter 3115 designated the Department of Human Services as the state information agency and required that it maintain a list of courts of record within Ohio and a registry of courts of record of other states.[9] (These functions are now performed by the Department of Job and Family Services.[10]) When the proper responding court is unknown, counsel may resort to these registries. It may be easier, however, to contact the local prosecutor's office, which should have a registry of courts. This list has the name and address of each jurisdiction within the United States and any foreign countries with which reciprocal jurisdiction exists. The court must accept and forward the petition even if there is another pending action, such as an action for divorce, separation, annulment, dissolution, habeas corpus, adoption, or custody,

---

[3]McMullen v. Muir, 34 Ohio App. 3d 241, 517 N.E.2d 1381 (8th Dist. Cuyahoga County 1986).

[4]Former RC 3115.08(B).

[5]Former RC 3115.09(A).

[6]McMullen v. Muir, 34 Ohio App. 3d 241, 517 N.E.2d 1381 (8th Dist. Cuyahoga County 1986).

[7]Former RC 3115.12.

[8]Former RC 3115.12.

[9]Former RC 3115.15(A).

[10]RC 3115.21(B).

or where another court has already issued a support order and retained jurisdiction for its enforcement.[11]

RURESA requires that the initiating and responding courts accept a petition without a prepaid filing fee or other costs; however, costs incurred in the initiating court may, on request, be taxed to the obligor by the responding court.[12] RC 3123.17(B) specifically permits the assessment of attorney fees when any support order, original or modification, is obtained, including all actions under former RC Chapter 3115. To preserve this claim, counsel should submit an affidavit as to reasonable attorney fees and should specifically set forth a demand for attorney fees in the petition. In addition, the court is required to assess interest on amounts found to be in arrears when the failure to comply with a prior order is willful.[13]

§ 23:44 RURESA—Ohio as a responding state

Upon receipt of a petition from an initiating state, the responding Ohio court is required to docket the action and notify the prosecuting attorney.[1] It is the obligation of the prosecuting attorney to prosecute the case diligently, to take all necessary steps to gain jurisdiction over the obligor or his or her property, to request that the court set a hearing, and to give notice to the obligor.[2] He or she must also conduct a diligent search for assets.[3] If the obligor or his or her property are located elsewhere, the prosecutor must so inform the clerk of court; the clerk must then forward all documents to an appropriate court in that location.[4] A failure by the trial court to ensure representation of the obligee at all stages has been ruled reversible error.[5]

A common procedure used in Ohio is to issue a notice of hearing consisting of a citation setting the time and place for a hearing.[6] Service may be done by certified mail or personal service under the Civil Rules.[7] Hearings are conducted under evidence rules that apply in juvenile court.[8] To maximize information available to the responding court, RURESA specifically disallows the husband-wife privilege,[9] permits the court to grant use immunity whenever a party claims a privilege against

---

[11]Former RC 3115.09(B).

[12]Former RC 3115.13.

[13]RC 3123.17(A).

[Section 23:44]

[1]Former RC 3115.16(A).

[2]Former RC 3115.16(B).

[3]Former RC 3115.17(A).

[4]Former RC 3115.17(B).

[5]Brown v. Brown, 16 Ohio App. 3d 26, 474 N.E.2d 613 (12th Dist. Warren County 1984).

[6]Robinson v. Robinson, 8 Ohio App. 2d 235, 37 Ohio Op. 2d 218, 221 N.E.2d 598 (10th Dist. Franklin County 1964).

[7]Civ. R. 4 to Civ. R. 4.6.

[8]Former RC 3115.21(A).

[9]Former RC 3115.20.

self-incrimination,[10] and provides that participation in a RURESA proceeding does not confer jurisdiction over that party in a different proceeding.[11]

Once service of process is perfected, discovery is permitted. Interrogatories and depositions upon written questions are recommended discovery tools for effective and affordable disclosure of necessary information. Given the interstate nature of RURESA actions, response time for interrogatories or other discovery devices should be extended when reasonable. Dismissal, however, would be appropriate under Civ. R. 37(B) if the obligee fails or refuses to comply with discovery requests. In a typical RURESA action, the obligee will not be able to appear at a hearing in the responding state. Thus, in cases where the obligor denies liability or offers evidence of a defense, former RC 3115.18 permits the court to continue the hearing so that the obligee may offer evidence by deposition in the initiating state.[12]

The hearing process is relatively simple. The court reviews the petition. If the action is based on a support order issued by another court, a certified copy of the order constitutes prima facie evidence of the obligor's duty of support.[13] If there is no prior support order, the obligee must go through the more burdensome process of establishing a duty of support under the law of the obligor's residence, subject, of course, to the choice of law limitations imposed by the FFCCSOA. If no defense is present, the court will enter appropriate findings and order the obligor to pay support or reimbursement.[14]

Enforcement of RURESA support orders is quite similar to enforcement of intrastate orders. Former RC 3115.22(D) requires that the RURESA court comply with RC 3113.21 to RC 3113.219 (now RC Chapter 3121) when entering or modifying a support order. The same section specifically incorporates the requirement of former RC 3113.21(A)(1) that a support order have a general provision requiring withholding or deduction of wages or assets or other provisions as required by former RC 3113.21(D). Hence, customary procedures such as automatic wage withholding, attachment of assets or benefits, and bond posting are available in RURESA actions. Payments are made to the child support enforcement agency.[15] Courts are also permitted to require the posting of a bond.[16] More significantly, former RC 3115.23(C) empowers courts to hold obligors in contempt for violation of court orders. Presumably a RURESA court would have the same power under the general contempt statute.[17] In addition to penalties imposed under a contempt sanction, the court must award all court costs plus reasonable

---

[10]Former RC 3115.19.

[11]Former RC 3115.29.

[12]Former RC 3115.18.

[13]Former RC 3115.21(A).

[14]Former RC 3115.22(A).

[15]Former RC 3115.22(C).

[16]Former RC 3115.23(A).

[17]RC 2705.031(B)(1).

attorney fees arising from the contempt proceeding to the obligee.[18] Any support payments collected are transmitted by the responding court to the initiating court,[19] which in turn disburses the money.[20] Finally, RURESA courts are empowered to encourage compliance by suspending an obligor's visitation rights. Former RC 3115.21(B) permits the court to suspend visitation rights if it finds a willful failure to support. This provision is an exception to the general rule of former RC 3115.21(A) that support and custody matters are separate.[21] As a practical matter, however, the obligee in a RURESA proceeding relies on the "kindness of strangers." Results in a RURESA action depend upon on forces beyond the obligee's control, such as the prosecuting attorney's diligence in finding the obligor and serving him or her with process to appear. Results have been mixed.[22]

§ 23:45 RURESA—Modifications—Ohio courts

An Ohio court's power to modify a prior order in a RURESA action has been a remarkably opaque subject. The leading case is the Ohio Supreme Court's decision in *San Diego County v. Elavsky.*[1] Construing former RC 3115.27, the Court held that a support award in an *initial* RURESA proceeding must conform to the amount decreed in the prior order. Relying on former RC 3115.28, the Court went on to hold that subsequent modifications by the court issuing the prior order did not automatically work a modification of the Ohio RURESA order; rather, the prior court must specifically provide for the modification of any subsequent RURESA order. *Elavsky* runs counter to the majority of other jurisdictions, which would permit modifications by responding courts to modify support awards in initial RURESA proceedings.[2]

The key factor in applying the *Elavsky* rule is the support specified in the prior order. In *Minnesota ex rel. Monroe v. Monroe,*[3] a public agency sought reimbursement for public assistance paid to a child. The obligor's support obligation had been suspended by a Minnesota court due to interference with visitation rights. Applying the *Elavsky* rule that a responding court must conform its support order to the amount determined in the previous support action, the Ninth District held that the rights of the state furnishing support under public assistance are no

---

[18]Former RC 3115.22(D).

[19]Former RC 3115.25(A).

[20]Former RC 3115.26.

[21]See In re Byard, 74 Ohio St. 3d 294, 1996-Ohio-163, 658 N.E.2d 735 (1996).

[22]Blueprint for Reform at 227-237.

[Section 23:45]

[1]San Diego County v. Elavsky, 58 Ohio St. 2d 81, 12 Ohio Op. 3d 88, 388 N.E.2d 1229 (1979).

[2]In re Keighley, 1999-Ohio-947, 1999 WL 1084269 (Ohio Ct. App. 3d Dist. Union County 1999) (citing Note, *Interstate Enforcement of Support Obligations Through Long Arm Statutes and URESA*, 18 J. Fam. L. 537, 549 n. 50 (1980)).

[3]State of Minn. ex rel. Monroe v. Monroe, 1995 WL 411393 (Ohio Ct. App. 9th Dist. Summit County 1995).

greater than the rights of the obligee as defined by the prior order. Thus, *Elavsky* required that no relief be granted in *Monroe*. The court did not declare that the other state was prohibited from bringing an action outside of RURESA for reimbursement of necessaries, just that RURESA was not the proper vehicle.[4]

Elavsky does not require that a responding court dismiss an action when the prior award is unclear. In *Linville v. Marshall*,[5] the obligor claimed that the Kentucky decree which awarded custody of one child to each parent and was silent as to support for either child implicitly provided that the custodial parent assumed the duty of support for the child in that parent's custody and, thus, that the trial court did not have subject matter jurisdiction to modify. The First District held that since the trial court had jurisdiction over the obligor's person and the decree was silent as to support, the court could exercise jurisdiction to set a support order.

Elavsky did not address the issue of modification of a RURESA order after the entry of the initial order. The courts of appeals have reached inconsistent results on this issue. One group of decisions takes the position that *Elavsky* also disallows subsequent modification of the Ohio RURESA order.[6] Another group would permit modification after entry of an initial, conforming order.[7] The distinction appears to be that the foreign support orders in the latter group were registered under former RC 3115.32 and hence became Ohio orders modifiable under Ohio law. The controversy, as it concerns child support orders, has been mooted by the federal Full Faith and Credit for Child Support Orders Act. The Act requires state courts to enforce sister state support orders according to their own terms, and disallows modifications under most circumstances.[8] Hence, a RURESA order must conform to a prior order both initially and subsequently.[9]

§ 23:46 RURESA—Modifications—Other states

Prior to the enactment of the Full Faith and Credit for Child Support Orders Act, an obligee ran the risk that the responding court would

---

[4]State of Minn. ex rel. Monroe v. Monroe, 1995 WL 411393 (Ohio Ct. App. 9th Dist. Summit County 1995).

[5]Linville v. Marshall, 1995 WL 84075 (Ohio Ct. App. 1st Dist. Hamilton County 1995).

[6]See, e.g., State ex rel. Scioto County Child Support Enforcement Agency v. Adams, 1999 WL 597257 (Ohio Ct. App. 4th Dist. Scioto County 1999) (initial, conforming order not modifiable); Colston v. Colston, 1990 WL 127045 (Ohio Ct. App. 4th Dist. Ross County 1990) (same); Jacobs v. Jacobs, 62 Ohio App. 3d 271, 575 N.E.2d 480 (6th Dist. Lucas County 1988) (same); Briggs v. Briggs, 1987 WL 7177 (Ohio Ct. App. 12th Dist. Clermont County 1987) (same).

[7]See, e.g., Hudgins v. Hudgins, 80 Ohio App. 3d 707, 610 N.E.2d 582 (3d Dist. Henry County 1992); Storey v. Storey, 1990 WL 119262 (Ohio Ct. App. 2d Dist. Greene County 1990).

[8]See § 23:21, Full Faith and Credit for Child Support Orders Act—In general.

[9]See Paton v. Brill, 104 Ohio App. 3d 826, 663 N.E.2d 421 (10th Dist. Franklin County 1995).

enter a child support order that provided less support. Former RC
3115.28 and its equivalents in other states provide that the award by
the initiating state "does not nullify and is not nullified by . . . a support order made by a court of any other state pursuant to [RURESA]."
Moreover, RURESA contemplates that a responding state will enter a
support order based on the law of the obligor's residence which may be
different from the support award or obligation in the initiating state.[1] As
a result, the jurisdiction in the best position to enforce an award, i.e.,
the obligor's current home state, may collect at a much lower rate than
required by the initiating state. FFCCSOA now severely restricts a
court's power to modify an out-of-state support award.[2]

Obligees also take a risk that the public representatives in the
responding state may compromise their claims unfavorably. In *Wyatt v.
Wyatt*,[3] a former wife initiated a RURESA action to recover a total of
$29,000 in child support arrearages owed by an Alaska resident. The ar-
rearages had been reduced to four judgments by the Franklin County
Court of Common Pleas. The Alaska Attorney General reached a settlement for less than $7,000. An appeal brought by the ex-wife was later
dismissed for want of prosecution; orders reflecting satisfaction of judgment were then filed in the Ohio trial court. Later, the ex-wife brought
an action to revive the Ohio judgments for $29,000. The Ohio Supreme
Court held that the wife was bound by the Alaska judgment under
principles of full faith and credit and res judicata. The decision turns on
the fact that the wife made an actual appearance in the Alaska proceeding and on a finding of fact by the Alaska trial court that she had given
authority to the attorney general to compromise the claim. The Court
reasoned that since the Alaska court had personal jurisdiction and
subject matter jurisdiction over the claim, the court's findings were res
judicata and could not be attacked collaterally in Ohio. Even if the
Alaska court had made an incorrect ruling, its judgment was owed full
faith and credit. Justice Resnik wrote a strong dissent arguing that
under former RC 3115.28 and its Alaska counterpart, the Alaska court
had no authority to "nullify" the Ohio judgments.

Lower courts have applied *Wyatt* sparingly.[4] In *Homewood v. Homewood*,[5] the Eleventh District held that, absent evidence that the
petitioner had given anyone in the responding state the authority to
reduce the monthly support obligation or to reduce the obligor's arrearage, the original decreed amount would be used to compute the
arrearage. The appellate court focused on the specific finding in *Wyatt*

---

[1]Former RC 3115.06.

[2]See § 23:21, Full Faith and Credit for Child Support Orders Act—In general.

[3]Wyatt v. Wyatt, 65 Ohio St. 3d 268, 602 N.E.2d 1166 (1992).

[4]Homewood v. Homewood, 1993 WL 548061 (Ohio Ct. App. 11th Dist. Geauga
County 1993); Kelley v. Kelley, 1994 WL 90378 (Ohio Ct. App. 9th Dist. Summit County
1994), dismissed, appeal not allowed, 70 Ohio St. 3d 1425, 638 N.E.2d 87 (1994); Bobbs
v. Cline, 116 Ohio App. 3d 46, 686 N.E.2d 556 (7th Dist. Jefferson County 1997).

[5]Homewood v. Homewood, 1993 WL 548061 (Ohio Ct. App. 11th Dist. Geauga
County 1993).

that the obligee had given the enforcement division in Alaska the "actual authority" to enter into a settlement. Mere representation by a prosecutor in a RURESA action does not constitute authorization to settle without specific consent by the petitioner. Otherwise the petitioner would be in the "unconscionable position of having to waive her rights to the full amount of ordered support in order to pursue collection through an URESA action."[6] Thus, it appears that the holding in *Wyatt* has been restricted to its narrow and unusual facts. It is also doubtful that the Alaska court in *Wyatt* would now have subject matter jurisdiction under the FFCCSOA to modify the Ohio judgments.[7]

§ 23:47 RURESA—Defenses

In keeping with the informal nature of RURESA proceedings, responding courts are not required to permit the defendant to file an answer.[1] Defenses are normally raised during hearings provided for under former RC 3115.16(B). So long as the defendant has an opportunity to raise defenses then, or after a continuance under former RC 3115.18, no error has been committed.[2]

Under RURESA, an obligor may raise only two defenses to enforcement of a prior order. He may argue that he is not the father of the child or that the underlying order is void.[3] Former RC 3115.24(B) permits the obligor to plead non-paternity as a defense so long as there is no prior determination by any court or administrative tribunal in Ohio or elsewhere. Prior determinations of parentage are owed full faith and credit.[4] The trial court must, of course, have sufficient evidence to support a finding of parentage.[5] As a practical matter, however, the requirement that a RURESA court order genetic testing[6] means that in most cases the evidence will be so definite that a dismissal or settlement will quickly follow. Even when prior parentage proceedings are defective, the Ohio court must adjudicate parentage on the merits rather than dismiss

---

[6]Homewood v. Homewood, 1993 WL 548061, at *4 (Ohio Ct. App. 11th Dist. Geauga County 1993).

[7]See § 23:21, Full Faith and Credit for Child Support Orders Act—In general.

[Section 23:47]

[1]McMullen v. Muir, 34 Ohio App. 3d 241, 517 N.E.2d 1381 (8th Dist. Cuyahoga County 1986); cf. Civ. R. 1(C)(5) (Civil Rules do not apply in RURESA proceeding when inappropriate).

[2]McMullen v. Muir, 34 Ohio App. 3d 241, 517 N.E.2d 1381 (8th Dist. Cuyahoga County 1986).

[3]Former RC 3115.21(A). See Greenfield v. Cobb, 90 Ohio App. 3d 618, 630 N.E.2d 66 (3d Dist. Allen County 1993); Brown v. Brown, 16 Ohio App. 3d 26, 474 N.E.2d 613 (12th Dist. Warren County 1984). For cases decided under UIFSA, see § 23:33, UIFSA—Civil provisions of general application—Procedural and evidentiary rules.

[4]Former RC 3115.24(A).

[5]Stacey v. Lacey, 1988 WL 81341 (Ohio Ct. App. 11th Dist. Lake County 1988); Bobbs v. Cline, 116 Ohio App. 3d 46, 686 N.E.2d 556 (7th Dist. Jefferson County 1997).

[6]Former RC 3115.24(B).

the action.[7] Former RC 3115.21(A) also permits obligors to defend against a prior support order on the basis of "defenses available . . . to a defendant in an action or proceeding to enforce a foreign money judgment." Thus, the obligor must demonstrate that the prior order was defective for want of personal or subject matter jurisdiction, or for fraud.[8] The merits of the prior order may not be re-examined.

Interference with the custodial or visitation rights of an obligor is not a defense to payment of support.[9] Former RC 3115.21(A) creates a general rule that support and parental rights are separate issues entitled to separate enforcement.[10] The Ohio Supreme Court held in *In re Byard*[11] that a court in a RURESA proceeding lacks subject matter jurisdiction to consider issues of visitation or custody. While one may quarrel about the fairness of allowing a RURESA court to suspend visitation rights as an enforcement tool[12] but not to consider a obligee's wrongdoing, it is clearly established that an obligor must assume the burden of a separate enforcement action. Perhaps the chief beneficiaries of former RC 3115.21(A) are public agencies whose claims for reimbursement are unaffected by a parent's misconduct.

The existence of a pending or concurrent proceeding elsewhere is also not a defense to a RURESA claim.[13] Former RC 3115.27 instructs responding courts not to stay proceedings in such a case. Instead, the court must proceed and enter a support order pendente lite. If necessary, the court may require the obligor to give a bond to ensure the prompt prosecution of the pending action. The responding court must also conform its order to the amount awarded in the pending proceeding if the latter is concluded before the hearing in the Ohio RURESA action. Retention of jurisdiction by another court is not grounds for staying enforcement of the Ohio RURESA order.[14]

Expiration of the statute of limitations is not a defense to enforcement of arrearages whether reduced to judgment or not.[15] Under some circumstances, however, an obligor may be able to employ a defense of laches. Laches is an equitable defense available when the petitioner has failed

---

[7]Campbell v. McCampbell, 1992 WL 185672 (Ohio Ct. App. 10th Dist. Franklin County 1992).

[8]Wyatt v. Wyatt, 65 Ohio St. 3d 268, 602 N.E.2d 1166 (1992). See also § 23:49, Uniform Enforcement of Foreign Judgments Act.

[9]Former RC 3115.24(A); see, e.g., Greenfield v. Cobb, 90 Ohio App. 3d 618, 630 N.E.2d 66 (3d Dist. Allen County 1993).

[10]Hammitt v. Howard, 99 Ohio App. 3d 463, 651 N.E.2d 20 (10th Dist. Franklin County 1994).

[11]In re Byard, 74 Ohio St. 3d 294, 1996-Ohio-163, 658 N.E.2d 735 (1996).

[12]Former RC 3115.21(B).

[13]Former RC 3115.27.

[14]See, e.g., Casale v. Casale, 61 Ohio App. 3d 118, 572 N.E.2d 192 (8th Dist. Cuyahoga County 1989) (enforcement of prior New Jersey decree during pending New Jersey modification proceedings).

[15]Williams v. Williams, 1987 WL 6814 (Ohio Ct. App. 8th Dist. Cuyahoga County 1987); DeCamp v. Beard, 94 Ohio App. 367, 52 Ohio Op. 32, 115 N.E.2d 403 (3d Dist. Hancock County 1953).

to assert a claim in a timely fashion. The respondent must show both that the petitioner has delayed the prosecution of a claim unreasonably and that the respondent has been materially prejudiced; in addition, the petitioner must have had an opportunity to assert the claim.[16] Ohio courts have on occasion applied laches to defeat claims for arrearages. For example, in *Fiskness v. Partin*,[17] the Fourth District Court of Appeals found that a mother's failure to assert support rights for nearly seven years while she concealed the child was an unreasonable delay. The court found that the denial of the father's visitation rights was sufficiently prejudicial to justify laches. *Arvin v. Arvin*[18] reaches a similar conclusion. The use of laches in *Fiskness* and *Arvin* may be a sympathetic court's answer to the lack of a defense under RURESA for interference with parental rights.[19] Other courts have declined to apply laches in spite of lengthy delays in asserting RURESA claims and obvious interference with parental rights or other expectations of the parties.[20]

§ 23:48 RURESA—Registration

RURESA provides the additional remedy of direct registration of a foreign support order. Former RC 3115.32 permits an obligee to bypass the two-state petition process described previously and file an existing order in the forum where enforcement is sought. As a practical matter, foreign support orders should be registered in Ohio when an obligor resides or owns property here; otherwise enforcement through wage withholding or attachment of assets is likely to be futile. By its terms, former RC 3115.32 does not require that an obligor live or own property in Ohio.

To register a foreign support order under RURESA, the obligee must file the following documents with the clerk:

(1) Three certified copies of the order with all modifications thereof.
(2) One copy of the rendering state's reciprocal enforcement of support act.
(3) A statement verified and signed by the obligee, showing the post office address of the obligee, the last known place of residence and post office address of the obligor, the amount of sup-

---

[16]Kinney v. Mathias, 10 Ohio St. 3d 72, 461 N.E.2d 901 (1984).

[17]Fiskness v. Partin, 1989 WL 17282 (Ohio Ct. App. 5th Dist. Richland County 1989); see also State ex rel. State of Florida v. Hays, 1993 WL 148785 (Ohio Ct. App. 4th Dist. Athens County 1993) (laches applied to bar claims for arrearages even though delay may have been caused by administrative process).

[18]Arvin v. Arvin, 1995 WL 70176 (Ohio Ct. App. 12th Dist. Warren County 1995) (citing Ferree v. Sparks, 77 Ohio App.3d 185, 601 N.E.2d 568 (Warren 1991)).

[19]Former RC 3115.21(A).

[20]See, e.g., Kinney v. Mathias, 10 Ohio St. 3d 72, 461 N.E.2d 901 (1984); Greenfield v. Cobb, 90 Ohio App. 3d 618, 630 N.E.2d 66 (3d Dist. Allen County 1993); Johnson v. Johnson, 71 Ohio App. 3d 713, 595 N.E.2d 388 (11th Dist. Portage County 1991); accord Genessee County v. Christenson, 1999 WL 1071564 (Ohio Ct. App. 5th Dist. Delaware County 1999) (denying laches in UIFSA case where mother failed to assert support rights for ten years and concealed child).

port remaining unpaid, a description and the location of any property of the obligor available upon execution, and a list of the states in which the order is registered.[1]

There is no requirement that arrearages be reduced to judgment before registration.[2]

Upon receipt of these documents, the clerk files them in the registry of foreign support orders. The filing constitutes registration. The prosecuting attorney has the duty to represent the obligee.[3] The Sixth District Court of Appeals, however, has ruled that while former RC 3115.32(D) requires the prosecuting attorney, on request of the court, to represent the obligee, the obligee may still employ private counsel.[4] Upon registration, the clerk issues process by certified or registered mail to the obligor at the address given in the registration with a copy of the registration order and post office address of the obligee.[5] The obligor has 20 days after the mailing of the notice to petition the court to vacate the registration or for other relief. If the obligor fails to petition the court, the registration is confirmed.[6]

At the hearing, the obligor is limited to presenting matters that would be available as defenses to enforce a foreign money judgment.[7] In other words, the obligor is limited to arguing that the registered order is void for want of personal or subject matter jurisdiction, or for some other denial of due process. If an appeal is pending or a stay has been granted in the rendering state, the Ohio court must stay proceedings so long as the obligor offers proof that security for payment has been furnished in the rendering state.[8] Likewise, if the obligor shows any basis for staying enforcement of an Ohio order, then the Ohio court must grant a stay contingent upon the obligor furnishing adequate security.[9]

Counsel should not overlook the significance of RURESA's decision to treat a registered order as an order of the registering state. Former RC 3115.32(G) provides that registered orders are to be treated as Ohio orders "subject to the same procedures, defenses, and proceedings for reopening, vacating, or staying a support order of this state and may be enforced and satisfied in like manner." Some, but not all, lower courts have construed this language to permit modification of a registered or-

---

[Section 23:48]

[1]Former RC 3115.32(E).

[2]Lambright v. Pullen, 1988 WL 57506 (Ohio Ct. App. 6th Dist. Lucas County 1988).

[3]Former RC 3115.32(D).

[4]Lambright v. Pullen, 1988 WL 57506 (Ohio Ct. App. 6th Dist. Lucas County 1988).

[5]Former RC 3115.32(F).

[6]Former RC 3115.32(H).

[7]Former RC 3115.32(I).

[8]Former RC 3115.32(I).

[9]Former RC 3115.32(I).

der on the grounds that Ohio orders are modifiable.[10] Lack of personal jurisdiction may prove a greater impediment to modification of a registered order. While registration itself does not require personal jurisdiction over the obligor,[11] an Ohio court must have personal jurisdiction over the obligor before it can modify an in personam support order.[12] Thus, registrations based solely on the presence of obligor's property in the forum are unlikely to support a finding of personal jurisdiction. Counsel should also remember that even if personal jurisdiction is present, a RURESA court's power to modify a registered child support order has been severely restricted by the Full Faith and Credit for Child Support Orders Act.

§ 23:49 Uniform Enforcement of Foreign Judgments Act

Judgments in support actions may be collected under the Uniform Enforcement of Foreign Judgments Act (UEFJA). Creditors may use UEFJA to enforce any judgment which is entitled to full faith and credit under Article IV of the United States Constitution.[1] UEFJA applies to judgments which are final and nonmodifiable.[2] Since Title IV-D rules require the states to treat support obligations when they fall due as vested, nonmodifiable judgments entitled to full faith and credit,[3] UEFJA may be used to collect any accrued support obligations. Courts are divided on the applicability of UEFJA to unaccrued support obligations.[4] No Ohio case appears to consider this point. Given the availability of RURESA, and now UIFSA, there should be little reason to use UEFJA to collect current support.

Ohio's version of the UEFJA, codified at RC 2329.021 to RC 2329.027, serves as an illustration of the mechanics of the Act. A copy of a foreign judgment authenticated in compliance with 28 U.S.C.A. § 1738, which

---

[10]Lewis v. Lewis, 1997 WL 128566 (Ohio Ct. App. 10th Dist. Franklin County 1997); Hudgins v. Hudgins, 80 Ohio App. 3d 707, 610 N.E.2d 582 (3d Dist. Henry County 1992); Storey v. Storey, 1990 WL 119262 (Ohio Ct. App. 2d Dist. Greene County 1990); Peterson v. Peterson, 101 Ohio Misc. 2d 34, 721 N.E.2d 515 (C.P. 1999) (look to Nebraska law to see if spousal support is modifiable, but to Ohio law to determine whether modification occurs); but see Colston v. Colston, 1990 WL 127045 (Ohio Ct. App. 4th Dist. Ross County 1990) (registered order not modifiable).

[11]See, e.g., Culbertson v. Reed, 1994 WL 262515 (Ohio Ct. App. 6th Dist. Lucas County 1994); Hudgins v. Hudgins, 80 Ohio App. 3d 707, 610 N.E.2d 582 (3d Dist. Henry County 1992); but see Bigley v. Bigley, 90 Ohio App. 3d 310, 629 N.E.2d 45 (9th Dist. Wayne County 1993) (personal jurisdiction necessary for registration).

[12]See, e.g., Chacon v. Chacon, 1995 WL 527669 (Ohio Ct. App. 10th Dist. Franklin County 1995); Hudgins v. Hudgins, 80 Ohio App. 3d 707, 610 N.E.2d 582 (3d Dist. Henry County 1992).

[Section 23:49]

[1]RC 2923.021; Rion v. Mom and Dad's Equipment Sales and Rentals, Inc., 116 Ohio App. 3d 161, 687 N.E.2d 311 (3d Dist. Mercer County 1996).

[2]Sistare v. Sistare, 218 U.S. 1, 30 S. Ct. 682, 54 L. Ed. 905 (1910); see also § 23:8, Impediments to interstate support actions—Full faith and credit.

[3]42 U.S.C.A. § 666(a)(9).

[4]See Annot., Validity, Construction, and Application of Uniform Enforcement of Foreign Judgments Act, 1 A.L.R. 4th 706, 775-78 (1984) (collecting cases).

requires attestation by the clerk of the original court and a certificate by the original judge, is filed with the clerk of any common pleas court, including a domestic relations court. An affidavit of the judgment creditor or his attorney must be filed, setting forth the names and last known addresses of the judgment debtor and judgment creditor, along with a praecipe instructing the clerk to issue a notice of the filing of the foreign judgment to the judgment debtor. It is also good practice to mail a notice of the filing of the foreign judgment to the judgment debtor, and to file proof of the mailing with the clerk. The foreign judgment can be enforced or satisfied in the same manner as any judgment rendered by a common pleas court, except that no execution or other process for the enforcement of the judgment will issue until 30 days after the filing of the foreign judgment. Collection of a foreign judgment may be stayed on a showing that the original action is still on appeal, or that a stay of execution has been granted in the rendering jurisdiction. It is not necessary, however, to reduce the foreign obligation to a judgment so long as the original state lacks jurisdiction to modify past support amounts.[5]

Obligors may not seek modification of accrued support payments in a UEFJA proceeding. The text of UEFJA does provide that foreign judgments are "subject to the same procedures, defenses, and proceedings for reopening, vacating, or staying as a judgment of a court of common pleas."[6] However, this formulation does not mean that final foreign support judgments can be re-opened under any ground specified in Civil Rule 60(B) or any other basis available under the law of the enforcing forum. There appears to be no Ohio case dealing precisely with this point.[7] However, the Minnesota Supreme Court, construing an identical provision in that state's UEFJA, held that the Act permitted challenges of final, nonmodifiable foreign judgments only on the grounds of lack of personal or subject matter jurisdiction in the issuing court, fraud, satisfaction, or lack of due process.[8] Hence, Civil Rule 60(B) may not be used to re-examine the merits or even to correct errors by the issuing court.[9] Any other interpretation of the UEFJA would place it in conflict with the requirements of the Full Faith and Credit Clause.[10] Also, the United States Supreme Court has recently held that there is no public policy

---

[5]See Darnell v. Darnell, 1987 WL 18284 (Ohio Ct. App. 11th Dist. Trumbull County 1987) (construing similar provision in RC 1901.19).

[6]RC 2329.022.

[7]Compare Speyer v. Continental Sports Cars, Inc., 34 Ohio App. 3d 272, 518 N.E.2d 39 (10th Dist. Franklin County 1986) (Ohio must recognize Texas judgment which violates public policy of Ohio).

[8]Matson v. Matson, 333 N.W.2d 862, 31 A.L.R.4th 696 (Minn. 1983); see also Annot., Validity, Construction, and Application of Uniform Enforcement of Foreign Judgments Act, 31 A.L.R. 4th 706.

[9]See, e.g., Fauntleroy v. Lum, 210 U.S. 230, 28 S. Ct. 641, 52 L. Ed. 1039 (1908) (court must enforce final judgment in spite of errors by rendering court).

[10]See, e.g., Morris v. Jones, 329 U.S. 545, 67 S. Ct. 451, 91 L. Ed. 488, 168 A.L.R. 656 (1947).

exception to the requirements of the full faith and credit.[11] Ohio's UEFJA should be subject to a correspondingly narrow interpretation. Conversely, any arrearages accumulating under a valid Ohio decree will be enforceable elsewhere without the burden of re-litigating the merits.[12]

§ 23:50   Criminal sanctions

Ohio follows the universal rule that willful nonsupport is a crime. RC 2919.21(B) criminalizes willful failures to pay support orders issued by a court. Interestingly, the latter section refers only to court orders and not administrative actions. RC 2919.21(A) prohibits abandonment or failure to "provide adequate support" to a spouse, a child under 18 or a handicapped child under 21, or to an "aged or infirm" parent who is incapable of self-support. The latter provision, due to its juxtaposition with RC 2919.12(B) and the absence of reference to court orders, would seem to apply only to situations where no support order is in place. However, reports of prosecutions under RC 2919.12(A) for failure to pay court-ordered support are common.[1] A defendant may raise the affirmative defense that he or she has provided support to the extent of his or her means.[2] Failure to support a parent is subject to a defense that the parent abandoned or failed to support the child while the latter was under 18, or under 21 in the case of a handicapped child.[3] It is no defense that the obligee was supported by someone else.[4]

Criminal sanctions for nonsupport of dependents vary with the degree of nonsupport. Anyone who fails to meet the support obligations of RC 2919.21(A) and (B) has committed a misdemeanor of the first degree.[5] However, if the obligor has previously been convicted of or pleaded guilty to nonsupport of a child under RC 2919.21(A)(2) or of failing to comply with a support order under RC 2919.21(B), or has failed to provide support under the same statutory sections for an accumulated total of 26 of the prior 104 weeks, then the penalty is increased to a felony of the fifth degree.[6] If the obligor has previously been convicted of or pleaded guilty to nonsupport constituting a felony of the fifth degree, then the next such violation is punished as a felony of the fourth degree.[7]

A separate provision criminalizes nonsupport of children under 18 (or under 21 in the case of handicapped children) who are legally wards of a

---

[11]Baker by Thomas v. General Motors Corp., 522 U.S. 222, 118 S. Ct. 657, 139 L. Ed. 2d 580 (1998).

[12]See Annot., Validity, Construction, and Application of Uniform Enforcement of Foreign Judgments Act, 31 A.L.R. 4th 706, 768-75 (1984) (collecting cases).

[Section 23:50]

[1]See, e.g., State v. Taylor, 2001-Ohio-1642, 2001 WL 1280226 (Ohio Ct. App. 9th Dist. Lorain County 2001).

[2]RC 2919.21(D).

[3]RC 2919.21(E).

[4]RC 2919.21(F).

[5]RC 2919.21(G)(1).

[6]RC 2919.21(G)(1).

[7]RC 2919.21(G)(1).

public children services agency, or are recipients of public assistance under RC Chapter 5107 or disability assistance under RC Chapter 5115. Here, the agency may bring charges under RC 3113.06 if proceedings have not already been brought under RC 2919.21 or RC Chapter 3115.

Pursuing criminal charges against an out-of-state obligor is problematic. Both RURESA and UIFSA have extradition provisions. The RURESA statute, former RC 3115.04, authorized the governor to demand and respond to demands for the surrender of defendants criminally charged with nonsupport. It was unnecessary to demonstrate that the defendant was in the demanding state when the offense was allegedly committed or that he or she had fled from the demanding jurisdiction. The governor, however, had considerable discretion in requesting extradition. Under former RC 3115.05(A), the governor of the demanding state could require the prosecuting attorney to demonstrate that a RURESA action had been brought 60 days prior to any demand or that the action would be futile.

Conversely, when reacting to demands from other states, former RC 3115.05(B) allowed the governor to require any prosecuting attorney to investigate whether a RURESA proceeding has been brought or would be effective. If a RURESA action might be effective, the governor was then permitted to delay extradition to permit the initiation of an action. If the obligor prevailed in such an action, former RC 3115.05(C) authorized the governor to decline to extradite. The same subsection also permitted non-extradition if the obligor lost but was complying with the resulting support order.

UIFSA's rules for extradition are codified at RC 3115.53 and RC 3115.54. Sections 801 and 802 of UIFSA, as promulgated by the National Conference of Commissioners on Uniform State Laws, carried over the RURESA extradition provisions without substantive changes.[8] For reasons that are not apparent, the Ohio General Assembly opted to limit the governor's extradition power under RC 3115.53 to making and responding to demands for the extradition of persons criminally charged with "having failed to pay support under a support order."[9] This formulation is much narrower than the RURESA provisions for extradition of persons charged with nonsupport. A literal application of RC 3115.53 would be that persons charged with failure to pay support under a support order under RC 2919.21(B) are subject to extradition demand but those charged with general nonsupport under RC 2919.21(A) are not.

Although the exceptions to extradition under RURESA and UIFSA may appear to make extradition unlikely, the overall effect is beneficial. Permitting the governor to condition demand or surrender on the pursuit of an interstate action, to delay extradition while an action is pending, or to refuse extradition after compliance is verified serves to route nonsupport cases into a preferred civil setting. Except in rare cases, jailing an obligor does nothing to produce support payments. The same philosophy is seen in RC 3113.04(A) which permits suspension of sentences

---

[8]UIFSA 801 (Comment); UIFSA 802 (Comment).
[9]RC 3115.53(B).

imposed for violation of RC 2919.21 if the defendant posts a bond of between $500 and $1,000 to secure performance of support obligations. The most important effect of the RURESA and UIFSA extradition provisions is to add the threat of criminal sanction to other means of enforcing civil orders.

Obligees may also benefit from Ohio's general extradition statute. RC 2963.21 provides that a prosecuting attorney may present to the governor a written application for a "requisition of the return of the person charged." The application must include the name of the person charged, the crime charged, the approximate time place and circumstances of its commission, the state where the defendant is believed to be located, and the defendant's location within that state. The prosecutor must further certify that the ends of justice require the arrest and return of the defendant and that extradition is not sought to enforce a private claim. The application must be verified by affidavit, executed in duplicate, and include two certified copies of the charging document (indictment or information), a complaint made to a judge, or a judgment of conviction, as is appropriate. If the governor concurs with the application, then he or she transmits a requisition for return of the person charged to the appropriate executive authority in the other state.[10]

Like RURESA and UIFSA, the general extradition statute does not require that the defendant be a fugitive from justice.[11] RC 2963.21 does lack RURESA's and UIFSA's elaborate schemes for granting the governor discretion to decline extradition requests from prosecutors seeking the return of persons to Ohio.[12] However, a decision to reject an extradition request on these grounds undoubtedly lies within the governor's inherent discretion.[13]

Bringing criminal charges against an out-of-state obligor requires foremost the cooperation of the prosecuting attorney. While RURESA, UIFSA, and the general extradition statute draw no distinctions between felony and misdemeanor charges, some prosecuting attorneys may be reluctant to pursue extradition if nonsupport is merely a misdemeanor.

§ 23:51 Actions in federal court

Although federal courts are barred from hearing most family law cases under the "domestic relations exception" to federal jurisdiction,[1] a federal forum is available under limited circumstances. Under 42

---

[10]See generally Ohio Jur. 3d, Criminal Law § 806.

[11]In re Roma, 82 Ohio App. 414, 38 Ohio Op. 66, 81 N.E.2d 612 (6th Dist. Lucas County 1948) (construing GC 109-1 to 109-32, later recodified as RC 2963.01 to RC 2963.27).

[12]RC 3115.05(A); UIFSA 801-802.

[13]State ex rel. Corbett v. Common Pleas Court of Stark County, 168 Ohio St. 468, 7 Ohio Op. 2d 288, 155 N.E.2d 923 (1959).

[Section 23:51]

[1]See, e.g., Ankenbrandt v. Richards, 504 U.S. 689, 112 S. Ct. 2206, 119 L. Ed. 2d 468 (1992); Ex parte Burrus, 136 U.S. 586, 10 S. Ct. 850, 34 L. Ed. 500 (1890).

U.S.C.A. § 660, federal district courts have jurisdiction over interstate child support enforcement actions when the matter is certified by the Secretary of Health and Human Services (HHS). Certification is a potentially effective remedy when a responding court or tribunal fails to execute its responsibilities under RURESA or UIFSA.

The Secretary may grant permission to use the federal courts only when an initiating state has requested the assistance of a responding state, the latter has not acted to enforce a sister state judgment against an absent parent within a reasonable time, and recourse to the federal courts is the only reasonable way to achieve enforcement.[2] In Ohio, the process begins when the child support enforcement agency identifies a IV-D case as appropriate for certification.[3] CSEA then prepares all necessary forms and forwards them to the Ohio Office of Child Support Enforcement.[4] The state office will send a notice to the responding state's IV-D agency that it intends to file a request for certification within 30 days; the 30-day notice, however, may not be sent until at least 60 days have passed since the request for assistance was directed to the responding jurisdiction.[5] If there is no response, the state office files a request for certification, normally through a regional office of HHS.

Certification is rarely sought and certification cases are rare. Perhaps the 30-day notices sent by the initiating states are sufficient to dislodge cases from their bureaucratic inertia in the responding states. Perhaps the certification requirements are so cumbersome that they discourage use of the process. Nonetheless, there is no reason why 42 U.S.C.A. § 660 should not be employed in an appropriate circumstance.

It is also possible to invoke the diversity jurisdiction of the federal district courts. So long as the amount in controversy exceeds $75,000 and there is complete diversity of citizenship between the parties, diversity jurisdiction will be available.[6] The domestic relations exception to federal jurisdiction is not an impediment so long as the action involves collection of support payments and not an adjudication of status.[7] Venue lies in the district in which all the plaintiffs or all the defendants reside, or where the claim arose.[8] The court must also be able to secure personal jurisdiction over the defendant.[9] Due to the $75,000 threshold for jurisdiction, diversity actions will be unavailable in the majority of cases.

There is no obvious advantage to pursuing a claim in federal court. In enforcing a federal judgment, federal district courts are required to use

---

[2]42 U.S.C.A. § 652(a)(8).

[3]OAC 5101:1-30-75(B).

[4]OAC 5101:1-30-75(B).

[5]OAC 5101:1-30-75(C).

[6]28 U.S.C.A. § 1332.

[7]See, e.g., Barber v. Barber, 62 U.S. 582, 21 How. 582, 16 L. Ed. 226 (1858); see generally Homer Harrison Clark, Jr., The Law of Domestic Relations in the United States § 12.2 at 414 (2d ed. 1988).

[8]28 U.S.C.A. § 1391.

[9]See §§ 23:2-23:7, Impediments to interstate support actions—Personal jurisdiction.

the rules of the state in which they sit.[10] Likewise, federal courts exercising diversity jurisdiction must apply the law of the state where they sit.[11] Hence, the plaintiff theoretically faces the same defenses to enforcement and the same techniques for execution as in state court. Any advantage would lie with the individual federal court, such as a short docket or an accommodating bench. Under the former URESA system, there was one situation where an action in federal court might make a difference. In *Sheres v. Engelman*,[12] a Texas URESA order had set support at a lower level than in the original New York divorce decree, and had retroactively modified arrearages. The federal district court granted a judgment for arrearages which amounted to the difference between the two orders.

Still, resorting to the federal courts may now be necessary. State courts are constitutionally obligated to extend full faith and credit to any nonmodifiable arrearage under a sister state's order.[13] Thanks to Title IV-D, child support orders become vested, nonmodifiable judgments when they fall due;[14] spousal support orders may also be nonmodifiable under the law of an issuing state. Perhaps the advantage of a federal forum in a *Sheres* situation is that proceedings can focus on full faith and credit issues instead of the confusing multiple order rules of RURESA. Certainly a federal forum is an attractive option when a state court mistakenly believes that its own RURESA order supersedes the order of the issuing state. Any such advantage in *Sheres*, however, should disappear now that the one-order system of the Full Faith and Credit for Child Support Orders Act[15] and UIFSA is in place.[16]

§ 23:52 Criminal sanctions—Federal court

Willful nonsupport may also be a federal crime. In 1992, Congress enacted the Child Support Recovery Act[1] (CSRA), which criminalizes a willful failure to pay a past due child support obligation in interstate situations.[2] First, the CSRA reaches obligors whose unpaid obligation for a child residing in another state remains unpaid for a year or is greater than $5,000 (18 U.S.C.A. § 228(a)(1)). Second, the Act covers obligors who travel in interstate or foreign commerce with the intent to evade a support obligation, provided that the obligation has remained

---

[10]28 U.S.C.A. § 1962.

[11]Erie R. Co. v. Tompkins, 304 U.S. 64, 58 S. Ct. 817, 82 L. Ed. 1188, 114 A.L.R. 1487 (1938).

[12]Sheres v. Engelman, 534 F. Supp. 286 (S.D. Tex. 1982).

[13]See § 23:8, Impediments to interstate support actions—Full faith and credit; § 23:49, Uniform Enforcement of Foreign Judgments Act.

[14]See § 23:49, Uniform Enforcement of Foreign Judgments Act.

[15]See § 23:21, Full Faith and Credit for Child Support Orders Act—In general.

[16]See § 23:37, UIFSA—Registration of foreign orders for enforcement—Procedures for registration.

[Section 23:52]

[1]Pub. L. No. 102-520, 106 Stat. 3403 (1992) (codified at 18 U.S.C.A. § 228).

[2]18 U.S.C.A. § 228(a).

unpaid for a period longer than one year or is greater than $5,000 (18 U.S.C.A. § 228(a)(2)). Third, the Act applies to obligors who willfully fail to pay a support obligation which has remained unpaid for a period longer than two years or is greater than $10,000 (18 U.S.C.A. § 228(a)(3)). Although the third situation is logically subsumed by the first, the two are distinct for purposes of sentencing, as noted below.

Willfulness and intent are notoriously difficult to establish. The legislative history from the CSRA's enactment in 1992[3] indicates that, in construing the willfulness requirement, courts were to compare it to the statutes which criminalize the willful failure to file federal income tax returns, provide information, or pay taxes. The burden of proof to show willfulness was met when the prosecutor provided evidence that an obligor failed to pay a past due support obligation that he was aware of, and that he had the ability to pay some amount during the relevant period, even if not the whole amount.[4] The 1998 amendments to the Act (the Deadbeat Parents Punishment Act of 1998) facilitated prosecutions by providing that the existence of a support order raises a rebuttable presumption that an obligor has the ability to pay.[5]

A first conviction under § 228(a)(1) is a misdemeanor punishable by up to six months imprisonment, a fine, or both.[6] All other convictions under the Act are punishable by a fine, imprisonment for up to two years, or both.[7] After a conviction, the court must order restitution in the amount of support due at the time of sentencing.[8] Payment of restitution may be a condition of probation.[9] Restitutory orders may be enforced either by the United States or by the obligee.[10]

Federal criminal prosecution will be an effective option in few cases. The threshold amounts for enforcement are relatively high. More importantly, enforcement lies with the discretion of the federal prosecuting authorities. Defendants have argued that the CSRA violates the Tenth Amendment limitations on Congressional power. So far, most courts have rejected this challenge on the theory that interstate child support payments are things within interstate commerce and thus within the Commerce Clause power of Congress.[11]

§ 23:53 Foreign country proceedings, judgments, and parties

Any support controversy with an international dimension is likely to

---

[3]H.R. Rep. No. 102-771, 1992 WL 187429.

[4]U.S. v. Mathes, 151 F.3d 251 (5th Cir. 1998).

[5]18 U.S.C.A. § 228(b).

[6]18 U.S.C.A. § 228(c)(1).

[7]18 U.S.C.A. § 228(c)(2).

[8]18 U.S.C.A. § 228(d).

[9]18 U.S.C.A. § 3563(b)(20).

[10]18 U.S.C.A. § 3664(m)(1)(A) and (m)(1)(B).

[11]See, e.g., U.S. v. Faasse, 265 F.3d 475 (6th Cir. 2001); U.S. v. Mussari, 95 F.3d 787 (9th Cir. 1996) (CSRA does not exceed commerce power); U.S. v. Parker, 108 F.3d 28 (3d Cir. 1997) (same); U.S. v. Bongiorno, 106 F.3d 1027 (1st Cir. 1997) (same). Compare U.S. v. Bailey, 902 F. Supp. 727 (W.D. Tex. 1995), rev'd, 115 F.3d 1222 (5th Cir. 1997) (CSRA unconstitutional).

pose difficulties for an obligee. There are several international conventions which are intended to facilitate establishment and enforcement of support obligations across international boundaries. The United Nations Convention on the Recovery of Maintenance Abroad[1] resembles RURESA and UIFSA. It creates a reciprocal obligation among the signatory nations to prosecute support claims and relies on transmission of requests to each nation's designated agency. The latter resembles a state information agency under RURESA or UIFSA. There is also a series of Hague Treaties which attempt to set standards for international recognition of support orders and the provision of free legal assistance.[2] As yet, the United States has not ratified any of these instruments, as it did the Hague Treaty on child custody issues.[3] To some degree, the unwillingness to ratify these agreements reflects the fact that many foreign support judgments do not meet the due process requirement of personal jurisdiction over non-residents.[4]

The 1996 amendments to Title IV-D promise to increase federal involvement in international support matters. Section 371 of the Personal Responsibility and Work Opportunity Reconciliation Act[5] authorizes the Secretary of State, with the concurrence of the Secretary of Health and Human Services, to declare a foreign nation a "foreign reciprocating country." To qualify, the foreign jurisdiction must: (1) have procedures in effect whereby U.S. residents may establish paternity or support orders and enforce support orders; (2) offer such procedures, including legal and administrative assistance, at no cost; and (3) establish a "Central Authority" which facilitates support enforcement activities for U.S. residents and ensures compliance with these standards.[6] The Secretaries of State and HHS are permitted to establish additional standards in consultation with the states.[7]

On the domestic side, the Secretary of HHS is designated as the Central Authority for the United States and must develop forms and procedures for facilitating cases involving reciprocating foreign

---

[Section 23:53]

[1]United Nations Convention on the Recovery of Maintenance Abroad, 268 UNTS 3 (New York, 1956).

[2]Hague Convention Concerning the Recognition and Enforcement of Decisions Relating to Maintenance Obligations Toward Children, 539 UNTS 27 (1958); Hague Convention on the Recognition and Enforcement of Decisions Relating to Maintenance Obligations of Children and Spouses, reprinted in, 21 Am. J. Comp. L. 156 (1973); Hague Convention on the Law Applicable to Maintenance Obligations, reprinted in, 21 Am. J. Comp. L. 596 (1973); Hague Convention on International Access to Justice, reprinted in, 19 Int'l Legal Materials 1501 (1980).

[3]See Uniform Child Custody Jurisdiction Act; Parental Kidnapping Prevention Act; International Child Abduction Remedies Act Ch 17.

[4]Philip Schwartz, International Support Remedies in Interstate Child Support Remedies 244 (Margaret C. Haynes ed. 1989).

[5]Pub. L. No. 104-193 § 371, 110 Stat. 2252 (1996) (codified at 42 U.S.C.A. § 654(32), 659a).

[6]42 U.S.C.A. § 659a(b)(1).

[7]42 U.S.C.A. § 659a(b)(2).

jurisdictions.[8] Individual states are permitted to enter reciprocal arrangements with foreign jurisdictions which have not been declared reciprocating foreign countries by the Secretary of State, so long as the agreement is consistent with federal law.[9] If a state does enter a reciprocal agreement with a foreign nation, the following rules apply: (1) the state must treat a request from that jurisdiction for Title IV-D services as a request from an American state; (2) the state may, at its option, provide for spousal support enforcement not otherwise required by Title IV-D; and (3) the state may not require an application or assess costs against a foreign reciprocating country or a foreign obligee although it may impose costs on an obligor.[10] As of mid-2002, neither the Department of State nor HHS had issued implementing regulations.

Reciprocal arrangements are, in some cases, presently available under RURESA and UIFSA. These Acts filled part of the gap left by the United States' traditional unwillingness to participate in the international treaty system. RURESA includes in its definition of a state a "foreign jurisdiction in which [RURESA] or a substantially similar reciprocal law is in effect."[11] UIFSA has a similar provision. RC 3115.01(U) defines a state to include "a foreign jurisdiction that has enacted a law or established procedures for issuance and enforcement of support orders that are substantially similar to the procedures under [UIFSA]." A footnote in *Poljakov v. Kshywonis*[12] questioned whether the Federal Republic of Germany was a state within the meaning of RC 3115.01(T)(2).[13] Since no party had raised the issue, the court presumed regularity.

Pursuant to these definitions, American states and territories have entered into de facto reciprocal agreements with foreign nations for the enforcement of agreements. Since these agreements are separate (but mutual) declarations of the state's intention to honor the support orders of a foreign state, they do not violate the federal constitutional restriction against a state concluding treaties with foreign nations.[14] Inquiries about what nations qualify as "states" under UIFSA or RURESA are best directed to the Ohio Department of Job and Family Services.

When attempting to enforce or establish an Ohio or other American support order in a foreign nation, the most reliable strategy may be to employ foreign counsel to pursue the claim in that nation's courts or agencies. Obviously, this option is available only to clients of means. Private referral by a reliable source is the best method of obtaining foreign counsel. Lists of foreign counsel may also be obtained from the Office of Citizens Counselor Services in the State Department or from

---

[8]42 U.S.C.A. § 659a(c).

[9]42 U.S.C.A. § 659a(d).

[10]42 U.S.C.A. § 654(32); see, e.g., RC 3121.92 (implementing 42 U.S.C.A. § 654).

[11]Former RC 3115.01(B)(1).

[12]Poljakov v. Kshywonis, 2000 WL 960960 (Ohio Ct. App. 9th Dist. Summit County 2000).

[13]Former RC 3115.01(T)(2) was renumbered RC 3115.01(U)(2) in 2000 S.B. 180, eff. 3-22-01.

[14]U.S. Const. art. I § 10.

the U.S. Consulate in the foreign country. In the event that private counsel is not a realistic option, counsel may initiate a UIFSA action in an Ohio court. Acting as an initiating tribunal, the court will transmit the request to the appropriate agency in a reciprocating foreign nation. Typically, services are provided free in the receiving nation. In some nations, locator services are more efficient than in the United States due to centralized record-keeping.[15] Presumably, requests for services in many cases will shift to HHS once the federal apparatus for reciprocal enforcement is operating.

In cases where Ohio has no arrangement with a foreign country, counsel at present has rather limited options. One approach is to request that the child support enforcement agency or the Department of Job and Family Services take steps to establish a relationship with the foreign nation. This option may or may not produce results within an acceptable length of time. (Federal reciprocal agreements will certainly alleviate much of the inconvenience once they are in place.) Another possibility is to bring an action under Ohio law against the foreign obligor. Of course, this approach depends entirely on being able to gain personal jurisdiction over the obligor. The obligor would have to satisfy one of the long-arm provisions in Civ. R. 4.3 or RC 3115.03. Service of process would also have to comply with Civ. R. 4.3, Civ. R. 4.4, or Civ. R. 4.5, and meet due process standards under the Fourteenth Amendment.

Once jurisdiction is established, however, an Ohio court may adjudicate a support claim and enter an order. Domestic support enforcement techniques may then be used. For example, if the obligor is employed by an American entity or a foreign entity with an office in the United States, it will be possible to serve an income withholding notice on the entity's designated agent for service of process. If the employer is located in Ohio, withholding could proceed under RC Chapter 3121; if located in another state, the obligee could forward an order to a responding state for enforcement under RURESA or UIFSA or could attempt direct enforcement under that state's version of RC 3115.32. Any property or benefits located in the United States could be attached in a similar fashion.

Foreign obligees may also proceed against United States citizens and residents in American state courts. For the most part, the strategies and procedures used here are the reverse of those used by U.S. residents seeking relief abroad. Any foreign obligee has the option of retaining local counsel to bring a support action in an Ohio (or other U.S.) court which has jurisdiction over the obligor or the obligor's assets. If no support order has been entered previously, the Ohio proceeding could result in the entry of a support order and enforcement under Ohio law. The same order could then be transmitted to other states which would serve as responding jurisdictions under RURESA or UIFSA for purposes of enforcement. Obligees who are unable to afford private counsel may also invoke the mechanisms of RURESA or UIFSA if their own nation has a

---

[15]Philip Schwartz, International Support Remedies in Interstate Child Support Remedies 246 (Margaret C. Haynes ed. 1989).

reciprocal arrangement with Ohio. Under these circumstances, Ohio will act as a responding state for the purposes of establishing or enforcing an award. Actual results, of course, will depend on the diligence of the prosecuting attorney or the child support enforcement agency. Counsel should note that, while RURESA remains applicable, a foreign award registered under former RC 3115.32 may be subject to subsequent modification under Ohio law.[16] Obligees whose nations have no reciprocal agreements with any American state may simply have no practical recourse. Finally, foreign obligees in reciprocating countries will eventually be able to take advantage of any procedures established by the Secretary of HHS.

If there is no reciprocal arrangement with the obligor's nation, then the only basis for recognition of a foreign order is comity. There is no constitutional requirement that American courts give foreign country judgments full faith and credit. There is, however, a tendency among courts to recognize and enforce foreign judgments so long as certain standards are met. Comity is less likely when the courts of the rendering nation are not willing to give effect to American judgments.[17] Courts are also less likely to grant comity when the foreign order is defective (by American standards) due to a lack of notice, want of subject matter or personal jurisdiction, or fraud, or produces a result which is repugnant to the public policy of the forum. Once an American court chooses to recognize a foreign order and enters a domestic judgment, that judgment is owed full faith and credit by sister states, at least as to its final, non-modifiable aspects.

---

[16]See § 23:48, RURESA—Registration.

[17]See, e.g., Hilton v. Guyot, 159 U.S. 113, 16 S. Ct. 139, 40 L. Ed. 95 (1895) (refusing recognition of French money judgment on ground of non-reciprocity).

Chapter 24

Relief from Judgment

By Stanley Morganstern, Esq.

> **KeyCite®:** Cases and other legal materials listed in KeyCite Scope can be researched through West Group's KeyCite service on Westlaw®. Use KeyCite to check citations for form, parallel references, prior and later history, and comprehensive citator information, including citations to other decisions and secondary materials.

§ 24:1   Election of remedy

A substantial difference exists between a motion for modification and a motion for relief from judgment.[1] Modification is primarily based upon a change of circumstances occurring subsequent to the original decree;[2]

[Section 24:1]

[1]See Civ. R. 60(B), Civ. R. 75(I). See also § 25:51, Motions by obligor regarding enforcement of judgments—Motion for relief from judgment; § 25:56, Post-decree motions—Motion to modify.

[2]Loetz v. Loetz, 63 Ohio St. 2d 1, 17 Ohio Op. 3d 1, 406 N.E.2d 1093 (1980); Drossman v. Drossman, 48 Ohio App. 2d 81, 2 Ohio Op. 3d 63, 355 N.E.2d 891 (6th Dist. Erie

it is not contemplated at the time of the divorce nor at the negotiations leading to a separation agreement incorporated into a decree.[3] Relief from judgment in most cases is a request to set aside a judgment for reasons of substantive error existing at the time of the decree.[4]

The choice of remedy, whether modification or relief from judgment, requires a clear understanding of the alternatives. The choice must be made with consideration of the particular relief sought, subject matter of the desired change, timeliness of the action, and nature of the change of circumstances.

Rule 60(B) of the Ohio Rules of Civil Procedure which governs relief from judgment, differs from Civ. R. 59(A) in that relief granted under Civ. R. 60(B) relieves a party from the final judgment. Civ. R. 59 permits the trial court to amend findings of fact and conclusions of law, or make new findings and conclusions, thus entering a new judgment.[5] Civ. R. 60(B) does not speak to the amendment of the final judgment but rather to the vacation of same, but "vacate" means to annul, set aside, or render void.[6]

Relief from judgment as provided by Civ. R. 60(B) originates from the inherent right of a court to review its own decisions.[7] The filing and service requirements of such a motion are likewise governed by the Civil Rules.[8]

In *Dzina*, wife sought to unseal the record in the parties' 1998 divorce case. The trial court granted wife's motion and, in effect, vacated its prior order which sealed the record. On appeal, the Eighth District Court of Appeals characterized wife's motion as one brought under Civil Rule 60(B) and applied the law thereto. The order to seal the record was a final and appealable order. A motion to vacate is not a substitute for a timely appeal. The matter was, however, remanded to the trial court for consideration of possible changed circumstances which might justify relief under Civil Rule 60(B)(4) or presentation of the reasons why wife sought access to the records which might establish the essential element of a meritorious defense.[9]

Civ. R. 60(B) motions address substantive matters and Civ. R. 60(A)

County 1975) (wife's remarriage, contemplated at time of permanent alimony decree, not sufficient change of circumstance for modification); Peters v. Peters, 14 Ohio St. 2d 268, 43 Ohio Op. 2d 441, 237 N.E.2d 902 (1968); Anderson v. Anderson, 71 Ohio L. Abs. 558, 118 N.E.2d 214 (Ct. App. 8th Dist. Cuyahoga County 1954).

[3]Stauffer v. Stauffer, 4 Ohio App. 2d 339, 33 Ohio Op. 2d 395, 212 N.E.2d 622 (4th Dist. Pickaway County 1965).

[4]Civ. R. 60(B).

[5]Civ. R. 59(A) ("On a motion for a new trial in an action tried without a jury, the court may open the judgment if one has been entered, take additional testimony, amend findings of fact and conclusions of law or make new findings or conclusions, and enter a new judgment.").

[6]Black's Law Dictionary (6th ed.) p 1548.

[7]RC 2325.01 (repealed).

[8]See Civ. R. 60(B).

[9]Dzina v. Dzina, 2002-Ohio-2753, 2002 WL 1265585 (Ohio Ct. App. 8th Dist. Cuyahoga County 2002).

motions address clerical errors. Civ. R. 60(A) may not be used to correct substantive mistakes. An error not apparent from the court's record may not be corrected by a Civ. R. 60(A) motion although, factually, the error existed.[10] A trial court need not allow a party an opportunity to respond to a Civ. R. 60(A) request to correct a clerical error.[11] A trial court has jurisdiction to correct a clerical error in a QDRO as to the date of division of the pension plan. Civ. R. 60(A) corrections do not amount to modifications of property division.[12]

§ 24:2 Jurisdiction

It is axiomatic in Ohio domestic relations law that the court granting the divorce or dissolution has continuing jurisdiction to modify that decree in such matters as parental rights,[1] visitation[2] child support,[3] and, under certain circumstances, spousal support.[4]

Continuing jurisdiction for modification or relief from judgment is specifically provided for under Civ. R. 75(J).[5] Continuing jurisdiction is invoked by the filing of a motion and properly serving it upon the adverse party.[6] Service of a motion must be made in accordance with Civ. R. 4.[7] Service of a motion after judgment cannot be made upon the attorney of record.[8] It must be served in a manner guaranteeing actual notice to satisfy due process requirements.

Civil Rule 75(J) does not specifically grant continuing jurisdiction, but

---

[10]Hiles v. Veach, 1998 WL 823802 (Ohio Ct. App. 4th Dist. Pike County 1998).

[11]McFarland v. McFarland, 1999 WL 436820 (Ohio Ct. App. 5th Dist. Licking County 1999).

[12]Peterson v. Peterson, 1998 WL 166475 (Ohio Ct. App. 12th Dist. Butler County 1998).

[Section 24:2]

[1]RC 3105.65, RC 3109.04(E). See also § 16:1, Jurisdiction.

[2]RC 3105.65, RC 3109.051; Schwartz v. Schwartz, 1 Ohio App. 2d 451, 30 Ohio Op. 2d 447, 203 N.E.2d 249 (8th Dist. Cuyahoga County 1964). See also § 18:20, Modifying visitation—Jurisdiction.

[3]RC 3105.21, RC 3109.05; Van Divort v. Van Divort, 165 Ohio St. 141, 59 Ohio Op. 207, 134 N.E.2d 715, 62 A.L.R.2d 538 (1956). See also §§ 19:16–19:19, Modification of prior orders.

[4]RC 3105.18(E); Wolfe v. Wolfe, 46 Ohio St. 2d 399, 75 Ohio Op. 2d 474, 350 N.E.2d 413 (1976). See also § 14:2, Procedure; §§ 14:20–14:35, Requirements for modification.

[5]Civ. R. 75(J) ("The continuing jurisdiction of the court shall be invoked by motion filed in the original action."). See also Loetz v. Loetz, 63 Ohio St. 2d 1, 17 Ohio Op. 3d 1, 406 N.E.2d 1093 (1980); § 25:55, Post-decree motions—Motion for continuing jurisdiction.

[6]See § 25:55, Post-decree motions—Motion for continuing jurisdiction. Yonally v. Yonally, 45 Ohio App. 2d 122, 74 Ohio Op. 2d 134, 341 N.E.2d 602 (9th Dist. Summit County 1974); Reynolds v. Reynolds, 12 Ohio App. 63, 1919 WL 1204 (1st Dist. Hamilton County 1919); Davis v. Davis, 1992 WL 47299 (Ohio Ct. App. 8th Dist. Cuyahoga County 1992).

[7]See Civ. R. 4 to Civ. R. 4.6 in conjunction with Civ. R. 75(I).

[8]See Civ. R. 4 to Civ. R. 4.6 in conjunction with Civ. R. 75(J). See also Yonally v. Yonally, 45 Ohio App. 2d 122, 74 Ohio Op. 2d 134, 341 N.E.2d 602 (9th Dist. Summit County 1974) (court of appeals held it is without power to conduct hearing on motion for return of personal property when service is upon attorney only).

it directs how such jurisdiction is to be invoked. Since there is no exclusion as to domestic matters, there is by implication continuing jurisdiction.

It initially appears that continuing jurisdiction under Civ. R. 75(J) and Civ. R. 60(B) is nearly the same. Civ. R. 75(J) provides, however, that "[t]he continuing jurisdiction of the court shall be invoked." Civ. R. 60(B) provides that "the court may relieve a party." Thus, while the court must consider a motion brought under Civ. R. 75(J), Civ. R. 60(B) only requires the court to use its discretion in accepting for hearing a Civ. R. 60(B) motion. A court must consider the principal Civ. R. 60(B) motion, but may (1) grant a hearing; or (2) consider it on the pleadings; and (3) after consideration, grant or deny relief.

While the motion is treated as a new complaint for purposes of service, jurisdiction of the court over the parties continues even though both parties are no longer residents of the state. Service is authorized outside of Ohio pursuant to Civ. R. 4.3.[9] Note that venue is still resolved by Civ. R. 3, and where a court has the case, it remains the proper forum unless and until there is a change of forum pursuant to Civ. R. 3(C) or Civ. R. 3(D).

§ 24:3 Procedure

A motion filed must be in writing. It must set forth the relief sought and grounds for seeking such relief with particularity.[1] Motions filed under Civ. R. 60(B) are subject to determination without oral hearing,[2] since the determination is based on the law or uncontroverted factual merits expressed in the motion, brief, affidavits, and exhibits. The motion invoking the continuing jurisdiction of the court under Civ. R. 75(J) may also be dismissed or determined with or without oral hearing but solely on the issue of proper service, not on the merits, where questions of fact are to be tried by the court.[3] Obviously, the motion is filed as a continuation of the original case and not as a separate matter.

Although divorce is purely statutory in nature, judgments which result from such actions should not in all regards be distinguished from judgments in other types of actions. Divorce judgments may, therefore, be so

---

[9]See also Weinberger v. Weinberger, 43 Ohio App. 2d 129, 72 Ohio Op. 2d 325, 334 N.E.2d 514 (9th Dist. Summit County 1974).

[Section 24:3]

[1]See Civ. R. 7(B)(1). See also Pleading and Practice Ch 25.

[2]See Civ. R. 7(B)(2).

[3]Jacks v. Jacks, 1994 WL 476549 (Ohio Ct. App. 5th Dist. Licking County 1994), dismissed, appeal not allowed, 71 Ohio St. 3d 1427, 642 N.E.2d 635 (1994); Coulson v. Coulson, 5 Ohio St. 3d 12, 448 N.E.2d 809 (1983), citing Adomeit v. Baltimore, 39 Ohio App. 2d 97, 105, 68 Ohio Op. 2d 251, 316 N.E.2d 469 (8th Dist. Cuyahoga County 1974) ("If the movant files a motion for relief from judgment and it contains allegations of operative facts which would warrant relief under Civil Rule 60(B), Civ. R. 60(B), the trial court should grant a hearing to take evidence and verify these facts before it rules on the motion.").

indefinite and uncertain as to render them null and void.[4] Litigants are entitled to relief from divorce decrees as they would be from any other judgment.

In those cases where there is an omission in the original judgment entry, neither a Civ. R. 60(B) motion nor a motion to modify would be appropriate. A nunc pro tunc entry may be used to supply omissions in a final judgment entry so long as they are corrections and are truly clerical corrections as opposed to a modification. The Ohio Rules of Civil Procedure do not provide for a motion for reconsideration or a motion to amend a judgment entry.

To obtain relief under Civ. R. 60(B), the movant must submit material containing operative facts sufficient to demonstrate (1) the timeliness of the motion, (2) the reason for seeking relief, (3) one of the grounds stated in Civ. R. 60(B), and (4) a defense.[5] If the motion is brought under subsections (1), (2), or (3) of Civ. R. 60(B), it must be brought no later than one year after the judgment, order, or proceeding was entered or taken.[6]

It is imperative to allege operative facts sufficient to sustain the granting of such a motion. Allegations must be made by way of affidavit, deposition, answers to interrogatories, stipulations, admissions, or other sworn testimony. It is not sufficient to submit unsworn statements or only a brief in support of a motion.[7] *Adomeit v. Baltimore*[8] clearly sets forth the proposition that if the motion for relief from judgment filed under Civ. R. 60(B) does not contain the appropriate operative facts, it is not an abuse of discretion for the trial court to overrule and refuse even to grant an oral hearing.[9] The Eleventh District Court of Appeals held that the trial court did not abuse its discretion in denying husband's Civil Rule 60(B) motion without a hearing. Husband's affidavit merely said that he read the brief attached to the motion and that the facts stated therein were true. The court found husband's allegation that at the time of the divorce he was not in the right state of mind because "he was taking prescription psychotropic drugs, he was under the care of a psychiatrist, he had not seen his children, he was in bankruptcy, and he

---

[4]Hardin v. Hardin, 65 Ohio L. Abs. 538, 115 N.E.2d 167 (Ct. App. 2d Dist. Franklin County 1952).

[5]GTE Automatic Elec., Inc. v. ARC Industries, Inc., 47 Ohio St. 2d 146, 1 Ohio Op. 3d 86, 351 N.E.2d 113 (1976); Adomeit v. Baltimore, 39 Ohio App. 2d 97, 68 Ohio Op. 2d 251, 316 N.E.2d 469 (8th Dist. Cuyahoga County 1974).

[6]Civ. R. 60(B); GTE Automatic Elec., Inc. v. ARC Industries, Inc., 47 Ohio St. 2d 146, 1 Ohio Op. 3d 86, 351 N.E.2d 113 (1976).

[7]East Ohio Gas Co. v. Walker, 59 Ohio App. 2d 216, 13 Ohio Op. 3d 234, 394 N.E.2d 348 (8th Dist. Cuyahoga County 1978); Tom McSteen Contracting Co. v. Thomas Maloney & Sons, Inc., 39 Ohio App. 2d 31, 68 Ohio Op. 2d 173, 314 N.E.2d 392 (8th Dist. Cuyahoga County 1974). See also §§ 25:65–25:69, Briefs.

[8]Adomeit v. Baltimore, 39 Ohio App. 2d 97, 68 Ohio Op. 2d 251, 316 N.E.2d 469 (8th Dist. Cuyahoga County 1974).

[9]See also Tom McSteen Contracting Co. v. Thomas Maloney & Sons, Inc., 39 Ohio App. 2d 31, 68 Ohio Op. 2d 173, 314 N.E.2d 392 (8th Dist. Cuyahoga County 1974); Pisani v. Pisani, 1996 WL 532077 (Ohio Ct. App. 8th Dist. Cuyahoga County 1996).

was losing his business" to be base allegations insufficient to grant him an evidentiary hearing.[10] A trial court may deny a Civ. R. 60(B) motion even though it appears that the movant did not receive notice of the hearing at which the judgment was rendered against him. He must exhibit a meritorious defense or establish that the court lacked jurisdiction over him.[11] A hearing on a Civ. R. 60(B) motion need not be granted if the trial court finds, within its discretion, that it is meritless. The entry denying the motion and hearing should so specify.[12] Any doubt, however, as to the granting of such a motion should be resolved in favor of the movant.[13]

The granting of such a motion where the record does not demonstrate the claimed ground for relief as well as the other prerequisites for the granting of such motion constitutes a breach of discretion by the trial court.[14] One must initially convince the court that there are operative facts establishing a valid claim, and that the movant is entitled to relief.[15] In *Driggers v. Driggers*,[16] the trial court properly denied the deceased wife's mother's motion to intervene and vacate order of dismissal of divorce action where the wife's mother lacked a meritorious claim or defense to justify the granting of her motion. Failure to file a compulsory counterclaim in which the same defenses and claims sought to be asserted through a motion for relief from judgment in a domestic relations case was a bar to the granting of the motion for relief.[17] A motion to vacate and reopen a judgment, which is not supported by an affidavit or other evidence supporting relief, will be denied.[18] Father filed two separate motions for relief from different portions of a judgment. Both motions were based on the same grounds of fraud and lack of notice. The trial court did not err in dismissing the second motion as moot after

---

[10]LaRosa v. LaRosa, 2002-Ohio-1170, 2002 WL 408074, at *4 (Ohio Ct. App. 11th Dist. Geauga County 2002).

[11]Mihovk v. Paulson, 1996 WL 532079 (Ohio Ct. App. 8th Dist. Cuyahoga County 1996).

[12]Jacks v. Jacks, 1994 WL 476549 (Ohio Ct. App. 5th Dist. Licking County 1994), dismissed, appeal not allowed, 71 Ohio St. 3d 1427, 642 N.E.2d 635 (1994).

[13]GTE Automatic Elec., Inc. v. ARC Industries, Inc., 47 Ohio St. 2d 146, 1 Ohio Op. 3d 86, 351 N.E.2d 113 (1976).

[14]Mount Olive Baptist Church v. Pipkins Paints and Home Imp. Center, Inc., 64 Ohio App. 2d 285, 18 Ohio Op. 3d 319, 413 N.E.2d 850 (8th Dist. Cuyahoga County 1979); Bates & Springer, Inc. v. Stallworth, 56 Ohio App. 2d 223, 10 Ohio Op. 3d 227, 382 N.E.2d 1179, 26 U.C.C. Rep. Serv. 1181 (8th Dist. Cuyahoga County 1978).

[15]Gatto v. Gatto, 1993 WL 107837 (Ohio Ct. App. 9th Dist. Summit County 1993); Schwartz v. Seibert, 1993 WL 524292 (Ohio Ct. App. 2d Dist. Montgomery County 1993).

[16]Driggers v. Driggers, 115 Ohio App. 3d 229, 685 N.E.2d 252 (11th Dist. Portage County 1996).

[17]Bowman v. Bowman, 2001 WL 28663 (Ohio Ct. App. 2d Dist. Montgomery County 2001), dismissed, appeal not allowed, 91 Ohio St. 3d 1524, 747 N.E.2d 250 (2001).

[18]White v. White, 1993 WL 26773 (Ohio Ct. App. 2d Dist. Montgomery County 1993).

denying the first motion on the merits.[19] However, in *Gholston v. Gholston*,[20] the trial court erred in striking, on its own motion or initiative, a second Civ. R. 60(B) motion. The first motion, overruled by the trial court, was not supported by an affidavit, while the second one was. Civ. R. 60(A) is only available to correct clerical mistakes in judgments arising from oversight or omission, or "blunders in execution." Substantive mistakes must be addressed through Civ. R. 60(B) motions.[21] The right to an evidentiary hearing on a motion for relief from judgment may be waived.[22]

An evidentiary hearing on a motion for relief from judgment is not required when appellant fails to support his Civ. R. 60(B)(1) motion with sufficient operative facts to establish that he was entitled to relief on the basis of excusable neglect.[23] A Civ. R. 60(B) motion, though timely filed with evidentiary materials supporting a claim for attorney misconduct, is properly overruled without hearing when there are no allegations of operative facts that support a meritorious claim or defense in the underlying divorce action.[24] In *Wukovich v. Wukovich*,[25] husband's Civ. R. 60(B) motion was properly denied without a hearing. He did not demonstrate a meritorious defense or claim that he was entitled to relief on one of the grounds stated in the rule. "Whenever a motion to vacate does not find support on the face of the record or is not accompanied by an affidavit or other evidence to support a vacation, it is not error to deny the motion without a hearing."[26] In *Caron v. Manfresca*,[27] the father failed to demonstrate operative facts to allow an evidentiary hearing on his Civ. R. 60(B) motion, claiming that DNA tests subsequent to divorce conclusively excluded him as the father of a child found to be of the marriage. In *Costakos v. Costakos*,[28] the trial court erred in denying wife's Civ. R. 60(B) motion without an evidentiary hearing. She presented sufficient operative facts by way of affidavit to allow her an opportunity to be heard in an attempt to vacate an entry which caused an

---

[19]Balogh v. Balogh, 1998 WL 355854 (Ohio Ct. App. 8th Dist. Cuyahoga County 1998).

[20]Gholston v. Gholston, 1999 WL 172876 (Ohio Ct. App. 2d Dist. Montgomery County 1999).

[21]Musson v. Musson, 1995 WL 477567 (Ohio Ct. App. 3d Dist. Hardin County 1995).

[22]Straker v. Straker, 2001 WL 253143 (Ohio Ct. App. 10th Dist. Franklin County 2001).

[23]Angel v. Angel, 1993 WL 49456 (Ohio Ct. App. 4th Dist. Scioto County 1993).

[24]Hatfield v. Hatfield, 1995 WL 332234 (Ohio Ct. App. 4th Dist. Ross County 1995).

[25]Wukovich v. Wukovich, 2000 WL 1038192 (Ohio Ct. App. 8th Dist. Cuyahoga County 2000).

[26]Tom McSteen Contracting Co. v. Thomas Maloney & Sons, Inc., 39 Ohio App. 2d 31, 34, 68 Ohio Op. 2d 173, 314 N.E.2d 392 (8th Dist. Cuyahoga County 1974).

[27]Caron v. Manfresca, 1998 WL 832163 (Ohio Ct. App. 10th Dist. Franklin County 1998), dismissed, appeal not allowed, 85 Ohio St. 3d 1455, 708 N.E.2d 1010 (1999).

[28]Costakos v. Costakos, 1997 WL 607477 (Ohio Ct. App. 10th Dist. Franklin County 1997).

acceleration of a decrease in her spousal support. In *Rundle v. Rundle*,[29] the father's Civ. R. 60(B)(1), Civ. R. 60(B)(4) and Civ. R. 60(B)(5) motion to set aside the trial court's order which determined an arrearage in child support was denied without hearing. The court of appeals dismissed the appeal from that ruling. The father attempted to use the Civ. R. 60(B) motion as a substitute for a direct and timely appeal. Arguments and statements of counsel alone are not sufficient to satisfy a trial court's obligation to hear evidence on a Civ. R. 60(B) motion when it holds a hearing on the motion.[30]

On the other hand, the trial court does not abuse its discretion when it grants a motion for relief without an evidentiary hearing when the record otherwise reflects sufficient facts for the granting of the motion.[31] The trial court did not err in granting appellant-wife's Civil Rule 60(B)(3) motion, where the husband had not disclosed that he had "gifted" a $60,000 bonus to his fiancee before his divorce from appellant was final. The Ninth District Court of Appeals held that the bonus was a marital asset and subject to division under RC 3105.171(E)(3), due to the husband's financial misconduct,[32] because the asset had been concealed.[33] A party seeking to set aside a separation agreement must prove by clear and convincing evidence that the agreement was executed under the influences of duress or mental incompetency.[34]

If the motion contains sufficient operative facts which if true would serve as a basis for relief, that is, a prima facie case, then it is error to refuse to grant the hearing to verify the asserted facts before ruling on the motion.[35] A full evidentiary hearing should have been granted where the trial court allowed some evidence and then denied the motion.[36] Failure to file a compulsory counterclaim in which the same defenses and claims sought to be asserted through a motion for relief from judgment in a domestic relations case was a bar to the granting of the motion for relief.[37] Where the motion and accompanying affidavits set forth allegations of operative facts that would warrant relief under Civ. R. 60(B), a

---

[29]Rundle v. Rundle, 123 Ohio App. 3d 304, 704 N.E.2d 56 (8th Dist. Cuyahoga County 1997).

[30]Conley v. Conley, 1994 WL 530745 (Ohio Ct. App. 5th Dist. Stark County 1994).

[31]Doddridge v. Fitzpatrick, 53 Ohio St. 2d 9, 7 Ohio Op. 3d 5, 371 N.E.2d 214 (1978). See also Wright, Miller & Cooper, Federal Practice and Procedure p 140 § 2851.

[32]See Spychalski v. Spychalski, 80 Ohio App. 3d 10, 608 N.E.2d 802 (6th Dist. Lucas County 1992).

[33]Hines v. Hansford, 1993 WL 218204 (Ohio Ct. App. 9th Dist. Summit County 1993).

[34]Davis v. Davis, 1996 WL 191785 (Ohio Ct. App. 8th Dist. Cuyahoga County 1996).

[35]Coulson v. Coulson, 5 Ohio St. 3d 12, 448 N.E.2d 809 (1983). See also Adomeit v. Baltimore, 39 Ohio App. 2d 97, 68 Ohio Op. 2d 251, 316 N.E.2d 469 (8th Dist. Cuyahoga County 1974).

[36]Urban v. Urban, 2001 WL 842026 (Ohio Ct. App. 5th Dist. Stark County 2001).

[37]Bowman v. Bowman, 2001 WL 28663 (Ohio Ct. App. 2d Dist. Montgomery County 2001), dismissed, appeal not allowed, 91 Ohio St. 3d 1524, 747 N.E.2d 250 (2001).

trial court must conduct an evidentiary hearing.[38] In *Offenberg v. Offenberg*,[39] the trial court erred in overruling the wife's Civ. R. 60(B)(5) motion without an evidentiary hearing. By affidavit, she alleged that her husband substantially misrepresented his income in prior proceedings. In *Taylor v. Taylor*,[40] the husband failed to appear in court due to the alleged misconduct of the wife. He properly set forth that misconduct in an affidavit, and the allegations presented a colorable case for misrepresentation. The appellate court held that the trial court abused its discretion in failing to hold a hearing on the motion for vacation of judgment. A subsequent change in law does not, however, constitute grounds for obtaining relief from final judgment under Civ. R. 60(B).[41] Failure to receive notice of the granting of a continuance and thus failure to take depositions as to values of assets did not constitute excusable neglect so as to justify the granting of Civ. R. 60(B) motion.[42]

Failure to appear for hearing after a hearing has been granted may result in a dismissal of the motion without notice or compliance by the court with Civ. R. 41(B)(1) or Civ. R. 37.[43] A claim of lack of notice of a trial date may be grounds for vacating a judgment under Civ. R. 60(B) if the movant also demonstrates a meritorious defense that he intended to argue at trial. In the absence of such, the motion must fail.[44]

Sufficient facts are stated to constitute a meritorious claim when affidavits and evidence indicate that testimony given at the time of the divorce as to the value of the marital home was false.[45] If sufficient operative facts are presented, it is error to grant the motion without a hearing. Respondent must be given an opportunity to cross-examine witnesses and to present evidence in opposition to the motion.[46] A Civ. R. 60(B) motion may not be used as an alternative to either filing objections to a referee's report or an appeal.[47] The mere filing of a Civ. R. 60(B) motion does not assure an opportunity to do discovery.[48]

---

[38]Salyers v. Salyers, 1993 WL 240084 (Ohio Ct. App. 2d Dist. Montgomery County 1993).

[39]Offenberg v. Offenberg, 1998 WL 274511 (Ohio Ct. App. 8th Dist. Cuyahoga County 1998).

[40]Taylor v. Taylor, 1993 WL 52065 (Ohio Ct. App. 2d Dist. Montgomery County 1993).

[41]Gotshall v. Gotshall, 1993 WL 34514 (Ohio Ct. App. 5th Dist. Stark County 1993).

[42]Schialdone v. Schialdone, 1995 WL 301458 (Ohio Ct. App. 11th Dist. Trumbull County 1995).

[43]Montano v. Montano, 1993 WL 526940 (Ohio Ct. App. 8th Dist. Cuyahoga County 1993).

[44]Mozena v. Mozena, 1995 WL 366064 (Ohio Ct. App. 9th Dist. Lorain County 1995).

[45]Longstreet v. Longstreet, 57 Ohio App. 3d 55, 566 N.E.2d 708 (8th Dist. Cuyahoga County 1989).

[46]Bolle v. Bolle, 1991 WL 26678 (Ohio Ct. App. 2d Dist. Clark County 1991).

[47]Conover v. Conover, 1988 WL 118012 (Ohio Ct. App. 11th Dist. Geauga County 1988).

[48]Salem v. Salem, 61 Ohio App. 3d 243, 572 N.E.2d 726 (9th Dist. Summit County 1988).

The Tenth District Court of Appeals in *Pokrass v. All Security, Inc.*[49] interpreted that portion of the rule which provides for relief of judgment upon such terms as the court finds just to include the imposition of attorney's fees and costs as a condition to the granting of a Civ. R. 60(B) motion.

§ 24:4 Parental rights

The Third District Court of Appeals held that the trial court did not err in denying wife's Civil Rule 60(B)(3) & (5) motion to set aside a shared parenting plan. She claimed that she did not understand the terms, especially those that designated husband as the residential parent for school purposes. Although wife was not represented by counsel, she acknowledged at the dissolution hearing that she understood the terms and believed the plan to be in the best interests of the children. The Civil Rule 60(B)(3) claim alleged misconduct on husband's part for failing to provide her with certified copies of the dissolution documents. The evidence did not support the claim. The Civil Rule 60(B)(5) claim asserted a lack of mutuality regarding the terms of the plan. Although there was some confusion over the specific provision regarding residential parent for school purposes, wife had ample opportunity to address the issue before judgment and at the hearing. There were no extraordinary or unusual circumstances justifying relief under Civil Rule 60(B)(5).[1]

§ 24:5 Parentage

The Second District Court of Appeals in *Johnson v. Johnson*[1] considered a request based on Civ. R. 60(B)(4) to vacate a judgment which had, by agreement of the parties, determined paternity some five years before. The court held that the rationale of *Wolfe v. Wolfe*[2] did not confer on the court continuing jurisdiction in issues of paternity. Even if the court could vacate the order under Civ. R. 60(B)(4), it would not do so as the motion was not timely filed, both parties were party to the fraud on the court, and the child was not represented and stood to lose its judicially decreed paternity. That rationale does not, however, seem to preclude the possibility of granting a Civ. R. 60(B) motion in a

---

[49]Pokrass v. All Sec., Inc., 1 Ohio App. 3d 47, 439 N.E.2d 422 (10th Dist. Franklin County 1980).

[Section 24:4]
[1]Roberts v. Roberts, 2002-Ohio-3388, 2002 WL 1433914 (Ohio Ct. App. 3d Dist. Hancock County 2002).

[Section 24:5]
[1]Johnson v. Johnson, 1985 WL 7849 (Ohio Ct. App. 2d Dist. Montgomery County 1985).

[2]Wolfe v. Wolfe, 46 Ohio St. 2d 399, 75 Ohio Op. 2d 474, 350 N.E.2d 413 (1976).

paternity situation where appropriate.[3] The Ohio Supreme Court, however, has held that a determination of parentage in previous litigation, including dissolution proceedings, is res judicata to any other paternity action.[4]

The proper procedural way to attempt to delegitimize a child who was previously determined to be born of the marriage in a divorce action is to timely file a Civ. R. 60(B) motion.[5] A Civ. R. 60(B) motion generally operates as an exception to the doctrine of res judicata. It may be used to vacate a finding of paternity. An oral hearing should be granted if a meritorious claim or defense is presented and the motion is timely brought.[6] Even if medical evidence of the father's infertility and of the mother's untruthfulness becomes available after the judgment of paternity, a Civ. R. 60(B) motion and a request for blood tests may still be properly overruled.[7]

A year's delay in filing a Civ. R. 60(B) motion after voluntarily acknowledging paternity without genetic testing was deemed to be unreasonable.[8] A Civ. R. 60(B) motion for relief from judgment from certain aspects of a divorce decree as it relates to paternity and child support is untimely filed when filed more than one year after judgment and more than one year after the new evidence upon which it is based became admissible. In *Strack v. Pelton*,[9] the parties were divorced in 1978. The father obtained HLA testing which excluded him as the father of the child in 1987. The father filed his Civ. R. 60(B)(2) motion in 1990. A Civ. R. 60(B)(2) motion claiming new evidence must be filed not more than one year after the judgment. Accordingly, the motion was denied. A party's delay in asserting rights is a critical consideration and must be weighed against the competing principle that litigation must be brought to an end.[10]

Even though genetic test results excluded an alleged father as the child's father, the First District Court of Appeals reversed the trial court's granting of a Civ. R. 60(B) motion vacating a 1992 order establishing paternity. The motion, brought as a result of newly discovered evidence under Civ. R. 60(B)(2) should have been filed within the one-year period.[11] A Civ. R. 60(B) motion attempting to vacate a paternity judgment entered nine years earlier was found to have been

---

[3]Keeney v. Lawson, 19 Ohio App. 3d 318, 484 N.E.2d 745 (1st Dist. Hamilton County 1984) (movant may be entitled to relief under Civ. R. 60(B) even after delay of two and one-half years).

[4]In re Gilbraith, 32 Ohio St. 3d 127, 512 N.E.2d 956 (1987).

[5]Matter of Springer, 1992 WL 389943 (Ohio Ct. App. 2d Dist. Clark County 1992).

[6]Matter of Belden, 1993 WL 179254 (Ohio Ct. App. 2d Dist. Miami County 1993).

[7]Gilbraith v. Gilbraith, 1989 WL 62900 (Ohio Ct. App. 4th Dist. Athens County 1989).

[8]Davis v. Nikitin, 1994 WL 11023 (Ohio Ct. App. 9th Dist. Summit County 1994).

[9]Strack v. Pelton, 1994 -Ohio- 107, 70 Ohio St. 3d 172, 637 N.E.2d 914 (1994).

[10]State ex rel. Minnis v. Lewis, 1993 WL 546584 (Ohio Ct. App. 10th Dist. Franklin County 1993).

[11]Gosink v. Hamm, 111 Ohio App. 3d 495, 676 N.E.2d 604 (1st Dist. Hamilton County 1996), dismissed, appeal not allowed, 77 Ohio St. 3d 1487, 673 N.E.2d 146 (1996).

not timely filed.[12] Relief was granted to a child who sought to set aside a paternity settlement entered into eight years before. The court found that the young child could not have been expected to have sought relief earlier.[13]

Parental rights orders are final orders but never "final" to the extent they cannot be modified.[14] Inadvertence, mistake, newly discovered evidence, fraud, or neglect, existing at the time of the original judgment, may be addressed by a Civ. R. 60(B) motion.[15] All evidence relevant to the issue of parental rights may be reserved upon the hearing of the Civ. R. 60(B) motion. The court is not limited to hearsay events which occurred since the last order.[16]

In a case certified to the Ohio Supreme Court to resolve conflicting appellate rulings, the Court held that genetic test results obtained after a final parentage adjudication do not constitute newly discovered evidence under Civil Rule 60(B)(2) or (4), and, thus, do not justify vacating a parentage finding. However, the Court held that under former RC 3111.16, a trial court does have authority to vacate a paternity finding upon proper evidence, and to grant relief from a prospective support obligation. A court may not, however, retroactively relieve an obligor of a support duty or eliminate an arrearage that accrued while the support order was in effect.[17]

Appellee-father was granted Civil Rule 60(B)(5) relief from a 1978 divorce decree ordering him to pay child support when, in 1999, he presented evidence of a zero percent probability that he was the father of the child for who he was ordered to pay support.

The Sixth District Court of Appeals, citing *Strack v. Pelton*,[18] reversed the trial court's holding that Civil Rule 60(B)(5) was not the appropriate way to grant relief in this case where father sought relief because of newly discovered evidence.

The matter was, however, remanded to the trial court for review pursuant to RC 3119.961, RC 3119.962, and RC 3119.967, which could give father retroactive relief under the circumstances of a zero percent probability of paternity.[19]

---

[12]In re Adkins, 109 Ohio App. 3d 518, 672 N.E.2d 715 (8th Dist. Cuyahoga County 1996), dismissed, appeal not allowed, 76 Ohio St. 3d 1434, 667 N.E.2d 984 (1996).

[13]Ransome v. Lampman, 103 Ohio App. 3d 8, 658 N.E.2d 313 (2d Dist. Miami County 1995), dismissed, appeal not allowed, 73 Ohio St. 3d 1449, 654 N.E.2d 985 (1995).

[14]See Modification of Parental Rights and Responsibilities Ch 16.

[15]Sexton v. Sexton, 60 Ohio App. 2d 339, 14 Ohio Op. 3d 297, 397 N.E.2d 425 (5th Dist. Morrow County 1978) (wife's motion to modify treated as motion under Civ. R. 60(B)(4) so that evidence of facts surrounding execution of separation agreement could be introduced).

[16]Wade v. Wade, 10 Ohio App. 3d 167, 461 N.E.2d 30 (9th Dist. Wayne County 1983).

[17]Cuyahoga Support Enforcement Agency v. Guthrie, 1999 -Ohio- 362, 84 Ohio St. 3d 437, 705 N.E.2d 318 (1999).

[18]Strack v. Pelton, 70 Ohio St. 3d 172, 1994-Ohio-107, 637 N.E.2d 914 (1994).

[19]Poskarbiewicz v. Poskarbiewicz, 2002-Ohio-3666, 2002 WL 445058 (Ohio Ct. App. 6th Dist. Lucas County 2002).

§ 24:6 Child support

Inadvertence, mistake, newly discovered evidence, fraud, or neglect, existing at the time of the original judgment would make a Civ. R. 60(B) motion appropriate in a request for change in a child support order. An attempt to eliminate arrearages in child support, not normally modifiable,[1] might be attempted by a Civ. R. 60(B) motion.

§ 24:7 Visitation

It is hard to conceive of Civ. R. 60(B) being the appropriate procedure in an attempt to affect visitation. Continuing jurisdiction of the court under Civ. R. 75(J) clearly gives the litigant a proper procedure for modifying visitation. Unquestionably, the court has continuing jurisdiction in visitation matters, but it must be properly invoked.[1] The best interests of the minor children are paramount in determining changes in visitation.[2] While in most cases a change of circumstances will have occurred, a change of circumstances is not required for the court to modify a prior visitation order.[3] The trial court has jurisdiction to correct a clerical error in a QDRO as to the date of division of the pension plan. Civ. R. 60(A) corrections do not amount to a modification of property division.[4]

§ 24:8 Division of property

Change of circumstances has no application in an attempted modification of a division of marital property.[1] A long line of cases before and after *Wolfe* clearly holds that a division of property is not modifiable under

---

[Section 24:6]
    [1]Wedebrook v. Wedebrook, 51 Ohio Misc. 81, 5 Ohio Op. 3d 342, 367 N.E.2d 937 (C.P. 1977); Asztalos v. Fortney, 48 Ohio App. 2d 66, 2 Ohio Op. 3d 45, 355 N.E.2d 517 (6th Dist. Lucas County 1975); Rhoades v. Rhoades, 40 Ohio App. 2d 559, 69 Ohio Op. 2d 488, 321 N.E.2d 242 (1st Dist. Hamilton County 1974); Smith v. Smith, 168 Ohio St. 447, 7 Ohio Op. 2d 276, 156 N.E.2d 113, 70 A.L.R.2d 1241 (1959).

[Section 24:7]
    [1]Schwartz v. Schwartz, 1 Ohio App. 2d 451, 30 Ohio Op. 2d 447, 203 N.E.2d 249 (8th Dist. Cuyahoga County 1964); Hotchkiss v. Hotchkiss, 85 Ohio L. Abs. 375, 174 N.E.2d 293 (Ct. App. 7th Dist. Geauga County 1960). See also RC 3109.05 (modification of child support when visitation denied); RC 3105.65 (pursuant to a dissolution); Hill v. Hill, 40 Ohio App. 2d 1, 69 Ohio Op. 2d 1, 317 N.E.2d 250 (1st Dist. Hamilton County 1973); Johnson v. Johnson, 52 Ohio App. 2d 180, 6 Ohio Op. 3d 170, 368 N.E.2d 1273 (9th Dist. Summit County 1977). See also § 25:55, Post-decree motions—Motion for continuing jurisdiction.
    [2]Kay v. Kay, 51 Ohio Op. 434, 65 Ohio L. Abs. 472, 112 N.E.2d 562 (C.P. 1953). See also §§ 18:26–18:33.
    [3]Appleby v. Appleby, 24 Ohio St. 3d 39, 492 N.E.2d 831 (1986). See Visitation Ch 18.
    [4]Peterson v. Peterson, 1998 WL 166475 (Ohio Ct. App. 12th Dist. Butler County 1998).

[Section 24:8]
    [1]Wolfe v. Wolfe, 46 Ohio St. 2d 399, 75 Ohio Op. 2d 474, 350 N.E.2d 413 (1976).

any circumstances.[2] Further, RC 3105.171(I) prohibits modification of a property division made under RC 3105.171.[3]

A serious question arises as to what constitutes a division of property as opposed to spousal support.[4] In those cases where it is clear that the decree is a true division of property, the only avenue open is Civ. R. 60(B). The original order must be vacated or set aside before there can be any adjustment of division of property.[5]

Where an asset has been excluded from the property division because the parties were unaware of its existence, Civ. R. 60(B)(5) may be appropriately applied. The Tenth District Court of Appeals in *Hellwege v. Hellwege*[6] so ruled. Additionally, the court in *Hellwege* indicated that a motion under this rule would be appropriate both in divorce and dissolution proceedings. Citing *In re Murphy*,[7] the court in *Hellwege* reasoned that RC 3105.18, as then in effect, requires a court to consider all the assets and liabilities of the parties in making an equitable division. Such may not be the case, however, if the motion is not timely filed.[8]

If the trial court did consider the existence or nonexistence of the asset, a Civ. R. 60(B)(5) motion would not be granted, as in the case of *Ewing v. Ewing*.[9] Other courts have held that where parties are aware of the particular asset, there are no grounds for a Civ. R. 60(B)(5) motion.[10]

In *Snyder v. Snyder*,[11] the appellant was aware that appellee participated in a pension fund and owned an insurance policy. Accordingly, she could not claim relief under Civ. R. 60(B)(2) or (3) because there was no evidence of fraud and/or newly discovered evidence as to

---

[2]Popovic v. Popovic, 45 Ohio App. 2d 57, 74 Ohio Op. 2d 94, 341 N.E.2d 341 (8th Dist. Cuyahoga County 1975); Korb v. Korb, 1981 WL 9750 (Ohio Ct. App. 1st Dist. Hamilton County 1981); Hetzel v. Hetzel, No. CA 37210 (Ohio Ct. App. 8th Dist. Cuyahoga County 1978).

[3]1990 H.B. 514, eff 1-1-91.

[4]Wolfe v. Wolfe, 46 Ohio St. 2d 399, 75 Ohio Op. 2d 474, 350 N.E.2d 413 (1976); Dailey v. Dailey, 171 Ohio St. 133, 12 Ohio Op. 2d 161, 167 N.E.2d 906 (1960); Tasin v. Tasin, No. 37707 (Ohio Ct. App. 8th Dist. Cuyahoga County 1978); Meket v. Meket, No. CA 34479 (Ohio Ct. App. 8th Dist. Cuyahoga County 1975); De Milo v. Watson, 166 Ohio St. 433, 2 Ohio Op. 2d 433, 143 N.E.2d 707 (1957). See Marital Obligations and Property Rights Ch 4; Marital and Separate Property Ch 12; Spousal Support Ch 13; Modification of Spousal Support Ch 14.

[5]See In re Marriage of Kesler, 59 Ohio Misc. 33, 13 Ohio Op. 3d 105, 392 N.E.2d 905 (C.P. 1978) (court modified portion of separation agreement incorporated into decree of dissolution on basis that wife should have had representation in negotiating property settlement).

[6]Hellwege v. Hellwege, 1986 WL 6335 (Ohio Ct. App. 10th Dist. Franklin County 1986).

[7]In re Murphy, 10 Ohio App. 3d 134, 461 N.E.2d 910 (1st Dist. Hamilton County 1983).

[8]See, e.g., Adams v. Adams, 1982 WL 5276 (Ohio Ct. App. 8th Dist. Cuyahoga County 1982).

[9]Ewing v. Ewing, 1986 WL 6049 (Ohio Ct. App. 4th Dist. Meigs County 1986).

[10]See, e.g., Byrd v. Byrd, 1985 WL 8807 (Ohio Ct. App. 1st Dist. Hamilton County 1985).

[11]Snyder v. Snyder, 1992 WL 14946 (Ohio Ct. App. 8th Dist. Cuyahoga County 1992).

the existence of those assets. However, it is clear that those assets are to be considered in dividing marital property.[12] The trial court, therefore, erred in adopting the report and recommendation of the referee which had denied the appellant's request for relief from judgment with respect to the omitted assets. The court of appeals remanded the matter to the trial court for valuation of the omitted assets only. The trial court was not directed to redistribute those assets that were part of the original division of property.

In *Dhillon v. Dhillon*,[13] the trial court erred in overruling the husband's Civ. R. 60(B) motion where the parties' in-court agreement negotiated with counsel was inequitable. The wife had factually misrepresented her debt; her PERS account was not valued. The parties used the wife's contribution in negotiating the property division settlement. The trial court was directed to reexamine the entire property division.

Appellant-wife sought to vacate a 1998 divorce decree alleging that appellee-husband failed to disclose the existence of a supplemental retirement plan valued in excess of $400,000. The trial court denied wife's motion, as it found that at the time of the divorce, husband had no entitlement to the funds and that the plan was not a qualified retirement plan. The Fifth District Court of Appeals agreed that the evidence established that the supplemental retirement plan was entirely optional with husband's employer. The benefits were not vested, nor in existence at the time of the divorce. He had not paid anything into the plan. The payment of any benefit was purely speculative at the time of divorce and could not be considered as a marital asset. Since husband did not conceal a marital asset as alleged, wife's motion was properly overruled.[14]

In *McCollum v. McCollum*,[15] wife claimed that significant marital property had not been divided in their divorce. Husband had acquired a business during the marriage. It was given no value at the time of divorce. Later, however, husband was awarded a judgment in excess of $156,000 for his interest in the business. Wife immediately filed her Civ. R. 60(B) motion which asserted that neither party knew that the business had any value at the time of divorce. Husband, by way of affidavit, asserted that wife knew of the business, but elected not to pursue any interest as she mistakenly believed it had no value. Without addressing the merits of the claims, the Eleventh District Court of Appeals held that wife's assertion that the sizable lawsuit settlement constituted marital property that was not equitably divided did state a potentially meritorious claim.

---

[12]Holcomb v. Holcomb, 44 Ohio St. 3d 128, 541 N.E.2d 597 (1989) (assets must be valued and distributed).

[13]Dhillon v. Dhillon, 1997 WL 626008 (Ohio Ct. App. 8th Dist. Cuyahoga County 1997).

[14]Evans v. Evans, 2002-Ohio-2526, 2002 WL 992081 (Ohio Ct. App. 5th Dist. Delaware County 2002).

[15]McCollum v. McCollum, 1996 WL 586768 (Ohio Ct. App. 11th Dist. Trumbull County 1996).

One trial court erred in failing to grant a Civ. R. 60(B) motion alleging that the court failed to divide parties' personal property. Though there was no appeal from the original decree, the court of appeals deemed Civ. R. 60(B) to be appropriate under the facts and circumstances of the case.[16]

Citing *Wolfe v. Wolfe*,[17] the Fifth District Court of Appeals in *Moore v. Moore*[18] held that a trial court does not have continuing jurisdiction to modify a property division by converting it into a sustenance alimony award and characterizing it as nondischargeable in bankruptcy.[19]

Where a separation agreement incorporated into a decree of dissolution fails to address a substantial marital asset, the decree is voidable and can only be attacked by a Civ. R. 60(B) motion.[20]

In *Zulli v. Zulli*,[21] the Eighth District Court of Appeals stated:

> When a separation agreement omits assets that are both substantial in relative amount and material to an informed and deliberate agreement about an equitable division of the property, such omissions render the dissolution decree voidable, and the decree can be vacated by motion for relief filed under Civ.R. 60(B)(5).[22]

Two 1996 decisions questioned the appropriateness of a Civ. R. 60(B) motion in dissolution cases where either or both of the parties have remarried. Although a separation agreement omitted substantial and material assets, a dissolution decree should not have been vacated when one or both of the parties had remarried. Rather, the aggrieved party should have sought relief by an action for accounting, declaratory judgment, conversion, damages, or unjust enrichment.[23] The Second District Court of Appeals also held that a dissolution decree should not have been vacated when one or both of the parties had remarried because they acted in reliance on the dissolution.[24] The Supreme Court of Ohio, however, in *In re Whitman*,[25] held that under Civil Rule 60(B)(1), (2) or (3), a trial court may grant relief from judgment as to the property division in a separation agreement without vacating the decree of dissolution where the separation agreement expressly allows for modification by court order. Remarriage of the opposing party is not a complete bar

---

[16]Iafiglio v. Nowak, 1996 WL 75719 (Ohio Ct. App. 8th Dist. Cuyahoga County 1996).

[17]Wolfe v. Wolfe, 46 Ohio St. 2d 399, 75 Ohio Op. 2d 474, 350 N.E.2d 413 (1976).

[18]Moore v. Moore, 1984 WL 4965 (Ohio Ct. App. 5th Dist. Stark County 1984).

[19]See Bankruptcy Ch 33; Marital Obligations and Property Rights Ch 4.

[20]Morgan v. Morgan, 1994 WL 265899 (Ohio Ct. App. 7th Dist. Columbiana County 1994).

[21]Zulli v. Zulli, 1992 WL 2578 (Ohio Ct. App. 8th Dist. Cuyahoga County 1992).

[22]Zulli v. Zulli, 1992 WL 2578, at *2 (Ohio Ct. App. 8th Dist. Cuyahoga County 1992).

[23]Whitman v. Whitman, 1996 WL 276379 (Ohio Ct. App. 3d Dist. Hancock County 1996), appeal allowed, 77 Ohio St. 3d 1478, 673 N.E.2d 141 (1996) and judgment rev'd, 1998 -Ohio- 466, 81 Ohio St. 3d 239, 690 N.E.2d 535 (1998).

[24]Henry v. Edwards, 1996 WL 220885 (Ohio Ct. App. 2d Dist. Montgomery County 1996), dismissed, appeal not allowed, 77 Ohio St. 3d 1445, 671 N.E.2d 1284 (1996); Crews v. Crews, 1996 WL 685570 (Ohio Ct. App. 2d Dist. Montgomery County 1996).

[25]In re Whitman, 1998 -Ohio- 466, 81 Ohio St. 3d 239, 690 N.E.2d 535 (1998).

to relief, but may be considered by the trial court in determining whether relief is equitable.

§ 24:9 Divorce

Ohio still requires the finding of fault upon which the divorce can be granted in cases other than a dissolution or divorce based upon incompatibility or living separate and apart for one year.[1] An attack upon the granting of the divorce may be an effort to achieve the real objective of changing division of property, child support, etc. Civ. R. 60(B) might provide a means to an end if sufficient provable facts exist to convince the court to set aside the divorce in its entirety.

A common pleas court has inherent authority and jurisdiction to vacate its own judgment, especially when such judgment is procured by means of fraud.[2] A motion for relief from judgment should be granted where "intolerable inequity" of a separation agreement supports allegations that the movant was defrauded into signing it.[3] Misconduct after the judgment was sufficient to the Second District Court of Appeals to affirm the holding of the trial court that granted a hearing and modified its original decree based on such misconduct.[4] The Second District Court of Appeals has held that a motion for relief from judgment is properly granted where one of the parties made material misrepresentations of fact to the court.[5]

Such a motion based on alleged fraud on the court is not subject to the one-year limitation of Civ. R. 60(B)(3).[6] Civ. R. 60(B)(5) allows relief from judgment for any reason which encompasses fraud on the court. Such rule reflects the inherent power of the court to relieve a party from judgment procured by a fraud on the court.[7] A trial court does not abuse its discretion when it refuses to vacate a judgment for reason of fraud on

---

[Section 24:9]

[1]RC 3105.01. For a more detailed discussion see Divorce Ch 11.

[2]Hartford v. Hartford, 53 Ohio App. 2d 79, 7 Ohio Op. 3d 53, 371 N.E.2d 591 (8th Dist. Cuyahoga County 1977); Jelm v. Jelm, 155 Ohio St. 226, 44 Ohio Op. 246, 98 N.E.2d 401, 22 A.L.R.2d 1300 (1951); Older v. Older, 1988 WL 63936 (Ohio Ct. App. 9th Dist. Wayne County 1988) (trial court erred by applying contract principles rather than Civil Rules to domestic relations case when it held that separation agreement executed by parties could not be attacked; Civ. R. 60(B) motion provides bases for relief from divorce judgment); Good v. Good, 1988 WL 70893 (Ohio Ct. App. 5th Dist. Knox County 1988) (where fraud found, trial court authorized by Civ. R. 60 to modify original alimony award; appellate court cannot weigh credibility of trial witnesses).

[3]In Re the Marriage of Siedlecki v. Siedlecki, 1987 WL 11094, at *6 (Ohio Ct. App. 8th Dist. Cuyahoga County 1987).

[4]Whitaker v. Whitaker, 1991 WL 19356 (Ohio Ct. App. 2d Dist. Greene County 1991).

[5]Brown v. Brown, 1987 WL 11265 (Ohio Ct. App. 2d Dist. Montgomery County 1987).

[6]Hartford v. Hartford, 53 Ohio App. 2d 79, 7 Ohio Op. 3d 53, 371 N.E.2d 591 (8th Dist. Cuyahoga County 1977).

[7]Coulson v. Coulson, 5 Ohio St. 3d 12, 448 N.E.2d 809 (1983) (any fraud connected with presentation of case to court is fraud on court and party must resort to motion under Civ. R. 60(B)(3), where an officer of court actively participates in defrauding court, then court may entertain motion under Civ. R. 60(B)(5)). See also Jelm v. Jelm, 155

the court when the party seeking relief participated in the fraud.[8] The trial court abuses its discretion when it dismisses a Civ. R. 60(B) motion without a hearing when the allegations, if true, could constitute a fraud on the court. Such a motion must, of course, be filed within a reasonable time.[9] The Second District Court of Appeals held that the appellant, seeking to set aside an uncontested divorce decree on the basis that it did not accurately reflect the parties' oral agreement, had set forth sufficient operative facts to state a "palpable" claim for relief to justify an oral hearing.[10]

§ 24:10 In-court settlements

In-court settlements, both oral and written, have also been attacked under Civ. R. 60(B). The results are usually predictable. An in-court settlement of division of property, spousal support, etc., adopted by the court as its judgment, is enforceable even in the absence of a written agreement or a judgment entry approved by the party or his attorney.[1] The agreement need only be made prior to or at the time of the trial or hearing.[2]

Dissatisfaction with a settlement is not sufficient to render the judgment voidable.[3] The court may, however, modify part of a final judgment to conform to the terms of the agreement if it is not correctly reflected in the judgment entry either by reason of clerical mistake, oversight, or

---

Ohio St. 226, 44 Ohio Op. 246, 98 N.E.2d 401, 22 A.L.R.2d 1300 (1951); Hazel-Atlas Glass Co. v. Hartford-Empire Co., 322 U.S. 238, 64 S. Ct. 997, 88 L. Ed. 1250 (1944) (overruled as stated in, W. R. Grace & Co., Inc. v. Western U. S. Industries, Inc., 608 F.2d 1214 (9th Cir. 1979)); Longstreet v. Longstreet, 57 Ohio App. 3d 55, 566 N.E.2d 708 (8th Dist. Cuyahoga County 1989).

[8]Gambill v. Gambill, 1991 WL 10958 (Ohio Ct. App. 2d Dist. Miami County 1991).

[9]See Civ. R. 60(B)(5); Hartford v. Hartford, 53 Ohio App. 2d 79, 7 Ohio Op. 3d 53, 371 N.E.2d 591 (8th Dist. Cuyahoga County 1977); Miller v. Miller, 1988 WL 36510 (Ohio Ct. App. 8th Dist. Cuyahoga County 1988) (movant-wife did not make meritorious claim under Civ. R. 60(B); no independent evidence of value of marital claim introduced; incorrect diagnosis that she was terminally ill not mistake of fact; court found wife intentionally delayed filing of motion to gain pecuniary advantage); Justice v. Justice, 1989 WL 25568 (Ohio Ct. App. 12th Dist. Madison County 1989), dismissed, 44 Ohio St. 3d 709, 542 N.E.2d 347 (1989) (nine years held not to be reasonable time); Yingst v. Yingst, 1990 WL 113457 (Ohio Ct. App. 3d Dist. Union County 1990) (where judgment is void as being jurisdictionally defective, Civ. R. 60(B) motion may be filed at any time).

[10]Smith v. Smith, 1990 WL 42319 (Ohio Ct. App. 2d Dist. Montgomery County 1990).

[Section 24:10]
[1]See §§ 9:39–9:46, In-court agreements.

[2]See §§ 9:39–9:46, In-court agreements. See also Popovic v. Popovic, 45 Ohio App. 2d 57, 74 Ohio Op. 2d 94, 341 N.E.2d 341 (8th Dist. Cuyahoga County 1975); Robrock v. Robrock, 167 Ohio St. 479, 5 Ohio Op. 2d 165, 150 N.E.2d 421 (1958) (disapproved of by, Nokes v. Nokes, 47 Ohio St. 2d 1, 1 Ohio Op. 3d 1, 351 N.E.2d 174 (1976)); Mozden v. Mozden, 162 Ohio St. 169, 55 Ohio Op. 4, 122 N.E.2d 295 (1954).

[3]Spercel v. Sterling Industries, Inc., 31 Ohio St. 2d 36, 60 Ohio Op. 2d 20, 285 N.E.2d 324 (1972). See also §§ 9:39–9:46, In-court agreements.

omission.[4] Settlement agreements do not have to be fair and equitable to be binding and enforceable, as long as they are not produced by fraud, duress, overreaching, or undue influence. Haste or poor advice from counsel does not offer a defense to the enforceability of the contract.[5] In *Horvath v. Horvath*,[6] the trial court did not err in denying the wife's Civ. R. 60(B) motion which claimed that an agreed arrearage in support was omitted from the decree of divorce. No direct appeal was filed and the record revealed that the parties had never reached an agreement as to the arrearage.

A trial court did not abuse its discretion in granting a wife's Civ. R. 60(B) motion where the wife met the elements necessary to establish that she signed a separation agreement while under duress. The separation agreement was drafted by her husband and his counsel. Her husband threatened to take all three children away from her unless she agreed, and the husband made repeated acts of actual and threatened abuse during the marriage. A separation agreement that is the product of duress will be held to be unenforceable.[7]

§ 24:11 Spousal support

The Tenth District Court of Appeals in *McKinnon v. McKinnon*[1] held that Civ. R. 60(B)(4) could be used to modify a spousal support award if the court found that the award was no longer equitable and the judgment should no longer have prospective application. The court in *McKinnon* further held that it could modify the spousal support portion of the prior order without vacating it. A contrary opinion was rendered in *Stump v. Stump*[2] where the Fifth District Court of Appeals held that the trial court was correct in ruling that it must vacate an entire judgment when granting a Civ. R. 60(B) motion regarding a spousal support award. A Civ. R. 60(B) motion failed where the court reserved jurisdiction over spousal support for thirty days. The husband did not timely file an appeal, and the Civ. R. 60(B) motion could not substitute for an appeal or give the trial court jurisdiction over spousal support after the thirty days expired.[3]

Civ. R. 60(A) authority may be used to correct an order of divorce

---

[4]Cadwell v. Cadwell, No. 41294 (Ohio Ct. App. 8th Dist. Cuyahoga County 1980); Coulson v. Coulson, 5 Ohio St. 3d 12, 448 N.E.2d 809 (1983) (new facts alleged in subsequent motion for relief from judgment, issues on appeal not res judicata and court may consider them).

[5]Vasilakis v. Vasilakis, 1996 WL 340010 (Ohio Ct. App. 8th Dist. Cuyahoga County 1996).

[6]Horvath v. Horvath, 1997 WL 728650 (Ohio Ct. App. 6th Dist. Lucas County 1997).

[7]See Young v. Young, 8 Ohio App. 3d 52, 455 N.E.2d 1360 (10th Dist. Franklin County 1982).

[Section 24:11]

[1]McKinnon v. McKinnon, 9 Ohio App. 3d 220, 459 N.E.2d 590 (10th Dist. Franklin County 1983).

[2]Stump v. Stump, 1983 WL 7064 (Ohio Ct. App. 5th Dist. Stark County 1983).

[3]Henderson v. Rolfert-Henderson, 1998 WL 241794 (Ohio Ct. App. 1st Dist. Hamilton County 1998).

which omitted an award of permanent spousal support when the omission was clerical.[4]

§ 24:12 Timeliness of motion

The first three subdivisions of Civ. R. 60(B) require the filing of a motion to vacate within one year of the entry of judgment.[1] Reliance on grounds under Civ. R. 60(B)(4) and (5) requires the filing to be within a reasonable time after the entry of judgment.[2]

A Civ. R. 60(B) motion was deemed untimely, although brought within eleven months from the date of divorce. The movant offered no explanation for the delay in filing.[3] A Civil Rule 60(B) motion on the basis of newly discovered evidence was deemed time-barred. The movant claimed that she only recently discovered that the attorney she consulted for advice regarding an antenuptial agreement was the partner of the attorney who represented husband. The trial court held that the parties' Antenuptial Agreement was valid and wife had independent counsel.[4]

Where a wife failed to disclose her employment at the time of final hearing, the husband's Civ. R. 60(B)(5) motion filed more than one year after the ruling was properly denied. Fraud on the court must be narrowly interpreted. In this case, the husband knew of his wife's employment at the time of the final hearing.[5] While Civ. R. 60(B)(5) cannot be used as a substitute for any specific provisions of Civ. R. 60(B), it "reflects the inherent power of the court to relieve an individual from the unjust operation of a judgment."[6] Reasonable time may be within the one-year period or beyond.[7]

When a party fails to seek relief from an alleged mistake within one year, a court is without authority to grant a motion to amend that judgment entry on a motion filed under Civ. R. 60(B)(5).[8] The motion should properly have been filed under Civ. R. 60(B)(1) within one year of the

---

[4]Wise v. Wise, 1997 WL 626027 (Ohio Ct. App. 8th Dist. Cuyahoga County 1997).

[Section 24:12]

[1]See Civ. R. 60(B)(1) to (3).

[2]Hartford v. Hartford, 53 Ohio App. 2d 79, 7 Ohio Op. 3d 53, 371 N.E.2d 591 (8th Dist. Cuyahoga County 1977).

[3]Schmuhl v. Schmuhl, 1997 WL 47645 (Ohio Ct. App. 8th Dist. Cuyahoga County 1997).

[4]Todd v. Todd, 2002-Ohio-2394, 2002 WL 992389 (Ohio Ct. App. 10th Dist. Franklin County 2002).

[5]Heltzel v. Heltzel, 1987 WL 18032 (Ohio Ct. App. 11th Dist. Trumbull County 1987).

[6]Klingman v. Klingman, 1984 WL 14432 (Ohio Ct. App. 6th Dist. Ottawa County 1984) (five-year delay reasonable where coercion had continued); In re Marriage of Watson, 13 Ohio App. 3d 344, 469 N.E.2d 876 (9th Dist. Lorain County 1983) (four-year period).

[7]Klingman v. Klingman, 1984 WL 14432, at *4 (Ohio Ct. App. 6th Dist. Ottawa County 1984) (five-year delay reasonable where coercion had continued); In re Marriage of Watson, 13 Ohio App. 3d 344, 469 N.E.2d 876 (9th Dist. Lorain County 1983) (four-year period). See also In re Marriage of Watson, 13 Ohio App. 3d 344, 469 N.E.2d 876 (9th Dist. Lorain County 1983).

[8]Hamlin v. Hamlin, 1993 WL 32010 (Ohio Ct. App. 2d Dist. Darke County 1993).

judgment. A reasonable time may be less than one year. Ill health, illiteracy, and advanced years were deemed insufficient reasons for an eight-month delay in attacking a judgment.[9]

Civ. R. 60(B)(5) is a "catch all" provision. However, if cannot be used as a substitute for any of the more specific provisions of Civ. R. 60(B).[10] Laches may be a defense to such action even if the motion is brought in what appeared to be a timely manner.[11] Wife's motion was brought under the "catch all" category of Civil Rule 60(B)(5), more than six months after the court granted a dissolution of marriage. Wife claimed an omission of assets from the separation agreement and affidavit of property, but failed to address the reasonableness of the delay in filing or to identify when she learned of the alleged omissions. Wife offered no excuse for the delay in filing. A movant has the burden of establishing the timeliness of the motion.[12]

In *Woods v. Woods*,[13] the wife's Civ. R. 60(B)(5) motion filed approximately two and one-half years after a decree of divorce was entered by the trial court was properly overruled. Appellant's motion alleged fraud and misrepresentation by her husband during the negotiations which lead to a separation agreement. The Third District Court of Appeals concluded that the trial court had not erred in denying appellant the relief she sought. Her motion, though brought under the provisions of Civ. R. 60(B)(5) could have been brought under Civ. R. 60(B)(3) and within one year after the judgment was rendered.

Even if the ground for relief from judgment is evident and not controverted, the trial court would have no authority to vacate a judgment subject to relief under Civ. R. 60(B)(1), (2), or (3), if the motion was not filed within the one-year time requirement.[14] A motion alleging fraud under Civ. R. 60(B)(3) filed six years after entry of judgment is untimely and will not be granted.[15]

Husband's Civil Rule 60(B)(3) motion filed 41 months after the divorce decree was properly dismissed as being untimely. He claimed that documents signed by the parties prior to the divorce contained "latent time bombs" which were not apparent until appellee-wife attempted to terminate her contract. However, the appellate court found the documents to be clear and unambiguous, and was therefore unpersuaded by appellant-husband's contention that he did not understand the docu-

---

[9]Derricoatte v. Hope, 1993 WL 536074 (Ohio Ct. App. 8th Dist. Cuyahoga County 1993).

[10]Woods v. Woods, 1991 WL 259560 (Ohio Ct. App. 3d Dist. Henry County 1991), citing Caruso-Ciresi, Inc. v. Lohman, 5 Ohio St. 3d 64, 448 N.E.2d 1365 (1983); Hornyak v. Brooks, 16 Ohio App. 3d 105, 474 N.E.2d 676 (8th Dist. Cuyahoga County 1984).

[11]Van DeRyt v. Van DeRyt, 6 Ohio St. 2d 31, 35 Ohio Op. 2d 42, 215 N.E.2d 698, 16 A.L.R.3d 271 (1966).

[12]Haley v. Helay, 2002-Ohio-1976, 2002 WL 701937 (Ohio Ct. App. 9th Dist. Summit County 2002) citing Youssefi v. Youssefi, 81 Ohio App. 3d 49, 610 N.E.2d 455 (9th Dist. Summit County 1991).

[13]Woods v. Woods, 1991 WL 259560 (Ohio Ct. App. 3d Dist. Henry County 1991).

[14]Luscre v. Luscre, 45 Ohio Misc. 9, 74 Ohio Op. 2d 18, 340 N.E.2d 854 (C.P. 1974).

[15]Cotton v. Cotton, 1993 WL 9717 (Ohio Ct. App. 3d Dist. Union County 1993).

ments' contents.

Husband's claim under Civil Rule 60(B)(5) was not filed within a reasonable time, when the evidence disclosed that the documents he claimed that he did not understand at the time of the divorce were discussed through counsel shortly after the divorce.[16]

A motion to vacate filed over two years after the judgment entry of divorce was journalized was overruled as not timely filed. Appellant knew of the entry within one year of its entry. A first Civ. R. 60(B) motion filed eight months after the decree was dismissed when appellant's fourth attorney withdrew.[17] Where husband purposely concealed and denied receipt of substantial bonus from his employer, a closely held corporation which he and his relatives controlled, it was error for the trial court to deny wife's Civ. R. 60(B)(3) motion although brought five years after the decree.[18] A Civ. R. 60(B) motion to vacate an adoption decree brought by the adopted child 24 years later was deemed not be timely filed despite emotional distress and financial hardship. If an adopted child could bring such an action, the time for filing would not commence until the child reached majority.[19]

A 2½-year delay in filing a motion for relief under Civ. R. 60(B) did not prevent review of paternity proceedings in *Keeney v Lawson*,[20] where the defendant alleged that he was borderline mentally retarded and had been unconstitutionally deprived of his rights to counsel and a blood grouping test, both to be provided by the state. Likewise, a Civ. R. 60(B)(5) motion filed more than four years after a ruling granting an adoption petition was properly granted where the adoptive parents failed to use reasonable diligence to ascertain the biological mother's address.[21] A motion to vacate a divorce decree, entered six years previously, was held not to be filed within a reasonable time. The movant's request for interrogatories to be answered by the referee and the attorney was not proper as they were not parties to the action.[22] A Civ. R. 60(B) motion to vacate a support order was deemed untimely filed where appellant waited four years after a disability had lowered his income.[23]

---

[16]Granneman v. Granneman, 2002-Ohio-1867, 2002 WL 602740 (Ohio Ct. App. 6th Dist. Huron County 2002).

[17]Kerns v. Kerns, 87 Ohio App. 3d 698, 622 N.E.2d 1149 (10th Dist. Franklin County 1993).

[18]Andrews v. Andrews, 1994 WL 581480 (Ohio Ct. App. 6th Dist. Fulton County 1994).

[19]Matter of Spine, 1995 WL 78044 (Ohio Ct. App. 10th Dist. Franklin County 1995).

[20]Keeney v. Lawson, 19 Ohio App. 3d 318, 484 N.E.2d 745 (1st Dist. Hamilton County 1984).

[21]In re Adoption of Knipper, 30 Ohio App. 3d 214, 507 N.E.2d 436 (1st Dist. Hamilton County 1986).

[22]Zuchniak v. Zuchniak, 1989 WL 1665 (Ohio Ct. App. 9th Dist. Medina County 1989), cause dismissed, 43 Ohio St. 3d 709, 540 N.E.2d 731 (1989).

[23]Perdew v. Perdew, 1990 WL 1354 (Ohio Ct. App. 6th Dist. Fulton County 1990).

In *Loew v. Loew*,[24] the ex-wife filed a motion to vacate a divorce decree which failed to credit her with a portion of her former husband's railroad pension. The trial court did not err in denying her motion to vacate. The motion was filed more than eight years after the divorce decree. The wife did not specify a ground or submit evidence which would constitute grounds pursuant to Civ. R. 60(B)(5). In *Dillard-Davis v. Dillard*,[25] the trial court correctly granted the wife's Civ. R. 60(B) motion which set aside a decree granting the husband dependency exemptions for the minor children. The wife claimed that the order was in error; it should have only been for one tax year. The wife demonstrated a meritorious defense other than excusable neglect. The motion was timely brought, although beyond one year. In *Sinsky v. Matthews*,[26] husband's Civ. R. 60(B) motion was denied as being untimely when filed 364 days after judgment. He was aware of the grounds for vacating one week after the judgment, but delayed the filing.

While Civ. R. 60(B) should be liberally applied so as to avoid extreme hardship in extraordinary circumstances, it cannot be used as a substitute for appeal. The filing of a Civ. R. 60(B) motion does not enlarge the time for filing of a notice of appeal.[27] A husband's motion for relief from judgment filed five months after judgment was properly denied and the appeal was dismissed as untimely. Civ. R. 60(B) cannot be used as a substitute for direct appeal or to circumvent time requirements for an appeal.[28]

Although a Civ. R. 60(B)(5) motion was filed within one year of DNA testing that rendered a 0.00% probability that movant was the biological father, the trial court properly denied the motion. Father knew he was not the biological father well before the DNA tests and was bound to file his motion under Civ. R. 60(B)(2) within one year of the agreed judgment.[29] In *Welter v. Welter*,[30] the trial court did not err in vacating a decree of divorce and conducting further hearings. The wife's claim that the decree was vacated only for the purpose of providing the husband with COBRA coverage under her insurance policy was not directly appealed and was improperly raised in a Civ. R. 60(B) motion. Procedurally, it can be used simultaneously. It is important to note the jurisdictional aspects between the trial court and the court of appeals while such dual procedures are pending and after the court of appeals

---

[24]Loew v. Loew, 114 Ohio App. 3d 632, 683 N.E.2d 847 (11th Dist. Trumbull County 1996).

[25]Dillard-Davis v. Dillard, 1997 WL 711254 (Ohio Ct. App. 8th Dist. Cuyahoga County 1997).

[26]Sinsky v. Matthews, 2001 WL 888378 (Ohio Ct. App. 9th Dist. Summit County 2001).

[27]Town & Country Drive-In Shopping Centers, Inc. v. Abraham, 46 Ohio App. 2d 262, 75 Ohio Op. 2d 416, 348 N.E.2d 741 (10th Dist. Franklin County 1975).

[28]Rundle v. Rundle, 123 Ohio App. 3d 304, 704 N.E.2d 56 (8th Dist. Cuyahoga County 1997).

[29]Shaffer v. Rusnak, 1998 WL 429624 (Ohio Ct. App. 5th Dist. Guernsey County 1998), dismissed, appeal not allowed, 84 Ohio St. 3d 1408, 701 N.E.2d 1018 (1998).

[30]Welter v. Welter, 1998 WL 254944 (Ohio Ct. App. 9th Dist. Summit County 1998).

has returned jurisdiction to the trial court.

§ 24:13 Appeal

When a motion for relief from judgment has been denied and a notice of appeal from such ruling is filed, the trial court loses its jurisdiction to hear a subsequent motion for relief. The court of appeals, however, may remand the matter of the second motion to the trial court for hearing.[1]

There is a dispute between appellate districts as to whether the trial court has jurisdiction to grant a motion for relief from judgment while an appeal is pending.[2] The Court of Appeals of Fayette County held that a trial court may hear a Civ. R. 60(B) motion even though an appeal is pending. Issues raised on a direct appeal and those raised in a Civ. R. 60(B) motion are necessarily different. There is no overlap of issues between the courts and judicial economy is best served.[3] Such a motion can be filed during the appeal. If the appeal is dismissed, or if the matter is partially remanded to the trial court, the motion may be considered.[4] Thus, it may be wise to file simultaneously a notice of appeal and a motion to vacate with the trial court. *Majnaric v. Majnaric*[5] provides a procedure whereby a motion in the court of appeals can be made to partially remand the matter to the trial court for hearing on the motion. In that way, the appeal is protected while the motion to vacate is considered. However, the Tenth District Court of Appeals will not entertain such a motion for remand to consider a Civ. R. 60(B) matter, holding that the trial court retains its jurisdiction to consider the Civ. R. 60(B) motion without remand.[6]

If the motion is denied, the appeal is still available for possible relief. The partial remand order should contain a provision that the appeal will be reinstated without the necessity of filing a new appeal on the overrul-

---

[Section 24:13]

[1]Garrett v. Garrett, 54 Ohio App. 2d 25, 8 Ohio Op. 3d 41, 374 N.E.2d 654 (1st Dist. Hamilton County 1977); Bosco v. City of Euclid, 38 Ohio App. 2d 40, 67 Ohio Op. 2d 209, 311 N.E.2d 870 (8th Dist. Cuyahoga County 1974). For further discussion of some of the appellate problems, see Appeals Ch 32.

[2]Dempsey v. Chicago Title Ins. Co., 20 Ohio App. 3d 90, 484 N.E.2d 1064 (8th Dist. Cuyahoga County 1985) (motion for relief filed before notice of appeal; appellate court held trial court loses jurisdiction absent request for remand); contra Matter of Appeal of Neff v. City of Westerville, 1986 WL 2928 (Ohio Ct. App. 10th Dist. Franklin County 1986).

[3]Beechler v. Beechler, 95 Ohio App. 3d 121, 641 N.E.2d 1189 (12th Dist. Fayette County 1994).

[4]Majnaric v. Majnaric, 46 Ohio App. 2d 157, 75 Ohio Op. 2d 250, 347 N.E.2d 552 (9th Dist. Summit County 1975); Vavrina v. Greczanik, 40 Ohio App. 2d 129, 69 Ohio Op. 2d 146, 318 N.E.2d 408 (8th Dist. Cuyahoga County 1974).

[5]Majnaric v. Majnaric, 46 Ohio App. 2d 157, 75 Ohio Op. 2d 250, 347 N.E.2d 552 (9th Dist. Summit County 1975).

[6]See, e.g., Matter of Appeal of Neff v. City of Westerville, 1986 WL 2928 (Ohio Ct. App. 10th Dist. Franklin County 1986); In re Estate of Davis, No. 79AP-731 (Ohio Ct. App. 10th Dist. Franklin County 1979); Bourque v. Bourque, 34 Ohio App. 3d 284, 518 N.E.2d 49 (12th Dist. Clermont County 1986). See also § 32:25, Jurisdiction during appeal—Relief from judgment during appeal.

ing of the motion for relief from judgment. Likewise, a lengthy wait for a decision on an appeal may place a Civ. R. 60(B) motion past the one-year limitation of 60(B)(1) to (3).

A pending motion to vacate under Civ. R. 60(B) does not stay execution of the judgment nor extend the time for filing a notice of appeal.[7] The filing of a notice of appeal will not stay execution.[8] A separate motion to stay execution should be filed either with a Civ. R. 60(B) motion or an appeal. The granting of such motion is within the discretion of the court.

An order overruling a motion brought under Civ. R. 60(B) is a final appealable order.[9] It has likewise been held that the granting of a motion to vacate a judgment is a final appealable order.[10] If an appeal is to be taken on that order, it must be done within thirty days. It would be a procedural error to wait until after the trial court has heard the merits of the case before claiming error in the granting of the motion. The appeal would, of course, be limited to consideration of whether the motion was properly granted. The merits of the case could not be considered.

An appellate court's scope of review of the denial of a Civ. R. 60(B) motion is to determine whether the trial court acted arbitrarily, unreasonably, or unconscionably. When allegations of misrepresentations of value are responded to by competent, credible evidence, a court of appeals cannot conclude that the denial of the motion was an abuse of discretion.[11]

A judgment corrected pursuant to Civ. R. 60(A) does not create or deny existing rights. The subsequent entry relates back to the time of filing the original entry and does not extend the time for an appeal.[12]

§ 24:14   Civil Rule 60(B)(1)

Obviously, finality of judgment is an objective of litigation. The Ohio Supreme Court in *Wolfe v. Wolfe*[1] specifically stated that

the General Assembly has directed that alimony be awarded in specific personal or real property or in a specific "sum of money," which is payable in installments or in a lump sum (in gross). We read that particular language as enjoining the court, at the time of decreeing the divorce, to settle all property rights *with certainty*. [Emphasis added]

---

[7]App. R. 4(A) (only timely motion under Civ. R. 50(B) or Civ. R. 59 has this effect). See Appeals Ch 32; Civ. R. 60(B) ("A motion under this subdivision (B) does not affect the finality of a judgment or suspend its operation.").

[8]White v. White, 50 Ohio App. 2d 263, 4 Ohio Op. 3d 225, 362 N.E.2d 1013 (8th Dist. Cuyahoga County 1977).

[9]App. R. 1; Tom McSteen Contracting Co. v. Thomas Maloney & Sons, Inc., 39 Ohio App. 2d 31, 68 Ohio Op. 2d 173, 314 N.E.2d 392 (8th Dist. Cuyahoga County 1974).

[10]Bates & Springer, Inc. v. Stallworth, 56 Ohio App. 2d 223, 10 Ohio Op. 3d 227, 382 N.E.2d 1179, 26 U.C.C. Rep. Serv. 1181 (8th Dist. Cuyahoga County 1978).

[11]Boos v. Boos, 1992 WL 337471 (Ohio Ct. App. 6th Dist. Lucas County 1992).

[12]Soroka v. Soroka, 1993 WL 215395 (Ohio Ct. App. 8th Dist. Cuyahoga County 1993).

[Section 24:14]
[1]Wolfe v. Wolfe, 46 Ohio St. 2d 399, 411, 75 Ohio Op. 2d 474, 350 N.E.2d 413 (1976).

The judgment, however, can be vacated for errors either of a clerical or substantive nature. Civ. R. 60(B) speaks to those of a substantive nature.

Civ. R. 60(B)(1) encompasses mistake, inadvertence, surprise, or excusable neglect. Civ. R. 75(L) provides litigants with notice of hearing if they are not represented. Lack of notice, therefore, would be difficult to raise as a successful Civ. R. 60(B)(1) allegation in cases where judgment was taken by default.[2] It must be demonstrated that the party seeking vacation of judgment has a meritorious defense to the action and that the judgment will be different if a retrial is had. It has been held, however, that the necessity of presenting a valid defense pertains only to those cases where the judgment was taken by default.[3] The rule does not provide for the vacation of a judgment simply because the judgment was taken by default, but the power to do so is inherent in the court.[4] Generally, the neglect of an attorney is imputed to the litigant and will not be sufficient grounds for the granting of a motion for relief.[5] A Civ. R. 60(B)(1) motion was properly denied by the trial court when there was no evidence of "mistake." If the terms of the QDRO in question were erroneous, it was due to neglect and not mistake.[6] The Eighth District Court of Appeals held that the trial court abused its discretion in granting relief to a party who claimed he misunderstood the procedures of the divorce court and had acted pro se. A misunderstanding of the proceedings and failure to obtain counsel did not constitute excusable neglect.[7] In *Moore v. Moore*,[8] however, the trial court properly granted husband's Civ. R. 60(B) motion and modified its judgment entry as to the commencement date of support obligation where there had been a miscommunication between husband and his attorney and a long delay between settlement and journalization of the decree. A Civ. R. 60(B) motion seeking relief on the basis of "ineffective counsel" is appropriately denied in the absence of extraordinary circumstances such as abandonment by counsel.[9]

A mathematical mistake by one party's attorney in computing an equal division of property which is immediately called to the court's at-

---

[2]King v. King, 55 Ohio App. 2d 43, 9 Ohio Op. 3d 205, 379 N.E.2d 251 (9th Dist. Summit County 1977) (overruled by Siler v. Siler, 1994 WL 386106 (Ohio Ct. App. 12th Dist. Warren County 1994).

[3]Advance Mortg. Corp. v. Novak, 53 Ohio App. 2d 289, 7 Ohio Op. 3d 338, 373 N.E.2d 400 (8th Dist. Cuyahoga County 1977).

[4]Westmoreland v. Valley Homes Mut. Housing Corp., 42 Ohio St. 2d 291, 71 Ohio Op. 2d 262, 328 N.E.2d 406 (1975).

[5]GTE Automatic Elec., Inc. v. ARC Industries, Inc., 47 Ohio St. 2d 146, 1 Ohio Op. 3d 86, 351 N.E.2d 113 (1976); Link v. Wabash R. Co., 370 U.S. 626, 82 S. Ct. 1386, 8 L. Ed. 2d 734, 6 Fed. R. Serv. 2d 831 (1962).

[6]Childs v. Kinder, 1998 WL 817608 (Ohio Ct. App. 12th Dist. Butler County 1998), dismissed, appeal not allowed, 85 Ohio St. 3d 1442, 708 N.E.2d 208 (1999).

[7]Tyukodi v. Tyukodi, 2001 WL 470172 (Ohio Ct. App. 8th Dist. Cuyahoga County 2001).

[8]Moore v. Moore, 1998 WL 473341 (Ohio Ct. App. 7th Dist. Belmont County 1998).

[9]Office v. Office, 2001 -Ohio- 1477, 2001 WL 958935 (Ohio Ct. App. 2d Dist. Montgomery County 2001).

tention after an in-court agreement of the parties was held to be excusable neglect under Civ. R. 60(B)(1) by the Second District Court of Appeals, which reversed the trial court's overruling of an appellant's Civ. R. 60(B) motion.[10] The Eighth District Court of Appeals held that a wife's Civ. R. 60(B) motion was properly granted by the trial court, where she alleged her trial counsel made a mathematical error in calculating the total value of the marital estate. Counsel inadvertently failed to include the value of husband's business and wife's pension in the calculation. Exclusion of these asset values led to a further miscalculation of the amount necessary to be paid by husband to wife to equalize the division of marital assets.[11] In *Rennie v. Rennie*,[12] the trial court erred in overruling the wife's Civ. R. 60(B) motion where it appeared that both parties relied upon a mutual mistake of pension value in arriving at a settlement.

In *Kern v. Kern*,[13] the appellee claimed that she was entitled to relief because her attorney failed to appear for trial. The negligence of an attorney cannot be "excusable neglect" so as to justify relief from judgment.[14] As in *Kern*, the Eighth District Court of Appeals in *Snyder v. Snyder*,[15] concluded that the appellant-wife was not entitled to relief from judgment as a result of omissions by her attorney. The fact that an attorney fails to adequately represent a client in a dissolution does not entitle the client to relief under Civ. R. 60(B)(1).[16] A party's failure to respond to a motion for default, however, may be found to be "excusable neglect" under some circumstances.[17]

The Ohio Supreme Court in *Moore v. Emmanuel Family Training Center*[18] reversed two older rulings on 60(B) motions. The court held that the trial court's dismissal of an action for failure to comply with a discovery order was improper where counsel had no actual knowledge of the discovery order. Failure to discover the order constituted excusable neglect.

In *Moore v. Emmanuel Family Training Center*[19] which was consolidated for purposes of appeal with *Moore*, failure to appear at a pretrial

---

[10]DeCurtins v. DeCurtins, 1993 WL 211348 (Ohio Ct. App. 2d Dist. Miami County 1993).

[11]Krysa v. Sieber, 113 Ohio App. 3d 572, 681 N.E.2d 949 (8th Dist. Cuyahoga County 1996), dismissed, appeal not allowed, 77 Ohio St. 3d 1490, 673 N.E.2d 147 (1996).

[12]Rennie v. Rennie, 1997 WL 640607 (Ohio Ct. App. 6th Dist. Lucas County 1997).

[13]Kern v. Kern, No. 59748 (Ohio Ct. App. 8th Dist. Cuyahoga County 1992).

[14]Kern v. Kern, No. 59748 (Ohio Ct. App. 8th Dist. Cuyahoga County 1992).

[15]Snyder v. Snyder, 1992 WL 14946 (Ohio Ct. App. 8th Dist. Cuyahoga County 1992).

[16]Snyder v. Snyder, 1992 WL 14946 (Ohio Ct. App. 8th Dist. Cuyahoga County 1992), citing Argo Plastic Products Co. v. City of Cleveland, 15 Ohio St. 3d 389, 474 N.E.2d 328 (1984).

[17]Harris v. Fifth Quarter, Inc., 1993 WL 32086 (Ohio Ct. App. 6th Dist. Lucas County 1993).

[18]Moore v. Emmanuel Family Training Center, Inc., 18 Ohio St. 3d 64, 479 N.E.2d 879 (1985).

[19]Moore v. Emmanuel Family Training Center, Inc., 18 Ohio St. 3d 64, 479 N.E.2d 879 (1985).

resulted in dismissal of the action, although the court's scheduler had advised counsel that the matter would be continued. The trial court did not send a Civ. R. 41(B)(1) notice. Such failure justified the granting of the Civ. R. 60(B)(1) motion.

The Eighth District Court of Appeals in following the precepts of *Moore* held in *Angelo v. Angelo*[20] that reliance upon the representations of a court employee as to when a decision would be mailed was excusable neglect under Civ. R. 60(B)(1). These rulings have modified, to some extent, the previous general rule that failure to discover a journal entry or final judgment does not entitle one to relief under Civ. R. 60(B)(1) or (5).

Civil Rule 60(B)(1) is the appropriate section to assert in attempting to set aside a judgment for procedural reasons. The failure of a court to give a party notice of judgment is a sufficient basis for granting relief from judgment.[21]

A mistake in a stipulation is not a clerical, but rather a substantive, mistake. Civ. R. 60(A) is not available to correct a mistake of fact. Civ. R. 60(B)(1) is available, but a motion must be brought within the one-year period.[22]

Correction of clerical mistakes after the filing of a notice of appeal requires leave of the court of appeals.[23]

§ 24:15   Civil Rule 60(B)(2)

Civil Rule 60(B)(2) allows vacation of judgment based upon newly discovered evidence. It is difficult, however, to imagine where newly discovered evidence, not obtained within the time frame provided under Civ. R. 59, would be significant enough to vacate a divorce decree. Civ. R. 60(B)(2) can be used, however, to obtain relief in collateral issues such as spousal support and division of property.

In *Moser v. Moser*,[1] the Ninth District Court of Appeals upheld a trial court decision that the discovery of a benign tumor "did not qualify as newly discovered evidence so as to warrant relief from judgment." The appellate court noted a lack of due diligence on the part of the appellant, who was uncooperative with her treating physician, and also noted that the appellant could still obtain employment. Newly discovered evidence refers to evidence of facts in existence at the time of trial of which the aggrieved party was excusably ignorant.[2]

Evidence which could have been discovered with due diligence at the

---

[20]Angelo v. Angelo, 1986 WL 4391 (Ohio Ct. App. 8th Dist. Cuyahoga County 1986).

[21]Connolly v. Connolly, 70 Ohio App. 3d 738, 591 N.E.2d 1362 (8th Dist. Cuyahoga County 1990).

[22]Hamlin v. Hamlin, 1993 WL 32010 (Ohio Ct. App. 2d Dist. Darke County 1993).

[23]Elsass v. Elsass, 1993 WL 541610 (Ohio Ct. App. 2d Dist. Greene County 1993).

[Section 24:15]

[1]Moser v. Moser, 1984 WL 3977, at *3 (Ohio Ct. App. 9th Dist. Lorain County 1984).

[2]Schwenk v. Schwenk, 2 Ohio App. 3d 250, 441 N.E.2d 631 (8th Dist. Cuyahoga County 1982).

time of trial is not grounds for relief from judgment, whether filed under Civ. R. 60(B)(2) or Civ. R. 60(B)(5).[3] In *Ogrizek v. Ogrizek*,[4] the wife's motion for a new trial was properly denied where the newly discovered evidence of a higher value of real estate than that which was presented at trial was available to her at the time of trial had she sought to introduce it. Likewise, the omission of trial evidence because of neglect of counsel is insufficient grounds for granting a Civ. R. 60(B) motion.[5]

§ 24:16   Civil Rule 60(B)(3)

Allegations of fraudulent testimony in support of a Civ. R. 60(B) motion must not only be exhibited by the record, but must relate to matters that were unknown to the movant at the time the testimony was given.[1]

Both intrinsic and extrinsic fraud are covered by Civ. R. 60(B)(3). There are differences between fraud upon a court and intrinsic and extrinsic fraud contemplated under Civ. R. 60(B)(3).

An independent contractual agreement of paternity between a husband and wife was made part of an agreed voluntary dissolution of marriage and an agreed modification of the decree in *Johnson v. Johnson*.[2]

Five years later, the husband/father moved to vacate the agreed judgment entry on the basis that both parties knew the representations as to paternity were erroneous. The Second District Court of Appeals held that its modification jurisdiction under *Wolfe v. Wolfe*[3] could not be extended to cover this issue. The court held that the husband/father's motion was properly denied where both parties were party to the fraud, the child was not represented and stood to lose its judicially decreed paternity, and the motion was not filed within a reasonable time.

An uncounseled party to a dissolution may not seek to vacate the decree unless there was undue influence, fraud, or duress and less than full disclosure.[4] The vacation of a decree of dissolution is proper where a husband, without aid of counsel, agrees to grant the wife the entire amount of equity in the marital home and all of his pension benefits. The court was informed by wife's counsel that the husband would be "taken care of" by his new girlfriend who owned a business. In fact, the

---

[3]Ackerman v. Ackerman, 1993 WL 19621 (Ohio Ct. App. 7th Dist. Monroe County 1993).

[4]Ogrizek v. Ogrizek, 1997 WL 772824 (Ohio Ct. App. 9th Dist. Summit County 1997).

[5]Quillen v. Quillen, 1997 WL 226209 (Ohio Ct. App. 12th Dist. Warren County 1997).

[Section 24:16]

[1]Chester v. Chester, 1993 WL 438795 (Ohio Ct. App. 5th Dist. Licking County 1993).

[2]Johnson v. Johnson, 1985 WL 7849 (Ohio Ct. App. 2d Dist. Montgomery County 1985).

[3]Wolfe v. Wolfe, 46 Ohio St. 2d 399, 75 Ohio Op. 2d 474, 350 N.E.2d 413 (1976), superseded by statute as stated in Heslep v. Heslep, 2000 WL 818909 (Ohio Ct. App. 7th Dist. Monroe County 2000).

[4]Swartzentruber v. Swartzentruber, 1991 WL 43321 (Ohio Ct. App. 9th Dist. Wayne County 1991).

girlfriend was a recipient of public assistance.[5]

In *In re Wood*,[6] the terms of a separation agreement gave rise to an inference that the agreement was the product of undue influence. The unfairness of the bargain, unavailability of independent advice and the susceptibility of the person persuaded should be considered. Relief under Civ. R. 60(B)(3) was appropriate. In *Perkins v. Perkins*,[7] the trial court erred by granting Civ. R. 60(B)(3) relief. The record did not reflect any fraudulent statements. Although a stipulation as to the value of a pension was not accurate, the correct information was available at the time of trial.

§ 24:17   Civil Rule 60(B)(4)

Although Civ. R. 60(B)(4) and (5) are, to some extent, catch-alls, they cannot be invoked when the reality of the grounds for the motion is one which falls within the preceding sections of Civ. R. 60.[1] The reason set forth in the motion must be such as to justify relief outside of the application of the previous sections.[2] They will have the most application in attempts to modify spousal support awards.

Civil Rule 60(B)(4) provides for the vacation of a judgment if it has been satisfied, released, discharged, or should no longer have prospective application. It is in this area that there may be more expansion into domestic relations. While few applications to domestic relations matters have been found, the annotations to the federal rule provide logic which seems to apply though the facts are not analogous.[3] When the decree has produced hardship so extreme and unexpected so as to make the decree oppressive, it should be modified. The change of circumstances which now renders the decree so oppressive must, of course, not have been contemplated.[4]

Traditionally, Civ. R. 60(B)(4), especially under the federal rules, applied to equitable orders such as permanent injunctions.[5] Circumstances may certainly change which would direct a court to reverse or modify a permanent injunction.[6]

Civ. R. 60(B)(4) applies in situations where a person has been

---

[5]Stice v. Stice, 1990 WL 187472 (Ohio Ct. App. 2d Dist. Montgomery County 1990).

[6]In re Wood, 1999 WL 430710 (Ohio Ct. App. 10th Dist. Franklin County 1999), dismissed, appeal not allowed, 87 Ohio St. 3d 1440, 719 N.E.2d 4 (1999).

[7]Perkins v. Perkins, 2001 WL 773238 (Ohio Ct. App. 9th Dist. Medina County 2001).

[Section 24:17]
[1]Adomeit v. Baltimore, 39 Ohio App. 2d 97, 68 Ohio Op. 2d 251, 316 N.E.2d 469 (8th Dist. Cuyahoga County 1974).

[2]See 6A Moore's Federal Practice 266 § 60.21[1] (1983).

[3]Equal Employment Opportunity Commission v. Safeway Stores, Inc., 611 F.2d 795 (10th Cir. 1979).

[4]Safe Flight Instrument Corp. v. United Control Corp., 576 F.2d 1340 (9th Cir. 1978); Huk-A-Poo Sportswear, Inc. v. Little Lisa, Ltd., 74 F.R.D. 621 (S.D. N.Y. 1977).

[5]See Fed. Civ. R. 60(B).

[6]Marshall v. Board of Ed., Bergenfield, N. J., 575 F.2d 417, 25 Fed. R. Serv. 2d 252 (3d Cir. 1978).

prospectively subjected to circumstances which they had no opportunity to foresee or control. Specific events occurring after the judgment which had an adverse effect on the prospective application of the judgment must be proved.[7] Relief is not appropriate under Civ. R. 60(B)(4) if the events relied upon did not occur subsequent to the order sought to be vacated.[8]

Parental rights would not normally be a matter to fall within the parameters of Civ. R. 60(B). In *Sexton v. Sexton*,[9] however, the trial court held it has inherent authority to vacate a prior custody order under Civ. R. 60(B)(4). The original order had been by separation agreement signed by the wife who apparently convinced the court she had consented to her husband's custody under duress. The motion to modify filed by the wife was treated as a Civ. R. 60(B)(4) motion as the trial court decided that it was appropriate that the prior custody order should no longer have prospective application.

In *Knapp v. Knapp*,[10] the Fourth District Court of Appeals acknowledged the Ohio Supreme Court's decision in *McClain v. McClain*[11] and then held that while a court has no jurisdiction to modify periodic alimony under a dissolution decree, it can enforce or *refuse to enforce* periodic alimony under Civ. R. 60(B)(4), where enforcement would be inequitable. On appeal, the Ohio Supreme Court reversed the application of Civ. R. 60(B)(4) to evade the application of *McClain*, saying that "litigants, armed with the knowledge that [Civil Rule 60(B)(4)] would relieve them of the consequences of their voluntary choices would be encouraged to litigate ceaselessly."[12] The Court found that "Ohio's public policy as established by the General Assembly is to deprive the courts of jurisdiction to modify periodic alimony payments in dissolution decrees."[13] A court does not retain jurisdiction over spousal support awards to the same extent as over other final orders because of the limitations of RC 3105.18(E), but still has the inherent power to vacate the order like any other order.

In *Crouser v. Crouser*,[14] the Ohio Supreme Court did not allow an appellant, whose attempt to increase the alimony award under RC 3105.18 was unsuccessful, to circumvent the judgment procedurally by a motion under Civ. R. 60(B)(4) and/or Civ. R. 60(B)(5). In contrast, the Cuyahoga

---

[7]Clemons v. Clemons, 1993 WL 271000 (Ohio Ct. App. 10th Dist. Franklin County 1993).

[8]Schafrath v. Schafrath, 1998 WL 417474 (Ohio Ct. App. 9th Dist. Wayne County 1998).

[9]Sexton v. Sexton, 60 Ohio App. 2d 339, 14 Ohio Op. 3d 297, 397 N.E.2d 425 (5th Dist. Morrow County 1978).

[10]Knapp v. Knapp, 1985 WL 8303 (Ohio Ct. App. 4th Dist. Pickaway County 1985), judgment rev'd, 24 Ohio St. 3d 141, 493 N.E.2d 1353 (1986).

[11]McClain v. McClain, 15 Ohio St. 3d 289, 473 N.E.2d 811 (1984).

[12]Knapp v. Knapp, 24 Ohio St. 3d 141, 493 N.E.2d 1353 (1986).

[13]Knapp v. Knapp, 24 Ohio St. 3d 141, 493 N.E.2d 1353 (1986).

[14]Crouser v. Crouser, 39 Ohio St. 3d 177, 529 N.E.2d 1251 (1988).

County Court of Appeals ruled, in *Popovic v. Popovic*,[15] that it would not consider the request to modify alimony, stating that to do so would give retroactive effect to *Wolfe*.

There must be a distinction between decrees adjudicating accrued rights and those adjudicating prospective rights. Those governing prospective rights must necessarily involve supervision of changed circumstances, conduct, or conditions that are tentative and provisional. Accrued rights at the time of the decree cannot be modified by change of circumstances. Such considerations would be res judicata. Applying such reasoning to domestic relations and specifically spousal support, the question is whether spousal support rights accrued at the time of the decree can be modified.

Civ. R. 60(B)(4) provides for the granting of relief in situations where "it is no longer equitable that the judgment should have prospective application."[16] That provision may serve as a basis for relief from judgment when events subsequent to the judgment render prospective application of the judgment inequitable.[17] The vacation of such judgment cannot work an undue hardship on other persons or the court.[18] It would appear then that Civ. R. 60(B)(4) would be the closest and most analogous situation to a change of circumstances under which a court could conceivably grant a modification of spousal support even if such spousal support was by agreement concluded prior to the decision in *Wolfe*.

As is consistent with modification for changed circumstances in any other area, under Civ. R. 60(B)(4) they must not have been within the knowledge or contemplation of the court or parties when the decree was entered.[19] The changed circumstances must be continuous and not temporary or frivolous.[20]

Civ. R. 60(B)(4) relief is not available to a party who had an opportunity to negotiate a separation agreement, but failed to diligently

---

[15]Popovic v. Popovic, 45 Ohio App. 2d 57, 74 Ohio Op. 2d 94, 341 N.E.2d 341 (8th Dist. Cuyahoga County 1975).

[16]Wurzelbacher v. Kroeger, 40 Ohio St. 2d 90, 69 Ohio Op. 2d 440, 320 N.E.2d 666 (1974).

[17]Wurzelbacher v. Kroeger, 40 Ohio St. 2d 90, 69 Ohio Op. 2d 440, 320 N.E.2d 666 (1974); Sexton v. Sexton, 60 Ohio App. 2d 339, 14 Ohio Op. 3d 297, 397 N.E.2d 425 (5th Dist. Morrow County 1978); Blanchard v. St. Paul Fire & Marine Ins. Co., 341 F.2d 351 (5th Cir. 1965); Whitacre v. Board of Ed., 42 Ohio App. 2d 19, 71 Ohio Op. 2d 126, 326 N.E.2d 696 (2d Dist. Miami County 1974).

[18]Wurzelbacher v. Kroeger, 40 Ohio St. 2d 90, 69 Ohio Op. 2d 440, 320 N.E.2d 666 (1974).

[19]Equal Employment Opportunity Commission v. Safeway Stores, Inc., 611 F.2d 795 (10th Cir. 1979).

[20]Equal Employment Opportunity Commission v. Safeway Stores, Inc., 611 F.2d 795 (10th Cir. 1979); Wurzelbacher v. Kroeger, 40 Ohio St. 2d 90, 69 Ohio Op. 2d 440, 320 N.E.2d 666 (1974); Kahoe v. Kahoe, 1981 WL 4691 (Ohio Ct. App. 8th Dist. Cuyahoga County 1981) (motion for relief from judgment under Civ. R. 60(B) requesting relief from dissolution and agreement on grounds he was distraught at time, and had to get out of marriage, denied with court observing this appeal borders on frivolous).

protect his rights.[21] A trial court does not err in denying a party's Civ. R. 60(B) motion when that motion seeks to vacate a judgment based on the other party's failure to follow the order. Contempt is the proper process.[22] Where a substantial change in circumstances occurred between May 1993 when the case was heard and March 1994 when the decree was entered, the trial court did not err in granting the husband's Civ. R. 60(B)(4) motion. The court concluded that it was unjust for the decree to have further prospective application.[23]

Further, a trial court did not err in granting a Civ. R. 60(B) motion where a change of circumstances occurred between the time a settlement agreement was reached and the time it was incorporated into a judgment entry, and the court had been notified of the change. The filing of a Civ. R. 60(B) motion does not relieve a party from obligations imposed by the underlying judgment, however, until it is actually vacated.[24]

§ 24:18   Civil Rule 60(B)(5)

Parties seeking relief under Civ. R. 60(B)(5) must establish that the fraud claimed was upon the court and not the type of fraud contemplated by Civ. R. 60(B)(3). Such fraud constitutes only that type of conduct which defiles the court itself or fraud practiced by officers of the court so as to prevent the judicial system from functioning in an impartial manner.[1] Examples of such fraud include "egregious misconduct," a bribery of judge or jury, fabrication of evidence by counsel, or misrepresentation to the court.[2] The prevention of an opposing party from fairly presenting his case would, likewise, constitute such fraud.[3] Perjury by a witness is not, however, sufficient to constitute fraud upon the court but

---

[21]Lenzer v. Lenzer, 1993 WL 468271 (Ohio Ct. App. 9th Dist. Lorain County 1993). But see Goode v. Goode, 89 Ohio App. 3d 405, 624 N.E.2d 788 (10th Dist. Franklin County 1993) (court of appeals reversed trial court's denial of Civ. R. 60(B) motion stating that party had affirmative duty to disclose income even though complaining party apparently did not preform even minimal discovery).

[22]Hickman v. Hickman, 1994 WL 530690 (Ohio Ct. App. 3d Dist. Hancock County 1994).

[23]Butts v. Butts, 1995 WL 470246 (Ohio Ct. App. 1st Dist. Hamilton County 1995).

[24]Spitler v. Spitler, 1995 WL 353870 (Ohio Ct. App. 2d Dist. Darke County 1995).

[Section 24:18]

[1]Equal Employment Opportunity Commission v. Safeway Stores, Inc., 611 F.2d 795 (10th Cir. 1979); Wurzelbacher v. Kroeger, 40 Ohio St. 2d 90, 69 Ohio Op. 2d 440, 320 N.E.2d 666 (1974); Kahoe v. Kahoe, 1981 WL 4691 (Ohio Ct. App. 8th Dist. Cuyahoga County 1981) (motion for relief from judgment under Civ. R. 60(B) requesting relief from dissolution and agreement on grounds he was distraught at time, and had to get out of marriage, denied with court observing this appeal borders on frivolous); Coulson v. Coulson, 5 Ohio St. 3d 12, 448 N.E.2d 809 (1983). See 6A Moore's Federal Practice 360 § 60.33 (1983).

[2]In re Coordinated Pretrial Proceedings in Antibiotic Antitrust Actions, 538 F.2d 180 (8th Cir. 1976). See also Coulson v. Coulson, 5 Ohio St. 3d 12, 448 N.E.2d 809 (1983).

[3]Keys v. Dunbar, 405 F.2d 955 (9th Cir. 1969). See Restatement of Judgments § 118–124 (1942).

rather would fall within the limits of Civ. R. 60(B)(3).[4] Therefore, the one-year limitation would apply.

Where an uncontested divorce was granted, and the judgment included a finding of paternity and an order of child support obtained upon wife's testimony, husband's attempt to terminate child support and disclaim paternity could not be sustained when the motion was brought under Civ. R. 60(B) three years after the judgment. Husband was not prevented from presenting a defense in the original action. Wife's misrepresentations, if any, would have constituted fraud under Civ. R. 60(B)(3) and not under the narrowly construed provision of Civ. R. 60(B)(5).[5]

Civ. R. 60(B)(5), the catch-all provision, allows the court to vacate its judgment for any other reason justifying relief. The relief sought must not be sought for reasons really encompassed in the other sections of the rule. Failure of an attorney to file a required affidavit or any excusable or willful neglect no matter how disguised will not fall within Civ. R. 60(B)(5) for the purposes of expanding the timeliness provision of the rule. Civ. R. 60(B)(5) has been, in conformity with application of the comparable federal rule, applied very rarely. It may not be used as a substitute for any other portion of the rule for the purposes of obtaining additional time for the filing of a motion. Thus, where a decree of divorce failed by mistake to include proper reference to real estate, it could not be modified through the use of Civ. R. 60(B) after the one-year time limitation had passed.[6]

The Ohio Supreme Court, in reviewing the applicability of Civ. R. 60(B)(5) to a domestic relations matter, held, in *Volodkevich v. Volodkevich*,[7] that a judge's participation in a case such as to give an appearance of impropriety and bias could constitute grounds under Civ. R. 60(B)(5) for relief from judgment. The motion, however, must be timely brought. Fraud on the court is limited to instances where an officer of the court perpetrates or participates in the fraud.[8] Civ. R. 60(B)(5) is a proper vehicle to challenge jurisdiction.[9] Civ. R. 60(B)(5) may be appropriate where marital assets are omitted from an agreement when both parties

---

[4]Hazel-Atlas Glass Co. v. Hartford-Empire Co., 322 U.S. 238, 64 S. Ct. 997, 88 L. Ed. 1250 (1944) (overruled as stated in, W. R. Grace & Co., Inc. v. Western U. S. Industries, Inc., 608 F.2d 1214 (9th Cir. 1979)); Hartford v. Hartford, 53 Ohio App. 2d 79, 7 Ohio Op. 3d 53, 371 N.E.2d 591 (8th Dist. Cuyahoga County 1977).

[5]Hartford v. Hartford, 53 Ohio App. 2d 79, 7 Ohio Op. 3d 53, 371 N.E.2d 591 (8th Dist. Cuyahoga County 1977); Adomeit v. Baltimore, 39 Ohio App. 2d 97, 105, 68 Ohio Op. 2d 251, 316 N.E.2d 469 (8th Dist. Cuyahoga County 1974) ("Civil Rule 60(B)(5) is only to be used in an extraordinary and unusual case when the interest of justice warrants it.").

[6]Luscre v. Luscre, 45 Ohio Misc. 9, 74 Ohio Op. 2d 18, 340 N.E.2d 854 (C.P. 1974).

[7]Volodkevich v. Volodkevich, 35 Ohio St. 3d 152, 518 N.E.2d 1208 (1988), on reconsideration, 36 Ohio St. 3d 612, 522 N.E.2d 521 (1988).

[8]Turoczy v. Turoczy, 30 Ohio App. 3d 116, 506 N.E.2d 942 (8th Dist. Cuyahoga County 1986); Imes v. Imes, 1989 WL 716 (Ohio Ct. App. 6th Dist. Lucas County 1989) (seeking Civ. R. 60(B) relief, appellant did not meet burden of proving fraud or that court approved agreement between parties in reliance on misrepresentation).

[9]Matter of Marsh, 1988 WL 135372 (Ohio Ct. App. 11th Dist. Trumbull County 1988).

are ignorant of their existence.[10] Where an asset is, however, omitted by the neglect of one party, especially if that party drew the agreement, a trial court errs in granting a Civ. R. 60(B) motion brought by the negligent party.[11]

The key words are, however, extraordinary circumstances and undue hardship.[12] An error by the court in sending notice of judgment dismissing an action together with the court's oversight and error in ruling on a motion for continuance which ultimately led to the dismissal was held to be sufficient reason to justify relief from judgment under Civ. R. 60(B)(5).[13] A finding that original service was improper, thus depriving the court of jurisdiction, may also be a Civ. R. 60(B)(5) reason for the vacating of a judgment.[14]

Civ. R. 60(B)(5) is available as a remedy for the unjust operation of a judgment and in the proper circumstances may be invoked several years after entry of a decree.

In *Klingman v. Klingman*,[15] relief was granted where a separation agreement containing a blatantly inequitable division of property was obtained by threats and violence and where the violence and harassment continued after the dissolution, when the parties were living together and attempting to reconcile their differences. The motion for relief was filed over 4½ years after the decree, and the decision was not rendered until 2½ years after that (7 years after the decree).

> To hold otherwise would invite individuals to obtain, by coercive measure, inequitable and unfair agreements by judicial process. The offending party would, then, only have to continue to exercise dominance over the other party for a period of one year so as to prevent the dominated party from initiating a motion for relief from judgment.[16]

In *Warrick v. Warrick*,[17] a wife was denied a motion for relief from judgment, even though she first saw the separation agreement only ten minutes prior to the divorce hearing, was not aware of the amount of her husband's pension and profit sharing funds with his employer, and was informed by her attorney that she was not entitled to any of the money in these accounts and that the separation agreement represented

---

[10]Millbon v. Millbon, No. 89AP-592 (Ohio Ct. App. 10th Dist. Franklin County 1989); Hellwege v. Hellwege, 1986 WL 6335 (Ohio Ct. App. 10th Dist. Franklin County 1986).

[11]In re Marriage of Wise, 46 Ohio App. 3d 82, 545 N.E.2d 1314 (10th Dist. Franklin County 1988).

[12]Caruso-Ciresi, Inc. v. Lohman, 5 Ohio St. 3d 64, 448 N.E.2d 1365 (1983) (grounds for invoking Civil Rule 60(B)(5) should be substantial).

[13]State ex rel. Gyurcsik v. Angelotta, 50 Ohio St. 2d 345, 4 Ohio Op. 3d 482, 364 N.E.2d 284 (1977).

[14]Fasick v. Fasick, Nos. 37826 & 37875 (8th Dist. Ct. App., Cuyahoga, 11-4-78), unreported.

[15]Klingman v. Klingman, 1984 WL 14432 (Ohio Ct. App. 6th Dist. Ottawa County 1984).

[16]Klingman v. Klingman, 1984 WL 14432 (Ohio Ct. App. 6th Dist. Ottawa County 1984) (three-pronged test for relief under Civ. R. 60(B) met here: lack of voluntary consent; necessity for relief in interest of justice; motion made within reasonable time).

[17]Warrick v. Warrick, 1985 WL 9082 (Ohio Ct. App. 3d Dist. Seneca County 1985).

the most equitable settlement she could expect. The Third District Court of Appeals found that the denial of the wife's motion was not an abuse of discretion because she had heard the interrogatories discussed and they had disclosed the amounts of the pension and profit sharing funds.

In *Khoshbin v. Khoshbin*,[18] the trial court did not err in granting the wife's Civ. R. 60(B)(5) motion for relief from judgment. The divorce was uncontested and the wife was unable to participate. The separation agreement incorporated into the decree was "unconscionable." On the other hand, in *Tsangaris v. Tsangaris*,[19] the husband's Civ. R. 60(B) motion was properly denied. The record did not support his claims that the parties' agreement was unconscionable or that he entered into the agreement under duress or in reliance upon misrepresentations by the wife or her attorney.

A Civ. R. 60(B)(5) motion was properly denied when husband sought to vacate a decree of dissolution. Although unrepresented by counsel, the agreement was not unconscionable nor did husband prove fraud, coercion, or duress.[20] In *Becker v. Becker*,[21] the wife's Civ. R. 60(B)(5) motion was not timely. Although knowing of the existence of husband's pension, she did nothing to ascertain its value when the parties dissolved their marriage. Civ. R. 60(B)(5) relief is not available if an asset, although not disposed of by the prior decree, was known to the parties at the time of the agreement but not incorporated into the decree.[22]

Relief under Civ. R. 60(B)(5) may be applied to any judgment, equitable or at law. It differs from Civ. R. 60(B)(4) in that it would be applicable to a judgment whether it has prospective and/or retroactive application. Civ. R. 60(B)(4) would, of course, only apply to prospective application of judgments.

Research References

Text References

2 Klein and Darling, Baldwin's Ohio Practice, Civil Practice Authors' Text 60–61 to 60–71, Rule 60(B)(5)

§ 24:19   Void judgments

A Civ. R. 60(B) motion is sufficient without an affidavit or supporting documentation when the judgment is void for lack of jurisdiction or fail-

---

[18]Khoshbin v. Khoshbin, 1997 WL 626584 (Ohio Ct. App. 9th Dist. Summit County 1997).

[19]Tsangaris v. Tsangaris, 1997 WL 391297 (Ohio Ct. App. 7th Dist. Mahoning County 1997).

[20]Biscardi v. Biscardi, 133 Ohio App. 3d 288, 727 N.E.2d 949 (7th Dist. Mahoning County 1999).

[21]Becker v. Becker, 1999 WL 126068 (Ohio Ct. App. 12th Dist. Butler County 1999).

[22]Straker v. Straker, 2001 WL 253143 (Ohio Ct. App. 10th Dist. Franklin County 2001).

ure of service.[1]

A court granting a void judgment may vacate it, whether or not the requirements of Civ. R. 60(B) have been satisfied. Civ. R. 60(B) provides for equitable relief from an otherwise valid judgment and does not apply to void judgments. In *Demianczuk v. Demianczuk*,[2] the Eighth District Court of Appeals was not disturbed by a six-year delay in seeking relief, since a void judgment does not change with time. In the absence of proper service, a valid judgment may only be entered if a party has voluntarily submitted himself to the court's jurisdiction or waived jurisdictional defenses.[3] Waiver may be evidenced by such acts as defending a motion on its merits.[4], requesting discovery,[5] or by filing one's own motion in response. The test to determine waiver appears to be whether or not the party exhibited a clear intent to defend the motion on its merits.[6]

An order which adopts a modified QDRO, which is inconsistent with the terms of the parties' divorce decree, is void *ab initio*. The requisites of Civ. R. 60(B) do not have to be met.[7]

§ 24:20 Motion for relief from judgment—Form⊚

[Title of Court]

[Caption]   Case No. [_____]
                                            MOTION FOR RELIEF FROM
                                            JUDGMENT

Defendant moves that this Court *[set aside / set aside in part]* the judgment entry/decree entered in this case on *[date]* on the ground that *[ground for relief under Civil Rule 60(B)]* as is more fully set forth in the affidavit of Defendant attached hereto as Exhibit "A" and the memorandum attached hereto as Exhibit "B."

_____
                                      Attorney for Defendant

[Notice of hearing]

[Exhibits "A" and "B"—Affidavit of movant and memorandum in sup-

---

[Section 24:19]

[1]Stokes v. Meimaris, 1993 WL 548447 (Ohio Ct. App. 11th Dist. Trumbull County 1993).

[2]Demianczuk v. Demianczuk, 20 Ohio App. 3d 244, 485 N.E.2d 785 (8th Dist. Cuyahoga County 1984) (defective service).

[3]Maryhew v. Yova, 11 Ohio St. 3d 154, 464 N.E.2d 538 (1984).

[4]Garnett v. Garnett, 1986 WL 8625 (Ohio Ct. App. 8th Dist. Cuyahoga County 1986).

[5]Joseph v. Lastoria, 1988 WL 117792 (Ohio Ct. App. 12th Dist. Clermont County 1988), dismissed, 41 Ohio St. 3d 714, 535 N.E.2d 306 (1989).

[6]Cooper v. Cooper, 10 Ohio App. 3d 143, 460 N.E.2d 1137 (3d Dist. Van Wert County 1983); Longshore v. White, 1994 WL 197209 (Ohio Ct. App. 8th Dist. Cuyahoga County 1994).

[7]Doolin v. Doolin, 123 Ohio App. 3d 296, 704 N.E.2d 51 (6th Dist. Lucas County 1997).

port of motion]

[Proof/certificate of service]

NOTES TO FORM

Drafter's Notes

A proof/certificate of service is only necessary when there is opposing counsel. Where the respondent is unrepresented by counsel at the time of filing the motion, the motion papers will be served by the clerk of court pursuant to written instructions filed with the motion. Counsel should be aware that on post-decree motions service on the respondent will be required unless the respondent has a pending motion.

Under his/her signature on the motion, counsel should list his or her Supreme Court registration number, business address, and phone number.

§ 24:21   Judgment entry granting relief from judgment—Form⊚

[Title of Court]

[Caption]   Case No. *[_____]*

                                   JUDGMENT ENTRY

This matter came on for hearing on *[date]*, upon Defendant's motion to vacate the judgment pursuant to Civil Rule 60(B), and the Court having heard the argument of counsel and the evidence, and being fully advised, it is

Ordered, adjudged, and decreed that Defendant's motion is hereby granted, the judgment entered on *[date]* is hereby set aside, and *[set forth relief granted]*.

                              _____

                                    Judge

Approved:

_____

Attorney for Movant

Chapter 25

Pleading and Practice[*]

By Joyce E. Barrett, Esq.

KeyCite®: Cases and other legal materials listed in KeyCite Scope can be researched through West Group's KeyCite service on Westlaw®. Use KeyCite to check citations for form, parallel references, prior and later history, and comprehensive citator information, including citations to other decisions and secondary materials.

---

[*]Updated for the Fourth Edition by Andrew Zashin, Esq.

§ 25:1   Pleadings—Complaint

The complaint in a divorce or annulment action must allege six months' residency in Ohio and proper venue.[1] In fact, a trial court lacks subject matter jurisdiction to grant a divorce if residency is not both

---

[Section 25:1]

[1]There has been no attempt to cover all of Ohio civil procedure in this text. The motions discussed herein are the ones unique to domestic relations matters or are standard common pleas motions included because of unique domestic relations implications. Motions not included are either not unique to domestic relations practice or have no special use in the domestic relations context such that discussion is warranted here.

pleaded and proven.[2] There is no similar residency requirement for a legal separation action. There must also be a recitation of the date and place of marriage and of the names and dates of birth of any minor children. It is good practice to include the total number of children and then to indicate whether any are emancipated.[3]

Next, there must be an allegation of one or more of the statutory grounds for divorce, legal separation, or annulment. It is not good practice to allege only incompatibility under RC 3105.01(K), because that section provides that incompatibility is only viable "unless denied by either party."

Finally, the complaint must contain a demand for the relief to which the plaintiff feels entitled. Mention should here be made of everything that is being sought, including temporary restraining orders, allocation of parental rights and responsibilities, spousal support, child support, division of property, attorney fees, and court costs. A catch-all phrase of "and for such other and further relief as the court may deem equitable" is customarily added to cover any unexpected contingencies.[4] In *Avis v. Avis*,[5] the Eighth District Court of Appeals held that a trial court errs in awarding attorney fees where there has been no request for fees in the cross-complaint and no other notice that fees will be sought. It should also be noted that it has been held that attorney fees can only be granted prospectively from the date of the request therefore.[6]

§ 25:2   Pleadings—Answer

In the answer, the defendant must admit or deny each and every averment set forth in the complaint. Otherwise, pursuant to Civil Rule 8(D), they will be deemed to be admitted. Normally, the first two paragraphs of the complaint reciting the jurisdiction and venue, date and place of the marriage, and dates of birth of children are admitted. If the one-year separation (RC 3105.01(J)) is alleged and factual, it may as well be admitted, since other grounds may be alleged by counterclaim. If the only ground alleged in the complaint is incompatibility, then a denial of that ground in the answer would pave the way for a motion to dismiss the complaint.

Civil Rule 12(A) provides that the defendant shall serve his or her answer within twenty-eight days after service of the summons and

---

[2]McMaken v. McMaken, 96 Ohio App. 3d 402, 645 N.E.2d 113 (2d Dist. Montgomery County 1994); Polakova v. Polak, 107 Ohio App. 3d 745, 669 N.E.2d 498 (1st Dist. Hamilton County 1995).

[3]See Form 20, Appendix of Official Forms, Rules of Civil Procedure.

[4]Martin v. Martin, 54 Ohio L. Abs. 369, 87 N.E.2d 499 (Ct. App. 8th Dist. Cuyahoga County 1949) (rules of pleading and other procedural matters should be liberally construed in domestic relations cases); Greene v. Greene, 54 Ohio L. Abs. 490, 87 N.E.2d 891 (Ct. App. 8th Dist. Cuyahoga County 1949). See also Annulment Ch 7; Legal Separation Ch 8; Divorce Ch 11; Jurisdiction and Venue Ch 27.

[5]Avis v. Avis, 1985 WL 9027 (Ohio Ct. App. 8th Dist. Cuyahoga County 1985).

[6]Seagraves v. Seagraves, 125 Ohio App. 3d 98, 707 N.E.2d 1165 (2d Dist. Montgomery County 1997).

complaint. However, since Civil Rule 75(F) provides that default judgments under Civil Rule 55 are not permissible in divorce proceedings, an answer to a divorce complaint can generally be filed at any time prior to trial, if leave of court is granted. While such an answer might be generally acceptable, it is not good practice. There is always the possibility that a judge or court may elect not to accept the late answer and proceed as if it were an uncontested divorce. Merely because Civil Rule 75(F) does not permit a default judgment does not mean that it does not permit an uncontested judgment, as long as plaintiff's testimony is corroborated. In such an event, it would not be improper for the court to refuse the defendant permission to testify on his or her own behalf, because no answer has been filed. However, at least one reviewing court has held that it is an abuse of discretion and reversible error to exclude a nonanswering party's evidence concerning property division during trial.[1]

§25:3 Pleadings—Counterclaim

Some local domestic relations court rules specifically provide that the defendant in a divorce action may file a counterclaim asserting any claims which he or she has against the plaintiff, pursuant to Civil Rule 13. The counterclaim may be for divorce on the same or different grounds from those set forth in the complaint, may ask for a legal separation, or in certain rare instances, may ask for an annulment.

It should be noted that Civil Rule 13(A) through Civil Rule 13(F) specifically deals with counterclaims. Civil Rule 13(A) defines a compulsory counterclaim as one which arises out of the same transaction or occurrence that is the subject matter of the opposing party's claim and does not require for its adjudication the presence of third-parties of whom the court cannot acquire jurisdiction. In determining whether a claim arises out of the same transaction or occurrence, a court is to use the "logical relation" test; i.e., whether a separate trial of the claim would involve substantial duplication of effort and time by the parties and the court. In a divorce proceeding, a counterclaim for divorce would have to be considered as a compulsory counterclaim.[1] Also, since jurisdiction is fixed by the service of the complaint, the counterclaimant need not separately allege jurisdiction or venue but may incorporate those allegations of the complaint by admission.

In most divorce cases, it is good strategy to file a counterclaim, even though the defendant may not be actively seeking a divorce or may not want the divorce at all. If the defendant later has a change of heart, then the action will continue even though the plaintiff may subsequently choose to dismiss the complaint.

If the defendant does not really want a divorce, then, in addition to

---

[Section 25:2]

[1]Skaggs v. Skaggs, 1995 WL 368838 (Ohio Ct. App. 3d Dist. Marion County 1995).

[Section 25:3]

[1]Rettig Enterprises, Inc. v. Koehler, 68 Ohio St. 3d 274, 1994-Ohio-127, 626 N.E.2d 99 (1994).

the counterclaim, he or she may wish to consider a conciliation procedure. Defendant's aggressive tactics and preparation will be fruitful if pretrial negotiations, discovery, or even the commencement of the trial are not favorable to the plaintiff and he or she voluntarily dismisses the case. Counsel should remain ever aware that two voluntary dismissals act as an adjudication on the merits.[2]

§ 25:4   Pleadings—Cross-complaint

According to Civil Rule 75(K), the domestic relations counterclaim may be designated as a cross-complaint. Choice of the latter rather than the former designation would depend upon local custom. There is no legal significance in the different terminology.[1]

§ 25:5   Pleadings—Cross-claim

"Cross-claim" is the appropriate designation for the claim of any defendant against any other defendant. It has no special application to a domestic relations action. Also Civil Rule 13(G) expressly provides for the filings of cross-claim against a co-party.

§ 25:6   Pleadings—Reply to counterclaim

Even though Civil Rule 7(A) provides that a reply need only be filed to a counterclaim denominated as such, it is good practice to file a reply to a cross-complaint also, as it is really a counterclaim by another name, not a separate pleading. That way, there can be no doubt that the allegations are denied. Also, the Civil Rules provide that service of the reply shall be made upon the plaintiff within twenty-eight days after service.

§ 25:7   Pleadings—Answer to cross-claim

Since Civil Rule 7(A) lists an answer to a cross-claim as a permitted pleading, it must be assumed that an answer is required lest counsel be obstructed by Civil Rule 8(D) and the unanswered cross-claim be construed as admitted.[1]

§ 25:8   Pleadings—Joining additional parties

The rules concerning joinder of parties, namely Civil Rules 14, 19,

---

[2]Civ. R. 41(A)(1).

[Section 25:4]

[1]Lampe v. Lampe, 74 Ohio L. Abs. 122, 136 N.E.2d 470 (C.P. 1954) (defendant, a resident of Michigan, was allowed to cross-petition for divorce in an annulment action filed by plaintiff, a resident of Ohio); Rubaszny v. Rubaszny, 46 Ohio L. Abs. 55, 70 N.E.2d 905 (Ct. App. 7th Dist. Ashtabula County 1945).

[Section 25:7]

[1]Ridgeway v. Ridgeway, 69 Ohio L. Abs. 341, 118 N.E.2d 845 (Ct. App. 8th Dist. Cuyahoga County 1954) (failure to answer cross-complaint did not constitute admission of allegations so as to render original complainant ineligible for a divorce on the complaint).

19.1, and 24, do not apply to divorce, annulment, or legal separation actions, being expressly excluded by Civil Rule 75(B). However, pursuant to that same rule, the following may be made parties defendant:

    (1) A person or corporation having possession of, control of, or claiming an interest in property, whether real, personal, or mixed, out of which another seeks an award of spousal support or other support. . . .

    (2) [T]he child of the parties . . . [with the] appoint[ment of] a guardian ad litem and legal counsel, if necessary. . . .

    (3) [The employer of a party who has been] ordered to pay child support.

Because of the express limitation of the applicability of Civil Rule 14, joinder of a third party in a divorce, annulment, or legal separation action must be pursuant to Civil Rule 75(B). In such cases, because Civil Rule 19 does not apply, it is not necessary to file a separate complaint and then ask for joinder. In fact, it is expressly prohibited. Because Civil Rule 24 does not apply, third parties have no right to intervene. A reading of Civil Rule 75(B) makes it clear that the parties have complete control over third party intervention or joinder. In fact, although a person or corporation having property of either party may wish to become a party to the proceedings, it appears to be a matter solely in the control of the parties. If new parties are added, a motion for leave to join them must be made.

There is, however, no prohibition against permissive joinder of parties pursuant to Civil Rule 20. It is this rule that courts use, inferentially or explicitly, when allowing a third party, such as a grandparent[1] or a stepparent,[2] interested in obtaining visitation to become a party, even post decree.

Civil Rule 75(B) governing third parties in such actions does not impose any procedural or time limitations, so the pleadings would have to be governed by initial or amended pleadings. It should also be noted, however, that the rights of third-parties who have a vested legal interest in marital or separate property of the spouses cannot be divested thereof unless they are properly joined as parties to the divorce action.[3]

§ 25:9 Pleadings—Amended and supplemental pleadings

These pleadings are alike in that they are submitted after the initial pleadings, and they are different because an amended pleading alters and a supplemental pleading amplifies the pleading to which it relates.

[Section 25:8]

    [1]Hollingsworth v. Hollingsworth, 34 Ohio App. 3d 13, 516 N.E.2d 1250 (10th Dist. Franklin County 1986) (court held that a trial court's jurisdiction to modify a visitation order includes the authority to add persons not parties to the original visitation order).

    [2]Hutton v. Hutton, 21 Ohio App. 3d 26, 486 N.E.2d 129 (9th Dist. Lorain County 1984).

    [3]Huener v. Huener, 110 Ohio App. 3d 322, 674 N.E.2d 389 (3d Dist. Henry County 1996).

Amended complaints are governed by Civil Rule 15(A) to (D). These are permitted as to facts or circumstances arising prior to the filing of the original complaint and may include a different claim for relief. For example, Jill believes Jack to have a mistress but cannot prove it. Attorney Al elects to file for gross neglect and extreme cruelty. Subsequently, Jill discovers the mistress' name and address. Attorney Al can now amend the original complaint to include adultery, as the alleged adultery was prior to the initial filing.

Assume the same complaint for divorce as discussed above, except that after Jack received the complaint, he went out and committed adultery. Jill discovered this subsequent act. Attorney Al can file a supplemental complaint to include the subsequent adultery.

The distinction is that the pleadings will determine relevance. In the second situation, if Attorney Al had used an amended complaint rather than a supplemental complaint, Jack's attorney could properly exclude any testimony of the subsequent adultery as not within the scope of the complaint, except to demonstrate a continuing course of conduct.

Attorney Al may suggest to the court that he be permitted to take advantage of Civil Rule 15(B) and amend his pleadings to conform to the evidence of the adultery, but note that the improper pleading prevented the evidence from being introduced in the first place; thus, there was no evidence on which to base an amendment pursuant to Civil Rule 15(B).

Suppose, on the other hand, that Jill discovered the name and address of the prior mistress, now permitting her attorney to allege adultery via an amended complaint. Assume, however, that Attorney Al alleged adultery by a supplemental complaint rather than an amended complaint. Jack's attorney may have evidence of the adultery excluded, based on the improper pleading, because the supplemental complaint only applies to acts subsequent to the original filing, and the adultery was prior.

Attorney Al was negligent and filed the wrong pleading, but he may be able to point out that although the adultery cannot be proven as a separate ground for divorce because of the improper pleading, evidence of the adultery is additional evidence of the gross neglect and/or extreme cruelty. Since the parties owe to each other obligations of mutual respect, fidelity, and support,[1] the duty of fidelity is certainly neglected by infidelity, and grossly so.

This distinction between amended and supplemental applies to all other pleadings, as well as complaints.[2]

If grounds other than those alleged originally ripen during the

---

[Section 25:9]

[1]RC 3103.01.

[2]Tompkins v. Tompkins, 107 Ohio App. 229, 8 Ohio Op. 2d 129, 157 N.E.2d 755 (2d Dist. Montgomery County 1958) (not an abuse of discretion for trial court to permit plaintiff to amend complaint to include acts of defendant up to time of trial which plaintiff claimed constituted grounds for divorce; court is given wide discretion in all matters of pleading and admission and evaluation of evidence in a divorce action); Perry v. Perry, 100 Ohio App. 15, 59 Ohio Op. 450, 135 N.E.2d 427 (4th Dist. Pickaway County 1955) (Rules of Civil Procedure as to amendment of pleadings apply to divorce actions,

pendency of the action (the most common being one year living separate and apart without cohabitation), the pleadings should be amended. However, pursuant to Civil Rule 15(B), if issues not raised in the pleadings are tried by express or implied consent of the parties, they must be treated in all respects as if they had been raised in the pleadings. If this occurs, an oral motion to amend the pleadings to conform to the evidence should be made at the conclusion of the trial.

Testimony relating to the conduct of a party in a divorce action subsequent to the filing of the complaint or counterclaim is not admissible in the absence of a supplemental complaint alleging such subsequent misconduct.[3] Thus, it is important to file supplemental pleadings if acts of aggression continue to be committed after the initial pleadings are filed, particularly where this evidence may be necessary to bolster grounds for divorce. Evidence of acts subsequent to the filing of a divorce complaint is admissible for the purpose of determining fitness for allocation of residential parent and legal custodian status.

Finally, it is the nature of the claim, not the form in which it is presented that is determinative.[4] Also, cases are to be decided on their merits rather than on mere procedural technicalities.[5] Therefore, a claim that is actually a supplemental claim should not be dismissed because it is denominated as an amended claim.

§ 25:10 Pleadings—Amendment to conform to the evidence

At trial, if issues not raised in the pleadings are tried by express or implied consent of the parties, they shall be treated in all respects as if they had raised in the pleadings. A motion may be made pursuant to Civil Rule 15(B) to amend the pleadings to conform to that evidence. This will normally be done orally at the conclusion of the trial.

In domestic relations, because of common confusion as to which evidence supports the various grounds, this motion may be a valuable tool.

---

so that when a party to a divorce action amends a pleading and it does not appear that the adverse party is taken by surprise or is unprepared to meet the issue made by the amended pleading, and the adverse party fails to request a continuance, the trial court may continue with the trial); Cassaro v. Cassaro, 50 Ohio App. 2d 368, 4 Ohio Op. 3d 320, 363 N.E.2d 753 (8th Dist. Cuyahoga County 1976) (party in a divorce action may file an amended complaint during the proceedings alleging other grounds, if the period of separation required by [then] RC 3105.01(K) matures during that time); Zatko v. Zatko, 100 Ohio App. 223, 60 Ohio Op. 200, 136 N.E.2d 358 (6th Dist. Lucas County 1953) (testimony relating to the conduct of a party in a divorce case subsequent to the filing of the complaint is not admissible in the absence of a supplemental complaint alleging such subsequent conduct); Weinstein v. Weinstein, 27 Ohio Op. 2d 115, 90 Ohio L. Abs. 199, 185 N.E.2d 56 (Ct. App. 8th Dist. Cuyahoga County 1962) (evidence of acts subsequent to the filing of a divorce complaint is admissible for the purpose of determining fitness for custody).

[3]Weinstein v. Weinstein, 27 Ohio Op. 2d 115, 90 Ohio L. Abs. 199, 185 N.E.2d 56 (Ct. App. 8th Dist. Cuyahoga County 1962).

[4]Hunter v. Shenango Furnace Co., 38 Ohio St. 3d 235, 527 N.E.2d 871 (1988).

[5]Peterson v. Teodosio, 34 Ohio St. 2d 161, 63 Ohio Op. 2d 262, 297 N.E.2d 113 (1973); State ex rel. Wilcox v. Seidner, 76 Ohio St. 3d 412, 1996-Ohio-390, 667 N.E.2d 1220 (1996).

Suppose, for example, that a party had complained of gross neglect of duty. At trial, evidence to support such neglect was not forthcoming, but in fact the elicited evidence did support extreme cruelty. As long as the evidence is in the record, the plaintiff may make this motion.

Assume, as another example, that counsel complained of adultery, but that the evidence instead established only gross neglect of duty. Without an amendment to assert this ground, the case must be dismissed for failure of proof.[1]

Because of the existence of this motion, and the admonition in the rule that the motion should be granted freely, trial counsel should be very cautious in permitting testimony not in conformity with the pleadings, lest the generous or negligent treatment of these irrelevant matters become the basis for application of this rule. Change of parental rights and responsibilities proceedings present a very common arena for the application of this rule, as typical practice in making a motion for change of the allocation of parental rights and responsibilities involves alleging incomplete grounds, or grounds "to be brought out at hearing."

Even though the motion may be made orally, or after judgment, it would always be better practice to supplement the oral motion immediately with the written motion as soon as possible, to keep the record "appeal proof."[2]

§ 25:11 Pleadings—Signing of pleadings

While the party verification of pleadings is no longer the rule, it is important in domestic relations practice that counsel be aware of its substitute. Civil Rule 11 now permits counsel to sign on behalf of the client. However, the rule also imposes a potentially severe sanction.

The signature of counsel is a statement that he has read the pleading and that to the best of his knowledge, information, and belief there is good ground to support it; and that it is not interposed for delay.

Often in domestic relations cases, there is pressure to file pleadings where counsel knows there may not be, or are not, grounds to support the allegations. Frequently, a complaint/answer/temporary restraining order (TRO) is filed solely for the purpose of obtaining a favorable negotiated settlement from the other party. Possibly the most flagrant violations involve ex parte TROs, designed for tactical advantage, or to annoy and harass, with little or no grounds to support them. However, since an affiant on an ex parte TRO motion will never be called upon to support

---

[Section 25:10]

[1]Moser v. Moser, 5 Ohio App. 3d 193, 450 N.E.2d 741 (9th Dist. Lorain County 1982) (where complaint alleged gross neglect of duty and extreme cruelty, and where evidence of adultery was presented, divorce on grounds of adultery not error).

[2]Cassaro v. Cassaro, 50 Ohio App. 2d 368, 4 Ohio Op. 3d 320, 363 N.E.2d 753 (8th Dist. Cuyahoga County 1976) (party in divorce action may file an amended complaint during the proceedings alleging other grounds, if the period of separation required by [then] RC 3105.01(K) matures during that time); Tompkins v. Tompkins, 107 Ohio App. 229, 8 Ohio Op. 2d 129, 157 N.E.2d 755 (2d Dist. Montgomery County 1958) (court has wide discretion in all matters of pleading and evidence in a divorce action).

the veracity of the affidavit, it is a no-risk situation for the party. While this may be true as to the client, it is not true as to the attorney who did the filing, and Civil Rule 11 leaves the attorney open for the sanctions available under the rule.

While the grounds for sanctions under Civil Rule 11 are scattered throughout the section, they may be summarized thus:

(1) There is not good ground to support the allegations;

(2) It was interposed for delay;

(3) The pleading was not signed;

(4) It was signed for the purpose of defeating the rule; or

(5) Scandalous or indecent matter was included.

For a violation, the matter may be stricken; for a willful violation, the attorney may be sanctioned. As strong as the asserted sanction may be, the burden remains on the accuser to show that the allegation had no good ground to support it at the time it was made, and for an attorney sanction, the additional burden to show that the attorney's action was willful. Construction of the term "willful" is open, and may include anything from "knowingly" to "maliciously."[1]

Besides Civil Rule 11, a court can award attorney fees in a domestic relations case under the attorney fee statute, RC 3105.18(H); the frivolous conduct statute, RC 2323.51; or the court's inherent power to award fees for bad faith conduct.[2] Also, a voluntary dismissal of a claim does *not* terminate the jurisdiction of a court to award attorney fees pursuant to RC 2323.51 or Civil Rule 11.[3] Finally, an award of attorney fees pursuant to RC 2323.51 can be awarded against a party, his or her counsel, or both.[4]

§ 25:12 Dissolution—Petition

RC 3105.63 identifies the appropriate pleading with which to initiate a dissolution as a "petition." In the rules, the term petition is never used.

The spirit of the procedure is in keeping with this neutral terminology. A dissolution is a no-fault termination of a marriage. There is no complaint and answer, because there is no plaintiff and no defendant. The

---

[Section 25:11]

[1]See Divorce Ch 11; Spousal Support Ch 13; § 25:18, Motions regarding pleadings—Motion to strike; § 25:26, Motions regarding temporary relief—Motion for temporary restraining order; § 25:28, Motions regarding temporary relief—Motion for temporary spousal support.

[2]Curtis v. Curtis, 140 Ohio App. 3d 812, 749 N.E.2d 772 (1st Dist. Hamilton County 2000), dismissed, appeal not allowed, 91 Ohio St. 3d 1489, 745 N.E.2d 437 (2001) and (overruled by, Riston v. Butler, 2002-Ohio-2308, 2002 WL 948536 (Ohio Ct. App. 1st Dist. Hamilton County 2002)).

[3]Burrell v. Kassicieh, 128 Ohio App. 3d 226, 714 N.E.2d 442 (3d Dist. Seneca County 1998).

[4]Ron Scheiderer & Assoc. v. London, 81 Ohio St. 3d 94, 1998-Ohio-453, 689 N.E.2d 552 (1998).

rationale is that neither party is at fault, neither party is a wrongdoer. Thus, the proper initial pleading is a petition.

This raises two interesting pleading questions. Custom and practice denominate one party to a judicial proceeding as the plaintiff (the "injured" party) and the other as the defendant or respondent (the alleged "wrongdoer"). However, neither of these designations is proper in a dissolution. In the caption of a dissolution action, it is correct to denominate each party as a petitioner.

In subsequent proceedings, such as a motion to show cause, it is proper to denominate one party as petitioner-wife and the other as petitioner-husband, even though they are no longer husband and wife. On appeal, one party becomes the petitioner-appellant and the other the petitioner-appellee.

RC 3105.62 indicates that for purposes of service of process, both parties shall be deemed to be defendants. This does not convert one of them to a plaintiff and the other to a defendant. The parties may be referred to as defendant 1 and defendant 2. This item is solely to assure that there is proper service. As a practical matter, service in a dissolution action should be waived pursuant to Civil Rule 4(D), because both parties are in agreement, and there is no practical reason why service should not be waived in the initial petition.

An affidavit for each party is strictly a stylistic device wherein the parties state all operative facts. There is no legal reason for inclusion of all this material in the petition per se, as it is not needed in this pleading any more than it is needed in any other petition or motion. Granted, it is necessary in a formal complaint, but this is not a complaint. In a motion, the operative facts are in the brief and/or the affidavit.

The petition need only state what is required by RC 3105.62 and RC 3105.63: the fact of a marriage, jurisdiction, the agreement, and the request for the dissolution. With the abbreviated petition, other matters may be placed on a separate page, but there is no reason for notarization. It is recommended only because it acts to remind the parties of the seriousness of the situation and that their actions have great legal significance.

While individual jurisdictions may vary somewhat, ordinarily one original executed agreement must be included with the petition and another with the decree. Thus, it is good practice to execute at least two agreements. Local practice may dictate whether there should be an original executed agreement for each party. If the agreement was the result of protracted negotiation, and the dissolution the consequence of bad feeling, it may be good practice to have a copy of the agreement for each party. Whether each should be executed is a judgment call.

With respect to an agreement executed in advance, it should be noted that RC 3105.63 permits amendments at any time prior to the hearing. In the event that amendments are made, a new executed agreement or at least an addendum, should be prepared for the hearing, with executed copies optional, as above. Some judges require that the executed agreement for the decree be one that was executed before the court.

Counsel should be aware of local practice customs and prepare accordingly.

If the agreement contemplates future action regarding realty, it may be appropriate to have the agreement witnessed and notarized, in case the agreement is intended to survive a dismissal, and the statute of frauds may become an issue.

Finally, it is good practice to have all documents available at the hearing, rather than leave matters to subsequent action by the parties. Since the documents (e.g., a deed) must be done sometime, there is no valid reason to leave them for a later time. Deeds, transfers of stock, checks, etc., can easily be brought to the court pending the results of the hearing. If the case goes to judgment, then the appropriate documents can be immediately given to the proper party. If the matter is dismissed, then each party can retrieve his or her documents, with no harm done. Again, it is good practice not to leave anything to be done after judgment, as this is an open invitation to post-decree show cause motions, which, with a little care, may be avoided.[1]

§ 25:13 Dissolution—Hearing

If, at the time of the hearing, either spouse is not satisfied with the separation agreement or does not wish a dissolution of the marriage, and if neither spouse files a motion pursuant to RC 3105.65(C) to convert the action to an action for divorce, the court shall dismiss the petition and refuse to validate the proposed separation agreement.

If, upon review of the testimony of both spouses, and of the report, if any, of the investigator pursuant to the Rules of Civil Procedure, the court approves the separation agreement and any amendments to it agreed upon by the parties, it shall grant a decree of dissolution of marriage that incorporates the separation agreement. A decree of dissolution of marriage has the same effect upon the property rights of the parties, including rights of dower and inheritance, as a decree of divorce. The court has full power to enforce its decree, and retains jurisdiction to modify all matters pertaining to the allocation of parental rights and responsibilities for the care of the minor children and the designation of a residential parent and legal custodian of the minor children, child support, and visitation, and, only in accordance with RC 3105.18(E)(2), has authority to modify the amount or terms of spousal support. It should be noted that RC 3105.18(E)(2) requires the consent of both petitioners.

At any time before a decree of dissolution of marriage has been granted under RC 3105.65(B), either spouse may convert the action for dissolution of marriage into a divorce action by filing a motion with the court in which the action for dissolution of marriage is pending for conversion of the action for dissolution of marriage. The motion shall contain a complaint for divorce that contains grounds for a divorce and that otherwise complies with the Rules of Civil Procedure and RC

[Section 25:12]
[1]See Dissolution of Marriage Ch 10.

Chapter 3105. The complaint should have a standard caption, including the addresses of all parties. The divorce action then shall proceed in accordance with the Rules of Civil Procedure in the same manner as if the motion had been the original complaint in the action, including, but not limited to, the issuance and service of summons pursuant to Civil Rules 4 to 4.6, except that no court fees shall be charged upon conversion of the action for dissolution of marriage into a divorce action under this division.

§ 25:14 Uncontested divorce actions

Civil Rule 75(F) specifically excludes Civil Rule 55 (on defaults) from divorce, annulment, and legal separation actions.

In place of a motion for a default judgment, plaintiff uses RC 3105.10 and Civil Rule 75(M) and merely presents evidence sufficient to establish a prima facie case, so that judgment can be given. Prior to the creation of the dissolution, this was the usual procedure in negotiated divorces. Part of the agreed testimony was the fact of a separation agreement, which was then incorporated into the judgment. The procedure is still used today but is generally limited to cases that begin as divorces, which are then followed by negotiated settlements. As part of the agreement, one party withdraws his or her complaint or answer and assumes the guilt, usually for gross neglect of duty, or both parties sign and agree they are incompatible. This is an optional tactic, and the parties may use this procedure rather than a refiling for a dissolution and waiting the additional time (especially if the trial date on the complaint is close, or where one party has a prospective spouse impatiently waiting).

§ 25:15 Motions regarding pleadings—Motion for leave to plead

It is not uncommon for the recipient of a common pleas complaint to wait until the approach of "rule time" before consulting an attorney. In practice, the motion for leave to plead is the law's recognition of this common human frailty, and the granting of the motion is generally a matter of intercounsel courtesy, a secretary-to-secretary exchange, at least the first time, and maybe even the second. To keep the record complete, counsel requesting and obtaining the leave to plead from opposing counsel should file a judgment entry concerning the agreed extension. If counsel does not grant the extension, the applicant can move the court for more time pursuant to Civil Rule 6(B)(1), so opposition to an informal request is likely to have only nuisance value. This motion is appropriate for any document requiring a response, including pleadings, motions, interrogatories, admissions, etc. This motion differs from the one permitted under Civil Rule 6(B)(2), since this motion is one made while the movant is still within rule time. Civil Rule 6(B)(2) permits a motion for a leave to plead after rule time has expired, for excusable neglect, and the motion should be so labeled. The more proper procedure in this latter situation is to file a motion for leave to plead instanter, with the motion being accompanied by the proposed responsive pleading.[1]

§ 25:16 Motions regarding pleadings—Motion for leave to plead instanter

Civil Rule 6(B)(1) covers the leave to plead where the movant is still within rule time; Civil Rule 6(B)(2) covers the situation where the movant is beyond rule time, but does not apply to motions filed in regard to a matter covered by Civil Rules 50(B), 59(B), or 60(B).

If counsel needs additional time to plead, then the leave to plead is the correct motion. If counsel has the time to file a responsive pleading with the motion (e.g., a boilerplate answer and counterclaim), then the instanter is the more correct motion, as it is a signal to the judge that this is not merely a request for more time to respond but that a proposed response has been filed, which acts to induce a favorable result.

In practice, it may also be a signal to the judge that leave has not been requested of opposing counsel, but this may be of no consequence because of the excusable neglect described in the accompanying brief and affidavit.

The Civil Rule 6(B)(2) motion differs from the Civil Rule 6(B)(1) motion in that the latter is essentially a motion for more time to prepare and draft appropriate pleadings and is made within rule time. The Civ. R. 6(B)(2) motion is appropriate when a party has exceeded rule time. It is filed with the answer (and/or counterclaim, etc.), and the only real problem may be with a clerk who is unfamiliar with the motion and demands a judgment showing that the motion has been granted before accepting the pleading. As with any such motion, the judgment entry should be included with the package and used according to local custom, which may permit the filing of all three, or the filing of the proposed pleading and the judgment entry, with a copy of the motion to be brought to the judge personally for ex parte action, before filing it with the clerk.

This is essentially a general common pleas procedure, the granting of which is contingent upon the moving party giving good cause for the delay. In domestic relations matters, the brief is also essential, and the motion is not certain to succeed, since Civil Rule 75(F) states that Civil Rule 55 (defaults) does not apply in the domestic relations context.

As a matter of practice, when a divorce complaint is filed and rule time passes without an answer, it may be advanced on the docket as an uncontested divorce. It is imperative that the attorney who plans this motion do so before the scheduled hearing, lest the matter be moot.[1]

[Section 25:15]

[1]See §§ 25:16–25:17, Motions regarding pleadings—Motion for leave to plead instanter.

[Section 25:16]

[1]See § 25:15, Motions regarding pleadings—Motion for leave to plead.

§ 25:17   Motions regarding pleadings—Motion for leave to plead instanter with entry—Form ⊚

[Title of Court]

[Caption]   Case No. *[_____]*
                                         MOTION FOR LEAVE TO PLEAD
                                         INSTANTER

Defendant moves this Court for an order, pursuant to Civil Rule 6(B), permitting *[him/her]* to file an answer *[within [_____] days/ instanter].*

This motion is supported by the memorandum below.

_____

Attorney for Defendant

[Memorandum in support of motion]

[Proof/certificate of service]

[Title of Court]

[Caption]   Case No. *[_____]*
                                         JUDGMENT ENTRY

Upon application of Defendant and for good cause shown, Defendant is permitted to file *[his/her]* answer out of rule instanter.

_____

Judge

Approved:

_____

Attorney for Movant

NOTES TO FORM

Drafter's Notes

The proposed pleading should be filed with the motion and entry.

§ 25:18   Motions regarding pleadings—Motion to strike

Civil Rule 12(F) permits the striking of matters, or pleadings that are "insufficient . . . or . . . redundant, immaterial, impertinent, or scandalous" from the files.

It is often true that the heated combat of a domestic relations case is further complicated by pleadings and allegations that are exaggerated or even false, designed for tactical position, or revenge. Although most attorneys, in representing a client, are forced to believe that client until the truth becomes known, it is also true that many of the exaggerations and claims commonly objected to are boilerplate or tactical poses created by and for lawyers. Civil Rule 11 imposes sanctions for abuse of the legal process, permitting matters to be stricken as "sham or false," and subjects the attorney involved to sanctions. These sanctions apply when the attorney signs a pleading without believing that there are good grounds to support it or for purposes of delay.

Exaggeration and fabrication are not uncommon, and domestic relations judges have traditionally shown great tolerance and understanding in these matters. Even so, there must come a point at which counsel perceives that an allegation is outrageous and should be stricken.

If the allegation is untrue and was inserted to persuade the trier of fact (judge or magistrate), note that the hearing on the motion to strike will put on record the material that counsel did not want in the record. This motion may then be beneficial to opposing counsel. Even without a hearing, the court will have its attention drawn to the matter.

§ 25:19 Motions regarding parties—Motion to join minor as party

Civil Rule 75(B)(2) provides that when it is essential to protect the interests of a child, the court may join him or her as a party defendant. The rule also provides that a guardian ad litem and legal counsel may also be appointed for said child by the court and the costs thereof taxed. This procedure is frequently used in contested parental rights and responsibilities cases. More often than not, the guardian ad litem is also an attorney and acts in a dual capacity.

The joining of the minor child as a party and appointment of a guardian ad litem bring before the court an element which both contesting parents may have forgotten or may not be able to consider rationally: the best interests of their minor child. The guardian ad litem can also be used as a buffer to insulate the minor child from the turmoil of the custody battle.

A frequent problem in joining the minor child and appointing a guardian ad litem is finding competent counsel, since the fee of the guardian is taxed as costs, and court costs are frequently not paid. Cuyahoga County was among the first to initiate a model guardian ad litem program which provides training for the guardian as well as a fund out of which the guardian can be assured payment.[1]

The trial court also has discretion and broad authority under Civ. R. 75(B)(2) to tax the costs equally to the parties in the action and, absent an abuse of discretion, the lower court's judgment as to the taxing of the fees of the guardian ad litem will not be reversed.[2]

[Section 25:19]

[1]See §§ 15:63–15:68, Guardian ad litem; § 25:21, Motions regarding parties—Motion to appoint guardian ad litem.

[2]Schulte v. Schulte, 1993 WL 197413 (Ohio Ct. App. 6th Dist. Wood County 1993), judgment aff'd, 1994 -Ohio- 459, 71 Ohio St. 3d 41, 641 N.E.2d 719 (1994).

§ 25:20   Motions regarding parties—Motion to join minor as party and appoint guardian ad litem—Form⊚

[Title of Court]

[Caption]   Case No. [_____]

MOTION TO JOIN MINOR AS
PARTY AND TO APPOINT

GUARDIAN AD LITEM

[Name of spouse] respectfully moves this Court for an order joining the minor *[child/children]*, namely *[name(s) and date(s) of birth of children]* of the parties as *[a party/parties]* Defendant, pursuant to Civil Rule 75(B)(2) as it is essential to protect the interests of said *[child/children]*.

[Movant] moves this Court for an order appointing a guardian ad litem for such minor *[child/children]* and for an order taxing the costs thereof *[equally between the parties/to the other party]*.

This motion is supported by the *[memorandum/affidavit]* below.

_____

Attorney for Movant

[Affidavit/memorandum in support of motion]

[Proof/certificate of service]

NOTES TO FORM

Drafter's Notes

When parental rights and responsibilities or visitation is contested, when a parentage action is filed, when a child is involved in a divorce, annulment, or legal separation action, or when support is being waived, this motion is justified.

Cross Reference

1 Klein and Darling, Baldwin's Ohio Practice, Civil Practice Rules 17, 19

§ 25:21   Motions regarding parties—Motion to appoint guardian ad litem

Civil Rule 17(B) states in relevant part, "When a minor . . . is not otherwise represented in an action the court shall appoint a guardian ad litem or shall make such other order as it deems proper for the protection of such minor or incompetent person." However, Civil Rule 75(B)(2) modifies this requirement by not considering a child in the divorce context as a party, so that the appointment of a guardian ad litem (GAL) is not mandatory.

Civil Rule 75(B)(2) permits the appointment of a GAL but does not require it. As a condition precedent to such appointment, the court must first make a finding that "it is essential to protect the interests of [the] child." The major reason for this is that the parents are recognized to be the natural guardians, and it is presumed that they will do all that is necessary to protect the interests of their children. Practitioners in this area generally agree that the children of divorcing parents are well provided for and that so long as both parents have agreed on a disposition with respect to the child, the courts are reluctant to intervene. On the other hand, children are often forgotten parties, and parents sometimes are more concerned about their own rights and problems than those of their children.

When it appears to the court that such is the case, the court on its own motion may make the appropriate finding, make the appointment, and join the child as a party. Alternatively, either party may file the motion to appoint a guardian ad litem. RC 3109.04(B) provides that the court should, upon the motion of either parent, appoint a guardian ad litem for a child if the court interviews any child in chambers regarding their wishes and concerns with respect to the allocation of parental rights and responsibilities.

Sometimes, one of the parties will recognize the unfortunate situation where the child's interests have been ignored, and a third party protector may be necessary to safeguard them. This will rarely occur in a dissolution or uncontested divorce but should be a primary consideration in a contest, especially if the child is the basis of the dispute. Counsel may then want to use Civil Rule 75(B)(2) and request the appointment of a GAL. In the supporting brief, counsel should clearly state the reasons why it is in the best interests of the child that a GAL be appointed.

While it is unlikely that moving counsel would also request the appointment of legal counsel for the child and thus turn a two-party litigation into a three-party litigation, the court has the right to do so on its own.

One party may not serve as both the attorney and guardian ad litem (GAL) where a conflict between such duties exists. Such conflict exists where a child desires to live with one parent while the guardian ad litem believes that it is in the child's best interests to live with the other parent. However, such conflict will rarely arise in young children who are incapable of making an informed choice of which parent to live with. Thus, the determination of when such a conflict exists is often, as a practical matter, up to the GAL.[1]

The rule also permits the court to "tax the costs thereof," which include the cost of the GAL and legal counsel. This of course means that the costs will be taxed at the end of the hearing to either or both parties, as is customary and traditional locally.[2] The court may require the posting of a deposit for guardian's fees.[3]

§ 25:22 Motions regarding parties—Motion to join employer

Civil Rule 75(B)(3) provides that the court may, on its own motion or that of an interested person, after notice to the party ordered to pay

---

[Section 25:21]

   [1]In re Baby Girl Baxter, 17 Ohio St. 3d 229, 479 N.E.2d 257 (1985).

   [2]See §§ 15:63–15:68, Guardian ad litem; §§ 25:19–25:20, Motions regarding parties—Motion to join minor as party.

   [3]See, for example, Frank. R. 15.

support and to his or her employer, make the employer a party defendant. It is not necessary for an employer to be named as a party defendant in order for an income source notice to be issued to the employer to deduct support from an obligor's pay and forward it to the child support enforcement agency for transmittal to the custodial parent.[1]

§ 25:23 Motions regarding parties—Motion to join employer as defendant—Form ⊚

[Title of Court]

[Caption]

Case No. *[_____]*

MOTION TO JOIN EMPLOYER

AS

NEW PARTY DEFENDANT

Now comes Plaintiff, pursuant to Civ. R. 75(B)(3), and moves this Court for an order making *[name]*, Defendant's employer, a new party Defendant the reasons for which are set forth in the Affidavit attached hereto as "Exhibit A" and incorporated herein.

_____

Attorney for Plaintiff

[Exhibit "A"—Affidavit of plaintiff, giving reasons/justifications for the motions]

[Proof/certificate of service]

NOTES TO FORM

Drafter's Notes

Service to be made on Defendant and Defendant's employer.

For purposes of RC 3113.21 withholding, there is no requirement that the employer be made a party defendant; only notice of the order to withhold must be given the employer. There may be other reasons for making the employer a party pursuant to Civ. R. 75(B)(3).

Cross Reference

1 Klein and Darling, Baldwin's Ohio Practice, Civil Practice Rule 19
3 Klein and Darling, Baldwin's Ohio Practice, Civil Practice, Ch 7

§ 25:24 Motions regarding parties—Motion to join additional parties

Civil Rules 14, 19, 19.1, and 24 do not apply in divorce, annulment, or legal separation actions, having been specifically excluded by Civil Rule 75(B). However, it may become necessary during the course of litigation to restrain certain assets which may be in the hands of third parties. Since those parties are not parties to the action, they cannot be restrained by motion. This can be done only by joining them as defendants and imposing upon them an order restraining them from

---

[Section 25:22]
[1]See Child Support Enforcement Agencies Ch 22.

releasing any of those assets.

The motion must be accompanied by an affidavit reciting the existence of the asset and the allegation that, unless restrained, the opposing party will in some way dissipate it. Thus, banks, brokerage houses, insurance companies, and other financial institutions are made parties to the action, and the economic status quo can be maintained.

§ 25:25 Motions regarding parties—Motion to join new party defendant—Form☉

[Title of Court]

[Caption]

Case No. *[_____]*

MOTION TO ADD NEW PARTY
DEFENDANT

Now comes Plaintiff and moves this Court for an order adding *[name]*, whose address is *[address]*, as a new party Defendant under Civ. R. 75(B)(1) for the reason that said new party Defendant has possession and control of funds out of which Plaintiff seeks spousal support and/or property settlement, as is more fully shown by the Affidavit attached hereto as "Exhibit A," which is incorporated herein by reference.

_____
Attorney for Plaintiff

[Exhibit "A"—Affidavit of plaintiff, giving reasons/justifications for the motion]

[Proof/certificate of service]

I hereby certify that a copy of the foregoing Request and Notice was *[mailed/delivered]* to *[Defendant/Defendant's attorney]* at *[full address]* on *[date]*.

_____
Attorney for Plaintiff

NOTES TO FORM

Drafter's Notes

This motion should be filed with an entry.

A proof/certificate of service is only necessary when there is opposing counsel. Where the respondent is unrepresented by counsel at the time of filing the motion, the motion papers will be served by the clerk of court pursuant to written instructions filed with the motion.

Under his/her name on the motion, counsel should list his or her business address, Supreme Court registration number, and phone number.

Cross Reference

1 Klein and Darling, Baldwin's Ohio Practice, Civil Practice Rule 19

§ 25:26 Motions regarding temporary relief—Motion for temporary restraining order

Civil Rule 75(I) authorizes two kinds of temporary restraining orders

(TROs) and the courts have created a third:

(1) Against disposing of marital property, so as to defeat a claim for support or division of property;

(2) Against abusing or annoying the other party; and

(3) Against entering premises (the judicially created eviction which is available under certain conditions and only in some counties).

All three types of TROs may be requested by motion at any time during the course of an action. Following good motion practice, a brief and affidavit should accompany the motion, along with a judgment entry, unless local practice involves use of the clerk of court's rubber stamp on such motions.

All three types of TROs are also available from the initial pleading and may be appended to the complaint or counterclaim. It makes no difference whether the request is added to a pleading or is presented in a separate motion. This must be decided on the basis of local custom and practice. If counsel wants to restrain third parties who hold marital property, then these third parties must be named as party defendants in the pleading. Local custom and practice may permit a blanket restraining order against all defendants named in the pleading. It is often very efficient to join third parties, such as banks and insurance companies, and restrain them all in one motion.

If there are bank accounts to be restrained, it is good practice to have immediate personal service on the banks rather than wait for certified mail service, as it may be important to restrain the banks before the assets can be removed and the motion rendered moot.

The TRO is usually granted ex parte, on the accompanying affidavit, and continues until further order of the court, or until the hearing on the complaint, whichever is earlier. The restrained party may have some relief from the TRO by subsequent motion for relief, to vacate, to reconsider, to modify, or to cancel, whichever is used locally.

In Cuyahoga County,[1] requests for restraining orders will be granted ex parte if accompanied by an affidavit, whether in the complaint, counterclaim, or by separate motion, without bond, in the following instances:

(1) To restrain a spouse from abusing, harassing, molesting, threatening, or physically injuring his or her spouse or child or the children.

(2) To restrain a spouse from communicating with the employer, business associates, and patients or customers of a party or of his or her employer and/or from entering upon the premises of said party's employer (unless both parties have the same employer).

(3) To restrain the removal of a child or the children of the parties from the jurisdiction of the court other than temporarily (fourteen days or less) for vacation, travel, visitation with the extended family, camp, or recreation.

[Section 25:26]

[1]As each jurisdiction relies on local custom and practice in the issuance of ex parte restraining orders, local rules and practice must be consulted.

(4) To restrain a party from changing the place of a child's education (secular or religious) or worship.

(5) To restrain a spouse from obstructing or interfering with visitation or communication by a party with a child of the parties.

(6) To restrain a spouse from disparaging, denigrating, or otherwise speaking ill of a party to or in the presence or hearing of a child of the parties.

(7) To restrain a spouse from withdrawing funds from a bank, savings and loan association, credit union, retirement or pension fund, trust, brokerage house, or financial institution, provided, however, that no business account will be so restrained.

(8) To restrain any bank, savings and loan association, credit union, retirement or pension fund, brokerage house, or other financial agency, fund, trust, or institution from disbursing funds to or on the account of a spouse.

(9) To restrain the removal from the marital home of tangible property other than (a) the clothing and personal effects of a spouse, and (b) tools, equipment, books, and papers incidental to the conduct of the trade, business, or profession of a spouse from the marital home.

(10) To restrain the sale, gift, transfer, conveyance, or encumbrance of any tangible property, or the disposition or delivery thereof, by a spouse or by a third party holding such property for or on behalf of a spouse.

(11) To restrain payment of a discretionary annual, semiannual, or quarterly bonus to a spouse, provided however, that said bonus is not a commission, draw, or other predetermined amount by which said spouse is regularly and customarily paid for his or her services in the ordinary course of his or her employment.

(12) To restrain the sale of a spouse's business or of his or her partnership, stock, or other interest in a business enterprise wherein he or she is employed or in which he or she is an officer, director, executive, or manager.

(13) To restrain a party from entering a safe deposit box and/or from removing any of the contents of a safe deposit box.

(14) To restrain a party from permitting a spouse or other person to enter a safe deposit box, vault, locked drawer, closet, or other place of safekeeping or storage located on a premises controlled by that party.

(15) To restrain a party from charging his or her purchase of goods or services to the account of his or her spouse and from using the credit (including credit cards) of his or her spouse.

(16) To restrain a spouse from returning to the marital residence after an uninterrupted absence of thirty or more days immediately prior to the filing of the motion.

(17) To restrain a spouse from interfering with a party's use of an automobile previously allocated to his or her general use when there is more than one automobile available for use by the parties.

(18) To restrain a spouse from terminating, modifying, or changing beneficiaries of any policies of insurance: automobile, life, health, or otherwise.[2]

The Eighth District Court of Appeals has held that any order, including a restraining order, must be granted by the judge to whom the case is assigned. No judge other than the assigned judge has any authority to so act. Such rulings are voidable upon the timely objection of either party.[3]

A TRO will not be granted ex parte for the following reasons:

(1) To restrain the removal of a child from the marital home or to any particular place (other than outside the jurisdiction of the court).

(2) To restrain a party from visiting or communicating with a child of the parties.

(3) To restrain the free movement of a party or the children of the parties.

(4) To order a spouse to return property to a party.

(5) To restrain a spouse from communicating with a party.

(6) To restrain disbursement or withdrawal from a business account.

(7) To restrain business or investment transactions.

(8) To direct or otherwise control the conduct of a spouse in relation to the care or supervision of a child of the parties.

(9) To restrain a public official or agency, including but not limited to a clerk of court, county recorder, auto title bureau, or government pension fund.

(10) To restrain a spouse from associating with any person.

(11) To restrain a spouse from remaining in or entering the marital home (unless absent thirty consecutive days immediately prior to the filing of the motion).

(12) To restrain a spouse from removing his or her clothing and other personal effects from the marital home.

(13) To restrain a spouse from removing his tools, equipment, books, and papers necessary to the conduct of his trade, business, or profession from the marital home.

If a restraining order is sought which does not fall within the categories enumerated, applications must be made directly to the court. If the judge declines to grant the order ex parte, a hearing will be set at the court's discretion.

---

[2]Hook v. Hook, 35 Ohio App. 3d 51, 519 N.E.2d 687 (8th Dist. Cuyahoga County 1987) (life insurance proceeds were properly payable to a named beneficiary even though that beneficiary was designated in violation of an ex parte order prohibiting a change during the pendency of the action; order was abated by the insured's death); Mack v. Allstate Life Ins. Co., 42 Ohio App. 3d 101, 536 N.E.2d 671 (1st Dist. Hamilton County 1987) (death of insured, who was under an order restraining him from changing beneficiaries, did not abate the divorce action or the restraining order; defendant-insured's attempt to change the beneficiary on his life insurance was not effective because his right or authority to make any changes was inhibited by the temporary restraining order).

[3]Leone v. Leone, 1991 WL 144183 (Ohio Ct. App. 8th Dist. Cuyahoga County 1991).

In all cases, whenever a restraining order is sought, that which is to be restrained must be specifically stated; unidentified assets may not be restrained.

A request for temporary restraining orders may be made in the demand clause of a complaint for divorce, counterclaim, answer, or by separate motion. The orders sought must be asked for specifically in the "wherefore" clause or demand of the complaint. The persons or assets to be restrained must be specified. The person to be restrained must be a party to the action. Other persons may be joined pursuant to Civil Rule 75(B). All requests must be accompanied by an affidavit as prescribed by Civil Rule 75(I)(2).

The TRO restraining a party from disposing of marital property is not really directed toward preservation of marital property per se but toward protection of marital property interests. Civil Rule 75(I)(2) is aimed at the disposition of any property that may defeat the interest of the other party in obtaining spousal or child support or a division of property.

If the termination is to be unpleasant, it is possible that the parties will seek to restrain each other into a state of total economic immobility. On the other hand, the parties may already have disposed of their assets so that there is nothing left for the TRO to act upon. The most difficult situation is where a party, usually the husband, has engaged in clandestine preparation for the combat and has quietly hidden assets. It often happens that the husband, who managed the marital finances, has left the wife unaware of the nature and extent of marital assets. Unfortunately, if assets cannot be identified, they cannot be restrained.

When representing a spouse who is economically dependent, there should be some careful preparation for the inevitable TRO if the termination is to be contested. Once the TRO and temporary spousal and child support awards are in place, the mutual marital support obligations are immediately suspended and replaced by the terms of the order. It is a rare award that will provide for adequate family support. Where a residential parent is involved, it is not unusual to compile necessities for the family, via the family charge accounts, in preparation for prolonged proceedings. Until the defendant has filed a restraining order upon the plaintiff, there is no order being violated by the plaintiff by using charge accounts. The court may, however, require the charging party to pay obligations incurred subsequent to filing unless it can be shown such charges were required to maintain the household. Once the temporary spousal support and restraining orders are in place, however, this self-help remedy is terminated as a matter of law. More than likely, the other spouse, on his or her initiative or the advice of counsel, will immediately cancel all outstanding charge accounts.

Civil Rule 75(I)(2) provides authority for an ex parte TRO where there has been an allegation by affidavit that a party or child is about to suffer physical abuse, annoyance, or bodily injury. Given the frequent occurrence of domestic violence, this TRO is an essential tool for counsel representing a spouse where there is a history and/or potential for domestic violence.

The TRO itself orders the defendant/respondent to refrain from such acts under penalty of contempt. Its effectiveness varies, depending on the situation. Where the allegations are mere sham, and used solely to gain tactical advantage, it is likely that a spouse, who has been wrongly accused, will certainly obey, unless he or she is so angered at the false allegations that the TRO precipitates the precise act it was designed to prevent.

If a spouse is a violent person but has never actually engaged in violence, it is likely that there will be compliance. Where a spouse is violent, and the TRO may precipitate the violence it was designed to control, the subsequent contempt proceedings will be of little value to the other spouse or children who have already suffered. The most common judicial reaction to such violations is to find the abusive spouse to be in contempt of court and order him or her not to repeat his or her actions on pain of liability for the victim's attorney fees. While this may be suitable for the attorney, it does the victim little good. Occasionally, the contempt order will threaten the abusive spouse with jail, which is a more effective deterrent.

Because of domestic relations judges' general reluctance to impose strong penalties, the most effective weapon against an abusive spouse is not the TRO, but the Domestic Violence Act,[4] which brings the abusive spouse before the local municipal court judge on a criminal charge, and which is much more likely to result in incarceration. The most complete remedy involves a four-pronged "paper attack" on the abusive spouse: the domestic violence (DV) complaint in municipal court, a DV complaint in domestic relations court, the TRO against violence, and the TRO eviction.

The existence of an ex parte restraining order incident to a divorce action is not a bar to a court issuing a civil protection order under RC 3113.31.[5]

The rule does not authorize the court to evict a husband from the marital premises. This authority has been found by the court to be inherent in the power of injunction, which is the essence of a TRO. Some judges will refuse to grant eviction TROs at all; some will grant them needlessly.

While it is essential to grant them where there is reasonable cause to believe that there may be violence, note that the TRO is granted on an unsubstantiated affidavit, with no need for a hearing on the just cause.

The due process required for cases involving actual violence under the Domestic Violence Act is a higher standard than for cases involving reasonable fear of it in the domestic relations context, which is clearly an inequitable, if not unconstitutional, arrangement. In fact, the legislature has provided a remedial device which can protect both parties. Where there is domestic violence but no contemplated divorce, the domestic violence criminal remedy is available. In some counties, where there is a

---

[4]RC 2919.25 et seq.

[5]Thomas v. Thomas, 44 Ohio App. 3d 6, 540 N.E.2d 745 (10th Dist. Franklin County 1988).

concurrent divorce, the victim's counsel can file a two-count complaint (complaint for divorce and a domestic violence complaint), triggering the Domestic Violence Act and permitting an emergency ex parte TRO, while simultaneously demanding an immediate hearing for the defendant.

If the DV-TRO is granted, the motion for a TRO may be moot. If the DV-TRO is denied, the motion for a TRO would probably also be denied.

When counsel represents a party who is the object of an eviction TRO, he or she should immediately file a motion for a hearing, for modification, vacation, and/or cancellation, and should demand an immediate deposition to prepare for the hearing on the TRO, and to determine whether there are grounds for sanctions under Civil Rule 11 against opposing counsel.[6]

A trial court has no jurisdiction to issue a post-decree temporary restraining order under Civil Rule 65(A) to persons not parties to the action. In *Van Ho v. Van Ho*,[7] the court had tried to restrain a county auditor from making a payment to one of the parties.

§ 25:27 Motions regarding temporary relief—Motion for temporary restraining order—Form⊚

[Title of Court]

[Caption]   Case No. *[_____]*

MOTION FOR TEMPORARY RESTRAINING ORDER

Now comes *[Plaintiff/Defendant]* and respectfully moves this Court for an order restraining *[Plaintiff/Defendant]* during the pendency of this action from selling, mortgaging, moving, destroying, or otherwise disposing of or attempting to dispose of any of the household goods and furnishings, or personal or real property of the parties whether jointly or individually owned until further order of the Court.

Further, *[Plaintiff/Defendant]* moves this Court for an order restraining *[Plaintiff/Defendant]* from molesting, threatening, harassing, or bothering *[him/her]* and from interfering with *[him/her]* at any place or any time during the pendency of this action.

Further, *[Plaintiff/Defendant]* moves this Court for an order restraining *[Plaintiff/Defendant]* from terminating or modifying any policies of insurance, life, health, or otherwise, during the pendency of this action.

Further, *[Plaintiff/Defendant]* moves this Court for an order restraining *[Plaintiff/Defendant]* from removing the *[child/children]* of the parties from the jurisdiction of the Court during the pendency of this action.

[Plaintiff/Defendant] further moves the Court that no bond be

---

[6]See Marital Obligations and Property Rights Ch 4; Domestic Violence Ch 5; Marital and Separate Property Ch 12.

[7]Van Ho v. Van Ho, 17 Ohio App. 3d 108, 477 N.E.2d 659 (3d Dist. Seneca County 1984).

required of *[him / her]*. This motion is supported by the affidavit attached hereto and incorporated herein by reference.

_____

Attorney for *[Plaintiff / Defendant]*

[Affidavit of movant, giving reasons / justification for the motion]

[Proof / certificate of service]

§ 25:28 Motions regarding temporary relief—Motion for temporary spousal support

Whether this motion is labeled "pendente lite" or "temporary spousal support" is not important, so long as it conforms to local custom or rule. It is generally filed with the initial complaint (or counterclaim) for divorce, annulment, or legal separation. When filed with the initial complaint or counterclaim, it is questionable practice to join them together in the same pleading. It may escape immediate processing if so combined. It is better practice to submit these motions separately. Death of a party abates the divorce action and any temporary order.[1] Interlocutory orders are merged with the final decree. Unless there has been a separate judgment on temporary spousal support arrearages or the final decree specifically mentions such amounts, there can be no enforcement of a temporary order subsequent to the final divorce decree.[2]

The motion should have sufficient data to permit the court to make an appropriate determination of need for spousal support, amount necessary, and ability to pay. According to Civil Rule 75(N)(1), this information must be provided by affidavit which may be on a form designed by counsel or on a court-developed form. Either way is adequate, and local custom will control. Note, however, that the rule requires such award to be on the basis of "good cause shown," which highlights the necessity for appropriate data content. As to the possibility of exaggeration, extravagance, or misstatements, petitioner's counsel should be aware of the impact of Civil Rule 11 on misleading or false information.

Also, the provisions of Civil Rule 75(N)(2) permit the filing of counter affidavits within 14 days of the filing of the motion. A court or magistrate can issue an order based solely upon the affidavits. However, upon the request of either party, an oral hearing must be held within 28 days of the journalization of the temporary order.

Again, following general practice, this motion (which is really a motion for support of the spouse and children pendente lite) need not be accompanied by a separate motion for child support, as such amount will generally be included in the total award. In practical effect, it is neither

_____

[Section 25:28]

[1]See Hook v. Hook, 35 Ohio App. 3d 51, 519 N.E.2d 687 (8th Dist. Cuyahoga County 1987) (life insurance proceeds were properly payable to a named beneficiary even though that beneficiary was designated in violation of an ex parte order prohibiting a change during the pendency of the action; order was abated by the insured's death).

[2]Colom v. Colom, 58 Ohio St. 2d 245, 12 Ohio Op. 3d 242, 389 N.E.2d 856 (1979); see also Coad v. Coad, 52 Ohio St. 3d 702, 556 N.E.2d 526 (1990).

exclusively spousal support nor child support, but an award for family support. Civil Rule 75(N), which pertains to spousal support pendente lite, permits such an order to cover custody and support of minor children as well. The motion and affidavit should therefore include a request for such total amount, although tax considerations may influence the allocation.

In those places where ex parte is the practice, defendant/respondent's counsel must be prepared to file an answer affidavit or brief in opposition as soon as possible but, even more important, without waiting for the expiration of the time to answer the complaint or counterclaim. While that latter period is twenty-eight days, it does not change the fourteen-day period provided in Civil Rule 75(N)(2) in which to file an answer affidavit on the temporary spousal support motion.

As a final problem, with respect to a challenge to the award, counsel should be aware of local custom and practice in determining permanent spousal support based on the pendente lite award. In some places, the awards may be parallel, on the theory that the effort to set the pendente lite award should not be duplicated, while in others, there may be a belief that a permanent award deserves much more consideration.[3]

It should be noted that the purpose of temporary alimony is to preserve the status quo between the parties. For example, a court may require a spouse to use his bonus payment to make current the mortgage on the marital residence.[4]

§25:29 Motions regarding temporary relief—Motion for temporary child support

Civil Rule 75(N) provides the domestic relations court with jurisdiction over child support. RC 3109.05 provides authorization for the court to grant child support and a list of standards to be considered in awarding it.

As a practical matter, a motion for spousal support pendente lite usually includes a request for child support. The court can and does consider these requests independently and will generally allocate in the award, not only to avoid objections because of a lack of precision, but also

---

[3]Rahm v. Rahm, 39 Ohio App. 2d 74, 68 Ohio Op. 2d 225, 315 N.E.2d 495 (8th Dist. Cuyahoga County 1974) (authority to grant alimony pendente lite is based on Civ. R. 75); Garnet v. Garnet, 1981 WL 4840 (Ohio Ct. App. 7th Dist. Mahoning County 1981) (temporary custody order not a final order and can be modified without a showing of changed circumstances); Sizemore v. Sizemore, 1981 WL 6560 (Ohio Ct. App. 5th Dist. Delaware County 1981) (temporary alimony award not a final order); Lowman v. Lowman, 98 Ohio App. 254, 57 Ohio Op. 284, 129 N.E.2d 213 (6th Dist. Lucas County 1955) (alimony pendente lite not a final order); Fields v. Fields, 88 Ohio App. 149, 42 Ohio Op. 427, 57 Ohio L. Abs. 225, 94 N.E.2d 7 (8th Dist. Cuyahoga County 1950) (alimony pendente lite not a final order); Englund v. Englund, 92 Ohio App. 527, 50 Ohio Op. 136, 63 Ohio L. Abs. 552, 110 N.E.2d 35 (8th Dist. Cuyahoga County 1952) (not an abuse of discretion to award alimony pendente lite while the parties were still living together). See Marital Obligations and Property Rights Ch 4.

[4]DiLacqua v. DiLacqua, 88 Ohio App. 3d 48, 623 N.E.2d 118 (9th Dist. Summit County 1993).

because there may be significant tax considerations. Further, an award of $100 per week, denominated as spousal support, but which was meant to be half spousal support and half child support, is subject to attack, both for failure to provide for child support and as an excessive spousal support award. Thus, while the motion for temporary spousal support may include a motion for temporary child support, the award pursuant thereto must specify the amount awarded for each.

Temporary spousal and child support awards may be made even though both the payor and payee are residing under the same roof. These orders also should address the payment of fixed household expenses such as mortgage, taxes, interest, insurance, and utilities on the marital home.

§ 25:30   Motions regarding temporary relief—Motion for allocation of parental rights and responsibilities pendente lite

A motion for allocation of parental rights and responsibilities may be filed at any time during the pendency of the domestic relations action, pursuant to Civil Rule 75(N). Where both parties remain in the marital home during the pendency of the action, there is probably no need for a temporary order since everyone is living under one roof. However, where the parties intend to live separate and apart during the pendency of the action, a temporary order should be sought to prevent the children from being shuttled from one home to another or snatched by one parent or the other. As with a permanent order, pursuant to RC 3109.04(A), the sole criterion for a temporary order is what is in the best interest of the children.

The other tactical use of this motion is a slight concession to the judicial practice of adhering to the status quo. Thus, if the allocation of parental rights and responsibilities for the care of minor children is to be an issue, one parent should not leave the marital home, so that the other becomes the de facto "residential parent." Both parents stand on equal footing pursuant to RC 3109.03 as relates to their parental rights and responsibilities for the care of their children.

In theory, a temporary allocation is not a final order, so that in the subsequent final hearing the only consideration is the best interest of the child, rather than changed circumstances, which standard applies when a change of allocation is sought.[1] It is bad practice to rely on this rule, however, because by the time the permanent motion comes on for hearing, the judge will be greatly persuaded by the status quo, i.e., that it is better for the child to remain in the existing stable environment. Practitioners in this field are generally aware that if the time between the temporary order and the final hearing has been prolonged by the temporary residential parent's counsel sufficiently, the status quo will

---

[Section 25:30]

[1]Schoffner v. Schoffner, 19 Ohio App. 3d 208, 483 N.E.2d 1190 (3d Dist. Auglaize County 1984) (change of custody factors is not required for court to change custodian under temporary orders at final hearing).

likely prevail.

Note that where the child has been located and has some stability, however temporary, the courts are reluctant to disturb this apparent stability in order to satisfy parental demands. When the child has been integrated into the home of the temporary residential parent, this may dispose of the allocation of parental rights and responsibilities upon final hearing.[2]

§ 25:31 Motions regarding temporary relief—Motion to vacate temporary order

Civil Rule 60, which deals with relief from judgment, applies only to final orders, judgments, or proceedings; motions under that rule cannot be made when relief is sought from a temporary order because a motion to vacate may be filed. Examples of temporary orders include orders for support, allocation of parental rights and responsibilities, and visitation. The motion would more accurately be styled as one for modification since such issues as support, allocation of parental rights and responsibilities, and visitation are always before the court. It should be noted that a denial of the motion will not be a final order since a temporary, nonfinal order cannot be converted into a final order by filing a motion to vacate it.[1]

§ 25:32 Motions for study and guidance of parties—Motion for psychological evaluation

Pursuant to RC 3109.04(C), where allocation of parental rights and responsibilities is an issue, the court may order the parties and their minor children to submit to medical, psychological, and psychiatric examinations. The report of such examinations must be made available to either party or his counsel of record not less than five days before trial.

A request may also be made under this section for an investigation to be made of the character, family relations, past conduct, earning ability,

---

[2]Garnet v. Garnet, 1981 WL 4840 (Ohio Ct. App. 7th Dist. Mahoning County 1981) (temporary custody order not a final order and can be modified without a showing of changed circumstances); Metro v. Metro, 1981 WL 4968 (Ohio Ct. App. 8th Dist. Cuyahoga County 1981) (where divorce decree resolved the issues of alimony and property settlement but awarded only temporary custody pending psychological evaluation, the order was not a final, appealable one); Spence v. Spence, 2 Ohio App. 3d 280, 441 N.E.2d 822 (10th Dist. Franklin County 1981) (order for custody pendente lite is temporary by its very nature and is subject to modification in the final divorce decree). See also Parental Rights and Shared Parenting Ch 15; Modification of Parental Rights and Responsibilities Ch 16; § 25:28, Motions regarding temporary relief—Motion for temporary spousal support.

[Section 25:31]
[1]Sizemore v. Sizemore, 1981 WL 6560 (Ohio Ct. App. 5th Dist. Delaware County 1981) (no appeal lies from the granting of temporary orders for alimony and child support); See Modification of Spousal Support Ch 14; Modification of Parental Rights and Responsibilities Ch 16; Visitation Ch 18; Child Support Ch 19; Relief from Judgment Ch 24.

and financial worth of the parties. The court's investigation unit makes the investigation and issues a report which must be made available to the parties or counsel not less than five days before trial.

Civil Rule 35(A), as explained by the Sixth District Court of Appeals in *Brossia v. Brossia*,[1] requires that (1) the physical and mental condition of a party or one in a party's custody be in controversy; (2) the order be made for good cause; and (3) the order specify the time, place, manner, conditions, and scope of the examination.

§ 25:33   Motions for study and guidance of parties—Motion for investigation

Where minor children are involved in a domestic relations dispute, RC 3109.04(C) and Civil Rule 75(D) authorize the court to make an investigation as to the character, family relations, past conduct, earning ability, and financial worth of the parties to the action. In some counties this will be done automatically upon the filing of the divorce, annulment, or legal separation action, or modification of the allocation of parental rights and responsibilities motion. In others, it will be necessary to file a formal written motion requesting same. If counsel wants it, it is better practice to file the motion, rather than rely on local custom which, according to "Murphy's law," will not operate at the time expected.

The rule provides that the report of such investigation shall be made available to either party or his or her counsel of record upon written request not less than seven days before trial. The investigator making the report shall be subject to cross-examination by either party.

Counsel should be aware of the precise nature of this investigation, as being a social and environmental history, and not a medical, physical, or psychological examination. Since the investigator is court appointed, there is only one such investigation because the investigator theoretically is neutral as to the parties, in a sense, an "amicus" that either party may examine the investigator "as on cross."

If counsel wishes to have a medical, physical, or psychological examination of the other party, then a motion for such examination is appropriate under Civil Rule 35.[1]

§ 25:34   Motions for study and guidance of parties—Motion for conciliation

RC 3105.091 provides that the court may, sua sponte or upon motion of a party, order the parties to undergo conciliation for a period of up to ninety days. This motion may be filed at any time after thirty days from the date of service in an action for divorce, annulment, or legal separa-

---

[Section 25:32]
[1]Brossia v. Brossia, 65 Ohio App. 3d 211, 583 N.E.2d 978 (6th Dist. Wood County 1989).

[Section 25:33]
[1]See § 15:34, Procedure for allocating parental rights—Investigation and report.

tion or at any time after filing a petition for dissolution. The granting of such a motion stays all proceedings during the pendency of the conciliation efforts.[1]

The statute sets forth the variety of referrals available to the court, that is, to a conciliation judge, if any, appointed pursuant to RC Chapter 3117, plus other named agencies and professionals.

§ 25:35 Motions regarding court proceedings—Motion to advance

It is probably a gross understatement to say that divorce litigants are governed more by emotion than logic. Men and women enmeshed in the painful experience of terminating a marriage, with the attendant legal and nonlegal decisions which must accompany it, often want an almost instant resolution of all their problems. The divorce practitioner is thus more times than not harassed by phone calls, many of which concern nonlegal matters. A question frequently asked is, "When will my case be heard?"

If there is a real need to have the case heard quickly, a motion to advance may be filed.[1] Compelling reasons should be set forth in the motion to convince the court that this particular case should be taken out of order and heard before others.

Civil Rule 75(K) provides that an action for divorce, annulment, or legal separation may not be heard until the expiration of forty-two days after the service of process or twenty-eight days after the last publication of notice of the complaint; nor can such an action be heard earlier than twenty-eight days after service of a counterclaim, unless the plaintiff files a written waiver of said period.

The affidavit and/or brief appended to the motion must demonstrate that the party seeking the relief has a meritorious claim and that the motion was made within a reasonable time.

§ 25:36 Motions regarding court proceedings—Motion to bifurcate

If there are multiple claims or multiple parties, a motion to bifurcate may be filed in a domestic relations action. This motion is, of course, more common in personal injury litigation to separate the issue of liability from damages. In the same way, it is possible to separate the issue of divorce grounds from that of support, allocation of parental rights and responsibilities, visitation, and division of property.

If there is a bifurcation of issues in a domestic relations action, the practitioner must be cognizant of Civil Rule 54(B), which provides that

---

[Section 25:34]
[1]See Mediation and Conciliation Ch 6.

[Section 25:35]
[1]There is no statutory or Civil Rule authority for this type of motion. Local practice or local rules may permit, such as Local Rule 3, Cuyahoga Common Pleas Court, Domestic Relations Division.

if judgment is not rendered on all claims, the order is not a final, appealable one unless the court makes a finding that there is no just cause for delay. Also, the practitioner must be cognizant of Civil Rule 75(F), which provides that for purposes of Civil Rule 54(B), the court shall not enter a final judgment for divorce, dissolution or legal separation unless one of the following applies:

(1) The judgment also divides the property of the parties, determines the appropriateness of an order of spousal support, and, where applicable, either allocates parental rights and responsibilities, including payment of child support, between the parties or orders shared parenting of minor children;

(2) Issues of property division, spousal support, and allocation of parental rights and responsibilities or shared parenting have been finally determined in orders, previously entered by the court, that are incorporated into the judgment;

(3) The court includes in the judgment the express determination required by Civ. R. 54(B) and a final determination that either of the following applies:

(a) The court lacks jurisdiction to determine such issues;

(b) In a legal separation action, the division of the property of the parties would be inappropriate at that time.

There are both advantages and disadvantages to the use of this motion, depending on the circumstances in the case at hand. In an action for divorce, spousal support, and division of property, for instance, assume the defendant requests bifurcation because he or she really believes there are no grounds. If the movant is correct, it would be a great saving of judicial time to litigate the divorce and then, if warranted, litigate the spousal support and property matters, which would most likely involve a lengthy hearing. If the trial is not bifurcated, then all the time spent on RC 3105.171 and RC 3105.18 analyses would be wasted time.

Another appropriate issue for bifurcation is the validity of a antenuptial agreement. Bifurcation should be seriously considered where the validity of a antenuptial agreement would be dispositive of such division of property issues as premarital property and appreciation therein being considered the separate property of the party owning it at the time of marriage.

It does not make sense to request bifurcation where the action is one for divorce and allocation of parental rights and responsibilities, however, because even if the grounds for divorce are denied, the court still has jurisdiction to make an order regarding the children, pursuant to RC 3105.21(B). In this case, it would be better not to bifurcate the matter, since the evidence as to the grounds for divorce would parallel that pertaining to the best interest of the child.

As a tactical matter, if counsel is seeking a divorce on extreme cruelty and is also seeking to be residential parent and legal custodian, he or she would certainly want all the evidence to be presented together, while opposing counsel would want to bifurcate.

If the case were to be tried before a judge who subscribed to the theory that fault is a factor to be considered in awarding spousal support, then the party representing the spouse seeking spousal support would certainly want to present evidence of grounds together with evidence on the spousal support issue, while the other side would certainly want a bifurcation.

Most situations will fall somewhere in between these extreme examples. In many cases, bifurcation may be a good idea for tactical reasons, or for reasons of judicial economy. It should not be dismissed out of hand.[1]

§ 25:37   Motions regarding court proceedings—Motion to consolidate

Occasionally, a party files an action unaware that the other party has filed, service not having been completed. Both cases should be consolidated with the court specifying under which case number it will proceed and whether the other case will be considered a counterclaim.

Where there are a number of motions outstanding, it may be important to have them all consolidated for a single hearing. As a matter of scheduling routine, motions are generally scheduled for hearing as they arrive at the scheduling office. As a result, it is possible to have a number of hearings scattered over time. For example, it is not unusual to have a temporary spousal support order followed by objections and request for hearing, possibly countered by nonpayment, precipitating a show cause. Under the system, each is scheduled in its turn, and likely all will be scheduled for a time after the hearing on the divorce itself.

The practical solution is to request a consolidation of all outstanding motions at the earliest possible time. One cannot merely rely on logic and expect all motions to be heard at the same time. The motion to consolidate, often combined with a motion to advance, is designed to impose logic on the system. Counsel who files this motion should be certain to bring it to the attention of the scheduler, lest it be scheduled for hearing in its turn, after all the other motions pending in the case.

[Section 25:36]
[1]Eligado v. Eligado, 1981 WL 4644 (Ohio Ct. App. 8th Dist. Cuyahoga County 1981) (where decree resolves the issues of divorce and custody but reserves the issues of alimony and child support for a later date, this does not constitute a final, appealable order); Ameritrust Company, Trustee, Etc. v. Wright, 1983 WL 4753 (Ohio Ct. App. 8th Dist. Cuyahoga County 1983) (parties were divorced in 1971, the judgment granting the divorce but bifurcating and reserving the issues of property division, alimony, custody, and support; husband remarried in 1976 and died in 1980; court of appeals found that the judgment granting the divorce was not a final order); Cooley v. Cooley, 1981 WL 5486 (Ohio Ct. App. 6th Dist. Lucas County 1981) (an appeal based on the assertion that a trial was unfair because it took thirteen months to complete the proceedings was denied because there was nothing to demonstrate that appellant was denied a fair hearing even though it took an inordinate amount of time).

§ 25:38   Motions regarding court proceedings—Motion to consolidate motions—Form⊙

[Title of Court]

[Caption]   Case No. *[_____]*
                                 <u>MOTION TO CONSOLIDATE</u>
                                 <u>MOTIONS</u>

[Plaintiff/Defendant] moves this Court to consolidate the motion filed herein on *[date]* by *[Respondent]*, presently scheduled for hearing on *[date and time]* and the motions of the *[other party]*, filed on *[date]* presently scheduled for hearing on *[date and time]*, to permit all motions to proceed on *[date and time]*. Said hearings will require the presence of the same parties and some of the same witnesses, and all matters should be resolved at the same time in the interest of the judicial economy and efficiency.

                 _____

                 Attorney for *[Plaintiff/Defendant]*

[Memorandum in support of motion]

[Proof/certificate of service]

NOTES TO FORM

Drafter's Notes

In most instances, informal contact with the attorney representing the other party, and with the court to assign motions, will be sufficient and the above motion will not be necessary.

Cross Reference

1 Klein and Darling, Baldwin's Ohio Practice, Civil Practice Rule 13

3 Klein and Darling, Baldwin's Ohio Practice, Civil Practice, Ch 7

§ 25:39   Motions regarding court proceedings—Motion to refer to magistrate

Civil Rule 75(C) permits the court to refer matters to a magistrate either on its own motion or on motion of either party. As a practical matter, most courts have established rules of court or rules of custom and practice to refer some or all of the matters that come before them to magistrates. It is difficult to conceive of a situation where counsel would want to use this motion, unless he or she were "forum-shopping."

§ 25:40   Motions regarding court proceedings—Motion to have magistrate expedite

Civil Rule 75(C) indicates that Civil Rule 53 controls proceedings before a magistrate. Prior to the 1995 amendment, Civil Rule 53(D)(1) provided that any party could file a motion requesting the magistrate to expedite the proceedings and/or issue a decision. The 1995 amendment removed this specific language, but Civil Rule 53(D)(1) now provides that all proceedings before a magistrate are to be in accordance with the

Civil Rules and all applicable statutes.

§ 25:41 Motions regarding court proceedings—Motion for findings by court

Even with full use of liberal discovery civil rules and full and extensive trial preparation, an undesirable outcome may result at trial. If this is the case, and an appeal seems indicated, the practitioner should move at once for the trial court to express in writing its findings of fact and conclusions of law, pursuant to Civil Rule 52. The request may be made in any of the various ways described in the rule but must be made prior to journalization of the decree. In this way, a reviewing court will have before it the basis of the trial court's decision. Moreover, Civil Rule 52 is quite clear in its mandate that the court "shall state in writing" its findings, such that failure or refusal to do so is error.

If findings are not requested, a reviewing court may find it difficult to determine the basis for a trial court's decision, particularly where the record may contain conflicting evidence on valuation of assets and other financial data.

When findings are requested, and the court imposes the burden of preparing the findings on the party requesting them,[1] this should never be viewed as a burden by that party, as the one who controls the wording may control the outcome on appeal. An untimely request for Civil Rule 52 findings does not toll the appeal period.[2] The majority of the Seventh District Court of Appeals concluded that a trial court is under no obligation to provide findings of fact and conclusions of law though requested under Civil Rule 52, if the issue was strictly limited to visitation. In *In re Thrush*,[3] Judge Wise, dissenting, suggested that findings would be most helpful to a reviewing court in all domestic matters.

As a tactical matter, where a decision appears to be close, it may be to the advantage of all parties, including the judge, to force a precise evaluation of the evidence by the trier of fact, in order to have the findings necessary to support the judgment.

It should be noted that Civil Rule 53(E)(2) permits the request for Findings of Fact and Conclusions of Law to be made following the decision of a magistrate. If a timely request therefore is made pursuant to Civil Rule 52, the time for the filing of Objections to the magistrate's decision does not begin until an amended magistrate's decision is filed which contains Findings of Fact and Conclusions of law.[4] A magistrate's decision, except in limited circumstances, does not need to contain Findings of Fact and Conclusions of Law unless so requested by a party.

[Section 25:41]

[1]Newman v. Industrial Glove Cleaning Co., 34 Ohio App. 3d 41, 516 N.E.2d 1278 (8th Dist. Cuyahoga County 1986).

[2]Turner v. Turner, 1989 WL 135309 (Ohio Ct. App. 2d Dist. Clark County 1989).

[3]In re Thrush, 44 Ohio App. 3d 40, 541 N.E.2d 119 (5th Dist. Tuscarawas County 1988), cause dismissed, 39 Ohio St. 3d 729, 534 N.E.2d 351 (1988); Hurchanik v. Hurchanik, 1991 WL 69357 (Ohio Ct. App. 12th Dist. Warren County 1991).

[4]Civil Rule 53(E)(3)(a).

Thus, when the hearing is before a magistrate, findings of fact must be made upon request, and appellate rights are preserved should the findings not be supported by the record.

Civil Rule 53 requires that the trial court enter its own judgment even if the trial court is adopting the magistrate's decision. Civil Rule 53(E)(4) provides that a judgment entry made subsequent to a magistrate's decision must show that the trial court entered its own judgment on the issues submitted for action and decision by the magistrate. The entry made by the court must have sufficient detail that the parties can ascertain their rights and obligations by referring to the judgment entry and no other document.[5] The decision of a magistrate becomes effective upon adoption of the decision by the trial court, pursuant to Civil Rule 53(E)(4)(a).

Failure to make a timely request for findings of fact and conclusions of law pursuant to Civil Rule 52 relieves the court of the duty to provide them.[6]

Where properly requested and necessary for appellate court determination, it is error to fail to make findings of fact.[7]

A timely motion for findings of fact and conclusions of law delays the period for filing a notice of appeal until findings and conclusions are filed.[8]

Findings of fact are now required by statute in the following situations:

(1) Where a court does not disburse a spouse's separate property to that spouse;[9]

(2) In any order for the division or disbursement of property or a distributive award to support the determination that the marital property has been equitably divided, and to specify the dates it used in determining the meaning of "during the marriage";[10]

(3) If the court finds that the calculated child support amount pursuant to the guidelines would be unjust or inappropriate and not in the best interest of the child;[11]

(4) If the child has sufficient reasoning ability but due to special circumstances it is not in the best interest of the child to determine the

---

[5]Lavelle v. Cox, 1991 WL 35642 (Ohio Ct. App. 11th Dist. Trumbull County 1991).

[6]Dooley v. Jenkins, 1985 WL 11120 (Ohio Ct. App. 4th Dist. Highland County 1985); Houck v. Houck, 1991 WL 224524 (Ohio Ct. App. 10th Dist. Franklin County 1991).

[7]Hawkins v. Hawkins, 1985 WL 10479 (Ohio Ct. App. 10th Dist. Franklin County 1985). But see Launsbach v. Launsbach, 1988 WL 128237 (Ohio Ct. App. 8th Dist. Cuyahoga County 1988) (trial court did not err in denying request pursuant to Civ. R. 52 when court issued a decision containing a step-by-step evaluation of the case).

[8]Walker v. Doup, 36 Ohio St. 3d 229, 522 N.E.2d 1072 (1988).

[9]RC 3105.171(D).

[10]RC 3105.171(G).

[11]RC 3113.215(B)(2)(c).

child's wishes and concerns regarding allocation of parental rights and responsibilities;[12]

(5) Where the perpetrator of an abusive act against a child nevertheless is being designated a residential parent;[13]

(6) If the court approves a separate plan for allocation of parental rights and responsibilities or denies a request for shared parenting;[14]

(7) When the court approves a plan under this division either as originally filed or with submitted changes or if the court denies the parent's request for shared parenting under this division and proceeds as if the request had not been made;[15]

(8) When the court determines it would not be in the best interest of the child to permit visitation;[16]

(9) When the court denies visitation to a parent who is not the residential parent or denies a motion for companionship and visitation rights brought under RC 3109.051(B) by a relative or other person, and the parent, relative or other person files a request for written findings of fact;[17]

(10) When the court determines that it is in the best interests of the parties to order mediation despite the fact that either parent has been found guilty of or convicted of an abusive act with respect to a family member or household member or other acts or offenses involving a victim who at the time of the commission of the offense was a member of the family or household that is the subject of the proceedings;[18] and

(11) When the trial court deviates from the child support guidelines pursuant to RC 3113.215(B)(1)(b).[19] A trial court must also make factual findings regarding child support even where it does not deviate from the child support guidelines, if requested to do so by a party under Civil Rule 52.[20]

§ 25:42   Motions regarding court proceedings—Motion to continue hearing

A trial court does not err in failing to grant a motion to continue nor in proceeding to hearing without the party or his counsel who sought the continuance. Cuyahoga County Local Rule 3(B) provides in relevant part that "[i]f the motion is not granted by the assigned judge, the case

---

[12]RC 3109.04(B)(2)(b).

[13]RC 3109.04(C).

[14]RC 3109.04(D)(1)(a)(ii).

[15]RC 3109.04(D)(1)(a)(iii).

[16]RC 3109.051(A).

[17]RC 3109.051(F)(1).

[18]RC 3109.052(A).

[19]Johnson v. Johnson, 86 Ohio App. 3d 433, 621 N.E.2d 530 (2d Dist. Greene County 1993).

[20]Johnson v. Emigh, 1993 WL 35667 (Ohio Ct. App. 5th Dist. Stark County 1993).

shall proceed as originally scheduled."[1] Denial of a motion to continue is within the discretion of the court. Where there is no constitutionally protected right to counsel, a motion to continue may be denied even if it requires a litigant to proceed pro se.[2]

Nor does the trial court err in proceeding with a hearing that had been continued by a party when that party claims he or she did not receive actual notice of the rescheduled hearing; it is incumbent upon the party seeking the continuance to apprise him or herself of the rescheduled date.[3]

The doctrine of a motion to continue is within the sound discretion of the trial court and involves a balancing test between the court's interest is controlling its docket and any potential prejudice to the moving party.[4] The factors to be considered by the court are: the length of the requested delay; whether other continuances have been requested and received; the inconvenience to the litigants, witnesses, opposing party and the court, whether the request is for legitimate reasons or is dilatory, purposeful or contrived; whether the moving party contributed to the circumstances which gave rise to the request; and, any other relevant factors.[5]

§ 25:43 Motions by obligee regarding enforcement of judgments—Motion to reduce to judgment

Judgments and awards are not self-executing. The court relies on the party in whose favor the award was made to advise it about compliance or upon the administrative process through the child support enforcement agency.

Continuing support (spousal or child support) is usually enforced by contempt or request for lump-sum judgment. Accrued arrearages are generally brought to the attention of the court by the motion to show cause. The best practice is to join a motion in contempt for failure to comply with a motion for judgment on arrearages and for attorney fees. Multi-branch motions heard at one hearing save both time and money. Whether to request payments on the arrearage or a judgment depends upon the collectibility of a judgment. Of course, the parties can agree, as in any civil action, to a judgment in whatever amount being not subject to execution so long as specified payments are made to reduce the

---

[Section 25:42]

[1]Holop v. Holop, 59 Ohio App. 3d 51, 570 N.E.2d 305 (8th Dist. Cuyahoga County 1989).

[2]Applegate v. Applegate, 2000 WL 1358063 (Ohio Ct. App. 10th Dist. Franklin County 2000), dismissed, appeal not allowed, 91 Ohio St. 3d 1428, 741 N.E.2d 892 (2001).

[3]Freeman v. Freeman, 1993 WL 35326 (Ohio Ct. App. 5th Dist. Fairfield County 1993).

[4]Ham v. Park, 110 Ohio App. 3d 803, 675 N.E.2d 505 (8th Dist. Cuyahoga County 1996).

[5]Ham v. Park, 110 Ohio App. 3d 803, 675 N.E.2d 505 (8th Dist. Cuyahoga County 1996).

judgment.

At the show cause hearing, continuing support payments may be rescheduled and total arrearages determined. The defendant/respondent may be found to be in contempt of court for having been in arrears. Finally, a judgment may be issued. Support orders are judgments when due and interest should be requested in the motion for judgment on the arrears.[1]

Assume, for example, that there is a judgment for an arrearage of $5,000. The object is to get those funds to the payee. In most instances, the funds will not be turned over to the payee merely because of the judgment. Remember that the payor has probably been in contempt of court for quite some time and will not be easily intimidated. If the reason for the contempt/arrearage was lack of funds, obtaining a judgment is not going to solve the problem.

If the reason for the contempt/arrearage was reluctance to pay or outright defiance, a judgment of contempt is not going to suddenly create a model citizen.

To protect the judgment and to make it practically enforceable, the court reduces the arrearage to a money judgment enforceable like any other money judgment. This judgment may also be filed in any state under the full faith and credit doctrine and may be enforced in that other state where the payor resides or has attachable assets.[2]

A judgment may become dormant if not executed upon. A dormant judgment, including one for support arrearages, can be revived within 21 years from the time it became dormant.[3] If the judgment provided for interest, the interest is also revived. Unless there is an agreement to compound interest, it is to be calculated as simple interest. Interest continues to run on a judgment although it is dormant.[4]

§ 25:44 Motions by obligee regarding enforcement of judgments—Motion for order to show cause

This motion would be better denominated "a motion for an order directed to respondent to appear before the court to show cause why he should not be held in contempt of court for violation of a valid court order."

Whether the motion is captioned "motion to show cause" or " motion for contempt" is a matter of local practice. The only noteworthy concern is the practical difficulty involved in putting the full title in the caption.

The motion requests an order directing the respondent to appear. The motion should be accompanied by an entry ordering the alleged contem-

---

[Section 25:43]

[1]Allen v. Allen, 62 Ohio App. 3d 621, 577 N.E.2d 126 (9th Dist. Summit County 1990).

[2]See Enforcement of Spousal and Child Support Ch 20; Interstate and Foreign Support Practice Ch 23.

[3]RC 2325.15.

[4]Ucker v. Ucker, 1999 WL 253439 (Ohio Ct. App. 5th Dist. Fairfield County 1999).

nor to appear on a date and time certain. These orders are issued ex parte upon the accompanying affidavit.

There is no specific rule covering this motion, but Civil Rule 70 permits such motions with respect to real and personal property that was to be delivered to the petitioner, where the respondent has failed to do so. For most common pleas actions, this is probably adequate. For domestic relations matters, however, it causes jurisdictional problems with respect to the enforcement of spousal support, child support, parental rights, and visitation provisions, since it is a post-judgment motion. Contempt motions in domestic matters are brought pursuant to RC 2705.031.

The problem can be easily resolved by viewing the motion as an invocation of the inherent power of a court to enforce its own orders or of the court's continuing jurisdiction under Civil Rule 75(J). Note the essential elements that must be averred in the brief, affidavit, and exhibits that must accompany such a motion. There must be a valid, outstanding court order, the specific act in default must be in the order, and the respondent must be in default. For purposes of this motion, interim orders, such as spousal support and allocation of parental rights and responsibilities pendente lite, restraining orders, etc., are valid and enforceable orders.

Refusal to comply with discovery requests is not punishable by contempt as they are not court orders but interparty matters covered by Civil Rule 37.

If the matter has not reached final judgment, service will be the usual interparty service affidavit by counsel pursuant to Civil Rule 5. The First District Court of Appeals has, however, recently held that a motion for contempt filed during the pendency of the divorce case should be served as a new action and not upon counsel under Civil Rule 5(B).[1] If the matter has reached final judgment, jurisdiction must be obtained by service appropriate for the invocation of continuing jurisdiction pursuant to Civil Rule 75(J). The majority of the Tenth District Court of Appeals concluded, however, that jurisdiction was properly invoked by service on the alleged contemnor's attorney when other post decree motions were pending and the contempt motion was defended.[2]

Once the respondent has been found to be in contempt of court, a judgment entry can be made to that effect. All terms of the contempt, including any purge orders, should be included in the entry.

An order in a contempt case becomes a final appealable order when the court has made a finding of contempt and imposed a sanction.[3]

Assuming that the petitioner's motivation was the failure of the re-

---

[Section 25:44]

[1]Hansen v. Hansen, 132 Ohio App. 3d 795, 726 N.E.2d 557 (1st Dist. Hamilton County 1999).

[2]Kennedy v. Talley, 1999 WL 177565 (Ohio Ct. App. 10th Dist. Franklin County 1999).

[3]Harshbarger v. Harshbarger, 1993 WL 221269 (Ohio Ct. App. 5th Dist. Licking County 1993); but see Ningard v. Ningard, 1993 WL 19592 (Ohio Ct. App. 8th Dist. Cuyahoga County 1993) (order denying attorney fees on show cause motion and failing

spondent to stay current on child or spousal support, a decree of contempt does not solve the problem. In practice, the court should determine the amount of the arrearages and have this recorded as a money judgment, if money was involved, in the contempt judgment. Now the petitioner can proceed to satisfy the judgment unless respondent is judgment-proof.

Where the contempt is for violation of parental rights and responsibilities or visitation orders, petitioner should suggest a proposed solution to the problem that can be incorporated into the contempt judgment. A finding of contempt will not automatically resolve the problem.

Other show cause motions should include proposed remedies or should be accompanied by simultaneous motions suggesting revisions in the order.[4]

Punishment for multiple violations heard in one proceeding is limited to one jail sentence or one fine of up to the statutory amount or both. However, the number of different contempt actions that may be brought is not limited.[5]

The movant need only show failure of compliance with a valid court order. Proof of intent to violate a court order is not a prerequisite to a finding of civil contempt. The burden of proving the defense of inability to comply is on the party asserting it.[6]

Intentional disregard of a court order is not a prerequisite for a finding of civil contempt.

---

to find contempt because motion to show cause premature was not a final appealable order).

[4]Flatter v. Flatter, 71 Ohio L. Abs. 89, 130 N.E.2d 145 (Ct. App. 2d Dist. Darke County 1954) (a motion for contempt dismissed where husband had failed to obey order to pay certain debts and hold wife harmless, because there was no evidence that wife had been called upon to pay debts in question); Fredericks v. Fredericks, 76 Ohio L. Abs. 296, 146 N.E.2d 153 (Ct. App. 7th Dist. Columbiana County 1956) (husband not in contempt for failure to pay amount ordered where wife showed that she had been called upon to pay the debt); Phillips, Nka Carter v. Phillips, 1982 WL 2312 (Ohio Ct. App. 8th Dist. Cuyahoga County 1982); McGill v. McGill, 3 Ohio App. 3d 455, 445 N.E.2d 1163 (2d Dist. Montgomery County 1982) (case includes discussion of civil and criminal contempt, imprisonment for contempt, and application of statutory contempt procedure); Rahm v. Rahm, 39 Ohio App. 2d 74, 68 Ohio Op. 2d 225, 315 N.E.2d 495 (8th Dist. Cuyahoga County 1974) (motion to show cause is not proper vehicle for obtaining alimony pending appeal); Wood v. Wood, 1982 WL 6563 (Ohio Ct. App. 6th Dist. Lucas County 1982) (where bureau of support begins contempt proceedings without giving statutorily required notice, proceedings are void.). See also Enforcement of Spousal and Child Support Ch 20; §§ 25:43–25:53, Motions by obligee regarding enforcement of judgments.

[5]Pugh v. Pugh, 15 Ohio St. 3d 136, 472 N.E.2d 1085 (1984). For the penalties in effect for contempt, see RC 2705.05, as amended by 1986 H.B. 509, eff. 12-1-86.

[6]Pugh v. Pugh, 15 Ohio St. 3d 136, 472 N.E.2d 1085 (1984). For the penalties in effect for contempt, see RC 2705.05, as amended by 1986 H.B. 509, eff. 12-1-86.

§ 25:45   Motions by obligee regarding enforcement of judgments—Motion to show cause—Form⊛

[Title of Court]

[Caption]   Case No. *[_____]*

MOTION TO SHOW CAUSE

Now comes *[Plaintiff/Defendant]*, by and through *[his/her]* counsel, and respectfully moves this Court for an order requiring *[Defendant/Plaintiff]* to appear before it and show cause why *[he/she]* should not be held in contempt for failing to comply with the Court's order regarding *[describe prior order]*, as is more fully set forth in the affidavit of *[Plaintiff/Defendant]* attached hereto and incorporated herein by reference.

[Plaintiff/Defendant] further moves the Court for an award of attorney fees, in the amount of *[$_____]*, same being the amount *[Plaintiff/Defendant]* has incurred as expenses in *[his/her]* efforts to enforce the Court's order of *[date]* as is more fully set forth in the affidavit of movant's counsel which is attached hereto and incorporated herein by reference.]

or

[Plaintiff/Defendant] further moves the Court for an award of attorney fees in an amount to be ascertained at hearing, incurred by *[Plaintiff/Defendant]* in enforcing this Court's order.]

_____

Attorney for *[Plaintiff/Defendant]*

[Notice of hearing]

[EXHIBIT "A"—Affidavit of movant, describing court's prior order and *[Defendant's/Plaintiff's]* noncompliance]

[EXHIBIT "B"—Affidavit of movant's counsel, explaining fees and expenses incurred]

[Proof/certificate of service]

NOTES TO FORM

Drafter's Notes

This motion may be combined with other motions, including a request for interest on unpaid support amounts if the contempt relates to support, motion for judgment on arrearages, and motion for modification.

Consult your local court rules for joinder of motions with separate branches.

§ 25:46   Motions by obligee regarding enforcement of judgments—Judgment entry and order to appear and show cause—Form⊛

[Title of Court]

[Caption]   Case No. *[_____]*

JUDGMENT ENTRY

This day this cause came on to be heard upon the Motion of *[name of movant]* for an order requiring *[Respondent]* to appear personally before this Court to show cause why *[he/she]* should not be punished for failure to comply with the former order of this Court. The Court, being fully advised in the premises, finds said Motion well taken and hereby sustains the same.

IT IS THEREFORE ORDERED, ADJUDGED, AND DECREED that *[Respondent]* appear personally before *[name of judge]* at *[address]* on *[date]* at *[time]* to show cause why *[he/she]* should not be punished for failure to comply with the former order of this Court.

_____
                                              Judge

APPROVED:

_____

Attorney for Movant

NOTES TO FORM

Drafter's Notes

The entry should be filed with the motion in contempt/to show cause and the affidavit in support of it.

Where the alleged contumacious behavior is failure to pay any support or comply with a visitation order, the court must also issue a summons with statutory notice (RC 2705.031(C)).

§ 25:47 Motions by obligee regarding enforcement of judgments—Judgment entry and order finding contempt—Form⊚

[Title of Court]

[Caption]   Case No. *[_____]*

JUDGMENT ENTRY

This cause came before the Court on *[date]* for an order finding *[name of party]* in contempt of a prior order of Court.

[Both parties appeared, represented by counsel./The Court advised *[Respondent]* who was unrepresented and waived the right to counsel.]

Wherefore, the Court finds the motion is well taken and finds that: *[Contemnor]* has failed to comply with a prior order of Court requiring *[him/her]* to *[describe prior order]* and is in contempt of this Court's order.

[Wherefore it is ordered that *[Respondent]* is sentenced to *[_____]* days in the county jail, such sentence to be suspended if *[Respondent]*[*describe action required to purge action]*.]

or

[Respondent] is fined *[$_____]*.]

[Respondent] shall purge *[himself/herself]* of said contempt by *[de-*

scribe action required to purge action, i.e., paying all arrearages within fourteen days, etc.], and attorney fees incurred by *[_____]* in the amount of *[$_____]* to be paid to *[Plaintiff/Defendant]* within fourteen days.

_____
Judge

Approved:

_____
Attorney for Movant

NOTES TO FORM

Drafter's Notes

This form is applicable where the contemnor appears at the hearing on the motion in contempt/to show cause.

§ 25:48 Motions by obligee regarding enforcement of judgments—Motion for capias

Where there has been an order or entry to appear, personally served upon the alleged contemnor, based upon a motion in contempt supported by an affidavit, and the alleged contemnor does not appear at the hearing, the court may issue a capias for his appearance. Obviously, this is an extreme remedy and would be used after other forms of reason have failed to curb the defendant/respondent's contumacious behavior.

The use of the capias by a domestic relations court may be the only way of insuring the presence of the contemnor who fails to appear after having due notice.[1]

Whether the local deputy sheriff will execute the capias with much effort depends upon the locale. However, if a person is stopped for a traffic offense and the outstanding warrant is noted, the person may find himself in jail without a scheduled bond.

§ 25:49 Motions by obligee regarding enforcement of judgments—Judgment entry to issue capias—Form⊛

[Title of Court]

[Caption]   Case No. *[_____]*
                                     JUDGMENT ENTRY

This cause came before the Court on *[date]* at *[time]* on the motion of *[Plaintiff/Defendant]* for a finding of contempt against *[Respondent]* and the order of the court requiring *[Respondent]* to appear. Said *[Respondent]* having been personally served with said order to appear and having failed to appear as ordered, it is hereby ORDERED that a capias issue for the arrest of *[Respondent]*.

_____

[Section 25:48]

[1]See § 25:49, Motions by obligee regarding enforcement of judgments—Judgment entry to issue capias—Form.

_____

                                        Judge

Approved:

_____

Attorney for Movant

NOTES TO FORM

Drafter's Notes

Instructions for service should be filed with the clerk's office when the entry is filed.

This form is applicable when the contemnor disregards the order to appear at the hearing on the motion in contempt/to show cause.

§ 25:50 Motions by obligee regarding enforcement of judgments—Motion for order enforcing judgment by specific act

Where property was ordered to be sold or conveyed in the decree, and there has been a failure to comply or perform a specific act, a motion pursuant to Civil Rule 70 can accomplish the deed. The court may decree the act be done by some other person appointed by the court or may enter judgment divesting the title of a party and vesting it in others. Typically, this relates to automobiles and real estate.

When property is to be sold, the court may appoint someone to cause the sale. Civil Rule 70, and not a partition action, is the proper method of enforcing decree provisions for sale and distribution of proceeds.[1]

An order of the trial court enforcing an order of divorce, or the terms thereof, does not constitute a modification and will not violate Ohio law prohibiting the trial court from modifying a judgment which is the subject of a judgment on appeal.[2]

A trial court's order of sale of marital assets at public auction was not an abuse of discretion where the spouse made no attempts at private sale over the course of many months and thwarted efforts to have the property appraised and assessed.[3]

§ 25:51 Motions by obligor regarding enforcement of judgments—Motion for relief from judgment

Civil Rule 60(B) provides that upon motion made and on such terms as are just, a court may relieve a party from a final judgment or order. The grounds for relief from judgment, as stated in the rule, include (1) mistake, inadvertence, surprise or excusable neglect, (2) newly

_____

[Section 25:50]

[1]Hagensick v. Hagensick, 1985 WL 10496 (Ohio Ct. App. 10th Dist. Franklin County 1985).

[2]Bartak v. Bartak, 1993 WL 311375 (Ohio Ct. App. 8th Dist. Cuyahoga County 1993).

[3]Winkler v. Winkler, 117 Ohio App. 3d 247, 690 N.E.2d 109 (7th Dist. Monroe County 1997).

discovered evidence which by due diligence could not have been discovered in time to move for a new trial under Civil Rule 59(B), (3) fraud or misrepresentation, (4) that it is no longer equitable that the judgment have prospective application, and (5) another reason for relief from judgment. The rule further provides that the motion must be made within a reasonable time and, for grounds under Civil Rule 60(B)(1), (2), and (3), that it must be filed within a year after entry of the judgment.

An attorney's failure to represent a client adequately is not grounds for relief under Civil Rule 60(B).[1] The failure of a court to give a party notice of judgment is a sufficient basis for granting a Civil Rule 60(B) motion.[2]

This motion is frequently used where one party has not been represented by counsel and upon reflection feels that he or she has been at a disadvantage in the proceedings. However, in-court settlement agreements do not have to be equitable or fair;[3] and will ordinarily not be vacated except upon a showing of fraud, duress, overreaching or undue influence in the procurement thereof.[4]

This motion may also be used where assets, hidden at the time of the divorce, are subsequently discovered, on the theory that those assets have never been subject to court scrutiny or order.

Courts have held that the failure of a spouse to fully or falsely disclose the nature, extent and value of his or her assets may provide grounds for relief from judgment under Civil Rule 60(B)(5).[5] Also, the Ohio Supreme Court has repeatedly held that the provisions of Civil Rule 60(B)(4) are applicable only when events subsequent to the judgment for which the moving party had no opportunity to foresee or control make the judgment inequitable.[6]

Requested relief can range from slight modification of the judgment to vacation of it. This motion is most commonly used to seek relief from continuing spousal support and child-related orders. Civil Rule 60(B)(4) provides that the motion is appropriate where "it is no longer equitable

---

[Section 25:51]

[1]Snyder v. Snyder, 1992 WL 14946 (Ohio Ct. App. 8th Dist. Cuyahoga County 1992).

[2]Connolly v. Connolly, 70 Ohio App. 3d 738, 591 N.E.2d 1362 (8th Dist. Cuyahoga County 1990).

[3]Walther v. Walther, 102 Ohio App. 3d 378, 657 N.E.2d 332 (1st Dist. Hamilton County 1995).

[4]Proctor v. Proctor, 122 Ohio App. 3d 56, 701 N.E.2d 36 (3d Dist. Allen County 1997). See also "The Enforceability of Settlement Agreements (In-Court Agreements)" and "A closer Look at Separation Agreement and Settlement Agreements in Divorce and Dissolution Proceedings" by Andrew A. Zashin, Esq., Domestic Relations Journal of Ohio, Volume 13, Issues 1 and 6.

[5]Lanzara v. Lanzara, 2000 WL 336540 (Ohio Ct. App. 8th Dist. Cuyahoga County 2000).

[6]Knapp v. Knapp, 24 Ohio St. 3d 141, 493 N.E.2d 1353 (1986); Crouser v. Crouser, 39 Ohio St. 3d 177, 529 N.E.2d 1251 (1988); Cuyahoga Support Enforcement Agency v. Guthrie, 84 Ohio St. 3d 437, 1999-Ohio-362, 705 N.E.2d 318 (1999).

that the judgment should have prospective application."[7]

§ 25:52 Motions by obligor regarding enforcement of judgments—Motion for relief pending appeal

A judgment is only effective when journalized. A trial court may not punish a party for failure to comply with a decision that is not yet legally binding.[1]

After judgment, a party may move for a stay of execution on provisions in the judgment relating to divorce or division of property. Pursuant to Civil Rule 75(H), however, spousal support, allocation of parental rights and responsibilities, and child support may not be stayed.

The substantive equivalent of a stay for these matters can be achieved by filing a motion for relief pending appeal pursuant to Civil Rule 75(H), which permits the trial judge to make any orders (including modification) pending appeal, and additionally permits the appellate court to make similar orders, and to modify or vacate the trial court's order. Note that this motion must be filed first in the trial court, either before or after the filing of the notice of appeal and that it is subject to all rules governing motions in general.[2] A motion filed with the appellate court must disclose what occurred in the trial court regarding the relief requested.

The filing of a motion for temporary spousal support prior to the filing of a notice of appeal properly will invoke the continuing jurisdiction of the lower court on the issue of spousal support after an appeal is filed.[3]

As a practical matter, the trial judge making the initial determination with respect to the modification sought may not be particularly receptive to a request for an immediate modification of his or her own order.

---

[7]Stuart v. Stuart, 1982 WL 2308 (Ohio Ct. App. 8th Dist. Cuyahoga County 1982) (neither a motion for reconsideration nor a motion under Civ. R. 60(B) stays the thirty-day time to appeal); Curtis v. Curtis, No. 42076 (Ohio Ct. App. 8th Dist. Cuyahoga County 1980) (motion for relief from judgment under Civ. R. 60(B) cannot be used as substitute for appeal where appeal was not perfected within thirty days); Caruso-Ciresi, Inc. v. Lohman, 5 Ohio St. 3d 64, 448 N.E.2d 1365 (1983) (Civ. R. 60(B)(5) is not to be used as substitute for any of the more specific provisions of Civ. R. 60(B); grounds for invoking Civ. R. 60(B)(5) should be substantial); Adomeit v. Baltimore, 39 Ohio App. 2d 97, 68 Ohio Op. 2d 251, 316 N.E.2d 469 (8th Dist. Cuyahoga County 1974) (mere filing of a motion does not guarantee requested relief, nor even a hearing, unless accompanying brief establishes a prima facie case for relief); Coulson v. Coulson, 5 Ohio St. 3d 12, 448 N.E.2d 809 (1983) (if movant files a motion under Civ. R. 60(B), with allegations of facts which would warrant relief, the court should grant a hearing on the motion). See also Relief From Judgment Ch 24.

[Section 25:52]
[1]Evans v. Cole, 2001 -Ohio- 2486, 2001 WL 688594 (Ohio Ct. App. 4th Dist. Jackson County 2001).

[2]Civ. R. 75(H), as amended eff. 7-1-98.

[3]Wittine v. Wittine, 1993 WL 172965 (Ohio Ct. App. 8th Dist. Cuyahoga County 1993).

§ 25:53   Motions by obligor regarding enforcement of judgments—Motion for stay of execution

The use of this motion in domestic relations matters is governed by Civil Rule 75(H), which expressly states that it does not apply to matters of allocation of parental rights and responsibilities, child support, and spousal support, and that the correct procedure in these matters is the motion for relief pending appeal.

§ 25:54   Post-decree motions—Motion for new trial

A motion for a new trial under Civil Rule 59 must be served not later than fourteen days after the entry of judgment. While there are numerous grounds for this motion, few are applicable to domestic relations actions. The only ones which have application are irregularity in the proceedings, accident or surprise, weight of the evidence, judgment contrary to law, newly discovered evidence, and errors of law occurring at the trial. The motion should contain a detailed brief and/or affidavit setting forth the reasons why the new trial should be granted.

A motion for new trial under Civil Rule 59 is properly granted on the grounds of new evidence where subsequent to trial but prior to judgment a party is injured, thus substantially lowering his earning capacity and thus his ability to pay nonmodifiable alimony.[1] Courts have held that it is an abuse of discretion to deny a Motion for New Trial when changed circumstances have occurred which substantially affects a spouse's earning capacity between the lengthy period between a trial and a judgment.[2]

While normally there is little chance that the same judge who just conducted the trial is going to do all or part of it over again, at least the filing of the motion serves to stay the time for filing a notice of appeal. Thus, even if the motion is not granted, the movant gains valuable time to regroup and perhaps negotiate a settlement rather than face the time and expense of an appeal.[3]

The granting of a motion for new trial is a final appealable order.[4]

Filing a motion for a new trial is not a condition precedent to the fil-

---

[Section 25:54]

[1]Marksbury v. Marksbury, 46 Ohio App. 3d 17, 545 N.E.2d 651 (6th Dist. Erie County 1988).

[2]Knox v. Knox, 26 Ohio App. 3d 17, 498 N.E.2d 236 (5th Dist. Stark County 1986); Bender v. Bender, 1994 WL 149247 (Ohio Ct. App. 9th Dist. Medina County 1994).

[3]Klump v. Klump, 96 Ohio App. 93, 54 Ohio Op. 202, 121 N.E.2d 273 (6th Dist. Lucas County 1954) (new trial was ordered where defendant's testimony was false and misleading); Schindler v. Schindler, 49 Ohio L. Abs. 476, 77 N.E.2d 363 (Ct. App. 7th Dist. Geauga County 1947) (motion for new trial must be timely filed or reviewing court will be precluded from reviewing evidence); Schwenk v. Schwenk, 2 Ohio App. 3d 250, 441 N.E.2d 631 (8th Dist. Cuyahoga County 1982) (motion for new trial was denied where newly discovered evidence occurred after trial but before judgment was entered).

[4]Nelson v. Nelson, 1992 WL 125234 (Ohio Ct. App. 8th Dist. Cuyahoga County 1992).

ing of a notice of appeal.[5]

§ 25:55 Post-decree motions—Motion for continuing jurisdiction

Civil Rule 75(J) states that the continuing jurisdiction of the court may be invoked by a motion filed in the original action. This simple statement needs translation. Assuming that the original action has already gone to judgment, one party is requesting the court to enforce or modify that judgment. The case is reopened by motion rather than by a new filing. The motion presumes that a court has continuing jurisdiction to modify its own decrees. Relief may also be sought through a Civil Rule 60(B) motion, which follows this same procedure.

Use of the term "in the original action" merely means that the movant shall use the original captions and case number and, in a multi-judge court, the same judge.

No separate motion needs to be filed other than the motion for enforcement or relief. That motion is construed to be the invocation of the court's continuing jurisdiction. If counsel wishes to be more formal, an additional sentence requesting such continuing jurisdiction can be added to the motion, such as: "Now comes Petitioner Paul A. White and invokes the continuing jurisdiction of this court, and moves this court for an order."

The complicated aspect of this motion involves service of process. While motions are usually sent to opposing counsel by regular or certified mail (Civil Rule 5), the procedure here is slightly different. As a matter of courtesy, a copy may be sent to the former counsel.

The court in *Rondy v. Rondy*[1] found that "the continuing jurisdiction of the court cannot be properly invoked by motion pursuant to Civ. R. 75(J) in the absence of service of notice on the opposing party. . . . Lacking such jurisdiction, the court is without power to issue a valid, binding judgment."

Where a post-decree movant fails to serve the other party with a copy of the motion, pursuant to Civil Rule 75(J), the court does not acquire continuing jurisdiction and any action taken on the motion is a nullity.[2] Service on a party's attorney is insufficient to invoke jurisdiction.[3]

---

[5]Dunn v. Westlake, 61 Ohio St. 3d 102, 573 N.E.2d 84 (1991).

[Section 25:55]

[1]Rondy v. Rondy, 13 Ohio App. 3d 19, 22, 468 N.E.2d 81 (9th Dist. Summit County 1983)(footnote omitted)(no notice of motions to modify support or hearings on motions).

[2]Hansen v. Hansen, 21 Ohio App. 3d 216, 486 N.E.2d 1252 (3d Dist. Seneca County 1985) (father's motion to change custody never served on mother, court granted motion erroneously).

[3]Szymczak v. Szymczak, 136 Ohio App. 3d 706, 737 N.E.2d 980 (8th Dist. Cuyahoga County 2000) (But see dissenting opinion which would have held wife waived objection of improper service by participating in the process and accepting benefits therefrom).

Following *Yonally v. Yonally*,[4] the Second District Court of Appeals in *Price v. Price*[5] held that continuing jurisdiction is not invoked under Civil Rule 75(I) where a motion is served by a means other than those specified in Civil Rule 4 to 4.6. Since service of process is jurisdictional, there is a lack of jurisdiction to act where it is not made in accordance with the rule.

In *Price*, the plaintiff-appellee's attorney served the defendant-appellant by certified mail. Civil Rule 4.1 provides for service by certified mail by the clerk of courts. If the return receipt shows that a party has received the certified mail, due process has been satisfied.

§ 25:56 Post-decree motions—Motion to modify

This is usually a post-decree motion filed for the modification of spousal or child support, allocation of parental rights and responsibilities, or visitation arrangements.

The motion must allege that a change in circumstances since the date of the final order sought to be modified makes that order no longer fair and equitable, and, in the case of allocation of parental rights and responsibilities and visitation, no longer in the best interest of the children.

In a request for modification of child support, the affidavit should contain allegations that the earnings of the obligor have increased and that the needs of the obligee and the minor children have likewise increased.

RC 3109.05 indicates that, in cases where the residential parent interferes with the visitation rights of the other parent, the order may be modified, thus resolving the matter of the proper motion to address that issue.

§ 25:57 Motions regarding attorneys—Motion for attorney fees

Generally, attorney fees are considered an aspect of spousal support.[1] A motion for attorney fees as additional spousal support may be made pendente lite pursuant to Civil Rule 75(N) and RC 3105.18(H), or at final hearing. When representing the wife, the request for attorney fees is normally included as part of the relief requested in the complaint. A domestic relations court does not have jurisdiction to award attorney fees to an attorney from his client.[2] A separate action must be

---

[4]Yonally v. Yonally, 45 Ohio App. 2d 122, 74 Ohio Op. 2d 134, 341 N.E.2d 602 (9th Dist. Summit County 1974).

[5]Price v. Price, 1985 WL 7633 (Ohio Ct. App. 2d Dist. Miami County 1985).

[Section 25:57]

[1]Munroe v. Munroe, 119 Ohio App. 3d 530, 695 N.E.2d 1155 (8th Dist. Cuyahoga County 1997).

[2]Zeefe v. Zeefe, 125 Ohio App. 3d 600, 709 N.E.2d 208 (8th Dist. Cuyahoga County 1998).

commenced.[3]

A two-pronged test has been established for the granting of attorney fees as spousal support in divorce cases. First, the award must be justified under the fourteen factors set forth in RC 3105.18. Second, the guidelines set forth in D.R. 2-106(B) of the Code of Professional Responsibility must be followed. Thus, the movant should be prepared to introduce into evidence carefully prepared time records indicating the precise nature of the services performed and the time spent. There may also be testimony by a corroborating witness, possibly a domestic relations practitioner, as to the validity of the services rendered and the reasonable value thereof.[4]

An order for payment of attorney fees is reversible error where no evidence is presented regarding the amount of the fees.[5]

It is good practice to include an affidavit detailing the hours, fee rate, and nature of the services performed, as well as an affidavit of the moving party that such liability was incurred (or paid). It would be better if not paid, since, if paid, it may be evidence of a lack of need. It is ironic that time must be put into a case and mere fees generated in order to support a claim for them.

The object here is to request the fees pursuant to RC 3105.18(H), which now provides a legal basis for payment of attorney fees. Interestingly, some attorneys insert in the judgment a clause which provides that such sum shall be paid directly to the attorney. This is reversible error.[6] Since there is a question as to whether such a judgment/order is a valid order, it would be better not to place such clause in the judgment/order. The general rule of "no spousal support, no fees" used to come into play here since the court was consistent in seeing that fees were awarded only as spousal support. Fees in pendente lite matters can be justified as part of the marital support obligation, whether the case is dismissed or not. In post-judgment situations, they are also available as necessary for enforcement of child and spousal support, child-related issues, and failure to transfer property.[7] RC 3109.05(C) statutorily requires the court, upon finding a contempt for failure to pay child sup-

---

[3]Maloof v. Hollingsworth, 1999 WL 1087492 (Ohio Ct. App. 8th Dist. Cuyahoga County 1999).

[4]Humphrey v. Humphrey, 2002-Ohio-3121, 2002 WL 1357108 (Ohio Ct. App. 11th Dist. Ashtabula County 2002), citing Swanson v. Swanson, 48 Ohio App. 2d 85, 2 Ohio Op. 3d 65, 355 N.E.2d 894 (8th Dist. Cuyahoga County 1976).

[5]Harshbarger v. Harshbarger, 1993 WL 221269 (Ohio Ct. App. 5th Dist. Licking County 1993). But see Gearig v. Gearig, 1993 WL 93525 (Ohio Ct. App. 6th Dist. Lucas County 1993) (trial court may award attorney fees using its own knowledge and experience to determine necessity for and reasonableness of fees without any testimony offered concerning fees). McCoy v. McCoy, 91 Ohio App. 3d 570, 632 N.E.2d 1358 (8th Dist. Cuyahoga County 1993) (holding that trial court is precluded from determining the reasonableness of a requested attorney fee when the party's attorney provides no evidence to the court showing the nature of the services rendered, the difficulty of the services performed or any other required information).

[6]Stout v. Stout, 3 Ohio App. 3d 279, 445 N.E.2d 253 (1st Dist. Hamilton County 1982) (attorney fees must be paid to defendant rather than defendant's attorney).

[7]RC 3105.18(G), RC 3109.05(C), RC 3109.051(K).

port, to "assess all court costs . . . and require the person to pay any reasonable fees of any adverse party." RC 3105.18(G) makes the same provision with respect to spousal support, and RC 3109.051(K) applies to failure to comply with visitation.

Attorney fees are a frequently contested issue in both original proceedings and subsequent actions to modify or enforce decrees.

The provisions of Section 3105.18(H) specifically require a showing as to whether either party will be prevented from fully litigating that party's rights and protecting that party's interests if [the court] does not award reasonable attorney fees. Therefore, the payment of attorney fees is normally the function of the party who retains the attorney.[8]

Additionally, compare *Demo v. Demo*,[9] where the court found that the wife was able to litigate her rights and to protect her interests without an award of attorney fees, with *Glick v. Glick*,[10] where the court held that the wife was not able to litigate her rights and protect her interests without an attorney fee award.

Moreover, an award of attorney fees cannot be based solely upon an inability of a party to pay his or her attorney fees.[11] Rather, it must be determined that the other party has the ability to pay an award.[12]

Finally, an attorney fee award cannot be computed by a mechanical computation of multiplying the number of hours expended by the attorney's hourly rate.[13]

Rather, a court must consider many factors in determining a reasonable award of attorney fees, including those established by the Ohio Supreme Court in Disciplinary Rule 2-106(B).[14]

§ 25:58 Motions regarding attorneys—Motion for leave to withdraw

Most attorney-client relationships are terminated like other agency relationships, by mutual or unilateral action. Sometimes, a party may not want to permit a counsel to withdraw and may refuse to recognize attempted withdrawal. This leaves the attorney in a predicament.

If the withdrawal is prior to any scheduled hearings, a motion to

---

[8]Bowen v. Bowen, 132 Ohio App. 3d 616, 725 N.E.2d 1165 (9th Dist. Medina County 1999), dismissed, appeal not allowed, 86 Ohio St. 3d 1402, 711 N.E.2d 231 (1999).

[9]Demo v. Demo, 101 Ohio App. 3d 383, 655 N.E.2d 791 (12th Dist. Butler County 1995).

[10]Glick v. Glick, 133 Ohio App. 3d 821, 729 N.E.2d 1244 (8th Dist. Cuyahoga County 1999).

[11]Layne v. Layne, 83 Ohio App. 3d 559, 615 N.E.2d 332 (2d Dist. Champaign County 1992).

[12]Shaffer v. Shaffer, 109 Ohio App. 3d 205, 671 N.E.2d 1317 (3d Dist. Crawford County 1996).

[13]Farley v. Farley, 97 Ohio App. 3d 351, 646 N.E.2d 875 (8th Dist. Cuyahoga County 1994).

[14]See Farley v. Farley, 97 Ohio App. 3d 351, 646 N.E.2d 875 (8th Dist. Cuyahoga County 1994); citing Swanson v. Swanson, 48 Ohio App. 2d 85, 2 Ohio Op. 3d 65, 355 N.E.2d 894 (8th Dist. Cuyahoga County 1976), supra.

withdraw filed with the court, copies to the party and opposing counsel, should suffice to terminate the relationship. However, if matters are at a sensitive point, i.e., in the middle of a hearing, the judge may refuse to grant the motion.

Local rules may also regulate an attorney's motion to withdraw in terms of timing, procedure, or both. The Twelfth District Court of Appeals held that a trial court erred when it granted a motion to withdraw filed less than one week prior to trial, and then refused to grant a continuance of that trial. Butler County Local Domestic Relations Rule 28 provides that a court may not grant a motion to withdraw within 30 days of a scheduled trial, absent extraordinary circumstances. While the trial court found that the attorney had good cause to withdraw, the court failed to find extraordinary circumstances as required by the local rule. Its refusal to continue the trial where appellant had arranged to meet with and retain new counsel was also held to be in error.

In *Stratton v. Stratton*,[1] the trial court erred and abused its discretion by granting appellant's counsel leave to withdraw and one week later denying appellant's motion for a continuance of a trial. A Local Rule of Butler County requires a showing of extraordinary circumstances before the court shall grant an attorney permission to withdraw within 30 days of a scheduled trial. The combined actions of the court in granting the withdrawal but denying a continuance were an abuse of discretion. However, the Sixth District Court of Appeals in *Teresa S. v. Sylvester W.*[2] held that the trial court did not err by allowing counsel to withdraw and then refusing to continue a hearing where the party failed to appear or provide sufficient evidence of an inability to attend.

§ 25:59   Miscellaneous motions—Motion to vacate premises

This is a very involved procedure. As an eviction procedure, it is founded on RC 3103.04, which states in relevant part, "Neither can be excluded from the other's dwelling, except upon a decree or order of injunction made by a court of competent jurisdiction."

Note first of all that this is the marital rights statute and not the divorce statute. Note too that it applies to eviction from the other's dwelling, not the defendant's own dwelling. By custom and tradition, in some counties, a plaintiff-wife usually filed a motion to vacate against the defendant-husband, which was customarily granted ex parte. The procedure for eviction now requires more than an ex parte order and generally requires a hearing. In spite of these changes, eviction tends not to be a viable remedy for a husband but is generally used only by the wife.

This motion does not affect ownership of real property in any way, as the statute refers only to the other spouse's dwelling, not to ownership

---

[Section 25:58]

[1]Stratton v. Stratton, 1998 WL 372394 (Ohio Ct. App. 12th Dist. Butler County 1998).

[2]Teresa S. v. Sylvester W., 1999 WL 316896 (Ohio Ct. App. 6th Dist. Lucas County 1999).

or title. Also, whether it is owned, rented, or leased is irrelevant, as long as it is the dwelling.

It should be noted that Cuyahoga County Court of Common Pleas, Division of Domestic Relations, Local Rule 22(C) permits the issuance of an ex parte restraining order preventing a party from returning to the marital residence if the opposing party has been absent therefrom for more than 30 continuing days.

§ 25:60 Miscellaneous motions—Motion to vacate premises—Form⊙

[Title of Court]

[Caption]   Case No. *[_____]*
                                                    MOTION TO VACATE

Now comes Plaintiff and moves this Court for an order requiring Defendant to vacate the premises at *[address]* and to present the key of said residence to Plaintiff and that Defendant be enjoined from entering or attempting to enter said premises or interfering with Plaintiff's exclusive use and occupancy of the home during the pendency of this action.

_____
                                                    Attorney for Plaintiff

MEMORANDUM

Testimony will be adduced at the hearing herein to show that Defendant should be ordered as requested by Plaintiff.

_____
                                                    Attorney for Plaintiff

[Notice of hearing]

[Proof/certificate of service]

NOTES TO FORM

Cross Reference
   1 Klein and Darling, Baldwin's Ohio Practice, Civil Practice Rule 13
   3 Klein and Darling, Baldwin's Ohio Practice, Civil Practice, Ch 9

§ 25:61 Miscellaneous motions—Motion to dismiss

Civil Rule 12(B) applies to domestic relations actions. Thus, a motion to dismiss is appropriate where there is lack of jurisdiction over the subject matter or the person, improper venue, insufficiency of process, insufficiency of service of process, or failure to state a claim upon which relief can be granted.

Probably the most common uses of this motion in the domestic relations context involve disputes with regard to jurisdiction over the person and venue. Often, an out-of-state defendant will challenge the court's jurisdiction over him or her. Civil Rule 4.3(A)(8) clearly addresses this circumstance. It provides that the court acquires "long-arm" jurisdiction over an absent defendant who has lived in the marital relationship within the state, notwithstanding subsequent departure from the state, with respect to spousal support, allocation of parental rights and responsibilities, child support, or property settlement, if the other party to the marital relationship continues to reside in the state.

If the parties have never lived together in the marital relationship in Ohio, the court could acquire only in rem jurisdiction, i.e., jurisdiction over the marriage, the plaintiff, the children if they are in the state, and any assets in the state that may be used for division of property or payment of spousal or child support.

Since there is no personal jurisdiction over the defendant, there can be no personal judgment against him or her. Thus, a judgment for spousal or child support, to be paid in the future from the defendant personally, is void for lack of jurisdiction. The named defendant may appear specially to point out the lack of jurisdiction and request that the complaint be dismissed as to him or her. While the court may dismiss the defendant personally, it will not dismiss as to property within the state from which spousal and child support could be obtained.

Counsel should remain aware that two voluntary dismissals act as an adjudication on the merits.[1]

§ 25:62 Miscellaneous motions—Motion to dismiss for lack of personal jurisdiction—Form ⊚

[Title of Court]

[Caption]   Case No. *[_____]*
                                              MOTION TO DISMISS

Now comes *[attorney for Defendant]* and without submitting to the jurisdiction of this Court, and for the sole and limited purpose of denying the jurisdiction of this Court over the person of the Defendant, hereby moves this Court pursuant to Civil Rule 12(B)(2) to find and order that it has no "in personam" jurisdiction against *[Defendant]*.

This motion is supported by the *[memorandum / affidavit]* below.

_____
Attorney for Defendant

[Notice of hearing]
[Memorandum / affidavit in support of motion]
[Proof / certificate of service]

NOTES TO FORM

Cross Reference
1 Klein and Darling, Baldwin's Ohio Practice, Civil Practice Rule 12
3 Klein and Darling, Baldwin's Ohio Practice, Civil Practice, Ch 2

_____

[Section 25:61]
[1] Civ. R. 41. See Jurisdiction and Venue Ch 27.

§ 25:63   Miscellaneous motions—Motion to dismiss for lack of subject matter jurisdiction—Form⊚

[Title of Court]

[Caption]   Case No. *[_____]*
MOTION TO DISMISS

Defendant moves the Court to dismiss the action herein for lack of jurisdiction over the subject matter, Plaintiff not having been a resident of the State of Ohio for six months prior to filing this action for divorce.

This motion is supported by the affidavit below.

_____

Attorney for Defendant

[Notice of hearing]

[Affidavit of movant in support of motion]

[Proof/certificate of service]

NOTES TO FORM

Cross Reference
  1 Klein and Darling, Baldwin's Ohio Practice, Civil Practice Rule 12
  3 Klein and Darling, Baldwin's Ohio Practice, Civil Practice, Ch 2

§ 25:64   Miscellaneous motions—Motion for summary judgment

Civil Rule 56, on summary judgments, is not mentioned in Civil Rule 75 and is therefore available for use in domestic relations proceedings.

As a practical matter, since Civil Rule 75(L) and RC 3105.10(A) require specific and corroborated testimony in actions for divorce, annulment, or legal separation, there is very little left for Civil Rule 56.

The parties may stipulate with respect to allocation of parental rights and responsibilities, visitation, and property division, the stipulated terms being contingent on the divorce itself. In fact, most courts appreciate this saving of judicial time.

In *Zimmie v. Zimmie*,[1] the Ohio Supreme Court held that it was not error to grant summary judgment in divorce proceedings. In *Zimmie*, the request was for partial summary judgment on the grounds. If a court grants partial summary judgment without an express finding (pursuant to Civil Rule 54(B)) that there is "no just reason for delay," then the judgment is not a final appealable order.

§ 25:65   Briefs—General format

In the brief in support or in opposition, counsel presents a concise summary statement of the law and facts applicable to the matter in issue. The brief should contain a statement of all operative facts ap-

_____

[Section 25:64]
   [1]Zimmie v. Zimmie, 11 Ohio St. 3d 94, 464 N.E.2d 142, 53 A.L.R.4th 75 (1984).

plicable to the matter in issue and a statement of all operative facts necessary to support (or oppose) the motion. It is not good practice to include lengthy quotations or extractions which would be better presented as exhibits. This does not mean it should not be done but merely suggests that any matters that can be better located in the affidavits or exhibits should be located there, with only a summary of their contents, effect, or interpretation in the argument/brief.

Brevity is the essence of a brief. While weight and volume may be viewed as essential elements of appellate briefs, this is not so with trial briefs submitted in support of a motion. If the trial judge wants more expository detail, he or she can request a trial brief from one or both counsels. Until such request is made, counsel must assume some judicial knowledge of the law and civil rules, as well as domestic relations practice, and limit the argument/brief to two or three pages. If counsel exceeds this length, he or she runs the risk that the brief will not be read.

If counsel determines that a trial brief is necessary in a particular situation, then it should of course be submitted, although it will rarely approach an appellate brief in weight or volume.

However, it is important for counsel to include in the narrative the purpose or effect of the items incorporated by reference. It is not wise to assume that the brief as well as the affidavits and exhibits will be read. The assumption should be that the argument/brief will be read, and that the affidavits and exhibits will not be read, as they are (or should be) more in the nature of supporting documentation of matters discussed in the argument/brief. Considering the narrow legal issues encountered in domestic relations practice and the repetitive nature of the factual issues involved in most divorce cases, a good practitioner can quite easily and rapidly develop a file of boilerplate reviews of applicable law for ready incorporation as exhibits. Practically, the issues of fact are likely to be even narrower, but because of changes in names, dates, circumstances, etc., these cannot be put into boilerplate.

If a particular motion requires certain facts be alleged and proven, then those facts, which will certainly become issues in the case, should be incorporated into the brief from a supporting affidavit. Some attorneys shortcut the process by including lengthy affidavits in place of an argumentative brief. In addition to being bad form, this is technically an incomplete motion, since it does not state the facts and law by brief as it should (an affidavit is not a brief), nor does it tell the judge of the reasons for the motion. It is economy pleading.

A supporting affidavit should include only those facts necessary to establish a prima facie case. The principal affidavit should be that of the petitioner or respondent. Affidavits from additional witnesses are a matter of style, tactics, and strategy. If there is to be a hearing, the affidavits of witnesses may be unnecessary, but if there is no hearing or no response, then they can be used to support the prima facie case.

As a general rule, motions should always include affidavits. Respondent should follow the same general rule and should be certain to cover each affidavit with one of his or her own, to guarantee that the other side does not prevail because the judge elected to view an unopposed affidavit as being the whole truth and act on it.[1]

With respect to format, the most common practice is to enter each item in a separate line, although there is really no reason for this, and no apparent reason why the affidavit could not be a simple narrative in a single paragraph format.

Sometimes a statement is included in the affidavit to the effect that the affiant has read the brief, agrees with it, and incorporates it into the affidavit by reference. There may be a problem with this language when the brief includes a discussion of the law. This could put the affiant in the position of asserting competence in the law. The legal affirmations should be in the legal brief, with the affidavits of the parties containing only operative facts.

Whenever a motion relies on a statute, letter, bill, invoice, or judgment, a copy of that writing should be included in the motion package as an exhibit.[2] Not only is this necessary to establish the case, but it provides both the opposition and the court with an essential fact. While an original should never be attached, given the advanced state of the copy machine, there is no excuse for failure to include copies of any and all writings that are to be in issue. A close reading of Civil Rule 7(B)(3) suggests that Civil Rule 10(D), requiring the inclusion of copies of relevant writings, applies to motions.

It is also good practice to include copies of relevant rules, statutes, etc., rather than to assume that the trial judge knows them completely. Failure to include this material merely forces the judge to find it, which wastes judicial time and causes unnecessary annoyance.

§ 25:66 Briefs—Brief in support of motion

Civil Rule 7(B) governs motion practice. It does not require a separate brief in support. This is simply a matter of good practice.[1] It provides the court with the additional information needed to make an informed analysis of the motion and relief requested.

Local court rules should be consulted with respect to the proper content and format for briefs in support of or in opposition to motions.

The brief in support of a motion generally must be separate from the motion itself, must state in detail the reasons for the motion and any legal grounds therefor, and must also state the relief or order requested and, as a practical matter, any alternative relief or orders that the petitioner will accept.[2]

Affidavits and exhibits may be essential to the establishment of a prima facie case and should be included where appropriate. Local court

---

[Section 25:65]
[1]Zimmie v. Zimmie, 11 Ohio St. 3d 94, 464 N.E.2d 142, 53 A.L.R.4th 75 (1984).
[2]Zimmie v. Zimmie, 11 Ohio St. 3d 94, 464 N.E.2d 142, 53 A.L.R.4th 75 (1984).

[Section 25:66]
[1]Zimmie v. Zimmie, 11 Ohio St. 3d 94, 464 N.E.2d 142, 53 A.L.R.4th 75 (1984).
[2]Zimmie v. Zimmie, 11 Ohio St. 3d 94, 464 N.E.2d 142, 53 A.L.R.4th 75 (1984).

rules should be consulted in this connection.

§ 25:67   Briefs—Brief in opposition to motion

A brief in opposition is not appended to a motion but follows immediately after the caption. It should contain a statement that it is a brief in opposition and should describe the particular motion to which it is presented in opposition.

If a motion format is used, this information can be presented on the first page, together with the service affidavit, with the facts of the brief beginning on the second page. This style makes easy boilerplate. If a motion format is not used, counsel must be certain to include the service affidavit at the end of the brief.

If the motion brief includes an affidavit, the opposition brief should include a counteraffidavit, lest the court view the lack of one as an admission of the allegations in the motion affidavit and rule accordingly.

The opposition brief must be limited to the subject matter of the original motion and brief and must not include any extraneous matter. Of course, when relevant facts or cases are omitted from the initial motion, they should be included in the opposition brief.

§ 25:68   Briefs—Brief in opposition to objections

Either party may submit objections to a magistrate's decision under Civil Rule 53(E)(3). Although the rule does not expressly authorize a brief in opposition to objections by opposing counsel, it indicates that objections should be treated like motions, and since briefs in opposition are permitted to motions, they are permitted in opposition to objections as well.

Following a magistrate's decision, either party may file objections thereto, and good practice requires that counsel overcome any issues or problems raised by an opponent's objections, lest the court find there is no opposition to the statements in the objections. Note that there is nothing to prevent a party from filing objections and then, upon receipt of the other party's objections, electing to respond to them with a brief in opposition to the objections. Upon receipt of the brief in opposition, the receiving party may elect to file a reply brief.[1]

§ 25:69   Briefs—Reply brief

A reply brief is written in response to a brief in opposition to a motion, or to a brief in opposition to objections to a magistrate decision. There is no specific authorization for a reply brief in the rules, but it is usually permitted by local court rule or custom. Civil Rule 7(A) mentions reply briefs, but seems to exclude them unless they are requested by the court.

In practice, however, it would be difficult to find an attorney who

[Section 25:68]
[1]See Magistrates Ch 31.

would rely on the rules on this issue. Though preparing a reply brief involves more work, it may prevent a judgment based on lack of response to a brief in opposition (where the court may presume that failure to reply is the equivalent of acquiescence).[1]

§ 25:70   Objections to magistrate's decision

Effective July 1, 1995, the Ohio Supreme Court revised Civ. R. 53. Referees are now known as "magistrates" pursuant to Civ. R. 53(A). Civil Rule 53(E) was entirely reworked. Most of the drafting considerations still apply. However, if findings of fact are desired to be included in the magistrate's decision, a request for such must be made prior to the decision being entered.[1] If the request is not made until after a decision has been filed, the magistrate must file an amended decision.[2]

While the rule states that a party may submit objections, counsel should note that if objections are not filed, then the magistrate's decision will probably be adopted. If no one has objected, the court might not use its precious time to scrutinize a magistrate's decision. The real purpose of objections is that they force a judicial review.

Often, the objections are routed to the same magistrate against whom the objections are made, so counsel must be sure to be accurate in stating such objections in case he or she wishes to take further action at the trial or appellate level. Frequently, counsel filing objections includes with the objections a motion for a hearing on the objections.

As a practical matter then, if the magistrate's decision is in any way objectionable, good practice demands the filing of objections.[3]

The format for objections should follow motion format (front page containing a statement as to the nature of the document, etc., with service at the bottom, the brief beginning on the next page) or the traditional format (narrative beginning immediately after the caption). The choice of one or the other format would depend on local custom and style.

It may be wise to preface the narrative on the specific objections with a series of brief statements in the style of statements of error in an appellate brief. This will aid counsel in preparing an appellate brief when and if it is needed.[4]

Also, it must be noted that pursuant to Civil Rule 53(E)(3)(b), a party shall not assign as error on appeal the court's adoption of any Finding of Fact or Conclusion of Law by a magistrate unless that party has objected to that Finding of Fact or Conclusion of Law.

[Section 25:69]
　　[1]See § 25:68, Briefs—Brief in opposition to objections.

[Section 25:70]
　　[1]Civ. R. 53(E)(2).
　　[2]Civ. R. 53(E)(2).
　　[3]See §§ 31:8–31:12, Objections to magistrate's decision.
　　[4]See §§ 31:8–31:12, Objections to magistrate's decision.

§ 25:71 Objections to judgment entry

Former Rule 13 of the Rules of Superintendence for Courts of Common Pleas was amended by the Supreme Court effective February 6, 1995. This amendment added division (B) to C.P. Sup. R. 13 in response to the holding in *Paletta v. Paletta*.[1] The language was unchanged by the 1997 revision and consolidation of the Rules of Superintendence of the Courts of Ohio. Now set forth in Sup. R. 7, Filing of judgment entries, it provides:

> (B) Approval of a judgment entry by a counsel or party indicates that the entry correctly sets forth the verdict, decree, or decision of the court and does not waive any objection or assignment of error for appeal.

§ 25:72 Notices—Notice of appearance

When there is a change in counsel while a matter is pending, a procedural problem arises. The court file has the name of the former attorney as the attorney of record, and the mailing section will continue to send notices to him or her.

Filing a notice of appearance will not only clear the record but assure subsequent counsel that court notices will be received. Copies of the notice should be sent to former counsel, as a matter of courtesy, and to opposing counsel, so he or she will know with whom he or she should do business.

The notice requests the clerk of courts to change the record. Counsel should check with the mailing service some time after filing to be sure that the mailing list has been changed as well.

§ 25:73 Notices—Notice of withdrawal

If the attorney-client relationship is terminated while a matter is pending, the attorney of record should place on the record the fact of the termination. Not only does this let the court know, but it may save the retiring attorney in the event some future activity in the case gives rise to a malpractice claim.

§ 25:74 Service of process—In general

Where both parties are residents of the same county, service is ordinarily by certified mail from the clerk, unless sheriff's service is requested. Civil Rule 4.1(3) provides that process must be served on someone residing in the household who is of suitable age and discretion.

The practitioner should check the docket to make sure that service has been perfected. If the certified mail is returned unclaimed, regular mail service must be requested through the clerk's office.

If counsel would prefer service other than clerk's certified mail ser-

---

[Section 25:71]

[1]Paletta v. Paletta, 68 Ohio App. 3d 507, 589 N.E.2d 76 (8th Dist. Cuyahoga County 1990).

vice, or sheriff service, generally by his or her own private process server, Civil Rule 4.1(2) permits such alternate service, so long as the process server is over age eighteen, not a party, and has been so designated by the court. The rule is not specific as to whether such alternate service is totally optional or is only available on a showing of special circumstances. Local rule or custom would control. In either event, a motion should be filed to obtain the order designating the process server/permitting special service.

Of particular importance to the domestic relations practitioner is the waiver of service provision contained in Civil Rule 4(D), which provides that service of a summons may be waived in writing by any person entitled thereto under Civil Rule 4.2 who is at least eighteen years of age and not under any disability. The filing of the waiver constitutes service for the purpose of computing the waiting period of forty-two days before the action can be heard. Waivers are most commonly used in dissolution actions.

The same service procedure applies where the defendant is a resident of another county within the state. The only exception involves sheriff's service; the summons must be transferred by the county in which the action is commenced to the sheriff of the county in which the defendant resides. Usually, certified mail service or a process server would be quicker in these cases.

Civil Rule 4.3 provides for service of process on a non-resident of the state or a resident of the state who is absent therefrom, where the defendant falls in one of eight categories. The category applicable in the domestic relations context involves a person who has lived "in the marital relationship within this state notwithstanding subsequent departure from this state, as to all obligations arising for spousal support, custody, child support, or property settlement, if the other party to the marital relationship continues to reside in this state." Thus, in personam jurisdiction may be obtained over an absent defendant, and support obligations can be imposed upon him or her. If the parties have not lived together in the marital relationship within the state and the defendant is not in this state but his or her residence is known, certified mail service may be made. In such a case, the court will not thereby acquire in personam jurisdiction but only in rem jurisdiction to grant the divorce. Thus, no child or spousal support can be ordered. Allocation of parental rights and responsibilities of minor children may, however, be awarded where the minor children and the plaintiff are residents of the jurisdiction.

If certified mail service on an out-of-state defendant is returned "unclaimed," then regular mail service is appropriate pursuant to Civil Rule 4.6.[1]

Where the address of the defendant is unknown, Civil Rule 4.4 provides for service by publication. Before this can be initiated, an affi-

---

[Section 25:74]

[1]Olezewski v. Niam, 1993 WL 372234 (Ohio Ct. App. 2d Dist. Montgomery County 1993).

davit of a party or his or her counsel must be filed with the court aver-
ring that the address of the defendant is unknown and with reasonable
diligence cannot be obtained. Upon the filing of the affidavit, notice is
published in a newspaper of general circulation in the county in which
the complaint is filed. The publication must appear at least once a week
for six successive weeks. Service is complete upon the date of the last
publication. It should be noted that service by publication creates in rem
jurisdiction only.

Civil Rule 75(L) requires that, when there is no counsel of record, service of the notice of a trial on the merits must be made by regular mail
to the party's last known address.[2] Service of notice to the marital residence, where the party no longer resides, will not be sufficient notice
under Civil Rule 75(L) when the court has been given information
regarding the party's change of address.[3]

Once judgment has been entered, the case is closed. Domestic relations cases are unique in the number of post-decree motions regularly
filed, which account for about half of the court's activity. Service of these
motions must be in the manner provided in Civil Rule 75(J).[4]

§ 25:75   Service of process—Service by publication—General affidavit—Form⊚

[Title of Court]

[Caption]   Case No. [_____]

AFFIDAVIT FOR SERVICE BY
PUBLICATION

[Name], being first duly sworn, deposes and says that *[he/she]* is the
Plaintiff in the within action; that this is an action for *[annulment/
divorce/legal separation]* against *[name]*; that the Defendant's last
known address is *[street address]*; that Defendant's present whereabouts
are unknown to Plaintiff; that by reasonable diligence, inquiry of former
associates and family members, and by correspondence, it has been
ascertained that service can only be had on Defendant by publication;
that this affidavit is made in pursuance to law in such cases under RC
3105.06.

The following efforts have been made by affiant to ascertain the residence of Defendant: *[here list efforts]*.

_____

Affiant

[Jurat]

_____

[2]Inboden v. Inboden, 1994 WL 321058 (Ohio Ct. App. 10th Dist. Franklin County
1994).

[3]Williams v. Williams, 1993 WL 310394 (Ohio Ct. App. 10th Dist. Franklin County
1993).

[4]See Uniform Child Custody Jurisdiction Act; Parental Kidnapping Prevention Act;
International Child Abduction Remedies Act Ch 17; Jurisdiction and Venue Ch 27.

NOTES TO FORM

Drafter's Notes

Civil Rule 4.4(A), as amended effective July 1, 1991, requires the affidavit for service by publication to aver all the efforts made to locate the residence of the defendant.

Cross Reference

1 Klein and Darling, Baldwin's Ohio Practice, Civil Practice Rule 4.4

3 Klein and Darling, Baldwin's Ohio Practice, Civil Practice, Ch 1

§ 25:76   Service of process—Service by publication—Real property affidavit—Form⊙

[Title of Court]

[Caption]   Case No. *[_____]*

AFFIDAVIT FOR SERVICE BY
PUBLICATION

[Name], being first duly sworn, deposes and says that:

(1) *[He/She]* is the Plaintiff in the within action for *[annulment/ divorce/legal separation]* against *[name]*;

(2) The parties are the joint owners of the following described real property: *[here provide description]*;

(3) The Plaintiff seeks the award of all of defendant's interest in said property in addition to other relief;

(4) The Defendant's last known address is *[street address]*;

(5) The Defendant's present whereabouts are unknown to Plaintiff;

(6) By reasonable diligence, inquiry of former associates and family members, and by correspondence, it has been ascertained that service can only be had on Defendant by publication; and

(7) This affidavit is made in pursuance to law in such cases under RC 3105.06.

The following efforts have been made by affiant to ascertain the residence of Defendant: *[here list efforts]*.

_____
Affiant

[Jurat]

NOTES TO FORM

Drafter's Notes

Civil Rule 4.4(A), as amended effective July 1, 1991, requires the affidavit for service by publication to aver all the efforts made to locate the residence of the defendant.

The common pleas courts have statewide jurisdiction over all property located in Ohio. To give the court jurisdiction over specific real property, the complaint should describe the property. Where divorce will be by publication, the publication notice should contain the full property description so that the court may make an award of the property.

Cross Reference

1 Klein and Darling, Baldwin's Ohio Practice, Civil Practice Rule 4.4

3 Klein and Darling, Baldwin's Ohio Practice, Civil Practice, Ch 1

§ 25:77 Service of process—Service by publication—Military affidavit—Form⊚

[Title of Court]

[Caption]

Case No. *[_____]*

AFFIDAVIT FOR SERVICE BY
PUBLICATION; MILITARY
AFFIDAVIT

[Name of Plaintiff], being first duly sworn, deposes and says that *[he/ she]* is the Plaintiff in the within action; that this is an action for *[annulment/divorce/legal separation]* against *[name of Defendant]*; that Defendant's last known address is *[street/city]*; that Defendant's present whereabouts are unknown to Plaintiff; that by reasonable diligence, inquiry of former associates and family members, and by correspondence, it has been ascertained that service can only be had on Defendant by publication; that *[Defendant]* is not now a member of the US Armed Forces to the best of affiant's knowledge and belief; that this affidavit is made pursuant to law in such cases under RC 3105.06 and the Civil Rules.

The following efforts have been made by affiant to ascertain the residence of Defendant: *[here list efforts]*.

_____
Affiant

[Jurat]

NOTES TO FORM

Drafter's Notes

Civil Rule 4.4(A), as amended effective July 1, 1991, requires the affidavit for service by publication to aver all the efforts made to locate the residence of the defendant.

§ 25:78 Service of process—Military duty—Defendant not in service affidavit—Form⊚

[Title of Court]

[Caption]

Case No. *[_____]*

AFFIDAVIT AS TO MILITARY
SERVICE; DEFENDANT NOT IN
SERVICE

[Name], being first duly sworn, deposes and says that:

(1) *[He/She]* is the *[Plaintiff/attorney for Plaintiff]* in the within action and makes this affidavit pursuant to the provisions of the Soldiers' and Sailors' Civil Relief Act, 50 U.S.C.A. App. 501 et seq.

(2) Upon lawful investigation, to wit: *[state nature, persons, and date of investigation]* affiant believes that Defendant, *[name]*, is not in the military service of the United States.

_____

Affiant

[Jurat]

§ 25:79 Service of process—Military duty—Defendant in service affidavit—Form⊚

[Title of Court]

[Caption]   Case No. [_____]
                                         AFFIDAVIT AS TO MILITARY
                                         SERVICE; DEFENDANT IN
                                         SERVICE

[Name], being first duly sworn, deposes and says that:

(1) *[He/She]* is the *[Plaintiff/attorney for Plaintiff]* in the within action and makes this affidavit pursuant to the provisions of the Soldiers' and Sailors' Civil Relief Act, 50 U.S.C.A. App 501 et seq.

(2) That, after investigation, affiant believes that Defendant, *[name]*, is in the military service of the United States.

(3) Defendant is not represented in this cause by an attorney and has not answered or defended.

(4) Defendant was served with summons on *[date]*.

(5) It is necessary to appoint counsel for Defendant and affiant requests that the court appoint *[an attorney/attorney's name]* to represent Defendant herein.

_____

Affiant

[Jurat]

§ 25:80 Service of process—Military duty—Entry appointing attorney to represent defendant in service—Form⊚

[Title of Court]

[Caption]   Case No. [_____]
                                         JUDGMENT ENTRY

It appearing to the Court that *[name]*, Defendant herein, is a member of the United States military service and that he has not entered an appearance although duly served, it is hereby ordered that *[name and address of attorney]* is hereby appointed to represent Defendant in this action and to protect *[his/her]* interests.

_____

Judge

§ 25:81 Service of process—Military duty—Appearance, answer, and waiver under Soldiers' and Sailors' Civil Relief Act—Form⊙

[Title of Court]

[Caption]

Case No. [_____]

APPEARANCE, ANSWER, AND
WAIVER PURSUANT TO
SOLDIERS' AND SAILORS' CIVIL
RELIEF ACT

(1) Defendant has been served with summons and a copy of the complaint in the above action against *[him / her]* and hereby submits to the jurisdiction of this court.

(2) Defendant neither admits nor denies the allegations contained in the complaint.

(3) Defendant is on active duty with the Armed Forces of the United States and *[he / she]* understands that *[he / she]* is entitled to the benefits of the Soldiers' and Sailors' Civil Relief Act of 1940, as amended and re-enacted.

(4) Defendant waives all benefits to which *[he / she]* may be entitled under the Soldiers' and Sailors' Civil Relief Act of 1940, as amended and re-enacted.

WHEREFORE, Defendant asks that any relief which is granted to Plaintiff be fair and equitable to Defendant.

_____

Defendant

§ 25:82 Filing decree from another state

RC 3109.32 provides that a certified copy of a parenting decree from another state may be filed in the office of the clerk of any court of this state that renders parenting decrees, and that the clerk must treat the decree in the same manner as the parenting decree of an appropriate court of this state. The statute further provides that the parenting decree so filed has the same effect and must be enforced in like manner as the parenting decree rendered by a court of this state. While this provision is part of the UCCJA,[1] many times it becomes necessary to attempt to transfer jurisdiction where the parties are no longer residing in the jurisdiction which originally entered the divorce decree. This is no problem where both parties consent to the transfer. However, where one party does not consent to the transfer, a motion must be filed seeking adoption of the foreign decree. If the court does adopt the foreign decree, appropriate motions may then be made with respect to modifications of all

---

[Section 25:82]
[1]RC 3109.21 et seq.

issues subject to further order of court.[2]

§ 25:83   Evidence

Evidence Rule 803(4) provides for an exception to the hearsay rule, which can be useful in a domestic relations case, by allowing statements made for purposes of medical diagnosis or treatment to be admitted into evidence. Statements need not be made to a treating physician to fall under this exception. Statements made to a social worker in child abuse situations,[1] and to a mental health professional during an evaluation conducted for the specific purpose of determining sexual abuse,[2] will be admissible under Evidence Rule 803(4).

---

[2]But see Johnson v. Johnson, 86 Ohio App. 3d 433, 621 N.E.2d 530 (2d Dist. Greene County 1993) (foreign decree of divorce not given full faith and credit due to failure of service).

[Section 25:83]

[1]Presley v. Presley, 71 Ohio App. 3d 34, 593 N.E.2d 17 (8th Dist. Cuyahoga County 1990).

[2]Schulte v. Schulte, 1993 WL 197413 (Ohio Ct. App. 6th Dist. Wood County 1993), judgment aff'd, 1994 -Ohio- 459, 71 Ohio St. 3d 41, 641 N.E.2d 719 (1994).

Chapter 26

Discovery

By Herbert Palkovitz, Esq.

> **KeyCite®:** Cases and other legal materials listed in KeyCite Scope can be researched through West Group's KeyCite service on Westlaw®. Use KeyCite to check citations for form, parallel references, prior and later history, and comprehensive citator information, including citations to other decisions and secondary materials.

§ 26:1   Introduction to discovery

In matrimonial law cases, broad discovery is vital to achieve equitable child and spousal support orders and an equitable distribution of marital property. Several jurisdictions have pre-trial forms on which each party must include information about income, assets, debts, and expenses. Each pre-trial form must be filed with the court before trial. Ideally, counsel for each party will obtain full disclosure from his or her client. The information disclosed is then made available to opposing counsel in the form of an affidavit signed by the client. Absent such pre-trial cooperation, the methods of discovery utilized in all civil cases are available in domestic relations cases as well. Those methods are discussed below.

Discovery in domestic relations cases is governed by Rules 26 through 37 of the Ohio Rules of Civil Procedure. Civ. R. 75(D), discussed in greater depth later in this chapter, applies solely to domestic relations cases and may be used in discovery. The application of the Rules of Civil Procedure may be modified by local rules of court. Therefore, it is important for the practitioner to be familiar with any local rules that may apply.

§ 26:2   Methods of discovery

The methods of discovery set forth in Civ. R. 26(A) are all available in domestic relations cases:

    (1) Deposition upon oral examination or written questions;
    (2) Written interrogatories;
    (3) Production of documents or things, or permission to enter upon land and/or other property for inspection and other purposes;
    (4) Physical and mental examinations; and
    (5) Requests for admissions.

Civ. R. 26(D) provides that, unless otherwise ordered, discovery methods may be used in any sequence. Further, the fact that one party is conducting discovery shall not operate to delay another party's discovery.

§ 26:3   Scope of discovery—In general

The scope of discovery in domestic relations cases is very broad. Relevance and privilege limit the scope of discovery pursuant to Civ. R. 26(B)(1). However, due to the subject matter of domestic relations cases, almost anything can be argued as relevant, and privilege does not usually provide much of a hurdle to discovery.[1] Achieving an equitable division of the marital property requires total disclosure of each party's earning ability, assets, and debts. Failure to make a full disclosure of

---

[Section 26:3]
    [1]Holmes v. Holmes, 1990 WL 1034310 (Ohio Ct. App. 1990) (diary of husband-attorney was held to be admissible when it did not fall within work product doctrine and

this information can result in an unbinding agreement.[2] Similarly, in a determination of what is in the best interest of a child in a parental rights case, or whether there has been a change in circumstances in a modification of spousal support or child support case, for example, a great deal of information is discoverable as being relevant or calculated to lead to admissible evidence. Although privilege may be a bar to discovery in some domestic relations cases, the relevance of privileged information may outweigh the privilege and may result in the court's permitting access thereto by opposing counsel.

"Mediation communications" are confidential as provided in RC 2317.023, and therefore are exempt from disclosure under RC 149.43 regarding release of public records.[3] Discovery of confidential material post judgment is permitted if the material requested is relevant to the case at hand, and in furtherance of the executed judgment.[4]

§26:4 Scope of discovery—Discovering value of a business

Full disclosure of each party's finances is vital for a fair support order or a division of property. Each party is entitled to access to corporate and partnership records in any business in which the other spouse has an interest. However, the degree of access to a corporation's books and records may depend on the nature of the party's interests.[1] If the party is not a majority shareholder, access to corporate records may be limited. The determination of the value of closely held corporations and corporate holdings is essential in matrimonial cases. As a practical matter, however, the cost of making such a determination may be prohibitive in cases where the business is a small one and the parties have no other substantial assets. Such valuation often entails depositions, interrogatories, the review of records, and the retaining of an expert by each party

---

did not contain privileged information, even though it was taken by wife without his consent).

[2]See Rossman v. Rossman, 47 Ohio App. 2d 103, 1 Ohio Op. 3d 206, 352 N.E.2d 149 (8th Dist. Cuyahoga County 1975) (abuse of discretion for trial judge to end party's pre-trial discovery on critical issue, i.e., a spouse's earning capacity, solely to hasten conclusion of case). See also Snyder v. Snyder, 1992 WL 14946 (Ohio Ct. App. 8th Dist. Cuyahoga County 1992) (pursuant to Civ. R. 60(B)(5), appellant was granted relief from judgment because separation agreement failed to disclose existence of appellee's pension fund and insurance policy); Erb v. Erb, 1991 WL 271412 (Ohio Ct. App. 8th Dist. Cuyahoga County 1991) (court held that trial court abused its discretion in failing to determine present value of husband's pension plan before evaluating fairness of separation agreement); In re Murphy, 10 Ohio App. 3d 134, 461 N.E.2d 910 (1st Dist. Hamilton County 1983) (court held that plaintiff was entitled to relief from judgment under Civ. R. 60(B)(5) because separation agreement failed to divulge existence of substantial, material assets owned by defendant-spouse).

[3]State ex rel. Schneider v. Kreiner, 1998 -Ohio- 271, 83 Ohio St. 3d 203, 699 N.E.2d 83 (1998).

[4]Van-Am. Ins. Co. v. Schiappa, 132 Ohio App. 3d 325, 724 N.E.2d 1232 (7th Dist. Jefferson County 1999).

[Section 26:4]
[1]Majestic Steel Service, Inc., 1999 WL 1206573 (Ohio Ct. App. 8th Dist. Cuyahoga County 1999) (trade secrets not discoverable).

to appraise the business and its holdings. In contested trials, these experts are often called upon to testify.[2]

One method to begin determining the value of a business is to discover information as to the existence, description, nature, custody, condition, and locations of any books, documents, or other tangible things and the identity and location of persons having knowledge of any discoverable matter as provided by Civ. R. 26(B)(1).

§ 26:5   Scope of discovery—Discovering expert testimony

Civ. R. 26(B)(4)(a) places limitations on discovery of facts known or opinions held by an expert retained in anticipation of trial. These limitations on the party seeking discovery are as follows:

(1) A showing must be made that he or she is unable, without undue hardship, to obtain facts and opinions on the same subject by other means; or

(2) A showing must be made of other exceptional circumstances indicating that denial of discovery would cause manifest injustice.

Civ. R. 26(B)(4)(b) provides that a party may use interrogatories to discover the identity of an opposing party's witnesses and the subject matter on which each expert is expected to testify. Thereafter, a party may discover from the expert or another party facts known or opinions held by the expert which are relevant to the stated subject matter.

§ 26:6   Scope of discovery—Protection from discovery

From time to time situations may arise where a party or a witness in a domestic relations matter requires protection from discovery. Civ. R. 26(C) is designed to balance the broad scope of discovery provided for in Civ. R. 26(B) by limiting discovery abuse through a broad protective order provision. Civ. R. 26(C) governs the method by which a protective order may be sought, the purpose for which it may be sought, and the protection which a court may afford. Generally, a protective order may be sought to avoid annoyance, embarrassment, oppression, or undue burden or expense. The rule indicates that the court may allow the following protections:

(1) That the discovery not be had;

(2) That the discovery may be had only on specified terms and conditions, and at a designated time and/or place;

(3) That the discovery may be had by way of a different method of discovery;

(4) That the scope of discovery be limited to certain matters;

(5) That the court may designate who may be present while discovery is being conducted;

(6) That a deposition be sealed and may be reopened only by order

---

[2]See Bernard Agin, *When Experts Disagree,* 4 Dom. Rel. J. Ohio 67 (July/Aug. 1992).

of the court;

(7) That trade secrets or other confidential research, development, or commercial information be disclosed only in a designated way or may not be disclosed at all; and

(8) That specified documents or information enclosed in sealed envelopes by each party and filed simultaneously be opened as directed by the court.

Before seeking a protective order from discovery, Civ. R. 26(C) provides that the person seeking protection must: (1) make a "reasonable effort" to resolve the problem without court intervention; and (2) submit a "statement" with any motion for a protective order indicating the efforts made to resolve the problem.[1]

§ 26:7   Scope of discovery—Protection from discovery—Motion for protective order—Form ⊚

[Title of Court]

[Caption]

Case No. [_____]

MOTION FOR A PROTECTIVE
ORDER

Defendant moves this Honorable Court for an Order, pursuant to Civil Rule 26(C), relieving him from the request of Plaintiff in [his/her] Notice to Take Deposition served upon Defendant's counsel on or about [date], for the reasons contained in the Brief attached hereto and made a part hereof as if fully rewritten herein.

_____
Attorney for Defendant

[Notice of hearing]

BRIEF

Defendant, on or about [date], filed a Motion to reduce child support for the parties' two minor children, [name], born [date], and [name], born [date].

Plaintiff has requested Defendant's deposition and has attached a duces tecum, a copy of which is attached as Exhibit "A," requesting items which are not applicable to the instant modification action.

It is, therefore, respectfully requested that this Honorable Court grant this motion and quash the subpoena.

[Section 26:6]

[1]Hattie v. Sherman, 1998 WL 318464 (Ohio Ct. App. 9th Dist. Lorain County 1998); Dennis v. State Farm Ins. Co., 2001 -Ohio- 3178, 143 Ohio App. 3d 196, 757 N.E.2d 849 (7th Dist. Mahoning County 2001), cause dismissed, 93 Ohio St. 3d 1401, 752 N.E.2d 983 (2001).

Respectfully submitted,

_____

Attorney for Defendant

[Proof/certificate of service]

§ 26:8 Scope of discovery—Supplementing discovery

A party who provides a complete response to a discovery request has no duty to supplement his or her response subsequently. However, an exception to Civ. R. 26(E) requires that a response be supplemented under the following circumstances:

  (1) When a question is directly addressed to:
     (a) the identity and location of persons having knowledge of discoverable matters; and
     (b) the identity of each person expected to be called as an expert witness and the subject matter on which he is to testify to at trial;[1]
  (2) To correct a response known or later learned to be incorrect; and
  (3) By order of the court, by agreement of the parties, or by requests for supplementation of prior responses at any time before trial.

§ 26:9 Depositions—General rules for depositions

Depositions may be taken within Ohio as well as outside of Ohio. Civ. R. 28(A) authorizes the taking of depositions in the state where the action is pending before a person authorized to administer oaths; a person appointed by the court in which the action is pending; or a person agreed upon by written stipulation of all the parties. A deposition may be taken outside of Ohio pursuant to Civ. R. 28(B). The deposition may be taken before a person authorized to administer oaths in the foreign state; a person appointed by the court in which the action is pending; a person agreed upon by all parties by written stipulation; or by a district consular officer of the United States situated in the foreign country. Further, Rule 28(C) provides that absent agreement by the parties, depositions may not be taken before any person with an interest in the action, including a relative, employee, or attorney of any of the parties, or a relative or employee of such an attorney.

Civ. R. 29 provides that the parties may, by written stipulation, modify the procedures provided by these rules for depositions or for other methods of discovery. The stipulation may provide that depositions may be taken before any person, at any time or place, upon any notice, and in any manner, and may be used like other depositions. The practitioner

_____

[Section 26:8]
  [1]Jones v. Jones, 1990 WL 107458 (Ohio Ct. App. 11th Dist. Geauga County 1990) (trial court did not abuse its discretion by allowing the testimony of a surprise witness because the testimony was not prejudicial).

should also be aware of certain objections provided in Civ. R. 32(D)(3)(a) and (b), and the timely manner in which they may be asserted.

Civ. R. 45 was amended in July 1993, to reduce the differences between deposition and trial subpoenas. Nonparties may now be subpoenaed for deposition. Each subpoena must contain the information provided in Sections (C) and (D) of Rule 45. Section (C) sets forth the rights of witnesses. It is meant to protect witnesses from undue burden or expense while not diluting other rights of protection under Rules 26 to 37. Under Civ. R. 45(A)(2), attorneys may now serve subpoenas for deposition and trial. Procedures to quash and/or modify a subpoena are addressed in Section (C)(3). According to Civ. R. 45(D)(1), subpoenaed documents kept in the ordinary course of business must be produced, organized, and labeled to correspond with the categories in the subpoena.

§ 26:10   Depositions—Perpetuating testimony before action is filed

A situation may arise where a person wants to perpetuate his own testimony or that of another person before an action is filed. Civ. R. 27 allows this and requires that a petition be filed in the common pleas court of the county in which the expected adverse party resides. The petitioner must verify that the contents of petition are true and the petition must contain the following:

(1) That the petitioner may be a party to an action or proceeding cognizable in a court but is unable to bring or defend the action;

(2) The subject matter of the action or proceeding and the petitioner's interest therein;

(3) The facts which the petitioner wishes to establish and his reasons for perpetuating those facts; and

(4) The names and addresses of the persons to be examined, and the subject matter of the testimony the petitioner expects to elicit from each person.

The petitioner must then request an order from the court allowing the deposition of the persons identified in his petition for the purpose of perpetuating their testimony. This discovery method may also be used while an appeal is pending. Although this method of discovery may be valuable in a civil case, its usefulness to a domestic relations practitioner may be limited.

§ 26:11   Depositions—Depositions upon oral questions

One of the most valuable and frequently used methods of discovery is the deposition. A deposition can provide immediate information in the least amount of time, which is important to every legal practitioner. Civ. R. 30 allows for the taking of depositions after the commencement of an action. Any party may take the testimony of any person by deposition upon oral examination. The witness's attendance may be compelled by the use of a subpoena as provided in Civ. R. 45. Civ. R. 30(B) requires that reasonable notice of the deposition be given to all parties. The notice must state the time and place for the taking of the deposition and the name and address of the person to be deposed. If a subpoena duces tecum is to be served on the person to be examined, the notice must designate the materials to be produced.

Civ. R. 30(B)(2) provides that if a party shows that he used due diligence and yet is unable to obtain counsel to represent him at the taking of the deposition, the deposition may not be used against him.

If the party taking the deposition intends to have the testimony recorded by other than stenographic means, Civ. R. 30(B)(3) requires that the notice specify the manner of such recording, preserving, and filing of the deposition. A notice of deposition may be accompanied by a request for production of documents made pursuant to Civ. R. 34. A corporation, partnership, or association may be named in the notice accompanied by a description of the matters on which examination is requested. The named organization must then appoint a proper person duly authorized to testify to those matters on its behalf.

The examination and cross-examination of the witness may proceed as allowed at trial. Civ. R. 30(C) provides that the witness must be put under oath by the officer before whom the deposition is taken. The testimony shall be recorded and must be transcribed when requested by one of the parties. Any objection to the manner of the taking of the deposition or to the conduct of any party must be noted by the officer taking the deposition. Evidence objected to must be taken subject to the objections. In lieu of participating in oral examination, parties may serve written questions on the deponent. This requires transmission of the questions to the officer who must then propound them to the witness. The answers must be recorded verbatim.

In the course of a deposition, a party may wish to limit or terminate the examination. Civ. R. 30(D) provides that upon motion of any party or of the deponent at any time during the taking of the deposition, upon a showing that the examination is being conducted in bad faith, or in a manner as to unreasonably annoy, embarrass, or oppress the deponent or party, the court may order the officer conducting the examination to immediately cease from taking the deposition, or may limit its scope pursuant to Civ. R. 26(C). The taking of the deposition may be suspended by the objecting party upon demand for the purpose of seeking a protective order. This provision is particularly useful in domestic relations cases which are, by their nature, subject to extreme emotions. The option of seeking a court order limiting the scope of a deposition or the manner in which it is being taken may be used by counsel to control the course of a deposition.

After the testimony of the deponent has been fully transcribed, Civ. R. 30(E) requires that the transcript be submitted to the deponent to be read and examined. This is done unless the deponent has waived signature. Any changes in form or substance made by the deponent must be entered upon the deposition by the officer with a statement of the reasons given by the deponent for the changes. The deponent must then sign the deposition. If the deponent has not signed the deposition within seven days of its submission to him, the officer who took the deposition must sign it, and, absent a motion to suppress, the deposition may be used as though it were signed. Upon a request by any party or the court, the officer before whom the deposition was taken must transcribe, certify, seal, and file it with the court in accordance with Civ. R. 30(F).[1] However, Civ. R. 5(D) states that depositions must not be filed unless on order of the court, or for use as evidence or for consideration of a motion in the proceeding. The officer must retain the original notes of the deposition for five years from the date of the deposition. After five years, the officer is permitted to discard the original notes so long as an archival copy is retained.

The failure of the party who initiated the deposition to attend or serve a subpoena on a witness may result in an award of fees and expenses by virtue of Civ. R. 30(G). If the party who gave the notice of the deposition fails to attend and proceed, and another party attends pursuant to the notice, the court may order the party who gave the notice to pay to the other party reasonable fees and expenses incurred in attending the failed deposition. If the party who gave the notice fails to serve a subpoena on a witness who for that reason fails to attend, the party who gave the notice may be ordered to pay reasonable fees and expenses incurred by other parties who attended the deposition.

§ 26:12   Depositions—Depositions upon oral questions—Notice to take deposition—Form⊚

[Title of Court]

[Caption]

Case No. *[_____]*

NOTICE TO TAKE DEPOSITION

NOTICE TO TAKE DEPOSITION UPON ORAL EXAMINATION:

To Attorney:

Please take notice that on *[date]* at *[time]* at the offices of *[name and address]*, *[Plaintiff/Defendant]* in the above entitled action will take the following depositions: *[here list depositions]*.

The oral examination will continue from day to day until completed. You are invited to attend and cross-examine.

_____

Attorney for *[Plaintiff/Defendant]*

[Proof/certificate of service]

[Section 26:11]

[1]See, e.g., Trimble-Weber v. Weber, 119 Ohio App. 3d 402, 695 N.E.2d 344 (11th Dist. Geauga County 1997).

§ 26:13 Depositions—Depositions upon oral questions—Notice to take deposition duces tecum—Form⊚

[Title of Court]

[Caption]   Case No. *[_____]*
                                               NOTICE TO TAKE DEPOSITION

To *[name of deponent]*:

Please take notice that at *[time]* on *[date]*, at the offices of *[name]*, located at *[address]*, counsel for *[Plaintiff/Defendant/Petitioner (name)]* will take deposition on oral examination of the following:

[Name of deponent].

[Name of deponent] shall bring with *[him/her]* the documents and things set forth on Exhibit "A" attached hereto and made a part hereof. *[Deponent]* will further take notice that said deposition will be conducted as if on cross-examination and pursuant to the Ohio Rules of Civil Procedure before a Notary Public or other officer authorized to take depositions and will be continued from day to day until completed.

[Deponent] shall further take notice that this Notice to Take Deposition upon a party shall not require further subpoena, it being the duty of counsel for *[deponent]* to produce *[deponent]* at said time and place.

_____

Attorney for *[Plaintiff/Defendant/Petitioner]*

[EXHIBIT A]

Bring with you any and all of the following items in your possession or under your control which existed or originated in the period *[date]* to present:

(a) Copies of all personal federal income tax returns, including all schedules, attachments, W-2 forms, and 1099 forms relating to each such return for each year and whether you filed individually or jointly and all data necessary to the preparation and filing of your 19[_____] return and a copy of such return, if the same be in existence;

(b) All check books, check stubs, canceled checks, bank statements and savings account passbooks, canceled or active, for any and all checking and/or savings accounts wherein you are or were a depositor, beneficiary or drawer, whether individually or jointly or otherwise with any other person;

(c) All agreements, records, books of account, corporate records, balance sheets, financial statements, and other writings pertaining to any business venture in which you have an interest;

(d) All records relating to the purchase or sale by you of any securities or intangible property, including periodic statements of account from any broker or brokers, confirmation slips and correspondence;

(e) All agreements, notes, personal financial statements and other writings pertaining to any loan or debt to which you became or are presently obligated, whether jointly or severally, and whether directly or indirectly as surety, co-signer or guarantor;

(f) All records pertaining to each employment of yours in the above period, including all employment contracts, pension or retirement plans, expense accounts or otherwise; including also all pay stubs;

(g) All other books, documents, records, accounts, lists, instruments, certificates, copies, deeds, bills of sale, contracts, financial statements and all other writings or things evidencing your ownership, legal interest, equitable interest, power or control in the above period in and to any and all property, real or personal, tangible or intangible, of whatever kind, nature and description, and wherever situated;

(h) All contracts, agreements, papers and documents pertaining to any corporation, partnership or association where you are one of the parties thereto as a principal, agent or employee;

(i) All Certificates of Title and Memorandum Certificates of Title for motor vehicles, recreational vehicles, trailers and boats in which you have an interest or which you operate on a regular basis;

(j) All canceled checks, credit applications, contracts, vouchers, invoices, statements and all other documents and records pertaining to the purchases of tangible or intangible personal property whether financed or purchased for cash;

(k) All invoices, billings and other indicia of the purchase of major items of personal property including furniture, carpeting and the like;

(l) Records and receipts of all out-of-town travel whether for business or pleasure;

(m) All contracts of insurance, certificates of insurance, certificates of coverage, statements of cash value upon insurance or other documents or writings in your possession concerning insurance for your benefit or for the benefit of your designee, including, specifically, any and all life insurance, medical or hospitalization insurance, disability insurance or any other type of insurance coverage which is for you or your designee;

(n) All notes, leases, contracts or other written instruments entered into, executed, endorsed or guaranteed by you whether such writings are for your benefit or the benefit of others;

(o) All correspondence with regard to applications by you for Social Security retirement and/or disability benefits;

(p) Wage or pay stubs for past three months; and

(q) All trust agreements for any trust of which you are a donor or grantor, a beneficiary, or a trustee, together with records of account and records of receipts, distributions, and payments.

[Proof/certificate of service]

§ 26:14 Depositions—Depositions upon written questions

Civ. R. 31 provides for depositions of witnesses upon written questions. This discovery tool is valuable when distance provides an obstacle to direct, in-person witness questioning. After an action has been commenced, the party wishing to take a deposition upon written questions must serve a notice upon every party in the action. The notice must state, if known, the name and address of the person who is to answer the questions, and if the name and address are unknown, a general description must be given to identify the person who is to be deposed. The notice must also state the name or descriptive title and address of the officer before whom the deposition is to be taken. This method may be used to take the deposition of a public or private corporation, a partnership, or an association in accordance with Civ. R. 30(B)(5). Civ. R. 31(A) further provides that within twenty-one days after service, a party may serve cross-questions upon all other parties. Within fourteen days after service of these questions, a party may serve redirect questions upon all other parties. Recross questions may be served upon all other parties within fourteen days after the redirect questions have been served. The questions must be taken by the witness to the officer named in the notice who will take the testimony of the witness in response to the questions as provided in Civ. R. 30(C), (E), and (F).

This discovery tool may be quite useful to domestic relations practitioners when, for example, assets of the parties are located out of state and it becomes necessary to depose an appraiser of those assets.

§ 26:15   Depositions—Depositions upon written questions— Notice to take deposition upon written questions—Form⊚

[Title of Court]

[Caption]   Case No. [_____]
                                             NOTICE TO TAKE DEPOSITION
                                             UPON WRITTEN QUESTIONS

TO: _____
                                                   Attorney for Plaintiff

Please take notice that the attached questions will be propounded on Defendant's behalf to: *[deponent]*, whose address is *[address]*, at the taking of his deposition before *[name and address of court reporter]*.

1. State your full name and address.

2. What is your profession or occupation?

3. What is your educational background?

4. What experience and training have you had in real estate appraising?

5. Have you done any teaching of real estate appraisal?

6. Have you made an appraisal of real property and any and all structures thereon on which *[name(s)]* are owners or co-owners, specifically:

[a. Cabin and land located one-fourth mile west of Allison's Gap about 150 yards up the side of wooded ridge south of State Road 613;

b. Lot 52, Plat Book 7, Page 39, intersection of roads 107 and 610;

c. Lot 25, Plat Book 7, Page 99, Deed Book 251, Page 383, Pleasant Heights Subdivision;

d. Sallie Terry land, consisting of 27 acres, more or less, Deed Book 228, Page 598, Plat Book 4, Page 58;]

all of said property being in [_____].

7. In whose name does Tract 1 stand?

    a. Describe said property.

    b. Do you have an opinion as to the current fair market value of said property?

    c. What is the current fair market value of said property?

8. In whose name does Tract 2 stand?

    a. Describe said property.

    b. Do you have an opinion as to the current fair market value of said property?

    c. What is the current fair market value of said property?

9. In whose name does Tract 3 stand?

    a. Describe said property.

    b. Do you have an opinion as to the current fair market value of said property?

    c. What is the current fair market value of said property?

10. In whose name does Tract 4 stand?

    a. Describe said property.

    b. Do you have an opinion as to the current fair market value of said property?

    c. What is the current fair market value of said property?

11. Have you made a written report concerning these four parcels of real estate? Please mark it Defendant's Deposition Exhibit "A" and give it to the Court Reporter to be attached to and made a part of the deposition.

[Proof/certificate of service]

§ 26:16   Depositions—Use of depositions in court proceedings

Civ. R. 32 governs the use of depositions in court proceedings. A deposition must be filed at least one day before the day of trial or hearing, absent leave of court. A trial court has wide discretion in determining the admissibility of evidence. The court may enforce a discovery cut off date. In *Lieberman v. Lieberman*,[1] the Eighth District Court of Appeals held that the trial court did not abuse its discretion by excluding deposition testimony taken after its imposed discovery deadline. Admissibility and any objections thereto are determined under the rules of evidence applied as though the witness were then present and testifying. The deposition may be used against any party who was present or represented at the deposition, or who had reasonable notice thereof, in accordance with any one of the following:

    (1) For the purpose of impeaching the testimony of the deponent as

---

[Section 26:16]

[1]Lieberman v. Lieberman, 1999 WL 342238 (Ohio Ct. App. 8th Dist. Cuyahoga County 1999).

a witness;

(2) For any purpose where the deponent, an officer of a corporation or partnership, testified on behalf of the corporation or partnership;

(3) For any purpose where the court finds that the witness is dead, beyond subpoena power of the court, is unable to attend because of age, sickness, or imprisonment,[2] is unable to be subpoenaed, or is an attending physician or medical expert; that oral examination of a witness is not required; or that exceptional circumstances exist as to allow the deposition to be used in the interest of justice; or

(4) Where only part of a deposition is offered into evidence by a party and an adverse party requires him to introduce all which is relevant to the offered portion.

Civ. R. 32(C) provides that a party does not make a person his own witness by taking his deposition. If a party introduces the deposition into evidence for any purpose other than that of impeaching the deponent, then the deponent is the witness of that party, unless the witness is the adverse party.

Civ. R. 32(D) relates to the effect of errors and irregularities in depositions. Any error or irregularity in the notice of deposition is waived unless written objections stating the reasons therefore are promptly served. Any objections to the qualifications of the officer before whom the deposition is taken are waived unless they are made prior to the commencement of the deposition or as soon thereafter as they become known.

Civ. R. 32(D)(3)(a) provides that any objections to the competency of a witness or to the competency, relevancy, or materiality of testimony are not waived by failure to make the objection before or during the deposition, unless the ground is one which might have been abbreviated or removed if presented at that time.

Error and irregularities occurring at the deposition in the form of questions or answers, in the oath or affirmation, or in the conduct of parties, or errors of any kind which might be cured or removed if promptly presented, are waived unless reasonable objections are made at the deposition.

Objections to written questions submitted under Civ. R. 31 are waived unless served in writing upon the propounding party.

§ 26:17 Interrogatories

Civ. R. 33 sets out the procedure for the use of interrogatories. Any party may be served with forty written interrogatories, after the commencement of an action, without leave of court. A party must obtain leave of court to serve written interrogatories in excess of forty. Any

---

[2]Wernert v. Wernert, 61 Ohio Misc. 2d 436, 579 N.E.2d 800 (C.P. 1991) (incarcerated divorce complainant permitted to present case through deposition).

subpart propounded under an interrogatory is considered a separate interrogatory for purposes of this rule. Each interrogatory must be fully answered in writing under oath. If the interrogatory is objected to, the reason for the objection may be stated in lieu of an answer. The answering party must sign the answers, and the attorney must sign any objections made. The answering party must serve the answers and objections within the time period specified by the submitting party, but the time specified may not be less than twenty-eight days after service. The submitting party may move for an order to compel answers pursuant to Civ. R. 37 if the answers are not forthcoming within the required time.

The scope of interrogatories is broad; they may relate to any matters relevant to the subject matter of the action that are not privileged.[1] If the interrogatories inquire about information contained in business records, the answering party should specify the records where the information may be found and make those records available to the party serving the interrogatories.[2] Sufficient space between each question should be left where the answering party may type his answer. This space must be at least one inch. It is often useful to serve interrogatories with the complaint for divorce in order to obtain fundamental information upon which to build a case. If a party fails to supplement the answers provided to written interrogatories as information becomes available, any answers, documents, and witnesses not identified may be excluded at trial.[3]

§ 26:18 Interrogatories—Form◉

[Title of Court]

[Caption]   Case No. [_____]
                              INTERROGATORIES TO
                              [DEFENDANT / PLAINTIFF]

To *[Defendant / Plaintiff]*,

The following Interrogatories are submitted herewith to you to be answered in writing, under oath, twenty-eight days after the date of service thereof upon you.

INSTRUCTIONS FOR ANSWERING:

(1) All information is to be divulged that is in your possession or

---

[Section 26:17]

[1]Wyrick v. Wyrick, 1982 WL 3505 (Ohio Ct. App. 4th Dist. Lawrence County 1982).

[2]But see Majestic Steel Service, Inc., 1999 WL 1206573 (Ohio Ct. App. 8th Dist. Cuyahoga County 1999) (trade secrets not discoverable).

[3]Jones v. Murphy, 12 Ohio St. 3d 84, 465 N.E.2d 444 (1984) (exclusion of plaintiff's expert medical testimony proper as sanction for plaintiff's violation of civil rule requiring supplementation of interrogatory responses with respect to identity of each expert witness expected to be called at trial). But see Sivillo v. Dreig & Krump Mfg. Co., 1986 WL 6114 (Ohio Ct. App. 8th Dist. Cuyahoga County 1986) (allowing expert witness to testify where defendant was provided with expert opinion and knew of expert's identity prior to trial, and the expert was available for deposition, yet defendant never deposed expert, nor made requests for production, nor asked for expert's name).

control or within the possession or control of your attorney, agents, or other representatives of you.

(2) Where an Interrogatory calls for an answer in more than one part, each part should be separate in the answer so that the answer is clearly understandable.

(3) You are reminded that all answers must be made separately and fully and that any incomplete or evasive answers are a failure to answer.

(4) Interrogatories are continuing in nature so as to require amendments, supplementation, or correction of answers should information become known to you which would change them in any manner.

INTERROGATORIES

Note: Civil Rule 33(A) limits the total number of interrogatories to forty, and counts subparts as a separate question.

(1) What is your full name?

ANSWER

(2) What is you social security number?

ANSWER

(3) What is your date of birth?

ANSWER

(4) What is your present address?

ANSWER

(5) How long have you resided at such address?

ANSWER

(6) Do you live alone? If not, give name of person or persons with whom you reside.

ANSWER

(7) Are you married? If so, state: *[include if post-decree]*

    a. The date of the marriage.

    b. The city, county and state of marriage.

ANSWERS

(8) Are there any living children that were born of your marriage to *[name of spouse]*? If so, for each child, state:

    a. The full name.

    b. The date and place of birth.

    c. The present address.

ANSWERS

(9) Except for your spouse and children, do you have any other dependents? If so, for each dependent, state:

    a. The name and address.

    b. The date and place of birth.

    c. Your relation to such dependent.

    d. The amount of money expended per month in the support of such dependent.

ANSWERS

(10) Were you married at any time prior to your present marriage? If so, for each former marriage, state:

a. The date of marriage.

b. The name and last known address of the former spouse.

c. The date on which the marriage was legally terminated.

d. Names and dates of birth of any children born of the marriage.

e. A description of the result of the action, including spousal support, custody awards, and determinations of parental rights and responsibilities.

ANSWERS

(11) If you will do so without a motion to produce, attach a copy of each divorce and annulment decree or judgment to your answers to these interrogatories.

ANSWER

(12) Have you been employed since the date of your marriage? If so, state:

a. Inclusive dates of employment.

b. Employer's name and address.

c. Position held.

d. Annual salary.

e. Reason for termination.

ANSWERS

(13) State your pay period and your gross pay each pay period and itemize all deductions.

ANSWER

(14) If you will do so without a motion to produce, attach a copy of your three past pay check stubs.

ANSWER

(15) Do you have payroll deductions for a stock or bond purchase plan? If so, state:

a. The amounts deducted.

b. The times of deductions.

c. The period of time you have been enrolled in such a plan.

d. Name of owner shown on bond.

ANSWERS

(16) Do you have a payroll deduction for a credit union savings account? If so, state:

a. The amounts deducted.

b. The time of deductions.

c. The period of time you have been enrolled in such a plan.

ANSWERS

(17) Do you have any savings or commercial accounts in your name solely or jointly with others, with any bank or financial institution? If so, for each account state:

a. The name and address of the bank or financial institution.

b. The names on the account.

c. The persons authorized to draw on the account.

d. The date the account was opened.

e. The account number.

f. The amount of the present balance, if any.

g. The date the account was closed.

h. The amount of the balance before the account was closed.

i. The disposition of funds after account was closed.

j. The date and amount of the largest balance in said account.

ANSWERS

(18) Are there any safe deposit boxes, vaults, safes or other places of deposit in safekeeping, in which you deposited money, documents or other items of personal property since *[date]*. If so, state:

a. The name and address of the depositor or institution.

b. The number of the means of identification of deposit.

c. The name and address of each person authorized to enter deposit.

d. The date deposit was commenced.

e. The item or items deposited.

f. The date the deposit was terminated.

ANSWERS

(19) Do you now own interest in any real property? If so, for each parcel of property, state:

a. The address.

b. A description of each building, structure or improvement on the property.

c. The method of acquisition of title.

d. The source of funds for the acquisition of title.

e. The date of acquisition.

f. The name and address of the seller or person from which title was acquired.

g. The date and place the deed was recorded.

h. How the property was titled.

i. The present location of the deed or other document of title.

j. Who has the outstanding mortgage, if any.

k. The amount of monthly payments, if any.

l. What portion of the purchase price was financed.

m. What was the interest rate.

n. What is the present balance due on the mortgage note.

ANSWERS

(20) Since *[date]* have you sold or transferred any interest in real property? If so, for each sale or transfer, state:

a. The address and description of the property.

b. The date of sale or transfer.

c. The method of transfer.

d. The name and address of each purchaser or person receiving title and the interest received by such person.

e. The purchase price or consideration received for the transfer.

f. The amount of the purchase price due and unpaid.

g. The amount of the proceeds of the transfer received by you.

h. The interest you presently have in such property.

ANSWERS

(21) Have you and your spouse filed joint tax returns? If so, state:

a. Whether since *[date]* there were any refunds.

b. The amount of each refund.

c. The disposition of each refund.

d. Whether a joint tax return is to be filed.

e. The anticipated disposition of any refund.

ANSWERS

(22) Does any person, executor, or estate hold any property, real or personal, or future interest for your benefit, in trust or otherwise? If so, for each item, past, present or future, state:

a. The name and address of any such person, firm or estate.

b. A description of the property and the past, present or future interest held for your benefit.

c. The conditions under which the property is held for your benefit.

d. The approximate value of the property.

ANSWERS

(23) Have you been examined or treated by any doctor or physician since *[date]*? If so, for each occasion, state:

a. The name and last known address of each doctor or physician.

b. The date that each doctor or physician was seen.

c. The nature of the disease or disorder for which each doctor or physician was seen.

d. The type of treatment received from each doctor or physician.

e. What was the duration of your treatment?

f. Are you fully recovered?

ANSWERS

(24) List your current monthly living expenses, in detail.

ANSWER

(25) Do these expenses include the support of any person other than yourself? If so, state the name of each such person and the monthly expenses contributed to such person.

ANSWER

(26) Do you have any outstanding obligations, including mortgages, conditional sales contracts, promissory notes or credit card accounts? If so, for each obligation, state specifically:

a. The name and address of the creditor.

b. The form of the obligation.

c. The date the obligation was incurred.

d. The consideration received for each obligation.

e. The amount of the original obligation.

f. A description of any security given for the obligation.

g. The rate of interest on the obligation.

h. The present unpaid balance on the obligation.

i. The date and amount of required installment repayment.

ANSWERS

(27) Please detail the number of trips taken by you outside of [_____] County] within the last [_____] months. Specify for each of such trips the date of departure and return, destination, mode of travel, purposes, where you stayed when you got there, with whom you stayed, name and address of anyone who may have accompanied you. Further state the name and address of any party who paid part or all of the expenses involved in any of such trips.

ANSWER

(28) Please specify any sources of income other than wages listed above which you have had within the last *[specify period of time]*. Specify in detail the dates and nature of such other income received by you.

ANSWER

(29) Does anybody owe you any money? If so, for each debtor, state:

a. The name and address of the debtor.

b. The amount owed.

c. The form of the obligation.

d. The date the obligation was incurred.

e. The date the obligation becomes due and owing.

f. The conditions for payment of the obligation.

g. The consideration given for the obligation.

ANSWERS

(30) Do you own any automobiles or other vehicles of transportation? If so, for each automobile or such vehicle of transportation, state:

a. The year, make, model, and license number.

b. The name and address of the registered owner.

c. The date of purchase.

d. The name and address of the person or firm from whom the automobile or vehicle was purchased.

e. The purchase price of the automobile or vehicle.

f. How long you have been driving this automobile or vehicle.

ANSWERS

(31) Does your employer provide you with an automobile?

ANSWER

(32) Do you presently own or have any interest in any life insurance or annuity policy? If so, for each policy, state:

a. The name and address of the insurance company.

b. The number of the policy.

c. The type of policy, that is, term, straight life, etc.

d. The day the policy was issued.

e. The face amount of the policy.

f. The amount of the annual premium.

g. The total amount of the premiums paid on the policy.

h. The name and address of each person making such payments.

i. The name and address of each owner of the policy.

j. The name and address of each beneficiary named in the policy.

k. The date of any change of beneficiary; the name of each beneficiary added or deleted.

l. The date of assignment of the policy; the name of each assignee, if the policy has been assigned.

m. The name and address of the insurance agent or broker for the policy.

n. The amount and date of each loan made on the policy.

o. The present cash surrender value of the policy.

ANSWERS

(33) Do you have any interest in any kind of retirement or pension fund? If so, state:

a. Name or description of said fund.

b. Name and address of custodian of the fund.

c. Name of employer contributing to said fund.

d. Total amount of your contributions to the fund to date.

e. Total amount of your employer's contributions to date.

f. Present balance of your interest in the fund.

g. Date you are entitled to receive retirement or pension benefits.

h. Amount of benefits receivable per month on retirement.

i. Amount of funds available to you and method of obtaining them without retirement.

ANSWERS

(34) List all stocks or other securities that you have owned during the past [specify period of time].

ANSWER

(35) List the stock which you have sold within the past [specify period of time] and the date sold and sale price.

ANSWER

(36) Have you moved from the marital home? If so, state:

a. When you moved.

b. What sums you have given for the support of your wife and children and dates given.

ANSWERS

(37) Have you in the past resided away from the marital home? If so, state:

a. Dates.

b. Where resided.

c. With whom you resided.

ANSWERS

(38) Have you ever committed adultery at any time during your marriage? If so, state for each act:

a. The date.

b. The address of the place.

    c. The name and address of the other person involved.
ANSWERS
(39) Have you ever asked your spouse for a divorce? If so, state:
    a. The date of the request.
    b. The reason for the request.
ANSWERS
(40) Have you ever sought help from a professional counselor? If so,
state:
    a. Name and address of counselor.
    b. Dates when consulted.
    c. Whether you received a written evaluation.
    d. The names of individuals to whom you disclosed details.
    e. Why you sought counseling.
    f. Who advised you to seek counseling.
ANSWERS
(41) Have you ever beaten, slapped, struck or kicked your spouse?
If so, for each incident, state:
    a. The date and place.
    b. The reason for your actions.
    c. A description of the injury caused to your spouse.
    d. Whether you were intoxicated.
ANSWERS
(42) Has your spouse ever required medical attention due to injuries
caused by you? If so, for each occasion, state:
    a. The date.
    b. The injuries involved.
    c. The manner in which injuries were received.
ANSWERS
(43) Have you ever accused your spouse of having sexual relations
with another person? If so, for each accusation, state:
    a. The date.
    b. The substance of the accusation.
    c. The name and address of the other person.
    d. The dates you claim that each act occurred.
    e. The place of each such act.
    f. The name and address of each person present when you made
the accusation.
    g. The facts on which you rely to support the accusation.
ANSWERS
(44) In your [paper filed with court], you allege that your spouse has
been guilty of gross neglect of duty. State with particularity:
    a. The acts of which you complain.
    b. The dates of each act.
    c. Where each act took place.
    d. Names and addresses of witnesses to each act.
    e. Whether you discussed these acts with your spouse.

ANSWERS

(45) In your *[paper filed with court]*, you allege that your spouse has been guilty of extreme cruelty. State with particularity:

 a. The acts of which you complain.

 b. The date of each act.

 c. Where each act took place.

 d. Names and addresses of witnesses to each act.

 e. Whether you discussed these acts with your spouse.

ANSWERS

(46) Have you obtained written or recorded statements concerning the issues in this action? If so, for each statement, state:

 a. The name and address of the person who took the statement.

 b. The name and address of the person who made the statement.

 c. Whether the statement is written or recorded.

 d. The name and address of the person who has custody of this statement.

 e. The substance of the statement.

ANSWERS

(47) Do you own any other personal property not referred to above? If so, for each item, state:

 a. A complete description.

 b. The present location of the property.

 c. The estimated present value of the property.

 d. The name and address of each other person who has possession of the property.

ANSWERS

Respectfully submitted,

_____

Attorney for *[Plaintiff/Defendant]*

[Proof/certificate of service]

NOTES TO FORM

Drafter's Notes

Neither the original or a copy of the interrogatories nor the answers thereto are to be filed with the court except pursuant to Civ. R. 5(D).

Sufficient space must be provided between each interrogatory for an answer. The minimum space between interrogatories pursuant to Civ. R. 33(D) is one inch.

The above are suggestions only. Since Civil Rule 33(A) limits interrogatories to forty in number, with each subpart counted as a separate interrogatory, select only necessary questions.

§ 26:19   Request for production of documents

The request for production of documents, provided for in Civ. R. 34, is quite useful in domestic relations cases. Like interrogatories, and distinct from depositions, this request may be made on the parties only. The request should set forth those items to be inspected and describe each item and category with reasonable particularity. Further, a specified reasonable time, place, and manner of making the inspection must be provided in the request. A written response by the party served with the request must be made within the period designated in the request, but the time specified may not be less than twenty-eight days after service. The response to each item or category must state that inspection will be allowed unless objections are raised. If such objections are raised, the reasons for the objections must be stated.

A request for production of documents may be very useful in a domestic relations matter, especially where one of the parties has an interest in a business. It is vital to name the business for whom a party works or in which he or she has an interest as a party to the divorce action, since business records are often vital in ascertaining the assets of the parties in domestic relations cases. However, interrogatories and requests for production of documents from businesses are only available if the organization is named as a party. These requests may be served with the initial complaint for divorce and are useful in combination with restraining orders where there is a fear that assets will be sequestered or disposed of by a party.

Civ. R. 34(B) provides a party producing documents with the option of producing the documents "as they are kept in the usual course of business or organized and labeled to correspond with the categories in the request." The Advisory Committee commentary to Civ. R. 34(B) indicates that this section was designed to prevent the commingling of "critical" documents with other documents in a deliberate effort to disguise the significance of the former.

§ 26:20 Request for production of documents—Form⊚

[Title of Court]

[Caption]

Case No. *[_____]*

REQUEST FOR PRODUCTION
OF
DOCUMENTS

Plaintiff requests that Defendant permit *[him / her]* to inspect and copy the documents attached hereto and for identification purposes marked Exhibit "A."

It is requested that this inspection take place in the office of *[name]* attorney for Plaintiff, *[address]*, on *[date]*, at *[time]*.

_____

Attorney for Plaintiff

[EXHIBIT "A"]

1. Copies of your federal income tax returns, including all schedules and attachments, W-2 forms and 1099 forms relating to such returns *[for calendar years [_____], [_____]]/for the past five years]*.

2. All records indicating any and all income received by you from any and all sources from *[date]* to date, including nontaxable income.

3. All employment information including, without limitation, wages,

salaries, bonuses, stock options, commissions, earnings, pay check stubs, employment contracts, letters or memoranda of terms of employment, pay raises, promotions, payroll deductions, other deductions of any kind, credit union accounts, pension plan, pension fund, retirement plan, retirement fund, annuity and other benefits or deductions of any kind which are, were previously, or which may be in the future, paid, available, accepted, rejected, credited, offered, withheld for any purpose by any individual, agency, department, company, or otherwise, or to which you are, were, or may become entitled in the future at any time from *[date]* to date.

4. Records that relate to any secured or unsecured personal loan made to you from *[date]*, whether from a member of your family, a banking institution, or any individual or entity.

5. All savings accounts, credit union, or other passbooks of yours, including those held by you in your name or in your name jointly with any person or entity, or in your name as trustee for any other person or over which you have a right of withdrawal, from *[date]* to date (regardless of whether or not the account or accounts have been closed), including any such accounts in your name as custodian for any minor under the Uniform Gift to Minors Act or otherwise, and showing any and all savings deposits of every kind and nature.

6. All checking accounts in your name individually, with another as trustee or guardian, or in which you may have an interest or a right of withdrawal, including checkbooks or their registers, deposit slips, monthly statements and canceled checks, regardless of whether or not the account or accounts have been closed, from *[date]* to date.

7. All records pertaining to real estate in which you have acquired or may have acquired an interest during the period of your marriage, including any leases or mortgages related thereto (including monthly payments and present outstanding balance of principal and interest), together with any evidence showing all contributions in cash or otherwise made by you to the acquisition of such real estate.

8. Copies of all sales agreements and/or options for any real estate owned by you and those held by you in your name or in your name jointly with any other person, or in your name in trust, or in your name as guardian for any other person.

9. Copies of any and all brokerage account statements or securities owned by you individually, jointly with any person or entity, or as trustee, guardian or custodian, from *[date]* to date, including in such records dates of purchase and amounts paid for such securities.

10. Copies of any securities and investments owned by you and not reflected in any brokerage account records or statements.

11. All records indicating all interest of any kind held by you in any and all corporations (foreign or domestic) or any other entities not evidenced by certificates or other instruments.

12. All records pertaining to stock options in any corporation or other entity, exercised or not yet exercised.

13. Copies of all mortgages, notes received, or other evidence of debts

due you individually, or otherwise, executed or payable from *[date]*, to date.

14. All records relative to all inter vivos trusts from which benefits have been received, are being received, or will be received by you, whether such trusts are revocable or irrevocable.

15. All records of all estates of decedents from which you have received, are receiving, or will receive any inheritance in either personal property, real property, assets, in trust or otherwise, or monetary assets of any kind during the period of your marriage to *[name of spouse]*.

16. Copies of all financial statements, balance sheets and income statements received by you with respect to any and all proprietorships, joint ventures, partnerships, realty trusts, corporation or other legal entities in which you hold a legal or equitable ownership interest, individually or otherwise, from *[date]*.

17. Copies of all partnership and/or joint venture agreements in which you are a party.

18. Copies of declarations of trust, and minute books for all trusts, to which you are a party.

19. Copies of all corporate records (articles of incorporation, by-laws and minute books) for every corporation in which you have a legal or equitable ownership interest.

20. All books and records showing any fringe benefits available to you from any business entity in which you have a legal or equitable ownership interest or by whom you are or have been employed, including without limitation, auto expenses, travel expenses, personal living and entertainment expenses, life insurance bonuses, health, accident and medical and dental insurance.

21. All records and statements pertaining to any interest which you may have in any pension, retirement, annuity or profit-sharing plans, or contracts, or Civil Service accounts, including copies of the plans, contracts or accounts.

22. All records, statements and documents regarding Individual Retirement Accounts (IRA) showing amount or value of account and beneficiary designation.

23. Copies of all loan applications and statements of loan accounts for all loans applied for by you, whether or not taken or approved, from *[date]*.

24. Copies of any and all personal financial statements prepared by an accountant or any other person for you for any business in which you have or had an interest, from *[date]*.

25. Copies of personal property tax returns for the years *[list of years]*.

26. Any and all documents, memoranda or writing relating to any interest you may have in real estate, whether as owner, co-owner, fiduciary, trust beneficiary (vested or contingent), partner, limited partner, shareholder, joint venturer, mortgagee, developer, manager, or otherwise.

27. Life insurance policies or certificates of life insurance currently in existence insuring your life and any disability insurance currently in ex-

istence, life insurance policies or certificates of life insurance currently in existence insuring the life of any other person in which you are named as either primary or contingent beneficiary.

28. All credit cards and charge accounts held by you and all statements and receipts received by you in connection with the use of such credit cards and charge accounts, from *[date]*, together with a list of all businesses where you are authorized to charge purchases to the account of another person or entity.

29. Copies of all financial statements or records containing financial information of any nature which have been submitted by you to banks or lending institutions or to any person or entities in connection with your application for credit or loans, from *[date]*.

30. All registrations to motor vehicles and water crafts currently being used by you or owned by you.

31. All records pertaining to the transfer by sale or gift or otherwise of any personal property with a value over $100 from *[date]*.

32. All records pertaining to the acquisition, transfer and sale of all securities from *[date]*, such records to include any and all information relative to gains or losses realized from transactions involving such securities.

33. All ledgers, books, accounts, cash receipt journals, accounts receivable, accounts payable, and all other accounts kept or maintained by you (or under your supervision and direction) in connection with any business or businesses, from *[date]*.

34. Any and all books, receipts, records, checks or other tangible evidence of charitable donations made by you or on your behalf, from *[date]*.

35. All records pertaining to gifts of any kind made by you to any person, firm, trust, corporation, or other entity, from *[date]*.

36. A list setting forth the names and addresses of all persons who were witnesses to or have knowledge or information of any relevant facts relating to this action or who possess proof of incidents or acts involved, their relationship to you, and indicating which were eyewitnesses, all written memoranda and reports and photographs submitted to you or your attorney by any such person, and all tape recordings or other evidence prepared from tape recordings made in connection with any wiretapping or other electronic surveillance conducted by you or others on your behalf.

37. A list of names and addresses of any and all proposed expert witnesses, and certified copies of all written reports rendered to you or your attorney by any such proposed expert witness.

38. Copies of any and all Wills and/or trusts wherein you are named, and/or wherein you are given any beneficial interest, and/or wherein you are named as trustee and/or executor, including but not limited to the Wills and/or trusts of your mother and/or close relatives.

39. All records pertaining to any account or accounts of every kind and nature whatsoever in which you have deposited or withdrawn funds or incurred debits or credits, including certificates of deposit.

40. Copies of all records of all transactions involving assets of any

kind, including without limitation, stocks, bonds, real and personal property of whatever nature and kind and wherever situated held by others for your benefit from *[date]*.

41. A list of all gifts received by you from any person or entity, including the amount and date of each such gift from *[date]*.

NOTES TO FORM

Drafter's Notes

A proof/certificate of service is only necessary when there is opposing counsel. Where the respondent is unrepresented by counsel at the time of filing the request, the request will be served by the clerk of court pursuant to written instructions filed with it. The original of these papers is to be served upon the party or counsel. A copy should not be filed with the court except pursuant to Civ. R. 5(D).

§ 26:21 Physical and mental examinations

Civ. R. 35 provides for the physical and/or mental examination of a person when a party's mental or physical condition is in controversy. Such an order may be made on motion for good cause shown.[1] The order must specify the time, place, manner, conditions, and scope of the examination and the person by whom it is to be made. The party against whom an order is made or the person examined may request a copy of the detailed written report submitted by the examiner which should state the findings, test results, diagnoses, and conclusions of the examinations.

The procedure in Civ. R. 35 has broad application in a domestic relations practice, since the mental and physical conditions of the parties are vital in parental rights, child support, and parentage actions.[2] RC 3109.04(C) has a parallel provision which states that the court may order the parties and their minor children to submit to medical, psychological, and psychiatric examinations.

§ 26:22 Motion for a medical/psychiatric exam—Form⊚

[Title of Court]

[Caption]

Case No. *[_____]*

MOTION FOR
MEDICAL/PSYCHIATRIC
EXAMINATION

[Party] moves this Court for an Order requiring the *[party/minor*

[Section 26:21]

[1]Wayne M. Shoff v. Andrea J. Shoff, 1995 WL 450249 (Ohio Ct. App. 10th Dist. Franklin County 1995).

[2]See, e.g., Brossia v. Brossia, 65 Ohio App. 3d 211, 583 N.E.2d 978 (6th Dist. Wood County 1989) (reversing trial court's order that former spouses and their children submit to psychiatric evaluations where neither party filed a motion pursuant to Civ. R. 35(A)); Williamson v. Williamson, 1997 WL 746425 (Ohio Ct. App. 10th Dist. Franklin County 1997) (reversing trial court's order that defendant submit to psychological evaluation where the only matter before the court was a motion for new trial, not a request for modification of the visitation order).

child of the party / all parties] to submit to a *[medical / psychological / psychiatric]* examination and evaluation to assist the Court in determining *[parental rights and responsibilities for / visitation rights with]* the minor children, pursuant to RC 3109.04(C).

This motion is supported by the Memorandum below.

_____

Attorney for Movant

[Memorandum in support of motion]

[Notice of hearing]

[Proof / certificate of service]

NOTES TO FORM

Drafter's Notes

This motion is often made in connection with a motion for modification of custody, parental rights and responsibilities, or visitation.

§ 26:23   Request for admission

Request for admission is another method of discovery available among parties only. Civ. R. 36(A) provides that a written request may be served upon any other party for admission of the truth of any matters set forth in the request that are within the scope of Civ. R. 26(B), including the genuineness of any documents described. Copies of any documents must be served with the request. Each matter on which an admission is requested must be separately stated and sufficient space of not less than one inch must be provided for the answer. The matter is admitted unless the answering party serves a written answer or objection addressed to the matter within the designated period in the request. The time period, however, shall not be less than twenty-eight days after service. The written answers or objections must be signed by the party or by his attorney. If an objection is made, the reasons should be stated. In answering the request, the rule provides as follows:

(1) The answer shall specifically deny the matter or provide in detail the reasons why the answering party cannot truthfully admit or deny the matter.

(2) A denial shall fairly meet the substance of the required admission.

(3) If a party must qualify his answer, he shall specify so much of it as is true and qualify or deny the remainder of the request.

(4) Lack of information or knowledge may not be given as a reason for failure to admit or deny the request, unless the answering party states that he has made reasonable inquiry and the information obtainable by him is insufficient to enable him to admit or deny.

Civ. R. 36(B) provides that any matter admitted in a request for admission is conclusively established unless the court permits withdrawal or amendment of the admission.

The procedure in Civ. R. 36 is useful to compare the issues before trial and may have grave consequences for the unwary practitioner who fails to file a timely response to the requests, or who fails to properly answer each request.[1] In addition to having the truth of the matter admitted for purposes of the action, Civ. R. 37(C) provides that the expenses of making the proof may be levied against the nonresponding party.

§ 26:24 Request for admissions—Form⊚

[Title of Court]

[Caption]   Case No. *[_____]*
                                           REQUEST FOR ADMISSIONS

[Plaintiff/Defendant] propounds the following requests for admissions to *[Defendant/Plaintiff]* pursuant to Civil Rule 36 to be responded to within twenty-eight days from the date of service hereof in accordance with the Rules of Civil Procedure and subject to the provisions of Rule 37:

1. That the parties were married on *[date]* at *[place]*;

2. That there are *[no/number]* minor *[child/children]* of the marriage, namely, *[name(s) and date(s) of birth of children]*;

3. That the grounds as stated in the complaint/cross-complaint are true;

4. That Plaintiff and Defendant are joint owners of the marital home, located at *[street address, city, state]* and that the marital home has a present fair market value of *[$_____]*;

5. That Plaintiff and Defendant own the following securities, all of which constitute marital assets:

[List securities including certificate numbers and number of shares]; and

6. That Plaintiff and Defendant are jointly responsible on the following marital debts:

[List creditors and amount of each debt]

_____
                                           Attorney for *[Plaintiff/Defendant]*

[Proof/certificate of service]

NOTES TO FORM

Drafter's Notes

Counsel should not file original or any copy of this discovery request before or after answered, except pursuant to Civ. R. 5(D).

§ 26:25 Compelling discovery

Civ. R. 37 provides the methods for compelling discovery and sanc-

---

[Section 26:23]

[1]Dobbelaere v. Cosco, Inc., 120 Ohio App. 3d 232, 697 N.E.2d 1016 (3d Dist. Paulding County 1997) (unanswered requests for admission render the matter requested conclusively established for the purpose of the suit).

tions for failure to make discovery. A party may move for an order compelling discovery if a deponent fails to answer a question propounded or submitted under Civ. R. 30 or 31, if a party fails to answer an interrogatory submitted under Civ. R. 33, or if a party fails to respond that inspection will be permitted under Civ. R. 34 or fails to permit the requested inspection. An evasive or incomplete answer constitutes a failure to answer.

If the court grants the motion to compel, the court must, after an opportunity for a hearing, require the party who opposed the motion or the attorney who advised such conduct, or both, to pay the moving party the reasonable expenses incurred in obtaining the order unless the court finds that an award of expenses would be unjust. If the motion is denied, the court must, after an opportunity for a hearing, require the moving party or the attorney advising the motion, or both, to pay the expenses incurred in opposing the motion, unless such an award would be unjust.

Civ. R. 37(E) is similar to Civ. R. 26(C) in that it requires parties to make efforts to resolve discovery disputes prior to seeking court intervention. A motion pursuant to Civ. R. 37 must be accompanied by a statement indicating the efforts made to resolve the matter between the parties.[1]

Civ. R. 37(B) further provides that if a party fails to be sworn or to answer a question after being directed to do so by the court, the failure to comply may be considered a contempt of that court. If a party fails to obey an order made pursuant to this rule to provide or permit discovery, the court may make any just order, including the following:

(1) An order finding the facts to be established according to the claim of the party who obtained the order;

(2) An order prohibiting the offending party from opposing claims or defenses or from introducing certain matters into evidence;[2]

(3) An order striking out pleadings or parts of pleadings, staying further proceedings, dismissing the action, or rendering a judgment by default against the offending party;[3] or

(4) May treat the failure to obey the order granted pursuant to this rule as contempt of court, with the exception of the failure to obey an order to submit to a physical or mental examination.

[Section 26:25]

[1]Jones v. Lackey, 2000 WL 840497 (Ohio Ct. App. 9th Dist. Summit County 2000); Dewey L. Tackett Builders v. Casey, 2001 -Ohio- 2674, 2001 WL 803016 (Ohio Ct. App. 4th Dist. Pike County 2001).

[2]Nakoff v. Fairview Gen. Hosp., 1996 -Ohio- 159, 75 Ohio St. 3d 254, 662 N.E.2d 1 (1996) (trial court's exclusion of defendant's expert's trial testimony and disallowance of defendant's impeachment of plaintiff's expert with authoritative texts were proper sanctions for abuse of discretion by the trial court due to defendant's continued failure to comply with plaintiff's discovery requests).

[3]Evans v. Smith, 75 Ohio App. 3d 160, 598 N.E.2d 1287 (1st Dist. Hamilton County 1991) (plaintiff's bad faith behavior and evasive answers at deposition justified dismissal with prejudice). See also Levorchick v. DeHart, 119 Ohio App. 3d 339, 695 N.E.2d 303 (2d Dist. Miami County 1997) (trial court must give noncomplying party notice of intention to dismiss with prejudice and one last chance to fully comply with discovery).

Again, the court may impose the expenses caused by the failure to obey the order upon the offending party. Further, Civ. R. 37(C) provides similar sanctions for failure to admit the genuineness of any documents or truth of the matter asserted in response to a request for admission under Civ. R. 36. Civ. R. 37(D) imposes sanctions for the failure to attend a deposition, serve answers to interrogatories, or respond to a request for inspection. The court may also impose sanctions if the surrounding facts and circumstances of the noncompliance suggest an abuse of discovery.[4]

There must be a protective order before sanctions can be imposed.[5] The precise sanction imposed will vary depending on the circumstances involved in each case, and lies within the sound discretion of the trial court.[6] An aggrieved party must inform the trial court of discovery problems, however, or any resulting error will be deemed to have been waived on appeal.[7]

§ 26:26 Motion for order compelling discovery—Form⊚

[Title of Court]

[Caption]   Case No. [_____]
                                       MOTION FOR ORDER
                                       COMPELLING DISCOVERY

[Movant] moves this Court for an Order, pursuant to Civil Rule 37(A) compelling:

[Respondent] to answer questions [numbers] of the Interrogatories submitted on [date].]

or

[Respondent] to permit inspection of documents as requested.]

or

[Name] to answer questions propounded in Deposition scheduled on [date].]

or

[Respondent] to answer completely questions [numbers], which were evasively or incompletely answered.]

Further, [Movant] moves Court to require [Respondent] to pay the rea-

---

[4]Short v. St. Luke's Hosp., 1990 WL 156082, at *6 (Ohio Ct. App. 8th Dist. Cuyahoga County 1990).

[5]Dafco, Inc. v. Reynolds, 9 Ohio App. 3d 4, 457 N.E.2d 916 (10th Dist. Franklin County 1983).

[6]See, e.g., Boller v. Boller, 1996 WL 393858 (Ohio Ct. App. 12th Dist. Clermont County 1996) ($440 sanction imposed for failure to produce tax returns); Sergi v. Sergi, 1996 WL 425914 (Ohio Ct. App. 9th Dist. Summit County 1996), dismissed, appeal not allowed, 77 Ohio St. 3d 1490, 673 N.E.2d 147 (1996) (continuance offered to party prejudiced by surprise expert witness).

[7]Johnson v. Johnson, 1995 WL 516467 (Ohio Ct. App. 2d Dist. Montgomery County 1995).

sonable expenses and attorney fees of *[Movant]* incurred in obtaining this Order.

A copy of the *[Interrogatories / Request for Production of Documents / Transcript of Depositions / etc.]* is attached hereto, pursuant to Civ. R. 5(D).

Attorney for Movant

[Memorandum in support of motion]

[Notice of hearing]

[Proof / certificate of service]

NOTES TO FORM

Drafter's Notes

Civil Rule 37(A) requires that a party obtain a court order compelling compliance before seeking sanctions. If there is a failure to obey the order, then Civil Rule 37(B) sanctions can be sought.

§ 26:27   Motion for sanctions—Form⊚

[Title of Court]

[Caption]   Case No. *[_____]*
MOTION FOR SANCTIONS

[Movant] hereby moves the Court for an Order, pursuant to Civil Rule 37(B), imposing all sanctions appropriate to the cause upon *[name of party / respondent]*, and requiring the *[party / respondent]* and his attorney to pay the reasonable expenses plus attorney fees incurred by *[Movant]*.

This motion is supported by the *[memorandum / affidavit]* below.

Attorney for Movant

[Memorandum / affidavit in support of motion]

[Notice of hearing]

[Proof / certificate of service]

NOTES TO FORM

Drafter's Notes

This motion should be supported by a memorandum/affidavit describing all efforts of movant to obtain compliance with the prior court order and respondent's unjustified failure to comply.

§ 26:28   Court-ordered investigations

Civ. R. 75(D) provides that, in divorce, annulment, or legal separation cases where minor children are involved, or upon the filing of a post-decree motion for modification of parental rights and responsibilities for the care of children, the court may cause an investigation to be made as to the character, family relations, past conduct, earning ability, and financial worth of the parties to the action. The rule is clear that the report of such an investigation shall be made available to the parties or their counsel at least seven days before trial, but it does not address the issue of the admissibility of the report at trial.[1]

§ 26:29 Filing with court

Civ. R. 5(D) provides that depositions upon oral examination, interrogatories, requests for documents, requests for admission, and answers and responses to such requests shall not be filed with the court unless ordered or unless provided as evidence or for use as evidence or for consideration of a motion in the proceeding. Thus, if interrogatories are properly served and not answered, attaching the unanswered interrogatories to a motion to compel answers is a means of getting the questions, but not the answers, into the court file.

Any improperly filed discovery documents would be subject to a motion to strike from the file, but not a motion under Civ. R. 12(F) because it relates only to pleadings.

Depositions for use at trial, with the limitations of Civ. R. 32(A), must be filed at least one day prior to trial.

[Section 26:28]

[1]See, e.g., Derr v. Derr, 1996 WL 131156 (Ohio Ct. App. 12th Dist. Preble County 1996); Black v. Black, 1995 WL 516476 (Ohio Ct. App. 2d Dist. Darke County 1995); Roach v. Roach, 79 Ohio App. 3d 194, 607 N.E.2d 35 (2d Dist. Montgomery County 1992); Stone v. Stone, 9 Ohio App. 3d 6, 457 N.E.2d 919 (12th Dist. Warren County 1983).

Chapter 27

Jurisdiction and Venue

By Beatrice K. Sowald, Esq.

> **KeyCite®:** Cases and other legal materials listed in KeyCite Scope can be researched through West Group's KeyCite service on Westlaw®. Use KeyCite to check citations for form, parallel references, prior and later history, and comprehensive citator information, including citations to other decisions and secondary materials.

§ 27:1 Subject matter jurisdiction—Source of authority

To hear a divorce action, the court must have jurisdiction of the subject matter, which the Ohio Supreme Court has held connotes the power to hear and to decide a case on its merits.[1] Subject matter jurisdiction has also been characterized as the authority to determine the general class of cases to which the action belongs.[2]

The prevailing view is that courts in the United States have no common law jurisdiction to decree divorce or alimony, now called spousal support in Ohio.[3] The structure of matrimonial jurisdiction in eighteenth century England is cited as the principal reason for this doctrine.[4] An absolute divorce (divorce a vinculo matrimonii) could be granted only by Parliament. Power to decree a legal separation (divorce a mensa et thoro) was vested in the ecclesiastical courts (which followed canon law, not equity principles).[5] As it is generally presumed, English chancery courts had no authority to grant divorce or alimony and had no cognizance of matrimonial matters,[6] although the historical accuracy of this notion has been questioned.[7]

There are no courts in this country which are regarded as successors of the ecclesiastical courts of England.[8] Jurisdiction over the subject of divorce is therefore said not to exist unless conferred by constitution or

---

[Section 27:1]

[1]Morrison v. Steiner, 32 Ohio St. 2d 86, 61 Ohio Op. 2d 335, 290 N.E.2d 841 (1972).

[2]Am. Jur. 2d, Divorce and Separation § 240.

[3]Jelm v. Jelm, 155 Ohio St. 226, 44 Ohio Op. 246, 98 N.E.2d 401, 22 A.L.R.2d 1300 (1951). See also Am. Jur. 2d, Divorce and Separation § 240.

[4]Marleau v. Marleau, 95 Ohio St. 162, 115 N.E. 1009 (1917); De Witt v. De Witt, 67 Ohio St. 340, 66 N.E. 136 (1902); Soyk v. Soyk, 45 Ohio App. 2d 319, 74 Ohio Op. 2d 532, 345 N.E.2d 461 (9th Dist. Summit County 1975); Wolfe v. Wolfe, 46 Ohio St. 2d 399, 75 Ohio Op. 2d 474, 350 N.E.2d 413 (1976).

[5]Maynard v. Hill, 125 U.S. 190, 8 S. Ct. 723, 31 L. Ed. 654 (1888); Wolfe v. Wolfe, 46 Ohio St. 2d 399, 75 Ohio Op. 2d 474, 350 N.E.2d 413 (1976); De Witt v. De Witt, 67 Ohio St. 340, 66 N.E. 136 (1902).

[6]De Witt v. De Witt, 67 Ohio St. 340, 66 N.E. 136 (1902); Fickel v. Granger, 83 Ohio St. 101, 93 N.E. 527 (1910). See also Wolfe v. Wolfe, 46 Ohio St. 2d 399, 75 Ohio Op. 2d 474, 350 N.E.2d 413 (1976).

[7]Spindel v. Spindel, 283 F. Supp. 797 (E.D. N.Y. 1968). See also Solomon v. Solomon, 516 F.2d 1018, 1030 (3d Cir. 1975) (Gibbons, J., dissenting).

[8]De Witt v. De Witt, 67 Ohio St. 340, 66 N.E. 136 (1902).

statute.[9] Furthermore, because chancery courts are viewed as having no authority over divorce and alimony, it is considered that Ohio courts cannot exercise general equity powers in such matters, in the absence of equity legislation.[10]

In *Wolfe v. Wolfe*,[11] the Ohio Supreme Court stated that insofar as Ohio courts have adopted common law rules regarding divorce and alimony, such rules were derived from the ecclesiastical courts. The rationale supplied was that the English chancery had no cognizance of matrimonial controversies.[12] However, although widely assumed,[13] the view that chancery courts lacked divorce and alimony jurisdiction has been disputed. In *Spindel v. Spindel*,[14] in a scholarly opinion by Judge Weinstein, numerous English authorities are cited to demonstrate that English chancery courts did exercise matrimonial jurisdiction in a broad range of areas. If Judge Weinstein is correct, then the Ohio Supreme Court's restriction of divorce "common law" precepts to ecclesiastical rules would appear to be unwarranted.

§ 27:2   Subject matter jurisdiction—Statutory powers—In general

In Ohio, subject matter jurisdiction over divorce matters is prescribed

---

[9]Miller v. Miller, 154 Ohio St. 530, 43 Ohio Op. 496, 97 N.E.2d 213 (1951). See also Durham v. Durham, 104 Ohio St. 7, 135 N.E. 280 (1922); Marleau v. Marleau, 95 Ohio St. 162, 115 N.E. 1009 (1917); Dougherty v. Dougherty, 97 Ohio App. 232, 56 Ohio Op. 19, 125 N.E.2d 15 (9th Dist. Summit County 1954); Purdy v. Purdy, 41 Ohio App. 411, 10 Ohio L. Abs. 401, 179 N.E. 698 (5th Dist. Holmes County 1931).

[10]Marleau v. Marleau, 95 Ohio St. 162, 115 N.E. 1009 (1917). See also De Milo v. Watson, 166 Ohio St. 433, 2 Ohio Op. 2d 433, 143 N.E.2d 707 (1957); Miller v. Miller, 154 Ohio St. 530, 43 Ohio Op. 496, 97 N.E.2d 213 (1951) (Impact of statute's enactment upon the decision was noted in Robinson v. Robinson, 26 Ohio Op. 2d 426, 95 Ohio L. Abs. 205, 198 N.E.2d 491 (C.P. 1964).); Durham v. Durham, 104 Ohio St. 7, 135 N.E. 280 (1922); Dougherty v. Dougherty, 97 Ohio App. 232, 56 Ohio Op. 19, 125 N.E.2d 15 (9th Dist. Summit County 1954); Purdy v. Purdy, 41 Ohio App. 411, 10 Ohio L. Abs. 401, 179 N.E. 698 (5th Dist. Holmes County 1931).

[11]Wolfe v. Wolfe, 46 Ohio St. 2d 399, 405 n.15, 75 Ohio Op. 2d 474, 350 N.E.2d 413 (1976) (the role of the English "common law" is noted at footnote 15:

> The relationship between the Ohio common law and the English common law was best explained by Bloom v. Richards, 2 Ohio St. 387, 390, 1853 WL 105 (1853), as follows: "The English common law, so far as it is reasonable in itself, suitable to the condition and business of our people, and consistent with the letter and spirit of our federal and state constitutions and statutes, has been and is followed by our courts, and may be said to constitute a part of the common law of Ohio. But wherever it has been found wanting in either of these requisites, our courts have not hesitated to modify it to suit our circumstances, or, if necessary, to wholly depart from it." (footnotes omitted.) Thacker v. Board of Trustees of Ohio State University, 35 Ohio St. 2d 49, 64 Ohio Op. 2d 28, 298 N.E.2d 542 (1973) (William B. Brown, J., dissenting).

[12]Wolfe v. Wolfe, 46 Ohio St. 2d 399, 405, 75 Ohio Op. 2d 474, 350 N.E.2d 413 (1976), citing De Witt v. De Witt, 67 Ohio St. 340, 66 N.E. 136 (1902).

[13]State ex rel. Popovici v. Agler, 119 Ohio St. 484, 7 Ohio L. Abs. 29, 164 N.E. 524 (1928), cert. granted, 279 U.S. 828, 49 S. Ct. 265, 73 L. Ed. 979 (1929) and aff'd, 280 U.S. 379, 50 S. Ct. 154, 74 L. Ed. 489 (1930); Maynard v. Hill, 125 U.S. 190, 8 S. Ct. 723, 31 L. Ed. 654 (1888).

[14]Spindel v. Spindel, 283 F. Supp. 797 (E.D. N.Y. 1968).

and determined by statute.[1] The Ohio Supreme Court has portrayed divorce as a statutorily created privilege. The power of the legislature over the civil status of marriage and its dissolution has been depicted by the court as "unlimited," except as restricted by the Ohio and the United States Constitutions.[2] The necessary corollary is that being a creature of statute, divorce jurisdiction is circumscribed by legislative enactment. Accordingly, the court's powers are viewed as no greater than those expressly conferred by the General Assembly.[3]

The Ohio statutes designate which tribunals have cognizance of divorce matters, define the causes of action, and delineate the powers of the court. Each of these will be addressed in turn.

§ 27:3 Subject matter jurisdiction—Statutory powers—Tribunal

In Ohio, divorce proceedings are judicial functions, involving the exercise of judicial power.[1] The Ohio legislature has no authority to grant a divorce.[2] Section 4, Article IV of the Ohio Constitution provides that the courts of common pleas shall have such original jurisdiction over domestic relations matters as may be provided by law.[3]

In certain enumerated counties, a division of domestic relations is established which is given jurisdiction over divorce matters.[4] While the issue of custody for never marrieds may be heard in some counties as probate, juvenile, or domestic court, the domestic relations division of the Court of Common Pleas of Licking County has the exclusive jurisdiction, by statute, to determine the allocation of parental rights.[5]

[Section 27:2]

[1]Jelm v. Jelm, 155 Ohio St. 226, 44 Ohio Op. 246, 98 N.E.2d 401, 404, 22 A.L.R.2d 1300 (1951); Marleau v. Marleau, 95 Ohio St. 162, 115 N.E. 1009 (1917); De Witt v. De Witt, 67 Ohio St. 340, 66 N.E. 136 (1902); Purdy v. Purdy, 41 Ohio App. 411, 10 Ohio L. Abs. 401, 179 N.E. 698 (5th Dist. Holmes County 1931). See Coleman v. Coleman, 32 Ohio St. 2d 155, 61 Ohio Op. 2d 406, 291 N.E.2d 530, 57 A.L.R.3d 213 (1972).

[2]Coleman v. Coleman, 32 Ohio St. 2d 155, 61 Ohio Op. 2d 406, 291 N.E.2d 530, 57 A.L.R.3d 213 (1972).

[3]Mark v. Mark, 145 Ohio St. 301, 30 Ohio Op. 534, 61 N.E.2d 595, 160 A.L.R. 608 (1945); Marleau v. Marleau, 95 Ohio St. 162, 115 N.E. 1009 (1917); Soyk v. Soyk, 45 Ohio App. 2d 319, 74 Ohio Op. 2d 532, 345 N.E.2d 461 (9th Dist. Summit County 1975); Purdy v. Purdy, 41 Ohio App. 411, 10 Ohio L. Abs. 401, 179 N.E. 698 (5th Dist. Holmes County 1931).

[Section 27:3]

[1]De Witt v. De Witt, 67 Ohio St. 340, 66 N.E. 136 (1902), as cited in Wolfe v. Wolfe, 46 Ohio St. 2d 399, 409, 75 Ohio Op. 2d 474, 350 N.E.2d 413 (1976).

[2]Bingham v. Miller, 17 Ohio 445, 1848 WL 125 (1848).

[3]RC 3105.01 (divorce); RC 3105.17 (legal separation); RC 3105.10 (annulment); RC 3105.61 (dissolution of marriage).

[4]RC 2301.03.

[5]RC 2301.03(S), Walters v. Johnson, 2002 WL 1162340 (Ohio Ct. App. 5th Dist. Licking County 2002).

§ 27:4 Subject matter jurisdiction—Statutory powers—Cause of action

The causes of action available in domestic relations matters are set forth in RC Chapter 3105. Residence in the state is a prerequisite to the institution of certain proceedings. Where neither party is a resident of the state of Ohio when an action for legal separation is commenced, the court has no jurisdiction to hear it.[1]

The elements of each action are defined. For example, the grounds for divorce, legal separation, and annulment actions are respectively specified.[2] The grounds listed are the only ones authorized; none may be implied.[3] Accordingly, a divorce may only be granted for a cause expressly provided. It has been held that proof of a cause not specified, such as irreconcilable estrangement or incompatibility, which is disputed, cannot be made the basis of a decree.[4]

Pursuant to RC 3105.03, it is not jurisdictionally necessary that the cause of the divorce arise in Ohio.[5] For example, if one spouse commits adultery in Nevada, the other may bring an action in Ohio on grounds of adultery, provided the complaining party is domiciled in this state. A divorce litigated in Ohio may thus be based on a cause which occurred elsewhere. Moreover, it is immaterial whether adultery constitutes a ground for divorce in Nevada, where the offense occurred, since the law controlling the divorce action is that of the forum.[6]

On the other hand, if the plaintiff is domiciled elsewhere, the fact that the marital offense was committed by the defendant in Ohio does not confer jurisdiction upon the court to hear the action.[7] This principle must be distinguished, however, from the due process question of whether the defendant's wrongful conduct in the state gives rise to in personam jurisdiction over him.

RC 3105.03 further provides that, for jurisdictional purposes, the mar-

---

[Section 27:4]

[1]Haylett v. Haylett, 1989 WL 56367 (Ohio Ct. App. 11th Dist. Portage County 1989).

[2]RC 3105.01 (Divorce); RC 3105.17 (Legal Separation); RC 3105.31 (Annulment).

[3]Mark v. Mark, 145 Ohio St. 301, 30 Ohio Op. 534, 61 N.E.2d 595, 160 A.L.R. 608 (1945); Ex parte Cattell, 146 Ohio St. 112, 32 Ohio Op. 43, 64 N.E.2d 416, 164 A.L.R. 312 (1945); Gage v. Gage, 101 Ohio App. 483, 1 Ohio Op. 2d 413, 73 Ohio L. Abs. 277, 129 N.E.2d 486 (8th Dist. Cuyahoga County 1955), judgment aff'd, 165 Ohio St. 462, 60 Ohio Op. 117, 136 N.E.2d 56 (1956).

[4]Slyh v. Slyh, 72 Ohio L. Abs. 537, 135 N.E.2d 675 (Ct. App. 2d Dist. Madison County 1955); Winnard v. Winnard, 62 Ohio App. 351, 16 Ohio Op. 51, 23 N.E.2d 977 (2d Dist. Franklin County 1939); Burke v. Burke, 36 Ohio App. 551, 8 Ohio L. Abs. 682, 173 N.E. 637 (6th Dist. Lucas County 1930); Vanatta v. Aten, 1995 WL 347903 (Ohio Ct. App. 5th Dist. Licking County 1995), dismissed, appeal not allowed, 73 Ohio St. 3d 1425, 652 N.E.2d 798 (1995).

[5]Coleman v. Coleman, 32 Ohio St. 2d 155, 61 Ohio Op. 2d 406, 291 N.E.2d 530, 57 A.L.R.3d 213 (1972); Cox v. Cox, 19 Ohio St. 502, 1869 WL 84 (1869).

[6]Am. Jur. 2d, Divorce and Separation § 23.

[7]See Van Fossen v. State, 37 Ohio St. 317, 1881 WL 101 (1881).

riage need not have taken place within the state.[8] Conversely, the fact that the marriage was celebrated in Ohio does not in itself confer any authority upon an Ohio court to hear the action.[9]

While RC 3105.03 requires that the plaintiff "shall have been a resident of the state at least six months immediately before filing" a complaint for divorce, the only statutory requirement for bringing an action for legal separation is that it be brought in the proper county for commencement of actions.[10]

§ 27:5 Subject matter jurisdiction—Equity powers of court

The court's exercise of general equity powers was unauthorized prior to 1951.[1] In that year, equity legislation (RC 3105.20) was adopted. Although this statute was subsequently repealed, a comparable provision (RC 3105.011) was enacted in 1975.[2] The current statute provides that the domestic relations court has full equity powers and jurisdiction appropriate to the determination of all domestic relations matters. It is thus now clear that, ancillary to its statutory powers, a domestic relations court has full equity jurisdiction. Additionally, any judge of the court of common pleas may order a case transferred to another judge or division of the court if that judge and division of the court has jurisdiction of the matter.[3]

During periods when Ohio did not have a statute authorizing equity jurisdiction, Ohio courts had repeatedly said that general equity powers could not be exercised in domestic relations matters.[4] For example, in the absence of a statute, it was held that the court has no authority to decree a division of property in an alimony only (now known as legal separation) action[5] or to make a division of property in a divorce case unless it is pursuant to an alimony award under RC 3105.18.[6] With the enactment of RC 3105.011, controversy over the existence of domestic relations equity jurisdiction presumably was eliminated, although

---

[8]Coleman v. Coleman, 32 Ohio St. 2d 155, 61 Ohio Op. 2d 406, 291 N.E.2d 530, 57 A.L.R.3d 213 (1972); Cox v. Cox, 19 Ohio St. 502, 1869 WL 84 (1869).

[9]Am. Jur. 2d, Divorce and Separation § 242. See Kulko v. Superior Court of California In and For City and County of San Francisco, 436 U.S. 84, 98 S. Ct. 1690, 56 L. Ed. 2d 132 (1978) (mere fact of marriage in forum state is insufficient to clothe a state with in personam jurisdiction over the non-resident).

[10]Taylor v. Taylor, 84 Ohio App. 3d 445, 616 N.E.2d 1199 (2d Dist. Montgomery County 1992) (error to dismiss when proper venue under Civ. R. 3(B)(10).)

[Section 27:5]
[1]De Milo v. Watson, 166 Ohio St. 433, 2 Ohio Op. 2d 433, 143 N.E.2d 707 (1957).

[2]RC 3105.20 was repealed in 1970, when the Civil Rules were adopted. The statute was originally enacted in 1951. Prior to that time, no comparable divorce equity statute existed.

[3]Mays v. Mays, 1993 WL 212697 (Ohio Ct. App. 2d Dist. Montgomery County 1993).

[4]Marleau v. Marleau, 95 Ohio St. 162, 115 N.E. 1009 (1917); Durham v. Durham, 104 Ohio St. 7, 135 N.E. 280 (1922).

[5]Durham v. Durham, 104 Ohio St. 7, 135 N.E. 280 (1922).

[6]Soyk v. Soyk, 45 Ohio App. 2d 319, 74 Ohio Op. 2d 532, 345 N.E.2d 461 (9th Dist. Summit County 1975) (prior to the enactment of RC 3105.011).

disputes over its appropriate application may continue to arise.

RC 3105.011 (and its predecessor) are generally viewed as expanding the court's authority.[7] Since the adoption of equity legislation, it has been held that the court has equity jurisdiction to make a division of property, which includes realty held in the name of only one spouse;[8] to provide that a spouse's support obligations should not abate upon the death of the payor, but continue as a charge against his estate;[9] to determine the equitable owner of property legally titled in the name of a third party;[10] and to consider the element of aggression in making an award of spousal support.[11] The Ohio Supreme Court has said that, in enacting the equity statute (former RC 3105.20), the apparent purpose of the legislature was to authorize trial courts "to exercise full equity powers and jurisdiction in adjudicating a complete dissolution of the marriage relationship," including a determination of rights to alimony or spousal support and division of property.[12]

The only limitation, expressed in the statute, on the court's full equity jurisdiction is that its exercise must be appropriate to the determination of domestic relations matters. The Ohio Supreme Court has also said that there must be a statutory basis upon which the court can exercise equity powers before they may come into play.[13]

Within those parameters, however, equity jurisdiction enlarges the court's authority in making a complete adjustment of the parties' rights. The Ohio Supreme Court in an unanimous opinion in *De Milo v. Watson*[14] described the combined effect of the revision of former alimony provisions and the adoption of equity legislation: "[T]heir effect is to permit the court a free and full exercise of its general equity powers to adjust property rights between opposing spouses as it determines will serve the ends of justice."[15]

The subject matter jurisdiction of the court commences when either party files a complaint for divorce.[16] The filing gives the court jurisdiction to formulate a division of the marital assets, award custody, and grant spousal support to either party.

---

[7]Clark v. Clark, 165 Ohio St. 457, 60 Ohio Op. 115, 136 N.E.2d 52 (1956).

[8]Clark v. Clark, 165 Ohio St. 457, 60 Ohio Op. 115, 136 N.E.2d 52 (1956).

[9]De Milo v. Watson, 166 Ohio St. 433, 2 Ohio Op. 2d 433, 143 N.E.2d 707 (1957).

[10]Dougherty v. Dougherty, 97 Ohio App. 232, 56 Ohio Op. 19, 125 N.E.2d 15 (9th Dist. Summit County 1954).

[11]Esteb v. Esteb, 173 Ohio St. 259, 19 Ohio Op. 2d 80, 181 N.E.2d 462 (1962).

[12]Clark v. Clark, 165 Ohio St. 457, 459, 60 Ohio Op. 115, 136 N.E.2d 52 (1956).

[13]Haynie v. Haynie, 169 Ohio St. 467, 8 Ohio Op. 2d 476, 159 N.E.2d 765 (1959).

[14]De Milo v. Watson, 166 Ohio St. 433, 436, 2 Ohio Op. 2d 433, 143 N.E.2d 707 (1957).

[15]See also Esteb v. Esteb, 173 Ohio St. 259, 19 Ohio Op. 2d 80, 181 N.E.2d 462 (1962).

[16]Bolinger v. Bolinger, 49 Ohio St. 3d 120, 551 N.E.2d 157 (1990).

§ 27:6 Subject matter jurisdiction—Express and implied powers of court

As discussed earlier, divorce is viewed in Ohio as a creature of statute.[1] Being a statutory proceeding, the court cannot exceed the limits of authority conferred on it by the legislature.[2] For example, a court has no power to order a spouse to support[3] or provide life insurance[4] for minor children beyond the date they reach majority, unless a parental agreement imposes such obligations. Statutes confer and determine the nature and extent of judicial authority over divorce, and the court has no greater jurisdiction or power than is given by the legislature.[5]

The rule that the domestic relations court may not exceed its statutory jurisdiction must be distinguished from the inherent authority of a court to implement the exercise of its jurisdiction. It is well settled that a grant of jurisdiction implies the necessary and usual incidental powers essential to effectuate it.[6] Thus, the domestic relations court has not only such authority as the statute explicitly gives, but also such incidental power as is necessary to make its orders and decrees effective.[7]

For instance, the court has inherent authority to modify, under certain circumstances, an alimony or spousal support award after the decree is entered;[8] to protect itself from perpetration of fraud;[9] to punish for contempt; to enforce its judgments and orders;[10] and to effectuate an orderly and efficient administration of justice.[11] In fact, a domestic relations court has jurisdiction to enforce its own orders after the death of a noncomplying party who violated a restraining order to maintain the

---

[Section 27:6]

[1]See Coleman v. Coleman, 32 Ohio St. 2d 155, 61 Ohio Op. 2d 406, 291 N.E.2d 530, 57 A.L.R.3d 213 (1972).

[2]Soyk v. Soyk, 45 Ohio App. 2d 319, 74 Ohio Op. 2d 532, 345 N.E.2d 461 (9th Dist. Summit County 1975); Purdy v. Purdy, 41 Ohio App. 411, 10 Ohio L. Abs. 401, 179 N.E. 698 (5th Dist. Holmes County 1931).

[3]Thiessen v. Moore, 105 Ohio St. 401, 1 Ohio L. Abs. 245, 137 N.E. 906 (1922).

[4]Miller v. Miller, 154 Ohio St. 530, 43 Ohio Op. 496, 97 N.E.2d 213 (1951).

[5]Ex parte Cattell, 146 Ohio St. 112, 32 Ohio Op. 43, 64 N.E.2d 416, 164 A.L.R. 312 (1945).

[6]Ex parte Cattell, 146 Ohio St. 112, 32 Ohio Op. 43, 64 N.E.2d 416, 164 A.L.R. 312 (1945); Hale v. State, 55 Ohio St. 210, 45 N.E. 199 (1896).

[7]Marleau v. Marleau, 95 Ohio St. 162, 115 N.E. 1009 (1917); De Witt v. De Witt, 67 Ohio St. 340, 66 N.E. 136 (1902); Jelm v. Jelm, 155 Ohio St. 226, 44 Ohio Op. 246, 98 N.E.2d 401, 22 A.L.R.2d 1300 (1951).

[8]Wolfe v. Wolfe, 46 Ohio St. 2d 399, 75 Ohio Op. 2d 474, 350 N.E.2d 413 (1976). See also Modification of Spousal Support Ch 14.

[9]Jelm v. Jelm, 155 Ohio St. 226, 44 Ohio Op. 246, 98 N.E.2d 401, 22 A.L.R.2d 1300 (1951). See also Coulson v. Coulson, 5 Ohio St. 3d 12, 448 N.E.2d 809 (1983).

[10]Hale v. State, 55 Ohio St. 210, 45 N.E. 199 (1896); Ohio Jur. 3d, Courts and Judges § 248.

[11]State ex rel. Johnston v. Taulbee, 66 Ohio St. 2d 417, 20 Ohio Op. 3d 361, 423 N.E.2d 80 (1981).

status quo of marital assets during divorce proceedings.[12] The court also has authority to determine the competency of an individual and the necessity for a guardian ad litem.[13] However, a domestic relations court has no jurisdiction to award a guardian's personal expenses as part of the divorce decree where the guardian was appointed by the probate court.[14]

The court can also enforce contractual obligations that exceed a spouse's statutory duties and the court's original authority. Once a separation agreement is incorporated into a decree, obligations imposed by contract are also imposed by decree and are enforceable as such, even though the court would otherwise lack jurisdiction to make the order. For example, although the court does not have the power to order a parent to pay for a child's college education, a parental agreement to that effect, incorporated into a decree, is fully enforceable by the court.[15]

§ 27:7   Subject matter jurisdiction—Concurrent jurisdiction—In general

When there are courts of concurrent jurisdiction, "the tribunal whose power is first invoked . . . acquires jurisdiction, to the exclusion of all other tribunals, to adjudicate upon the whole issue."[1]

The court first acquiring jurisdiction retains it until a final judgment on the merits is rendered. Once an action has been fully litigated in a domestic relations division, granting a divorce and providing for property division, exclusive domestic relations court jurisdiction terminates and there is concurrent jurisdiction with the general division for enforcement.[2] However, while the common pleas court would have concurrent jurisdiction after the matter had been finalized, where issues were pending in the domestic court regarding the enforcement of the

---

[12]Sherban v. Sherban, 1985 WL 4710 (Ohio Ct. App. 5th Dist. Stark County 1985); Taylor v. Taylor, 1992 WL 166076 (Ohio Ct. App. 1st Dist. Hamilton County 1992) (trial court can enforce temporary spousal support arrearages which accrued prior to death of obligee, even though divorce action abated).

[13]Wozniak v. Wozniak, No. L-85-147 (Ohio Ct. App. 6th Dist. Lucas County 1986).

[14]Caudill v. Caudill, 29 Ohio App. 3d 51, 502 N.E.2d 703 (10th Dist. Franklin County 1986).

[15]Robrock v. Robrock, 167 Ohio St. 479, 5 Ohio Op. 2d 165, 150 N.E.2d 421 (1958) (disapproved of by, Nokes v. Nokes, 47 Ohio St. 2d 1, 1 Ohio Op. 3d 1, 351 N.E.2d 174 (1976)); Grant v. Grant, 60 Ohio App. 2d 277, 14 Ohio Op. 3d 249, 396 N.E.2d 1037 (6th Dist. Erie County 1977); Ohio Jur. 3d, Family Law § 1150.

[Section 27:7]

[1]State ex rel. Racing Guild of Ohio, Local 304, Service Employees Internatl. Union, AFL-CIO, CLC v. Morgan, 17 Ohio St. 3d 54, 476 N.E.2d 1060 (1985).

[2]Jackman v. Jackman, 1986 WL 14082 (Ohio Ct. App. 12th Dist. Madison County 1986); Price v. Price, 16 Ohio App. 3d 93, 474 N.E.2d 662 (8th Dist. Cuyahoga County 1984). See also State Savings Bank v. Watts, 1997 WL 101658 (Ohio Ct. App. 10th Dist. Franklin County 1997) (municipal court has concurrent jurisdiction to enforce decree where cause of action is within original jurisdiction of municipal court).

divorce decree, the priority doctrine would apply.[3] When the power of the domestic relations division is invoked before a complaint is filed in the common pleas court, the domestic court acquires jurisdiction to the exclusion of all other courts.[4]

A court in one county may proceed to hear a complaint for divorce even though a court in a different county had heard and granted a decree of legal separation previously.[5]

Where two state courts have concurrent jurisdiction, the jurisdictional priority rule applies if the second case involves the same parties and causes of action. Where an employer sought a declaratory judgment in common pleas court to prevent the CSEA from enforcing a lump sum payment provision, at the same time that the CSEA was seeking show cause orders in the juvenile and domestic courts against employee-obligors and the employer, the common pleas court lacked jurisdiction to hear and grant relief.[6]

There is concurrent jurisdiction in the common pleas court, after the child support orders have terminated, to hear a complaint alleging a violation of state and federal laws by the CSEA and former spouse. The plaintiff claimed a malicious and harassing attempt to collect support under a terminated order where there were no arrearages.[7]

While there is concurrent jurisdiction in the general division to enforce a domestic relations court order, where the matter relates to the support of minor children, said matter should be determined by the domestic relations division.[8] Framing the complaint in the language showing a cause of action for fraud does not convert the matter from a child support proceeding.

§ 27:8 Subject matter jurisdiction—Concurrent jurisdiction— Enforcement

A municipal court has authority to enforce a domestic relations decree as long as it fits within the monetary jurisdiction of the court and the

---

[3]Dowling v. Schaser, 1993 WL 515596 (Ohio Ct. App. 8th Dist. Cuyahoga County 1993); Fronk v. Chung, 1999 WL 266571 (Ohio Ct. App. 11th Dist. Lake County 1999) (the jurisdictional priority rule applies where claims or causes of action are the same in both cases).

[4]Dowling v. Schaser, 1993 WL 515596 (Ohio Ct. App. 8th Dist. Cuyahoga County 1993).

[5]Payton v. Payton, 1997 WL 354797 (Ohio Ct. App. 4th Dist. Scioto County 1997).

[6]State ex rel. LTV Steel Co., Inc. v. Cuyahoga Child Support Enforcement, 1998 WL 213181 (Ohio Ct. App. 8th Dist. Cuyahoga County 1998).

[7]Thomas v. O'Connor, 2000 WL 296080 (Ohio Ct. App. 9th Dist. Summit County 2000).

[8]Kessler v. Warner, 2001 WL 127747 (Ohio Ct. App. 8th Dist. Cuyahoga County 2001); Ward v. Ward, 2001-Ohio-1358, 2001 WL 1141502 (Ohio Ct. App. 9th Dist. Lorain County 2001) (municipal court lacks subject matter jurisdiciton to determine ex-wife's obligation to husband for orthodontics charges for parties' son).

domestic relations court is not then exercising jurisdiction.[1] However, a county court does not have jurisdiction to enforce collection of any judgments other than its own, and thus does not have subject matter jurisdiction to enforce a common pleas court order from a divorce.[2]

The lack of subject matter jurisdiction of a court may be raised for the first time on appeal and may even be raised "sua sponte" by a court at any stage of the proceeding.[3]

§ 27:9 Subject matter jurisdiction—Concurrent jurisdiction—Jurisdictional priority rule

Even though there may be concurrent jurisdiction for enforcement among the domestic relations court, the common pleas general division, and a municipal court, where the power of the domestic relations court is invoked first, it has priority until the matter is completely disposed of under the jurisdictional priority rule.[1] The Supreme Court has held that the jurisdictional priority rule applies in divorce actions.[2]

§ 27:10 Subject matter jurisdiction—Concurrent jurisdiction—Same state

It is well settled that, as between courts having concurrent and coextensive jurisdiction, the court whose power is first invoked by the institution of proper proceedings and service of the required process acquires the right to adjudicate the whole issue and to settle the rights of the parties, to the exclusion of all other such tribunals.[1] Once a court acquires jurisdiction over the action, its authority continues until the matter is completely and finally disposed of. No other court having coordinate authority may interfere with its proceedings.[2]

This rule fully applies to divorce actions filed in the common pleas

---

[Section 27:8]

[1]Mitchell v. Georges, 1985 WL 7268 (Ohio Ct. App. 5th Dist. Stark County 1985).

[2]Allison v. Anderson, 2001 WL 575170 (Ohio Ct. App. 5th Dist. Holmes County 2001).

[3]Fox v. Eaton Corp., 48 Ohio St. 2d 236, 2 Ohio Op. 3d 408, 358 N.E.2d 536 (1976) (overruled by, Manning v. Ohio State Library Bd., 62 Ohio St. 3d 24, 577 N.E.2d 650 (1991)).

[Section 27:9]

[1]DuFresne v. DuFresne, 2000 WL 1545044 (Ohio Ct. App. 6th Dist. Erie County 2000).

[2]State ex rel. Largent v. Fisher, 43 Ohio St. 3d 160, 540 N.E.2d 239 (1989).

[Section 27:10]

[1]State ex rel. Miller v. Court of Common Pleas of Lake County, 151 Ohio St. 397, 39 Ohio Op. 232, 86 N.E.2d 464 (1949); Kane v. Kane, 146 Ohio St. 686, 33 Ohio Op. 166, 67 N.E.2d 783 (1946) (concurrent jurisdiction of common pleas court and probate court); Miller v. Court of Common Pleas of Cuyahoga County, 143 Ohio St. 68, 28 Ohio Op. 19, 54 N.E.2d 130 (1944). See also Hardesty v. Hardesty, 16 Ohio App. 3d 56, 474 N.E.2d 368 (10th Dist. Franklin County 1984) (domestic relations and juvenile courts regarding custody and support matters).

[2]John Weenink & Sons Co. v. Court of Common Pleas of Cuyahoga County, 150 Ohio St. 349, 38 Ohio Op. 189, 82 N.E.2d 730 (1948).

courts of Ohio counties.[3] As a general rule, pendency of a prior divorce action abates a subsequent action. Thus, a court may not exercise its jurisdiction where a prior case is pending in the same or another common pleas court.[4] Since a court has ancillary jurisdiction to grant spousal support, pendency of a divorce is said to preclude another court from acquiring jurisdiction over a subsequent action for spousal support.[5]

At what point does a court first acquire jurisdiction? Civil Rule 3(A) defines commencement of an action as "filing a complaint with the court, if service is obtained within one year from such filing."[6] It has been argued that under this rule the court in which the action is first commenced acquires exclusive jurisdiction if service is perfected within a year. In *State ex rel. Balson v. Harnishfeger,*[7] the Ohio Supreme Court rejected this proposition and held that completion of proper service is a prerequisite to vesting of exclusive jurisdiction. The court reiterated that not simply subject matter jurisdiction but in personam jurisdiction must be acquired to confer exclusivity.[8]

The facts in *Harnishfeger* were the following: The husband had filed a divorce action against his wife in Allen County Common Pleas Court on November 7. Summons was issued on the same date and was served by certified mail on November 10. The wife filed for divorce in Franklin County on November 9 and obtained service on the husband on the same day. The issue before the Supreme Court was which tribunal has exclusive jurisdiction to adjudicate—the court (Allen) in which the action is first filed or the court (Franklin) in which both filing of the action and service are first completed. The Supreme Court ruled that it was the latter. A writ of prohibition against the Allen County Common Pleas Court was accordingly granted.

Thus, as between courts of concurrent jurisdiction, exclusive jurisdiction vests in the court in which both the filing of the action and service are first completed and not necessarily in the court in which the proceedings were first filed.

Similarly, where the wife obtained personal service on the husband in

---

[3]Miller v. Court of Common Pleas of Cuyahoga County, 143 Ohio St. 68, 28 Ohio Op. 19, 54 N.E.2d 130 (1944).

[4]Miller v. Court of Common Pleas of Cuyahoga County, 143 Ohio St. 68, 28 Ohio Op. 19, 54 N.E.2d 130 (1944); Robinson v. Robinson, 79 Ohio App. 149, 34 Ohio Op. 500, 47 Ohio L. Abs. 409, 72 N.E.2d 466 (8th Dist. Cuyahoga County 1946).

[5]State ex rel. Hoffman v. Markey, 17 Ohio L. Abs. 444, 1934 WL 1751 (Ct. App. 2d Dist. Montgomery County 1934); Ohio Jur. 3d, Family Law § 1041.

[6]See staff notes to Civ. R. 3(A).

[7]State ex rel. Balson v. Harnishfeger, 55 Ohio St. 2d 38, 9 Ohio Op. 3d 21, 377 N.E.2d 750 (1978); State ex rel. Largent v. Fisher, 43 Ohio St. 3d 160, 540 N.E.2d 239 (1989) (writ of prohibition will issue to prevent judge from assuming jurisdiction where another court had acquired exclusive jurisdiction over the divorce).

[8]State ex rel. Balson v. Harnishfeger, 55 Ohio St. 2d 38, 9 Ohio Op. 3d 21, 377 N.E.2d 750 (1978). See also Hathorn v. Hathorn, 1988 WL 138503 (Ohio Ct. App. 5th Dist. Fairfield County 1988) (court held that where a husband filed for divorce only in Louisiana and the wife appeared but did not answer, the Louisiana decree is res judicata for divorce but not for issues of alimony, custody, and support).

a Cuyahoga County action before publication service was completed upon her in an Ashtabula County action by the husband, it was held that the incompleted service did not vest the Ashtabula court with jurisdiction. Thus, the court in which service was first perfected has precedence to determine the action.[9]

§ 27:11   Subject matter jurisdiction—Concurrent jurisdiction— Different states

The foregoing rules apply only to actions pending in courts of concurrent jurisdiction in the same state. They do not apply to cases pending in different states. In fact, the pendency of a suit in one state does not generally abate an action brought subsequently in a different state, even though the actions involve the same parties and concern the same subject matter.[1] However, as a matter of comity and in the exercise of discretion, some courts have declined to entertain or have stayed a local action, on the ground that another case between the same parties involving the same matter is pending in another state.[2]

Where the issue is one of custody or parental rights of a minor child, the provisions of the Uniform Child Custody Jurisdiction Act (UCCJA)[3] determine the jurisdiction between competing states over the subject matter.

§ 27:12   Subject matter jurisdiction—Jurisdiction to render judgment

The court must have jurisdiction to hear a divorce action as well as render a judgment in that action. The term of a common pleas judge is set for a fixed period of time; once that expires, the judge is without authority to act in an official capacity unless the judge is given a de facto status. Problems may arise when the trial judge in a divorce action is replaced by a successor judge before the final decree has been rendered. A successor judge cannot render judgment if the judge's predecessor had not filed findings of fact and conclusions of law and cannot render a judgment on the transcript when it is determined that the

---

[9]Gehelo v. Gehelo, 160 Ohio St. 243, 52 Ohio Op. 114, 116 N.E.2d 7 (1953), as cited in State ex rel. Balson v. Harnishfeger, 55 Ohio St. 2d 38, 9 Ohio Op. 3d 21, 377 N.E.2d 750 (1978).

[Section 27:11]

[1]Fox v. King Investment & Lumber Co., 22 Ohio App. 469, 4 Ohio L. Abs. 547, 153 N.E. 284 (1st Dist. Hamilton County 1926); Ohio Jur. 3d, Courts and Judges § 332. See also Weil v. Guerin, 42 Ohio St. 299, 1884 WL 241 (1884).

[2]Fraiberg v. Cuyahoga Cty. Court of Common Pleas, Domestic Relations Div., 1996 -Ohio- 384, 76 Ohio St. 3d 374, 667 N.E.2d 1189 (1996) (wife filed action for legal separation in Ohio, husband filed for divorce in Florida, Florida court stayed its action awaiting Ohio determination). See Ohio Jur. 3d, Actions § 140.

[3]RC 3109.21 to RC 3109.37.

witness's credibility is a factor.[1]

A court has inherent authority to clarify a judgment entry sua sponte where confusion exists as to its meaning.[2]

§ 27:13 Subject matter jurisdiction—Jurisdiction to render judgment—During appeal

◆ **NOTE:** See also § 32:23, Jurisdiction during appeal—Enforcement during appeal.

The Supreme Court has expressly held that an appeal divests a trial court of jurisdiction to consider Civ. R. 60(B) motions.[1] Therefore, when a court reconsiders its dismissal entry and grants a judgment while an appeal is pending, the trial court lacks the jurisdiction to reinstate and decide the divorce case.[2]

§ 27:14 Subject matter jurisdiction—Jurisdiction to reconsider

A motion for reconsideration made after final judgment in the trial court is a nullity.[1] Interlocutory orders are subject to motions for reconsideration whereas judgments and final orders are not.[2] The Supreme Court has held that "the Rules of Civil Procedure specifically limit relief from judgments to motions expressly provided for within the same Rules. A motion for reconsideration is conspicuously absent within the Rules. Rather the Civil Rules do allow for relief from final judgments by means of Civ.R. 50(B) . . ., Civ.R. 59 . . ., and Civ.R. 60(B)."[3] The filing of a motion for reconsideration does not toll the time for filing an appeal pursuant to App. R. 4(A).[4]

[Section 27:12]

[1]Vergon v. Vergon, 87 Ohio App. 3d 639, 622 N.E.2d 1111 (8th Dist. Cuyahoga County 1993).

[2]Long v. Long, 1999 WL 333215 (Ohio Ct. App. 5th Dist. Licking County 1999).

[Section 27:13]

[1]Howard v. Catholic Social Serv. of Cuyahoga Cty., Inc., 1994 -Ohio- 219, 70 Ohio St. 3d 141, 637 N.E.2d 890 (1994).

[2]McAuley v. Smith, 133 Ohio App. 3d 685, 729 N.E.2d 792 (7th Dist. Mahoning County 1999).

[Section 27:14]

[1]Horak v. Horak, 1997 WL 449976 (Ohio Ct. App. 8th Dist. Cuyahoga County 1997); Pitts v. Ohio Dept. of Transp., 67 Ohio St. 2d 378, 21 Ohio Op. 3d 238, 423 N.E.2d 1105 (1981).

[2]Civ. R. 54(B); In re Guardianship of Maurer, 108 Ohio App. 3d 354, 670 N.E.2d 1030 (6th Dist. Wood County 1995), cause dismissed, 74 Ohio St. 3d 1461, 656 N.E.2d 1297 (1995) and dismissed, appeal not allowed, 76 Ohio St. 3d 1405, 666 N.E.2d 565 (1996); Gibson v. Westfall, 1999 WL 809813 (Ohio Ct. App. 8th Dist. Cuyahoga County 1999).

[3]Pitts v. Ohio Dept. of Transp., 67 Ohio St. 2d 378, 380, 21 Ohio Op. 3d 238, 423 N.E.2d 1105 (1981).

[4]Ditmars v. Ditmars, 16 Ohio App. 3d 174, 475 N.E.2d 164 (10th Dist. Franklin County 1984).

§ 27:15 Subject matter jurisdiction—Loss of subject matter jurisdiction

The trial court loses its subject matter to make or enforce any orders over all issues after the divorce case is voluntarily dismissed under Civ. R. 41(A) by all parties to the case. A writ of mandamus or procedendo was granted where a trial court attempted to make custody orders to a nonparty after the husband and wife had voluntarily dismissed their divorce action.[1] A later "nunc pro tunc" entry purporting to join the nonparty, retroactive to a date preceding the dismissal, was held to be void.

After the trial court unconditionally dismisses a divorce case for failure of proof, it patently and unambiguously lacks jurisdiction to proceed in the case, and a writ of prohibition is the appropriate procedure to challenge the court's exercise of jurisdiction following the dismissal.[2]

The trial court loses jurisdiction and a divorce action abates where one of the parties to the action dies before the final decree is entered.[3] The court, lacking jurisdiction to proceed in the underlying divorce, has no authority to add parties or to impose or enforce restraining orders.[4]

Even though the domestic relations court is without jurisdiction to enforce an order restraining a change of beneficiaries of life insurance after the death of the insured, equities may arise in favor of the surviving spouse where there is fraud and improper conduct. Unjust enrichment, if found, may serve as the basis for imposing a constructive trust upon the proceeds.[5]

In *Starr v. Starr*,[6] the Twelfth District Court of Appeals held that the thirty-day waiting period prescribed in the dissolution statute (RC 3105.64) is mandatory, citing the public policy in favor of a "cooling-off period" and possible reconciliation. However, the court held that a dissolution decree entered before the expiration of thirty days was voidable, rather than void.

§ 27:16 Subject matter jurisdiction—Loss of subject matters jurisdiction—Assumption by juvenile court

Once complaints of abuse, neglect, or dependency are filed in juvenile court, the domestic relations court that previously awarded custody of

---

[Section 27:15]

[1]State ex rel. Fogle v. Steiner, 1995 -Ohio- 278, 74 Ohio St. 3d 158, 656 N.E.2d 1288 (1995).

[2]McAuley v. Smith, 1998 -Ohio- 402, 82 Ohio St. 3d 393, 696 N.E.2d 572 (1998).

[3]State ex rel. Litty v. Leskovyansky, 1996 -Ohio- 340, 77 Ohio St. 3d 97, 671 N.E.2d 236 (1996).

[4]Ondak v. Ondak, 1999 WL 179477 (Ohio Ct. App. 8th Dist. Cuyahoga County 1999).

[5]Concepcion v. Concepcion, 131 Ohio App. 3d 271, 722 N.E.2d 176 (3d Dist. Seneca County 1999).

[6]Starr v. Starr, 26 Ohio App. 3d 134, 498 N.E.2d 1092 (12th Dist. Madison County 1985).

the minor loses jurisdiction to proceed in matters affecting custody.[1] The juvenile court's assumption of jurisdiction is original and, while concurrent, it is in the interest of judicial economy for the juvenile court to address all related issues.[2]

The juvenile court does not have jurisdiction to determine "child" support for an adult child when the complaint is not brought until after the child is 18 years of age or older,[3] except in a parentage action.[4]

Once a child has attained the age of majority, as set forth in RC 3109.01, the court generally lacks subject matter jurisdiction to modify parental rights and responsibilities.[5]

§ 27:17 Subject matter jurisdiction—Jurisdiction after dismissal

While the trial court loses jurisdiction over the divorce itself when it dismisses the action due to failure of proof of the cause in the complaint, the court may make orders regarding the care and disposition of any minor child.[1]

A trial court has jurisdiction after dismissal of a case to impose sanctions under Civ.R. 11 after final judgment is ordered.[2] The court also has the authority to entertain a motion for sanctions brought under RC 2323.51 after a voluntary dismissal of underlying action. In *Flatinger v. Flatinger*[3] the appellate court held that the trial court erred in dismissing a motion for sanctions after the trial court dismissed the divorce complaint for lack of subject matter jurisdiction. The trial court had concluded that because it lacked jurisdiction over the underlying divorce action, it also lacked jurisdiction over the motion for sanctions.

[Section 27:16]

[1]Kovalak v. Kovalak, 1998 WL 456506 (Ohio Ct. App. 8th Dist. Cuyahoga County 1998), dismissed, appeal not allowed, 84 Ohio St. 3d 1468, 704 N.E.2d 577 (1999).

[2]In re Poling, 1992 -Ohio- 144, 64 Ohio St. 3d 211, 594 N.E.2d 589 (1992).

[3]In re Livingston, 115 Ohio App. 3d 613, 685 N.E.2d 1285 (8th Dist. Cuyahoga County 1996).

[4]Park v. Ambrose, 85 Ohio App. 3d 179, 619 N.E.2d 469 (4th Dist. Ross County 1993) (because juvenile court has jurisdiction to determine parentage, it has authority to make provisions for support retroactive to date of birth, more than twenty years after child's birth), appeal dismissed by 67 Ohio St.3d 1409, 615 N.E.2d 1043 (1993).

[5]Rohrbacher v. Rohrbacher, 83 Ohio App. 3d 569, 615 N.E.2d 338 (6th Dist. Lucas County 1992); State ex rel. Mandich v. Mandich, 1997 WL 537670 (Ohio Ct. App. 9th Dist. Medina County 1997).

[Section 27:17]

[1]RC 3105.21(B); State ex rel. Easterday v. Zieba, 58 Ohio St. 3d 251, 569 N.E.2d 1028 (1991).

[2]Stevens v. Kiraly, 24 Ohio App. 3d 211, 494 N.E.2d 1160 (9th Dist. Wayne County 1985).

[3]Flatinger v. Flatinger, 2002-Ohio-3781, 2002 WL 1724342 (Ohio Ct. App. 10th Dist. Franklin County 2002).

§ 27:18   Subject matter jurisdiction—Lack of subject matter jurisdiction

If the court does not have subject matter jurisdiction, any judgments rendered in that case are void "ab initio."[1] Lack of such jurisdiction may be raised at any time, including upon appeal.

The power to vacate a void judgment is not derived from Civ. R. 60(B) but is an inherent power possessed by the court.[2]

§ 27:19   Motion to dismiss—Lack of subject matter jurisdiction—Form⊚

[Title of Court]

[Caption]   Case No. [_____]

MOTION TO DISMISS

Defendant moves the Court to dismiss the action herein for lack of jurisdiction over the subject matter, Plaintiff not having been a resident of the State of Ohio for six months prior to filing this action for divorce.

This motion is supported by the affidavit below.

_____

Attorney for Defendant

[Affidavit of movant in support of motion]
[Notice of hearing]
[Proof/certificate of service]

§ 27:20   Jurisdiction over marital status—Domicile as element

It is well established that domicile is an essential element of divorce jurisdiction.[1] The reason for the doctrine becomes apparent in relation to traditional jurisdictional concepts. A divorce decree is regarded as a judgment in rem in the sense that it determines marital status.[2] To terminate a marriage, the court must have jurisdiction over the marital relationship.[3] It is considered that the marital status (the "res") follows

---

[Section 27:18]

[1]Patton v. Diemer, 35 Ohio St. 3d 68, 518 N.E.2d 941 (1988).

[2]Lincoln Tavern, Inc. v. Snader, 165 Ohio St. 61, 59 Ohio Op. 74, 133 N.E.2d 606 (1956); McCree v. McCree, 2000 WL 310319 (Ohio Ct. App. 7th Dist. Mahoning County 2000).

[Section 27:20]

[1]Spires v. Spires, 7 Ohio Misc. 197, 35 Ohio Op. 2d 289, 214 N.E.2d 691 (C.P. 1966). See also Williams v. State of N. C., 325 U.S. 226, 65 S. Ct. 1092, 89 L. Ed. 1577, 157 A.L.R. 1366 (1945); Andrews v. Andrews, 188 U.S. 14, 23 S. Ct. 237, 47 L. Ed. 366 (1903); Glassman v. Glassman, 75 Ohio App. 47, 30 Ohio Op. 352, 42 Ohio L. Abs. 385, 60 N.E.2d 716 (1st Dist. Hamilton County 1944).

[2]McGill v. Deming, 44 Ohio St. 645, 11 N.E. 118 (1887).

[3]Williams v. State of North Carolina, 317 U.S. 287, 63 S. Ct. 207, 87 L. Ed. 279, 143 A.L.R. 1273 (1942); Am. Jur. 2d, Divorce and Separation § 240.

the domiciles of the parties. In other words, domicile operates on the premise that the marriage moves from place to place with either spouse.[4] To insure the court's jurisdiction over the res, it is therefore required that one of the spouses be domiciled within the divorce-granting state.[5]

The United States Supreme Court has clearly endorsed the precept that judicial authority over matrimonial status is predicated on domicile. This is particularly evident in the landmark decisions, *Williams v. North Carolina (I) and (II)*.[6] In *Williams (I)*, the Court acknowledged that a state has a legitimate concern in the marital relations of persons within its borders. It emphasized, however, that the state's power to alter their marital status is dependent upon the relationship which domicile creates.[7]

In *Williams v. North Carolina (II)*, this principle was reiterated in unequivocal terms: "Under our system of law, judicial power to grant a divorce—jurisdiction, strictly speaking—is founded on domicil."[8] Speaking for the majority, Justice Frankfurter described the penetration of the doctrine: "The framers of the Constitution were familiar with this jurisdictional prerequisite, and since 1789 neither this Court nor any other court in the English-speaking world has questioned it."[9] The Court's identification of domicile and power was emphatic: "The domicil of one spouse within a State gives power to that State . . . to dissolve a marriage. . . [Domicile is a fact] upon which depends the power to exert judicial authority."[10] Jurisdiction over marital status is thus dependent upon domicile. Unless one spouse is domiciled within the state, the court lacks power to dissolve the marriage.

The rationale provided by the Court focused on the connection domicile creates between the individual and the forum. In the absence of domicile, the Court said, a state lacks a sufficient nexus between person and place of such permanence as to control the creation of legal relations and responsibilities.[11]

Ohio has codified the requirement of domicile in Ohio, in RC 3105.03.

---

[4]Rosenstiel v. Rosenstiel, 16 N.Y.2d 64, 262 N.Y.S.2d 86, 209 N.E.2d 709, 13 A.L.R.3d 1401 (1965) (court remarked that although domicile is not intrinsically an indispensable prerequisite to jurisdiction, it is pragmatically suitable to a highly mobile era).

[5]Am. Jur. 2d, Divorce and Separation § 240.

[6]Williams v. State of North Carolina, 317 U.S. 287, 63 S. Ct. 207, 87 L. Ed. 279, 143 A.L.R. 1273 (1942); Williams v. State of N. C., 325 U.S. 226, 65 S. Ct. 1092, 89 L. Ed. 1577, 157 A.L.R. 1366 (1945).

[7]See also Williams v. State of N. C., 325 U.S. 226, 65 S. Ct. 1092, 89 L. Ed. 1577, 157 A.L.R. 1366 (1945); Cox v. Cox, 19 Ohio St. 502, 1869 WL 84 (1869).

[8]Williams v. State of N. C., 325 U.S. 226, 229, 65 S. Ct. 1092, 89 L. Ed. 1577, 157 A.L.R. 1366 (1945).

[9]Williams v. State of N. C., 325 U.S. 226, 229, 65 S. Ct. 1092, 89 L. Ed. 1577, 157 A.L.R. 1366 (1945).

[10]Williams v. State of N. C., 325 U.S. 226, 229-30, 65 S. Ct. 1092, 89 L. Ed. 1577, 157 A.L.R. 1366 (1945) (footnotes omitted).

[11]Williams v. State of N. C., 325 U.S. 226, 65 S. Ct. 1092, 89 L. Ed. 1577, 157 A.L.R. 1366 (1945).

The statute provides that in an action for divorce and annulment the plaintiff must have been a resident of the state at least six months immediately before filing the complaint and must prove such residence by a preponderance of the evidence.[12]

"Resident," although not defined in RC 3105.03 or Civil Rule 3(B)(9), requires a "domicile" in the sense of a permanent home, where one actually resides with intent to remain.[13] Where a party fails to prove the allegation of her complaint as to residency, a trial court has no jurisdiction to determine the remaining issues in her complaint.[14] Although the word "domicile" does not appear in the Code, Ohio courts which have considered the question have determined that the word "residence," as used in the statute, means a domiciliary residence within the state.[15] If a bona fide residence has not been established, a divorce decree from that jurisdiction is void ab initio. A party cannot be estopped from challenging the validity of the decree.[16]

Ohio follows the prevailing view that a court has no jurisdiction to hear an action for divorce unless one of the spouses is a domiciliary resident of the state.[17] It is also generally agreed that a divorce decree granted by a sister state in which neither party was domiciled is not entitled to extra-territorial recognition.[18]

---

[12]Saunders v. Saunders, 1988 WL 34635 (Ohio Ct. App. 7th Dist. Columbiana County 1988). See also Reed v. Reed, 1993 WL 125435 (Ohio Ct. App. 2d Dist. Montgomery County 1993) (testimony of neighbor that she had been the parties' neighbor for four or five years supported the trial court's finding of jurisdiction).

[13]State ex rel. Saunders v. Court of Common Pleas of Allen County, 34 Ohio St. 3d 15, 516 N.E.2d 232 (1987); Hager v. Hager, 79 Ohio App. 3d 239, 607 N.E.2d 63 (2d Dist. Greene County 1992); Heath v. Heath, 1997 WL 103832 (Ohio Ct. App. 6th Dist. Lucas County 1997) (when challenged, it is plaintiff's burden to show he or she is domiciled within the state by a preponderance of the evidence).

[14]Sanor v. Sanor, 1989 WL 155727 (Ohio Ct. App. 5th Dist. Stark County 1989); Polakova v. Polak, 107 Ohio App. 3d 745, 669 N.E.2d 498 (1st Dist. Hamilton County 1995) ("J" status, non immigrant temporary visa holder found by trial court without sufficient proof of intent to reside).

[15]Saalfeld v. Saalfeld, 86 Ohio App. 225, 41 Ohio Op. 94, 55 Ohio L. Abs. 156, 89 N.E.2d 165 (1st Dist. Clermont County 1949); Glassman v. Glassman, 75 Ohio App. 47, 30 Ohio Op. 352, 42 Ohio L. Abs. 385, 60 N.E.2d 716 (1st Dist. Hamilton County 1944); Draper v. Draper, 107 Ohio App. 32, 7 Ohio Op. 2d 354, 78 Ohio L. Abs. 5, 151 N.E.2d 379 (10th Dist. Franklin County 1958); Spires v. Spires, 7 Ohio Misc. 197, 35 Ohio Op. 2d 289, 214 N.E.2d 691 (C.P. 1966). See also Coleman v. Coleman, 32 Ohio St. 2d 155, 61 Ohio Op. 2d 406, 291 N.E.2d 530, 57 A.L.R.3d 213 (1972).

[16]In re Estate of Newton, 65 Ohio App. 3d 286, 583 N.E.2d 1026 (5th Dist. Muskingum County 1989).

[17]Glassman v. Glassman, 75 Ohio App. 47, 30 Ohio Op. 352, 42 Ohio L. Abs. 385, 60 N.E.2d 716 (1st Dist. Hamilton County 1944); Ready v. Ready, 25 Ohio App. 432, 5 Ohio L. Abs. 629, 158 N.E. 493 (8th Dist. Cuyahoga County 1927); Smerda v. Smerda, 35 Ohio Op. 472, 48 Ohio L. Abs. 232, 74 N.E.2d 751 (C.P. 1947). See Van Fossen v. State, 37 Ohio St. 317, 1881 WL 101 (1881); Cox v. Cox, 19 Ohio St. 502, 510, 1869 WL 84 (1869).

[18]Van Fossen v. State, 37 Ohio St. 317, 1881 WL 101 (1881); Cox v. Cox, 19 Ohio St. 502, 1869 WL 84 (1869); Glassman v. Glassman, 75 Ohio App. 47, 30 Ohio Op. 352, 42 Ohio L. Abs. 385, 60 N.E.2d 716 (1st Dist. Hamilton County 1944); Neal v. Neal, 53 Ohio

§ 27:21 Jurisdiction over marital status—Domicile defined—Residence versus domicile

Although the words "domicile" and "residence" are sometimes used interchangeably, they are not synonymous. Mere residence, as distinguished from domicile, is legally inadequate to confer divorce jurisdiction upon a court.[1] The word "residence" imports actual physical presence within the state. It signifies an abode or place of dwelling.[2] "Domicile" ordinarily has a broader meaning than residence. Domicile conveys a fixed, permanent home. It is the place to which one intends to return and from which one has no present purpose to depart.[3] Domicile has been described as the relationship which the law creates between an individual and a particular locality.[4]

A party's domicile generally coincides with his place of residence. However, an individual may have several residences, but he can be domiciled in only one place at a given time.[5] Moreover, one could establish a residence without intending to remain there indefinitely. It is generally agreed that domicile is not acquired unless the residence is accompanied by an intention that the place be a fixed or permanent home.[6] The duration of the residence (whether for six months or six years) is not controlling. A temporary residence, no matter how long extended, does not constitute a domicile. Accordingly, it has been held that if one has had a temporary residence in Ohio, but has not formulated an intention that Ohio be a permanent home, the residence does not amount to a domiciliary residence and does not fulfill the requirements of RC 3105.03.[7]

On the other hand, a domicile may be retained, even though one does not currently reside in that locality. Thus, actual residence is not an es-

---

L. Abs. 329, 85 N.E.2d 147 (C.P. 1949); Smerda v. Smerda, 35 Ohio Op. 472, 48 Ohio L. Abs. 232, 74 N.E.2d 751 (C.P. 1947). See Williams v. State of N. C., 325 U.S. 226, 65 S. Ct. 1092, 89 L. Ed. 1577, 157 A.L.R. 1366 (1945).

[Section 27:21]

[1]Saalfeld v. Saalfeld, 86 Ohio App. 225, 41 Ohio Op. 94, 55 Ohio L. Abs. 156, 89 N.E.2d 165 (1st Dist. Clermont County 1949); Glassman v. Glassman, 75 Ohio App. 47, 30 Ohio Op. 352, 42 Ohio L. Abs. 385, 60 N.E.2d 716 (1st Dist. Hamilton County 1944); Smerda v. Smerda, 35 Ohio Op. 472, 48 Ohio L. Abs. 232, 74 N.E.2d 751 (C.P. 1947).

[2]Franklin v. Franklin, 5 Ohio App. 3d 74, 449 N.E.2d 457 (7th Dist. Mahoning County 1981); Jackman v. Jackman, 110 Ohio App. 199, 12 Ohio Op. 2d 464, 160 N.E.2d 387 (1st Dist. Hamilton County 1959).

[3]Smerda v. Smerda, 35 Ohio Op. 472, 48 Ohio L. Abs. 232, 74 N.E.2d 751 (C.P. 1947). See Sturgeon v. Korte, 34 Ohio St. 525, 1878 WL 57 (1878).

[4]Sturgeon v. Korte, 34 Ohio St. 525, 1878 WL 57 (1878).

[5]Spires v. Spires, 7 Ohio Misc. 197, 35 Ohio Op. 2d 289, 214 N.E.2d 691 (C.P. 1966). See also Foote v. Foote, 192 Misc. 270, 77 N.Y.S.2d 60 (Sup 1948).

[6]Glassman v. Glassman, 75 Ohio App. 47, 30 Ohio Op. 352, 42 Ohio L. Abs. 385, 60 N.E.2d 716 (1st Dist. Hamilton County 1944); Polakova v. Polak, 107 Ohio App. 3d 745, 669 N.E.2d 498 (1st Dist. Hamilton County 1995) ("J" status, non-proof of intent to reside).

[7]Glassman v. Glassman, 75 Ohio App. 47, 30 Ohio Op. 352, 42 Ohio L. Abs. 385, 60 N.E.2d 716 (1st Dist. Hamilton County 1944); Saalfeld v. Saalfeld, 86 Ohio App. 225, 41 Ohio Op. 94, 55 Ohio L. Abs. 156, 89 N.E.2d 165 (1st Dist. Clermont County 1949).

sential component of domicile once it has been established.[8] Accordingly, a party may live in different locations or wander from place to place for years without having abandoned his domicile.[9]

§ 27:22   Jurisdiction over marital status—Domicile defined— Permanent home

Ohio courts have frequently used the language "permanent home" in defining domiciliary intent. In applying this standard, one commentator has suggested that a requirement of intended "permanent" settlement in the state is unrealistic today. A sensible alternative, and one finding support in early analogous federal decisions, relies on the "absence of an intention to go elsewhere." Domicile would thus be acquired if the place is to be one's home for an indefinite period of time and if the party has no present intention to return to the former domicile or to go elsewhere.[1]

A similar definition of domiciliary residence was applied by the Ohio Supreme Court in an early case:

> It is not, however, necessary that [one] should intend to remain there for all time. If he lives in a place, with the intention of remaining for an indefinite period of time, as a place of fixed present domicile, and not as a place of temporary establishment, or for mere transient objects, it is to all intents, and for all purposes, his [domiciliary] residence.[2]

Under this criterion, a permanent home is established if it is the party's principal home, and he intends to remain there indefinitely, provided he has no present purpose to move elsewhere.

§ 27:23   Jurisdiction over marital status—Domicile defined— Wife's domicile

The common law rule, later codified, was that a wife takes the domicile of her husband on marriage.[1] Former RC 3103.02, which had designated the husband as head of the family and provided that he had the right to choose any reasonable domicile to which the wife was required to conform, was repealed in 1974. Since the statute has been abolished, it would appear that the rule which it incorporated has been abrogated in Ohio. Presumably, the marital domicile is now to be selected by mutual agreement of the spouses. If they are unable to agree, there seems to be no legal impediment to either spouse establishing a separate domicile.

Even before the repeal of the statute, the wife was permitted to select

---

[8]Smerda v. Smerda, 35 Ohio Op. 472, 48 Ohio L. Abs. 232, 74 N.E.2d 751 (C.P. 1947).

[9]Spires v. Spires, 7 Ohio Misc. 197, 35 Ohio Op. 2d 289, 214 N.E.2d 691 (C.P. 1966).

[Section 27:22]

[1]1 *Moore's Federal Practice* § .074 [3.-1] (1983) (domicile and federal diversity).

[2]Sturgeon v. Korte, 34 Ohio St. 525, 535, 1878 WL 57 (1878).

[Section 27:23]

[1]Sturgeon v. Korte, 34 Ohio St. 525, 535, 1878 WL 57 (1878); Glassman v. Glassman, 75 Ohio App. 47, 30 Ohio Op. 352, 42 Ohio L. Abs. 385, 60 N.E.2d 716 (1st Dist. Hamilton County 1944).

a new domicile in the event of the husband's desertion[2] or upon his aggression.[3] It was also recognized that neither the statute nor the common law legal fiction that the wife takes the husband's domicile should preclude the wife from asserting a separate domicile in an action to obtain matrimonial relief.[4] Moreover, RC 3105.04 provides that a divorce plaintiff's access to the courts is not foreclosed by the residence of the other spouse. Accordingly, for purposes of divorce jurisdiction, it is clear that a wife is entitled to demonstrate a separate domicile and that her right to institute proceedings is unaffected by the domicile of her husband.[5]

§ 27:24 Jurisdiction over marital status—Domicile—Armed services member

A member of the armed forces may claim residency wherever the member is stationed. In general the member may retain the residency where he or she entered the service, unless the person voluntarily selects a new residence. For purposes of jurisdiction to file a divorce, the marital status follows the domicile of the parties.

In *Hager v. Hager*,[1] the plaintiff, a major in the United States Air Force, had, as recently as one month before filing a divorce action, certified that his legal residence was in the state of Florida. In testifying as to his actual living situation in Ohio and his "intent to remain," he explained the Florida residency was only to avoid Ohio income tax consequences, and did not represent his domicile.

The spouse of a person in the military does not necessarily lose a former residency when living on base because of military service.[2]

§ 27:25 Jurisdiction over marital status—Change of domicile

It is said that the law ascribes a domicile to every person, and no one

---

[2]Cox v. Cox, 19 Ohio St. 502, 1869 WL 84 (1869); Malgras v. Malgras, 15 Ohio App. 335, 1921 WL 1143 (1st Dist. Clermont County 1921).

[3]Glassman v. Glassman, 75 Ohio App. 47, 30 Ohio Op. 352, 42 Ohio L. Abs. 385, 60 N.E.2d 716 (1st Dist. Hamilton County 1944).

[4]Glassman v. Glassman, 75 Ohio App. 47, 30 Ohio Op. 352, 42 Ohio L. Abs. 385, 60 N.E.2d 716 (1st Dist. Hamilton County 1944). See also Cox v. Cox, 19 Ohio St. 502, 1869 WL 84 (1869); Saalfeld v. Saalfeld, 86 Ohio App. 225, 41 Ohio Op. 94, 55 Ohio L. Abs. 156, 89 N.E.2d 165 (1st Dist. Clermont County 1949).

[5]Armstrong v. Armstrong, 99 Ohio App. 7, 58 Ohio Op. 79, 130 N.E.2d 710 (1st Dist. Hamilton County 1954), judgment aff'd, 162 Ohio St. 406, 55 Ohio Op. 234, 123 N.E.2d 267 (1954), cert. granted, 349 U.S. 915, 75 S. Ct. 604, 99 L. Ed. 1248 (1955) and judgment aff'd, 350 U.S. 568, 76 S. Ct. 629, 100 L. Ed. 705, 73 Ohio L. Abs. 514 (1956).

[Section 27:24]

[1]Hager v. Hager, 79 Ohio App. 3d 239, 607 N.E.2d 63 (2d Dist. Greene County 1992).

[2]Dobson v. Dobson, 1998 WL 519255 (Ohio Ct. App. 5th Dist. Stark County 1998).

can have more than one domicile at a given time.[1] As a logical extension of this rule, one's former domicile is not deemed lost unless and until a new domicile is acquired. In fact, the old domicile continues until another is established.[2]

Accordingly, a mere change of residence does not itself effect a change of domicile. Under the law of Ohio, a change of domicile contemplates both physical presence and intent to remain (factum and animus). Three elements are required: (1) a fixed intention to abandon the former domicile (animus non revertendi); (2) a fixed intention to acquire a new domicile, that is, to establish a permanent home elsewhere (animus manendi); and (3) an actual change of residence.[3] Until these factors concur, a new domicile is not acquired and the old domicile is presumed to continue.[4] Once a new domicile is established, the preceding one is terminated.[5]

One does not cease to be domiciled in a particular location because he intends to move elsewhere and prepares to do so; or because he is absent from the place of domicile for extended periods of time; or because he leaves and actually resides elsewhere, without intending to stay.[6] Conversely, the fact that one may entertain a fleeting intention to return to his former domicile at some future time does not defeat a change of domicile if he has moved to another place with the intention of remaining there indefinitely.[7]

To change domicile, physical residence in the new location must be coupled with an intention that the residence be a permanent, principal home and that the former domicile be abandoned.[8] It is not necessary, however, that the party intend to acquire a new domicile at the time he

---

[Section 27:25]

[1]Saalfeld v. Saalfeld, 86 Ohio App. 225, 41 Ohio Op. 94, 55 Ohio L. Abs. 156, 89 N.E.2d 165 (1st Dist. Clermont County 1949). See Sturgeon v. Korte, 34 Ohio St. 525, 1878 WL 57 (1878).

[2]Sturgeon v. Korte, 34 Ohio St. 525, 1878 WL 57 (1878); Glassman v. Glassman, 75 Ohio App. 47, 30 Ohio Op. 352, 42 Ohio L. Abs. 385, 60 N.E.2d 716 (1st Dist. Hamilton County 1944); Saalfeld v. Saalfeld, 86 Ohio App. 225, 41 Ohio Op. 94, 55 Ohio L. Abs. 156, 89 N.E.2d 165 (1st Dist. Clermont County 1949); Spires v. Spires, 7 Ohio Misc. 197, 35 Ohio Op. 2d 289, 214 N.E.2d 691 (C.P. 1966); Ohio Jur. 3d, Domicile § 11.

[3]Paparella v. Paparella, 74 A.D.2d 106, 426 N.Y.S.2d 610 (4th Dep't 1980). See also Saalfeld v. Saalfeld, 86 Ohio App. 225, 41 Ohio Op. 94, 55 Ohio L. Abs. 156, 89 N.E.2d 165 (1st Dist. Clermont County 1949); Smerda v. Smerda, 35 Ohio Op. 472, 48 Ohio L. Abs. 232, 74 N.E.2d 751 (C.P. 1947); Neal v. Neal, 53 Ohio L. Abs. 329, 85 N.E.2d 147 (C.P. 1949).

[4]Saalfeld v. Saalfeld, 86 Ohio App. 225, 41 Ohio Op. 94, 55 Ohio L. Abs. 156, 89 N.E.2d 165 (1st Dist. Clermont County 1949); Smerda v. Smerda, 35 Ohio Op. 472, 48 Ohio L. Abs. 232, 74 N.E.2d 751 (C.P. 1947); Reese v. Reese, 1997 WL 272368 (Ohio Ct. App. 8th Dist. Cuyahoga County 1997) (temporary absence from the state to avoid abuse by spouse does not cause loss of residence for jurisdiction).

[5]Sturgeon v. Korte, 34 Ohio St. 525, 1878 WL 57 (1878); Ohio Jur. 3d, Domicile § 11.

[6]Glassman v. Glassman, 75 Ohio App. 47, 30 Ohio Op. 352, 42 Ohio L. Abs. 385, 60 N.E.2d 716 (1st Dist. Hamilton County 1944); Spires v. Spires, 7 Ohio Misc. 197, 35 Ohio Op. 2d 289, 214 N.E.2d 691 (C.P. 1966).

[7]Redrow v. Redrow, 94 Ohio App. 38, 51 Ohio Op. 266, 114 N.E.2d 293 (1st Dist. Clermont County 1952). See also 3 Moore's Federal Practice § 74.

[8]Spires v. Spires, 7 Ohio Misc. 197, 35 Ohio Op. 2d 289, 214 N.E.2d 691 (C.P. 1966).

moves to the location; his intention to remain may be formed afterwards. Thus, residence may be acquired for temporary purposes only, but if the party later adopts the place as his home it may become his domicile. In such a case, the new domicile would be acquired at the point where the intention to adopt the new residence became fixed.[9]

§ 27:26 Jurisdiction over marital status—Proof of domicile

Domicile is a question of fact to be determined on the evidence submitted.[1] It has been described as essentially a matter of intent,[2] although both elements of "residence" and "intent to remain in the location" must be demonstrated.[3]

It has been said that the fact of residence in a location is prima facie evidence of domicile there, which is rebuttable by proof to the contrary.[4] The burden of proof rests on the party whose right to affirmative relief depends upon establishing his own domicile or that of another. In an original action, it is the plaintiff's burden to show that he is domiciled in the state.[5] The standard of proof is a preponderance of evidence.[6] In a collateral proceeding, however, the burden of proving that a spouse was not domiciled in the divorce granting state is upon the party challenging the legitimacy of the judgment.[7] According to the United States Supreme Court, the burden of undermining a finding of domicile and the "verity" which a decree imports "rests heavily upon the assailant."[8] Ohio courts have said that the party challenging a finding of domicile must sustain the burden by clear and convincing evidence.[9]

One writer has observed that it is impossible to lay down any positive

---

[9]Sturgeon v. Korte, 34 Ohio St. 525, 1878 WL 57 (1878) (citing Story's conflict of laws).

[Section 27:26]
[1]Redrow v. Redrow, 94 Ohio App. 38, 51 Ohio Op. 266, 114 N.E.2d 293 (1st Dist. Clermont County 1952); Sturgeon v. Korte, 34 Ohio St. 525, 1878 WL 57 (1878).

[2]Redrow v. Redrow, 94 Ohio App. 38, 51 Ohio Op. 266, 114 N.E.2d 293 (1st Dist. Clermont County 1952); Winnard v. Winnard, 62 Ohio App. 351, 16 Ohio Op. 51, 23 N.E.2d 977 (2d Dist. Franklin County 1939).

[3]Redrow v. Redrow, 94 Ohio App. 38, 51 Ohio Op. 266, 114 N.E.2d 293 (1st Dist. Clermont County 1952). See Franklin v. Franklin, 5 Ohio App. 3d 74, 449 N.E.2d 457 (7th Dist. Mahoning County 1981); E. Cleveland v. Landingham, 97 Ohio App. 3d 385, 646 N.E.2d 897 (8th Dist. Cuyahoga County 1994).

[4]Ohio Jur. 3d, Domicile § 19.

[5]Redrow v. Redrow, 94 Ohio App. 38, 51 Ohio Op. 266, 114 N.E.2d 293 (1st Dist. Clermont County 1952); Saalfeld v. Saalfeld, 86 Ohio App. 225, 41 Ohio Op. 94, 55 Ohio L. Abs. 156, 89 N.E.2d 165 (1st Dist. Clermont County 1949); Polakova v. Polak, 107 Ohio App. 3d 745, 669 N.E.2d 498 (1st Dist. Hamilton County 1995).

[6]Sturgeon v. Korte, 34 Ohio St. 525, 1878 WL 57 (1878); In re Hatt's Estate, 47 Ohio L. Abs. 603, 73 N.E.2d 107 (Ct. App. 8th Dist. Cuyahoga County 1947).

[7]In re Sayle's Estate, 51 Ohio L. Abs. 46, 80 N.E.2d 229 (Ct. App. 8th Dist. Cuyahoga County 1948).

[8]Williams v. State of N. C., 325 U.S. 226, 233–34, 65 S. Ct. 1092, 89 L. Ed. 1577, 157 A.L.R. 1366 (1945).

[9]Linck v. Linck, 31 Ohio Misc. 224, 60 Ohio Op. 2d 388, 288 N.E.2d 347 (C.P. 1972); In re Sayle's Estate, 37 Ohio Op. 167, 51 Ohio L. Abs. 33, 80 N.E.2d 221 (Prob. Ct.

rule with respect to the evidence necessary to establish domiciliary intent, since each case varies with the circumstances, and a fact of importance in one case may be accorded little weight in another.[10] An illustration of this is when a spouse attempts to establish residence in another state and then shortly obtains a divorce which he could not have otherwise secured in the state of his former residence. Some courts have adopted the position that if a spouse takes up residence in another state and soon afterward applies for a divorce, a "violent" if not "conclusive" presumption arises that he went there for that purpose; and no bona fide domicile is acquired in the state.[11] Other courts have said that the motive of removal to procure a divorce is immaterial, because there is no rule of law preventing one from changing domicile to facilitate a divorce, provided that the party has a bona fide intention to remain in the jurisdiction permanently.[12] A third view is that the party's purpose to obtain a divorce is not dispositive but is one factor which may be considered in determining whether he has established a bona fide residence in the state.[13]

Another example of differing views as to probative value concerns the testimony of the person whose domicile is in question. Some courts have said that a party's claim that he intended to establish a domiciliary residence will be accepted as true, unless facts and circumstances are so persuasive that his statements of intent cannot be believed.[14] Another view is that a party's conduct has greater evidential value and is more trustworthy than his declarations, especially where the declarations are not consistent with his actions.[15]

In determining whether a particular residence has become a domicile, courts have considered any number of factors that shed light on the party's intention. No one factor appears to be controlling. Some examples of behavior given weight in assessing domiciliary intent are length of stay in the foreign state; location of checking accounts; site and nature of business transactions; social and business connections in the foreign

---

1947), order aff'd, 51 Ohio L. Abs. 46, 80 N.E.2d 229 (Ct. App. 8th Dist. Cuyahoga County 1948).

[10]Spires v. Spires, 7 Ohio Misc. 197, 35 Ohio Op. 2d 289, 214 N.E.2d 691 (C.P. 1966).

[11]Smerda v. Smerda, 35 Ohio Op. 472, 48 Ohio L. Abs. 232, 74 N.E.2d 751 (C.P. 1947). See also Neal v. Neal, 53 Ohio L. Abs. 329, 85 N.E.2d 147 (C.P. 1949); Davis v. Davis, 42 Ohio L. Abs. 105, 57 N.E.2d 703 (Ct. App. 2d Dist. Franklin County 1944); Wolfe v. Wolfe, 45 Ohio App. 309, 14 Ohio L. Abs. 577, 187 N.E. 86 (6th Dist. Lucas County 1933), error dismissed, 127 Ohio St. 160, 187 N.E. 201 (1933).

[12]In re Sayle's Estate, 37 Ohio Op. 167, 51 Ohio L. Abs. 33, 80 N.E.2d 221 (Prob. Ct. 1947), order aff'd, 51 Ohio L. Abs. 46, 80 N.E.2d 229 (Ct. App. 8th Dist. Cuyahoga County 1948).

[13]Franklin v. Franklin, 5 Ohio App. 3d 74, 449 N.E.2d 457 (7th Dist. Mahoning County 1981).

[14]Winnard v. Winnard, 62 Ohio App. 351, 16 Ohio Op. 51, 23 N.E.2d 977 (2d Dist. Franklin County 1939).

[15]Redrow v. Redrow, 94 Ohio App. 38, 51 Ohio Op. 266, 114 N.E.2d 293 (1st Dist. Clermont County 1952); Neal v. Neal, 53 Ohio L. Abs. 329, 85 N.E.2d 147 (C.P. 1949).

state;[16] voting registration;[17] vehicle and driver's license registration;[18] where taxes are paid; where mail is addressed;[19] location of real and personal property (furniture and automobiles); site of club and church memberships;[20] where family is housed;[21] relative living accommodations;[22] involuntary nature of relocation, such as armed forces assignments;[23] and failing to take to new domicile a family member with whom the party had been living.[24]

§ 27:27 Jurisdiction over marital status—Residency statutes—In general[1]

The Ohio residency statutes require that the plaintiff in actions for divorce and annulment and one spouse in an action for dissolution shall have been a resident of the state for at least six months immediately before filing the complaint.[2] Residence within the state, for purposes of these statutes, must be actual. In other words, the word "resident" means one who has his place of abode in the state.[3]

As discussed earlier, the use of the term residence in RC 3105.03 is also deemed to import the requirement of domiciliary residence.[4] The

---

[16]Neal v. Neal, 53 Ohio L. Abs. 329, 85 N.E.2d 147 (C.P. 1949); Smerda v. Smerda, 35 Ohio Op. 472, 48 Ohio L. Abs. 232, 74 N.E.2d 751 (C.P. 1947).

[17]Saalfeld v. Saalfeld, 86 Ohio App. 225, 41 Ohio Op. 94, 55 Ohio L. Abs. 156, 89 N.E.2d 165 (1st Dist. Clermont County 1949).

[18]Neal v. Neal, 53 Ohio L. Abs. 329, 85 N.E.2d 147 (C.P. 1949).

[19]Franklin v. Franklin, 5 Ohio App. 3d 74, 449 N.E.2d 457 (7th Dist. Mahoning County 1981); Smerda v. Smerda, 35 Ohio Op. 472, 48 Ohio L. Abs. 232, 74 N.E.2d 751 (C.P. 1947).

[20]Neal v. Neal, 53 Ohio L. Abs. 329, 85 N.E.2d 147 (C.P. 1949); Smerda v. Smerda, 35 Ohio Op. 472, 48 Ohio L. Abs. 232, 74 N.E.2d 751 (C.P. 1947). See also Wolfe v. Wolfe, 45 Ohio App. 309, 14 Ohio L. Abs. 577, 187 N.E. 86 (6th Dist. Lucas County 1933), error dismissed, 127 Ohio St. 160, 187 N.E. 201 (1933).

[21]Redrow v. Redrow, 94 Ohio App. 38, 51 Ohio Op. 266, 114 N.E.2d 293 (1st Dist. Clermont County 1952).

[22]Spires v. Spires, 7 Ohio Misc. 197, 35 Ohio Op. 2d 289, 214 N.E.2d 691 (C.P. 1966). See also Wolfe v. Wolfe, 45 Ohio App. 309, 14 Ohio L. Abs. 577, 187 N.E. 86 (6th Dist. Lucas County 1933), error dismissed, 127 Ohio St. 160, 187 N.E. 201 (1933).

[23]Saalfeld v. Saalfeld, 86 Ohio App. 225, 41 Ohio Op. 94, 55 Ohio L. Abs. 156, 89 N.E.2d 165 (1st Dist. Clermont County 1949); Glassman v. Glassman, 75 Ohio App. 47, 30 Ohio Op. 352, 42 Ohio L. Abs. 385, 60 N.E.2d 716 (1st Dist. Hamilton County 1944); Spires v. Spires, 7 Ohio Misc. 197, 35 Ohio Op. 2d 289, 214 N.E.2d 691 (C.P. 1966).

[24]Neal v. Neal, 53 Ohio L. Abs. 329, 85 N.E.2d 147 (C.P. 1949).

[Section 27:27]

[1]See § 27:19, Motion to dismiss—Lack of subject matter jurisdiction—Form.

[2]RC 3105.03 (divorce and annulment), RC 3105.62 (dissolution).

[3]Franklin v. Franklin, 5 Ohio App. 3d 74, 449 N.E.2d 457 (7th Dist. Mahoning County 1981); Jackman v. Jackman, 110 Ohio App. 199, 12 Ohio Op. 2d 464, 160 N.E.2d 387 (1st Dist. Hamilton County 1959).

[4]Saalfeld v. Saalfeld, 86 Ohio App. 225, 41 Ohio Op. 94, 55 Ohio L. Abs. 156, 89 N.E.2d 165 (1st Dist. Clermont County 1949); Glassman v. Glassman, 75 Ohio App. 47,

Ohio Supreme Court reiterated this principle in *Coleman v. Coleman*:[5] "The word 'resident,' as used in R.C. § 3105.03, means one who possesses a domiciliary residence, a residence accompanied by an *intention* to make the state of Ohio a permanent home." The Ohio statute further mandates that the domiciliary residence exist for at least six months and that this requirement be met at the time of the filing.[6]

§ 27:28 Jurisdiction over marital status—Residency statutes— Validity

Arguably, a state could authorize granting a divorce on the basis of a party's domicile for any length of time, even for a day. However, most states have superimposed upon the requirement of domicile the additional qualification that the domiciliary residence continue for a specified period of time.[1]

Durational residency statutes, such as Ohio's, have successfully withstood constitutional attack. In *Sosna v. Iowa*,[2] a state's one-year waiting period was challenged on several grounds, including equal protection and due process. It was argued that the durational residence statute deprived the plaintiff of access to the courts and denied her the opportunity to make an independent showing of bona fide domicile. Rejecting this argument, the United States Supreme Court asserted that more compelling considerations are the state's interest in insulating its divorce decrees from collateral attack and in insuring that a party be genuinely attached to the state, as determined by a reasonable waiting period.[3]

The validity of Ohio's former one-year residency statute had been upheld earlier by the Ohio Supreme Court.[4] The rationale supplied by the court was that durational residency requirements tend to insure both that a party is domiciled in the state and that state divorce laws are not exercised over non-residents, thus furthering the state's obligation not to interfere with marital relationships over which it has no jurisdiction.

---

30 Ohio Op. 352, 42 Ohio L. Abs. 385, 60 N.E.2d 716 (1st Dist. Hamilton County 1944); Spires v. Spires, 7 Ohio Misc. 197, 35 Ohio Op. 2d 289, 214 N.E.2d 691 (C.P. 1966).

[5]Coleman v. Coleman, 32 Ohio St. 2d 155, 61 Ohio Op. 2d 406, 291 N.E.2d 530, 57 A.L.R.3d 213 (1972) (emphasis in original). See also Glassman v. Glassman, 75 Ohio App. 47, 30 Ohio Op. 352, 42 Ohio L. Abs. 385, 60 N.E.2d 716 (1st Dist. Hamilton County 1944).

[6]Coleman v. Coleman, 32 Ohio St. 2d 155, 61 Ohio Op. 2d 406, 291 N.E.2d 530, 57 A.L.R.3d 213 (1972). See RC 3105.03.

[Section 27:28]

[1]Am. Jur. 2d, Divorce and Separation § 248.

[2]Sosna v. Iowa, 419 U.S. 393, 95 S. Ct. 553, 42 L. Ed. 2d 532, 19 Fed. R. Serv. 2d 925 (1975).

[3]Am. Jur. 2d, Divorce and Separation § 248 (cases upholding the constitutionality of durational residence statutes); 57 A.L.R. 3d 221.

[4]Coleman v. Coleman, 32 Ohio St. 2d 155, 61 Ohio Op. 2d 406, 291 N.E.2d 530, 57 A.L.R.3d 213 (1972).

§ 27:29 Jurisdiction over marital status—Residency statutes—Effect of noncompliance with statute

As noted, RC 3105.03 provides that the plaintiff must have been a resident for six months at the time the action is commenced. What result obtains if the plaintiff did not meet this requirement at the time of filing, but has been an Ohio resident for six months by the time of trial?

In *Coleman v. Coleman*,[1] a divorce complaint was brought by a former New York resident who had not lived in Ohio for the requisite period (then one year) when she filed the complaint. By the time of trial, she had been living in Ohio for a year. No answer or appearance was made by the defendant. The trial judge, sua sponte, dismissed the divorce action at trial on the basis that plaintiff had not met the residency requirements at the time of filing. The Ohio Supreme Court affirmed, observing that the durational residence requirement is substantive and constitutionally valid. It should be noted, however, that the opinion explicitly reflects, although without comment, that no request for leave to amend the complaint had been filed by the plaintiff when the trial judge dismissed the action.[2]

Some Ohio courts appear to have expressed the view that the durational residence requirements of RC 3105.03 are jurisdictional. In one well-known opinion, *Glassman v. Glassman*,[3] the court said that if the plaintiff has not been a resident in the state for the statutory waiting period, the court has no jurisdiction over the action, and any decree rendered is "absolutely void" in this state and elsewhere.[4] A different view based on cases from other jurisdictions is that where the issue arises on appeal, compliance with durational requirements obviously should be regarded as mandatory; however, on collateral attack, noncompliance would not render the decree void if the plaintiff was domiciled in the state when the action was commenced.[5] Under the second approach, domiciliary residence is a jurisdictional prerequisite, but, strictly speaking, the statutory waiting period is not.

The Ohio Supreme Court does not appear to have directly determined whether the durational requirement is jurisdictional. However, two decisions of the highest court may suggest that it is not. In *Coleman*, the court stated in dicta that the term "residence," as used in the statute,

---

[Section 27:29]

[1]Coleman v. Coleman, 32 Ohio St. 2d 155, 61 Ohio Op. 2d 406, 291 N.E.2d 530, 57 A.L.R.3d 213 (1972).

[2]See Gieg v. Gieg, 16 Ohio App. 3d 51, 474 N.E.2d 626 (11th Dist. Trumbull County 1984) (amendment of alimony only to divorce complaint after residence requirement met).

[3]Glassman v. Glassman, 75 Ohio App. 47, 50, 30 Ohio Op. 352, 42 Ohio L. Abs. 385, 60 N.E.2d 716 (1st Dist. Hamilton County 1944); see also McMaken v. McMaken, 96 Ohio App. 3d 402, 645 N.E.2d 113 (2d Dist. Montgomery County 1994).

[4]Accord Maze v. Maze, 1985 WL 8757 (Ohio Ct. App. 2d Dist. Montgomery County 1985). See also Redrow v. Redrow, 94 Ohio App. 38, 51 Ohio Op. 266, 114 N.E.2d 293 (1st Dist. Clermont County 1952) (pre-Ohio Civil Rule venue provisions under RC 3105.03 are jurisdictional).

[5]Am. Jur. 2d, Divorce and Separation § 249.

means "domiciliary residence," and referred to the durational residency requirement as being substantive. However, the word "jurisdictional" was conspicuously not employed.[6] Also, in an early case, the Supreme Court held that a writ of prohibition is unwarranted to restrain a trial court from proceeding in a divorce action upon the sole ground that the plaintiff had not been a resident of the state for the statutory period before filing the complaint. Noting that the question involved a factual dispute, the court observed that where the court below has jurisdiction over the matter, a writ does not lie to determine whether it has erred in exercising its powers.[7]

The Tenth District Court of Appeals held that the trial court properly found that where the appellant had been properly served with process and did not file an answer, his failure to file an answer constituted an admission of the facts to establish subject matter jurisdiction.[8] The court recognized that the parties cannot confer jurisdiction upon a court by mutual consent where none would otherwise exist. The court found the decree established the finding of residency, and the decree was not appealed. The issue of subject matter jurisdiction could not be collaterally attacked.

◆ **Practice Tips:** Before advising a client, who has been served with divorce papers filed by his or her spouse in another state, to ignore the action where the filing spouse has not actually satisfied the residency requirements of the other state before filing, check with counsel in that state to verify if subject matter jurisdiction is admitted if not timely denied.

See § 27:19, Motion to dismiss—Lack of subject matter jurisdiction—Form.

§ 27:30 Jurisdiction over marital status—Residency statutes— Application to cause of action and parties

Ohio's durational residency requirements apply to proceedings for divorce, annulment, and dissolution.[1] However, the statutes do not impose any residence restrictions upon a legal separation (formerly alimony only) action.[2] As a result, the complaining party may initiate an action for legal separation without complying with a waiting period,

---

[6]Coleman v. Coleman, 32 Ohio St. 2d 155, 61 Ohio Op. 2d 406, 291 N.E.2d 530, 57 A.L.R.3d 213 (1972).

[7]Kelley v. State, 94 Ohio St. 331, 114 N.E. 255 (1916).

[8]Weightman v. Weightman, 1999 WL 354405 (Ohio Ct. App. 10th Dist. Franklin County 1999).

[Section 27:30]
[1]RC 3105.03 (divorce and annulment), RC 3105.62 (requiring that one of the spouses in a dissolution proceeding has been a resident of the state for a period of six months immediately preceding the filing).

[2]RC 3105.17, RC 3105.18.

thereby being afforded immediate recourse for support.[3] In *Gieg v. Gieg*,[4] the Eleventh District Court of Appeals held that the plaintiff husband, who had been an Ohio resident for less than six months, could file an alimony only action for division of marital assets and a determination of support for the defendant wife. Provided the court has jurisdiction over the defendant, there would appear to be no statutory impediment to a non-resident spouse filing an original action for legal separation. However, the court held, in *Haylett v. Haylett*,[5] where neither party was a resident of the state of Ohio when the action was commenced, the court had no jurisdiction over an alimony only action, in spite of the fact that there was property within the state.

It should also be noted that Ohio's residency statute is a limitation on the plaintiff's right to bring suit. It does not pertain to the defendant. Consequently, defendant need not be a domiciliary resident to vest jurisdiction over the marital status.[6] However, if neither spouse is a bona fide domiciliary of the state, the fact that both parties submit to the jurisdiction of the court does not confer authority to grant a divorce.[7]

A spouse cannot predicate his domicile on the Ohio residence of the defendant for the purpose of bringing a divorce action in this state. For example, where the wife has never lived in Ohio, she cannot use her husband's domicile in this state as a basis to file an action for divorce. She must first be able to demonstrate an Ohio domicile in her own right.[8]

As a logical extension of the rule that the residency statute governs the complaining party's right to bring suit, the provisions of RC 3105.03 are considered pertinent only to initiation of actions. Accordingly, it has been held that a non-resident can file a counterclaim for divorce in an Ohio annulment action brought by a resident spouse.[9] Similarly, a plaintiff's voluntary dismissal of the divorce complaint has been determined not to deprive the court of jurisdiction to proceed on the counterclaim of a non-resident.[10]

---

[3]RC 3105.18; Shaw v. Shaw, 10 Ohio App. 216, 1917 WL 1462 (6th Dist. Wood County 1917). See Coleman v. Coleman, 32 Ohio St. 2d 155, 61 Ohio Op. 2d 406, 291 N.E.2d 530, 57 A.L.R.3d 213 (1972).

[4]Gieg v. Gieg, 16 Ohio App. 3d 51, 474 N.E.2d 626 (11th Dist. Trumbull County 1984).

[5]Haylett v. Haylett, 1989 WL 56367 (Ohio Ct. App. 11th Dist. Portage County 1989).

[6]RC 3105.03. See also Cox v. Cox, 19 Ohio St. 502, 1869 WL 84 (1869).

[7]Van Fossen v. State, 37 Ohio St. 317, 1881 WL 101 (1881).

[8]Malgras v. Malgras, 15 Ohio App. 335, 1921 WL 1143 (1st Dist. Clermont County 1921).

[9]Lampe v. Lampe, 74 Ohio L. Abs. 122, 136 N.E.2d 470 (C.P. 1954).

[10]Lincoln v. Lincoln, 33 Ohio Misc. 213, 62 Ohio Op. 2d 384, 294 N.E.2d 254 (C.P. 1973) (court determined it had jurisdiction to proceed on non-resident's counterclaim after the complaint was dismissed by the plaintiff, even though the plaintiff had not been an Ohio resident for the statutory period at the time the action was commenced). See Childers v. Childers, 112 Ohio App. 229, 12 Ohio Op. 2d 491, 165 N.E.2d 477 (1st Dist. Hamilton County 1959); Payer v. Payer, 74 Ohio L. Abs. 124, 133 N.E.2d 620 (Ct. App. 8th Dist. Cuyahoga County 1956).

§ 27:31   Jurisdiction over property—Lis pendens

Common pleas courts have state-wide jurisdiction and thus have jurisdiction over property located within the state. To obtain primary jurisdiction over real estate, to the exclusion of subsequent claimants or lien creditors, there must be a "sufficient" and "specific" description of the property concerning which relief is sought to invoke the protection by RC 2703.26.[1] That statute, providing for "lis pendens," states:

> When summons has been served or publication made, the action is pending so as to charge third persons with notice of its pendency. While pending, no interest can be acquired by third persons in the subject of the action, as against the plaintiff's title.

The purpose of the "lis pendens" doctrine is to protect a party's interest in property that is the subject of litigation. A third party acquiring an interest in the property while a lawsuit is pending takes the interest subject to the outcome of the suit, regardless of whether the third party was a party to the suit or had notice of the suit.[2]

In *Bowles v. Middletown Collateral Loan Co.*,[3] the plaintiff husband set forth the property description in his complaint. The wife did not repeat it in her counterclaim. Later, the jointly held property was transferred to her in the divorce. Applying the statute to invalidate a subsequent lien claimant's interest in the property, the appellate court held that

> in a domestic relations case where relief is sought under R.C. § 3105.18, the protection of the lis pendens statute will extend to property which, as here, has been sufficiently described and expressly submitted for action by the court at some point in the body of pleadings considered as a whole.

In the event the real or tangible personal property is located in a county other than where the action is commenced, Civil Rule 3(F) requires a certified copy of the complaint to be filed with the clerk of the common pleas court in such counties, or third persons will not be charged with notice.

The trial court has jurisdiction over real and personal property of a defendant which property is situated in the state, where the property is legally seized at the commencement of the case, by virtue of actual seizure (possession) of tangible property, lis pendens for real property, and restraining orders. Such jurisdiction is sometimes referred to as "quasi in rem." Even though a defendant may receive only constructive notice by publication, the court may reach the defendant's property for purposes of property division or spousal support.

In a case that pre-dated the Ohio Rules of Civil Procedure (which now

---

[Section 27:31]

[1]Cook v. Mozer, 108 Ohio St. 30, 1 Ohio L. Abs. 436, 1 Ohio L. Abs. 845, 140 N.E. 590 (1923).

[2]Third Federal Sav. and Loan Association of Cleveland v. Hayward, 1998 WL 488642 (Ohio Ct. App. 9th Dist. Summit County 1998).

[3]Bowles v. Middletown Collateral Loan Co., 71 Ohio Op. 2d 110, 328 N.E.2d 821, 822 (Ct. App. 1st Dist. Butler County 1974).

allow long arm "in personam" jurisdiction over non-resident defendants upon proper service, if the requirements of Civ. R. 4.3(A)(1) to (10) are met), and which predated the separation of the alimony statute into spousal support and property division sections, the Lorain County Common Pleas Court analyzed the jurisdiction of the court over property located in the state.[4] Even though the affidavit for service by publication failed to set forth a property description, the trial court found that the real property was brought within the jurisdiction of the court by virtue of the plaintiff's allegation in the petition of the ownership by the parties of the home and its street address.

Clearly it is better practice and less subject to challenge to set forth a complete property description, not only in the complaint, but also in the affidavit for service by publication.[5]

A decree incorporating a separation agreement that orders one spouse's interest in real property to be conveyed to the other spouse operates to create an equitable lien in the recipient spouse. The appellate court in *Padgett v. Home Federal Bank*[6] affirmed the trial court's order giving priority to the equitable lienholder spouse ahead of later judgment creditors of the non-complying spouse who failed to transfer by deed.

◆ **Practice Tips:** The litigation in *Padgett* could have been avoided by having the transferring spouse execute the quitclaim deed or limited warranty deed at the same time as signing the separation agreement. Or, at the very least, the separation agreement could have provided that it, or the decree, could be used as a conveyance. Counsel representing a spouse who is to receive an interest in real property at present should not close the file until the property transfer has been duly recorded.

§ 27:32 Jurisdiction over children

Chapter 3109 defines the age of majority and governs parental rights and responsibilities. RC 3109.04 requires the court, in any divorce, legal separation or annulment procedure, or any proceeding where the allocation of parental rights are in issue, to follow specific procedures and consider specific factors. In general, the court hearing domestic relations maters will be the court deciding parental rights pursuant to the Uniform Child Custody Jurisdiction Act.[1]

Where, however, the juvenile court has taken jurisdiction pursuant to RC 2151.23(A), the juvenile court has exclusive jurisdiction. The juvenile court has original jurisdiction under RC 2151.23(B) for parentage, interstate matters and child support and can, in some circumstances,

---

[4]Shonk v. Shonk, 16 Ohio Misc. 123, 45 Ohio Op. 2d 86, 241 N.E.2d 178 (C.P. 1968).

[5]See § 25:76, Service of process—Service by publication—Real property affidavit—Form.

[6]Padgett v. Home Federal Bank, 1998 WL 204943 (Ohio Ct. App. 12th Dist. Butler County 1998).

[Section 27:32]
[1]See Ch 17.

hear child related matters certified to it.[2]

Where a domestic relations division has issued a decree terminating the marriage, and issues a decree which involves the custody, care, and control of the minor children, a probate court cannot, as between the parties, legally interfere with that custody by letters of guardianship.[3]

§ 27:33   Personal jurisdiction—In general

Although a court may have in rem jurisdiction to terminate a marriage, the court must have in personam jurisdiction over the person of the defendant before it can impose a personal obligation or duty or terminate the defendant's rights.[1]

A claim of lack of personal jurisdiction can be waived if a party fails to assert the defense in responsive motions.[2] In *Olezewski v. Niam*,[3] the defendant asserted in a Civil Rule 60(B) motion that he had never been properly or effectively served. The appellate court affirmed the trial court's finding that service upon the non-resident defendant by ordinary mail, pursuant to Civil Rule 4.6(D), following the return of certified mail service marked "unclaimed" was sufficient service. The appellate court noted that the record did not reflect that the trial court had personal jurisdiction over the defendant, nor "in rem" jurisdiction sufficient to grant a monetary judgment, but that these defenses had not been raised.

A legal fiction exists that regards the marital status as a res present at the permanent home of either of the spouses. Ex parte divorces are an exception to the rule that the court must have personal jurisdiction over a party before it may adjudicate substantive rights.

Since the constitutional rule is that a court cannot adjudicate a personal claim or obligation unless it has jurisdiction over the person of the defendant, the court is without power to cut off a non-resident, non-participating spouse's right to support; nor can it order a non-resident spouse to pay alimony.[4] An ex parte divorce results in a divisible divorce. The ex parte decree cannot impose orders of support or alimony where the court lacks personal jurisdiction over the defendant.[5] *Estin v. Estin*

---

[2]RC 2151.23(C).

[3]Hoffman v. Hoffman, 15 Ohio St. 427, 1864 WL 51 (1864); Herron v. Herron, 2001-Ohio-2304, 2001 WL 1338828 (Ohio Ct. App. 3d Dist. Allen County 2001).

[Section 27:33]

[1]Pennoyer v. Neff, 95 U.S. 714, 24 L. Ed. 565 (1877) (overruled in part by, Shaffer v. Heitner, 433 U.S. 186, 97 S. Ct. 2569, 53 L. Ed. 2d 683 (1977)). See also Meadows v. Meadows, 73 Ohio App. 3d 316, 596 N.E.2d 1146 (3d Dist. Hancock County 1992) (the trial court erred as matter of law in holding notice by publication sufficient to make award of child support since personal service must be obtained to award money judgment). Greene v. Greene, 1997 WL 82814 (Ohio Ct. App. 2d Dist. Montgomery County 1997).

[2]Kries v. Kries, 1992 WL 126095 (Ohio Ct. App. 6th Dist. Lucas County 1992).

[3]Olezewski v. Niam, 1993 WL 372234 (Ohio Ct. App. 2d Dist. Montgomery County 1993).

[4]Estin v. Estin, 334 U.S. 541, 68 S. Ct. 1213, 92 L. Ed. 1561, 1 A.L.R.2d 1412 (1948).

[5]Rice v. Rice, 336 U.S. 674, 69 S. Ct. 751, 93 L. Ed. 957 (1949).

made the divorce divisible to give effect to the Nevada decree insofar as it affected marital status, and made it ineffective on the issue of alimony. Therefore, a valid unilateral ex parte divorce with proper jurisdictional requirements of residency, while not being in personam against the defendant spouse to fix or terminate rights of support, can terminate both the legal status and the right to claim as a surviving spouse.

§ 27:34 Personal jurisdiction—Long-arm jurisdiction

States have enacted long-arm statutes or rules to establish personal jurisdiction over non-resident defendants. Such rules generally place perimeters around such extension of jurisdiction, with limitations greater than merely that the parties may "at any time have lived together within the state."[1]

Ohio provides for long-arm jurisdiction in Civil Rule 4.3, which determines upon whom process may be made out of state. Civil Rule 4.3(A) states:

> Service of process may be made outside of this state, . . . in any action in this state, upon a person who, at the time of service of process is, a non-resident of this state or is a resident of this state who is absent from this state. "Person," includes an individual, . . . who, . . . has caused an event to occur out of which the claim which is the subject of the complaint arose, from the person's:
>
> . . .
>
> (8) Living in the marital relationship within this state notwithstanding subsequent departure from this state, as to all obligations arising for spousal support, custody, child support, or property settlement, if the other party to the marital relationship continues to reside in this state.

In *Brown v. Pugh*,[2] the defendant-husband, seven years after the divorce, entered a written special appearance in response to a motion to show cause. The plaintiff-wife had obtained a divorce in November 1980. The decree made the following findings and orders: (1) the plaintiff had proper residency in Ohio and in Hancock County; (2) the date and place of the marriage were established; (3) there were two children as issue; (4) custody was granted to the wife; and (5) the defendant was ordered to pay child support of $35 per week through the bureau of support, plus the children's medical bills.

Service by certified mail had been made on the defendant in North Carolina. In 1987, plaintiff filed for contempt for failure to pay support and requested a lump-sum judgment for arrearages in excess of $22,000. Service of the motion and the court's order to appear were made on the defendant by certified mail addressed to him in North Carolina. Accompanying defendant's motion to dismiss was his affidavit which stated that the parties were married in New Jersey, that defendant had never resided in Ohio, that the parties last lived together in Fayetteville,

---

[Section 27:34]

[1]See Interstate and Foreign Support Practice Ch 23, for discussion of UIFSA's definition of long-arm jurisdiction for child support establishment and collection.

[2]Brown v. Pugh, 1989 WL 77017 (Ohio Ct. App. 3d Dist. Hancock County 1989).

North Carolina, and that he had not responded to the original action on advice of counsel. The decree stated that the defendant "has been duly served with a copy of the Complaint as required by law and entered his appearance in this action and said service is hereby approved."[3]

However, the Third District Court of Appeals noted that the transcript of the docket and journal entries and original papers did not otherwise reflect any entry of appearance by the defendant or any participation by the defendant in the divorce proceeding. The trial court had concluded that since the defendant knew of the divorce complaint, and because his income tax refund had been attached for support, that such was sufficient contact. The court of appeals held that notwithstanding the fact that the trial court had found that defendant entered his appearance, that jurisdiction over the defendant's person must affirmatively appear in the record of the action for the court to be able to proceed to order child support. The court found that the child support order was void ab initio for lack of jurisdiction, and thus it could not support a lump-sum judgment thereafter rendered. Service by publication does not create in personam jurisdiction; a trial court may not make child support or spousal support orders against a defendant served only by publication.

In determining whether there could be any validity to the lump-sum judgment, the appellate court applied three United States Supreme Court cases: *Pennoyer v. Neff*,[4] *International Shoe Co. v. Washington*,[5] and *Kulko v. Superior Court of Cal.*.[6] In *Pugh*, the court stated that the first two of those cases

> establish and confirm the long standing rule under the due process clause of the Fourteenth Amendment that a valid judgment imposing a personal obligation or duty in favor of the plaintiff may be entered only by a court having jurisdiction over the person of the defendant. Citing *International Shoe*, the Supreme Court held in *Kulko* that a "defendant to be bound by a judgment against him must 'have certain minimum contacts with [the forum state] such that the maintenance of the suit does not offend "traditional notions of fair play and substantial justice."[7]

In *Kulko*, the Court stated:

> The unilateral activity of those who claim some relationship with a non-residential defendant cannot satisfy the requirement of contact with the forum State. . . . [I]t is essential in each case that there be some act by

---

[3]Brown v. Pugh, 1989 WL 77017, at *3 (Ohio Ct. App. 3d Dist. Hancock County 1989).

[4]Pennoyer v. Neff, 95 U.S. 714, 24 L. Ed. 565 (1877) (overruled in part by, Shaffer v. Heitner, 433 U.S. 186, 97 S. Ct. 2569, 53 L. Ed. 2d 683 (1977)).

[5]International Shoe Co. v. State of Wash., Office of Unemployment Compensation and Placement, 326 U.S. 310, 66 S. Ct. 154, 90 L. Ed. 95, 161 A.L.R. 1057 (1945).

[6]Kulko v. Superior Court of California In and For City and County of San Francisco, 436 U.S. 84, 98 S. Ct. 1690, 56 L. Ed. 2d 132 (1978).

[7]Brown v. Pugh, 1989 WL 77017, at *4 (Ohio Ct. App. 3d Dist. Hancock County 1989) (citing Hanson v. Denckla, 357 U.S. 235, 253, 78 S. Ct. 1228, 2 L. Ed. 2d 1283 (1958).

which the defendant purposely avails [him]self of the privilege of conducting activities within the forum State . . ..[8]

The *Pugh* court found that *Kulko* did not differ greatly in its essential facts. In *Kulko*, the United States Supreme Court stated that the California court had not relied on the appellant's fleeting presence in the state some thirteen years earlier during his military stopovers, or on the fact that the parties were actually married in California on one of the husband's two visits.

The act that the California court believed warranted exercise of personal jurisdiction was appellant's active and full consent to sending his daughter to California to live with the mother for the school year. The Supreme Court objected to the proposition that the husband's acquiescence in his daughter's desire to live with her mother conferred jurisdiction over him to the California courts. The husband had remained in New York, the state of the marital domicile, while the wife had moved across the continent. California had argued that it had a substantial interest in protecting the welfare of its minor residents and promoting a healthy and supportive family environment. The mere fact that the marriage occurred in the forum state, or that property or family is located in the forum state is insufficient to give the state in personam jurisdiction over a non-resident.

A non-resident defendant who is properly served with a divorce complaint and fails to raise the defense of lack of jurisdiction over the person by motion or responsive pleading as required by Civ. R. 12(H)(1) waives the defense.[9]

◆ **Practice Tips:** Before advising a client who has been sued for divorce in another state to disregard the action, check with counsel in that state if failure to raise the defense of lack of personal jurisdiction is waived if it is not timely and appropriately made.

Different minimum contacts must exist with the state in order to justify personal jurisdiction. The fact that a party's wife and children received welfare in Ohio cannot alone justify personal jurisdiction over one who had no other contact with the state of Ohio.[10]

Long-arm jurisdiction is also provided under Civ.R. 4.3(A)(9), based on causing tortious injury within the state. Where a child is not conceived within the state, acquiring personal jurisdiction over a non-resident to establish parentage cannot be based upon the failure to support the child. The Ohio Supreme Court reasoned that support was ancillary to the issue of parentage and failure to support could not support personal

---

[8]Kulko v. Superior Court of California In and For City and County of San Francisco, 436 U.S. 84, 92, 98 S. Ct. 1690, 56 L. Ed. 2d 132 (1978), quoting Hanson v. Denckla, 357 U.S. 235, 78 S. Ct. 1228, 2 L. Ed. 2d 1283 (1958).

[9]Crozier v. Hafer, 1999 WL 194205 (Ohio Ct. App. 9th Dist. Wayne County 1999).

[10]Brown v. Pugh, 1989 WL 77017 (Ohio Ct. App. 3d Dist. Hancock County 1989).

jurisdiction.[11]

Trial courts frequently stretch reason to find "in personam" jurisdiction over a non-resident defendant. In *Depaulitte v. Depaulitte*[12] the parties had traveled to Dayton from their home in Wyoming and spent a week looking for a house. The husband, who was in the service, then left to go to Japan and was not in Ohio again. The wife moved to Dayton and two years later filed for divorce in Montgomery County. The court granted the divorce and entered orders regarding spousal support, child support, and property division. A later 60(B) motion based on lack of personal jurisdiction was overruled. The appellate court reversed all but the divorce itself. Likewise, in *Kvinta v. Kvinta*[13] the trial court found "in personam" jurisdiction based on the defendant's owning real property in Ohio. The appellate court found that the trial court erred in finding personal jurisdiction pursuant to Civ. R. 4.3(A)(6) "Having an interest in, using, or possessing real property in this state." There was no nexus between the legal separation action and the real property to give personal jurisdiction.

§ 27:35   Motion to dismiss for lack of personal jurisdiction—Form⊚

[Title of Court]

[Caption]   Case No. [_____]

MOTION TO DISMISS, LACK OF PERSONAL JURISDICTION

Now comes *[attorney for Defendant]* and without submitting to the jurisdiction of this Court, and for the sole and limited purpose of denying the jurisdiction of this Court over the person of the Defendant, hereby moves this Court pursuant to Civil Rule 12(B)(2) to find and order that it has no "in personam" jurisdiction against *[Defendant]*.

This motion is supported by the *[memorandum/affidavit]* below.

_____

Attorney for Defendant

[Memorandum/affidavit in support of motion]
[Notice of hearing]
[Proof/certificate of service]

_____

[11]State ex rel. Stone v. Court of Common Pleas of Cuyahoga County, Juvenile Div., 14 Ohio St. 3d 32, 470 N.E.2d 899 (1984); State ex rel. Wayne Cty. Child Support Enforcement Agency v. Tanner, 146 Ohio App. 3d 765, 2001-Ohio-1722, 768 N.E.2d 679 (9th Dist. Wayne County 2001).

[12]Depaulitte v. Depaulitte, 138 Ohio App. 3d 780, 742 N.E.2d 659 (2d Dist. Montgomery County 2000), appeal allowed, 89 Ohio St. 3d 1429, 729 N.E.2d 1199 (2000) and appeal dismissed as improvidently allowed, 2001 -Ohio- 229, 91 Ohio St. 3d 1201, 740 N.E.2d 1103 (2001).

[13]Kvinta v. Kvinta, 2000 WL 197461 (Ohio Ct. App. 10th Dist. Franklin County 2000), dismissed, appeal not allowed, 89 Ohio St. 3d 1427, 729 N.E.2d 1197 (2000).

§27:36 Personal jurisdiction—Transient presence

The cases on long-arm jurisdiction deal with situations where the defendant receives service outside of the state. Civil Rule 4.1 describes the method of service within Ohio. Service within the state can confer in personam jurisdiction over the defendant even if defendant's presence does not meet the requirement of minimum contacts. The concept of transient presence may be enough to confer personal jurisdiction, even though a party is served while in Ohio solely for visitation.

Lonigro v. Lonigro[1] concerned a defendant who had never lived in Ohio, but had visited the plaintiff and minor child in Ohio. The parties had last lived together in Indiana, and all of the defendant's assets were located in Indiana. The defendant was personally served by a special process server at or near the plaintiff's residence. The trial court had granted the defendant's motion to dismiss, without a hearing, based on the affidavits filed by the parties upon a finding of lack of personal jurisdiction. The court of appeals concluded that "transient presence," without more, is insufficient to support the court's exercise of personal jurisdiction, but reversed for purposes of requiring the trial court to conduct an evidentiary hearing to determine whether the defendant's contacts with the state were such that maintenance of the suit basically would "'offend traditional notions of fair play and substantial justice.'"[2]

In reaching its decision in *Lonigro*, the Second District Court of Appeals analyzed the above-mentioned United States Supreme Court cases, and held that "all questions of personal jurisdiction must be resolved by minimum contacts analysis."[3] It also concluded that transient presence was "no longer a viable basis for the assertion of personal jurisdiction."[4] Transient presence jurisdiction is based solely on the fact that service is made upon a person while physically present in the forum state. The *Lonigro* court did not have the advantage, or disadvantage, of the subsequent pronouncement of the United States Supreme Court on this issue.

In *Burnham v. California*,[5] the Court considered whether service founded upon transient presence was consistent with due process. In *Burnham*, Mr. Burnham and his wife last lived together in New Jersey. By agreement, the wife and children moved to California, while Mr. Burnham remained in New Jersey. Burnham was served with divorce papers while he was in California visiting his children. His efforts to

---

[Section 27:36]

[1]Lonigro v. Lonigro, 1988 WL 79315 (Ohio Ct. App. 2d Dist. Montgomery County 1988).

[2]Lonigro v. Lonigro, 1988 WL 79315, at *7 (Ohio Ct. App. 2d Dist. Montgomery County 1988).

[3]Lonigro v. Lonigro, 1988 WL 79315, at *3 (Ohio Ct. App. 2d Dist. Montgomery County 1988).

[4]Lonigro v. Lonigro, 1988 WL 79315, at *5 (Ohio Ct. App. 2d Dist. Montgomery County 1988).

[5]Burnham v. Superior Court of California, County of Marin, 495 U.S. 604, 110 S. Ct. 2105, 109 L. Ed. 2d 631 (1990).

quash service were rejected at all levels through the state courts and he appealed to the Supreme Court, which granted certiorari. The state courts had held that the defendant's presence in the state and the personal service of process upon him while he was in the state constituted a valid jurisdictional predicate for in personam jurisdiction.

Distinguishing the cases where a court had to measure concepts of fair play and substantial justice to determine whether a non-resident served by long-arm process was subject to the court's jurisdiction, the Court opined that a defendant who is voluntarily present in a state has "reasonable expectation" that he may be subject to being sued. One need not look at minimum contacts when asserting in personam jurisdiction based upon physical presence.[6]

The Court in *Burnham* rejected the contention that defendant's presence alone is insufficient to establish jurisdiction stating:

> Among the most firmly established principles of personal jurisdiction in American tradition is that the courts of a State have jurisdiction over non-residents who are physically present in the State. The view developed early that each State had the power to hale before its courts any individual who could be found within its borders, and that once having acquired jurisdiction over such a person by properly serving him with process, the State could retain jurisdiction to enter judgment against him, no matter how fleeting his visit.[7]

The husband in *Van Kan v. Mattheus*[8] traveled from South Africa to Chardon, Ohio, to see his daughter. He claimed the trial court lacked personal jurisdiction over him because he was induced to come by false representations or wrongful device and that service was invalid. The trial and appellate courts concluded he had not been improperly served and that the wife's attorney had merely taken advantage of his presence to serve him, rather than fraudulently inducing.

Each state can legislate methods of service, and so long as they do not offend traditional notions of fair play, they will be upheld. This decision does not mean that every court must or will declare in-state service alone a sufficient basis for jurisdiction. A state may require more than defendant's voluntary presence in the state, i.e., evidence that he was not brought into the state by force, fraud, or as a party or witness in an unrelated proceeding.

§ 27:37   Personal jurisdiction—Service by publication

Where the defendant's residence is unknown, constructive service by publication is necessary to commence the case. Civil Rule 3(A) states that a civil action is commenced by filing a complaint with the court, if service is obtained within one year from such filing upon the named

---

[6]Burnham v. Superior Court of California, County of Marin, 495 U.S. 604, 110 S. Ct. 2105, 109 L. Ed. 2d 631 (1990).

[7]Burnham v. Superior Court of California, County of Marin, 495 U.S. 604, 610, 110 S. Ct. 2105, 109 L. Ed. 2d 631 (1990).

[8]Van Kan v. Mattheus, 1999 WL 476139 (Ohio Ct. App. 11th Dist. Geauga County 1999), dismissed, appeal not allowed, 87 Ohio St. 3d 1440, 719 N.E.2d 4 (1999).

defendant. Service by publication, however, will not effect in personam jurisdiction over the defendant. It may affect property within the state if the court has jurisdiction over such property when the action is commenced. A court obtains "in rem" jurisdiction over real property located within the state, where the property is properly described in the pleadings and also in the affidavit for service by publication.[1]

In *Salyer v. Salyer*,[2] the appellate court found, although the issue was not raised by either party, that the trial court did not have jurisdiction to make an alimony award, since by virtue of publication service, jurisdiction over the person of the defendant was never obtained. The trial court was found, however, to have jurisdiction to grant the divorce.[3]

Conversely, in *Lindeman v. Lindeman*,[4] the granting by the trial court of a motion to vacate the entire divorce decree based on the failure of the plaintiff-husband to exercise due diligence, or any kind of diligence, in obtaining an address for the defendant-wife was upheld.[5]

§ 27:38 Personal jurisdiction—Continuing jurisdiction

To invoke the continuing jurisdiction of the court, Civ. R. 75(J) requires notice to be served in the manner provided for service of process under Civ. R. 4 to Civ. R. 4.6. Civ. R. 4.1(1) requires that certified mail service be made by the clerk of court with a return receipt requested and requires the clerk to enter the mailing and return receipt on the docket. Since the rule does not provide for the service by certified mail to be mailed by an attorney for the parties, such service by the attorney is defective.[1]

Service after a decree must be made upon the party, not the party's attorney, even though other motions are pending, where the subject matter of the post-decree motion is different from the pending motion.[2]

Normally, post-decree proceedings invoking the continuing jurisdiction of the court will be brought in the forum which rendered the underlying order. It has been held that under the venue provisions of Rule 3(B), the common pleas court which granted the original decree

---

[Section 27:37]

[1]See § 27:31, Jurisdiction over property—Lis pendens.

[2]Salyer v. Salyer, 1990 WL 16510 (Ohio Ct. App. 3d Dist. Marion County 1990).

[3]Salyer v. Salyer, 1990 WL 16510 (Ohio Ct. App. 3d Dist. Marion County 1990) (citing Rousculp v. Rousculp, 17 Ohio App. 2d 101, 46 Ohio Op. 2d 125, 244 N.E.2d 512 (10th Dist. Franklin County 1968)).

[4]Lindeman v. Lindeman, 1990 WL 6270 (Ohio Ct. App. 5th Dist. Stark County 1990).

[5]Salyer v. Salyer, 1990 WL 16510 (Ohio Ct. App. 3d Dist. Marion County 1990) (citing Sizemore v. Smith, 6 Ohio St. 3d 330, 453 N.E.2d 632 (1983)).

[Section 27:38]

[1]Price v. Price, 1985 WL 7633 (Ohio Ct. App. 2d Dist. Miami County 1985).

[2]Yonally v. Yonally, 45 Ohio App. 2d 122, 74 Ohio Op. 2d 134, 341 N.E.2d 602 (9th Dist. Summit County 1974); Hansen v. Hansen, 21 Ohio App. 3d 216, 486 N.E.2d 1252 (3d Dist. Seneca County 1985); Walsh v. Walsh, 1988 WL 62966 (Ohio Ct. App. 6th Dist. Wood County 1988) (child support order entered after service on appellee's attorney, although other motions pending, was void ab initio and unenforceable).

may transfer its continuing custody jurisdiction to a juvenile court in another county where a parent or child resides.[3] However, the decision whether to transfer or retain jurisdiction over post-decree matters is within the sound discretion of the original divorce-granting court.[4]

Special venue problems arise in enforcing a divorce judgment when both plaintiff and defendant live outside of Ohio. For example, assume that H has left Ohio and that, after obtaining an Ohio divorce against H, W also moves out of state. W wishes to bring an Ohio action to enforce the divorce against H.

Where both parties have left Ohio, the Ohio court which granted the divorce decree retains jurisdiction over the controversy and is a proper forum to enforce the decree.[5] With regard to venue, it is logical that an enforcement action is properly venued in the county where the decree was granted as (if nothing else) the county where the claim for relief arose.[6]

Suppose that W left Ohio without obtaining a divorce from H. Later, W secures a divorce against H in another state and obtains an in personam judgment against him for spousal support and property division. H has property in Ohio County M which W wants to attach to satisfy her claims. W has a choice of venue.

Where the parties are no longer residents of the state and there is no other available forum in Ohio, plaintiff could use the provisions of Civ. R. 3(B)(12). Under this subsection, an action would be properly venued in a county where the defendant's property is located or there are debts owing to him. Where both parties reside out of state and plaintiff W is attempting to reach defendant's Ohio property to satisfy an out-of-state judgment, plaintiff may bring the action in County M, where the property is located. To invoke the venue provisions of Civ. R. 3(B)(12), it is not necessary that the cause of action arose in Ohio.[7]

In *Gottberg v. Gottberg*,[8] the former wife had alleged child abuse and because she did not want her former husband to have her address, the court permitted all notifications to be sent to the wife's counsel. Months following the decree a motion was served upon the wife's counsel to name the paternal grandparents as parties and for an increase in visitation. The appellate court vacated the order that ensued, holding that service through the wife's counsel's office did not obviate the rule that *service* must be made upon the party, absent a waiver in writing or

---

[3]Pylant v. Pylant, 61 Ohio App. 2d 247, 15 Ohio Op. 3d 407, 401 N.E.2d 940 (6th Dist. Huron County 1978).

[4]Bieniek v. Bieniek, 27 Ohio App. 3d 28, 499 N.E.2d 356 (9th Dist. Medina County 1985).

[5]Weinberger v. Weinberger, 43 Ohio App. 2d 129, 72 Ohio Op. 2d 325, 334 N.E.2d 514 (9th Dist. Summit County 1974).

[6]See Civ. R. 3(B)(6).

[7]Penrod v. Baltimore & O. R. Co., 64 Ohio App. 2d 216, 18 Ohio Op. 3d 164, 412 N.E.2d 949 (10th Dist. Franklin County 1979).

[8]Gottberg v. Gottberg, 1994 WL 313770 (Ohio Ct. App. 5th Dist. Tuscarawas County 1994).

an appearance in court, even though notification through counsel had been permitted during the pendency of the divorce.

Research References

Text References
1 Klein and Darling, Baldwin's Ohio Practice, Civil Practice Rule 3

§ 27:39   Venue versus jurisdiction

It is important that venue be distinguished from jurisdiction. Venue connotes the locality or geographic division where the lawsuit should be heard.[1] Jurisdiction has reference to the power to adjudicate.[2]

Venue does not affect the power of a court to render a valid judgment.[3] If a case is not properly venued, and the court nevertheless proceeds to hear the matter, the judgment is not void or subject to collateral attack.[4] In other words, the jurisdiction of a court is not affected by venue. The following language of Civil Rule 3(G) emphasizes this distinction: "The provisions of this rule relate to venue and are not jurisdictional. No order, judgment, or decree shall be void or subject to collateral attack solely on the ground that there was improper venue."

Venue is a procedural matter.[5] Improper venue is waived unless asserted by timely objection during an initial phase of the action.[6] In contrast, subject matter jurisdiction defines the competency of a court to hear the suit. Consequently, lack of subject matter jurisdiction may be asserted at any stage in the proceedings.[7]

§ 27:40   Motion to change venue—Form⊙

[Title of Court]

[Caption]   Case No. [_____]

MOTION TO CHANGE VENUE

Now comes _____, Defendant by and through counsel, and moves this court for an order transferring the above captioned action to _____ County as a more convenient and proper forum.

Grounds for said motion are set forth below.

[Section 27:39]

[1]Morrison v. Steiner, 32 Ohio St. 2d 86, 61 Ohio Op. 2d 335, 290 N.E.2d 841 (1972).

[2]Fireproof Const., Inc. v. Brenner-Bell, Inc., 152 Ohio St. 347, 40 Ohio Op. 375, 89 N.E.2d 472 (1949).

[3]Staff notes Civ. R. 3(G).

[4]Civ. R. 3(G).

[5]Morrison v. Steiner, 32 Ohio St. 2d 86, 61 Ohio Op. 2d 335, 290 N.E.2d 841 (1972).

[6]Civ. R. 12.

[7]Fox v. Eaton Corp., 48 Ohio St. 2d 236, 2 Ohio Op. 3d 408, 358 N.E.2d 536 (1976) (overruled by, Manning v. Ohio State Library Bd., 62 Ohio St. 3d 24, 577 N.E.2d 650 (1991)). See also Civ. R. 12(H); § 27:51, Improper venue and remedies.

Respectfully Submitted,

_____

Attorney for Defendant
Sup. Ct. Reg. No.

MEMORANDUM

Pursuant to Civil Rule 3(B) _____ venue is appropriate in _____ county, and is not proper in _____ county because _____. For these reasons, and others, which may be elicited at a hearing of this matter, the Defendant respectfully requests that this court transfer the within action to the _____ County Court of Common Pleas, Division of Domestic Relations.

Respectfully Submitted,

_____

Attorney for Defendant
Sup. Ct. Reg. No.

NOTICE OF HEARING
CERTIFICATE OF SERVICE

§ 27:41　Judgment entry granting venue transfer—Form◉

[Title of Court]

[Caption]　　　　　　　　　　　　　　　Case No. *[_____]*

JUDGMENT ENTRY

This matter came before the court on (date), upon Defendant's Motion to Transfer Venue. The court finds defendant's motion to be well taken, and, grants said motion to transfer the case to _____ County.

Therefore, the above captioned case shall be transferred forthwith to the clerk of _____ County Common Pleas Court, Division of Domestic Relations, _____, for docketing and further assignment to that court.

IT IS SO ORDERED.

_____

Judge

Approved:

_____

Attorney for

§ 27:42 Choice of venue—In general

Prior to the enactment of the Ohio Rules of Civil Procedure, venue in domestic relations matters was governed by RC 3105.03. The only two forums available in divorce actions were the county of plaintiff's residence and the county where the cause of action arose. If statutory requirements for proper venue were not carefully met, the decree was considered a nullity and subject to collateral attack. When venue was challenged successfully, dismissal was deemed necessary.

As in any civil action, venue in domestic relations actions is now governed by Civil Rule 3.[1] Rule 3(B) expressly provides that "proper venue lies in any one or more" of the counties listed.[2]

Counties deemed conclusively proper forums for a lawsuit are enumerated in Civil Rule 3(B)(1) to (11).[3] In a given case, the plaintiff must first determine whether venue lies in any of the counties specified in the first nine subsections of Civil Rule 3(B). For purposes of venue under Civil Rule 3(B)(2), principal place of employment does not equal principal place of business; merely being employed in a county does not give that county venue in a divorce action.[4] If there is an available forum in only one county, plaintiff must bring the action in that county.[5]

However, where more than one county listed in Rule 3(B)(1) to (9) is a proper forum, plaintiff may choose the county in which he or she prefers to file the action. As explained by the court in *Varketta v. General Motors Corp.*:[6]

> The first nine provisions of 3(B) are alternatives, and each may be a proper basis for venue, but they do not have to be followed in any order. Plaintiff has a choice where the action will be brought if any of the counties specified in C.R. 3(B)(1) through (9) are a proper forum under the facts of the case.

Accordingly, none of the forums in Rule 3(B)(1) to (9) is considered to have priority over any other.[7] As emphasized by the Ohio Supreme Court in *Morrison v. Steiner*,[8] "The first nine provisions of Civ. R. 3(B) are on an equal status, and any court specified therein *may* be a proper and initial place of venue." Under the venue provisions of Rules 3(B)(1) to (9), plaintiff is thus entitled to choose where the action will be brought,

---

[Section 27:42]

[1]RC 3105.62; Civ. R. 75(A); Fuller v. Fuller, 32 Ohio App. 2d 303, 61 Ohio Op. 2d 400, 290 N.E.2d 852 (10th Dist. Franklin County 1972).

[2]Fuller v. Fuller, 32 Ohio App. 2d 303, 305, 61 Ohio Op. 2d 400, 290 N.E.2d 852 (10th Dist. Franklin County 1972). See staff notes Civ. R. 3(B).

[3]Staff notes Civ. R. 3(B).

[4]Owens v. Owens, 1993 WL 307477 (Ohio Ct. App. 3d Dist. Union County 1993).

[5]General Motors Acceptance Corp. v. Jacks, 27 Ohio Misc. 115, 56 Ohio Op. 2d 93, 56 Ohio Op. 2d 343, 268 N.E.2d 833 (Mun. Ct. 1971).

[6]Varketta v. General Motors Corp., 34 Ohio App. 2d 1, 6, 63 Ohio Op. 2d 8, 295 N.E.2d 219 (8th Dist. Cuyahoga County 1973).

[7]Morrison v. Steiner, 32 Ohio St. 2d 86, 61 Ohio Op. 2d 335, 290 N.E.2d 841 (1972).

[8]Morrison v. Steiner, 32 Ohio St. 2d 86, 89, 61 Ohio Op. 2d 335, 290 N.E.2d 841 (1972) (emphasis by the court).

if more than one forum listed is proper.[9]

If there is no available forum under Civil Rules 3(B)(1) to (9), then plaintiff must determine if an appropriate county can be selected from Civil Rule 3(B)(11) (county of plaintiff's residence or business).[10] Only if subsection 3(B)(11) is inapplicable may plaintiff use the provisions of 3(B)(12) (county in which defendant has property or debts owing or has appointed a statutory agent).[11]

In some instances, Civil Rule 3(B) lists a specific forum in connection with a particular kind of action. It should be noted that these references are not exclusionary. Civil Rule 3(B)(9), for example, provides that in an action for divorce, proper venue lies in the county where the plaintiff has resided for ninety days immediately preceding the filing. This provision does not restrict the plaintiff's selection of a forum for the divorce case. In general, the county of plaintiff's residence is not favored for venue purposes. Rule 3(B)(9) merely sets forth the divorce action as a special circumstance in which the county of the plaintiff's residence can constitute a proper venue.[12] The same principle applies to Rule 3(B)(7), which designates the county of plaintiff's residence as a proper venue for Rule 4.3 actions (out-of-state service). The point is that neither Rule 3(B)(7) nor (9) is a limitation on the availability of other forums for a domestic relations action.[13]

In fact, at least four forums are always potentially available in any divorce case: (1) residence of defendant;[14] (2) residence of plaintiff for ninety days immediately preceding the filing;[15] (3) place where defendant conducted activity giving rise to the claim for relief;[16] and (4) place where claim for relief arose.[17] In addition to these four, any other available forum may be selected by the plaintiff from the various counties

---

[9]Varketta v. General Motors Corp., 34 Ohio App. 2d 1, 63 Ohio Op. 2d 8, 295 N.E.2d 219 (8th Dist. Cuyahoga County 1973); General Motors Acceptance Corp. v. Jacks, 27 Ohio Misc. 115, 56 Ohio Op. 2d 93, 56 Ohio Op. 2d 343, 268 N.E.2d 833 (Mun. Ct. 1971). See Morrison v. Steiner, 32 Ohio St. 2d 86, 61 Ohio Op. 2d 335, 290 N.E.2d 841 (1972); Fuller v. Fuller, 32 Ohio App. 2d 303, 61 Ohio Op. 2d 400, 290 N.E.2d 852 (10th Dist. Franklin County 1972).

[10]Varketta v. General Motors Corp., 34 Ohio App. 2d 1, 63 Ohio Op. 2d 8, 295 N.E.2d 219 (8th Dist. Cuyahoga County 1973). See, e.g., Gieg v. Gieg, 16 Ohio App. 3d 51, 474 N.E.2d 626 (11th Dist. Trumbull County 1984); Taylor v. Taylor, 84 Ohio App. 3d 445, 616 N.E.2d 1199 (2d Dist. Montgomery County 1992) (legal separation action filed in county where plaintiff lived for eighteen days was proper when there was no other proper county under Civ. R. 3(B)(1) to Civ. R. 3(B)(10)).

[11]Varketta v. General Motors Corp., 34 Ohio App. 2d 1, 63 Ohio Op. 2d 8, 295 N.E.2d 219 (8th Dist. Cuyahoga County 1973). See, e.g., Gieg v. Gieg, 16 Ohio App. 3d 51, 474 N.E.2d 626 (11th Dist. Trumbull County 1984).

[12]Fuller v. Fuller, 32 Ohio App. 2d 303, 61 Ohio Op. 2d 400, 290 N.E.2d 852 (10th Dist. Franklin County 1972).

[13]Fuller v. Fuller, 32 Ohio App. 2d 303, 61 Ohio Op. 2d 400, 290 N.E.2d 852 (10th Dist. Franklin County 1972). See also staff notes Civ. R. 3(B).

[14]Civ. R. 3(B)(1).

[15]Civ. R. 3(B)(9).

[16]Civ. R. 3(B)(3).

[17]Civ. R. 3(B)(6).

listed as proper under the rule.

In reality, since venues are places inhabited by courts and judges, considerations other than geography may influence the selection of venue. That the rule indulges forum shopping seems apparent. Nonetheless, if a county is listed as a proper venue for an action, albeit less than substantially connected to the parties or the claim, an objection that another county is more substantially connected will not carry the day.

The Ohio Supreme Court has reaffirmed that venue lies in the county where service of process is first accomplished when there is concurrent and coextensive jurisdiction.[18] While the provisions of Civil Rules 3(B)(1) to (9) are equal in status, the specific provision should take precedence over the general. Where Civil Rule 3(B)(9) does not apply, venue should be determined under the more specific rather than more general provisions of Civil Rule 3(B).[19]

§ 27:43   Choice of venue—Domestic violence victim

In an action for a civil protection order[1] proper venue can, in addition to any other proper venue provision, be in the county where the petitioner currently or temporarily resides.[2] Thus, even if the alleged victim is in a shelter in another county, the action for relief could properly be brought in that county.

§ 27:44   Choice of venue—Residence of plaintiff

All examples which follow assume that plaintiff has satisfied Ohio's six-month residency requirement for divorce and annulment actions, and that an Ohio court has jurisdiction of the subject matter and the parties.

To illustrate the selection of proper venue in a divorce case, assume that H and W are residents of the same County A, where they have lived for four months. Either may bring a divorce action against the other in County A on the basis of Civil Rule 3(B)(9), which provides that proper venue lies in the county where the plaintiff has resided for ninety days immediately preceding the filing.

Suppose H and W have lived in County A for only a week. Either may file a divorce action against the other in County A. Although venue may not be based on Rule 3(B)(9), other provisions of Rule 3(B) may be applied. Proper venue lies in A, as the county of defendant's residence under Rule 3(B)(1) or as the county where the claim for relief arose under Rule 3(B)(6). Neither of these provisions imposes a waiting period. Accordingly, it is immaterial that the plaintiff has not resided in County

---

[18]State ex rel. Largent v. Fisher, 43 Ohio St. 3d 160, 540 N.E.2d 239 (1989); State ex rel. Balson v. Harnishfeger, 55 Ohio St. 2d 38, 9 Ohio Op. 3d 21, 377 N.E.2d 750 (1978).

[19]Glover v. Glover, 66 Ohio App. 3d 724, 586 N.E.2d 159 (12th Dist. Brown County 1990).

[Section 27:43]
[1]See Ch 5.
[2]Civ. R. 3(B)(10).

A for ninety days before bringing the action, as is required under Rule 3(B)(9).[1] Residency means an intent to remain.

W leaves H and takes up residence in County B. Until she has lived in County B for ninety days, W cannot bring an action there on the basis of her residence. However, W may file a divorce action at once in County A, as the county where defendant resides, pursuant to Rule 3(B)(1), or as the place where the claim for relief arose, pursuant to Rule 3(B)(6). Of course, once she has complied with the requisite waiting period, W can bring the action in County B, as the county of plaintiff's residence under Rule 3(B)(9).

A prison inmate is not a resident of the county in which he is incarcerated so as to satisfy Civil Rule 3(B).[2]

§ 27:45　Choice of venue—Residence of defendant

If H and W reside in the same county, either may always bring an action for divorce in that county. The basis for venue is Civil Rule 3(B)(1), which provides that proper venue lies in the county of defendant's residence. No waiting period is required.

Suppose W moves to County B and wants to bring a divorce action at once. H continues to live in County A. W may immediately file in A as the county where defendant resides under Rule 3(B)(1). However, County B is not an available forum as the county of plaintiff's residence until the expiration of ninety days.

H wants to initiate divorce proceedings. Once W moves to County B, H may commence a divorce action immediately in either County A or B. H may bring the action in County B, as the place of defendant's residence under Rule 3(B)(1). H may also directly file in County A under Rule 3(B)(3) or (6), on the basis that defendant W's conduct in County A gave rise to his divorce claim.

If H and W were to file a dissolution action, the county where either resides would be a proper forum. RC 3105.62 provides that petitioners in a dissolution are considered "defendants" for purpose of service. Consequently, a dissolution action could be brought by the parties in either County A or B, under Rule 3(B)(1).

§ 27:46　Choice of venue—Cause of action

Civil Rule 3(B)(3) states that proper venue lies where defendant conducted activity giving rise to the claim for relief. Rule 3(B)(6) provides for venue in the county where the claim for relief arose. Neither provision imposes a waiting period.

The forum where the cause of action arose will often coincide with the location of the marital residence as being the situs of the breach of mar-

---

[Section 27:44]

[1]Fuller v. Fuller, 32 Ohio App. 2d 303, 61 Ohio Op. 2d 400, 290 N.E.2d 852 (10th Dist. Franklin County 1972).

[2]State ex rel. Saunders v. Court of Common Pleas of Allen County, 34 Ohio St. 3d 15, 516 N.E.2d 232 (1987).

ital duties. However, this is not necessarily true. For example, suppose W learns that H has been having an extramarital affair in County C. W may commence divorce proceedings at once in County C. C is a proper venue for the action under Rule 3(B)(3) as the county where defendant H engaged in activity giving rise to the claim.

In order to bring the action in County C, W need not live in that county. In fact, it is immaterial whether W (or H) is a resident of County A, B, or C, for the purposes of Rule 3(B)(3) and (6).

§ 27:47 Choice of venue—Multiple parties

In addition to the above scenario, where H is having an extramarital affair in County C, suppose H has a savings account at a Bank doing business in County D. H also has an interest in a Pension and Profit Sharing Plan by virtue of his job with the Employer, who acts as trustee for the plan and who is located in County E. H and W have a child who has been living with H's Elderly Mother in County F. To protect W's marital claims to the property, W joins Bank and Employer as third-party defendants under Rule 75(B). In order to obtain jurisdiction over the physical custodian of the child, W joins Elderly Mother as a defendant also. W files the divorce action in County C. Employer, Elderly Mother, and H file objections to venue; Bank does not.

The first issue to be determined is whether the court may consider a motion to change venue if fewer than all the defendants join in the motion. The answer is yes. Where there are multiple defendants, if any defendant timely objects to venue, and venue is in fact improper, the court must transfer the action.[1]

The second issue is whether County C is a proper venue for the action as to Bank, Employer, and Elderly Mother. The answer is yes. Since the defendant conducted activity in County C giving rise to the divorce claim, the action is properly venued in that county. Civil Rule 3(E) provides that, where there are multiple parties, if venue is proper as to any one of the parties or as to any claim for relief, it is proper as to all parties.[2]

The result would be different if W had filed an action in County D, where Bank is located. County D is a proper forum only as to Bank, a nominal party to the action. Upon timely objection, the case should be transferred to a county proper to the main action.[3]

Assume that Elderly Mother timely files a motion to change venue from County C to F where she and the child reside, on the basis that there are substantial contacts between that county and the child, whose custody is to be determined. Elderly Mother's motion should be denied,

---

[Section 27:47]

[1]Ohio Bell Telephone Co. v. BancOhio Nat. Bank, 1 Ohio Misc. 2d 11, 440 N.E.2d 69 (C.P. 1982).

[2]Civ. R. 3(E); Varketta v. General Motors Corp., 34 Ohio App. 2d 1, 63 Ohio Op. 2d 8, 295 N.E.2d 219 (8th Dist. Cuyahoga County 1973).

[3]See Civ. R. 3(E).

since it is the plaintiff's prerogative to choose where the action will be brought, if more than one county is proper under the rule. Since County C is a proper forum, plaintiff W has the right to have the matter heard in that county.

§ 27:48 Choice of venue—Property in third county

W wants to file the divorce action in County C, where the claim for relief arose. Assume that there is real or personal property located in County M, which is titled in H's name. W need not bring the divorce action in County M in order to adjudicate her claims to that property. Where an action is properly venued and the court has subject matter jurisdiction, service of process may be issued any place in Ohio.[1] Therefore, the fact that the property is located outside County C does not prevent the County C court from obtaining jurisdiction over the property or over any person having control of or an interest in the property.[2] Moreover, to further protect her claims to the property in M, W may give notice of the divorce litigation pending in County C to third parties not joined in the action by filing a certified copy of the divorce complaint with the common pleas court in County M.[3] When the cause is properly venued as to the main action, W's rights to property in another county may thus be fully adjudicated from any forum in Ohio.

Despite the fact that her property claims can be protected by the County C court, W wants to bring the divorce action in County M for tactical reasons. She perhaps may do so on the basis that the defendant (or she) has property in County M.

Under Civil Rule 3(B)(11), the county where defendant has property or debts owing to him is listed as a proper forum, but this subsection may be used only where there is no other available forum in the state.[4] Where either or both parties are residents of the state, another forum is available and Rule 3(B)(11) may not be applied.[5] Therefore, under the fact pattern, W may not rely on this provision as a basis for venue.[6]

Still looking for a vehicle to bring the action in County M, W turns to Civil Rule 3(B)(5), which provides that venue is proper in a county where "the property is situated, if the subject of the action is real or tangible personal property." The question is whether the subject of a divorce action is the real or tangible personal property of the parties. W contends that the subject of the action is the parties' marital rights and obligations and that these are property rights. Assuming, arguendo, the correctness of W's assertion, she should not prevail on the venue claim.

[Section 27:48]

[1]Civ. R. 4.6(A); staff notes Civ. R. 4.6; Morrison v. Steiner, 32 Ohio St. 2d 86, 61 Ohio Op. 2d 335, 290 N.E.2d 841 (1972).

[2]Civ. R. 75(B).

[3]Civ. R. 3(F).

[4]See Varketta v. General Motors Corp., 34 Ohio App. 2d 1, 63 Ohio Op. 2d 8, 295 N.E.2d 219 (8th Dist. Cuyahoga County 1973).

[5]See Civ. R. 3(B)(1), (9), (10).

[6]See § 27:49, Choice of venue—Party out of state.

Marital property rights are "intangible" rights. The express language of Rule 3(B)(5) refers to "real or tangible personal property" as being the subject of the action. It should therefore be concluded that the presence of real or tangible personal property in the county is itself insufficient to create proper venue.

§ 27:49 Choice of venue—Party out of state

H leaves his residence in County A and moves to California. W remains in County B. When the defendant is out of state, the action may be brought in the county of plaintiff's residence under Civil Rule 3(B)(7). Accordingly, W may directly bring a divorce action against H in County B, where she resides. No residential waiting period is required for venue purposes. However, W is not restricted to County B. W may also file the action in any other available forum under the rule, such as the county where the cause of action arose.[1]

The converse does not apply to H, residing in California. Where the plaintiff resides outside the state, he cannot commence an action for divorce in an Ohio court. The impediment is not because of lack of venue. H cannot bring the divorce action in this state because he must be an Ohio domiciliary resident to establish jurisdiction.[2]

However, since there is no residency requirement for a legal separation action, H could arguably bring such an action against W in Ohio. Available forums include the county of defendant W's residence or the county where the claim for relief arose.[3]

§ 27:50 Choice of venue—Post-decree enforcement

Where both parties have left Ohio, the Ohio court which granted the divorce decree retains jurisdiction over the controversy and is a proper forum to enforce the decree.[1] With regard to venue, it is logical that an enforcement action is properly venued in the county where the decree was granted as (if nothing else) the county where the claim for relief arose.[2]

§ 27:51 Improper venue and remedies

Research References

3 Klein and Darling, Baldwin's Ohio Practice, Civil Practice, Ch 3

Where an action has been brought in a county which is not a proper

---

[Section 27:49]

[1]Civ. R. 3(B)(6).

[2]See §§ 27:27–27:30, Jurisdiction over marital status—Residency statutes.

[3]Civ. R. 3(B)(6). But see Haylett v. Haylett, 1989 WL 56367 (Ohio Ct. App. 11th Dist. Portage County 1989).

[Section 27:50]

[1]Weinberger v. Weinberger, 43 Ohio App. 2d 129, 72 Ohio Op. 2d 325, 334 N.E.2d 514 (9th Dist. Summit County 1974).

[2]See Civ. R. 3(B)(6). For discussion of venue in post-decree and enforcement issues, § 27:38, Personal jurisdiction—Continuing jurisdiction.

venue, the court may not dismiss the action on the basis of improper venue.[1] Civil Rule 3(C)(2) states that, under these circumstances and where the defense of improper venue is timely asserted, the court must transfer the action to a proper county, and it may assess costs, including attorney fees, against the party who improperly brought the action. Needless to say, the moving party has the burden of establishing that the forum is improper.

Aside from the ground of improper venue, the court may transfer the case, when it appears that a fair and impartial trial cannot occur in the county where the lawsuit is pending. In such a situation, the court has authority to transfer the action to an adjoining county. Transfer may be undertaken upon motion of a party or on the court's own motion.[2]

Venue is a waivable defense.[3] Accordingly, unless improper venue is challenged in a timely fashion, it is deemed waived. The defense must be raised by either motion or answer.[4] Pursuant to Rule 12(H), improper venue is waived if not asserted by pre-answer motion or by answer or by amendment of the answer within the time permitted for amendment under Rule 15(A).[5]

Where the objection is properly preserved, error of the court in overruling a motion to change venue may be the subject of appeal.[6] It has been held, however, that since a proceeding for change of venue is not a special proceeding and since an order changing venue does not determine the action or prevent a judgment, a change of venue order is not a final appealable order under RC 2505.02.[7] The order is reviewable at such time as a final judgment is entered in the case.[8]

§ 27:52   Full faith and credit—History and purpose

Under Article IV, Section 1 of the United States Constitution, full faith and credit must be given in each state to the judicial proceedings of every other state.[1] The full faith and credit clause and its implement-

---

[Section 27:51]

[1]Civ. R. 3(C); Fuller v. Fuller, 32 Ohio App. 2d 303, 61 Ohio Op. 2d 400, 290 N.E.2d 852 (10th Dist. Franklin County 1972).

[2]Civ. R. 3(C).

[3]See Civ. R. 12(H).

[4]Civ. R. 12(B). Civil Rule 12(G) requires the moving party to include in a Rule 12 motion all defenses and objections available under Civil Rule 12(B); no waivable defense or objection which is omitted from the motion can thereafter be asserted in an answer.

[5]Wurz v. Santa Fe Intern. Corp., 423 F. Supp. 91 (D. Del. 1976).

[6]See Civ. R. 3(G).

[7]Timson v. Young, 70 Ohio App. 2d 239, 24 Ohio Op. 3d 309, 436 N.E.2d 538 (10th Dist. Franklin County 1980).

[8]Timson v. Young, 70 Ohio App. 2d 239, 24 Ohio Op. 3d 309, 436 N.E.2d 538 (10th Dist. Franklin County 1980).

[Section 27:52]

[1]U.S. Const. art. IV § 1 ("Full Faith and Credit shall be given in each State to the public Acts, Records, and judicial Proceedings of every other State. And the Congress may by general Laws prescribe the Manner in which such Acts, Records and Proceed-

ing legislation require that a state give to the judgments of sister states the same credit, validity, and effect as they have in the state where they were rendered.[2]

These provisions have been substantially the same since 1792. Virtually no legislative history is available to explain their meaning and purpose.[3] According to judicial interpretation, the framers intended the clause to help weld the aggregation of independent, sovereign states into a nation, while avoiding centralization.[4] The constitutional mandate, as implemented by Congress, thus leaves each state with power over its own courts but binds litigants wherever they may be in the nation by prior orders of other courts.[5]

On the subject of interstate divorce litigation, the Supreme Court has said that, even though the regulation of family relations has traditionally been reserved to the separate states, a collateral attack on an out-of-state judgment presents considerations that go beyond a state's right to regulate its domiciliaries. Such a situation involves inconsistent assertions of power by courts of two states of the federal union. In the application of the full faith and credit clause, the interests of local policy must at times be required to give way: "[S]uch 'is part of the price of our federal system.' "[6]

§ 27:53   Full faith and credit—Scope and limitations

One application of Article IV, Section 1 is that a decree of divorce which was granted by a state having jurisdiction is entitled to validity and effect in every other state.[1] The dictates of full faith and credit require that a state submit even to hostile policies reflected in the judgment of a sister state.[2]

For instance, a decree of another state must be given effect, even

---

ings shall be proved, and the Effect thereof."); 28 U.S.C.A. § 1738 ("Such Acts, records and judicial proceedings or copies thereof, so authenticated, shall have the same full faith and credit in every court within the United States and its Territories and Possessions as they have by law or usage in the courts of such State, Territory or Possession from which they are taken.").

[2]Aldrich v. Aldrich, 378 U.S. 540, 84 S. Ct. 1687, 12 L. Ed. 2d 1020 (1964); Johnson v. Muelberger, 340 U.S. 581, 71 S. Ct. 474, 95 L. Ed. 552 (1951).

[3]Johnson v. Muelberger, 340 U.S. 581, 71 S. Ct. 474, 95 L. Ed. 552 (1951).

[4]Johnson v. Muelberger, 340 U.S. 581, 71 S. Ct. 474, 95 L. Ed. 552 (1951); Sherrer v. Sherrer, 334 U.S. 343, 68 S.Ct. 1087, 92 L.Ed. 1429 (1948). See Estin v. Estin, 334 U.S. 541, 68 S. Ct. 1213, 92 L. Ed. 1561, 1 A.L.R.2d 1412 (1948); Williams v. State of North Carolina, 317 U.S. 287, 63 S. Ct. 207, 87 L. Ed. 279, 143 A.L.R. 1273 (1942).

[5]Johnson v. Muelberger, 340 U.S. 581, 71 S. Ct. 474, 95 L. Ed. 552 (1951). See also Davis v. Davis, 305 U.S. 32, 59 S. Ct. 3, 83 L. Ed. 26, 118 A.L.R. 1518 (1938).

[6]Sherrer v. Sherrer, 334 U.S. 343, 355, 68 S.Ct. 1087, 92 L.Ed. 1429 (1948).

[Section 27:53]

[1]Johnson v. Muelberger, 340 U.S. 581, 71 S. Ct. 474, 95 L. Ed. 552 (1951); Williams v. State of North Carolina, 317 U.S. 287, 63 S. Ct. 207, 87 L. Ed. 279, 143 A.L.R. 1273 (1942); Van Fossen v. State, 37 Ohio St. 317, 1881 WL 101 (1881); Barber v. Barber, 62 U.S. 582, 21 How. 582, 16 L. Ed. 226 (1858).

[2]Estin v. Estin, 334 U.S. 541, 68 S. Ct. 1213, 92 L. Ed. 1561, 1 A.L.R.2d 1412 (1948).

though its enforcement offends the public policy of the state in which recognition is sought. Thus, the fact that Nevada's divorce practices may have been obnoxious to North Carolina did not suspend the operation of full faith and credit in *Williams v. North Carolina (I)*.[3] Similarly, a divorce is entitled to recognition, even though it was granted by another state for a cause not permitted as a ground for divorce in the reviewing state.[4]

However, a divorce which is binding within the confines of the issuing state is not necessarily entitled to extraterritorial effect. Several bases are recognized for the refusal of a forum to accord full faith and credit to an out-of-state decree.

The permissible restrictions on the scope of the full faith and credit clause are governed by federal law.[5] The most significant qualification of the doctrine is the jurisdictional proviso: To be entitled to recognition, the judgment must have been rendered by a court having jurisdiction over the parties and the matters litigated. As the Supreme Court stated in *Williams v. North Carolina (II)*:[6] "A judgment in one State is conclusive upon the merits in every other State, but only if the court of the first State had power to pass on the merits—had jurisdiction, that is, to render the judgment." Thus, it is only a judgment which the tribunal had authority to issue that must be given full faith and credit in another state.

As *Williams (II)* also established, the decree is not a conclusive adjudication of the jurisdictional facts upon which it is based. The state in which recognition is sought is entitled to reexamine whether the issuing forum had authority to render the judgment. If it finds that the granting court lacked jurisdiction, the reviewing state need not give full faith and credit to the judgment.[7]

Thus, a state is not bound to enforce a divorce decree based on constructive service if it finds that neither spouse was domiciled in the foreign state, since the divorce court had no authority to render the decree.[8] For the same reason, a state is not required to recognize a sister

---

[3]Williams v. State of North Carolina, 317 U.S. 287, 63 S. Ct. 207, 87 L. Ed. 279, 143 A.L.R. 1273 (1942).

[4]Larrick v. Walters, 39 Ohio App. 363, 10 Ohio L. Abs. 508, 177 N.E. 642 (7th Dist. Noble County 1930); Am. Jur. 2d, Divorce and Separation § 948.

[5]Williams v. State of North Carolina, 317 U.S. 287, 63 S. Ct. 207, 87 L. Ed. 279, 143 A.L.R. 1273 (1942). See Johnson v. Muelberger, 340 U.S. 581, 71 S. Ct. 474, 95 L. Ed. 552 (1951).

[6]Williams v. State of N. C., 325 U.S. 226, 229, 65 S. Ct. 1092, 89 L. Ed. 1577, 157 A.L.R. 1366 (1945).

[7]Williams v. State of N. C., 325 U.S. 226, 229, 65 S. Ct. 1092, 89 L. Ed. 1577, 157 A.L.R. 1366 (1945).

[8]Aldrich v. Aldrich, 378 U.S. 540, 84 S. Ct. 1687, 12 L. Ed. 2d 1020 (1964); Rice v. Rice, 336 U.S. 674, 69 S. Ct. 751, 93 L. Ed. 957 (1949); Cook v. Cook, 342 U.S. 126, 72 S. Ct. 157, 96 L. Ed. 146 (1951); Sutton v. Leib, 342 U.S. 402, 72 S. Ct. 398, 96 L. Ed. 448 (1952); Van Fossen v. State, 37 Ohio St. 317, 1881 WL 101 (1881). See Glassman v. Glassman, 75 Ohio App. 47, 30 Ohio Op. 352, 42 Ohio L. Abs. 385, 60 N.E.2d 716 (1st Dist. Hamilton County 1944); Neal v. Neal, 53 Ohio L. Abs. 329, 85 N.E.2d 147 (C.P.

state's adjudication of personal rights, such as custody[9] or alimony,[10] where the rendering court lacked in personam jurisdiction over the defendant. Before a state may honor a sister state's adjudication, proper service pursuant to constitutional mandates must be observed.[11]

The impeachment of a sister state's judgment for lack of jurisdiction is restricted, however, by the doctrine of res judicata. Three years after *Williams (II)* was decided, the Supreme Court held that a collateral attack on a sister state's decree for want of jurisdiction can be barred by res judicata.[12] For example, a defendant is precluded from collaterally impeaching a divorce decree on jurisdictional grounds where he participated in the foreign proceeding, was accorded full opportunity to contest the jurisdictional issues, and where the decree is not susceptible to such collateral attack in the courts of the rendering state.[13]

It should also be noted that the holding in *Williams (II)* does not apply to voidable judgments. As a general rule, collateral impeachment may not be based on errors or irregularities committed by the foreign court in the exercise of its jurisdiction. It has been held that where a court of competent jurisdiction renders a final decision which is erroneous under the laws of the forum, the judgment is not subject to collateral attack in a sister state while it stands unreversed and in force.[14] Such a decree must be treated as if it were correct under the substantive law of the rendering state and must be afforded as broad a scope by a sister state as it has in the original forum.[15]

Aside from the jurisdictional proviso, other bases for refusing to accord full faith and credit have been recognized. The full faith and credit

---

1949); Smerda v. Smerda, 35 Ohio Op. 472, 48 Ohio L. Abs. 232, 74 N.E.2d 751 (C.P. 1947).

[9]May v. Anderson, 345 U.S. 528, 73 S. Ct. 840, 97 L. Ed. 1221, 67 Ohio L. Abs. 468 (1953); Pasqualone v. Pasqualone, 63 Ohio St. 2d 96, 17 Ohio Op. 3d 58, 406 N.E.2d 1121 (1980). See Uniform Child Custody Jurisdiction Act; Parental Kidnapping Prevention Act; International Child Abduction Remedies Act Ch 17.

[10]Vanderbilt v. Vanderbilt, 354 U.S. 416, 77 S. Ct. 1360, 1 L. Ed. 2d 1456 (1957); Estin v. Estin, 334 U.S. 541, 68 S. Ct. 1213, 92 L. Ed. 1561, 1 A.L.R.2d 1412 (1948). See Slapp v. Slapp, 143 Ohio St. 105, 28 Ohio Op. 47, 54 N.E.2d 153 (1944); Cox v. Cox, 19 Ohio St. 502, 1869 WL 84 (1869).

[11]Johnson v. Johnson, 86 Ohio App. 3d 433, 621 N.E.2d 530 (2d Dist. Greene County 1993) (Ohio did not recognize an Illinois decree of divorce where service by publication and regular mail were insufficient because best possible method was by certified mail).

[12]Sherrer v. Sherrer, 334 U.S. 343, 68 S.Ct. 1087, 92 L.Ed. 1429 (1948). See Johnson v. Muelberger, 340 U.S. 581, 71 S. Ct. 474, 95 L. Ed. 552 (1951); Rice v. Rice, 336 U.S. 674, 69 S. Ct. 751, 93 L. Ed. 957 (1949). See also Winkler v. Stowe, 1997 WL 30947 (Ohio Ct. App. 4th Dist. Jackson County 1997), dismissed, appeal not allowed, 78 Ohio St. 3d 1512, 679 N.E.2d 308 (1997) (Michigan determination of validity of Ohio divorce decree bars Ohio court from later finding it had no jurisdiction).

[13]Sherrer v. Sherrer, 334 U.S. 343, 68 S.Ct. 1087, 92 L.Ed. 1429 (1948). See Johnson v. Muelberger, 340 U.S. 581, 71 S. Ct. 474, 95 L. Ed. 552 (1951); Rice v. Rice, 336 U.S. 674, 69 S. Ct. 751, 93 L. Ed. 957 (1949).

[14]Aldrich v. Aldrich, 378 U.S. 540, 84 S. Ct. 1687, 12 L. Ed. 2d 1020 (1964); Southard v. Southard, 305 F.2d 730 (2d Cir. 1962). See also Am. Jur. 2d, Divorce and Separation § 477.

[15]Aldrich v. Aldrich, 378 U.S. 540, 84 S. Ct. 1687, 12 L. Ed. 2d 1020 (1964).

clause only requires a state to accord a judgment the same validity and effect as it has in the rendering state.[16] It does not compel a state to give a decree greater effect than it has in the state of its issuance. Therefore, if a decree is invalid and may be collaterally attacked in the rendering state, full faith and credit does not preclude such an attack in another forum.[17]

A corollary of this rule is that, if a judgment is not final and conclusive in the state of its origin, it is not entitled to recognition under the full faith and credit doctrine.[18] This principle has most often been applied to the enforcement in another state of alimony or spousal support and child support arrearages that have not been reduced to judgment in the state which granted the award.

It has been held, for example, that an order for spousal or child support, payable in installments and subject to retroactive modification under the laws of the rendering state, is not entitled to full faith and credit because it is considered to lack sufficient finality.[19] Of course, once a money judgment on the arrearage has been obtained, the judgment is entitled to recognition.

On the other hand, it is firmly established that a sister state's decree for periodic spousal or child support is entitled to recognition as to accrued installments if the law of the rendering state does not permit retroactive modification of the arrearages and provided that no modification of the decree has actually been made prior to the maturity of the installments.[20] Future periodic payments, which are not modifiable by

---

[16]Johnson v. Muelberger, 340 U.S. 581, 71 S. Ct. 474, 95 L. Ed. 552 (1951); Sherrer v. Sherrer, 334 U.S. 343, 68 S.C.t 1087, 92 L.Ed. 1429 (1948); People of State of N.Y. ex rel. Halvey v. Halvey, 330 U.S. 610, 67 S. Ct. 903, 91 L. Ed. 1133 (1947). See Aldrich v. Aldrich, 378 U.S. 540, 84 S. Ct. 1687, 12 L. Ed. 2d 1020 (1964).

[17]Williams v. State of North Carolina, 317 U.S. 287, 63 S. Ct. 207, 87 L. Ed. 279, 143 A.L.R. 1273 (1942). See Sherrer v. Sherrer, 334 U.S. 343, 68 S.Ct. 1087, 92 L.Ed. 1429 (1948); People of State of N.Y. ex rel. Halvey v. Halvey, 330 U.S. 610, 67 S. Ct. 903, 91 L. Ed. 1133 (1947).

[18]Yarborough v. Yarborough, 290 U.S. 202, 54 S. Ct. 181, 78 L. Ed. 269, 90 A.L.R. 924 (1933); Sistare v. Sistare, 218 U.S. 1, 30 S. Ct. 682, 54 L. Ed. 905 (1910); Armstrong v. Armstrong, 117 Ohio St. 558, 6 Ohio L. Abs. 14, 160 N.E. 34, 57 A.L.R. 1108 (1927); Price v. Price, 4 Ohio App. 3d 217, 447 N.E.2d 769 (8th Dist. Cuyahoga County 1982); Restatement (Second) of Conflict of Laws § 107 (1971); Am. Jur. 2d, Divorce and Separation § 979. But see People of State of N.Y. ex rel. Halvey v. Halvey, 330 U.S. 610, 67 S. Ct. 903, 91 L. Ed. 1133 (1947) (concurring opinion).

[19]Sistare v. Sistare, 218 U.S. 1, 30 S. Ct. 682, 54 L. Ed. 905 (1910); Lynde v. Lynde, 181 U.S. 183, 21 S. Ct. 555, 45 L. Ed. 810 (1901); Armstrong v. Armstrong, 117 Ohio St. 558, 6 Ohio L. Abs. 14, 160 N.E. 34, 57 A.L.R. 1108 (1927); Gilbert v. Gilbert, 83 Ohio St. 265, 94 N.E. 421 (1911); Price v. Price, 4 Ohio App. 3d 217, 447 N.E.2d 769 (8th Dist. Cuyahoga County 1982).

[20]Barber v. Barber, 323 U.S. 77, 65 S. Ct. 137, 89 L. Ed. 82, 157 A.L.R. 163 (1944); Sistare v. Sistare, 218 U.S. 1, 30 S. Ct. 682, 54 L. Ed. 905 (1910); Barber v. Barber, 62 U.S. 582, 21 How. 582, 16 L. Ed. 226 (1858); McPherson v. McPherson, 153 Ohio St. 82, 41 Ohio Op. 151, 90 N.E.2d 675 (1950); Armstrong v. Armstrong, 117 Ohio St. 558, 6 Ohio L. Abs. 14, 160 N.E. 34, 57 A.L.R. 1108 (1927).

the granting state, will also be accorded full faith and credit.[21]

Where enforcement is not required by the full faith and credit clause, any state is free to enforce the judgment of another state by comity.[22] For instance, if it elects to do so, a court may give effect to an out-of-state support decree, even though it is subject to modification under the laws of the rendering state.[23]

Finally, the scope of the full faith and credit clause only extends to questions which were adjudicated by the sister state. The doctrine does not prohibit subsequent litigation of matters left undecided by the foreign court. For example, if the defendant's right to spousal support was not determined by the court granting the divorce, full faith and credit does not preclude a subsequent action for spousal support in the state of the defendant's residence.[24]

For purposes of full faith and credit, out-of-state divorce judgments are sometimes classified into two types, ex parte and bilateral. Each of these will be addressed in turn.

§ 27:54   Full faith and credit—Ex parte decree—In general

The United States Supreme Court has applied the phrase "ex parte divorce" to a decree rendered by a court lacking personal jurisdiction over the defendant.[1] The landmark cases of *Williams v. North Carolina (I) and (II)* both involved ex parte proceedings.

Abandoning the restrictive concepts of matrimonial domicile,[2] the Supreme Court in *Williams (I)* overruled the venerable *Haddock v. Haddock*[3] and declared that any state has the power to grant a divorce, without obtaining personal jurisdiction over the defendant, provided that one spouse has established a bona fide domicile in the state.

On this basis, the court held that a divorce obtained against a nonresident upon constructive service, where such service is authorized in the rendering state, is conclusive and binding under full faith and credit

---

[21]Price v. Price, 4 Ohio App. 3d 217, 447 N.E.2d 769 (8th Dist. Cuyahoga County 1982); Ades v. Ades, 70 Ohio App. 487, 25 Ohio Op. 214, 37 Ohio L. Abs. 58, 45 N.E.2d 416 (1st Dist. Hamilton County 1942).

[22]Am. Jur. 2d, Divorce and Separation § 964.

[23]Am. Jur. 2d, Divorce and Separation § 983.

[24]Armstrong v. Armstrong, 350 U.S. 568, 76 S. Ct. 629, 100 L. Ed. 705, 73 Ohio L. Abs. 514 (1956).

[Section 27:54]

[1]Sherrer v. Sherrer, 334 U.S. 343, 68 S.Ct. 1087, 92 L.Ed. 1429 (1948); Rice v. Rice, 336 U.S. 674, 69 S. Ct. 751, 93 L. Ed. 957 (1949) (Jackson, J., dissenting).

[2]Williams v. State of North Carolina, 317 U.S. 287, 63 S. Ct. 207, 87 L. Ed. 279, 143 A.L.R. 1273 (1942) (the limitation of ex parte divorces to the matrimonial domicile was rejected as being based on "fiction"). Case overruled Haddock v. Haddock, 201 U.S. 562, 26 S. Ct. 525, 50 L. Ed. 867 (1906) (overruled in part by, Williams v. State of North Carolina, 317 U.S. 287, 63 S. Ct. 207, 87 L. Ed. 279, 143 A.L.R. 1273 (1942).

[3]Haddock v. Haddock, 201 U.S. 562, 26 S. Ct. 525, 50 L. Ed. 867 (1906) (state of matrimonial domicile could disregard a decree of divorce obtained by the husband after constructive service in another state), overruled by Williams v. State of North Carolina, 317 U.S. 287, 63 S. Ct. 207, 87 L. Ed. 279, 143 A.L.R. 1273 (1942).

as to the termination of the marriage, provided that the service complies with due process and that the plaintiff was a domiciliary of the state granting the decree.

In *Williams (I)*, the record contained no evidence that the state granting the divorce was not the complaining party's state of domicile. After a retrial, a second appeal was taken to the Supreme Court. Reasoning that domicile is essential to divorce jurisdiction, the court in *Williams v. North Carolina (II)*[4] established that an ex parte divorce is not entitled to recognition if the complaining party was not domiciled in the state granting the decree.

The facts in *Williams (II)* were these. Mr. Williams and Mrs. Hendrix, longtime residents of North Carolina, left their respective spouses and went to Nevada, where they stayed in an auto court for transients. Each filed a divorce action in Nevada as soon as state law permitted. Although copies of the complaint were delivered to the defendant spouses in North Carolina, service of process was not made within Nevada, and neither defendant appeared in the Nevada proceedings.

The Nevada court granted a divorce to both Mr. Williams and Mrs. Hendrix on the ground of extreme cruelty. Each decree recited that the plaintiff was a bona fide resident of the state of Nevada. As soon as their divorces were final, Mr. Williams and Mrs. Hendrix were married in Nevada. When they returned to North Carolina to live, they were arrested for bigamy.

As a defense to the indictments, the defendants argued that, under the full faith and credit clause, North Carolina was bound to recognize the Nevada divorce decree and marriage license. The issue which emerged was whether North Carolina had the power to refuse recognition to the Nevada decrees on the basis that, contrary to the findings of the Nevada court, North Carolina had determined that the defendants had not acquired a bona fide domicile in Nevada.

The Supreme Court declared that full faith and credit need not be afforded a divorce decree obtained upon constructive service where neither spouse was domiciled in the state and the non-resident spouse did not appear or participate in the proceedings.[5] It also established that the court in which recognition is sought may determine whether the state granting the divorce had jurisdiction to render the judgment.

The Court reasoned that a state's finding that it has jurisdiction cannot foreclose reexamination of this question by another state. Otherwise, said the Court, a court's record would establish its own power, and its power would be proved by its own record.

Consequently, the decree of a sister state is a conclusive adjudication except as to the jurisdictional facts upon which it is based. Domicile be-

---

[4]Williams v. State of N. C., 325 U.S. 226, 65 S. Ct. 1092, 89 L. Ed. 1577, 157 A.L.R. 1366 (1945).

[5]Williams v. State of N. C., 325 U.S. 226, 65 S. Ct. 1092, 89 L. Ed. 1577, 157 A.L.R. 1366 (1945). Accord Rice v. Rice, 336 U.S. 674, 69 S. Ct. 751, 93 L. Ed. 957 (1949); Cook v. Cook, 342 U.S. 126, 72 S. Ct. 157, 96 L. Ed. 146 (1951); Sutton v. Leib, 342 U.S. 402, 72 S. Ct. 398, 96 L. Ed. 448 (1952).

ing a jurisdictional fact, Nevada's finding of domicile is not foreclosed from reexamination by another state. If the reviewing court finds that no domicile was acquired by the plaintiff, despite the foreign court's findings to the contrary, full faith and credit need not be given.[6]

However, the Court added, Nevada's finding that the parties were domiciliaries "is entitled to respect, and more." The burden of undermining the "verity" which the decree imports "rests heavily" upon the party challenging the legitimacy of the decree.[7] The judgment of a sister state evokes a presumption that the rendering court had jurisdiction over the parties and over the subject matter.[8] The party attempting to impeach the decree has the burden of overcoming this presumption.[9] According to some authorities, the burden must be sustained by clear and convincing evidence.[10]

§ 27:55 Full faith and credit—Ex parte decree—Res judicata

Res judicata may preclude a party from relitigating the existence of the jurisdictional facts underlying an ex parte divorce. Once a court of competent jurisdiction has determined the validity of the decree, the parties will be denied a second opportunity to litigate the question.

This restriction upon the rule of *Williams (II)* is illustrated by the following case. A Nevada divorce was obtained ex parte upon a finding that the plaintiff was domiciled in Nevada. The defendant later brought suit in another state attacking the divorce for lack of jurisdiction. The second state found that the plaintiff had not been domiciled in Nevada and, under *Williams (II)*, held that the divorce was void. The original plaintiff then filed a third action in federal district court, attacking the second judgment on the ground that it failed to give full faith and credit to the Nevada decree. The Second Circuit held that the principles of res judicata barred relitigation of the issue and that the decision of the second state court was binding.[1]

---

[6]Williams v. State of N. C., 325 U.S. 226, 65 S. Ct. 1092, 89 L. Ed. 1577, 157 A.L.R. 1366 (1945). Accord Smerda v. Smerda, 35 Ohio Op. 472, 48 Ohio L. Abs. 232, 74 N.E.2d 751 (C.P. 1947); Hamilton v. Dillon, 110 Ohio App. 489, 13 Ohio Op. 2d 246, 82 Ohio L. Abs. 606, 167 N.E.2d 356 (10th Dist. Franklin County 1959).

[7]Williams v. State of N. C., 325 U.S. 226, 233–34, 65 S. Ct. 1092, 89 L. Ed. 1577, 157 A.L.R. 1366 (1945).

[8]Cook v. Cook, 342 U.S. 126, 72 S. Ct. 157, 96 L. Ed. 146 (1951).

[9]Cook v. Cook, 342 U.S. 126, 72 S. Ct. 157, 96 L. Ed. 146 (1951); Sutton v. Leib, 342 U.S. 402, 72 S. Ct. 398, 96 L. Ed. 448 (1952); Southard v. Southard, 305 F.2d 730 (2d Cir. 1962).

[10]In re Sayle's Estate, 37 Ohio Op. 167, 51 Ohio L. Abs. 33, 80 N.E.2d 221 (Prob. Ct. 1947), order aff'd, 51 Ohio L. Abs. 46, 80 N.E.2d 229 (Ct. App. 8th Dist. Cuyahoga County 1948); Linck v. Linck, 31 Ohio Misc. 224, 60 Ohio Op. 2d 388, 288 N.E.2d 347 (C.P. 1972).

[Section 27:55]
[1]Southard v. Southard, 305 F.2d 730 (2d Cir. 1962).

§ 27:56   Full faith and credit—Ex parte decree—Death or remarriage of divorced plaintiff

After *Williams (II)* was decided, the Supreme Court had occasion to consider whether an ex parte divorce could be questioned in a collateral proceeding brought after the divorced plaintiff's death and remarriage.

In *Rice v. Rice*,[1] the husband had obtained an ex parte divorce from his wife and later married another woman. At his death, the former wife initiated an action to invalidate the divorce and to determine the inheritance of the decedent's property. Adhering to the doctrine of *Williams (II)*, the court held that the ex parte divorce obtained by the deceased husband could be collaterally attacked on grounds of lack of domicile in an action by the former wife to establish herself as the surviving spouse and to invalidate the decedent's subsequent marriage to another woman.

§ 27:57   Full faith and credit—Ex parte decree—Third parties

The right of a third party to collaterally impeach an ex parte divorce has also been addressed by the US Supreme Court. In *Cook v. Cook*,[1] the court held that, under the ruling in *Williams (II)*, a stranger to the divorce action may reopen the question of whether the divorce court had jurisdiction if the defendant spouse neither appeared nor was personally served in the original proceeding.[2]

According to one Ohio court, *Williams (II)* permits reexamination of an ex parte decree without limitation as to time or remoteness of the impeaching party's interest. The court allowed the decedent's sons to attack for lack of domicile a Nevada divorce obtained ex parte twenty years earlier by the first husband of the decedent's wife. The invalidity of the decree was alleged by the sons in their action to remove the decedent's wife as the administratrix of the decedent's estate on the ground that she was not the surviving spouse.[3]

§ 27:58   Full faith and credit—Ex parte decree—Divisible divorce

As discussed earlier, the dictates of *Williams (I)* require that sister state recognition be accorded an ex parte divorce based on domicile. It is important to note, however, that full faith and credit may extend to an

---

[Section 27:56]

[1]Rice v. Rice, 336 U.S. 674, 69 S. Ct. 751, 93 L. Ed. 957 (1949).

[Section 27:57]

[1]Cook v. Cook, 342 U.S. 126, 72 S. Ct. 157, 96 L. Ed. 146 (1951).

[2]See Johnson v. Muelberger, 340 U.S. 581, 71 S. Ct. 474, 95 L. Ed. 552 (1951).

[3]In re Sayle's Estate, 37 Ohio Op. 167, 51 Ohio L. Abs. 33, 80 N.E.2d 221 (Prob. Ct. 1947), order aff'd, 51 Ohio L. Abs. 46, 80 N.E.2d 229 (Ct. App. 8th Dist. Cuyahoga County 1948) criticizing Williams v. State of N. C., 325 U.S. 226, 65 S. Ct. 1092, 89 L. Ed. 1577, 157 A.L.R. 1366 (1945) for permitting reexamination of sister state decrees without limitation as to time, estoppel, remoteness of interest, or ultimate effects. Court then ruled that on the evidence presented, decedent's sons had failed to overcome the presumptive validity of the Nevada decree, affirmed by 51 Ohio Law Abs. 46, 80 N.E.2d 229 (App., Cuyahoga 1948).

ex parte divorce only insofar as it adjudicates marital status. Because in rem jurisdiction cannot be used to decide personal claims, an ex parte judgment is not effective to determine questions such as spousal or child support.

Where an ex parte decree adjudicates both marital status and support claims, full faith and credit will be accorded the marriage dissolution, but not the determination of personal rights. This result is known as divisible divorce.[1]

§ 27:59　Full faith and credit—Bilateral decree—In general

The term "bilateral decree" has been used by text writers to describe a judgment based on the non-resident's appearance and participation in the original proceeding.[1]

Although the term is useful to describe a general category, it should not be mechanically applied as a rule of collateral impeachment. Aside from the fact of the defendant's appearance, a number of other factors affect the question of whether a bilateral decree may be collaterally attacked, such as the extent of the defendant's participation in the proceeding; the opportunity afforded him to litigate the question; the nature of the matter in issue; and the law of the rendering forum.[2] Moreover, where the defendant appeared in the prior case, relitigation of matters which were in issue in the original action is governed by the rules of res judicata.[3]

§ 27:60　Full faith and credit—Bilateral decree—Jurisdictional questions

As discussed earlier, *Williams (II)* made it clear that full faith and credit must be accorded a sister state's divorce decree only if the rendering state is actually the domicile of one spouse, and that the divorce court's finding on the issue of domicile is not conclusive and can be readjudicated by another state.

However, later cases established that the right to relitigate jurisdictional facts under *Williams (II)* can be lost by a party's participation in the original divorce proceeding. If the defendant in the original action appeared and unsuccessfully contested the issue of domicile, or appeared in the proceeding and admitted or conceded domicile, the defen-

---

[Section 27:58]

　[1]Estin v. Estin, 334 U.S. 541, 68 S. Ct. 1213, 92 L. Ed. 1561, 1 A.L.R.2d 1412 (1948). See § 27:63, Full faith and credit—Divisible divorce—Doctrine.

[Section 27:59]

　[1]Ohio Jur. 2d, Divorce and Separation § 317.

　[2]See Aldrich v. Aldrich, 378 U.S. 540, 84 S. Ct. 1687, 12 L. Ed. 2d 1020 (1964); Sutton v. Leib, 342 U.S. 402, 72 S. Ct. 398, 96 L. Ed. 448 (1952); Johnson v. Muelberger, 340 U.S. 581, 71 S. Ct. 474, 95 L. Ed. 552 (1951); Cook v. Cook, 342 U.S. 126, 72 S. Ct. 157, 96 L. Ed. 146 (1951); Sherrer v. Sherrer, 334 U.S. 343, 68 S.Ct. 1087, 92 L.Ed. 1429 (1948).

　[3]See generally Johnson v. Muelberger, 340 U.S. 581, 71 S. Ct. 474, 95 L. Ed. 552 (1951); Sherrer v. Sherrer, 334 U.S. 343, 68 S.Ct. 1087, 92 L.Ed. 1429 (1948).

dant will be barred from collaterally impeaching the divorce decree on jurisdictional grounds in a sister state, at least where a collateral attack would not be permitted under the law of the rendering forum.[1]

The holding in *Williams (II)* was restricted further in *Sherrer v. Sherrer*,[2] where both parties appeared in the original action but did not litigate the matter of domicile. The Supreme Court held that, if the defendant made an appearance in the original proceedings and was afforded "full opportunity" to contest the jurisdictional issue, he is precluded from collaterally impeaching the foreign decree for lack of domicile, unless it is subject to collateral attack in the rendering state.

Relitigation was foreclosed in *Sherrer* even though the divorce court's finding of domicile did not result from a hearing where the issue was actually litigated and determined. The court said that, since the defendant was given full opportunity to contest the matter, if he failed to take advantage of the opportunities afforded him, "the responsibility is his own."[3]

§ 27:61 Full faith and credit—Bilateral decree—Personal claims and obligations

As a general rule, if the non-resident has generally appeared in the foreign action or has otherwise submitted himself to the jurisdiction of the court, he must litigate in the foreign court any matter there in issue. Where the defendant participated in the action, the foreign judgment is res judicata as to all questions existing between the parties arising out of their marital relationship.[1] Under the full faith and credit doctrine, the defendant is bound by the sister state's determination, and he may be foreclosed from relitigating the same claim or cause of action in another jurisdiction.[2]

A corollary of this rule is that a divorce decree rendered by a sister

---

[Section 27:60]

[1]Cook v. Cook, 342 U.S. 126, 72 S. Ct. 157, 96 L. Ed. 146 (1951); Johnson v. Muelberger, 340 U.S. 581, 71 S. Ct. 474, 95 L. Ed. 552 (1951); Coe v. Coe, 334 U.S. 378, 68 S. Ct. 1094, 92 L. Ed. 1451, 1 A.L.R.2d 1376 (1948); Davis v. Davis, 305 U.S. 32, 59 S. Ct. 3, 83 L. Ed. 26, 118 A.L.R. 1518 (1938).

[2]Sherrer v. Sherrer, 334 U.S. 343, 68 S.Ct. 1087, 92 L.Ed. 1429 (1948).

[3]Sherrer v. Sherrer, 334 U.S. 343, 352, 68 S.Ct. 1087, 92 L.Ed. 1429 (1948).

[Section 27:61]

[1]Stephenson v. Stephenson, 54 Ohio App. 239, 6 Ohio Op. 559, 22 Ohio L. Abs. 580, 6 N.E.2d 1005 (8th Dist. Cuyahoga County 1936). See Wood v. Wood, 174 Ohio St. 318, 22 Ohio Op. 2d 378, 189 N.E.2d 54 (1963); Hamilton v. Hamilton, 81 Ohio App. 330, 37 Ohio Op. 183, 49 Ohio L. Abs. 275, 73 N.E.2d 820 (2d Dist. Franklin County 1947); Whitaker v. Whitaker, 52 Ohio App. 223, 6 Ohio Op. 316, 21 Ohio L. Abs. 599, 3 N.E.2d 667 (8th Dist. Cuyahoga County 1936); Johnson v. Muelberger, 340 U.S. 581, 71 S. Ct. 474, 95 L. Ed. 552 (1951).

[2]Wood v. Wood, 174 Ohio St. 318, 22 Ohio Op. 2d 378, 189 N.E.2d 54 (1963); Ashley v. Ashley, 118 Ohio App. 155, 25 Ohio Op. 2d 13, 193 N.E.2d 535 (6th Dist. Lucas County 1962); Hamilton v. Hamilton, 81 Ohio App. 330, 37 Ohio Op. 183, 49 Ohio L. Abs. 275, 73 N.E.2d 820 (2d Dist. Franklin County 1947). See also Weidman v. Weidman, 57 Ohio St. 101, 48 N.E. 506 (1897).

state having personal jurisdiction over the parties and authority over the matters litigated is conclusive and binding as to any personal rights or obligations of the parties that could have been litigated in the proceeding, even if they were not.[3]

Thus, where the sister state had personal jurisdiction over the parties, a non-resident spouse who generally appears in the original divorce will be estopped from later litigating in another state any support or property claim which could have been litigated in the foreign court.[4] Under such circumstances the divisible divorce doctrine may not be invoked in a subsequent suit for support in another jurisdiction.

The foregoing rules extend to any incidental claims that either spouse has against the other which were actually litigated or which could have been litigated in the foreign action.[5] For example, a party may lose the right to enforce spousal support arrearages by failing to vindicate the arrearage claim in a suit for divorce brought by the other spouse in another state.

In *Gilbert v. Gilbert*,[6] a wife, an Ohio resident, had obtained an alimony decree against her husband in this state. The husband left Ohio and failed to comply with the alimony order. Later, the wife entered an appearance in a divorce action which the husband brought against her in another state, and she obtained an alimony award in that proceeding. She then brought suit in Ohio to recover the installments owed under the original alimony decree. The Ohio court ruled that where the wife had submitted her support claims against the husband to the foreign court, she was bound by the judgment of the foreign state and could not collect unpaid arrearages due under the prior Ohio alimony order.

§ 27:62 Full faith and credit—Bilateral decree—Third parties

If the defendant appeared in the original proceeding, a stranger who was not a party, who did not appear in the action, and who has independent interests may be barred from collaterally attacking the decree.

As a general rule, where the original defendant appeared in the divorce action and contested or admitted the issue of the plaintiff's domicile or where he was personally served in the rendering state, a stranger to the proceeding is precluded from attacking the decree collaterally for want of jurisdiction, unless such an attack by the stranger

---

[3]Williams v. Williams, 44 Ohio St. 2d 28, 73 Ohio Op. 2d 121, 336 N.E.2d 426 (1975); Wood v. Wood, 174 Ohio St. 318, 22 Ohio Op. 2d 378, 189 N.E.2d 54 (1963). See Coe v. Coe, 334 U.S. 378, 68 S. Ct. 1094, 92 L. Ed. 1451, 1 A.L.R.2d 1376 (1948); Hasselschwert v. Hasselschwert, 103 Ohio App. 202, 3 Ohio Op. 2d 269, 145 N.E.2d 224 (3d Dist. Defiance County 1956); Whitaker v. Whitaker, 52 Ohio App. 223, 6 Ohio Op. 316, 21 Ohio L. Abs. 599, 3 N.E.2d 667 (8th Dist. Cuyahoga County 1936).

[4]Wood v. Wood, 174 Ohio St. 318, 22 Ohio Op. 2d 378, 189 N.E.2d 54 (1963). See Estin v. Estin, 334 U.S. 541, 68 S. Ct. 1213, 92 L. Ed. 1561, 1 A.L.R.2d 1412 (1948).

[5]Whitaker v. Whitaker, 52 Ohio App. 223, 6 Ohio Op. 316, 21 Ohio L. Abs. 599, 3 N.E.2d 667 (8th Dist. Cuyahoga County 1936). See Gilbert v. Gilbert, 83 Ohio St. 265, 94 N.E. 421 (1911).

[6]Gilbert v. Gilbert, 83 Ohio St. 265, 94 N.E. 421 (1911).

would be permitted in the original forum.[1]

§ 27:63 Full faith and credit—Divisible divorce—Doctrine

The phrase "divisible divorce," as used here, signifies that, under certain circumstances, a divorce judgment of a sister state may only be entitled to partial recognition.[1]

The concept is an accommodation of two jurisdictional principles. It is well established that a court can dissolve a marriage on the basis of inrem jurisdiction if one spouse is domiciled in the forum.[2] However, a court cannot adjudicate a personal claim or obligation, such as spousal support, property division, or parental rights and responsibilities, unless it has jurisdiction over the person of the defendant.[3]

Where a judgment entered by a court lacking personal jurisdiction purports to adjudicate both marital status and personal rights, full faith and credit need be only partially afforded that judgment by another state. Recognition will be given to the foreign court's severance of the marital relationship but not to its disposition of personal rights. The result is to make the divorce divisible.[4] The underlying rationale is that, although the decree is valid insofar as it dissolves the marriage, it is invalid to the extent that it determines a personal claim or obligation.[5]

The doctrine of divisible divorce was first enunciated by the United States Supreme Court in *Estin v. Estin*.[6] In that case, the wife had obtained a New York decree for separation and alimony against the husband. Thereafter, he obtained a divorce in a state in which he was

---

[Section 27:62]

[1]Cook v. Cook, 342 U.S. 126, 72 S. Ct. 157, 96 L. Ed. 146 (1951); Johnson v. Muelberger, 340 U.S. 581, 71 S. Ct. 474, 95 L. Ed. 552 (1951). See Aldrich v. Aldrich, 378 U.S. 540, 84 S. Ct. 1687, 12 L. Ed. 2d 1020 (1964).

[Section 27:63]

[1]See Estin v. Estin, 334 U.S. 541, 68 S. Ct. 1213, 92 L. Ed. 1561, 1 A.L.R.2d 1412 (1948); Armstrong v. Armstrong, 350 U.S. 568, 76 S. Ct. 629, 100 L. Ed. 705, 73 Ohio L. Abs. 514 (1956) (concurring opinion).

[2]Williams v. State of North Carolina, 317 U.S. 287, 63 S. Ct. 207, 87 L. Ed. 279, 143 A.L.R. 1273 (1942); Armstrong v. Armstrong, 99 Ohio App. 7, 58 Ohio Op. 79, 130 N.E.2d 710 (1st Dist. Hamilton County 1954), judgment aff'd, 162 Ohio St. 406, 55 Ohio Op. 234, 123 N.E.2d 267 (1954), cert. granted, 349 U.S. 915, 75 S. Ct. 604, 99 L. Ed. 1248 (1955) and judgment aff'd, 350 U.S. 568, 76 S. Ct. 629, 100 L. Ed. 705, 73 Ohio L. Abs. 514 (1956).

[3]Vanderbilt v. Vanderbilt, 354 U.S. 416, 77 S. Ct. 1360, 1 L. Ed. 2d 1456 (1957); May v. Anderson, 345 U.S. 528, 73 S. Ct. 840, 97 L. Ed. 1221, 67 Ohio L. Abs. 468 (1953); Estin v. Estin, 334 U.S. 541, 68 S. Ct. 1213, 92 L. Ed. 1561, 1 A.L.R.2d 1412 (1948); Pasqualone v. Pasqualone, 63 Ohio St. 2d 96, 17 Ohio Op. 3d 58, 406 N.E.2d 1121 (1980). See Beatrice K. Sowald, *Jurisdiction, Misunderstood and Abused,* 2 Dom. Rel. J. Ohio 49 (July/Aug. 1990).

[4]Estin v. Estin, 334 U.S. 541, 68 S. Ct. 1213, 92 L. Ed. 1561, 1 A.L.R.2d 1412 (1948).

[5]Estin v. Estin, 334 U.S. 541, 68 S. Ct. 1213, 92 L. Ed. 1561, 1 A.L.R.2d 1412 (1948). See Vanderbilt v. Vanderbilt, 354 U.S. 416, 77 S. Ct. 1360, 1 L. Ed. 2d 1456 (1957); Armstrong v. Armstrong, 350 U.S. 568, 76 S. Ct. 629, 100 L. Ed. 705, 73 Ohio L. Abs. 514 (1956).

[6]Estin v. Estin, 334 U.S. 541, 68 S. Ct. 1213, 92 L. Ed. 1561, 1 A.L.R.2d 1412 (1948).

domiciled without personal service on the wife or a personal appearance by her.

The divorce court made no provision for alimony, although it was advised of the New York alimony order. The husband then ceased all payments to the wife. She brought an enforcement action in a New York court, which rejected the husband's contention that the alimony order was terminated by the subsequent divorce decree.

On certiorari, the Supreme Court held that the preexisting order for periodic alimony survived the ex parte divorce granted to the husband. As the court reasoned, sovereign concern for the regularity and integrity of marriage justifies the power of a state in which one spouse is domiciled to alter marital status by an ex parte proceeding. However, the support of the absent spouse is a matter in which her community has a legitimate interest. Moreover, since the state granting the divorce had no personal jurisdiction over the defendant, it had no power to terminate the husband's obligations under the prior order.

The court thus concluded that the divorce was divisible. The foreign decree was effective insofar as it adjudicated marital status, but ineffective on the issue of property rights. Therefore, New York was not bound to give full faith and credit to the alimony phase of the foreign decree, and the survival of the wife's support rights could be determined under New York law.

In *Estin*, the wife's alimony claim had been incorporated into a court order before the divorce was granted. Suppose, however, that the defendant first seeks an order for spousal support or property division after the marriage has been ended by divorce. In *Armstrong v. Armstrong*,[7] decided eight years after *Estin*, Justice Black stated in a concurring opinion that if the divorce court had no personal jurisdiction over the absent spouse, there is no "meaningful distinction" between a spousal support claim that has been reduced to judgment and one that has not.[8]

A majority of the court adopted this view in *Vanderbilt v. Vanderbilt*,[9] which extended the divisible divorce doctrine to inchoate support rights. Prior to their separation, Mr. and Mrs. Vanderbilt were both residents of California. Mrs. Vanderbilt then moved to New York, and her husband moved to Nevada. Mr. Vanderbilt obtained a Nevada divorce upon constructive service, releasing him from all the duties and obligations of matrimony. The wife was not served in Nevada and did not enter an appearance in the divorce proceedings.

Thereafter, Mrs. Vanderbilt instituted a New York action for separation and alimony. Mr. Vanderbilt had property located in the state of New York. New York had not been the marital domicile, and the court had no in personam jurisdiction over Mr. Vanderbilt. However, it sequestered his New York property (under *Pennington v. Fourth*

---

[7]Armstrong v. Armstrong, 350 U.S. 568, 76 S. Ct. 629, 100 L. Ed. 705, 73 Ohio L. Abs. 514 (1956).

[8]Armstrong v. Armstrong, 350 U.S. 568, 577, 76 S. Ct. 629, 100 L. Ed. 705, 73 Ohio L. Abs. 514 (1956).

[9]Vanderbilt v. Vanderbilt, 354 U.S. 416, 77 S. Ct. 1360, 1 L. Ed. 2d 1456 (1957).

National Bank)[10] to satisfy his support obligations, if any, to Mrs. Vanderbilt.

Mr. Vanderbilt entered a limited appearance and contended that the full faith and credit clause required New York to treat the Nevada decree as having ended the marriage and as having discharged any duty of support which he owed to Mrs. Vanderbilt.

The New York court found the Nevada divorce decree valid. It nevertheless ordered the ex-husband to pay alimony to the wife. While recognizing Nevada's dissolution of the marriage, New York thus refused to give full faith and credit to that aspect of the Nevada judgment which terminated support obligations.

The New York decision was upheld by the United States Supreme Court. It was not material, said the court, that no support order against Mr. Vanderbilt had existed prior to the divorce. Since a tribunal cannot adjudicate personal claims or obligations unless it has in personam jurisdiction, the Nevada divorce court had no power to extinguish any right which Mrs. Vanderbilt may have had under the law of New York to financial support from her husband. The Nevada decree was therefore void "to the extent it purported to affect the wife's right to support."[11] Consequently, even if the full faith and credit clause applied to the marriage dissolution, it did not require New York to recognize Nevada's adjudication of the incidents of the marriage dissolution.

In summary, according to the doctrine of divisible divorce, a nonresident defendant's support rights under the law of his domicile are not necessarily terminated by a valid ex parte divorce granted in another state. Although marital status may have been extinguished by the ex parte divorce, the survival of incidental rights and obligations is a matter to be decided under state law. As extended by *Vanderbilt*, this rule obtains even though the support rights have not been incorporated into a judgment before the end of the marital relation. The doctrine also applies, notwithstanding the fact that the defendant's action to enforce spousal claims is brought in a state which had not been marital domicile.[12]

The rationale for the divisible divorce doctrine has been assailed in some quarters.[13] Even Justice Douglas, writing for the majority in *Estin*, acknowledged that the logic behind the concept was less than tidy:

An absolutist might quarrel with the result and demand a rule that once a

---

[10]Pennington v. Fourth Nat. Bank of Cincinnati, Ohio, 243 U.S. 269, 37 S. Ct. 282, 61 L. Ed. 713 (1917).

[11]Vanderbilt v. Vanderbilt, 354 U.S. 416, 419, 77 S. Ct. 1360, 1 L. Ed. 2d 1456 (1957).

[12]The domiciliary state's exertion of jurisdiction over the former divorce plaintiff must, of course, comport with the requirements of due process. Under Shaffer v. Heitner, 433 U.S. 186, 97 S. Ct. 2569, 53 L. Ed. 2d 683 (1977), the minimum contacts standard governs actions quasi in rem as well as in personam.

[13]Vanderbilt v. Vanderbilt, 354 U.S. 416, 77 S. Ct. 1360, 1 L. Ed. 2d 1456 (1957) (Frankfurter, J., dissenting); Rice v. Rice, 336 U.S. 674, 678, 69 S. Ct. 751, 93 L. Ed. 957 (1949) (Jackson, J., dissenting) ("[E]x parte divorce is a concept as perverse and unrealistic as an ex parte marriage."). See *Divisible Divorce*, 76 Harv. L. Rev. 1233 (1963).

divorce is granted, the whole of the marriage relation is dissolved, leaving no roots or tendrils of any kind. But there are few areas of the law in black and white. The greys are dominant and even among them the shades are innumerable. For the eternal problem of the law is one of making accommodations between conflicting interests.[14]

Nonetheless, divisible divorce seems firmly established as a pragmatic adaptation to conflicting interests.[15] In a nation of over fifty jurisdictions, the ex parte divorce is an inevitable legal development.[16] But notions of fundamental fairness proscribe a unilateral disposition of the incidents of marriage. Consequently, under divisible divorce, the cause of action for the termination of marital status and for the determination of rights and obligations arising from that status has been divided,[17] with each part being subject to separate adjudications.

§ 27:64 Full faith and credit—Divisible divorce—Personal claims not adjudicated by ex parte divorce

If the in rem foreign decree does not purport to adjudicate spousal support or property division, resorting to the doctrine of divisible divorce may not be necessary. This was the situation in *Armstrong v. Armstrong*.[1] The husband, a Florida resident, obtained an ex parte divorce from his wife, who resided in Ohio. The Florida decree recited that the wife had not made a claim for relief or a showing of any need for alimony, and therefore no award of alimony would be made to her.

Later, the wife filed suit in Ohio for divorce and alimony. The husband set up the Florida divorce, asserting that that court had denied alimony to the wife. The Ohio court refused to grant a divorce to the wife, finding that Florida had already issued a valid divorce decree to the husband. However, the Ohio court awarded the wife alimony, taking into account the total property owned by the husband.

On certiorari, the United States Supreme Court affirmed. As the majority interpreted the decree, the Florida court did not purport to adjudicate the absent wife's right to alimony but merely asserted that it would not pass on the question. Therefore, in awarding alimony to the wife, Ohio did not fail to give full faith and credit to the Florida judgment. Consequently, the court did not reach the constitutional issue,[2] and the divisible divorce rule did not have to be invoked.

---

[14]Estin v. Estin, 334 U.S. 541, 545, 68 S. Ct. 1213, 92 L. Ed. 1561, 1 A.L.R.2d 1412 (1948).

[15]Estin v. Estin, 334 U.S. 541, 68 S. Ct. 1213, 92 L. Ed. 1561, 1 A.L.R.2d 1412 (1948).

[16]*Divisible Divorce,* 76 Harv. L. Rev. 1233 (1963).

[17]See generally Vanderbilt v. Vanderbilt, 354 U.S. 416, 77 S. Ct. 1360, 1 L. Ed. 2d 1456 (1957) (Frankfurter, J., dissenting).

[Section 27:64]

[1]Armstrong v. Armstrong, 350 U.S. 568, 76 S. Ct. 629, 100 L. Ed. 705, 73 Ohio L. Abs. 514 (1956).

[2]Armstrong v. Armstrong, 350 U.S. 568, 76 S. Ct. 629, 100 L. Ed. 705, 73 Ohio L. Abs. 514 (1956).

§ 27:65 Full faith and credit—Divisible divorce—Appearance by defendant in foreign suit

If the non-resident defendant has generally appeared in the divorce action or has otherwise submitted himself to the jurisdiction of the out-of-state court, he may be precluded from invoking the divisible divorce doctrine. Consistent with the rules of res judicata, a defendant who participates in the proceedings is bound to litigate in the foreign court all matters there in issue. If he was afforded an opportunity to litigate personal claims in the divorce action, he may be barred in a subsequent suit from asserting any right, including support claims, which could have been litigated in the earlier proceeding.[1]

Wood v. Wood[2] demonstrates how a non-resident defendant may lose the opportunity to enforce an inchoate right to alimony. The husband brought a divorce action in Florida, where he was domiciled, and served the wife, an Ohio resident, by publication. The wife filed a general denial in the Florida suit but did not actually appear in the proceedings.

On the same day she filed an answer in the Florida case, the wife also commenced an Ohio divorce action, seeking the husband's real property in Ohio as alimony. The husband filed a motion to dismiss the Ohio action, which was granted by the trial court on the basis of res judicata.

The Supreme Court of Ohio affirmed the trial court's dismissal of the wife's divorce action. It held that the wife's general appearance in the Florida proceedings had submitted her person to the jurisdiction of that court. She was therefore estopped in the Ohio action from litigating any matter, including her right to support, which could have been litigated in the Florida proceeding.

The result in *Wood* can be avoided. If a spouse has instituted a divorce action in another state, there are several ways for the spouse residing in Ohio to preserve support claims. First, he may enter an appearance (thus foregoing the right to relitigate the jurisdictional question) and move to enforce his spousal support and property rights in the foreign court. A second but potentially dangerous alternative is to ignore the foreign proceeding and later seek to relitigate its validity under more favorable conditions. Another alternative, to protect against a court's making an order beyond a termination of marriage, is entering an appearance for the sole purpose of challenging the court's jurisdiction over the person.[3] Finally, if the state where the defendant resides recognizes the divisible divorce doctrine (as does Ohio), the defendant may concede

---

[Section 27:65]

[1]Wood v. Wood, 174 Ohio St. 318, 22 Ohio Op. 2d 378, 189 N.E.2d 54 (1963); Weidman v. Weidman, 57 Ohio St. 101, 48 N.E. 506 (1897). See also Sherrer v. Sherrer, 334 U.S. 343, 68 S.Ct. 1087, 92 L.Ed. 1429 (1948); Coe v. Coe, 334 U.S. 378, 68 S. Ct. 1094, 92 L. Ed. 1451, 1 A.L.R.2d 1376 (1948); Estin v. Estin, 334 U.S. 541, 68 S. Ct. 1213, 92 L. Ed. 1561, 1 A.L.R.2d 1412 (1948).

[2]Wood v. Wood, 174 Ohio St. 318, 22 Ohio Op. 2d 378, 189 N.E.2d 54 (1963).

[3]Civ. R. 12(B).

the divorce and proceed to vindicate support claims in his own domicile.[4]

§ 27:66 Full faith and credit—Divisible divorce—Alimony or spousal support

Ohio courts, even prior to the *Estin* and *Vanderbilt* decisions, have held that support rights survive an ex parte decree. The Ohio Supreme Court first decided this question in the 1869 case of *Cox v. Cox*.[1] The issue presented was whether a valid divorce decree, obtained without personal jurisdiction over the wife, could defeat her rights to alimony and support. The court reasoned that a foreign state which lacks personal jurisdiction over the defendant has no power to adjudicate the question of alimony. Accordingly, it held that the foreign decree was not entitled to recognition beyond its dissolution of the marriage, and that a subsequent alimony action could be maintained by the defendant in this state. It is not essential to the allowance of alimony, explained the court, that the marriage relation exist up to the time it is granted.

Many Ohio decisions subsequent to *Cox* have reiterated this principle.[2] In fact, in *Armstrong v. Armstrong*,[3] the United States Supreme Court expressly recognized that Ohio case law authorizes the prosecution of an alimony action after a marriage has been terminated by a valid ex parte decree.

§ 27:67 Full faith and credit—Divisible divorce—Property and custody rights

Aside from spousal support, other incidents of marriage, such as the right to custody and property division, have been protected by the divisible divorce doctrine.[1] For example, Ohio courts have held that where a spouse has obtained a valid ex parte divorce from an Ohio resident after

---

[4]*Divisible Divorce,* 76 Harv. L. Rev. 1233 (1963).

[Section 27:66]

[1]Cox v. Cox, 19 Ohio St. 502, 1869 WL 84 (1869).

[2]Armstrong v. Armstrong, 162 Ohio St. 406, 55 Ohio Op. 234, 123 N.E.2d 267 (1954), cert. granted, 349 U.S. 915, 75 S. Ct. 604, 99 L. Ed. 1248 (1955) and judgment aff'd, 350 U.S. 568, 76 S. Ct. 629, 100 L. Ed. 705, 73 Ohio L. Abs. 514 (1956); Slapp v. Slapp, 143 Ohio St. 105, 28 Ohio Op. 47, 54 N.E.2d 153 (1944); Woods v. Waddle, 44 Ohio St. 449, 8 N.E. 297 (1886); Hasselschwert v. Hasselschwert, 103 Ohio App. 202, 3 Ohio Op. 2d 269, 145 N.E.2d 224 (3d Dist. Defiance County 1956); Wick v. Wick, 58 Ohio App. 72, 11 Ohio Op. 463, 15 N.E.2d 780 (2d Dist. Montgomery County 1938); Linck v. Linck, 31 Ohio Misc. 224, 60 Ohio Op. 2d 388, 288 N.E.2d 347 (C.P. 1972); Melnyk v. Melnyk, 49 Ohio Op. 22, 66 Ohio L. Abs. 102, 107 N.E.2d 549 (C.P. 1952); Harrison v. Harrison, 214 F.2d 571, 70 Ohio L. Abs. 252 (4th Cir. 1954); Rousculp v. Rousculp, 17 Ohio App. 2d 101, 46 Ohio Op. 2d 125, 244 N.E.2d 512 (10th Dist. Franklin County 1968); Davis v. Davis, 80 Ohio L. Abs. 303, 156 N.E.2d 494 (C.P. 1959).

[3]Armstrong v. Armstrong, 350 U.S. 568, 76 S. Ct. 629, 100 L. Ed. 705, 73 Ohio L. Abs. 514 (1956).

[Section 27:67]

[1]May v. Anderson, 345 U.S. 528, 73 S. Ct. 840, 97 L. Ed. 1221, 67 Ohio L. Abs. 468 (1953); Slapp v. Slapp, 143 Ohio St. 105, 28 Ohio Op. 47, 54 N.E.2d 153 (1944); Rousculp v. Rousculp, 17 Ohio App. 2d 101, 46 Ohio Op. 2d 125, 244 N.E.2d 512 (10th Dist. Fran-

constructive service in another state, the Ohio resident may thereafter maintain an action in this state to determine the property rights of the parties and for a division of their property.[2]

Real property rights, such as dower, have been treated in similar fashion. Although an ex parte decree may terminate the marriage, a divorce obtained without personal jurisdiction over the defendant spouse has been deemed not to extinguish the defendant's right to dower in Ohio realty or affect his right to property located in Ohio.[3]

Notions of fundamental fairness have been advanced to justify permitting a subsequent action for division of property. As stated by the Ohio Supreme Court in *Slapp v. Slapp*,[4] where one spouse has obtained an ex parte divorce in another state, to relegate the non-resident defendant to a subsequent decree for alimony alone, thus depriving her of an equitable division of marital property, while the divorce plaintiff enjoys the status of a foreign marriage dissolution, would work a fraud and injustice on the non-resident spouse.

§ 27:68   Full faith and credit—Divisible divorce—Divorce plaintiff brings subsequent action

Suppose that the ex parte divorce was initiated by the same spouse who then files a subsequent spousal support or property division action. Most Ohio courts have concluded that the consequences of the fact that the complaining party was the plaintiff in the divorce action depend upon whether the court granting the divorce had the power to adjudicate personal claims. If the divorce court lacked in personam authority over the defendant, the spouse who obtained the divorce has ordinarily been permitted to maintain a subsequent action for spousal support and property division.[1]

It has been held, for example, that if a wife receives a valid divorce in another state having no personal jurisdiction over the non-resident

---

klin County 1968); Wick v. Wick, 58 Ohio App. 72, 11 Ohio Op. 463, 15 N.E.2d 780 (2d Dist. Montgomery County 1938); Davis v. Davis, 80 Ohio L. Abs. 303, 156 N.E.2d 494 (C.P. 1959). See also Ex parte Elliott, 114 Ohio App. 533, 20 Ohio Op. 2d 85, 183 N.E.2d 804 (10th Dist. Franklin County 1961). The interstate adjudication of custody matters is now governed by the Uniform Child Custody Jurisdiction Act. See Uniform Child Custody Jurisdiction Act; Parental Kidnapping Prevention Act; International Child Abduction Remedies Act Ch 17.

[2]Slapp v. Slapp, 143 Ohio St. 105, 28 Ohio Op. 47, 54 N.E.2d 153 (1944); Wick v. Wick, 58 Ohio App. 72, 11 Ohio Op. 463, 15 N.E.2d 780 (2d Dist. Montgomery County 1938). See also Rousculp v. Rousculp, 17 Ohio App. 2d 101, 46 Ohio Op. 2d 125, 244 N.E.2d 512 (10th Dist. Franklin County 1968).

[3]Doerr v. Forsythe, 50 Ohio St. 726, 35 N.E. 1055 (1893); Snyder v. Buckeye State Bldg. & Loan Co., 26 Ohio App. 166, 6 Ohio L. Abs. 203, 160 N.E. 37 (4th Dist. Pickaway County 1927). See Melnyk v. Melnyk, 49 Ohio Op. 22, 66 Ohio L. Abs. 102, 107 N.E.2d 549 (C.P. 1952).

[4]Slapp v. Slapp, 143 Ohio St. 105, 28 Ohio Op. 47, 54 N.E.2d 153 (1944).

[Section 27:68]

[1]Weidman v. Weidman, 57 Ohio St. 101, 48 N.E. 506 (1897); Hasselschwert v. Hasselschwert, 103 Ohio App. 202, 3 Ohio Op. 2d 269, 145 N.E.2d 224 (3d Dist. Defiance County 1956).

husband, she may thereafter maintain a spousal support or property division action against the husband in a jurisdiction in which he resides or has property.[2]

This test has been applied even where the divorce and the subsequent spousal support or property division action were filed in the same state.[3] For instance, an alimony action was instituted in Ohio by a spouse who had earlier obtained a divorce after service by publication in this state. At the time the divorce was granted, the defendant's whereabouts were unknown to the plaintiff and the court had no jurisdiction over his person or property. The court said that it made no difference whether the divorce was granted in the same forum or another forum, since the criterion was whether the question of alimony could have been determined by the court granting the divorce.[4]

In a similar case, at the time the husband obtained the original divorce, the wife did not own any property which could have been brought within the jurisdiction of the court and was not amenable to personal service. In a subsequent alimony action by the husband, the court determined that the original divorce decree was not res judicata as to the husband's alimony claims against his wife, because the divorce court had no authority to pass on the question of alimony. Accordingly, the husband was permitted to recover alimony out of property belonging to the former wife.[5]

The outcome is different, however, where the spouse seeking spousal support or property division has obtained a divorce in a forum having personal jurisdiction over the defendant. Consistent with the rules of res judicata, an in personam divorce decree bars a subsequent action for spousal support or property division.[6] It also extinguishes any preexisting order for spousal support or property division rendered in Ohio.[7] Furthermore, the foreign decree is binding as to all questions which could have been litigated as well as those which actually were litigated.

[2]Woods v. Waddle, 44 Ohio St. 449, 8 N.E. 297 (1886); Stephenson v. Stephenson, 54 Ohio App. 239, 6 Ohio Op. 559, 22 Ohio L. Abs. 580, 6 N.E.2d 1005 (8th Dist. Cuyahoga County 1936).

[3]Hasselschwert v. Hasselschwert, 103 Ohio App. 202, 3 Ohio Op. 2d 269, 145 N.E.2d 224 (3d Dist. Defiance County 1956); Wick v. Wick, 58 Ohio App. 72, 11 Ohio Op. 463, 15 N.E.2d 780 (2d Dist. Montgomery County 1938); Stephenson v. Stephenson, 54 Ohio App. 239, 6 Ohio Op. 559, 22 Ohio L. Abs. 580, 6 N.E.2d 1005 (8th Dist. Cuyahoga County 1936).

[4]Stephenson v. Stephenson, 54 Ohio App. 239, 6 Ohio Op. 559, 22 Ohio L. Abs. 580, 6 N.E.2d 1005 (8th Dist. Cuyahoga County 1936). See generally Cox v. Cox, 19 Ohio St. 502, 1869 WL 84 (1869).

[5]Hasselschwert v. Hasselschwert, 103 Ohio App. 202, 3 Ohio Op. 2d 269, 145 N.E.2d 224 (3d Dist. Defiance County 1956).

[6]Weidman v. Weidman, 57 Ohio St. 101, 48 N.E. 506 (1897). See Stephenson v. Stephenson, 54 Ohio App. 239, 6 Ohio Op. 559, 22 Ohio L. Abs. 580, 6 N.E.2d 1005 (8th Dist. Cuyahoga County 1936). But see Metzger v. Metzger, 32 Ohio App. 202, 7 Ohio L. Abs. 298, 167 N.E. 690 (4th Dist. Pickaway County 1929).

[7]Whitaker v. Whitaker, 52 Ohio App. 223, 6 Ohio Op. 316, 21 Ohio L. Abs. 599, 3 N.E.2d 667 (8th Dist. Cuyahoga County 1936). See Gilbert v. Gilbert, 83 Ohio St. 265, 94 N.E. 421 (1911).

Therefore, if the plaintiff fails to ask for spousal support or property division or to bring existing orders to the foreign court's attention, he will be deemed to have waived such claims including those for due and unpaid installments.[8]

§ 27:69 Full faith and credit—Divisible divorce—Grounds requirements

Ohio courts have said that in order to maintain an action for spousal support or property division after an ex parte divorce has been granted, the plaintiff must make a proper showing of grounds.[1] In a typical case, the plaintiff files an action for divorce or spousal support, attacking the foreign decree on the basis of domicile. Even where the court upholds the foreign decree, it may nevertheless grant the plaintiff incidental relief if evidence is presented to sustain grounds for divorce or spousal support. As explained by the Ohio Supreme Court, if the evidence warrants the granting of a divorce and spousal support to the plaintiff, except for the fact that the defendant has already procured a foreign divorce, the court has jurisdiction to determine the property rights of the parties just as though it had granted a divorce to the plaintiff.[2]

At least one appellate court has adopted the position that the plaintiff is entitled to maintain a subsequent spousal support action solely by virtue of the fact that the defendant has obtained a foreign divorce.[3] In *Rousculp v. Rousculp*,[4] the trial court upheld the validity of a foreign divorce previously obtained by the husband yet granted the wife custody, support, and property division. On appeal, the husband argued that the trial court lacked authority to give relief to the wife because she had failed to prove grounds.[5]

The court of appeals agreed that the wife had not established grounds for alimony only under RC 3105.17 or for divorce under RC 3105.01. Nevertheless, the appeals court applied a seldom used ground for divorce to justify the trial court's award to the wife. RC 3105.01(I) provides that a court may grant a divorce where one of the parties procures "a divorce outside this state . . . by virtue of which the party who procured it is released from the obligations of the marriage, while those obligations

---

[8]Whitaker v. Whitaker, 52 Ohio App. 223, 6 Ohio Op. 316, 21 Ohio L. Abs. 599, 3 N.E.2d 667 (8th Dist. Cuyahoga County 1936).

[Section 27:69]

[1]Slapp v. Slapp, 143 Ohio St. 105, 28 Ohio Op. 47, 54 N.E.2d 153 (1944).

[2]Slapp v. Slapp, 143 Ohio St. 105, 28 Ohio Op. 47, 54 N.E.2d 153 (1944).

[3]Linck v. Linck, 31 Ohio Misc. 224, 60 Ohio Op. 2d 388, 288 N.E.2d 347 (C.P. 1972), citing Rousculp v. Rousculp, 17 Ohio App. 2d 101, 46 Ohio Op. 2d 125, 244 N.E.2d 512 (10th Dist. Franklin County 1968).

[4]Rousculp v. Rousculp, 17 Ohio App. 2d 101, 46 Ohio Op. 2d 125, 244 N.E.2d 512 (10th Dist. Franklin County 1968).

[5]Although *Rousculp* involved the decree of a foreign nation, full faith and credit principles were applied by the court to resolve the issues presented. The decision has been cited with approval by other Ohio courts in connection with sister state decrees. See Linck v. Linck, 31 Ohio Misc. 224, 60 Ohio Op. 2d 388, 288 N.E.2d 347 (C.P. 1972).

remain binding upon the other party." Although changes in the concept of full faith and credit have made this provision an anomaly, the intent of the Ohio General Assembly at the time of its adoption was, according to the court, that the statute contemplated a divorce granted one spouse by a foreign state which had not obtained personal jurisdiction over the other spouse.

The court found that this ground for divorce had been established by the evidence. Accordingly, it concluded that the trial court had the power under RC 3105.18 to grant subsequent relief to the wife.

§ 27:70   Full faith and credit—Res judicata—Relationship to full faith and credit

The United States Supreme Court has explained that one of the functions of the full faith and credit clause is to avoid the relitigation in other states of adjudicated issues.[1] Accordingly, the doctrine of res judicata, as a bar and as a collateral estoppel, applies fully to a final judgment of a foreign court having jurisdiction of the parties and the matters litigated.[2] Full faith and credit requires each state to give to a judgment at least the res judicata effect which the judgment would be accorded in the rendering forum.[3] Thus, a state must enforce a foreign divorce by barring each party who was personally served, who appeared in the original proceeding, and his privies, from collaterally attacking the decree, at least where the assailant could not collaterally attack the judgment in the original forum.[4]

§ 27:71   Full faith and credit—Res judicata—Nonjurisdictional questions

As a general rule, if a cause of action is adjudicated by a sister state court having jurisdiction, res judicata operates as a bar to the relitigation of a subsequent action upon the same claim, demand, or cause of action in another state between the same parties or those in privity with them under full faith and credit.[1] If the same material fact or issue arises in two different causes of action, and if such fact or issue was

---

[Section 27:70]

[1]Sutton v. Leib, 342 U.S. 402, 72 S. Ct. 398, 96 L. Ed. 448 (1952).

[2]See Johnson v. Muelberger, 340 U.S. 581, 71 S. Ct. 474, 95 L. Ed. 552 (1951); Sistare v. Sistare, 218 U.S. 1, 30 S. Ct. 682, 54 L. Ed. 905 (1910); Gilbert v. Gilbert, 83 Ohio St. 265, 94 N.E. 421 (1911); Am. Jur. 2d, Divorce and Separation § 949.

[3]Durfee v. Duke, 375 U.S. 106, 84 S. Ct. 242, 11 L. Ed. 2d 186 (1963); Aldrich v. Aldrich, 378 U.S. 540, 84 S. Ct. 1687, 12 L. Ed. 2d 1020 (1964).

[4]Johnson v. Muelberger, 340 U.S. 581, 71 S. Ct. 474, 95 L. Ed. 552 (1951).

[Section 27:71]

[1]Am. Jur. 2d, Divorce and Separation § 949. See also Whitehead v. General Tel. Co., 20 Ohio St. 2d 108, 49 Ohio Op. 2d 435, 254 N.E.2d 10, 41 A.L.R.3d 526 (1969) (overruled by, Grava v. Parkman Twp., 1995 -Ohio- 331, 73 Ohio St. 3d 379, 653 N.E.2d 226 (1995)); Norwood v. McDonald, 142 Ohio St. 299, 27 Ohio Op. 240, 52 N.E.2d 67 (1943) (overruled by, Grava v. Parkman Twp., 1995 -Ohio- 331, 73 Ohio St. 3d 379, 653 N.E.2d 226 (1995)).

actually litigated and determined in the former action by a court of competent jurisdiction, the first adjudication is deemed conclusive and the parties and their privies are estopped from relitigating the fact or issue.[2]

It has been held, for example, that where a divorce is obtained by the husband after service by publication and bars the non-resident wife from alimony and any right in the husband's property, res judicata precludes the wife from prosecuting an action for alimony and division of property in her home state after she has unsuccessfully instituted a separate action to vacate the decree and obtain alimony in the state where the decree was rendered.[3] Also, a finding of paternity made in a support proceeding between the same parties in a sister state has been adjudged conclusive on the issue of adultery, as well as paternity, in their subsequent Ohio divorce action.[4]

In a later action involving the same claim or cause of action in another state, res judicata as a bar applies to those issues which could have been litigated in the foreign proceeding, as well as to those which were actually litigated.[5] A party is bound by the original decree, regardless of whether he actually availed himself of the opportunity to litigate the question in the sister state.[6]

For example, a divorce action was initiated in the state of the husband's domicile. The non-resident wife, after being served by publication, filed an answer denying the allegations in the complaint but requested no affirmative relief. The foreign court granted a divorce to the husband, although it did not award alimony to the wife. The wife's subsequent suit for divorce and alimony in the state of her residence was dismissed by the court, on the basis that the foreign decree was conclusive of the wife's right to support. The court said that the plaintiff was estopped from relitigating any issue which could have been litigated

---

[2]Am. Jur. 2d, Divorce and Separation § 949. See Aldrich v. Aldrich, 378 U.S. 540, 84 S. Ct. 1687, 12 L. Ed. 2d 1020 (1964); Ashley v. Ashley, 118 Ohio App. 155, 25 Ohio Op. 2d 13, 193 N.E.2d 535 (6th Dist. Lucas County 1962). See also Johnson v. Norman, 66 Ohio St. 2d 186, 20 Ohio Op. 3d 196, 421 N.E.2d 124 (1981); Whitehead v. General Tel. Co., 20 Ohio St. 2d 108, 49 Ohio Op. 2d 435, 254 N.E.2d 10, 41 A.L.R.3d 526 (1969) (overruled by, Grava v. Parkman Twp., 1995 -Ohio- 331, 73 Ohio St. 3d 379, 653 N.E.2d 226 (1995)).

[3]Hamilton v. Hamilton, 81 Ohio App. 330, 37 Ohio Op. 183, 49 Ohio L. Abs. 275, 73 N.E.2d 820 (2d Dist. Franklin County 1947).

[4]Ashley v. Ashley, 118 Ohio App. 155, 25 Ohio Op. 2d 13, 193 N.E.2d 535 (6th Dist. Lucas County 1962).

[5]Aldrich v. Aldrich, 378 U.S. 540, 84 S. Ct. 1687, 12 L. Ed. 2d 1020 (1964); Johnson v. Muelberger, 340 U.S. 581, 71 S. Ct. 474, 95 L. Ed. 552 (1951); Sherrer v. Sherrer, 334 U.S. 343, 68 S.Ct. 1087, 92 L.Ed. 1429 (1948); Wood v. Wood, 174 Ohio St. 318, 22 Ohio Op. 2d 378, 189 N.E.2d 54 (1963); Gilbert v. Gilbert, 83 Ohio St. 265, 94 N.E. 421 (1911); Whitaker v. Whitaker, 52 Ohio App. 223, 6 Ohio Op. 316, 21 Ohio L. Abs. 599, 3 N.E.2d 667 (8th Dist. Cuyahoga County 1936).

[6]Johnson v. Muelberger, 340 U.S. 581, 71 S. Ct. 474, 95 L. Ed. 552 (1951); Sherrer v. Sherrer, 334 U.S. 343, 68 S.Ct. 1087, 92 L.Ed. 1429 (1948); Coe v. Coe, 334 U.S. 378, 68 S. Ct. 1094, 92 L. Ed. 1451, 1 A.L.R.2d 1376 (1948); Southard v. Southard, 305 F.2d 730 (2d Cir. 1962); Wood v. Wood, 174 Ohio St. 318, 22 Ohio Op. 2d 378, 189 N.E.2d 54 (1963).

in the foreign divorce action.[7]

In the preceding example, the foreign court originally lacked jurisdiction to determine the non-resident's spousal support rights. However, by entering a general appearance, the defendant submitted her person to the jurisdiction of the divorce court, conferring authority on that court to adjudicate her personal rights and obligations. The judgment of the foreign court, which has thus acquired personal authority over the parties and which has jurisdiction of the controversy, is res judicata as to all matters in issue, including the parties' personal claims and obligations.[8]

Another aspect of res judicata is that the final judgment of a sister state may be conclusive as to the parties and their privies, even though the decision is patently erroneous under the laws of the rendering forum. As a general rule, where a court of competent jurisdiction renders an erroneous judgment which is final and unreversed, the judgment must be afforded the same validity and effect by a sister state as it has in the rendering forum.

For example, a divorce decree which was granted by a Florida court made alimony payments a charge on the husband's estate, even though such an award was not proper under Florida law. The husband died intestate in West Virginia, which refused full faith and credit on the basis that the decree was invalid in Florida.

The Supreme Court reversed, relying on Florida's certification that, since the husband had failed to appeal, the judgment had become final and was not subject to collateral attack in Florida. As a result, the Florida judgment was held binding on the husband and on those whom Florida law considers to be in privity with him.[9]

§ 27:72 Full faith and credit—Res judicata—Authority of forum

It is well settled that res judicata does not bar relitigation of a sister state's determination of personal claims or obligations where the foreign court had no jurisdiction to pass on these questions.[1] For example, an ex parte divorce rendered by another state is not conclusive as to any right which the non-resident defendant has under the law of his domicile to

---

[7]Wood v. Wood, 174 Ohio St. 318, 22 Ohio Op. 2d 378, 189 N.E.2d 54 (1963).

[8]Wood v. Wood, 174 Ohio St. 318, 22 Ohio Op. 2d 378, 189 N.E.2d 54 (1963).

[9]Aldrich v. Aldrich, 378 U.S. 540, 84 S. Ct. 1687, 12 L. Ed. 2d 1020 (1964). See Johnson v. Muelberger, 340 U.S. 581, 71 S. Ct. 474, 95 L. Ed. 552 (1951); Southard v. Southard, 305 F.2d 730 (2d Cir. 1962).

[Section 27:72]

[1]Armstrong v. Armstrong, 162 Ohio St. 406, 55 Ohio Op. 234, 123 N.E.2d 267 (1954), cert. granted, 349 U.S. 915, 75 S. Ct. 604, 99 L. Ed. 1248 (1955) and judgment aff'd, 350 U.S. 568, 76 S. Ct. 629, 100 L. Ed. 705, 73 Ohio L. Abs. 514 (1956); Woods v. Waddle, 44 Ohio St. 449, 8 N.E. 297 (1886). See *Divisible Divorce,* 76 Harv. L. Rev. 1233 (1963).

spousal support or division of property.[2] This result obtains even if support rights do not survive an ex parte divorce under the laws of the rendering forum.[3]

A corollary of this rule is that a spouse who has obtained a valid divorce in a state having no personal jurisdiction over the defendant may maintain a subsequent action for spousal support and property division in another jurisdiction where the defendant resides or has property. The original divorce is not res judicata as to spousal support and property rights because the divorce court had no authority to adjudicate personal claims.[4]

In contrast, regardless of whether the issue of spousal support was actually litigated, if the divorce was granted by a state having personal jurisdiction over the defendant, res judicata bars a subsequent action for spousal support or for enforcement of a preexisting spousal support decree.[5]

§ 27:73   Full faith and credit—Res judicata—Jurisdictional questions

Res judicata also applies to sister state adjudications of jurisdiction over the person and subject matter.[1] As a general rule, a finding by a foreign court that it has jurisdiction, after actual litigation of the question, is conclusive on the parties in the divorcing state and, under full faith and credit, in other states as well.

For example, in *Davis v. Davis*,[2] an out-of-state resident appeared in a Virginia divorce action brought by her husband and challenged the court's jurisdiction by asserting that the plaintiff was not domiciled in the state. The Virginia court decided that it had jurisdiction and granted a divorce. The wife did not appeal the court's ruling, but in a later proceeding elsewhere she attempted to assert that the Virginia decree was void for lack of domicile.

On certiorari, the United States Supreme Court held that the issue of domicile was res judicata. The "*Davis* rule," as it has come to be known, is that, after actual litigation of the issue of domicile in the foreign

---

[2]Vanderbilt v. Vanderbilt, 354 U.S. 416, 77 S. Ct. 1360, 1 L. Ed. 2d 1456 (1957); Estin v. Estin, 334 U.S. 541, 68 S. Ct. 1213, 92 L. Ed. 1561, 1 A.L.R.2d 1412 (1948); Slapp v. Slapp, 143 Ohio St. 105, 28 Ohio Op. 47, 54 N.E.2d 153 (1944).

[3]Estin v. Estin, 334 U.S. 541, 68 S. Ct. 1213, 92 L. Ed. 1561, 1 A.L.R.2d 1412 (1948).

[4]Hasselschwert v. Hasselschwert, 103 Ohio App. 202, 3 Ohio Op. 2d 269, 145 N.E.2d 224 (3d Dist. Defiance County 1956). See Stephenson v. Stephenson, 54 Ohio App. 239, 6 Ohio Op. 559, 22 Ohio L. Abs. 580, 6 N.E.2d 1005 (8th Dist. Cuyahoga County 1936).

[5]Gilbert v. Gilbert, 83 Ohio St. 265, 94 N.E. 421 (1911); Whitaker v. Whitaker, 52 Ohio App. 223, 6 Ohio Op. 316, 21 Ohio L. Abs. 599, 3 N.E.2d 667 (8th Dist. Cuyahoga County 1936). See also Weidman v. Weidman, 57 Ohio St. 101, 48 N.E. 506 (1897).

[Section 27:73]

[1]Sherrer v. Sherrer, 334 U.S. 343, 68 S.Ct. 1087, 92 L.Ed. 1429 (1948). See Johnson v. Muelberger, 340 U.S. 581, 71 S. Ct. 474, 95 L. Ed. 552 (1951); Winkler v. Stowe, 1997 WL 30947 (Ohio Ct. App. 4th Dist. Jackson County 1997), dismissed, appeal not allowed, 78 Ohio St. 3d 1512, 679 N.E.2d 308 (1997).

[2]Davis v. Davis, 305 U.S. 32, 59 S. Ct. 3, 83 L. Ed. 26, 118 A.L.R. 1518 (1938).

court, if a decree is rendered with a finding of domicile, the decree is entitled to full faith and credit and cannot be collaterally questioned in another state.

Res judicata applies equally to a collateral proceeding in which jurisdictional issues are litigated and determined. In one case, an ex parte divorce was obtained by the plaintiff upon a finding of domicile. The defendant later brought a collateral action in Connecticut attacking the divorce on jurisdictional grounds. The Connecticut court, having jurisdiction to decide the question, determined that the divorce decree was void. The original plaintiff did not appeal this judgment but filed another action in a third court, asserting that Connecticut unconstitutionally failed to give full faith and credit to the ex parte decree.

On appeal, the action was dismissed on the basis that Connecticut's determination was res judicata between the parties: "The appellant's opportunity to attack the Connecticut decree on the merits died with his failure to appeal, unless the laws of that jurisdiction afford some opportunity to reopen the proceedings there."[3]

As a result, the appellate court held that it was precluded from considering not only the constitutional question, but also the alleged denial of various procedural rights by the Connecticut court.

Consistent with the foregoing rules, the non-resident defendant may be able to choose whether to make a direct attack in the divorce state or a collateral attack elsewhere. If the defendant litigates the jurisdictional question in the divorce court and loses, under the ruling in *Davis* the court's decision upholding the decree is res judicata when the defendant tries to raise the issue in a subsequent collateral proceeding.

If the defendant ignores the foreign action and litigates the jurisdictional question for the first time in a collateral proceeding and the decree is held valid (or void), the ruling of the court in the collateral proceeding will be conclusive between the parties on a second collateral attack.[4]

Res judicata has been extended to the situation where a party had, but did not use, a "full opportunity" to litigate jurisdictional issues. In *Sherrer v. Sherrer*,[5] a non-resident defendant received notice by mail of Florida divorce proceedings instituted by his wife, who had left the state of their marital domicile ninety days earlier. The wife's complaint had alleged that she was a bona fide resident of Florida. The husband, who was represented by counsel throughout the proceeding, filed an answer and entered a general appearance. He personally appeared and testified at the Florida hearing.

The United States Supreme Court said that the husband was foreclosed from relitigating the validity of the decree. It established that, where the defendant participated in the divorce proceedings, was afforded full opportunity to contest the jurisdictional issues, and where the decree was not susceptible to such a collateral attack in the granting

---

[3]Southard v. Southard, 305 F.2d 730, 732 (2d Cir. 1962).

[4]Am. Jur. 2d, Divorce and Separation § 972.

[5]Sherrer v. Sherrer, 334 U.S. 343, 68 S.Ct. 1087, 92 L.Ed. 1429 (1948).

state, full faith and credit prevents the defendant from collaterally impeaching the decree on jurisdictional grounds in a sister state.

The court explicitly distinguished the judicial re-examination of jurisdictional facts permitted in *Williams (II)*. The court said that *Williams (II)* involved an ex parte proceeding, whereas the finding of jurisdictional facts made by the Florida court involved a hearing in which Mr. Sherrer appeared and participated.[6] Due process, said the court, does not require that a party be afforded a "second opportunity" to litigate jurisdictional facts.[7]

§ 27:74 Full faith and credit—Third parties

A third party who did not appear in the original proceeding and who has independent interests may nevertheless be barred from collaterally attacking the decree on jurisdictional grounds, if both spouses appeared in the original proceeding.

In *Cook v. Cook*,[1] the wife's second husband brought an action for annulment of their marriage on the ground that his wife was not a bona fide domiciliary of the state where she had obtained a divorce from her first husband. When the case reached the Supreme Court, there was no finding in the record as to whether the wife's first husband had made an appearance in the divorce case, either generally or specially, to contest the jurisdictional issue. Stating that the vulnerability of the divorce decree to a collateral attack by the second husband depended upon the first husband's participation in the original proceeding, the court remanded the case for a determination of whether the defendant had appeared or had been personally served in the divorce action.

The court set forth two rules that govern the collateral impeachment of a foreign divorce by a stranger to the judgment. If the defendant spouse has been personally served or has appeared in the original divorce action and contested the issue of the plaintiff's domicile, or has appeared and admitted domicile, a third party to the action is barred from collaterally attacking the decree, unless under the law of the divorcing state the issue of jurisdiction would not be res judicata as to the third party.

Conversely, under the ruling in *Williams (II)*, if the defendant spouse had neither appeared nor been personally served in the original proceeding, a stranger could reopen the issue of domicile in a collateral attack on the foreign judgment.

The right of a child to attack the validity of a parent's divorce was

---

[6]Sherrer v. Sherrer, 334 U.S. 343, 68 S.Ct. 1087, 92 L.Ed. 1429 (1948); Williams v. State of N. C., 325 U.S. 226, 65 S. Ct. 1092, 89 L. Ed. 1577, 157 A.L.R. 1366 (1945). See Rice v. Rice, 336 U.S. 674, 69 S. Ct. 751, 93 L. Ed. 957 (1949).

[7]Sherrer v. Sherrer, 334 U.S. 343, 348, 68 S.Ct. 1087, 92 L.Ed. 1429 (1948).

[Section 27:74]
[1]Cook v. Cook, 342 U.S. 126, 72 S. Ct. 157, 96 L. Ed. 146 (1951).

considered in *Johnson v. Muelberger*.[2] In a New York probate proceeding, the deceased husband's daughter and sole legatee attempted to collaterally impeach a Florida divorce obtained against her father by his former wife. The decedent, a New York resident, had filed a general denial through counsel in his wife's Florida divorce action but had not contested the wife's domicile. In the New York proceeding, it was undisputed that the decedent's wife had not complied with Florida residency requirements in bringing the divorce.

However, the Supreme Court held that the husband's daughter was barred from collaterally attacking the divorce decree as beyond the jurisdiction of the Florida court, because she would not be permitted to question the decree collaterally under Florida law. Since the original parties had the opportunity to contest the jurisdictional issues in the divorce court, the Florida residency requirement as a jurisdictional basis for the Florida divorce was "no longer open as an issue."[3]

A foreign decree may be conclusive as to some questions, such as marital status, but not others, such as a stranger's rights or duties incident to the decree. Although an out-of-state divorce may be binding upon a stranger, as to the marital status of the husband and wife, another state may apply its own laws to decide what effect the marital dissolution has upon the stranger's obligations.

The duty of a former husband to pay alimony after a foreign court has annulled his wife's subsequent marriage was the subject of *Sutton v. Leib*.[4] The wife had obtained an Illinois divorce decree requiring Leib to pay her alimony for so long as she remained unmarried. She later went to Nevada and married Henzel. Henzel's Nevada divorce from his first wife was subsequently declared void in a New York proceeding, which Henzel unsuccessfully defended. On this basis, the wife obtained an annulment of her marriage to Henzel in a New York action in which both she and Henzel appeared.

Later, the wife instituted diversity proceedings against her first husband Leib to collect alimony installments due after her second marriage was declared a nullity. The lower courts decided in favor of Leib on the theory that, since the wife's marriage to Henzel was valid in Nevada, it was entitled to full faith and credit in Illinois (the state of Leib's residence) and terminated Leib's liability for alimony.

The Supreme Court reversed,[5] stating that the wife's claim had to be resolved by giving the various proceedings the effect to which the Constitution entitles them. The court ruled that Henzel's Nevada divorce

---

[2]Johnson v. Muelberger, 340 U.S. 581, 71 S. Ct. 474, 95 L. Ed. 552 (1951).

[3]Johnson v. Muelberger, 340 U.S. 581, 583, 71 S. Ct. 474, 95 L. Ed. 552 (1951).

[4]Sutton v. Leib, 342 U.S. 402, 72 S. Ct. 398, 96 L. Ed. 448 (1952).

[5]The Supreme Court rejected the lower court's conclusion that the marriage was valid in Nevada, observing that full faith and credit would thereby be given to the Nevada marriage rather than the New York annulment. The court said that the marriage ceremony between the wife and Henzel could not be deemed valid because Henzel had a living wife, by reason of his invalid divorce. Moreover, the New York annulment, to which full faith and credit must be given, held the Nevada marriage void; and under Nevada law bigamous marriages are void.

from his first wife was void and not entitled to full faith and credit. Since both parties were before the court, the New York decree annulling the marriage between the wife and Henzel was conclusive everywhere as to their marriage status. Full faith and credit to the new York annulment required Illinois to treat the Nevada marriage ceremony as void, also.

However, full faith and credit does not require that the effect of the New York annulment decree on a stranger's duties be the same in every state. Since Leib was a stranger to the New York annulment proceeding, the court said that the effect of the annulment on Leib's duty to pay alimony should be determined under Illinois law. The case was therefore remanded for a determination of the Illinois rule on the obligation of a former husband to pay alimony where the wife's subsequent marriage is declared invalid.

§ 27:75   Full faith and credit—Decree of foreign nation

The full faith and credit clause does not apply to judicial acts of another country. States are therefore not obliged to recognize a divorce decree rendered by a foreign nation.

However, judgments of foreign courts may be given recognition in the United States on the basis of the deference and respect due the courts of one country from another.[1] This doctrine is known as comity. Since there is no constitutional compulsion upon a state to give effect to a foreign nation's decree, comity is regarded as a matter of privilege.[2] It is generally agreed that a state, if it elects to do so, is empowered to recognize the validity of a judicial decree of a foreign government where such decree is valid under the law of the foreign country and where recognition is harmonious with the public policy of the forum state.[3]

Accordingly, the validity of a divorce granted by a country in which both parties were domiciled is usually determined by the laws of that country, unless recognition offends some positive law or policy of the forum state.[4] Hence, comity has been extended to a foreign divorce between spouses who were domiciled in the foreign country, even though the marriage was dissolved by proceedings other than a judicial decree.[5] For example, a religious divorce between persons residing in a foreign nation, which is valid under the laws of that nation, has been given ef-

---

[Section 27:75]

[1]Yoder v. Yoder, 24 Ohio App. 2d 71, 53 Ohio Op. 2d 193, 263 N.E.2d 913 (5th Dist. Holmes County 1970).

[2]Bobala v. Bobala, 68 Ohio App. 63, 20 Ohio Op. 45, 33 Ohio L. Abs. 440, 33 N.E.2d 845 (7th Dist. Mahoning County 1940); Smith v. Smith, 72 Ohio App. 203, 27 Ohio Op. 79, 38 Ohio L. Abs. 531, 50 N.E.2d 889 (1st Dist. Hamilton County 1943).

[3]Yoder v. Yoder, 24 Ohio App. 2d 71, 53 Ohio Op. 2d 193, 263 N.E.2d 913 (5th Dist. Holmes County 1970).

[4]Machransky v. Machransky, 31 Ohio App. 482, 6 Ohio L. Abs. 315, 166 N.E. 423 (8th Dist. Cuyahoga County 1927).

[5]Am. Jur. 2d, Divorce and Separation § 964.

fect in courts of the United States.[6]

As a general rule, the divorce decree of a foreign court having jurisdiction over the parties and the matters litigated will be given effect under principles of comity, as to both the dissolution of the marriage and the determination of personal rights.[7] Where one party was domiciled in the foreign country, recognition will normally be given to the decree, insofar as it adjudicates marital status, even if the foreign court lacked personal jurisdiction over the defendant.[8]

However, a decree will not be recognized under principles of comity where the foreign court lacked jurisdiction;[9] or where neither spouse was domiciled in the foreign country;[10] or if the decree was obtained by a procedure which denied due process or was obtained by perjury or fraud;[11] or where important factual recitals in the decree are found by the forum state to be false;[12] or where the divorce offends the public policy of the state in which recognition is sought.[13]

For instance, regardless of its validity in the nation awarding it, a divorce granted by a foreign country will not normally be recognized in the United States as a valid termination of a marriage, unless at least one of the spouses was a bona fide domiciliary in the foreign nation at the time the decree was rendered.[14] This rule has been applied by American courts even in cases where domicile is not a jurisdictional requirement under the laws of the foreign nation.[15] Moreover, a foreign decree which is based upon the ex parte application of one spouse and constructive service upon the other will not be permitted (by application of the principles of comity) to extinguish the defendant spouse's rights to

---

[6]Machransky v. Machransky, 31 Ohio App. 482, 6 Ohio L. Abs. 315, 166 N.E. 423 (8th Dist. Cuyahoga County 1927). See Kapigian v. Der Minassian, 212 Mass. 412, 99 N.E. 264 (1912) (trial court stretched to find comity for divorce because husband had remarried).

[7]Am. Jur. 2d, Divorce and Separation § 964; Annot., 13 A.L.R. 3d 1419; Ahmad v. Ahmad, 2001 WL 1518116 (Ohio Ct. App. 6th Dist. Lucas County 2001).

[8]Rousculp v. Rousculp, 17 Ohio App. 2d 101, 46 Ohio Op. 2d 125, 244 N.E.2d 512 (10th Dist. Franklin County 1968); Davis v. Davis, 80 Ohio L. Abs. 303, 156 N.E.2d 494 (C.P. 1959).

[9]Bobala v. Bobala, 68 Ohio App. 63, 20 Ohio Op. 45, 33 Ohio L. Abs. 440, 33 N.E.2d 845 (7th Dist. Mahoning County 1940).

[10]Bobala v. Bobala, 68 Ohio App. 63, 20 Ohio Op. 45, 33 Ohio L. Abs. 440, 33 N.E.2d 845 (7th Dist. Mahoning County 1940); Smith v. Smith, 72 Ohio App. 203, 27 Ohio Op. 79, 38 Ohio L. Abs. 531, 50 N.E.2d 889 (1st Dist. Hamilton County 1943). See Annot., 13 A.L.R. 3d 1419.

[11]Am. Jur. 2d, Divorce and Separation §§ 968 and 969.

[12]Yoder v. Yoder, 24 Ohio App. 2d 71, 53 Ohio Op. 2d 193, 263 N.E.2d 913 (5th Dist. Holmes County 1970) (recitals as to mutual consent and appearance of both spouses were false).

[13]Yoder v. Yoder, 24 Ohio App. 2d 71, 53 Ohio Op. 2d 193, 263 N.E.2d 913 (5th Dist. Holmes County 1970).

[14]Smith v. Smith, 72 Ohio App. 203, 27 Ohio Op. 79, 38 Ohio L. Abs. 531, 50 N.E.2d 889 (1st Dist. Hamilton County 1943); Bobala v. Bobala, 68 Ohio App. 63, 20 Ohio Op. 45, 33 Ohio L. Abs. 440, 33 N.E.2d 845 (7th Dist. Mahoning County 1940).

[15]Annot., 13 A.L.R. 3d 1419.

spousal support, custody, and child support under state law.[16]

Reciprocity is regarded as an important issue in determining whether a foreign decree will be recognized under the principles of comity. If, under similar circumstances, the foreign country would not recognize the judgment of a court of the United States as conclusive, the American court need not give effect to such a judgment by the foreign court.[17]

Some courts have not strictly adhered to the principles of res judicata in deciding whether to uphold the judgment of a foreign nation. A Mexican divorce instituted by the husband and defended by his wife through an attorney in Mexico was held invalid in *Bobala v. Bobala.*[18] Even though the wife had filed an answer and had unsuccessfully prosecuted an appeal through counsel in Mexico, since the husband never established a bona fide residence in that country, the Mexican decree obtained by the husband against the wife was held not to be res judicata as to her Ohio divorce action. The court reasoned that, because the husband was not a bona fide resident of the country, and jurisdiction cannot be conferred by consent, the Mexican court lacked jurisdiction to grant a divorce. Thus, in the Ohio proceeding, the wife was granted a divorce, custody, and was awarded alimony and attorney fees, without regard to the Mexican decree.

Some courts have taken the position that a presumption of legitimacy attaches to a foreign judgment. The burden of proving that a decree is invalid is upon the party challenging it.[19] Thus, a Mexican ex parte divorce, which was attacked on the basis that the husband was not domiciled in Mexico, was given recognition under principles of comity, because the Ohio court found that the wife had not sustained the burden of undermining the verity which the foreign decree imports.[20]

The divisible divorce doctrine has been applied to a judgment of a foreign country. Consistent with the general rule, an ex parte foreign divorce, based upon constructive service, is deemed not to extinguish the rights of a non-resident spouse to spousal support, custody, and child

---

[16]Rousculp v. Rousculp, 17 Ohio App. 2d 101, 46 Ohio Op. 2d 125, 244 N.E.2d 512 (10th Dist. Franklin County 1968); Davis v. Davis, 80 Ohio L. Abs. 303, 156 N.E.2d 494 (C.P. 1959).

[17]In re Vanderborght, 57 Ohio L. Abs. 143, 91 N.E.2d 47 (C.P. 1950); Am. Jur. 2d, Divorce and Separation § 964.

[18]Bobala v. Bobala, 68 Ohio App. 63, 20 Ohio Op. 45, 33 Ohio L. Abs. 440, 33 N.E.2d 845 (7th Dist. Mahoning County 1940) (although in refusing to recognize the Mexican decree, the trial court relied in part upon the husband's violation of its restraining order enjoining him from further prosecuting his Mexican divorce action, the court of appeals affirmance rested on the Mexican court's lack of jurisdiction).

[19]Davis v. Davis, 80 Ohio L. Abs. 303, 156 N.E.2d 494 (C.P. 1959); Am. Jur. 2d, Divorce and Separation § 964; Annot., 13 A.L.R. 3d 1419. See generally Machransky v. Machransky, 31 Ohio App. 482, 6 Ohio L. Abs. 315, 166 N.E. 423 (8th Dist. Cuyahoga County 1927).

[20]Davis v. Davis, 80 Ohio L. Abs. 303, 156 N.E.2d 494 (C.P. 1959).

support.[21] Where a divorce has been granted by a foreign nation in which the plaintiff was domiciled, a state may recognize the foreign court's dissolution of the marriage, yet ignore its adjudication of personal rights and obligations. The defendant spouse has therefore been permitted to bring a subsequent action for spousal support, custody, and child support in Ohio, even though the marriage was terminated by the foreign proceeding.[22]

---

[21]Davis v. Davis, 80 Ohio L. Abs. 303, 156 N.E.2d 494 (C.P. 1959); Rousculp v. Rousculp, 17 Ohio App. 2d 101, 46 Ohio Op. 2d 125, 244 N.E.2d 512 (10th Dist. Franklin County 1968).

[22]Davis v. Davis, 80 Ohio L. Abs. 303, 156 N.E.2d 494 (C.P. 1959); Rousculp v. Rousculp, 17 Ohio App. 2d 101, 46 Ohio Op. 2d 125, 244 N.E.2d 512 (10th Dist. Franklin County 1968); Ahmad v. Ahmad, 2001 WL 1518116 (Ohio Ct. App. 6th Dist. Lucas County 2001) (trial court has jurisdiction to award spousal support and property division where foreign country decree did not address).

Chapter 28

Tax Considerations

By Michael J. Johrendt, Esq.

> **KeyCite®:** Cases and other legal materials listed in KeyCite Scope can be researched through West Group's KeyCite service on Westlaw®. Use KeyCite to check citations for form, parallel references, prior and later history, and comprehensive citator information, including citations to other decisions and secondary materials.

§ 28:1   Impact of tax laws in domestic relations matters

The federal tax treatment of property division and support payments can have substantial economic consequences. Because the division of marital assets incident to a divorce is now almost always a non-taxable event under I.R.C. § 1041, the economic consequences of tax issues may not be recognized until after the marriage has been terminated. However, as with all tax planning, consideration of the tax costs or corresponding benefits available to the parties can avoid unintended tax consequences. Conversely, failure to consider the tax consequences of property division and support payments may be considered akin to overlooking marital assets in the termination of a marriage.

The tax consequences of the property division to be made to each spouse must be considered by the court.[1] Unless there are no tax consequences associated with a distributive award, or any tax consequences are de minimis, it is error for the court to fail to address tax consequences in Ohio.[2]

Terminology for tax purposes is not always consistent with state law.[3] State law is often determinative of federal tax consequences and proper consideration of the impact of one on the other is required. Substance controls over form for tax purposes, and labels placed by the parties will not necessarily be given the desired tax effect.

Separate and careful documentation of the consideration of tax consequences provides an additional benefit. Assuming proper allocation, it is possible for the parties to deduct a portion of the total legal fees paid in a domestic relations proceeding.[4]

The Tax Reform Act of 1984 radically altered the prior tax rules relating to the division of property and the payment of support. The Tax Reform Act of 1986 made additional changes. Since the rules do not apply retroactively, except under limited circumstances, it may still be necessary to refer to the law in effect at the time of the decree. Reference to prior tax law has been included where it has been thought to be helpful or instructive.

§ 28:2   Alimony—Before tax reform acts of 1984 and 1986

Prior to 1985, there was a general rule for taxability of divisions of property, and another rule for taxability of periodic alimony. These rules were quite clear. The recipient of a property division did not pay tax on property received. The transferor of property could not deduct the value of property transferred in property division.

The tax consequences of the payment of periodic alimony essentially were the reverse. Periodic alimony payments were includable in the

---

[Section 28:1]

[1]RC 3105.171(F)(6).

[2]Browning v. Browning, 1995 WL 23367 (Ohio Ct. App. 4th Dist. Gallia County 1995).

[3]The tax term "alimony" has not been changed, although RC 3105.18 now refers to the obligation as "spousal support."

[4]See § 28:22, Attorney fees.

gross income of the recipient and deductible by the payor.[1] No payment would be characterized as periodic alimony unless it met two tests: (1) it must have been periodic, and (2) it must have resulted from a legal obligation arising from the marital relationship. The second test was construed by the regulations and the courts to mean that the payment must have discharged a legal obligation of the payor to support the recipient.[2]

As the tax treatment indicates, distinguishing property division from periodic alimony was critical. There were circumstances, however, where the distinction was inconsequential from a tax point of view because the tax consequences were identical. If a payment was not periodic, it was not deductible by the payor and was not taxable to the recipient, even if it was made to discharge the payor's obligation to support the recipient.

Divorce decrees or separation agreements entered into prior to 1985 can be modified to take advantage of the post-1984 rules.[3] Only payments made after this type of modification will qualify for the post-1984 tax treatment.

§ 28:3   Alimony—Effect of tax reform acts

Neither the Tax Reform Act of 1984[1] nor the Tax Reform Act of 1986[2] changed the basic rule: Alimony payments are deductible by the payor in arriving at adjusted gross income and are includable in the gross income of the recipient. However, virtually every other corollary of this basic rule has been changed by the 1984 and 1986 Acts. For example, the previous requirement that payments must be periodic to be deductible has been eliminated, as has the requirement that deductible payments must be made in discharge of a legal obligation of support. The six-year minimum term rule was completely eliminated from the I.R.C. by the Tax Reform Act of 1986. No minimum term rule exists.[3]

§ 28:4   Alimony—Payments as deductible—In general

I.R.C. § 71(b)(1) lists the criteria which must be met before payments can be construed as deductible alimony. Payments must be made in cash and must be made under a decree of divorce or separate maintenance, or a written instrument incident to a decree, a written separation instrument, or a decree requiring the payor to support and maintain the

---

[Section 28:2]

[1]I.R.C. § 62(a)(10) (the deduction is allowed irrespective of whether the payor itemizes deductions, i.e., the payments are deductible in arriving at adjusted gross income, rather than from adjusted gross income; since Ohio's income tax starts with adjusted gross income, the payments reduce the payor's Ohio taxable income and increase the recipient's Ohio taxable income).

[2]Treas. Reg. § 1.71-1(b)(4).

[3]I.R.C. § 71; Treas. Reg. § 1.71-1T.

[Section 28:3]

[1]Pub. L. No. 98-369 (1984).

[2]Pub. L. No. 99-514 (1986).

[3]I.R.C. § 71.

payee (i.e., a temporary spousal support decree). The payments do not have to be made directly to the recipient to be deductible; they may be made to a third party for the benefit of the recipient.[1] RC 3105.18(A) defines spousal support as payments made to a spouse or former spouse, or to a third party for the benefit of a spouse or a former spouse. However, payments which constitute a division or distribution of property are not spousal support under Ohio law.

§ 28:5 Alimony—Payments as deductible—Cash payment required

To qualify as deductible for tax purposes, payments must be made in cash or cash-like form (e.g., checks or money orders). Payments made by in-kind distributions of property or by promissory note do not qualify.[1]

§ 28:6 Alimony—Payments as deductible—Writing required

Installments must be made subsequent to and pursuant to a divorce or support decree (or a written instrument incident to such divorce or support decree), or a written separation agreement, to satisfy the writing requirement. This requirement clearly is met in the case of a divorce decree or separation agreement, or a decree of support, if the court's decree, by its terms, requires the parties to make installment payments meeting the other requirements of deductible alimony. Problems generally arise with respect to written instruments incident to the divorce or support decree and written separation agreements.

In order for a written instrument incident to a divorce or a written separation agreement to meet the writing requirement, the parties must be legally bound by the written instrument or separation agreement. Generally, under Ohio law, the parties must sign the written instrument or written separation agreement.

In *Auerbach v. Commissioner*,[1] a husband sent a letter to his wife after they were separated and living apart, declaring that the payments made to the wife were alimony payments. The court held that the letter was not a sufficient written agreement because both parties had not consented to the terms of the letter by signing it. Therefore, the letter was not a binding and enforceable agreement between the parties.[2] However, in *Ducar v. Commissioner*,[3] a letter sent by one party's attorney to the other party's attorney was held to be a sufficient written agreement even though neither party signed the letter. Notwithstanding

---

[Section 28:4]
[1]Treas. Reg. § 1.71-1T; H. Rep. 98-432, Part 2, 98th Cong., 2d Sess., 1496 (1984).

[Section 28:5]
[1]I.R.C. § 71(b)(1); Treas. Reg. § 1.71-1T, Q & A 5.

[Section 28:6]
[1]Auerbach v. C.I.R., T.C. Memo. 1975-219, 1975 WL 2839 (1975).

[2]See Greenfield v. C.I.R., T.C. Memo. 1978-386, 1978 WL 3060 (1978); Saniewski v. C.I.R., T.C. Memo. 1979-337, 1979 WL 3395 (1979).

[3]Ducar v. C.I.R., T.C. Memo. 1977-316, 1977 WL 3044 (1977).

cases like *Ducar*,[4] counsel should have the parties sign a written agreement specifying the terms and the intent with respect to the alimony payments.

§ 28:7 Alimony—Payments as deductible—Payments to third party

Alimony payments may be made as premium payments on life insurance, if the payee owns the policy, and as mortgage payments, if the payee owns the real estate. The payee must receive an economic benefit from the payment made to the third party. Payments to satisfy rent, tax, or medical obligations of the payee may also qualify if all the other required elements are present.

§ 28:8 Alimony—Payments as deductible—Termination on death of recipient

The Tax Reform Act of 1984 requires that alimony terminate on the death of the recipient to be deductible. Payments may qualify as alimony only if:

> [T]here is no liability to make any such payment for any period after the death of the payee spouse and there is no liability to make any payment (in cash or property) as a substitute for such payments after the death of the payee spouse.[1]

The 1986 Act eliminated the requirement that, in order to be deductible, payments provided for in a divorce decree or separation agreement contain the "magic language" that they would terminate on the death of the payee spouse. Local law can supply the termination requirement, and RC 3105.18(B) provides that "[a]ny award of spousal support made under this section shall terminate upon the death of either party, unless the order containing the award expressly provides otherwise." Nevertheless, prudence dictates that counsel specifically negate the requirement to pay alimony beyond the death of the payee spouse when drafting agreements, and not rely solely on local law.

Prior to January 1, 1991, the effective date of RC 3105.18(B), if a separation agreement stated that a husband was to pay $300 per month as and for alimony to his wife until further order of the court, then no payments made pursuant to the agreement (whether made before or after the death of the recipient) were deductible. The separation agreement failed to comply with I.R.C. § 71(b)(1)(D) in two respects. First, it is not clear that payments would terminate on the death of the recipient.[1] Second, the separation agreement itself did not negate any obligation to

---

[4]See, e.g., Estate of Hill v. Commissioner of Internal Revenue, 59 T.C. 846, 1973 WL 2535 (1973), acq., 1973-2 C.B. 1; Garner v. C. I. R., T.C. Memo. 1973-79, 1973 WL 2282 (1973).

[Section 28:8]
[1]I.R.C. § 71(b)(1)(D).
[1]Treas. Reg. § 1.71-1T(b)Q-10.

make payments beyond the death of the recipient.[2] To insure that the payments would be deductible, a separation agreement prior to 1991 should have tracked the language of I.R.C. § 71(b)(1)(D):

> There is no liability to make such payment for any period after the death of the wife and there is no liability to make any such payment (in cash or property) as a substitute for such payments after the death of the wife.

Although the temporary regulations do not require the separation agreement specifically to negate substitute payments,[3] counsel should consider doing so because provisions construed as requiring payments to continue beyond the payee's death negate corresponding alimony treatment during life.

The temporary regulations provide that the determination as to whether substitute payments exist is a question of fact. The regulations provide: "To the extent that one or more payments are to begin to be made, increase in amount, or become accelerated in time as a result of the death of the payee spouse, such payments may be treated as [substitute payments]."[4]

The rule requiring that alimony terminate on the death of the payee in order to be deductible does not preclude a payor from obligating his estate to continue making alimony payments after his own death; rather, it only precludes payments after the death of the recipient.

Pursuant to I.R.C. § 71(b)(1)(D), separation agreements should be drafted to comply with this provision and specifically to negate the payor's liability after the death of the recipient. Careful counsel will not only routinely include this language, but will also be wary of any payment made after the death of a recipient which could be construed as alimony.

§ 28:9   Alimony—Payments as deductible—Living separate and apart

I.R.C. § 71(b)(1)(C) states that the payor and the recipient may not be members of the same household. However, the legislative history[1] and the temporary regulations retreat from the unambiguous statutory language by providing as follows: "The spouses will not be treated as members of the same household if one spouse is preparing to depart from the household of the other spouse, and does depart not more than one month after the date the payment is made."[2]

Even if the spouses are not legally separated or divorced, a payment under a written separation agreement or a decree of separate maintenance may qualify as deductible alimony, notwithstanding that the

---

[2]Treas. Reg. § 1.71-1T(b)Q-11.

[3]Treas. Reg. § 1.71-1T(b)Q-13.

[4]Treas. Reg. § 1.71-1T(b)Q-14.

[Section 28:9]

[1]Treas. Reg. § 1.71-1T; H. Rep. 98-432, Part 2, 98th Cong., 2d Sess., 1496 (1984).

[2]Treas. Reg. § 1.71-1T Q & A 9.

spouses are members of the same household at the time the payment is made.[3]

§ 28:10   Alimony—Payments as deductible—Election of tax treatment

To qualify for deductibility, the separation agreement or decree can not designate the payments as nondeductible by the payor or as excludable from the payee's income.[1]

Under some circumstances, the parties may elect to have the payment, that would in all other respects qualify as deductible alimony, treated as nondeductible and nonincludable. If the payor has no need for the deduction, as in the situation where his income is primarily tax free or otherwise sheltered, no benefit results from creating taxable income to the recipient. The parties may elect to have such payments nondeductible and nonincludable by reciting their intention in the separation agreement or consent entry. A copy of the written designation must be attached to the payee's tax return for each year in which the designation applies.[2]

The legislative history of the 1984 Act indicates that this provision was enacted to give the parties the flexibility to structure payments in accordance with their wishes.[3]

§ 28:11   Alimony—Payments as deductible—Separate return required

Alimony is only deductible if the parties file separate federal income tax returns. Parties subject to a decree of support or a written separation agreement are required to file separate federal income tax returns before payments under the decree or agreement will be treated as deductible alimony.[1]

I.R.C. § 7703 determines the taxpayer's marital status for a given tax year at the end of that tax year. Taxpayers who are legally divorced or separated are not considered married, and therefore, cannot file a joint return and take advantage of the joint tax rates under I.R.C. § 1(a).

The effective date of the decree should be timed, wherever possible, to achieve the lowest overall tax for the parties. Tax savings may be available by filing a final joint return. The trial court may consider a party's refusal to file a joint tax return, resulting in higher taxes to the other,

---

[3]Treas. Reg. § 1.71-1T, Q & A 9.

[Section 28:10]
　[1]I.R.C. § 71(b)(1)(B).
　[2]Treas. Reg. § 1.71-1T, Q & A 8.
　[3]See § 28:23, Innocent spouse rule.

[Section 28:11]
　[1]I.R.C. § 71(e) specifically provides, "This section . . . shall not apply if the spouses make a joint return with each other."

as a factor when equitably dividing the marital estate.[2] Tax planning should consider both federal and state law. RC 5747.08 requires that taxpayers file using the same status (joint or separate) for Ohio as for federal income tax purposes. Where the taxable incomes of the spouses are approximately equal, a lower total tax (federal plus Ohio) may result from electing to file separate returns.[3]

The parties may choose to share or allocate the tax savings resulting from the joint return. Consideration should be given to the proportionate sharing of the refund if the parties' earnings are disproportionate. In situations where there is only one significant wage earner, separate returns by unmarried individuals may be more beneficial than a joint return. A single parent may also qualify for a head of household status which will further tax savings over that gained by filing a joint return. Where the option exists, effective tax planning requires the timing of the termination of the marriage to coincide with the greatest tax savings.

§ 28:12   Alimony—Payments as deductible—Payments cannot be child support

Alimony payments will not be deductible to the extent they are deemed as being for the support of payor's children. For these purposes, if the alimony payment is reduced on the occurrence of a contingency relating to a child (such as attaining a specified age, marrying, dying, leaving school, etc.), or at a time which clearly can be associated with such a contingency, the amount of the reduction will be treated as nondeductible child support rather than deductible alimony.[1]

§ 28:13   Alimony—Payments as deductible—Reporting requirements

Alimony payments are reported and deducted on Form 1040. I.R.C. § 215 provides that an alimony recipient must supply his taxpayer identification number to the payor, who in turn must include the recipient's number on his federal income tax return. I.R.C. §§ 6673 and 6724 impose a $50 penalty for failure of either party to comply.

§ 28:14   Alimony—Payments as deductible—Voluntary payments

To be considered deductible alimony, the installment payments cannot be made voluntarily. They must be made under a decree of divorce, decree of support, or a written separation agreement. Payments made in excess of the amount specified in the decree or written separation agree-

---

[2]Cromberg v. Cromberg, 1995 WL 316526 (Ohio Ct. App. 6th Dist. Lucas County 1995).

[3]See § 28:23, Innocent spouse rule.

[Section 28:12]
[1]I.R.C. § 71(c)(2).

ment are voluntary payments and are not deductible.[1] Payments made after the occurrence of a contingency terminating the obligation to pay spousal support, or after the expiration of the period over which payment of spousal support was required, are also voluntary and nondeductible. Payments made prior to the entry of the decree or the signing of the written separation agreement are voluntary and nondeductible.

To insure deductibility, the decree or written separation agreement should be modified if payments are increased over the amount specified in the original decree or written separation agreement, or continued beyond the payment period or after the occurrence of a contingency specified in the original decree or written separation agreement.

Payment of temporary spousal support should be made pursuant to a written separation agreement between the parties or under a court order. Numerous cases have held that where a court refused to order payment of temporary spousal support because the voluntary payments made by a party were sufficient support of party's spouse, the payments were nondeductible.[2] Spousal support payments made under a temporary decree are deductible. Those payments made before the effective date of the decree are not. Payments may not be made retroactively deductible by a subsequent decree.

§ 28:15 Alimony—Recomputation

The 1986 Tax Reform Act not only eliminated the "minimum term" rule, but modified the recomputation, or recapture, rule. Recomputation is now limited to the third post-separation year. The 1986 Tax Reform Act only applies to agreements or orders entered into in 1985 and 1986 if the agreement or order is modified specifically to provide for the application of the 1986 Act. If such modification is made, recomputation will occur only in the third post-separation year.

I.R.C. § 71(f) provides for the recomputation of alimony.

(1) In general—If there are excess alimony payments—

(A) the payor spouse shall include the amount of such excess payments in gross income for the payor spouse's taxable year beginning the 3rd post-separation year, and

(B) the payee spouse shall be allowed a deduction in computing adjusted gross income for the amount of such excess payments for the payee's taxable year beginning in the 3rd post-separation year.

Recapture of alimony can only occur in the third post-separation year. The computation is based on amounts actually paid, not the amounts scheduled. Excess alimony in the second year is the amount by which

---

[Section 28:14]

[1]Wondsel v. C. I. R., 350 F.2d 339, 65-2 (2d Cir. 1965).

[2]Sharp v. C. I. R., 15 T.C. 185, 1950 WL 43 (T.C. 1950); Taylor v. Commissioner of Internal Revenue, 55 T.C. 1134, 1971 WL 2609 (1971), recommendation regarding acquiescence, 1971 WL 29247 (I.R.S. AOD 1971); Shapiro v. C.I.R., T.C. Memo. 1979-427, 1979 WL 3563 (1979); Dean v. C.I.R., T.C. Memo. 1981-554, 1981 WL 10983 (1981).

the second year payments exceed those for the third year by more than $15,000. Excess payment for the first year is the amount by which the first year payment exceeds the average of the second year, reduced by excess payments, and the third year amounts by more than $15,000.

Assuming that, either by agreement or court order, an obligor was required to pay and did pay alimony in the amount of $60,000 the first year, $40,000 the second year, and $20,000 the third year, the following is a computation of the recapture using a typical worksheet for such computation:

WORKSHEET FOR RECAPTURE OF ALIMONY

(For Instruments Executed After 1986)

Note: Do not enter less than zero on any line.

1.	Alimony paid in 2nd year	$40,000
2.	Alimony paid in 3rd year	$20,000
3.	Floor	$15,000
4.	Add lines 2 and 3	$35,000
5.	Subtract line 4 from line 1	$5,000
6.	Alimony paid in 1st year	$60,000
7.	Adjusted alimony paid in 2nd year (line 1 less line 5)	$35,000
8.	Alimony paid in 3rd year	$20,000
9.	Add lines 7 and 8	$55,000
10.	Divide line 9 by 2	$27,500
11.	Floor	$15,000
12.	Add lines 10 and 11	$42,500
13.	Subtract line 12 from line 6	$17,500
14.	*Recapture alimony.* Add lines 5 and 13	$22,500

* **If you deducted alimony paid**, report this amount as income on line 11, Form 1040

If you reported alimony received, deduct this amount on line 29, Form 1040

Unless the parties and/or the court intend a recapture of alimony, it is clear that the tax consequences anticipated by the agreement or the court order will be greatly affected by recapture. The payor must include the recaptured amount in his gross taxable income in the year of recapture and the payee will receive a commensurate deduction from gross income.[1]

I.R.C. § 71(f)(6) defines "post-separation years" as calendar years. Thus, if payments are made on December 31, 1992, January 1, 1993, and January 1, 1994, all of the payments would have actually occurred within one year and two days, but were made over three calendar years.

[Section 28:15]

[1] I.R.C. § 71(f)(1)(A), (B).

Temporary support payments are not considered for purposes of recapture as the payments must be made under a decree of divorce or separate maintenance or a voluntary separation agreement.[2]

Payments that terminate by reason of the death of either party or remarriage of the obligee will not trigger recapture nor will payments that cause an excess of more than $15,000 if such payments are made pursuant to a continuing liability to pay a fixed portion or portions of the income from a business, property, or from compensation from employment or self-employment.[3]

While recapture may be purposely triggered if there is anticipation of a significant change in income between the first and third years so as to result in a net tax savings to the parties, more often than not, recapture will be the result of failure of the parties, counsel, or the court to consider the recapture rule.

§28:16 Alimony—Alimony trusts

Notwithstanding the elimination of trusts as a source of alimony payments under the 1984 Act, the use of alimony trusts remains an option available under current tax law. The tax treatment to the parties will be determined under the rules relating to the taxation of trust income, rather than the usual rules relating to the tax treatment of alimony.[1] The payor will not receive a corresponding deduction, but under appropriate circumstances, that loss may not be significant. Funding spousal payments through a trust also provides the potential for avoiding the recapture rule of I.R.C. § 71(f), the requirement that spousal payments terminate upon the death of the recipient under I.R.C. § 71(b)(1)(D), and limitations on the reduction or termination of support based upon occurrences relating to a child under I.R.C. § 71(c)(2).

§28:17 Property division

With the enactment of I.R.C. § 1041 in 1984, the 1962 holding in *United States v. Davis*[1] and the potential for capital gain to result from the division of property have been virtually eliminated. I.R.C. § 1041, which was enacted as part of the Tax Reform Act of 1984, creates two new black letter rules regarding property division and the federal income tax. First, no gain or loss is recognized to the transferor in a property division. Second, the recipient of a property division assumes the transferor's adjusted basis in the asset.

I.R.C. § 1041(a) protects the transferor of appreciated property from recognizing, and being taxed on, any gain on the transfer to a spouse, former spouse, or a trust for the benefit of either, provided that the re-

---

[2]I.R.C. § 71(f)(5)(B).

[3]I.R.C. § 71(f)(5)(C).

[Section 28:16]
[1]I.R.C. § 682.

[Section 28:17]
[1]U.S. v. Davis, 370 U.S. 65, 82 S. Ct. 1190, 8 L. Ed. 2d 335 (1962).

cipient is not a non-resident alien.[2]

This provision statutorily overrules the United States Supreme Court's decision in *United States v. Davis*, so that the transfer of appreciated property during marriage or incident to a divorce will not result in gain to the transferor. The House Report indicates that "for purposes of this provision, annulment is treated as a divorce."[3] The 1986 Act added new I.R.C. § 267(g), which states that the loss disallowance rules under I.R.C. § 267 do not apply to any transfer incident to a divorce decree or separation agreement pursuant to I.R.C. § 1041(a).

"Incident to a divorce" is defined as within one year after the date on which the marriage ceases, or if later, is related to the cessation of the marriage.[4] If the transfer occurs within one year of the divorce, the motive for the transfer has no bearing on I.R.C. § 1041 application. If the transfer occurs later than one year, it must have been related to the cessation of the marriage to receive nonrecognition treatment. If the transfer occurs after six years from the cessation of the marriage, it will be presumed not to have been made in connection with the cessation of the marriage and, therefore, will be taxable.[5]

Because I.R.C. § 1041(b)(1) treats such transfers as gifts, the depreciation recapture rules and other rules such as those found in I.R.C. § 1245, I.R.C. § 1250, and I.R.C. § 1254, do not apply.[6] Although depreciation recapture is not triggered by gift, investment tax credit recapture generally is. To prevent the mere transfer of property between a spouse and a former spouse from triggering investment tax credit recapture, the Tax Reform Act of 1984 also amended I.R.C. § 47(e)(2) to provide that the transferee in a property division will receive the same tax treatment with respect to the property transferred as the transferor. This means that the transferor in a property division will not recognize investment tax credit recapture on a transfer of property. However, it also means that if the recipient of property division does not use the property in a qualified fashion, i.e., in business, then the recipient will have to pay the investment tax credit recapture tax.

Under new I.R.C. § 1041(c), added by the 1986 Act, gain will be recognized by the transferor on a transfer into trust incident to a decree of divorce or separate maintenance to the extent that the trust assumes liabilities in excess of the transferor's basis in the transferred property. Under I.R.C. § 453B, as amended by the 1986 Act, a transfer of an installment obligation will trigger recognition of deferred income.

Prior to the Tax Reform Act of 1984, whenever appreciated property was transferred to a spouse at a gain, that gain was characterized as ordinary income rather than as capital gain. Since the 1984 Act precludes the recognition of gain on the transfer of appreciated property to a spouse, a conforming amendment was made to I.R.C. § 1239 to elim-

---

[2]I.R.C. § 1041(d).

[3]H. Rep. 98-432, Part 2, 98th Cong., 2d Sess., 1492 (1984).

[4]I.R.C. § 1041(c).

[5]Treas. Reg. § 1.1041-1T(b) Q & A 7.

[6]See I.R.C. § 1245(b)(1), I.R.C. § 1250(d)(1), I.R.C. § 1254(b)(1).

inate the ordinary income characterization rule. In other words, there is now no need to characterize the gain on a property division because no gain will be recognized.

Prior to the Tax Reform Act of 1984, it was possible to structure a property division so that the transferor would be entitled to deduct his loss, where the basis of the property exceeded its fair market value. The 1984 Act has totally eliminated this possibility. Now, no gain or loss will be recognized to the transferor from a transfer incident to a divorce.

Two other rules relating to taxation of property division were changed by the 1984 Act. First, life insurance proceeds received by reason of the death of the insured generally are exempt from federal income taxes.[7] However, the transfer for value rule provides that if the life insurance policy is sold or otherwise transferred for valuable consideration, then only a portion of the proceeds received on the death of the insured may be excluded from the recipient's gross income. Under the old law, if a life insurance policy was transferred pursuant to a property division, a portion of the proceeds received by the recipient on the death of the insured would be subject to federal income tax. The new rule provides that the transfer of a life insurance policy in a property division will not cause the proceeds of the policy to be included in the recipient's income upon the death of the insured.

Second, the 1984 Act included a carryover basis rule. The recipient of property in a property division will recognize gain and be required to pay a tax on the sale of the property, to the extent the amount realized from the sale exceeds the transferor's adjusted basis.[8]

If title to property is not transferred incident to a divorce but only a right to share in sales proceeds is created, the party who retained title to the property may be liable for the entire top on disposition.[9] Careful drafting to provide for subsequent distribution of sales proceeds "not of all applicable taxes resulting from sale" should alleviate this concern.

Division of retirement benefits can have substantial economic consequences without current income tax consequences if properly structured. Although a comprehensive discussion of the tax consequences of distributions from retirement plans is beyond the scope of this chapter, a number of principles bear mentioning.

The Retirement Equity Act of 1984[10] created an exception to the anti-alienation provisions of ERISA for interest transfer pursuant to a qualified domestic relations order (QDRO).[11] The QDRO must be drafted to meet the statutory requirements and, in practice, must be submitted for the review and approval of the retirement benefit plan administrator to avoid issues regarding its acceptability. Once a qualified QDRO has been created, I.R.C. § 402(e)(1)(A) provides that the alternate payee,

---

[7]I.R.C. § 101(a)(1).

[8]I.R.C. § 1015 has been amended to create this special basis rule, which is different from the general rule with respect to gifted property in the hands of a recipient.

[9]Suhr v. C.I.R., T.C. Memo. 2001-28, T.C.M. (RIA) ¶ 2001-028 (2001).

[10]Pub. L. No. 98-397.

[11]I.R.C. §§ 401(a)(13)(B) and 414(p).

rather than the participant, will be taxed on the plan distribution made thereunder. Similarly, the alternate payee can defer taxation on the distribution from the retirement plan by depositing the amount received into another eligible retirement plan or an IRA within sixty days of the receipt of the distribution.[12]

The division of IRAs is provided for in I.R.C. § 408(d)(6), which permits a distribution from an IRA to a spouse or former spouse under a divorce or separation instrument without being considered a taxable transfer. The requirement that the transfer be pursuant to a decree or an instrument incident to a decree such as a separation agreement (but only after the decree has been entered) is mandatory, and once the transfer has been completed the IRA will be considered that of the transferee. In *Mukhopadhyay v. Mookerjee*,[13] the trial court did not err by failing to consider tax implications of an IRA fund awarded to the husband. There was no evidence that the husband closed, or planned to prematurely close, the account and there was no evidence of applicable tax rates.

While the transfer of a marital residence is a non-recognition event between spouses or former spouses, the subsequent tax consequences held potential substantial tax consequences to the transferee unless he or she could take advantage of the tax deferral or exclusion provisions of Sec. 1034 and Sec. 121.

The 1997 amendments to Sec. 121 greatly expanded the exclusion, and the deferral provisions of Sec. 1034 were eliminated.

After May 6, 1997, a single taxpayer may exclude up to $250,000 of gain on the sale of a principal place of residence. For those who are married and file a joint return, the excluded gain may be as high as $500,000 if either spouse meets the ownership and use tests and has not used the exclusion during the applicable period.

The ownership test is met if, during a five-year period prior to the sale, the home has been owned for at least a total of two years. The use test is met if, during that five-year period, the home was used for at least two years as the principal place of residence. The ownership and use tests do not have to be met in the same two-year period so long as both fall within the five years prior to the sale. A person who becomes mentally or physically ill and must reside in a qualifying facility may still meet the use test if he lived in the home being sold for a total of one year of the five before sale.

Each spouse is treated as owning the property for any period in which either spouse owned it.

Significantly, a former spouse is now deemed to have used the property as a principal place of residence, in meeting the use test, during that period of time in which the other spouse was granted use of the property under a divorce or separation instrument as defined in Sec. 71(b)(2). Generally, the exclusion may only be used once during any two-

---

[12]I.R.C. § 402(e)(1)(B) and 402(c).

[13]Mukhopadhyay v. Mookerjee, 1997 WL 638816 (Ohio Ct. App. 8th Dist. Cuyahoga County 1997).

year period. Unlike the former Sec. 121, however, it is not a once in a lifetime exclusion. It applies to exchanges as well as sales. The two-year period may be reduced if the transfer was required by a change in place of employment or health, or required by other unforeseen circumstances.

If a home was used partially for business and partially as a principal place of residence, the gain attributable to the business portion may not be excluded. A sale or exchange of the home may not qualify for the exclusion if the transfer is to a related person as defined in Sec. 267(b) or Sec. 707(b). A taxpayer may also elect not to have the exclusion apply, and it does not apply if the taxpayer's spouse or former spouse is a non-resident alien.

§ 28:18   Child support payments—Before tax reform act of 1984

Prior to its being effectively overruled by the Tax Reform Act of 1984, the US Supreme Court in *Commissioner v. Lester*[1] laid down a very specific rule that payments must be expressly designated as child support payments in the text of the written instrument in order to be characterized as child support (i.e., nondeductible by the payor and nontaxable to the recipient) rather than as periodic alimony (i.e., deductible by the payor and taxable to the recipient). In *Lester*, the written instrument provided in pertinent part:

[I]n the event that any of the [three] children of the parties hereto shall marry, become emancipated, or die, then the payment herein specified shall . . . be reduced in a sum equal to one-sixth of the payments which would thereafter otherwise accrue.[2]

The commissioner argued that this language sufficiently identified one-half of the payments (one-sixth times three children) as having been paid for the support of the parties' minor children, as child support, which was nondeductible by the payor. The Court held, however, that the Code's requirement that the written instrument fix the portion of the payment which is to go to the support of the children prevented any inference from the language of the written instrument that the amounts were to be one-half alimony and one-half child support. In other words, the Court held that all of the payments made pursuant to the written instrument were periodic alimony, because they were not specifically fixed in the instrument as child support. The Court relied on the fact that under the language of the written instrument, the recipient of the installment payments could spend the money received as she saw fit and was not required to expend the funds in support of the minor children, and that taxing the recipient on the payments complied with the philosophy of the Code that the power to dispose of income is the equivalent of

---

[Section 28:18]

[1]C.I.R. v. Lester, 366 U.S. 299, 81 S. Ct. 1343, 6 L. Ed. 2d 306 (1961) (overruling recognized by, Trout v. Patterson, 1994 WL 151442 (Tex. App. Houston 14th Dist. 1994)).

[2]C.I.R. v. Lester, 366 U.S. 299, 300, 81 S. Ct. 1343, 6 L. Ed. 2d 306 (1961) (overruling recognized by, Trout v. Patterson, 1994 WL 151442 (Tex. App. Houston 14th Dist. 1994)).

ownership of it.

The decision in *Lester* resulted in the strict rule that periodic payments received for the support of the spouse and minor children of the payor spouse would be treated as periodic alimony unless the written instrument specifically fixed the amount attributable to child support.

As a practical matter, the decision in *Lester* also permitted the parties the freedom to determine themselves by agreement whether child support would be considered taxable or not. Since the enactment of the Tax Reform Act of 1984, such freedom has been greatly curtailed and reference to what the payments actually, or in substance, constitute is now more important than the labels which the parties themselves place on the payments.

§ 28:19　Child support payments—Effect of tax reform acts

Payments representing child support are neither taxable to the payee nor deductible by the payor.[1] If a payment is deemed to represent both child support and spousal support, the payment is first treated as child support with the balance treated as spousal support.[2] Payments exclusively for child support are, generally, not deductible as alimony.

I.R.C. § 71(c)(1) sets forth the general rule that payments or portions of payments "fixed" as child support by a qualifying divorce instrument will be treated as child support. A payment is "fixed" as payable for the support of a child of the payor spouse if the payment is reduced (a) on the happening of a contingency relating to a child of the payor, or (b) at a time which can clearly be associated with such a contingency. Examples of such contingencies include the following: the child's attaining a specific age or income level, dying, marrying, leaving school, leaving the spouse's household, or gaining employment.[3]

Conversely, child support payments will be includable in the gross income of the payee and deductible by the payor if all the requirements for taxable alimony are met and the following three additional requirements are satisfied:

    (1) the instrument does not actually "fix" a sum which is payable for the support of the child.[4]

    (2) the instrument does not provide that the amount will be reduced "on the happening of a contingency relating to a child."[5]

    (3) the instrument does not provide that the amount payable will be reduced "at a time which can clearly be associated with such a contingency."[6]

[Section 28:19]
[1]I.R.C. §§ 71(c), 215(b).
[2]I.R.C. § 71(c)(3).
[3]Treas. Reg. § 1.71-1T(c).
[4]I.R.C. § 71(c)(1).
[5]I.R.C. § 71(c)(2)(A).
[6]I.R.C. § 71(c)(2)(B).

The regulations outline only two types of situations involving reductions in payments that will be presumed to have occurred at a time clearly associated with the happening of a contingency relating to a child: (a) reductions six months before or after the child is to attain the age of eighteen, twenty-one, or a local age of majority, and (b) two or more occasions which occur one year before or after a different child of the payor attains a certain age between the ages of eighteen and twenty-four, inclusive. Such age must be the same for each such child.[7]

It should be noted that if the child for whom support is being paid is a step-child of the payor, the payments will be treated as taxable alimony since I.R.C. § 71(c)(1) only applies with respect to a child of the payor spouse.

§ 28:20 Filing status

The parties' filing status determines which tax rate schedule or tax table will be used to calculate their tax liability. For the year in which the parties obtain a final decree of divorce or support, they are considered unmarried for the entire taxable year and cannot file a joint return.[1] Temporary orders for support or separate living arrangements are insufficient to establish single status.[2]

Even if the parties are eligible to file a joint return, they may pay an overall lower state and federal tax by filing separate returns. This is often the case when both parties have independent sources of income which are approximately equal and live in a state, such as Ohio, which requires that the filing status on the state tax return be the same as on the federal tax return.

In situations where the parties remain married at the end of their taxable year, but the relationship between them makes filing a joint return impossible, one or both of the parties may be able to avoid the higher, married filing separately[3] tax rates if he or she meets the special rule for married people living apart, often referred to as "the Abandoned Spouse Rule."[4] Under this rule, a spouse may file as an unmarried taxpayer (i.e., using single taxpayer rates)[5] if the following conditions apply:

(1) The party paid more than one-half the cost to keep a home;
(2) The party's spouse did not live in the party's home at any time during the tax year; and
(3) The party's home was, for more than six months of the year, the principal residence of the party's child qualifying as a

---

[7]Treas. Reg. § 1.71-1T(c) Q & A 18.

[Section 28:20]
[1]I.R.C. § 7703.
[2]Haase v. United States, 91-1 U.S.T.C. ¶ 50,116 (ND Ohio 1991).
[3]I.R.C. § 1(d) (the highest income tax rates in the Code).
[4]I.R.C. § 7703(b).
[5]I.R.C. § 1(c).

dependent.

No spouse need actually be "abandoned" to qualify for this favorable tax treatment, nor does one spouse's qualification necessarily preclude the other from similar treatment should they otherwise qualify.

A married party deemed unmarried under I.R.C. § 7703(b) can also often qualify as head of household and obtain the advantage of even more favorable rates.[6]

Note that parties separated under a written separation agreement are still considered married for filing status purposes and must file jointly or as married, filing separately, unless the Abandoned Spouse Rule applies. A trial court may direct the parties to a divorce action to file joint or separate tax returns. The court cannot, however, delegate that decision to an accountant under Civ. R. 53 or Civ. R. 75.[7]

§ 28:21 Dependency exemptions

A dependency exemption is available for each dependent child of a taxpayer.[1] In general, for a child to qualify as a taxpayer's dependent, the taxpayer must supply over one-half of the child's support, and the child's income must be less than the exemption amount for that year, unless the child is under nineteen years of age or is under twenty years of age and a full-time student at an educational institution for at least five calendar months during the calendar year.[2] An educational institution is defined as a school maintaining a regular faculty and an established curriculum, and having an established body of students in attendance. A full-time student is one who is enrolled for some part of five calendar months for the number of hours considered full-time attendance by the educational institution.[3]

Under the Tax Reform Act of 1984, as under prior law, the parent having custody of a child for the greater portion of the year (known as the "custodial parent" under the I.R.C.) will generally be treated as having provided more than one-half of the child's support and will, therefore, be entitled to the dependency exemption.[4] The general rule under the 1984 Act applies to children of parents who have lived apart for the last six months of the calendar year, even where there is no divorce or written separation agreement, as well as to children of parents who are divorced or living apart under a decree of divorce or separate maintenance or written separation agreement. As under prior law, the 1984

---

[6]See I.R.C. § 2(b).

[7]Younkman v. Younkman, 1990 WL 119291 (Ohio Ct. App. 2d Dist. Montgomery County 1990).

[Section 28:21]

[1]I.R.C. § 151(c) ($2,050 in 1990, $2,150 in 1991, $2,300 in 1992); I.R.C. § 151(d)(3) provides for a cost-of-living increase in the dependency exemption.

[2]I.R.C. § 151, I.R.C. § 152.

[3]Treas. Reg. § 1.151-3(c).

[4]I.R.C. § 152(e)(1).

Act provides exceptions to the general rule.[5]

The custodial parent may release the exemption to the noncustodial parent. To do so, the custodial parent must sign a written declaration releasing the exemption, and the noncustodial parent must attach the written declaration to his tax return. The written declaration may be permanent, may be given annually, or may be given for a limited number of taxable years (to insure future payment of child support). The declaration must be attached to the noncustodial parent's tax return for each year that such parent claims the dependency exemption. IRS Form 8332 *Release of Claim to Exemption for Child of Divorced or Separated Parents* or a "similar statement" must be attached to the tax return for each year the exemption is being claimed. Copies of IRS Form 8332 attached to subsequent year returns will suffice. However, the use of any "similar statements" which fail to conform to the substance of IRS Form 8332 will result in denial of the dependency exemption.[6]

RC 3119.82, effective March 3, 2002, now requires the court to designate which parent may claim dependency exemptions for federal income tax purposes. If the parties agree on which parent should claim dependency exemptions, the court shall adopt such agreement in its order.

The Ohio Supreme Court, by split decision, resolved the question of whether a trial court could award the dependency exemption to a noncustodial parent as part of its division of marital property.[7] While the courts of appeals for the Fourth and Ninth Districts had held that a trial court had no authority to do so because of federal preemption,[8] the Sixth District Court of Appeals held that such an award was within the authority of the trial court.[9] The Supreme Court affirmed the decision of the Sixth District Court.[10] The Supreme Court has also allowed an award of the dependency exemption to a noncustodial parent in a paternity ac-

---

[5]I.R.C. § 152(e)(2).

[6]White v. C.I.R., T.C. Memo. 1996-438, T.C.M. (RIA) ¶ 96438 (1996).

[7]Hughes v. Hughes, 35 Ohio St. 3d 165, 518 N.E.2d 1213 (1988).

[8]Leunenberger v. Leuenberger, 1987 WL 9824 (Ohio Ct. App. 9th Dist. Lorain County 1987); Bobo v. Jewell, 1987 WL 12245 (Ohio Ct. App. 4th Dist. Athens County 1987), judgment aff'd, 38 Ohio St. 3d 330, 528 N.E.2d 180 (1988) (Supreme Court stated that parentage court could award tax dependency if in child's best interest).

[9]Hughes v. Hughes, 1987 WL 5559 (Ohio Ct. App. 6th Dist. Lucas County 1987), judgment aff'd, 35 Ohio St. 3d 165, 518 N.E.2d 1213 (1988).

[10]Hughes v. Hughes, 35 Ohio St. 3d 165, 518 N.E.2d 1213 (1988). See also Hodges v. Hodges, 43 Ohio App. 3d 113, 539 N.E.2d 709 (2d Dist. Clark County 1988) (following *Hughes*, the court held that the authority to award dependency exemptions as part of the property division extends to state tax exemptions); Kozloski v. Kozloski, 1988 WL 71617 (Ohio Ct. App. 12th Dist. Butler County 1988) (where a father's job was changed due to physical problems and depression and his salary was lowered, and the court ordered modification of support based on the father receiving the income tax dependency exemption, the court abused its discretion and the amount should be recalculated; exemption in the divorce decree was a property division, not part of child support); Ridenour v. Ridenour, 1988 WL 83516 (Ohio Ct. App. 5th Dist. Richland County 1988) (*Hughes* does not require the court to award a tax dependency exemption to the noncustodial parent; where the court's "standard order" regarding noncustodial support,

tion where the parties were not married.[11] There was no property division; thus, the award of the exemption must have been in consideration of the best interests of the child. The Ninth District Court of Appeals, citing *Bobo v. Jewell*, concluded that, at least where the exemption had not been allocated in the original proceeding, it was subject to the continuing jurisdiction of the court as a support item.[12] The Supreme Court later modified the syllabus in *Hughes* by deleting reference to marital property. A dependency exemption is now clearly an item of support.[13] The Tenth District Court of Appeals in *Houck v. Reasoner*[14] held that a trial court in a paternity action had continuing jurisdiction to modify an award of the dependency exemption. Appellate courts have not been consistent in their holdings as to continuing jurisdiction to modify such awards in both paternity and divorce actions.[15]

RC 3113.21(C)(1)(e) grants authority to trial courts to modify awards of dependency exemptions while considering motions to modify child support because of changed circumstances. There must, however, be a finding by the trial court that a substantial change of circumstances has occurred and that it is in the best interest of the child to modify the dependency exemption allocation.[16] A trial court should consider the following factors:

    (1) the relative tax brackets of the parties;

    (2) the gross incomes of the parties;

    (3) other exemptions and deductions available to each party; and

    (4) the relevant federal state, and local income tax rates of each party.[17]

A trial court may enforce its order requiring a party to execute the necessary IRS form to allow the noncustodial parent to take the dependency exemption by contempt proceedings. Any financial loss

---

insurance, and visitation expenses leaves a party unable to meet bare necessities, the order constitutes an abuse of discretion); Gunkel v. Gunkel, 1989 WL 52895 (Ohio Ct. App. 6th Dist. Lucas County 1989); Mettler v. Mettler, 61 Ohio App. 3d 14, 572 N.E.2d 127 (4th Dist. Ross County 1988); Lamberjack v. Lamberjack, 1988 WL 100614 (Ohio Ct. App. 3d Dist. Seneca County 1988), cause dismissed, 41 Ohio St. 3d 713, 535 N.E.2d 316 (1989).

[11]Bobo v. Jewell, 1987 WL 12245 (Ohio Ct. App. 4th Dist. Athens County 1987), judgment aff'd, 38 Ohio St. 3d 330, 528 N.E.2d 180 (1988).

[12]Esber v. Esber, 63 Ohio App. 3d 394, 579 N.E.2d 222 (9th Dist. Medina County 1989).

[13]Singer v. Dickinson, 63 Ohio St. 3d 408, 588 N.E.2d 806 (1992).

[14]Houck v. Reasoner, 1990 WL 41786 (Ohio Ct. App. 10th Dist. Franklin County 1990).

[15]See Helm v. Helm, 1990 WL 15736 (Ohio Ct. App. 2d Dist. Montgomery County 1990); Esber v. Esber, 63 Ohio App. 3d 394, 579 N.E.2d 222 (9th Dist. Medina County 1989); Gunkel v. Gunkel, 1989 WL 52895 (Ohio Ct. App. 6th Dist. Lucas County 1989); Mettler v. Mettler, 61 Ohio App. 3d 14, 572 N.E.2d 127 (4th Dist. Ross County 1988).

[16]Hoban v. Hoban, 64 Ohio App. 3d 257, 580 N.E.2d 1175 (9th Dist. Wayne County 1990).

[17]Singer v. Dickinson, 63 Ohio St. 3d 408, 588 N.E.2d 806 (1992).

incurred because of a party's failure to execute the form may be reimbursed by judgment.[18] So long as the child qualifies as a dependent under the federal income tax laws, a trial court has jurisdiction to enforce its order allocating the exemption, even though the child has reached majority.[19]

The right to claim a dependency exemption may be subject to compliance with the support order. It is within the discretion of the trial court to determine if compliance has been satisfactory.[20] A trial court cannot make an award of dependency exemption when considering a motion to modify custody until it determines a sufficient change of circumstances has occurred and it considers the best interests of the child.[21] When a trial court finds substantial change of circumstances to justify a modification of child support, it then may reallocate the federal income tax dependency exemptions pursuant to RC 3113.21(C)(1)(f). Payments for child support must be current if the obligor is to receive the exemption.[22]

A trial court must consider the parties' respective exemptions and deductions, the best interest of the children, and the relevant federal, state, and local income tax rates in allocating dependency exemptions.[23] The record must demonstrate that the trial court considered all pertinent factors, including the parents' gross income, other exemptions and deductions, and relevant federal, state and local income tax rates when awarding dependency exemptions to either parent.[24] The trial court must make a sufficient legal and factual analysis to determine the best interest of the children when awarding dependency exemptions.[25] In *Corple v. Corple*,[26] the trial court erred in awarding federal tax dependency exemption to the husband. There was no finding of a net tax savings and no showing that the award was in the best interests of the child. In *Goff v. Goff*,[27] the trial court concluded that awarding the dependency exemptions to the mother was more beneficial to the children than awarding them to the father. Additionally, as the father owed

---

[18]Hughes v. Hughes, 72 Ohio App. 3d 286, 594 N.E.2d 653 (6th Dist. Lucas County 1991).

[19]Casey v. Casey, 1990 WL 71587 (Ohio Ct. App. 6th Dist. Lucas County 1990). See Stanley Morganstern, *Tax Tips: Award of Dependency Exemptions,* 3 Dom. Rel. J. of Ohio 89 (July/Aug. 1991).

[20]Contini v. Contini, 1993 WL 221257 (Ohio Ct. App. 5th Dist. Tuscarawas County 1993).

[21]Inbody v. Inbody, 1995 WL 328095 (Ohio Ct. App. 3d Dist. Hancock County 1995).

[22]Presutti v. Presutti, 1997 WL 433527 (Ohio Ct. App. 7th Dist. Belmont County 1997).

[23]Maitlen v. Maitlen, 1993 WL 564220 (Ohio Ct. App. 5th Dist. Stark County 1993).

[24]Wolfangel v. Wolfangel, 1995 WL 312697 (Ohio Ct. App. 9th Dist. Summit County 1995).

[25]Saunders v. Saunders, 1995 WL 98956 (Ohio Ct. App. 9th Dist. Lorain County 1995).

[26]Corple v. Corple, 123 Ohio App. 3d 31, 702 N.E.2d 1234 (7th Dist. Columbiana County 1997).

[27]Goff v. Goff, 2001 WL 726716 (Ohio Ct. App. 2d Dist. Greene County 2001).

a substantial support arrearage, he was not entitled to the exemptions. A trial court may reallocate dependency exemptions as part of a modified support order even if the reallocation controverts the provisions of an adopted shared parenting plan.[28] The pertinent factors of gross income, other exemptions, deductions, and relevant tax rates must be fully considered. Failure to do so is error.[29]

The best interest of the child is the proper legal standard for determining which parent should have the dependency exemptions.[30] A trial court errs when it reallocates dependency exemptions without evidence demonstrating that it would be in the best interests of the children to do so.[31] The record must demonstrate that the trial court considered all pertinent factors, including the parents' gross income, other exemptions and deductions, and relevant federal, state, and local income tax rates when awarding dependency exemptions to either parent.[32] A trial court did not abuse its discretion in awarding the dependency tax exemption to the appellant-mother, even though the appellee-father was in a higher tax bracket.[33] Under *Singer v. Dickinson*,[34] a trial court may allocate a dependency exemption to a non-residential parent when that allocation would produce a net tax savings for the parents, thus furthering the best interests of the child. In *Madden v. Madden*,[35] although the trial court did not review the parents' gross income in light of exemptions and deductions, the award of the dependency exemption to each parent in alternating years was not an abuse of discretion. The mother's income for raising the minor child exceeded that of the father. The award to each parent produced nearly the same net tax savings. Accordingly, the child's best interests were furthered regardless of which parent received the dependency exemption. Beginning in 2002 federal personal exemption is $3000 per person. The value of the personal exemption to a parent will depend on his or her tax bracket. For a person in the 15% bracket, the tax savings is $450 ($3000 times 15%); for a person in the 27% bracket, the tax savings is $810 ($3000 times 27%). The personal exemption is phased out if the taxpayer's adjusted gross income (hereafter AGI) is above a threshold amount: $137,300 for single and $171,650 for head of household. The dollar amount of the exemption is reduced by 2% of each $2500 that AGI exceeds the phase out amount. Thus the value of the personal exemption is eliminated if AGI exceeds the threshold amount by $122,500 or more.

---

[28]Bender v. Bender, 2001 WL 808975 (Ohio Ct. App. 9th Dist. Summit County 2001).

[29]Handlovic v. Handlovic, 2000 WL 1335072 (Ohio Ct. App. 5th Dist. Ashland County 2000).

[30]Hurchanik v. Hurchanik, 110 Ohio App. 3d 628, 674 N.E.2d 1260 (12th Dist. Warren County 1996).

[31]Mills v. Mills, 1995 WL 234351 (Ohio Ct. App. 3d Dist. Wyandot County 1995).

[32]Wolfangel v. Wolfangel, 1995 WL 312697 (Ohio Ct. App. 9th Dist. Summit County 1995).

[33]Pryor v. Nye, 1995 WL 477600 (Ohio Ct. App. 3d Dist. Marion County 1995).

[34]Singer v. Dickinson, 63 Ohio St. 3d 408, 588 N.E.2d 806 (1992).

[35]Madden v. Madden, 1997 WL 675449 (Ohio Ct. App. 8th Dist. Cuyahoga County 1997).

As under prior law, the general rule will not apply to multiple support agreements[36] and, under the 1984 Act, will not apply to decrees of divorce or separate maintenance or written separation agreements in effect on or before December 31, 1984.[37] Prior law will control the availability of the exemption to the noncustodial parent, but it appears the waiver may still be required.

In the case of remarriage of a child's parent, the Tax Reform Act of 1984 also added a provision that treats support provided by the remarried parent's spouse as support provided by the remarried parent.[38]

A trial court has discretion to consider a party's new spouse's income for the purpose of reallocating the federal income tax dependency exemption.[39] The Supreme Court decision in *Singer v. Dickinson* does not mandate the award of dependency exemptions to the party with the greatest increase in income even though it may result in the net tax savings to the parties combined. An increase in the net spendable income of a custodial parent may be in the best interest of a child even though tax savings are not maximized.[40]

The determination of a child's status as a dependent also affects other Internal Revenue Code provisions. In general, the 1984 Act provides that a custodial parent who releases his dependency exemption with respect to a child will still be treated as the parent of such child for all other purposes under the Code, including:

(1) *Medical expenses*: For purposes of the medical expense deduction, any child subject to a waiver of dependency exemption by the custodial parent will be considered as a child of both parents. Therefore, both the custodial and noncustodial parents may deduct their respective medical expenses paid on behalf of the child, even though the dependency exemption is claimed by the noncustodial parent.[41]

(2) *Child care credit*: The custodial parent may claim a tax credit for eligible expenses for the care of children under age thirteen, even though that parent has released his dependency exemption.[42] A parent receives a federal child care tax credit if he or she pays for work-related child care. There is a limit on the amount which can be used to figure the credit; $2400 for one child and $4800 for two or more children. The percentage of the credit decreases as the payor's adjusted gross income (AGI) increases. To claim the child care credit, a parent need not claim the minor child as a dependent on the federal income tax return provided the other tests are met. The child care credit is nonrefundable so there must be a tax liability to use this credit.

A parent receives an Ohio child care tax credit if his/her AGI is less

---

[36]I.R.C. § 152(e)(3).

[37]I.R.C. § 152(e)(4).

[38]I.R.C. § 152(e)(5).

[39]Hutchinson v. Hutchinson, 85 Ohio App. 3d 173, 619 N.E.2d 466 (4th Dist. Jackson County 1993).

[40]Stafford v. Stafford, 1994 WL 30515 (Ohio Ct. App. 6th Dist. Lucas County 1994).

[41]I.R.C. § 105(b).

[42]I.R.C. § 21(e)(5).

than $40,000. The credit is 35% of the federal child care tax credit if AGI is less than $20,000 and 25% of the federal child care tax credit if AGI is between $20,000 and $40,000. If AGI is more than $40,000 there is no State of Ohio child care credit.

(3) *Earned income credit*: Under the Tax Reform Act of 1984, the earned income credit will be available to the custodial parent who releases his right to a dependency exemption.[43] Low income wage earners qualify for an earned income credit if AGI is less than $29,201 with one qualifying child and $33,178 for more than one qualifying child. The qualifying child does not need to be claimed as a dependent but must have lived with the parent for more than half the year.

A wife's federal earned income credit was deemed to be marital property, even though it was for a child from a previous marriage, where the husband had assumed complete financial responsibility for the child and the natural father had no relationship with the child.[44]

The deduction available for the dependency exemption may be reduced, or phased out, depending on the taxable amount of the income of the parent claiming the exemption.[45] A careful tax analysis may conclude that a custodial parent with significantly less income should retain the exemption(s), so as to maximize the overall tax savings, and could be in consideration of a reduced or lower monthly contribution from the noncustodial parent. The dependency exemption should be awarded to the parent who will be most able to use it for the best interest of the minor child.[46]

The changes discussed above are generally effective for taxable years commencing after December 31, 1984. Decrees of divorce or separate maintenance and written separation agreements that comply with prior law are not affected by the 1984 Act. However, if a pre-1985 instrument is amended, the new rules will apply.

A $600 tax credit is available for each qualifying child under the age of seventeen.[47] The child tax credit is linked to the dependency exemption and cannot be separated. A qualifying child is generally defined as one for whom the taxpayer can claim a dependency exemption. There is a limit on the child tax credit if the taxpayer's adjusted gross income is above a certain amount: $75,000 for single or head of household ($110,000 for married filing joint). The credit is reduced by $50 for each $1000 (or fraction of $1000) that AGI exceeds the phase-out limit. Thus if the taxpayer's AGI is $87,000 and there is only one child, he or she

---

[43]Former I.R.C. § 43(c)(1)(A), recodified as I.R.C. § 32, and former I.R.C. § 44A(f)(5), recodified as I.R.C. § 21.

[44]Derr v. Derr, 1996 WL 131156 (Ohio Ct. App. 12th Dist. Preble County 1996).

[45]For 1995, the phase-out begins at $86,025 for married taxpayers filing separate returns, $114,700 for single taxpayers, $143,350 for unmarried heads of household and $172,050 for married taxpayers filing jointly. The threshold amounts for subsequent years are adjusted annually for inflation. 26 U.S.C.A. § 151(d)(3).

[46]Gosiewski v. Gosiewski, 1990 WL 140685 (Ohio Ct. App. 10th Dist. Franklin County 1990); Brant v. Brant, 1991 WL 11395 (Ohio Ct. App. 9th Dist. Medina County 1991).

[47]I.R.C. § 24.

does not benefit from the credit. If there are two children and the taxpayer's AGI is $99,000, the credit is totally phased out.

Originally, the child tax credit was limited to the amount of federal income tax liability unless there were three or more qualifying children. If the taxpayer owed no federal tax because of the earned income credit and/or the child care credit, the child tax credit could not be used to increase the tax refund. If there were three or more qualifying children, the disallowed portion of the child tax credit could be refundable up to the amount that social security taxes exceed the earned income credit. Beginning in 2001, the child tax credit is refundable, whether or not federal tax is owed, to the extent of 10% of earned income in excess of $10,350. The Taxpayer Relief Act of 1997 also makes available tax credit for qualified tuition and related expenses paid on behalf of dependents of up to $1,500 per year.[48] The educational tax credits are phased out as modified adjusted gross income exceeds $40,000 ($80,000 in the case of joint return) and not available to married taxpayers unless they file a joint return.[49] There are two tax credits for higher education, the Hope scholarship credit and the lifetime learning credit. The Hope credit is up to $1500 for qualified tuition and related expenses paid for each student attending at least half time, but can only be claimed for two years. The lifetime learning credit is 20% of expenses paid up to a maximum of $1000 per year, but there is no restriction on the number of years the credit can be claimed nor must the student attend at least half time. Taxpayers that qualify for both credits may only claim one. Both these credits are phased out or reduced if the taxpayer's AGI is between $40,000 and $50,000. If AGI is over $50,000 the taxpayer cannot claim any credit.

§ 28:22 Attorney fees

Generally, attorney fees in a divorce case are nondeductible.[1] However, a portion of the attorney fees paid by a party may be allowable as a deduction. Code Section 212 provides:

> In the case of an individual, there shall be allowed as a deduction all the ordinary and necessary expenses paid or incurred during the taxable year—
>
> (1) for the production or collection of income;
>
> (2) for the management, conservation, or maintenance of property held for the production of income; or
>
> (3) in connection with the determination, collection, or refund of any tax.

Since the recipient of periodic alimony must include the payments received in gross income under Section 71, that portion of the total attorney fees paid by the recipient which relate to "the production . . . of

---

[48]I.R.C. § 25A.

[49]I.R.C. § 25A(d) and I.R.C. § 25A(g)(6).

[Section 28:22]

[1]Treas. Reg. § 1.262-1(b)(7).

income" are therefore deductible by the periodic alimony recipient.[2]

The recipient of periodic alimony should be entitled to deduct attorney fees incurred in a modification proceeding, at least where the periodic alimony payments are increased. Also, the recipient of periodic alimony should be entitled to deduct attorney fees incurred as a result of appellate court actions which relate to the production of taxable income (i.e., periodic alimony).[3]

Section 212(1) permits a deduction for costs attributable to the production or collection of income. The payor of periodic alimony is usually not entitled to any attorney fee deductions under Section 212(1). Fees paid by the payor of periodic alimony to defend against an action for the enforcement of an alimony award, to defend against an increase in periodic alimony, to seek a decrease in the amount of periodic alimony, and related appellate matters are nondeductible personal expenses.[4]

In a divorce case, virtually no attorney fees will be deductible by either party under Section 212(2) which allows a deduction for the "management, conservation, or maintenance of property held for the production of income." In 1963, the United States Supreme Court in companion cases denied such deductions and established the "origin of the claim" test for determining whether attorney fees are deductible under Section 212(2).

United States v. Gilmore[5] involved a husband who spent substantial sums successfully defending against his wife's claim that his interest in three franchise car dealerships was community property. The trial court found that the husband's principal object in the divorce case was to protect the dealership property from his wife's claim that she was entitled to a significant portion of it. The court found that the husband's defense was motivated in substantial part by a desire to continue to earn a livelihood and also by a fear that the damaging allegations made by his wife would cause the franchisors to terminate the dealership franchises.

The government argued that the attorney fees paid by the husband were not deductible, in spite of the likely result if his wife were successful in the divorce case, because the origin and nature of his wife's claims were inherently personal in nature. The Supreme Court adopted the government's view and held that the question of whether the amounts paid for attorney fees were personal and therefore nondeductible or were business related and therefore deductible turned on "the origin and character of the claim with respect to which the expenses [were] incurred, rather than . . . [the] potential consequences upon the fortunes of the taxpayer."[6]

The Court held that the wife's claims did not arise in connection with

---

[2]I.R.C. § 212(1); Treas. Reg. § 1.262-1(b)(7).

[3]Treas. Reg. § 1.262-1(b)(7).

[4]Sunderland v. C.I.R., T.C. Memo. 1977-116, 1977 WL 3417 (1977).

[5]U.S. v. Gilmore, 372 U.S. 39, 83 S. Ct. 623, 9 L. Ed. 2d 570 (1963).

[6]U.S. v. Gilmore, 372 U.S. 39, 49, 83 S. Ct. 623, 9 L. Ed. 2d 570 (1963).

the husband's profit-seeking activities because her claims "stemmed entirely from the marital relationship."[7] The wife's claim that the car dealerships were community property "could not have existed but for the marital relationship,"[8] and the wife's claim that she was entitled to more than one-half of the community property depended upon "the wife making good her charges of [the husband's] marital infidelity."[9]

In *United States v. Patrick*,[10] the husband and the wife each owned twenty-eight percent of the common stock issued by a close corporation which was in the business of publishing a newspaper. The remaining stock was owned directly or indirectly by the couple's children. The wife also owned a portion of the real property which the close corporation used in its business. The husband conveyed some publicly traded securities to his wife for her interest in the close corporation, and a new lease was arranged with regard to the real property used by the close corporation. The attorney fees paid by the husband were allocated in part to rearranging the stock interests in the close corporation and arranging the new lease.

The trial court allowed a deduction for the attorney fees so paid because it found that the fees were not incurred "to resist a liability, but to arrange how it could be met without depriving [the husband] of income-producing property, the loss of which would have destroyed his capacity to earn income."[11]

The United States Supreme Court reversed and held for the government. The Court stated, "These matters were incidental to litigation brought by [the] wife, whose claims arising from [the husband's] personal and family life were the origin of the property arrangements."[12]

In short, a claim by either spouse in a divorce case that attorney fees are deductible because the fees were incurred for the "conservation, or maintenance of property held for the production of income" will only rarely, if ever, be successful.[13]

If attorney fees are awarded to a party, the taxability of the award to the recipient turns on whether or not the award is itself periodic alimony. If attorney fees are awarded in a lump sum to a party, they should not be taxable to the recipient or deductible by the payor. Conversely, if an award of attorney fees is blended into a stream of periodic alimony payments, presumably they are taxable to the recipient and deductible by the payor as periodic alimony.

Prior to the Tax Reform Act of 1984, an alimony payor could not deduct as alimony his spouse's legal fees. The 1984 Act permits a deduction of

---

[7]U.S. v. Gilmore, 372 U.S. 39, 51, 83 S. Ct. 623, 9 L. Ed. 2d 570 (1963).

[8]U.S. v. Gilmore, 372 U.S. 39, 52, 83 S. Ct. 623, 9 L. Ed. 2d 570 (1963).

[9]U.S. v. Gilmore, 372 U.S. 39, 52, 83 S. Ct. 623, 9 L. Ed. 2d 570 (1963).

[10]U.S. v. Patrick, 372 U.S. 53, 83 S. Ct. 618, 9 L. Ed. 2d 580 (1963).

[11]U.S. v. Patrick, 372 U.S. 53, 56, 83 S. Ct. 618, 9 L. Ed. 2d 580 (1963).

[12]U.S. v. Patrick, 372 U.S. 53, 57, 83 S. Ct. 618, 9 L. Ed. 2d 580 (1963).

[13]U.S. v. Patrick, 372 U.S. 53, 53 fn.1, 83 S. Ct. 618, 9 L. Ed. 2d 580 (1963).

any payment made to or on behalf of an alimony recipient.[14]

Any portion of the attorney fees which relate to "the determination, collection, or refund of any tax" are deductible under Section 212(3). Presumably, both the husband and the wife receive some tax advice with regard to the divorce. All such fees are deductible in full by reason of Section 212(3) if paid by the recipient of the tax advice.[15]

The attorney should make an allocation of the total fee to deductible and nondeductible items. When an attorney renders tax advice, it is proper to allocate a portion of the total fee to such advice so that his client can deduct that portion under Section 212. Revenue Ruling 72-545 indicates that if a sole practitioner allocates a total fee between tax and nontax matters based "on the amount of the attorney's time attributable to each, the fee customarily charged in the locality for similar services, and the results obtained in the divorce," then that portion of the fee allocated to tax advice will be deductible.

Examples of deductible tax planning issues arising in domestic matters may be summarized as follows:

(a) Costs of allocating dependency exemptions.

(b) Costs of maximizing the deduction of spousal support required to be paid.

(c) Alternatively, the costs of minimizing the taxable portion of spousal support to be received.

(d) Costs associated with preparing the written separation agreement required to assure deductible support payments.

(e) Costs associated with estate planning which relate to assuring proper estate and gift tax treatment for the payment of support or the receipt of property distributed.

(f) Costs incurred in determining the adjusted basis of assets which are distributed as part of the property settlement.

(g) Costs of assuring that either or both spouses secure rollover treatment for retirement plan benefit distributions.

(h) Costs of preparing a written QDRO to assure proper tax treatment.

(i) Costs of assuring rollover treatment for the sale of the personal residence in connection with the divorce.

(j) Costs associated with planning an alimony trust to avoid restrictions limiting the deductibility of alimony.

(k) Costs allocated to properly planning and structuring the property division to produce the intended tax results.

Counsel should maintain time records which support the itemizations. Note that the allocations need not be purely mathematical; rather, allocations may be based on the degree of difficulty of the issues presented

---

[14]I.R.C. § 71(b)(1)(A); Burkes v. C.I.R., T.C. Memo. 1998-61, T.C.M. (RIA) ¶ 98061 (1998); Berry v. C.I.R., T.C. Memo. 2000-373, T.C.M. (RIA) ¶ 2000-373 (2000), judgment aff'd, 36 Fed. Appx. 400 (10th Cir. 2002).

[15]U.S. v. Davis, 370 U.S. 65, 82 S. Ct. 1190, 8 L. Ed. 2d 335 (1962).

and the amount of tax at issue as well as time.[16] Even where expenses are not currently deductible, they may be added to the basis of assets acquired in the property division. In *Serriani v. Commissioner*,[17] for example, the Tax Court permitted $200,000 of a $236,000 legal fee to be capitalized and added to the basis of the property acquired from the spouse.

Fees allocable either to disclaiming or defending title to particular items of property while not currently deductible may be added to the basis of the asset and utilized to reduce taxable gain on subsequent disposition. For example, where one spouse claims rights to an asset acquired prior to the marriage in defense of claims that it was subsequently transmuted into marital property, legal fees allocable to the defense of title may be added to the basis of that property.

§ 28:23   Innocent spouse rule

Joint tax liability, including interest and penalty, is created by the signing and filing of a joint tax return. Each spouse is responsible for the tax liability resulting for a tax year in which a joint return was filed even if the income or expense is attributable to only one spouse. Joint liability continues for any subsequent audit adjustments which may result. Divorce does not relieve a party from joint liability and individual responsibility created on a joint return for any year prior to the divorce.

A trial court has jurisdiction to allocate possible tax liability between the parties. In *Halpern v. Halpern*,[1] the husband ran an insurance agency, even though the wife owned one-half. The amount of liability which was unknown at the time of trial was assessed to the husband primarily because of his greater involvement.

A provision in a separation agreement incorporated into a decree of divorce requiring one party to hold the other harmless from any tax liability in any year in which the parties filed a joint tax return will not relieve that party of the responsibility for unpaid taxes, interest, and penalties as between that party and the Internal Revenue Service.

There does exist, however, an exception to the general rule of joint responsibility. I.R.C. § 6013(e) sets forth the exception and the requirements for innocent spouse relief. An "innocent spouse" may escape liability if the tax on a joint tax return was understated by more than $500 because the other spouse (1) omitted an item of gross income; or (2) claimed a deduction, credit, or property basis for which there was no basis in fact or law.

Prior to the 1984 Tax Reform Act, I.R.C. § 6013(e) generally provided

---

[16]Rev. Rul. 72-545.

[17]Serianni v. Commissioner of Internal Revenue, 80 T.C. 1090, 1983 WL 14842 (1983), decision aff'd, 765 F.2d 1051 (11th Cir. 1985).

[Section 28:23]

[1]Halpern v. Halpern, 1993 WL 266904 (Ohio Ct. App. 8th Dist. Cuyahoga County 1993).

that a party to a joint tax return could escape liability if that spouse was unaware of an omission of gross income in excess of 25% of the total gross income, so long as the spouse claiming to be innocent had (1) no knowledge of the omission, (2) no reason to know of the omission, and (3) under all circumstances existing, it would be inequitable to hold the innocent spouse liable for the tax, penalties, and interest. The innocent spouse had the burden of proving by a preponderance of the evidence that these factors existed and also that he or she had not received any benefit from the omission.

The 1984 Tax Reform Act changed the innocent spouse provisions to include relief from any "grossly erroneous" items, including claims for deductions, credits, or property basis, which had no basis in fact or in law.[2]

A substantial understatement is one that creates an understatement of tax by more than $500. If the tax liability was created by the omission of income, then the tax must be understated by more than $500 before a party is entitled to relief under the innocent spouse doctrine.

However, if the understatement of tax was created by a false claim for deduction, credit, or property basis, then the innocent spouse relief will be subject to the following limitations:

(1) If the innocent spouse's adjusted gross income is less than $20,000 for the year immediately before the year in which the adjustment is sought, relief will be allowed only if the liability attributable to the understatement exceeds 10% of that spouse's adjusted gross; and

(2) If adjusted gross income of the innocent spouse was more than $20,000 for the year immediately preceding the year in which the adjustment is sought, relief will only be allowed if the liability attributable to the understatement exceeds 25% of such spouse's adjusted gross income.[3]

The limitations of relief apply only to cases of understatement resulting from deductions, credits, or basis unfounded in law and fact and not to omissions of income.

While the 1984 Tax Reform Act liberalized the innocent spouse doctrine by expanding the circumstances in which relief could be granted, as under the prior law, relief may only be granted when it would be inequitable to hold the innocent spouse liable.[4]

The disallowance of a deduction in and of itself is not sufficient to satisfy the requisites of the innocent spouse doctrine. The deduction must have been taken when there was no basis in fact or in law for claiming it. As was the case before the 1984 Tax Reform Act, an innocent spouse must establish that he or she had no knowledge of nor reason to know that income was omitted or deductions improperly

---

[2]I.R.C. § 6103(e)(2)(B).

[3]I.R.C. § 6013(e)(4)(A).

[4]See generally Wren, Gabinet and Carrad, Tax Aspects of Marital Dissolution § 6:18.

claimed. These are questions of fact and a reasonably prudent person standard applies: "whether a reasonably prudent person with knowledge of the facts possessed by the person claiming innocent spouse status should have been alerted to the possibility of a substantial understatement."[5]

Significant factors to be considered include whether the alleged innocent spouse participated in the business affairs or bookkeeping of the other spouse; whether the guilty spouse refused to be forthright concerning his or her income; whether there was unusual or lavish expenditures made as compared to the reported income; and whether the couple's standard of living improved significantly during the years for which innocent spouse status is sought.

Knowledge of a spouse's gambling activities may be sufficient to establish that the claimed innocent spouse had knowledge or should have known of unreported income.[6]

An innocent spouse must be one who does not significantly benefit from the omission or claimed deduction. Normal support is not a significant benefit. Direct or indirect benefits obtained through the transfer of property or traceable to property that should have been included in gross income may preclude innocent spouse status. Each case must be decided on its own factual situation to determine whether the claimed innocent spouse benefitted from the omission.

Specific examples of innocent spouse doctrine include the following:

(1) Protection denied:
    (a) Wife signed blank returns;[7]
    (b) Wife's personal debts paid from refunds;[8]
    (c) Wife knew of husband's finances;[9]
    (d) Family unit spent more than reported income;[10] and
    (e) Wife did not review tax return although having had the opportunity.[11]

(2) Protection granted:

---

[5]Mertens Law of Federal Income Taxation § 55.186 (citing Shea v. C.I.R., 780 F.2d 561, 566 (6th Cir. 1986)).

[6]Swofford v. C.I.R., T.C. Memo. 1975-148, 1975 WL 2775 (1975) (failure of spouse to show claimed innocent spouse's books and records may be sufficient to put that spouse on notice); Adams v. Commissioner of Internal Revenue, 60 T.C. 300, 1973 WL 2541 (1973) (unusual and lavish expenditures by spouse as compared to reported income may be sufficient to disqualify claimed innocent spouse); Mysse v. Commissioner of Internal Revenue, 57 T.C. 680, 1972 WL 2536 (1972), recommendation regarding acquiescence, 1972 WL 33093 (I.R.S. AOD 1972) and acq., 1972-2 C.B. 1.

[7]Ewell v. C.I.R., T.C. Memo. 1988-265, 1988 WL 62047 (1988).

[8]Schlosser v. C.I.R., T.C. Memo. 1992-233, T.C.M. (RIA) ¶ 92233 (1992), aff'd, 2 F.3d 404 (11th Cir. 1993).

[9]Hill v. C. I. R., T.C. Memo. 1990-367, 1990 WL 99422 (1990).

[10]Estate of Jackson v. Commissioner of Internal Revenue, 72 T.C. 356, 1979 WL 3737 (1979).

[11]Skelton v. C.I.R., T.C. Memo. 1988-136, 1988 WL 25334 (1988).

(a) Husband did not know of wife's embezzlement of funds;[12]

(b) Wife ignorant of husband's criminal activities;[13]

(c) Wife did not sign 1040 form;[14]

(d) Parties lived apart, wife did not know of husband's drug dealings; and

(e) Wife ignorant of business or family finances.[15]

The Taxpayer Relief Act of 1997 expanded the application of the innocent spouse rule by granting special administrative relief to spouses of partners in the context of partnership tax proceedings.[16]

While counsel may not always be able to protect a client from tax liability that may arise after a termination of marriage, the innocent spouse rule may be available to accord relief for liability attributable to tax filings made during the marriage. Laying the ground work for such a claim through discovery during the divorce process should be considered if the circumstances warrant.

Potential liability for back taxes on prior returns and liability for estimated tax liability for current periods should also be considered by counsel. The non-income-producing spouse should consider seeking indemnification for taxes assessed because of a change in a prior joint return and for penalties assessed for underpayment of estimated taxes before agreeing to sign a joint return, since both spouses are jointly and severally liable for all tax, penalty, and interest which may be due for a tax year in which a joint return was filed.[17]

I.R.C. § 6015 now provides relief from joint and several liability on joint returns. This new innocent spouse provision has been held to apply retroactively to the full amount of any pre-existing tax liability.[18] In order to qualify for such relief, the following factors must exist:

(1) A joint return was filed;

(2) There was an understatement of tax because of erroneous items of *one* of the joint files;

(3) The innocent spouse did not know and had no reason to know of the understatements; and

(4) Under all of the facts and circumstances, it would be inequitable to hold the innocent spouse liable.

The claim for relief on the appropriate form must be filed within two (2) years after collection activities commenced. Generally, the burden of proof rests with the claimant.

Although wife was barred from presenting an innocent spouse claim

---

[12]Klimenko v. C.I.R., T.C. Memo. 1993-340, T.C.M. (RIA) ¶ 93340 (1993).

[13]Jones v. C.I.R., T.C. Memo. 1977-51, 1977 WL 3356 (1977).

[14]Leggett v. C.I.R., T.C. Memo. 1976-7, 1976 WL 3205 (1976).

[15]Estate of Brown v. C.I.R., T.C. Memo. 1988-297, 1988 WL 70611 (1988).

[16]Sec. 1237 of the Act (H.R. 2014).

[17]I.R.C. § 6013; Treas. Reg. § 1.6013-1 to Treas. Reg. § 1.6013-7.

[18]Flores v. U.S., 51 Fed. Cl. 49 (2001).

to the Internal Revenue Service, she was not barred by res judicata from asserting the defense against husband in the trial of their divorce case.[19]

---

[19]Prohaska v. Prohaska, 2000 WL 530359 (Ohio Ct. App. 9th Dist. Medina County 2000).

§ 28:24   Request for innocent spouse relief—Form

Form **8857**	**Request for Innocent Spouse Relief**	
(Rev. December 1998)	(And Separation of Liability and Equitable Relief)	OMB No. 1545-1596
Department of the Treasury Internal Revenue Service	▶ Do not file with your tax return. ▶ See instructions.	

Your name	Your social security number

Your current address	Apt. no.

City, town or post office, state, and ZIP code. If a foreign address, see instructions.	Daytime phone no. (optional) ( )

Before you begin, you need to understand the following terms. See instructions for descriptions.

- Separation of Liability
- Joint and Several Liability
- Innocent Spouse Relief
- Understatement of Tax
- Equitable Relief
- Underpayment of Tax

TIP *The IRS can help you with your request. If you are working with an IRS employee, you can ask that employee, or you can call 1-800-829-1040.*

1 Enter the year(s) for which you are requesting relief from liability of tax (see instructions) . ▶ ....

2 Information about your spouse (or former spouse) to whom you were married at the end of the year(s) on line 1.

Name	Social security number

Current home address (number and street). If a P.O. box, see instructions.	Apt. no.

City, town or post office, state, and ZIP code. If a foreign address, see instructions.	Daytime phone no. (if known) ( )

TIP *If you only have an **underpayment of tax** (tax shown on your joint return that was not paid), you may only request **equitable relief.** Skip lines 3 and 4 and see line 5 and its instructions.*

3 If you have an **understatement of tax,** you may request **Separation of Liability.** You may be relieved of liability for your spouse's (or former spouse's) part of the liability. However, this relief is available only if you and your spouse (or former spouse):
- Are no longer married, or
- Are legally separated, or
- Have lived apart at all times during the 12-month period prior to the date you file this form.

If one of the above conditions apply, attach a statement as explained on page 3 and check here . . . ▶ ☐

4 If you have an **understatement of tax** due to erroneous items of your spouse (or former spouse), you may be allowed **Innocent Spouse Relief.** Attach a statement as explained on page 4 and check here . . . . . ▶ ☐

5 If you have an **underpayment of tax** or you do not qualify for relief under **3** or **4** above, we will automatically consider whether you qualify for **Equitable Relief.** Attach a statement as explained on page 4 and check here . . . . ▶ ☐

Where To File: Generally, send this form to: **Internal Revenue Service Center, Cincinnati, OH 45999-0857.** But if you are meeting with an IRS employee or you received an IRS notice of deficiency, see page 2.

Under penalties of perjury, I declare that I have examined this form and any accompanying schedules and statements, and to the best of my knowledge and belief, they are true, correct, and complete. Declaration of preparer (other than taxpayer) is based on all information of which preparer has any knowledge.

Sign Here Keep a copy of this form for your records.	Your signature ▶		Date

Paid Preparer's Use Only	Preparer's signature ▶	Date	Check if self-employed ☐	Preparer's social security no.
	Firm's name (or yours if self-employed) and address ▶			EIN
				ZIP code

For Privacy Act and Paperwork Reduction Act Notice, see page 4.   Cat. No. 24647V   Form **8857** (Rev. 12-98)

§ 28:25   Estate and gift taxes

Transfers between spouses may have gift tax implications. If the parties are divorced within two years after entering into a separation agreement, or within one year prior to entering into the agreement to transfer property, there will be no gift tax. The agreement must settle their property rights or provide a reasonable allowance for the support of minor children. The transfer is then deemed to be for full consideration.[1]

A transferor's gross estate may include property transferred under the terms of a separation agreement or divorce decree if the transferor is deemed to have retained control over or an interest in the property. Specific instances of includability for estate tax purposes could result from the transfers made within three years of the transferor's death,[2] transfers made with a retained life estate,[3] transfers taking effect at death,[4] or revocable transfers.[5] Generally speaking, complete transfers which were made for full and adequate consideration will not be included.

§ 28:26   Reconciliation Act of 2001

Marginal tax rates for individuals have been reduced. A new 10% rate bracket has been established. Effective July 1, 2001, the marginal rates will decline through 2006. The top rate of 39.6% will be reduced to 35%. The limitation on itemized deductions will be gradually eliminated beginning in 2006. Likewise, in 2006, the personal exemption phase-out will begin to be reduced and entirely eliminated in 2010.

Beginning in 2005, the marriage penalty will be addressed. Joint filers will receive a standard deduction twice the amount of single filers.

The child tax credit will be doubled to $1,000. The phase-in begins in tax year 2001 and extends for ten years. The adoption credit is increased to $10,000 effective in 2002.

Effective in 2002 the dependent care tax credit is increased from 30% to 35%, and the amount of eligible employment-related expenses is raised from $2,000 to $3,000.

The act also affects estate taxes, gift taxes, college tuition deductions, education savings accounts, student loan interest, and retirement savings and pension plans.

[Section 28:25]
   [1]I.R.C. § 2516.
   [2]I.R.C. § 2035.
   [3]I.R.C. § 2036.
   [4]I.R.C. § 2037.
   [5]I.R.C. § 2038.

Chapter 29

Government Retirement Benefits

By Melissa Graham-Hurd, Esq.

> **KeyCite®:** Cases and other legal materials listed in KeyCite Scope can be researched through West Group's KeyCite service on Westlaw®. Use KeyCite to check citations for form, parallel references, prior and later history, and comprehensive citator information, including citations to other decisions and secondary materials.

§ 29:1 Social security benefits—In general

RC 3105.171(A)(3)(a)(i), (ii), and RC 3105.18(C)(1) require a court to consider the parties' financial resources, including retirement benefits, when dividing marital property and when determining the appropriateness of awarding spousal support. A failure to do so is plain error, subjecting the orders of the offending court to reversal.[1]

This section will explain briefly the operation of the social security system and highlight those areas of particular relevance to domestic relations law. Specifically, the two major programs of the system to be examined are Title II of the Social Security Act, 42 U.S.C.A. § 401, and Title XVI, 42 U.S.C.A. § 1381.

§ 29:2 Social security benefits—Worker's Title II benefits— Retirement

A worker becomes entitled to collect retirement benefits through the social security system when he or she attains the age of sixty-two years, has filed an application for benefits, and has worked in employment covered by the system for a required number of years or quarters.[1] Generally, the rule is that any worker born after January 2, 1929 must have at least forty quarters of covered employment in order to have full benefits under the system.[2] This means that the employment had to be covered by the social security system and that the worker earned a minimum amount in each calendar quarter or earned a minimum amount yearly.[3]

All payments are based on the earning history of the worker. Although a worker can begin to receive benefits at age 62, the amount of the monthly benefit will increase if the worker continues to contribute to the system and delays retirement up to age 70. Retirement benefits claimed prior to full retirement age will result in a reduction of the monthly benefit, between 54.8% for persons born in 1938 to 50% for persons born in 1960. For persons born in 1937 and prior years, full retirement age is 65 years, and for each year of birth thereafter, through birth dates in 1942, two months are added. For example, a person born in 1938 must be age 65 plus two months, a person born in 1939 must be age 65 plus four months, and so on. For persons born 1943 through 1954, age 66 is full retirement age. Persons born in 1955 must be age 66 plus two months, and again there are two additional months for persons

---

[Section 29:1]

[1]Beyer v. Beyer, 64 Ohio App. 2d 280, 18 Ohio Op. 3d 267, 413 N.E.2d 844 (8th Dist. Cuyahoga County 1979); Brown v. Brown, 32 Ohio App. 2d 139, 61 Ohio Op. 2d 162, 288 N.E.2d 852 (8th Dist. Cuyahoga County 1972); Eickelberger v. Eickelberger, 93 Ohio App. 3d 221, 638 N.E.2d 130 (12th Dist. Butler County 1994); Schaefers v. Schaefers, 1994 WL 631660 (Ohio Ct. App. 7th Dist. Columbiana County 1994).

[Section 29:2]

[1]42 U.S.C.A. § 402(a)(2).

[2]20 C.F.R. § 101.

[3]20 C.F.R. § 101. The amount changes each year. For example, in 1978 the required yearly earnings were $250, and by 1995, the amount had risen to $630.

born each year thereafter through 1959. For persons born in 1960 and beyond, full retirement age is 67 years. Delaying retirement beyond full retirement age will result in a higher monthly benefit, again depending on the year of birth, and the increase in benefits ranges between 4% for persons born from 1927 to 1928 and 8% for persons born in 1943 or later.RSDHI retirement benefits will continue unless the worker begins working and earns over the maximum allowable amount, is convicted of a subversive act, is deported, or dies.[4] A cost of living adjustment is determined with reference to the Consumer Price Index and is effective on January 1 each year.

§ 29:3   Social security benefits—Worker's Title II benefits— Disability

Prior to receiving a monthly social security benefit ("old age pension"), a worker may be eligible to receive a monthly benefit from the Social Security Disability Insurance (SSDI) program if he or she becomes disabled.[1] Basically, if a worker under age sixty-five years is unable to engage in substantial gainful activity because of a medically determinable physical or mental impairment that has lasted or can reasonably be expected to last for more than twelve months or end in death, and has the required number of quarters of coverage under the Social Security Act, he or she will be eligible for disability benefits.[2] "Substantial gainful activity" is a term of art and is defined in 42 U.S.C.A. § 423(e).

The amount of these disability benefits depends on the earnings record of the worker. The monthly benefits will continue in full until the worker is able to engage in substantial gainful activity, receives workers' compensation, refuses to accept vocational rehabilitation, is deported, dies, fails to follow proper treatment, or for other causes.[3]

Once disability benefits are awarded, a review takes place every six to 18 months thereafter if improvement of the disabling condition is expected, or every five to seven years if improvement is not expected. Benefits can be reduced depending on the amount and regularity of income, number of hours worked, and work duties of the recipient.

A person may receive both SSDI benefits and payments from an employer or a private disability policy at the same time. A person may collect SSDI benefits and workers' compensation benefits at the same time, as long as the total is not more than 80% of the person's average wage before he or she was disabled.

Medicare benefits are available to SSDI recipients after 24 months of receiving benefits or at age 65, whichever comes first. Hospitalization benefits under Medicare are free, but a premium payment is required for medical insurance. Special rules apply for married disabled persons

---

[4]1 Unempl. Ins. Rep. 12451.

[Section 29:3]
   [1]42 U.S.C.A. § 423.
   [2]42 U.S.C.A. § 423.
   [3]42 U.S.C.A. § 423.

who are covered by their spouses' medical insurance. Details are available at 1-800-MEDICARE.

§ 29:4 Social security benefits—Worker's Title II benefits—Children's benefits

The child of a worker with a sufficient number of quarters of coverage under the social security system may be eligible for a monthly benefit of one-half of the insured worker's monthly benefit amount,[1] under certain conditions,[2] if the parent or person in the place of a parent retires or becomes disabled. The benefit increases to 75% in the case of a deceased worker.

To obtain benefits, the child or person acting on behalf of the child must file an application and be recognized as the "legal" child of the worker. A "legal" child is defined in the Social Security Act as a natural child, adopted child, step-child (if child has been so for at least one year prior to date of application), grandchild or step-grandchild (if there was no natural or adoptive parent living at the time of application), or equitably adopted child (where the parents went through a marriage ceremony which would have been a legal marriage but for a legal impediment).[3]

When there is ambiguity as to whether a child qualifies as a child of the worker entitled to benefits, the Act requires reference to state law where the worker was domiciled at the time of application for benefits.[4] If the child has the right to inherit under the laws of intestate succession, he or she will be deemed to be a "legal child" for purposes of the Social Security Act, regardless of actual or adoptive status.[5]

In Ohio, the general rule is that an illegitimate child is not entitled to inherit through his or her father until there is a final acknowledgment of paternity, a marriage to the mother, an adoption of the child, a provision for the child by last will and testament, or a judicial or administrative establishment of paternity.[6]

Another requirement for the child to receive benefits is that the child must live with the worker or be dependent on the worker for at least one-half of the child's support.[7] In order to receive benefits, the child must be unmarried and must be under the age of eighteen unless the child is a full-time student, in which case the benefits continue until age nineteen,[8] or be disabled prior to attaining age twenty-two.

If all of these conditions are met, the child will receive monthly

---

[Section 29:4]

[1]20 C.F.R. § 353, 20 C.F.R. § 404.407(c).

[2]42 U.S.C.A. § 402(d); 20 C.F.R. § 404.350.

[3]42 U.S.C.A. § 416(e).

[4]42 U.S.C.A. § 416(h)(2)(A).

[5]See Parentage Ch 3.

[6]RC 5101.314.

[7]42 U.S.C.A. § 402(d)(1)(C), 42 U.S.C.A. § 402(d)(4).

[8]42 U.S.C.A. § 402(d)(1)(B).

benefits until he or she attains the maximum age (except if the child is disabled), is married, dies, or is convicted of a subversive act.[9] The child's benefit amount may be affected by a family maximum amount,[10] usually 150% to 180% of a retired worker's benefits, or 150% of a disabled worker's benefits.

Although the social security administration determines the right to receive benefits and the amount of those benefits, it will not oversee the use of the funds in the hands of the representative payee for the child.

Trial courts have determined that trust funds should be established for children's social security benefits, and that those funds can be used for current maintenance as opposed to being kept in trust throughout the child's minority.[11]

The Ohio Supreme Court resolved the division of authority between the various courts of appeals on the issue of how to treat a child's receipt of disability social security benefits in the case of *Williams v. Williams*[12] See § 29:11 following.

§ 29:5 Social security benefits—Worker's Title II benefits—Spouse's retirement benefits

A wife is defined in the Social Security Act as an individual who, in addition to being married to the worker: is the mother of his child; or was married to the worker for more than one year before applying for benefits; or, prior to marrying the worker, was otherwise entitled to annuity benefits as a spouse, parent, or child under 42 U.S.C.A. § 402(b) or the Railroad Retirement Act, or, in the month prior to her marriage to the worker, was entitled to social security benefits as a wife, widow, parent, or child.[1] A husband is defined similarly to a wife in the Act.[2] The qualifications, regulations, and benefits flowing to a husband are the same as they are to a wife under the Social Security Act.[3]

The spouse of a worker entitled to receive benefits may be entitled to a monthly amount equal to one-half of the worker's benefit under certain conditions.[4]

First, the spouse must have reached the age of sixty-two years, or have a child in his or her care who is entitled to social security benefits in his or her own right based on the worker's social security status.[5]

---

[9]42 U.S.C.A. § 402(d)(1).

[10]42 U.S.C.A. § 403.

[11]Catlett v. Catlett, 55 Ohio App. 3d 1, 561 N.E.2d 948 (12th Dist. Clermont County 1988).

[12]Williams v. Williams, 88 Ohio St. 3d 441, 2000-Ohio-375, 727 N.E.2d 895 (2000).

[Section 29:5]

[1]42 U.S.C.A. § 416(b).

[2]42 U.S.C.A. § 416(f).

[3]42 U.S.C.A. § 402(c).

[4]20 C.F.R. § 404.333.

[5]42 U.S.C.A. § 402(b)(1)(B), 42 U.S.C.A. § 402(c)(1)(B).

Second, he or she must file an application for benefits[6] and not be entitled on his or her own earnings record to an amount greater than the one-half of the spouse's benefit amount that she or he will receive.[7]

A wife's survivor's benefit, if she is at least age sixty, is 71.5% of the worker's retirement benefit, and this percentage increases 5.7% per year until the benefit reaches 100% at age 65.

§ 29:6 Social security benefits—Worker's Title II benefits— Former spouse's retirement benefits

A divorced wife is defined as a woman who is divorced from a worker, and who had been married to that worker for more than ten years immediately prior to the date on which the divorce became effective.[1] A divorced husband is defined similarly to a divorced wife, requiring ten years of marriage.[2] Additionally, the divorce must have taken place at least two years prior to the application for benefits, unless the worker qualified for social security benefits prior to the decree.

If the spouse of a fully insured worker meets the definition of divorced wife or divorced husband, he or she is treated in the same manner as a present spouse.[3] If the former spouse qualifies for benefits because of the duration of the marriage, he or she also has the ability to continue to receive benefits if he or she remarries after attaining age sixty. Remarriage before age sixty will end benefits.

An important exception in consideration of a divorced spouse's benefits is that his or her benefits will be excluded from computation of maximum family benefits. Therefore, payments to a divorced spouse, or any number of divorced spouses, do not cause a reduction of benefits to any other person, and payments to others will not reduce a divorced spouse's benefits.[4]

It is important to note that a divorced spouse may apply for benefits when his or her former spouse reaches age 62, whether or not that former spouse has applied for benefits for himself or herself.

The most important distinction between a spouse and a divorced spouse for purposes of social security benefits is the requirement that a divorced spouse must be at least sixty-two years of age to receive benefits based on the former spouse's earnings record, whereas a current spouse can either be sixty-two or more years old, or have a minor child in his or her care.[5] This distinction has been ruled constitutionally valid, rationally supported by the fact that divorced persons are forced to lead independent lives, while married spouses have a greater dependency

---

[6]42 U.S.C.A. § 402(b)(1)(A), 42 U.S.C.A. § 402(c)(1)(A).

[7]42 U.S.C.A. § 402(b)(1)(D), 42 U.S.C.A. § 402(c)(1)(D).

[Section 29:6]

[1]42 U.S.C.A. § 416(d)(1).

[2]42 U.S.C.A. § 416(d)(4).

[3]42 U.S.C.A. § 402(b).

[4]42 U.S.C.A. § 403(a)(3)(C).

[5]42 U.S.C.A. § 402(b)(1)(B).

and need for support when they have minor children and their spouses become disabled, retire, or die.[6]

For survivor benefits, divorced spouses who were married to the worker for at least 10 years can apply for divorced widow's or widower's benefits as early as age 60, and receive 100% of the worker's social security benefit, which would be reduced by a percentage for each year before full retirement age.

§ 29:7   Social security benefits—Worker's Title II benefits— Eligibility under more than one program

If a person is eligible to receive RSDHI benefits from more than one source, whether they are survivor's benefits, disability benefits, retirement benefits, or dependent's benefits, a person can only collect one at a time the highest benefit paid under any of the programs for which the person meets all the criteria. A person may collect one RSDHI benefit and SSI at the same time.

§ 29:8   Social security benefits—Offset for public employment pension

If a person is entitled to both a social security benefit under RSDHI and a public employment pension on his or her own work record, the social security benefits are reduced dollar for dollar by two-thirds of the amount of the public pension. In other words, for every three dollars of government employment pension received, two dollars of social security benefits are lost. However, if a person is entitled to survivor's benefits under both RSDHI and a public pension, no offset is made. The pension offset rule does not apply if the person was eligible for RSDHI survivors benefits before December 1, 1977 or if the person was eligible to receive a public pension before December 1, 1982 and the pre-1977 rules which required 20 years of marriage, instead of the current ten years, were met. The Social Security Administration has a fact sheet entitled "Windfall Eliminations Provisions" which can be obtained by calling 1-800-772-1213.

§ 29:9   Social security benefits—Supplemental security income (SSI)

In 1972, Congress enacted Title XVI of the Social Security Act, initiating the Supplemental Security System.[1] Supplemental security income, or SSI, as the program is commonly known, is intended to provide aged (over 65 years), blind, and disabled individuals, who do not qualify for a sizable benefit under Title II, the RSDHI program, with a minimum income. In effect, it is a form of federal welfare operated through the social security system. In 1996, the maximum federal benefit under SSI

---

[6]Mathews v. de Castro, 429 U.S. 181, 97 S. Ct. 431, 50 L. Ed. 2d 389 (1976).

[Section 29:9]

[1]42 U.S.C.A. § 1381.

was $484 per month.

Although the rules defining disability are the same as SSDI, financial rules as to income and assets must be met for SSI. The rules for eligibility are complex, including guidelines of "countable" income.[2]

For example, the "countable" assets must be below $2,000 per individual or $3,000 per married couple. Assets which are not counted include: a house and lot, if the applicant lives in the house; an automobile worth less than $4,500 or no limit on value if used for work purposes, medical treatment, or is specially adapted; personal property and household goods valued up to $2,000; wedding and engagement rings; medical equipment; trade tools valued up to $6,000; life insurance policies with face values under $1,500 per person, or term life insurance policies; and burial spaces.

"Countable" incomes or wages must be under $500 per month per person at the time of application for SSI benefits, unless the person is engaged in subsidized employment. Total countable income for a single individual cannot exceed $484 per month in 1997 to be eligible for SSI. Income not counted includes: the first $20 per month from any source except public assistance; the first $65 per month in wages or self-employment, and one-half of earnings over $65 per month; food stamps; energy assistance vouchers or payments; housing assistance; certain one-time payments; and 1/3 of court-ordered child support received for children.

For children to receive SSI benefits, it must be shown that they meet the requirements of at least one of the listed disabilities, taking into consideration the functioning level of the child. The rules for application had relaxed for children to receive SSI, resulting in a threefold increase in the number of recipients between 1989 and 1994. Now, however, changes to the SSI laws have made it again more difficult for children with Attention Deficit/Hyperactivity Disorder to qualify. The child's parent's "countable" income and assets must meet the strict rules.

Ohio has a special supplement to SSI, as do many states, providing additional monies for eligible SSI recipients, which are applied for through the Ohio Department of Job and Family Services.

SSI benefits cease when the recipient dies, obtains income or assets above the allowable minimums, ceases to be disabled, or lives outside of the United States.[3]

Domestic relations courts and practitioners should be particularly sensitive to how a division of property or a spousal support award will affect the right to receive SSI benefits, because most SSI benefit recipients are eligible to receive a Medicaid card, which is usually a valuable asset. The exclusion of 1/3 of court-ordered child support payments in the SSI program is intended as an incentive for parents to pursue such support for their disabled children.

Unlike social security benefits, supplemental security income is not

---

[2]42 U.S.C.A. § 1382.
[3]42 U.S.C.A. § 1382.

classified as "gross income" for purposes of computing child support.[4] A discussion of the application of a child's receipt of SSI benefits and its effect on child support is found in *Oatley v. Oatley*[5] and *Smith v. Smith*.[6]

§ 29:10   Social security benefits—Benefits as marital property

Trial courts in Ohio are required, in divorce proceedings, to determine what property constitutes "marital property," including the parties' interests in retirement benefits, both for the purpose of dividing property interests[1] and in determining whether spousal support is appropriate and reasonable under the circumstances.[2] The Ohio Supreme Court, in the case of *Hoyt v. Hoyt*,[3] held that when a trial court decides how to divide retirement benefits in a divorce, the court must apply its discretion based upon the "status of the parties, the nature, terms and conditions of the pension or retirement plan, and the reasonableness of the result; the trial court should attempt to preserve the pension or retirement asset in order that each party can procure the most benefit."[4] The Court further states that "any given pension or retirement fund is not necessarily subject to direct division but is subject to evaluation and consideration in making an equitable distribution of both parties' marital assets,"[5] noting that social security benefits cannot be directly divided.

In *Hisquierdo v. Hisquierdo*,[6] the United States Supreme Court ruled that benefits paid under the Railroad Retirement Act of 1974[7] could not be considered "property" under California's community property law, reasoning that the state could not order a division of a federal benefit designed for an individual which is not a "property right" and, unless the invasion of the benefit was a garnishment for the purpose of child support or spousal support, which ostensibly are based on need, no invasion of the federal benefit would be permitted, citing 42 U.S.C.A. § 407(a) and 42 U.S.C.A. § 659(a), where the garnishment provisions are detailed.

The case of *Cornbleth v. Cornbleth*[8] upheld the consideration of social security benefits in offsetting the present value of a hypothetical social security benefit from the present value of a pension of a government employee who did not participate in the social security system, thereby tak-

---

[4]RC 3113.215(A)(2).

[5]Oatley v. Oatley, 57 Ohio App. 2d 226, 11 Ohio Op. 3d 260, 387 N.E.2d 245 (6th Dist. Lucas County 1977).

[6]Matter of Smith v. Smith, 1996 WL 71068 (Ohio Ct. App. 7th Dist. Jefferson County 1996).

[Section 29:10]

[1]RC 3105.171(A)(3)(a)(ii).

[2]RC 3105.18(C)(1)(d).

[3]Hoyt v. Hoyt, 53 Ohio St. 3d 177, 559 N.E.2d 1292 (1990).

[4]Hoyt v. Hoyt, 53 Ohio St. 3d 177, 559 N.E.2d 1292 (1990).

[5]Hoyt v. Hoyt, 53 Ohio St. 3d 177, 559 N.E.2d 1292 (1990).

[6]Hisquierdo v. Hisquierdo, 439 U.S. 572, 99 S. Ct. 802, 59 L. Ed. 2d 1 (1979).

[7]45 U.S.C.A. § 231.

[8]Cornbleth v. Cornbleth, 397 Pa. Super. 421, 580 A.2d 369 (1990).

ing away the potential disadvantage the government employee would face without such an offset. A government employee's entire pension, including the portion which is a replacement of sorts for social security, would be subject to an equal division of marital property property, when a non-government employee's social security benefit would not be subject to division, without considering the offset. The steps are first to determine the present value of the government pension, then to determine the hypothetical value of that person's social security benefit if he or she had contributed to the social security system, and then subtract the hypothetical social security value from the government pension value.

Ohio courts have followed this philosophy, notably in the cases of *Stovall v. Stovall*,[9] *Walker v. Walker*,[10] and *Neel v. Neel*,[11] but have differed on how best to approach the problem. The *Walker, Neel*, and *Stovall* courts followed *Cornbleth* and subtracted the present value of the hypothetical social security benefit from the present value of the government retirement plan. Failure of a trial court to take social security benefits into consideration when valuing state retirement funds was held to be error in the case of *Biggs v. Biggs*.[12]

---

[9]Stovall v. Stovall, 1992 WL 236770 (Ohio Ct. App. 9th Dist. Summit County 1992).

[10]Walker v. Walker, 112 Ohio App. 3d 90, 677 N.E.2d 1252 (1st Dist. Hamilton County 1996).

[11]Neel v. Neel, 113 Ohio App. 3d 24, 680 N.E.2d 207 (8th Dist. Cuyahoga County 1996), dismissed, appeal not allowed, 77 Ohio St. 3d 1514, 674 N.E.2d 369 (1997). See also Streeter v. Streeter, 1991 WL 151215 (Ohio Ct. App. 10th Dist. Franklin County 1991); Simmons v. Simmons, No. 91-04-0834 (Ohio Ct. C.P. 9th Dist. Summit County 1992); Dye v. Dye, No. 91-06-1096 (Ohio Ct. C.P. 12th Dist. Butler County 1992); Smith v. Smith, 91 Ohio App. 3d 248, 632 N.E.2d 555 (10th Dist. Franklin County 1993); Eickelberger v. Eickelberger, 93 Ohio App. 3d 221, 638 N.E.2d 130 (12th Dist. Butler County 1994); Schaefers v. Schaefers, 1994 WL 631660 (Ohio Ct. App. 7th Dist. Columbiana County 1994); Risner v. Risner, 1995 WL 767360 (Ohio Ct. App. 4th Dist. Jackson County 1995); Dockus v. Dockus, 1996 WL 243689 (Ohio Ct. App. 5th Dist. Stark County 1996); Walker v. Walker, 112 Ohio App. 3d 90, 677 N.E.2d 1252 (1st Dist. Hamilton County 1996); Black v. Black, 1996 WL 752885 (Ohio Ct. App. 5th Dist. Stark County 1996); Stewart v. Stewart, 1998 WL 177558 (Ohio Ct. App. 2d Dist. Montgomery County 1998), dismissed, appeal not allowed, 83 Ohio St. 3d 1428, 699 N.E.2d 945 (1998); Rinehart v. Rinehart, 1999 WL 1232876 (Ohio Ct. App. 4th Dist. Washington County 1999); Back v. Back, 2000 WL 1622 (Ohio Ct. App. 5th Dist. Richland County 1999); and Bauer v. Bauer, 2000 WL 281718 (Ohio Ct. App. 6th Dist. Lucas County 2000), on reconsideration, 2000 WL 390173 (Ohio Ct. App. 6th Dist. Lucas County 2000).

[12]Biggs v. Biggs, 1996 WL 464163 (Ohio Ct. App. 6th Dist. Lucas County 1996); Allen v. Allen, 1998 WL 118055 (Ohio Ct. App. 4th Dist. Scioto County 1998); Stewart v. Stewart, 1998 WL 177558 (Ohio Ct. App. 2d Dist. Montgomery County 1998), dismissed, appeal not allowed, 83 Ohio St. 3d 1428, 699 N.E.2d 945 (1998); Guthrie v. Guthrie, 1998 WL 336905 (Ohio Ct. App. 6th Dist. Lucas County 1998); Mullen v. Mullen, 1998 WL 391385 (Ohio Ct. App. 12th Dist. Warren County 1998); Simon v. Simon, 1999 WL 63667 (Ohio Ct. App. 6th Dist. Sandusky County 1999); Fannin v. Fannin, 1999 WL 450205 (Ohio Ct. App. 12th Dist. Preble County 1999); Levine v. Levine, 1999 WL 729262 (Ohio Ct. App. 4th Dist. Washington County 1999), dismissed, appeal not allowed, 87 Ohio St. 3d 1476, 721 N.E.2d 121 (1999); Burroughs v. Burroughs, 2000 WL 262366 (Ohio Ct. App. 1st Dist. Hamilton County 2000); Bourjaily v. Bourjaily, 2000 WL 968509 (Ohio Ct. App. 5th Dist. Licking County 2000).

The Cuyahoga County Common Pleas Court, in *Coats v. Coats*,[13] added the present value of the actual social security benefit to the non-government employee spouse's private pension plan, and compared the combination with the government employee spouse's entire retirement plan. Subtracting the actual social security present value from the government pension present value yielded the portion of the public pension subject to equal division. The court was careful to point out that this method was to be used strictly on a case-by-case basis, and was especially useful when the parties were near retirement age and/or the marriage was one of long duration.

The courts in the *Smith v. Smith*,[14] *Eickelberger v. Eickelberger*,[15] *Dockus v. Dockus*,[16] and *Black v. Black*[17] cases took an income approach, subtracting the potential monthly social security benefit of the non-governmental employee spouse from the potential monthly benefit amount of the governmental benefit.

A valuation of a person's social security benefits can be obtained from the Social Security Administration at no charge by filling out a Request for Earnings and Benefit Estimate Statement, designated Form OMB No. 0960-0466.

You may also obtain your benefit information via the Internet at http://www.ssa.gov and request that your statement be mailed to you. It takes about four weeks for the statement to arrive.

In *Bauser v. Bauser*,[18] the Second District Court of Appeals held that a disability social security pension is not marital property because there was no evidence that any of the disability income received was provided "in lieu of old-age retirement pay, in which event they are marital property to the extent that such retirement pay is included in the disability pension benefit." This reasoning was also applied in *Carnifax v. Carnifax*,[19] *Johnson v. Johnson*,[20] and *Okos v. Okos*.[21]

§ 29:11   Social security benefits—Attachment of benefits

While the Social Security Act does exempt benefits from garnishment,

---

[13]Coats v. Coats, 63 Ohio Misc. 2d 299, 626 N.E.2d 707 (C.P. 1993).

[14]Matter of Smith v. Smith, 1996 WL 71068 (Ohio Ct. App. 7th Dist. Jefferson County 1996).

[15]Eickelberger v. Eickelberger, 93 Ohio App. 3d 221, 638 N.E.2d 130 (12th Dist. Butler County 1994).

[16]Dockus v. Dockus, 1996 WL 243689 (Ohio Ct. App. 5th Dist. Stark County 1996).

[17]Black v. Black, 1996 WL 752885 (Ohio Ct. App. 5th Dist. Stark County 1996).

[18]Bauser v. Bauser, 118 Ohio App. 3d 831, 694 N.E.2d 136 (2d Dist. Clark County 1997).

[19]Carnifax v. Carnifax, 2000 WL 557875 (Ohio Ct. App. 11th Dist. Trumbull County 2000).

[20]Johnson v. Johnson, 2001 WL 108767 (Ohio Ct. App. 6th Dist. Wood County 2001), appeal allowed, 92 Ohio St. 3d 1418, 748 N.E.2d 550 (2001).

[21]Okos v. Okos, 137 Ohio App. 3d 563, 739 N.E.2d 368 (6th Dist. Lucas County 2000).

levy, execution, assignment, or any operation of legal process,[1] an express statutory exception was created for collection of alimony and child support.[2]

A court may not divide the social security entitlement itself, but once child support or alimony (spousal support) is properly awarded, the court may enforce such award by attaching the obligor's social security benefits.[3] Spousal support, or alimony as it is still called for the purposes of the Social Security Act, is considered to be periodic payments made for the support of a spouse, not payments made in a lump sum or on a periodic basis designed to effectuate a property division.[4] Payments to a former spouse may be treated differently by the Ohio domestic relations court, the federal tax court, and the Social Security Administration.

§ 29:12 Social security benefits—Dependents' benefits as offset to court-ordered support

Authority had been split regarding whether credit toward court-ordered child support or spousal support should be given when social security benefits are being received by a spouse or children until the Ohio Supreme Court issued its decision in *Williams v. Williams.*[1]

In *Williams*, the Court stated that the courts which permitted an offset from an obligor parent's child support obligation when the obligee parent receives social security payments on behalf of a child as a result of the obligor's disability were recognizing that the underlying intent of the social security payments to a child of a disabled parent is to provide support in lieu of support which would have been paid from wages, but for the disability, and the courts allowing the offset have characterized the social security payments as a substitute for wages rather than a gratuity from the federal government. The Court cited *Pride v. Nolan*,[2] *Stephenson v. Stephenson*,[3] *McClure v. McClure*,[4] and *Cervone v. Cervone*,[5] as so doing.

The Ohio Supreme Court, in its discussion, cited the other position on the issue, which had been followed by the Warren County Court of Ap-

---

[Section 29:11]

[1] 42 U.S.C.A. § 407.

[2] 42 U.S.C.A. § 659.

[3] Knox v. Knox, 1981 WL 6629 (Ohio Ct. App. 3d Dist. Union County 1981).

[4] 42 U.S.C.A. § 662.

[Section 29:12]

[1] Williams v. Williams, 2000 -Ohio- 375, 88 Ohio St. 3d 441, 727 N.E.2d 895 (2000).

[2] Pride v. Nolan, 31 Ohio App. 3d 261, 511 N.E.2d 408 (1st Dist. Hamilton County 1987).

[3] Stephenson v. Stephenson, 1996 WL 133000 (Ohio Ct. App. 7th Dist. Mahoning County 1996).

[4] McClure v. McClure, 1996 WL 562793 (Ohio Ct. App. 2d Dist. Greene County 1996).

[5] Cervone v. Cervone, 2000 WL 126583 (Ohio Ct. App. 7th Dist. Mahoning County 2000), cause dismissed, 88 Ohio St. 3d 1511, 728 N.E.2d 400 (2000) and cert. denied, 121 S. Ct. 657, 148 L. Ed. 2d 560 (U.S. 2000).

peals when it reviewed the *Williams* case,[6] that a disabled parent was not permitted an offset from his or her support obligation, of the entire amount which was received by the child, but said benefits were instead deducted from the total combined child support obligation of both parents, and referred to *Fruchtnicht v. Fruchtnicht*,[7] *In re Ehritz*,[8] *Previte v. Previte*,[9] *Slowbe v. Slowbe*,[10] and *Barnett v. Hanson*[11] as so doing. The Court cited to the leading case on the issue, *McNeal v. Cofield*[12] and referred to the rationale for allocating the offset between the parents as seeing the benefits as going to the benefit of the child rather than to only one parent because not doing so would be a windfall to the parent receiving the benefits.

In *Williams*, the Ohio Supreme Court discussed the reasoning employed by the majority of other states which permitted a disabled parent's child support obligation to be directly set off by social security payments received on behalf of the minor child, and rejected the reasoning of the Twelfth District Court of Appeals. The Court found that social security payments received because of a parent's disability are tantamount to earnings by the disabled parent. The Court further found that the windfall to the recipient argument was illogical, stating that the offset merely changes the source of payments for child support and does not retroactively modify the disabled parent's child support obligation. The Ohio Supreme Court held that "a disabled parent is entitled to a full credit in his or her child support obligation for Social Security payments received by a minor child. Accordingly, [obligor's] child support obligation shall be set off by those Social Security payments received on [the child's] behalf. Since the amount of Social Security payments [the child] received exceeds what [obligor] owed, the trial court shall enter judgment reflecting that no child support is owed from the time [the child] first received Social Security benefits."[13]

A child's receipt of Supplemental Security Income (SSI), however, has been determined to be very different in nature and purpose from a child's receipt of benefits due to the retirement or disability of a parent. In

---

[6]Williams v. Williams, 1999 WL 172826 (Ohio Ct. App. 12th Dist. Warren County 1999), appeal allowed, 86 Ohio St. 3d 1466, 715 N.E.2d 568 (1999) and judgment rev'd and remanded, 2000 -Ohio- 375, 88 Ohio St. 3d 441, 727 N.E.2d 895 (2000).

[7]Fruchtnicht v. Fruchtnicht, 122 Ohio App. 3d 492, 702 N.E.2d 145 (12th Dist. Butler County 1997).

[8]In re Ehritz, 1998 WL 295550 (Ohio Ct. App. 12th Dist. Butler County 1998).

[9]Previte v. Previte, 99 Ohio App. 3d 347, 650 N.E.2d 919 (11th Dist. Lake County 1994).

[10]Slowbe v. Slowbe, 1995 WL 723333 (Ohio Ct. App. 8th Dist. Cuyahoga County 1995), dismissed, appeal not allowed, 75 Ohio St. 3d 1495, 664 N.E.2d 1291 (1996).

[11]Barnett v. Hanson, 1997 WL 679630 (Ohio Ct. App. 6th Dist. Erie County 1997).

[12]McNeal v. Cofield, 78 Ohio App. 3d 35, 603 N.E.2d 436 (10th Dist. Franklin County 1992).

[13]Williams v. Williams, 2000 -Ohio- 375, 88 Ohio St. 3d 441, 444-45, 727 N.E.2d 895 (2000).

Oatley v. Oatley,[14] the court stated that the purpose of SSI benefits was to provide a base minimum income to eligible individuals in their own right, and other income and assets, such as child support paid on behalf of the child, are used by the Social Security Administration in determining the amount of SSI benefits to be received. "The amount of supplemental security income received is modified as the amount of the recipient's other income changes, not vice versa."[15]

The Fourth District Court of Appeals held that "[s]upplemental security income is intended to supplement, not replace, other income; it is based upon *need* and is supplemental in name and nature."[16] The reasoning of *Oatley* has been followed by the Third District Court of Appeals in *Paton v. Paton*,[17] which stated that it was improper for the trial court to subtract the yearly amount of SSI received from the basic combined child support obligation of both parents, and then multiply the remainder of the obligation by the income percentages as shown on the worksheet, and held that supplemental security income should not be used to decrease the parent's support obligation.

§ 29:13 Social security benefits—Supplemental security income—Dependent's benefits do not offset court-ordered support

A child's receipt of Supplemental Security Income (SSI) has been determined to be very different in nature and purpose from a child's receipt of benefits due to the retirement or disability of a parent. In *Oatley v. Oatley*,[1] the court stated that the purpose of SSI benefits was to provide a base minimum income to eligible individuals in their own right, and other income and assets, such as child support paid on behalf of the child, are used by the Social Security Administration in determining the amount of SSI benefits to be received. "The amount of Supplemental Security Income received is modified as the amount of the recipient's other income changes, not vice versa."[2]

The Fourth District Court of Appeals held that "Supplemental Security Income is intended to supplement, not replace, other income; it is

---

[14]Oatley v. Oatley, 57 Ohio App. 2d 226, 11 Ohio Op. 3d 260, 387 N.E.2d 245 (6th Dist. Lucas County 1977).

[15]Oatley v. Oatley, 57 Ohio App. 2d 226, 228, 11 Ohio Op. 3d 260, 387 N.E.2d 245 (6th Dist. Lucas County 1977).

[16]Lattimore v. Lattimore, 1997 WL 643581 (Ohio Ct. App. 4th Dist. Scioto County 1997).

[17]Paton v. Paton, 1999 WL 181188 (Ohio Ct. App. 3d Dist. Allen County 1999), appeal allowed, 86 Ohio St. 3d 1465, 715 N.E.2d 568 (1999) and judgment aff'd, 2001 -Ohio-291, 91 Ohio St. 3d 94, 742 N.E.2d 619 (2001).

[Section 29:13]

[1]Oatley v. Oatley, 57 Ohio App. 2d 226, 11 Ohio Op. 3d 260, 387 N.E.2d 245 (6th Dist. Lucas County 1977).

[2]Oatley v. Oatley, 57 Ohio App. 2d 226, 228, 11 Ohio Op. 3d 260, 387 N.E.2d 245 (6th Dist. Lucas County 1977).

based on *need* and is supplemental in name and nature."[3]

The reasoning of *Oatley* has been followed by the Third District Court of Appeals in *Paton v. Paton*,[4] which stated that it was improper for the trial court to subtract the yearly amount of SSI received from the basic combined child support obligation of both parents, and then multiply the remainder of the obligation by the income percentages as shown on the worksheet, and held that Supplemental Security Income should not be used to decrease the parent's support obligation. The Fourth District Court of Appeals' decision was affirmed by the Ohio Supreme Court,[5] holding that Supplemental Security Income benefits received by a child are intended to supplement other income, not substitute for it, and that SSI benefits received by a disabled child are not considered to be a "financial resource of the child" for purposes of deviation from the basic child support schedule.

§ 29:14   Social security benefits—Award of benefits as basis for post-decree modification

Generally, an Ohio court may modify an order of child support, or spousal support where jurisdiction to modify is reserved, upon the demonstration of changed circumstances that make a modification of the previous order just under the circumstances as they currently exist.[1]

Courts must consider social security benefits received by a parent as part of gross income.[2] If the income of a parent has changed from the prior calculation of child support due to the receipt of such benefits, and the change results in a computation under the guidelines which deviates by more than ten percent from the existing support order, the court must consider that change to constitute a change of circumstances.[3]

§ 29:15   Social security benefits—Practical applications—In general

Knowledge of the social security considerations in a domestic relations case is not only useful information, but can also be an essential element of effective representation by counsel. Such information as to how the parties will be affected by the social security laws, by choosing one course of action or another, gives the creative and intelligent practitioner a decided advantage.

---

[3]Lattimore v. Lattimore, 1997 WL 643581 (Ohio Ct. App. 4th Dist. Scioto County 1997).

[4]Paton v. Paton, 1999 WL 181188 (Ohio Ct. App. 3d Dist. Allen County 1999), appeal allowed, 86 Ohio St. 3d 1465, 715 N.E.2d 568 (1999) and judgment aff'd, 2001 -Ohio-291, 91 Ohio St. 3d 94, 742 N.E.2d 619 (2001).

[5]Paton v. Paton, 91 Ohio St.3d 94, 742 N.E.2d 6190 (2000).

[Section 29:14]

[1]Bright v. Collins, 2 Ohio App. 3d 421, 442 N.E.2d 822 (10th Dist. Franklin County 1982), superseded by statute as stated in Todd v. Augustin, 1999 WL 615382 (Ohio Ct. App. 4th Dist. Scioto County 1999).

[2]RC 3113.215(A)(2).

[3]RC 3113.215(B)(4).

Probably the closest analogy to social security law in virtually all domestic relations cases is the consideration of tax implications on a termination of a marriage. Effective advocates will use all of these laws to maximize benefits for their clients.

An additional consideration, and an important one for the practitioner, is that failure by an attorney to learn, understand, and adequately advise a client on the ramifications of a divorce, including the social security effects, could well be viewed as legal malpractice.[1] Again, one can analogize to tax law implications in domestic relations cases, where a growing number of courts have adopted the view that a failure to understand and disclose tax implications to a client prevents the attorney from effective representation, thereby constituting malpractice.[2]

A four-step process should be used in every domestic relations case, to insure that counsel effectively carries out their duty of adequate representation. Usually, questions concerning social security benefits are not asked unless a specific problem presents itself, such as when the parties are already receiving some form of disability or retirement benefits, are of advanced age, or have made application for benefits.

The practitioner must address four questions, and use the answers to provide the client with the greatest possible advantage under the social security laws.

    (1) "Does either party have any rights to social security or SSI benefits presently, or will he or she have any such rights in the future?"

    (2) "What effect will a divorce or dissolution, and what effect will a division of assets and liabilities, or receipt or payment of spousal support have on my client's rights to receive social security or SSI benefits?"

    (3) "What alternatives are available to maximize my client's rights to such benefits as may be available now or in the future?"

    (4) "How can I use my knowledge of the social security laws as a bargaining tool in negotiations?"

§ 29:16 Social security benefits—Practical applications—Effects of divorce

A wife or husband may be entitled to retirement or disability income because of a spouse's work record, whereas the same spouse may lose those benefits upon obtaining a divorce.[1] For example, if parties are receiving social security benefits based on their own earnings records, a divorce will not affect their rights to continue receiving such benefits.

[Section 29:15]

  [1]See generally Ohio Jur. 3d, Attorneys at Law §§ 143 to 146.

  [2]Smith v. Lewis, 13 Cal. 3d 349, 118 Cal. Rptr. 621, 530 P.2d 589, 78 A.L.R.3d 231 (1975).

[Section 29:16]

  [1]See § 29:4, Social security benefits—Worker's Title II benefits—Children's benefits.

However, if a spouse under the age of sixty-two and without a child in his or her custody is divorced before the marriage has lasted ten years, he or she will lose the ability to receive benefits on the other spouse's account.

The practitioner must ascertain what the effect on the client will be if a divorce, dissolution, or property settlement is obtained. Frequently, timing is going to be as important as any other factor in this area. Since a ten-year marriage is required for benefits to vest in many instances, it may be more prudent to file a legal separation action,[2] especially in those cases where the parties have few liquid assets and little prospect of future income except social security. It is possible for the parties to remain married for an additional period of time to allow the spouse not eligible for retirement or disability benefits in his or her own right to obtain those rights after the ten-year vesting period has run. Of course, clients should be made aware that, when opting for this course of conduct, the other side has the right to counterclaim for a divorce, so serious consideration should also be given to taking absolutely no legal action until the ten years has elapsed. This should be considered if there is no evidence of abuse and if the retirement benefits to be obtained by waiting outweigh the necessity for immediate legal action.

Counsel may want to use social security considerations in negotiating a settlement, especially in marriages of seven, eight, or nine years, in which the timing issue may be critical. For example, if the spouse who is entitled to the benefits threatens to move quickly to obtain a divorce before the other spouse's rights have vested, or to move slowly in order to allow the other party to qualify, he or she may be able to obtain a favorable result in negotiating a settlement of the case.

A difficult problem arises when trying to negotiate a separation agreement where one party is receiving SSI, because the SSI system has limitations on the assets and income a recipient may have, eliminating many possible methods of arriving at a favorable and acceptable separation agreement.[3]

The attorney representing a spouse in a domestic relations matter where one spouse or both spouses are receiving SSI benefits has the added problem of negotiating an agreement that will give the SSI recipient maximum assets and income, while at the same time not forcing him or her to give up the SSI income he or she receives, or a Medicaid card that pays hospital expenses and is often more valuable than the SSI payments the party may be receiving.

Some attorneys have opted to use trusts and gift devices to hide a recipient's actual income and assets. This approach is definitely not recommended, as it may subject the recipient, as well as the attorney, to civil and/or criminal sanctions for overpayments and/or fraud. A far easier and more practical solution is to use the system itself, and the exception provisions built right into the SSI law, to achieve equity and maximize benefits for both parties.

---

[2]RC 3105.17.

[3]See § 29:8, Social security benefits—Supplemental security income (SSI).

For example, certain income can be excluded from the computation of monthly income determinations of an SSI recipient, and certain resources, such as personal clothing and furniture up to a limit, can be excluded from the maximum resource limitation permitted. One very important exclusion is the value of an automobile up to a limit, or the entire value of the car no matter what its fair market value if it is used in obtaining medical treatment or is modified for operation or transportation of the handicapped. In addition, the cash surrender value of a life insurance policy is also excluded if it has a value of less than $1,500.

Probably the most important exclusion from resources, especially when considering domestic relations matters, is the entire fair market value of a house used as the principal residence of the recipient.[4] Thus, in cases where the parties' sole asset consists of a marital residence, it may be advisable to grant the SSI recipient a life estate in the mansion house rent free, which life estate would terminate upon his or her death. This provision would allow the parties to maintain their equity in the home without having to go through a distress sale and also provides the SSI recipient, who normally has very little income, with an adequate and inexpensive place to reside without cutting off the SSI benefits. The nonrecipient spouse maintains his equity in the property, and again, this manipulation of the property division maximizes benefits without threatening the SSI recipient's benefits.

§ 29:17 Social security benefits—Practical applications—Social security issues in perspective

Obviously, social security should not be the only factor, or even the major factor, in deciding if, when, and how to pursue the legal termination of a marriage. Nonetheless, it is an important factor that should always be considered in every case.

Old age and a lengthy marriage should not be the only signals to the practitioner, who should consider social security as a potentially important aspect in any divorce. In marriages of slightly less than ten years, the creative practitioner will have the greatest potential for manipulation, and hence, the best opportunity to use social security as an important bargaining tool. It is true that the social security and SSI systems are complex; however, they are not nearly as complex as most advocates imagine, and the potential benefits to the clients involved certainly warrant the careful attention of the domestic relations practitioner.

§ 29:18 Civil Service Retirement System—In general

The Federal Civil Service Retirement System (CSRS) provides disability and survivorship benefits to persons employed by the federal govern-

---

[4]20 C.F.R. § 416.110.

ment and hired prior to January 1, 1984.[1] CSRS participants do not participate in the social security system. Persons hired before January 1, 1984 also had the opportunity to switch to the Federal Employees' Retirement System (FERS).[2]

A CSRS participant must have at least five years of federal service in order to receive benefits, and the five years do not have to be consecutive or with the same federal agency.[3] A participant usually can begin to receive monthly pension benefits at age 55 with 30 years of service,[4] or at age 60 with 20 years of service,[5] or at age 62 with five years of service.[6] Air traffic controllers can receive full retirement benefits at age 50 with 20 years of service, or at any age with 25 years of service.[7] Federal law enforcement and firefighter personnel can retire at age 50 with 20 years of service.[8]

An employee separated from service before retirement age can elect to leave the contributions in the system or can withdraw them in a lump sum. If an election is made to leave the contributions in the system, the former employee can claim a retirement annuity at age 62 or take a lump-sum benefit at any time prior to attaining age 62.

Monthly benefits are calculated on the participant's highest three years of earnings, called the "high three average," and are not dependent on the total amount contributed to the system. Benefits are not increased for dependents of the retiree. Cost of living adjustments (COLAs) do attach to CSRS pension annuities.

Under the CSRS system, the calculation of benefits is as follows: 1.5% of the high three average multiplied by 5 (for the first five years of service), plus 1.75% of the high three average times 5 (for years six through ten of service), plus 2% of the high three average times the number of years of service beyond ten.[9] For example: highest three years' earnings average equals $40,000 with 25 years of service:

$$1.5\% \times \$40,000 \times 5 = \$3,000$$
$$1.75\% \times \$40,000 \times 5 = \$3,500$$
$$2\% \times \$40,000 \times 15 = \$12,000$$

Total yearly pension 18,500

[Section 29:18]

[1] 5 U.S.C.A. § 8331.

[2] Federal Employees' Retirement Contribution Temporary Adjustment Act of 1983, P.L. 98-168, Section 208.

[3] 5 U.S.C.A. § 8333(a).

[4] 5 U.S.C.A. § 8336(a).

[5] 5 U.S.C.A. § 8336(b).

[6] 5 U.S.C.A. § 8336(f).

[7] 5 U.S.C.A. § 8336(e).

[8] 5 U.S.C.A. § 8336(c).

[9] 5 U.S.C.A. § 8339(a).

§ 29:19 Civil Service Retirement System—Benefits to former spouse

A former spouse's right to civil service benefits is set forth in Title V of the United States Code Annotated, which defines who is an employee under the title, computes annuities, survivor's annuities, and lump-sum benefits, and directs payment of benefits.

In 1978, civil service benefits became subject to state court orders directing payment of a retiree's annuity to a former spouse.[1]

Under 5 U.S.C.A. § 8339(j)(3), an employee entitled to civil service benefits may elect, under the procedures provided, to have an annuity computed for a former spouse. The election for the annuity must be made at the time of retirement or, if later, within two years after the date on which the marriage of the former spouse and the employee was dissolved. The employee may elect one of the following options: a full retirement annuity with zero benefits to survivors after death; a full survivor benefit in which the retirant's annuity is reduced, and the survivor's benefit is paid to the named survivor until the survivor's death or remarriage prior to age 55; or a reduced survivor benefit in which the retirant's annuity is reduced, but not as much as it is under the full survivor benefit option. Under CSRS, the reduction for the full survivor benefit is 2.5% of the first $3,600 per year, plus 10% of the amount over $3,600 per year.[2] The annuity of the employee may not be reduced more than forty percent.[3] The survivor then receives 55% of the full benefit amount (calculated before reduction),[4] plus cost of living adjustments (COLAs),[5] and commencing on the day after the retired employee dies and continuing until the surviving spouse dies or remarries prior to attaining age 55.[6]

Further, if the employee is remarried at the time of making the election, the written consent of the present spouse is required.[7] A former spouse is eligible for benefits so long as the employee was a participant of CSRS for a period of at least eighteen months, and the former spouse was married to the employee for at least nine months.[8] The consent of the present spouse is required because the annuity of that spouse is affected by other annuities being granted.

Any reduction in an annuity that results from a survivor annuity paid to a former spouse of a retired employee will be terminated for each full month after the former spouse remarries before reaching the age of

---

[Section 29:19]

[1]Pub. L. No. 95-366, 92 Stat. 600 (1978).

[2]5 U.S.C.A. § 8339(j)(3).

[3]5 U.S.C.A. § 8339(k)(1).

[4]5 U.S.C.A. § 8341(b)(1).

[5]5 U.S.C.A. § 8340.

[6]5 U.S.C.A. § 8341(b)(3).

[7]5 U.S.C.A. § 8339(j)(1)(B).

[8]5 U.S.C.A. § 8331(23).

fifty-five or dies.[9] Further, the employee, at the time of retirement may elect the reduced annuity, instead of the full annuity as it would be computed, in the interest of providing for an individual, including a former spouse, after the death of the retired employee. If there is a former spouse and a surviving spouse, the combination of benefits will not exceed the fifty-five percent limit.[10]

If an employee under CSRS dies before reaching retirement age, but after having at least 18 months of service, a surviving spouse receives an annuity equal to 55% of what the employee's benefits would have been at age 60, or 40% of the high three average salary, whichever is less.[11] If an employee under CSRS dies having at least 18 months of service and a surviving spouse or former spouse who is the parent of a surviving child, CSRS pays to each child 60% of the average pay of the employee divided by the number of children, or $900, or $2700 divided by the number of children.[12] If there is no spouse or parent of surviving children, CSRS pays to the children 75% of the high three average divided by the number of children, or $1,080, or $3240 divided by the number of children.[13] A child is dependent if he or she is under age 18, or is a full time student and under age 22, or is disabled.[14]

§ 29:20   Civil Service Retirement System—Lump-sum benefits

An employee may elect to receive payment of benefits in a lump sum.[1] Payment of the lump-sum amount will only be made if the current spouse and any former spouse of the employee have been notified of the application for lump-sum credit.[2] The application will be subject to the terms of a court decree of divorce, annulment, or legal separation, or any court-ordered or court-approved property settlement incident to such decree if the decree relates to any portion of the lump-sum credit involved and payment of the lump-sum credit would extinguish entitlement of the spouse or former spouse to a survivor annuity.[3]

§ 29:21   Civil Service Retirement System—Payment of benefits

Payments that would otherwise be made to the employee can be made to another person if, and to the extent expressly provided for in the terms of any decree of divorce, annulment, or legal separation, or any court-ordered or court-approved property settlement incident to a decree of divorce, annulment, or legal separation, provided that the federal Of-

---

[9]5 U.S.C.A. § 8339(a)(5)(B).

[10]5 U.S.C.A. § 8341(f)(2).

[11]5 U.S.C.A. § 8341(c).

[12]5 U.S.C.A. § 8341(e)(2)(A), (B), (C).

[13]5 U.S.C.A. § 8341(e)(2)(C)(i), (ii), (iii).

[14]5 U.S.C.A. § 8341(e)(3).

[Section 29:20]

[1]5 U.S.C.A. § 8342(a).

[2]5 U.S.C.A. § 8342(j).

[3]5 U.S.C.A. § 8342(j).

fice of Personnel Management (OPM) has had written notice of such decree,[1] and provided that a properly drafted Court Order Acceptable for Processing (COAP) is approved by OPM. The United States Office of Personnel Management, Retirement and Insurance Group offers a publication that contains model language acceptable for court orders regarding federal employees under CSRS and FERS.[2] The approved form language can be found at 5 C.F.R. pt. 838.[3]

§ 29:22 Civil Service Retirement System—COAP for CSRS pensions—Form⊚

IN THE COURT OF COMMON PLEAS
DOMESTIC RELATIONS DIVISION
————————COUNTY, OHIO

[Name], Plaintiff	)	Case No. [_____]
vs.	)	Judge
[Name], Defendant	)	**QUALIFYING COURT ORDER ACCEPTABLE FOR PROCESSING**

This cause came before the Court on the _____ day of _____, 20__. The Court found as follows:

1. *[Name]* (Husband) and *[Name]* (Wife) were married on *[Date of Marriage]*;

2. The parties have separated and have obtained, in these proceedings, a Decree of Divorce/ Dissolution of Marriage on *[Date of Decree]*;

3. The Court has, pursuant to such decree, divided the marital estate and all other property, including their respective interests in the retirement plan as provided for herein and the Decree requires the entry of a Court Order Acceptable for Processing by this court providing for the division and distribution of the marital portion of the benefits and benefit rights of the Plaintiff/Defendant under the Civil Service Retirement System (CSRS);

4. The terminology used in the provisions of this Order concerning benefits under CSRS are governed by and were drafted in accordance with the standard conventions established in Part 8 of Title 5 of the Code of Federal Regulations (5 CFR 838);

5. This order is issued in connection with the Divorce/Dissolution of a Federal employee or retiree, is a "court order" as that term is defined in 5 CFR 838.103, and is intended to be a "court order acceptable for processing" as that term is defined in 5 CFR 838.103; and

---

[Section 29:21]

[1]5 U.S.C.A. § 8345(j)(1).

[2]United States Office of Personnel Management, Retirement and Insurance Group, *A Handbook for Attorneys on Court-Ordered retirement and health benefits under the Civil Service Retirement System, Federal Employees Retirement System, and Federal Employees Health Benefits Program.*

[3]See § 29:22.

6. Husband and Wife wish to settle all issues with respect to their interest in such plan.

NOW, THEREFORE, in consideration of the foregoing premises and the mutual promises hereunder specified, Husband and Wife do agree, and the Court does order, as follows:

1. Authority for Order: This order is entered pursuant to the authority granted under the domestic relations laws of the State of Ohio.

2. Employee Information: The Employee is alive and has not retired under CSRS. The information below is found to be correct as of the date of this order:

Name of Employee:
Address:
Date of Birth:
Social Security Number:
CSRS Claim Number:

3. Former Spouse Information: The Former Spouse is alive and has not remarried. The information below is found to be correct as of the date of this order:

Name of Former Spouse:
Address:
Date of Birth:
Social Security Number:

4. Identification of Retirement System: The Employee is or will be eligible for retirement benefits under the Civil Service Retirement System (CSRS) based on employment with the United States Government.

5. Entitlement to Benefits: The Former Spouse is found to be entitled to share in the Employee's gross monthly annuity under CSRS awarded in Paragraph 6 of this order. The Former Spouse is also found to be entitled to a former spouse survivor annuity should the Employee predecease the Former Spouse. The United States Office of Personnel Management is hereby directed to pay the benefits awarded or assigned to the Former Spouse directly to the Former Spouse, except as provided in Paragraph 8 of this Order.

[Select one of the following, as appropriate]

[Alt #1] 6. Amount of Former Spouse's Share of Employee Annuity: The Former Spouse is entitled to and is hereby assigned and awarded and amount equal to fifty percent (50%) of the marital portion of Employee's gross monthly annuity determined as of the Employee's date of retirement. The marital portion of the Employee's gross monthly annuity shall be determined by multiplying the gross monthly annuity by a fraction, the numerator of which is the total number of months of the Employee's creditable service under CSRS during the marriage if the parties and the denominator of which is the Employee's total number of months of creditable service accrued under CSRS, including military service credited to CSRS. The marriage of the parties began on *[Date of*

Marriage] and ended on *[Date of Decree]*. The Former Spouse's share of the Employee's gross monthly annuity shall be calculated without regard to any amounts that are withheld from the Employee's annuity for any reason, including amounts withheld for the purpose of providing Former Spouse with a survivor annuity. The United States Office of Personnel Management is directed to make payment directly to Former Spouse.

[Alt #2] 6. Amount of Former Spouse's Share of Employee Annuity: The Former Spouse is entitled to and is hereby assigned and awarded the amount of _____ U.S. dollars ($_____US) per month from the Employee's civil service retirement benefits. The marriage of the parties began on *[Date of Marriage]* and ended on *[Date of Decree]*. The United States Office of Personnel Management is directed to make payment directly to Former Spouse.

[Alt #3] 6. Amount of Former Spouse's Share of Employee Annuity: The Former Spouse is entitled to and is hereby assigned and awarded a pro rata share of the Employee's gross monthly retirement annuity accrued under the CSRS. The marriage of the parties began on *[Date of Marriage]* and ended on *[Date of Decree]*. The United States Office of Personnel Management is directed to make payment directly to Former Spouse.

[Alt #4] 6. Amount of Former Spouse's Share of Employee Annuity: The Former Spouse is entitled to and is hereby assigned and awarded a share of the Employee's gross monthly annuity under CSRS that is computed as follows: *[Calculation method]*. The marriage of the parties began on *[Date of Marriage]* and ended on *[Date of Decree]*. The United States Office of Personnel Management is directed to make payment directly to Former Spouse.

7. Payment of Former Spouse's Share of Employee Annuity: The Former Spouse shall begin receiving his/her share of the Employee Annuity benefits as soon as administratively feasible after the date this order is approved as a Court Order Acceptable for Processing or on the date that the Employee begins receiving benefits, if that date is later. Such payments shall continue to Former Spouse for the remainder of Employee's lifetime except as provided in Paragraph 8 of this order. The Employee is ordered to arrange or execute all forms necessary for the commencement of payments to the Former Spouse in accordance with the terms of this Order.

8. Payment of Employee Annuity of Former Spouse Predeceases Employee: Should the Former Spouse die before the Employee, the United States Office of Personnel Management is directed to pay the Former Spouse's share of the Employee's annuity, as described in Paragraph 6 of the order, to *[the surviving children of the parties in equal shares]*. Upon the death of any child, that child's share shall be paid to the then surviving children of the parties in equal shares. *[Name Beneficiary at Address/ the Court issuing this Order]*.

9. Cost of Living Adjustments. The Employee is or will be entitled to cost of living adjustments to his/her retirement benefits. When cost of living adjustments are applied to the Employee's retirement benefits, the same cost of living adjustments shall be applied to the Former

Spouse's share of the benefits. The United States Office of Personnel Management is directed to pay the Former Spouse's share of any such adjustments directly to Former Spouse except as provided in Paragraph 8 of this Order.

[Select one of the following, as appropriate]

[Alt #1] 10. Refunds of Employee's Contributions: If Employee leaves the Federal service before retirement and applies for a refund of employee contributions, the United States Office of Personnel Management is directed <u>not</u> to pay the Employee a refund of employee contributions.

[Alt #2] 10. Refunds of Employee's Contributions: If Employee leaves the Federal service before retirement and applies for a refund of employee contributions, the United States Office of Personnel Management is directed to pay to Former Spouse fifty percent (50%) of the marital portion of any such refund. The marriage of the parties began on *[Date of Marriage]* and ended on *[Date of Decree]*. The United States Office of Personnel Management is directed to make payment directly to Former Spouse.

[Select one of the following, as appropriate]

[Alt #1] 11. Former Spouse Survivor Annuity: Under the authority of Section 8341(h)(1) of Title 5, United States Code, Former Spouse is hereby awarded the maximum possible former spouse survivor annuity under CSRS. The cost of the annuity shall be paid from Employee's annuity and not from Former Spouse's share of the employee annuity.

[Alt #2] 11. Former Spouse Survivor Annuity: Under the authority of Section 8341(h)(1) of Title 5, United States Code, Former Spouse is hereby awarded the maximum possible former spouse survivor annuity under CSRS in the same amount to which Former Spouse would have been entitled had the divorce not occurred. The cost of the annuity shall be paid from Employee's annuity and not from Former Spouse's share of the employee annuity.

[Alt #3] 11. Former Spouse Survivor Annuity: Under the authority of Section 8341(h)(1) of Title 5, United States Code, Former Spouse is hereby awarded the a former spouse survivor annuity under CSRS in an amount equal to a pro rata share of the maximum possible survivor annuity. The marriage began on *[Date of Marriage]* and ended on *[Date of Decree]*.

[Alt #4] 11. Former Spouse Survivor Annuity: Under the authority of Section 8341(h)(1) of Title 5, United States Code, Former Spouse is hereby awarded a former spouse survivor annuity under CSRS in an amount equal to _____U.S. dollars ($_____U.S.). The United States Office of Personnel Management is ordered not to increase this amount by cost of living adjustments that occur before death of the Employee.

[Alt #5] 11. Former Spouse Survivor Annuity: Under the authority of Section 8341(h)(1) of Title 5, United States Code, Former Spouse is hereby awarded a former spouse survivor annuity under CSRS in an amount equal to fifty percent (50%) of Employee's gross Employee annuity.

[Alt #6] 11. Former Spouse Survivor Annuity: Under the authority of Section 8341(h)(1) of Title 5, United States Code, Former Spouse is hereby awarded a former spouse survivor annuity under CSRS in an amount equal to seventy-five percent (75%) of the maximum possible survivor annuity.

[Alt #7] 11. Former Spouse Survivor Annuity: Under the authority of Section 8341(h)(1) of Title 5, United States Code, Former Spouse is hereby awarded the maximum possible former spouse survivor annuity under CSRS unless Employee remarries before retirement. If Employee remarries before retirement, Former Spouse is hereby awarded a former spouse survivor annuity under CSRS in the amount of a pro rata share of the maximum possible survivor annuity. The marriage began on *[Date of Marriage]* and ended on *[Date of Decree]*.

[Alt #8] 11. Former Spouse Survivor Annuity: Under the authority of Section 8341(h)(1) of Title 5, United States Code, Former Spouse is hereby awarded the maximum possible former spouse survivor annuity under CSRS unless Employee elects to provide a survivor annuity for a new spouse acquired after retirement. If the Employee elects to provide a survivor annuity to a new spouse acquired after retirement, the Former Spouse is hereby awarded a former spouse survivor annuity under CSRS in an amount equal to a pro rata share of the maximum possible survivor annuity. The marriage began on *[Date of Marriage]* and ended on *[Date of Decree]*.

12. Transfer to FERS: If the employee makes a one-time irrevocable election to transfer from CSRS to the Federal Employee's retirement System (FERS), before retirement, the Former Spouse shall then be entitled to a share of Employee's basic annuity under FERS calculated in the manner set forth in Paragraph 6 of this Order. The Former Spouse shall also be entitled to a former spouse survivor annuity payable under FERS in the maximum amount allowable under FERS.

13. Military Retired Pay: If the Employee waives military retired pay to credit military service under CSRS, the Former Spouse shall be entitled to a pro rata share of the portion of the Employee's gross monthly annuity under CSRS attributable to the military retired pay. The United States Office of Personnel Management is directed to pay the Former Spouse's share directly to Former Spouse.

14. Reimbursement: Of the benefits awarded or assigned to Former Spouse in this Order are inadvertently or erroneously paid by CSRS or FERS to Employee, Employee shall immediately reimburse Former Spouse for such benefits inadvertently or erroneously paid.

15. Construction of this Order: This Order is not intended, and shall not be construed so as to require the United States Office of Personnel Management to: (a) pay the Former Spouse a portion of the Employee annuity before it begins to accrue; (b) pay Former Spouse amounts in excess of the Employee's net annuity; or (c) pay a former spouse survivor annuity in excess of the maximum amounts payable under CSRS or FERS, whichever is applicable.

16. Continued Jurisdiction: The Court shall retain jurisdiction with respect to this Order for the purposes of maintaining the status of this

Order as a Court Order Acceptable for Processing and interpreting and enforcing the provisions of this Order.

IT IS SO ORDERED.

_____
Judge

Approved:

_____   _____
[Name] - Employee   [Name] - Former Spouse

_____   _____
Name of Attorney   Name of Attorney
Attorney for [Employee Name]   Attorney for [Former Spouse Name]
Ohio Supreme Court ID   Ohio Supreme Court ID
No._____   No._____
Address   Address
City, State, Zip   City, State, Zip
Telephone   Telephone

§ 29:23   Civil Service Retirement System—Health insurance

An employee covered by CSRS may enroll either himself or herself individually, or his or her family, in an approved health benefits plan when he becomes an annuitant, so long as certain conditions are met. In addition, a former spouse may, within sixty days after the dissolution of the marriage or within sixty days after an election is made for the former spouse by the retired employee, enroll in an approved health benefits plan so long as the former spouse agrees to pay the full subscription charge of the enrollment. Further, the former spouse must submit an enrollment application and make premium payments either to the agency which originally employed the employee or to the OPM if appropriate.[1] Continuation of health insurance coverage regulations are contained in 5 U.S.C.A. § 8905a, providing that an employee separating from service, a child ceasing to qualify as a dependent child, or a former spouse may apply for a continuation of benefits within 60 days of separation from service or receipt of the notice from OPM, and those benefits can continue for 18 months or 36 months, depending on the circumstances.

§ 29:24   Civil Service Retirement System—Practical effects

The practitioner should be concerned with benefits available to an employee in the civil service and the ensuing spousal benefits. It is additionally important that, once provisions are made for spousal annuity, there is written notification sent to the Office of Personnel Management; a properly drafted "Court Order Acceptable for Processing," or COAP,

_____
[Section 29:23]
[1]5 U.S.C.A. § 8905(c)(1).

much like a QDRO for the federal OPM; an application letter with the required contents; and a certified copy of the decree, so that any attempt in the future to modify the annuity will come to the attention of the spouse.[1]

§29:25 Federal Employees' Retirement System—In general

The Federal Employees Retirement System (FERS)[1] provides disability and survivorship benefits to persons employed by the federal government and hired after January 1, 1984. Unlike CSRS participants, FERS participants also pay into and participate in the social security system.[2]

A FERS participant usually can begin to receive monthly pension benefits at age 55 with 30 years of service,[3] at age 60 with 20 years of service,[4] or at age 62 with five years of service.[5] The minimum retirement age is 55, and the minimum number of years of service as a Federal employee is five.[6] For law enforcement officers and firefighters, the number of years of service at age 55 drops to 25,[7] or they can retire at age 50 with 20 years of service.[8] Air traffic controllers can retire at age 50 with 20 years of service,[9] or at any age after 25 years of service.[10]

The monthly annuity benefit is basically 1% of the high three average times the number of years of service.[11] For example, where there are 25 years of service and high three average is $40,000: $40,000 × 1% × 25 = $10,000 annual retirement benefit. The full retirement annuity is reduced by 5% for every year the participant is under the age of 62 at time of retirement. There is a very complex set of rules for FERS retirement benefits including contributions from the employee and the employing federal agency, COLAs, and annuity supplements.

[Section 29:24]

[1]See § 29:22, Civil Service Retirement System—COAP for CSRS pensions—Form and Gary A. Shulman, Qualified Domestic Relations Order Handbook (Wiley Law Pubs. 1993) for proper form. See also United States Office of Personnel Management, Retirement and Insurance Group, *A Handbook for Attorneys on Court-Ordered retirement and health benefits under the Civil Service Retirement System, Federal Employees Retirement System, and Federal Employees Health Benefits Program.*

[Section 29:25]

[1]5 U.S.C.A. §§ 8401 et seq.

[2]5 U.S.C.A. § 8403.

[3]5 U.S.C.A. § 8412(a).

[4]5 U.S.C.A. § 8412(b).

[5]5 U.S.C.A. § 8412(c).

[6]5 U.S.C.A. § 8410.

[7]5 U.S.C.A. § 8412(d)(1).

[8]5 U.S.C.A. § 8412(d)(2).

[9]5 U.S.C.A. § 8412(e)(2).

[10]5 U.S.C.A. § 8412(e)(1).

[11]5 U.S.C.A. § 8415(a).

§ 29:26   Federal Employees' Retirement System—Benefits to former spouse

A former spouse's right to FERS benefits is set forth in Title V of the United States Code Annotated, which defines who is an employee under the title, computes annuities, survivor's annuities, and lump-sum benefits, and directs payment of benefits.

Under 5 U.S.C.A. § 8417, a participant of FERS may elect, under the procedures provided, to have an annuity computed for a former spouse. The election for the annuity must be made at the time of retirement or, if later, within two years after the date on which the marriage of the former spouse and the employee was dissolved.[1]

At the time of retirement, the employee may elect one of the following options: a full retirement annuity with zero benefits to survivors after death; a full survivor benefit in which the retirant's annuity is reduced, and the survivor's benefit is paid to the named survivor until his/her death or remarriage prior to age 55; or a reduced survivor benefit in which the retirant's annuity is reduced, but not as much as it is under the full survivor benefit option.[2] Under FERS, the reduction for the full survivor benefit is 10% of the annuity benefit,[3] and the survivor receives 50% of the full benefit (computed before the 10% reduction) plus all COLAs.

Further, if the employee is remarried at the time of making the election, the written consent of the present spouse is required.[4] A former spouse is eligible for benefits until the former spouse dies or remarries prior to attaining age 55.[5] Further, the employee, at the time of retirement, may elect the reduced annuity instead of the full annuity, as it would be computed, in the interest of providing for an individual, including a former spouse, after the death of the retired employee. If there is a former spouse and a surviving spouse, the combination of benefits will not exceed the fifty-five percent limit.[6] FERS adds additional protections for spouses and former spouses regarding notification of changes in elections under 5 U.S.C.A. § 8434.

If a FERS participant dies before retirement, and was employed by the federal government for at least 18 months but less than ten years, FERS pays to the surviving spouse a lump sum, plus 50% of the employee's yearly pay at death or 50% of the high three average, whichever is more, plus $15,000.[7] If the employee had been employed for more than 10 years, the surviving spouse would receive an additional annuity

---

[Section 29:26]

[1] 5 U.S.C.A. § 8416(c).

[2] 5 U.S.C.A. § 8418.

[3] 5 U.S.C.A. § 8419.

[4] 5 U.S.C.A. § 8416.

[5] 5 U.S.C.A. § 8419(b)(2).

[6] 5 U.S.C.A. § 8341(f)(2).

[7] 5 U.S.C.A. § 8442(b)(1)(A).

valued at 50% of the employee's retirement annuity.[8] The amounts due to a surviving spouse can be received in monthly installments or in a lump sum.

If a FERS employee dies having attained required age and years of service to be eligible for a deferred annuity, but before having established a claim by making an application for that annuity, the surviving spouse will receive 50% of the employee's annuity,[9] beginning on the day after the employee dies and continuing until the surviving spouse dies or marries prior to attaining age 55.[10] If a former spouse's benefit is lost due to remarriage prior to age 55, it can resume again if that later marriage is dissolved by death, divorce, or annulment if a reapplication is made for the benefit.[11] A supplementary annuity is also available, but is reduced by a formula based on survivor's benefits received under social security.[12]

§ 29:27 Federal Employees' Retirement System—Surviving dependent child's benefits

A dependent child surviving a FERS worker who was employed for at least 18 months will receive a benefit equal to the same benefit as a surviving spouse, minus social security benefits paid to the child.

§ 29:28 Federal Employees' Retirement System—Lump-sum benefits

An employee may elect to receive payment of benefits in a lump sum.[1] Payment of the lump-sum amount will be made only if the current spouse and any former spouse of the employee have been notified of the application for lump-sum credit.[2] The application will be subject to the terms of a court decree of divorce, annulment, or legal separation, or any court-ordered or court-approved property settlement incident to such decree, if the decree relates to any portion of the lump-sum credit involved and payment of the lump-sum credit would affect any entitlement of the spouse or former spouse to a survivor annuity.[3]

§ 29:29 Federal Employees' Retirement System—Benefits to other persons

Payments which would otherwise be made to the employee can be made to another person, if and to the extent expressly provided for in

---

[8]5 U.S.C.A. § 8442(b)(1)(B).

[9]5 U.S.C.A. § 8441(c).

[10]5 U.S.C.A. § 8442(d)(1).

[11]5 U.S.C.A. § 8442(d)(2).

[12]5 U.S.C.A. § 8442(f).

[Section 29:28]

[1]5 U.S.C.A. § 8424(a).

[2]5 U.S.C.A. § 8424(b).

[3]5 U.S.C.A. § 8424(b).

the terms of any decree of divorce, annulment, or legal separation, or any court-ordered or court-approved property settlement incident to a decree of divorce, annulment, or legal separation, provided that the federal Office of Personnel Management (OPM) has had written notice of such decree,[1] and provided that a properly drafted COAP is approved by OPM.[2]

§ 29:30   Federal Employees' Retirement System—COAP for FERS pensions—Form⊚

IN THE COURT OF COMMON PLEAS

DOMESTIC RELATIONS DIVISION

_____ COUNTY, OHIO

[Name], Plaintiff	) Case No. [_____]
vs.	) Judge
[Name], Defendant	) **QUALIFYING COURT ORDER ACCEPTABLE FOR PROCESSING**

This cause came before the Court on the_____day of_____, 200_____. The Court found as follows:

1. *[Name]* (Husband) and *[Name]* (Wife) were married on *[Date of Marriage]*;

2. The parties have separated and have obtained, in these proceedings, a Decree of Divorce/ Dissolution of Marriage on *[Date of Decree]*;

3. The Court has, pursuant to such decree, divided the marital estate and all other property, including their respective interests in the retirement plan as provided for herein and the Decree requires the entry of a Court Order Acceptable for Processing by this court providing for the division and distribution of the marital portion of the benefits and benefit rights of the Plaintiff/Defendant under the Federal Employees Retirement System (FERS);

4. The terminology used in the provisions of this Order concerning benefits under FERS are governed by and were drafted in accordance with the standard conventions established in Part 8 of Title 5 of the Code of Federal Regulations (5 CFR 838);

5. This order is issued in connection with the Divorce/Dissolution of a Federal employee or retiree, is a "court order" as that term is defined in 5 CFR 838.103, and is intended to be a "court order acceptable for processing" as that term is defined in 5 CFR 838.103; and

6. Husband and Wife wish to settle all issues with respect to their interest in such plan.

NOW, THEREFORE, in consideration of the foregoing premises and

---

[Section 29:29]

[1]5 U.S.C.A. § 8345(j)(1).

[2]5 C.F.R. §§ 838.101 et seq.

the mutual promises hereunder specified, Husband and Wife do agree, and the Court does order, as follows:

1. Authority for Order: This order is entered pursuant to the authority granted under the domestic relations laws of the State of Ohio.

2. Effect of this Order as a Court Order Acceptable for Processing: This Order creates and recognizes the existence of Former Spouse's right to receive a portion of the Employee's benefits under the Federal Employees Retirement System (FERS). Such benefits may represent a portion of the employee annuity, a refund of employee contributions or may award a former spouse survivor annuity to the Former Spouse. It is intended to constitute a Court Order Acceptable for Processing under the final regulations issued by the United States Office of Personnel Management. The provisions of this Order are drafted in accordance with the terminology used in Part 838 of Title 5, Code of Federal Regulations.

3. Employee Information: The Employee is alive and has not retired under FERS. The information below is found to be correct as of the date of this order:

Name of Employee:
Address:
Date of Birth:
Social Security Number:
CSRS Claim Number:

4. Former Spouse Information: The Former Spouse is alive and has not remarried. The information below is found to be correct as of the date of this order:

Name of Former Spouse:
Address:
Date of Birth:
Social Security Number:

5. Identification of Retirement System: The Employee is or will be eligible for retirement benefits under the Federal Employees Retirement System (FERS) based on employment with the United States Government.

6. Entitlement to Benefits: The Former Spouse is found to be entitled to share in the Employee's gross monthly annuity under FERS awarded in Paragraph 7 of this order. The Former Spouse is also found to be entitled to a former spouse survivor annuity should the Employee predecease the Former Spouse. The United States Office of Personnel Management is hereby directed to pay the benefits awarded or assigned to the Former Spouse directly to the Former Spouse, except as provided in Paragraph 9 of this Order.

[Select one of the following, as appropriate]

[Alt #1] 7. Amount of Former Spouse's Share of Employee Annuity: The Former Spouse is entitled to and is hereby assigned and awarded and amount equal to fifty percent (50%) of the marital portion of

Employee's gross monthly annuity determined as of the Employee's date of retirement. The marital portion of the Employee's gross monthly annuity shall be determined by multiplying the gross monthly annuity by a fraction, the numerator of which is the total number of months of the Employee's creditable service under FERS during the marriage if the parties and the denominator of which is the Employee's total number of months of creditable service accrued under FERS, including military service credited to FERS. The marriage of the parties began on *[Date of Marriage]* and ended on *[Date of Decree]*. The Former Spouse's share of the Employee's gross monthly annuity shall be calculated without regard to any amounts that are withheld from the Employee's annuity for any reason, including amounts withheld for the purpose of providing Former Spouse with a survivor annuity. The United States Office of Personnel Management is directed to make payment directly to Former Spouse.

[Alt #2] 7. Amount of Former Spouse's Share of Employee Annuity: The Former Spouse is entitled to and is hereby assigned and awarded the amount of _____ U.S. dollars ($_____US) per month from the Employee's civil service retirement benefits. The marriage of the parties began on *[Date of Marriage]* and ended on *[Date of Decree]*. The United States Office of Personnel Management is directed to make payment directly to Former Spouse.

[Alt #3] 7. Amount of Former Spouse's Share of Employee Annuity: The Former Spouse is entitled to and is hereby assigned and awarded a pro rata share of the Employee's gross monthly retirement annuity accrued under the FERS. The marriage of the parties began on *[Date of Marriage]* and ended on *[Date of Decree]*. The United States Office of Personnel Management is directed to make payment directly to Former Spouse.

[Alt #4] 7. Amount of Former Spouse's Share of Employee Annuity: The Former Spouse is entitled to and is hereby assigned and awarded a share of the Employee's gross monthly annuity under FERS that is computed as follows: *[Calculation method]*. The marriage of the parties began on *Date of Marriage* and ended on *[Date of Decree]*. The United States Office of Personnel Management is directed to make payment directly to Former Spouse.

8. Payment of Former Spouse's Share of Employee Annuity: The Former Spouse shall begin receiving his/her share of the Employee Annuity benefits as soon as administratively feasible after the date this order is approved as a Court Order Acceptable for Processing or on the date that the Employee begins receiving benefits, if that date is later. Such payments shall continue to Former Spouse for the remainder of Employee's lifetime except as provided in Paragraph 8 of this order. The Employee is ordered to arrange or execute all forms necessary for the commencement of payments to the Former Spouse in accordance with the terms of this Order.

9. Payment of Employee Annuity of Former Spouse Predeceases Employee: Should the Former Spouse die before the Employee, the United States Office of Personnel Management is directed to pay the Former Spouse's share of the Employee's annuity, as described in Paragraph 6

of the order, to *[the surviving children of the parties in equal shares. Upon the death of any child, that child's share shall be paid to the then surviving children of the parties in equal shares.] [Name Beneficiary at Address.] [the Court issuing this Order.]*

10. Cost of Living Adjustments. The Employee is or will be entitled to cost of living adjustments to his/her retirement benefits. When cost of living adjustments are applied to the Employee's retirement benefits, the same cost of living adjustments shall be applied to the Former Spouse's share of the benefits. The United States Office of Personnel Management is directed to pay the Former Spouse's share of any such adjustments directly to Former Spouse except as provided in Paragraph 8 of this Order.

[Select one of the following, as appropriate]

[Alt #1] 11. Refunds of Employee's Contributions: If Employee leaves the Federal service before retirement and applies for a refund of employee contributions, the United States Office of Personnel Management is directed <u>not</u> to pay the Employee a refund of employee contributions.

[Alt #2] 11. Refunds of Employee's Contributions: If Employee leaves the Federal service before retirement and applies for a refund of employee contributions, the United States Office of Personnel Management is directed to pay to Former Spouse fifty percent (50%) of the marital portion of any such refund. The marriage of the parties began on *[Date of Marriage]* and ended on *[Date of Decree.]* The United States Office of Personnel Management is directed to make payment directly to Former Spouse.

[Select one of the following, as appropriate]

[Alt #1] 12. Former Spouse Survivor Annuity: Under the authority of Section 8341(h)(1) of Title 5, United States Code, Former Spouse is hereby awarded the maximum possible former spouse survivor annuity under FERS. The cost of the annuity shall be paid from Employee's annuity and not from Former Spouse's share of the employee annuity.

[Alt #2] 12. Former Spouse Survivor Annuity: Under the authority of Section 8341(h)(1) of Title 5, United States Code, Former Spouse is hereby awarded the maximum possible former spouse survivor annuity under FERS in the same amount to which Former Spouse would have been entitled had the divorce not occurred. The cost of the annuity shall be paid from Employee's annuity and not from Former Spouse's share of the employee annuity.

[Alt #3] 12. Former Spouse Survivor Annuity: Under the authority of Section 8341(h)(1) of Title 5, United States Code, Former Spouse is hereby awarded the a former spouse survivor annuity under FERS in an amount equal to a pro rata share of the maximum possible survivor annuity. The marriage began on *[Date of Marriage]* and ended on *[Date of Decree]*.

[Alt #4] 12. Former Spouse Survivor Annuity: Under the authority of Section 8341(h)(1) of Title 5, United States Code, Former Spouse is hereby awarded a former spouse survivor annuity under FERS in an amount equal to _____U.S. dollars ($_____U.S.). The United States Office of Personnel Management is ordered not to increase this amount by cost of living adjustments that occur before death of the Employee.

[Alt #5] 12. Former Spouse Survivor Annuity: Under the authority of Section 8341(h)(1) of Title 5, United States Code, Former Spouse is hereby awarded a former spouse survivor annuity under FERS in an amount equal to fifty percent (50%) of Employee's gross Employee annuity.

[Alt #6] 12. Former Spouse Survivor Annuity: Under the authority of Section 8341(h)(1) of Title 5, United States Code, Former Spouse is hereby awarded a former spouse survivor annuity under FERS in an amount equal to seventy-five percent (75%) of the maximum possible survivor annuity.

[Alt #7] 12. Former Spouse Survivor Annuity: Under the authority of Section 8341(h)(1) of Title 5, United States Code, Former Spouse is hereby awarded the maximum possible former spouse survivor annuity under FERS unless Employee remarries before retirement. If Employee remarries before retirement, Former Spouse is hereby awarded a former spouse survivor annuity under FERS in the amount of a pro rata share of the maximum possible survivor annuity. The marriage began on *[Date of Marriage]* and ended on *[Date of Decree]*.

[Alt #8] 12. Former Spouse Survivor Annuity: Under the authority of Section 8341(h)(1) of Title 5, United States Code, Former Spouse is hereby awarded the maximum possible former spouse survivor annuity under FERS unless Employee elects to provide a survivor annuity for a new spouse acquired after retirement. If the Employee elects to provide a survivor annuity to a new spouse acquired after retirement, the Former Spouse is hereby awarded a former spouse survivor annuity under CSES in an amount equal to a pro rata share of the maximum possible survivor annuity. The marriage began on *[Date of Marriage]* and ended on *[Date of Decree]*.

13. Transfer to CSRS: If the employee makes a one-time irrevocable election to transfer from FERS to the Civil Service Retirement System (CSRS), before retirement, the Former Spouse shall then be entitled to a share of Employee's basic annuity under FERS calculated in the manner set forth in Paragraph 6 of this Order. The Former Spouse shall also be entitled to a former spouse survivor annuity payable under CSRS in the maximum amount allowable under CSRS.

14. Military Retired Pay: If the Employee waives military retired pay to credit military service under FERS, the Former Spouse shall be entitled to a pro rata share of the portion of the Employee's gross monthly annuity under FERS attributable to the military retired pay. The United States Office of Personnel Management is directed to pay the Former Spouse's share directly to Former Spouse.

15. Reimbursement: Of the benefits awarded or assigned to Former Spouse in this Order are inadvertently or erroneously paid by FERS or CSRS to Employee. Employee shall immediately reimburse Former Spouse for such benefits inadvertently or erroneously paid.

16. Construction of this Order: This Order is not intended, and shall

not be construed so as to require the United States Office of Personnel Management to: (a) pay the Former Spouse a portion of the Employee annuity before it begins to accrue; (b) pay Former Spouse amounts in excess of the Employee's net annuity; or (c) pay a former spouse survivor annuity in excess of the maximum amounts payable under CSRS or FERS, whichever is applicable.

17. Continued Jurisdiction: The Court shall retain jurisdiction with respect tot his Order for the purposes of maintaining the status of this Order as a Court Order Acceptable for Processing and interpreting and enforcing the provisions of this Order.

IT IS SO ORDERED.

_____

Judge

Approved:

_____   _____

[Name] - Employee   *[Name]* - Former Spouse

_____   _____

Name of Attorney   Name of Attorney

Attorney for *[Employee Name]*   Attorney for *[Former Spouse Name]*

Ohio Supreme Court ID No._____   Ohio Supreme Court ID No._____

Address   Address

City, State, Zip   City, State, Zip

Telephone   Telephone

§ 29:31 Federal Employees' Retirement System—Health insurance

An employee covered by FERS may enroll either himself or herself individually, or his or her family, in an approved health benefits plan when he becomes an annuitant, so long as certain conditions are met. In addition, a former spouse may, within sixty days after the dissolution of the marriage, or within sixty days after an election is made for the former spouse by the retired employee, enroll in an approved health benefits plan so long as the former spouse agrees to pay the full subscription charge of the enrollment. Further, the former spouse must submit an enrollment application and make premium payments either to the agency that originally employed the employee or to the OPM if appropriate.[1]

[Section 29:31]

[1]5 U.S.C.A. § 8905(c)(1). See also United States Office of Personnel Management, Retirement and Insurance Group, *A Handbook for Attorneys on Court-Ordered retirement and health benefits under the Civil Service Retirement System, Federal Employees Retirement System, and Federal Employees Health Benefits Program.*

§ 29:32   Federal Employees' Retirement System—Practical considerations

The practitioner should be concerned with the benefits available to an employee employed by the federal government and the ensuing spousal benefits. It is additionally important that once provisions are made for spousal annuity, there be written notification to the Office of Personnel Management and a properly drafted "Court Order Acceptable for Processing," or COAP, much like a QDRO for the federal OPM, an application letter with the required contents, and a certified copy of the decree, so that any attempt in the future to modify of the annuity will come to the attention of the spouse.[1]

§ 29:33   Federal thrift savings plans

Federal employees may also contribute to a Thrift Savings Plan (TSP), which is similar to a 401(k) plan, a defined contribution plan, rather than a defined benefit plan like FERS and CSRS.

For employees who participate in CSRS, their TSPs are funded solely by themselves, and they can contribute up to 5% of gross annual wages.[1] FERS employees, however, can contribute up to 10% of their gross annual wages, and the government also contributes dollar-for-dollar for the first 3% of wages, and can contribute up to a total of 5% of the employee's basic pay.[2]

Withdrawals may be made from a TSP upon retirement by equal payments over time or in a lump sum, beginning no later than the attainment of age 70½ years.[3]

Withdrawals are taxable upon receipt if received prior to minimum age unless they are transferred to an IRA or a different kind of purchased annuity. Withdrawals may also be made if the employee is separated from service, but there is a 10% penalty attached unless the entire amount is rolled over into an IRA. Loans may also be taken against a TSP account upon application.[4]

[Section 29:32]

[1]See § 29:30, Federal Employees' Retirement System—COAP for FERS pensions—Form for proper form and Gary A. Shulman, Qualified Domestic Relations Order Handbook (Wiley Law Pubs. 1993).

[Section 29:33]

[1]5 U.S.C.A. § 8351(b)(2).

[2]5 U.S.C.A. § 8432.

[3]5 U.S.C.A. § 8432.

[4]See § 29:34, Federal thrift savings plan—Court order to divide federal thrift savings plan ("TSP")—Form.

§ 29:34   Federal thrift savings plan—Court order to divide federal thrift savings plan ("TSP")—Form◎

IN THE COURT OF COMMON PLEAS

DOMESTIC RELATIONS DIVISION

_____COUNTY, OHIO

[Name], Plaintiff	)	Case No. [_____]
vs.	)	Judge
[Name], Defendant	)	**QUALIFYING RETIREMENT BENEFITS COURT ORDER**

This cause came before the Court on the _____ day of _____, 200_____. The Court found as follows:

1. *[Name]* (Husband) and *[Name]* (Wife) were married on *[Date of Marriage]*;

2. The parties have separated and have obtained, in these proceedings, a Decree of Divorce/ Dissolution of Marriage on *[Date of Decree]*;

3. The Court has, pursuant to such decree, divided the marital estate and all other property, including their respective interests in the retirement plan as provided for herein and the Decree requires the entry of a Qualified Retirement Benefits Court Order by this court providing for the division and distribution of the marital portion of the benefits and benefit rights of the Plaintiff/Defendant under the Thrift Savings Plan;

4. This order is issued in connection with the Divorce/Dissolution of a Federal employee or retiree, is a "court order"; and

5. Husband and Wife wish to settle all issues with respect to their interest in such plan.

NOW, THEREFORE, in consideration of the foregoing premises and the mutual promises hereunder specified, Husband and Wife do agree, and the Court does order, as follows:

1. Effect of This Order As a Qualifying Retirement Benefits Court Order: This order creates and recognizes the existence of an Alternate Payee's right to receive a portion of the Participant's benefits payable under the Thrift Savings Plan, which is administered by the Federal Retirement Thrift Investment Board.

2. Participant Information: The name, last-known address, Social Security Number, and date of birth of the Participant are:

Name:
Address:
Social Security Number:
Date of Birth:

3. Alternate Payee Information: The name, last-known address, Social Security Number, and date of birth of the Alternate Payee are:

Name:
Address:
Social Security Number:
Date of Birth:

The Alternate Payee shall have the duty to notify the United States Office of Personnel Management in writing of any changes in the Alternate Payee's mailing address subsequent to the entry of this Order.

4. Plan Name: The name of the Plan to which this Order applies is the Thrift Savings Plan ("TSP") (hereinafter referred to as "Plan")

5. Pursuant to State Domestic Relations Law: This Order is entered pursuant to the authority granted in the applicable domestic relations laws of the State of Ohio.

6. For Provisional of Marital Property Rights: This Order relates to the provision of the marital property rights and/or spousal support to the Alternate Payee as a result of the Order of Divorce between the Participant and the Alternate Payee.

7. Amount of the Alternate Payee's Benefit: This Order assigns to the Alternate Payee an amount equal to Fifty Percent (50%) of the Participant's total account balance accumulated under the plan as of _____ (or the closest valuation date thereto), plus any interest and investment earnings or losses attributable thereon for periods subsequent to _____, until the date of total distribution. Further, such total account balance shall include all amounts maintained under all of the various accounts and/or sub-accounts established on behalf of the Participant.

8. Commencement Date and Form Payment to the Alternate Payee: The Alternate Payee shall be paid benefits as soon as administratively feasible following the date this Order is approved as a Qualifying Retirement Benefits Court Order by the Plan Administrator.

9. Savings Clause: This Order is not intended , and shall not be construed in such a manner as to require the Plan:

(a) to provide any type or form of benefit option not otherwise provided under the terms of the Plan;

(b) to require the Plan to provide increased benefits determined on the basis of actual value; or

(c) to require the payment of any benefits to the Alternate Payee which are required to be paid to another Alternate Payee under another order which was previously deemed to be a Qualifying Retirement Benefits Court Order.

10. Constructive Receipt: In the event that the Plan Trustee inadvertently pays to the Participant and benefits that are assigned to the Alternate Payee pursuant to the terms of this Order, the Participant shall immediately reimburse the Alternate Payee to the extent that the Participant has received such benefit payments, and shall forthwith pay such amounts so received directly to the Alternate Payee within ten (10) days of receipt.

11. Continued Jurisdiction: The court shall retain jurisdiction with respect to this Order to the extent required to maintain its qualified status and the original intent of the parties stipulated herein. The Court shall also retain jurisdiction to enter such further orders as are necessary to enforce the assignment of benefits to the Alternate Payee as set forth herein, including the re-characterization thereof as a division of benefits under another plan, as applicable, or to make an award of alimony, if applicable, in the event that the Participant fails to comply with the provisions contained above requiring said payments to the Alternate Payee.

12. Actions by Participant: The Participant shall not take any actions, affirmative or otherwise, that can circumvent the terms and provisions of this Qualified Domestic Relations Order, or that could diminish or extinguish the rights and entitlements of the Alternate Payee as set forth herein. Should the Participant take any action or inaction to the detriment of the Alternate Payee, the Participant shall be required to make sufficient payments directly to the Alternate Payee to the extent necessary to neutralize the effects of the Participant's actions or inactions and to the extent of the Alternate Payee's full entitlements hereunder.

13. Death of Participant: In the event the Participant predeceases the Alternate Payee before the Alternate Payee receives distribution, the Participant's death shall have no effect on the Alternate Payee's assigned portion of the benefits, as stipulated herein. If necessary to secure assigned benefits, the Alternate Payee shall be treated as the beneficiary of the Participant, but to the extent of the Alternate Payee's assigned interest hereunder.

IT IS SO ORDERED.

_____
Judge

Approved:

_____   _____
[Name] - Employee   *[Name]* - Former Spouse

_____   _____
Name of Attorney   Name of Attorney
Attorney for *[Employee Name]*   Attorney for *[Former Spouse Name]*

Ohio Supreme Court ID   Ohio Supreme Court ID
No._____   No._____
Address   Address
City, State, Zip   City, State, Zip
Telephone   Telephone

§ 29:35 Railroad retirement benefits

The Railroad Retirement Act[1] provides retirement benefits for railroad employees. The benefits are determined by Congress and are not contractual. Tier I benefits are not divisible because they are equivalent to social security for railroad workers. Tier II benefits are subject to equal division upon divorce. Tier II benefits consist of retirement and survivors' basic benefits, vested dual benefits (not available to persons employed after 1974), and supplemental benefits. Under Tier II there are no surviving spouse annuities, but separate retirement benefits are provided for the non-employee spouse, equal to 45% of the employee's annuity.

The entitlement of a spouse of an employee to an annuity under Tier I terminates when the spouse and the employee are absolutely divorced.[2] 45 U.S.C.A. § 231m provides that the annuity shall not be assignable or be subject to garnishment, attachment, or other legal process, except for satisfying child support or alimony (spousal support) obligations. Although the benefits are determined at the federal level through Congress, the United States Supreme Court consistently has been reluctant to review cases involving property and alimony rights in a divorce, reasoning that those considerations are best left to the states. However, the Supreme Court will invoke the Supremacy Clause[3] when it determines that state family or property law conflicts with clear federal interests. In *Hisquierdo v. Hisquierdo*,[4] the Supreme Court held that "(t)he pertinent questions are whether the right as asserted conflicts with the express terms of federal law and whether its consequences sufficiently injure the objectives of the federal program to require nonrecognition." In *Hisquierdo*, the Court found that the community property laws of California did in fact conflict with the intent of the Railroad Retirement Act, and held that benefits payable under the Act could not be divided under the state law.

Just as *McCarty v. McCarty*,[5] was legislatively overruled by the Uniformed Services Former Spouse's Protection Act,[6] so *Hisquierdo* was legislatively overruled by the Railroad Retirement Solvency Act.[7] Benefits under Tier II must be distributed in accordance with court decrees of divorce, annulment, legal separation, or court-approved property agreements incident thereto. The administrators of Tier II will accept a marriage coverture formula in determining the part to be paid to the former spouse.

[Section 29:35]

[1]45 U.S.C.A. § 231.

[2]45 U.S.C.A. § 231d(c)(3).

[3]U.S. Const. art. VI.

[4]Hisquierdo v. Hisquierdo, 439 U.S. 572, 583, 99 S. Ct. 802, 59 L. Ed. 2d 1 (1979).

[5]McCarty v. McCarty, 453 U.S. 210, 101 S. Ct. 2728, 69 L. Ed. 2d 589 (1981).

[6]Pub. L. No. 97-252, 96 Stat. 737 (1982).

[7]Pub. L. No. 98-76, 97 Stat. 434 (1983).

Tarbet v. Tarbet[8] held that Tier I benefits are exempt from the state court's power to divide upon a divorce. Just as with the value of social security benefits, however, the Tier I benefits still have a value and should be evaluated and presented to the Court for consideration, not division, upon a divorce. In addition, railroad employees are usually covered by a defined benefit plan from the employer as well as under the Railroad Retirement Act.

§ 29:36 Railroad retirement benefits—Court order for tier II railroad retirement board pensions—Form⊚

IN THE COURT OF COMMON PLEAS

DOMESTIC RELATIONS DIVISION

———————COUNTY, OHIO

[Name], Plaintiff	)	Case No. [———————]
vs.	)	Judge
[Name], Defendant	)	**QUALIFYING COURT ORDER**

This cause came before the Court on the ———————— day of ————————, 200————————. The Court found as follows:

1. *[Name]* (Husband) and *[Name]* (Wife) were married on *[Date of Marriage]*;

2. The parties have separated and have obtained, in these proceedings, a Decree of Divorce/ Dissolution of Marriage on *[Date of Decree]*;

3. The Court has, pursuant to such decree, divided the marital estate and all other property, including their respective interests in the retirement plan as provided for herein and the Decree requires the entry of a Court Order Acceptable for Processing by this court providing for the division and distribution of the marital portion of the benefits and benefit rights of the Plaintiff/Defendant under the Railroad Retirement Board;

4. The terminology used in the provisions of this Order concerning benefits under the Railroad Retirement Board are governed by and were drafted in accordance with the standard conventions established in the Railroad Retirement Act, 45 U.S.C.A. § 231, et seq.

5. This order is issued in connection with the Divorce/Dissolution of a Railroad employee or retiree, is a "court order"; and

6. Husband and Wife wish to settle all issues with respect to their interest in such plan.

NOW, THEREFORE, in consideration of the foregoing premises and the mutual promises hereunder specified, Husband and Wife do agree, and the Court does order, as follows:

1. Authority for Order: This order is entered pursuant to the authority granted under the domestic relations laws of the State of Ohio.

---

[8]Tarbet v. Tarbet, 97 Ohio App. 3d 674, 647 N.E.2d 254 (9th Dist. Summit County 1994).

2. Employee Information: The Employee is alive and has not retired under the Railroad Retirement Board. The information below is found to be correct as of the date of this order:

Name of Employee:
Address:
Date of Birth:
Social Security Number:

3. Former Spouse Information: The Former Spouse is alive and has not remarried. The information below is found to be correct as of the date of this order:

Name of Former Spouse:
Address:
Date of Birth:
Social Security Number:

4. Assignment of Benefits: The employee assigns to the Former Spouse an interest in the Employee's Railroad Retirement Benefits payable under the Railroad Retirement Act. The Former Spouse is entitled to direct payments of the amount specified in Paragraph 5 below from the Railroad Retirement Board and which will be payable from the divisible portion of the Employee's benefits (including, but not limited to the Employee's Tier II Annuity, as applicable, as well as any vested dual benefit payments, supplemental annuity, or overall minimum increases payable to the Employee).

5. Amount of Payments: The Former Spouse shall receive the following amount from each monthly payment of the Employee's divisible portion of the Employee's retirement benefits (i.e., the non-Tier I benefits):

The Former Spouse shall receive fifty percent (50%) of the marital portion of Employee's total divisible portion of the Employee's monthly retirement benefits determined as of the Employee's date of retirement.. The marital portion shall be calculated by multiplying such total divisible portion by a fraction, the numerator of which is the number of years and months of the Employee's service earned under the Plan during the marriage to the Former Spouse (from _____to_____), and the denominator of which is the Employee's total number of years and months of service earned under the Plan as of his date of retirement.

Except for the amount assigned to the Former Spouse above, the Employee shall maintain as his the Employee's sole and separate property all other pension benefits that the Employee shall maintain as his the Employee's sole and separate property all other pension benefits that the Employee may be eligible to receive from the Railroad Retirement Board based on the Employee's years of service with a railroad employer.

6. Commencement of Benefits: The monthly payments under Paragraph 5 shall commence when the Employee commences benefits and upon completion of the necessary paperwork. The Former Spouse shall continue to receive assigned benefits for as long as the Employee has the right to receive Railroad Retirement Benefits and shall cease at the death of either party.

7. Overpayments: The Former Spouse agrees that any future overpayments to the Former Spouse are recoverable and subject to involuntary collection from the Former Spouse or the estate of the Former Spouse.

8. Notification: The Former Spouse agrees to notify the Railroad Retirement Board about any changes in the Qualifying Court Order or the order affecting these provisions of it, or in the eligibility of any recipient receiving benefits pursuant to it.

9. Continued Cooperation of the Employee: The Employee agrees to cooperate with the Former Spouse to prepare an application for direct payment to the Former Spouse from the Employee's Railroad Retirement Benefits, if necessary. The Employee agrees to execute all documents that the Railroad Retirement Board may require to certify that the specified portion of the Employee's Railroad Retirement Benefits can be provided to the Former Spouse.

10. As part of Property Division: The division of Railroad Retirement Benefits in this Order represents a final disposition of property between the Employee and the Former Spouse in compliance with a community property settlement, equitable distribution of property, or other distribution of property which is intended as a present and complete settlement of the property rights of the parties.

11. Jurisdiction: The parties agree that the Court of Common Pleas, Division of Domestic Relations, _____County, Ohio, is a court of competent jurisdiction in this action. This order bears the certification of _____ of the Court of Common Pleas, Division of Domestic Relations, _____ County, Ohio, and has not been amended, superseded or set aside by any subsequent order.

12. Qualifying Court Order Under the Railroad Retirement Board: The Employee and the Former Spouse intend that this Order qualify under the Railroad Retirement Act, 45 U.S.C. Section 231(m). All provisions of this Order shall be construed and/or modified to the extent necessary to conform with the requirements of the Railroad Retirement Board for the division of an Employee's Railroad Retirement Benefits.

13. Merger of Benefits and Indemnification: The Employee agrees not to merge the Employee's Tier II Railroad Retirement Benefits with any other pension and not to pursue any course of action that would defeat the Former Spouse's right to receive a portion of the Employee's benefits as stipulated herein. The Employee agrees not to take any action by merger of the Employee's Railroad Retirement pension so as to cause a limitation in the amount of the benefits in which the Employee has a vested interest, and , therefore, the Employee will not cause a limitation of the former Spouse's monthly payments as set forth above. The Employee agrees to indemnify Former Spouse for any breach of this paragraph as follows: If the Employee becomes employed or otherwise has his Tier II Railroad Retirement pension merged, which employment or other condition causes a merger of the Employee's Tier II Railroad Retirement Benefits, the Employee will pay to the Former Spouse Tier II Railroad Retirement Benefits, the Employee will pay to the Former Spouse directly the monthly amount provided in Paragraph 5, under the same terms and conditions as if those payments were made pursuant to the terms of this order.

14. Continued Jurisdiction: The Court retains limited jurisdiction to amend this order for the purposes of maintaining the original intent of the parties and of meeting any requirements to create, conform, and maintain this order as a Qualifying Court Order for the division of the Employee's Railroad Retirement Benefits, as stipulated herein. The court shall also retain jurisdiction to enter such further orders are necessary to enforce the assignment of benefits to Former Spouse as set forth herein, including the recharacterization thereof as a division of benefits under another plan, as applicable.

15. Actions by Employee: The Employee shall not take any actions, affirmative or otherwise, that can circumvent the terms and provisions of this Qualified Domestic Relations Order, or that could diminish or extinguish the rights and entitlements of the Former Spouse as set forth herein. Should the Employee take any action or inaction to detriment of the Former Spouse, the Employee shall be required to make sufficient payments directly to the Former Spouse to the extent necessary to neutralize the effects of the Employee's actions or inactions and to the extent of the Former Spouse's full entitlements hereunder.

16. Notice of Pending Retirement: The Employee shall be required to notify the Former Spouse, in writing within thirty (30) days prior to the Employee's actual date of retirement. Such notice shall indicate the Employee's intention to retire and the Employee's elected benefit commencement date. The notice shall be sent via regular, first-class mail. For this purpose, the Former Souse shall notify the Employee of any changes in the Former Spouse's mailing address.

IT IS SO ORDERED.

_____
Judge

Approved:

_____
[Name] - Employee

_____
Name of Attorney
Attorney for [Employee Name]

Ohio Supreme Court ID
No._____
Address
City, State, Zip
Telephone

_____
[Name] - Former Spouse

_____
Name of Attorney
Attorney for [Former Spouse Name]

Ohio Supreme Court ID
No._____
Address
City, State, Zip
Telephone

§ 29:37   Foreign service benefits

Benefits payable to former spouses of employees of the foreign service are addressed in Title 22 of the United States Code Annotated. 22 U.S.C.A. § 4054(a)(1) provides that if the former spouse was married to the employee for at least 10 years of the employee's employment in the foreign service, the spouse is entitled to a benefit equal to fifty percent of the annuity of the employee, or to a prorated share of fifty percent based on the duration of the marriage in relation to the employee's length of service. As in other federal entitlement programs, the former spouse will still be eligible for benefits even after remarriage, so long as the spouse is at least sixty years of age.[1]

The spousal support or property division order cannot award more than the annuity of the participant, and must be issued within twenty-four months of the decree or divorce.[2] Further, since the annuity is calculated based on the term of the marriage in relation to the number of years of service, it will reduce the annuity payable to the employee.[3]

Finally, should the former spouse survive the employee, the former spouse's share of the monthly annuity will be increased from fifty to fifty-five percent of the full amount of the employee's annuity or, depending upon the duration of the marriage, a prorated share of the fifty-five percent.[4]

§ 29:38   Military benefits—Uniformed Services Former Spouses Protection Act

Although the United States Supreme Court has traditionally been reluctant to consider cases involving division of property upon divorce or annulment, it did so in *McCarty v. McCarty*,[1] where it held that there was a conflict between the terms of the federal military retirement statutes and the community property right asserted by a California spouse. The Court recognized that the plight of an ex-spouse of a retired service member is often a serious one, but held that application of community property principles to the division of retirement pay threatened grave harm to clear and substantial federal interests. Congress, in 1982, addressing the problem created by the *McCarty* case, enacted the Uniformed Services Former Spouses Protection Act[2] establishing former spouses' rights to military benefits.

Under the provisions of 10 U.S.C.A. § 1408(c), effective February 1, 1983, a court may now treat disposable retired or retainer pay, payable to a member of the armed services, either as property solely of the member, or as property of the member and his spouse in accordance with the law of the jurisdiction of such court.[3] However, this section does not authorize a court to order a member of the armed services to apply for retirement or to retire at a particular time to effectuate a payment

[Section 29:37]
   [1]22 U.S.C.A. § 4054(a)(2).
   [2]22 U.S.C.A. § 4054(a)(4).
   [3]22 U.S.C.A. § 4054(a)(5).
   [4]22 U.S.C.A. § 4054(b).

[Section 29:38]
   [1]McCarty v. McCarty, 453 U.S. 210, 101 S. Ct. 2728, 69 L. Ed. 2d 589 (1981).
   [2]Uniformed Services Former Spouses Protection Act, Pub. L. No. 737 (1982).
   [3]10 U.S.C.A. § 1408(c)(1).

under a court order. For a court order to be effective, jurisdiction over the member of the armed services is required either by his residence being in the territorial jurisdiction of the court (other than because of military assignment), his domicile being in the jurisdiction of the court, or by his having consented to the jurisdiction of the court. Failure to consider a military pension earned during the marriage, even where unvested, was error requiring reversal.[4]

Service of the court order must be made either personally on the secretary of the branch of the service in which the member was enlisted or through a designated agent of the secretary, and should include the social security number of the member.[5] If, on the date of effective service of the order, the member is entitled to receive retirement or retainer pay, the payments to the spouse will begin not later than ninety days after the date of service. In the case of a member not entitled to receive such pay on the date of effective service of the court order, such payments will begin not later than ninety days after the date on which the member first becomes entitled to the benefits.[6]

§ 29:39 Military benefits—Benefits as marital property

Direct payments by the federal government of court-ordered spousal or child support payments are authorized by 10 U.S.C.A. § 1408(d)(1). However, 10 U.S.C.A. § 1408(d)(2) prevents direct payment of amounts that are property settlement payments where the payee-spouse was not married to the service member for ten years or more while the service member performed ten years of service. That provision does not limit the trial court's authority to require an armed forces member to pay a portion of his retirement income to his former spouse, even if it is a property division.[1]

A trial court, in awarding a spouse a coverture fraction of retirement pay, may also award a percentage of any severance pay, continuation pay, and Voluntary Separation Incentive (VSI) pay.[2] In affirming the trial court's award of the VSI payments to the wife, the Second District Court of Appeals in *Denny v. Denny*[3] distinguished its prior refusal to award a portion of the former service member's VSI in *McClure v. McClure*[4] by stating that where the separation from service is voluntary, the VSI pay is in lieu of retirement benefits which are divisible upon divorce, as opposed to where the separation from service and VSI election are, in reality, involuntary, and actually are intended to replace

---

[4]Siler v. Siler, 1994 WL 386106 (Ohio Ct. App. 12th Dist. Warren County 1994).

[5]10 U.S.C.A. § 1408(c)(1).

[6]10 U.S.C.A. § 1408(d)(1).

[Section 29:39]

[1]Canales v. Canales, 1989 WL 24187 (Ohio Ct. App. 2d Dist. Greene County 1989).

[2]Denny v. Denny, 1996 WL 173397 (Ohio Ct. App. 2d Dist. Greene County 1996).

[3]Denny v. Denny, 1996 WL 173397 (Ohio Ct. App. 2d Dist. Greene County 1996).

[4]McClure v. McClure, 98 Ohio App. 3d 27, 647 N.E.2d 832 (2d Dist. Greene County 1994).

compensation for future services.

The trial court's interpretation of the provisions of a separation agreement that included a wife's entitlement to a percentage of the husband's "net retirement" from the Air Force was reversed in *Meinke v. Meinke*.[5] The retirement benefits were held to be so low as to render it foreseeable by the parties that the husband would seek and obtain additional income from nonretirement sources. Such additional income would put him in a higher tax bracket than without the second income. Since the wife's entitlement was based on "net," she argued that the net after taxes should be calculated based only on retirement income. The appellate court reversed the trial court's acceptance of that interpretation, finding dispositive and persuasive the holding in *Mansell v. Mansell*[6] that the Uniformed Services Former Spouse's Protection Act[7] only gave state courts the authority to treat "disposable retired pay," and not total military retired pay, as community property, and an appropriate deduction from "total" to "disposable" would be the taxes calculated according to the retirant's actual bracket for that year. An additional complicating factor in *Mansell* was that retirement benefits were waived in order for the member to receive disability pay, and once waived, the state court was precluded from treating that waived benefit as marital property. *Clauson v. Clauson*[8] held that even though military disability pension was not subject to direct division by the state court because of the holding in *Mansell*, the value of the disability pension should still be considered.

In *Alexander v. Alexander*,[9] a former spouse, who had been divorced while *McCarty* prevailed, returned to court after enactment of the Uniformed Services Former Spouse's Protection Act[10] to obtain division of retirement benefits. The Tenth District Court of Appeals found that because RC 3105.18 required the trial court to consider retirement benefits, even at the time the case was originally decided, these benefits had been taken into account, even if they were not specifically divided.

A trial court can find a spouse in contempt of court and impose purge conditions to satisfy the harm caused by a voluntary relinquishment of retirement benefits upon separation from service. In *Collins v. Collins*,[11] husband and wife had agreed in their decree of divorce to use a formula to determine the amount each owed the other from military retirement benefits earned during the marriage. However, before husband became eligible to retire, he was honorably discharged and forfeited his military pension. At the time of the divorce husband had been in the military for

---

[5]Meinke v. Meinke, 1990 WL 187548 (Ohio Ct. App. 2d Dist. Miami County 1990).

[6]Mansell v. Mansell, 490 U.S. 581, 109 S. Ct. 2023, 104 L. Ed. 2d 675 (1989).

[7]10 U.S.C.A. § 1408.

[8]Clauson v. Clauson, 831 P.2d 1257 (Alaska 1992).

[9]Alexander v. Alexander, 20 Ohio App. 3d 94, 484 N.E.2d 1068 (10th Dist. Franklin County 1985).

[10]Pub. L. No. 97-252, 96 Stat. 737 (1982).

[11]Collins v. Collins, 139 Ohio App. 3d 900, 746 N.E.2d 201 (2d Dist. Montgomery County 2000).

thirteen years and argued that the trial court imposed involuntary servitude upon him. The Court of Appeals for the Second District found that there was no unconstitutional involuntary servitude by requiring him to purge his contempt of the decree's retirement provisions. Although the husband was free to leave the military and forfeit his retirement, he was obligated to reimburse his former wife for the financial consequences of his decision because he was under an order to protect his former spouse's benefit yet took a unilateral action to destroy her interest in his retirement benefit.

The Ohio Supreme Court reversed a decision of the Court of Appeals of Summit County in *Mackey v. Mackey*[12] when it held that benefits received by a member under the VSI program qualify as marital property under RC 3105.171 and as such are divisible upon divorce.[13] In doing so, the Court relied on the Colorado case of *In re Marriage of Heupel*[14] which held that "unilateral control to transform marital property into separate property could inappropriately sway a service member's decision to opt for the SSB or VSI program. This would have the undesirable consequence of divesting the nonemployee spouse of a valuable asset."[15]

§ 29:40   Military benefits—Benefits as spousal support

The total amount of the disposable retired or retainer pay of a member payable to the former spouse may not exceed fifty percent of the net pay. In the event of effective service of more than one court order that provides for payment to a spouse, or one or more former spouses, the disposable retired or retainer pay of the member will be used to satisfy the court orders on a first-come, first-served basis. In other words, any subsequent orders of court will be paid out of that amount of disposable pay which remains after all previous court orders have been satisfied.[1] The total amount of disposable benefits of a member payable by the secretary concerned under all court orders may not exceed sixty-five percent of the disposable benefits. The benefits will be adjusted for amounts paid during each month pursuant to legal process served under section 459 of the Social Security Act.[2] A court order which exceeds the benefits because of previously served court orders is not considered irregular on its face solely because of the excess but rather will be considered fully satisfied for purposes of the military retirement benefits due under it by payment to the former spouse of the maximum amount of disposable benefit available.[3] While the Act places limits calculated on the basis of net pay or disposable retired or retainer pay, the Act does not preclude parties

---

[12]Mackey v. Mackey, 95 Ohio St. 3d 396, 2002-Ohio-2429, 768 N.E.2d 644 (2002).

[13]Mackey v. Mackey, 95 Ohio St. 3d 396, 2002-Ohio-2429, 768 N.E.2d 644 (2002).

[14]In re Marriage of Heupel, 936 P.2d 561 (Colo. 1997).

[15]In re Marriage of Heupel, 936 P.2d 561, 569 (Colo. 1997).

[Section 29:40]

[1]10 U.S.C.A. § 1408(e)(2).

[2]10 U.S.C.A. § 1408(e)(4)(B).

[3]10 U.S.C.A. § 1408(e)(5).

to a divorce from using gross military retired pay to calculate an agreed upon sum for spousal support.[4]

It should be understood that even if the full amount of the court order cannot be satisfied out of the military retirement benefits, the payor or member of the armed services is not relieved of his obligation under the court order to make full payment under that order. Any remaining obligation of a member can be enforced through any other means available.[5] Therefore, even though a benefit to a subsequent former spouse may exceed the sixty-five percent limit imposed by federal law, a domestic relations court in Ohio can and should take into consideration the income available to the member of the armed services in relation to the needs of the spouse and make appropriate orders with regard to methods for providing for those needs. It is important to consider RC 3105.18 in this regard; the Tenth District Court of Appeals in *Alexander v. Alexander*[6] determined that the *McCarty* case did not preempt the trial court's right to consider benefits and property settlement as set forth in Ohio law.

A spouse or former spouse receiving benefits under 10 U.S.C.A. § 1408 is still entitled to receive medical and dental care, to use commissary and exchange stores, and to have other benefits provided to dependents of retired members.[7]

§ 29:41   Military benefits—Obtaining information

For active duty military personnel, information as to benefits estimates can be obtained by inquiring of the current duty station's commander. For reserve personnel, information can be obtained from military personnel centers, as follows:

Army Reserve:
HQ ARPC/PAC
US Army Reserve Personnel Center
9700 Pahe Blvd.
St. Louis, MO 63132-5200
1-800-325-8311
314-538-3567
fax 314-538-3567

Navy Reserve:
HQ NRPC/N211 or N212
Navy Reserve Personnel Center
4400 Dauphine St.

---

[4]Blissit v. Blissit, 122 Ohio App. 3d 727, 702 N.E.2d 945 (2d Dist. Greene County 1997); Jordan v. Jordan, 2000 WL 282305 (Ohio Ct. App. 2d Dist. Greene County 2000).

[5]10 U.S.C.A. § 1408(e)(6); Blissit v. Blissit, 122 Ohio App. 3d 727, 702 N.E.2d 945 (2d Dist. Greene County 1997).

[6]Alexander v. Alexander, 20 Ohio App. 3d 94, 484 N.E.2d 1068 (10th Dist. Franklin County 1985).

[7]10 U.S.C.A. § 1408(h)(9).

New Orleans, LA 70149
1-800-535-2699
504-678-1812
fax 504-678-5470

Air Force Reserve:
HQ ARPC/DPK
Air Force Reserve Personnel Center
6760 E. Irvington Place #2100
Denver, CO 80280-2100
1-800-525-0102 ext 403 points, ext 402 retired pay
303-676-7151 points, 303-676-6369 retired pay
fax 303-676-6793

§ 29:42   Military benefits—Procedure

A DFAS Form 2293 should accompany a court order requiring division of military retired pay. Copies of Form 2293 can be acquired from DFAS in Cleveland. Procedurally, notice and a certified copy of the court order directing division of retirement benefits should be mailed by certified mail to the following:

Army, Navy, Marines and Air Force:

Director
Defense Finance & Accounting Service
Garnishment Department
P O Box 998002
Attn.: CODE LF
Cleveland Ohio 44191-8002
(800) 321-1080 (inquiries)
(216) 522-5301 (legal department)
DfasLane@Cleveland.Dfas.Mil
homepage: http://www.dfas.mil

U.S. Coast Guard:

Commanding Officer (L)
Pay and Personnel Center
444 S.E. Quincy Street
Topeka KS 66683-3591
(785) 357-3600
homepage: http://www.cjnetworks.com/~usguard/index.html

While the military services will accept a decree that clearly specifies what is to be assigned, they will also accept a separate order.[1]

[Section 29:42]
[1]See §§ 29:43 to 29:45.

§ 29:43   Military qualifying order—Active service—Form⊚

IN THE COURT OF COMMON PLEAS
DOMESTIC RELATIONS DIVISION
_____COUNTY, OHIO

[Name], Plaintiff	)	Case No. [_____]
vs.	)	Judge
[Name], Defendant	)	**QUALIFYING COURT ORDER**

This cause came before the Court on the _____ day of _____, 200_____. The Court found as follows:

1. *[Name]* (Husband) and *[Name]* (Wife) were married on *[Date of Marriage]*;

2. The parties have separated and have obtained, in these proceedings, a Decree of Divorce/ Dissolution of Marriage on *[Date of Decree]*;

3. The Court has, pursuant to such decree, divided the marital estate and all other property, including their respective interests in the retirement plan as provided for herein; and

4. Husband and Wife wish to settle all issues with respect to their interest in such plan.

NOW, THEREFORE, in consideration of the foregoing premises and the mutual promises hereunder specified, Husband and Wife do agree, and the Court does order, as follows:

1. Acknowledgement: The parties acknowledge that *[Name Military Member]* is currently accruing a military retirement benefit based on his/her service in the United States *[Branch of Service]*. The parties further agree that his/her Former Spouse, *[Name Spouse]*, has an interest in *[Name Military Member's]* disposable military retirement pay in an amount set forth herein. Further, *[Name Military Member]* shall assist *[Name Spouse]* in submitting any applications necessary to secure his/her share of his/her disposable military retired pay as awarded herein.

2. Member Information: The "Member" as referred to herein is *[Name Military Member]*, Social Security Number *[SSN]*.

3. Former Spouse Information: The "Former Spouse" as referred to herein is *[Name Spouse]*, Social Security Number *[SSN]*.

4. Assignment of Benefits: The Member assigns to Former Spouse an interest in the Member's disposable military retired pay. The Former Spouse is entitled to a direct payment in the following specified amount and shall receive payments at the same times as the member.

5. Observance of Member's Rights under Soldier's and Sailor's Civil Relief Act of 1940: The Member's rights under the Soldier's and Sailor's Civil Relief Act of 1940 (50 USC § 521) were observed by the Court as evidence by *[his/her presence at and participation in the hearings giving rise to this Order/ the presence of his/her legal counsel at the hearings giving rise to this Order/ his/her signature on the Separation Agreement/Decree.]*

[Select one of the following, as appropriate]

[Alt #1] 6. Amount of Payments: This Order assigns to Former Spouse an amount equal to fifty percent (50%) of the marital portion of Member's disposable military retired pay under this plan as of his/her benefit commencement date. The marital portion shall be determined by multiplying the Member's disposable military retired pay by a fraction (less than or equal to 1.0), the numerator of which is the number of months of the Member's creditable service in the plan earned during the marriage, defined as _____ months, and the denominator of which is the total number of months of the Member's total creditable service in the plan as of his/her date of retirement.

[Alt #2] 6. Amount of Payments: This Order assigns to Former Spouse a portion of the Member's disposable military retired pay in the amount $_____ per month.

[Alt #3] 6. Amount of Payments: This Order assigns to Former Spouse an amount equal to _____ percent (_____ %) of the Member's disposable retired pay.

6.1. In addition, the Former Spouse shall receive a pro rata share of any postretirement cost of living adjustments made to the Member's benefits on or after the date of his/her retirement. Such pro rata share shall be calculated in the same manner as the Former Spouse's share of the Member's retired pay benefit is calculated pursuant to Section 6.

7. Survivor Benefit Plan (SBP) Protection to Former Spouse: The Member agrees to elect to make the Former Spouse, and such Former Spouse shall be deemed, as the irrevocable beneficiary of the survivor's Survivor Benefit Plan (SBP) Annuity through the Member's military retirement, and the Member shall execute such documents as may be required to make or extend the election of Former Spouse as such beneficiary.

[Select one of the following, as appropriate]

[ALT #1] Member agrees to pay any charge associated with naming Former Spouse as beneficiary of the SBP annuity.

[ALT#2] Former Spouse agrees to pay any charge associated with naming Former Spouse as beneficiary of the SBP annuity.

[ALT#3] The parties agree to pay any charge associated with naming Former Spouse as beneficiary of the SBP annuity equally.

8. Duration of Payments: The monthly payments under Section 6 shall be paid to Former Spouse as soon as administratively feasible following the commencement of the Member's retirement benefits and shall continue through the joint lives of Member and Former Spouse and, to the extent permitted under law, irrespective of the future marital status of either of them; they shall terminate only upon the death of wither Member or Former Spouse.

9. Jurisdiction: The jurisdictional requirements of 10 USC § 1048 have been complied with, and this order has not been amended, superceded or set aside by any subsequent order.

10. Duration of Marriage Acknowledgement (Compliance with 10/10 Rule): The Member and the Former Spouse acknowledge that they have been married for a period of more than ten years during which time the Member performed more than ten years of creditable military service. The parties were married from *[Date of Marriage to Date of Decree.]*

11. Overpayments: The Former Spouse agrees that any future overpayments made to him/her are recoverable and subject to involuntary collection from Former Spouse or his/her estate.

12. Notification: Former Spouse agrees to notify DFAS about any changes in this Qualifying Court Order or the order affecting these provisions of it or in the eligibility of any recipient receiving benefits pursuant to it.

13. Qualification: The Member and the Former Spouse intend that this order qualify under the Uniformed Services Former Spouses' Protection Act, 10 U.S.C.A. Section 1408 et seq. All provisions shall be construed and modified to the extent necessary in order to qualify as a Qualifying Court Order.

14. Continued Cooperation of Member: The Member agrees to cooperate with the Former Spouse to prepare an application for direct payment to the Former Spouse from the Member's retired or retainer pay pursuant to 10 U.S.C.A. Section 1408. The Member agrees to execute all documents required by the United States *[Name of Service Branch]* may require to certify that the disposable military retired pay can be provided to the Former Spouse.

15. Merger of Benefits and Indemnification: The Member agrees not to merge the Member's disposable military retired pay with any other pension and not to pursue any course of action that would defeat the Former Spouse's right to receive a portion of the disposable military retired pay of the Member. The Member agrees not to take any action by merger of the military pension so as to cause a limitation in the amount of the total retired pay in which the Member has a vested interest and therefore the member will not cause a limitation of the Former Spouse's monthly payments as set forth above. The Member agrees to indemnify Former Spouse for any breach of this paragraph as follows: If Member becomes employed or otherwise has his/her military pension merged, which employment or other condition causes a merger of the Member's disposable military retired pay, the Member will pay to Former Spouse directly the monthly payment amount provided in Section 6 under the same terms and conditions as if those payments were made pursuant to the terms of this order.

16. Allotment: If the amount paid by the military pay center to Former Spouse is less than the amount specified, Member shall initiate an allotment to Former Spouse in the amount of any such difference to be paid from any federal entitlements due to Member, with said allotment to be initiated by Member immediately upon receipt of notice of such difference.

17. Direct Payment by Member: If in any month, direct payment is not made to Former Spouse by the appropriate military pay center, and no federal entitlement exists against which an allotment as set forth in Section 16 may be initiated, or for whatever reason full payment by allotment is not made in that month, or if the amount paid through the allotment is insufficient to pay the difference specified, Member shall pay the amounts called for herein directly to Former Spouse by the fifth day of each month in which the military pay center and/or allotment fails to

satisfy the amounts called for under Section 6, beginning upon Member's eligibility for military retired pay.

18. Actions by Member: If Member takes any action that prevents, decreases or limits the collection by Former Spouse of the sums to be aid hereunder, he/she shall make payments to Former Spouse directly in an amount sufficient to neutralize, as to Former Spouse, the effects of the actions taken by Member.

19. Submission of Information: The parties acknowledge that the following items must be sent by Former Spouse to DFAS (Cleveland Center), located at PO Box 998002, Cleveland OH 44199-8002. Member agrees to provide any of this information to the Former Spouse at the Former Spouse's request and to make all necessary efforts to obtain any of this information that the Former Spouse is unable to obtain.

a. A copy of this Qualifying Court Order that divides retired pay and any decree that approves this order certified within ninety (90) days immediately preceding its service on the applicable military pay center for the United States *[Name of Service]*.

b. A statement by the Former Spouse hat verified that the divorce decree has not been modified, superceded or set aside.

c. The parties' marriage certificate.

d. The Member's name, Social Security number, date of birth and name of the military service.

e. The Former Spouse's name, address and Social Security Number.

20. Continued Jurisdiction: The Court shall retain jurisdiction to enter such further orders as necessary to enforce the award to Former Spouse of the military retirement benefits awarded herein, including the recharacterization thereof as a division of Civil Service or other retirement benefits, or to make an award of spousal support payments (in the sum of benefits payable plus future cost of living adjustments) in the event that Member fails to comply with the provisions of this order requiring such payments to Former Spouse by any means, including but not limited to the application for a disability award or filing for protection under the Bankruptcy Code, or if military or governmental regulations or other restrictions interfere with payments to Former Spouse as set forth herein, or if Member fails to comply with the provisions contained herein requiring said payments to Former Spouse.

21. Discovery: Member hereby waives any privacy or other rights as may be required of Former Spouse to obtain information relating to Member's date and time of retirement, last unit assignment, final rank, grade and pay, present or past military retired pay or other such information as may be required to enforce this order, or required to revise this order so as to make it enforceable.

22. Notice of Pending Retirement: Member shall notify the Former Spouse, in writing, within thirty (30) days prior to the Member's actual date of retirement. Such notice shall be sent via regular first-class mail. For this purpose, Former Spouse shall notify Member of all changes of mailing address.

23. Definition of Military Retirement: For the purposes of interpreting

this court's intention in making the division as set forth in this order, "military retirement" includes retired pay paid or to which Member would be entitled for longevity of active duty and/or reserve component military service and all payments pad or payable under the provisions of Chapter 38 or Chapter 61 of Title 10 of the United States Code, before any statutory, regulatory or elective deductions are applied. It also includes all amounts of retired pay Member actually or constructively waives or forfeits in any manner and for any reason or purpose, including but not limited to any waiver made in order to qualify for Veterans Administration benefits and any waiver arising from Member electing not to retire despite being qualified to retire. It also includes any sum taken by Member in addition to or in lieu of retirement benefits, including but not limited to exit bonuses, voluntary separation incentive pay, special separation benefit, or any other form of compensation attributable to separation from military service instead of or in addition to payment of the military retirement benefits normally payable to a retired member.

IT IS SO ORDERED.

_____
Judge

Approved:

_____   _____
[Name] - Member   *[Name]* - Former Spouse

_____   _____
Name of Attorney   Name of Attorney
Attorney for *[Member Name]*   Attorney for *[Former Spouse Name]*

Ohio Supreme Court ID   Ohio Supreme Court ID
No._____   No._____
Address   Address
City, State, Zip   City, State, Zip
Telephone   Telephone

§ 29:44 Military qualifying order—Reserve service—Form⊚

IN THE COURT OF COMMON PLEAS

DOMESTIC RELATIONS DIVISION

_____COUNTY, OHIO

[Name], Plaintiff	)	Case No. [_____]
vs.	)	Judge
[Name], Defendant	)	**QUALIFYING COURT ORDER**

This cause came before the Court on the _____ day of _____, 200_____. The Court found as follows:

1. *[Name]* (Husband) and *[Name]* (Wife) were married on *[Date of Marriage]*;

2. The parties have separated and have obtained, in these proceedings, a Decree of Divorce/ Dissolution of Marriage on *[Date of Decree]*;

3. The Court has, pursuant to such decree, divided the marital estate and all other property, including their respective interests in the retirement plan as provided for herein; and

4. Husband and Wife wish to settle all issues with respect to their interest in such plan.

NOW, THEREFORE, in consideration of the foregoing premises and the mutual promises hereunder specified, Husband and Wife do agree, and the Court does order, as follows:

1. Acknowledgement: The parties acknowledge that *[Name Military Member]* is currently accruing a military retirement benefit based on his/her service in the United States *[Branch of Service]*. The parties further agree that his/her Former Spouse, *[Name Spouse]*, has an interest in *[Name Military Member's]* disposable military retirement pay in an amount set forth herein. Further, *[Name Military Member]* shall assist *[Name Spouse]* in submitting any applications necessary to secure his/her share of his/her disposable military retired pay as awarded herein.

2. Member Information: The "Member" as referred to herein is *[Name Military Member]*, Social Security Number *[SSN]*.

3. Former Spouse Information: The "Former Spouse" as referred to herein is *[Name Spouse]*, Social Security Number *[SSN]*.

4. Assignment of Benefits: The Member assigns to Former Spouse an interest in the Member's disposable military retired pay. The Former Spouse is entitled to a direct payment in the following specified amount and shall receive payments at the same times as the member.

5. Observance of Member's Rights under Soldier's and Sailor's Civil Relief Act of 1940: The Member's rights under the Soldier's and Sailor's Civil Relief Act of 1940 (50 USC § 521) were observed by the Court as evidence by *[his/her presence at and participation in the hearings giving rise to this Order/ the presence of his/her legal counsel at the hearings giving rise to this Order/ his/her signature on the Separation Agreement/Decree]*.

[Select one of the following, as appropriate]

[ALT#1] 6. Amount of Payments: This Order assigns to Former Spouse an amount equal to fifty percent (50%) of the marital portion of Member's disposable military retired pay under this plan as of his/her benefit commencement date. The marital portion shall be determined by multiplying the Member's disposable military retired pay by a fraction (less than or equal to 1.0), the numerator of which is the number of months of the Member's creditable service in the plan earned during the marriage, defined as _____ months, and the denominator of which is the total number of months of the Member's total creditable service in the plan as of his/her date of retirement.

[ALT#2] 6. Amount of Payments: This Order assigns to Former Spouse a portion of the Member's disposable military retired pay in the amount $_____ per month.

[ALT#3] 6. Amount of Payments: This Order assigns to Former Spouse an amount equal to _____ percent (_____ %) of the Member's disposable retired pay.

6.1. In addition, the Former Spouse shall receive a pro rata share of any postretirement cost of living adjustments made to the Member's benefits on or after the date of his/her retirement. Such pro rata share shall be calculated in the same manner as the Former Spouse's share of the Member's retired pay benefit is calculated pursuant to Section 6.

7. Survivor Benefit Plan (SBP) Protection to Former Spouse: The Member agrees to elect to make the Former Spouse, and such Former Spouse shall be deemed, as the irrevocable beneficiary of the survivor's Survivor Benefit Plan (SBP) Annuity through the Member's military retirement, and the Member shall execute such documents as may be required to make or extend the election of Former Spouse as such beneficiary.

[Select one of the following, as appropriate]

[ALT #1] Member agrees to pay any charge associated with naming Former Spouse as beneficiary of the SBP annuity.

[ALT#2] Former Spouse agrees to pay any charge associated with naming Former Spouse as beneficiary of the SBP annuity.

[ALT#3] The parties agree to pay any charge associated with naming Former Spouse as beneficiary of the SBP annuity equally.

8. Duration of Payments: The monthly payments under Section 6 shall be paid to Former Spouse as soon as administratively feasible following the commencement of the Member's retirement benefits and shall continue through the joint lives of Member and Former Spouse and, to the extent permitted under law, irrespective of the future marital status of either of them; they shall terminate only upon the death of wither Member or Former Spouse.

9. Jurisdiction: The jurisdictional requirements of 10 USC § 1048 have been complied with, and this order has not been amended, superceded or set aside by any subsequent order.

10. Duration of Marriage Acknowledgement (Compliance with 10/10 Rule): The Member and the Former Spouse acknowledge that they have been married for a period of more than ten years during which time the Member performed more than ten years of creditable military service. The parties were married from *[Date of Marriage to Date of Decree.]*

11. Overpayments: The Former Spouse agrees that any future overpayments made to him/her are recoverable and subject to involuntary collection from Former Spouse or his/her estate.

12. Notification: Former Spouse agrees to notify DFAS about any changes in this Qualifying Court Order or the order affecting these provisions of it or in the eligibility of any recipient receiving benefits pursuant to it.

13. Qualification: The member and the Former Spouse intend that this order qualify under the Uniformed Services Former Spouses' Protection Act, 10 USC Section 1408 et seq. All provisions shall be construed and modified to the extent necessary in order to qualify as a Qualifying Court Order.

14. Continued Cooperation of Member: The Member agrees to cooperate with the Former Spouse to prepare an application for direct payment to the Former Spouse from the Member's retired or retainer pay pursuant to 10 USC Section 1408. The Member agrees to execute all documents required by the United States *[Name of Service Branch]* may require to certify that the disposable military retired pay can be provided to the Former Spouse.

15. Merger of Benefits and Indemnification: The Member agrees not to merge the Member's disposable military retired pay with any other pension and not to pursue any course of action that would defeat the Former Spouse's right to receive a portion of the disposable military retired pay of the Member. The Member agrees not to take any action by merger of the military pension so as to cause a limitation in the amount of the total retired pay in which the Member has a vested interest and therefore the member will not cause a limitation of the Former Spouse's monthly payments as set forth above. The Member agrees to indemnify Former Spouse for any breach of this paragraph as follows: If Member becomes employed or otherwise has his/her military pension merged, which employment or other condition causes a merger of the Member's disposable military retired pay, the Member will pay to Former Spouse directly the monthly payment amount provided in Section 6 under the same terms and conditions as if those payments were made pursuant to the terms of this order.

16. Allotment: If the amount paid by the military pay center to Former Spouse is less than the amount specified, Member shall initiate an allotment to Former Spouse in the amount of any such difference to be paid from any federal entitlements due to Member, with said allotment to be initiated by Member immediately upon receipt of notice of such difference.

17. Direct Payment by Member: If in any month, direct payment is not made to Former Spouse by the appropriate military pay center, and no federal entitlement exists against which an allotment as set forth in Section 16 may be initiated, or for whatever reason full payment by allotment is not made in that month, or if the amount paid through the allotment is insufficient to pay the difference specified, Member shall pay the amounts called for herein directly to Former Spouse by the fifth day of each month in which the military pay center and/or allotment fails to satisfy the amounts called for under Section 6, beginning upon Member's eligibility for military retired pay.

18. Actions by Member: If Member takes any action that prevents, decreases or limits the collection by Former Spouse of the sums to be aid hereunder, he/she shall make payments to Former Spouse directly in an amount sufficient to neutralize, as to Former Spouse, the effects of the actions taken by Member.

19. Submission of Information: The parties acknowledge that the following items must be sent by Former Spouse to DFAS (Cleveland Center), located at PO Box 998002, Cleveland OH 44199-8002. Member agrees to provide any of this information to the Former Spouse at the Former Spouse's request and to make all necessary efforts to obtain any of this information that the Former Spouse is unable to obtain.

a. A copy of this Qualifying Court Order that divides retired pay and any decree that approves this order certified within ninety (90) days immediately preceding its service on the applicable military pay center for the United States *[Name of Service]*.

b. A statement by the Former Spouse hat verified that the divorce decree has not been modified, superceded or set aside.

c. The parties' marriage certificate.

d. The Member's name, Social Security number, date of birth and name of the military service.

e. The Former Spouse's name, address and Social Security Number.

20. Continued Jurisdiction: The Court shall retain jurisdiction to enter such further orders as necessary to enforce the award to Former Spouse of the military retirement benefits awarded herein, including the recharacterization thereof as a division of Civil Service or other retirement benefits, or to make an award of spousal support payments (in the sum of benefits payable plus future cost of living adjustments) in the event that Member fails to comply with the provisions of this order requiring such payments to Former Spouse by any means, including but not limited to the application for a disability award or filing for protection under the Bankruptcy Code, or if military or governmental regulations or other restrictions interfere with payments to Former Spouse as set forth herein, or if Member fails to comply with the provisions contained herein requiring said payments to Former Spouse.

21. Discovery: Member hereby waives any privacy or other rights as may be required of Former Spouse to obtain information relating to Member's date and time of retirement, last unit assignment, final rank, grade and pay, present or past military retired pay or other such information as may be required to enforce this order, or required to revise this order so as to make it enforceable.

22. Notice of Pending Retirement: Member shall notify the Former Spouse, in writing, within thirty (30) days prior to the Member's actual date of retirement. Such notice shall be sent via regular first-class mail. For this purpose, Former Spouse shall notify Member of all changes of mailing address.

23. Definition of Military Retirement: For the purposes of interpreting this court's intention in making the division as set forth in this order, "military retirement" includes retired pay paid or to which Member would be entitled for longevity of active duty and/or reserve component military service and all payments pad or payable under the provisions of Chapter 38 or Chapter 61 of Title 10 of the United States Code, before any statutory, regulatory or elective deductions are applied. It also includes all amounts of retired pay Member actually or constructively waives or forfeits in any manner and for any reason or purpose, including but not limited to any waiver made in order to qualify for Veterans Administration benefits and any waiver arising from Member electing not to retire despite being qualified to retire, It also includes any sum taken by Member in addition to or in lieu of retirement benefits, including but not limited to exit bonuses, voluntary separation incentive pay, special separation benefit, or any other form of compensation attribut-

able to separation from military service instead of or in addition to payment of the military retirement benefits normally payable to a retired member.

IT IS SO ORDERED.

_____

Judge

Approved:

_____   _____

[Name] - Employee   *[Name]* - Former Spouse

Name of Attorney   Name of Attorney
Attorney for *[Employee Name]*   Attorney for *[Former Spouse Name]*

Ohio Supreme Court ID   Ohio Supreme Court ID
No._____   No._____
Address   Address
City, State, Zip   City, State, Zip
Telephone   Telephone

§ 29:45 Military qualifying order—Retired military member— Form⊚

IN THE COURT OF COMMON PLEAS

DOMESTIC RELATIONS DIVISION

_____COUNTY, OHIO

[Name], Plaintiff	) Case No. [_____]
vs.	) Judge
[Name], Defendant	) **QUALIFYING COURT ORDER**

This cause came before the Court on the _____ day of _____, 200_____. The Court found as follows:

1. *[Name]* (Husband) and *[Name]* (Wife) were married on *[Date of Marriage]*;

2. The parties have separated and have obtained, in these proceedings, a Decree of Divorce/ Dissolution of Marriage on *[Date of Decree]*;

3. The Court has, pursuant to such decree, divided the marital estate and all other property, including their respective interests in the retirement plan as provided for herein; and

4. Husband and Wife wish to settle all issues with respect to their interest in such plan.

NOW, THEREFORE, in consideration of the foregoing premises and the mutual promises hereunder specified, Husband and Wife do agree, and the Court does order, as follows:

1. Acknowledgement: The parties acknowledge that *[Name Military Member]* is currently receiving a military retirement benefit based on

his/her service in the United States *[Branch of Service]*. The parties further agree that his/her Former Spouse, *[Name Spouse]*, has an interest in *[Name Military Member's]* disposable military retirement pay in an amount set forth herein. Further, *[Name Military Member]* shall assist *[Name Spouse]* in submitting any applications necessary to secure his/her share of his/her disposable military retired pay as awarded herein.

2. Member Information: The "Member" as referred to herein is *[Name Military Member]*, Social Security Number *[SSN]*.

3. Former Spouse Information: The "Former Spouse" as referred to herein is *[Name Spouse]*, Social Security Number *[SSN]*.

4. Assignment of Benefits: The Member assigns to Former Spouse an interest in the Member's disposable military retired pay. The Former Spouse is entitled to a direct payment in the following specified amount and shall receive payments at the same times as the member.

[Select one of the following, as appropriate]

[Alt #1] 5. Amount of Payments: This Order assigns to Former Spouse an amount equal to fifty percent (50%) of the marital portion of Member's disposable military retired pay under this plan as of his/her benefit commencement date. The marital portion shall be determined by multiplying the Member's disposable military retired pay by a fraction (less than or equal to 1.0), the numerator of which is the number of months of the Member's creditable service in the plan earned during the marriage, defined as _____ months, and the denominator of which is the total number of months of the Member's total creditable service in the plan as of his/her date of retirement.

[Alt #2] 5. Amount of Payments: This Order assigns to Former Spouse a portion of the Member's disposable military retired pay in the amount $_____ per month.

[Alt #3] 5. Amount of Payments: This Order assigns to Former Spouse an amount equal to _____ percent (_____ %) of the Member's disposable retired pay.

5.1. In addition, the Former Spouse shall receive a pro rata share of any postretirement cost of living adjustments made to the Member's benefits on or after the date of his/her retirement. Such pro rata share shall be calculated in the same manner as the Former Spouse's share of the Member's retired pay benefit is calculated pursuant to Section 5.

For the purposes of interpreting this court's intention in making the division as set forth in this order, "military retirement" includes retired pay paid or to which Member would be entitled for longevity of active duty and/or reserve component military service and all payments pad or payable under the provisions of Chapter 38 or Chapter 61 of Title 10 of the United States Code, before any statutory, regulatory or elective deductions are applied. It also includes all amounts of retired pay member actually or constructively waives or forfeits in any manner and for any reason or purpose, including but not limited to any waiver made in order to qualify for Veterans Administration benefits and any waiver arising from Member electing not to retire despite being qualified to retire. It also includes any sum taken by Member in addition to or in lieu of retirement benefits, including but not limited to exit bonuses, voluntary separation incentive pay, special separation benefit, or any other form of compensation attributable to separation from military service instead of or in addition to payment of the military retirement benefits normally payable to a retired member.

6. Duration of Payments: The monthly payments under Section 5 shall be paid to Former Spouse as soon as administratively feasible following the commencement of the Member's retirement benefits and shall continue through the joint lives of Member and Former Spouse and, to the extent permitted under law, irrespective of the future marital status of either of them; they shall terminate only upon the death of wither Member or Former Spouse.

7. Overpayments: The Former Spouse agrees that any future overpayments made to him/her are recoverable and subject to involuntary collection from Former Spouse or his/her estate.

8. Notification: Former Spouse agrees to notify DFAS about any changes in this Qualifying Court Order or the order affecting these provisions of it or in the eligibility of any recipient receiving benefits pursuant to it.

9. Qualification: The member and the Former Spouse intend that this order qualify under the Uniformed Services Former Spouses' Protection Act, 10 U.S.C.A. § 1408 et seq. All provisions shall be construed and modified to the extent necessary in order to qualify as a Qualifying Court Order.

10. Continued Cooperation of Member: The Member agrees to cooperate with the Former Spouse to prepare an application for direct payment to the Former Spouse from the Member's retired or retainer pay pursuant to 10 U.S.C.A. Section 1408. The Member agrees to execute all documents required by the United States *[Name of Service Branch]* may require to certify that the disposable military retired pay can be provided to the Former Spouse.

11. Jurisdiction: The parties agree that the Court of Common Pleas, Domestic Relations Division _____ County, Ohio, is a court of competent jurisdiction in this action pursuant to 10 USC Section 1408(a)(1). This order bears the certification of the Clerk of Courts for the Common Pleas Court, _____ County, Ohio, and has not been amended, superceded or set aside by any subsequent order.

12. Merger of Benefits and Indemnification: The Member agrees not to merge the Member's disposable military retired pay with any other pension and not to pursue any course of action that would defeat the Former Spouse's right to receive a portion of the disposable military retired pay of the Member. The Member agrees not to take any action by merger of the military pension so as to cause a limitation in the amount of the total retired pay in which the Member has a vested interest and therefore the member will not cause a limitation of the Former Spouse's monthly payments as set forth above. The Member agrees to indemnify Former Spouse for any breach of this paragraph as follows: If Member becomes employed or otherwise has his/her military pension merged, which employment or other condition causes a merger of the

Member's disposable military retired pay, the Member will pay to Former Spouse directly the monthly payment amount provided in Section 5 under the same terms and conditions as if those payments were made pursuant to the terms of this order.

13. Allotment: If the amount paid by the military pay center to Former Spouse is less than the amount specified, Member shall initiate an allotment to Former Spouse in the amount of any such difference to be paid from any federal entitlements due to Member, with said allotment to be initiated by Member immediately upon receipt of notice of such difference.

14. Direct Payment by Member: If in any month, direct payment is not made to Former Spouse by the appropriate military pay center, and no federal entitlement exists against which an allotment as set forth in Section 16 may be initiated, or for whatever reason full payment by allotment is not made in that month, or if the amount paid through the allotment is insufficient to pay the difference specified, Member shall pay the amounts called for herein directly to Former Spouse by the fifth day of each month in which the military pay center and/or allotment fails to satisfy the amounts called for under Section 6, beginning upon Member's eligibility for military retired pay.

15. Actions by Member: If Member takes any action that prevents, decreases or limits the collection by Former Spouse of the sums to be aid hereunder, he/she shall make payments to Former Spouse directly in an amount sufficient to neutralize, as to Former Spouse, the effects of the actions taken by Member.

16. Submission of Information: The parties acknowledge that the following items must be sent by Former Spouse to the appropriate military pay center. Member agrees to provide any of this information to the Former Spouse at the Former Spouse's request and to make all necessary efforts to obtain any of this information that the Former Spouse is unable to obtain.

a. A copy of this Qualifying Court Order that divides retired pay and any decree that approves this order certified within ninety (90) days immediately preceding its service on the applicable military pay center for the United States [Name of Service].

b. A statement by the Former Spouse hat verified that the divorce decree has not been modified, superceded or set aside.

c. The parties' marriage certificate.

d. The Member's name, Social Security number, date of birth and name of the military service.

e. The Former Spouse's name, address and Social Security Number.

17. Survivor Benefit Plan (SBP) Protection to Former Spouse: The Member agrees to elect to make the Former Spouse, and such Former Spouse shall be deemed, as the irrevocable beneficiary of the survivor's Survivor Benefit Plan (SBP) Annuity through the Member's military retirement, and the Member shall execute such documents as may be required to make or extend the election of Former Spouse as such beneficiary. Member shall elect the Former Spouse Only option and

shall select as the base amount the full amount of his/her monthly retired pay.

[Select one of the following, as appropriate]

[ALT #1] Member agrees to pay any charge associated with naming Former Spouse as beneficiary of the SBP annuity.

[ALT#2] Former Spouse agrees to pay any charge associated with naming Former Spouse as beneficiary of the SBP annuity.

[ALT#3] The parties agree to pay any charge associated with naming Former Spouse as beneficiary of the SBP annuity equally.

18. Continued Jurisdiction: The Court shall retain jurisdiction to enter such further orders as necessary to enforce the award to Former Spouse f the military retirement benefits awarded herein, including the recharacterization thereof as a division of Civil Service or other retirement benefits, or to make an award of spousal support payments (in the sum of benefits payable plus future cost of living adjustments) in the event that Member fails to comply with the provisions of this order requiring such payments to Former Spouse by any means, including but not limited to the application for a disability award or filing for protection under the Bankruptcy Code, or if military or governmental regulations or other restrictions interfere with payments to Former Spouse as set forth herein, or if Member fails to comply with the provisions contained herein requiring said payments to Former Spouse.

19. Discovery: Member hereby waives any privacy or other rights as may be required of Former Spouse to obtain information relating to Member's date and time of retirement, last unit assignment, final rank, grade and pay, present or past, military retired pay or other such information as may be required to enforce this order, or required to revise this order so as to make it enforceable.

IT IS SO ORDERED.

	Judge
Approved:	
[Name] - Member	*[Name]* - Former Spouse
Name of Attorney	Name of Attorney
Attorney for *[Member Name]*	Attorney for *[Former Spouse Name]*
Ohio Supreme Court ID No._____	Ohio Supreme Court ID No._____
Address	Address
City, State, Zip	City, State, Zip
Telephone	Telephone

§ 29:46   State benefits—In general

Each of the Ohio retirement systems has its own statutes, systems, and procedures. These include the Public Employees Retirement System (PERS),[1] the State Teachers Retirement System (STRS),[2] the School Employees Retirement System (SERS),[3] the Police and Fireman's Disability and Pension Fund (PFDPF),[4] and the Highway Patrol Retirement System (HPRS).[5] The current contribution by the employee rates for HPRS is 10%, PERS is 8.5%, STRS is 9.3%, and SERS is 9%.

An employee who has participated in each of the state's systems may choose to combine the benefits and service credits of each of his terms of employment for computation of disability retirement, total years of service, and his single benefit.[6] PERS members may be granted up to 10 years of free service credit if, after one year of qualifying PERS service, they left public employment, entered active duty in the armed forces within three months of separation from employment, and within three years of leaving the armed forces with an honorable discharge return to public employment for at least one year to a position that is covered by PERS, STRS, or SERS. PFDPF and HPRS service can also be used when determining whether the one-year return to service has occurred.[7]

STRS members who took a leave of absence or resigned due to pregnancy prior to July 1, 1982 may purchase up to two years' of service credit for the prior leave of absence or resignation.[8]

All of the Ohio retirement systems now have their own web pages. The HPRS page is located at http://www.state.oh.us/ohiostatepatrol, the STRS page is located at http://www.strsoh.org, the SERS is located at http://www.ohsers.org, the PERS is located at http://www.opers.org, and the PFDPF is located at http://www.pfdpf.org.

§ 29:47   State benefits—Benefits as marital asset

An interest in a state retirement plan accumulated during the marriage must be considered in dividing marital assets, even when being paid out to the beneficiary.[1] Because of anti-alienation provisions of the statutes creating Ohio governmental pension and retirement plans, and the fact that they are not subject to the Employee Retirement Income Security Act (ERISA),[2] court orders cannot divide or assign the funds, except for payment of child or spousal support after payments are being

---

[Section 29:46]

   [1]RC Ch. 145.

   [2]RC Ch. 3307.

   [3]RC Ch. 3309.

   [4]RC Ch. 742.

   [5]RC Ch. 5505.

   [6]RC 145.295 (PERS); RC 3307.32 (STRS); RC 3309.351 (SERS); RC 742.379 (PFDPF); RC 5505.201 (HPRS).

   [7]RC 145.30(B).

   [8]RC 3307.514.

[Section 29:47]

   [1]Erb v. Erb, 75 Ohio St. 3d 18, 661 N.E.2d 175 (1996).

   [2]29 U.S.C.A. § 1002(32), 29 U.S.C.A. § 1003(b)(1).

received.[3] Despite the prohibition against dividing a spouse's interest in such a fund, the value of the fund still must be considered when dividing property interests, although there is not full agreement in Ohio courts as to the manner in which the fund is to be valued.[4]

In *Province v. Province*,[5] even though all of the pension benefits accumulated by the husband were awarded to him in the decree, and no interest was awarded to the wife, the trial court was authorized to enforce its support judgments by using RC 3113.21 to require withholding from husband's police retirement benefits.

Whether or not "vesting" of a state pension had occurred prior to the actual receipt of benefits was discussed at length in the case of *Erb v. Erb*[6] both at the appellate level and in the Ohio Supreme Court's decision. The Ohio Supreme Court discussed whether the retirement benefit had matured (which it defined as whether the benefits were currently due and payable to the employee), finding that actual retirement was a condition precedent to the receipt of retirement benefits, and concluding that the husband's benefits, although "mature" because he had attained the required number of years of service, were not yet payable because he was still working.

§ 29:48 State benefits—Social Security offset

When a person is employed by a state, he or she does not pay into the social security system. Some courts will allow the value of a hypothetical social security benefit of the governmental worker to offset the governmental pension value.[1] Other courts will allow a valuation of the social security benefit of the non-governmental employee spouse to be calculated and compared to the total calculated value of the governmental employee's pension plan.[2]

---

[3]RC 3113.21(P)(9), as amended by 1997 H.B. 352, includes state retirement programs within the definition of "payor" for purposes of RC 3113.21 to RC 3113.217.

[4]Klamfoth v. Schwarz, 1994 WL 369423 (Ohio Ct. App. 5th Dist. Fairfield County 1994); Reitano v. Reitano, 1994 WL 369412 (Ohio Ct. App. 5th Dist. Fairfield County 1994); Zuschak v. Zuschak, 1998 WL 254932 (Ohio Ct. App. 9th Dist. Summit County 1998).

[5]Province v. Province, 1989 WL 24237 (Ohio Ct. App. 9th Dist. Summit County 1989).

[6]Erb v. Erb, 1994 WL 245676, at *6 (Ohio Ct. App. 8th Dist. Cuyahoga County 1994), appeal allowed, 71 Ohio St. 3d 1406, 641 N.E.2d 203 (1994) and judgment rev'd, 75 Ohio St. 3d 18, 661 N.E.2d 175 (1996).

[Section 29:48]

[1]Smith v. Smith, 91 Ohio App. 3d 248, 632 N.E.2d 555 (10th Dist. Franklin County 1993).

[2]Coats v. Coats, 63 Ohio Misc. 2d 299, 626 N.E.2d 707 (C.P. 1993).

§ 29:49 State benefits—Methods of division

In *Sprankle v. Sprankle*,[1] the court noted four methods by which state retirement benefits can be divided: (1) order a withdrawal from the fund, (2) offset the present value of the non-employee's share of the pension with other property, (3) offset the present value by ordering installment payments, or (4) order that a percentage of the pension be paid to the non-employee once the pension matures.

Option number four will not work in a state pension as a division of assets because QDROs are not recognized by the state plans, because they are not subject to ERISA.[2] Option number one will often reduce the present value to much less in "real" dollars to be divided, as the withdrawing member can only receive his or her own contributions, and not those of the employer, prior to reaching age and service years thresholds. The most common method courts use to divide these state retirement interests is to order the employee spouse to pay to the non-employee spouse a monthly amount once benefits are received, and to retain jurisdiction over the marital portion of the retirement fund to assure there is no dissipation of assets prior to such time.

The Ohio Supreme Court stated in *Hoyt v. Hoyt*[3] that the "trial court should attempt to preserve the pension or retirement asset in order that each party can procure the most benefit, and should attempt to disentangle the parties' economic partnership so as to create a conclusion and finality to their marriage." The Fourth District Court of Appeals quoted that holding in the case of *Evans v. Cole*[4] for the proposition that it was error for the trial court to retain jurisdiction over a PERS retirement benefit when the parties were "so far removed from a retirement date" and held that the trial court should have determined the present values and to make an award of the wife's share rather than waiting until the husband retires.

The Ninth District Court of Appeals stated in *Bakota v. Bakota*[5] that:

[G]overnment retirement systems, such as the STRS are not subject to the Employee Retirement Income Security Act of 1974 ("ERISA"), codified primarily at Sections 1101 et seq., Title 29, U.S. Code, and R.C. 3307.01– 3307.12. The terms and conditions of STRS do not recognize a Qualified Domestic Relations Order ("QDRO") to divide the retirement fund. See Sections 1002 (32) and 1003(b)(1), Title 29, U.S. Code, Sprankle v. Sprankle, 87 Ohio App. 3d 129, 133, 621 N.E.2d 1310, 86, 86 Ed. Law Rep. 387 (9th Dist. Medina County 1993). As such, a trial court's options in dividing unvested or unmatured public pension benefits are limited.

The appellate court affirmed a trial court's order to pay out 41% to the

---

[Section 29:49]

[1]Sprankle v. Sprankle, 87 Ohio App. 3d 129, 133, 621 N.E.2d 1310, 86, 86 Ed. Law Rep. 387 (9th Dist. Medina County 1993).

[2]29 U.S.C.A. § 1002(32), 29 U.S.C.A. § 1003(b)(1).

[3]Hoyt v. Hoyt, 53 Ohio St. 3d 177, 559 N.E.2d 1292 (1990) (syl., para. 2).

[4]Cole v. Cole, 2000 WL 33256638 (Ohio Ct. App. 4th Dist. Jackson County 2000).

[5]Bakota v. Bakota, 2001 WL 542330, at *1 (Ohio Ct. App. 9th Dist. Summit County 2001).

non-member spouse after commencement of benefits, secured by life insurance and reserving jurisdiction.

§ 29:50   State benefits—Methods of division—QDRO

◆ **Note:** See also § 29:55, State benefits—Methods of division—Legislative changes—DOPO.

A number of attempts have been made by trial courts to impose QDROs on state pension plans, none of which have been met with success. The Seventh District Court of Appeals overturned a QDRO placed on the Police and Firemen's Disability and Pension Fund in *Ciavarella v. Ciavarella*,[1] as did the Eighth District Court of Appeals in *Erb v. Erb (Erb I)*[2] and in *Erb v. Erb (Erb III)*.[3]

The Second District Court of Appeals in *Davis v. Davis*[4] also attempted to place a QDRO on a state retirement system, as did the Fifth District Court of Appeals in *Volz v. Volz*.[5] The trial court in *Barnes v. Barnes*[6] attempted to impose a QDRO on the State Employees Retirement System, and was reversed on appeal. The *Barnes* appeals court appreciated the trial court's attempt and sensed its frustration, but held that "for better or worse, public pensions in Ohio remain exempt from QDROs."[7]

The most recent decision in *Erb v. Erb*[8] expressly abrogated the *Davis*, *Volz*, *Ciavarella*, and *Ricketts* cases.

The Ohio Supreme Court heard the appeal from *Erb v. Erb*[9] and decided the case on May 30, 2001. In the five years since the Ohio Supreme Court last heard the *Erb* case, husband retired, and husband

---

[Section 29:50]

[1]Ciavarella v. Ciavarella, 1999 WL 979238 (Ohio Ct. App. 7th Dist. Columbiana County 1999), dismissed, appeal not allowed, 88 Ohio St. 3d 1424, 723 N.E.2d 1112 (2000) and abrogated by Erb v. Erb, 2001 -Ohio- 104, 91 Ohio St. 3d 503, 747 N.E.2d 230 (2001).

[2]Erb v. Erb, 1991 WL 271412 (Ohio Ct. App. 8th Dist. Cuyahoga County 1991) (case remanded due to no finding of the value of the PFDPF pension); Erb v. Erb, 1994 WL 245676 (Ohio Ct. App. 8th Dist. Cuyahoga County 1994), appeal allowed, 71 Ohio St. 3d 1406, 641 N.E.2d 203 (1994) and judgment rev'd, 75 Ohio St. 3d 18, 661 N.E.2d 175 (1996) (case affirmed a QDRO placed against the PFDPF pension).

[3]Erb v. Erb, 2000 WL 426544 (Ohio Ct. App. 8th Dist. Cuyahoga County 2000), appeal allowed, 90 Ohio St. 3d 1417, 735 N.E.2d 456 (2000) and rev'd, 2001 -Ohio- 104, 91 Ohio St. 3d 503, 747 N.E.2d 230 (2001) (held RC 742.47 does not permit QDROs on such member's benefit until the member retires from the plan), reversed by 91 Ohio St.3d 503, 747 N.E.2d 230 (2001).

[4]Davis v. Davis, 131 Ohio App. 3d 686, 723 N.E.2d 599 (2d Dist. Montgomery County 1998), abrogated by Erb v. Erb, 2001 -Ohio- 104, 91 Ohio St. 3d 503, 747 N.E.2d 230 (2001).

[5]Volz v. Volz, 1999 WL 770728 (Ohio Ct. App. 5th Dist. Richland County 1999), abrogated by Erb v. Erb, 2001 -Ohio- 104, 91 Ohio St. 3d 503, 747 N.E.2d 230 (2001).

[6]Barnes v. Barnes, 2000 WL 817082 (Ohio Ct. App. 7th Dist. Columbiana County 2000).

[7]Barnes v. Barnes, 2000 WL 817082, at *2 (Ohio Ct. App. 7th Dist. Columbiana County 2000).

[8]Erb v. Erb, 2001 -Ohio- 104, 91 Ohio St. 3d 503, 747 N.E.2d 230 (2001).

[9]Erb v. Erb, 2001 -Ohio- 104, 91 Ohio St. 3d 503, 747 N.E.2d 230 (2001).

and wife agreed that wife would receive $1,000 per month directly from the PFDPF, and the trial court issued an order to the fund to pay the sums. The PFDPF appealed, alleging that the anti-alienation provisions of the statute which created the fund, RC 742.47, would not permit payments to be made to a non-member; and the Eighth District Court of Appeals agreed.[10] The Ohio Supreme Court held that a former spouse is not a creditor, but a person who has a property interest in the fund, and RC Ch. 742 does not prohibit payments to satisfy a former spouse's interest in the fund; that when the trial court issued a "qualified" order, it did so only to ease any tax burden upon husband and not for the purpose of making the PFDPF an ERISA plan; per RC 742.27, the fund has the ability to pay sums due to *any person*, and does not state any *member*; the payments were vested and matured because husband's benefits were in payout status, and the new Am. H.B. merely codifies a clarification of the authority the fund already had to make payments because the legislature was aware of conflicting interpretations of the law by several courts of appeal. The dissent was quite vociferous in its opposition to this holding, finding that Am. H.B. 535 was designed as a new tool to effectuate property divisions and make legal that which had previously been illegal.

§29:51 State benefits—Methods of division—Cash payment at time of divorce

A distributive award was made in the case of *Stewart v. Stewart*,[1] where the trial court ordered payments for one year to compensate for the wife's one-half of a PERS account, but that ruling was overturned on appeal, as the court of appeals found that the trial court failed to consider the statutory requirements of RC 3105.171(E)(2) and RC 3105.171(F), and cited the case of *Smith v. Smith*[2] which held that it was inequitable to order a distributive award from current income to divide a nonliquid pension benefit absent a substantial amount of other assets.

The trial court in *Corbett v. Corbett*[3] attempted to equitably distribute the PERS pension by means of a cash payment within sixty days of the decree of divorce, and the appellate court reversed, finding that the PERS asset was the only marital asset still remaining and there was inadequate income and inadequate collateral with which the PERS member would be able to make such a large lump-sum payment, stating

---

[10]Erb v. Erb, 2000 WL 426544 (Ohio Ct. App. 8th Dist. Cuyahoga County 2000), appeal allowed, 90 Ohio St. 3d 1417, 735 N.E.2d 456 (2000) and rev'd, 2001 -Ohio- 104, 91 Ohio St. 3d 503, 747 N.E.2d 230 (2001).

[Section 29:51]
[1]Stewart v. Stewart, 1998 WL 177558 (Ohio Ct. App. 2d Dist. Montgomery County 1998), dismissed, appeal not allowed, 83 Ohio St. 3d 1428, 699 N.E.2d 945 (1998).

[2]Smith v. Smith, 91 Ohio App. 3d 248, 632 N.E.2d 555 (10th Dist. Franklin County 1993).

[3]Corbett v. Corbett, 1999 WL 436727 (Ohio Ct. App. 5th Dist. Coshocton County 1999).

"to force the spouse who lacks significant financial resources to pay the value of a delayed benefit from current income ordinarily is inequitable as the payee/spouse enjoys a present benefit, at the expense of the payor/spouse's reduction in current available funds, especially in view of the fact that the pension can be divided in an alternative manner."[4]

§ 29:52 State benefits—Methods of division—Cash payment over a term of years

A payment of a non-member spouse's marital interest in a state pension over a term of years was attempted in *Patsey v. Patsey*,[1] where the trial court ordered the member spouse to pay to the non-member spouse one-half of the present value of the STRS pension over a period of fifteen years with interest at 7%. The Seventh District Court of Appeals, while sympathetic to the trial court's dilemma in arriving at a method by which to disentangle the financial affairs of the parties while not being able to order a QDRO and not being able to make an offset award of other marital property, found that ordering such installment payments constituted an abuse of discretion when viewed in light of the other financial circumstances of the parties, and recommended that the trial court exercise its option to retain jurisdiction to order a percentage of future benefit to be paid to the member spouse when the pension has vested and matured and the member spouse retires in the future.

§ 29:53 State benefits—Methods of division—Present offset

The Eleventh District Court of Appeals found no error in awarding a lump-sum distribution to a nonmember spouse in a PERS pension when it was an enhancement of an equity share in real estate in *Frederick v. Frederick*,[1] a case involving two public pension plans. The appellate court stated that because husband's Police and Fireman's Disability and Pension Fund was both vested and matured, the amount due was currently payable. Therefore, the wife's share was currently fixed and readily ascertainable and therefore an offset of that value against husband's interest in the real estate was proper. However, because husband's Public Employees Retirement System benefits were vested but unmatured (a right to receive an undetermined amount of money in the future), and there was no right to immediately receive payments, an offset of a reduced cash value was used for that asset. The court stated that to retain jurisdiction some ten years hence would have been unacceptable as that would entail making the nonmember spouse bear the

---

[4]Corbett v. Corbett, 1999 WL 436727, at *3 (Ohio Ct. App. 5th Dist. Coshocton County 1999).

[Section 29:52]

[1]Patsey v. Patsey, 1998 WL 896455 (Ohio Ct. App. 7th Dist. Columbiana County 1998).

[Section 29:53]

[1]Frederick v. Frederick, 2000 WL 522170 (Ohio Ct. App. 11th Dist. Portage County 2000).

risk of the member's death prior to distribution.

The Eighth District Court of Appeals saw no abuse of discretion in allocating almost all of the marital debt to the STRS member, and considering that allocation as a setoff of the nonmember's interest in the pension plan, as the dollar amounts of the two sums were nearly equal.[2]

§ 29:54 State benefits—Methods of division—Retention of jurisdiction

In a division of property, where premature distribution of Public Employees Retirement System (PERS) benefits is unavailable as long as the party is still employed, the trial court may delay the division until retirement, maintaining the court's jurisdiction to some unspecified date in the future.[1]

In *Patsey v. Patsey*,[2] the court of appeals reversed a payment over a term of years as an abuse of discretion when viewed in light of the other financial circumstances of the parties, and recommended that the trial court exercise its option to retain jurisdiction to order a percentage of the future benefit to be paid to the member spouse when the pension has vested and matured and the member spouse retires in the future.

The Twelfth District Court of Appeals in *Schiavone v. Schiavone*[3] found the trial court to be in error when it reserved jurisdiction to make further disposition of retirement benefits if the member spouse attempted to file bankruptcy to discharge his obligation to make the property settlement payments imposed by the trial court to make an equal division of PERS benefits.

If the court retains jurisdiction to make a division of state pension benefits until they are about to be paid out to the member spouse, there is a risk that the member spouse will not live until benefits are received. That risk of death prior to distribution of benefits is just what occurred in the case of *Cosby v. Cosby*.[4] By the terms of their 1989 decree, upon husband's retirement from STRS, wife was to receive 40% of the monthly benefit he received, not less than $1,000 per month. Ten days after the decree was journalized, husband remarried. Husband died in 1997 before retiring. Husband had designated his second wife as his surviving spouse, and as such, "death benefits" were payable to his second wife per RC 3307.48. The first wife sued the second wife, claiming a right to receive 40% of the monthly benefits that STRS was paying to the second

[2]Braylock Braylock, 1999 WL 1249558 (Ohio Ct. App. 8th Dist. Cuyahoga County 1999).

[Section 29:54]
[1]McIntire v. McIntire, 1989 WL 137205 (Ohio Ct. App. 7th Dist. Carroll County 1989).

[2]Patsey v. Patsey, 1998 WL 896455 (Ohio Ct. App. 7th Dist. Columbiana County 1998).

[3]Schiavone v. Schiavone, 126 Ohio App. 3d 780, 711 N.E.2d 694 (12th Dist. Butler County 1998).

[4]Cosby v. Cosby, 2001 -Ohio- 4205, 141 Ohio App. 3d 320, 750 N.E.2d 1207 (12th Dist. Butler County 2001), appeal allowed, 93 Ohio St. 3d 1435, 755 N.E.2d 356 (2001).

wife on a theory of unjust enrichment. The trial court rejected that claim, finding that the right of the first wife to receive payment was conditioned on husband's retirement, and since he had died prior to retirement, there was no satisfaction of the condition precedent. The Twelfth District Court of Appeals reversed and vacated, finding that husband's rights to his STRS account were limited by the decree and he could not give his second wife rights which were not his to give. The appellate court stated that marital property rights cannot be made subject to a contingency, citing *Zimmie v. Zimmie*,[5] and stated that "conversion of his retirement account into a death benefit occasioned by his unanticipated death prior to retirement cannot change its identity for purposes of the prior divorce decree. Nor can it defeat the division of the respective rights of the parties in the retirement account asset that the court awarded in the decree."

In a 4-3 decision, the Ohio Supreme Court rejected the reasoning of the court of appeals and reversed.[6] The majority of the Ohio Supreme Court Justices agreed with the dissenter at the appellate level, who reasoned that former husband's pension benefits never vested under RC 3307.42[7] The Supreme Court stated that because the member died before retiring, no pension benefits were available, leaving only survivor benefits under RC 3307.562 and RC 3307.66. Survivor benefits are provided to a designated beneficiary, or, if there is no person so designated by the member, to a surviving spouse. A former spouse cannot qualify as "surviving spouse" because a divorce automatically revokes the designation as "spouse" under RC 3307.562(B). The Supreme Court disagreed with the appellate court dissenter, stating that survivor benefits are not death benefits because death benefits are paid if a member dies after retiring and receiving benefits under RC 3307.661, and in this case, the husband had not yet begun to receive benefits at the time of his death. The Court held that the STRS could only pay benefits as authorized by statute, the surviving spouse is the only possible beneficiary permitted under RC 3307.562, and the constructive trust as recommended by the court of appeals was contrary to the statutory mandates governing STRS. The Court concluded "[a]lthough we may not like the result, a different solution lies only with the General Assembly"[8] The dissenting opinion argues that an equitable solution such as a constructive trust is especially well suited in a situation where statutory construction erases the express intent of the parties. Because former husband could have designated former wife as a survivor (by name and not by "wife") of 40% of his survivor benefits and chose not to do so despite the court ordered agreement, a constructive trust was necessary to enforce the obligations former husband assumed in the decree

---

[5]Zimmie v. Zimmie, 11 Ohio St. 3d 94, 464 N.E.2d 142, 53 A.L.R.4th 75 (1984).

[6]Cosby v. Cosby, 96 Ohio St. 3d 228, 2002-Ohio-4170, 773 N.E.2d 516 (2002).

[7]See RC 3307.42, STRS retirement benefits do not vest until a member qualifies and applies for benefits; and State ex rel. Horvath v. State Teachers Retirement Bd., 83 Ohio St. 3d 67, 1998-Ohio-424, 697 N.E.2d 644, 127 Ed. Law Rep. 1017 (1998).

[8]Cosby v. Cosby, 96 Ohio St. 3d 228, 2002-Ohio-4170, 773 N.E.2d 516 (2002).

of divorce.

§ 29:55 State benefits—Methods of division—Legislative changes—DOPO

Am. Sub. H.B. 535, effective January 1, 2002, amends RC 3307.21 to permit division of public retirement accounts by orders entered into pursuant to RC 3105.171. An order is permitted by RC 3307.41 to be placed on state pensions, giving effect to a property division, and directing the state plan to make direct payments of either a fixed monthly dollar amount or a percentage of the coverture fraction of the retirement pension.

There is great controversy regarding that proposed law, however, as it does not provide for survivorship benefits to the former spouse, nor would a member spouse's share of the pension benefit be permitted to go below 50% of the total benefit, nor would it allow COLA to inure to the benefit of the nonmember spouse, nor would a former spouse be able to begin receiving payments until the participant files for retirement benefits.

Without pre-retirement survivorship protection, as is available under ERISA plans, nonmember former spouses are still bearing the risk of death, especially in the case of remarriage such as the *Cosby* case.[1] The best practice will continue to be requiring life insurance on the member spouse until actual retirement.

The plans have formulated an acceptable form order.[2]

§ 29:56 State benefits—Methods of division—Division of property order for state retirement plans—Form⊚

IN THE COURT OF COMMON PLEAS

DOMESTIC RELATIONS DIVISION

_____COUNTY, OHIO

_____,	)	Case No.
Plaintiff/Petitioner,	)	Judge
vs.	)	Magistrate
_____,	)	
Defendant/Petitioner	)	

DIVISION OF PROPERTY ORDER

The Court finds the following facts and issues the following Order pursuant to Revised Code Sections 3105.80 to 3105.90:

I. Terms:

[Section 29:55]

[1]See § 29:44.

[2]See § 29:56, State benefits—Methods of division—Division of property order for state retirement plans—Form.

A. The "Plan Participant" or "Participant" means ___, Social Security number_____, whose date of birth is _____, whose current address is _____, and whose current mailing address is _____.

B. The "Alternate Payee" means _____, Social Security number, whose date of birth is _____, whose current address is _____, and whose current mailing address is _____.

C. The "Public Retirement Program(s)" means (please check the name and address of the public retirement program(s) and/or University/College Alternative Retirement Plan Administrator):

☐ Public Employees Retirement System of Ohio
277 East Town Street. Columbus. Ohio 43215-4642
☐ State Teachers Retirement System of Ohio
275 East Broad Street, Columbus, Ohio 43215-3771
☐ School Employees Retirement System of Ohio
300 East Broad Street, Suite 100, Columbus, Ohio 43215-3746
☐ Ohio Police and Fire Pension Fund
140 East Town Street, Columbus, Ohio 43215
☐ Ohio Highway Patrol Retirement System
6161 Busch Boulevard, Suite 119, Columbus, Ohio 43229-2553
☐ University/College Alternative Retirement Plan
Name and address of University/College Plan Administrator:

_____

_____

D. Obligation of Plan Participant and Alternate Payee: The Plan Participant and the Alternate Payee are ordered to notify in writing the Public Retirement Program of a change in the individual's mailing address.

II. Amount Payable to the Alternate Payee: Upon the Plan Participant receiving a benefit payment or a lump sum payment from the Public Retirement Program, the court orders that the Alternate Payee shall receive payment in accordance with and subject to the limitations set forth in Revised Code Sections 3105.82 to 3105.90. If the Plan Participant is a reemployed retiree contributing to a money purchase annuity or is eligible to receive or is receiving monthly benefits or a lump sum payment from a money purchase annuity, the Alternate Payee shall receive payment in a monthly or one-time dollar amount as specified in Paragraph ll(B)(l) below. If the Plan Participant is a member of the State Teachers Retirement System and is participating in the defined contribution program established pursuant to Revised Code Section 3307.81, or any of its constituent plans, the Alternate Payee shall receive payment in a percentage of a fraction as specified in Paragraph II(B)(2) below. If the Plan Participant is participating in any other plan in a

Public Retirement Program, the Alternate Payee shall receive payment in either a dollar amount or a percentage of a fraction as specified below (please check the type and the method of payment):

A. <u>Type of Payment</u>: If the Participant is eligible to receive more than one benefit payment or more than one lump sum payment, please check the benefit or lump sum payment from which payment to the Alternate Payee shall be made. If no benefit or lump sum payment is designated, the Alternate Payee shall receive payment from the first benefit payment or lump sum payment for which the Participant is eligible to apply and to receive. Please check ALL APPLICABLE BENEFIT(S) OR LUMP SUM PAYMENT(S):

☐ Age and service monthly retirement benefit

☐ Disability monthly retirement benefit

☐ Account refund

☐ Additional money purchase monthly annuity or lump sum refund

☐ Reemployed retiree money purchase monthly annuity (when monthly payment exceeds $25.00) or lump sum refund

☐ Defined contribution plan benefit (STRS only)

B. <u>Method of Payment</u>:

1. <u>Dollar Amount</u>: Please check the appropriate box:

☐ $_____ per month from the Participant's monthly benefit upon the Participant's receipt of the monthly benefit.

☐ $_____from the Participant's lump sum payment upon the Participant's receipt of the payment.

2. <u>Percentage</u>: If the Plan Participant elects to receive a monthly benefit or a one-time lump sum payment, the Public Retirement Program shall pay directly to the Alternate Payee per month or in a one-time lump sum payment ____ percent (__%) of a fraction as set forth below of the Plan Participant's monthly benefit or one-time lump sum payment.

a. The numerator of the fraction shall be ____ which is the number of years during which the Plan Participant was both a member of the Public Retirement Program and married to the Alternate Payee. The date of marriage is _____

b. The denominator, which shall be determined by the Public Retirement Program at the time that the Plan Participant elects to take a monthly benefit or a one-time lump sum payment, shall be the Participant's total years of service credit with the Public Retirement Program or, in the case of a Participant in a retirement plan established under Chapter 3305, Revised Code, the years of participation in the plan.

C. <u>Applicable Benefit</u>: The monthly benefit amount used to determine the amount paid to the Alternate Payee from the Participant's monthly benefit shall be whichever applies:

1. If the Participant is receiving a monthly benefit, the monthly benefit shall be the benefit the Participant is receiving at the time the decree of divorce or dissolution becomes final. The effective date of the decree of divorce or dissolution is _____.

2. If the Participant has applied for but is not yet receiving a monthly benefit, the monthly benefit shall be the benefit for which the Participant is eligible;

3. If the Participant has not applied for a benefit, the monthly benefit shall be the benefit calculated at the time the Participant elects to take the benefit.

D. Minimum Benefit Notice: The total amount paid to the Alternate Payee pursuant to this order plus any administrative fee charged to the Participant and Alternate Payee as authorized by Revised Code Section 3105.84, shall not exceed fifty percent of the amount of a benefit or lump sum payment that the Plan Participant is to receive or, if withholding is to be made from more than one benefit or lump sum payment, fifty percent of the total of the benefits or lump sum payments that the Plan Participant is to receive. If the Plan Participant's benefit or lump sum payment is or will be subject to more than one order issued pursuant to Revised Code Section 3105.81, the Public Retirement Program shall not withhold an aggregate amount for all the orders plus the administrative fee(s) charged to the Participant and Alternate Payee as authorized by Revised Code Section 3105.84, that exceeds fifty percent of the benefit or lump sum payment.

III. Notification to Alternate Payee: The Alternate Payee is hereby notified of the following:

The Alternate Payee's right to payment under this Order is conditional on the Plan Participant's right to a benefit payment or lump sum payment from the Public Retirement Program;

A. When the Plan Participant's benefit or lump sum payment is subject to more than one order under Revised Code Section 3105.81, or to an order described in Revised Code Section 3105.81, and a withholding order under Revised Code Section 3121.03, the amount paid to the Alternate Payee under this order may be reduced based on the priority of the other orders;

B. The Alternate Payee's right to receive an amount from the benefit payment or lump sum payment to the Plan Participant shall terminate upon:

1. The death of the Plan Participant;
2. The death of the Alternate Payee;
3. The termination of a benefit pursuant to the governing laws of the Public Retirement Program.

IV. Administrative Fee: Pursuant to Revised Code Section 3105.84, this order authorizes the Public Retirement Program that is or will be paying the benefit or lump sum payment to withhold from any benefit or payment that is subject to this order an amount determined by the Public Retirement Program to be necessary to defray the cost of administering the order. This amount shall be divided equally between the Plan Participant and the Alternate Payee.

V. Application of Order: This order applies to payments made by the Public Retirement Program after retention of the Order under Revised Code Sections 145.571, 742.462, 3305.21, 3307.371, 3309.671, or 5505.261.

VI. Additional Limitations on Order

A. Payments under this order shall commence as provided under Revised Code Sections 145.571, 742.462, 3305.21 3307.371, 3309.671, or 5505.261.

B. The Alternate Payee has no right or privilege under the law governing the Public Retirement Program that is not otherwise provided in the governing law.

C. This order shall not require the Public Retirement Program to take any action or provide any benefit, allowance, or payment not authorized under the law governing the Public Retirement Program.

VII. Notice of Order:

A. The clerk of courts shall transmit a certified copy of this order to the Public Retirement Program(s) named in the order.

B. On receipt of this order, the Public Retirement Program shall determine whether the order meets the requirements as set forth in Revised Code Sections 3105.80 to 3105.90.

C. The Public Retirement Program shall retain the order in the Plan Participant's record if the order meets the requirements in Sections 3105.80 to 3105.90, Revised Code.

D. The Public Retirement Program shall return, by regular mail, to the clerk of courts of the court that issued the order any order the Public Retirement Program determines does not meet the requirements in Revised Code Sections 3105.80 to 3105.90, no later than sixty days after the Public Retirement Program's receipt of the order.

VIII. Jurisdiction of the Court: The Court shall retain jurisdiction to modify, supervise, or enforce the implementation of this order notwithstanding Revised Code Section 3105.171 (1).

APPROVED:

_____

Attorney for Plaintiff/Petitioner

_____

Attorney for Defendant/Petitioner

_____

Retirement System

_____

Retirement System

_____

Retirement System

SO ORDERED

_____

Judge

§ 29:57   State benefits—Methods of calculation and valuation

Calculation of the value of the state retirement system benefits for purposes of property division, allocation, or set-off requires expert testimony at trial because the "values" provided by the various plans only reflect the member's accumulated contributions and does not state the value of any of the state employer's contributions. The State Teachers Retirement System, for example, has two alternate methods to calculate a participant's projected monthly retirement benefit, the money-purchase plan and the salary-related formula, and the member is entitled to the higher of the monthly benefits achieved by the two methods. Service retirement is available when the member has met the specified age and years of service requirements. Eligibility occurs when a member has at least thirty years of public service credit at any age, or twenty-five years of service at age 55, or five years of service at age 60.

Calculation of the value of a state employee's retirement fund may be offset by the calculation of the nonparticipant's social security benefits.[1]

§ 29:58   State benefits—Beneficiary designation

A member in any of the state retirement programs may designate, by proper form filed with the appropriate board, a beneficiary or beneficiaries to share in retirement benefits. The last designation of any beneficiary revokes all previous designations, and the member's marriage, divorce, marriage dissolution, legal separation, withdrawal of account, or the birth or adoption of child constitutes an automatic revocation of his previous designation.[1] Therefore, in the case of a divorce, the ex-spouse is automatically terminated as a designated beneficiary upon the termination of the marriage. A member may redesignate the former spouse as beneficiary of death benefits with the proper forms and the court may order that such be done,[2] and this designation will remain until terminated or until revoked by another change in status. A provision in a separation agreement should be enforceable by the court, as any other order.

Benefits to a designated beneficiary continue until terminated by that beneficiary's marriage, remarriage, abandonment, adoption, or active military service. However, benefits terminated due to a first remarriage can resume if the remarriage ceases within two years due to divorce, annulment, dissolution, or death.[3] Therefore, the practitioner should be aware, in dealing with a case where the marriage has been of relatively short duration and is not the first marriage for both parties, that the client may be eligible for benefits once terminated. A surviving spouse receiving benefits under PFDPF, STRS, PERS, or SERS can remarry at

---

[Section 29:57]

   [1]See § 29:9, Social security benefits—Benefits as marital property.

[Section 29:58]

   [1]RC 145.43, RC 1339.63.

   [2]RC 1339.63(B)(1).

   [3]RC 145.45.

age 55 or older without losing monthly benefits.

The member also has the option of electing to receive a retirement benefit in a lesser amount, based on the actuarial equivalent of his retirement allowance, paid either in part or in whole to a designated beneficiary.[4] Various options are available for retirees. If they are married at the time of election of benefits, they must give notice to the spouse if any election other than joint and survivorship is selected, and the spouse is to sign an acknowledgment of having received such notice. It is possible, then, for a member to designate an ex-spouse upon his retirement for payments of a part of his retirement benefit, those payments to continue after his death, but not to exceed the amount payable to the retiree during his life. The annuity option selected by the member must be considered. If a member selects an annuity with survivorship rights of specified percentages, such election reduces the monthly annuity payable to the retiree. Selecting an annuity with rights of reversion reduces the monthly benefit even more, but allows the retiree the option of reverting to and receiving a greater monthly amount in the form of a single life annuity upon either the death of the named payee of survivor benefits or divorce from such payee prior to the member's death. This ability to revert or "pop-up" to a single life annuity is to be considered in negotiating an agreement. If the member has selected an annuity with rights of reversion upon death or divorce, unless a decree provides otherwise, the member can file for a divorce, "pop-up" his or her benefits, and eliminate the other spouse's rights to a survivor annuity.

1996 House Bill 586, effective March 3, 1997, requires STRS to pay interest on a member's contributions, when distribution is made due to death or separation from employment. If the member had fewer than three years of service, STRS is to pay up to 4% interest; if the member had between three and five years of service credit, STRS is to pay up to 6% interest; and if the member had five or more years of service credit, STRS is to pay up to 6% interest *plus* an amount equal to one-half of the member's accumulated contributions, including payments for the purchase of canceled service, approved leaves of absence, and additional annuity income, *plus* annual compound interest on that 50% of accumulated contributions, at a rate not to exceed 6%.

§ 29:59   State benefits—Cost of living adjustments

Do not forget that a cost of living adjustment (COLA) attaches to all of the state pension plans. The first COLA in the non-uniformed state plans (STRS, SERS, and PERS) was authorized in 1971, and provided that in any year in which the Consumer Price Index (CPI) rose more than 3%, the pensioners would receive a COLA of a certain percentage, at first 1.5%, which increased to 3%. In 1981, HPRS was granted authority to grant a COLA to any retiree over age 62, which was lowered to age 53 as of 1996. The first 3% COLA was authorized under PFDPF in 1988 and awarded a flat $360 to individuals retiring before July 24,

---

[4]RC 145.46.

1986.

Since 1971, there have been five years in which the CPI did not rise by more than 3%, and in those years, the COLA was not paid to the retirees, but was saved in the fund balances. Any percentage change over 3% is "banked" for each employee based on the effective date of the benefit, so those who have been retired longer have larger banks. The actuaries maintaining the state plans for each retirement system assume that the 3% COLA will be paid each year, and the cost to fund these additional payments has been calculated in the current contribution rates for employees and their state employers. 1996 House Bill 365, effective July 1, 1996, permits payments of a COLA equal to the actual change of the CPI, or such change plus any prior accumulations, up to a maximum of 3% whenever the average change in the CPI is less than 3%.

Some courts have refused to include the COLA portion of the valuation of a state pension, stating that such is too speculative, thereby awarding the entire COLA portion of the marital pension to the employee-spouse. Ninety-seven percent of all retired teachers have received COLAs over all years since 1971, and 95% of SERS members have received COLAs.[1]

Courts of appeals have held there to be no error, however, when trial courts have elected to use a value for a state retirement benefit without including the COLA in Corbett v. Corbett[2] and Cross v. Cross.[3]

§ 29:60   State benefits—Health insurance

Medical insurance coverage for spouses of retirees ordinarily will cease upon divorce, although some plans have provisions for continuation, similar to COBRA, for former spouses, which should be investigated. Counsel should verify whether continuation of benefits can be achieved. The medical insurance provider must be contacted to obtain information available, conversion benefits, as well as to alert plan so it can give proper notification of benefits.[1] The Public Health Service Act amendments of state and local government employees for group health plans (comparable to COBRA for private employees) applies to employees and not retirees.

[Section 29:59]

[1]See Gary A. Shulman and David I. Kelley, Dividing Pensions in Divorce: Learning from the Pension Experts (Wiley Law Pubs. 1993).

[2]Corbett v. Corbett, 1999 WL 436727 (Ohio Ct. App. 5th Dist. Coshocton County 1999).

[3]Cross v. Cross, 2001 WL 688890 (Ohio Ct. App. 9th Dist. Wayne County 2001).

[Section 29:60]

[1]See § 29:61, State benefits—Health insurance—Continuation of health benefits—Form letters.

§ 29:61 State benefits—Health insurance—Continuation of health benefits—Form letters

277 East Town Street   Columbus, Ohio 43215-4642

Public Employees Retirement System of Ohio
1-800-222-PERS (7377) • www.opers.org

When replying please give the number below.
This is used to identify your account in PERS.

For:
Effective:

Our records show that the above-named individual will no longer be eligible for the PERS Health Care Plan, administered by Aetna U.S. Healthcare, including the PERS Prescription Plan, administered by Merck-Medco Managed Care, Inc.

As an alternative to the PERS Health Care Plan, the above-named individual may apply for the Aetna U.S. Healthcare Direct Bill Plan or the Aetna Basic Conversion Option. We have enclosed a brief summary of each plan along with general cost information.

If enrollment information is desired, please do the following no later than 30 days following the date of this letter. Application can only be made for either the Direct Bill Plan or the Basic Conversion Option.

• To obtain enrollment information on the Basic Conversion Option, indicate the applicant's name and address on the enclosed Notice of Conversion Privilege (request form) and send it to: Aetna U.S. Healthcare
Attn: Conversion Department
P. O. Box 2117
Fall River, MA 02722

• To obtain enrollment information on the Aetna Direct Bill Option, complete the lower portion of this letter and send it to:
Aetna U.S. Healthcare
Sales and Marketing
7400 West Campus Road
New Albany, OH 43054

_____   _____   _____
Date   Applicant's Telephone Number   Applicant's Birth Date

Is the applicant eligible for Medicare A (hospital) insurance?   YES   NO (Circle one)

Is the applicant eligible for Medicare B (medical) insurance?   YES   NO (Circle one)

Laurie Fiori Hacking
Executive Director

Danny L. Drake
Director
Benefits Administration

Mark Snodgrass
Director
Finance

Blake W. Sherry
Director
Information Technology

Neil V. Toth
Director
Investments

277 East Town Street   Columbus, Ohio 43215-4642

Public Employees Retirement System of Ohio
1-800-222-PERS (7377) • www.opers.org

When replying please give the number below.
This is used to identify your account in PERS.

For:
Effective:

Our records show that the above-named individual will no longer be eligible for the PERS Health Care Plan, administered by Medical Mutual, including the PERS Prescription Plan, administered by Merck-Medco Managed Care, Inc.

As an alternative to the PERS Health Care Plan, the above-named individual may wish to apply for the Medical Mutual conversion plan. The conversion plan is subject to the policies and procedures established by Medical Mutual. We are enclosing a brief summary of the benefit plan and general cost information.

If enrollment information is desired, complete the lower portion of this letter and send the entire letter to:

Medical Mutual
Firstar Bank Building
175 S. Third Street, Suite 330
Columbus, Ohio 43215
Telephone inquiries: 1-800-242-1936

The request for enrollment in the conversion plan must be received by Medical Mutual no later than 30 days from the date of this letter.

_____
Date

_____
Birth Date of Applicant

_____
Telephone Number of Applicant

Is applicant eligible for Medicare A (hospital) insurance?

Is applicant eligible for Medicare B (medical) insurance?

___   ___
yes   no

___   ___
yes   no

Laurie Fiori Hocking   Danny L. Drake   Mark Snodgrass   Blake W. Sherry   Neil V. Toth
Executive Director   Director   Director   Director   Director
                              Benefits Administration Finance   Information Technology   Investments

§ 29:62   Ohio Public Employees Deferred Compensation Fund

RC 145.75 provides that income deferred under a deferred compensation program offered by the Ohio Public Employees Deferred Compensation is subject to a marital property division order in a divorce, legal separation, or dissolution action, under certain circumstances. The circumstances must be consistent with the plan, and the assignment or attachment must not be available prior to the time that the spouse in whose name the participant account is maintained begins to receive the moneys and income credited to the account.[1] In effect, the legislature has made an exception to the anti-alienation provisions of the deferred compensation funds for domestic relations orders. Ostensibly, the court order would be sufficient to alert the fund to the necessity of a later transfer if the participant account was not ripe for transfer when the order is issued, and not require an order similar to the QDRO for private defined contribution plans.[2]

§ 29:63   Ohio Public Employees Deferred Compensation Fund— Qualified Domestic Relations Order—Form◉

QUALIFIED DOMESTIC RELATIONS ORDER

IT IS HEREBY ORDERED AS FOLLOWS:

1. **Effect of This Order as a Qualified Domestic Relations Order:** This Order creates and recognizes the existence of an Alternate Payee's right to receive a portion of the Participant's benefits payable under a government-sponsored retirement plan that is qualified under Section 457 of the Internal Revenue Code (the "Code"). It is intended to constitute a Qualified Domestic Relations Order ("QDRO") under Section 414(p) of the Code and Section 206(d)(3) of ERISA.

2. **Participant Information:** The name, last known address, birth date and social security number of the plan "Participant" are:

Name:
Address:
Social Security Number:
Birth Date:

3. **Alternate Payee Information:** The name, last known address, social security number and date of birth of the "Alternate Payee" are:

Name:
Address:
Social Security Number:
Birth Date:

[Section 29:62]

[1]RC 3105.171, RC 3105.63.

[2]See § 29:63, Ohio Public Employees Deferred Compensation Fund—Qualified Domestic Relations Order—Form

The Former Spouse shall have the duty to notify in writing the Ohio Public Employees Deferred Compensation Program (located at 250 Civic Center Drive, Suite 350, Columbus, Ohio 43215-5450) of any changes in her mailing address subsequent to the entry of this Order and within thirty (30) days of any such change of address.

4. **Plan Name:** The name of the Plan to which this Order applies is the **Ohio Public Employees Deferred Compensation Program** (hereinafter referred to as "Plan"). Further, any successor plan to the Plan or any other plan(s) to which liability for provision of the Participant's benefits described above is incurred, shall also be subject to the terms of this Order.

5. **Pursuant to State Domestic Relations Law:** This Order is entered pursuant to the authority granted in the applicable domestic relations laws of the State of Ohio.

6. **For Provision of Marital Property Rights:** This Order relates to the provision of marital property rights and/or spousal support to the Alternate Payee as a result of the Order of Divorce between Participant and Alternate Payee.

7. **Amount of Alternate Payee's Benefit:** This Order assigns to Alternate Payee ***(1) (\$ _____) **or*****(2) (an amount equal to **Fifty Percent (50%)**) of the Participant's Total Account Balance accumulated under the Plan as of *** date *** (or the closest valuation date thereto), plus any interest and investment earnings or losses attributable thereon subsequent to the date of acknowledged receipt of this order by OPEDCP, until the date of total distribution. Such Total Account Balance shall include all amounts maintained under all of the various accounts and/or investment funds established on behalf of the Participant. The Alternate Payee's share of the benefits shall be allocated on a "pro-rata" basis among all of the Participant's accounts maintained on his behalf under the Plan.

8. **Commencement Date and Form of Payment to Alternate Payee:** If the Alternate Payee so elects, she shall be paid her benefits as soon as administratively feasible following the date this Order is approved as a QDRO by the Plan Administrator, or at the earliest date permitted under the Plan or Section 414(p) of the Internal Revenue Code, if later. Benefits will be payable to the Alternate Payee in any form or permissible option otherwise available to participants and alternate payees under the terms of the Plan, including, but not limited to, a single lump-sum cash payment.

9. **Alternate Payee's Rights and Privileges:** On or after the date that this Order is deemed to be a Qualified Domestic Relations Order, but before the Alternate Payee receives her total distribution under the Plan, the Alternate Payee shall be entitled to all of the rights and election privileges that are afforded to Plan beneficiaries, including, but not limited to, the rules regarding the right to designate a beneficiary for death benefit purposes.

10. **Death of Alternate Payee:** In the event of Alternate Payee's death prior to Alternate Payee receiving the full amount of benefits

called for under this Order, such Alternate Payee's beneficiary(ies), as designated on the appropriate form provided by the Plan Administrator (or in the absence of a beneficiary designation, her estate), shall receive the remainder of any unpaid benefits under the terms of this Order.

11. **Death of Participant:** In the event that the Participant dies **before** the Alternate Payee receives her distribution in accordance with the terms of this QDRO, or before the establishment of separate account(s) in the name of the Alternate Payee, such Alternate Payee shall be treated as the surviving spouse of the Participant for any death benefits payable under the Plan to the extent of the full amount of her benefits as called for under Paragraph 7 of this Order. Should the Participant predecease the Alternate Payee **after** the new account(s) have been established in her behalf, such Participant's death shall not affect Alternate Payee's right to the portion of her benefits as stipulated herein.

12. **Savings Clause:** This Order is not intended, and shall not be construed in such a manner as to require the Plan:

(a) to provide any type or form of benefit option not otherwise provided under the terms of the Plan:

(b) to require the Plan to provide increased benefits determined on the basis of actuarial value; or

(c) to require the payment of any benefit to the Alternate Payee which are required to be paid to another alternate payee under another death order which was previously deemed to be a QDRO.

13. **Tax Treatment of Distributions Made Under This Order:** For purposes of Sections 402(a)(1) and 72 of the Internal Revenue Code, any Alternate Payee who is the spouse or former spouse of the Participant shall be treated as the distributee of any distribution or payments made to the Alternate Payee under the terms of this Order, and as such, will be required to pay the appropriate federal income taxes on such distribution.

14. **Constructive Receipt:** In the event that the Plan Trustee inadvertently pays to the Participant any benefits which are assigned to the Alternate Payee pursuant to the terms of this Order, the Participant shall immediately reimburse the Alternate Payee to the extent that he has received such benefit payments, and shall forthwith pay such amounts so received directly to the Alternate Payee within ten (10) days of receipt.

15. **Continued Jurisdiction:** The Court shall retain jurisdiction with respect to this Order to the extent required to maintain its qualified status and the original intent of the parties as stipulated herein. The Court shall also retain jurisdiction to enter such further orders as are necessary to enforce the assignment of benefits to Alternate Payee as set forth herein.

16. **Plan Termination:** In the event of a Plan termination, the Alternate Payee shall be entitled to receive her portion of Participant's benefits as stipulated herein in accordance with the Plan's termination provisions for participants and beneficiaries.

17. **Actions By Participant:** The Participant shall not take any actions, affirmative or otherwise, that can circumvent the terms and provisions of this Qualified Domestic Relations Order, or that could diminish or extinguish the rights and entitlements of the Alternate Payee as set forth herein. Should the Participant take any action or inaction to the detriment of the Alternate Payee, he shall be required to make sufficient payments **directly** to the Alternate Payee to the extent necessary to neutralize the effects of his actions or inactions and to the extent of her full entitlements hereunder.

   IT IS SO ORDERED.

_____

JUDGE

APPROVED:

_____

Attorney for Participant

_____

Attorney for Alternate Payee

§ 29:64   Government retirement benefits—Conclusion

Federal entitlements programs provide, almost uniformly, a percentage formula for awarding to nonparticipating spouses under divorce decrees some portion of benefits accruing to their participating spouses during the term of the marriage. In most cases, these benefits are available to former spouses even upon remarriage, if the successive marriage takes place in the spouse's later years. It is therefore incumbent upon the domestic relations practitioner to examine the complete work history of each party to a divorce action so that the attorney, not the client, can make a determination as to whether benefits have accrued. Exploration of this nature, conducted at the onset of the case, can help to determine the course of discovery and expedite a complete and equitable resolution of the case.

For Ohio state retirement systems, there is no provision for complete benefits to be payable to divorced spouses under divorce decrees. Benefits are only available at the initiation of the participating member through the filing of the appropriate forms with his or her retirement board. Further, because designations are automatically revoked upon changes of status, continual redesignation is necessary. For the domestic relations practitioner whose client is a beneficiary of a state plan by designation, it is imperative that the client be made aware that continuing vigilance is necessary.

Chapter 30

Dividing Private Retirement Benefits in Divorce

By David I. Kelley, CFP Pension Evaluators, and Gary A. Shulman, Esq., QDRO Consultants Medina, Ohio

> **KeyCite®:** Cases and other legal materials listed in KeyCite Scope can be researched through West Group's KeyCite service on Westlaw®. Use KeyCite to check citations for form, parallel references, prior and later history, and comprehensive citator information, including citations to other decisions and secondary materials.

§ 30:1   Private retirement benefits as marital property—In general

Because a retirement plan represents deferred wages earned during the marriage, it is settled law in Ohio that such a benefit "accumulated during marriage is a marital asset that *must* be considered in arriving at an equitable division of property."[1] Courts do not have the discretion to ignore retirement benefits or to accept the parties' oral agreement. Instead, trial courts must conduct an independent review if not presented with documentation on the value of retirement benefits.[2] The retirement benefit must be valued and then divided.[3] It is error for a trial court to fail to consider retirement benefits in the distribution of marital property. It is also error to award the benefits to a party when the award renders the total property division inequitable without findings to justify the award. A trial court should also consider allocation of available survivor benefits under the plan.[4] A formula for division of retirement benefits that gives the non-participant any portion of the participant's after divorce contributions is in error. Those contributions are the participant's separate property.[5] The calculation of the marital portion of a retirement plan should consider the premarital component and appreciation on that separate property.[6]

This principle was codified in 1990 when the legislature enacted RC

[Section 30:1]

[1]Bisker v. Bisker, 1994 -Ohio- 307, 69 Ohio St. 3d 608, 609, 635 N.E.2d 308 (1994) (emphasis added).

[2]Bisker v. Bisker, 1994 -Ohio- 307, 69 Ohio St. 3d 608, 635 N.E.2d 308 (1994).

[3]Allen v. Allen, 109 Ohio App. 3d 640, 672 N.E.2d 1056 (12th Dist. Butler County 1996).

[4]McClelland v. McClelland, 2001 -Ohio- 3302, 2001 WL 674200 (Ohio Ct. App. 7th Dist. Jefferson County 2001), dismissed, appeal not allowed, 93 Ohio St. 3d 1447, 756 N.E.2d 112 (2001).

[5]Hamlin v. Hamlin, 1999 WL 397328 (Ohio Ct. App. 2d Dist. Darke County 1999).

[6]Couts v. Couts, 2001 WL 278174 (Ohio Ct. App. 5th Dist. Tuscarawas County 2001).

3105.171. The definition of marital property expressly includes "the retirement benefits of the spouses" to the extent they were acquired during the marriage.[7] These benefits must be included and divided as with any other marital asset the parties own.

In *Karguljiac v. Karguljiac*,[8] the trial court concluded that a waiver of wife's rights in husband's 401K plan was not to be considered a "separation agreement" so as to entitle husband to the 401K as separate property.

Retirement benefits may also be accessed through a qualified domestic relations order to satisfy both spousal and child support payments.[9]

§ 30:2 Private retirement benefits as marital property— Pensions in pay status

A pension in pay status constitutes an asset and may not be excluded as merely a stream of income.[1]

§ 30:3 Private retirement benefits as marital property— Unvested pensions

Unvested pensions acquired during the marriage are also considered marital assets that must be valued and divided during the divorce.[1] In determining what portion of an unvested pension is marital property, and in determining its value as an asset, the court should consider the present value of the pension, the percentage of the value that accrued during the marriage, and what conditions must be met for the fund to vest. The court then divides and distributes the marital portion pursuant to RC 3105.171.

§ 30:4 Retirement benefits excluded from property—In general

Some types of pensions or retirement benefits may be exclusions to this general rule. Social security benefits, disability retirement pay, and railroad benefits are three possible exclusions.[1] . The term "may" is used advisedly because various trial courts and courts of appeals have allowed at least some consideration of such benefits at various times.

Some types of pensions or retirement benefits may be excluded from

---

[7]RC 3105.171(A)(3)(a)(i).

[8]Lingenfelter v. Lingenfelter, 2001 WL 881787 (Ohio Ct. App. 5th Dist. Stark County 2001).

[9]See, e.g. Taylor v. Taylor, 44 Ohio St. 3d 61, 541 N.E.2d 55 (1989); Lyddy v. Lyddy, 1990 WL 157289 (Ohio Ct. App. 6th Dist. Lucas County 1990).

[Section 30:2]
[1]Holcomb v. Holcomb, 44 Ohio St. 3d 128, 541 N.E.2d 597 (1989); Jackson v. Jackson, 1997 WL 158097 (Ohio Ct. App. 11th Dist. Geauga County 1997).

[Section 30:3]
[1]RC 3105.171(A)(3)(a). See Lemon v. Lemon, 42 Ohio App. 3d 142, 537 N.E.2d 246 (4th Dist. Hocking County 1988).

[Section 30:4]
[1]Hoyt v. Hoyt, 53 Ohio St. 3d 177, 559 N.E.2d 1292 (1990).

the statutory definition of marital property, or may not be subject to the court's jurisdiction to distribute. Social security benefits, disability retirement pay, and railroad benefits are three types of benefits that have been excluded by courts in the past.[2] While an asset may not be within the court's power to award, many trial courts and courts of appeals have allowed at least some consideration of such benefits when dividing the marital estate as a whole.

§ 30:5   Retirement benefits excluded from property—Social security issues

Social security frequently enters the marital equation when one party is employed under social security and the other party has earned a retirement benefit from a government plan which takes the place of Social Security. The rationale behind the many appellate court cases on this issue lies with the offset provisions of social security in which participants in Ohio's public pension plans (as well as participants in the Civil Service Retirement System) lose two dollars of their independent spousal Social Security benefit for every three dollars they receive from their public pension.[1]

The second social security issue arises when one or both parties are covered solely by social security. The disparity of benefits between a worker covered under social security or Tier I of the Railroad Retirement Act and that worker's spouse has been addressed by one court of appeals in *Tarbet v. Tarbet*.[2] Keep in mind that a worker compensated under covered employment may earn a retirement benefit up to $1,326 per month (1997 maximum benefit), while a former spouse who was married to the participant for more than 10 years and has not remarried has the right to an independent benefit 50% the size of the worker's benefit up to a maximum of $663 in 1997. The *Tarbet* court ruled that the U.S. Supreme Court in *Hisquierdo v. Hisquierdo*,[3] precluded Social Security or Tier I of the Railroad Retirement Act from consideration as a marital asset.

However, the consideration of the differing social security entitlements of a worker and spouse has met with some success nationally.[4] These courts held that while courts may not directly partition social security or Tier I benefits, these benefits may be considered in the totality of relevant factors in reaching a property division. The Iowa Supreme Court dismissed the federal preemption issue in *Boyer* stating, "We do not think the federal preemption legislation requires state courts under these circumstances to purge so obvious an economic reality in its

---

[2]Hoyt v. Hoyt, 53 Ohio St. 3d 177, 559 N.E.2d 1292 (1990).

[Section 30:5]

[1]See Government Retirement Benefits Ch 29.

[2]Tarbet v. Tarbet, 97 Ohio App. 3d 674, 647 N.E.2d 254 (9th Dist. Summit County 1994).

[3]Hisquierdo v. Hisquierdo, 439 U.S. 572, 99 S. Ct. 802, 59 L. Ed. 2d 1 (1979).

[4]In re Marriage of Boyer, 538 N.W.2d 293 (Iowa 1995); Matter of Marriage of Brane, 21 Kan. App. 2d 778, 908 P.2d 625 (1995).

assessment."[5] The closer the parties are to retirement, the more likely it is that this issue will crop up.

§ 30:6 Disability pensions: Are they a marital asset?

Argument focuses on the income replacement versus retirement component. The issue of disability pensions is a confusing one in Ohio and nationally. For several years, courts relied on Footnote 3 in *Hoyt v. Hoyt*[1] which noted exceptions to the assumption that pension or retirement benefits earned during the marriage are marital.[2] In *Hoyt*, the footnote reads: "See exclusions to the general rule, such as (1) social security benefits, (2) disability retirement pay, and (3) railroad benefits." However, that broad rule has been dramatically refined by courts in the intervening decade. Now courts typically attempt to distinguish between the income replacement function of a disability pension and the retirement component of the pension. There are two unreported court of appeals cases: *Bauser v. Bauser*,[3] and *Okos v. Okos*.[4] *Okos* is very much a minority opinion of Ohio courts while *Bauser* is more in alignment with most Ohio and national case law. *Bauser* held that a Public Employees Retirement System of Ohio (PERS) disability retirement pension was not a marital asset because:

> the record contains no evidence demonstrating that any of the disability pension income that Mr. Bauser receives is paid in lieu of old-age retirement benefits or that the amount of old-age retirement benefits that he would otherwise be entitled to receive is diminished by the current payment of disability pension benefits.[5]

The court reiterated a distinction they made in *Elsass*[6] (explained later) that:

> disability pension benefits are not marital property unless they are accepted in lieu of old-age retirement pay, in which event they are marital property to the extent that the retirement pay is included in the disability pension benefit.[7]

In a warning to attorneys for nonparticipant spouses, the court noted:

---

[5]In re Marriage of Boyer, 538 N.W.2d 293, 296 (Iowa 1995).

[Section 30:6]
[1]Hoyt v. Hoyt, 53 Ohio St. 3d 177, 559 N.E.2d 1292 (1990).

[2]Parr v. Parr, No. 70300, unreported (Ohio Ct. App. 8th Dist. Cuyahoga County 3-06-97), where the court of appeals relied on the footnote in excluding the wife's disability pension as a marital asset.

[3]Bauser v. Bauser, 118 Ohio App. 3d 831, 694 N.E.2d 136 (2d Dist. Clark County 1997).

[4]Okos v. Okos, 137 Ohio App. 3d 563, 739 N.E.2d 368 (6th Dist. Lucas County 2000).

[5]Bauser v. Bauser, 118 Ohio App. 3d 831, 835, 694 N.E.2d 136 (2d Dist. Clark County 1997).

[6]Elsass v. Elsass, 1993 WL 541610 (Ohio Ct. App. 2d Dist. Greene County 1993).

[7]Bauser v. Bauser, 118 Ohio App. 3d 831, 694 N.E.2d 136 (2d Dist. Clark County 1997).

It was Mrs. Bauser's burden to prove the statutory exception for marital earnings in order to have the court classify some or all of Mr. Bauser's disability pension benefit as marital property.[8]

Must prove disability exchanged for retirement pension. The necessity for the non-participant spouse to prove that the disability benefits either eliminate or reduce voluntary or old age retirement benefits is also evidenced in *Criswell v. Criswell*.[9] In *Criswell* the court of appeals reversed and remanded the trial court's order, which held the husband in contempt for failing to pay his wife a share of the disability benefits that he received from General Motors. The court found that the wife failed to meet her burden of proof demonstrating that the retirement component of the disability pay.

In *Motter v. Motter*,[10] the court of appeals held that the trial court correctly classified the appellant's disability retirement benefits as marital property, where the appellant's retirement pay was completely absorbed by his decision to take the disability prior to becoming eligible for retirement. In other words, the court decided that one party should not be able to unilaterally surrender a marital asset and in doing so convert it into separate property. In *Fannin v. Fannin*,[11] the court of appeals found appellant's retirement benefits to be "essentially all retirement benefits" because they were soon to be normal retirement benefits as the trial court had correctly determined. *Potter v. Potter*[12] held that it was an abuse of discretion not to assign any value to the wife's PERS disability benefits. The court of appeals asserted that "the benefits certainly represent either a retirement benefit or a payment is lieu of old-age retirement pay as of [wife's] retirement date. As such, these benefits should be considered a marital asset to be given a value. . ."[13]

Disability is not a marital asset. In *Okos v. Okos*,[14] the court found that appellee's disability retirement payments were, in reality, a wage continuation necessitated by his physical condition which lead to a premature retirement. This finding was made despite the fact that the husband was eligible for a pension of exactly the same amount from the Ohio Police and Fire Pension Fund. The court of appeals upheld the trial court stating that there was ample evidence to decide that the plan participant's retirement payments were in reality a wage continuation, not a marital asset subject to division. However, other Ohio cases that

---

[8]Bauser v. Bauser, 118 Ohio App. 3d 831, 694 N.E.2d 136 (2d Dist. Clark County 1997).

[9]Criswell v. Criswell, Nos. 18101, 18111, unreported (Ohio Ct. App. 2d Dist. Montgomery County 9-22-00).

[10]Motter v. Motter, No. 16-99-14, unreported (Ohio Ct. App. 3d Dist. Wyandot County 7-27-00).

[11]Fannin v. Fannin, No. CA98-09-015, unreported (Ohio Ct. App. 12th Dist. Preble County 6-1-99).

[12]Potter v. Potter, No. O 1 CA0033, unreported (Ohio Ct. App. 9th Dist. Wayne County 11-14-01).

[13]Potter v. Potter, No. O 1 CA0033, unreported (Ohio Ct. App. 9th Dist. Wayne County 11-14-01).

[14]Okos v. Okos, 137 Ohio App. 3d 563, 739 N.E.2d 368 (6th Dist. Lucas County 2000).

have held that disability benefits are not a marital asset have normally not been that expansive. For example, in *Kimmey v. Kimmey*[15] the court of appeals reversed the trial court's decision which divided husband's Federal Employees Retirement System pension (FERS). This was another case of failing to obtain expert pension testimony. As in *Bauser*, the court of appeals did not rule that disability pensions could not be a marital asset, but that there was no evidence in the record indicating that the disability pension was paid in lieu of old age retirement benefits, or that the amount of the retirement pension was diminished by the receipt of disability benefits. Moreover, "where old age retirement benefits are impacted by the disbursement of current disability benefits, disability benefits are marital property only to the extent that such retirement pay value is included in the disability pension benefit."[16]

The majority viewpoint: distinguish disability from retirement. Another court of appeals case, *Koba v. Koba*,[17] dealt with the interpretation of a separation agreement which had not specifically mentioned a disability pension, which was in pay status at the time of the divorce. Interestingly, the agreement did mention the retirement pension that would start at age 60 and distinguished that pension from the disability pension. The section of the separation agreement dividing the retirement pension was untouched by the court. The court determined that a School Employees Retirement System (SERS) disability pension in pay status at the time of the divorce and which was not mentioned in the separation agreement was not overlooked in the agreement and was not a marital asset. The court examined a similar situation considered by the Second District Court of Appeals in *Elsass v. Elsass*.[18] In *Elsass* the court also distinguished between disability and old age pensions deciding that the disability retirement benefit was separate property because "disability benefits such as those received by appellee are a form of wage continuation designed to compensate the recipient for wages that he would otherwise receive but for the disability."[19] Several trial courts have agreed with this logic.[20]

The national perspective. Distinguishing between income replacement and the retirement component of a pension is also the prevailing case law nationally. However, the issue is not always that simple. In the *Equitable Distribution of Property* (2d Ed.) published in 1994 by

[15]Kimmey v. Kimmey, No. 1-01-68, unreported (Ct. App. 3d Dist. Allen County 10-31-01).

[16]See Carnifax v. Carnifax, No. 97-T-0189, unreported (Ct. App. 11th Dist. Trumbull County 5-14-00), where the court of appeals reversed the trial court because the wife had not met the burden to prove that the disability benefits were paid in lieu of old age benefits.

[17]Koba v. Koba, 1996 WL 732547 (Ohio Ct. App. 8th Dist. Cuyahoga County 1996).

[18]Elsass v. Elsass, 1993 WL 541610 (Ohio Ct. App. 2d Dist. Greene County 1993).

[19]Elsass v. Elsass, 1993 WL 541610, at *5 (Ohio Ct. App. 2d Dist. Greene County 1993). See also, Kutzke v. Kutzke, 1996 WL 173399 (Ohio Ct. App. 2d Dist. Greene County 1996).

[20]See, for example, Jones v. Jones, No. 95-DR-16592, unreported (Ohio Ct. App. 12th Dist. Warren County 3-1-95).

Shepard's/McGraw Hill at page 384, author Brett R. Turner suggests:

> The first step in classifying disability benefits is to determine whether they are really benefits awarded for disability. Most employees who receive disability benefits must give up all or part of their retirement benefits, and as a result many disability plans include elements of retirement pay. To the extent a particular benefit was acquired in compensation for prior service and not in compensation for a work-related injury, it will be treated as a retirement benefit even if it takes the form of disability pay.
>
> Separating retirement and disability pay is not always an easy process. If the owning spouse gave up certain specific retirement benefits in order to obtain disability benefits, the amount of the retirement benefit given up will be treated as if it still existed. The retirement benefit itself is not marital property, of course, but an equivalent amount of the disability plan was acquired in exchange for the retirement plan, and thus has the same classification. The excess of the disability pay over the former retirement pay will be treated as true disability pay, and divided under the principles set forth in this section.
>
> Where there was no formal exchange of retirement benefits for disability benefits, but the disability benefits are still based in part upon length of service, the court has discretion to treat some part of the disability pay as compensation for prior service. The rationale is that a given work related injury inflicts the same damage regardless of how long the employee has been with the employer. Thus, the actual compensation for the injury should be the same for all employees. If the compensation is greater for employees with more service, then the additional amount is not compensation for the injury, but rather compensation for the prior service. It is therefore more in the nature of retirement pay than disability pay.

What does the court need? The disability provisions of a defined benefit pension are specific to each plan. Some plans re-characterize the disability pension as a regular plan pension when the participant attains normal retirement age. Some plans provide payments for the participant's entire lifetime, while others may change once he or she reaches retirement age. To determine the marital portion of a disability pension, the court needs evidence on the following:

(1) the age and service requirements of disability pension compared to the age and service requirements of the retirement pension;

(2) the amount and duration of the disability payments; and

(3) whether future service is included in the formula the extent to which the disability pension is paid in lieu of retirement benefits.

Social security disability. Social Security Disability Benefits are far more difficult to receive than disability payments under the typical ERISA or government pension. The main distinction is that Social Security has a demanding final threshold question to qualify for benefits: Does the impairment prevent the individual from doing any other work?

Social Security disability is defined as the inability to engage in any substantial gainful activity by reason of any medically determinable physical or mental impairment which can be expected to result in death or which has lasted or can be expected to last for a continuous period of not less than 12 months. A person must be not only unable to do his/her previous work but cannot, considering, age, education, and work experience, engage in any other substantial work which exists in the national economy. It is immaterial whether such work exists in the immediate area, or whether a specific job vacancy exists, or whether the worker would be hired if he/she applied for work.

In insurance parlance, Social Security is an "AnyOc" definition while corporate and government disability pensions have different forms of "YourOc" definition.

Typical large corporate disability program. Typical large company disability programs include a stand-alone short and long-term plan which focuses on income replacement. However, once an employee has 15 years of service and suffers a disability, he or she may be able to retire immediately under their pension plan. Thus, a 37 year-old with the requisite 15 years of credited service may start his or her pension immediately rather than having to wait until reaching either 60 or 65. The pension is the greater of the regular pension reduced for early commencement, with various early retirement supplements added, or the guaranteed pension reduced by 2% a year if payments start before age 60. The disability pension, therefore, is a highly subsidized pension benefit that is greater than the regular pension benefit.GE is typical of a large company disability program. Part of their disability plan is a stand-alone short and long-term plan, which focuses on income replacement. However, once an employee has 15 years of service and suffers a disability, he or she may be able to retire immediately under their pension plan. Thus, a 37 year-old with the requisite 15 years of credited service may start his or her pension immediately rather than having to wait until reaching either 60 or 65. The pension is the greater of the regular pension reduced for early commencement, with various early retirement supplements added, or the guaranteed pension reduced by 2% a year if payments start before age 60. The disability pension, therefore, is a highly subsidized pension benefit that is greater than the regular pension benefit.

Sample of Large Corporate Disability Program*

Personal Illness Program

When Coverage Starts	Your Cost	When Benefits Begin	What You Receive	How Long Benefits Last
After 1 year of continuous Service.	Corporation pays full cost	On the date of your absence	Full pay	Up to 20 days in a 12-month period; additional days may be available subject to management approval

Short-Term Disability Income Plan

When Coverage Starts	Your Cost	When Benefits Begin	What You Receive	How Long Benefits Last
Automatically on your first day of work	Corporation pays full cost; except in some areas where you pay for coverage mandated by state law	In most cases, after you've received 20 days of pay from the Personal Illness Program	60% of your pay, up to $350 a week (for disabilities beginning on or after January 1, 1995)	As long as your disability continues; up to age 65 (or longer, depending when your disability begins)

Long-Term Disability Income Plan

When Coverage Starts	Your Cost	When Benefits Begin	What You Receive	How Long Benefits Last
On the date your enrollment is accepted	You pay the full cost	After you have been disabled for 26 weeks	Coverage of 50%, 60%, or 70% of your pay, based on your election, or the scheduled benefit, if greater	As long as your disability continues; up to 26 weeks

Disability Pension

When Coverage Starts	Your Cost	When Benefits Begin	What You Receive	How Long Benefits Last
You become eligible after 15 years of PQS; notify Human Resources if you need to apply	Paid through the corporation pension plan	Generally after STD benefits end, depending on your disability	Monthly disability pension benefits	As long as your disability continues

- *Depending on the nature of your disability, you may be eligible for benefits from other sources, such as Social Security and/or Workers' Compensation. You must meet the application plan definition of disability to be eligible for benefits from each plan.*

§ 30:7   Survivorship issues

Valuing survivorship in a pension: tale of the tail. Should survivorship "tails" be actuarially valued when dividing pensions and placed in the appropriate asset column? Under at least two circumstances, it may make sense. Incidentally, when we refer to the "tail" of a pension, we are talking about the survivor annuity payable to an eligible surviving spouse upon the death of the plan participant. In virtually all ERISA defined benefit pension plans, once a participant retires and elects a form of benefit option, such as a 50% joint and survivor annuity (50% J&S), the election is irrevocable.[1]

[Section 30:7]

[1]One rare exception exists: plans with "pop up" provisions where the death of the alternate payee or the divorce of the couple cause the benefit to return to a single life annuity.

Thus, the election is case in stone, even upon a subsequent divorce after retirement. Also keep in mind that there is a cost for electing survivorship for a second person. The maximum benefit is payable under a single life form and is reduced to extend survivorship for another individual to cover the statistical odds of paying out the benefits for a longer period of time. The reduction to the single life annuity increases, of course, with the size of the survivorship election, i.e. a 75% J&S election would cost 50% more than a 50% J&S election. In *Wylie v. Wylie,*[2] the Court of Appeals reversed the trial court for not valuing the wife's survivorship interest in her husband's pension. "[Wife] has been granted an undetermined amount of money that was not included in the property division," noted the court, which went on to say, "[T]he fact that no evidence concerning the value of the survivorship interest was submitted to the trial court does not detract from the necessity of valuation. When parties fail to submit appropriate evidence on an issue that must be determined, the trial court should direct them to do so."

"Excess" survivorship. "Excess" survivorship is a fairly common occurrence with pensions in pay status but infrequently valued. It occurs in marriages when the entire pension was not earned during the marriage, yet a 50% J&S (or greater!) election was made. It may also occur when the entire pension was earned during the marriage but a survivorship election greater than a 50% J&S is made. The concept of "excess" survivorship is predicated on the belief that a non-participant deserves survivorship on 50% of the pension *earned during the marriage.* Thus, an alternate payee under the QDRO has a right to a survivorship half the size of the coverture fraction (years in plan while married/years in plan at retirement). For example, if 20% of the pension was earned during the marriage, the non-participant has a right to a 10% J&S. If a 50% J&S election is extended to the non-participant, 80% of the value of the survivorship is "excess" (50% actual election - 10% "earned" survivor benefit during marriage = 40%/50% of the full value of the survivorship is "excess" =; 80% X value of full survivorship = value of "excess").

Even when the entire pension is earned during the marriage, "excess" survivorship can occur. Thus, a 75% J&S election in such a case would end up with 33% of the value of the entire survivorship ending up in the asset column of the non-participant (75% actual election - 50% earned survivor benefit during marriage = 25%/75% of the full value is "excess" = 33% X value of the full survivorship = value of "excess").

Age disparity survivorship. The second scenario is more complex but still commonplace. It occurs when:

(1) Each party has their own pension plan;
(2) There is a significant age difference; and
(3) One party is already retired (or near retirement) and has elected a joint and survivor annuity for the soon-to-be former spouse.

Let's look at an example. Bill retired last year at age 65 from ABC

---

[2]Wylie v. Wylie, 1996 WL 292044 (Ohio Ct. App. 4th Dist. Lawrence County 1996).

Company with an accrued pension of $2,400 per month payable on a life-only basis. However, because he was married when he retired, he elected the automatic 50% joint and survivor annuity, which pays him a reduced monthly pension for life in the amount of $1,920. Under this method of payment, should he predecease his wife, Mary, she will receive a survivor annuity for the remainder of her life in the amount of $960 per month. Because Mary was only 45 years-old when Bill retired last year, she could receive a survivor annuity for perhaps 26 years if the actuarial tables hold true.[3]

Now that Bill and Mary are divorcing, many attorneys contact the plan in order to have Bill's pension annuity "pop-up" to the larger single life annuity of $2,400 per month. But it's too late. Generally, under ERISA, once a participant retires, he can no longer change his elected form of benefit. Even absent a QDRO, Mary would still be entitled to receive the full survivor annuity upon Bill's death. Essentially, she has her own separate property interest in this survivorship "tail". Based upon an expert's calculations, the actuarial present value of Bill's monthly pension of $1,920 is $246,000, while the present value of Mary's potential 26-year survivor annuity is calculated to be $73,000. Assume further that Mary is covered by a state teacher's pension, with an accrued benefit of $1,800 at age 60, which has a present value of $140,000 at the time of divorce.

These pension assets should be analyzed as follows:

Present value of Bill's reduced lifetime annuity:	$246,000
Minus present value of Mary's survivorship tail:	$ 73,000
Minus present value of Mary's teacher's pension:	$140,000
Equals:	$ 33,000
Divided by two equals:	$16,500

Bill could write Mary a check for $16,500 immediately, and retain his entire pension. If you want to provide Mary with her equitable share of his pension plan through a QDRO, you must divide $16,500 by the total present value of his reduced pension benefit, or $246,000. Remember, we are only determining what percentage of his defined benefit pension plan should be payable to Mary while both parties are alive. Because Bill has already retired, it is too late to draft a "separate interest" QDRO which would provide Mary with an actuarially adjusted lifetime benefit. Rather, you must utilize the "shared" approach, whereby Mary will receive 6.7% of Bill's accrued monthly pension, as calculated below:

Mary's immediate equitable share of Bill's pension:	$16,500

---

[3]Bill is expected to live to approximately age 80 under the GAM-83 mortality table for healthy males, another 15 years, while Mary to live to age 86 under the female table, another 41 years. Thus, the 26 year tail (41 yrs. - 15 yrs. = 26 yr. "tail").

Divided by the present value of Bill's pension:	$246,000
Equals:	6.7%

Therefore, instead of preparing a QDRO that provides Mary with 50% of the marital portion of Bill's pension, the QDRO should provide her with 6.7% of his final pension.

This survivorship tail analysis is necessary because Bill is 20 years older than Mary and is unlikely to enjoy any of the fruits of her teacher's pension. Because Mary will enjoy both Bill's pension during his lifetime as well as 26 years more of survivorship benefits under his pension, it seems more reasonable to value her pension as well as the survivorship tail, and offset those against his pension.

§ 30:8 Are retirement health benefits marital property?

"Marital property" under the RC 3105.17.1(A)(3)(a)(ii) is "All interest that either or both of the spouses currently has in any real or personal property, including but not limited to, the *retirement benefits* of the spouses, and that was acquired by either or both of the spouses during the marriage." (emphasis added)

Retirement health care benefits, even those for "30 year-and-out" type retirees, have typically been ignored as marital property by Ohio courts despite the equitable distribution statute and huge potential lump sum values—values which may exceed $100,000. Even when considered, they have normally only been factored into spousal support and not into the property division. That may be changing as two unreported trial court decisions have now attached a lump sum value to retirement health benefits and offset them against other assets. More on those cases later.

Too large an asset to ignore? With yearly coverage costs that may exceed $6,000 and present values that routinely reach $50,000, retiree health care is too large an asset to ignore. The General Motors Health Insurance Plan, for example, pays some $6,092 a year in coverage pre-age 65 for retirees. In fact, ERISA retirement plans must actuarially value their promised retiree health care benefits just as they do their pensions under Standard No. 106 promulgated by the Fair Accounting Standards Board in 1990.

For a 50 year-old male GM retiree, the health care is worth $69,290 using the PBGC interest rates of March 2002.

"The New Equitable Distribution Frontier." Valuing health care is not new. In 1994, the *Family Law Quarterly* published "Division of Retiree Health Benefits on Divorce: The New Equitable Distribution Frontier." In the article, authors William R. Horbatt and Alan M. Grossman laid out compelling reasons for inclusion of health care in the marital estate. The crux of their argument was: Retiree health benefits are a form of deferred compensation, earned by the employed spouse during the course of the marriage. Intrinsically, they are no different from pensions and 401(k) savings plans.

Why has the lump sum value of health care been ignored? As the last eight years ticked by without a rush to health care judgments, five obstacles have emerged:

(1) Many attorneys are unfamiliar with the prodigious present values of the retirement health benefit.

(2) It appears a non-issue in most cases because both parties have, or are likely to have, health care as a result of their employment.

(3) Precious little winning case law exists even on the national level. Opponents seem to possess the upper hand when they point out that the contingent nature of a health care benefit renders it too speculative to value and offset against other "real" assets. Further, they argue that health care benefits are not explicitly guaranteed the same way that the PBGC guarantees ERISA-governed defined benefit pensions.

(4) Valuing health care appears more daunting than determining the present value of a pension where one need only obtain an accrued pension benefit and enter it on a software program or submit it to a number of present value services. Discovering the cost of retiree health care may challenge even the best attorney. Some companies and state plans will simply not share the information or claim they would if only they knew the cost. And even if the company is forthcoming with the benefit information, who will do the present value?

(5) Clients faced with slim prospects for success may be reluctant to pay for the necessary evaluation.

Two Ohio pro-health care cases. But the "New Frontier" may have arrived. Two Ohio cases have placed a present value on a plan participant's health care: *Becker v. Becker*,[4] and *Bradley v. Bradley*.[5] The courts recognized that the parties would be on an unequal footing if the health coverage was ignored, as well as the nature of health care as deferred wages similar to pensions. The *Becker* court explained, "[t]he plaintiff does not have any health insurance and will have to buy coverage in the market place or do without coverage. The medical insurance benefit which defendant receives through SERS is a valuable part of her retirement package."[6]

Anti-health care questions. As history has shown, winning the health care battle challenges even the best of attorneys. For example, if one is arguing for including the value of health care benefits, opposing counsel will likely ask questions similar to the following:

Q. Are health care costs increasing dramatically even in this pe-

---

[4]Becker v. Becker, No. 00-DR-0531, unreported (Ohio Ct. App. 9th Dist. Wayne County 9-21-01).

[5]Bradley v. Bradley, No. D-238058, unreported (Ohio Ct. App. 8th Dist. Cuyahoga County 12-13-99).

[6]Becker v. Becker, No. 00-DR-0531, unreported (Ohio Ct. App. 9th Dist. Wayne County 9-21-01); Bradley v. Bradley, No. D-238058, unreported (Ohio Ct. App. 8th Dist. Cuyahoga County 12-13-99).

riod of low inflation?

Q. Can you unequivocally guarantee that the health care benefits you talk about will be delivered?

Q. Do the lousy investment returns of the last several years have any impact on the funding of health care benefits?

Q. Isn't it a fair characterization to describe health care benefits as a "contingency?"

Q. Are the employees of LTV now receiving health care benefits?

Q. Is there a chance you might have been standing in court some years ago arguing for including the lump sum value of LTV health care coverage for retirees into the marital estate?

Q. Are you familiar with a company called Enron?

Q. How many Wall Street analysts saw the shifting sands beneath Enron two years ago?

Q. When benefits don't come from an actuarially funded, separate trust fund but instead flow from the company's general fund there is an additional level of risk isn't there?

Q. This risk doesn't exist with the pension does it?

Q. If an ERISA-governed company fails financially, who guarantees the pension?

Q. Does the Pension Benefit Guaranty Corporation guarantee retiree health care benefits?

Health care coverage is a "third rail" like Social Security. Health care coverage for state plans is much like Social Security: While it is not "guaranteed" it would start a political firestorm to eliminate it once people have grown dependent on it. In assessing whether state plan health care coverage will be around for the next 40 years, one must recognize that politicians view well-established retiree programs much like the subway's third rail: touch it and die.

Rising health care costs: proof of its value. Do rising health care costs make health care more speculative? Not at all. While the exact cost of the medical care is certainly speculative, the basic funding of the coverage is not. In fact, the rising costs point out how valuable the generous levels of coverage are. Keep in mind that the plans have actuarially funded "trend line" increases in the range of 3%. While expenses far in excess of that may not be covered, current levels of coverage with modest inflationary increases are anticipated and will be covered.

Method 1: valuing the actual costs of the health care coverage. Two methods exist for actuarially valuing health care benefits. As we explained earlier, the greatest challenge for the attorney is to obtain the monthly costs of the health care coverage. The first method is to value the actual cost of the coverage. This method was laid out in the 1994 Grossman and Horbatt article and requires an understanding court (and company). It examines the actual costs of the retiree health care coverage by reviewing the assumptions used in establishing the current company liability. A court order may be required to compel the company to divulge its projected health care costs. Companies may be reluctant to disclose such internal information on the grounds that it may be used by others in situations not nearly so benign.

Fortunately, this is not a problem with most state pensions and union-obtained coverage, and is, therefore, the most common method.

Additional costs might crop up with this method if a review of company records is necessary. Numerous assumptions must be employed by the evaluator, including the future growth rate for health care costs. Called the *trend line*, this assumption guesses at the unknowable by projecting past increases. Whether a company will continue to cover all increases or move toward cost-sharing is a legitimate objection to making robust growth assumptions in health care costs. Clearly, a modest cost-of-living increase may be borne by the company and should be included in valuing retiree health care benefits.

Method 2: valuing a replacement policy. The second method of valuing retiree health care benefits is similar to dealing with pensions and requires valuing the cost of replacement health insurance. The attorney wishing to value the health care benefits should simply obtain plan coverage information. That plan coverage should be submitted to a health care professional to determine the approximate current replacement costs. Much like a pension, the evaluator can then make modest cost-of-living assumptions as well as interest and mortality reductions. At times there may also have to be an assessment of the likelihood of continued employment under the plan.

The attorney's standard of care. Domestic relations attorneys must, at a minimum, examine the health care coverage of the parties in a divorce. At the very least both parties should sign authorizations and all employers should be contacted to see if retiree health care coverage is offered as well as the qualifying thresholds. If the plan is not forthcoming or does not wish to reveal monthly costs, it may be necessary to obtain a court order that asks for the following:

(1) All health care booklets, pamphlets or brochures furnished to employees as well as copies of the medical plans themselves; and

(2) Copies of financial reports related to health care costs and valuations made pursuant to FASB Standard No. 106.

§ 30:9 Overlooked retirement benefits

In Ohio, the failure to value and divide retirement benefits appears to allow a reopening of the case at any reasonable point after the omission is discovered. In *Bisker v. Bisker*,[1] the Ohio Supreme Court faced a situation where a couple was first married in 1959, divorced in 1983, and remarried two months later. At the time of the first divorce, the trial court merely noted that the parties had agreed to a division of assets yet

---

[Section 30:9]

[1]Bisker v. Bisker, 1994 -Ohio- 307, 69 Ohio St. 3d 608, 635 N.E.2d 308 (1994).

never enumerated those assets. The Chrysler pension was never mentioned. At the second entry of divorce, the antenuptial agreement was ruled invalid and the court divided the marital property. Again, the Chrysler pension was not assigned a value or even mentioned.

The Supreme Court, in reversing the court of appeals noted that the pension "*issue remained unsettled at the time of the second divorce* and again was not addressed. Instead of rectifying an earlier omission, the trial court compounded it."[2]

The failure to address the retirement benefits may start with the separation agreement. One court of appeals held that the separation agreement must list all substantial assets so that the parties can make an informed and deliberate agreement.[3] Failure to enumerate the retirement benefits renders the decree voidable, and the decree can be vacated by motion for relief under Civ. R. 60(B)(5). It is important to note that the catch-all clause (5) of "any other reason justifying relief from judgment" is *not* subject to the one year limitation as are the first three clauses of 60(B).

In *Gearhart v. Gearhart*, the Second District Court of Appeals held that a trial court did not err in granting wife's Civ. R. 60(B) motion when she received substantially less of husband's retirement benefits than contemplated by the parties. Husband's early retirement and the employers interpretation of the qualified domestic relations order resulted in an inequitable division of the asset.[4] Civil Rule 60(B) motions have been denied when brought to set aside property divisions which did not address pension benefits. Two Stark County cases held that the motions were not timely brought and that evidentiary hearings were not required.[5]

§ 30:10 Types of plans—The "defined contribution" plan

From a QDRO or plan valuation perspective, a defined contribution plan is the simpler of the two types of plans, and is usually referred to as an individual account plan. That is, separate accounts are established and maintained on behalf of each plan participant. The most popular defined contributions plans are 401(k) plans, profit-sharing plans, employee stock ownership plans (ESOPs), savings plans, and thrift savings plans. While there are exceptions, a defined contribution plan can usually be identified by its name, such as the ABC Company Retirement Savings Plan, or the ABC Company 401(k) Plan. Generally, the word "pension" does not appear in the official name of the plan.

A defined contribution plan can often contain several different ac-

---

[2]Bisker v. Bisker, 1994 -Ohio- 307, 69 Ohio St. 3d 608, 609, 635 N.E.2d 308 (1994) (emphasis added).

[3]In re Murphy, 10 Ohio App. 3d 134, 461 N.E.2d 910 (1st Dist. Hamilton County 1983).

[4]Gearhart v. Gearhart, 23 Employee Benefits Cas. (BNA) 2256, 1999 WL 1043894 (Ohio Ct. App. 2d Dist. Montgomery County 1999).

[5]See Fronimo v. Fronimo, 2001 WL 91731 (Ohio Ct. App. 5th Dist. Stark County 2001); Harris v. Harris, 2001 WL 109128 (Ohio Ct. App. 5th Dist. Stark County 2001).

counts and/or investment funds for each plan participant. Therefore, when referring to a participant's defined contribution plan under a separation agreement, you should always refer to the participant's "total account balance under all of the accounts and/or subaccounts maintained on his or her behalf under the plan."

Many defined contribution plans offer employees the choice to contribute either on a pre-tax or on an after-tax basis, or both. It is, therefore, important to include language when dividing benefits under a defined contribution plan regarding the allocation of benefits to the nonparticipant spouse. For example, it may not be in the best interests of the nonparticipant spouse to receive her equitable dollar interest in the benefit solely from the pre-tax portion of the plan. It is common (and equitable) to use language that provides the alternate payee with a "pro-rata" share of the benefits from each account and/or investment fund maintained on behalf of the participant.

It is also important to remember that a participant's benefits under a defined contribution plan are usually made up of his or her own contributions to the plan as well as matching employer contributions. A participant is always 100% vested in his or her own employee contributions. However, the plan may include a *vesting schedule* with respect to the employer contributions. For example, a participant may become vested in the employer contributions after satisfying a stated number of years of service with the company. While multi-employer plans may have a vesting schedule as long as 10 years, most ERISA plans have a five- to seven-year vesting period. The word "vesting" refers to the nonforfeitability of the participant's right to receive the benefits. Once vested, he or she has earned a nonforfeitable right to receive such vested benefits even if he or she is terminated from the company prior to retirement.

At any point in time, it is relatively easy to determine the value of a participant's benefits under a defined contribution plan. Often referred to as a "what you see is what you get" type of plan, one can merely look at the participant's total account balance under the plan as of a specified date to determine its value.

◆ **Practice Tips:** One word of caution, however. If you represent a nonparticipant spouse whose divorce is final on November 1, 1997, for example, be careful not to simply include language in the separation agreement that provides the alternate payee with 50% of the total account balance as of November 1, 1997. For tax purposes, many companies do not make their contributions to the plan until sometime during the next plan year. It may not be until April 1998, before the company makes its contributions to the accounts of participants for the 1997 plan year. As a result, in this example, the participant's total account balance on November 1, 1997 would not include benefits that have been accrued or earned previously to that date and the alternate payee would not share in almost a year's worth of benefits leading up to the date of divorce.

You should therefore include language in your separation agreement that provides the alternate payee a pro-rata share of any contributions made after November 1, 1997, that are attributable to periods before November 1, 1997.

One of the features of a defined contribution plan that facilitates settlement is the fact that a participant can generally receive his or her distributions under the plan in the form of a single lump-sum distribution. These are relatively easy benefits to divide during a divorce. The nonparticipant spouse can be assigned his or her equitable share of the total account balance plus any gains or losses associated with his or her share of the benefits until the date of distribution. Because it is pursuant to a property settlement, there is no 10% early withdrawal penalty that is associated with retirement plans that are used before age 59 and a half. Immediate income taxes, though, remain a tax obligation if the distribution is not rolled into an IRA by the recipient. Remember, though, not all defined contribution plans will provide alternate payees with immediate distributions upon approval of the QDRO.

Most plan administrators prefer to avoid the costly burden of maintaining records on alternate payees for ten or twenty years following the date of divorce. They are permitted, depending on the terms of the plan, to allow alternate payees to receive immediate distributions upon approval of the QDRO even though the participant is not yet eligible to receive a distribution.

Be careful. Before telling your client that they can receive the funds immediately upon approval of the QDRO, check with the plan administrator.

§ 30:11 Types of plans—The "defined benefit" plan

A defined benefit pension plan is the second type of ERISA-governed pension plan. From a family law attorney's perspective, this type of plan is much more difficult to deal with, both from a QDRO and a valuation standpoint. A defined benefit pension plan is just that—a plan whereby the participant's benefit is *defined* by a plan formula that provides for the payment of a monthly pension check for life upon the participant's retirement. Keep in mind that while the benefit is defined as a stream of income, a lump-sum payment may be available in lieu of the payments, just as a defined contribution plan may allow the account balance to be annuitized—that is turned into a pension upon retirement.

Generally, there are no separate accounts established for participants under a defined benefit pension plan. Further, there are no interest or investment earnings attributable to any participant accounts. In essence, the plan makes a contractual promise to pay a plan participant a pension for life in accordance with the terms of the pension plan formula. The plan benefits are aggregately funded on an actuarial basis that incorporates many assumptions, including mortality and interest rate factors.

A defined benefit pension plan usually presents the most difficult asset to value and split. It is uncommon for a plan participant to be able to readily explain the extent of their benefits and even more uncommon for a nonparticipant to be able to detail the plan's entitlements. Unlike a defined contribution plan, they do not receive annual statements regarding the amount or value of their benefits accrued under the plan. Generally, all they know is that if they work a certain number of years, and then retire at a certain age, they can receive a pension for the rest of their lives. They are often unfamiliar with the plan's specific formula for calculating the accrued benefit. And they are also not aware of the plan's provisions for calculating early retirement subsidies, vesting, and joint and survivorship annuities.

§ 30:12   Types of plans—Distinction between service pension and deferred vested pension

Defined benefit plans must be carefully reviewed. Especially critical to the attorney for the nonparticipant spouse is a thorough understanding of the difference in the entitlements of the participant who retires from active service and begins receiving benefits immediately, versus the benefit available on a deferred basis when retirement begins at a later time. *Always obtain a summary plan description and review the early retirement section of the plan!*

It is common that a plan administrator's calculation of pension present values is based on the assumption that the plan participant will terminate employment contemporaneous with the divorce but will not begin to receive the accrued benefits until a later date. However, the value of this "Deferred Vested Pension" may vary significantly from a "Service Pension," in which the participant begins to receive benefits from active employment and begins to receive benefits immediately without any deferral period.

Many plans have special thresholds which allow immediate retirement far before the normal retirement age. Sometimes special supplements are added to the basic pension. United Auto Worker pensions with the major car manufacturers stand out as one of the most common examples. A participant with 30 years of work is eligible for an immediate unreduced monthly pension of approximately $1,200, along with a significant supplement of over $900 each month until age 62 when social security benefits begin.

However, the typical plan response to a letter of discovery only lists the benefit the participant has earned at the time of the normal retirement age of 65. A worker, therefore, with 28 years of service might be described in the plan response as having only a deferred vested pension of some $1,120 payable at age 65. However, within two years, the participant could retire with a service pension of $2,295 a month until age 62, when the benefit would drop to $1,200.

Clearly, the present value of this "Service Pension" is far greater than the present value of the "Deferred Vested Pension" because the basic pension is received sooner and over a longer period of time. In addition, there is a significant supplement which is not valued in the "Deferred Vested Pension." For a 48-year-old worker with 28 years of credited UAW service, the present value of the pension would increase five-fold. While the nonparticipant may not receive a present value based on the future service,[1] it is likely that the nonparticipant spouse could obtain a QDRO giving him or her a proportionate share of the pension when it is received.

§ 30:13   Valuing pension plans—Defined contribution plans

The value of a defined contribution plan is the account balance at any given moment in time. The only common valuation problem centers on determining the amount subject to equitable distribution if the participant was in the plan prior to the marriage. In that case, it is important for the participant to detail the passive growth on the nonmarital component.[1] This is typically done by obtaining at least every annual statement during the marriage. First, the value of the account at the time of the marriage (or interpolated from the statement date closest to the marriage) must be established. Next, the growth attributable to the premarital account balance must be calculated by determining growth rates. If the plan does not provide growth rates, the annual statement is used to determine a growth rate for that year. Finally, the premarital account balance and its passive growth are subtracted from the current account balance to determine the marital part of the defined contribution plan.

Warning: Because of changes in administrators or record keepers, or the expenses associated with dredging through archives of microfiche, annual (sometimes quarterly or semi-annual) statements can be extremely difficult if not impossible to obtain from plans.

As with other assets, if the nonparticipant can indicate that the growth of the marital asset is not passive in nature but the result of marital labors, then it is possible that the entire plan account, with the exception of the premarital account balance, would be judged to be marital. None of the growth may be considered to be separate property.

Determining the difference between passive and active management of a defined contribution plan is problematic at best. How active is "active"? Does the mere act of changing investment options after the marriage render the investment gains as totally marital property? Is the court to consider the potentially significant growth in the premarital component of a defined contribution plan to be totally marital property if the participant spends less time on making the choices than he or she did with the morning sports page? Compounding the complexity of this issue are the well researched tenets of modern portfolio theory which demonstrate that active money management is less efficient than diversified "buy-and-hold" strategies. If index funds and dart board throwers are more productive money management systems than active money

---

[Section 30:12]
    [1]Potts v. Potts, 1994 WL 693527 (Ohio Ct. App. 8th Dist. Cuyahoga County 1994).

[Section 30:13]
    [1]Mitchell v. Mitchell, 1998 WL 225043 (Ohio Ct. App. 9th Dist. Summit County 1998) (a trial court errs when it divides husband's pension and does not exclude the portion of that pension as separate property that was accumulated between the parties' two marriages).

management, should plan participants who make investment changes suffer a double injury? Besides suffering from lower than average returns should they also have all growth on their nonmarital asset characterized as marital property?

§ 30:14 Valuing pension plans—Defined benefit plans—In general

Present values are snapshots frozen in time. Reducing a stream of income to a current lump-sum value depends on two variables: the length of the payments and the assumed interest discounting rate. With defined benefit pension plans that offer monthly payments for life, the number of payments depends on the mortality table that is employed. Because only slight changes in interest rates can have significant impact on the present value, interest rates have been a central issue in many present value battles. This also explains the volatility of present value calculations. As bond yields change, so do present values.

The mortality table valuation issue is straightforward: the more payments the recipient is likely to receive, the greater the present value. Interest rates, however, have an inverse relationship to the present value, i.e., the higher the interest discounting factor, the lower the present value. Conversely, if the pension payments are discounted ("uncompounded") by a lower interest rate, a larger lump sum must be invested at the present time to insure the benefit.

Determining which mortality tables and interest rates to use in the present value calculation depends on one's definition of what a present value should measure. That definition will then circumscribe the present value calculation method and resulting present value. Typically, Ohio and other state courts have found that the fair market value of a pension is best measured by the cost of a replacement vehicle in the financial market. Because the only financial vehicle that offers a lifetime of income from the liquidation of principal and income is an insurance annuity, the use of the insurance annuity definition has emerged as the dominant definition of present value for pensions.[1] The value of a pension under the annuity definition must correspond, therefore, to the actual cost of a replacement annuity in the marketplace. This is a decidedly non-speculative exercise because the annuity marketplace can be surveyed to find the range of possible present values.

If one adopts a different definition, the result could vary dramatically from the answer obtained from annuity quotes. For example, using the fixed life expectancies of the U.S. Bureau of Health Statistics Mortality table in the Revised Code would significantly understate the value of commercially obtained annuities.

Use of the new "GATT Method" promulgated by the Retirement

[Section 30:14]

[1]Conant v. Conant, 1994 WL 122193 (Ohio Ct. App. 9th Dist. Summit County 1994).

Protection Act[2] also significantly understates the annuity replacement value of a pension for younger plan participants. The GATT Method is a simplified present value system which is now being used by companies to determine lump-sum payments which a participant may elect to receive in lieu of the pension. The GATT Method does approximate current annuity plan costs for participants near retirement.

Almost invariably, the services and experts who use the annuity definition for pension present values use what is known as the "PBGC Method." PBGC stands for the Pension Benefit Guaranty Corporation which is directed by the secretaries of labor, treasury, and commerce. The PBGC was established by the Employee Retirement Income Security Act (ERISA) to safeguard the pensions of American workers by carefully delineating participant rights including vesting and providing for adequate funding on an ongoing basis for those entitlements.[3] ERISA standardized plan funding requirements around the annuity concept. If a company fell into bankruptcy and the PBGC had to insure the pension payments, the cost of that liability could be measured by subtracting the plan's current assets from the cost of buying replacement annuities in the insurance market.

To aid in determining adequate funding, the PBGC has a quarterly survey of insurance companies that write annuities conducted to determine current market interest rates. These rates are fine tuned on a monthly basis and, in conjunction with the mortality tables used by the PBGC, enable experts and services across the country to calculate present values with precision and consistency.

While widely employed across the country because of its objectivity and its ability to reflect annuity company prices, the PBGC system is not without problems. Two major concerns are possible inconsistencies with current interest rates, and an inability to accurately reflect the value of an annuity for an individual with a health problem. While it does depend on actuarial statistics and does reflect the interest yield curve on bonds, it can sometime lag behind changes in the interest rate marketplace. For example, if the Federal Reserve were to change interest rates late in the month, the rates employed by the PBGC for the next month and a half might be out of sync with the annuity marketplace because the PBGC announces rates for the coming month on the 15th of the preceding month.

The PBGC employs only three gender specific mortality tables: Healthy, Disabled Not Receiving Social Security Disability Payments, and Disabled Receiving Social Security Disability Payments. For any given individual with health problems, the present value determined under the various mortality tables may bear little relationship to the actual value of the benefits the specific individual might receive.

---

[2]Pub. L. No. 103-465, 108 Stat. 4809 (part of General Agreement on Tariffs and Trade legislation).

[3]ERISA, Pub. L. No. 93-406, 88 Stat. 829 1 et seq., codified at 29 U.S.C.A. §§ 1001 et seq. (1974).

§ 30:15 Valuing pension plans —Defined benefit plans—Pitfalls

Defined benefit plans are fickle, dangerously changing creatures that can bite even the most experienced practitioners. Every defined benefit plan must be scrutinized for early retirement options as well as possible supplements and subsidies. In order to do that, a summary plan description (SPD) is essential. A benefit statement from the plan does not provide the longitudinal view of the plan that is essential. It infrequently reveals when a pension threshold is about to occur that would cause the present value of the plan to jump five- and six-fold in value—sometimes in just weeks.

An example from an Ameritech Non-Management Pension will illustrate what the practitioner must watch for. In this case, it was a pension plan that doubled in three months and increased four-fold in two and a half years after the divorce was started. In October 1995, a 49.8-year-old Ameritech plan participant initiated divorce proceedings against his spouse. His attorney furnished opposing counsel with a statement indicating that the worker had earned an age 65 monthly benefit of $1,317 for his 27 years and six months of service. The immediate lump sum that the plan would currently offer in lieu of the pension was $66,198, and was clearly indicated on a pension calculation printout from the plan. The nonparticipant's share was $33,099 (half of $66,198).

The proceedings slowed because of other issues. Then came the initial red flag for the attorney for the nonparticipant. The attorney requested and received another statement from the plan that showed the lump sum offered by the plan increased to $113,091 a scant three months later. Clearly, his client could have received $23,447 less if an agreement had been reached three months earlier.

Upon studying the plan, the attorney unraveled the mystery. The Ameritech Non-Management plan assumes a normal retirement age of 65. If a 49-year-old writes to the plan for an accrued pension statement, the plan will indicate the size of the age 65 benefit—in this case $1,317 a month—and also indicate that if the pension started immediately the pension would only be $303 a month for life. However, age 50 is one of those magic thresholds. As soon as the participant reaches age 50 and has 25 years of credited service, they can retire with a service pension rather than a deferred vested pension. The pension will then be actuarially adjusted from an age 55 retirement because the participant has less than 30 years of credited service.

When the plan participant reached the required age of 50 or more, and the number of required years of service of 30, all actuarial reductions to the service pension disappeared. In other words, in February 1998 the Ameritech pension ratcheted up to $238,932 in value when the worker had 30 years of credited service. The nonparticipant could easily have lost some $86,367 in the property settlement without careful analysis of the plan by her attorney.

The example is not an esoteric one. It is common for companies to offer 30-year-and-out incentives encouraging early retirement by plan participants. They are especially common in the utility, auto, manufacturing, and trucking industries.

Also keep in mind that a qualified domestic relations order can not access the early retirement subsidies for an alternate payee if the plan participant does not actually retire. The participant must retire before the subsidies come into play. Otherwise, the alternate payee will only receive the actuarially adjusted pension discounted from the normal retirement age.

The rising standard of care in present values requires that attorneys know the value of the current accrued deferred pension as well as the potential increases possible with a service pension. This information will allow the parties to make informed decisions regarding present values and deferred distributions with a QDRO.

§30:16 Discovery of retirement benefits

Obtaining the summary plan description (SPD) should always be the first course of business. Following that, an attorney should obtain the accrued benefit information from the plan for defined benefit plans, and the account balances for defined contribution plans. In addition, information about possible service pensions should be requested in the letter as well as any possible enhancements to the plan that are being contemplated. Under ERISA, a plan participant has the right to this information as least once a year without charge.

When the other side will not provide a signed authorization, the plan should be named as a party to the action and a subpoena duces tecum issued for the same information. Be wary of the paternalistic attitude of many smaller plans towards their participants. While outright deception is uncommon, less than forthright answers are not.

Because many workers, especially electricians and plumbers, may be covered by various local and national defined benefit and defined contribution plans, always have a disclosure statement signed by the worker detailing all retirement entitlements, or conduct a deposition to obtain the worker's sworn testimony if the case does not come to trial. It is very easy to miss a pension plan with workers in the building trades. These statements should allow the case to be reopened at any future date when a missed pension asset is discovered.

§30:17 Electing present value or QDRO

Advising a client about the advantages and disadvantages of accepting assets to offset the present value as represented versus accepting a deferred distribution of the pension by drafting a QDRO should be done cautiously—if at all—by an attorney. A simple exercise it is not. It is best to present the possible values and options to the client and have the client make the choice.

The general advice offered by attorneys for plan participants early in their working careers is to "cash out" the nonparticipant to preclude them from sharing in future enhancements to the plan. This is only true if the participant believes he or she will continue working under the plan. The attorney for the nonparticipant will typically work to gain a higher "cash out" offer than that based on the employee's immediate termination of employment, or opt for a QDRO.

Aggressive advocacy by the attorney for one position over the other, or an inflexible "I always get the cash" or "I always draft a QDRO" should be avoided. Client choices that seem unreasonable should be covered with a disclaimer letter to the client and maintained in the file along with their signed response.

The strengths of using present values instead of a QDRO when dividing a defined benefit plan are:

(1) Parties disentangle their economic affairs.

(2) Nonparticipant builds an estate. Remember that few plans allow an alternate payee to name another individual, and certainly not their estate, for a continuation of their benefits if they die before the participant.

(3) Intelligent investing of the lump sum may exceed the value of the QDRO.

Point three should be carefully reviewed. Because a present value is based on an assumed interest rate (as of October 1997, 6.3% for the next 25 years and 5.0% for all years thereafter), any investment performance which "beats" that rate will result in a larger pension for the alternate payee. While beating PBGC interest rates may seem simple in light of the robust stock market for the last several decades, it is by no means guaranteed.

Conversely, keep in mind that a "Coverture" QDRO which splits a pension based on final average salary or a benefit multiplier will allow the alternate payee's share to grow over time.[1] In other words, a worker's continued participation in the pension plan will typically recast the value of the entire pension, including the marital portion, because the salary increases with inflation or the plan increases the monthly amount of the pension for each year of service. Remember that in 1980, a UAW pension offered participants $15 a month at retirement for each year of service. That rate has now increased to $40 for current plan participants.

The strengths of using a QDRO are:

(1) Nonparticipant will (with proper survivorship wording) obtain a lifetime of income.

(2) Coverture QDRO will allow for significant growth in the pension.

(3) Expensive battles over the pension's present value may be avoided. This is especially true with plans offering early retirement options.

(4) Both parties share the risks associated with the pension while also sharing in all other tangible assets.

A trial court may order a QDRO to divide husband's pension even though there are sufficient assets to accomplish an immediate offset of

---

[Section 30:17]
[1]See § 30:24, Drafting the QDRO—Defined benefit plans—The "coverture approach."

wife's interest in a pension.[2] When the terms of the QDRO are contested, it is error for a trial court to accept a QDRO submitted by one party as its order without allowing both parties an opportunity to be heard.[3]

Trial court did not err in ordering husband to pay wife one-half of his pension benefits in monthly installments for her life, even though such payments might exceed one-half of the present dollar value.[4] A QDRO was appropriately modified to include survivorship rights where those rights had been part of the calculation in arriving at each party's share of the marital estate. The modification reflected the original intent of the parties.[5]

A QDRO must conform to the language of the separation providing for it. Where the parties agreed that wife would receive 50% of the marital portion of husband's defined benefit plan, a QDRO providing that wife's benefit would be "equal to the actuarial equivalent of Fifty Percent (50%) of the Marital Portion of the Participant's Accrued Benefit" was appropriate. The actual amount of wife's portion could only be determined when husband retired.[6]

§ 30:18 QDRO requirements under I.R.C. 414(p)

Section 414(p) of the Internal Revenue Code contains the criteria necessary for qualified domestic relations orders. Rather than reciting all of the qualification requirements for QDROs in piecemeal fashion verbatim, section 414(p) in its entirety is set forth in the Appendix to Ch 30 for the reader's review. We will focus our attention on some QDRO drafting tips and horror stories to assist you in your representation of the nonparticipant spouse. Remember, the federal pension law, ERISA, has many built-in protections designed for the plan participant. But only a good QDRO will help protect and secure the alternate payee's entitlement to his or her equitable share of the benefit.

In *Egelhoff v. Egelhoff ex rel. Breiner*,[1] the U.S. Supreme Court held that ERISA, under 29 U.S.C.A. § 1144(a), preempts state laws which provide for automatic revocation of beneficiary designations on non-probate assets such as retirement plans and insurance policies. Ohio's statute, RC 1139.63, provides that unless a decree of divorce or dissolution or annulment provides otherwise, the designation of a beneficiary under a life insurance policy, annuity, individual retirement plan, employee death benefit plan, or any other contract providing for a death

---

[2]Haynes v. Haynes, 1998 WL 114424 (Ohio Ct. App. 9th Dist. Summit County 1998).

[3]McGeorge v. McGeorge, 2001 WL 537037 (Ohio Ct. App. 10th Dist. Franklin County 2001).

[4]Perorazio v. Perorazio, 1999 WL 159218 (Ohio Ct. App. 7th Dist. Columbiana County 1999).

[5]Gordon v. Gordon, 144 Ohio App. 3d 21, 759 N.E.2d 431 (8th Dist. Cuyahoga County 2001).

[6]Ferris v. Ferris, 2001 WL 194779 (Ohio Ct. App. 5th Dist. Fairfield County 2001).

[Section 30:18]

[1]Egelhoff v. Egelhoff ex rel. Breiner, 532 U.S. 141, 121 S. Ct. 1322, 149 L. Ed. 2d 264 (2001).

benefit is deemed revoked as a result of the divorce, dissolution of marriage or annulment. RC 1339.63 can no longer be relied upon when dealing with ERISA plans.

An antenuptial agreement is not a sufficient waiver of a spouse's rights under an ERISA retirement plan. An antenuptial agreement does not meet the requirements of ERISA for a waiver of a spouse's rights. The court in *Bowman v. Bowman*[2] noted that ERISA preempts state law. An antenuptial agreement is not a waiver by a spouse, but rather by a spouse-to-be.

§ 30:19   The separation agreement—In general

Ideally, your QDRO should be drafted concurrently with the separation agreement and then incorporated by reference into the agreement. In reality though, it seems that very few family law attorneys draft the QDRO at the same time as the separation agreement. This can lead to considerable problems for you and the nonparticipant spouse. If you do not draft the QDRO right away, be sure that your separation agreement contains specific language regarding the division of the pension and/or savings plan benefits. A simple sentence such as "Wife will get one-half of the pension, QDRO shall issue." is not good enough. Your separation agreement should include specific language depending on the type of plan involved.

The Eleventh District Court of Appeals held that a trial court did not err in awarding a wife a share of the lump sum payment received by the husband when he elected early retirement. The parties entered into a separation agreement which provided that wife would receive a share of the "ultimate value" of husband's retirement benefits. The trial court properly interpreted that this encompassed special early retirement payment and was not limited to what husband would have received at normal retirement age.[1]

A trial court may interpret ambiguity in a separation agreement which gives rise to a QDRO. In *McKinney v. McKinney*,[2] the trial court interpreted the term "present value" as permitting the "coverture formula" to be applied when the plan participant retired rather than at the termination of the marriage.

Wife's award of 50% of funds paid to husband from his retirement plan was interpreted by the trial court and affirmed by the court of appeals as including early retirement benefits.[3]

An agreement which provided that wife would receive 36% of

---

[2]Bowman v. Bowman, 2001 WL 28663 (Ohio Ct. App. 2d Dist. Montgomery County 2001), dismissed, appeal not allowed, 91 Ohio St. 3d 1524, 747 N.E.2d 250 (2001).

[Section 30:19]

[1]Kincaid v. Kincaid, 117 Ohio App. 3d 148, 690 N.E.2d 47 (11th Dist. Ashtabula County 1997).

[2]McKinney v. McKinney, 142 Ohio App. 3d 604, 756 N.E.2d 694 (2d Dist. Montgomery County 2001).

[3]Peters v. Peters, 2001 WL 173214 (Ohio Ct. App. 2d Dist. Montgomery County 2001).

husband's retirement benefits, accrued as of the date of final hearing, was also deemed to include early retirement benefits.[4]

An award of a stated dollar amount of a plan participant's pension without provision for growth or interest is not ambiguous. In *Thomas v. Thomas*,[5] the trial court erred when it adopted a QDRO that provided for interest on the alternative payee's portion when none was provided for in the entry.

An alternate payee was, however, held to be entitled to interest on her share of the retirement funds when the distribution to her was delayed because of a dispute as to how her share was to be calculated.[6]

§ 30:20 The separation agreement—Checklist for defined contribution plans

- The specific percentage or dollar amount payable to the alternate payee
- The effective date of assignment
- A statement regarding the allocation of benefits among the various accounts maintained on behalf of the participant
- Gains/losses to be applied to alternate payee's share of the benefits for periods subsequent to the effective date of assignment until the date of distribution
- A statement that contributions made to the plan after the effective date of assignment, but that are attributable to periods before such date, should be incorporated into calculation of alternate payee's share of the benefits
- Effect of previous loans taken by participant, if any
- Survivorship protection for the alternate payee in the event of the death of the participant
- Provision for benefits to beneficiary of alternate payee in the event of his or her death before receipt of benefits
- Continued jurisdiction
- Constructive receipt language in the event the plan administrator inadvertently pays benefits to participant rather than alternate payee
- Anticircumvention language preventing participant from taking any actions to the detriment of the alternate payee

§ 30:21 The separation agreement—Checklist for defined benefit pension plans

- Specific formula or dollar amount of accrued benefit to be payable

---

[4]Reed v. Reed, 2001 WL 127873 (Ohio Ct. App. 2d Dist. Greene County 2001).

[5]Thomas v. Thomas, 26 Employee Benefits Cas. (BNA) 1081, 2001 WL 422967 (Ohio Ct. App. 10th Dist. Franklin County 2001).

[6]Mattice v. Mattice, 2001 WL 726780 (Ohio Ct. App. 2d Dist. Montgomery County 2001).

to alternate payee (coverture formula recommended)
- Whose life expectancy the benefits are to be payable over (i.e., alternate payee's or participant's)
- Pre-retirement survivorship protection for the alternate payee in the event of the death of the participant before retirement
- Post-retirement survivorship protection for the alternate payee in the event the QDRO utilizes the participant's life expectancy for payment of benefits to the alternate payee
- Early retirement subsidy benefits for the alternate payee
- Post-retirement cost-of-living adjustments for the alternate payee
- Continued jurisdiction
- Constructive receipt language in the event the plan administrator inadvertently pays benefits to participant rather than alternate payee
- Anticircumvention language preventing participant from taking any actions to the detriment of the alternate payee

§ 30:22   Drafting the QDRO—Defined contribution plans

When drafting a QDRO for a defined contribution plan, you should refer to the participant's "total account balance" rather than his or her accrued benefit. Additionally, you should include an effective date of assignment and an affirmative statement providing the alternate payee with any gains or losses associated with his or her share of the benefits from the effective date of assignment to the date of distribution. If you fail to include the proper investment growth or appreciation language, the plan administrator may interpret the alternate payee's share of the benefits to be *frozen* as of the assignment date.

For example, if the QDRO states that the alternate payee is assigned the amount of $10,000 from the participant's 401(k) plan, the plan administrator may simply distribute $10,000 to the alternate payee even though the parties divorced in 1992. Further, if the plan does not permit alternate payees to receive immediate distributions upon approval of the QDRO, the alternate payee may have to wait ten or twenty years before receiving the $10,000. Without an effective date of assignment and growth language included in the QDRO, the alternate payee could miss out on twenty years of growth on his or her assigned share of the benefits.

Many attorneys automatically include language in a QDRO for a defined contribution plan that permits the alternate payee to receive his or her distribution on or after the participant's earliest retirement age under the plan. While this language is necessary for a defined benefit pension plan, you should include language in your defined contribution plan QDRO that also permits the alternate payee to receive benefits *as soon as administratively feasible following the date the QDRO is approved by the plan administrator*, or upon the date that the participant is first eligible to receive benefits, if later. In this manner, the alternate payee will be entitled to an immediate distribution should the company permit this.

Under most defined contribution plans, an alternate payee may designate a beneficiary to receive his or her share of the benefits in the event of his or her death before receiving them. You should always include language in your QDRO that provides such a beneficiary designation, or payable to the alternate payee's estate in the absence of a designation.

§ 30:23 Drafting the QDRO—Defined benefit plans—In general

Because there are no account balances under a defined benefit pension plan, never refer to a participant's "account" when drafting the QDRO. You should always refer to the participant's *accrued benefit*. Generally, a participant's accrued benefit can be calculated at any point in time during his or her working career. A participant's accrued benefit is usually payable in the form of a monthly annuity for life commencing at his or her normal retirement age, usually age 65. In other words, if the participant is age 35 at his divorce date, it is possible for the plan administrator to calculate his accrued benefit as of that date, but this amount generally would not become payable to the participant (or the alternate payee) on an unreduced basis until he or she attains the plan's normal retirement age.

Many attorneys that represent the plan participant attempt to draft a QDRO that freezes the alternate payee's share of the benefit at 50% of the participant's accrued benefit under the plan *as of the date of divorce*. While a plan administrator will certainly accept this language (and may even recommend it in one of their model QDROs), it can be extremely hazardous to the financial health of the alternate payee. This is another good reason for an attorney that represents the alternate payee not to arbitrarily use the company's model QDRO. A company provides model QDROs for one reason only—to expedite the QDRO review process. And from a paternalistic standpoint, they do not really care whether the alternate payee's rights are secured in an "equitable" manner. It is all right to use some of the boilerplate nonsubstantive language from a model QDRO, but be sure to complement it with language that will properly secure the benefits for your client.

§ 30:24 Drafting the QDRO—Defined benefit plans—The "coverture approach"

To best represent the rights of the nonparticipant spouse, you should utilize the "coverture approach" for dividing benefits under a defined benefit pension plan. Under this coverture approach, the alternate payee's share of the benefit is not based on the participant's accrued benefit under the plan at the date of divorce. Rather, the alternate payee's share is based on the participant's benefit at the participant's *date of retirement*, when it is the highest. However, the alternate payee does not simply receive 50% of the participant's ultimate retirement benefit.

Once the participant's final benefit is calculated at retirement, the marital portion is then determined by multiplying the accrued benefit by a coverture fraction. The coverture fraction is the ratio of the number of years of plan participation during the marriage to the total number of years of participation. This fraction is described as one in which the numerator of which is equal to the participant's years of service under the plan that were earned during the marriage and the denominator of which is equal to the participant's total service under the plan as of his date of retirement. The alternate payee would then be entitled to 50% of the marital portion of the ultimate pension.

The use of the coverture approach is the only way to provide the alternate payee with inflationary protection on her ownership share of the pension. Under a QDRO, the numerator of the coverture fraction remains constant. It always represents the number of years of service earned under the plan by the participant while married. Remember, it is not a measurement of the duration of the marriage, but rather the years of service earned by the participant during the marriage. Therefore, if the participant accrued ten years of service during a thirty-year marriage, the numerator would equal ten years.

The denominator of the coverture fraction represents all of the participant's years of service at retirement. Therefore, as the participant continues to earn additional years of credited service after the divorce, the denominator continues to grow by one each year. In reality, as the denominator grows by one each year, the percentage share of the alternate payee's pension (i.e., the coverture fraction) decreases. But this ever-decreasing coverture fraction is applied to a larger pension as the participant's accrued benefit continues to grow. In essence, with each passing year after the divorce, the alternate payee is earning a smaller percentage of a larger pie. This is how the alternate payee receives his or her inflationary protection under a pension plan.

This coverture approach is widely recommended as the only means of providing inflationary protection for an alternate payee under a defined benefit pension plan. In 1990, the Supreme Court of Ohio in the case of *Hoyt v. Hoyt*,[1] held that:

> In determining the proportionality of the pension or retirement benefits, the nonemployed spouse, in most instances, is only entitled to share in the actual marital asset. The value of this asset would be determined by computing the ratio of the number of years of employment of the employed spouse during the marriage to the total years of his or her employment.

With respect to addressing the alternate payee's co-ownership interest in the participant's pension utilizing the coverture approach, one Ohio appellate court said it best in *Layne v. Layne*:[2]

> Because the ultimate value of a pension benefit, and of the respective shares of the spouses, increases with the number of years of service credit, an argument is frequently made that a former spouse is unjustly enriched when the value of his or her share is increased by post-divorce participation in a plan by the other spouse.

[Section 30:24]

[1]Hoyt v. Hoyt, 53 Ohio St. 3d 177, 559 N.E.2d 1292 (1990).

[2]Layne v. Layne, 83 Ohio App. 3d 559, 566-67, 615 N.E.2d 332 (2d Dist. Champaign County 1992).

. . . a retirement plan is an investment made by both spouses during marriage to provide for their later years. They anticipate that the value of the investment will increase with time. At divorce, each spouse is entitled to the value of his or her investment. When the investment has not yet matured, each is entitled to its value at maturity in proportion to the years of marriage. The nonemployed former spouse is not entitled to share in the direct contributions made by the participant former spouse after divorce. However, the nonemployed former spouse is entitled to the benefit of any increase in the value of his or her unmatured proportionate share after divorce attributable to the continued participation of the other spouse in the retirement plan. That increase was contemplated when the investment was made. It would be inequitable to deprive the owner of its value. So long as each former spouse is limited to his or her proportionate right to share, there is neither unjust enrichment of the nonparticipant nor an inequitable deprivation of his or her rights.

In viewing the nonparticipant as a co-owner of the pension, the *Layne* court logically found that the co-owner of an asset must be allowed to share in the inevitable growth of that asset. This perspective was, of course, in marked contrast to the trial court which froze the pension as of the date of the divorce. This would be like freezing the nonparticipant's share of a defined contribution plan at a current dollar figure, and then insisting that the amount would remain the same no matter when it was distributed. To do so would deprive the nonparticipant of the passive growth on their marital share of the account. A similar situation crops up with defined benefit plans when the nonparticipant spouse is "frozen out" from receiving the natural (and funded!) growth in the plan.

§ 30:25 Drafting the QDRO—Defined benefit plans—The "coverture approach"—Form ⓔ

Amount of Alternate Payee's Benefit: This Order assigns to Alternate Payee an amount equal to the actuarial equivalent of *Fifty Percent (50%) of the Marital Portion of the Participant's Accrued Benefit* under the Plan as of the Participant's benefit commencement date, or the Alternate Payee's benefit commencement date, if earlier. The Marital Portion shall be determined by multiplying the Participant's Accrued Benefit by a fraction (less than or equal to 1.0), the numerator of which is the number of months of the Participant's participation in the Plan earned during the marriage (*from date of marriage to date of divorce*), and the denominator of which is the total number of months of the Participant's participation in the Plan as of the earlier of Participant's date of cessation of benefit accruals or the date that Alternate Payee commences his/her share of the benefits.

NOTES TO FORM

Drafter's Notes

This paragraph can be incorporated in a QDRO to implement the coverture approach.

§ 30:26 Drafting the QDRO—Defined benefit plans—Whose life expectancy?—In general

Choosing whose life expectancy to use is one of the most overlooked issues that can lead to failed QDROs. Or even worse, it could lead to a QDRO that is accepted, but is not understood by the parties. For the alternate payee, it's a life and death situation; for the alternate payee's attorney, it could be much worse. There are two basic ways to draft a QDRO for a defined benefit pension plan. The sole distinction between the two basic approaches lies totally on whose life expectancy the alternate payee's share of the benefits are based.

§ 30:27 Drafting the QDRO—Defined benefit plans—Whose life expectancy?—"Separate interest" QDRO based on alternate payee's life expectancy: approach number 1

Your QDRO could base the alternate payee's share of the benefits on his or her own life expectancy. In this case, the alternate payee's benefits would have to be *"actuarially adjusted"* to his or her own lifetime. For example, a participant retires with an accrued benefit of $2,000 per month and, assuming it is all marital, the intent of the parties is for the participant to get $1,000 per month and the alternate payee to get $1,000 per month. One must remember that pension plans are funded to provide the "participant" with a lifetime of benefits upon retirement. They are not designed to provide an alternate payee with a lifetime of benefits.

In this example, if the alternate payee was ten years younger than the participant, the plan would likely have to pay the alternate payee's $1,000 share of the benefit for a longer period of time if the actuarial tables hold true. If the QDRO included language that simply required the alternate payee to receive $1,000 per month (1/2 of the pension) for the remainder of her lifetime, this would increase the value of the participant's benefit and the QDRO would be rejected by the plan administrator. Under a separate interest QDRO, the alternate payee's benefits are actuarially adjusted to reflect his or her own life expectancy. In this example, the alternate payee who is ten years younger than the participant may receive only $800 per month, rather than $1,000, for the rest of her life, to reflect her longer life expectancy.

This life expectancy issue is also important from a QDRO survivorship perspective. If your QDRO utilizes the separate interest approach and instructs the plan administrator to pay the alternate payee on an actuarially adjusted basis for the rest of her lifetime, the *death of the participant after the alternate payee's benefit commencement date* should not affect the alternate payee's rights to continued benefits. It is critical for family law attorneys to understand the ramifications of ERISA's joint and survivor benefits depending on whose life expectancy the alternate payee's benefits are based.

If you use the separate interest approach, where the alternate payee's benefits are actuarially adjusted to his or her own lifetime, you do *not* have to include post-retirement joint and survivor protection in the QDRO for the benefit of the alternate payee. In other words, because the alternate payee is already guaranteed a lifetime of benefits, the QDRO does not have to require that the participant elect benefits in the form of a reduced joint and survivor annuity for the benefit of the alternate payee. The participant is free to elect any form of benefits available under the plan with respect to his or her share of the benefits including perhaps a single-life annuity without any reduction. If the participant is remarried, he or she can elect a joint and survivor benefit for the new spouse. This is one of the advantages of the "separate interest" QDRO. It provides a lifetime of benefits for the alternate payee while at the same time permitting the participant to elect any form of benefits for his or her remaining share.

Warning: Some plan administrators vary in their treatment of separate interest QDROs.

Under a separate interest QDRO, the alternate payee's benefits are actuarially adjusted to his or her own life expectancy. Therefore, once they begin, the alternate payee will continue to receive them for the remainder of his or her lifetime. It is not necessary for the participant to elect a reduced post-retirement joint and survivor annuity for the benefit of the alternate payee. In most cases, however, it is still necessary to include pre-retirement survivorship protection for the alternate payee. This qualified pre-retirement survivor annuity (QPSA) protection will help secure the alternate payee's benefits until her benefit commencement date should the participant die before then.

Generally, if a QDRO includes language that provides the alternate payee with pre-retirement survivorship protection, the alternate payee will receive the QPSA benefits in lieu of his or her regular assigned share of the benefits in the event of the participant's death before retirement. That is, the alternate payee will not generally receive both his or her assigned interest *and* the QPSA benefits. It is one or the other.

However, some plan administrators that utilize the separate interest approach (or severed approach), do not require pre-retirement survivorship protection in the QDRO. Once it is clear that the QDRO provides the alternate payee with an actuarially adjusted benefit, the alternate payee's benefits are "secure." That is, the participant's death, either before or after retirement, will not impact the alternate payee's rights to continued benefits. Further, they do not require any survivorship language in the separate interest QDRO whatsoever.

A word of caution. If you determine that a plan administrator in a particular case does not require any pre-retirement survivorship language in their separate interest QDROs, you should include an affirmative statement in the QDRO that "the participant's death, either before or after retirement will not affect the alternate payee's rights to his or her benefits as set forth herein."

In cases where the plan administrator does not require pre-retirement survivorship language in order to secure the alternate payee's benefits, they may nonetheless accept this language in the QDRO. For these plan administrators, if your separate interest QDRO includes pre-retirement survivorship coverage, the alternate payee would be entitled to his or her separate interest in the participant's pension regardless of the participant's death, and would in addition to his or her assigned interest, receive a pre-retirement survivor annuity in the event of the death of the participant before retirement.

Warning: Reversionary issues as potential drawback for participant of separate interest QDRO.

In many cases, the separate interest approach can be an advantage for the participant. It allows the participant to elect any form of benefit under the plan. However, under the separate interest approach, once the plan administrator actuarially adjusts the alternate payee's benefits to his or her own lifetime, the chance for a reversion to the participant is lost once the alternate payee's benefits go into pay status. In other words, if the alternate payee predeceases the participant *after* the alternate payee's benefit commencement date, the alternate payee's share of the benefits evaporates rather than reverts back to the participant.

This is where some strategy should enter the picture when you negotiate QDRO issues for your client. If you represent the participant who has a former spouse in ill-health, for example, you should probably not use a separate interest QDRO. The "shared interest" QDRO, discussed below, could be in your client's best interests. Under the shared interest QDRO, the alternate payee's share of the benefits would revert back to the participant in the event of the premature death of the alternate payee. This is true even if the alternate payee predeceases the participant after the alternate payee's benefit commencement date.

§ 30:28   Drafting the QDRO—Defined benefit plans—Whose life expectancy?—"Shared interest" QDRO based on participant's life expectancy: approach number 2

The shared interest approach is the second type of QDRO for a defined benefit pension plan. In essence, the alternate payee simply shares a portion of the participant's benefits when they go into pay status. Generally, under this approach, the alternate payee must wait until the participant retires before he or she can begin to receive their portion of the benefits. Because the alternate payee's share of the benefits is not actuarially adjusted to the alternate payee's life expectancy, it will always revert to the participant upon the alternate payee's death.

While this reversion issue could play an important part in the negotiation strategy, the participant should understand that there is a trade-off. In order to maintain full reversionary rights in the event of the alternate payee's death, the participant would typically be required to elect benefits in the form of a reduced joint and survivor annuity upon retirement. Because the alternate payee's share of the benefits is not actuarially adjusted, the only means of securing the alternate payee's benefits (i.e., providing a lifetime of benefits to the alternate payee) is to require the participant to elect a reduced joint and survivor annuity at retirement for the benefit of the alternate payee. Without a post-retirement joint and survivor election by the participant, the alternate payee's share of the benefits would cease at the death of the participant. In this case, if the participant died just one month after retirement, the alternate payee would not receive any benefits unless the participant had elected a reduced joint and survivor annuity and the QDRO included proper language that treated the alternate payee as the participant's surviving spouse.

§ 30:29   QDRO survivorship benefits—In general

There are generally just two types of survivor benefits offered under ERISA-governed defined benefit pension plans. One is a survivor annuity that "kicks in" if the participant dies before retirement, and the other provides a survivor annuity based on the participant's election at retirement. In other words, one is a "pre-retirement" death benefit (the "QPSA") and the other is a "post-retirement" death benefit (the "QJSA"). Under Section 414(p) of the Internal Revenue Code, an alternate payee under a QDRO could be treated as a surviving spouse of the participant for either or both the QPSA or the QJSA. It is critical that family law attorneys understand the distinction and address them separately, as applicable, under a QDRO.

§ 30:30   QDRO survivorship benefits—Qualified pre-retirement survivor annuity (QPSA)

Regardless of the QDRO approach you utilize (separate interest approach or shared interest approach), your QDRO should include qualified pre-retirement survivorship protection for the alternate payee. This is the only way to secure the alternate payee's benefits in the event of the death of the participant before their benefit commencement date. Even for QDROs that utilize the separate interest approach (i.e., those that actuarially adjust the alternate payee's benefits to his or her own life expectancy), the alternate payee could forfeit his or her rights to any benefits should the participant die before the alternate payee commences benefits. The key issue here is whether the alternate payee has already commenced benefits. If the alternate payee has already commenced benefits under a separate interest QDRO, the QPSA is a moot point. The alternate payee's benefits should continue for life in any event. However, if the alternate payee has not yet commenced benefits, the QPSA is the only means of protecting the alternate payee's interest in the pension.

Many attorneys simply include language in their QDRO that states "the alternate payee is treated as a surviving spouse for purposes of the plan's pre-retirement survivor annuity." This language is rather vague and could be rejected by the plan administrator. It is not good enough simply to state that the alternate payee is entitled to such pre-retirement survivorship protection. A QDRO must also include the extent to which the alternate payee is to receive such pre-retirement survivor benefits. In other words, how much of the QPSA benefit will the alternate payee receive? Your QDRO could provide that the alternate payee receives any and all QPSA benefits that may become payable under the plan in the event of the participant's death before retirement. However, this may not be considered "equitable." For example, if the participant is remarried, perhaps some of the pre-retirement death benefits should become payable to the new spouse, while a proportionate share becomes payable to the alternate payee based on the marital portion of the participant's benefits.

Alternatively, you could include language in the QDRO that provides the alternate payee with a pre-retirement survivor annuity "to the extent of her assigned interest." Then, any remaining survivor annuity benefits could become payable to the participant's subsequent surviving spouse. To take it one step further, you could include language in the QDRO that provides the alternate payee with *all* of the QPSA benefits if the participant is not remarried on the date of his death and then limit the alternate payee's QPSA benefits to the extent of his or her assigned interest if the participant is remarried. Usually, QPSA benefits under a pension plan are based on a 50% joint and survivor annuity. The plan would base such benefits on the amount that the participant would have received had he retired on the day before his death and elected his benefits in the form of a reduced 50% joint and survivor annuity. If you limit an alternate payee's benefits to the extent of his or her assigned interest, and the participant is not remarried on the date of death, any QPSA benefits in excess of the alternate payee's assigned share will inure to the plan. It may make sense in this case to provide the alternate payee with maximum QPSA benefits rather than having the excess benefits evaporate.

Usually the QPSA benefit is a "free" benefit. In other words, the participant's benefits are not reduced to reflect the fact that he or she had this coverage in place during his or her working career. In the pension vernacular, this is considered a fully subsidized benefit. The reasons are simple. If the plan were to administer a charge for this QPSA coverage, they would have to allow the participant to opt into and out of this coverage at any point during his career and as many times as he or she may elect. This would pose a huge administrative burden for the plan administrator. They would have to maintain records for plan participants for their entire careers to monitor their QPSA elections, and then calculate the charges accordingly upon their dates of retirement. Because the "insurance-type" charge for a QPSA is relatively small (i.e., a participant's benefits might only be reduced by .2% for each year of coverage) most companies believe that subsidizing this small charge outweighs the time and expense associated with monitoring the QPSA election procedures.

§ 30:31 QDRO survivorship benefits—Qualified pre-retirement survivor annuity (QPSA)—Form⊚

Death of Participant Before Benefit Commencement Date: Treatment of Alternate Payee as Surviving Spouse for Purposes of Determining Qualified Preretirement Survivor Annuity as Such Term is defined in Section 417 of the Code: In the event that the Participant predeceases the Alternate Payee, and *neither* the Participant nor the Alternate Payee has commenced receiving benefits under the Plan, such Alternate Payee shall be designated as the surviving spouse of the Participant for purposes of establishing Alternate Payee's entitlement to receipt of this monthly pre-retirement survivor annuity. For purposes of determining the eligibility for such surviving spouse benefits, the Alternate Payee and the Participant have satisfied the one (1) year marriage requirement as enumerated in Sections 401(a)(11) and 417(d) of the Code and as may be required under the provisions of the Plan.

This designation applies to the Martial Portion of the Participant's accrued benefit as set forth in Section 7. As a result, the Alternate Payee shall be treated as the surviving spouse for purposes of any pre-retirement survivor annuity benefits that are attributable to the Marital Portion of the Participant's benefits as stipulated herein and any subsequent spouse of the Participant shall **not** be treated as a surviving spouse for such purposes.

In the event that the costs associated with providing this pre-retirement survivor annuity benefit are not fully subsidized by the Participant's employer, then Participant must make an affirmative election for such pre-retirement survivor annuity benefit coverage in a timely manner and in accordance with his/her employer's election procedures.

NOTES TO FORM

Drafter's Notes

This paragraph can be incorporated in a QDRO using the coverture approach to include pre-retirement survivorship protection for the alternate payee.

§ 30:32 QDRO survivorship benefits—Qualified (post-retirement) joint and survivor annuity (QJSA)

This is the form of survivor benefit that most attorneys are familiar with. When a participant retires, he or she elects a form of benefit from among several options available under the plan. Under federal law, a married participant at retirement must elect his or her benefits in the automatic form of a 50% qualified joint and survivor annuity (the "QJSA"). The participant could elect an alternative form of benefit with the written, notarized consent of the spouse. Under the 50% joint and survivor annuity, the participant will receive a reduced monthly benefit during his or her lifetime, and upon his or her death, the surviving spouse will receive 50% of such reduced amount for the remainder of the spouse's lifetime.

Under section 414(p) of the Internal Revenue Code, an alternate payee under a QDRO could be treated as the surviving spouse of the participant with respect to any or all of this post-retirement survivor coverage. If you utilize the "shared interest" approach for your QDRO, and you represent the alternate payee, it also better include QJSA protection for the alternate payee. Without proper post-retirement survivorship language, the alternate payee will forfeit all rights to any benefits upon the death of the participant.

If your QDRO utilizes the "separate interest" approach, you do not have to include post-retirement survivorship protection for the alternate payee. This is because the alternate payee's benefits are actuarially adjusted to his or her own lifetime and the participant's death after the alternate payee's benefit commencement date will not affect the alternate payee's rights to continued benefits.

Like the qualified pre-retirement survivor annuity (the "QPSA"), your QDRO must also include the extent to which the alternate payee is entitled to such post-retirement joint and survivor annuity coverage. You could include language that provides the alternate payee with post-retirement survivorship protection "to the extent of his or her assigned interest." Any remaining QJSA benefits could then become payable to the subsequent spouse of the participant.

In situations where the alternate payee is younger than the participant (and will likely, from an actuarial perspective, out-live the participant) it may be in the best interests of the participant to utilize the "separate interest" or actuarially adjusted QDRO. In this manner, the participant will not be required to elect a reduced joint and survivor annuity upon retirement and will be free to elect from any other available options under the plan. Here, it may make sense for the participant to forfeit any reversionary interests he or she would otherwise have in favor of receiving a higher benefit during his or her life.

§ 30:33 Government's model QDRO language

On December 30, 1996, the Internal Revenue Service issued Notice 97-11 in an attempt, in their words, "to assist domestic relations attorneys, plan participants, spouses and former spouses of participants, and plan administrators in drafting and reviewing a qualified domestic relations order."[1] In fact, it offered little help on many of the substantial issues involved in QDROs. Below is a portion of their model QDRO language:

PART II. SAMPLE LANGUAGE FOR INCLUSION IN QDRO

A. SAMPLE LANGUAGE FOR IDENTIFICATION OF PARTICIPANT AND ALTERNATE PAYEE

The "Participant" is [insert name of Participant]. The Participant's address is [insert Participant's address]. The Participant's social security number is [insert Participant's social security number].

The "Alternate Payee" is [insert name of Alternate Payee]. The Alternate Payee's address is [insert Alternate Payee's address]. The Alternate Payee's social security number is [insert Alternate Payee's social security number]. The Alternate Payee is the [describe the Alternate Payee's relationship to Participant] of the Participant.

B. SAMPLE LANGUAGE FOR IDENTIFICATION OF RETIREMENT PLAN

This order applies to benefits under the [insert formal name of retirement plan] ("Plan").

C. AMOUNT OF BENEFITS TO BE PAID TO ALTERNATE PAYEE

Instruction: The QDRO should clearly specify the amount or percentage of benefits assigned to the Alternate Payee or the manner in which the amount or percentage is to be determined, and the number of payments or period to

---

[Section 30:33]

[1]Notice 97-11, 1997-2 I.R.B. 49, 1996 WL 747904.

which the Order applies. There are many different forms in which benefits may be paid from a qualified plan. *Because of the diversity of factors that should be considered, and the need to tailor the assignment of benefits under a QDRO to meet the needs of the parties involved, specific sample language regarding the assignment of benefits has not been provided.*[2]

Clearly, the government's QDROs gloss over the all important benefit clause language. In reality, the government's model QDRO language is of minimal help. It certainly does not help the attorney to carry out the intentions of the separation agreement. While it does go on to distinguish between the two types of QDROs for defined benefit pension plans (separate interest and shared interest), it gives no practical guidance necessary for the attorney to best represent his or her client, be it the participant or alternate payee. It does not discuss the various approaches to assigning benefits under a defined benefit QDRO, such as coverture. It is also silent on many other substantive issues such as early retirement subsidy recalculations, cost-of-living adjustments, or reversionary aspects.

---

[2]Italics added for emphasis.

APPENDIX 30-A

I.R.C. § 414(p)

§ I.R.C. § 414(p)

(p) Qualified domestic relations order defined.—For purposes of this subsection and section 401(a)(13)—

(1) In general.—

(A) Qualified domestic relations order.—The term "qualified domestic relations order" means a domestic relations order—

(i) which creates or recognizes the existence of an alternate payee's right to, or assigns to an alternate payee the right to, receive all or a portion of the benefits payable with respect to a participant under a plan, and

(ii) with respect to the requirements of paragraphs (2) and (3) are met.

(B) Domestic relations order.—The term "domestic relations order" means any judgment, decree, or order (including approval of a property settlement agreement) which—

(i) relates to the provision of child support, alimony payments, or marital property rights to a spouse, former spouse, child, or other dependent of a participant, and

(ii) is made pursuant to a State domestic relations law (including a community property law).

(2) Order must clearly specify certain facts.—A domestic relations order meets the requirements of this paragraph only if such order clearly specifies—

(A) the name and last known mailing address (if any) of the participant and the name and mailing address of each alternate payee covered by the order,

(B) the amount or percentage of the participant's benefits to be paid by the plan to each such alternate payee, or the manner in which such amount or percentage is to be determined,

(C) the number of payments or period to which such order applies, and

(D) each plan to which such order applies.

(3) Order may not alter amount, form, etc., of benefits.—A domestic relations order meets the requirements of this paragraph only if such order—

(A) does not require a plan to provide any type or form of benefit, or any option not otherwise provided under the plan,

(B) does not require the plan to provide increased benefits (determined on the basis of actuarial value), and

(C) does not require the payment of benefits to an alternate payee which are required to be paid to another alternate payee under another order previously determined to be a qualified domestic relations order.

(4) Exception for certain payments made after earliest retirement age.—

(A) In general.—A domestic relations order shall not be treated as failing to meet the requirements of subparagraph (A) of paragraph (3) solely because such order requires that payment of benefits be made to an alternate payee—

(i) in the case of any payment before a participant has separated form service, on or after the date on which the participant attains (or would have attained) the earliest retirement age,

(ii) as if the participant had retired on the date on which such payment is to begin under such order (but taking into account only the preset value of the benefits actually accrued and not taking into account the preset value of any employer subsidy for early retirement), and

(iii) in any form in which such benefits may be paid under the plan to the participant (other than in the form of a joint and survivor annuity with respect to the alternate payee and his or her subsequent spouse).

For purposes of clause (ii), the interest rate assumption used in determining the preset value shall be the interest rate specified in the plan or, if no rate is specified, 5 percent.

(B) Earliest retirement age.—For purposes of this paragraph, the term "earliest retirement age" [means earlier of] means the earlier of—

(i) [in] the date on which the participant is entitled to a distribution under the plan, or

(ii) [in] the later of—

(I) the date the participant attains age 50, or

(II) the earliest date on which the participant could begin receiving benefits under the plan if the participant separated from service.

(5) Treatment of former spouse as surviving spouse for purposes of determining survivor benefits.—To the extent provided in any qualified domestic relations order—

(A) the former spouse of a participant shall be treated as a surviving spouse of such participant for purposes of section 410(a)(11) and 417 (and any spouse of the participant shall not be treated as a spouse of the participant for such purposes), and

(B) is married for at least 1 year, the surviving former spouse shall be treated as meeting the requirements of section 417(d).

(6) Plan procedures with respect to orders.—

(A) Notice and determination by administrator.—In the case of any domestic relations order received by a plan—

(i) the plan administrator shall promptly notify the participant and such alternate payee of the receipt of the order and the plan's procedures for determining the qualified statue of domestic relations orders, and

(ii) within a reasonable period after receipt of such order, the plan administrator shall determine whether such order is a qualified domestic relations order and notify the participant of such determination.

(B) Plan to establish reasonable procedures.—Each plan shall establish reasonable procedures to determine the qualified status of domestic relations orders and to administer distributions under such qualified orders.

(7) Procedures for period during which determination is being made.—

(A) In general.—During any period in which the issue of whether a domestic relations order is a qualified domestic relations order is being determined (by the plan administrator, by a court of competent jurisdiction, or otherwise), the plan administrator shall separately account for the amounts (hereinafter in this paragraph referred to as the "segregated amounts") which would have been payable to the alternate payee during such period if the order had been determined to be a qualified domestic relations order.

(B) Payment to alternate payee is order determined to be qualified domestic relations order.—If within the 18-month period described in subparagraph (E) the order (or modification thereof) is determined to be a qualified domestic relations order, the plan administrator shall pay the segregated amounts (including any interest thereon) to the person or persons entitled thereto.

(C) Payment to plan participant in certain cases.—If within the 18-month period described in subparagraph (E)—

(i) it is determined that the order is not a qualified domestic relations order, or

(ii) the issue as to whether such order is a qualified domestic relations order is not resolved, then the plan administrator shall pay the segregated amounts (including any interest thereon) to the person or persons who would have been entitled to such amounts if there had been no order.

(D) Subsequent determination or order to be applied prospectively only.—Any determination that an order is a qualified domestic relations order which is made after the close of the 18-month period described in subparagraph (E) shall be applied prospectively only.

(E) Determination of 18-month period.—For purposes of this paragraph, the 18-month period described in this subparagraph is the 18-month period beginning with the date on which the first payment would be required to be made under the domestic relations order.

(8) Alternate Payee defined.—The term "alternate payee" means any spouse, former spouse, child, or other dependent of a participant who is recognized by a domestic relations order as having a right to receive all, or a portion of, the benefits payable under a plan with respect to such participant.

(9) Subsection not to apply to plans to which section 401(a)(13) does not apply.—This subsection shall not apply to any plan to which section 401(a)(13) does not apply. For purposes of this title, except as provided in regulations, any distribution from an annuity contract under section 403(b) pursuant to a qualified domestic relations order shall be treated in the same manner as distribution form a plan to which section 401(a)(13) applies.

(10) Waiver of certain distribution requirements.—With respect to the requirements of subsections (a) and (k) of section 401, section 403(b), and section 409(d), a plan shall not be treated as failing to meet such requirements solely by reason of payments to an alternative payee pursuant to a qualified domestic relations order.

(11) Application of rules to governmental and church plans.—For purposes of this title, a distribution or payment from a governmental plan (as described in subsection (e)) shall be treated as made pursuant to a qualified domestic relations order if it is made pursuant to a domestic relations order which meets the requirement of clause (i) of paragraph (1)(A)).

[(11)] (12) Consultation with the Secretary.—In prescribing regulations under this subsection and section 401(a)(13), the Secretary of Labor shall consult with the Secretary.

Chapter 31

Magistrates

By Mary C. LoPresti, Esq. and Sherry A. Naegele[*]

> **KeyCite®:** Cases and other legal materials listed in KeyCite Scope can be researched through West Group's KeyCite service on Westlaw®. Use KeyCite to check citations for form, parallel references, prior and later history, and comprehensive citator information, including citations to other decisions and secondary materials.

§ 31:1   Appointment and jurisdiction

Magistrates (formerly called referees) have become invaluable to our family law court system in the disposition of the increasingly difficult caseload. In some of Ohio's counties, a magistrate's scope of power and authority is practically indistinguishable from that of the judge's power and authority.

The promulgation of the Ohio Rules of Civil Procedure under the 1968

---

[*]Sherry A. Naegele, formerly known as Sherry A. Tucker.

Courts Amendment to the Ohio Constitution[1] opened the way for the less restricted use of magistrates in general. Prior statutes governing the use of referees and masters[2] were replaced by Civil Rule 53, which permits a liberal use of magistrates to "aid the court in the expedition of the court's business."[3] In the field of domestic relations, the liberalization of social and legal conceptions concerning legal separation, annulment, dissolution, divorce, allocation of parental rights and responsibilities, support (child and spousal), domestic violence and related matters has led to a docket explosion often requiring the use of magistrates as a necessary component in an effective case management plan. Finally, many domestic proceedings lend themselves to a less formal hearing before a magistrate.

Magistrates' roles and powers are governed by revised Ohio Civil Rule 53, effective July 1, 1995, and amended thereafter. The revised rule expands the authority of the magistrate and, under some circumstances, reduces the red-tape and paperwork formerly involved in hearings and decisions of magistrates.

While much of the existing case law and commentary is still relevant, it must be carefully read in conjunction with the revisions to Ohio Civil Rule 53. Each precedent case should be independently reviewed in comparison to the amended language of Civil Rule 53 to which it relates, and to the local rules of court, to determine its applicability under the current version of the rule. Practitioners must also become familiar with the local rules of the court in which the case is pending. Further, some local rules of court limit and define the scope of magistrates' powers. Some local rules mandate orders of reference to be specific as to the hearing referred to a magistrate, or may allow general reference to the magistrate of all issues outstanding in a case.

Civil Rule 53(A) requires magistrates to be ". . . attorneys at law admitted to practice in Ohio." The power to appoint magistrates is expressly limited to courts of record, which includes the mayor's court pursuant to RC 1905.05.

As officers of the judicial system, performing judicial functions, magistrates must comply with the Code of Judicial Conduct[4] as well as with

---

[Section 31:1]

[1]Even though the Ohio Rules of Civil Procedure were promulgated in 1968, the Rules were not introduced to the Supreme Court until January of 1969 and were not in effect until the first day of July, 1970.

[2]Former RC 2315.26 to RC 2315.37.

[3]Civ. R. 53 (1970 Staff Note).

[4]See Compliance section of the Code of Judicial Conduct; see also Supreme Court of Ohio, Board of Commissioners on Grievance and Discipline, Op. No. 87-14 (part-time referees may not practice before court division in which they serve); Op. No. 87-36 (part-time referees practice of law before his appointing judge); Op. No. 87-38 (referees should disqualify themselves from any proceeding where their impartiality might reasonably be questioned); Op. No. 87-41 (referee's participation in continuing legal education); Op. No. 92-16 (referee's use of title in advertisements used in seeking judicial office); Op. No. 96-8 (magistrate's use of the title "magistrate" in campaign advertisements); Op No. 98-3 (part-time magistrate practicing law in the court in which he/she serves or in which

RC Chapter 102, codifying Ohio ethics law.

Civil Rule 53(B) requires that the compensation of magistrates be fixed by the court and paid by the taxpayers, rather than taxed as costs to the parties. This has always been true for magistrates who are full-time court employees. Formerly, however, the services of a magistrate, appointed in a specific case or on an interim basis, could be taxed as costs to be paid by the parties. This is no longer permitted.

§ 31:2 Reference and powers

Civil Rule 53(C) requires that the reference of any matter to a magistrate be done by court order. The scope of the magistrate's powers is defined in the order.

Civil Rule 53(C)(1) clarifies that magistrates have the authority to act only on matters referred to them by a judge in the order of reference. The order of reference may be specific to a particular case or motion, or may be general as to the entire case or a category of cases.[1] This subsection also permits a magistrate to preside over a jury trial with the unanimous written consent of the parties.[2] The referring judge may restrict the magistrate's general powers by specifying limits in the order of reference.

Civil Rule 53(C)(1) provides little guidance in defining the form of the reference. Rather, the rule focuses on the substance of the order, which may do all of the following:

(1) Specify or limit the magistrate's powers;

(2) Direct the magistrate to report only upon particular issues, to do or perform particular acts, or to receive and report evidence only, and/or

(3) Fix the time and place for beginning and closing the hearings and for the filing of the magistrate's decision.

Regardless of form, a court has a wide range of options in fashioning an order of reference. The magistrate may be ordered to function with broad powers or be subjected to severe limitations.

Whether the order of reference is general (granting full powers) or special (placing limitations on the magistrate's function), it is likely to appear in one of three forms: (1) an individual journalized order of reference in a particular case or several cases; (2) a blanket journalized order of reference in a particular type or types of cases, or (3) a local rule or

---

the appointing judge serves), and Op. No. 98-12 (magistrate's extra-judicial business activity limitations).

[Section 31:2]
  [1]See State ex rel. Allstate Ins. Co. v. Gaul, 131 Ohio App. 3d 419, 432-433, 722 N.E.2d 616 (8th Dist. Cuyahoga County 1999).
  [2]See Hartt v. Munobe, 1993 -Ohio- 177, 67 Ohio St. 3d 3, 5, 615 N.E.2d 617 (1993).

rules providing for automatic reference in certain types of cases.[3]

In the area of domestic relations, the practitioner is most likely to encounter a blanket order of reference, appearing either as a journal entry or as a local rule of court.[4] With the variety of form and content available to a court, it is necessary to consider separately each domestic court's order of reference. Orders will vary considerably from one locality to another.

In the absence of a blanket order of reference, the option of requesting a hearing before a magistrate is available to the domestic litigant.[5] If the court grants such a request, the litigants should consider what powers they would prefer in the order of reference. However, the court has the ultimate power to define or limit the powers of the magistrate.

The matter of reference is one of procedure not jurisdiction. Therefore, if the court does not fully comply with the procedural requirements of Civ. R. 53, the failure does not affect the jurisdiction of the court to hear the matter. Violation of said procedures has been held to constitute reversible error only when shown to effect substantial rights of the complaining party.[6]

Civil Rule 53(C)(2) sets forth the general powers of magistrates. Some local rules define or limit the powers of magistrates.

Absent specific limitations, the magistrate's powers in a domestic relations hearing are quite broad. A magistrate is directed to "regulate all proceedings in every hearing as if by the court and do all acts and take all measures necessary or proper for the efficient performance of the magistrate's duties under the order."[7] A magistrate's general powers, unless specifically limited, include the authority to:

(1) issue subpoenas for the attendance of witnesses and the production of evidence;

(2) rule upon the admissibility of evidence, unless otherwise directed by the order of reference;

(3) put witnesses under oath and examine them, and

(4) call the parties to the action and examine them under oath.

(5) In cases involving direct or indirect contempt of court, and when necessary to obtain the alleged contemnor's presence for hearing, issue an attachment for the alleged contemnor and set bail

---

[3]See, e.g., White v. White, 50 Ohio App. 2d 263, 267, 4 Ohio Op. 3d 225, 362 N.E.2d 1013 (8th Dist. Cuyahoga County 1977); Davis v. Reed, 2000 WL 1231462 (Ohio Ct. App. 8th Dist. Cuyahoga County 2000).

[4]See, e.g., Rule 37 of Cuyahoga County Domestic Relations; Rule 8 of Franklin County Domestic Relations; Rule 7.01 of Green County Domestic Relations; Rule 5.02 of Lucas County Domestic Relations; Rule 4.07 of Montgomery County Domestic Relations; Rule 15.06 of Stark County Family Court Division, and Rule 6.03 of Summit County Domestic Relations Division.

[5]Civ. R. 75(C).

[6]Hines v. Amole, 4 Ohio App. 3d 263, 265, 448 N.E.2d 473 (2d Dist. Greene County 1982).

[7]Civ. R. 53(C)(2). See also Stewart v. Stewart, 1991 WL 110216 (Ohio Ct. App. 4th Dist. Gallia County 1991).

to secure the alleged contemnor's appearance, considering the conditions of release prescribed in Crim. R. 46.[8]

In addition, Civil Rule 53(C)(3)(c) codifies the authority of the magistrate to impose appropriate civil or criminal contempt sanctions where the contempt takes place in the magistrate's presence. Such a contempt order must be in writing, and must recite the facts and certify that the magistrate saw or heard the conduct constituting contempt. The contempt order must be filed, and the clerk must immediately provide a copy to the appropriate judge of the court. The individual held in contempt may file a motion to obtain immediate review of the magistrate's contempt order by a judge. The judge or the magistrate may set bail pending judicial review.

Civil Rule 53(C)(3)(d) recognizes that there may be authority granted to magistrates by other areas of the Ohio Revised Code. Unless limited by the order of reference, the magistrate has those statutory powers conveyed throughout the laws of Ohio, and as defined by local rule.

§ 31:3 Proceedings

The framework for a domestic relations hearing before a court-appointed magistrate is found in Civil Rule 53(C) and (D). Civil Rule 53(D)(1) provides that all proceedings before a magistrate shall be in accordance with the Civil Rules and any applicable statutes. The procedures shall be the same as in other civil proceedings, as if before the court.[1] The precise nature of the hearing will vary from jurisdiction to jurisdiction. The starting point in determining the probable nature of a given hearing should be the order of reference and local rules.[2]

If the order of reference or a local rule places specific limitations on the magistrate's function, preparation for the hearing should be conducted with such limitations clearly in view. The magistrate's role may be restricted to simply receiving and reporting evidence,[3] leaving the court to determine the credibility of testimony and to apply the appropriate law.

In exercising its rule-making power, the Ohio Supreme Court has specifically applied the Ohio Rules of Evidence to "proceedings . . . before court-appointed referees and magistrates."[4] Evidence Rule 101(A) was amended effective July 1, 1996, to delete the specific reference to "referees and magistrates." The Staff Note to the amendment indicates that "no substantive change is intended" because proceedings before magistrates are "proceedings in the courts of this state," already included in Evidence Rule 101(A), and the specific reference is

---

[8]Civ. R. 53(C)(2).

[Section 31:3]
[1]Staff Note to 1995 amendment to Civ. R. 53(D).
[2]See § 31:2, Reference and powers.
[3]Civ. R. 53(C)(1)(c)(ii).
[4]Formerly Evid. R. 101(A).

redundant.[5]

The applicability of the Rules of Evidence may be limited in certain ways, however. Evidence Rule 101(C)(6) provides exclusions for "[p]roceedings in which other rules prescribed by the Supreme Court govern matters relating to evidence." Thus, as the Staff Note to Evidence Rule 101(A) contemplates, Civil Rule 53 may control evidentiary considerations if the order of reference limits the magistrate's powers to hearing and recording testimony. Similarly, the procedure set forth in Civil Rule 75(N),[6] permitting domestic magistrates to make orders pendente lite on the basis of affidavits, would supersede the more general Rules of Evidence.

Civil Rule 53(D)(2) provides that magistrates must conduct all proceedings before them on the record pursuant to procedures established by the court.[7] The Staff Note to the 1995 amendments points out that the rule is not meant to limit courts to particular recording methods. Proceedings may be recorded by whatever method a court deems appropriate.

A final consideration should be noted concerning domestic hearings before a court-appointed magistrate. If the order of reference grants the broadest possible powers to the magistrate, then the magistrate obviously will be functioning with many powers available to the court. These powers would no doubt include the full equity powers placed with the court pursuant to RC 3105.011. Thus, if the proper circumstances were to arise, a magistrate might substantially, and yet permissibly, deviate from the normal procedure in order to effect an equitable result.

§ 31:4 Magistrate's authority to enter orders

Civil Rule 53(C)(3)(a) authorizes a magistrate to enter an order which will take effect without judicial approval, unless the order of reference provides otherwise.[1]

Civil Rule 53(C)(3)(e) specifies that all magistrate's orders must be in writing, signed by the magistrate, and titled as a magistrate's order in the caption, which enables the parties and the docket to identify a magistrate's order more easily.[2] The orders must then be filed with the clerk and served on all parties or their attorneys.

The orders which a magistrate may enter include those in pretrial proceedings under Civil Rule 16; in discovery proceedings under Civil

---

[5]See 1 Giannelli and Snyder, Baldwin's Ohio Practice, Evidence §§ 101.1, 101.5.

[6]Formerly Civ. R. 75(M).

[7]Bell v. Bell, 1998 WL 332942 (Ohio Ct. App. 9th Dist. Medina County 1998) (court may, by local rule, require party to file request for a court reporter seven days in advance); Moyers v. Moyers, 1999 WL 418007 (Ohio Ct. App. 11th Dist. Ashtabula County 1999).

[Section 31:4]

[1]See Barker v. Barker, 118 Ohio App. 3d 706, 711, 693 N.E.2d 1164 (6th Dist. Lucas County 1997).

[2]Staff Note to 1995 amendment to Civ. R. 53 (C).

Rules 26 to 37; temporary restraining orders under Civil Rule 75(I);[3] in hearings held under Civil Rule 75(N); and any other orders that are necessary to regulate the proceedings.

Since many temporary orders are not final appealable orders,[4] the binding and interpreting law may be found in orders of reference, local rules and Civil Rule 53 more often than in case law.

While Civil Rule 53 has no provision for counsel to request findings of fact and conclusions of law from some orders, an order of reference may require the same under Civil Rule 53(C)(3). Without such a provision in the order of reference, a magistrate's interim child support order does not require findings of fact and conclusions of law even if requested. The trial court's decision denying the request for findings of fact and conclusions of law as not appropriate for interim order was further held not to be a final and appealable order.[5]

In some counties, temporary orders of support and/or custody are made without a hearing. Since local practice may vary, counsel should review both the order of reference and the local rules to ascertain the magistrate's powers and the requirements for decisions and orders.

In some courts, Civil Rule 75(N)(1) "hearing[s]" are on affidavit only, and may, therefore, not be considered hearings from which one may appeal.

Civil Rule 53(C)(3)(b) provides a safeguard for parties against whom a magistrate has entered an order under Civil Rule 53(C)(3)(a). Just as a party may file objections to a magistrate's decision, a party may appeal to the court from any magistrate's order under Civil Rule 53(C)(3) by filing a motion to set the order aside.[6] This motion must state with particularity the objection(s) to the magistrate's order.

The motion to set aside a magistrate's order differs in several key respects from objections filed to a magistrate's decision. First, a motion to set aside a magistrate's order must be filed no later than 10 days after the order is entered, as opposed to the 14 days allowed for objections to a decision.[7] Civ. R. 53(C)(3)(e) provides that magistrate's orders must be filed, so presumably an order is entered on the date it is filed. Second, the filing of a timely motion to set aside a magistrate's order does not operate as an automatic stay of the order as does the timely filing of objections to a magistrate's decision. Third, unlike the rule regarding objections, there is no provision for additional response time by one party after the other party files a motion to set aside. Therefore, a decision on whether to file a motion to set aside cannot depend upon the ac-

---

[3]Formerly Civ. R. 75(H).

[4]See Kelm v. Kelm, 93 Ohio App. 3d 686, 639 N.E.2d 842 (10th Dist. Franklin County 1994).

[5]Brooks v. Brooks, 1998 WL 212863 (Ohio Ct. App. 10th Dist. Franklin County 1998).

[6]Sagen v. Thrower, 1999 WL 195665 (Ohio Ct. App. 8th Dist. Cuyahoga County 1999), dismissed, appeal not allowed, 86 Ohio St. 3d 1462, 715 N.E.2d 565 (1999).

[7]Civ. R. 53(C)(3)(e) provides that magistrate's orders must be filed, so presumably an order is considered entered on the date it is filed.

tion of the other party.

§ 31:5   Motion to set aside magistrate's order—Form⊚

[Title of Court]

[Caption]

Case No. [_____]
MOTION TO SET ASIDE
MAGISTRATE'S ORDER

Pursuant to Civil Rule 53(C)(3)(b), [plaintiff/defendant] moves this court for an order setting aside the magistrate's order filed herein on [date], as to the following orders:

[Temporary child support/temporary spousal support/temporary parental rights/temporary restraining order/other].

[Plaintiff/Defendant] states that such orders should be set aside for the following reasons: [Here state with specificity the party's objections].

_____

Attorney for [Plaintiff/Defendant]

[Notice]

[Proof/Certificate of Service]

NOTES TO FORM

Drafter's Notes

Civil Rule 53(C)(3)(b) requires a party to file a "motion to set the order aside" rather than an "objection" as in Civil Rule 53(E)(3), although each requires the stating of objections with particularity. The time period for filing a motion to set an order aside (10 days from order) is not only shorter than that for filing objections to a magistrate's decision (14 days), but the latter also permits the opposing party an additional 10 days after first objection to file his or her objection. No corresponding protection for opposing counsel is present in Civil Rule 53(C)(3).

§ 31:6   Magistrate's decisions in referred matters

Civil Rule 53(E) underwent substantial modification in the July 1, 1995 amendment. Further, Civil Rule 53(E) underwent modifications on July 1, 1996 and July 1, 1998.[1] Because of these changes, practitioners need to pay close attention to the procedures set out in Civil Rule 53(E) governing the preparation of magistrate's decisions and the filing of objections to those decisions. Failure to do so can result in the loss of significant rights of review both at the trial and appellate levels.

Civil Rule 53(E)(1) provides that a magistrate must promptly conduct all proceedings necessary to decide referred matters. A magistrate's decision must then be prepared and signed by the magistrate. The decision must be filed with the clerk of courts, and served by the clerk on all par-

_____

[Section 31:6]
[1]Staff Notes to 1996 and 1998 amendments to Civ. R. 53(E).

ties or their attorneys.[2] In some jurisdictions, it may be possible for a magistrate to delegate the drafting of the decision to one of the attorneys, but only if there is a local rule of court authorizing such a procedure.[3]

A magistrate's decision must be distinguished from a magistrate's order. The inclusion of language purporting to be an "order" does not alter the procedure to challenge the magistrate's decision under Civ. R. 53(E). The Sixth District Court of Appeals recognized the potential for confusion in this area, and held that "magistrates do not have authority to issue 'orders' as part of their decisions."[4] In *Barker*, a magistrate entered a "Magistrate's Decision With Judgment Entry and Interim Order" that included findings of fact, conclusions of law, and several "orders." The document provided that it would take effect immediately, would become final if no objections were filed, and its application would not be stayed if objections were filed.

The appellate court found that the magistrate exceeded his authority in declaring that the decision would become a final order without action by the judge, and in declaring that it would be entered as an interim order. A judge may enter an interim order based on a magistrate's decision, but the magistrate has no authority to make that determination. Further, Civ. R. 53(E) provides that an interim order is to expire at the end of the twenty-eight day period. By simply adopting the magistrate's decision, the court in *Barker* entered only an interim, or temporary, order, which was not final and appealable.

Under Civil Rule 53(E), a magistrate "is not required to prepare any report other than the magistrate's decision." The magistrate's decision must include findings of fact and conclusions of law only if a party requests them under Civil Rule 52, or if they are otherwise required by law or by the order of reference.[5] The procedures for entering, disputing, adopting, and modifying a magistrate's decision are set forth in revised Civil Rule 53(E).

The previous version of Civil Rule 53(E)(1) provided that upon written consent of the parties, if permitted by the order of reference, the require-

---

[2]Swarmer v. Swarmer, 1998 WL 964575 (Ohio Ct. App. 11th Dist. Trumbull County 1998) (party unable to file timely objections due to clerk's failure to properly serve the magistrate's decision on counsel of record); see Prenatt v. Prenatt, 1998 WL 543741 (Ohio Ct. App. 2d Dist. Montgomery County 1998); See Alldred v. Alldred, 1998 WL 769814 (Ohio Ct. App. 2d Dist. Montgomery County 1998); See Swain v. Swain, 2000 WL 1729472 (Ohio Ct. App. 9th Dist. Summit County 2000); See State v. Hayes, 2002-Ohio-751, 2002 WL 242115 (Ohio Ct. App. 9th Dist. Medina County 2002) and Capitol Mortgage Services, Inc. v. Hummel, 2001 WL 170594 (Ohio Ct. App. 10th Dist. Franklin County 2001) (Given the limited review of the magistrate's decision by both the trial court and the appellate court when proper objections are not filed, proper service of the magistrate's decision pursuant to the mandatory language in Civ. R. 53(E)(1) is necessary so that objections, if any, may be timely and properly filed.).

[3]Matter of Slavey, 1998 WL 546580 (Ohio Ct. App. 3d Dist. Crawford County 1998).

[4]Barker v. Barker, 118 Ohio App. 3d 706, 711, 693 N.E.2d 1164 (6th Dist. Lucas County 1997).

[5]Thomas v. Thomas, 2000-Ohio-2598, 2000 WL 1672879 (Ohio Ct. App. 7th Dist. Jefferson County 2000).

ment of a report could be waived, and the referee could instead submit an agreed form, order, or judgment to the court. Since the filing of objections is tied to the filing of a report, the waiver of the need for a report would also obviate the need for a fourteen day objection period with respect to the findings of fact.

Now, under Civil Rule 53(E)(3)(b), parties can stipulate in writing that the magistrate's findings of fact shall be final, in which case, the parties may object only to errors of law in the decision. Civil Rule 53(E)(4)(c) provides that "[t]he court may adopt a magistrate's decision . . . without waiting for timely objections"[6] and therefore, where the parties have stipulated to the magistrate's factual findings and waived the right to file objections to said findings of fact, the court's order would take effect much as it would have under the waiver provision in the former version.

§ 31:7   Findings of fact and conclusions of law—Request by a party; Required by law

Instead of the report required under the previous rule, Civil Rule 53(E)(2), now provides for findings of fact and conclusions of law to be included in the magistrate's decision if requested by a party, or otherwise required by law or by the order of reference.[1] Civil Rule 53(E)(2) provides that a request for findings of fact and conclusions of law under Civil Rule 52 may be made either before or after the magistrate's decision is filed.[2] If the request for findings of fact and conclusions of law is made before the decision is filed, Civil Rule 53(E)(2) states that "the magistrate's decision shall include findings of fact and conclusions of law." The July 1, 1996 amendment to this division of the rule deleted the word "proposed" which inadvertently appeared in the initial version. The Staff Note to the 1996 amendment explains that no substantive change is intended, and that it is a technical amendment to delete the word included in error by the 1995 amendment. If a party's request for findings of fact and conclusions of law under Civil Rule 52 is made after the decision is filed, the magistrate must include the findings of fact and conclusions of law in an amended magistrate's decision.[3]

Civil Rule 52 requires a request for findings of fact and conclusions of law to be filed within seven days after the filing of the magistrate's decision. Under Civil Rule 52, when a request for findings of fact and conclusions of law is made, the court may choose to require any or all of

---

[6]See Weitz v. Paulik, 1998 WL 429906 (Ohio Ct. App. 5th Dist. Stark County 1998).

[Section 31:7]

[1]See Thomas v. Thomas, 2000-Ohio-2598, 2000 WL 1672879 (Ohio Ct. App. 7th Dist. Jefferson County 2000).

[2]Banks v. Banks, 1998 WL 156999 (Ohio Ct. App. 11th Dist. Trumbull County 1998).

[3]Hanley v. Hanley, 1998 WL 372685 (Ohio Ct. App. 4th Dist. Pickaway County 1998).

the parties to submit their own proposed findings and conclusions.[4] The court may then draw from or use those findings and conclusions as its order, thereby alleviating the need for the magistrate to prepare a lengthy report as under the former Civil Rule 53. Assuming that all the provisions of Civil Rule 52 apply, a magistrate's decision must state "the conclusions of fact found separately from the conclusions of law."[5]

Findings of fact may be required by law even in the absence of a request by either party. There are many sections of the Revised Code that require a court to make findings of fact on specific issues. For example, RC 3105.171(D) requires written findings of fact if separate property is not disbursed to the spouse who owns it, and RC 3109.04(B)(2)(b) requires written findings of fact if a court declines to interview a child to determine wishes and concerns. In addition, there are a number of sections in the child support statute, RC 3119.01 et seq., requiring a court to enter specific findings of fact on the journal. One is RC 3119.01(B)(11) which requires a finding of "voluntary unemployment or underemployment" before imputing income. It is reasonable to assume a magistrate's decision would have to include an ultimate finding of fact on any of these issues even in the absence of a request under Civ. R. 53(E)(2).

The main purpose of a report, under the former Civ. R. 53(E), was to provide the trial court with a record on which to base an independent analysis of the matter referred to, heard, and reported on by the referee.[6] The rule required that the "findings of fact must be sufficient for the court to make an independent analysis of the issues and to apply appropriate rules of law in reaching a judgment order."[7] The requirement that the trial court conduct an independent analysis was not tied to the filing of objections and had to be done whether or not objections were filed.

On July 1, 1995, Civ. R. 53(E) was amended. The current version does not contain the same language concerning independent analysis. The Staff Notes to the 1995 amendment explain that, as to magistrate's decisions to which no objections have been filed, ". . . the judge is no longer required to conduct an independent review and make a determination himself or herself."[8] The Ohio Supreme Court recently affirmed this in

---

[4]See Ferguson v. Ferguson, 2000 WL 1724294 (Ohio Ct. App. 5th Dist. Knox County 2000), and Simpson v. Byrider, 2000 WL 222048 (Ohio Ct. App. 5th Dist. Stark County 2000).

[5]Civ. R. 52.

[6]Logue v. Wilson, 45 Ohio App. 2d 132, 136, 74 Ohio Op. 2d 140, 341 N.E.2d 641 (10th Dist. Franklin County 1975) and Brownell v. Brownell, 1985 WL 17450 (Ohio Ct. App. 4th Dist. Athens County 1985).

[7]Former Civ. R. 53(E)(5).

[8]Capitol Mortgage Services, Inc. v. Hummel, 2001 WL 170594 (Ohio Ct. App. 10th Dist. Franklin County 2001); In re Putka, 2001 WL 210027 (Ohio Ct. App. 8th Dist. Cuyahoga County 2001); Weber v. Weber, No. 2846-M (Ohio Ct. App. 9th Dist. Medina County 1999); Lowery v. Keystone Bd. of Educ., 2001 WL 490017 (Ohio Ct. App. 9th Dist. Lorain County 2001); Bontempo v. Miles, 2002-Ohio-487, 2002 WL 192100 (Ohio

Miele v. Ribovich,[9] which involved a forcible entry and detainer proceeding and a magistrate's decision to which no objections were filed. The Supreme Court stated that ". . . in the absence of written objections or an erroneous or patently defective magistrate's decision, a judge is no longer required 'to make an independent analysis of the issues,' as required under the former version of the rule."

However, where objections are filed, appellate courts considering cases decided under the current rule, still emphasized the need for the trial court to independently review a magistrate's decision.[10] Therefore, cases decided under previous versions of Civ. R. 53, which address the issue of the adequacy of findings of fact in referee's reports, would be equally applicable to magistrate's decisions.

A magistrate's decision must set forth clearly and concisely the controlling facts, the applicable law (if requested by a party or otherwise required by law or by the order of reference) and a decision.[11] Controlling facts would include names and addresses and other relevant personal data about the parties; jurisdiction and venue factors, and the salient facts about the matter in controversy derived from testimony and other evidence presented to the magistrate.

Findings of fact should be findings of ultimate facts.[12] Ultimate facts are deduced from evidentiary facts only after the magistrate has determined relevancy, materiality, and credibility. These facts must

---

Ct. App. 8th Dist. Cuyahoga County 2002), and Chrin v. Thudium, 1999 WL 689900 (Ohio Ct. App. 9th Dist. Summit County 1999).

[9]Miele v. Ribovich, 90 Ohio St. 3d 439, 2000-Ohio-193, 739 N.E.2d 333 (2000).

[10]Spring Works, Inc. v. Sarff, 1996 WL 339991 (Ohio Ct. App. 10th Dist. Franklin County 1996) and Loges v. England, 1996 WL 631399 (Ohio Ct. App. 2d Dist. Montgomery County 1996).

[11]Former Civ. R. 53(E)(5). See Miller v. Miller, 1987 WL 32749 (Ohio Ct. App. 12th Dist. Warren County 1987) (former Civ. R. 53(E)(5) required report to contain as much factual information as necessary to support the findings of fact and recommendations made). See also State, ex rel. Bedard, v. Lockbourne, 69 Ohio App. 3d 452, 459, 590 N.E.2d 1327 (10th Dist. Franklin County 1990) (although not "model of clarity," report sufficient because it contained two findings essential to conclusion reached; conclusion sufficiently stated for court to know what final recommendation was); Garcia v. Tillack, 9 Ohio App. 3d 222, 222, 459 N.E.2d 918 (9th Dist. Lorain County 1983); Freeman v. Westland Builders, Inc., 2 Ohio App. 3d 212, 214, 441 N.E.2d 283 (8th Dist. Cuyahoga County 1981); Harrower v. Aker, 1988 WL 94015 (Ohio Ct. App. 5th Dist. Tuscarawas County 1988) (trial court erred in adopting referee's report where it presented no recitation of facts and the trial court could make no "independent analysis" as required by former Civ. R. 53(E)(5) as then in effect; referee did not consider the child support guidelines, effective 10-1-87, when the motion to modify child support was filed 10-9-87), and Zimmerman v. Zimmerman, 1988 WL 89651 (Ohio Ct. App. 12th Dist. Clermont County 1988) (where the referee's report did not include the findings of fact as required by former Civ. R. 53(E)(5), the court could not make the independent judgment mandated by the Civil Rules to adopt the report; report was rendered totally defective even absent objections by either party).

[12]Buzinski v. Buzinski, 1993 WL 544358 (Ohio Ct. App. 5th Dist. Stark County 1993); In re Spears, No. 96 CA 1718 (Ohio Ct. App. 4th Dist. Adams County 1996); Quality Supply Co., Inc. v. D'S Drive Thru, 1996 WL 631385 (Ohio Ct. App. 2d Dist. Montgomery County 1996), and Columbus City School Dist. Bd. of Edn. v. Zaino, 90 Ohio St. 3d 496, 498-99, 2001-Ohio-5, 739 N.E.2d 783 (2001).

then be tied to the applicable law, conclusions drawn, and a decision set forth.[13] Without this record, the trial court would not have a basis of review. One court of appeals has held: "[t]he ultimate test of adequacy of findings of fact is whether they are sufficiently comprehensive and pertinent to the issue to form a basis for the decision reached. . . . The adequacy of those findings is critical to the decision of a party whether to file objections, and to the independent review of the magistrate's decision that Civ. R. 53 requires the trial court to perform."[14]

Occasionally, an appellate court has allowed for something less than a full written report/decision. One court held that the factual record was the requisite part of a report and that the absence of a written report could have been cured by a transcript of proceedings before the referee.[15] In a similar vein, another court held that the failure of a referee to make specific factual findings in a report did not preclude a trial court from adopting the recommendation, where exhibits were attached to the report and were available for the court's review.[16] However, these cases are the exceptions. If the report under the old rule did not satisfy the requirement of sufficiency, it had to be referred back by the trial court for clarification. The trial court could take this action independently[17] or after there was an objection.

Civil Rule 53(E)(4)(b) still provides for the court, when considering and ruling on any objections, among other things, to recommit the matter to the magistrate with instructions. Failure to rectify a deficient decision, either by independent action by the trial judge, or on objections, would not render a judgment based on such a report void, but voidable.[18] The judgment could be reversed on appeal. This same reasoning has been applied to judgments made when there was no report, on the basis that if the trial court has jurisdiction of the matter, its judgment is not void, but voidable.[19]

Where Civil Rule 52 request is properly made of a trial court, the court "does not abuse its discretion when it fails to make separate findings of fact and conclusions of law . . . but instead issues an order

---

[13]Brownell v. Brownell, 1985 WL 17450 (Ohio Ct. App. 4th Dist. Athens County 1985).

[14]Quality Supply Co., Inc. v. D'S Drive Thru, 1996 WL 631385, at *2-3 (Ohio Ct. App. 2d Dist. Montgomery County 1996).

[15]Bernard v. Bernard, No. 9443 (Ohio Ct. App. 9th Dist. Summit County 1980).

[16]Kilroy v. B.H. Lakeshore Co., 111 Ohio App. 3d 357, 359-360, 676 N.E.2d 171 (8th Dist. Cuyahoga County 1996).

[17]Staggs v. Staggs, 9 Ohio App. 3d 109, 109-110, 458 N.E.2d 904 (8th Dist. Cuyahoga County 1983).

[18]Eisenberg v. Peyton, 56 Ohio App. 2d 144, 146-147, 10 Ohio Op. 3d 158, 381 N.E.2d 1136 (8th Dist. Cuyahoga County 1978).

[19]State ex rel. Lesher v. Kainrad, 65 Ohio St. 2d 68, 19 Ohio Op. 3d 261, 417 N.E.2d 1382 (1981); Russell v. Russell, 1992 WL 67094 (Ohio Ct. App. 8th Dist. Cuyahoga County 1992) (referee's failure to file report harmless error because issue before court one of jurisdiction under statutes and case law which trial court correctly applied).

adopting the findings and conclusions of the court's referee."[20] Where the trial court did not adopt the referee's report, a failure to comply with the request for findings of fact and conclusions of law was held to be prejudicial error.[21]

Because current Civil Rule 53(E)(2) specifically refers to Civil Rule 52, and provides that the magistrate must include findings of fact and conclusions of law in a decision or amended decision, many of the issues arising in this context will be resolved by following the revised procedures.

§ 31:8 Objections to magistrate's decision—In general

The procedure for objecting to magistrate's decisions under the 1995 amendment to Civil Rule 53 is substantially the same as the objection procedure had been under the former rule. Therefore, cases construing the former rule, although referring to "referee" and "reports," are still applicable under the current rule.

Civil Rule 53(E)(3)(a) requires a party to file any written objections to the magistrate's decision within 14 days after the decision is filed.[1] The opposing party may file objections no later than 10 days after the first objections are filed.[2] If a party has filed a request for findings of fact and conclusions of law under Civil Rule 52, the time for filing objections begins to run when a decision, which includes the findings and conclusions, is filed.[3]

The time period for filing objections remains the same under the current version of Civil Rule 53 as it was under the former version. Accordingly, the case law dealing with the issue of timely filing remains applicable. Objections to a decision must be filed within fourteen days after date of filing. The fourteen-day period can be extended in the man-

---

[20]Dunson v. Aldrich, 54 Ohio App. 3d 137, 138, 561 N.E.2d 972 (10th Dist. Franklin County 1988); Johnson v. Johnson, 1992 WL 209320, at *6 (Ohio Ct. App. 3d Dist. Crawford County 1992) ("[i]t would be unreasonable to require the trial court to rewrite the referee's findings of fact and conclusions of law when the court has reached the same factual and legal conclusions, as it specifically indicated"); Whitson v. Whitson, 1992 WL 211938 (Ohio Ct. App. 2d Dist. Miami County 1992) (after adopting referee's findings of fact and conclusions of law it is not abuse of discretion for trial court to decline to make separate findings of fact and conclusions of law).

[21]Stocker v. Stocker, 1987 WL 28447 (Ohio Ct. App. 1st Dist. Hamilton County 1987).

[Section 31:8]

[1]See Sellers v. Sellers, 1999 WL 770257 (Ohio Ct. App. 5th Dist. Licking County 1999).

[2]Davis v. Davis, 1996 WL 430868 (Ohio Ct. App. 2d Dist. Montgomery County 1996), cause dismissed, 76 Ohio St. 3d 1480, 669 N.E.2d 861 (1996) and dismissed, appeal not allowed, 77 Ohio St. 3d 1519, 674 N.E.2d 372 (1997) and Mathers v. Mathers, 1992 WL 86564 (Ohio Ct. App. 11th Dist. Geauga County 1992).

[3]Green v. Lemarr, 139 Ohio App. 3d 414, 420-421, 744 N.E.2d 212 (2d Dist. Greene County 2000), and Dean v. Dean, 1999 WL 211828 (Ohio Ct. App. 12th Dist. Fayette County 1999).

ner provided by Civil Rule 6(B).[4] Objections filed after the Civil Rule 53(E)(3) time period can, within the discretion of the trial court, be considered.[5] Leave of court can be granted to file objections, otherwise excusable neglect may justify their consideration.[6] When one party has timely filed an objection, any other party then has an additional ten days to file objections, or can file them within the original period, whichever is longer.[7]

A trial court may adopt a magistrate's decision prior to the timely filing of objections.[8] Timely objections, however, stay the order except when the order is an interim order entered pursuant to Civil Rule 53(E)(4)(c).[9] If a party fails to timely object after the adoption of the order, he/she waives the right to appeal issues of fact.[10]

The fact that the decision must be served on the parties does not require the application of Civil Rule 6(E) to extend the fourteen-day objection period by another three days. Civil Rule 6(E) is inapplicable because the time limit for filing objections "begins to run on the date the report is filed and not the date a party receives notice of the report or is served a copy of it."[11] This view was supported in the 1975 Staff Notes to Civil Rule 53 wherein it was noted that "[t]he time period for objections is keyed to the filing of the report and not to its receipt by the objecting party." While untimely filing of objections or failure to file can be the result of causes beyond the control of the parties, such as the court's failure to mail a copy of the report or lost mail, the fact remains that responsible practice of law requires vigilance and checks of the court's docket to determine the date of filing of the report to insure timely filing of objections.

§ 31:9 Objections to magistrate's decision—Purpose and content of objections

Civil Rule 53(E)(3) does not set forth a formula for preparing objec-

---

[4]Russell v. Russell, 14 Ohio App. 3d 408, 471 N.E.2d 810 (12th Dist. Warren County 1984).

[5]Sellers v. Sellers, 1999 WL 770257 (Ohio Ct. App. 5th Dist. Licking County 1999).

[6]Conroy v. Conroy, 1993 WL 310421 (Ohio Ct. App. 10th Dist. Franklin County 1993).

[7]Civ. R. 53(E)(3)(a).

[8]Civ. R. 53(E)(4)(c); Wood Manor Furniture, Inc. v. Miken, Inc., 2000 WL 1158752 (Ohio Ct. App. 5th Dist. Stark County 2000), and Abate v. Abate, 2000 WL 327227 (Ohio Ct. App. 9th Dist. Summit County 2000).

[9]McCown v. McCown, 145 Ohio App. 3d 170, 171, 762 N.E.2d 398 (12th Dist. Fayette County 2001); see King v. King, 2002-Ohio-1060, 2002 WL 398716, 2002 (Ohio Ct. App. 4th Dist. Adams County 2002), and see Tulley v. Tulley, 2001-Ohio-4307, 2001 WL 1216974 (Ohio Ct. App. 11th Dist. Portage County 2001).

[10]Huffman v. Huffman, 2001 WL 799882 (Ohio Ct. App. 11th Dist. Trumbull County 2001); Berry v. Pate, 1997 WL 727492 (Ohio Ct. App. 12th Dist. Butler County 1997); Zahn v. Zahn, 1997 WL 625482 (Ohio Ct. App. 9th Dist. Summit County 1997), and Gearhart v. Gearhart, 1997 WL 359320 (Ohio Ct. App. 4th Dist. Ross County 1997).

[11]Hucke v. Hucke, 1990 WL 125700, at *2 (Ohio Ct. App. 2d Dist. Montgomery County 1990).

tions, except to require they be in writing, be specific, and state with particularity the grounds for the objections. A general objection is insufficient to preserve an issue for judicial consideration.[1] Since the purpose is to focus the trial court's attention on alleged errors, a mere statement of difference of opinion not supported by specific reference to error in fact, law, recommendation, or other irregularity would not provide the trial court with necessary information concerning the objection.[2]

At one time, the rule of law, established in the case of *Normandy Place Assocs. v. Beyer*,[3] was that the filing of objections was not a prerequisite to appellate review of a referee's report. The Ohio Supreme Court drew this conclusion from the language in Civil Rule 53 as it existed at that time. As a result of the amendments to Civil Rule 53 since that time, the opposite is now true.

Compliance with the requirements as to the filing and content of objections to a magistrate's decision is critical to preserving rights of review both at the trial and appellate levels. Civil Rule 53(E)(4)(a) provides that, if no written objections are filed, the trial court may adopt the magistrate's decision absent error of law or other defect on the face of the decision.[4] The 1995 Staff Note to Civil Rule 53(E)(4) makes it clear that, when no objections are filed, "the judge is no longer required to conduct an independent review and make a determination himself or herself."[5] A 1998 amendment, however, clarified that the trial court is to consider and rule on, not merely to consider, properly filed objections.[6] In *Hulcher*,[7] the Second District Court of Appeals could not address the merits of husband's appeal of the trial court's denial of a motion to terminate spousal support by reason of cohabitation. Husband did not file objections to the magistrate's order pursuant to Civil Rule 53(E)(4)(c).

Civil Rule 53(E)(3)(b) addresses the effect, at the appellate level, of the failure to file objections. A party may not assign as error on appeal the court's adoption of any finding of fact or conclusion of law unless the

---

[Section 31:9]

[1]1995 Staff Notes to Civ. R. 53(E); King v. King, 2002-Ohio-1060, 2002 WL 398716, 2002 (Ohio Ct. App. 4th Dist. Adams County 2002), and Youngstown Metropolitan Housing Authority v. Scott, 2001-Ohio-3308, 2001 WL 744496 (Ohio Ct. App. 7th Dist. Mahoning County 2001).

[2]Bolli v. Bolli, 1990 WL 152104 (Ohio Ct. App. 7th Dist. Mahoning County 1990) (appellant failed to state with specificity particular grounds on which she relied for objections).

[3]Normandy Place Associates v. Beyer, 2 Ohio St. 3d 102, 443 N.E.2d 161 (1982).

[4]Haas v. Haas, 1997 WL 835077 (Ohio Ct. App. 11th Dist. Geauga County 1997) and Matter of Williams, 1997 WL 84659 (Ohio Ct. App. 10th Dist. Franklin County 1997).

[5]See also Pacific v. Interstate Ford, Inc., 1996 WL 257434 (Ohio Ct. App. 2d Dist. Montgomery County 1996) and Miele v. Ribovich, 90 Ohio St. 3d 439, 2000-Ohio-193, 739 N.E.2d 333 (2000).

[6]1998 Staff Notes to Civ. R. 53(E).

[7]Hulcher v. Hulcher, 2000 WL 543315 (Ohio Ct. App. 2d Dist. Montgomery County 2000).

party has objected to that finding or conclusion under the rule.[8] By failing to file any objection, a party "is foreclosed from assigning any error in this Court to the trial court's adoption of the magistrate's decision."[9]

A party who does file objections must take care to raise any and all arguments in those objections. Arguments not made at the trial level will not be entertained by the court of appeals.[10]

Objections can be made to factual findings or to conclusions of law, or both. Objections to factual findings must be accompanied by a transcript or an affidavit concerning the evidence if a transcript is not available.[11] In the case of objections alleging only error of law in a magistrate's decision, no transcript is necessary.[12] Nevertheless, one appellate court has cautioned: "because so many issues of family law involve the application of law to specific facts, the prudent practitioner seeking review of a referee's proposed conclusions of law should still provide the trial court with pertinent parts of the transcript of the . . . hearing or proper substitute therefor."[13] Otherwise, there is the risk that the court of appeals will disagree with appellant that the issue is solely one of law and not an issue of fact and law requiring a transcript.[14]

§ 31:10 Objections to magistrate's decision—Need for transcript

If a party objects to a magistrate's findings of fact, it is essential that the objections be supported by relevant portions of the transcript or, if no transcript is available, by an affidavit. Civil Rule 53(E)(3)(b) acknowledges the principle that, absent an adequate record of the

---

[8]See Walker v. J.W. Automotive, 2001 WL 726803 (Ohio Ct. App. 2d Dist. Montgomery County 2001); Doane v. Doane, 2001 WL 474267 (Ohio Ct. App. 5th Dist. Guernsey County 2001); Pletcher v. Pletcher, 2000 WL 1886291 (Ohio Ct. App. 5th Dist. Muskingum County 2000); Handwerker v. Handwerker, 1998 WL 801351 (Ohio Ct. App. 2d Dist. Montgomery County 1998); Flax v. Flax, 1998 WL 128402 (Ohio Ct. App. 2d Dist. Greene County 1998); Rush v. Schlagetter, 1997 WL 193169 (Ohio Ct. App. 4th Dist. Ross County 1997), and Chrin v. Thudium, 1999 WL 689900 (Ohio Ct. App. 9th Dist. Summit County 1999).

[9]See Donnelly v. Donnelly, 1996 WL 688165 (Ohio Ct. App. 9th Dist. Summit County 1996); Hanshaw v. Hanshaw, 1996 WL 368232 (Ohio Ct. App. 3d Dist. Marion County 1996), and Asad v. Asad, 131 Ohio App. 3d 654, 656, 723 N.E.2d 203 (8th Dist. Cuyahoga County 1999).

[10]Towne v. Towne, 1996 WL 688155 (Ohio Ct. App. 9th Dist. Summit County 1996); Hansen v. Hansen, 1998 WL 666763 (Ohio Ct. App. 5th Dist. Morrow County 1998), and Cottle v. Cottle, 1998 WL 964582 (Ohio Ct. App. 11th Dist. Portage County 1998).

[11]In re Cooper Brown, 2002-Ohio-395, 2002 WL 125690 (Ohio Ct. App. 2d Dist. Montgomery County 2002); Lovas v. Mullett, 2001 WL 735726 (Ohio Ct. App. 11th Dist. Geauga County 2001); Brown v. Brown, 2001 WL 324391 (Ohio Ct. App. 9th Dist. Summit County 2001); Wantz v. Wantz, 2001 WL 285864 (Ohio Ct. App. 11th Dist. Geauga County 2001); Priester v. Priester, 2000 WL 1733689 (Ohio Ct. App. 11th Dist. Lake County 2000), and Link v. Link, 2000 WL 234866 (Ohio Ct. App. 11th Dist. Lake County 2000).

[12]Syal v. Singh, 1996 WL 556913 (Ohio Ct. App. 9th Dist. Summit County 1996).

[13]Helton v. Helton, 102 Ohio App. 3d 733, 737, 658 N.E.2d 1 (1st Dist. Hamilton County 1994).

[14]See Kalnoki v. Kalnoki-Kis, 1997 WL 156715 (Ohio Ct. App. 8th Dist. Cuyahoga County 1997).

proceedings before the trial court, a reviewing court must presume regularity and affirm.[1] Since the requirements of a transcript or affidavit to support objections to findings of fact is the same under the 1995 amendments to Civil Rule 53 as it was under the former version, the case law which had developed around that issue remains applicable.[2]

Objections to a magistrate's decision may be supported by a partial transcript as long as the partial transcript provides testimony relevant to each objection.[3] However, proceed with caution if choosing to provide the trial court with only a partial transcript. Without a complete transcript, a trial court does not know if a record of all the relevant facts was submitted. Therefore, a trial court may presume that the magistrate's evidentiary rulings are valid and overrule the objections.[4]

It has been held that if an objecting party files only a partial transcript in support of the objections, it is incumbent on the other party to file additional relevant portions of the transcript if necessary to a proper adjudication.[5]

However, more recent decisions have placed the burden solely on the objecting party to provide the trial court with a complete account of the evidence.[6] One court refused to consider the full transcript on appeal where the appellant had provided the trial court with only isolated por-

---

[Section 31:10]

[1]Deluca v. Goldstein, 2000 WL 284088 (Ohio Ct. App. 8th Dist. Cuyahoga County 2000); Nicholson v. Starcher, 2000 WL 1658 (Ohio Ct. App. 5th Dist. Stark County 1999); Glazer v. Glazer, 1999 WL 608795 (Ohio Ct. App. 8th Dist. Cuyahoga County 1999); Shannon v. Shannon, 122 Ohio App. 3d 346, 349-350, 701 N.E.2d 771 (9th Dist. Summit County 1997), and Spring Works, Inc. v. Sarff, 1996 WL 339991 (Ohio Ct. App. 10th Dist. Franklin County 1996).

[2]See Proctor v. Proctor, 48 Ohio App. 3d 55, 548 N.E.2d 287 (3d Dist. Allen County 1988); Waltimire v. Waltimire, 55 Ohio App. 3d 275, 564 N.E.2d 119 (3d Dist. Henry County 1989) (appellant could not assign as error abuse of discretion of trial court instead of filing objections to referee's report); Ankrom v. Ankrom, 30 Ohio App. 3d 47, 506 N.E.2d 259 (8th Dist. Cuyahoga County 1985) (party who failed to attend hearing and to file objection waived right to appeal review of findings); Frizzell v. Frizzell, 1991 WL 271705 (Ohio Ct. App. 3d Dist. Logan County 1991) (where party's written objections did not address referee's decision to limit number of witnesses, alleged error was waived); Richardson v. Richardson, 1990 WL 37433 (Ohio Ct. App. 8th Dist. Cuyahoga County 1990) (failure to appear at hearing and to file objections waived right to appeal on weight of evidence); Jeter v. Allen, 1990 WL 95375 (Ohio Ct. App. 10th Dist. Franklin County 1990) (failure to file objections and transcript prevented trial court from determining whether referee's recommendations were against weight of evidence and waived right to appeal trial court's adoption of findings); Bisbee v. Bisbee, 1992 WL 193686 (Ohio Ct. App. 12th Dist. Madison County 1992) (failure to object to exclusion of findings precluded raising issue on appeal).

[3]Kozlevchar v. Kozlevchar, 2000 WL 640614 (Ohio Ct. App. 8th Dist. Cuyahoga County 2000).

[4]Carro v. Carro, 2001 WL 637492 (Ohio Ct. App. 8th Dist. Cuyahoga County 2001); Deluca v. Goldstein, 2000 WL 284088 (Ohio Ct. App. 8th Dist. Cuyahoga County 2000), and Chrin v. Thudium, 1999 WL 689900 (Ohio Ct. App. 9th Dist. Summit County 1999).

[5]Zadzilka v. Zadzilka, 1989 WL 151286 (Ohio Ct. App. 8th Dist. Cuyahoga County 1989).

[6]Haley v. Haley, 2001-Ohio-3083, 2001 WL 1590170 (Ohio Ct. App. 6th Dist. Lucas County 2001); Molnar v. Molnar, 2001 WL 688898 (Ohio Ct. App. 9th Dist. Medina

tions of it, making it "impossible to discern whether the testimony was later rebutted, contradicted, or impeached in any fashion."[7] Similarly, another court termed it "disingenuous for a party to submit only those portions of the evidence presented that supports his position, while omitting all evidence that was contrary to his position."[8] Further, a trial court erred in adopting the finding of a referee's report before reviewing a transcript that was timely ordered by a party filing objections.[9]

If no transcript is available and an affidavit is submitted, it must purport to comprise all the relevant evidence submitted on the issue, not just the evidence the objecting party believes was disregarded.[10] In *Witriol v. Witriol*,[11] the trial court properly accepted the referee's findings without further consideration. In this 1987 case, the party objected to the findings on the basis that the findings were against the manifest weight of the evidence, but failed to present contrary evidence beyond unsupported statements in an affidavit.

A record provides the trial court with an objective basis on which to analyze the decision and the objections which have been made to it, and it preserves the record for appeal. Civil Rule 53(D)(2) requires that ". . . all proceedings before the magistrate shall be recorded in accordance with procedures established by the court."[12] Even though parties agree that a proceeding which determines the effective date of modification of child support should not be recorded, Civ. R. 53(D)(2) requires it. The magistrate should not have relied upon unsworn statements of counsel and stipulations only signed by counsel to determine the issue.[13] At least one appellate court has considered the cost of a transcript to support objections as a necessary litigation expense and thus taxable as costs in the action.[14] However, the Eighth District Court of Appeals does not

---

County 2001), and Stewart v. Stewart, 1998 WL 177558 (Ohio Ct. App. 2d Dist. Montgomery County 1998), dismissed, appeal not allowed, 83 Ohio St. 3d 1428, 699 N.E.2d 945 (1998).

[7]Medoff v. Medoff, 1995 WL 363811, at *2 (Ohio Ct. App. 8th Dist. Cuyahoga County 1995).

[8]Wade v. Wade, 113 Ohio App. 3d 414, 418, 680 N.E.2d 1305 (11th Dist. Lake County 1996); see also Oatey v. Oatey, 1997 WL 47658 (Ohio Ct. App. 8th Dist. Cuyahoga County 1997) (it is the appellant's burden to provide an adequate record demonstrating claimed error).

[9]Fabry v. Kral, 1993 WL 6676 (Ohio Ct. App. 9th Dist. Summit County 1993).

[10]Blinsky v. Protain, 2001-Ohio-3321, 2001 WL 772244 (Ohio Ct. App. 7th Dist. Mahoning County 2001); Pappenhagen v. Payne, 48 Ohio App. 3d 176, 549 N.E.2d 208 (8th Dist. Cuyahoga County 1988); Wagner v. Wagner, 1989 WL 21419 (Ohio Ct. App. 8th Dist. Cuyahoga County 1989); Lapp v. Lapp, 1989 WL 112997 (Ohio Ct. App. 8th Dist. Cuyahoga County 1989).

[11]Witriol v. Witriol, 1987 WL 12624 (Ohio Ct. App. 8th Dist. Cuyahoga County 1987).

[12]Civ. R. 53(D)(2); Moyers v. Moyers, 1999 WL 418007 (Ohio Ct. App. 11th Dist. Ashtabula County 1999).

[13]Leopard v. Leopard, 1999 WL 333247 (Ohio Ct. App. 10th Dist. Franklin County 1999).

[14]Zittkowski v. Zittkowski, 70 Ohio App. 3d 484, 591 N.E.2d 396 (11th Dist. Lake County 1990).

concur with said decision.[15]

Civ. R. 53(E)(3)(b) does not establish a time within which the objecting party must file the transcript. Procedures for filing may be provided by local rule.[16] Counsel may rely upon audio transcripts in order to prepare proposed findings of fact and conclusions of law. In *Dean v. Dean*,[17] the trial court waited nearly three months before adopting the magistrate's decision during which time the objecting party neither ordered a transcript nor requested an extension of time to obtain the transcript. The court has no obligation to provide the transcript.

The failure to file a transcript in support of otherwise properly filed objections to findings of fact does not totally preclude appellate review of the trial court's adoption of the findings of fact. Where no transcript or affidavit was provided to the trial court, however, appellate review will be limited to determining whether the trial court's adoption of the findings constituted an abuse of discretion.[18] The appellate court may not consider a transcript of the proceedings before a magistrate, which was not provided to the trial court, but was submitted to the court of appeals

---

[15]Carro v. Carro, 2001 WL 637492 (Ohio Ct. App. 8th Dist. Cuyahoga County 2001).

[16]Motoycka v. Motycka, 1999-Ohio-963, 1999 WL 1215322 (Ohio Ct. App. 3d Dist. Van Wert County 1999); Shull v. Shull, 135 Ohio App. 3d 708, 710, 1999-Ohio-950, 735 N.E.2d 496 (3d Dist. Union County 1999), and In re Guardianship of Allen, 2000 WL 522282 (Ohio Ct. App. 11th Dist. Trumbull County 2000).

[17]Dean v. Dean, 1999 WL 211828 (Ohio Ct. App. 12th Dist. Fayette County 1999).

[18]Purpura v. Purpura, 33 Ohio App. 3d 237, 515 N.E.2d 27 (8th Dist. Cuyahoga County 1986) (court could accept referee's factual findings where objecting party did not provide transcript or other evidentiary material to contest referee's findings); Proctor v. Proctor, 48 Ohio App. 3d 55, 548 N.E.2d 287 (3d Dist. Allen County 1988); Slota v. Slota, 1991 WL 172898 (Ohio Ct. App. 9th Dist. Medina County 1991) (no transcript provided on objection or appeal; reviewing court could not overturn findings of referee and trial court absent complete record of evidence); Luthman v. Luthman, 1991 WL 199914 (Ohio Ct. App. 9th Dist. Summit County 1991) (failure to support objections with transcript constrained appellate court to review solely face of referee's report for abuse of discretion); Ritchhart v. Phillips, 1991 WL 136742 (Ohio Ct. App. 4th Dist. Ross County 1991) (reversed on abuse of discretion even though no transcript provided with objection to referee report because a finding critical to conclusion was totally lacking in report); Staats v. Staats, 1991 WL 97765 (Ohio Ct. App. 2d Dist. Montgomery County 1991) (facts not clearly inconsistent with conclusion so as to require reversal); Stange v. Stange, 1991 WL 26763 (Ohio Ct. App. 11th Dist. Lake County 1991) (since appellant did not file transcript or affidavit with objections he was precluded from raising factual questions on appeal); MacDonald v. MacDonald, 62 Ohio St. 3d 1432, 578 N.E.2d 824 (1991) (failure to file transcript or affidavit with objections precluded appellate review of findings of fact on child support modification); Davis v. Davis, 1996 WL 430868 (Ohio Ct. App. 2d Dist. Montgomery County 1996), cause dismissed, 76 Ohio St. 3d 1480, 669 N.E.2d 861 (1996) and dismissed, appeal not allowed, 77 Ohio St. 3d 1519, 674 N.E.2d 372 (1997) (correctness of referee's report presumed even given parties' joint objection that recommendation was in opposition to agreement, absent transcript being filed with objections submitted to trial court); Spring Works, Inc. v. Sarff, 1996 WL 339991 (Ohio Ct. App. 10th Dist. Franklin County 1996); Jones v. Holbert, 1998 WL 6947 (Ohio Ct. App. 8th Dist. Cuyahoga County 1998); Hobt v. Hobt, No. 99-G-2223 (Ohio Ct. App. 11th Dist. Geauga County 2000); In re Guardianship of Visnich, 2000 WL 1488081 (Ohio Ct. App. 11th Dist. Trumbull County 2000); In re Cooper Brown, 2002-Ohio-395, 2002 WL 125690 (Ohio Ct. App. 2d Dist. Montgomery County 2002), and Love v. Rable, 147 Ohio App. 3d 63, 2001-Ohio-2174, 768 N.E.2d 1185 (3d Dist. Van Wert County 2001).

to support objections to said magistrate's decision.[19]

Civil Rule 53(E)(4)(b) sets forth the procedures for the consideration of objections. In 1998, this rule was amended to clarify that "[t]he court shall rule on any objections." The Staff Notes to this amendment explain that the previous language—"[u]pon consideration of any objections . . ." led some courts to consider objections without ruling on them when acting on a magistrate's decision.

The Rule provides that the court may adopt, reject, or modify the magistrate's decision, hear additional evidence, send the matter back to the magistrate with further instructions, or hear the matter itself. The court may refuse to consider additional evidence proffered unless the objecting party demonstrates that, with reasonable diligence, he or she could not have produced that evidence for the magistrate's consideration.[20] Because an appellate court cannot consider evidentiary materials that were not before the trial court, if a transcript or affidavit is not provided to the trial court, the deficiency cannot be cured by the provision of the transcript or an Appellate Rule 9(C) statement on appeal.[21] Absent a transcript of the magistrate's proceedings, the court of appeals in *Hale v. Hale*[22] could not conclude that the trial court improperly modified the parties' division of property or that the parties had not agreed to modify the agreement in writing. A transcript that contains only the facts supportive of objections is inadequate. The trial court may, in its discretion, order a complete transcript. The costs should be assessed against the objecting party.[23]

Former Civil Rule 53(E)(7) entitled "Permanent and Interim Orders" gave the trial court the right to enter judgment on the basis of the findings of fact in the referee's report without waiting for objections. However, if timely written objections were filed by either party, the filing of them operated as a stay of execution of the judgment until the court ruled on the objections.[24] Because proceedings are stayed until the court rules on objections, a judgment entry under the former rule that failed to dispose of the objections was interlocutory and not a final ap-

---

[19]Schafrath v. Schafrath, 1997 WL 422779 (Ohio Ct. App. 9th Dist. Wayne County 1997); Chew v. Gribble, 1998 WL 103329 (Ohio Ct. App. 9th Dist. Summit County 1998).

[20]McClain v. McClain, 1999 WL 960969 (Ohio Ct. App. 11th Dist. Portage County 1999) (trial court must first give offering party an opportunity to demonstrate that the evidence could not have been produced before the magistrate); Cox v. Cox, 1999 WL 74573 (Ohio Ct. App. 12th Dist. Fayette County 1999).

[21]Nicholson v. Starcher, 2000 WL 1658 (Ohio Ct. App. 5th Dist. Stark County 1999); Girves v. Girves, 1990 WL 108759 (Ohio Ct. App. 9th Dist. Medina County 1990); Mothes v. Mothes, 1991 WL 147412 (Ohio Ct. App. 11th Dist. Lake County 1991) (appellate court will not consider evidentiary materials that were not before the trial court); Medoff v. Medoff, 1995 WL 363811 (Ohio Ct. App. 8th Dist. Cuyahoga County 1995).

[22]Hale v. Hale, 2000 WL 109101 (Ohio Ct. App. 9th Dist. Medina County 2000).

[23]Carro v. Carro, 2001 WL 637492 (Ohio Ct. App. 8th Dist. Cuyahoga County 2001).

[24]O'Connor v. O'Connor, 1990 WL 14811 (Ohio Ct. App. 10th Dist. Franklin County 1990).

pealable order under RC 2505.02.[25] Amended Civil Rule 53(E)(4)(c) provides a similar process, and is likely to have the same result.[26]

Alternatively, where immediate relief is justified, the court may make an interim order on the basis of findings of fact contained in the magistrate's decision without waiting for or ruling on timely objections, and such an interim order is not subject to the automatic stay caused by the filing of objections.[27] However, interim orders extend no more than twenty-eight days from the date of entry unless, within that time for good cause shown, the court extends the interim order for one additional twenty-eight day period.[28]

§ 31:11   Objections to magistrate's decision—Basic—Form⊚

[Title of Court]

[Caption]   Case No. *[_____]*
                                                   OBJECTIONS TO DECISION OF
                                                   MAGISTRATE

[Plaintiff/Defendant] hereby objects to the Decision of Magistrate *[name]*, filed on *[date]*, for the reasons set forth in the *[affidavit/ memorandum]* of *[Plaintiff/Defendant]* *[attached hereto/as set forth below]*.

It is respectfully requested that the Magistrate's Decision be modified in the following manner: *[here state]*.

_____

Attorney for *[Plaintiff/Defendant]*

[Attach memorandum/affidavit of objecting party specifying and sup-porting objections]

[Notice]

[Proof/Certificate of Service]

NOTES TO FORM

Drafter's Notes

The Objections must state with particularity the grounds of objection.

Check court's Local Rules to verify if a hearing on the objections will be provided.

---

[25]Gainor v. Gainor, 1991 WL 147416 (Ohio Ct. App. 11th Dist. Lake County 1991).

[26]Weitz v. Paulik, 1998 WL 429906 (Ohio Ct. App. 5th Dist. Stark County 1998); Mc-Cown v. McCown, 145 Ohio App. 3d 170, 171, 762 N.E.2d 398 (12th Dist. Fayette County 2001); Barker v. Barker, 118 Ohio App. 3d 706, 711-712, 693 N.E.2d 1164 (6th Dist. Lucas County 1997); Tulley v. Tulley, 2001-Ohio-4307, 2001 WL 1216974 (Ohio Ct. App. 11th Dist. Portage County 2001); Lade v. Wheeler, 2000 WL 525717 (Ohio Ct. App. 12th Dist. Clermont County 2000), and Abate v. Abate, 2000 WL 327227 (Ohio Ct. App. 9th Dist. Summit County 2000).

[27]Brown v. Cummins, 120 Ohio App. 3d 554, 556, 698 N.E.2d 501 (6th Dist. Lucas County 1997).

[28]Civ. R. 53(E)(4)(c), formerly Civ. R. 53(E)(7); Barker v. Barker, 118 Ohio App. 3d 706, 711-712, 693 N.E.2d 1164 (6th Dist. Lucas County 1997); Walker v. Estate of Walker, No. 00 CA 208 (Ohio Ct. App. 7th Dist. 2001); LeFever v. Cornnuts, Inc., 1999 WL 22664 (Ohio Ct. App. 2d Dist. Champaign County 1999), and In Re Poole, No. 1997CA00163 (Ohio Ct. App. 5th Dist. 1998).

Franklin County Local Rule 9 requires that a party filing objections provide notice of date the matter is to be heard or submitted to opposing party or his attorney.

§ 31:12   Objections to magistrate's decision—Detailed—Form⊚

[Title of Court]

[Caption]   Case No. [_____]

OBJECTIONS TO DECISION OF
MAGISTRATE

This cause was heard before Magistrate [name] upon [Plaintiff's / Defendant's] motion to [describe motion]. All proceedings were duly heard before a court reporter, and the entire transcript of proceedings will be ordered and submitted to the Court upon receipt thereof for consideration with the Objections of the [Plaintiff / Defendant] herein filed. Upon receipt of the transcript of proceedings, it may be necessary for [Plaintiff / Defendant] to supplement these Objections based upon counsel's review of the transcript of proceedings.

Without limiting any further Objections that may be deemed necessary in supplemental filings upon review of the transcript of proceedings, [Plaintiff / Defendant] objects to the Decision of Magistrate [name], filed [date], as follows: [list objections].

It is respectfully submitted that the Magistrate has erroneously decided several significant issues against [Plaintiff / Defendant] and has not based [his / her] decision upon the evidence including testimony and exhibits. The Magistrate's findings that [list objectionable findings] should be reversed, and it is respectfully submitted that [describe requested relief] should be awarded based upon the trial of this cause.

[Plaintiff / Defendant] respectfully requests that this Court withhold ruling on the within Objections until the transcript of proceedings has been prepared and reviewed and any appropriate supplemental objections or briefs are filed with the Court.

Respectfully submitted,

_____
Attorney for [Plaintiff / Defendant]

[Notice]

[Proof / Certificate of Service]

NOTES TO FORM

Drafter's Notes

The Objections must state with particularity the grounds of objection.

Check court's Local Rules to verify if a hearing on the objections will be provided. Franklin County Local Rule 9 requires that a party filing objections provide notice of date the matter is to be heard or submitted to opposing party or his attorney.

§ 31:13   Effect of decision

Under the prior version of Civil Rule 53, a report was not a judgment and could not be presented as such.[1] It was a report of facts, applicable law, and the referee's recommendation. If a judgment was entered, it was to be the judgment of the court.[2] The journalized judgment may or may not have adopted the report as the basis of its judgment. The report standing alone was not effective as a judgment or binding on the parties.[3]

If a referee's report, under the prior rule, was never adopted by the court, will not become an order and will not be effective or binding.[4] A magistrate's decision is to be affected in the same way.

§ 31:14   Standard of review of magistrate's decisions; adoption of decision by court; permanent and interim orders

The power of a trial court to adopt, reject, or modify the decision of the magistrate, or any findings or conclusion that the magistrate makes, is a plenary power, and the review the trial court conducts must be de novo.[1] The standards of appellate review do not apply to the trial court's acceptance or rejection of the magistrate's findings or proposed decision.[2] The deferential review that is accorded the trial court by a reviewing court does not apply to a trial court's review of a magistrate's decision.[3] The trial court ". . . must undertake the equivalent of a *de novo* determination, in light of any filed objections, when independently assessing the facts and conclusions . . ." of the magistrate.[4] A trial court, having full power to review, including the power to conduct a trial de novo, was

---

[Section 31:13]

[1]Logue v. Wilson, 45 Ohio App. 2d 132, 74 Ohio Op. 2d 140, 341 N.E.2d 641 (10th Dist. Franklin County 1975).

[2]Wellborn v. K-Beck Furniture Mart, Inc., 54 Ohio App. 2d 65, 8 Ohio Op. 3d 93, 375 N.E.2d 61 (10th Dist. Franklin County 1977).

[3]Logue v. Wilson, 45 Ohio App. 2d 132, 74 Ohio Op. 2d 140, 341 N.E.2d 641 (10th Dist. Franklin County 1975); Eisenberg v. Peyton, 56 Ohio App. 2d 144, 10 Ohio Op. 3d 158, 381 N.E.2d 1136 (8th Dist. Cuyahoga County 1978); Nolte v. Nolte, 60 Ohio App. 2d 227, 14 Ohio Op. 3d 215, 396 N.E.2d 807 (8th Dist. Cuyahoga County 1978).

[4]Holton v. Holton, 1985 WL 9356 (Ohio Ct. App. 6th Dist. Lucas County 1985).

[Section 31:14]

[1]Loges v. England, 1996 WL 631399 (Ohio Ct. App. 2d Dist. Montgomery County 1996) and Cox v. Cox, 1999 WL 74573 (Ohio Ct. App. 12th Dist. Fayette County 1999).

[2]Mealey v. Mealey, 1996 WL 233491 (Ohio Ct. App. 9th Dist. Wayne County 1996); Breece v. Breece, 1999 WL 999759 (Ohio Ct. App. 2d Dist. Darke County 1999), and Goetze v. Goetze, 1998 WL 136164 (Ohio Ct. App. 2d Dist. Montgomery County 1998).

[3]Rhoads v. Arthur, 1999 WL 547574 (Ohio Ct. App. 5th Dist. Delaware County 1999), Quick v. Kwiatkowski, 2001-Ohio-1498, 2001 WL 871406 (Ohio Ct. App. 2d Dist. Montgomery County 2001) (the trial court errs when applying the abuse of discretion standard of review in ruling on Civil Rule 53(E)(3) objections to the decision of a magistrate).

[4]Klamfoth v. Klamfoth, 1996 WL 180939, at *6 (Ohio Ct. App. 10th Dist. Franklin County 1996); Harbeitner v. Harbeitner, 94 Ohio App. 3d 485, 641 N.E.2d 206 (8th Dist. Cuyahoga County 1994), dismissed, appeal not allowed, 70 Ohio St. 3d 1465, 640 N.E.2d 527 (1994); DeSantis v. Soller, 70 Ohio App. 3d 226, 232, 590 N.E.2d 886 (10th Dist. Franklin County 1990); Amos Suburban Newspapers v. Platt, 1996 WL 257213 (Ohio Ct. App. 2d Dist. Montgomery County 1996), and Holland v. Holland, 1998 WL 30179 (Ohio Ct. App. 10th Dist. Franklin County 1998).

to make its own independent analysis.[5]

As was true under the former version, the current version of Civil Rule 53 requires a court, before adopting a magistrate's decision, to determine whether there is any error of law or other defect on the face of the report/decision.[6] Civil Rule 53(E)(4)(a) provides, in pertinent part, that "[t]he court may adopt the magistrate's decision if no written objections are filed unless it determines that there is an error of law or other defect on the face of the magistrate's decision." The court's obligation to review a decision for error of law or other defects on the face of the decision exists regardless of whether objections are filed.[7]

What has been eliminated as a result of the 1995 amendments to Civil Rule 53 is the requirement that the court, in all cases, make an independent analysis of the issues. Under the current rule, the requirement of an independent analysis applies only in the event objections are filed. According to the 1995 Staff Notes to section Civil Rule 53(E)(4), if there is no apparent error and no objections are filed, "the judge is no longer required to conduct an independent review and make a determination himself or herself." The Ohio Supreme Court recently considered this issue in Miele v. Ribovich, 90 Ohio St. 3d 439, 2000-Ohio-193, 739 N.E.2d 333 (2000), which involved a forcible entry and detainer proceeding and a magistrate's decision to which no objections were filed. The Court, interpreting Civil Rule 53(E)(4), concluded that independent analysis is not required where no objections are filed.

Where a party does file objections to a magistrate's decision, the requirements for review by the trial court are the same as they were under the former rule. Prior to the 1995 amendments to Civil Rule 53, much had been said about the responsibility of the trial court to make an independent analysis of the referee's report and not to simply "rubber stamp" it.[8] The principles and rationales discussed by the various courts when considering cases decided under the former rule continues

---

[5]Tucke v. Tucke, 1991 WL 189174 (Ohio Ct. App. 5th Dist. Stark County 1991).

[6]Rush v. Schlagetter, 1997 WL 193169 (Ohio Ct. App. 4th Dist. Ross County 1997); Cheatham v. Cheatham, 1992 WL 371846 (Ohio Ct. App. 2d Dist. Greene County 1992); Lucas Metropolitan Housing Authority v. Kincade, 1995 WL 112963 (Ohio Ct. App. 6th Dist. Lucas County 1995) (overruled by, Sabrina J. v. Robbin C., 2001 WL 85157 (Ohio Ct. App. 6th Dist. Lucas County 2001)), and Williams v. Mark IV Apartments, 1994 WL 521136 (Ohio Ct. App. 8th Dist. Cuyahoga County 1994).

[7]Miele v. Ribovich, 90 Ohio St. 3d 439, 443, 2000-Ohio-193, 739 N.E.2d 333 (2000); Chrin v. Thudium, 1999 WL 689900 (Ohio Ct. App. 9th Dist. Summit County 1999); Asad v. Asad, 131 Ohio App. 3d 654, 656, 723 N.E.2d 203 (8th Dist. Cuyahoga County 1999); Seo v. Austintown Twp., 131 Ohio App. 3d 521, 525, 722 N.E.2d 1090 (7th Dist. Mahoning County 1998); Group One Realty, Inc. v. Dixie Internatl. Co., 125 Ohio App. 3d 767, 769, 709 N.E.2d 589 (10th Dist. Franklin County 1998); In re Weingart, 2002-Ohio-38, 2002 WL 68204 (Ohio Ct. App. 8th Dist. Cuyahoga County 2002); Cahill v. Phelps, 2001 WL 1561130 (Ohio Ct. App. 11th Dist. Lake County 2001); Thompson v. Thompson, 2001 WL 901252 (Ohio Ct. App. 11th Dist. Portage County 2001) (failure of magistrate's decision to address factors in 3105.18(C)(1) constitutes an "error of law or other defect on the face of the magistrate's decision"), and Thomas v. Thomas, 2001 WL 409533 (Ohio Ct. App. 11th Dist. Trumbull County 2001).

[8]Normandy Place Associates v. Beyer, 2 Ohio St. 3d 102, 105, 443 N.E.2d 161 (1982); Logue v. Wilson, 45 Ohio App. 2d 132, 136, 74 Ohio Op. 2d 140, 341 N.E.2d 641 (10th

to be instructive. A judgment which incorporates the trial court's own decision on objections to the magistrate's decision meets the requirements of a final order under Civil Rule 54(A).[9] A trial court erred in adopting a referee's report when it appeared to simply "rubber stamp" it.[10] The court must enter its own judgment on an issue submitted by the referee.[11] A referee's report which contained enough factual detail to permit a court to exercise independent review of the issues was sufficient despite its conclusory language.[12] Where a transcript of evidence before a referee was filed with the court, former Civil Rule 53 required the trial court to make its own independent determination of factual issues.[13]

Civil Rule 54(A) provides that "[a] judgment entry shall not contain a recital of pleadings, the magistrate's decision in a referred matter, or the record of prior proceedings." A 1996 amendment to Civil Rule 54(A) replaced "report of a referee" with "magistrate's decision in a referred matter," with no substantive change intended.[14] A trial court must render its own separate judgment and may not simply state that it approves, adopts, or incorporates a magistrate's decision. A judgment entry is not sufficient if it merely recites that a recommendation/decision is approved and adopted thereby requiring the parties to refer to another document in order to determine exactly what their rights and obligations are. It has been said that ". . . the judgment entry must be worded in such a manner that the parties can readily determine what is necessary to comply with the order of the court" and need not resort to any other documents.[15]

Cases interpreting the former version of Civil Rule 53 (and still ap-

---

Dist. Franklin County 1975); Eisenberg v. Peyton, 56 Ohio App. 2d 144, 146, 10 Ohio Op. 3d 158, 381 N.E.2d 1136 (8th Dist. Cuyahoga County 1978), and Lane v. Lane, 1986 WL 1107 (Ohio Ct. App. 12th Dist. Clinton County 1986).

[9]Harrison v. Harrison, 2001 WL 838991 (Ohio Ct. App. 10th Dist. Franklin County 2001), dismissed, appeal not allowed, 93 Ohio St. 3d 1484, 758 N.E.2d 185 (2001).

[10]In re Swain, 68 Ohio App. 3d 737, 741, 589 N.E.2d 483 (11th Dist. Portage County 1991). See also Pamela J. MacAdams Referees' Reports Must Not Be "Rubber Stamped," 3 Dom. Rel. J. Ohio 91 (July/Aug. 1991).

[11]Delombard v. DeLombard, 1988 WL 38020 (Ohio Ct. App. 5th Dist. Richland County 1988); In re Michael, 71 Ohio App. 3d 727, 729, 595 N.E.2d 397 (11th Dist. Portage County 1991); Lear v. Brown, 1993 WL 452010 (Ohio Ct. App. 2d Dist. Miami County 1993); White v. White, 1991 WL 6019 (Ohio Ct. App. 11th Dist. Trumbull County 1991); Stewart v. Huchison, 1991 WL 229316 (Ohio Ct. App. 2d Dist. Montgomery County 1991), and Tyron v. Tyron, No. 90-T-4444 (Ohio Ct. App. 11th Dist. 1991).

[12]Zellner v. Turner, 1993 WL 15640 (Ohio Ct. App. 2d Dist. Greene County 1993).

[13]Columbus Window Co. v. American K & K Window, 1993 WL 19947 (Ohio Ct. App. 10th Dist. Franklin County 1993).

[14]Staff Note to 1996 Amendment to Civ. R. 54(A).

[15]Lavelle v. Cox, 1991 WL 35642 (Ohio Ct. App. 11th Dist. Trumbull County 1991) (Ford, J. concurring); Tyron v. Tyron, No. 90-T-4444 (Ohio Ct. App. 11th Dist. 1991) (wording of entry must be such that the parties can understand the order without resorting to referee's report); Carroll v. Carroll, 1990 WL 40225 (Ohio Ct. App. 7th Dist. Columbiana County 1990) (judgment entry which read that the court "adopts the findings of fact and conclusions of law of the referee and enters judgment thereon" was not sufficient as judgment could not be understood without looking to referee's report; case

plicable today) held it to be solely in the discretion of the trial court to decide what use to make of the report (now decision), the court having the authority to adopt, reject, or modify, hear additional evidence,[16] return the report to the referee with instructions[17] or hear the matter itself. An objection to the referee's report was not necessary to preserve the matter for review in a case where a trial court, rather than adopting a referee's report, instead conducted a complete independent review of the evidence and determined the issues itself.[18] Where a trial court modified a referee's report or an award of child support, it was to make findings of fact to support its deviation from the recommendation and basic child support schedule and worksheet as mandated by then section 3113.215(B)(1)(b).[19] If there was no report, or if there were irregularities in the report, and judgment was nevertheless entered by the trial court, the judgment was voidable—not void.[20] If a voidable judgment was not appealed, it would be valid and not subject to collateral attack.[21] These decisions were based on the view that Civil Rule 53 is procedural, not jurisdictional, and that if the jurisdictional facts are present and procedure is not challenged, a judgment based on faulty procedure will be valid.[22] A judgment which may or may not have approved and adopted a report, became effective and binding when journalized. As stated above, a report/decision standing alone is not effective as a judgment or binding on the parties.

---

remanded for court to "frame its judgment entry to specifically state its orders"); In re Michael, 71 Ohio App. 3d 727, 729, 595 N.E.2d 397 (11th Dist. Portage County 1991) (trial court's entry which merely found referee's report to be well taken and overruled objections did not satisfy Civ. R. 54(A) and was not final appealable order), and Seitz v. Seitz, 1992 WL 171273 (Ohio Ct. App. 2d Dist. Greene County 1992) (overruling objections to referee's report without separately stating own judgment did not constitute final order).

[16]Freeman v. Freeman, 1987 WL 12962 (Ohio Ct. App. 2d Dist. Greene County 1987) (trial court erred in refusing to consider fact that potential support obligor had become employed after case had been submitted to referee), and Polen v. Prines, 69 Ohio App. 3d 631, 636, 591 N.E.2d 731, 17 U.C.C. Rep. Serv. 2d 1035 (11th Dist. Lake County 1990).

[17]Dietz v. Dietz, 1991 WL 163501 (Ohio Ct. App. 6th Dist. Ottawa County 1991) (where report contained no findings of fact or conclusions of law, only several recommendations, trial court reviewing report should have ordered deficiencies corrected).

[18]Keil v. Keil, 1991 WL 253925 (Ohio Ct. App. 6th Dist. Ottawa County 1991).

[19]Stephens v. Stephens, 1993 WL 221345 (Ohio Ct. App. 5th Dist. Tuscarawas County 1993); Grant v. McNeil, 1993 WL 221290 (Ohio Ct. App. 5th Dist. Stark County 1993), and Junke v. Junke, 1993 WL 204619 (Ohio Ct. App. 8th Dist. Cuyahoga County 1993).

[20]State ex rel. Lesher v. Kainrad, 65 Ohio St. 2d 68, 71, 19 Ohio Op. 3d 261, 417 N.E.2d 1382 (1981); Hines v. Amole, 4 Ohio App. 3d 263, 265, 448 N.E.2d 473 (2d Dist. Greene County 1982); Morrow v. Family & Community Services of Catholic Charities, Inc., 28 Ohio St. 3d 247, 504 N.E.2d 2 (1986); Haponek v. Charter Realty, Inc., 1984 WL 4730 (Ohio Ct. App. 9th Dist. Lorain County 1984), and Mcdonough v. Noble, 1981 WL 4728 (Ohio Ct. App. 7th Dist. Mahoning County 1981).

[21]Eisenberg v. Peyton, 56 Ohio App. 2d 144, 10 Ohio Op. 3d 158, 381 N.E.2d 1136 (8th Dist. Cuyahoga County 1978).

[22]Eisenberg v. Peyton, 56 Ohio App. 2d 144, 10 Ohio Op. 3d 158, 381 N.E.2d 1136 (8th Dist. Cuyahoga County 1978). See also State ex rel. Lesher v. Kainrad, 65 Ohio St. 2d 68, 71, 19 Ohio Op. 3d 261, 417 N.E.2d 1382 (1981)

It was not error for the trial court to adopt the recommendation of a successor referee where (1) both parties agreed to the successor referee, (2) the successor referee heard the parties' testimony and read the testimony of other witnesses, and (3) the trial court had transcripts of all proceedings and the successor referee's summary of all the testimony.[23]

Civil Rule 53(E)(4)(c) entitled "Permanent and Interim Orders" allows the court to adopt a magistrate's decision and enter judgment without waiting for objections. The filing of timely written objections, however, operates as an automatic stay of the judgment until the court disposes of the objections, and either vacates, modifies, or affirms the judgment.[24] Where immediate relief is justified, the court may enter an interim order based on a magistrate's decision without waiting for the filing of or ruling on objections. Such an interim order is not stayed by the filing of timely objections.[25] An interim order may not extend more than twenty-eight days from the date of its entry unless, within the first twenty-eight day time period and for good cause shown, the court extends the interim order for an additional twenty-eight days.[26] An interim order is, by definition, not a final appealable order.[27]

§ 31:15 Temporary orders

A variation from the general powers of a magistrate, found solely in

---

[23]Apgar v. Apgar, 21 Ohio App. 3d 193, 486 N.E.2d 1181 (8th Dist. Cuyahoga County 1984).

[24]Rheude v. Rheude, 1997 WL 226207 (Ohio Ct. App. 12th Dist. Clermont County 1997) (court did not err by filing its judgment one hour before magistrate filed amended decision; objections filed within fourteen days would stay execution of the judgment under Civil Rule 53(E)(4)(c); McCown v. McCown, 145 Ohio App. 3d 170, 171, 762 N.E.2d 398 (12th Dist. Fayette County 2001); Barker v. Barker, 118 Ohio App. 3d 706, 711-712, 693 N.E.2d 1164 (6th Dist. Lucas County 1997); Riolo v. Navin, 2002-Ohio-1551, 2002 WL 502408 (Ohio Ct. App. 8th Dist. Cuyahoga County 2002); State ex rel. Nalls v. Russo, 2002-Ohio-583, 2001 WL 1772191 (Ohio Ct. App. 8th Dist. Cuyahoga County 2001), judgment aff'd, 96 Ohio St. 3d 410, 2002-Ohio-4907, 775 N.E.2d 522 (2002); Tulley v. Tulley, 2001-Ohio-4307, 2001 WL 1216974 (Ohio Ct. App. 11th Dist. Portage County 2001); Chapman v. Adkins, 2001 WL 1098037 (Ohio Ct. App. 10th Dist. Franklin County 2001); Wright v. Wright, 2001 WL 1769939 (Ohio Ct. App. 5th Dist. Stark County 2001); Huffman v. Huffman, 2001 WL 799882 (Ohio Ct. App. 11th Dist. Trumbull County 2001); Abate v. Abate, 2000 WL 327227 (Ohio Ct. App. 9th Dist. Summit County 2000), and West v. West, No. 99-CA-31 (Ohio Ct. App. 2d Dist. 1999), unreported.

[25]Barker v. Barker, 118 Ohio App. 3d 706, 708, 711-712, 693 N.E.2d 1164 (6th Dist. Lucas County 1997); Simpkins v. Simpkins, 2000 WL 920314 (Ohio Ct. App. 6th Dist. Lucas County 2000), and In Re Poole, No. 1997CA00163 (Ohio Ct. App. 5th Dist. 1998).

[26]Brown v. Cummins, 120 Ohio App. 3d 554, 555, 698 N.E.2d 501 (6th Dist. Lucas County 1997); Barker v. Barker, 118 Ohio App. 3d 706, 711-712, 693 N.E.2d 1164 (6th Dist. Lucas County 1997); Walker v. Estate of Walker, No. 00 CA 208 (Ohio Ct. App. 7th Dist. 2001), and LeFever v. Cornnuts, Inc., 1999 WL 22664 (Ohio Ct. App. 2d Dist. Champaign County 1999); Kocher v. Blair, 1988 WL 61048 (Ohio Ct. App. 9th Dist. Summit County 1988). See also Nolte v. Nolte, 60 Ohio App. 2d 227, 230-231, 14 Ohio Op. 3d 215, 396 N.E.2d 807 (8th Dist. Cuyahoga County 1978).

[27]LeFever v. Cornnuts, Inc., 1999 WL 22664 (Ohio Ct. App. 2d Dist. Champaign County 1999).

the domestic relations setting, is contained in Civil Rule 75(N)(1)[1] governing the allowance of spousal support, child support, and custody pendente lite. Civil Rule 75(N)(1) provides:

(1) When requested in the complaint, answer, or counterclaim, or by motion served with the pleading, upon satisfactory proof by affidavit duly filed with the clerk of the court, the court or magistrate, without oral hearing and for good cause shown, may grant spousal support pendente lite to either of the parties for the party's sustenance and expenses during the suit and may make a temporary order regarding the support, maintenance, and allocation of parental rights and responsibilities for the care of children of the marriage, whether natural or adopted, during the pendency of the action for divorce, annulment, or legal separation.

This procedure for the award of temporary spousal support, child support, or allocation of parental rights and responsibilities based on affidavits is applicable only to domestic relations proceedings. It is intended to streamline the processing of these cases by the court and to expedite the issuance of temporary orders so that domestic relations litigants and their children are not disadvantaged by economic inequities during the initial stages of a domestic relations proceeding. Due process is afforded in this setting by a further provision which states that any pendente lite award, based on affidavits and counter-affidavits, can be reviewed at an oral hearing if an objecting party requests a hearing by written motion.[2] While there is no time within which such a request must be filed, the person disadvantaged by and unhappy with a temporary order does not gain anything by delay. The rule provides that the court must grant a hearing within twenty-eight days.[3] This is clearly intended to give the complaining party quick access to a hearing. Depending on local practice, that oral hearing may take place before either a magistrate or a judge.

Civil Rule 75(N)(2) further provides that the request for an oral hearing to review the temporary orders issued on affidavits and counter-affidavits ". . . shall not suspend or delay the commencement of spousal support or other support payments previously ordered or change the allocation of parental rights and responsibilities until the order is modified by journal entry after the oral hearing."[4] The need for certainty regarding the allocation of parental rights and responsibilities, along with the need to balance the parties' economics during the initial stages of a domestic relations proceeding, necessitates this provision with regard to the continued efficacy of the temporary order after an oral hearing has been requested.

The most interesting aspect of Civil Rule 75(N) as it affects the role of

---

[Section 31:15]

[1]Formerly Civ. R. 75(M)(1).

[2]Civil Rule 75(N)(2) and Biscello v. Biscello, 2000 WL 552188 (Ohio Ct. App. 10th Dist. Franklin County 2000).

[3]Drumm v. Drumm, 1999 WL 198120 (Ohio Ct. App. 2d Dist. Montgomery County 1999).

[4]Simpkins v. Simpkins, 2000 WL 920314 (Ohio Ct. App. 6th Dist. Lucas County 2000).

magistrate in the area of domestic relations concerns the extent of a magistrate's powers in granting orders pendente lite. The language of the rule indicates that ". . . the court *or* magistrate, without oral hearing and for good cause shown, may grant spousal support pendente lite . . . and may make a temporary order regarding the support, maintenance, and allocation of parental rights and responsibilities for the care of children."[5] This language suggests that, in a Civil Rule 75(N) setting, a magistrate acting without approval of a judge, may order temporary spousal support, child support, and allocation of parental rights and responsibilities on affidavits.[6] When the magistrate is the official who holds the oral hearing described in Civil Rule 75(N)(2), the magistrate must then file the decision required by Civil Rule 53(E). Either party may then file objections to the judge as outlined in that rule.

Ohio case law unanimously supports the conclusion that under no circumstances can a magistrate issue final orders affecting the rights and obligations of litigants. For example, the Eighth District Court of Appeals, in *Nolte v. Nolte*,[7] held as follows:

> Nevertheless, we stress that referees serve only in an advisory capacity to the court and have no authority to render final judgments affecting the rights of parties. Allowing the referees . . . to hear cases and occupy the trial bench in regular courtrooms does not confer upon them the powers reserved to the judges.

In *Normandy Place Assocs. v. Beyer*,[8] the Ohio Supreme Court made the following observation:

> It is the primary duty of the court, and not the referee, to act as a judicial officer. Indeed, the court must approve the referee's report and enter it upon its own record in order for that report to have any validity or binding effect.

The court then referred to the 1970 Staff Note to Rule 53 of the Ohio Rules of Civil Procedure indicating that it is the function of a referee to aid a court and not to be a substitute for the court.

In light of the functional necessity for the provisions of Civil Rule 75(N), the purpose of this rule is to permit a magistrate to aid the court in a quick resolution of the issues of temporary spousal support, child support, and/or allocation of parental rights and responsibilities unfettered by the procedural aspects of Civil Rule 53. The magistrate's function in this setting is to review the large volume of motions and affidavits filed requesting or opposing temporary orders and to provide the court with findings and conclusions regarding the same. On receipt of the magistrate's decision, the judge may immediately adopt it and enter judgment ordering spousal support, child support, and allocation of

---

[5]Civ. R. 75(N)(1) (emphasis added).

[6]Stewart v. Stewart, 1998 WL 177558 (Ohio Ct. App. 2d Dist. Montgomery County 1998), dismissed, appeal not allowed, 83 Ohio St. 3d 1428, 699 N.E.2d 945 (1998).

[7]Nolte v. Nolte, 60 Ohio App. 2d 227, 231, 14 Ohio Op. 3d 215, 396 N.E.2d 807 (8th Dist. Cuyahoga County 1978).

[8]Normandy Place Associates v. Beyer, 2 Ohio St. 3d 102, 443 N.E.2d 161 (1982).

parental rights and responsibilities pendente lite, which controls the parties' rights and obligations during the pendency of the domestic relations proceeding.[9]

The use of magistrates has been increased by the statutes pertaining to the child support enforcement agency (formerly called the bureau of support) and regarding wage withholding for child support and spousal support. RC 3125.60(A)[10] states that the court may appoint a magistrate to deal with support enforcement, and RC 3125.60(B)[11] gives the magistrates authority to perform any of the following functions: (1) taking testimony and keeping a record; (2) evaluating evidence and issuing a recommendation; (3) accepting voluntary acknowledgments of support liability and stipulated agreement; (4) entering default orders (not just reports) in Title IV-D cases, and (5) any other function considered necessary by the court. The right of parties to request a court hearing after the completion of the administrative processes provided under RC 3123.01 through RC 3123.071[12] (default proceedings) and RC 3119.64 through RC 3119.66[13] (review of child support orders) further expands the need for magistrates.

---

[9]Simpkins v. Simpkins, 2000 WL 920314 (Ohio Ct. App. 6th Dist. Lucas County 2000).

[10]Formerly RC 3113.21(L)(3)(a).

[11]Formerly RC 3113.21(L)(3)(b)(iv).

[12]Formerly RC 3113.21(B).

[13]Formerly RC 3113.216 and 3113.21(C).

Chapter 32

Appeals

By Douglas R. Jennings, Esq.[*]

> **KeyCite®:** Cases and other legal materials listed in KeyCite Scope can be researched through West Group's KeyCite service on Westlaw®. Use KeyCite to check citations for form, parallel references, prior and later history, and comprehensive citator information, including citations to other decisions and secondary materials.

---

[*]The author gratefully acknowledges the invaluable assistance of Judge Alba L. Whiteside during the preparation of this chapter.

§ 32:1　Jurisdiction—In general

The purpose of an appeal is to permit a court of superior jurisdiction to review issues of law upon the record after a final order, judgment, or decree has been rendered by a lower court. The jurisdiction of the Ohio Supreme Court and the courts of appeals is limited to the review of final appealable orders, judgments, and decrees.[1] The existence of a final appealable order is jurisdictional, and an appeal may be dismissed at any stage of the proceedings for lack of such an order. Jurisdiction may be challenged by motion or in the briefs upon the merits. Jurisdiction may also be raised by the court of appeals upon its own motion,[2] though typically after having given the parties notice of the court's intent to consider the issue.[3]

A final appealable order has three essential characteristics: it is *final* under Civil Rule 54(B); *appealable* under RC Ch. 2505; and meets the definition of an *order, judgment, or decree*. Each of these characteristics is a separate requirement, the absence of any of which will deprive the court of jurisdiction to hear the appeal. Accordingly, an appeal may be taken only from:

(1) An order, judgment or decree,

[Section 32:1]

[1]RC 2505.03(A).

[2]Chef Italiano Corp. v. Kent State University, 44 Ohio St. 3d 86, 541 N.E.2d 64, 54 Ed. Law Rep. 947 (1989); Farrow Restoration, Inc. v. Kowalski, 81 Ohio App. 3d 54, 610 N.E.2d 458 (9th Dist. Summit County 1991).

[3]C. Miller Chevrolet, Inc. v. City of Willoughby Hills, 38 Ohio St. 2d 298, 67 Ohio Op. 2d 358, 313 N.E.2d 400 (1974).

(2) which is appealable under RC Ch. 2505, and

(3) which is final under Civ. R. 54(B), if applicable.

§ 32:2 Jurisdiction—Order, judgment, or decree

Appeal may be taken only from orders, judgments, and decrees.[1] Decisions, reports, and other findings of a domestic relations court are not appealable. The essential elements of a judgment are set forth in Civ. R. 58(A). For this purpose, the term "judgment" includes a decree and any final order from which an appeal lies.[2] A judgment must be signed by the trial judge and filed by the clerk.[3] A judgment should not contain a recital of pleadings, a decision of a magistrate, or a record of prior proceedings.[4]

An order, judgment, or decree must also contain a clear pronouncement of the court's ruling and manifest an intention to finally terminate the case or a separate and distinct portion thereof.[5] Use of the words "ordered," "adjudged," or "decreed" are evidence of that intention. Nevertheless, there is no single form, and the title of the document is not determinative.[6] Decisions and entries may be combined, or set forth in separate documents.[7] But where the decision or entry calls for the preparation of an additional document, a hearing, or the submission of additional evidence, it is not a judgment.[8] Likewise, the mere approval of a magistrate's decision without a clear pronouncement of the court's order does not qualify as a judgment under Civ. R. 58(A).[9]

§ 32:3 Jurisdiction—Appealable orders—In general

The appellate jurisdiction of the court of appeals extends to final

---

[Section 32:2]

[1] RC 2505.03.

[2] Civ. R. 54(A).

[3] Civ. R. 58(A); In re Hopple, 13 Ohio App. 3d 54, 468 N.E.2d 129 (6th Dist. Wood County 1983); In re Mitchell, 93 Ohio App. 3d 153, 637 N.E.2d 989 (8th Dist. Cuyahoga County 1994).

[4] Civ. R. 54(A).

[5] Brackmann Communications, Inc. v. Ritter, 38 Ohio App. 3d 107, 526 N.E.2d 823 (12th Dist. Clermont County 1987); Peters v. Arbaugh, 50 Ohio App. 2d 30, 4 Ohio Op. 3d 17, 361 N.E.2d 531 (10th Dist. Franklin County 1976).

[6] St. Vincent Charity Hosp. v. Mintz, 33 Ohio St. 3d 121, 515 N.E.2d 917 (1987).

[7] L.T.M. Builders Co. v. Village of Jefferson, 61 Ohio St. 2d 91, 15 Ohio Op. 3d 127, 399 N.E.2d 1210 (1980); Shore v. Chester, 40 Ohio App. 2d 412, 69 Ohio Op. 2d 368, 321 N.E.2d 614 (10th Dist. Franklin County 1974) (preferred practice is to use a decision and entry for interlocutory orders, and separate documents for the final judgment).

[8] Prod. Credit Assn. v. Hedges, 87 Ohio App. 3d 207, 621 N.E.2d 1360 (4th Dist. Pickaway County 1993); In re Zakov, 107 Ohio App. 3d 716, 669 N.E.2d 344 (11th Dist. Geauga County 1995).

[9] In re Michael, 71 Ohio App. 3d 727, 595 N.E.2d 397 (11th Dist. Portage County 1991).

orders, judgments, and decrees.[1] The term "final order" is further defined in RC 2505.02(B). Orders that do not qualify as final orders are interlocutory and subject to revision or modification by the trial court until such time that a final order, judgment or decree is granted. To be successfully appealed, an order, judgment, or decree of a domestic relations court must fit into one of the following categories of *appealable* orders:

(1) Final judgments and decrees.[2]
(2) Orders which determine the action and prevent a judgment.[3]
(3) Orders issued in special proceedings.[4]
(4) Orders issued in post-decree proceedings.[5]
(5) Orders vacating or setting aside a judgment.[6]
(6) Orders granting a new trial.[7]
(7) Orders granting or denying a provisional remedy.[8]

Final judgments and decrees that terminate the entire case are specifically appealable pursuant to RC 2505.03. Orders that both determine the action and prevent a judgment are appealable under RC 2505.02(B)(1) where a substantial right is affected.[9] These include orders granting summary judgment or dismissing an action for lack of jurisdiction.[10] Because it does not determine the action or prevent a judgment, an order denying summary judgment is not similarly appealable upon this ground.[11]

An order made in a special proceeding or upon summary application after judgment is also appealable if it affects a substantial right.[12] A special proceeding is defined as an "action or proceeding that is specifically created by statute and that prior to 1853 was not denoted as an action at law or suit in equity."[13] Actions for divorce as well as ancillary claims for custody and support were unknown at common law and have been recognized as special proceedings.[14] Orders issued in special

---

[Section 32:3]

[1]RC 2505.03.

[2]RC 2505.03.

[3]RC 2505.02(B)(1).

[4]RC 2505.02(B)(2).

[5]RC 2505.02(B)(2).

[6]RC 2505.02(B)(3).

[7]RC 2505.02(B)(3).

[8]RC 2505.02(B)(4).

[9]Stewart v. Midwestern Indem. Co., 45 Ohio St. 3d 124, 543 N.E.2d 1200 (1989).

[10]Wisintainer v. Elcen Power Strut Co., 67 Ohio St. 3d 352, 1993-Ohio-120, 617 N.E.2d 1136 (1993); City of Tiffin v. Board of Review, Ohio Bureau of Employment Services, 3 Ohio App. 3d 467, 446 N.E.2d 207 (10th Dist. Franklin County 1982).

[11]Balson v. Dodds, 62 Ohio St. 2d 287, 16 Ohio Op. 3d 329, 405 N.E.2d 293 (1980).

[12]RC 2505.02(B)(2).

[13]RC 2505.02(A)(2); Polikoff v. Adam, 67 Ohio St. 3d 100, 616 N.E.2d 213 (1993).

[14]State ex rel. Papp v. James, 69 Ohio St. 3d 373, 1994-Ohio-86, 632 N.E.2d 889 (1994).

proceedings also include post-decree custody and support modification as well as contempt proceedings. Orders issued upon summary application after judgment include ancillary proceedings necessary to carry a judgment into effect and orders denying relief from judgment under Civ. R. 60(B).[15]

Orders that determine the action and prevent a judgment or that were made in a special or post-decree proceeding may be appealed only where a substantial right is affected.[16] A substantial right is defined as a "right that the United States Constitution, the Ohio Constitution, a statute, the common law, or a rule of procedure entitles a person to enforce or protect."[17] A substantial right is affected where denial of an immediate appeal would effectively preclude appropriate relief in the future.[18] Orders that have been found to affect a substantial right include orders compelling disclosure of privileged medical records[19] , requiring submission to a psychological examination[20] , or ordering disqualification of counsel.[21] In each of these cases, a substantial right was affected because the harm caused by the trial court's order could not be corrected unless an immediate appeal was permitted.

With the amendment of RC 2505.02 in 1998, orders granting or denying provisional remedies are now appealable under certain circumstances. This amendment superceded prior case law, which had virtually eliminated the right of interlocutory appeal in ordinary civil actions.[22] Under the statute, a "provisional remedy" is defined as a "proceeding ancillary to an action, including but not limited to, a proceeding for a preliminary injunction, attachment, discovery of a privileged matter, or suppression of evidence."[23] An order granting or denying a provisional remedy is appealable if it: (1) determines the request for the remedy and prevents a judgment upon the remedy in favor of the appealing party, and; (2) effectively precludes meaningful remedy by an appeal following final judgment as to all proceedings, issues, claims, and parties in the action.[24]

Whether denominated as an appeal from a special proceeding or an

---

[15]Colley v. Bazell, 64 Ohio St. 2d 243, 18 Ohio Op. 3d 442, 416 N.E.2d 605 (1980) (order denying relief from judgment).

[16]RC 2505.02(B)(1); RC 2505.02(B)(2).

[17]RC 2505.02(A)(1). See also, Noble v. Colwell, 44 Ohio St. 3d 92, 540 N.E.2d 1381 (1989).

[18]Bell v. Mt. Sinai Med. Ctr., 67 Ohio St. 3d 60, 616 N.E.2d 181 (1993), modified on other grounds by Moskovitz v. Mt. Sinai Med. Ctr., 69 Ohio St. 3d 638, 1994-Ohio-324, 635 N.E.2d 331, 35 A.L.R.5th 841 (1994).

[19]Whiteman v. Whiteman, 1995 WL 375848 (Ohio Ct. App. 12th Dist. Butler County 1995).

[20]Wayne M. Shoff v. Andrea J. Shoff, 1995 WL 450249 (Ohio Ct. App. 10th Dist. Franklin County 1995).

[21]Hollis v. Hollis, 124 Ohio App. 3d 481, 706 N.E.2d 798 (8th Dist. Cuyahoga County 1997).

[22]Polikoff v. Adam, 67 Ohio St. 3d 100, 616 N.E.2d 213 (1993).

[23]RC 2505.02(A)(3).

[24]RC 2505.02(B)(4).

appeal from a provisional order, there is little practical difference between the tests applied by the courts of appeals in determining whether an appeal from an otherwise interlocutory order will be permitted. The test is whether enforcement of the order will cause irreparable harm that will preclude a meaningful remedy in an appeal from the final judgment. Many appellate courts screen notices of appeal for jurisdiction and they have the authority to dismiss non-appealable orders *sua sponte*. Accordingly, the appellant may want to include a statement in support of jurisdiction with the notice of appeal when an appeal is taken from a provisional order prior to final judgment.

§ 32:4 Jurisdiction—Appealable orders—Discovery orders

Orders granting or denying demands for discovery are generally considered interlocutory and not subject to immediate appeal.[1] Like other interlocutory orders issued during the case, discovery orders may be appealed with the appeal of the final judgment. However, if the order affects a substantial right or precludes meaningful or effective remedy by appeal, it may be a final appealable order. The same standard applies to sanctions awarded for failure to comply with discovery.

Discovery orders in domestic relations actions may be appealed if the order affects a substantial right or precludes a meaningful and effective remedy in an appeal following final judgment. For example, an order requiring the disclosure of privileged medical records in a domestic relations action has been recognized as a final appealable order.[2] Likewise, an order requiring a spouse to submit to psychological testing in a divorce action pursuant to Civ. R. 35 may be a final appealable order.[3] While these cases were analyzed as appeals from orders issued in special proceedings, the same result would follow were the cases treated as appeals from provisional remedies under RC 2505.02(B)(4). In each case, the appeal will be allowed if enforcement of the order will affect the case in a manner which cannot be corrected if appeal is delayed until final judgment.

The imposition of sanctions under Civ. R. 37 for failure to make discovery is not typically a final appealable order.[4] This is typically true even where the sanction is associated with a provisional remedy for which appeal may be allowed. In *Miller v. Anthem, Inc.*[5] , the appellate court allowed an appeal from an order compelling disclosure of privileged

---

[Section 32:4]

[1]Kennedy v. Chalfin, 38 Ohio St. 2d 85, 67 Ohio Op. 2d 90, 310 N.E.2d 233 (1974).

[2]Whiteman v. Whiteman, 1995 WL 375848 (Ohio Ct. App. 12th Dist. Butler County 1995).

[3]Wayne M. Shoff v. Andrea J. Shoff, 1995 WL 450249 (Ohio Ct. App. 10th Dist. Franklin County 1995).

[4]Kennedy v. Chalfin, 38 Ohio St. 2d 85, 67 Ohio Op. 2d 90, 310 N.E.2d 233 (1974); Miller v. Anthem, Inc., 2000 WL 1808322 (Ohio Ct. App. 10th Dist. Franklin County 2000).

[5]Miller v. Anthem, Inc., 2000 WL 1808322 (Ohio Ct. App. 10th Dist. Franklin County 2000).

documents, but found it was without jurisdiction to review the sanction until final judgment was rendered. However, where the monetary sanction is so large that appeal after judgment would not afford an effective remedy, an award of sanctions under Civ. R. 37 may be a final appealable order.[6] Under the same reasoning, an order granting other sanctions authorized by Civ. R. 37, such as staying the proceedings until the order is obeyed, dismissing the action, or rendering judgment by default, might also present a final appealable order. Finally, any sanction that leads to a final judgment of contempt is immediately reviewable within the appeal of the contempt judgment.[7]

§ 32:5 Jurisdiction—Appealable orders—Temporary orders

Orders granting temporary custody, child support or spousal support are generally considered interlocutory orders not subject to immediate appeal.[1] Likewise, the denial of a motion for temporary orders is considered interlocutory.[2] However, where a substantial right is affected or the order effectively precludes meaningful review upon an appeal after final judgment, immediate appeal may be allowed.

Like discovery orders, temporary orders issued in domestic relations case may be subject to immediate appeal when they affect substantial rights. This was the analysis in *Kelm v. Kelm*[3] Though observing that temporary orders were ordinarily not considered final and appealable, the *Kelm* court went on to find that confirmation of a temporary spousal and child support award rendered in an arbitration was an order made in a special proceeding. The court dismissed the appeal only because it found that the order did not affect a substantial right, as denial of an immediate appeal would not foreclose appropriate relief in the future.

While temporary orders do not typically affect substantial rights, in the unusual case where a substantial right is affected, an immediate appeal may be allowed. *Oatey v. Oatey*[4] may be an example of such a case. In *Oatey*, the trial court ordered that interim attorney fees be paid during the pendency of the case from the immediate liquidation of marital property. Finding that there was a likelihood of extreme and irreparable harm which would make relief practically impossible if appeal was not

---

[6]White v. Aztec Catalyst Co., 2000 WL 1636023 (Ohio Ct. App. 9th Dist. Lorain County 2000) (sanctions of $22,414 awarded for failure to attend depositions).

[7]See § 32:9, Jurisdiction—Appealable orders—Contempt.

[Section 32:5]

[1]Daughtry v. Daughtry, 47 Ohio App. 2d 195, 1 Ohio Op. 3d 275, 353 N.E.2d 641 (9th Dist. Summit County 1973) (temporary spousal support); In re Devlin, 78 Ohio App. 3d 543, 605 N.E.2d 467 (10th Dist. Franklin County 1992) (temporary custody); In re Boehmke, 44 Ohio App. 3d 125, 541 N.E.2d 630 (8th Dist. Cuyahoga County 1988) (visitation).

[2]Cassim v. Cassim, 98 Ohio App. 3d 576, 649 N.E.2d 28 (10th Dist. Franklin County 1994).

[3]Kelm v. Kelm, 93 Ohio App. 3d 686, 639 N.E.2d 842 (10th Dist. Franklin County 1994).

[4]Oatey v. Oatey, 83 Ohio App. 3d 251, 614 N.E.2d 1054 (8th Dist. Cuyahoga County 1992).

permitted, the court concluded that the order affected a substantial right. These same facts would also demonstrate the absence of a meaningful and effective remedy after final judgment necessary to appeal a provisional remedy under RC 2505.02(B)(4).

In the event a temporary order is not immediately appealable, or an immediate appeal is not filed, review may be obtained in an appeal of the final judgment. Interlocutory custody and support orders are merged into the final judgment and may be reviewed on appeal from that judgment. Accordingly, either spouse may obtain review of temporary support and custody orders in an appeal from final judgment. Even if the temporary order might have qualified as an immediately appealable provisional order, a spouse may choose to reserve the issue for appeal from final judgment. App. R. 4(B)(5) provides that an appeal which is permitted from a judgment entered in a case in which the court has not disposed of all claims of all parties may be taken within 30 days of the temporary order or within 30 days of the final judgment. Accordingly, such an appeal is not lost by failing to take an immediate appeal unless the order is entered under Civ. R. 54(B) with an express determination that there is not just reason for delay.

§ 32:6   Jurisdiction—Appealable orders—Partial judgments

Partial judgments upon some but fewer than all of the claims in a divorce case or post-decree motion generally are not considered appealable orders. For instance, a judgment upon custody or property division which reserves support for further proceedings does not qualify as a final appealable order under RC 2505.02.[1] While recognizing the actions as special proceedings, these courts hold that a substantial right is not typically affected until a judgment is rendered upon all issues before the court. This is true even where the trial court has certified that there is no just reason for delay under Civ. R. 54(B).[2] The same approach has been applied to judgments upon fewer than all of the issues or motions in a post-decree modification proceeding.[3] Accordingly, an appeal of a judgment upon some but fewer than all of the pending claims or motions in a domestic relations case must typically await resolution of all of the issues before the court.

In addition, Civ. R. 75(F) provides that most judgments in an action for divorce, dissolution, annulment or legal separation are not final for purposes of Civ. R. 54(B) unless the judgment also determines property division, spousal support, and allocation of parental rights. The only exceptions are cases where the court lacks jurisdiction to determine the issues or where division of property in a legal separation action would

---

[Section 32:6]

[1]Tismo v. Tismo, 1990 WL 127064 (Ohio Ct. App. 4th Dist. Lawrence County 1990), cause dismissed, 59 Ohio St. 3d 702, 571 N.E.2d 137 (1991).

[2]Benson v. Heskett, 1995 WL 557003 (Ohio Ct. App. 5th Dist. Fairfield County 1995).

[3]Kouns v. Pemberton, 84 Ohio App. 3d 499, 617 N.E.2d 701 (4th Dist. Lawrence County 1992).

be inappropriate.[4]

§ 32:7　Jurisdiction—Appealable orders—Consent decrees

Contested divorce cases are frequently resolved in whole or in part by consent agreements. They may be reached on the eve of trial, at court after protracted negotiations, in the middle of or even at the end of trial. The Ohio Supreme Court has long held that a "judgment of a court of competent jurisdiction, rendered by consent of parties, will not be reversed on error."[1] Relying on this principle, appellate courts have dismissed appeals from agreed final entries even when the entries incorporate previous decisions upon contested issues.

In *Chase v. Chase*,[2] the appellate court applied this rule to an appeal from the denial of a motion to join a third party. Finding that the parties had entered into an agreed final judgment and decree of divorce, the court ruled that no appeal would lie from a prior interlocutory order absent an explicit reservation of the right to appeal. A notation in the entry that "the court notes Plaintiff's objection" to the refusal to join the third party was found insufficient to overcome the presumption that the consent decree operated as a waiver of the right to appeal.

This rule was subsequently applied to a final divorce decree which incorporated both a contested decision on custody and a separation agreement settling matters pertaining to property division. In *Sharp v. Sharp*,[3] the appellate court construed the entry incorporating the separation agreement as a consent decree. Absent the express preservation of the right to appeal from the portion of the entry reflecting the custody decision, the appellate court ruled that no appeal could be taken from the final decree.

§ 32:8　Jurisdiction—Appealable orders—Contempt

Contempt actions have long been recognized as special statutory proceedings subject to immediate appeal.[1] Judgments and orders of contempt are also specifically reviewable on appeal pursuant to RC 2705.09. However, a judgment of contempt must be complete before it can be appealed. A judgment of contempt of court includes both a finding of contempt and a sanction.[2] Accordingly, a judgment in a contempt action is not a final appealable order unless there has been both a find-

---

[4]Civ. R. 75(F)(3) (as effective 7-1-98).

[Section 32:7]

[1]Wells v. Martin & Co., 1 Ohio St. 386, 1853 WL 40 (1853).

[2]Chase v. Chase, 2001 WL 579804 (Ohio Ct. App. 10th Dist. Franklin County 2001), dismissed, appeal not allowed, 93 Ohio St. 3d 1428, 755 N.E.2d 352 (2001).

[3]Sharp v. Sharp, 2002-Ohio-1040, 2002 WL 378090 (Ohio Ct. App. 10th Dist. Franklin County 2002).

[Section 32:8]

[1]State v. Timson, 38 Ohio St. 2d 122, 67 Ohio Op. 2d 140, 311 N.E.2d 16 (1974).

[2]Chain Bike Corp. v. Spoke 'N Wheel, Inc., 64 Ohio App. 2d 62, 18 Ohio Op. 3d 43, 410 N.E.2d 802 (8th Dist. Cuyahoga County 1979).

ing of contempt and imposition of a sanction.³ A contempt judgment containing both a finding of contempt and a sanction is immediately appealable whether or not the court has finally resolved any other pending claims.

§ 32:9   Jurisdiction—Finality—In general

Under RC 2505.03(A), only *final* orders, judgments, or decrees may be reviewed on appeal. A judgment or decree which disposes of all of the claims of all of the parties is, by its very nature, a final judgment. However, a judgment, decree, or order resolving fewer than all of the claims of all of the parties in a multi-claim or multi-party case is final and immediately appealable only if the requirements of both Civ. R. 54(B), Civ. R. 75(F), and RC 2505.02 are met.¹ Under Civ. R. 54(B), a partial judgment or decree is not final unless the court expressly determines that there is no just reason for delay. The use of this language puts the parties on notice that the order, judgment, or decree has become final and appealable.²

Civ. R. 54(B) is a procedural rule which defines when a partial judgment as to fewer than all of the claims or parties may be treated as final for purposes of appeal. It can neither abridge or enlarge the substantive right to appeal.³ The mere incantation of Civ. R. 54(B) language will not transform an otherwise non-appealable order into a final appealable order.⁴ The rule applies only to orders, judgments, and decrees which dispose of fewer than all of the claims or parties in an action. Accordingly, a judgment which resolves fewer than all of the claims in the action may be appealed despite the absence of Civ. R. 54(B) language where the remaining claims or parties are dismissed after the judgment or the claims are rendered moot by the judgment.⁵

Where the words "no just reason for delay" are omitted from an order, judgment, or decree to which Civ. R. 54(B) applies, the order is subject to revision at any time before entry of final judgment disposing of all the claims and parties in the case.⁶ Appellate review in this case must wait until the entire case is completed, at which time all interlocutory orders

---

³Cooper v. Cooper, 14 Ohio App. 3d 327, 471 N.E.2d 525 (8th Dist. Cuyahoga County 1984); Garrison v. Garrison, 1994 WL 285915 (Ohio Ct. App. 9th Dist. Summit County 1994).

[Section 32:9]

¹Chef Italiano Corp. v. Kent State University, 44 Ohio St. 3d 86, 541 N.E.2d 64, 54 Ed. Law Rep. 947 (1989); State ex rel. A & D Limited Partnership v. Keefe, 1996 -Ohio-95, 77 Ohio St. 3d 50, 671 N.E.2d 13 (1996).

²Noble v. Colwell, 44 Ohio St. 3d 92, 540 N.E.2d 1381 (1989).

³General Acc. Ins. Co. v. Insurance Co. of North America, 44 Ohio St. 3d 17, 540 N.E.2d 266 (1989).

⁴Noble v. Colwell, 44 Ohio St. 3d 92, 540 N.E.2d 1381 (1989).

⁵Denham v. New Carlisle, 86 Ohio St. 3d 594, 1999-Ohio-128, 716 N.E.2d 184 (1999) (dismissal of remaining claims); General Acc. Ins. Co. v. Insurance Co. of North America, 44 Ohio St. 3d 17, 540 N.E.2d 266 (1989) (claims rendered moot by judgment).

⁶Civ. R. 54(B).

may be reviewed.[7] On the other hand, if the trial court certifies that there is "no just reason for delay," and the order is otherwise appealable under RC 2505.02, the opportunity for appeal will be lost if a notice of appeal is not filed within thirty days.[8]

§ 32:10 Jurisdiction—Finality—When required

Civ. R. 54(B) applies in any case in which a court renders judgment upon fewer than all of the claims or parties in a domestic relations action. It was once common in some courts to issue separate judgments upon one or more of the claims and issues in a domestic relations action. Effective July 1, 1998, Civ. R. 75(F) was amended to prevent separate appeals from these judgments.

Under Civ. R. 75(F), a judgment in a claim for divorce, dissolution, annulment, or legal separation is generally not final for purposes of Civ. R. 54(B) unless issues of property division, spousal support, allocation of parental rights and child support are all determined. This does not prevent a court from issuing separate decisions upon these issues, provided these determinations are all incorporated into one final judgment.[1] A judgment which resolves some but fewer than all of these claims may be separately appealed under Civ. R. 75(F)(3) only where the court lacks jurisdiction to determine the remaining issues or where division of property is left unresolved in a legal separation action.

There is not complete agreement among the appellate courts regarding the elements necessary to finally determine property division in accordance with Civ. R. 75(F). All courts agree that the judgment must identify, value and provide for the division of marital property. However, several courts have held that where the judgment provides for preparation of a Qualified Domestic Relations Order, the judgment does not become final for purposes of Civ. R. 75(F) until the Qualified Domestic Relations Order is issued by the trial court.[2] Given the difficulties sometimes encountered in preparing such an order and getting it approved by plan administrator, this can result in a significant delay.

Other courts have permitted immediate review of a final judgment of divorce without preparation of the Qualified Domestic Relations Order, reasoning that the division specified in the underlying decree affects a substantial right.[3] Under this approach, the subsequent approval of a Qualified Domestic Relations Order would qualify as a order granted upon summary application after judgment, appealable in the event if affected a substantial right. By treating the Qualified Domestic Relations

---

[7]Bobko v. Sagen, 61 Ohio App. 3d 397, 572 N.E.2d 823 (8th Dist. Cuyahoga County 1989), dismissed, 45 Ohio St. 3d 716, 545 N.E.2d 901 (1989).

[8]App. R. 4(B)(5).

[Section 32:10]

[1]Civ. R. 75(F)(2).

[2]Carestia v. Carestia, 2000 WL 277916 (Ohio Ct. App. 9th Dist. Wayne County 2000); Scott v. Scott, 2000-Ohio-1636, 2000 WL 140844 (Ohio Ct. App. 3d Dist. Allen County 2000).

[3]Wright v. Wright, 1994 WL 649271 (Ohio Ct. App. 4th Dist. Hocking County 1994).

Order as an ancillary order analogous to withholding orders or orders vesting title pursuant to Civ. R. 70, this approach permits a prompt appeal and eliminates the need to fully execute an order that may be reversed or modified on appeal.

Because it applies only to *claims* in an action for divorce, dissolution, annulment, or legal separation action, Civ. R. 75(F) does not prevent entry of final judgment upon one but fewer than all of the parties in a domestic relations action. Accordingly, a judgment resolving all of the claims against one but fewer than all of the *parties* may be considered final with certification that there is no just cause for delay. Such a judgment might resolve ancillary claims by grandparents in a custody dispute, or against employers, persons or corporations having possession of property from which a spouse seeks an order of support. As Civ. R. 75(F) makes no reference to judgments as to fewer than all of the parties, it is inapplicable to these judgments. With certification that there is no just reason for delay, judgments dismissing individual parties should still be final appealable orders under RC 2505.02(A)(1) and Civ. R. 54(B) prior to final judgment upon all claims in the action.

§ 32:11 Jurisdiction—Finality—When not required

Certification that there is no just reason for delay is required to appeal an order, judgment, or decree only where Civ. R. 54(B) is applicable.[1] Civ. R. 54(B) applies only to final judgments rendered upon one or more *claims* or *parties*. Where a final order does not dispose of a claim for relief, but is otherwise appealable under RC 2505.02, finality may not be required under Civ. R. 54(B). This includes contempt proceedings, appeals from certain orders issued in special proceedings, and appeals from provisional orders.

Civ. R. 54(B) language is not required to take an appeal from an otherwise final judgment of contempt issued in an action involving other unresolved claims. One court explained that a finding of contempt is "in and of itself final and appealable," notwithstanding the lack of Civ. R. 54(B) certification.[2] However, the judgment of contempt must be complete. A judgment of contempt is not final until there has been both a finding of contempt and imposition of a sanction. Even the inclusion of Civ. R. 54(B) language will not change this result.[3]

Certification is also not required to take an appeal from certain orders affecting substantial rights and made in special proceedings. For example, appeals have been taken from orders compelling production of documents or submission to psychological examinations without any ref-

---

[Section 32:11]

[1]Chef Italiano Corp. v. Kent State University, 44 Ohio St. 3d 86, 541 N.E.2d 64, 54 Ed. Law Rep. 947 (1989).

[2]Roberts v. Roberts, 1995 WL 432612, at *3 (Ohio Ct. App. 10th Dist. Franklin County 1995).

[3]Cooper v. Cooper, 14 Ohio App. 3d 327, 471 N.E.2d 525 (8th Dist. Cuyahoga County 1984).

erence to Civ. R. 54(B).[4] In *Amato v. General Motors Corp*[5] the Supreme Court of Ohio explained that Civ. R. 54(B) did not apply to orders which did not dispose of a claim for relief, such as an order certifying a class action under Civ. R. 23.[6] Accordingly, orders issued in special proceedings that affect substantial rights, but do not resolve claims for relief, are not subject to Civ. R. 54(B).

So long as appeals from contempt judgments and orders issued in special proceedings are not subject to Civ. R. 54(B), it logically follows that orders granting or denying provisional remedies may be appealed under RC 2505.02(B)(4) without a certification that there is no just reason for delay. Defined as proceedings ancillary to an action, provisional remedies are separate and distinct from claims for relief. Like contempt actions and special proceedings, provisional orders do not dispose of claims for relief. Thus, Civ. R. 54(B) certification is not required to appeal from orders granting or denying provisional remedies.

While Civ. R. 54(B) certification may not be required to take an appeal from orders that do not resolve claims for relief, App. R. 4(B)(5) provides that an appeal is generally not lost for failure to take an immediate appeal from such an order. Where appeal is permitted from a judgment or order entered in a case in which the trial court has not disposed of the entire case, other than an order entered under Civ. R. 54(B), a party may appeal within thirty days of either the judgment or order appealed, or the judgment or order disposing of the remaining claims.[7] Only orders, judgments or decrees which expressly provide that there is no just cause for delay are excluded from the rule.[8] Where otherwise appealable under RC 2505.02, these orders must be appealed within 30 days of the entry of the order or not at all.[9]

§ 32:12   Jurisdiction—Finality—Certification under Civil Rule 54(B)

Where Civ. R. 54(B) is applicable, the use of the language "there is no just reason for delay" is mandatory.[1] If this language does not appear in a judgment to which Civ. R. 54(B) applies, the judgment is not final or appealable. However, it is not necessary that the language be included

---

[4]Wayne M. Shoff v. Andrea J. Shoff, 1995 WL 450249 (Ohio Ct. App. 10th Dist. Franklin County 1995); Whiteman v. Whiteman, 1995 WL 375848 (Ohio Ct. App. 12th Dist. Butler County 1995). See § 32:5, Final appealable orders—Appealable orders—Discovery orders.

[5]Amato v. General Motors Corp., 67 Ohio St. 2d 253, 21 Ohio Op. 3d 158, 423 N.E.2d 452 (1981) (overruled by, Polikoff v. Adam, 67 Ohio St. 3d 100, 616 N.E.2d 213 (1993)).

[6]See also Voss v. Voss, 62 Ohio App. 3d 200, 574 N.E.2d 1175 (8th Dist. Cuyahoga County 1989).

[7]App. R. 4(B)(5).

[8]Staff Note to July 1, 1992 Amendment to App. R. 4(B)(5).

[9]State ex rel. A & D Limited Partnership v. Keefe, 77 Ohio St. 3d 50, 1996-Ohio-95, 671 N.E.2d 13 (1996).

[Section 32:12]

[1]Noble v. Colwell, 44 Ohio St. 3d 92, 540 N.E.2d 1381 (1989).

in the original judgment. An order may be amended nunc pro tunc to include Civ. R. 54(B) language.[2] In this instance, the time for filing the notice of appeal runs from the date of the nunc pro tunc order, not the underlying order.[3]

A trial court's decision to include "no just reason for delay" language in a judgment is reviewable for abuse of discretion. However, the trial court is given wide latitude in making this judgment. In *Wisintainer v. Elcen Power Strut Co.*,[4] the Supreme Court ruled that Civ. R. 54(B) certification is essentially a factual determination, one which should be accorded a presumption of correctness. "Where the record indicates that the interests of sound judicial administration could be served by a finding of 'no just reason for delay,' the trial court's certification determination must stand."[5]

§ 32:13   Jurisdiction—Table of appealable and non-appealable orders

The following table includes examples of judgments and orders which have or have not been recognized as final appealable orders by the courts of Ohio.

Type of order	Appealable?	Case name and citation
Grant/Deny Change of Venue	No	Timson v. Young, 70 Ohio App. 2d 239, 24 Ohio Op. 3d 309, 436 N.E.2d 538 (10th Dist. Franklin County 1980); Tandon v. Tandon, 1999 WL 1279166 (Ohio Ct. App. 7th Dist. Jefferson County 1999); Johnson v. Warner, 2000 WL 1460079 (Ohio Ct. App. 5th Dist. Muskingum County 2000)
Grant/Deny Continuance	No	Venable v. Venable, 3 Ohio App. 3d 421, 445 N.E.2d 1125 (8th Dist. Cuyahoga County 1981)

---

[2]Hughes v. Miner, 15 Ohio App. 3d 141, 473 N.E.2d 53 (11th Dist. Portage County 1984).

[3]Wisintainer v. Elcen Power Strut Co., 1993 -Ohio- 120, 67 Ohio St. 3d 352, 617 N.E.2d 1136 (1993).

[4]Wisintainer v. Elcen Power Strut Co., 1993 -Ohio- 120, 67 Ohio St. 3d 352, 617 N.E.2d 1136 (1993).

[5]Wisintainer v. Elcen Power Strut Co., 1993 -Ohio- 120, 67 Ohio St. 3d 352, syl. 2, 617 N.E.2d 1136 (1993).

Type of order	Appealable?	Case name and citation
Deny motion to dismiss	No	Haskins v. Haskins, 104 Ohio App. 3d 58, 660 N.E.2d 1260 (2d Dist. Montgomery County 1995)
Grant motion to dismiss	Yes	City of Tiffin v. Board of Review, Ohio Bureau of Employment Services, 3 Ohio App. 3d 467, 446 N.E.2d 207 (10th Dist. Franklin County 1982)
Deny motion to join third party	No	Briggs v. Briggs, 1997 WL 24882 (Ohio Ct. App. 10th Dist. Franklin County 1997)
Deny motion for relief from judgment	Yes	Colley v. Bazell, 64 Ohio St. 2d 243, 18 Ohio Op. 3d 442, 416 N.E.2d 605 (1980)
Grant motion for relief from judgment	Yes	Ashley v. Ashley, 1 Ohio App. 3d 80, 439 N.E.2d 911 (8th Dist. Cuyahoga County 1981); Welter v. Welter, 1998 WL 254944 (Ohio Ct. App. 9th Dist. Summit County 1998)
Approve magistrate's report, without rendering judgment	No	In re Michael, 71 Ohio App. 3d 727, 595 N.E.2d 397 (11th Dist. Portage County 1991)
Reject magistrate's report and set hearing	No	Lambert v. Lambert, 1988 WL 51502 (Ohio Ct. App. 8th Dist. Cuyahoga County 1988)
Discovery rulings, generally	No	Kennedy v. Chalfin, 38 Ohio St. 2d 85, 67 Ohio Op. 2d 90, 310 N.E.2d 233 (1974); Voss v. Voss, 62 Ohio App. 3d 200, 574 N.E.2d 1175 (8th Dist. Cuyahoga County 1989)
Compel disclosure of psychological records	Yes	Whiteman v. Whiteman, 1995 WL 375848 (Ohio Ct. App. 12th Dist. Butler County 1995). See also RC 2505.02(B)(4)

Type of order	Appealable?	Case name and citation
Compel submission to psychological exam	Yes	Wayne M. Shoff v. Andrea J. Shoff, 1995 WL 450249 (Ohio Ct. App. 10th Dist. Franklin County 1995); Williamson v. Williamson, 1997 WL 746425 (Ohio Ct. App. 10th Dist. Franklin County 1997)
Compel disclosure of medical records	Yes	Neftzer v. Neftzer, 140 Ohio App. 3d 618, 748 N.E.2d 608 (12th Dist. Clermont County 2000)
Compel testimony protected by attorney-client privilege	Yes	Tandon v. Tandon, 1999 WL 1279162 (Ohio Ct. App. 7th Dist. Jefferson County 1999) (no discussion of appealability, but reversed trial court)
Grant or deny expenses under Civil Rule 37, generally	No	Kennedy v. Chalfin, 38 Ohio St. 2d 85, 67 Ohio Op. 2d 90, 310 N.E.2d 233 (1974) (deny order for expenses); Miller v. Anthem, Inc., 2000 WL 1808322 (Ohio Ct. App. 10th Dist. Franklin County 2000) (grant order for expenses).
Temporary custody orders, generally	No	In re Devlin, 78 Ohio App. 3d 543, 605 N.E.2d 467 (10th Dist. Franklin County 1992); In re Boehmke, 44 Ohio App. 3d 125, 541 N.E.2d 630 (8th Dist. Cuyahoga County 1988)
Temporary custody orders, post-decree	No	Brooks v. Brooks, 117 Ohio App. 3d 19, 689 N.E.2d 987 (10th Dist. Franklin County 1996)

Type of order	Appealable?	Case name and citation
Temporary support orders, generally	No	Daughtry v. Daughtry, 47 Ohio App. 2d 195, 1 Ohio Op. 3d 275, 353 N.E.2d 641 (9th Dist. Summit County 1973); Cassim v. Cassim, 98 Ohio App. 3d 576, 649 N.E.2d 28 (10th Dist. Franklin County 1994)
Award of attorneys fees funded by immediate sale of marital assets	Yes	Oatey v. Oatey, 83 Ohio App. 3d 251, 614 N.E.2d 1054 (8th Dist. Cuyahoga County 1992)
Pretrial motion to disqualify counsel	Yes	Hollis v. Hollis, 124 Ohio App. 3d 481, 706 N.E.2d 798 (8th Dist. Cuyahoga County 1997)
Contempt finding with penalty	Yes	Cooper v. Cooper, 14 Ohio App. 3d 327, 471 N.E.2d 525 (8th Dist. Cuyahoga County 1984)
Contempt without finding of penalty	No	Garrison v. Garrison, 1994 WL 285915 (Ohio Ct. App. 9th Dist. Summit County 1994)
Parentage determination without child support established	No	State ex rel. Dixon v. Clark Cty. Court of Common Pleas, Juv. Div., 103 Ohio App. 3d 523, 660 N.E.2d 486 (2d Dist. Clark County 1995); Mullins v. Roe, 1998 WL 282974 (Ohio Ct. App. 4th Dist. Scioto County 1998); Berends v. Pearn, 2000 WL 85351 (Ohio Ct. App. 8th Dist. Cuyahoga County 2000)

Type of order	Appealable?	Case name and citation
Final consent decree without reservation of right to appeal	No	Chase v. Chase, 2001 WL 579804 (Ohio Ct. App. 10th Dist. Franklin County 2001), dismissed, appeal not allowed, 93 Ohio St. 3d 1428, 755 N.E.2d 352 (2001); Sharp v. Sharp, 2002-Ohio-1040, 2002 WL 378090 (Ohio Ct. App. 10th Dist. Franklin County 2002)
Final decree ordering Q.D.R.O., without Q.D.R.O. having been filed	No	Carestia v. Carestia, 2000 WL 277916 (Ohio Ct. App. 9th Dist. Wayne County 2000); Scott v. Scott, 2000-Ohio-1636, 2000 WL 140844 (Ohio Ct. App. 3d Dist. Allen County 2000); Bohl v. Bohl, 2000 WL 697455 (Ohio Ct. App. 9th Dist. Lorain County 2000)
Final Decree ordering Q.D.R.O., without Q.D.R.O. having been filed	Yes	Wright v. Wright, 1994 WL 649271 (Ohio Ct. App. 4th Dist. Hocking County 1994)
Appoint Receiver	Yes	Prudential Ins. Co. of Am. v. Corporate Circle, Ltd., 103 Ohio App. 3d 93, 658 N.E.2d 1066 (8th Dist. Cuyahoga County 1995)

§ 32:14 Notice of appeal—Time limit to file

An appeal is commenced by filing a notice of appeal in the court in which the judgment was entered within thirty days of the judgment or order appealed.[1] This period is jurisdictional and can be extended only as provided by rule.[2] The thirty-day period runs from the date of filing, provided notice of the entry is served within three days under Civ. R. 58. In the event notice of the entry is not served within three days as required by Civ. R. 58, the time for filing an appeal runs from service of

---

[Section 32:14]

[1]App. R. 3(A).

[2]Bosco v. City of Euclid, 38 Ohio App. 2d 40, 67 Ohio Op. 2d 209, 311 N.E.2d 870 (8th Dist. Cuyahoga County 1974).

the notice.[3]

The thirty-day period is calculated like any other under the civil rules—the first day is excluded and the last day is included, unless it is a Saturday, Sunday, or a legal holiday.[4] Where the thirty-day period expires on a weekend or a legal holiday, the time for filing the appeal runs until the next working day.[5] Because the period for appeal generally runs from the date judgment is entered, not from service of the notice, the three day extension for service by mail does not ordinarily apply.[6]

A notice of appeal filed after the announcement of a decision but before the entry of final judgment, or while the time for appeal is tolled under App. R. 4(B)(2), will be treated as filed immediately after the entry.[7] However, such an appeal will often be dismissed sua sponte for lack of a final appealable order if it is docketed in the court of appeals before the time for appeal has commenced. Accordingly, counsel should ensure that the notice in such a "premature" appeal is retained by the clerk until final judgment is entered.

§ 32:15 Notice of cross-appeal—When required—Time limit to file

Within ten days after a notice of appeal is filed, or within the period otherwise permitted for filing an appeal, any other party may file a cross-appeal. Like the period for filing an appeal, this period is mandatory and jurisdictional.[1] A cross-appeal must be filed if the appellee seeks to change or modify the judgment in any way.[2] In many cases, an appellee may urge a change in the judgment only in the event of reversal on the appellant's assignments of error. Nevertheless, these issues cannot be raised unless a notice of appeal is filed.[3] Where, however, a party merely intends to defend the judgment upon grounds not relied upon by the trial court, a notice of appeal need not be filed. Provided the appellee does not seek to change or modify the judgment, App. R. 3 and RC 2505.22 permit an appellee to assert such issues in order to prevent reversal without filing a notice of appeal.[4]

Where appellee seeks remand on issues that were not decided in his favor, assignments of error raised in his brief are not properly before the

---

[3]App. R. 4(A); See Atkinson v. Grumman Ohio Corp., 37 Ohio St. 3d 80, 523 N.E.2d 851 (1988).

[4]App. R. 14(A).

[5]Lewis v. Chardon, 64 Ohio St. 3d 463, 597 N.E.2d 87 (1992); App. R. 14(A).

[6]See App. R. 14(C).

[7]App. R. 4(C).

[Section 32:15]

[1]Kaplysh v. Takieddine, 35 Ohio St. 3d 170, 519 N.E.2d 382 (1988).

[2]App. R. 3(C)(1).

[3]App. R. 3(C)(1).

[4]Duracote Corp. v. Goodyear Tire & Rubber Co., 2 Ohio St. 3d 160, 443 N.E.2d 184, 35 U.C.C. Rep. Serv. 471 (1983).

court if no cross appeal is filed.[5]

§ 32:16   Notice of appeal—When time to file is tolled

App. R. 4(B)(2) allows an extension of time to file the notice of appeal where one of the following motions has been filed:

(1) Motion for judgment notwithstanding the verdict (Civ. R. 50).

(2) Motion for new trial (Civ. R. 59).

(3) Motion to vacate or modify a judgment which adopted a magistrate's decision without waiting for timely objections to be filed (Civ. R. 53).

(4) Request for findings of fact and conclusions of law (Civ. R. 52).

Where timely and properly filed, any of the foregoing motions will toll the period for filing a notice of appeal until the motion is resolved. The appeal is stayed for all parties to the case, not just the party who filed the motion.[1] However, the time for filing an appeal is tolled under App. R. 4(B)(2) only if the motion is both properly and timely filed. Neither an untimely[2] nor an improperly filed motion is effective to suspend the period.[3] When in doubt about the application of App. R. 4(B)(2), counsel should consider filing a premature notice of appeal under App. R. 4(C).

A timely motion for a new trial in a domestic relations case will suspend the period for filing an appeal where the trial court's judgment was predicated upon an evidentiary hearing. Any proceeding in which indicia of trial substantially predominate is a trial from which a party may move for a new trial under Civ. R. 59.[4] However, a new trial motion cannot be taken from a summary judgment or similar order entered without an evidentiary hearing.[5]

A timely motion for findings of fact and conclusions of law under Civ. R. 52 will also suspend the time for filing an appeal. However, Civ. R. 52 applies only to final judgments where questions of fact are tried by the court. Findings of facts and conclusions of law are unnecessary upon motions, in contempt proceedings, in post-decree domestic relations mat-

---

[5]Knight v. Knight, 2000 WL 426167 (Ohio Ct. App. 4th Dist. Washington County 2000).

[Section 32:16]

[1]Winters v. Beitler, 67 Ohio App. 2d 163, 21 Ohio Op. 3d 459, 426 N.E.2d 524 (10th Dist. Franklin County 1980).

[2]R-H-L Advertising Co. v. Americo Wholesale Plumbing Supply Co., 69 Ohio App. 2d 61, 23 Ohio Op. 3d 67, 430 N.E.2d 472 (8th Dist. Cuyahoga County 1980).

[3]L.A. & D., Inc. v. Board of Lake County Com'rs, 67 Ohio St. 2d 384, 21 Ohio Op. 3d 242, 423 N.E.2d 1109 (1981) (motion for new trial); Henderson v. Brost Foundry Co., 74 Ohio App. 3d 78, 598 N.E.2d 62 (8th Dist. Cuyahoga County 1991) (motion for findings of fact and conclusions of law).

[4]First Bank of Marietta v. Mascrete, Inc., 1997 -Ohio- 158, 79 Ohio St. 3d 503, 684 N.E.2d 38 (1997); see also Haase v. Haase, 64 Ohio App. 3d 758, 582 N.E.2d 1107 (8th Dist. Cuyahoga County 1990).

[5]L.A. & D., Inc. v. Board of Lake County Com'rs, 67 Ohio St. 2d 384, 21 Ohio Op. 3d 242, 423 N.E.2d 1109 (1981).

ters, or where questions of fact were not tried by the court.[6] In addition, a court need not make additional findings where it has previously filed an opinion containing findings of fact and conclusions of law.[7]

A motion to vacate a judgment which adopts a magistrate's decision without waiting for timely objections by the parties under Civ. R. 53(E)(4)(c) also suspends the time for filing an appeal. Objections to a magistrate's decision filed before final judgment is entered do not typically suspend the time for filing an appeal because the magistrate's decision is not an appealable judgment. But where the court exercises its discretion to adopt the magistrate's decision and enter judgment immediately under Civ. R. 53(E)(4)(c), without waiting for the filing of timely objections, a motion to vacate the judgment with objections to the magistrate's decision will suspend the time for filing an appeal until the objections are resolved. Finally, a motion for judgment notwithstanding the verdict in a paternity action will also suspend the time for filing an appeal.

No motion other than those specifically listed in App. R. 4(B)(2) will stay, suspend, or enlarge the thirty-day period. Neither a motion to correct an entry under Civ. R. 60(A)[8] nor a motion for relief from judgment under Civ. R. 60(B)[9] can extend the time in which to file an appeal. Likewise, a motion for reconsideration of a final appealable judgment or order will not extend the period.[10]

§ 32:17 Notice of appeal—Contents

Timely filing of a notice of appeal in the trial court is the only act necessary to invoke the jurisdiction of the court of appeals.[1] Nevertheless, nearly every court of appeals requires the preparation and filing of additional documents by local rule. Because the court of appeals retains discretion to dismiss an appeal for defects in the notice of appeal, it is important to ensure that the notice and other papers are properly prepared and filed. A notice of appeal should do all of the following:

(1) Identify each party appealing

---

[6]Paramount Supply Co. v. Sherlin Corp., 16 Ohio App. 3d 176, 475 N.E.2d 197, 40 U.C.C. Rep. Serv. 447 (8th Dist. Cuyahoga County 1984) (summary judgment); Miller v. Barker, 64 Ohio App. 3d 649, 582 N.E.2d 647 (8th Dist. Cuyahoga County 1989) (contempt); Hughes v. Hughes, 65 Ohio App. 2d 193, 19 Ohio Op. 3d 139, 417 N.E.2d 121 (2d Dist. Miami County 1979) (post-decree domestic relations motions); Henderson v. Brost Foundry Co., 74 Ohio App. 3d 78, 598 N.E.2d 62 (8th Dist. Cuyahoga County 1991) (questions of fact not tried to the court).

[7]Civ. R. 52; Peck v. Peck, 96 Ohio App. 3d 731, 645 N.E.2d 1300 (12th Dist. Butler County 1994).

[8]Morton v. Morton, 19 Ohio App. 3d 212, 483 N.E.2d 1192 (8th Dist. Cuyahoga County 1984).

[9]Bosco v. City of Euclid, 38 Ohio App. 2d 40, 67 Ohio Op. 2d 209, 311 N.E.2d 870 (8th Dist. Cuyahoga County 1974).

[10]Pitts v. Ohio Dept. of Transp., 67 Ohio St. 2d 378, 21 Ohio Op. 3d 238, 423 N.E.2d 1105 (1981).

[Section 32:17]
[1]Transamerica Ins. Co. v. Nolan, 72 Ohio St. 3d 320, 649 N.E.2d 1229 (1995).

(2) Identify each case appealed

(3) Designate the final order appealed

(4) Be filed in the trial court

(5) Comply with local rules

The notice of appeal must individually designate each party appealing a judgment.[2] Reversal as to one party typically does not justify reversal as to other parties who are not designated as appellants.[3] While App. R. 3(B) permits use of a joint notice of appeal in cases involving multiple parties, each party must be individually named. Use of terms such as "et al." in the pleadings may not extend the jurisdiction of the court of appeals to parties not individually identified.[4]

The notice of appeal must also designate the court from which the appeal is taken, and identify each case being appealed.[5] The style of the case is the same as in the trial court, with the designation of appellant or appellee added as appropriate.[6] Where several cases are consolidated in the trial court, the local rules of several courts of appeals require that a separate notice of appeal be filed for each consolidated case. Other local rules permit use of joint notices. Failure to properly identify consolidated cases may preclude review or prevent reversal.[7]

The notice of appeal must also specifically designate the final order, judgment, or decree from which the appeal is taken. The court of appeals lacks jurisdiction to review final judgments not individually designated in the notice of appeal.[8] Where several final judgments are issued within a thirty day period, the appellant should ensure that each final judgment or order is separately identified in the notice of appeal.

The notice of appeal must be filed in the trial court. This step is jurisdictional. In some counties, the clerk of the court of appeals can simultaneously file the notice in both courts. In other counties, the appellant is responsible for separately filing the notice in the trial court and forwarding it to the court of appeals for docketing.

Finally, the notice of appeal should comply with the applicable local rules of the court of appeals.[9] Some courts require attachment of the decision and entry being appealed, while others require that the notice

---

[2]App. R. 3(D).

[3]Wigton v. Lavender, 9 Ohio St. 3d 40, 457 N.E.2d 1172 (1984).

[4]Seipelt v. Motorists Mut. Ins. Co., 81 Ohio App. 3d 530, 611 N.E.2d 917 (12th Dist. Brown County 1992) ("et al." insufficient to extend jurisdiction to unnamed parties); but see Grand Council of Ohio v. Owens, 86 Ohio App. 3d 215, 620 N.E.2d 234 (10th Dist. Franklin County 1993) (use of "et al." not a jurisdictional defect).

[5]App. R. 3(D).

[6]App. R. 3(D).

[7]Shaw v. Shaw, 72 Ohio App. 3d 546, 595 N.E.2d 500 (8th Dist. Cuyahoga County 1991) (court refused to consider record in an unappealed consolidated case); see also National Mut. Ins. Co. v. Papenhagen, 30 Ohio St. 3d 14, 505 N.E.2d 980 (1987) (court erred by dismissing appeal for combining consolidated appeals in a single notice).

[8]Parks v. Baltimore & Ohio RR., 77 Ohio App. 3d 426, 602 N.E.2d 674 (8th Dist. Cuyahoga County 1991).

[9]Ivery v. Ivery, 2000 WL 46108 (Ohio Ct. App. 9th Dist. Summit County 2000).

include a certification of counsel, or that it be in a certain form. In addition, nearly every court of appeals requires that the notice be accompanied by a praecipe or docketing statement. These forms permit classification of the appeal, aid in any court-annexed mediation program, and, in most cases, satisfy the requirement under App. R. 9(B) that the appellant file a statement regarding the portions of the record to be included on appeal.

App. R. 3(E) requires the clerk of the trial court to serve a copy of the notice of appeal and docketing statement upon each party. In addition, the appellant should make service of both the notice of appeal and any additional filings upon each party pursuant to App. R. 13(B).

§ 32:18   Notice of appeal—Form⊚

[Title of Court]

[Caption]   Case No. *[_____]*
NOTICE OF APPEAL

Notice is hereby given that Defendant, *[name]*, appeals to the Court of Appeals of *[_____]* County, Ohio, *[number]* Appellate District, from the final judgment *[describe]* entered in this action on *[date]*.

_____

Attorney for Defendant

§ 32:19   Jurisdiction during appeal—Stay of execution pending appeal

An appeal does not stay proceedings to execute upon a judgment unless a stay has been first obtained.[1] A request for a stay must ordinarily be made in the first instance in the trial court.[2] Typically, a request for stay of execution in the court of appeals will be considered only after such a motion has been filed in the trial court.

Under Civ. R. 62(B), a trial court may stay execution of a judgment or any proceedings to enforce a judgment, upon the giving of an adequate supersedeas bond. However, Civ. R. 75(H) directs that Civ. R. 62(B) does not apply to orders allocating parental rights and responsibilities, or to spousal or child support orders. The trial court retains broad discretion to grant stays of these matters with or without bond.

Where conditioned on a bond, a stay is effective only when the bond is approved by the trial court. Whether the stay is granted by the trial court or by the court of appeals, the bond is filed in the trial court and the trial court retains limited jurisdiction to rule upon the adequacy of the bond filed. Where a trial or appellate court grants a stay conditioned on the posting of a supersedeas bond, failure to post the required bond permits the trial court to exercise jurisdiction, including proceedings in

_____

[Section 32:19]
[1]RC 2505.09.
[2]App. R. 7(A).

aid of judgment.[3]

Stays of judgments in contempt are separately governed by RC 2705.09. That section provides that while the bond is filed with the trial court, the amount of the bond is fixed by the appellate court. Accordingly, appeals from contempt citations are an exception to the general rule that applications for a stay must ordinarily be made in the trial court.

If the trial court denies or fails to rule upon the request for a stay, or it is impractical to apply to the trial court, the appellant may move the court of appeals to stay execution of the judgment. The motion should include all of the following:

(1) Showing that relief was sought in the trial court, or an explanation why such an application was not practicable.

(2) Showing that the trial court has denied the application or failed to afford the relief requested.

(3) The reasons the relief is requested and the security proposed, supported by affidavits or relevant parts of the record where facts are in dispute.

(4) Certificate of service demonstrating that reasonable notice was given to all parties.

§ 32:20 Jurisdiction during appeal—Motion for stay pending appeal—Form ⊚

[Title of Court]

[Caption]   Case No. [_____]
                                   MOTION FOR A STAY PENDING
                                   APPEAL

Now comes [Appellant], pursuant to App. R. 7, and respectfully moves this Court for an order [suspending/modifying] during the pendency of this appeal, the order filed in the [name of court] on [date]. Application to the trial court [has been denied by Journal Entry, a copy of which is attached hereto/fails to afford relief requested/is not practicable due to time to be consumed].

The relief requested is necessary due to [inability to pay/necessity for continuation of previous order].

This motion is further supported by [affidavits/memoranda] and will be further supplemented with parts of the record when made available.

Further [Appellant] requests no bond be required.

_____
                                   Attorney for Appellant

[Affidavits in support of the motion]
[Proof/certificate of service]

---

[3]Lash v. Lash, 1990 WL 15329 (Ohio Ct. App. 8th Dist. Cuyahoga County 1990) (citing Pugh v. Pugh, 15 Ohio St. 3d 136, 472 N.E.2d 1085 (1984).

NOTES TO FORM

Drafter's Notes

This motion is to be filed in the appellate court.

§ 32:21 Jurisdiction during appeal—Enforcement during appeal

Enforcement of an order is the reciprocal of a stay. Upon appeal, a trial court retains all jurisdiction not inconsistent with the reviewing court's jurisdiction to reverse, modify, or affirm the judgment.[1] Accordingly, the trial court retains jurisdiction to proceed with any part of the case not appealed. For this purpose, the appellate rules provide that the trial court, upon its own order or the stipulation of the parties, may retain any part of the record required for its use during the appeal.[2]

Unless a stay has been granted, the trial court retains jurisdiction over execution, aid of execution, contempt, or other proceedings to enforce a judgment while it is on appeal. Likewise, the child support enforcement agency will continue to be responsible for enforcement during appeal of spousal and child support orders that have been filed and registered with it.

In domestic relations cases, the trial court also retains limited jurisdiction to modify judgments allocating parental rights and responsibilities, or awarding spousal or child support, during appeal.[3] Recognizing that family circumstances do change and that the need may arise to enter or modify an order during appeal, Civ. R. 75(H) authorizes a trial court to make temporary orders modifying custody, spousal support or child support for the pendency of the appeal. Whether made before or after the notice of appeal was filed, such a motion should be directed in the first instance to the trial court. The appellate court retains jurisdiction to vacate or modify any order granted under this rule, or to enter its own order in the event the trial court has failed or refused to act.

§ 32:22 Jurisdiction during appeal—Motion for relief pending appeal—Form⊚

[Title of Court]

[Caption]   Case No. *[_____]*

MOTION FOR RELIEF PENDING APPEAL

Now comes *[Plaintiff/Defendant]*, pursuant to Civ. R. 75(H), and respectfully requests this Court to modify the order of *[parental rights and responsibilities/child support/spousal support]* entered herein on

---

[Section 32:21]

[1]In re Kurtzhalz, 141 Ohio St. 432, 25 Ohio Op. 574, 48 N.E.2d 657 (1943); Howard v. Catholic Social Serv. of Cuyahoga Cty., Inc., 1994 -Ohio- 219, 70 Ohio St. 3d 141, 637 N.E.2d 890 (1994).

[2]App. R. 10(D), (E).

[3]Civ. R. 75(H).

[date], for the period of the pendency of the appeal. The order as filed requires *[Plaintiff/Defendant]* to pay the sum of *[$_____]* per *[week/month/year]*.

[Plaintiff/Defendant] further requests a stay of any execution.

[Plaintiff/Defendant] further requests that no bond be required of *[him/her]*.

This motion is supported by the memorandum below.

_____

Attorney for *[Plaintiff/Defendant]*

MEMORANDUM

[Movant] has filed an appeal from the decision of the *[court]*, which ordered *[him/her]* to pay the sum of *[$_____]* per week for support for *[duration]*. *[State reason, e.g., payment while the appeal is pending will impose unjust hardship on the movant and [his/her] family.][Movant]* requests that no bond be ordered, due to *[state reason]*.

Respectfully submitted,

_____

Attorney for *[Plaintiff/Defendant]*

[Notice of hearing]

[Proof/certificate of service]

NOTES TO FORM

Drafter's Notes

This motion is to be filed in the trial court.

A proof/certificate of service is only necessary when there is opposing counsel. Where the respondent is unrepresented by counsel at the time of filing the motion, the motion papers will be served by the clerk of court pursuant to written instructions filed with the motion.

Under his/her signature on the motion, counsel should list his/her business address, Supreme Court registration number, and phone number.

§ 32:23   Jurisdiction during appeal—Relief from judgment during appeal

While the trial court retains jurisdiction to proceed with any unappealed portion of the case, or to enforce the judgment where no stay is granted, the trial court's jurisdiction to grant relief from the judgment on appeal is more limited. Civ. R. 60(A) provides that clerical mistakes in a judgment or order may be corrected during the pendency of an appeal only with leave of the appellate court. Likewise, the Supreme Court has held that a trial court lacks jurisdiction to vacate or set aside any portion of a judgment pursuant to Civ. R. 60(B) after an appeal has been taken.

In *Howard v. Catholic Social Services of Cuyahoga County, Inc.*,[1] the Supreme Court ruled that an appeal divests a trial court of jurisdiction to consider a Civ. R. 60(B) motion for relief from judgment during the pendency of an appeal. Adopting the approach advocated in *Majnaric v. Majnaric*,[2] the Supreme Court also suggested that an appellate court could remand a matter to the trial court for consideration of a Civ. R. 60(B) motion before ruling on the merits of the appeal. Under this approach, a Civ. R. 60(B) motion may be filed during the pendency of an appeal, but the trial court is prohibited from granting relief upon the motion unless and until the matter is remanded by the appellate court. Since the trial court is divested of jurisdiction while an appeal is pending, except to clarify or enforce its own judgments, any judgment entered upon a 60(B) motion during appeal is null and void.[3]

§ 32:24 Record on appeal—In general

When reviewing the merits of an appeal, the court of appeals is limited to reviewing the record on appeal as defined by App. R. 9(A).[1] The record includes the original pleadings filed in the trial court, the transcript of proceedings and exhibits thereto, and a certified copy of the docket and journal entries.[2] Because it is the appellant's burden to demonstrate error by reference to the record, it is essential that every fact and ruling relevant to the appeal be included in the record.

§ 32:25 Record on appeal—Transcript of proceedings

With the notice of appeal, the appellant should file and serve on the appellee a docketing statement or praecipe indicating whether the record will include a complete transcript, a partial transcript, no transcript, or a statement pursuant to App. R. 9(C) or (D).[1] The precise form of the statement or praecipe is prescribed by the local rules of nearly every court of appeals. Typically, the 9(B) statement is incorporated into the docketing statement.[2] However, some courts require preparation of a separate praecipe,[3] and one court requires that the 9(B) statement be

---

[Section 32:23]

[1]Howard v. Catholic Social Serv. of Cuyahoga Cty., Inc., 70 Ohio St. 3d 141, 1994-Ohio-219, 637 N.E.2d 890 (1994).

[2]Majnaric v. Majnaric, 46 Ohio App. 2d 157, 75 Ohio Op. 2d 250, 347 N.E.2d 552 (9th Dist. Summit County 1975).

[3]Bishop v. Bishop, 2000 WL 757592 (Ohio Ct. App. 11th Dist. Portage County 2000).

[Section 32:24]

[1]App. R. 12(A)(1)(b).

[2]App. R. 9(A).

[Section 32:25]

[1]App. R. 9(B).

[2]See Local Rules of the First, Second, Fourth, Fifth, Ninth, Tenth and Twelfth District Courts of Appeals.

[3]See Local Rules of the Third, Sixth and Eighth District Courts of Appeals.

included in the notice of appeal.[4] Unless a complete copy of the available transcript is ordered, the appellant must also file and serve on the appellee a statement of the assignments of error the appellant intends to present on appeal.[5]

It is not always necessary to order a transcript, and if the appellant can demonstrate the error complained of without reference to testimony or exhibits introduced at trial, a transcript may be omitted. However, if the appellant intends to challenge the sufficiency or weight of the evidence, a transcript of the relevant testimony is required.[6] Likewise, if the transcript is necessary to demonstrate or otherwise resolve an error, the relevant portions must be produced.[7]

The transcript must be ordered when the notice of appeal is filed.[8] Separate and apart from the docketing statement or praecipe, an appellant must file a written request with the court, serve the request upon the reporter, and pay the necessary fee. Where only a small portion of a lengthy transcript is relevant to the appeal, the appellant may order a partial transcript. In this instance, the docketing statement or praecipe should describe the parts of the transcript which have been ordered.

Where the appellant orders a partial transcript, the appellee has ten days in which to request that additional parts of the transcript be ordered and included in the record on appeal. If the appellant fails to order the additional parts, the appellee may either apply to the court for an order requiring the appellant to order the additional parts, or order the additional parts directly from the reporter.[9]

§ 32:26   Record on appeal—Request to file transcript—Form⊚

[Title of Court]

[Caption]   Case No. *[_____]*
                                         REQUEST TO FILE
                                         TRANSCRIPT

To: *[Reporter]*

Please prepare and file with the Clerk of the Common Pleas Court the Transcript of Proceedings in the above entitled case. The Notice of Appeal was filed on *[_____]*; therefore the transcript must be filed on or before *[_____]*.

---

[4]Local Rule 5(D) of the Eleventh District Court of Appeals.

[5]App. R. 9(B).

[6]App. R. 9(B); Hartt v. Munobe, 1993 -Ohio- 177, 67 Ohio St. 3d 3, 615 N.E.2d 617 (1993).

[7]City of Columbus v. Hodge, 37 Ohio App. 3d 68, 523 N.E.2d 515 (10th Dist. Franklin County 1987).

[8]App. R. 9(B).

[9]See Jenks v. City of West Carrollton, 58 Ohio App. 3d 33, 567 N.E.2d 1338 (2d Dist. Montgomery County 1989).

Respectfully submitted,

Attorney for *[Appellant]*

[Proof/certificate of service]

§ 32:27 Record on appeal—Statement of evidence

Where a reporter was not present at a hearing, there is an alternate mechanism for making a record of the proceedings. Under App. R. 9(C), the appellant may prepare a statement of the evidence or proceedings and submit the statement to the trial court for approval. However, App. R. 9(C) is not a substitute for a transcript, and is not applicable where a transcript could be prepared but the appellant has simply chosen not to do so.

A statement of evidence may be prepared from the best available means, including the appellant's own recollection.[1] It may include a summary of testimony or proceedings, and attach relevant exhibits admitted into evidence during the hearing. The statement must be filed with the court and served upon the appellee no less than twenty days prior to the time for transmission of the record pursuant to App. R. 10. Upon service of the statement, the appellee has ten days to submit objections or an alternate statement.

A statement of evidence under App. R. 9(C) does not become part of the record on appeal until it is approved and signed by the trial judge.[2] The trial court may adopt the proposed statements or prepare its own. In either event, the trial court may not approve a statement containing evidence that was not actually part of the record before it.[3] App. R. 9(C) requires the trial court to act before the record is transmitted to the court of appeals by the clerk. Where the trial court does not act until after the record has been transmitted, the record may be supplemented pursuant to App. R. 9(E).

§ 32:28 Record on appeal—Transmission of the record

The time within which the clerk of the trial court is required to transmit or forward the record on appeal to the clerk of the court of appeals is set forth in App. R. 10(A). Where the appellate court has adopted an accelerated calendar, the period for filing the record is dependent upon which calendar the appeal is docketed:

[Section 32:27]

[1]App. R. 9(C).

[2]State v. Bell, 78 Ohio App. 3d 781, 605 N.E.2d 1335 (4th Dist. Scioto County 1992); Kotula v. Kotula, 1997 WL 381946 (Ohio Ct. App. 8th Dist. Cuyahoga County 1997).

[3]See Joiner v. Illuminating Co., 55 Ohio App. 2d 187, 9 Ohio Op. 3d 340, 380 N.E.2d 361 (8th Dist. Cuyahoga County 1978).

	Regular Calendar	Accelerated Calendar
Record Due	40 days after notice of appeal	20 days after notice of appeal

Where necessary to accommodate a lengthy transcript, either party may move for an extension of time for transmitting the record. Under App. R. 10(C), such motions are ordinarily directed to the trial court, unless the local rules of the court of appeals direct otherwise. Upon transmission of the record, the clerk must give notice to all parties.[1] This notice should be carefully reviewed to ensure that the entire record was transmitted. While it is the clerk's duty to assemble and transmit the record, an appellant is well advised to ensure that papers, exhibits, or transcripts essential to the appeal are in fact included in the record.[2]

§ 32:29 Record on appeal—Correction and supplementation of the record

Correction or supplementation of the record of appeal is governed by App. R. 9(E). Requests to correct omissions or misstatements in the trial court's record must generally be submitted to the trial court. Where there is conflicting evidence concerning the state of the record, only the trial judge can resolve such a dispute.[1] Only where the accuracy of the proposed changes is undisputed should a request for correction of the record be directed to the court of appeals.

Requests for supplementation of the record should be directed to the court of appeals. The record on appeal may be supplemented with pleadings, exhibits, transcripts, or statements of evidence filed after the record was transmitted to the court of appeals, or mistakenly omitted from the record by the clerk of the trial court. Nevertheless, appellate review on the merits is still limited to evidence before the trial court when the decision or judgment was entered.

§ 32:30 Basis of review—Briefs

The time for filing briefs upon the merits in an appeal runs from the date on which the clerk has mailed the notice that the record was filed with the court of appeals.[1] In districts which have adopted an accelerated calendar, the time for filing briefs is also dependent on whether the appeal was docketed on the regular or accelerated calendar. The time for filing the appellee's brief runs from service of the appellant's brief. In regular calendar cases, reply briefs may be filed within ten days after

---

[Section 32:28]

[1]App. R. 11(B).

[2]See Rose Chevrolet, Inc. v. Adams, 36 Ohio St. 3d 17, 520 N.E.2d 564 (1988) (duty of appellant to ensure that adequate record is filed).

[Section 32:29]

[1]State v. Schiebel, 55 Ohio St. 3d 71, 564 N.E.2d 54 (1990).

[Section 32:30]

[1]App. R. 18(A).

service of the appellee's brief. Four copies of the brief must be filed with the clerk on or before the date due.[2]

	Regular Calendar	Accelerated Calendar
Appellant's Brief	20 days after mailing of notice that the record was filed	15 days after record filed
Appellee's Brief	20 days after service of appellant's brief	15 days after service of appellant's brief
Reply Brief	10 days after service of appellee's brief	Not Permitted

Three days may be added to the period for filing a brief when it runs from service of a prior brief, and the brief is served by mail.[3] Because the time for filing the appellant's brief runs from the date the notice was mailed, not the date it was served, this rule is not applicable to appellants. Appellate briefs may also be filed with the court by mail, and are deemed filed on the day of mailing.[4] Briefs must be served on all other parties, and proof of service must be included in the brief.

The contents of an appellate brief are governed by App. R. 16 and 19, together with applicable local rules. App. R. 16 sets out the required elements of the brief, while App. R. 19 governs form and length. While App. R. 19 includes page limits, these are superseded by local rule in most jurisdictions. In addition, many courts have enacted local rules governing the substance and form of appellate briefs filed in that district. Unfortunately, briefs have been rejected by clerks and, in rare cases, appeals dismissed for failure to comply with these rules. Accordingly, the local rules should be consulted before preparing any brief.

§ 32:31 Basis of review—Preservation of error

The court of appeals is limited to reviewing that which transpired in the trial court as reflected in the record on appeal.[1] As a result, the burden naturally falls on the appellant to affirmatively demonstrate error on the record.[2] Every issue on appeal must be raised and preserved in the trial court and assigned as error in the court of appeals. Where the record on appeal does not affirmatively demonstrate the error complained of, the court of appeals will generally presume the regularity

---

[2]App. R. 18(E).

[3]App. R. 14(C).

[4]App. R. 13(A):

[Section 32:31]

[1]App. R. 12(A)(1)(b); State v. Ishmail, 54 Ohio St. 2d 402, 8 Ohio Op. 3d 405, 377 N.E.2d 500 (1978).

[2]Volodkevich v. Volodkevich, 48 Ohio App. 3d 313, 549 N.E.2d 1237 (9th Dist. Medina County 1989), dismissed, 47 Ohio St. 3d 705, 547 N.E.2d 987 (1989); City of Columbus v. Hodge, 37 Ohio App. 3d 68, 523 N.E.2d 515 (10th Dist. Franklin County 1987).

of the trial court's proceedings and affirm.[3]

Before it can become a basis for reversal, an error must be raised in the trial court. The only exception to this rule, the plain error doctrine, is rarely applied in civil cases. An error to which no objection was made at trial will be recognized as plain error only when it seriously affects the fairness, integrity, and reputation of the judiciary, effectively challenging the underlying judicial process.[4]

Unless it constitutes plain error, any issue of which a party was aware but did not bring to the trial court's attention is waived.[5]

Furthermore, the issue must be raised at the appropriate time in the proceedings. For example, an error in granting or denying a motion in limine may be appealed only where the record demonstrates that the issue was finally determined at trial.[6] Unless the record contains an objection to the admission or exclusion of the evidence at trial, any error in granting or denying a motion in limine is waived.[7]

In cases where facts are tried to a magistrate, error must be preserved by filing a timely objection to the magistrate's decision.[8] Absent such an objection, any error in the court's adoption of a magistrate's findings of fact or conclusions of law is waived.[9] Furthermore, the objection must be supported by relevant portions of the transcript of the proceedings before the magistrate, or an affidavit of evidence if no transcript is available.[10] Failure to provide the trial court with such a transcript will generally preclude the appellate court from reviewing or considering the transcript on appeal.[11]

Once raised, the issue and the court's decision must be preserved in the record. It is not unusual in domestic cases for issues to be discussed in chambers or off the record. Nevertheless, it is the appellant's burden to ensure that rulings made during these conferences are either recorded at the time, or repeated for the record.[12] Likewise, error may not be predicated upon the exclusion of evidence during direct examination unless the evidence is proffered for the record.[13] A proffer may take the form of a statement of counsel on the record, documentary evidence, or

---

[3]City of Columbus v. Hodge, 37 Ohio App. 3d 68, 523 N.E.2d 515 (10th Dist. Franklin County 1987).

[4]Goldfuss v. Davidson, 1997 -Ohio- 401, 79 Ohio St. 3d 116, 679 N.E.2d 1099 (1997).

[5]Varisco v. Varisco, 91 Ohio App. 3d 542, 632 N.E.2d 1341 (9th Dist. Medina County 1993).

[6]Gibson v. Gibson, 87 Ohio App. 3d 426, 622 N.E.2d 425 (4th Dist. Scioto County 1993).

[7]State v. Brown, 38 Ohio St.3d 305, 528 N.E.2d 523 (1988), cert. denied 489 U.S. 1040, 109 S.Ct. 1177, 103 L.Ed.2d 239 (1989).

[8]Civ. R. 53(E)(3)(b).

[9]Civ. R. 53(E)(3)(b); Shaffer v. Shaffer, 109 Ohio App. 3d 205, 671 N.E.2d 1317 (3d Dist. Crawford County 1996).

[10]Civ. R. 53(E)(3)(b).

[11]State ex rel. Duncan v. Chippewa Twp. Trustees, 1995 -Ohio- 272, 73 Ohio St. 3d 728, 654 N.E.2d 1254 (1995).

[12]State v. Gray, 85 Ohio App. 3d 165, 619 N.E.2d 460 (3d Dist. Allen County 1993).

[13]Evid. R. 103(A).

testimony, and should include the basis upon which the evidence is offered.

Where the alleged error goes to the weight or sufficiency of the evidence, the appellant must include all relevant portions of the transcript.[14] Where no transcript is available, a statement pursuant to App. R. 9(C) or (D) may be prepared in lieu of the transcript. If facts were found by a magistrate, the record must contain a transcript of the hearing before the magistrate, or an affidavit of all relevant evidence.[15]

If the trial court's decision does not contain separate findings of fact and conclusions of law, a request for separate findings under Civ. R. 52 may be required to preserve error in the court's decision. For example, the trial court is required to consider all applicable factors in making an award of spousal support under RC 3105.18. Failure to consider these factors may be grounds for reversal or remand.[16] However, absent a request for findings of fact and conclusions of law, some courts will presume that the trial court considered all relevant factors, effectively waiving any error therein.[17] If an appeal turns upon the application of one or more statutory factors, findings of fact should be requested in any case in which the trial court has not already included them in its decision.

Finally, each error must be assigned in the court of appeals. For this purpose, assignment of error refers to a specific ruling challenged on appeal, not to the legal grounds upon which the ruling is challenged.[18] The court of appeals need not rule upon any error in a ruling not separately assigned as erroneous.[19] Furthermore, errors must be separately argued, and the appellant must identify where in the record the error occurred.[20] Assignments of error which are not separately argued, or which do not identify the location of the error in the record, may be disregarded.[21]

§ 32:32 Basis of review—Standards of review—In general

Final orders, judgments, and decrees of domestic relations courts are reviewed by the courts of appeals on the same basis as any other final

---

[14]Hartt v. Munobe, 1993 -Ohio- 177, 67 Ohio St. 3d 3, 615 N.E.2d 617 (1993).

[15]Civ. R. 53(E)(3)(b).

[16]Kaechele v. Kaechele, 35 Ohio St. 3d 93, 518 N.E.2d 1197 (1988).

[17]Carman v. Carman, 109 Ohio App. 3d 698, 672 N.E.2d 1093 (12th Dist. Butler County 1996); Brown v. Brown, 1997 WL 411615 (Ohio Ct. App. 12th Dist. Butler County 1997).

[18]North Coast Cookies, Inc. v. Sweet Temptations, Inc., 16 Ohio App. 3d 342, 476 N.E.2d 388 (8th Dist. Cuyahoga County 1984).

[19]App. R. 12(A)(2).

[20]App. R. 12(A)(2).

[21]Contel Credit Corp. v. Rosenblatt, 43 Ohio App. 3d 113, 539 N.E.2d 708 (8th Dist. Cuyahoga County 1988).

judgment or order.[1] The basis for review in the courts of appeals is on questions of law, including the weight and sufficiency of the evidence.[2] Orders are reviewable upon the basis that they are unsupported by sufficient evidence, contrary to the weight of the evidence, contrary to law, or the product of an abuse of the trial court's discretion. However, these are not precise terms of art and, in fact, they are often used interchangeably by courts.

§ 32:33 Basis of review—Standards of review—Sufficiency and weight of the evidence

Factual determinations, including the characterization of the parties' property and its valuation, are subject to review for sufficiency and weight of the evidence.[1] Every judgment must be supported by sufficient evidence. In addition, a judgment may be reversed by an appellate court as against the manifest weight of the evidence. Though frequently treated together, sufficiency and weight of the evidence are distinct legal concepts.[2] Sufficiency is a test of adequacy—whether the evidence is legally sufficient to support the judgment.[3] Weight, on the other hand, implies a consideration of the greater weight of the evidence.

As a practical matter, most courts treat the two issues together. It is frequently said that "judgments supported by some competent credible evidence going to all the essential elements of the case will not be reversed by a reviewing court as being against the manifest weight of the evidence."[4] The evaluation of evidence and the credibility of witnesses is primarily for the trier of fact.[5] Where susceptible to multiple interpretations, the evidence will generally be construed consistently with the judgment.[6]

[Section 32:32]

[1]See Jelm v. Jelm, 155 Ohio St. 226, 44 Ohio Op. 246, 98 N.E.2d 401, 22 A.L.R.2d 1300 (1951).

[2]RC 2505.01(A)(1).

[Section 32:33]

[1]See Barkley v. Barkley, 119 Ohio App. 3d 155, 694 N.E.2d 989 (4th Dist. Pickaway County 1997).

[2]State v. Thompkins, 1997 -Ohio- 52, 78 Ohio St. 3d 380, 678 N.E.2d 541 (1997); Baxter v. Baxter, 27 Ohio St. 2d 168, 56 Ohio Op. 2d 104, 271 N.E.2d 873 (1971).

[3]State v. Thompkins, 1997 -Ohio- 52, 78 Ohio St. 3d 380, 678 N.E.2d 541 (1997); Hartford Cas. Ins. Co. v. Easley, 90 Ohio App. 3d 525, 630 N.E.2d 6 (10th Dist. Franklin County 1993).

[4]C. E. Morris Co. v. Foley Const. Co., 54 Ohio St. 2d 279, 8 Ohio Op. 3d 261, 376 N.E.2d 578 (1978); Fletcher v. Fletcher, 1994 -Ohio- 434, 68 Ohio St. 3d 464, 628 N.E.2d 1343 (1994); Smith v. Smith, 75 Ohio App. 3d 679, 600 N.E.2d 396 (4th Dist. Scioto County 1991).

[5]Seasons Coal Co., Inc. v. City of Cleveland, 10 Ohio St. 3d 77, 461 N.E.2d 1273, 38 U.C.C. Rep. Serv. 469 (1984); Moore v. Moore, 83 Ohio App. 3d 75, 613 N.E.2d 1097 (9th Dist. Summit County 1992).

[6]Karches v. City of Cincinnati, 38 Ohio St. 3d 12, 526 N.E.2d 1350 (1988).

§ 32:34 Basis of review—Standards of review—Magistrate's decisions

When a case or a portion thereof has been referred to a magistrate for decision, the appellate court's review of the resulting judgment is constrained by Civ. R. 53. The magistrate must prepare and file a written decision and include findings of fact and conclusions of law if properly requested or otherwise required. Objections to findings of fact must be supported by a transcript of the hearing or affidavit if the transcript is unavailable. A trial court must allow a reasonable time for preparation of the transcript.[1] In the event a transcript is not filed in the trial court prior to its ruling on the objections, the court of appeals may not review it as part of the appellate record.[2] Under Civ. R. 53, the appellate court is specifically prohibited from considering the adoption of any finding of fact or conclusion of law unless an objection has been filed in accordance with the rule.[3]

The standard of review applied by an appellate court when reviewing a trial court decision approving and adopting the decision of a magistrate is no different from the standard applied to any other case. In contrast, a trial court is required to review a magistrate's decision "de novo." The trial court must make its own factual determination from an independent examination of the record. A trial court judgment indicating that it will not substitute its judgment for that of the magistrate on questions of credibility or granting deference to the magistrate's findings of fact may be reversed.[4]

Several courts of appeal have held that "boilerplate" trial court orders overruling objections and adopting the decision of the magistrate do not qualify as judgments from which an appeal will lie.[5] These courts have held that a judgment must be a separate and distinct instrument, which articulates the outcome and sets forth the order of the court.

§ 32:35 Basis of review—Standards of review—Contrary to law

Judgments, orders, and decrees of a domestic relations court are also reviewable for errors of law. A trial court must correctly decide ques-

---

[Section 32:34]

[1]Shull v. Shull, 1999 -Ohio- 950, 135 Ohio App. 3d 708, 735 N.E.2d 496 (3d Dist. Union County 1999).

[2]State ex rel. Duncan v. Chippewa Twp. Trustees, 1995 -Ohio- 272, 73 Ohio St. 3d 728, 654 N.E.2d 1254 (1995).

[3]Civ. R. 53(E)(3)(b).

[4]DeSantis v. Soller, 70 Ohio App. 3d 226, 590 N.E.2d 886 (10th Dist. Franklin County 1990); Barker v. Barker, 2001 WL 477267 (Ohio Ct. App. 6th Dist. Lucas County 2001).

[5]In re Zakov, 107 Ohio App. 3d 716, 669 N.E.2d 344 (11th Dist. Geauga County 1995); In re Dortch, 135 Ohio App. 3d 430, 734 N.E.2d 434 (9th Dist. Summit County 1999); Reiter v. Reiter, No. 5-98-32 (Ohio Ct. App. 3d Dist. Hancock County 1999), unreported; Muzenic v. Muzenic, 2000 WL 748114 (Ohio Ct. App. 7th Dist. Mahoning County 2000).

tions of law—it has no discretion in this matter.[1] Accordingly, these issues are reviewed by the courts of appeals de novo.

Questions of law reversible on appeal include failure to hold an evidentiary hearing when required,[2] granting a motion to dismiss,[3] application of an erroneous standard,[4] or failure to comply with the applicable statutory standard.[5]

Errors of law in domestic relations cases frequently concern failure to comply with a statutory directive. While most domestic relations issues were traditionally committed to the sound discretion of the trial court, every year additional mandatory requirements are placed upon domestic relations judges. Where a statute provides that the court "shall" perform certain functions or make certain findings, these duties are often construed as mandatory. Failure to perform a mandatory duty is an error of law reversible on appeal.[6]

§ 32:36   Basis of review—Standards of review—Abuse of discretion

Once the facts are determined, domestic relations courts have traditionally been granted broad discretion to fashion equitable relief under the facts and circumstances of each case.[1] This discretion extends to orders granting spousal support,[2] orders dividing marital and separate property,[3] and orders allocating parental rights and responsibilities.[4] In each case, the equitable distribution of the rights or property at issue is a matter committed to the sound discretion of the trial court. In addi-

---

[Section 32:35]

[1]Wolfinger v. Ocke, 72 Ohio App. 3d 193, 594 N.E.2d 139 (3d Dist. Shelby County 1991).

[2]Aristech Chem. Corp. v. Carboline Co., 86 Ohio App. 3d 251, 620 N.E.2d 258 (4th Dist. Scioto County 1993).

[3]Wilson v. State, 101 Ohio App. 3d 487, 655 N.E.2d 1348 (4th Dist. Hocking County 1995), dismissed, appeal not allowed, 72 Ohio St. 3d 1538, 650 N.E.2d 479 (1995).

[4]Castlebrook, Ltd. v. Dayton Properties Ltd. Partnership, 78 Ohio App. 3d 340, 604 N.E.2d 808 (2d Dist. Montgomery County 1992).

[5]Connolly v. Connolly, 70 Ohio App. 3d 738, 591 N.E.2d 1362 (8th Dist. Cuyahoga County 1990).

[6]Marker v. Grimm, 65 Ohio St. 3d 139, 601 N.E.2d 496 (1992) (failure to include child support worksheet with judgment); Eisler v. Eisler, 24 Ohio App. 3d 151, 493 N.E.2d 975 (11th Dist. Geauga County 1985) (failure to value property); Haase v. Haase, 64 Ohio App. 3d 758, 582 N.E.2d 1107 (8th Dist. Cuyahoga County 1990) (spousal support withholding order in excess of statutory maximum).

[Section 32:36]

[1]See Booth v. Booth, 44 Ohio St. 3d 142, 541 N.E.2d 1028 (1989); Cherry v. Cherry, 66 Ohio St. 2d 348, 20 Ohio Op. 3d 318, 421 N.E.2d 1293 (1981).

[2]Kaechele v. Kaechele, 35 Ohio St. 3d 93, 518 N.E.2d 1197 (1988).

[3]Martin v. Martin, 18 Ohio St. 3d 292, 480 N.E.2d 1112 (1985).

[4]Miller v. Miller, 37 Ohio St. 3d 71, 523 N.E.2d 846 (1988).

tion, evidentiary rulings are subject to the discretion of the trial court.[5]

Abuse of discretion is typically defined in Ohio as more than an error of law or judgment, implying that the court's attitude was unreasonable, arbitrary, or unconscionable.[6] By requiring more than a mere difference of opinion, the standard preserves the authority of the domestic relations courts to fashion equitable relief under the specific facts and circumstances of each case. However, that discretion is not unlimited. Though high, the standard does not require proof of an ulterior motive, arbitrary conduct, or willful disregard of the rights of a litigant before a judgment may be reversed as an abuse of discretion.

A judgment is arbitrary when it lacks an adequate guiding principle.[7] A judgment is unreasonable when it lacks a rational basis.[8] A judgment is unconscionable when it is manifestly unfair, harsh, or unjust.[9] Furthermore, the standard applies only where the trial court has discretion to act as it did. Where the court's exercise of discretion was unauthorized by statute, it constitutes an error of law reviewable de novo.

The exercise of discretion must also be guided by the relevant statutory factors. An abuse of discretion may occur where a relevant factor is not considered or where an improper factor is given significant weight. Failure to take relevant factors into account or explain the application thereof may require reversal or remand.[10]

§ 32:37   Basis of review—Standards of review—Prejudice

No matter what standard of review is applicable, a judgment, order, or decree of a domestic relations court will not be reversed unless the appellant can demonstrate prejudice. The court of appeals may reverse a judgment only upon a finding of "prejudicial error committed by such lower court."[1] Where not immediately apparent, an appellant should always explain how the result would have been materially different were it not for the intervening error.

§ 32:38   Basis of review—Principles and presumptions of appellate review

In addition to the application of the appropriate standard of review, the court of appeals is guided by a series of long-standing presumptions. Chief among these is that the court of appeals will presume regularity

---

[5]State v. Combs, 62 Ohio St. 3d 278, 581 N.E.2d 1071 (1991); Ingalls v. Ingalls, 88 Ohio App. 3d 570, 624 N.E.2d 368 (8th Dist. Cuyahoga County 1993).

[6]Blakemore v. Blakemore, 5 Ohio St. 3d 217, 450 N.E.2d 1140 (1983).

[7]Cedar Bay Const., Inc. v. City of Fremont, 50 Ohio St. 3d 19, 552 N.E.2d 202 (1990).

[8]Rowe v. Rowe, 69 Ohio App. 3d 607, 591 N.E.2d 716 (6th Dist. Lucas County 1990).

[9]See *Webster's Third International Dictionary*, unabridged (1971).

[10]Kaechele v. Kaechele, 35 Ohio St. 3d 93, 518 N.E.2d 1197 (1988) (spousal support); Spychalski v. Spychalski, 80 Ohio App. 3d 10, 608 N.E.2d 802 (6th Dist. Lucas County 1992) (property division).

[Section 32:37]

[1]RC 2501.02; see also RC 2309.59, Civ. R. 62.

in the trial court's proceedings and correctness of the trial court's findings of fact.[1] A judgment will not be reversed merely because the trial court has assigned an erroneous basis for its decision.[2] The judgment must be affirmed if there is any valid basis which would support the judgment.[3]

Some presumptions assist the court of appeals in construing the actions or judgments of the lower court. Unless shown to the contrary, the appellate court will presume that the trial court considered only relevant, material, and competent evidence in rendering its judgment.[4] Where a motion or objection is not ruled upon, the court will presume that it was overruled.[5] The court of appeals reviews the case for errors in the judgment only, not in the decision.[6] Where there is an inconsistency between the decision and the judgment entry, the judgment controls.[7]

In addition to the presumptions, there are a variety of principles which ensure the orderly administration of justice. Under the doctrine of law of the case, a court of appeals will ordinarily adhere to conclusions on legal questions reached in prior appeals of the same case.[8] This rule is necessary to insure consistency of results in a case, and to avoid endless litigation. Under the invited error rule, a party will not be permitted to take advantage of an error invited or induced by that party's own conduct.[9] Where the law changes during the course of a case, the court of appeals will usually apply the substantive law which existed upon the date the case was commenced.[10]

§ 32:39   Basis of review—Decision and judgment

On every appeal not dismissed, the court of appeals is required to decide each assignment of error, unless an assignment of error is made

---

[Section 32:38]

[1]Hartt v. Munobe, 1993 -Ohio- 177, 67 Ohio St. 3d 3, 615 N.E.2d 617 (1993); Seasons Coal Co., Inc. v. City of Cleveland, 10 Ohio St. 3d 77, 461 N.E.2d 1273, 38 U.C.C. Rep. Serv. 469 (1984).

[2]Agricultural Ins. Co. v. Constantine, 144 Ohio St. 275, 29 Ohio Op. 426, 58 N.E.2d 658 (1944).

[3]Moore v. Moore, 83 Ohio App. 3d 75, 613 N.E.2d 1097 (9th Dist. Summit County 1992).

[4]Oatey v. Oatey, 83 Ohio App. 3d 251, 614 N.E.2d 1054 (8th Dist. Cuyahoga County 1992).

[5]Dozer v. Dozer, 88 Ohio App. 3d 296, 623 N.E.2d 1272 (4th Dist. Ross County 1993) (motion); Shaffer v. Shaffer, 109 Ohio App. 3d 205, 671 N.E.2d 1317 (3d Dist. Crawford County 1996) (objection).

[6]Economy Fire & Cas. Co. v. Craft General Contractors, Inc., 7 Ohio App. 3d 335, 455 N.E.2d 1037 (10th Dist. Franklin County 1982).

[7]Andrews v. Board of Liquor Control, 164 Ohio St. 275, 58 Ohio Op. 51, 131 N.E.2d 390 (1955).

[8]Nolan v. Nolan, 11 Ohio St. 3d 1, 462 N.E.2d 410 (1984).

[9]Hal Artz Lincoln-Mercury, Inc. v. Ford Motor Co., Lincoln-Mercury Div., 28 Ohio St. 3d 20, 502 N.E.2d 590 (1986).

[10]Lyon v. Lyon, 86 Ohio App. 3d 580, 621 N.E.2d 718 (4th Dist. Scioto County 1993).

moot by a ruling upon another assignment of error.[1] Where no error prejudicial to the appellant is found, the court of appeals must affirm. When an appeal from an action tried to the court is reversed upon the weight of the evidence, the court of appeals may either reverse and remand for further proceedings, or weigh the evidence in the record and render the judgment or final order that the trial court should have rendered.[2]

Upon finding prejudicial error, a judgment may be reversed, or affirmed in part and reversed in part. Where a judgment is reversed without qualification, the reversal leaves the matter as it was immediately before the judgment was rendered by the trial court.[3] Under these circumstances, the trial court must generally retry all issues upon remand.[4] On the other hand, the court of appeals retains discretion to limit the remand to only those issues affected by the error. In this case, the trial court must give effect to those portions of the judgment affirmed, and retry only those issues specifically reversed and remanded for further proceedings.[5]

§ 32:40 Basis of Review—Decision and Judgment—Effect of remand

Upon finding error, an appellate court may reverse a case in whole or in part, and remand the case to the trial court. In domestic relations matters, cases are frequently remanded to consider an issue, make findings, explain conclusions, exercise discretion, recalculate a figure, or determine an amount. While appellate courts sometimes provide specific instructions regarding the nature of the required proceedings, cases are frequently remanded for "further proceedings consistent with this opinion." Thus, it is not always clear, to the trial court nor the litigants, what is expected of the trial court when a case has been reversed and remanded.

Where a judgment is reversed and remanded for further proceedings, it must be taken up at the point where the first error was committed.[1] The reversal has the effect of reinstating the case upon the docket of the trial court at a point in the proceedings immediately before the error

---

[Section 32:39]

[1]App. R. 12.

[2]App. R. 12(C).

[3]Greene v. Woodland Ave. & W.S. St. R. Co., 62 Ohio St. 67, 56 N.E. 642 (1900).

[4]State ex rel. Smith v. O'Connor, 1995 -Ohio- 40, 71 Ohio St. 3d 660, 646 N.E.2d 1115 (1995).

[5]State ex rel. TRW, Inc. v. Jaffe, 78 Ohio App. 3d 411, 604 N.E.2d 1376 (8th Dist. Cuyahoga County 1992), cause dismissed, 63 Ohio St. 3d 1460, 590 N.E.2d 754 (1992); Nolan v. Nolan, 11 Ohio St. 3d 1, 462 N.E.2d 410 (1984) (trial court has no authority to extend or vary the mandate of the appellate court.)

[Section 32:40]

[1]Wilson v. Kreusch, 111 Ohio App. 3d 47, 675 N.E.2d 571 (2d Dist. Montgomery County 1996).

that caused the appeal and reversal.[2] A trial court has no discretion to disregard the mandate of an appellate court.[3] Accordingly, when a judgment is reversed and remanded for additional findings, a trial court cannot rely on its prior findings in making its judgment.[4]

The extent of the hearing required on remand depends on the nature of the error and the terms of the appellate court's mandate. Where the error had the effect of denying a hearing upon an issue, failing to provide notice or opportunity to be heard, or excluding evidence from the record, an evidentiary hearing will generally be required on remand.[5] On the other hand, unless the appellate court limits the nature of the hearing on remand, the trial court retains discretion to determine the scope or extent of the hearing.[6] Where the trial court is directed to re-calculate a figure or determine an amount, it may accept additional evidence on remand.[7] However, the trial court may not expand the scope of the hearing beyond the issues remanded or take evidence upon an issue that was affirmed by the court of appeals.[8]

Upon remand, the trial court must also adhere to the appellate court's determination of the applicable law. Known as "law of the case," this doctrine ensures consistency of results by requiring that subsequent courts apply the determination of legal questions reached in prior proceedings in the same case.[9] The rule is applicable to subsequent proceedings in the trial court as well as the appellate court. Thus, a trial court on remand may not deviate from the legal principles set forth in the appellate opinion.

Finally, the judgment may be reversed with express or implied instructions to enter a specific judgment for a party or upon an issue. In actions tried to the trial court, the court of appeals has the authority to reverse the judgment, independently weigh the evidence and render the judgment that the trial court should have rendered.[10] For instance, language requiring "disposition" in accordance with an opinion, or directing the trial court to "carry this judgment into execution," did not call for a new

---

[2]Armstrong v. Marathon Oil Co., 32 Ohio St. 3d 397, 513 N.E.2d 776 (1987).

[3]Nolan v. Nolan, 11 Ohio St. 3d 1, 462 N.E.2d 410 (1984).

[4]Steven M. v. Robin D., 2000 WL 569568 (Ohio Ct. App. 6th Dist. Lucas County 2000).

[5]State v. Thrower, 85 Ohio App. 3d 729, 621 N.E.2d 456 (9th Dist. Summit County 1993).

[6]State ex rel. Smith v. O'Connor, 71 Ohio St. 3d 660, 1995-Ohio-40, 646 N.E.2d 1115 (1995).

[7]Thomas v. Thomas, 1997 WL 762825 (Ohio Ct. App. 2d Dist. Greene County 1997); Dever v. Dever, 2000 WL 1902195 (Ohio Ct. App. 12th Dist. Clermont County 2000).

[8]State ex rel. TRW, Inc. v. Jaffe, 78 Ohio App. 3d 411, 604 N.E.2d 1376 (8th Dist. Cuyahoga County 1992), cause dismissed, 63 Ohio St. 3d 1460, 590 N.E.2d 754 (1992).

[9]Nolan v. Nolan, 11 Ohio St. 3d 1, 462 N.E.2d 410 (1984).

[10]App. R. 12(C).

hearing or the exercise of discretion.[11] Where the mandate of the appellate court is clear, the trial court has no discretion to fail to enter an order effectuating the requested relief.

§ 32:41 Basis of Review—Decision and Judgment—Motion for reconsideration

App. R. 26 permits the application for reconsideration of an appellate court's decision. The time limits require the motion to be filed in writing before the judgment has been approved and filed or within 10 days after the announcement of the decision. Filing of an application does not extend the time for filing a notice of appeal in the Supreme Court.

When a motion for reconsideration has been filed, the factors that the appellate court should consider include whether the motion calls to the attention of the court an obvious error in its decision, or raises an issue for consideration that was either not considered at all or was not fully considered by the court when it should have been.[1]

§ 32:42 Original actions—In general

While not constituting appeals, the extraordinary writs of mandamus, prohibition, procedendo, and habeas corpus may provide an additional avenue for review of domestic relations orders when appeal is unavailable. Each of the extraordinary writs provides a different remedy. Mandamus compels the performance of a legal duty; prohibition prevents the exercise of unlawful jurisdiction; procedendo directs a court to exercise jurisdiction; and habeas corpus frees a person from unlawful detention. Typically granted only where a court has clearly overstepped its jurisdiction or authority, the writs are designed to provide a remedy in extraordinary cases where a party would otherwise be denied an adequate remedy at law.

The Ohio Supreme Court and the courts of appeals share concurrent original jurisdiction to hear extraordinary writs.[2] Such an action is commenced by filing a complaint in the court of appeals or Supreme Court. Not limited to the record on appeal, original actions are decided on the evidence introduced in the court of appeals or the Supreme Court. The procedure is governed by the Civil Rules to the extent they are not clearly inapplicable. In addition, the Supreme Court and many courts of appeals have enacted specific rules of procedure. As a result, the pleadings and procedure in an original action vary significantly from standard appellate practice.

---

[11]In re Willhite, 85 Ohio St. 3d 28, 1999-Ohio-201, 706 N.E.2d 778 (1999); In re Willhite, 2000 WL 492065 (Ohio Ct. App. 1st Dist. Hamilton County 2000); State v. Lilly, 139 Ohio App. 3d 560, 744 N.E.2d 1222 (2d Dist. Montgomery County 2000).

[Section 32:41]
[1]Bauer v. Bauer, 2000 WL 390173 (Ohio Ct. App. 6th Dist. Lucas County 2000).
[2]O. Const. art. IV § 2(B)(1), O. Const. art. IV § 3(B)(1).

§ 32:43   Original actions—Mandamus

A writ of mandamus commands an inferior judicial tribunal or officer to perform an act required by law.[1] Relief in mandamus requires proof that the relator has a clear legal right to the relief requested, that the respondent has a clear legal duty to perform the act, and that the relator has no adequate remedy at law.[2] Limited to compelling performance of a clear legal duty, a writ of mandamus cannot control the exercise of a discretionary act.[3] Mandamus will not be issued as a substitute for appeal from an interlocutory order.[4] Generally, the availability of appeal is an adequate remedy at law which will preclude issuance of a writ of mandamus.

A writ of mandamus is an appropriate remedy to compel a lower court to comply with the mandate of an appellate court.[5] A party has a clear legal right, and a lower court has a clear legal duty to see that an appellate court's mandate is carried into execution. While available, appeal from a judgment or order entered in violation of a superior court's mandate is considered inadequate, warranting extraordinary relief in mandamus.[6]

A writ of mandamus is also an appropriate remedy to require a lower court to carry out certain other duties required by law. For example, a writ of mandamus will issue to require a court to rule upon a motion to correct the record under App. R. 9(E), or to rule upon a request for findings of fact and conclusions of law.[7] Because the right to appeal may depend upon the trial court's rulings upon these issues, the trial court's failure to act leaves the party without an adequate remedy at law.

Procedurally, the mandamus action must be captioned and brought in the name of the state on relation of the party seeking the writ as required by RC 2731.04. The judge, magistrate or court must be listed as respondent.[8]

§ 32:44   Original actions—Prohibition

A writ of prohibition is an order from a superior court issued to prevent

---

[Section 32:43]

[1]RC 2731.01.

[2]See State ex rel. Pressley v. Industrial Commission, 11 Ohio St. 2d 141, 40 Ohio Op. 2d 141, 228 N.E.2d 631 (1967).

[3]State ex rel. City of Niles v. Bernard, 53 Ohio St. 2d 31, 7 Ohio Op. 3d 119, 372 N.E.2d 339 (1978).

[4]State ex rel. Daggett v. Gessaman, 34 Ohio St. 2d 55, 63 Ohio Op. 2d 88, 295 N.E.2d 659 (1973).

[5]State ex rel. Potain v. Mathews, 59 Ohio St. 2d 29, 13 Ohio Op. 3d 17, 391 N.E.2d 343 (1979); State ex rel. Heck v. Kessler, 1995 -Ohio- 304, 72 Ohio St. 3d 98, 647 N.E.2d 792 (1995).

[6]State ex rel. Heck v. Kessler, 1995 -Ohio- 304, 72 Ohio St. 3d 98, 647 N.E.2d 792 (1995).

[7]State ex rel. Howard v. Ferreri, 70 Ohio St.3d 587, 639 N.E.2d 1189, 1994-Ohio-234 (Ohio, Oct 19, 1994); State ex rel. Jennings v. Nurre, 1995 -Ohio- 280, 72 Ohio St. 3d 596, 651 N.E.2d 1006 (1995).

[8]Pogoloff v. Pogoloff, 1998 WL 290235 (Ohio Ct. App. 6th Dist. Lucas County 1998).

an inferior court from proceeding without jurisdiction, or from unlawfully usurping jurisdiction it does not possess.[1] To obtain a writ of prohibition, the relator must generally show that the trial court is about to exercise judicial power, that the exercise of power is unauthorized by law, and that the relator has no adequate remedy at law.[2]

Generally, a trial court retains jurisdiction to determine its own jurisdiction.[3] However, where the lower court lacks any jurisdiction whatsoever to act, the availability of an adequate remedy of appeal is immaterial.[4] Where a statute plainly and unambiguously prevents a lower court from proceeding in a given manner, it is irrelevant that the court possesses subject matter jurisdiction over the cause in general.[5] In such cases, prohibition will lie both to prevent future unauthorized jurisdiction and to correct the results of previously unauthorized actions.[6]

Writs of prohibition have been granted where a domestic relations court continued to exercise jurisdiction following the dismissal of the action by both parties,[7] or following the death of a party and the abatement of the action.[8] A trial court may also be restrained from improperly transferring a matter from the general division to the domestic relations division,[9] or from unlawfully proceeding in a case in which another court has previously exercised concurrent jurisdiction.[10] Likewise, the writ will lie to prevent a juvenile court from unlawfully proceeding in a neglect action,[11] or from attempting to compel a pregnant women to take action for the benefit of her unborn child.[12]

Writs of prohibition will also issue to prevent a trial court from

---

[Section 32:44]

[1]State ex rel. Doe v. Tracy, 51 Ohio App. 3d 198, 555 N.E.2d 674 (12th Dist. Warren County 1988), cause dismissed, 39 Ohio St. 3d 713, 534 N.E.2d 95 (1988).

[2]Fraiberg v. Cuyahoga Cty. Court of Common Pleas, Domestic Relations Div., 1996 -Ohio- 384, 76 Ohio St. 3d 374, 667 N.E.2d 1189 (1996).

[3]State ex rel. Litty v. Leskovyansky, 1996 -Ohio- 340, 77 Ohio St. 3d 97, 671 N.E.2d 236 (1996).

[4]State ex rel. Adams v. Gusweiler, 30 Ohio St. 2d 326, 59 Ohio Op. 2d 387, 285 N.E.2d 22 (1972).

[5]State ex rel. Sanquily v. Court of Common Pleas of Lucas County, 60 Ohio St. 3d 78, 573 N.E.2d 606 (1991).

[6]State ex rel. Adams v. Gusweiler, 30 Ohio St. 2d 326, 59 Ohio Op. 2d 387, 285 N.E.2d 22 (1972).

[7]State ex rel. Fogle v. Steiner, 1995 -Ohio- 278, 74 Ohio St. 3d 158, 656 N.E.2d 1288 (1995).

[8]State ex rel. Litty v. Leskovyansky, 1996 -Ohio- 340, 77 Ohio St. 3d 97, 671 N.E.2d 236 (1996).

[9]State, ex rel. Lomaz v. Court of Common Pleas of Portage County, 36 Ohio St. 3d 209, 522 N.E.2d 551 (1988).

[10]State ex rel. Racing Guild of Ohio, Local 304, Service Employees Internatl. Union, AFL-CIO, CLC v. Morgan, 17 Ohio St. 3d 54, 476 N.E.2d 1060 (1985).

[11]State ex rel. Cuyahoga Cty. Dept. of Children & Family Serv. v. Ferreri, 96 Ohio App. 3d 660, 645 N.E.2d 837 (8th Dist. Cuyahoga County 1994).

[12]Cox v. Court of Common Pleas of Franklin County, Div. of Domestic Relations, Juvenile Branch, 42 Ohio App. 3d 171, 537 N.E.2d 721 (10th Dist. Franklin County 1988).

proceeding contrary to the prior mandate of an appellate court.[13] The writ will lie where a lower court unlawfully exercises jurisdiction during the pendency of an appeal.[14] On remand, the trial court must proceed consistently with the appellate court's opinion and judgment. Absent extraordinary circumstances, a trial court is without authority to extend or vary the mandate of an appellate court.[15] Where the trial court exceeds or deviates from the plain mandate of an appellate court, a writ of prohibition may issue.[16]

§ 32:45 Original actions—Procedendo

A writ of procedendo is an order from a superior court to an inferior court directing it to proceed to judgment.[1] The opposite of prohibition, procedendo lies when the trial court has jurisdiction, but refuses to exercise it. Like other extraordinary writs, a writ of procedendo will not control the discretion of the lower court, and will be granted only where the relator has a clear legal right to relief and the respondent has a clear legal duty to proceed.[2]

Writs of procedendo will be granted to require the lower court to enforce the mandate of an appellate court.[3] Mandamus or procedendo are also appropriate where the court has either refused to render judgment or has unnecessarily delayed proceeding to judgment.[4] While most delays or continuances would not merit relief in procedendo, the refusal upon repeated requests to set a trial date for a period of 15 months after remand was held to warrant relief in *State ex rel. Crandall, Pheils & Wisniewski v. DeCessna*.[5]

§ 32:46 Original actions—Habeas corpus

The writ of habeas corpus is available to any person unlawfully

---

[13]State ex rel. Crandall, Pheils & Wisniewski v. DeCessna, 1995 -Ohio- 98, 73 Ohio St. 3d 180, 652 N.E.2d 742 (1995).

[14]State ex rel. Republic Steel Corp. v. Environmental Bd. of Review, 54 Ohio St. 2d 75, 8 Ohio Op. 3d 79, 374 N.E.2d 1355 (1978).

[15]Nolan v. Nolan, 11 Ohio St. 3d 1, 462 N.E.2d 410 (1984).

[16]State ex rel. Crandall, Pheils & Wisniewski v. DeCessna, 1995 -Ohio- 98, 73 Ohio St. 3d 180, 652 N.E.2d 742 (1995); State ex rel. TRW, Inc. v. Jaffe, 78 Ohio App. 3d 411, 604 N.E.2d 1376 (8th Dist. Cuyahoga County 1992), cause dismissed, 63 Ohio St. 3d 1460, 590 N.E.2d 754 (1992).

[Section 32:45]

[1]State ex rel. Ratliff v. Marshall, 30 Ohio St. 2d 101, 59 Ohio Op. 2d 114, 282 N.E.2d 582 (1972).

[2]State ex rel. Ratliff v. Marshall, 30 Ohio St. 2d 101, 59 Ohio Op. 2d 114, 282 N.E.2d 582 (1972).

[3]State ex rel. Crandall, Pheils & Wisniewski v. DeCessna, 1995 -Ohio- 98, 73 Ohio St. 3d 180, 652 N.E.2d 742 (1995).

[4]State ex rel. Ney v. Niehaus, 33 Ohio St. 3d 118, 515 N.E.2d 914 (1987); State ex rel. Doe v. Tracy, 51 Ohio App. 3d 198, 555 N.E.2d 674 (12th Dist. Warren County 1988), cause dismissed, 39 Ohio St. 3d 713, 534 N.E.2d 95 (1988).

[5]State ex rel. Crandall, Pheils & Wisniewski v. DeCessna, 1995 -Ohio- 98, 73 Ohio St. 3d 180, 652 N.E.2d 742 (1995).

restrained of liberty or unlawfully deprived of the custody of another.[1] The writ commands the person in custody of the individual unlawfully restrained to appear before the court and explain the lawful basis for the detention. The writ is not available where the relator has an adequate remedy at law, nor is it a substitute for appeal.[2]

A writ of habeas corpus will lie in child custody matters where the order was entered by a court without basic statutory jurisdiction to proceed.[3] The Supreme Court has also suggested that, under extraordinary circumstances, habeas corpus would be granted where a court with jurisdiction to proceed has unlawfully deprived a person of custody. Such an instance might occur where a series of emergency orders are used to deprive a parent of custody. To the extent that the emergency orders are not final appealable orders, the relator would lack an adequate remedy at law and habeas corpus would lie to examine the basis for the detention.

§ 32:47   Attorney fees for appeals

The appellate court has the power to award attorney fees in an appeal. In *Lee v. Lee*[1] the appellee wife filed a motion in the appellate court for appellate attorney fees. Acknowledging that it had concurrent jurisdiction with the trial court in awarding attorney fees, the appellate court concluded that the trial court was the more appropriate forum to evaluate the attorney's services.

In so deciding, the court set forth five conditions that should exist before the trial court awards attorney fees as alimony: 1) the supported spouse needs assistance; 2) the supporting spouse has the ability to pay; 3) the appeal is taken or resisted by the supported spouse in good faith; 4) there was reasonable grounds for the supported spouse's appellate position; and 5) the amount of the fees allowed is reasonable.

Appellate Rule 23 also permits the appellate court to award reasonable fees and costs where an appeal appears frivolous.[2]

[Section 32:46]

[1]RC 2725.01.

[2]In re Davis, 18 Ohio St. 3d 226, 480 N.E.2d 775 (1985); McNeal v. Miami Cty. Children's Services Bd., 64 Ohio St. 3d 208, 594 N.E.2d 587 (1992).

[3]Howard v. Catholic Social Serv. of Cuyahoga Cty., Inc., 1994 -Ohio- 219, 70 Ohio St. 3d 141, 637 N.E.2d 890 (1994).

[Section 32:47]

[1]Lee v. Lee, 10 Ohio App. 3d 113, 460 N.E.2d 710 (8th Dist. Cuyahoga County 1983).

[2]Korn v. Korn, 1997 WL 770961 (Ohio Ct. App. 10th Dist. Franklin County 1997), dismissed, appeal not allowed, 81 Ohio St. 3d 1496, 691 N.E.2d 1058 (1998) (the court invited the appellee to file a motion for her reasonable attorney fees).

Chapter 33

Bankruptcy

By Sheldon Stein, Esq.

> **KeyCite®**: Cases and other legal materials listed in KeyCite Scope can be researched through West Group's KeyCite service on Westlaw®. Use KeyCite to check citations for form, parallel references, prior and later history, and comprehensive citator information, including citations to other decisions and secondary materials.

§ 33:1   Introduction to Bankruptcy

Divorce can have a devastating financial effect on the family unit. The large number of marriages ending in divorce or dissolution, the increased filing in the bankruptcy court, the general economic conditions in the country, and the fact that people are now filing bankruptcy in record numbers[1] combine to create a duty on the part of the family law practitioner to consider the relief afforded by the Bankruptcy Code as a part of effective client representation. No longer can an attorney effectively negotiate a separation agreement or advise a client with respect to post-decree matters without a working knowledge of the Bankruptcy Code.[2]

Domestic relations attorneys must be familiar with both Chapter 7 liquidation proceedings and Chapter 13 debt consolidations. Although most attorneys have at least a basic working knowledge of Chapter 7 liquidations, many lawyers need a better understanding of Chapter 13, how it works, and why, in many instances, Chapter 13 proceedings are

---

[Section 33:1]

[1]According to the American Bankruptcy Institute, the number of consumer bankruptcy filings doubled from 1984 to 1991, with almost 944,000 being filed nationally in 1991. Each subsequent year the number of filings has increased. By 1996, more than 1,125,006 individuals had filed bankruptcy. In 2001, more than $1,452,030 filings had taken place. About 71% of the filings were Chapter 7 cases.

[2]See Testa, *Bankruptcy: The Matrimonial Practitioner's Worst Nightmare*, 4 Trial Law 68 (March, 1992).

preferable to Chapter 7 cases.[3] Therefore, this chapter contains a great deal of basic information regarding the basics of Chapter 13, as well as a review of Chapter 7 proceedings, focusing on particular issues, such as the changing rules regarding the dischargeability of marital debts.

§ 33:2   Chapter 13—In general

A Chapter 13 filing involves a full or partial repayment of debts over a period of time not exceeding five years, during which time the debtor retains possession and use of nonexempt property. In enacting the Bankruptcy Code, Congress clearly intended to encourage individuals to make use of Chapter 13 whenever possible, and to file a Chapter 7 liquidation only as a last resort.[1]

Chapter 13 is available only to individuals with a regular income sufficiently stable to support a repayment program.[2] Such includes welfare, pension, social security payments, and exempt property.[3] Self-employed individuals are eligible for Chapter 13.[4] Spouses can file jointly or separately,[5] and where only one spouse files, the nondebtor spouse's income may supplant or supplement the debtor spouse's income with his or her income for funding purposes so long as such income is regular, steady, and stable.[6] Although 11 U.S.C.A. § 109(e) excludes stock brokers or commodity brokers from being debtors under Chapter 13, an account executive is not considered a stockbroker for purposes of the statute

---

[3]Drummond, *Chapter 13 Bankruptcy Offers Advantages over Chapter 7*, 21-SEP Mont.Law 11 (July/Aug., 1996). See, also, Jean Braucher, *Counseling Consumer Debtors to Make Their Own Informed Choices—A Question of Professional Responsibility*, 5 Am. Bank. L. Inst. L. Rev. 165 (Spring, 1997).

[Section 33:2]

[1]See H. Rep. 595, 89th Cong., 1st Sess (1977) at 118: ("The premises of the bill with respect to consumer bankruptcy are that use of the bankruptcy law should be a last resort; that it is used, debtors should attempt repayment under Chapter 13.").

[2]11 U.S.C.A. § 101(27). See, e.g., In re Murray, 199 B.R. 165 (Bankr. M.D. Tenn. 1996) (seven year old debtor was eligible for Chapter 13 because she received $908 per month social security survivor benefits. See, also, Matter of Kelly, 217 B.R. 273 (Bankr. D. Neb. 1997) (graduate student working towards Ph.D. who also works as a store clerk 32 hours per week, earns $5.85 per hour, has regular income and is eligible for Chapter 13).

[3]Such does not, however, include gratuitous payments to the debtor by family members or other third parties unless such payments are based upon moral or legal obligation as well as the contributor's joint liability for the debts, and where there is direct evidence of the actual assent of the contributor to make payments to fund the plan. In re Jordan, 226 B.R. 117 (Bankr. D. Mont. 1998).

[4]In re Estus, 695 F.2d 311 (8th Cir. 1982).

[5]11 U.S.C.A. § 302. But see In re Smith, 200 B.R. 213 (Bankr. E.D. Mo. 1996) (separate filings by spouses within days of each other held improper where purpose was to manipulate bankruptcy system to discharge large amounts of credit card debt).

[6]In re Bottelberghe, 253 B.R. 256, 261 (Bankr. D. Minn. 2000). See, also In re Murphy, 226 B.R. 601 (Bankr. M.D. Tenn. 1998) (unconditional written commitment to fund plan made by debtor's long-time "significant other" satisfied regular income requirement).

and, hence, may seek relief under Chapter 13.[7] A guardian may file a Chapter 13 on behalf of the ward if authorized by the Probate Court.[8] Only those individuals with noncontingent, liquidated, unsecured debts totaling less than $269,250, and noncontingent, liquidated, secured debts of less than $807,750 are eligible for relief under Chapter 13.[9]

The benefits of a Chapter 13 proceeding are substantial, and in many cases the filing of a Chapter 13 is preferable to the filing of the more traditional liquidation under Chapter 7 of the Bankruptcy Code.

§ 33:3 Chapter 13—Benefits—Expansive stay

The automatic stay provisions of 11 U.S.C.A. § 362 are the most basic element of protection afforded the debtor.[1] The purpose of the stay is to give a debtor a "breathing spell" from pursuit by his creditors and to prevent one creditor from rushing to enforce its lien to the detriment of other creditors.[2]

At the moment a debtor files a petition under either Chapter 7 or Chapter 13, creditors are prohibited from commencing or continuing collection action against the debtor, including the commencement or continuation of judicial proceedings,[3] the enforcement of judgments,[4] nonjudicial "self-help" collection actions,[5] including landlord-tenant

---

[7]In re Berry, 22 B.R. 950 (Bankr. N.D. Ohio 1982).

[8]In re Woods, 248 B.R. 322 (Bankr. W.D. Tenn. 2000).

[9]11 U.S.C.A. § 109(e).

[Section 33:3]

[1]In re Smith, 876 F.2d 524 19 Bankr.Ct.Dec. 1097, Bankr. L. Rep. P 72,936 (6th Cir.(Mich.), May 26, 1989).

[2]In re Smith, 876 F.2d 524, 525 (6th Cir. 1989).

[3]11 U.S.C.A. § 362(a)(1). In re Elegant Concepts, Ltd., 61 B.R. 723 (Bankr. E.D. N.Y. 1986); Compare In re Schock, 37 B.R. 399 (Bankr. D. N.D. 1984) (divorce action is not action to collect debt and therefore not subject to automatic stay) with In re Briglevich, 147 B.R. 1015 (Bankr. N.D. Ga. 1992) (equitable distribution provisions of divorce decree entered into after filing of Bankruptcy violated automatic stay and were null and void); In re Edge, 60 B.R. 690 (Bankr. M.D. Tenn. 1986) (automatic stay bars continued action in state court on medical malpractice claim which occurred pre-petition, but discovered post-petition).

[4]11 U.S.C.A. § 362(a)(2). In re Elder, 12 B.R. 491 (Bankr. M.D. Ga. 1981) (garnishment actions, levies, and other executions violate this section); In re Acorn Investments, 8 B.R. 506 (Bankr. S.D. Cal. 1981). See, also, In re Stephens, 43 B.R. 97 (Bankr. N.D. Ala. 1984) (section has special significance to litigants in state court post-decree domestic relations enforcement actions); In re O'Connor, 42 B.R. 390 (Bankr. E.D. Ark. 1984).

[5]11 U.S.C.A. § 362(a)(3). Compare In re Guinn, 102 B.R. 838 (Bankr. N.D. Ala. 1989) (credit union violated automatic stay when, in attempting to coerce the debtor into repaying unsecured debt with them, terminated the debtor's membership in the credit union, refused to accept the debtor's payment on an outstanding mortgage note, and thereafter declared the mortgage in default) with Brown vs. Pennsylvania State Employees Credit Union, 851 F.2d 81 (3d Cir. 1988) (credit union did not violate the automatic stay by informing the debtor that the failure to reaffirm a debt with them would result in the refusal of future services); In re Sechuan City, Inc., 96 B.R. 37 (Bankr. E.D. Pa. 1989) (credit violated automatic stay by posting signs around the debtor's restaurant, indicating that the debtor was not paying his bills).

disputes,[6] vehicle repossession,[7] denial of student transcripts,[8] set-off of funds on deposit by banks or credit unions,[9] post-petition collection letters,[10] the postpetition withholding of wages by an employer,[11] as well as the creation[12] and enforcement[13] of liens against the debtor's property. A foreclosure sale of real estate after the filing of a Chapter 13 violates the automatic stay, and is void.[14] 11 U.S.C.A. § 362 provides that the stay is applicable to all entities, including individuals, partnerships, corporations, estates, trusts, and governmental units,[15] but does not prohibit

---

[6]In re Davis, 62 B.R. 345 (Bankr. S.D. Ohio 1986) (landlord violates automatic stay by engaging in self-help remedies against tenant in arrears in rent).

[7]In re Sharon, 234 B.R. 676, 1999 FED App. 9P (B.A.P. 6th Cir. 1999) (violation of automatic stay for creditor not to turnover vehicle after demand by debtor and tender of adequate protection notwithstanding the fact that repossession took place just prior to filing of Chapter 13); In re Clark, 60 B.R. 13 (Bankr. N.D. Ohio 1986) (post-petition repossession of vehicle violates automatic stay).

[8]In re Merchant, 958 F.2d 738, 73 Ed. Law Rep. 619 (6th Cir. 1992) (denial of transcripts to debtor violates automatic stay); Loyola University vs. McClarty, 234 B.R. 386 (E.D. La. 1999) (same).

[9]Matter of Sumrall, 56 B.R. 134 (Bankr. M.D. Fla. 1985) (bank or credit union cannot remove funds from debtor's account to satisfy pre-petition debt). See, also, In re Brooks, 132 B.R. 29 (Bankr. W.D. Mo. 1991) (credit union cannot retain money obtained post-petition based upon pre-petition authorized waged deduction).

[10]In re Driggers, 204 B.R. 70 (Bankr. N.D. Fla. 1996); In re Olson, 38 B.R. 515 (Bankr. N.D. Iowa 1984);

[11]In re Hellums, 772 F.2d 379 (7th Cir. 1985); In re Ohning, 57 B.R. 714 (Bankr. N.D. Ind. 1986) (employer cannot, post-petition, withhold money from the debtor's pay for a prepetition debt owed the employer).

[12]11 U.S.C.A. § 362(a)(4). Matter of Gotta, 47 B.R. 198 (Bankr. W.D. Wis. 1985) (purpose of the prohibition against post-petition lien creation is to prevent some creditors from gaining an unfair advantage by becoming secured instead of unsecured); In re Funket, 127 B.R. 640 (Bank. M.D. Pa. 1982) (post-petition recording of mortgage violates the automatic stay); In re Ken Gardner Ford Sales, Inc., 10 B.R. 632, 32 U.C.C. Rep. Serv. 1281 (Bankr. E.D. Tenn. 1981), decision aff'd, 23 B.R. 743, 35 U.C.C. Rep. Serv. 1352 (E.D. Tenn. 1982), affirmed by 23 B.R. 743 (E.D. Tenn. 1982). However, it should be noted that where a creditor is given a grace period under state law to perfect a security interest which relates back to an earlier, pre-petition date, the creditor may perfect its lien post-petition. See Matter of Fiorillo & Co., 19 B.R. 21 (Bankr. S.D. N.Y. 1982).

[13]11 U.S.C.A. § 362(a)(5). Matter of Fernandez, 125 B.R. 317 (Bankr. M.D. Fla. 1991), aff'd in part, remanded in part, 132 B.R. 775 (M.D. Fla. 1991) (I.R.S. has a duty to insure the pre-petition tax lien levy does not result in a post-petition seizure of debtor's assets).

[14]In re Smith, 245 B.R. 622 (Bankr. W.D. Mo. 2000). See In re Bunch, 249 B.R. 667, 670-71 (Bankr. D. Md. 2000) (debtor's equitable interest in real estate sufficient to permit filing of complaint for violation of the automatic stay where mortgage lender foreclosed after the petition date with knowledge that the debtor was the personal representative and sole beneficiary of his deceased mother's estate and where the debtor was in possession of the real estate).

[15]U.S. Postal Service v. Hudson, 230 B.R. 542, 545 (W.D. Tenn. 1999) (automatic stay applied to U.S. Postal Service to prevent it from charging a $50 administrative fee for complying with the bankruptcy court wage order); In re Finley, 237 B.R. 890, 894 (Bankr. N.D. Miss. 1999) (forfeiture proceeding by Mississippi Department of Public Safety based upon debtor's third D.U.I. was in essence a civil action subject to the provisions of the automatic stay); In re Layton, 220 B.R. 508 (Bankr. N.D. N.Y. 1998) (taxing

the prosecution of criminal contempt proceedings against the debtor.[16]

The automatic stay requires a creditor to act affirmatively to reverse actions which, if not reversed, would result in a stay violation. The creditor must restore the *status quo*. For example, if a wage garnishment has been issued pre-petition, the creditor may not accept post-petition payment of garnished funds and must act to halt or suspend the garnishment.[17] Similarly, a creditor that refuses to return a vehicle repossessed prior to the filing of the Chapter 13 must return the vehicle to the debtor,[18] and violates the automatic stay by conditioning return of the vehicle on proof of insurance and adequate protection.[19]

An award of actual damages, including attorney's fees is mandated by 11 U.S.C.A. § 362(h) for willful violation of the automatic stay.[20] Such may include, for example, damages for emotional distress and punitive damages.[21]

The Bankruptcy Code expressly provides that the automatic stay does not apply to the collection of alimony, maintenance, or support from

---

agency violated automatic stay by refusing to accept the debtor's payment of post-petition taxes until delinquent pre-petition payments were paid; In re Tarrant, 190 B.R. 704 (Bankr. S.D. Ga. 1995) (city cannot terminate utility service after receiving notice of filing of Chapter 13 based upon pre-petition unpaid account. See, also, In re Parr Meadows Racing Ass'n, Inc., 880 F.2d 1540 (2d Cir. 1989), In re Shafer, 63 B.R. 194 (Bankr. D. Kan. 1986); In re McCullough, 63 B.R. 97 (Bankr. E.D. Pa. 1986); In re Burrow, 36 B.R. 960 (Bankr. D. Utah 1984) (I.R.S. cannot freeze debtor's tax refund because the debtor owes pre-petition taxes) (In re Nashville White Trucks, Inc., 731 F.2d 376 (6th Cir. 1984) (automatic stay prohibits post-petition state tax collection efforts); In re Mack, 46 B.R. 652 (Bankr. E.D. Pa. 1985); In re Ashby, 36 B.R. 976 (Bankr. D. Utah 1984); In re Blair, 62 B.R. 650 (Bankr. N.D. Ala. 1986) (state cannot institute post-petition efforts to collect pre-petition fine); In re Liss, 59 B.R. 556 (Bankr. N.D. Ill. 1986) (state cannot pursue restitution for its citizens based on pre-petition fraud).

[16]In re Perez, 220 B.R. 216 (Bankr. D. N.J. 1998), opinion aff'd, 1998 WL 2030664 (D. N.J. 1998); In re Altchek, 124 B.R. 944 (Bankr. S.D. N.Y. 1991).

[17]In re Sucre, 226 B.R. 340 (Bankr. S.D. N.Y. 1998); In re Walters, 219 B.R. 520 (Bankr. W.D. Ark. 1998).

[18]In re Sharon, 234 B.R. 676, 1999 FED App. 9P (B.A.P. 6th Cir. 1999); In re Bunton, 246 B.R. 851, 853 (Bankr. N.D. Ohio 2000).

[19]In re Jackson, 251 B.R. 597, 601 (Bankr. D. Utah 2000).

[20]In re Walsh, 219 B.R. 873 (B.A.P. 9th Cir. 1998).

[21]Fleet Mortg. Group, Inc. v. Kaneb, 196 F.3d 265 (1st Cir. 1999) (creditor and counsel willfully violated automatic stay and sanctioned $25,000 damages for emotional distress and $18,220.68 for attorney fees); In re Johnson, 253 B.R. 857 (Bankr. S.D. Ohio 2000) (actual damages of $6,669 plus $1,000 punitive damages, plus counsel fees awarded); In re Fridge, 239 B.R. 182, 190-191 (Bankr. N.D. Ill. 1999) (attorney and law firm violated automatic stay and sanctioned with fees of $6,484.37 and punitive damages of $2,000); In re Riddick, 231 B.R. 265 (Bankr. N.D. Ohio 1999) (collection agency ordered to pay $850 counsel fees and $3,000 punitive damages for violation of the automatic stay); In re Florio, 229 B.R. 606, 608 (S.D. N.Y. 1999) (Ford Motor Credit ordered to pay damages of $8,699.85 and counsel fees for repossessing vehicles in violation of a conditional order for relief from stay); In re Georgeff, 226 B.R. 852 (Bankr. S.D. Ohio 1998) (creditor willfully violated automatic stay justifying actual damages, attorney fees and punitive damages of $1,000 where creditor initiated garnishment while Chapter 13 case was pending); (In re Holden, 226 B.R. 809 (Bankr. D. Vt. 1998).

property that is not property of the bankruptcy estate.[22] Care must be taken, however, for the application of the Code in this area depends on the type of bankruptcy proceeding.

During the pendency of a Chapter 7 proceeding the former spouse is free to collect support arrearages from property that is not included with the Bankruptcy Code definition of "property of the estate",[23] such as exempt property, post-petition wages, property acquired by the debtor after the commencement of the case, and property abandoned by the Trustee.[24] Collection efforts may not be directed at pre-petition wages or other property owned by the debtor at the time that the case was filed.[25]

Upon the filing of a Chapter 13 case, the spouse or former spouse is prohibited from taking further action to collect support arrearages from post-petition earnings of the debtor.[26] However, such support arrearages are not dischargeable in Chapter 13 proceedings,[27] and the Bankruptcy Code requires that such arrearages be paid in full through the plan in the same manner as other priority obligations.[28]

Similarly, a Chapter 13 debtor's interest in a ERISA qualified pension and retirement plan is excluded from being property of the estate under § 541(c)(2) of the Bankruptcy Code. As such, the debtor cannot claim an exemption in such property, and the debtor's former spouse is entitled, without first obtaining relief from the automatic stay, to litigate her interest in same pursuant to a state court divorce decree.[29]

Furthermore, the modification of support obligations is prohibited by the automatic stay, and any modification obtained in violation of the automatic stay is void.[30] Like any other action taken in violation of the automatic stay, the offending party runs the risk of being held in contempt of court.[31] Anyone wishing to modify a support obligation during the pendency of a bankruptcy proceeding must first ask the bank-

---

[22]11 U.S.C.A. § 362(b)(2).

[23]11 U.S.C.A. § 541(a)(1) defines property of the estate to include all of the debtor's legal and equitable interests as of the commencement of the case.

[24]Matter of Daugherty, 117 B.R. 515, 517 (Bankr. D. Neb. 1990); In re Weidenhammer, 82 B.R. 383, 385 (Bankr. E.D. Pa. 1988).

[25]Matter of Daugherty, 117 B.R. 515, 517 (Bankr. D. Neb. 1990); In re Weidenhammer, 82 B.R. 383, 385 (Bankr. E.D. Pa. 1988).

[26]In re Walter, 153 B.R. 38, 40 (Bankr. N.D. Ohio 1993); In re Lackey, 148 B.R. 626, 629 (Bankr. N.D. Ala. 1992); In re Henry, 143 B.R. 811, 814 (Bankr. W.D. Pa. 1992)

[27]See 11 U.S.C.A. § 1328(a)(2).

[28]11 U.S.C.A. § 1322(a)(2). See Matter of Olson, 200 B.R. 40 (Bankr. D. Neb. 1996) and In re Beverly, 196 B.R. 128 (Bankr. W.D. Mo. 1996) (confirmation of Chapter 13 Plans denied where debtors failed to schedule support arrearages and provide of such claims in full, regardless of the treatment of other debts). It should be noted that the plan must also permit the former spouse to collect post-petition interest after confirmation. In re Jacobson, 231 B.R. 763, 765-767 (Bankr. D. Ariz. 1999).

[29]In re Miller, 224 B.R. 913 (Bankr. D. N.D. 1998).

[30]In re Stringer, 847 F.2d 549 (9th Cir. 1988); Matter of Dexter, 116 B.R. 92 (Bankr. S.D. Ohio 1990).

[31]Matter of Dexter, 116 B.R. 92 (Bankr. S.D. Ohio 1990) (former spouse held in contempt of court for prosecuting support modification action in state court without first obtaining relief from the automatic stay in accordance with 11 U.S.C.A. § 362(d).

ruptcy court to lift the automatic stay "for cause" before going to state court to obtain the modification.[32]

What distinguishes Chapter 13 from Chapter 7 in this area is the co-debtor stay of 11 U.S.C.A. § 1301(a), which, in Chapter 13 proceedings, extends the protection of the automatic stay to those who co-signed or guaranteed consumer debts[33] incurred by the debtor.[34] However, taxes are not consumer debts, and, hence, the co-debtor stay does not preclude the Internal Revenue Service from collecting jointly owed unpaid federal income taxes from a nondebtor wife.[35]

This relief is subject to the limitations contained in 11 U.S.C.A. § 1301(c), which permits a creditor to obtain relief from the stay to proceed against a co-obligor where (1) the co-obligor received the consideration for the claim,[36] (2) the proposed Chapter 13 does not provide for full payment of the claim,[37] or (3) the creditor will suffer irreparable harm if the stay is not lifted.[38] This protection is not available in a Chapter 7.

The co-debtor stay has significance to the debtor whose friends or relatives have guaranteed some of his debts, and where the debtor wishes to pay the debt in a longer period of time than the creditor will permit while protecting the co-signer from creditor pressure. By obtaining confirmation of a plan providing for repayment of the debt, the debtor stops collection action against a co-debtor even if the debt is presently due, the Chapter 13 plan provides for installment payments to the creditor, and the co-debtor is solvent and not in bankruptcy.[39]

Suppose a husband and wife jointly are indebted to a bank based

---

[32]11 U.S.C.A. § 362(d) permits the court to lift the automatic stay "for cause." See Matter of Daugherty, 117 B.R. 515, 517 (Bankr. D. Neb. 1990); In re Weidenhammer, 82 B.R. 383, 386 (Bankr. E.D. Pa. 1988); See, also In re Mac Donald, 755 F.2d 715, 717 (9th Cir. 1985) (the discretionary "cause" standard of section 362(d) permits debtor's former spouse to return to state court to modify final alimony and property award).

[33]See 11 U.S.C.A. § 101(7), which defines "consumer debts" to be a debt incurred by and for an individual for personal, family, or household purposes. Compare In re Haugland, 199 B.R. 125 (Bankr. D. N.J. 1996) (condominium association fees are a consumer debt), In re Bertolami, 235 B.R. 493, 4496-497 (Bankr. S.D. Fla. 1999) (mortgage loan on residence is a consumer debt) and In re Zersen, 189 B.R. 732, 740 (Bankr. W.D. Wis. 1995) (mortgage loan to purchase family residence is a consumer debt) with In re Izzi, 196 B.R. 727 (Bankr. E.D. Pa. 1996) (co-debtor stay does not protect wife from tort judgment because tort claims are not consumer debts) and In re Dye, 190 B.R. 566 (Bankr. N.D. Ill. 1995) (tax liability is not a consumer debt. I.R.S. can proceed against non-filing spouse to collect unpaid taxes).

[34]Harris v. Fort Oglethorpe State Bank, 721 F.2d 1052 (6th Cir. 1983).

[35]In re Westberry, 215 F.3d 589, 591-93, 2000 FED App. 189P (6th Cir. 2000), reversing In re Westberry, 219 B.R. 976 (Bankr. M.D. Tenn. 1998).

[36]In re Bradley, 705 F.2d 1409 (5th Cir. 1983); In re Ragin, 249 B.R. 118 (Bankr. D. S.C. 2000).

[37]In re Sandifer, 34 B.R. 507 (Bankr. W.D. La. 1983); In re Rondeau, 9 B.R. 403 (Bankr. E.D. Pa. 1981).

[38]In re Schaffrath, 214 B.R. 153, 155 (B.A.P. 6th Cir. 1997).

[39]In re Janssen, 220 B.R. 639 (Bankr. N.D. Iowa 1998). In re Singley, 233 B.R. 170, 173 (Bankr. S.D. Ga. 1999) (co-debtor stay violated where creditor caused to be noted on the non-debtor's credit record the fact that the debtor has filed Chapter 13); Matter of

upon a loan used to finance of a purchase of an automobile. A divorce follows, with the husband being awarded the car and ordered to pay the car note. On subsequent default by the husband, the bank can and will begin collection procedures against both of them. The former wife will probably respond with state court contempt proceedings against the husband. By obtaining confirmation of an appropriate Chapter 13 plan providing for payment in full of the deficiency judgment notwithstanding a smaller dividend to other unsecured creditors, the husband can prevent collection procedures against both of them and will also avoid having to defend the contempt proceedings.

But what about the situation where the debtor has made use of his or her parent's credit card? Can a Chapter 13 debtor protect a family member from collection efforts upon the account? It has been held that the co-debtor stay does not apply because the debtor does not have a direct contractual relationship with the credit card issuer, let alone, a joint, contractual liability upon the account with the family member.[40]

§ 33:4 Chapter 13—Benefits—Availability of relief

In a proceeding under Chapter 7, an individual may receive a discharge only once every six years.[1] Chapter 13 contains no such prohibition. An individual can file a Chapter 13 within six years after a Chapter 7 discharge. This filing is not, per se, bad faith so as to warrant denial of confirmation of a Chapter 13 plan.[2]

For example, suppose an individual files a bankruptcy and obtains a discharge. At such time, a debtor owned a home with a fair market value of $65,000 subject to a mortgage of $65,000, with all payments being current. Under such circumstances the trustee in the bankruptcy will probably abandon his or her interest in the property, and the mortgage holder will likely permit the debtor to keep the house because the mortgage is current.

Two years later, the debtor is laid off from work or becomes ill and does not work for a substantial period of time. The mortgage falls into arrears, and the debtor is also being pressed by other creditors. Chapter 7 relief is obviously not available to the debtor. However, the debtor can, upon return to work, turn to Chapter 13 for relief; the debtor can cure the mortgage arrearages during the life of the plan while providing for payment to his other creditors.[3]

Sommersdorf, 139 B.R. 700 (Bankr. S.D. Ohio 1991) (co-debtor stay violated where bank caused profit and loss write off notation to be entered on non-debtor's credit report).

[40]In re Hill, 268 B.R. 548 (B.A.P. 9th Cir. 2001).

[Section 33:4]
[1]11 U.S.C.A. § 727(a)(8).

[2]Johnson v. Home State Bank, 501 U.S. 78, 111 S. Ct. 2150, 115 L. Ed. 2d 66 (1991); In re Dixon, 241 B.R. 234 (Bankr. M.D. Fla. 1999); In re Waters, 227 B.R. 784, 787-788 (Bankr. W.D. Va. 1998).

[3]In re Lewis, 63 B.R. 90 (Bankr. E.D. Pa. 1986).

§ 33:5   Chapter 13—Benefits—Possession of property

In Chapter 7 proceedings all nonexempt property can be sold by the trustee. On the other hand, the debtor retains possession of all nonexempt property in a Chapter 13 proceeding.[1]

For example, presume that an individual owns a house, valued at $125,000, but subject to a mortgage of only $60,000. This person co-signs a loan for the purchase of a new car for his son. A year later the son loses his job, the car is repossessed, and the bank looks to the father for payment of an $8,500 deficiency balance.

If the individual cannot pay the deficiency in full or cannot reach agreement with the bank as to payment of this debt, the bank will likely place a judgment lien upon the real estate and begin a foreclosure proceedings, wage garnishments, or take other collection action against the father.

Because the father's house is worth more than the mortgage, the debtor's $5,000 Ohio homestead exemption,[2] and the costs of sale, the father will not want to seek relief under Chapter 7 because the Chapter 7 Trustee will take possession of, and sell, the house.

Through the use of a Chapter 13 the father can pay this debt over a three to five-year period upon terms that he can afford. At the same time he will retain the possession, use, and enjoyment of his house and other nonexempt property.

§ 33:6   Chapter 13—Benefits—Modifying rights of secured creditors

In a Chapter 7 case, unless the debtor redeems the collateral with a lump sum payment, the debtor is forced to either surrender the collateral or enter into a consensual reaffirmation agreement with the creditor which survives the bankruptcy.

In a Chapter 13 the debtor can, except as to mortgages on the debtor's principal residence, modify the rights of secured creditors.[1] Thus, a Chapter 13 debtor can, for example, reduce the monthly payments to the secured creditor, reduce the interest rate, or value the collateral securing the loan and provide for full payment to the extent of the value of the collateral and a lesser payment upon different terms on the

---

[Section 33:5]

[1]11 U.S.C.A. § 1306(b). See, also, 11 U.S.C.A. § 1322(a)(1).

[2]The Ohio exemption statute is contained in R.C. 2329.66. A discussion of exemptions is beyond the scope of this article, but every attorney contemplating the filing of a Chapter 7 or Chapter 13 proceeding should review this provision as well as the case law. Whether certain assets are exempt from turn-over to the Bankruptcy Trustee is an important factor that must be considered in advising a client as to whether to file Chapter 7 or Chapter 13.

[Section 33:6]

[1]11 U.S.C.A. § 1322(b)(2).

unsecured portion of the claim.[2] The value is determined as of the date of the filing of the petition.[3]

11 U.S.C.A. § 1322(b)(2) provides that a claim secured only by a real estate mortgage on the debtor's principal residence may not be modified except to cure payment default by decelerating the mortgage. This prohibition against modifying the rights of creditors holding valid mortgages upon the debtor' principal residence applies only in the situation where the debtor's residence is the *only* collateral securing the loan, and where sufficient equity in the real estate exists to secure at least a portion of the mortgage.[4]

Thus, the anti-modification language of 11 U.S.C.A. § 1322(b)(2) does *not* apply to a mortgage on a multi-family property even though the debtor occupies one of the units as his home,[5] , nor does it apply to a mobile home,[6] to houses purchased under land contract,[7] or to claims secured by other collateral in addition to the residence.[8]

It is now well established that the holder of a junior mortgage does not have a secured claim if no equity exists in the real estate beyond the claim of senior mortgages. Under such circumstances the prohibition against modifying the rights of a mortgage holder upon the debtor's res-

---

[2]See Associates Commercial Corp. v. Rash, 520 U.S. 953, 117 S. Ct. 1879, 138 L. Ed. 2d 148 (1997), wherein the court held that the collateral is to be valued at its replacement value, as opposed to its liquidation value. See In re Getz, 242 B.R. 916, 919-20 (B. A.P. 6th Cir. 2000) (After *Rash*, average of NADA wholesale and retail values is permissible starting and ending point for determining value of vehicle). Some courts have held that the property is to be valued as of the date of confirmation.

[3]In re Longbine, 256 B.R. 470 (Bankr. S.D. Tex. 2000). But see In re Crain, 243 B.R. 75, 82-83, (Bankr. C.D. Cal. 1999) (valuation determined as of effective date of plan).

[4]Lomas Mortg., Inc. v. Louis, 82 F.3d 1 (1st Cir. 1996) (multi-family home occupied by debtor and rent paying tenants held not protected from modification under 11 U.S.C.A. § 1322(b); See, generally, Comment, Lien Stripping after Nobleman vs. American Savings Bank: What is "Additional Collateral", 32 Hous. L. Rev. 201 (Summer, 1995).

[5]Lomas Mortg., Inc. v. Louis, 82 F.3d 1 (1st Cir. 1996) (multi-family home occupied by debtor and rent paying tenants held not protected from modification under 11 U.S.C.A. § 1322(b); In re Kimbell, 247 B.R. 35, 38 (Bankr. W.D. N.Y. 2000); In re Bookout, 231 B.R. 306, 308-309 (Bankr. E.D. Ark. 1999) (same); In re Falotico, 231 B.R. 35 (Bankr. D. N.J. 1999) (same); In re Maddaloni, 225 B.R. 277 (D. Conn. 1998) (same); In re Loper, 222 B.R. 431 (D. Vt. 1998) (anti-modification provisions of 11 U.S.C.A. § 1322(b)(2) does not apply to a home mortgage because it also reached to cover a satellite dish, stove, refrigerator, and carpeting. But see In re Marenaro, 217 B.R. 358 (B. A.P. 1st Cir. 1998) (debtor's home mortgage held subject to anti-modification provision of § 1322(b)(2) even though mortgage also covered "enhancements" such as mineral rights, fixtures, and the like); In re Mendez, 255 B.R. 143 (Bankr. D. N.J. 2000).

[6]In re Thompson, 217 B.R. 375 (B.A.P. 2d Cir. 1998); In re Stratton, 248 B.R. 177 (Bankr. D. Mont. 2000).

[7]Matter of Leazier, 55 B.R. 870 (Bankr. N.D. Ind. 1985).

[8]In re Larios, 259 B.R. 675 (Bankr. N.D. Ill. 2001) (second mortgage not protected from modification where lender also took a security interest in business assets); In re Loper, 222 B.R. 431, 437-39 (D. Vt. 1998); The Money Store Investment Corporation vs. Cummings, 214 B.R. 126 (D.N.J. 1997); In re Howard, 220 B.R. 716 (Bankr. S.D. Ga. 1998); In re Rodriguez, 218 B.R. 764, 774-77 (Bankr. E.D. Pa. 1998).

idence does not apply, and the lien can be stripped away.[9]

Similarly, judgment liens and statutory liens are not "security interests" within the meaning of the Bankruptcy Code. Accordingly, they are subject to the valuation rules of 11 U.S.C.A. § 506 and can be stripped away if no equity exists in the real estate to reach these liens.[10]

11 U.S.C.A. § 1322(c)(2) creates a statutory exception to the protection from modification for "short term" home mortgages in the debtor's principal residence in Chapter 13 cases, that is, mortgages which, by their terms, mature or become due before the date on which the final payment under the Chapter 13 plan is due. The debtor can bifurcate an under-secured second balloon mortgage, for example, and pay the allowable secured portion through the plan, with interest, while paying the unsecured portion of the mortgage upon the same terms as other unsecured creditors.[11]

Thus, because mortgage lenders necessarily accelerate the entire balance of the defaulted mortgage prior to commencing foreclosure proceedings, an argument can be made that an accelerated mortgage can be bifurcated provided the secured portion can be liquidated, with interest, through the plan.[12]

The ability to modify the rights of secured creditors has increased significance to the debtor. Many consumers borrow money from finance companies at interest rates approaching 25% per annum, and pledge their household goods and motor vehicles to secured payment of the loan. At these rates it does not take much for a loan balance to become two or three times the value of the collateral and otherwise impossible to liquidate. By valuing the lien, securing the loan and reducing the interest rate, the debtor will obtain title to the collateral free of the creditor's lien upon payment of the secured portion of the claim instead of when the entire balance of the loan is paid.

§ 33:7   Chapter 13—Benefits—Curing mortgage arrearages

Curing mortgage arrearages is perhaps the greatest benefit of a Chapter 13. A debtor who is behind in his mortgage payments faces the loss of his home, and a Chapter 7 filing will not change this fact. No provision of the Code permits a Chapter 7 debtor to decelerate the mortgage and to pay arrearages either in lump sum or by payments while making current payments.

The contrary is true in a Chapter 13 proceeding. 11 U.S.C.A.

---

[9]Lane vs. Western Bancorp (In re Lane), 280 F.3d 663 (6th Cir. 2002).

[10]In re Allard, 196 B.R. 402 (Bankr. N.D. Ill. 1996), decision aff'd, 202 B.R. 938 (N.D. Ill. 1996) (judgment liens).

[11]American General Finance, Inc. vs. Paschen (In re Paschen), 296 F.3d 1203 (11th Cir. 2002). See, also, In re Eubanks, 219 B.R. 468 (B.A.P. 6th Cir. 1998); In re Ibarra, 235 B.R. 204, 211 (Bankr. D. P.R. 1999); In re Sexton, 230 B.R. 346, 350 (Bankr. E.D. Tenn. 1999); In re Reeves, 221 B.R. 756, 760 (Bankr. C.D. Ill. 1998). See generally, Collier on Bankruptcy § 1322(c)(2) (Lawrence P. King, et al. eds., rev. 15th Ed. 2001).

[12]In re Nepil, 206 B.R. 72, 74-77 (Bankr. D. N.J. 1997). But see In re Rowe, 239 B.R. 44, 550-52 (Bankr. D. N.J. 1999) (holding to the contrary).

§ 1322(b)(5) expressly permits a Chapter 13 debtor to decelerate a home mortgage after acceleration by the mortgage holder and to reinstate the original payment terms of the mortgage while curing the arrearages during the life of the Chapter 13.[1]

11 U.S.C.A. § 1322(b)(5) provides that the arrearages must be cured and paid during the life of the Chapter 13 plan and within a "reasonable time." However, the Code provides no guidance as to what a reasonable period of time is, and relevant legislative history is of little assistance.[2] Thus, the determination of what is a "reasonable time" under 11 U.S.C.A. § 1322(b)(5) is left to the discretion of the court and is to be determined based upon the facts and circumstances of each particular case.

The factors for analysis include (1) the amount and reason for the arrearages; (2) the availability of the debtor's discretionary income to cure the default; (3) whether the debtors are acting in good faith and putting forth their best efforts to cure the default; and (4) the ability of the debtors to fund the plan while continuing current payments on the mortgage each month outside the plan.[3]

However, the fact is that one can learn very little from reading the reported decisions in this area because they are very much inconsistent. A practitioner contemplating the filing of a Chapter 13 to prevent a foreclosure sale should consult with attorneys familiar with court practice in the jurisdiction where the case will be filed to obtain a sense of what the court considers to be a "reasonable time" within the meaning of the Code.[4]

Attorneys faced with a pending foreclosure on a client's home must, therefore, be aware of the availability of relief to a Chapter 13 debtor. However, the right conferred by 11 U.S.C.A. § 1322(b)(5) to decelerate the mortgage is not without time constraints. The Chapter 13 must be filed **before** the actual foreclosure sale. Once the sale takes place, even if not yet confirmed by the Common Pleas Court, it is too late.[5]

[Section 33:7]

[1]See In re Glenn, 760 F.2d 1428 (6th Cir. 1985); In re Taddeo, 685 F.2d 24, 67 A.L.R. Fed. 207 (2d Cir. 1982); In re Threet, 60 B.R. 87 (Bankr. N.D. Ohio 1986); In re Thomas, 59 B.R. 758 (Bankr. N.D. Ohio 1986).

[2]In re Hickson, 52 B.R. 11 (Bankr. S.D. Fla. 1985).

[3]In re Hickson, 52 B.R. 11 (Bankr. S.D. Fla. 1985); In re Lynch, 12 B.R. 533 (Bankr. W.D. Wis. 1981); In re Acevedo, 9 B.R. 852 (Bankr. E.D. N.Y. 1981), decision aff'd, 26 B.R. 994 (E.D. N.Y. 1982).

[4]See, e.g., In re Ford, 221 B.R. 749, 754 (Bankr. W.D. Tenn. 1998); In re Hatcher, 202 B.R. 626 (Bankr. E.D. Okla. 1996), order aff'd in part, 208 B.R. 959 (B.A.P. 10th Cir. 1997), aff'd, 133 F.3d 932 (10th Cir. 1998) and the cases cited therein (60-month cure period approved); In re Lobue, 189 B.R. 216 (Bankr. S.D. Fla. 1995) (53 month cure approved). Compare, for example, In re LaCrue, 33 B.R. 569 (Bankr. D. Colo. 1983) (33-month cure period approved) with In re Mitchell, 27 B.R. 288 (Bankr. S.D. Fla. 1983) (32-month cure period not approved). The practitioner should also review PNC Mortg. Co. v. Dicks, 199 B.R. 674 (N.D. Ind. 1996) (debtor can add default to the principal balance and pay arrearages over the mortgage's 25 year term).

[5]In re Glenn, 760 F.2d 1428 (6th Cir. 1985).

§ 33:8 Chapter 13—Benefits—Unequal treatment of unsecured creditors

A common situation facing the practitioner is that of the co-signed debt, where the debtor wishes to protect a family member, friend, or co-worker from collection efforts while otherwise obtaining a fresh start.

Chapter 7 provides little solace to the debtor. In a Chapter 7 proceeding, all unsecured creditors receive a pro rata distribution from the estate. The debtor receives a discharge from his or debts, but the creditor is free to continue collection efforts against the joint obligor as to the unpaid balance of the account.

In a Chapter 13, on the other hand, the debtor can treat some unsecured creditors more favorably than others.[1] To the extent that this is attempted, however, the debtor "may not unfairly discriminate against any class so designated," and all claims within the class must receive the same treatment.[2] The Code is otherwise silent as to what classifications are permissible. There are, however, a great many cases on the subject.[3]

The cases indicate that four factors will be considered in determining whether the proposed classification of unsecured claims is permissible: (1) whether the discrimination has a reasonable basis; (2) whether the debtor can carry out the plan without such discrimination; (3) whether such discrimination is proposed in good faith; and (4) the treatment of the class discriminated against. These factors are not, however, rigid rules but are flexible guidelines for the court.[4] Each plan must necessarily be decided on its own merits.[5]

In the case of a co-debtor, the Code now expressly permits a Chapter 13 plan to provide for payment upon joint debts in full while paying other unsecured creditors at a less favorable rate.[6]

Thus, a divorced individual can protect himself or herself from

---

[Section 33:8]

[1]11 U.S.C.A. § 1322(b)(1), following Barnes vs. Whelan, 689 F.2d 193 (D.C. Cir. 1982).

[2]11 U.S.C.A. § 1322(b)(1), following Barnes vs. Whelan, 689 F.2d 193 (D.C. Cir. 1982).

[3]The cases are collected in Sepinuck, Rethinking Unfair Discrimination in Chapter 13, 74 Am. Bankr. L. J. 341 (2000).

[4]In re Bentley, 250 B.R. 475, 477, 146 Ed. Law Rep. 201 (Bankr. D. R.I. 2000), aff'd, 266 B.R. 229, 157 Ed. Law Rep. 190 (B.A.P. 1st Cir. 2001).

[5]Compare In re Janssen, 220 B.R. 639 (Bankr. N.D. Iowa 1998) (plan providing payment in full upon debts arising from obligations cosigned by the debtor's father and only a 40% distribution to other unsecured creditors approved by the court) with In re McNichols, 249 B.R. 160 (Bankr. N.D. Ill. 2000) (confirmation of Chapter 13 plan denied where plan provided for a 100% repayment upon debts co-signed by non-filing spouse and only a 10% repayment to other unsecured creditors where non-filing spouse had financial ability to pay the claims herself).

[6]11 U.S.C.A. § 1322(b)(1). In re Janssen, 220 B.R. 639 (Bankr. N.D. Iowa 1998); In re Perkins, 55 B.R. 422 (Bankr. N.D. Okla. 1985). But see In re McNichols, 249 B.R. 160 (Bankr. N.D. Ill. 2000) (confirmation of Chapter 13 plan denied where plan provided for a 100% repayment upon debts co-signed by spouse and only 10% repayment to other unsecured creditors where non-filing spouse had financial ability to pay the claims

contempt proceedings in state court and/or a costly dis-chargeability fight in a Chapter 7 proceeding by obtaining confirmation of a Chapter 13 plan which proposes full payment to creditors upon which the former spouse is also obligated; the other unsecured creditors need not paid in full, although the plan must still be fair, just and equitable in its treatment of these claims. However, the plan may not provide for the payment of interest of these separately classified obligations.[7]

In the past the Bankruptcy Code regarded spousal support and child support arrearages as unsecured claims which may or may not, depending upon the jurisdiction, be subject to classification and given preferential treatment as to other unsecured claims.[8]

However, a recent change to the Code now regards spousal support and child support arrearages as priority claims.[9] The Chapter 13 plan must now provide for payment in full of such arrearages, or the plan will not be confirmed.[10] As such, the practitioner can, under appropriate circumstances, obtain confirmation of a Chapter 13 plan which provides for payment in full of support arrearages but which provides for less favorable treatment to general unsecured creditors.

Student loans are another problem for the practitioner. Because of another recent change in the law, student loans not paid in full in a Chapter 13 proceeding, including unmatured interest, are not discharged, and survive to permit collection efforts by the creditor at a

---

himself); In re Martin, 189 B.R. 619 (Bankr. E.D. Va. 1995) (court recognized that the cases are split as to whether the unfair discrimination test applies to co-signed debts, and refused to confirm a plan providing for 100% payment to co-signed obligations and 6.5% to hold of a judgment for assault and battery) and In re Thompson, 191 B.R. 967 (Bankr. S.D. Ga. 1996) (confirmation denied where plan provided for 100% payment to co-signed debts and no payment to other unsecured debt). See, also, In re McKown, 227 B.R. 487, 492-494 (Bankr. N.D. Ohio 1998); In re Regine, 234 B.R. 4, 5-7 (Bankr. D. R.I. 1999); In re Markham, 224 B.R. 599, 601 (Bankr. W.D. Ky. 1998) and In re Chacon, 223 B.R. 917 (Bankr. W.D. Tex. 1998), subsequently aff'd, 202 F.3d 725 (5th Cir. 1999) and subsequently aff'd, 204 F.3d 595 (5th Cir. 2000). These cases illustrate the pitfalls of writing a Chapter 13 plan involving co-signed debts. The practitioner should review these cases before writing a plan, which contains a significant disparity in treatment for the co-signed and general unsecured creditors. Note, however, that even where permitted, a debtor cannot pay post-petition interest upon a co-signed unsecured debt. In re Alls, 238 B.R. 914, 920 (Bankr. S.D. Ga. 1999).

[7]In re Ramirez, 204 F.3d 595 (5th Cir. 2000).

[8]Compare In re Leser, 939 F.2d 669 (8th Cir. 1991) (classification permitted) with Caswell vs. Lang, 757 F.2d 608 (4th Cir. 1985) (classification not permitted).

[9]11 U.S.C.A. § 507(a)(7).

[10]11 U.S.C.A. § 1322(a)(2). See In re Olson, 200 B.R. 40 (Bank. D. Neb. 1996). See, also, In re Beverly, 196 B.R. 128 (Bankr. W.D. Mo. 1996) (support arrearages assigned to governmental agency entitled to priority status, and, hence, must be paid in full); In re Doe, 193 B.R. 12 (Bankr. N.D. Cal. 1996), rev'd, 210 B.R. 578 (B.A.P. 9th Cir. 1997), rev'd, 163 F.3d 1138 (9th Cir. 1998) (fees for court appointed attorney and neutral expert in paternity and custody litigation are actually in the nature of support, and are entitled to be paid in full in the Chapter 13).

later date.[11] Although the cases are split on this issue, most courts do **not** permit a separate classification of student loan obligations.[12] It is suggested that the reader review the *Williams*[13] and *Thibodeau*[14] decision for guidelines as to when and under what circumstances separate classification of student loans may be appropriate.

As a practical matter, it is very difficult to obtain confirmation of a Chapter 13 Plan which classifies unsecured claims other than co-debtor claims.[15] The courts have denied confirmation to plans which prefer consumer creditors over business creditors,[16] which offer to pay one creditor 100%, based upon a criminal court order of restitution while paying others 20%,[17] which treat the debtor's landlord differently from other creditors, which provide for full payment to a credit union and 26% to other creditors,[18] which treated unsecured creditors that received NSF checks differently from other unsecured creditors,[19] and which classify the debtor's physicians differently from other creditors.[20]

---

[11]11 U.S.C.A. § 1328(a)(2). In re Wagner, 200 B.R. 160, 112 Ed. Law Rep. 277, 31 U.C.C. Rep. Serv. 2d 1072 (Bankr. N.D. Ohio 1996).

[12]Labib-Kiyarash vs. McDonald (In re Labib-Kiyarash), 271 B.R. 189 (B.A.P. 9th Cir. 2001); In re Bentley, 266 B.R. 229, 239-42, 157 Ed. Law Rep. 190 (B.A.P. 1st Cir. 2001); In re Edwards, 263 B.R. 690, 691 (Bankr. D. R.I. 2001). But see In re Dodds, 140 B.R. 542 (Bankr. D. Mont. 1992) and In re Boggan, 125 B.R. 533, 66 Ed. Law Rep. 1135 (Bankr. N.D. Ill. 1991) (classification permitted). See generally, Note, *Separate Classification of Student Loans in Chapter 13*, 73 Wash U.L.Q. 269 (Spring, 1995). In this area counsel should be aware of In re Andersen, 179 F.3d 1253, 136 Ed. Law Rep. 135 (10th Cir. 1999) (student loan discharged -- unopposed confirmation of a plan had a res judicata effect with respect to the issue of undue hardship and discharge of student loan even if such plan provisions were inconsistent with the Code) and In re Pardee, 193 F.3d 1083 (9th Cir. 1999) (unmatured interest discharged based upon res judicata effect of confirmed plan even where plan provisions inconsistent with the Code.

[13]In re Williams, 253 B.R. 220, 228-233, 147 Ed. Law Rep. 179 (Bankr. W.D. Tenn. 2000).

[14]In re Thibodeau, 248 B.R. 699, 144 Ed. Law Rep. 273 (Bankr. D. Mass. 2000).

[15]See, however, In re Foster, 263 B.R. 688, 690 (Bankr. D. R.I. 2001) wherein the court held that it was not unfair discrimination to separately classify a portion of an unsecured line of credit for payment in full and for 2% to other unsecured creditors where line of credit was used to pay priority federal and state taxes that would have been entitled to payment ahead of unsecured creditors if not paid before the filing of the Chapter 13.

[16]In re Harris, 62 B.R. 391 (Bankr. E.D. Mich. 1986). See In re Sutherland, 3 B.R. 420 (Bankr. W.D. Ark. 1980) (discrimination permitted where business creditors favored); In re Perskin, 9 B.R. 626 (Bankr. N.D. Tex. 1981) (traveling salesman permitted to discriminate in favor of credit card creditors).

[17]In re Limbaugh, 194 B.R. 488 (Bankr. D. Or. 1996); In re Bowles, 48 B.R. 502 (Bankr. E.D. Va. 1985); In re Gay, 3 B.R. 336 (Bankr. D. Colo. 1980).

[18]In re Dziedzic, 9 B.R. 424 (Bankr. S.D. Tex. 1981).

[19]In re Brigance, 219 B.R. 486, 495 (Bankr. W.D. Tenn. 1998), judgment aff'd, 229 B.R. 739 (W.D. Tenn. 1999) and judgment aff'd, 234 B.R. 401, 39 U.C.C. Rep. Serv. 2d 1037 (W.D. Tenn. 1999); In re Hiner, 161 B.R. 688 (Bankr. D. Idaho 1993).

[20]Compare In re Hosler, 12 B.R. 395 (Bankr. S.D. Ohio 1981) with In re Sutherland, 3 B.R. 420 (Bankr. W.D. Ark. 1980) (plan confirmed).

§ 33:9   Chapter 13—Benefits—Flexibility

Proceedings under Chapter 13 are more flexible than Chapter 7 liquidations. Confirmed plans can be modified based upon a change in income or other circumstance.[1] Furthermore, the debtor can, at any time, convert the Chapter 13 to a Chapter 7 liquidation[2] or ask that it be dismissed.[3] It should be noted that a Chapter 13 debtor, other than a farmer, can be the subject of an involuntary conversion to Chapter 7 after notice and a hearing.[4]

In addition, 11 U.S.C.A. § 1328(b) provides for what is known as "hardship" discharge. At any time after confirmation, the debtor may obtain a discharge of his unsecured obligations where an adverse change in circumstances does not permit the debtor to complete the plan.[5] Priority and secured claims are not affected by a hardship discharge. Similarly, a hardship discharge does not discharge debts which are not dischargeable in a Chapter 7 liquidation as set forth in 11 U.S.C.A. § 523(a).[6]

A hardship discharge can only be granted after notice and a hearing. This discharge can be granted where (1) the failure to complete the plan is due to circumstances for which the debtor should not be held accountable,[7] (2) the unsecured creditors have already received through the plan the amount they would have received had the estate been liquidated under Chapter 7,[8] and where (3) modification of the plan is not practicable.[9]

§ 33:10   Chapter 13—Benefits—Broader discharge

Under Chapter 7, a debtor cannot obtain a discharge from certain tax obligations, student loans, willful torts, debts arising from fraudulent misrepresentations, and from alimony, maintenance, and support

---

[Section 33:9]

[1]11 U.S.C.A. § 1322(a)(2); 11 U.S.C.A. § 1329(a)(1). But see In re Brown, 219 B.R. 191, 195 (B.A.P. 6th Cir. 1998) (Chapter 13 Trustee may not require the debtor, through post-petition motion to modify confirmed plan, to pay proceeds of post-petition personal injury settlement to creditors).

[2]11 U.S.C.A. § 1307(a). In re Bistrian, 184 B.R. 678 (E.D. Pa. 1995).

[3]11 U.S.C.A. § 1307(b). In re Robinson, 196 B.R. 454 (Bankr. E.D. Ark. 1996); In re Harper-Elder, 184 B.R. 403 (Bankr. D. D.C. 1995).

[4]11 U.S.C.A. § 1307(e). See In re Molitor, 76 F.3d 218 (8th Cir. 1996); Matter of Love, 957 F.2d 1350 (7th Cir. 1992); In re Bistrian, 184 B.R. 678 (E.D. Pa. 1995); In re Gaudet, 132 B.R. 670 (D.R.I. 1991).

[5]11 U.S.C.A. § 1328(c). But see In re Bandilli, 218 B.R. 273, 274-75 (Bankr. D. R.I. 1998), aff'd, 231 B.R. 836 (B.A.P. 1st Cir. 1999) (hardship discharge denied three and one-half months after confirmation of the Chapter 13 plan, where the serious medical condition was permanent and pre-existed the filing of the case.

[6]See 11 U.S.C.A. § 1328(c)(2).

[7]11 U.S.C.A. § 1328(b)(1). See, e.g., In re Edwards, 207 B.R. 728 (Bankr. N.D. Fla. 1997); In re Nelson, 135 B.R. 304, 307 (Bankr. N.D. Ill. 1991); In re Bond, 36 B.R. 49 (Bankr. E.D. N.C. 1984).

[8]11 U.S.C.A. § 1328(b)(2).

[9]11 U.S.C.A. § 1328(b)(3).

obligations.[1]

Congress itself elected to make the Chapter 13 discharge broader than the Chapter 7 discharge.[2] In a Chapter 13 proceeding, a debtor may, provided that the case is otherwise prosecuted in good faith, obtain a discharge of all pre-petition debts, except those for alimony, maintenance, and support,[3] student loans to the extent not dischargeable in Chapter 7 proceedings,[4] restitution arising from criminal cases,[5] and for obligations arising from personal injuries or death resulting from driving while intoxicated. In addition, certain long-term obligations[6] and unscheduled debts are not discharged.[7]

However, the broader discharge available under Chapter 13 is only available to individuals acting in good faith, and not for an ulterior motive or purpose.[8] The debtor must be making an honest effort to repay

---

[Section 33:10]

[1]11 U.S.C.A. § 523(a). But see In re Andersen, 215 B.R. 792, 793-96 (B.A.P. 10th Cir. 1998), judgment aff'd, 179 F.3d 1253, 136 Ed. Law Rep. 135 (10th Cir. 1999) (student loan discharged where the creditor failed to object to a plan provision which provided for a 10% dividend to all unsecured creditors, including the student loan, and which further specifically provided for discharge of the student loan upon successful completion of all plan payments).

[2]In re Alicea, 199 B.R. 862 (Bankr. D. N.J. 1996).

[3]In re Jodoin, 196 B.R. 845 (Bankr. E.D. Cal. 1996), aff'd, 209 B.R. 132 (B.A.P. 9th Cir. 1997).

[4]In re Bell, 236 B.R. 426, 428-30, 136 Ed. Law Rep. 435 (N.D. Ala. 1999). Unsecured creditors are not permitted to receive post-petition unmatured interest. The holders of spousal and child support arrearage claims and student loan claims do not have an allowable claim for such post-petition unmatured interest during the Chapter 13, but such interest continues to accrue and survives the discharge upon completion of the Chapter 13. Thus, even a confirmed Chapter 13 plan providing for payment of 100% of claims may cause the debtor to be the subject of collection efforts by support or student loan creditors seeking to recover the post-petition unmatured interest not paid during the Chapter 13. In re Crable, 174 B.R. 62 (Bankr. W.D. Ky. 1994) (support arrearage claims. See, also, Leeper v. Pennsylvania Higher Educ. Assistance Agency, (PHEAA), 49 F.3d 98, 98 Ed. Law Rep. 30 (3d Cir. 1995); In re Boone, 215 B.R. 386 (Bankr. S.D. Ill. 1997); and In re Wagner, 200 B.R. 160, 112 Ed. Law Rep. 277, 31 U.C.C. Rep. Serv. 2d 1072 (Bankr. N.D. Ohio 1996) (student loan interest). But see In re Andersen, 179 F.3d 1253, 136 Ed. Law Rep. 135 (10th Cir. 1999) (student loan discharged—unopposed confirmation of a plan had a res judicata effect with respect to the issue of undue hardship and discharge of student loan even if such plan provisions were inconsistent with the Code) and In re Pardee, 193 F.3d 1083 (9th Cir. 1999) (unmatured interest discharged based upon res judicata effect of confirmed plan even where plan provisions inconsistent with the Code.

[5]In re Bryer, 227 B.R. 201 (Bankr. D. Me. 1998).

[6]11 U.S.C.A. § 1328(a).

[7]In re Trembath, 205 B.R. 909 (Bankr. N.D. Ill. 1997); In re Crites, 201 B.R. 277 (Bankr. D. Or. 1996).

[8]In re Altmann, 256 B.R. 468 (Bankr. S.D. Miss. 2000) (Chapter 13 dismissed where debtor attempted to use Chapter 13 as a substitute for appeal of state court judgment); In re Rodriguez, 248 B.R. 16 (Bankr. D. Conn. 1999) (Chapter 13 filed by a debtor not in financial distress, and who could comfortably pay his bills, dismissed where debtor attempted to use Chapter 13 solely for the purpose of stripping down the mortgage liens upon his real estate.

creditors, and not using Chapter 13 as a sword to thwart creditors.[9] Such does not mean, however, that the Chapter 13 plan must provide for a significant dividend to unsecured creditors. The amount to be repaid to unsecured creditors is but one factor to be considered by the court in deciding whether to confirm a Chapter 13 plan.

Thus, in *In re Fields*,[10] the court confirmed a plan which provided for payment in full of priority tax claims and mortgage arrearages, but provided for no dividend to unsecured creditors. The court said that a zero distribution plan is a relevant factor that the court may consider in deciding whether a plan is filed in good faith, but such fact does not require the denial of confirmation of such a plan.

Similarly, in *In re Goodrich*,[11] the court confirmed a Chapter 13 plan which provided for payment in full of priority tax claims and mortgage arrearages of $19,844.57, but provided for only nominal payments to unsecured creditors.[12]

Courts have also confirmed a number of plans providing for less than payment in full (and discharge) of claims not dischargeable in a Chapter 7 proceeding, where the court found that the Chapter 13 was not filed for the sole purpose of evading the non-dischargeable debt, and the debtor was making a sincere attempt to resolve financial problems.[13]

Thus, $17,000 claim based upon embezzlement was held dischargeable in Chapter 13,[14] as was a debt originating from willful misrepresentations to obtain money from the government,[15] debts which originated through conversion,[16] a debt arising from the omission of debts from a false financial statement,[17] debts arising from insurance fraud,[18] debts arising from the misappropriation of funds,[19] debts arising from an assault and battery,[20] and debts arising from breach of trust.[21]

Taxes can also be discharged in a Chapter 13. Although a Chapter 13 plan must provide for payment in full of all tax claims which are not

---

[9]In re Rodriguez, 248 B.R. 16, 20 (Bankr. D. Conn. 1999); In re Mattson, 241 B.R. 629, 636-37 (Bankr. D. Minn. 1999).

[10]In re Fields, 190 B.R. 16 (Bankr. D. N.H. 1995).

[11]In re Goodrich, 257 B.R. 101 (Bankr. M.D. Fla. 2000).

[12]See, In re Alicea, 199 B.R. 862 (Bankr. D. N.J. 1996) (0% plan submitted in good faith and confirmed); In re Weisser, 190 B.R. 453 (Bankr. M.D. Fla. 1995) (plan proposing to pay unsecured creditors 4% filed in good faith and confirmed).

[13]In re Young, 237 F.3d 1168, 1177-78 (10th Cir. 2001).

[14]In re Gregory, 705 F.2d 1118 (9th Cir. 1983); In re Corino, 191 B.R. 283 (Bankr. N.D. N.Y. 1995).

[15]In re Otero, 48 B.R. 704 (Bankr. E.D. Va. 1985).

[16]In re Freeman, 66 B.R. 610 (Bankr. W.D. Va. 1986); In re Vratanina, 22 B.R. 453 (Bankr. N.D. Ill. 1982).

[17]In re Little, 116 B.R. 615 (Bankr. S.D. Ohio 1990).

[18]In re Kazzaz, 62 B.R. 308 (Bankr. E.D. Va. 1986).

[19]In re Anadell, 190 B.R. 309 (Bankr. S.D. Ohio 1995).

[20]In re Gillespie, 266 B.R. 721, 727 (Bankr. N.D. Iowa 2001); In re Martin, 189 B.R. 619 (Bankr. E.D. Va. 1995); In re Vent, 188 B.R. 396 (Bankr. E.D. Ark. 1995) (assault with firearm).

[21]In re Wilcox, 251 B.R. 59, 61 (Bankr. E.D. Ark. 2000).

dischargeable in a Chapter 7,[22] the IRS must timely file a proof of claim in order to participate in the Chapter 13. The failure to do so will preclude distribution of funds to the IRS in the Chapter 13 and will result in the tax obligation being discharged upon successful completion of the Chapter 13 by the debtor.[23] However, statutory tax liens will survive a Chapter 13.[24] Where the IRS has perfected a lien, the debtor should file a proof of claim on behalf of the IRS to insure payment through the plan.

On the other hand, courts will not confirm a plan, regardless of the dividend being paid to unsecured creditors, where the debtor is not making a sincere attempt to repay creditors, is attempting to discharge debts not dischargeable in Chapter 7 proceeding, or where the debtor is using the Chapter 13 process as a financial planning tool.[25] The Chapter 13 plan must be proposed in a good faith attempt to obtain financial rehabilitation, and not for the purpose of thwarting creditors.[26]

Thus, a practitioner considering use of Chapter 13 for this purpose must be aware of the factors considered by the courts in determining the issue of good faith. No ironclad rules have evolved. The bankruptcy court will examine each case individually to determine if, after reviewing the totality of the circumstances confronting a debtor, the plan is proposed in good faith.[27]

The Sixth Circuit Court of Appeals has written extensively in this area. The 1988 decision in *In re Okoreeh-Baah*,[28] adopted as a measure of good faith the twelve-factor inquiry first postulated by the bankruptcy court in *Matter of Kull*.[29] The twelve factors are as follows:

> (1) The amount of the plan payments and the amount of the debtor's surplus income available for distribution to creditors;

---

[22]11 U.S.C.A. § 1322(a)(2).

[23]In re Thibodaux, 201 B.R. 827 (Bankr. N.D. Ala. 1996); Matter of Border, 116 B.R. 588 (Bankr. S.D. Ohio 1990); In re Richards, 50 B.R. 339 (Bankr. E.D. Tenn. 1985); In re Goodwin, 58 B.R. 75 (Bankr. D. Me. 1986). These cases must be compared to In re Tobias, 200 B.R. 412 (Bankr. M.D. Fla. 1996) and In re Maclean, 200 B.R. 417 (Bankr. M.D. Fla. 1996) wherein the court dismissed Chapter 13 filings upon bad faith grounds where the debtors failed to prepare and file tax returns after being ordered to do so by the court.

[24]In re Lovato, 203 B.R. 747 (Bankr. D. Wyo. 1996); Matter of Driscoll, 57 B.R. 322 (Bankr. W.D. Wis. 1986) (overruling recognized by, In re Blackerby, 1997 WL 30865 (Bankr. E.D. Pa. 1997)).

[25]In re Altmann, 256 B.R. 468 (Bankr. S.D. Miss. 2000) (Chapter 13 dismissed where debtor attempted to use Chapter 13 as a substitute for appeal of state court judgment); In re Rodriguez, 248 B.R. 16 (Bankr. D. Conn. 1999) (Chapter 13 filed by a debtor not in financial distress and who could comfortably pay his bills dismissed where debtor attempted to use Chapter 13 solely for the purpose of stripping down the mortgage liens upon his real estate).

[26]Memphis Bank & Trust Co. v. Whitman, 692 F.2d. 427 (6th Cir. 1982); Neufeld v. Freeman, 794 F.2d 149 (4th Cir. 1986); In re Chase, 43 B.R. 739 (D. Md. 1984).

[27]In re Okoreeh-Baah, 836 F.2d 1030 (6th Cir. 1988).

[28]In re Okoreeh-Baah, 836 F.2d 1030 (6th Cir. 1988).

[29]Matter of Kull, 12 B.R. 654, 659 (S.D. Ga. 1981), order aff'd, 702 F.2d 885 (11th Cir. 1983), aff'd. sub nom, In re Kitchens, 702 F.2d 885 (11th Cir. 1983).

(2) The debtor's employment history, ability to earn and likelihood of future increases in income;

(3) The expected duration of the plan;

(4) The extent of preferential treatment between classes of creditors;

(5) The extent to which secured claims are modified;

(6) The accuracy of the bankruptcy schedules filed by the debtor, and whether any inaccuracies are an attempt to mislead the court;

(7) Whether the debtor is seeking to discharge an debt which is non-dischargeable in a Chapter 7 proceeding;

(8) The existence of special circumstances, such as inordinate medical expense;

(9) The frequency which the debtor has sought relief in the bankruptcy court;

(10) The motivation and sincerity of the debtor in seeking Chapter 13 relief;

(11) Whether the debtor is attempting to abuse the spirit of the Bankruptcy Code; and

(12) The burden which the plan's administration would place upon the trustee.

Shortly thereafter, the Sixth Circuit cited these same factors in *In re Doersam*,[30] holding that a Chapter 13 plan was not proposed in good faith where 81% of the unsecured debt was comprised of student loans not yet due when the plan was filed, and which plan provided for a payment of only 19% to the unsecured creditors.

About a month after the decision in *Doersam*, another panel from the Sixth Circuit decided yet another Chapter 13 "good faith" decision. This time, in *In re Caldwell*,[31] the court indicated a preference for a list of eleven factors set forth in the Eighth Circuit case of *In re Estus*.[32] This panel reviewed the two lists of factors set forth in *Matter of Kull, supra*, and in *In re Estus, supra,* and concluded that the list provided in *Estus* is a "particularly succinct and clear statement of some of the factors that a court may consider in making its determination of good faith."[33]

The *Caldwell* court cited the following factors taken from the Estus case:[34]

(1) The amount of proposed payments and the amount of the debtor's surplus income;

(2) The debtor's employment history;

(3) The probable expected duration of the plan;

---

[30]In re Doersam, 849 F.2d 237, 47 Ed. Law Rep. 410 (6th Cir. 1988).

[31]In re Caldwell, 851 F.2d 852 (6th Cir. 1988).

[32]In re Estus, 695 F.2d 311 (8th Cir. 1982).

[33]In re Caldwell, 851 F.2d 852, 859 (6th Cir. 1988).

[34]In re Caldwell, 851 F.2d 852, 859 (6th Cir. 1988).

(4) The accuracy of the plan's statement of debts, expenses and percentage of repayment of unsecured debt, and whether any inaccuracies are an attempt to mislead the court;

(5) The extent of preferential treatment between classes of creditors;

(6) The extent to which secured claims are modified;

(7) The type of debt sought to be discharged and whether such debt is non-dischargeable in a Chapter 7;

(8) The existence of special circumstances such as inordinate medical expense;

(9) The frequency with which the debtor has sought relief under the Bankruptcy Code;

(10) The motivation and sincerity of the debtor in seeking Chapter 13 relief;

(11) The burden which the plan's administration would place upon the trustee.

To these factors the court in *Caldwell* added the following considerations:[35]

(1) Whether the debtor is attempting to abuse the spirit of the Bankruptcy Code;

(2) "Good faith" does not necessarily require substantial repayment of unsecured debt;

(3) The mere fact that a debt is non-dischargeable in a Chapter 7 does not make it non-dischargeable in a Chapter 13; and

(4) The fact that a debtor seeks to discharge an otherwise non-dischargeable debt is not, per se, evidence of bad faith, but may be considered as part of the totality of the circumstances analysis.

The lists in the two cases are nearly identical, and must be considered, along with the additional factors set forth in *Caldwell* in analyzing a particular debtor's good faith. What these cases demonstrate is that no one factor is determinative of the issue of good faith.[36] A great deal of case law exists in this area, and a thorough review of the authorities is necessary before advising a client.[37]

Thus, in a number of cases the courts have denied confirmation for failure to meet this good faith standard. These cases should be compared with those discussed earlier where plans were confirmed. The following cases are offered by way of example:

---

[35]In re Caldwell, 851 F.2d 852, 859-60 (6th Cir. 1988).

[36]The court in In re Caldwell, 851 F.2d 852, 860 (6th Cir. 1988) observed that ". . . [n]o list is exhaustive of all the conceivable factors which would be relevant when analyzing a particular debtor's good faith . . . . We also stress that no one factor should be viewed as being a dispositive indication of the debtor's good faith. . . ."

[37]See, In re Francis, 273 B.R. 87 (B.A.P. 6th Cir. 2002).

In *In re Banks*,[38] the court denied confirmation of a plan which was designed to last only 36 months, and to pay the debtor's former spouse less than 15% of her claim for her interest in the debtor's military pension, where the debtor admitted that his sole motivation in filing Chapter 13 was to avoid paying his former spouse.

In *In re Georgeff*,[39] the court refused to confirm a Chapter 13 plan filed by the debtor (who was an attorney) that proposed a 30% dividend where the majority of debt was based upon claims for professional malpractice and conversion where the debtor withdrew from his law partnership, used a former client's bank account to avoid garnishment, prepaid a motor vehicle lease, removed personal property from his residence, and failed to disclose an interest in real estate.

The courts in *In re White*,[40] *In re Holder*,[41] *In re Keach*,[42] and *In re Rasmussen*,[43] held that it was bad faith to file a Chapter 13 primarily designed to discharge, through a minimal payment plan, non-dischargeable debts arising out of a previous Chapter 7 case.

In *In re Norwood*,[44] the court refused to confirm a Chapter 13 plan where 76% of the total debt was owed to victims of sexual assaults, and the plan provided for no payments to unsecured creditors.

In *Matter of Scarborough*,[45] the court denied confirmation where the primary, if not sole, purpose of the filing of a Chapter 13 was to nullify a judgment lien for child support arrearages and for which a garnishment had issued.

In *In re Brock*,[46] the court denied confirmation to a plan which consisted of one creditor, whose claim was based upon embezzlement, and was therefore non-dischargeable in Chapter 7, and

[38]In re Banks, 248 B.R. 799, 804 (B.A.P. 8th Cir. 2000), aff'd, 267 F.3d 875 (8th Cir. 2001).

[39]In re Georgeff, 218 B.R. 403, 408 (Bankr. S.D. Ohio 1998) (applying the *Caldwell* decision).

[40]In re White, 255 B.R. 737 (Bankr. W.D. Mo. 2000).

[41]In re Holder, 263 B.R. 622 (Bankr. N.D. Ala. 2001).

[42]In re Keach, 225 B.R. 264 (Bankr. D. R.I. 1998).

[43]In re Rasmussen, 888 F.2d 703 (10th Cir. 1989).

[44]In re Norwood, 178 B.R. 683 (Bankr. E.D. Pa. 1995). See, also, In re Young, 237 B.R. 791 (B.A.P. 10th Cir. 1999), aff'd on other grounds, 237 F.3d 1168 (10th Cir. 2001) (B.A.P. affirms a denial of confirmation of a 4%, 60 month plan seeking to discharge a $300,000 punitive damage judgment for violation of civil rights and wrongful discharge); In re Thomas, 118 B.R. 421 (Bankr. D. S.C. 1990).

[45]Matter of Scarborough, 50 B.R. 1 (Bankr. S.D. Miss. 1985). See, also, In re Lewis, 227 B.R. 886, 889 (Bankr. W.D. Ark. 1998) (confirmation denied where "overwhelming evidence" indicated that the debtor's sole motive in filing Chapter 13 was to circumvent domestic relations orders).

[46]In re Brock, 47 B.R. 167 (Bankr. S.D. Cal. 1985). But see In re King, 131 B.R. 207 (Bankr. N.D. Fla. 1991) (not bad faith to file a Chapter 13 plan for the sole purpose of reinstating a defaulted mortgage to avoid a foreclosure.

which provided for a 10% payment to the creditor. Similarly, in *In re McLaughlin*,[47] the court held that under the totality of the circumstances it was bad faith for a debtor to file a Chapter 13 on the day that a $177,031.02 judgment for breach of fiduciary duty was entered.

In *In re Boyd*,[48] the debtor scheduled two unsecured creditors, with 97% of the unsecured debt belonging to the Illinois Department of Public Aid. The court denied confirmation to the plan, which proposed a 10% payment.

In *In re White*[49] the court refused to confirm a 0% plan that would discharge a $300,000 claim for malicious prosecution that had been declared non-dischargeable in the debtor's prior Chapter 7 case. The debtor had made no payments upon the debt from 1993 to 2000, and then filed a Chapter 7 in an unsuccessful attempt to discharge the debt. When that did not work, he filed the Chapter 13.

In *In re Greatwood*,[50] the dismissal of a Chapter 13 filed by a "tax protester" to deal solely with tax claims that survived discharge in prior Chapter 7 Case was affirmed by the appellate court.

Under the facts of particular cases, courts have also refused to confirm Chapter 13 plans which called for a 20% payment of debts brought about by unemployment insurance benefit misconduct,[51] plans precipitated by the debtor's fraudulent conduct,[52] and plans which attempted to eliminate debts based upon conversion.[53] The courts also take a dim view of a plan through which the debtor is attempting to misuse the system for a purpose other than rehabilitation.[54]

The bottom line is that the liberal discharge provisions of Chapter 13 can be used to great advantage where the discharge of a debt non-dischargeable in Chapter 7 is but one, and not the sole motivating factor in the filing of the Chapter 13.

---

[47]In re McLaughlin, 217 B.R. 772, 778 (Bankr. W.D. Tex. 1998). But see In re Keach, 243 B.R. 851 (B.A.P. 1st Cir. 2000) reaching a contrary result.

[48]In re Boyd, 57 B.R. 410 (Bankr. N.D. Ill. 1983).

[49]In re White, 255 B.R. 737 (Bankr. W.D. Mo. 2000).

[50]In re Greatwood, 194 B.R. 637 (B.A.P. 9th Cir. 1996), aff'd, 120 F.3d 268 (9th Cir. 1997). See, also, In re Hopkins, 201 B.R. 993 (D. Nev. 1996).

[51]In re Brown, 56 B.R. 293 (Bankr. N.D. Ill. 1985).

[52]In re Sanders, 28 B.R. 917 (Bankr. D. Kan. 1983); Matter of Stevens, 25 B.R. 664 (Bankr. S.D. Ohio 1982). See, also, In re Petersen, 228 B.R. 19, 22 (Bankr. M.D. Fla. 1998) (disapproved of by, In re Baker, 264 B.R. 759 (Bankr. M.D. Fla. 2001)) (confirmation denied to the debtor's 36 month, 2% plan that would discharge a $550,000 judgment for prepetition misconduct where the debtor "lived a luxurious lifestyle."

[53]In re Chura, 33 B.R. 558 (Bankr. D. Colo. 1983).

[54]In re Waldron, 785 F.2d 936 (11th Cir. 1986), cert. dismissed, 478 U.S. 1028, 106 S. Ct. 3343, 92 L. Ed. 2d 763 (1986); In re DeReus, 53 B.R. 362 (Bankr. S.D. Cal. 1985); In re Setzer, 47 B.R. 340 (Bankr. E.D. N.Y. 1985); In re Chase, 43 B.R. 739 (D. Md. 1984).

§ 33:11   Chapter 13—Contents of Chapter 13 plan

The Code delineates the mandatory and optional provisions of Chapter 13 plans. An attorney cannot properly advise a client without an understanding of what may and may not be included in a Chapter 13 plan.

First of all, the plan must provide for the submission of all of the debtor's future disposable income, not reasonably necessary for the support of the debtor and his or her dependents, to the Trustee for execution of the plan.[1] 11 U.S.C.A. § 1325(b) provides that upon objection of the trustee or an unsecured creditor, all of the debtor's projected disposable income for three years must be applied to the plan or unsecured creditors must be paid in full.[2] To apply these standards to a married debtor who files individually, the courts base their calculation of the debtor's disposable income on the debtor's family budget, including the income and expenses of the non-filing spouse.[3]

Regular income may include welfare, pension, social security payments and exempt property, but does not include gratuitous payments to the debtor by family or other third parties unless such payments are based upon a legal or moral obligation.[4] An unconditional written commitment to fund the Chapter 13 plan by the debtor's long-time "significant other" satisfies this rule.[5]

It should be noted that the courts do not consider the repayment of retirement plan or pension loans to be "debts" within the meaning of the Bankruptcy Code, and, hence, do not permit debtors to deduct from their budget the monthly repayment amount of these obligations.[6]

Careful attention must be given to the budget submitted to the court in support of the proposed Chapter 13 plan, for the court will not confirm a Chapter 13 plan where the budget contains excessive living expense

---

[Section 33:11]

[1]"Disposable income" is defined by 11 U.S.C.A. § 1325(b)(2) to include all income "not reasonably necessary to be expended . . . for the maintenance or support of the debtor or a dependent of the debtor." 11 U.S.C.A. § 1322(a)(1). See, e.g., In re Weiss, 251 B.R. 453, 146 Ed. Law Rep. 209 (Bankr. E.D. Pa. 2000).

[2]In re Greer, 60 B.R. 547 (Bankr. C.D. Cal. 1986).

[3]In re Bottelberghe, 253 B.R. 256, 263 (Bankr. D. Minn. 2000); In re Ehret, 238 B.R. 85, 88 (Bankr. D. N.J. 1999); In re Carter, 205 B.R. 733, 735 (Bankr. E.D. Pa. 1996); In re Pickering, 195 B.R. 759, 762 (Bankr. D. Mont. 1996). See, also, In re Bush, 120 B.R. 403 (Bankr. E.D. Tex. 1990) (holding that although a non debtor wife is not obligated to contribute any money to the Chapter 13 plan, it is evidence of bad faith for the debtor's budget to provide for the payment of all of the couples on-going living expenses while the spouse's income is not considered in determining the amount of the plan payments) and Matter of Saunders, 60 B.R. 187 (Bankr. N.D. Ohio 1986) (where only one spouse files Chapter 13, the income and expenses of the other spouse must be included in the debtor's budget and income statement). See, generally, Drummond, *Disposable Income Requirements under Chapter 13 of the Bankruptcy Code*, 47 Mont. L.Rev. 423 (1996).

[4]In re Jordan, 226 B.R. 117 (Bankr. D. Mont. 1998).

[5]In re Murphy, 226 B.R. 601 (Bankr. M.D. Tenn. 1998).

[6]In re Harshbarger, 66 F.3d 775, 1995 FED App. 286P (6th Cir. 1995). See, e.g., In re Estes, 254 B.R. 261, 263 (Bankr. D. Idaho 2000); In re Anes, 216 B.R. 514 (Bankr. M.D. Pa. 1998), subsequently aff'd, 195 F.3d 177 (3d Cir. 1999).

budget items,[7] even if the plan provides for payment in full to unsecured creditors.[8] However, a recent amendment to the Bankruptcy Code allows debtors to contribute upon to 15% of their gross income to qualified religious or charitable entities.[9]

The plan must also provide for payment in full to creditors holding priority claims, such as certain tax obligations and child and spousal support claims, as defined in 11 U.S.C.A. § 507.[10] Secured creditors must be paid at least the value of the collateral securing the claim, the collateral must be returned, or the consent of the creditor obtained as to a different treatment under the plan.[11] Unsecured creditors must receive, at a minimum, what they would receive if the estate were liquidated.[12] Also, the plan may provide for the concurrent payment of priority, secured, and unsecured claims.[13] If the plan classifies claims, each claim within a class must be treated the same.[14]

The plan must not last longer than three years, unless the court approves a longer period. In any event, it may not last longer than five years.[15] Given the inevitability of illness job layoff or termination, or personal tragedy, a practitioner who is considering writing a 60-month plan should do so only in extreme cases. A 55 or 56-month plan will usually work just as well and will also provide the debtor with time to resume working or to find other work should the need arise.

As noted above, the plan can provide for the modification of the rights of secured creditors and for the curing of prior default of long term debt.

Due to recent changes in the Bankruptcy Code, spousal and child support arrearage claims are now afforded priority status, and are nondischargeable in Chapter 13 proceedings. The Chapter 13 plan must provide

---

[7]In re Weiss, 251 B.R. 453, 462-63, 146 Ed. Law Rep. 209 (Bankr. E.D. Pa. 2000) (confirmation denied because of budget excess and extravagance); In re Williams, 201 B.R. 579 (Bankr. M.D. Fla. 1996) (same). See In re Hendricks, 250 B.R. 415, 421 (Bankr. M.D. Fla. 2000) (that debtor overstated many of her expenses, inflated costs of everyday items, and contrived to find a way to spend her money other than to pay creditors, and such is an indication of a lack of good faith).

[8]In re Smith, 196 B.R. 565 (Bankr. M.D. Fla. 1996).

[9]11 U.S.C.A. § 1325(b)(2)(A). However, a debtor may not begin tithing solely to prevent his or her creditors from receiving a distribution in the Chapter 13 case. In re Cavanagh, 250 B.R. 107, 111-14 (B.A.P. 9th Cir. 2000).

[10]11 U.S.C.A. § 1322(a)(2). In re Messinger, 241 B.R. 697 (Bankr. D. Idaho 1999) (child support arrearages are priority claims which must be paid in full through the Chapter 13 plan).

[11]11 U.S.C.A. § 1325(a)(5). Associates Commercial Corp. v. Rash, 520 U.S. 953, 117 S. Ct. 1879, 138 L. Ed. 2d 148 (1997) (creditor entitled to replacement value of collateral). See In re Getz, 242 B.R. 916 (B.A.P. 6th Cir. 2000) (construing *Associates Commercial Corporation vs. Rash* "replacement value" of vehicle to be the average of the wholesale and retail values of the vehicle as set forth in the N.A.D.A. guide to vehicle valuation).

[12]11 U.S.C.A. § 1325(a)(4). In re Brugger, 254 B.R. 321 (Bankr. M.D. Pa. 2000); In re Carter, 250 B.R. 454 (Bankr. S.D. Ga. 2000); In re Miller, 247 B.R. 795, 797 (Bankr. W.D. Mo. 2000).

[13]11 U.S.C.A. § 1322(b).

[14]11 U.S.C.A. § 1322(a)(3).

[15]11 U.S.C.A. § 1322(c).

for payment in full, inside the plan, of past due spousal and child support arrearages.[16] As noted above, a properly drafted Chapter 13 plan can now provide for payment in full of support arrearages while providing a smaller dividend to general unsecured creditors.

The plan can also provide for the payment of certain post-petition debts, such as certain taxes and consumer debts, necessary for the debtor's performance under the plan,[17] for the partial liquidation of the estate,[18] for the assumption or rejection of executory contracts,[19] and for any other provision consistent with the Bankruptcy Code.[20]

§33:12 Chapter 13—Confirmation of Chapter 13 plan— Requirements for confirmation

The bankruptcy court must confirm the Chapter 13 plan if it meets the six criteria set out in 11 U.S.C.A. § 1325(a).[1]

(1) The plan complies with the provisions of Chapter 13 and other applicable provisions of Title 11;

(2) The filing fee has been paid;

(3) The plan has been proposed in good faith and not by any means forbidden by law;

(4) The plan provides for payment to unsecured creditors to be not less than would be received if the estate were liquidated under Chapter 7 (commonly referred to as the "best interest of creditors test).[2] This means the liquidation value of the estate, **not** what would actually happen if the estate were converted; otherwise a composition plan would never be confirmed if it

---

[16]11 U.S.C.A. § 1322(a)(2). See Matter of Olson, 200 B.R. 40 (Bankr. D. Neb. 1996) and In re Beverly, 196 B.R. 128 (Bankr. W.D. Mo. 1996) (confirmation of Chapter 13 plans denied where debtors failed to schedule support arrearages and provide for such claims in full regardless of the treatment of other obligations).

[17]11 U.S.C.A. § 1322(b)(6). In re Bagby, 218 B.R. 878, 889-90 (Bankr. W.D. Tenn. 1998); In re King, 217 B.R. 623 (Bankr. S.D. Cal. 1998).

[18]11 U.S.C.A. § 1322(b)(8).

[19]11 U.S.C.A. § 1322(b)(7). In re Alexander, 670 F.2d 885 (9th Cir. 1982). But see In re Waldron, 785 F.2d 936 (11th Cir. 1986), cert. dismissed, 478 U.S. 1028, 106 S. Ct. 3343, 92 L. Ed. 2d 763 (1986) (Chapter 13 cannot be filed where the sole purpose is to reject an executory contract).

[20]11 U.S.C.A. § 1322(b)(10).

[Section 33:12]

[1]In re Estus, 695 F.2d 311 (8th Cir. 1982). In re Kazzaz, 62 B.R. 308 (Bankr. E.D. Va. 1986); In re Chase, 43 B.R. 739 (D. Md. 1984).

[2]In re Brugger, 254 B.R. 321 (Bankr. M.D. Pa. 2000) (plan fails best interest of creditors test because the debtor's business was worth more than the debtor proposes to pay through the plan); In re Carter, 250 B.R. 454 (Bankr. S.D. Ga. 2000) (plan not confirmed because liquidation value of real estate dictated payment in full, with interest, to unsecured creditors); In re Larson, 245 B.R. 609 (Bankr. D. Minn. 2000) (plan fails best interest of creditors test because a hypothetical Chapter 7 trustee would likely succeed in recovering a fraudulent conveyance not accounted for in payments being made through the plan to unsecured creditors).

contained nondischargeable debt under Chapter 7;[3]

(5) The holder of a secured claim has approved the plan, the secured creditor retains its lien and is paid the value of its collateral, the collateral is returned to the secured creditor, or the creditor consents;[4] and

(6) The debtor will be able to make all payments under the plan and to comply with the provisions of the plan.[5]

In addition to the above, a plan may not be confirmed *over the objection of the trustee or an unsecured creditor* unless it provides for payment of 100% of the allowed claims, or all of the debtor's disposable income for three years will be used to fund the plan.[6] However, the Bankruptcy Code otherwise imposes no minimum plan length, and in the absence of an objection by the trustee or an unsecured creditor, and provided that the plan is filed in good faith, the court may not deny confirmation based upon plan length.[7]

§ 33:13   Chapter 13—Confirmation of Chapter 13 plan—Effect of confirmation

The legal consequences of confirmation are threefold and are set forth in 11 U.S.C.A. § 1327. First, all creditors are bound by its terms, regardless of whether the claim of a creditor is provided for, or whether the creditor has accepted, rejected, or objected to the plan.[1]

When properly used, this code section can be a powerful tool in the arsenal of debtor's counsel. For example, most claims filed by the secured creditors can be bifurcated into their secured and unsecured portions based upon the value of the collateral securing the debt. These creditors are bound by the provisions of a confirmed plan which establish the secured portion of the claims to be significantly less that the entire outstanding balance, which reduce the interest rate paid upon the

---

[3]Matter of Akin, 54 B.R. 700 (Bankr. D. Neb. 1985); In re Jenkins, 4 B.R. 278 (Bankr. D. Colo. 1980).

[4]Matter of Spohn, 61 B.R. 264 (Bankr. W.D. Wis. 1986).

[5]In re Thornhill, 268 B.R. 570, 573 (Bankr. E.D. Cal. 2001) (plan not feasible and confirmation denied where the plan proposed to pay more than $90,000 to creditors based upon 36 monthly payments of $1,200). See, also, In re Hendricks, 250 B.R. 415, 421-22 (Bankr. M.D. Fla. 2000) and In re McNichols, 249 B.R. 160, 175-80 (Bankr. N.D. Ill. 2000) wherein the courts denied confirmation where the debtors failed to introduce evidence that they would be able to make, or obtain a loan to cover balloon payments to secured creditors in the 36th month of the plan.

[6]11 U.S.C.A. § 1325(b)(1).

[7]In re Torres, 193 B.R. 319 (Bankr. N.D. Cal. 1996).

[Section 33:13]

[1]11 U.S.C.A. § 1327(a). In re Sanders, 243 B.R. 326 (Bankr. N.D. Ohio 2000); In re Ferrante, 195 B.R. 990 (Bankr. N.D. N.Y. 1996). See, also, In re Pence, 905 F.2d 1107 (7th Cir. 1990) (secured creditor bound by terms of confirmed plan); In re Szostek, 886 F.2d 1405 (3d Cir. 1989); In re Bonanno, 78 B.R. 52 (Bankr. E.D. Pa. 1987) (unsecured creditors bound by terms of confirmed plan).

secured portion of the claim,[2] and which provide for a minimal dividend upon the unsecured portion of the claim.[3]

This code section is also of great significance to the practitioner having to deal with nondischargeable student loans. Where a student loan creditor failed to object to the confirmation of a Chapter 13 plan which provided for the discharge of otherwise nondischargeable post-petition interest on the student loan, it was held that such creditor was bound by the plan and such interest was discharged.[4]

Similarly, it was held that a student loan creditor was also bound the provisions of a confirmed plan which provided for the discharge of the entire loan. The confirmed plan said that ". . .[p]ursuant to 11 U.S.C.A. § 523(a)(8), excepting the aforementioned educational loan from discharge will impose an undue hardship on the debtor and debtor's dependents. Confirmation of the debtor's plan shall constitute a finding to that effect and that such debt is dischargeable. . .."[5]

A second effect of confirmation is that it vests all property of the estate, except wages, in the debtor unless the plan otherwise provides.[6]

The final effect of confirmation is that absent a provision in the plan or confirmation order, the property revesting in the debtor under 11 U.S.C.A. § 1327(b) is free and clear of any claim or interest of any creditor provided for by the plan.[7] A secured creditor who voluntarily accepts a plan must insist upon lien retention or it is lost.[8] Absent acceptance by the secured creditor, however, the plan must provide for lien retention or return of the collateral.[9]

§ 33:14 Chapter 7—In general

Most attorneys know that a Chapter 7 proceeding is a liquidation in which the trustee takes possession and liquidates the debtor's nonexempt property while the debtor discharges most or all of his or her

---

[2]In re Vincent, 252 B.R. 91, 94-96 (Bankr. E.D. Va. 2000).

[3]Green Tree Fin. Servicing Corp. vs. Karbel, 220 B.R. 108 (B.A.P. 10th Cir. 1998); Chevy Chase Bank v. Locke, 227 B.R. 68, 71 (E.D. Va. 1998) (car lender bound by plan which established secured value of claim to be $8,500 notwithstanding a proof of claim being filed in the amount of $12,004.25); In re Thomas, 222 B.R. 524, 525-526 (Bankr. E.D. Va. 1998) (furniture company bound by plan provision establishing secured value of claim to be $2,000 even though collateral worth significantly more than this amount).

[4]In re Pardee, 218 B.R. 916 (B.A.P. 9th Cir. 1998), judgment aff'd, 193 F.3d 1083 (9th Cir. 1999); In re York, 250 B.R. 842, 844-48, 145 Ed. Law Rep. 1063 (Bankr. D. Del. 2000), as amended, (Aug. 16, 2000).

[5]In re Andersen, 215 B.R. 792, 793-96 (B.A.P. 10th Cir. 1998), judgment aff'd, 179 F.3d 1253, 136 Ed. Law Rep. 135 (10th Cir. 1999). But see In re Fox, 249 B.R. 140 (Bankr. D.S.C. 2000) (holding that on preconfirmation objection to such provision in a Chapter 13 plan, such provision must be removed from the plan).

[6]11 U.S.C.A. § 1327(b). In re Fisher, 203 B.R. 958 (N.D. Ill. 1997); Matter of Clark, 207 B.R. 559 (Bankr. S.D. Ohio 1997); In re Strong, 203 B.R. 105 (Bankr. N.D. Ill. 1996).

[7]U.S.C.A. § 1327(c). In re Nale, , 238-239 (Bankr. D. Colo. 1999); In re Siemers, (Bankr. D. Minn. 1997).

[8]In re Harnish, 224 B.R. 91 (Bankr. N.D. Iowa 1998).

[9]11 U.S.C.A. § 1325(a).

indebtedness and receives a fresh start — "a new opportunity in life and a clear field for future effort, unhampered by pressure and discouragement of preexisting debt."[1] With limited exception, the Ohio exemption statute, R.C. 2329.66, dictates what property the debtor can retain and what property is subject to turnover to the trustee.

The domestic relations lawyer must consider a number of issues in advising a client as to relief under Chapter 7. The first issue is eligibility. Generally speaking, any individual that resides or has a domicile, a place of business, or property in the United States can be a debtor in a Chapter 7 case.[2] However, an individual can seek protection under Chapter 7 only once every six years.[3]

Once it has been determined that an individual is eligible for Chapter 7 relief, the attorney must conduct a sensitive inquiry into the facts of the case to determine if the filing of the case would be a substantial abuse of the bankruptcy system. If such is the case, the client must be alerted that the court can, and will, dismiss the case.[4]

Next, the practitioner must be aware of what debts will not be discharged in the Chapter 7 proceeding. Such information is especially important when a separation agreement is being negotiated and when commencing and defending post-decree matters.

Fourth, the attorney must be aware of the impact of the automatic stay provision of 11 U.S.C.A. § 362 as it relates to state court contempt proceedings. Specifically, the practitioner must have an understanding as to when a filing of a Chapter 7 or 13 stops contempt proceedings, what to do when the offending spouse takes refuge in the bankruptcy court, and what can happen when one party violates the stay.

Finally, counsel must be able to render appropriate advice when a client advises, for the first time after the Chapter 7 has been completed and the discharge issued, about an unscheduled and forgotten creditor now pressing for payment.

Each of these issues will be discussed below.

§ 33:15   Chapter 7—Substantial abuse

Section 707(b) of the Bankruptcy Code provides that the court may, on its own motion or upon the motion of the United States Trustee, dismiss a case filed by an individual debtor whose debts are *primarily consumer debts*, if the court finds that the granting of relief under Chapter 7

[Section 33:14]

[1]Local Loan Co. v. Hunt, 292 U.S. 234, 244, 54 S. Ct. 695, 78 L. Ed. 1230, 93 A.L.R. 195 (1934). See Elsnau, *The Chapter 7 Bankruptcy Case: An Overview for the General Practitioner,* 38 N.H.B.J. 56 (March, 1997).

[2]11 U.S.C.A. § 109(a).

[3]11 U.S.C.A. § 727(a)(8) (court shall grant a debtor a discharge unless the debtor had previously been granted a discharge in a Chapter 7 proceeding within six years before the filing of the case.

[4]11 U.S.C.A. § 707(b).

would be a substantial abuse of the bankruptcy system.[1]

Federal courts throughout the country are not in agreement as to what constitutes "substantial abuse."[2] Lawyers in Ohio, however, are bound by the Sixth Circuit holding in the *Krohn*[3] case, which holds that the purpose of section 707(b) is to deny Chapter 7 relief to the dishonest or non-needy debtor. *Krohn* requires an examination of the totality of the circumstances to determine whether the debtor is "honest" in the sense that his or her financial situation warrants a Chapter 7 discharge, or, rather, whether the debtor is attempting to use the bankruptcy system to obtain an unfair advantage over creditors.

The court in *Krohn* clearly stated that section 707(b) serves notice that those tempted by unprincipled accumulation of consumer debt will be held to a minimum standard of fair play and honorable dealings.[4] As such, a "substantial abuse" dismissal can be predicated upon either lack of honesty or want of need for a Chapter 7 discharge.[5] This section can serve as a basis for dismissal even if the debtor is not eligible to file a Chapter 13.[6]

This does not mean that an individual is automatically ineligible to file Chapter 7 if the debtors' family budget reflects an ability to repay creditors. The legislative history and cases following the *Krohn* decision indicate that section 707(b) *permits but does not require* dismissal based solely on the debtor's ability to repay his debts over a period of time.

The ability to pay creditors, standing without more, is not sufficient to justify a denial of relief under Chapter 7.[7] Rather, the ability to pay creditors is one of many factors the court must look at in viewing the totality of the circumstances in determining whether the debtor is

---

[Section 33:15]

[1]11 U.S.C.A. § 707(b). See *What are "primarily consumer debts"*under 11 U.S.C.A. § 707(b), authorizing dismissal of Chapter 7 bankruptcy if granting relief would be substantial abuse of Chapter's provision,, 101 A.L.R. 711 § 4 (West, 1991).

[2]See, generally, Bankruptcy: When Does Filing of Chapter 7 Petition Constitute "Substantial Abuse" Authorizing Dismissal of Petition Under 11 U.S.C.A. 707(b), 122 A.L.R. 141 § 6 et seq.. (West, 1994). See, also, Anthony, *"Substantial Abuse" under section 707(b) of the Bankruptcy Code: American Consumers Learn Declaring Bankruptcy May Cease to Be a Way Out*, 67 U. Cin. L. Rev. 535 (1999); Coulson, *Substantial Abuse of Bankruptcy Code Section 707(b): An Evolving Philosophy of Debtor Need*, 52 Consumer Fin. L.Q. Rep. 261 (1998). See, also, In re Adams, 206 B.R. 456 (Bankr. M.D. Tenn. 1997); In re Ontiveros, 198 B.R. 284 (C.D. Ill. 1996) and In re Mastromarino, 197 B.R. 171 (Bankr. D. Me. 1996).

[3]In re Krohn, 886 F.2d 123 (6th Cir. 1989).

[4]In re Krohn, 886 F.2d 123, 126 (6th Cir. 1989); In re Adams, 206 B.R. 456, 460 (Bankr. M.D. Tenn. 1997).

[5]In re Krohn, 886 F.2d 123, 126 (6th Cir. 1989).

[6]See, e.g., In re Stratton, 136 B.R. 804 (Bankr. C.D. Ill. 1991) (case dismissed for substantial abuse in spite of debtor not being eligible for Chapter 13 relief where the net income was $8,000 per month and the budget revealed living expenses of only $4,627).

[7]In re Browne, 253 B.R. 854, 856 (Bankr. N.D. Ohio 2000); In re Marshalek, 158 B.R. 704, 708 (Bankr. N.D. Ohio 1993).

genuinely in need of relief.[8] The debtor's choice of Chapter 7 relief should
be respected and the debtor granted a discharge if the debtor, notwithstanding a budget surplus that could be devoted to the repayment of
debt, did not deliberately construct the situation in anticipation of bankruptcy, lived a modest lifestyle, and continued to have genuine difficulty
in meeting his or her obligations as they became due.[9]

On the other hand, a Chapter 7 filing will be dismissed where a debtor
with significant income enjoys a lavish lifestyle but is not making an
honest effort to deal with creditors.[10]

Thus, in *In re Summer*,[11] the debtor, an attorney with a gross annual
salary of $210,000, and having more than $240,000 in unsecured debt,
was denied a discharge on the basis of substantial abuse even though
there was no hint of dishonesty or lack of full disclosure in the schedules.
While the debtor's budget reflected an annual net income of $8,551,80
and expenditures of $8,370, the court was obviously not impressed by
monthly budget expenditures of $889.76 per month for life insurance,
$160 per month for telephone service, $320 per month for maid service,

---

[8]In re Browne, 253 B.R. 854 (Bankr. N.D. Ohio 2000). See, also, In re Adams, 206
B.R. 456, 460 (Bankr. M.D. Tenn. 1997). The legislative history of this statute is
discussed in the case of In re Balaja, 190 B.R. 335 (Bankr. N.D. Ill. 1996).

[9]Several cases following *Krohn* have denied section 707(b) motions even where a
budget excess exits. See, e.g., In re Browne, 253 B.R. 854 (Bankr. N.D. Ohio 2000) ($500
budget surplus); In re McDonald, 213 B.R. 628 (Bankr. E.D. N.Y. 1997) ($400 budget
surplus). See, also, In re Adams, 206 B.R. 456 (Bankr. N.D. Tenn. 1997) (section 707(b)
motion to dismiss denied even though debtor had a net disposable income of $1,247.90
which could have funded a 93% plan. Cases should be dismissed under section 707 (B)
only to thwart unscrupulous debtors seeking to enlist the court's assistance in a scheme
to take unfair advantage of creditors); In re Higuera, 199 B.R. 196 (Bankr. W.D. Okla.
1996) (debtor had approximately $1,000 per month in disposable income, but plain
meaning of "substantial abuse" indicates something more than an ability to repay before
a case will be dismissed under section 707(b)); In re Gentri, 185 B.R. 368 (Bankr. M.D.
Fla. 1995) (debtor could have funded a 70% plan over 3 years, but court did not find that
the debtor's Chapter 7 filing constituted substantial abuse).

[10]In re Blum, 255 B.R. 9 (Bankr. S.D. Ohio 2000) (debtors not entitled to a discharge
given debtors lack of honesty in dealing with creditors in maintaining a consistent pattern of living beyond their means, as well as a lack of candor and honesty in filing their
bankruptcy schedules); In re Stallman, 198 B.R. 491 (Bankr. W.D. Mich. 1996) (debtor
failed "honesty" test because he purchased objects, such as a new truck, when he knew
he had no ability to repay and where he had unreasonable expenses); In re McCormack,
159 B.R. 491 (Bankr. N.D. Ohio 1993) (debtor failed "honesty" test where he charged
vacations on credit cards, and knowingly failed to schedule a credit card balance of
$2,800 used just prior to filing of case). See, also, In re Duncan, 201 B.R. 889 (Bankr.
W.D. Pa. 1996) (debtor's gross income was $260,000 per year and had more than
$179,000 in consumer debts); In re Mastromarino, 197 B.R. 171 (Bankr. D. Me. 1996)
(debtor's annual income exceeded $5,776, living expenses were only $2,656, and he had
more than $189,000 in unsecured debt); In re Braithwaite, 192 B.R. 882 (Bankr. N.D.
Ohio 1996) (debtor owed more than $60,000 on 16 different credit cards, and in the six
year period prior to filing, charged more than $37,000 in travel expenses, including
$1,795.24 in the three months prior to filing while on a spring vacation). See, also, In re
Stump, 280 B.R. 208 (Bankr. S.D. Ohio 2002) (case dismissed as a "bad faith" filing
under 11 U.S.C.A. § 707(a) where debtor and spouse continued to have significant
income, a lavish lifestyle, and made no effort to reduce lifestyle).

[11]In re Summer, 255 B.R. 555 (Bankr. S.D. Ohio 2000).

$800 per month for projected vehicle replacements, $410 per month in student loan repayments for a 24 year old daughter earning $40,000 per year, and $1,855 for school tuition for his two sons. The court no doubt believed that the debtor had not made a sufficient effort to moderate his lifestyle and deal with his debt problems.

Similarly, in *In re Blum*[12] the debtors, one of whom was a successful businessman, and the other an accountant, were denied discharges under § 707 (b) for much the same reasons as in *Summer*, namely having a significant income, leading a high lifestyle, and making little effort to deal with their debt problems. In *Blum* the debtors earned for the years 1997 through 1999 between $109,000 per year and $139,000 per year. Dating back to 1997, the debtors maintained nineteen credit cards having a total balance of more than $67,000. Nonetheless, in the spring of 1998, the debtors purchased a home for $375,000, and in 1999 financed the sum of $13,949 to purchase a tractor. They also entered into a lease of a new Ford Expedition at a monthly rental payment of $450. Significantly, in 1999, one of the debtors obtained a $46,120 loan from his 401(k) plan, but failed to use the funds to retire the credit card debt. The court had little trouble in finding substantial abuse, especially since during the course of the Chapter 7 proceedings, the debtors filed amended schedules reflecting a voluntary reduction in income and increased living expenses.

But what about the common situation where a newly married debtor, having accumulated a significant amount of debt before marriage, seeks to file Chapter 7 in spite of the fact that the debtor's income, when added to the nondebtor spouse, indicates an ability to pay the debtor's bills over a reasonable period of time? Here, again, the facts of the case must be closely examined.

In *In re Reese*,[13] for example, the debtor had significant debt prior to her marriage. About a year and a half later the debtor filed a Chapter 7. During the time period between her marriage and the bankruptcy filing the debtor and her husband maintained separate bank accounts. Although there was little doubt that the debtor could not afford to repay her creditors, the United States Trustee argued that the debtor' income, combined with her spouse's income, indicated an ability to repay.

The court denied the substantial abuse motion. Because the nondebtor spouse had not derived any benefit from his spouse's debt, the court held that the proper method to determine whether the debtor had an ability to repay her debt was to compare the debtor's income to one-half of the joint family expenses. Under this test the debtor was clearly unable to repay her debts.

It is not uncommon for an individual with a budget surplus to insist that the attorney file a Chapter 7 for them. Where the budget surplus is significant, the practitioner should advise the client about section 707(b), and strongly recommend that the client consider filing a Chapter 13.

---

[12]In re Blum, 255 B.R. 9 (Bankr. S.D. Ohio 2000).

[13]In re Reese, 236 B.R. 371 (Bankr. N.D. Ohio 1999).

§ 33:16   Chapter 7—Dischargeability—Taxes

Basically three types of taxes are nondischargeable in a Chapter 7 proceeding.[1]

First, taxes entitled to a priority in distribution above general creditors from the bankruptcy estate may not be discharged.[2] This includes, for example, income tax claims for which a return was due within three years of the filing of the case, property taxes, employment taxes, excise taxes, and withholding taxes.

Second, tax claims which relate to taxpayers who did not file a tax return, or where a tax return was filed late but within two years of the filing of the bankruptcy petition, may not be discharged.[3]

The final category of nondischargeable tax claims, involve tax evasion and fraud. A debtor may not discharge a tax claim if he made a fraudulent tax return or otherwise willfully attempted in any manner to evade or defeat the payment of such tax.[4]

Thus, where a debtor is faced with significant tax claims, a Chapter 7 may not be the answer. The attorney advising such client should investigate the possibility of filing a Chapter 13.

§ 33:17   Chapter 7—Dischargeability—Unscheduled debts

To be discharged, a debt must be scheduled so that creditors can receive notice of the proceedings and a chance to share in any distributions as well as to contest dischargeability.

If a debt is not properly scheduled, the Bankruptcy Code states that such debt will not be discharged.[1] This rule is subject to the very important exception that a debt not scheduled will still be discharged if the creditor received some form of notice or had actual knowledge of the case.[2]

It is, therefore, the better practice to require a client to make a list of

---

[Section 33:16]

   [1]11 U.S.C.A. § 523(a)(1).

   [2]11 U.S.C.A. § 523(a)(1)(A).

   [3]11 U.S.C.A. § 523(a)(1)(B). A substitute tax return filed by the IRS and installment agreement signed by the debtor does not constitute a tax return for purposes of 523(a)(1)(B). In order for a document to qualify as a tax return, it must (1) purport to be a tax return; (2) be executed under penalty of perjury; (3) contain sufficient data to allow calculation of tax; and (4) represent an honest and reasonable attempt to satisfy the requirements of the tax laws. In re Hatton, 220 F.3d 1057 (9th Cir. 2000). See In re Hindenland, 164 F.3d. 1029 (6th Cir. 1999) (Form 1040 filed by the debtor after assessment by the IRS, based upon substitute tax returns filed by the IRS, are not "tax returns" for § 523(a)(1)(B) purposes because the forms cannot, as a matter of law, qualify as an honest and reasonable attempt to satisfy the requirements of the tax laws).

   [4]11 U.S.C.A. § 523(a)(1)(C). See In re Fretz, 244 F.3d 1323 (11th Cir. 2001); Matter of Birkenstock, 87 F.3d 947 (7th Cir. 1996); In re Toti, 24 F.3d 806, 1994 FED App. 152P (6th Cir. 1994); Matter of Zuhone, 88 F.3d 469 (7th Cir. 1996).

[Section 33:17]

   [1]11 U.S.C.A. § 523(a)(3).

   [2]In re Heuring, 139 B.R. 856 (Bankr. N.D. Ohio 1992). Even if the creditor is not properly scheduled, the debt will still be discharged if the creditor was in possession of

all debts prior to the conference with the attorney. Counsel should also obtain the debtor's credit report. Once the schedule of creditors has been prepared, the client should be asked to review the creditor's list and initial each page of the bankruptcy creditors lists. Such precautions will save time and, more importantly, avoid a subsequent claim by the debtor that it was the attorney's fault that a certain debt was not scheduled and, hence, discharged.

What should be done when a client calls after the closing of his case and says an unscheduled creditor is now seeking payment? The traditional approach taken by attorneys was to move the court for an order reopening the case to add the omitted creditors to the appropriate schedules.

However, the Sixth Circuit recently indicated that such may not be necessary—at least cases involving unscheduled debts which are otherwise dischargeable. In the *Madaj*[3] case the court held that in the typical, no asset Chapter 7 case involving omitted but otherwise dischargeable debt, such debts are discharged *whether or not scheduled*.

Thus, under the holding in *Madaj* most courts will deny a motion to reopen the case to add a creditor, as no purpose would be served. When faced with such a situation, debtor's counsel should notify the omitted creditor of the filing of the Chapter 7, and if collection efforts persist, file an action in the bankruptcy based upon a violation of the discharge injunction.

A different approach must be taken where the unlisted creditor holds a claim which may not be dischargeable under 11 U.S.C.A. § 523(a)(2), (4), (6) or (15), that is, for example, debts of a kind based upon fraud, willful and malicious conduct, or as part of a domestic relations property order.

In such circumstances it is entirely proper for debtor's counsel to file a motion to reopen the bankruptcy, and to amend the schedules to reflect the existence of the unlisted debts. At such time the creditor will be afforded the opportunity to contest the dischargeability of their debt. If the creditor fails to thereafter act within the specified time, the debt will be discharged. If a complaint is thereafter timely filed, the court will proceed to the merits of the creditor' claim.[4]

§ 33:18 Chapter 7—Dischargeability—Student loans

The discharge granted under Chapter 7 does not include educational loans made, insured, or guaranteed by a governmental unit, or made under any program funded in whole or in part by a governmental unit

---

sufficient facts which would cause a reasonably prudent person to make further inquiry. In re Constantino, 80 B.R. 865, 868 (Bankr. N.D. Ohio 1987). But see In re Stratton, 29 B.R. 93 (Bankr. W.D. Ky. 1983) (unsubstantiated rumor does not constitute actual knowledge of bankruptcy filing).

[3]In re Madaj, 149 F.3d 467, 1998 FED App. 211P (6th Cir. 1998); In re Wells, 246 B.R. 268 (Bankr. E.D. Ky. 2000).

[4]U.S. v. Westley, 7 Fed. Appx. 393 (6th Cir. 2001).

or a nonprofit institution.[1]

On the other hand, an extension of credit by school to a debtor, without more, is not a student loan within the meaning of the Bankruptcy Code.[2] Thus, in the *Coole*[3] case the debtor was able to discharge charges incurred over four semesters of tuition, room, board, insurance and telephone expense totaling more than $10,000.

Where a parent co-signs the educational loan obligation or where the parent is the sole obligor on the child's student loan, this section applies to prevent the discharge of the obligation.[4]

The sole exception to the rule of nondischargeability of a student loan is when the court determines that excepting the debt from discharge will impose an "undue hardship" on the debtor or the debtor's dependents.[5]

The problem for practitioners is that neither the Code nor the legislative history defines "undue hardship"[6] As such, the determination of what constituted "undue hardship" must be made on a case-by-case basis.[7]

Undue hardship means more than unpleasantness associated with the payment of a just debt, but less than utter hopelessness or abject poverty, and is not based on a present inability to pay, for most debtors

---

[Section 33:18]

[1]11 U.S.C.A. § 523(a)(8). See TI Federal Credit Union v. DelBonis, 72 F.3d 921, 106 Ed. Law Rep. 33 (1st Cir. 1995) (federal credit union is a "governmental unit" for purposes of 11 U.S.C.A. § 523(a)(8); In re LaFlamme, 188 B.R. 867, 105 Ed. Law Rep. 185 (Bankr. D. N.H. 1995) ("parents plus" loan originated with private bank are funded under the Higher Education Act of 1965, and are thus "made, insured, or guaranteed by a governmental until" with the meaning of the statute). But see In re Segal, 57 F.3d 342, 101 Ed. Law Rep. 76 (3d Cir. 1995) (loan made pursuant to an employment contract, although used to repay educational loan, is not excepted from discharge under 11 U.S.C.A. § 523(a)(8).

[2]In re Renshaw, 222 F.3d 82, 146 Ed. Law Rep. 675 (2d Cir. 2000). In re Johnson, 222 B.R. 783 (Bankr. E.D. Va. 1998). But see In re Burks, 244 F.3d 1245, 152 Ed. Law Rep. 72 (11th Cir. 2001) (stipends issued by the state board of regents to assist debtor in obtaining graduate degree in return for either repayment with interest or a teaching commitment for three years constituted a nondischargeable student loan within the meaning of § 523(a)(8).

[3]In re Coole, 202 B.R. 518 (Bankr. D. N.M. 1996).

[4]In re Hamblin, 277 B.R. 676, 165 Ed. Law Rep. 199 (Bankr. S.D. Miss. 2002); In re Clark, 273 B.R. 207 (Bankr. N.D. Iowa 2002); In re Lawson, 256 B.R. 512 (Bankr. M.D. Fla. 2000); In re Stein, 218 B.R. 281, 125 Ed. Law Rep. 145 (Bankr. D. Conn. 1998); In re LaFlamme, 188 B.R. 867, 105 Ed. Law Rep. 185 (Bankr. D. N.H. 1995); In re Uterhark, 185 B.R. 39, 102 Ed. Law Rep. 600 (Bankr. N.D. Ohio 1995).

[5]11 U.S.C.A. § 523(a)(8)(B).

[6]In re Markley, 236 B.R. 242, 246, 136 Ed. Law Rep. 420 (Bankr. N.D. Ohio 1999). See, also, In re Garybush, 265 B.R. 587, 591 (Bankr. S.D. Ohio 2001).

[7]In re Foley, 204 B.R. 582, 584, 115 Ed. Law Rep. 367 (Bankr. M.D. Fla. 1996); In re D'Ettore, 106 B.R. 715, 718 (Bankr. M.D. Fla. 1989); This section embodies a policy decision that repayment of federally insured educational loans generally trumps provisions providing a fresh start to debtors. In re Merchant, 958 F.2d 738, 740, 73 Ed. Law Rep. 619 (6th Cir. 1992). However, this policy is tempered by the "undue hardship" exception. In re Elebrashy, 189 B.R. 922, 925, 105 Ed. Law Rep. 1083 (Bankr. N.D. Ohio 1995).

could make that assertion.[8] The fact that a debtor's budget may be tight for the foreseeable future is the norm rather than the exception.[9] A finding of undue hardship is reserved for those exceptional circumstances where it is unlikely that the debtor will ever be able to repay the loan.[10]

There are many cases involving the issue of what constitutes "undue hardship." The practitioner is advised to review them before advising a client because each case must be decided based upon a totality of the circumstances.[11] Note that the burden of proof rests with the creditor to prove that the loan is nondischargeable, while the burden of proving undue hardship, as would warrant discharge of the debt, is upon the debtor.[12]

Nonetheless, in the absence of a firm definition of undue hardship, courts within the Sixth Circuit have developed a three-part test for guidance in determining the issue of undue hardship based upon a test first announced by the Second Circuit in the *Brunner*[13] case.

Under the *Brunner* test, the debtor must establish the following:

(1) That the debtor cannot maintain, based on current income and expenses, a "minimal" standard of living for the debtor and the debtor's dependents if forced to repay the loan; and

(2) That additional circumstances exit indicating that this state of affairs is likely to persist for a significant portion of the repayment period; and

(3) That the debtor made a good faith effort to repay the loan.

Most debtors litigating the issue fail to meet their burden of proof under the *Brunner* test. For example, in *In re Smalley*,[14] the court refused to discharge the debtor's student loans where, although the debtor's circumstances demonstrated a temporary hardship, the debtor

---

[8]In re Hornsby, 144 F.3d 433, 437, 126 Ed. Law Rep. 643, 1998 FED App. 184P (6th Cir. 1998); In re Gammoh, 174 B.R. 707, 709, 96 Ed. Law Rep. 145 (Bankr. N.D. Ohio 1994); In re Johnson, 121 B.R. 91, 93, 64 Ed. Law Rep. 154 (Bankr. N.D. Okla. 1990); In re Berthiaume, 138 B.R. 516, 73 Ed. Law Rep. 986 (Bankr. W.D. Ky. 1992).

[9]In re Bakkum, 139 B.R. 680, 682, 74 Ed. Law Rep. 877 (Bankr. N.D. Ohio 1992).

[10]In re LaFlamme, 188 B.R. 867, 105 Ed. Law Rep. 185 (Bankr. D. N.H. 1995); In re Ballard, 60 B.R. 673, 32 Ed. Law Rep. 1001 (Bankr. W.D. Va. 1986).

[11]See Gargotta, *Undue Hardship and the Discharge of Student Loans*, 15 ABI J. 10 (May, 1996).

[12]In re Dolph, 215 B.R. 832 (B.A.P. 6th Cir. 1998). See, e.g., Barry Russell, Bankruptcy Evidence Manual, 2002 Ed., § 301.60(G) at 554 (West 2002). See, also, In re Fowler, 250 B.R. 828 (Bankr. D. Conn. 2000); In re Brown, 247 B.R. 228, 233 (Bankr. N.D. Ohio 2000); In re Cobb, 188 B.R. 22, 23 (Bankr. N.D. Ohio 1995); In re Healey, 161 B.R. 389, 393, 87 Ed. Law Rep. 495 (E.D. Mich. 1993).

[13]In re Hornsby, 144 F.3d 433, 126 Ed. Law Rep. 643, 1998 FED App. 184P (6th Cir. 1998) adopting modified "undue hardship" test found in Brunner v. New York State Higher Educ. Services Corp., 831 F.2d. 395, 396 (2d Cir. 1987). See, In re Ledbetter, 254 B.R. 714, 716, 148 Ed. Law Rep. 388 (Bankr. S.D. Ohio 2000), collecting cases. See, e.g., In re Fraley, 247 B.R. 417 (Bankr. N.D. Ohio 2000); In re Windland, 201 B.R. 178 (Bankr. N.D. Ohio 1996) and In re Elebrashy, 189 B.R. 922, 105 Ed. Law Rep. 1083 (Bankr. N.D. Ohio 1995).

[14]In re Smalley, 200 B.R. 318 (Bankr. N.D. Ohio 1996).

had an accounting decree and demonstrated earning ability, his dependents did not have any health problems, and the debtor had not demonstrated any good faith effort to repay the educational loans.

Similarly, in *In re Burgess*,[15] the debtor, a certified public accountant with many years of experience, was unable to discharge educational loans incurred by him in educating his children despite claims by the debtor that, due to unsubstantiated depression, he could not earn enough to repay the loans. The debtor lost this case due to a lack of proof because the court found that the debtor did not make a sincere effort to find employment until the eve of trial, and because the debtor failed to establish that he suffered from any permanent disability or deficiency which would diminish his earning potential.

In *In re McLeod*,[16] the debtor was not entitled to an undue hardship discharge even though the debtor made a good faith effort to repay the loan; it was not shown that the debtor would be unable to maintain a minimal standard of living if required to repay the loan given the fact that the debtor's dependent son had a monthly income which contributed to the household finances.

In *In re O'Flaherty*,[17] the court determined that the debtor was not entitled to discharge his student loan. Although the debtor could not fulfill his goal as ordination as a Catholic priest on which the student loan funds were spent, the debtor was single with no dependents, had an annual income of $31,000, had cash in his checking account in excess of the balance of the student loan, had a savings account, his living expenses were not extraordinary, and he received financial assistance from his mother.

In *In re Holtorf*,[18] the debtor was not able to discharge his student loans used to finance his medical education. Although the debtor suffered from depression and drug addiction, he did not exercise good faith in attempting to repay the loans, and did not make an attempt to make best use of his medical training and license. However, debtor made his mother's mortgage payments, which he was not legally obligated to do. Furthermore, the debtor worked only 20 hours per week at minimum wage jobs.[19]

In a few cases, however, the debtors were able to obtain a discharge of their student loans.[20]

In *In re Windland*,[21] the debtor, a single mother with two dependent children and limited education, was entitled to discharge her student loan where one of the debtor's children suffered from asthma, her living

---

[15]In re Burgess, 204 B.R. 521 (Bankr. N.D. Ohio 1997).

[16]In re McLeod, 197 B.R. 624 (Bankr. N.D. Ohio 1996).

[17]In re O'Flaherty, 204 B.R. 793, 115 Ed. Law Rep. 954 (Bankr. N.D. Ala. 1997).

[18]In re Holtorf, 204 B.R. 567 (Bankr. S.D. Cal. 1997).

[19]To the same effect, see In re Dennehy, 201 B.R. 1008, 113 Ed. Law Rep. 1254 (Bankr. N.D. Fla. 1996).

[20]In re Balaski, 280 B.R. 395 (Bankr. N.D. Ohio 2002) (discharge granted to profoundly handicapped debtor).

[21]In re Windland, 201 B.R. 178 (Bankr. N.D. Ohio 1996).

expenses exceeded her income, she had no savings, could not afford automobile insurance, and where she lived frugally, from paycheck to paycheck. The court found that it was unlikely that her situation would improve, and that she had made a good faith effort to repay the student loan.

In *In re Taylor*,[22] the court found that excepting the debtors' student loans from discharge would cause the debtors' financial situation to continue on a downward spiral. The debtors were 58 and 59 years of age, were both suffering from extensive health problems, lost retirement funds on an unsuccessful business venture, and, although took significant steps to obtain new employment, their income decreased over the last three years to about $13,300 per year.

In *In re Elebrashy*,[23] the court found that the debtor was entitled to a discharge of his student loan where debtor could not maintain a minimal standard of living for himself and his dependents if required to repay the loan. The court also found that the debtor's current circumstances were likely to persist into the foreseeable future because the debtor had no apparent prospect for advancement either in his current job or in a new position.

In *In re Harris*,[24] the debtor, a disbarred lawyer, was entitled to undue hardship discharge because the debtor was a convicted felon, had several years left to repay criminal restitution, was addicted to cocaine, and his living expenses exceeded his current income.

It should be noted that educational loan dischargeability litigation is not an "all or nothing" proposition.[25] Courts have discharged portions of a student loan obligation where the court determined that it would create an undue hardship to require payment in full,[26] and even, at times, crafted its own repayment schedule to lessen the financial burden

---

[22]In re Taylor, 198 B.R. 700, 111 Ed. Law Rep. 841 (Bankr. N.D. Ohio 1996).

[23]In re Elebrashy, 189 B.R. 922, 105 Ed. Law Rep. 1083 (Bankr. N.D. Ohio 1995).

[24]In re Harris, 198 B.R. 190 (Bankr. W.D. Va. 1996), vacated, 129 F.3d 1259 (4th Cir. 1997).

[25]Where a debtor has multiple student loans, the court applies the undue hardship test on a loan-by-loan basis. See In re Myers, 280 B.R. 416, 167 Ed. Law Rep. 217 (Bankr. S.D. Ohio 2002) (discharging some, but not all, of the debtor's student loans).

[26]In re Hornsby, 144 F.3d 433, 126 Ed. Law Rep. 643, 1998 FED App. 184P (6th Cir. 1998) (debtors not entitled to an undue hardship discharge but 11 U.S.C.A. § 105 would permit a remedy short of complete nondischargeability); In re Fraley, 247 B.R. 417 (Bankr. N.D. Ohio 2000) (declining based upon facts of case to grant partial discharge); In re Gammoh, 174 B.R. 707, 96 Ed. Law Rep. 145 (Bankr. N.D. Ohio 1994). See, In re Heckathorn, 199 B.R. 188 (Bankr. N.D. Okla. 1996), corrected, (Aug. 16, 1996); In re Hawkins, 139 B.R. 651, 74 Ed. Law Rep. 873 (Bankr. N.D. Ohio 1991) ($7,159 of $11,159 plus interest and collection costs discharged); In re Bakkum, 139 B.R. 680, 74 Ed. Law Rep. 877 (Bankr. N.D. Ohio 1992) ($34,000 of $75,000). In In re Cheesman, 25 F.3d 356, 361, 91 Ed. Law Rep. 858, 1994 FED App. 185P (6th Cir. 1994), the Sixth Circuit affirmed a lower court decision granting the debtor an undue hardship discharge, but withholding the final order of dischargeability for 18 months to see if the discharge was still warranted. The appellate court held that the Bankruptcy Court properly exercised its equitable authority under 11 U.S.C.A. § 105 in attempting to balance the Code's goal of a fresh start with Congress's goal of preventing abuse of the student loan program.

imposed by the repayment of the obligations.[27]

For example, in *In re Grine*,[28] the court required the debtor to repay only $18,000 of the $102,526.46 in question, with such debt being repaid at the rate of $100 per month. Likewise, in *In re Ledbetter*,[29] the court ordered the discharge of one of the debtor's two student loans. In *In re Boyd*,[30] the court would not discharge the student loan on the basis of undue hardship, but did discharge the obligation to pay past and future interest.

Similarly, in *In re Berthiaume*[31] both the husband and wife sought to discharge their student loan obligations. The court found the husband's student loan to be nondischargeable, but because of a limited amount of money available for repayment, permitted the loan to be repaid at the monthly amount of $65 for a period of time, with the amount increasing thereafter to $100 per month until the loans were paid. Because of health problems, which hampered the wife's ability to obtain or maintain permanent employment, the court discharged the wife's student loans.

§ 33:19   Chapter 7—Dischargeability—Debts incurred by fraud—Dealing with credit card abuse case

Only honest debtors may benefit from bankruptcy proceedings. Therefore, 11 U.S.C.A. § 523(a)(2) excepts from discharge debts incurred through fraud.

The Code suggests two categories of such nondischargeable debts. 11 U.S.C.A. § 523(a)(2)(A) excepts from discharge debts precipitated by false pretense, false representation, or actual fraud, other than by making a statement about the debtor's financial condition, while 11 U.S.C.A. § 523(a)(2)(B) excepts from discharge those debts obtained through the use of a materially false, written financial statement, made with the intent to deceive and on which the creditor reasonably relied.

---

[27]In re Garybush, 265 B.R. 587 (Bankr. S.D. Ohio 2001) (partial discharge of student loan, court eliminating all interest, costs, and collection fees and granting payment moratorium); In re Berry, 266 B.R. 359 (Bankr. N.D. Ohio 2000) (eliminating all interest and collection fees and permitting repayment at reduced monthly rate); In re Grine, 254 B.R. 191 (Bankr. N.D. Ohio 2000) (discharging all but $18,000 of student loans totaling $102,526.46); In re Dennehy, 201 B.R. 1008, 113 Ed. Law Rep. 1254 (Bankr. N.D. Fla. 1996) (student loan nondischargeable but repayment and accrual of interest deferred for two years); In re Bakkum, 139 B.R. 680, 74 Ed. Law Rep. 877 (Bankr. N.D. Ohio 1992) (loans repaid at $200 per month); In re Berthiaume, 138 B.R. 516, 73 Ed. Law Rep. 986 (Bankr. W.D. Ky. 1992) (husband's student loans to be repaid for two years at $65 per month, thereafter at $100 per month); In re Conner, 89 B.R. 744, 49 Ed. Law Rep. 224 (Bankr. N.D. Ill. 1988) (repayment deferred until debtor's daughter had graduated from college). See, also, In re Dennehy, 201 B.R. 1008, 113 Ed. Law Rep. 1254 (Bankr. N.D. Fla. 1996) (student loan not dischargeable, but repayment and accrual of interest "deferred" for 2 years) and In re O'Donnell, 198 B.R. 1, 111 Ed. Law Rep. 328 (Bankr. D. N.H. 1996) (student loan not dischargeable, but repayment deferred for 6 months to allow debtor to become settled in new job or to obtain more stable employment).

[28]In re Grine, 254 B.R. 191 (Bankr. N.D. Ohio 2000).

[29]In re Ledbetter, 254 B.R. 714 (Bank. S.D. Ohio 2000).

[30]In re Boyd, 254 B.R. 399 (Bankr. N.D. Ohio 2000).

[31]In re Berthiaume, 138 B.R. 516, 73 Ed. Law Rep. 986 (Bankr. W.D. Ky. 1992).

Under either section, the creditor must prove, by a preponderance of the evidence,[1] that the debtor made a material misrepresentation of fact with the purpose and intent of deceiving the creditor, and that the creditor justifiably and reasonably relied upon such misconduct to their detriment.[2]

For example, where the debtor obtains a loan to purchase a vehicle for another person, such as a boyfriend, girlfriend, or child who would otherwise not qualify for the loan, the vehicle is immediately turned over to the third person. If, thereafter, the vehicle cannot be located or is damaged in an accident, the debtor may have to deal with a dischargeability action based upon this section.

Such is exactly what happened in *In re Dobek*,[3] wherein the court excepted from discharge the debtor's obligation upon a loan used to purchase a motorcycle using her own good credit on behalf of the debtor's boyfriend who would not have qualified for the loan on his own.

It is these sections, and especially 11 U.S.C.A. § 523(a)(2)(A), that credit card issuers rely on in challenging the dischargeability of debtor's credit card balance to them.[4] The following sections will discuss the basics for defending a dischargeability action by a credit card lender.

§ 33:20 Chapter 7—Dischargeability—Debts incurred by fraud—Dealing with credit card abuse case—Subjective intent to defraud

First of all, it must be remembered that a credit card embodies a continuing invitation by the issuer to the cardholder to make purchases or take cash advances from funds loaned to him by the issuer. There is nothing intrinsically illegal or improper about a cardholder accepting this invitation during a period of adversity.[1]

Thus, there must be some fraudulent conduct on the part of the credit card user in order to justify or warrant excluding the debt from discharge. In order to prevail in an action under 11 U.S.C.A. § 523(a)(2)(A), the credit card issuer must prove by a preponderance of the evidence that: (1) the credit cardholder obtained money or credit by making materially false representations; (2) that at such time the cardholder knew such misrepresentations were false or made with gross

---

[Section 33:19]

[1]Grogan v. Garner, 498 U.S. 279, 111 S. Ct. 654, 112 L. Ed. 2d 755 (1991); In re Rembert, 141 F.3d 277, 281, 1998 FED App. 106P (6th Cir. 1998).

[2]In re Rembert, 141 F.3d 277, 280-281, 1998 FED App. 106P (6th Cir. 1998); In re Shartz, 221 B.R. 397 (B.A.P. 6th Cir. 1998); In re Kromar, 258 B.R. 692 (Bankr. N.D. Ohio 2001).

[3]In re Dobek, 278 B.R. 496 (Bankr. N.D. Ill. 2002).

[4]See In re Butterworth, 279 B.R. 31, 2002 BNH 18 (Bankr. D. N.H. 2002) (credit card application and credit increase request form held not to be a writing with respect to a debtor's financial condition under 11 U.S.C.A. § 523(a)(2)(B)).

[Section 33:20]

[1]In re McCreery, 213 B.R. 689, 694 (Bankr. N.D. Ohio 1997); In re Lippert, 206 B.R. 136, 141 (Bankr. N.D. Ohio 1997).

recklessness as to the truth; (3) the debtor intended to deceive the credit card issuer; (4) the credit card issuer actually and justifiably relied upon the false representations; and (5) the creditor's reliance was the proximate cause of loss.[2]

Traditionally, many courts deciding credit card dischargeability cases under 11 U.S.C.A. § 523(a)(2)(A) indulged in the legal fiction that the use of a credit card was an implied representation of intention *and* ability to pay on the part of the cardholder. Thus, insolvency at the time of usage constituted a breach of the implied representations of intent and ability to pay, and a resulted in nondischargeable debt.[3]

However, in *Field v. Mans*[4] the Supreme Court held that a credit card issuer relying on the fraud exception to dischargeability must satisfy the common law standard of fraud, which requires proof of a subjective intent to defraud.[5] That is, the card issuer must prove that the cardholder made the charges without any *actual* intent to repay. Proving subjective intent to defraud involves an analysis of all of the circumstances of the case, to look into the mind of the cardholder.[6]

Based upon the holding in *Field v. Mans* the Sixth Circuit held in *In re Rembert*,[7] that credit card debt will be held nondischargeable *only* if it appears that the debtor could not have realistically expected to pay the charges *and* that the debtor did not, in fact, intend to pay the charges.[8] Fraudulent intent *cannot* be inferred solely from the debtor's insolvency, unemployment, or financial condition at the time of use.[9] While the use of a credit card implies a promise to pay the charges, such promise of future payment are not actionable absent proof that that the cardholder intended to deceive when incurring the charges.[10]

---

[2]In re Rembert, 141 F.3d 277, 280-81, 1998 FED App. 106P (6th Cir. 1998). See, also, American Exp. Travel Related Services Co., Inc. v. Henein, 257 B.R. 702 (E.D. N.Y. 2001) requiring that in a credit card dischargeability case the alleged fraud must be pled with specificity.

[3]The cases are collected in In re Cox, 182 B.R. 626, 633 (Bankr. D. Mass. 1995) (disapproved of by, A.T.&T. Universal Card Service Corp. v. Nguyen, 208 B.R. 258 (D. Mass. 1997)).

[4]Field v. Mans, 516 U.S. 59, 116 S. Ct. 437, 133 L. Ed. 2d 351 (1995).

[5]In re Sziel, 206 B.R. 490, 493 (Bankr. N.D. Ill. 1997); In re Briese, 196 B.R. 440 (Bankr. W.D. Wis. 1996).

[6]See, generally, Credit card debt as nondischargeable under Bankruptcy Code provisions concerning nondischargeability of individual debt obtained through false pretenses, false representation, or actual fraud, other than statement respecting debtor's or insider's financial condition, 158 A.L.R. Fed. 189 § 6[a], et seq. (West, 1999); In re Sziel, 206 B.R. 490, 493 (Bankr. N.D. Ill. 1997); In re Murphy, 190 B.R. 327, 333-34 (Bankr. N.D. Ill. 1995).

[7]In re Rembert, 141 F.3d 277, 1998 FED App. 106P (6th Cir. 1998).

[8]In re Lippert, 206 B.R. 136, 140 (Bankr. N.D. Ohio 1997).

[9]In re Lippert, 206 B.R. 136, 140 (Bankr. N.D. Ohio 1997).

[10]In re Pantelias, 265 B.R. 788 (Bankr. E.D. Tenn. 2001); In re McCreery, 213 B.R. 689 (Bankr. N.D. Ohio 1997); In re Lippert, 206 B.R. 136 (Bankr. N.D. Ohio 1997); In re Briese, 196 B.R. 440, 451 (Bankr. W.D. Wis. 1996).

Under *Rembert*,[11] the representation made by a cardholder through use of the credit card is that the cardholder *intends* to repay the debt, *not* that the cardholder has an ability to repay the debt. The court in *Rembert* correctly observed that is not proper to measure the cardholder's intention to repay by looking solely to the cardholders ability to repay at the time of use. To do so, without more, would be contrary to one of the main reasons that consumers use credit cards, namely, the inability to pay in full at the time of a purchase.[12]

Rather, the focus of a credit card dischargeability case must be solely whether the cardholder maliciously and in bad faith incurred credit card debt with the intention of petitioning for bankruptcy and avoiding the debt. While the cardholder's overall financial condition is necessarily a part of inferring whether or not the cardholder incurred the debt maliciously and in bad faith, the state of the cardholder's financial condition at the time of use of the credit card can never be a substitute for an actual finding of bad faith on the part of the cardholder. The cardholder's intent must be ascertained from all of the relevant facts and circumstances, and cannot solely be inferred from the debtor's insolvency, unemployment or financial condition.[13]

As such, the proper inquiry to determine the cardholder's fraudulent intent is whether the cardholder subjectively intended to repay the debt.[14] An honest but mistaken belief by the debtor that the debt would be paid does not meet the fraudulent intent requirement, and will result in the debt being discharged.[15]

Thus, in *In re Shartz*,[16] the debtor was earning about $46,000 per year when she was laid off in April of 1995. At that time the debtor had about $8,000 in revolving debt. From that time until the debtor filed bankruptcy, the total credit card debt increased to about $67,000, including $12,500 owed to Providian.

After being laid off, the debtor's only income was $240 per week in unemployment benefits. In November, 1995, the debtor paid the entire Providian balance through a cash advance on another card. That was the last payment made on the card. From the date of payment until

---

[11]In re Rembert, 141 F.3d 277, 1998 FED App. 106P (6th Cir. 1998).

[12]In re Rembert, 141 F.3d 277, 281, 1998 FED App. 106P (6th Cir. 1998); In re Anastas, 94 F.3d 1280, 1287, 158 A.L.R. Fed. 699 (9th Cir. 1996); In re Feld, 203 B.R. 360, 368 (Bankr. E.D. Pa. 1996); In re Briese, 196 B.R. 440, 448 (Bankr. W.D. Wis. 1996).

[13]In re Rembert, 141 F.3d 277, 282, 1998 FED App. 106P (6th Cir. 1998); Chevy Case Bank FSB v. Kukuk (In re Kukuk), 255 B.R. 778, 786-87(10th Cir. B.A.P. 1998); In re McCreery, 213 B.R. 689 (Bankr. N.D. Ohio 1997).

[14]In re Rembert, 141 F.3d 277, 281, 1998 FED App. 106P (6th Cir. 1998); In re Grause, 245 B.R. 95 (B.A.P. 8th Cir. 2000).

[15]In re Pantelias, 265 B.R. 788 (Bankr. E.D. Tenn. 2001); In re Way, 260 B.R. 291 (Bankr. M.D. Fla. 2000); In re McCreery, 213 B.R. 689 (Bankr. N.D. Ohio 1997); In re Briese, 196 B.R. 440, 452 (Bankr. W.D. Wis. 1996). See, also, In re Stansel, 203 B.R. 339 (Bankr. M.D. Fla. 1996); Matter of Totina, 198 B.R. 673 (Bankr. E.D. La. 1996) (gambling debts).

[16]In re Shartz, 221 B.R. 397 (B.A.P. 6th Cir. 1998).

January, 1996, the debtor borrowed another $12,500 on the card. In August 1996, the debtor filed bankruptcy.

Thereafter, Providian sought to except their debt from discharge. The debtor testified at trial that during her unemployment she was using the credit cards to maintain payments and payoff balances on other credit cards, but that the debts only "snowballed", ultimately causing the debtor to file bankruptcy. The debtor further testified that she did not use the credit cards to buy jewelry, furs or other extravagant purchases, but was merely trying to preserve her credit until she found a job when she would begin paying off her credit cards.

The bankruptcy court found for the debtor and Providian appealed. The Sixth Circuit Bankruptcy Appellate Panel affirmed, finding no subjective intent on the part of the debtor to defraud. Rather, the court held that totality of the evidence indicated that the debtor was trying to tide herself over during her unemployment, and not seeking "one last hurrah" at the expense of her creditors.[17]

In a similar vane, the debtor in *In re Lippert*,[18] used cash advances from credit cards to pay balances in full on other cards. The debtor also used his credit card to pay for his wedding while he was insolvent. Although the debtor was unemployed for nine months, he was diligently searching for a new job. The court found for the debtor in the creditor's complaint to determine dischargeability, finding no subjective intent to defraud. Rather, the court found that the debtor's actions were simply an attempt to "tide himself over" during a difficult time, and not a "final splurge prior to writing off his debt in bankruptcy."[19]

In *In re Kong*,[20] the appellate court affirmed a finding by the bankruptcy court in favor of the debtor in a dischargeability suit brought by a credit card issuer against the debtor, based upon the use of a credit card to finance gambling. The trial court found that the debtor, a recreational gambler, lacked fraudulent intent based upon the debtor's history over a number of years of the repayment of credit card cash advances from winnings and in the absence of any evidence other than an objective inability to repay.[21]

Lastly, the *In re Stearns*[22] case involved an $8,700 balance upon a preapproved credit card used by the debtor within four months preceding the filing of the bankruptcy in order to gamble at local casinos. Here, again, the court found for the debtor in the subsequent dischargeability proceeding, find that, given all of the facts and circumstances, the debtor did not intend to induce the creditor to grant her credit without a corresponding subjective intent to repay. That is, the court found that the use of the credit cards was not an intentional plan to make use of credit in

---

[17]In re Shartz, 221 B.R. 397, 401 (B.A.P. 6th Cir. 1998). See, also, In re Blount, 276 B.R. 119 (Bankr. N.D. Miss. 2000).

[18]In re Lippert, 206 B.R. 136 (Bankr. N.D. Ohio 1997).

[19]In re Lippert, 206 B.R. 136, 141 (Bankr. N.D. Ohio 1997).

[20]In re Kong, 239 B.R. 815 (B.A.P. 9th Cir. 1999).

[21]To the same effect, see In re Alnajjar, 276 B.R. 844 (Bankr. N.D. Ohio 2002).

[22]In re Stearns, 241 B.R. 611 (Bankr. D. Minn. 1999).

contemplation of bankruptcy.

These cases must be contrasted with those cases where a debtor did intentionally incur credit card debt as part of a scheme to defraud a credit card company.

Thus, in *In re Hashimi*,[23] the debtor owed more than $300,00 in credit card debts when he financed a six-week trip for Europe for himself and his family. During the trip he made more than $60,000 in charges on his American Express Card, and upon return home, filed for bankruptcy. The court had little trouble finding the debt to be nondischargeable.

Similarly, in *In re Eashai*,[24] the debtor had accumulated more than $100,000 on 26 credit cards after becoming unemployed from a job that paid him only $26,000 per year. The debtor used cash advances from one card to make the minimum payments on his other cards, take a trip to Pakistan, and a $1,000 gambling spree. Here, again, the court had little trouble finding the debt to be excepted from discharge.

§33:21 Chapter 7—Dischargeability—Debts incurred by fraud—Dealing with credit card abuse case—Justifiable reliance

The decisions in *Field v. Mans*[1] and *In re Rembert*[2] also require the credit card issuer to prove that it *actually* and *justifiably* relied upon false representations made by the debtor as to intent to pay the charges. Under this standard, a creditor must "use his senses, and cannot recovery if he blindly relies upon a misrepresentation the falsity of which would be patent to him if he had utilized his opportunity to make a cursory examination or investigation."[3]

In order to establish justifiable reliance on the debtor's implied representation that he intends to pay the charges at issue, the credit card issuer must demonstrate that it conducted a credit check and evaluated the creditworthiness of the debtor, or that circumstances otherwise exist which demonstrate that credit was not extended blindly.[4]

As such, breach of the implied representation regarding intention to pay, standing by itself, does not generally give rise to a dischargeability action under 11 U.S.C.A. § 523(a)(2)(A). Credit cards are marketed by issuers and often used by consumers *because* the consumer lack the abil-

---

[23]In re Hashemi, 104 F.3d 1122 (9th Cir. 1996), as amended, (Jan. 24, 1997).

[24]In re Eashai, 87 F.3d 1082 (9th Cir. 1996).

[Section 33:21]

[1]Field v. Mans, 516 U.S. 59, 70-72, 116 S. Ct. 437, 133 L. Ed. 2d 351 (1995).

[2]In re Rembert, 141 F.3d 277, 1998 FED App. 106P (6th Cir. 1998).

[3]Field v. Mans, 516 U.S. 59, 71, 116 S. Ct. 437, 133 L. Ed. 2d 351 (1995).

[4]In re Cameron, 219 B.R. 531, 539 (Bankr. W.D. Mo. 1998); In re McCreery, 213 B.R. 689, 693 (Bankr. N.D. Ohio 1997); In re Akdogan, 204 B.R. 90, 97 (Bankr. E.D. N.Y. 1997).

ity to pay the charge when that they use the credit card.[5]

People use credit cards precisely because they do not have a present ability to pay, and it is this reality which makes the credit card industry extremely profitable. Such is also why many credit card companies often advertise their cards as just the right thing to use in an emergency.[6] It is this reality which caused one court to apt conclude that it is "audacious, oppressive and hypocritical" for a credit card issuer to accuse a customer of fraud for using the credit card in exactly the manner the issuer permits, and, in fact, encourages.[7]

Most credit card issues distribute their cards freely without performing any credit analysis. Under such circumstances, there can be no actual and justifiable reliance by the creditor so long as the lender takes no action to restrict card use.[8]

Thus, debtors have prevailed in credit card dischargeability contests where the creditor sent the debtor an unsolicited credit card and the debtor does not exceed the credit line,[9] where the creditor gave the debtor a credit card with a $7,700 credit line without a credit check which would have revealed that the debtor earned less than $10,000 per year and was receiving minimal disability income,[10] where the debtor had an honest but mistaken belief that the cash advances and charges would be repaid,[11] and where the debtor paid off the credit card and the creditor thereafter unilaterally raised the credit limit to entice him to use the card.[12]

Given the state of the law since *Field v. Mans* and *Rembert*, counsel should not automatically concede dischargeability actions by credit card companies. As shown by the above examples, courts have become increasingly reluctant to declare credit card debt nondischargeable in all but the most egregious situations.

---

[5]In re Rembert, 141 F.3d 277, 1998 FED App. 106P (6th Cir. 1998); In re Kukuk, 255 B.R. 778, 786-87(10th Cir. B.A.P. 1998); In re Kountry Korner Store, 221 B.R. 265, 274 (Bankr. N.D. Okla. 1998); In re Briese, 196 B.R. 440, 448 (Bankr. W.D. Wis. 1996).

[6]In re Briese, 196 B.R. 440, 448 (Bankr. W.D. Wis. 1996).

[7]In re Kountry Korner Store, 221 B.R. 265, 274 (Bankr. N.D. Okla. 1998).

[8]In re Feld, 203 B.R. 360, 370 (Bankr. E.D. Pa. 1996); In re Briese, 196 B.R. 440 (Bankr. W.D. Wis. 1996).

[9]In re Cameron, 219 B.R. 531 (Bankr. W.D. Mo. 1998) (unsolicited balance transfer of about $9,000 from other credit cards to account without any balance coupled with increase in credit line from $3,000 to $11,000); In re McCreery, 213 B.R. 689 (Bankr. N.D. Ohio 1997) ($8,000 credit line extended to debtor with an annual income of $12,000); In re Akdogan, 204 B.R. 90 (Bankr. E.D. N.Y. 1997) (use of preapproved credit card with $8,000 credit line); In re Briese, 196 B.R. 440 (Bankr. W.D. Wis. 1996) (unsolicited credit card with $11,700 credit line); In re Arroyo, 205 B.R. 984 (Bankr. S.D. Fla. 1997) (preapproved credit card with $5,000 credit line and no prior credit evaluation for credit worthiness).

[10]In re Feld, 203 B.R. 360, 370 (Bankr. E.D. Pa. 1996).

[11]In re Stansel, 203 B.R. 339 (Bankr. M.D. Fla. 1996); Matter of Totina, 198 B.R. 673 (Bankr. E.D. La. 1996) (gambling debts).

[12]In re McDaniel, 202 B.R. 74 (Bankr. N.D. Tex. 1996).

§ 33:22 Chapter 7—Dischargeability—Debts incurred by fraud—Dealing with credit card abuse case—Presumption of nondischargeability

The Code specifies that certain credit transactions are presumed to be nondischargeable. 11 U.S.C.A. § 523(a)(2)(C) provides that consumer debts owed to a single creditor and aggregating more than $1,075 for luxury goods or services incurred within 60 days before the filing of a petition, or cash advances aggregating more than $1,075 under an open end credit plan by an individual debtor within 60 before a case is filed, are presumed nondischargeable.

This presumption, however, can be rebutted, and, in any event, in the end each case will rise and fall on its own particular facts.[1] As shown by *In re Kitzmiller*,[2] discussed below, the practitioner should not automatically assume that significant credit card charges made within 60 days before the filing of the petition will automatically result in a nondischargeable debt.

In *In re Kitzmiller*[3] the debtors took cash advances of more than $5,500 within 60 days of the filing of the bankruptcy. Although employed at the time that they took the cash advances, the debtors were aware that the husband would soon no longer be working due to a plant closing.

In finding for the debtors, the court found that the credit card company offered no evidence of reliance upon any misrepresentations by the debtors as required by *Field v. Mans*. The wife made the cash advances, and the husband had little or no participation in the family's financial affairs. Therefore, according to the court, the husband could not, as a matter of law, have an intent to deceive when the wife took the cash advances.

As to the wife, the court found her explanation as to the use of the credit card credible, that she did not intend to deceive or defraud when she used the credit card. It was established that the wife knew that her husband would soon be out of a job, and that she was are of the fact that they would not be able to repay the credit card company on the resulting reduced income. However, her husband had been laid off before and she financed the family affairs with credit cards until he returned to work. The cash advances were used only for living expenses, and the wife honestly believed that her husband would soon return to work and that she would then be able to repay the credit card company.

A similar result was reached in *In re Manning*,[4] wherein the court held that balance transfers from one credit card account to another made within 60 days prior the filing of the bankruptcy were not excepted from discharge where the transfers were made to obtain lower interest

---

[Section 33:22]

[1]In re Koch, 83 B.R. 898 (Bankr. E.D. Pa. 1988); In re Faulk, 69 B.R. 743 (Bankr. N.D. Ind. 1986); In re Pittman, 41 B.R. 382 (Bankr. W.D. Mo. 1984) (after looking at facts, court found debts dischargeable).

[2]In re Kitzmiller, 206 B.R. 424 (Bankr. N.D. W. Va. 1997).

[3]In re Kitzmiller, 206 B.R. 424 (Bankr. N.D. W. Va. 1997).

[4]In re Manning, 280 B.R. 171 (Bankr. S.D. Ohio 2002).

rates in order to keep the debtor afloat financially until payments obligations imposed upon the debtor by a divorce court had ended.

In re Kitzmiller and *In re Manning* represent common fact patterns that the practitioner is likely to face. Credit card companies often use the threat of dischargeability proceedings and the knowledge that most debtors cannot afford to defend such cases as a hammer to force debtors into repaying otherwise dischargeable debt. These type of cases can be won, and in many cases the credit card company's position is not justified. Knowledgeable debtor's counsel should carefully consider all of the facts of the case and review the authorities before recommending settlement.

§ 33:23 Chapter 7—Dischargeability—Debts incurred by fraud—Dealing with credit card abuse case—Recovery of counsel fees

The practitioner should also be aware of 11 U.S.C.A. § 523(d), which provides that if a creditor requests a determination as to dischargeability of a consumer debt under 11 U.S.C.A. § 523(a)(2), and such debt is discharged, the court shall award the debtor his counsel fees and costs in defending the action if the court finds that the creditor's position was not substantially justified.[1]

Thus, in *In re Arroyo*,[2] the credit card company sent the debtor an unsolicited, pre-approved credit card with a credit line of $5,000. The credit card company never evaluated the debtor for credit worthiness, ability to pay, or whether or not he should, in fact, even be given the card in the first place. The credit card company presented no proof of a misrepresentation or intent not to pay, let alone any evidence as to their reliance.

On the other hand, the debtor testified that he always intended to repay the credit card company, but that two incidents in his life, a financially devastating divorce and subsequent heart attack which

---

[Section 33:23]

[1]See, e.g., In re Stahl, 222 B.R. 497 (Bankr. W.D. N.C. 1998) (creditor not justified in filing dischargeability action and ordered to pay debtor's counsel fees where original credit application indicated debtor was unemployed, debtor had no balance on the account, and where issuer raised credit limit and gave debtor unsolicited checks of $3,000 and $1,000 to draw upon credit card account); In re Cameron, 219 B.R. 531 (Bankr. W.D. Mo. 1998) (dischargeability complaint not substantially justified and counsel fees in the amount of $6,132.95, awarded where debtor, having no balance on a credit card with a $3,000 credit line, received an unsolicited increase in the credit line to $11,000 and a letter advising that a balance transfer of about $8,000 existing on debtor's other credit cards had been preapproved); In re Akins, 235 B.R. 866 (Bankr. W.D. Tex. 1999) (dischargeability complaint held not substantially justified and counsel fees awarded where credit card issuer send the debtor unsolicited checks to be drawn against her credit card account, and before using same, the debtor called the credit card issuer and formally obtained permission to use a check to obtain $4,000 to pay bills. The credit card company never asked about the nature or amount of the bills or the debtor's current financial situation, but, instead, granted permission based upon a credit report that they obtained).

[2]In re Arroyo, 205 B.R. 984 (Bankr. S.D. Fla. 1997).

impaired is ability to work, precipitated the bankruptcy.

The court held that the credit card was dischargeable because the credit card company did not present any evidence of a misrepresentation or intent not to pay. In addition, the court found that because the creditor did not investigate the credit worthiness of potential customers before issuing credit cards, and because it conducted minimal discovery before filing the adversary proceeding to deny discharge and Arroyo, the filing of the complaint was not substantially justified. It awarded the debtor counsel fees in the sum of $7,200, and a further fee enhancement in the sum of $5,000.

A similar result occurred in the case of *In re Stansel.*[3] Here, again, the credit card company not only failed to prevail in the dischargeability proceeding, but was ordered to pay the debtor's counsel fees in the amount of $3,340.

In *In re Stansel*, the credit card company sent the debtor a credit card with a credit limit of $3,200. Some two years later, the debtor and her fiance began living together. In June, 1995, they purchased a home together.

On September 12, 1995, the debtor took a $2,000 cash advance, and on September 15, 1995, she took an additional cash advance. Both of these cash advances were obtained after the credit card company's telephonic pre-approval. During the months of September and October 1995, the debtor also made charges totaling $561, thus giving her a balance of $3,639.95 inclusive of finance charges.

Prior to the cash advances the debtor's credit card account had a zero balance, and she had twice paid off her credit card balances in the past. The debtor testified that the cash advances were used to pay for wedding expenses. Although the debtor had exceeded her credit limit and thereafter missed some monthly payments, the credit card company did not terminate or revoke her credit card privileges.

The debtor and her husband jointly earned about $33,000 in 1995. The debtor testified that she first considered bankruptcy in November 1995, after returning from her honeymoon. The Chapter 7 was filed in January 1996.

The court found for the debtor. The court said that it could not imply a misrepresentation merely based upon an alleged inability to pay. There was no showing that when the debtor obtained the cash advances and made the charges that she intended at that time to later file bankruptcy and relieve herself of the debt. The court found that the debtor testified truthfully and honestly when she said that she believed that she was capable of repaying her credit card bill as she had done in the past. The credit card company presented little evidence of fraud other than the fact that the cash advances and charges were made within four months of the filing of the bankruptcy.

The court also found that the filing of the adversary proceeding was not substantially justified. The credit card company did not send a rep-

---

[3]In re Stansel, 203 B.R. 339 (Bankr. M.D. Fla. 1996).

resentative to the meeting of creditors to question the debtor about her credit use, and did not conduct a Rule 2004 examination of the debtor prior to filing the complaint. It filed the adversary proceeding solely upon the basis that the cash advances were taken within four months of the filing of the bankruptcy without first determining whether it could prove fraud on the part of the debtor.

In re Arroyo and *In re Stansel* represent common fact patterns that the practitioner is likely to face. As noted above, credit card companies often use the threat of dischargeability proceedings and the knowledge that most debtors cannot afford to defend such cases as a hammer to force debtors into repaying otherwise dischargeable debt. Given that counsel fees are available to debtor's counsel in these types of cases, counsel should carefully consider all of the facts of the case and review the authorities before recommending settlement.

§ 33:24   Chapter 7—Dischargeability—Debts incurred by fraud—Dealing with credit card abuse case—NSF checks

Another common problem which arises is that of the bad or NSF check. Here, again, *Fields v. Mann*[1] controls. The objecting creditor must prove that the debtor subjectively intended to defraud.[2] The mere utterance of a bad check, without more, is insufficient to except the debt from discharge under 11 U.S.C.A. § 523(a)(2)(A).[3] The determination of whether a debtor actually intended to defraud is a factual question resolved by reviewing all of the facts and circumstances of the case.[4] Thus, a knowing tender of a bad check by a hopelessly insolvent debtor will result in a finding of nondischargeability,[5] while liability upon an NSF check will be dischargeable when brought about by bookkeeping errors.[6]

§ 33:25   Chapter 7—Dischargeability—Alimony, maintenance, and support

It is an unfortunate but true fact that the financial distress that accompanies divorce can be so devastating that the former spouse must seek refuge from his or her creditors by filing for relief under Chapter 7.

Until 1994, the rules in bankruptcy were superficially simple: obligations in the nature of spousal and child support were nondischargeable

---

[Section 33:24]

[1]Field v. Mans, 516 U.S. 59, 116 S. Ct. 437, 133 L. Ed. 2d 351 (1995).

[2]In re Paul, 266 B.R. 686 (Bankr. N.D. Ill. 2001).

[3]In re Sanchez, 277 B.R. 904, 908 (Bankr. N.D. Ill. 2002); In re Paul, 266 B.R. 686, 694 (Bankr. N.D. Ill. 2001).

[4]In re Paul, 266 B.R. 686, 694 (Bankr. N.D. Ill. 2001).

[5]In re Levitsky, 137 B.R. 288 (Bankr. E.D. Wis. 1992); In re Feldman, 111 B.R. 481 (Bankr. E.D. Pa. 1990).

[6]In re Degraffenreid, 131 B.R. 178 (Bankr. N.D. Okla. 1991); In re Boyer, 62 B.R. 648 (Bankr. D. Mont. 1986); In re Burgstaler, 58 B.R. 508 (Bankr. D. Minn. 1986); In re Hammett, 49 B.R. 553 (Bank. M.D. Fla. 1985).

and obligations in the nature of property division were dischargeable.[1]

In 1994 Congress hastily amended 11 U.S.C.A. § 523 by excepting from discharge any debt which is *not* in the nature of support but which was incurred by the debtor in the course of a divorce or separation or in connection with a separation agreement or divorce decree *unless* the debtor does not have the ability to pay such debt or discharging such debt would result in a benefit to the debtor that outweighs the consequences to the spouse, former spouse, or child of the debtor.[2]

This new section is a trap for the unwary. It has been described as a "paving stone on a road to the region of Hades reserved for litigation nightmares."[3] A practitioner must now be acutely aware that even a formerly dischargeable property settlement *may* still be nondischargeable in a subsequent Chapter 7 proceeding.[4] Cases decided before the 1994 amendments, finding a certain obligation under a divorce decree or separation agreement to be dischargeable must be viewed with a jaundiced eye.

The practitioner must remember that the plaintiff bears the burden of proof to prove nondischargeability under § 523(a) by a preponderance of the evidence,[5] and that exceptions to discharge are to be strictly construed against the creditor.[6] However, one exception to this principle of statutory construction is found in § 523(a)(5), in which the term "support" has been given a broad construction by most courts in order to promote the Congressional policy that favors the enforcement of obligations for spousal and child support.[7]

§ 33:26 Chapter 7—Dischargeability—Alimony, maintenance, and support—Spousal and child support obligations

11 U.S.C.A. § 523(a)(5) expressly provides for the nondischargeability of debts owed to a spouse, former spouse, or child of the debtor for

---

[Section 33:25]

[1]In re Fitzgerald, 9 F.3d 517 (6th Cir. 1993).

[2]11 U.S.C.A. § 523(a)(15).

[3]In re Smither, 194 B.R. 102, 106 (Bankr. W.D. Ky. 1996).

[4]Wiggins, *Testing the Limits of Congressional Intent: Divorce Obligations in Bankruptcy After the 1994 Reform Act*, 6 J. Bankr. L. & Prac. 181 (1997); Hanson, *Protection for Family Support, and Maintenance in Consumer Bankruptcies Under the 1994 Reform Act*, 69 Wisc. Law. 14 (Feb. 1996); Anderson, *Family Law Matters Under the Bankruptcy Reform Act of 1994*, 25 Colo Law. 27 (June, 1996); Leahy, *Divorce Settlements Are Now Non-Dischargeable; Or Are They?*, 22 Vt.B.J. & L. Dig. 29 (June, 1996); Maloy, *Does the New Exception to Discharge in Bankruptcy Give the Marital Creditor a Benefit or a Trompe L'Oeil?*, 6 J. Bankr. L. & Prac. 51 (Nov.-Dec. 1996); White, *Divorce After the Bankruptcy Reform Act of 1994: Can You Stay Warm After You Split the Blanket?*, 29 Creighton L. Rev. 617 (1996). Snyder, *Did Congress Really Know What it Was Doing? Problems Arising From New Child Support, Alimony and Property Settlement Rules*, 114 ABI J. 16 (February, 1995).

[5]Grogan v. Garner, 498 U.S. 279, 290-91, 111 S. Ct. 654, 112 L. Ed. 2d 755 (1991).

[6]In re Ward, 857 F.2d 1082, 1083 (6th Cir. 1988) (overruling recognized by, In re Stockard, 216 B.R. 237 (Bankr. M.D. Tenn. 1997)).

[7]In re LaRue, 204 B.R. 531, 533 (Bankr. E.D. Tenn. 1997).

alimony to, maintenance for, or support of such spouse in connection with a separation agreement, divorce decree, or other order of a court or property settlement agreement.

To be nondischargeable under § 523(a)(5), the obligation must actually be in the nature of support, as opposed to being part of a division of marital assets.[1] Obligations to pay or receive money as part of a property settlement are not covered by § 523(a)(5).[2] So, too, support obligations lose nondischargeable status under section 523(a)(5) if the debt or obligation is assigned to another entity, whether voluntarily or by operation of law. This does not include assignment to the federal government or a state or other political subdivision; debts assigned to a governmental agency retain their nondischargeable status.[3]

The dischargeability issue arises not only when direct payments are to be made to a former spouse. It is now well established that the typical "hold harmless" clause involving the assumption of joint obligations found in most separation agreements and divorce decrees can, under certain circumstances, create nondischargeable debt to third parties.[4] The obligation to pay the mortgage on the house the former wife lives in, for example, may or may not be "in the nature of support" and, hence, may or may not be dischargeable under section § 523(a)(5).[5]

It is, therefore, most important to understand the criteria by which bankruptcy courts determine whether obligations are "in the nature" of support and, therefore, nondischargeable under § 523(a)(5). This is because the court is not bound by a state court's characterization or determination of an award as being either support or a property

---

[Section 33:26]

[1]11 U.S.C.A. § 523(a)(5)(B). In re Calhoun, 715 F.2d 1103 (6th Cir. 1983); See, for example, In re Szuch, 117 B.R. 296 (Bankr. N.D. Ohio 1990) (obligation to pay second mortgage on marital home and to hold harmless on obligations to the Internal Revenue Service held nondischargeable).

[2]See, e.g., In re Mallin, 137 B.R. 673 (Bankr. N.D. Ohio 1992) (obligation to hold former spouse harmless on debt secured by second mortgage on former marital residence held dischargeable); In re Lever, 137 B.R. 243 (Bankr. N.D. Ohio 1992) (judgment against debtor for failure to pay his share of escrow deficit resulting from sale of former marital residence held not exempt from discharge); In re Kreitzer, 130 B.R. 505 (Bankr. S.D. Ohio 1991) (obligation to pay former spouse specified amount in satisfaction of wife's interest in jointly owned marital stock held dischargeable); In re Cornett, 123 B.R. 776 (Bankr. N.D. Ohio 1990) (debt to pay mortgage held dischargeable as being part of a property settlement).

[3]11 U.S.C.A. § 523(a)(5)(A). Matter of Seibert, 914 F.2d 102 (7th Cir. 1990); See, also, In re Lhamon, 139 B.R. 649 (Bank. N.D. Ohio 1991) (child support arrearage obligation to county department of human services held nondischargeable even though debtor remarried his former wife); In re Jones, 94 B.R. 99 (Bankr. N.D. Ohio 1988) (debt owed to Ohio Bureau of support for ADC benefits paid as support for minor child held nondischargeable). See, generally, Fraas, *Assignment Makes Maintenance Dischargeable in Bankruptcy*, 7 Mo. Law Weekly 1 (May 3, 1993).

[4]In re Calhoun, 715 F.2d 1103 (6th Cir. 1983); In re Gibson, 291 B.R. 195, 199 (B. A.P. 6th Cir. 1998); In re Slygh, 244 B.R. 410, 414 (Bankr. N.D. Ohio 2000).

[5]Compare In re Szuch, 117 B.R. 296 (Bankr. N.D. Ohio 1990) (obligation to pay second mortgage nondischargeable) with In re Cornett, 123 B.R. 776 (Bankr. N.D. Ohio 1990) (obligation to pay mortgage held dischargeable).

settlement.[6] The issue of whether a debt is "in the nature of alimony, maintenance or support" as opposed to property settlement, is to be determined by federal bankruptcy law.[7]

The starting point for every practitioner in the area of dischargeability of alimony/support obligations under § 523(a)(5) is the case of *In re Calhoun*,[8] which involved the issue of whether the payment of joint obligations was "in the nature of alimony, maintenance and support" and, therefore, dischargeable. However, its holding has been extended to all forms of alimony, maintenance, and support.[9]

As set forth in *Calhoun*, the criteria for determining whether payments by a debtor are in the nature of alimony/support or are instead a property settlement are as follows:

(1) Whether the parties or the state court intended to create a support obligation;

(2) Whether the support provision has the effect of providing support;

(3) Whether the amount of support is so excessive so as to be unreasonable; and

(4) If the amount of support is unreasonable, how much should be characterized as nondischargeable for purposes of federal bankruptcy law.[10]

Some seven years later the Sixth Circuit had reason to reconsider its holding in *Calhoun* In the case of *In re Fitzgerald*,[11] the court retreated from its decision in *Calhoun* to the extent that it eliminated the "present needs" test set forth in *Calhoun*

The court in the *Fitzgerald* case eliminated the analytic framework in *Calhoun* which flowed from the "present needs" test. As a result, the issue in § 523(a)(5) litigation was limited to determining whether, at the time of the divorce, the state domestic relations court or, in the case of a separation agreement, the parties, intended to create a support obligation or to bring about a property settlement. The current financial condition and the "fairness" of the support obligation ceased to be at issue in

---

[6]In re Schultz, 204 B.R. 275 (D. Mass. 1996); Matter of Daugherty, 117 B.R. 515, 517 (Bankr. D. Neb. 1990).

[7]In re Calhoun, 715 F.2d 1103 (6th Cir. 1983); In re Slygh, 244 B.R. 410, 414 (Bankr. N.D. Ohio 2000).

[8]In re Calhoun, 715 F.2d 1103 (6th Cir. 1983).

[9]In re Singer, 787 F.2d 1033 (6th Cir. 1986); In re Helm, 48 B.R. 215 (Bankr. W.D. Ky. 1985), reconsideration overruled, 49 B.R. 573 (Bankr. W.D. Ky. 1985); In re Sullivan, 62 B.R. 465 (Bankr. N.D. Miss. 1986); In re Elder, 48 B.R. 414 (Bankr. W.D. Ky. 1985).

[10]See In re Singer, 787 F.2d 1033 (6th Cir. 1986); In re Helm, 48 B.R. 215 (Bankr. W.D. Ky. 1985), reconsideration overruled, 49 B.R. 573 (Bankr. W.D. Ky. 1985).

[11]In re Fitzgerald, 9 F.3d 517 (6th Cir. 1993).

§ 523(a)(5) litigation.[12]

Later, in *In re Sorah*,[13] the Sixth Circuit admonished bankruptcy courts not to sit as "super" divorce courts. Rather, the court said, the bankruptcy court must give substantial weight to the characterization of the financial arrangements as either support or property split made by the parties and the domestic relations court.[14]

Thus, where an award is designated as support and has all the indicia of a support obligation, it is conclusively presumed to be support. Under the holding in *Sorah*, the court order or separation agreement must be examined to determine if, for example, any of the follow indicia are present: (1) a label such as alimony, support or maintenance in the divorce decree or separation agreement; (2) a direct payment to a spouse as opposed to the assumption of debt owed to third parties; and (3) whether payments are contingent upon such events as death, remarriage, or eligibility for Social Security Benefits.[15]

An award that is designated as support by the state court and that has the indicia of a support obligation is conclusively considered to be a support obligation. However, where the award is not clearly labeled as support, the court may still inquire as to other factors in determining the intent of the parties or the state court. Such includes, for example: (1) the disparity of earning power between the parties; (2) the need for economic support and stability; (3) the presence of minor children; (4) marital fault; (5) the length of the marriage; (6) the age, health, and work skills of the parties; and (7) the adequacy of support absent the debt assumption.[16]

Once it is determined that the award is in the nature of support, the burden shifts to the debtor spouse to demonstrate that although the obligation is of the *type* that may not be discharged in bankruptcy, the *amount* of the obligation is unreasonable in light of the debtor's financial circumstances.[17] The debtor may not introduce evidence as to the non-debtor spouse's need for support or the fairness of the support award, either at the time the obligation arose or at the time of the bankruptcy proceeding.[18]

The debtor spouse is limited to demonstrating that the obligation is unreasonable in light of the *debtor's* financial circumstances. The court may consider evidence that the obligation is unreasonable and discharge it to *the extent* that is exceeds what the debtor can reasonably be

---

[12]But see In re Perlin, 30 F.3d 39, 1994 FED App. 241P (6th Cir. 1994), wherein a different panel of the Sixth Circuit cited the *Calhoun* case but ignored the *Fitzgerald* case in deciding a section 523(a)(5) dischargeability issue.

[13]In re Sorah, 163 F.3d 397, 1998 FED App. 375P (6th Cir. 1998).

[14]In re Sorah, 163 F.3d 397, 1998 FED App. 375P (6th Cir. 1998); In re Findley, 245 B.R. 526, 528 (Bankr. N.D. Ohio 2000).

[15]In re Sorah, 163 F.3d 397, 401, 1998 FED App. 375P (6th Cir. 1998).

[16]In re Luman, 238 B.R. 697, 706 (Bankr. N.D. Ohio 1999), cited with approval in In re Bailey, 254 B.R. 901, 2000 FED App. 13P (B.A.P. 6th Cir. 2000).

[17]In re Sorah, 163 F.3d 397, 401, 1998 FED App. 375P (6th Cir. 1998).

[18]In re Sorah, 163 F.3d 397, 401-02, 1998 FED App. 375P (6th Cir. 1998).

expected to pay. However, the bankruptcy court must not second guess the state domestic relations court absent evidence that the burden on the debtor spouse is excessive.[19]

It is evident that, given the comprehensive nature of these factors, each case must turn on its own facts.[20] Therefore, great care must be given when drafting separation agreement. Several examples are offered below.

For example, in *In re Hayes*,[21] the state court divorce decree, incorporating a separation agreement, required the debtor to assume and hold his former spouse harmless from liability upon certain credit card debts totaling about $29,000. The separation agreement specifically stated that ". . .the minimum payment required by the credit card companies shall be treated as spousal support. . . ." When the debtor failed to make these payments, the state court subsequently modified this payment obligation by requiring the debtor to make payments directly to the former spouse until the credit card debts were paid.

The court held that this obligation was in the nature of nondischargeable support. The court found that the first and second *Sorah* factors were satisfied in that the award was clearly labeled as support, and the obligation was payable directly to the former spouse.

Although the payment was not conditioned upon the death or remarriage of the former spouse, the court looked to other traditional indicia of support and determined that the parties intended a support obligation. Significantly, the former spouse was not employed at the time of the divorce. Although she had been a nursing student, a back injury prevented her from pursuing a career in nursing. Thereafter, the former spouse changed her major and obtained a degree in education. The court found the obligation was in the nature of temporary support payable while the former spouse obtained the necessary education to support herself.[22]

In *In re Chapman*,[23] the court found that the joint marital debts assumed by the debtor under a divorce judgment entry came within the discharge exception for support where the former wife's retention of the house was necessary as support for the minor children, nonpayment of the debts could result in attachment of the house by creditors, the former wife lacked sufficient income to enable her to pay the marital debts, and the hold harmless provision of the entry stated that bankruptcy should not be undertaken if it would affect the former wife's ownership of the house.

---

[19]In re Sorah, 163 F.3d 397, 401-02, 1998 FED App. 375P (6th Cir. 1998).

[20]69 A.L.R. Fed. 403 § 4.5 See, e.g., "Debtors for alimony, maintenance and support as exceptions to bankruptcy discharge, under § 523(a)(5) of the Bankruptcy Code, etc.".

[21]In re Hayes, 235 B.R. 885 (Bankr. W.D. Tenn. 1999). See, also, In re Findley, 235 B.R. 526 (Bankr. N.D. Ohio 2000).

[22]In re Hayes, 235 B.R. 885, 892-893 (Bank. W.D. Tenn. 1999).

[23]In re Chapman, 187 B.R. 573 (Bankr. N.D. Ohio 1995).

Similarly, in *In re Leslie*,[24] the debtor's obligation under the divorce decree to pay a credit line represented a nondischargeable support obligation where the credit line encumbered the marital home, the former wife lived in the marital home, the marriage was of long duration, the former wife had custody of the minor children, and where the former spouse testified that she would be unable to meet daily living expenses absent payment of the credit line by her former husband.[25]

In *In re Spangler*,[26] the debtor was unable to discharge the joint loan on an automobile where the payment of this loan was necessary to enable the former wife to maintain employment.[27]

On the other hand, in *In re Jones*,[28] the debtor was awarded, as part of the divorce proceedings, the marital residence and ordered to pay, and hold his former spouse harmless, from any liability arising out of the two mortgages upon the home. The separation agreement specifically stated that ". . . all payments called for in this Agreement, including payment of marital obligations, shall be construed as spousal support and shall not be dischargeable in bankruptcy under 11 U.S.C.A. § 523(a)(5). . . ."

The court found that the obligation arising under the divorce decree to assume and hold the former spouse harmless from payment of the mortgage obligations were not in the nature of support, and determined them to be discharged.

In reaching this conclusion, the court first looked to the three part test set forth in the *Sorah* decision. The court found that the first branch of the *Sorah* test was satisfied because the clause in question was clearly labeled as being in the nature of support. However, the court noted that the clause in question failed the second and third parts of the *Sorah* standard because the payment was not a direct payment to the former spouse, and because the payment of the obligations was not conditioned upon death, remarriage or eligibility for Social Security benefits.

The court then stated that, given the strong public policy against discharging marital obligations, that a party that satisfies only one of the three indicia enumerated in the *Sorah* case was not automatically

---

[24]In re Leslie, 181 B.R. 317 (Bankr. N.D. Ohio 1995).

[25]See In re Williams, 189 B.R. 678 (Bankr. N.D. Ohio 1995) wherein the court did not permit the debtor to discharge his obligation under the divorce decree to pay certain joint credit card debts incurred during their 14-year marriage because it was clear that the parties intended such to be a support obligation in light of the disparity in their financial circumstances. The former wife had custody of the minor child, and the payment of these credit card bills would have the effect of providing the former wife and child with necessary support because her monthly living expenses exceeded her income. See, also, In re Friedrich, 158 B.R. 675 (Bankr. N.D. Ohio 1993) where, although the obligation to pay joint debts was characterized in the separation agreement as being a property settlement, the disparity in the parties income and the wife's residential needs led the court to find that the debtor's assumption of the joint debts was in the nature of support.

[26]In re Spangler, 139 B.R. 684 (Bankr. N.D. Ohio 1992).

[27]See In re Keeran, 112 B.R. 881 (Bankr. N.D. Ohio 1990) (payment of household appliance bills held nondischargeable).

[28]In re Jones, 265 B.R. 746 (Bankr. N.D. Ohio 2001).

precluded from a holding of dischargeability under § 523(a)(5). The court then looked to other factors to determine the intent of the clause, and found that the vast majority of the factors cut against a finding of nondischargeability. Specifically, the court found that the disparity of earning power of the parties was not great, the former spouse was in better physical health than the debtor, the debtor did not have a great deal of marketable job skills, and the former spouse's financial situation, although not great, were better than the debtors.[29]

Similarly, in *In re Hodge*,[30] the court held that the debtor's obligation under a state court divorce decree incorporating a separation agreement signed by the parties, to pay a certain finance company debt and to hold the former spouse harmless from same, was not a nondischargeable support obligation.

The court held that the state court order failed the *Sorah* test in that it did not contain any of the traditional indicia of support. Specifically, the court found that the clause in question was not labeled as support, and, in fact, the separation agreement specifically stated that both of the parties waived any claims against the other for support. The court also noted that the debt in question was not payable directly to the former spouse, and the payment was not conditioned upon the death, remarriage or eligibility for Social Security benefits. The mere fact that the former spouse was in precarious financial position, and thus had need for the debt to be paid by the debtor, the court said, was insufficient to transform the debt into one excepted from discharge under § 523(a)(5).[31]

A similar result was also reached in *In re Davis*.[32] In that case the parties were married for three years when divorce ensued. The debtor was awarded the marital residence and ordered to pay the mortgage debts and other joint marital debts, and to hold the former spouse harmless therefrom. The former spouse was awarded custody of the two minor children and the debtor was required to pay $679 per month for child support. The court specifically ordered that neither party pay support to the other.

The court held that the debtor's hold harmless obligation was not in the nature of support, and discharged the obligations as not being in the nature of support. The court based its decision on the fact that because the debtor was awarded the marital residence, his assumption of mortgage debts does not have the effect of providing support to his former spouse. The court was also influenced by the fact that the divorce decree specifically provided that both parties waived spousal support, and that the payment of the obligations did not terminate upon the death or remarriage of the former spouse. The court also noted that the hold harmless provision was located with those sections of the divorce decree dealing with division and distribution of marital property.

---

[29]In re Jones, 265 B.R. 746, 751-52 (Bankr. N.D. Ohio 2001).

[30]In re Hodge, 265 B.R. 908 (Bankr. N.D. Ohio 2001).

[31]In re Hodge, 265 B.R. 908, 911-12 (Bankr. N.D. Ohio 2001).

[32]In re Davis, 261 B.R. 659 (Bankr. S.D. Ohio 2001).

So, too, the court in *In re Semler*,[33] found that the husband's obligation to pay joint marital debts and to hold his former wife harmless was not intended to be in the nature of alimony and support, and hence dischargeable where the marriage was of short duration, no children were born to them, the debt assumption was not styled as support, the parties were represented by counsel, and no marital or family circumstances or disparity in income indicated the necessity for support.

Last, is the issue of attorney fees. It is generally held that the obligation to pay attorney fees to the former spouse or directly to counsel[34] imposed by a divorce decree is "in the nature of" support for dischargeability purposes.[35] This rule has been extended to attorney fees incurred by a former husband in seeking to enforce visitation rights.[36] Nonetheless, the obligation to pay such attorney fees must be tested by the *Calhoun-Fitzgerald-Sorah* factors to determine if it will be nondischargeable under section 523(a)(5).[37] It should be noted that attorney fees owed to the debtor's own attorney in the domestic relations case *are* dischargeable.[38]

§ 33:27 Chapter 7—Dischargeability—Alimony, maintenance, and support—Nondischargeable property settlements

Even if the court determines that the debt is not in the nature of support and, thus, subject to discharge under section 523(a)(5), the court must then look at the debt to determine if it is excepted from discharge under section 11 U.S.C.A. § 523(a)(15)(A) and (B).

These sections except from discharge any debt which is not in the nature of support but which was incurred by the debtor in the course of a divorce or separation or in connection with a separation agreement or divorce decree unless the debtor does not have the ability to pay such debt or discharging such debt would result in a benefit to the debtor that outweighs the consequences to the spouse, former spouse, or child of the debtor.[1]

---

[33]In re Semler, 147 B.R. 137 (Bankr. N.D. Ohio 1992).

[34]In re Kline, 65 F.3d 749 (8th Cir. 1995).

[35]In re Pinkstaff, 163 B.R. 504 (Bankr. N.D. Ohio 1994); In re Hodges, 139 B.R. 846 (Bankr. N.D. Ohio 1991); In re Rudicil, 125 B.R. 747 (Bankr. N.D. Ohio 1991). See, generally, Annotation, Debts for Alimony, Maintenance and Support as Exceptions to Bankruptcy Discharge Under § 23(a)(5) of the Bankruptcy Code of 1978 (11 U.S.C.A.S (a)(5), 69 A.L.R. Fed. 403 § 6[b] at 419-30 (1984).

[36]In re Lever, 137 B.R. 243 (Bankr. N.D. Ohio 1992).

[37]Matter of Joseph, 16 F.3d 86 (5th Cir. 1994); Matter of Balvich, 135 B.R. 323 (N.D. Ind. 1991); See, e.g., In re Shaw, 66 B.R. 399 (Bankr. N.D. Ohio 1986) (attorney fees held dischargeable). See, also, Raven & Rosen, The Dischargeability in Bankruptcy of Alimony, Maintenance and Support Obligations, 60 Am Bankr. L. J. (1986).

[38]In re Klein, 197 B.R. 760 (Bankr. E.D. N.Y. 1996).

[Section 33:27]
[1]11 U.S.C.A. § 523(a)(15).

§ 33:28 Chapter 7—Dischargeability—Alimony, maintenance, and support—Nondischargeable property settlements— Burden of proof

In section 523(a)(15) litigation the objecting creditor bears the burden of proof to establish that the debt was incurred by the debtor in the course of a divorce proceeding, was imposed by the court in that proceeding, and did not qualify as maintenance or support under § 523(a)(5).[1]

The cases are split as to who has the burden of proof under § 523(a)(15)(A) and (B) (Ability to Pay and Detriment tests). The majority of courts have held that the burden then shifts to the debtor to prove either of the exceptions to nondischargeability contained in § 523(a)(15)(A) or (B).[2] The debtor must make these showings by a preponderance of the evidence.[3] A minority of the courts would shift the burden upon these two issue to the creditor.[4]

§ 33:29 Chapter 7—Dischargeability—Alimony, maintenance, and support—Nondischargeable property settlements— Ability to pay test

Under 11 U.S.C.A. § 523(a)(15)(A), the debt is discharged if the debtor does not have an ability to pay the debt.[1] If the debtor is found to have some disposable income available to pay the debt, the debt will still be discharged unless it is ascertained that the debtor can realistically pay, after considering the total amount of indebtedness involved, the marital debts within a reasonable amount of time.[2] However, a court may discharge only a portion of the debt if the circumstances of a particular case would make it equitable to do so.[3]

This presents a number of issues for the practitioner. First of all, how is the "ability to pay" measured?

The majority view followed throughout the country is that the ability to pay under § 523(a)(15) is measured by a consideration of the debtor's

---

[Section 33:28]

[1]Barry Russell, Bankruptcy Evidence Manual, 2002 Ed., § 301.60(F) at 548 (West Pub. 2002).

[2]In re Molino, 225 B.R. 904 (B.A.P. 6th Cir. 1998); See, generally, Barry Russell, Bankruptcy Evidence Manual, 2002 Ed., § 301.60(F) at 548 (West, 2002).

[3]Matter of Crosswhite, , 884-885 (7th Cir. 1998); Matter of Gamble, , 226 (5th Cir. 1998); In re Molino, , 907 (B.A.P. 6th Cir. 1998); In re Slygh, 244 B.R. 410 (Bankr. N.D. Ohio 2000).

[4]Barry Russell, Bankruptcy Evidence Manual, 2002 Ed., § 301.60(F) at 548 (West Pub. 2002).

[Section 33:29]

[1]In re Calabrese, 277 B.R. 357, 361 (Bankr. N.D. Ohio 2002).

[2]In re Romer, 254 B.R. 207, 212 (Bankr. N.D. Ohio 2000); In re Melton, 238 B.R. 686, 695 (Bankr. N.D. Ohio 1999).

[3]In re Romer, 254 B.R. 207, 212 (Bankr. N.D. Ohio 2000); In re Miller, 247 B.R. 412, 415-16 (Bankr. N.D. Ohio 2000).

financial situation at trial[4] and the debtor's future earning capacity.[5] The court may consider the debtor's prior employment, future employment opportunities, and health status to determine the current and future earning status of the debtor.[6] A debtor's income is measured by his realistic earning potential, not by lifestyle or other choices which restrict income. Where a debtor has chosen not to work or to work at a reduced salary, the court may measure the ability to pay by earning potential rather than actual income.[7] Only living expenses reasonably necessary for the support of the debtor and debtor's dependents will be considered in calculating whether the debtor is able to pay the debt arising from the divorce decree or separation agreement.[8]

In *In re Armstrong*,[9] the court listed nine factors that should be examined in determining whether a debtor has the ability to pay an obligation incurred in a divorce proceeding. These include (1) the debtor's disposable income as measured at the time of trial; (2) the presence of more lucrative employment opportunities which might enable the debtor to fully satisfy the divorce-related obligation; (3) the extent to which the debtor's burden of debt will be lessened in the near term; (4) the extent to which the debtor made a good faith effort towards satisfying the debt in question; (5) the amount of the debts which the debtor seeks to have held dischargeable and the repayment terms and conditions of these debts; (6) the value and nature of any property that the debtor retained after the bankruptcy filing; (7) the amount of reasonable and necessary expenses which the debtor must incur for the support of the debtor, the debtor's dependents and the continuation, preservation and operation of the debtor's business, if any; (8) the income of debtor's new spouse, as such income should be included in the calculation of the debtor's disposable income; and (9) any evidence of probable changes in debtor's expenses.

Second, should the income of the debtor's current spouse be considered? Some courts hold that income of the current spouse should not be considered in determining whether the debtor has the ability to pay the debt.[10] Many courts take a contrary view, holding that they cannot determine how much of the debtor's income is truly necessary for the debtor and his dependents without inquiring into whether or not, and

---

[4]In re Cordia, 280 B.R. 138, 146 (Bankr. N.D. Ohio 2001).

[5]In re Myrvang, 232 F.3d. 1116, 1120, fn. 3 (9th Cir. 2000); Matter of Gamble, 143 F.3d 223, 226 (5th Cir. 1998); In re Jodoin, 209 B.R. 132, 142 (B.A.P. 9th Cir. 1997) (disposable income test provides "excellent reference point" for determining ability to pay). See, also, In re Osborne, 262 B.R. 435 (Bankr. E.D. Tenn. 2001); In re Konick, 236 B.R. 524, 527 (B.A.P. 1st Cir. 1999); In re Greenwalt, 200 B.R. 909, 913 (Bankr. W.D. Wash. 1996).

[6]In re Molino, 225 B.R. 904, 908 (B.A.P. 6th Cir. 1998).

[7]In re Slygh, 244 B.R. 410, 416 (Bankr. N.D. Ohio 2000).

[8]In re Dunn, 225 B.R. 393, 399-400 (Bankr. S.D. Ohio 1998).

[9]In re Armstrong, 205 B.R. 386, 392 (Bankr. W.D. Tenn. 1996).

[10]In re Carter, 189 B.R. 521 (Bankr. M.D. Fla. 1995).

how much, the new spouse is contributing to the family's maintenance.[11]

Third, at what date is the debtor's income measured? The most courts measure from the time of trial,[12] although some courts have used the date of the complaint to determine dischargeability,[13] and the date of the bankruptcy petition.[14] Still other courts considered the debtor's current and future financial circumstances rather than at any one fixed point in time.[15]

§33:30 Chapter 7—Dischargeability—Alimony, maintenance, and support—Nondischargeable property settlements—Benefit/detriment balance test

Even if the court determines that the debtor has an ability to pay the debt, the inquiry does not end because discharge is still possible under 11 U.S.C.A. §523(a)(15)(B) if the court determines that the benefit to the debtor in getting a discharge outweighs the determent to the former spouse if such is granted. Stated another way, the benefit-detriment test requires the court to determine who will suffer more if the debt is discharged.[1]

In applying §523(a)(15)(B), courts generally review both parties financial statuses and standards of living. If the standards of living are relatively equal, or if the debtor enjoys a higher standard of living, the debt is not discharged. If, however, the repayment of the obligations would materially lessen the debtor's standard of living, the debt should be discharged.[2]

In conducting this analysis, the court must consider the current income, current expenses, current assets, current liabilities health, job skills, training, age and education of the debtor, objecting creditor, *and their respective spouses.*[3] An unreported decision of the Sixth Circuit

---

[11]In re Adams, 200 B.R. 630 (N.D. Ill. 1996); Matter of Cleveland, 198 B.R. 394 (Bankr. N.D. Ga. 1996); In re Slover, 191 B.R. 886 (Bankr. E.D. Okla. 1996); In re Woodworth, 187 B.R. 174 (Bankr. N.D. Ohio 1995).

[12]In re Cordia, 280 B.R. 138, 146 (Bankr. N.D. Ohio 2001); In re Christison, 201 B.R. 298 (Bankr. M.D. Fla. 1996); In re Greenwalt, 200 B.R. 909 (Bankr. W.D. Wash. 1996); In re Henderson, 200 B.R. 322 (Bankr. N.D. Ohio 1996); In re Morris, 197 B.R. 236 (Bankr. N.D. W. Va. 1996); In re Anthony, 190 B.R. 433 (Bankr. N.D. Ala. 1995); In re Hesson, 190 B.R. 229, 238 (Bankr. D. Md. 1995), as corrected, (Jan. 24, 1996).

[13]In re Hill, 184 B.R. 750, 754 (Bankr. N.D. Ill. 1995).

[14]In re Anthony, 194 B.R. 433 (Bank. N.D. Ala. 1995); In re Becker, 185 B.R. 567, 570 (Bankr. W.D. Mo. 1995).

[15]In re Craig, 196 B.R. 305 (Bankr. E.D. Va. 1996); In re Florez, 191 B.R. 112 (Bankr. N.D. Ill. 1995).

[Section 33:30]

[1]In re Shurelds, 276 B.R. 803, 808 (Bankr. N.D. Ohio 2001).

[2]In re Molino, 255 B.R. 904, 909 (6th Cir. BAP 1998); In re Cordia, 280 B.R. 138, 147 (Bankr. N.D. Ohio 2001).

[3]In re Smither, 194 B.R. 102 (Bankr. W.D. Ky. 1996). In re Celani, 194 B.R. 719 (Bankr. D. Conn. 1996); In re Gantz, 192 B.R. 932, 936, (Bankr. N.D. Ill. 1996) (income of debtor's new spouse may not be considered in determining ability to pay under section

Court of Appeals[4] adopted a nonexclusive list of eleven factors in determining the parties standard of living:

(1) The amount of debt involved, including payment terms

(2) The current income of the debtor, the objecting creditor and their respective spouses

(3) The current expenses of the debtor, the objecting creditor and their respective spouses

(4) The current assets, including exempt property, of the debtor, objecting creditor and their respective spouses

(5) The current liabilities, excluding those discharged by the debtor's bankruptcy, of the debtor, objecting creditor and their respective spouses

(6) The health, age, job skills, training and education of the debtor, the objecting creditor and their respective spouses

(7) The dependents of the debtor, objecting creditor and their respective spouses, their ages, and any special needs that they may have

(8) The amount of debt which has been or will be discharged in the debtor's bankruptcy

(9) Any change in the financial conditions of the debtor and the objecting creditor which may have occurred since the entry of the divorce decree

(10) Whether the objecting creditor is eligible for relief under the Bankruptcy Code

(11) Whether the parties have acted in good faith in the filing of the bankruptcy and the litigation under 11 U.S.C.A. § 523(a)(15) issues.

In addition, the financial contribution of any live-in companions must also be considered by the court.[5]

Based upon the foregoing, courts have discharged obligations where the former spouse is judgment proof or otherwise so deep in debt that a Chapter 7 filing by the former spouse is the only viable alternative.[6] However, as a general rule, each case must rise and fall upon its own particular facts.

§ 33:31 Chapter 7—Dischargeability—Fines and penalties

The Bankruptcy Code does not permit the discharge of a fine, penalty,

---

523(a)(15)(A) but may be considered in balancing the equities under section 523(a)(15)(B). See, also, In re Adams, 200 B.R. 630 (N.D. Ill. 1996) (error for the Bankruptcy Court not to consider the financial circumstances of the debtor's new wife).

[4]In re Patterson, 132 F.3d 33 (6th Cir. 1997), cited in and adopted by the court in In re Cordia, 280 B.R. 138, 147-48 (Bankr. N.D. Ohio 2001).

[5]Short v. Short, 232 F.3d 1018 (9th Cir. 2000); Matter of Crosswhite, 148 F.3d 879 (7th Cir. 1998).

[6]In re Morris, 193 B.R. 949, 955 (Bankr. S.D. Cal. 1996); In re Woodworth, 187 B.R. 174, 176-78 (Bankr. N.D. Ohio 1995); In re Hill, 184 B.R. 750, 756 (Bankr. N.D. Ill. 1995).

or forfeiture payable to or for the benefit of a governmental unit.[1] Thus, any obligation to pay a fine, penalty, or forfeiture owed to a governmental entity, such as traffic or parking fines, is nondischargeable,[2] as is restitution awards payable to the government Treasury for matters such as welfare fraud.[3]

On the other hand, criminal state court restitution awards to victims of crimes are not "for the benefit of a governmental unit", and hence, dischargeable.[4] Similarly, restitution payments ordered by a state court pursuant to state consumer protection laws are also dischargeable.[5]

Tax penalties are given separate treatment by the Code. They are nondischargeable only to the extent that the underlying tax is nondischargeable.[6] In addition, tax penalties imposed with respect to a transaction or event that occurred before three years before the filing of the bankruptcy are dischargeable.[7]

§ 33:32 Chapter 7—Dischargeability—Willful and malicious injury

11 U.S.C.A. § 523(a)(6) provides for the nondischargeability of debts arising out of the willful and malicious injury to the person or property of another. Recently the Supreme Court in *Kawaauhau v. Geiger*[1] indicated nondischargeability under this section requires a deliberate or intentional injury, not merely a deliberate or intentional act that leads to injury. This means that the actor must be shown to intend to cause the consequences of his actions or believes that the consequences are substantially certain to result from it.[2]

Thus, claims arising from intentional assault and battery will give rise to a nondischargeability[3] as do obligations flowing from the willful and malicious conversion of insurance checks due the debtor's physician

---

[Section 33:31]

[1]11 U.S.C.A. § 523(a)(7).

[2]11 U.S.C.A. § 523(a)(7). U.S. Dept. of Housing & Urban Development v. Cost Control Marketing & Sales Management of Virginia, Inc., 64 F.3d 920, 927-28 (4th Cir. 1995). This section applies to both civil and criminal fines. Pennsylvania Dept. of Public Welfare v. Davenport, 495 U.S. 552, 562, 110 S. Ct. 2126, 109 L. Ed. 2d 588 (1990) (overruling recognized by, In re Torwico Electronics, Inc., 131 B.R. 561 (Bankr. D. N.J. 1991)) and (overruling recognized by, People v. Kelley, 895 P.2d 1080 (Colo. Ct. App. 1994)).

[3]Kelly v. Robinson, 479 U.S. 36, 107 S. Ct. 353, 93 L. Ed. 2d 216 (1986).

[4]In re Rashid, 210 F.3d. 201 (3d Cir. 2000).

[5]Matter of Towers, 162 F.3d 952 (7th Cir. 1998).

[6]11 U.S.C.A. § 523(a)(7)(A).

[7]11 U.S.C.A. § 523(a)(7)(B).

[Section 33:32]

[1]Kawaauhau v. Geiger, 523 U.S. 57, 118 S. Ct. 974, 140 L. Ed. 2d 90 (1998).

[2]In re Markowitz, 190 F.3d 455, 1999 FED App. 343P (6th Cir. 1999). See In re Su, 259 B.R. 909 (B.A.P. 9th Cir. 2001), order aff'd, 290 F.3d 1140 (9th Cir. 2002).

[3]In re Baldwin, 245 B.R. 131 (B.A.P. 9th Cir. 2000), aff'd, 249 F.3d 912 (9th Cir. 2001); In re Smith, 270 B.R. 544 (Bankr. D. Mass. 2001) (judgment against debtor for sexual harassment); In re Mitchell, 256 B.R. 256 (Bankr. N.D. Ohio 2000).

per an assignment of insurance benefits.[4] On the other hand, debts arising from torts such as medical malpractice which are grounded in reckless or negligent conduct does not fall within the ambit of this section.[5]

Traditionally the deliberate sale of collateral and conversion of the proceeds by a debtor without paying the secured creditor gave rise to a nondischargeable debt.[6] However, since the decision in *Kawaahau*, these decisions may no longer represent good law.[7]

§ 33:33   Chapter 7—Dischargeability—Embezzlement, larceny, and fiduciary fraud

Another exception to discharge is based upon debts incurred through embezzlement or larceny, or for fraud or defalcation while acting in a fiduciary capacity.[1] The term "fiduciary" refers only to a trustee of an expressed trust, not to a constructive trust.[2] A fiduciary relationship also exists between shareholders of a corporation.[3] The attorney-client relationship also gives rise to a fiduciary relationship.[4]

§ 33:34   Chapter 7—Dischargeability—Driving while intoxicated

A recent amendment to 11 U.S.C.A. § 523(a)(9) excepts from discharge any debt for personal injuries or death caused by the debtor's operation of a motor vehicle if such was unlawful because the debtor was intoxicated from the use of alcohol, drugs, or any other substance.[1] For purposes of this statute, a snowmobile is considered a motor vehicle[2], as

---

[4]Compare In re Hopkins, 65 B.R. 967 (Bankr. N.D. Ill. 1986) (debt not dischargeable) with In re Kessnick, 174 B.R. 481 (S.D. Ohio 1994) (debt held dischargeable).

[5]Kawaauhau v. Geiger, 523 U.S. 57, 118 S. Ct. 974, 140 L. Ed. 2d 90 (1998); In re Markowitz, 190 F.3d 455, 1999 FED App. 343P (6th Cir. 1999); In re Su, 259 B.R. 909 (B.A.P. 9th Cir. 2001), order aff'd, 290 F.3d 1140 (9th Cir. 2002)

[6]Ford Motor Credit Co. v. Owens, 807 F.2d 1556 (11th Cir. 1987); Matter of Petsch, 82 B.R. 605 (Bankr. M.D. Fla. 1988); In re Lau, 140 B.R. 172 (Bankr. N.D. Ohio 1992). But see In re Crisafi, 205 B.R. 444 (Bankr. M.D. Fla. 1996) (goods purchased on Sears account) and In re Horldt, 86 B.R. 823 (Bankr. E.D. Pa. 1988) (debts discharged where consumer debtor did not understand the legal implications of a security agreement); Matter of Burdick, 65 B.R. 105 (Bankr. N.D. Ind. 1986) (debt not excepted from discharge as being a willful and malicious injury).

[7]In re Peklar, 260 F.3d. 1035 (9th Cir. 2001).

[Section 33:33]
[1]11 U.S.C.A. § 523(a)(4). In re Brady, 101 F.3d 1165, 1996 FED App. 379P (6th Cir. 1996); In re Needleman, 204 B.R. 524 (Bankr. S.D. Ohio 1997).

[2]In re Young, 91 F.3d 1367 (10th Cir. 1996); In re Long, 774 F.2d 875 (8th Cir. 1985).

[3]In re Frain, 230 F.3d 1014 (7th Cir. 2000).

[4]In re Hayes, 183 F.3d. 162 (2d Cir. 1999).

[Section 33:34]
[1]In re Barnes, 266 B.R. 397, 57 Fed. R. Evid. Serv. 938 (B.A.P. 8th Cir. 2001) (state law determines whether driver of vehicle legally intoxicated). In re Mellott, 187 B.R. 578 (Bankr. N.D. Ohio 1995).

[2]In re Dunn, 203 B.R. 414 (E.D. Mich. 1996).

is a motor boat.[3]

It should be noted that because of the wording of the statute, it appears that property damage claims are not excepted from discharge under this section; such may, however, still be nondischargeable as a willful and malicious injury under 11 U.S.C.A. § 523(a)(6).

§ 33:35 Chapter 7—Dischargeability—Multiple bankruptcies

A debtor cannot obtain a discharge in a Chapter 7 case if he or she was granted a discharge in a prior case commenced within six years of the filing of a current Chapter 7.[1]

Similarly, a debtor cannot obtain a discharge in a Chapter 7 if the debtor was granted a discharge in a prior Chapter 13 case commenced within six years of the present case unless all of the allowed unsecured claims were paid in full in such case, or, in the alternative, at least 70% of the allowed unsecured claims were paid and the plan was proposed in good faith and was the debtor's best efforts.[2]

Furthermore, even if more than six years passes before the filing of a second Chapter 7, a debtor cannot, on the grounds of res judicata and collateral estoppels, discharge a debt that was not discharged in a prior case. That is, if the debtor was denied a general discharge in the prior case, or if the court determined a particular debt to be excepted from discharge in such case, those debts cannot be discharged in a subsequent Chapter 7.[3] This exception does not, however, apply where the earlier denial of a discharge was based solely upon the failure to observe the six-year limitation on the filing of bankruptcy.

§ 33:36 Chapter 7—Dischargeability—Payment of restitution

11 U.S.C.A. § 523(a)(13) renders nondischargeable any ordered payment of restitution under Title 18, U.S.C.A., that is restitution ordered in federal criminal cases.

§ 33:37 Chapter 7—Dischargeability—Debts incurred to pay a federal tax

11 U.S.C.A. § 523(a)(14) exempts from discharge any debt incurred to pay a tax to the United States that would be otherwise nondischargeable. This section prohibits, for example, an individual from taking credit

---

[3]In re Soda, 261 B.R. 342 (Bankr. D. Conn. 2001).

[Section 33:35]
[1]11 U.S.C.A. § 727(a)(8). In re Belmore, 68 B.R. 889 (Bankr. M.D. Pa. 1987); Matter of Housler, 41 B.R. 455 (W.D. Pa. 1984). The six-year period is calculated from the date of the filing of the first case to the date of filing of the second case. The discharge date in the first case is irrelevant. In re Canganelli, 132 B.R. 369 (Bankr. N.D. Ind. 1991).

[2]11 U.S.C.A. § 727(a)(9).

[3]Matter of Housler, 41 B.R. 455, 456 (W.D. Pa. 1984).

card cash advances to pay nondischargeable taxes.[1]

§ 33:38 Chapter 7—Dischargeability—Debts for a condominium fee or assessment

11 U.S.C.A. § 523(a)(16) does not permit a fee or assessment that becomes due and payable after the filing of the petition to a membership organization with respect to a debtor's ownership in a dwelling unit that has condominium ownership to be discharged, but only if the debtor actually occupied the condominium, or rented the dwelling unit to a tenant and received payment from the tenant during such time period.

§ 33:39 Bankruptcy and the former spouse

A common situation which arises is that the husband is not meeting his obligations under the divorce decree and the former spouse files a motion for contempt in state court. The husband then files bankruptcy before the state court determines the contempt issues. The former spouse is properly scheduled as a creditor and is otherwise formally notified of the bankruptcy proceedings. Should she continue to prosecute the contempt proceedings?

The key to this problem lies in understanding what action is permitted by the automatic stay of 11 U.S.C.A. § 362(b)(2). The Bankruptcy Code expressly provides that the automatic stay does not apply to the collection of nondischargeable alimony, maintenance, or support from property that is not property of the bankruptcy estate.[1]

Thus, during the pendency of a Chapter 7 proceeding the former spouse is free to collect support arrearages from property that is not included with the Bankruptcy Code definition of "property of the estate", such as exempt property, post-petition wages, property acquired by the debtor after the commencement of the bankruptcy, and property abandoned by the Trustee. Collection efforts may not be directed at pre-petition wages or other property owned by the debtor at the time that the case was filed.[2]

In Chapter 13 cases post-petition wages are property of the estate.[3] The automatic stay precludes the collection of child or spousal support arrearages from post-petition earnings since such earnings are property

---

[Section 33:37]

[1]In re Chrusz, 196 B.R. 221 (Bankr. D. N.H. 1996) ($13,641.60 credit card access check deposited two days before check issued to I.R.S. in payment of taxes held nondischargeable.

[Section 33:39]

[1]11 U.S.C.A. § 362(b)(2).

[2]Matter of Daugherty, 117 B.R. 515, 517 (Bankr. D. Neb. 1990); In re Weidenhammer, 82 B.R. 383, 385 (Bankr. E.D. Pa. 1988).

[3]Carver v. Carver, 954 F.2d 1573, 1577 (11th Cir. 1992). See 11 U.S.C.A. § 541(a)(6) and 1306(a)(2).

of the estate.[4]

That does not mean that in the case of a Chapter 13 filing the former spouse is without a remedy. The Bankruptcy Code provides that unpaid support arrearages are priority obligations.[5] 11 U.S.C.A. § 1322(a)(2) requires that the Chapter 13 plan must provide for payment in full of all priority claims, including support arrearages.[6] Thus, a Chapter 13 plan cannot be confirmed unless it provides for payment of such claims in full.[7]

The Bankruptcy Code does not, however, permit collection efforts concerning nonsupport domestic relation obligations unless the debt is declared to be nondischargeable under section 11 U.S.C.A. § 523(a)(15). An individual that continues collection efforts regarding a dischargeable property settlement obligation runs the very real risk of being the subject of contempt proceedings in Bankruptcy Court for violating the automatic stay.

The practical problem for the former spouse of a debtor is that it is sometimes very difficult to determine whether a particular debt is for alimony, support, and maintenance, or, alternatively, whether it is a dischargeable or nondischargeable property settlement claim. The automatic stay would be violated by any attempt to collect any obligation other than for support or a nondischargeable property settlement obligation.

If there is any doubt as to whether 11 U.S.C.A. § 362(b)(2) applies, the prudent practitioner should seek a determination in the Bankruptcy Court that the obligation is, in fact, in the nature of support or a nondischargeable property settlement, and at the same time seek relief from the automatic stay prior to filing or continuing the action in state court.

For example, the case of *Brock*,[8] demonstrates what can happen when this advice is not heeded, and counsel incorrectly makes the judgment that the obligation is in the nature of support.

In *Brock*, a former a wife ignored the automatic stay of 11 U.S.C.A. § 362 and prosecuted the contempt matter in state court with the result that the debtor was incarcerated for three and one-half days.

The debtor thereafter filed a complaint in bankruptcy court to determine the dischargeability of the debt in question and to hold the former spouse in contempt for violating 11 U.S.C.A. § 362. The court found that the joint debt which the debtor failed to pay did not meet the *Calhoun* test and discharged the obligation to pay it. It also awarded the debtor damages from his former wife in the sum of $8,892.50 plus costs.

---

[4]In re Walter, 153 B.R. 38, 40 (Bankr. N.D. Ohio 1993); In re Lackey, 148 B.R. 626, 629 (Bankr. N.D. Ala. 1992); In re Henry, 143 B.R. 811, 814 (Bankr. W.D. Pa. 1992).

[5]11 U.S.C.A. § 507(a)(7).

[6]11 U.S.C.A. § 1322(a)(2).

[7]Matter of Olson, 200 B.R. 40 (Bankr. D. Neb. 1996); In re Beverly, 196 B.R. 128 (Bankr. W.D. Mo. 1996).

[8]Matter of Brock, 58 B.R. 797 (Bankr. S.D. Ohio 1986).

In a similar vane, in *In re Ray*,[9] a *pro se* spouse commenced and lost dischargeability proceedings in bankruptcy court, and, thereafter, with the help of counsel, prosecuted state court contempt proceeds against the debtor based upon the debtor's failure to pay those obligations which the bankruptcy court has ordered discharged. In subsequent contempt proceedings brought in the bankruptcy court against the former spouse and her counsel, the bankruptcy court found both the former and counsel to be in contempt of court for violating the discharge injunction and awarded monetary sanctions to the debtor. Because the former spouse acted upon the advice of counsel who had actual knowledge of the earlier dischargeability proceedings, the court ordered counsel to pay the sanction award.

In *In re Pody*,[10] a former wife made her own determination of dischargeability and continued to garnish her former husband's wages even after he filed bankruptcy and received his discharge. Upon timely filing of a complaint by the debtor to determine dischargeability and for contempt, the court held the underlying debt to be dischargeable as not being in the nature of support and ordered the wife to pay $500 in damages to the debtor.

Unfortunately, it is not always easy to determine the basis of the state court contempt proceedings. In *In re Maloney*,[11] for example, the court found that the automatic stay was not violated as to a Chapter 7 debtor ordered incarcerated for 90 days due to his failure to comply with terms of prior State Court contempt order requiring him to make payments to former wife as equitable distribution of marital property. The court held that the commitment order did not implicate any claim against the debtor by his former spouse, but was simply punishment for disregarding the state court's prior order.

One thing is clear, however, from the *Rollins* and *Maloney* cases discussed above. The wise course of action is to always seek relief from stay before proceeding. The case of *In re Weidenhammer*,[12] illustrates the proper procedure to be followed by an aggrieved former spouse. In that case the former wife filed a motion for relief from stay in the Bankruptcy Court asking that the stay be lifted so that she could commence state court proceedings to collect unpaid support. The court granted the motion, and the wife then presumably took the debtor back to state court.[13]

One final note. These same rules apply to the modification of nondischargeable support obligations during the bankruptcy proceedings. Modification proceedings cannot be commenced or litigated during the bankruptcy without first obtaining an order lifting the automatic stay

---

[9]In re Ray, 262 B.R. 580 (Bankr. D. Me. 2001).

[10]In re Pody, 42 B.R. 570 (Bankr. N.D. Ala. 1984).

[11]In re Maloney, 204 B.R. 671 (Bankr. E.D. N.Y. 1996).

[12]In re Weidenhammer, 82 B.R. 383 (Bankr. E.D. Pa. 1988).

[13]See, also, Matter of Daugherty, 117 B.R. 515 (Bankr. D. Neb. 1990),

from the Bankruptcy Court.[14]

Thus, in *In re Dexter*,[15] the former spouse brought an action in state court to both collect child support arrearages and to modify the support obligation. The debtor soon thereafter filed bankruptcy, but the former spouse continued to litigate in state court.

The debtor commenced contempt proceedings against his former wife. The court held that although the former wife's state court action to collect child support arrearages from the debtor was not barred by the automatic stay, her attempt to modify the support payment obligation was barred by the automatic stay, and she was adjudged to be in contempt of court. As all actions taken in violation of the automatic stay are void, the Bankruptcy Court voided the state court modification order.

---

[14]In re Stringer, 847 F.2d 549 (9th Cir. 1988). See Matter of Dexter, 116 B.R. 92 (Bankr. S.D. Ohio 1990). 11 U.S.C.A. § 362(d) permits the Bankruptcy Court to lift the automatic stay for "cause," and the modification of support may well be just cause for obtaining relief from the automatic stay. In re Weidenhammer, 82 B.R. 383, 386 (Bankr. E.D. Pa. 1988). Cf. In re Mac Donald, 755 F.2d 715, 717 (9th Cir. 1985) (the discretionary "cause" standard of section 362(d) permits debtor's former spouse to return to state court to modify final alimony and property award).

[15]Matter of Dexter, 116 B.R. 92 (Bankr. S.D. Ohio 1990).

Chapter 34

Role of Attorney: Ethics

By Beatrice K. Sowald, Esq.

> **KeyCite®:** Cases and other legal materials listed in KeyCite Scope can be researched through West Group's KeyCite service on Westlaw®. Use KeyCite to check citations for form, parallel references, prior and later history, and comprehensive citator information, including citations to other decisions and secondary materials.

§ 34:1   Code, canons, and rules

In the late 1960s, the American Bar Association promulgated a Code of Professional Responsibility to replace the Canons of Ethics which had been in existence for over half a century. This new Code, with some modifications and deletions, was adopted by the Ohio Supreme Court on October 5, 1970. Since then, the Court has adapted a number of amendments to the Ohio Code of Professional Responsibility.

This Code consists of canons, which are principles expressing general standards for professional conduct; ethical considerations (known as ECs), which are aspirational and provide guidance in many specific situations; and the disciplinary rules (D.R.s), which set forth the minimum levels of conduct and which are mandatory. If an attorney is found to have violated a disciplinary rule, one of four sanctions may be imposed. These include a public reprimand, a suspension from practice for a period of six months to two years, an indefinite suspension, or disbarment.[1] A lawyer who has been suspended for a specified period may also be placed on probation. If a lawyer who has been suspended for a specified period, placed on probation, or publicly reprimanded has a subsequent finding of misconduct, the discipline is upgraded to indefinite suspension or disbarment. A lawyer who has been suspended from the practice of law for an indefinite period may not file for reinstatement within two years from the date of the order suspending the lawyer from practice. A lawyer who is disbarred, and a lawyer who has voluntarily surrendered the license to practice law, shall never thereafter be admitted to practice law in Ohio.[2]

§ 34:2   Attorney disciplinary procedures

The procedure for a grievance brought against an attorney begins with the filing of a complaint by a grievant, either with a certified grievance committee as defined in the Rules for the Government of the Bar or with the Office of Disciplinary Counsel. Basically, a screening procedure occurs at various levels to determine if the matters of alleged misconduct are sufficiently serious to warrant investigation, and, after investigation, whether it is necessary to file a complaint. A complaint is a formal written allegation of misconduct.

Upon a demonstration of probable cause to believe a violation of a

---

[Section 34:1]
[1]Gov. Bar R. V § 7.
[2]Gov. Bar R. V § 8.

disciplinary rule has occurred, a complaint is filed by the certified grievance committee with the secretary of the Board of Commissioners on Grievances and Discipline of the Supreme Court. If no probable cause is found, the matter is dismissed, and the grievant or the judge or attorney is notified in writing.

Disciplinary Procedures are found in the Supreme Court Rules for the Government of the Bar, specifically Gov. Bar R. V. The rule sets forth the jurisdiction, power of board administration, investigation powers, proceedings, and sanctions. The procedural regulations of the Board of Commissioners on Grievance and Discipline (BCGD) are listed in Appendix II to the Rules for the Government of the Bar.

Until July 1, 1996, a certified grievance committee or the disciplinary counsel had the authority to determine that, while probable cause was not established, the grievance was "colorable," and that the conduct of the attorney, if repeated, could form the basis for a disciplinary violation. The grievance could then be retained on file for a period of two years from the date the grievance was received. This ability to retain a "colorable" grievance has been eliminated. Therefore, a dismissal is a dismissal with nothing remaining.

The Ohio Supreme Court cannot mandate that attorneys and judges read the canons, ethical considerations and disciplinary rules annually. The Supreme Court has mandated, however, that each attorney desiring to be in active practice have minimum continuing legal education of 24 credit hours each two-year reporting period, of which at least 2 hours of instruction are related to legal ethics and professional responsibility.[1] Those 2 hours should include at least 30 minutes of instruction on substance abuse. A publication of the list of names of attorneys who fail to obtain and maintain their continuing legal education requirement appears periodically in the Ohio Bar Association Reports.

A common mistake of an attorney under investigation, which can compound the attorney's problem, is a failure to cooperate or participate in the investigation. That failure violates Gov. Bar R. V § 4(G) which requires cooperation with a Certified Grievance Committee and provides "[n]o justice judge, or attorney shall neglect or refuse to assist or testify in an investigation or hearing."[2]

◆ **Practice Tip** If you, as an attorney, receive notice that a grievance has been made against you, do not delay in responding to all requests and inquiries from the grievance committee or Office of Disciplinary Counsel.

[Section 34:2]

[1]Gov. Bar R. X § 3(A).

[2]Cleveland Bar Assn. v. Harris, 96 Ohio St. 3d 138, 2002-Ohio-2988, 772 N.E.2d 621 (2002) (Attorney not only converted his client's alimony payments, he also repeatedly failed to respond to grievance committee inquiries during investigation); Columbus Bar Assn. v. Milless, 96 Ohio St. 3d 74, 2002-Ohio-3455, 771 N.E.2d 845 (2002) (failure to cooperate in relator's investigation).

§ 34:3 Attorney disciplinary procedures—Consent agreements

In an effort to permit resolution of certain complaints which are not egregious, and where all parties consent, Gov Bar R V Section 11(A)(3) permits the entering into a written agreement as to the existence of a disciplinary violation and a recommendation of discipline other than an indefinite suspension or disbarment. The regulations for the Consent to Discipline are listed in BCGD Reg section 11, effective May 1, 2001.

§ 34:4 Advertising by attorneys

A thorough and frequent reading of D.R. 2-101 is a must for the attorney practicing in the domestic area who chooses to advertise, especially since the advertising-related rules have been subject to change with each new pronouncement of the United States Supreme Court.[1]

The Ohio Supreme Court substantially modified the rules relating to advertising on March 1, 1986, and again on January 1, 1993. D.R. 2-101(A) bars a lawyer from using, in any form of public communication, false, fraudulent, misleading, deceptive, self-laudatory, or unfair statements. Public communication includes direct mail solicitation.

In an attempt to distinguish unacceptable fee advertising claims from acceptable ones, D.R. 2-101(A)(5) describes "cut rate," "lowest," "giveaway," "below cost," "discount," and "special" as being unacceptable and "reasonable" and "moderate" as being acceptable.

The rules of advertising are subject to constant modification. D.R. 2-105 provides that a lawyer may not hold himself out as a specialist (except in the areas of patent law, trademarks, and admiralty), but a lawyer may advertise that his practice is limited to a certain area.[2] The United States Supreme Court has held it is permissible for a lawyer to list areas of law in which he will accept cases.[3] D.R. 2-101(B) permits publication or broadcast of information as long as the information complies with D.R. 2-102 to D.R. 2-105, and is not false, fraudulent, misleading, or deceptive.

In 1993 D.R. 2-105 was amended to permit an attorney who is certified as a specialist in a particular field pursuant to Supreme Court Rules, to hold himself or herself out as a specialist in accordance with

---

[Section 34:4]

[1]Bates v. State Bar of Arizona, 433 U.S. 350, 97 S. Ct. 2691, 53 L. Ed. 2d 810 (1977) (blanket prohibition of advertising by attorneys is unconstitutional); Zauderer v. Office of Disciplinary Counsel of Supreme Court of Ohio, 471 U.S. 626, 105 S. Ct. 2265, 85 L. Ed. 2d 652 (1985) (restriction on use of illustrations in advertisement is unconstitutional); Shapero v. Kentucky Bar Ass'n, 486 U.S. 466, 108 S. Ct. 1916, 100 L. Ed. 2d 475 (1988) (states cannot ban personal letters from attorneys to potential clients known to need particular legal advice); Peel v. Attorney Registration and Disciplinary Com'n of Illinois, 496 U.S. 91, 110 S. Ct. 2281, 110 L. Ed. 2d 83 (1990) (attorney may use, on his letterhead, certification information if it represents an established and valid certifying institution).

[2]D.R. 2-105(A)(5).

[3]In re R. M. J., 455 U.S. 191, 102 S. Ct. 929, 71 L. Ed. 2d 64 (1982).

those rules.[4]

Television commercials including testimonials from former clients, along with statements regarding "no fee unless we win," violate D.R. 2-101(A)(3) and D.R. 2-101(E)(1)(c), resulting in a public reprimand.[5]

D.R. 2-101 permits a lawyer or law firm to advertise through newspapers, periodicals, trade journals, print media, outdoor advertising, radio and television, and written communication. Not specifically listed, but probably included in one of the above, would be marketing a firm or an attorney on a web site. Widespread use of the internet may actually lead to some specified policy regarding compliance with the ethical rules. If the communication reaches people who are represented by other counsel, it may violate another rule. In the event an attorney is engaging in direct mail solicitation, in addition to all disclaimers and standards, it must include in its text and on the envelope in red ink "advertisement only."

D.R. 2-101(F)(4) requires a lawyer, prior to making a solicitation of legal business to a defendant named in a law suit, to verify that the defendant has been served with notice of the action. In a domestic relations context, where ex parte restraining orders are commonly issued but are not effective until served, this provision may forestall dissipation or concealment of assets.

§ 34:5 Office sharing arrangements

Many lawyers in domestic practice enter office sharing arrangements with others; the savings in receptionist and book costs are worthwhile. However, it is not proper to list all lawyers party to this sort of arrangement on the letterhead unless they are in fact all partners. D.R. 2-102(C) is explicit. The reason for the rule is to avoid misleading the public. If the lawyer is a sole practitioner, the public should be aware of that. What happens if a lawyer, apparently in a partnership, commits malpractice? Are the apparent partners liable? RC 1775.15 states that any person holding himself out as a partner is liable to any creditor who extended credit to another partner and in doing so relied on the existence of a partnership.

§ 34:6 Letterhead

The name of a partnership and its letterhead may carry the names of deceased partners. However, there are different opinions as to whether it is improper to include names of laypersons, paralegals, investigators, and secretaries on the letterhead. A paralegal may sign a letter on the lawyer's letterhead, but only if the signer accurately identifies his

---

[4]See § 34:9, Specialization.

[5]Disciplinary Counsel v. Shane, 1998 -Ohio- 609, 81 Ohio St. 3d 494, 692 N.E.2d 571 (1998).

capacity.[1] The use of a lawyer's name on a letterhead followed by the words "and Associates" is proper only if there are associates. Also, before someone is listed as being "of counsel," it is prudent to be sure he meets the test set forth in D.R. 2-102(A)(4).

Under the Code, a lawyer may not practice under a trade name. Case law has modified D.R. 2-102(B) to the extent that the use of the term "Legal Clinic" in the name of a law firm was held not to be misleading or in violation of the D.R.s.[2] Now, D.R. 2-102(G) expressly allows the use of "legal clinic" as part of the name of a law office as long as all of the other requirements of the rule are met.

Letterhead information which is neither misleading nor deceptive is constitutionally protected commercial speech. In *Peel v. Attorney Registration and Disciplinary Commission of Illinois*,[3] the United States Supreme Court stated that the Illinois Commission improperly censured an attorney who indicated on his letterhead that he was certified by the National Board of Trial Advocacy as a civil trial specialist. In response to the *Peel* decision, D.R. 2-105(A)(5) now provides that, under certain enumerated conditions and circumstances, an attorney who has received certification from a private organization of special training, competence or experience may communicate that fact. The communication must disclose if the certifying organization has not been approved by the Ohio Supreme Court commission on Certification of Attorneys as Specialists.

§ 34:7 Organizational form of law firm

An attorney may practice law through a legal professional association, corporation, legal clinic, a limited liability company, or a partnership having limited liability. All of the above must be formed pursuant to the appropriate Revised Code sections[1] Attorneys who operate through a legal professional association or legal clinic must have their name end with the legend "Co., L.P.A." or immediately below it in legible form, the words "A Legal Professional Association." A firm operating as a corporation, limited liability company, or registered partnership must also include a descriptive designation as required under the appropriate sections of the Code.[2] Even if the attorney is participating in a legal professional association or other form, it will not relieve the attorney of the obligations under the ethics rules, and will not limit the attorney's liability for personal malpractice in violation of D.R. 6-102.[3]

It should be noted that while attorneys do not presently have any

---

[Section 34:6]

[1]American Bar Association Informal Opinion No. 1367 (June 15, 1976).

[2]Bates v. State Bar of Arizona, 433 U.S. 350, 97 S. Ct. 2691, 53 L. Ed. 2d 810 (1977).

[3]Peel v. Attorney Registration and Disciplinary Com'n of Illinois, 496 U.S. 91, 110 S. Ct. 2281, 110 L. Ed. 2d 83 (1990).

[Section 34:7]

[1]Gov. Bar R. III § 1.

[2]RC 1701.05(A), RC 1705.05(A), or RC 1775.62.

[3]Gov. Bar R. III § 3(C).

mandatory requirement to have professional liability insurance, an entity such as a legal professional association, corporation, legal clinic, limited liability company, or registered partnership, is required to maintain a specified amount of attorneys with professional liability insurance.[4] An attorney cannot practice law with more than one law firm, including a legal professional association, within the state at the same time.[5]

§ 34:8   Attorney liability insurance—Form[1] ⊙

Effective July 1, 2001, a lawyer who does not maintain professional liability insurance of at least one hundred thousand dollars per occurrence and three hundred thousand dollars in the aggregate, or if the lawyer's professional insurance is terminated, must inform the client of such non-coverage.[2]

The following notice, and accompanying client acknowledgement is set forth in the rule:

> Pursuant to D.R. 1-104 of the Ohio Code of Professional Responsibility, I am required to notify you that I do not maintain professional liability (malpractice) insurance of at least $100,000 per occurrence and $300,000 in the aggregate.

_____
Attorney's Signature

CLIENT ACKNOWLEDGMENT

I acknowledge receipt of the notice required by D.R. 1-104 of the Ohio Code of Professional Responsibility that *[insert attorney's name]* does not maintain professional liability (malpractice) insurance of at least $100,000 per occurrence and $300,000 in the aggregate.

_____
Client's Signature

_____
Date

NOTES TO FORM

Drafter's Notes

A copy of the notice signed by the client must be kept for five years. The rule does not apply to lawyers when acting as government employees or in-house counsel.

§ 34:9   Specialization

Effective January 1, 1993, the Supreme Court issued Gov. Bar R. XIV,

---

[4]Gov. Bar R. III § 4.

[5]Colaluca v. Climaco, Climaco, Seminatore, Lefkowitz & Garofoli Co., L.P.A., 1995 -Ohio- 70, 72 Ohio St. 3d 229, 648 N.E.2d 1341 (1995).

[Section 34:8]

[1]See also § 34:9, Specialization.

[2]D.R. 1-104, eff. 7-1-01.

Certification of Attorneys as Specialists. The stated purpose of the rule is to enhance the public access to appropriate legal services by regulating the certification of lawyers as specialists. The Supreme Court created the Commission on Certification of Attorneys as Specialists which established standards, called the Standards for Accreditation of Specialty Certification Programs for Lawyers, or ASCP Standards. By the middle of 1997, the Supreme Court had adopted standards that set forth the method by which a certifying organization can become an accredited organization. Some areas of specialization have been identified, but the list is not yet complete.

To become accredited as a certifying organization, the organization must apply to the Supreme Court of Ohio Commission on Certification, the organization that issues the accreditation. The appendix to the rules sets forth the regulations under which the certifying organization must operate, and what must be provided and completed prior to certifying that an individual attorney can hold himself or herself out as a specialist. The ASCP Standards require a statement of the organization's purpose, and the organization must be a not-for-profit organization with the purpose of identifying lawyers with enhanced level of skills. The organization will have a continuing responsibility to maintain the integrity of its speciality designation showing that it has a history of adequate financing, proof that the decision makers have competence, and that they apply uniform and nondiscriminatory requirements to the applicants. The certifying agency must require the lawyer seeking certification to demonstrate a satisfactory showing of experience through involvement in the speciality area; there must be peer review, educational experience, and a passing of a written examination.

It is interesting that while otherwise there is no state mandated requirement of liability insurance, an attorney wishing certification must show evidence of coverage by a professional liability insurance carrier in an amount of not less than $500,000 per loss.[1] There is an exception if the attorney can show that the lawyer's "practice relationship with the lawyer's clients will fully cover any professional liability claim made against the lawyer in an amount not less than [$500,000]."[2] It is unclear what that means. In addition, the attorney must furnish the certifying agency a signed certificate and acknowledgment of complying with all the requirements. An attorney wishing to be certified as a specialist, in addition to the requirements of the certifying agency, must have 12 hours of continuing legal education in each specialty area in addition to the 24 hours found in Gov. Bar R. X for every two-year period.

§ 34:10   Fees—In general

A large percentage of complaints against lawyers arise as a result of misunderstandings over fees. D.R. 2-106 addresses excessive fees, and

---

[Section 34:9]
[1]ASCP Std. 4.02(J).
[2]ASCP Std. 4.02(J)(4).

D.R. 2-107 provides rules for division of fees among lawyers. Generally, a lawyer shall not enter into an agreement for an illegal or clearly excessive fee, taking into account the guidelines set forth in D.R. 2-106.

Attorney fees are a matter of contract between the client and the client's attorney. While RC 3105.18 permits a trial court to award reasonable attorney fees from one party to another, it does not permit a court to determine the amount of the fees between the client and attorney. A domestic relations court exceeds its jurisdiction in limiting the fees attorneys can collect from their clients.[1]

§ 34:11 Fees—Retainer

The domestic practitioner runs the risk of violating D.R. 2-106 in the following situation. Assume the client comes in at 5:00 p.m. and wants a divorce. The lawyer interviews the client for an hour or so, takes down the pertinent information for the affidavits, and gets a retainer of $500. After the client leaves, the lawyer leaves also, planning to dictate the complaint and motions the next morning. At 8:30 a.m., before the lawyer proceeds on the complaint and motions, the client calls and says the divorce is no longer desired and asks if the $500 can be returned. In this situation the lawyer who refuses to return a portion of that money risks violation of D.R. 2-106.

This type of retainer must be distinguished from a retainer in the business world, for there the money is paid in advance to the lawyer in anticipation of future need. This prearranged employment insures the client that his lawyer will not be retained by a party which might result in a conflict of interest. Also, it compensates the lawyer for this assurance. In the domestic situation, the retainer is not really a retainer in that sense; it is "upfront" money to insure the lawyer's compensation. To the extent it is not earned by the lawyer, it should be returned to the client. There may be some justification for retaining part of the "retainer" under D.R. 2-106(B)(2), which reads as follows: "The likelihood . . . that the acceptance of the particular employment will preclude other employment by the lawyer." The attorney is at a disadvantage in that he or she is unable to represent the other spouse once having consulted with one party.

§ 34:12 Fees—Security for fees

Disciplinary Rule 5-103(A) permits an attorney to acquire a lien granted by law to secure the payment of fees and expenses. There are considered to be three types of liens: a retaining lien which attaches to a client's property in the lawyer's possession; a charging lien which is a lien on the proceeds of a claim; and a contractual lien which typically arises from a mortgage or security interest.

[Section 34:10]
[1]Zeefe v. Zeefe, 125 Ohio App. 3d 600, 709 N.E.2d 208 (8th Dist. Cuyahoga County 1998).

In *Foor v. Huntington National Bank*,[1] the court held that the attorney is entitled to a common law retaining lien, which attaches to all property, papers, documents, and moneys in the attorney's possession, for payment of fees and expenses. The retaining lien exists as leverage over the client and is generally discharged by payment, by voluntary relinquishment, or by wrongful termination of the attorney-client relationship or wrongful acts of the attorney. This lien must be balanced against D.R. 9-102(B)(4) and D.R. 2-110, both of which require the attorney to deliver to the client property to which the "client is entitled" when necessary to avoid foreseeable prejudice to the client. It could be argued that the client is not "entitled" until the fee is paid or security for the fee is posted.

However, the Supreme Court in *Reid, Johnson, Downs, Andrachik & Webster v. Lansberry*[2] , stated that "Along with the mandatory obligation to withdraw from a case when discharged, an attorney who is discharged must yield the case file. At the time appellant discharged the law firm, the firm was *required* to return his case file to him, and to cease any and all involvement in the case." The Court further stated that the law firm should not have imposed a requirement that the client execute a guarantee to obtain the release of the file, and that the guarantee was not enforceable.

The attorney-client relationship was found to be a consumer transaction, and the use of a cognovit note to secure the payment of fees was thus prohibited by RC 2323.13.[3] An attorney who takes a mortgage interest in real estate from his client to secure his fees, while a divorce case is pending and the attorney knows there is a restraining order on the client, acts improperly.[4]

§ 34:13   Fees—Contingent fees

There is no prohibition against contingency fees in domestic relations cases, and D.R. 5-103(A)(2) permits an attorney to contract with a client for a reasonable contingent fee in a civil case. Clearly, domestic relations cases are civil cases.

E.C. 2-19 states that contingent fees are rarely justified in the domestic area; however, justification for such fee arrangements may arise in instances in which the client is unable to pay a retainer or on an hourly basis.[1] In the Model Rules of Professional Conduct adopted by the American Bar Association, contingent fees measured by the amount of

---

[Section 34:12]

[1]Foor v. Huntington Nat. Bank, 27 Ohio App. 3d 76, 499 N.E.2d 1297 (10th Dist. Franklin County 1986).

[2]Reid, Johnson, Downes, Andrachik & Webster v. Lansberry, 1994 -Ohio- 512, 68 Ohio St. 3d 570, 574, 629 N.E.2d 431, 56 A.L.R.5th 813 (1994) (emphasis in original).

[3]Patton v. Diemer, 35 Ohio St. 3d 68, 518 N.E.2d 941 (1988).

[4]Van Hoy v. Van Hoy, 1992 WL 2912 (Ohio Ct. App. 6th Dist. Wood County 1992).

[Section 34:13]

[1]See also Gross v. Lamb, 1 Ohio App. 3d 1, 2, 437 N.E.2d 309 (10th Dist. Franklin County 1980) (fee contract for representation in a divorce action was for "the sum of ten

alimony, support, or property settlement are prohibited.[2] This seems to preclude a contingent agreement even for the collection of alimony and support arrearages.

§ 34:14   Fees—Division of fees

A lawyer cannot divide a fee with another lawyer who is not a partner or associate, unless the client first consents to such split fee after a full written disclosure of the proposed split. The fees are then divided in proportion to the work performed and responsibility assumed by each, assuming the total fee is not excessive.[1]

D.R. 2-107(A)(1) allows the fees to be split in any proportion if both lawyers assume full responsibility to the client and the client has signed a written agreement to that effect. The total fee must be reasonable. Payment of a referral fee must not increase the total sum beyond the standard of reasonableness. As in other areas of specialization, the ability of attorneys to "split a fee" should encourage the referral of family law cases to specialists. Additionally, it seems that the client need not be advised as to the precise fee splitting arrangement, presuming both lawyers are assuming full responsibility.

It is well established that a lawyer cannot compensate or give anything of value to a person or organization for recommending the lawyer to a client, except for dues to bar association referral services and similar organizations as set forth in D.R. 2-103.

In the event of a dispute between lawyers regarding division of fees, either between lawyers who have shared the work or when an attorney has left a firm, the attorneys must resolve the matter by mediation or arbitration. A dispute can also arise in the context of the firm first retained making claims to services under the original fee agreement which was probably on firm stationery. Pursuant to D.R. 2-107(B), disputed fees shall be divided in accordance with mediation or arbitration provided by a local bar association or the Ohio State Bar Association. This provision mandating referral to alternate dispute resolution, which was intended to prevent litigation between attorneys disputing fees, has been held to be constitutional.[2] The rationale is that the practice of law is a privilege, and the Supreme Court has the authority to enact rules for persons who wish to enjoy the privilege of practicing law in the State of Ohio.

---

percent (10%) of whatever financial settlement I receive . . . excluding awards of child support and personal property"; contract held not to be illegal nor violative of public policy; Model Rule 1.5(d)(1) prohibits a fee contingent on the securing of a divorce, or the amount of alimony or support awarded, or the size of the property settlement in lieu thereof).

[2]Rule 1.5(d)(1), Fees.

[Section 34:14]
[1]D.R. 2-107.

[2]Shimko v. Lobe, No. 96CVH02-1206 (Ohio Ct. C.P. 10th Dist. Franklin County 1996); see State ex rel. Shimko v. McMonagle, 92 Ohio St. 3d 426, 2001-Ohio-301, 751 N.E.2d 472 (2001) (for additional litigation and results).

D.R. 3-102 prohibits the division of legal fees with a non-lawyer except under the circumstances of payment to the estate of a decedent lawyer.

§ 34:15 Fees—Written agreement—In general

It is a good rule of practice that a lawyer, in all but very limited circumstances, present the client with the specific arrangements for the fees to be charged in writing. There is presently no requirement that a fee agreement be in writing, except if it is a contingent fee. RC 4705.15 requires an attorney, if representing a person in a tort action on a contingency fee basis, to provide the client with a written contingency fee agreement.

§ 34:16 Fees—Written agreement—Form⊚

FEE AGREEMENT

THIS AGREEMENT of legal representation is entered into by and between [_____] (hereinafter referred to as "Attorney") and [_____] (hereinafter referred to as "Client"), on this [_____] day of [_____], 20[_____].

1. Attorney agrees to represent Client relative to the following described activity:[_____]

2. Client agrees to pay Attorney on an hourly basis of [_____] [$_____]) per hour. Attorney will be charging for, but is not limited to, consultations, telephone calls, preparation of letters, pleadings and other documents, negotiations, case preparation, representation at depositions, hearings, trials and other court appearances; and any and all such other legal services as may be provided by Attorney. Further, work performed by Attorney's paralegal will be billed at [_____] [$_____]) Dollars per hour. Costs of copying, faxes, and postage on behalf of Client shall also be billed to Client.

3. Client shall pay to Attorney a refundable retainer of [_____] Dollars ($_____]). Said sum shall be applied toward the hourly fees set forth above. At such time as said retainer is exhausted during the representation of the Client then Client will be billed and pay an additional retainer or retainers in the same amount as the original retainer.

4. Attorney shall bill Client on a periodic basis for all fees then due and payable and Client agrees to make prompt and timely payments, in full, for said periodic billings. Unpaid delinquent bills will accrue interest at the statutory rate of interest. All billings are due upon receipt and Attorney reserves the right to withdraw as counsel for Client if any billing is not immediately paid.

5. Further, Client agrees to pay any and all costs and expenses of investigators, experts, expert witnesses, witness fees, filing fees, court costs, depositions, court reporters, and other such expenses as may be necessary and proper. Attorney shall, prior to incurring any such expense, obtain Client's approval for same and may require Client to deposit in Attorney's trust account a sum sufficient to cover all such

expenses prior to Attorney incurring same. Should Client refuse to deposit said sum, Attorney reserves the right to withdraw as counsel for Client.

6. Further, both parties understand and agree that the Attorney is only being hired to perform the task set forth above and Attorney's services do not include any representation or legal services which may hereafter be desired by Client relative to actions to enforce any judgments which may result herein, appeals to any court whether Client is appellee or appellant, post-judgment motions, or any other additional legal service, unless both Attorney and Client agree to such additional services being performed and a new Fee Agreement may be entered into for same. IN WITNESS WHEREOF, the above parties have hereunto set their hands on the day and date set forth above.

[————————————————] [————————————————]
Attorney   Client

§ 34:17 Withdrawal from employment—Prejudice to client

The rules for withdrawal from employment are set forth in D.R. 2-110. In withdrawing from a case, a lawyer must take reasonable steps to avoid foreseeable prejudice to the client's rights before withdrawing. The lawyer cannot withhold papers or matters to which the client is entitled. In addition, a lawyer must refund any part of a fee received from the client that has not been earned.

In addition to the attorney's responsibility for taking reasonable steps to avoid prejudice, a trial court abuses its discretion when it permits counsel to withdraw immediately prior to a show cause hearing and requires a party to proceed without benefit of counsel. In *Bennett v. Bennett*[1] the appellate court found that the trial court had a duty to enforce the mandates of D.R. 2-110(A)(1) and (2) D.R. 2-110(A)(2) and the trial court's own local rule, since the purpose of such rules was to assure that a client not be prejudiced as a result of withdrawal. There is, however, no constitutional right to counsel in a domestic relations matter, and thus a claim of ineffective assistance of counsel will fail.[2]

§ 34:18 Withdrawal from employment—Mandatory

A lawyer must withdraw from a case if (1) it is obvious the client is bringing the action to harass or injure a person maliciously; (2) it is obvious that continued representation will result in the lawyer violating a DR; (3) the lawyer cannot carry on for mental or physical reasons; or

---

[Section 34:17]

[1]Bennett v. Bennett, 86 Ohio App. 3d 343, 620 N.E.2d 1023 (8th Dist. Cuyahoga County 1993); Williams v. Williams, 2000 WL 678825 (Ohio Ct. App. 6th Dist. Lucas County 2000).

[2]Lynch v. Lynch, 1993 WL 35325 (Ohio Ct. App. 5th Dist. Fairfield County 1993).

(4) the lawyer is discharged by the client.[1]

§ 34:19 Withdrawal from employment—Permissive

A lawyer may withdraw only if (1) the client insists upon presenting a matter not warranted under existing law which cannot be supported by good faith argument; (2) the client insists the lawyer violate a law or DR; (3) the client renders it unreasonably difficult for the lawyer to operate effectively; (4) the client disregards the fee agreement; or (5) the client agrees to the withdrawal.[1]

§ 34:20 Confidences—In general

D.R. 4-101 sets forth the rules for the preservation of confidences and secrets of a client. Confidences are the matters protected by the attorney-client privilege[1] and include all communication made by a client to an attorney while the attorney-client relation exists, as well as the advice given. A secret is other information gained in the professional relationship that the client has requested not be revealed or the disclosure of which would embarrass or be detrimental to the client.

Generally, the rule is not to reveal anything, including the name of a client who has consulted with the lawyer, until such time as a case has been filed and the representation is then public knowledge.

A problem may arise for the family lawyer who has represented both spouses in separate matters in the past. For example, assume a lawyer represented the wife in setting up a small business and represented the husband in a drunk driving case; now, one of them has approached the lawyer for representation in a divorce action. In such a situation, the lawyer might find the opportunity to use matters learned in the prior representation of one spouse against the other spouse. In that event, the lawyer must withdraw.

It is of the utmost importance that the lawyer caution employees and others who may have access to protected information that they must abide by these rules as well.[2]

Care must also be given to the need for assuring secrecy and privacy in car and cellular phone communications. Attorneys like to make and return calls from their cars. If they are doing so with a client, they must be alert to the lack of privacy in such communications. Also, if an attorney receives a call from a client and it is clear he or she is calling from a car phone, it is recommended that clients be advised that they cannot be assured of privacy. The attorney and staff must be aware of

---

[Section 34:18]
   [1]D.R. 2-110(B).

[Section 34:19]
   [1]D.R. 2-110(C) contains a list of specific circumstances in which a lawyer may withdraw.

[Section 34:20]
   [1]RC 2317.02.
   [2]D.R. 4-101(D).

the danger when faxing a document or letter that the correct number is dialed and the recipient is the person intended to receive the document.

§ 34:21   Confidences—Exceptions

Confidences and secrets may be revealed under certain circumstances: (1) if the client gives consent; (2) if the Disciplinary Rules allow it or if a court so orders; (3) if the client intends to commit a crime and the matter revealed is necessary to prevent that crime from being committed; or (4) if it becomes necessary to collect fees or to defend the lawyer against an accusation of wrongful conduct.[1]

Practitioners should be aware of RC 2151.421, which requires attorneys to report cases of child abuse or neglect to the children services board. This can create a dilemma for an attorney who learns from his client that the client is abusing a child. While the obligation in the original statute for attorneys to report suspected or known abuse was absolute and carried the threat of a misdemeanor charge, pursuant to the current statute as amended, the attorney is absolved of the requirement of reporting any communication made to him in the attorney-client relationship, if the attorney could not testify with respect to that communication under the confidentiality provisions of RC 2317.02(A).[2] A client is deemed to have waived the privilege if the client is under eighteen years of age (twenty-one years of age if mentally or physically handicapped), the client has suffered or may suffer abuse or neglect, and the client has not consulted the attorney to attempt to have an abortion without parental consent.[3]

§ 34:22   Conflicts of interest—In general

Conflicts of interest matters are found in D.R. 5-101 et seq. The situation that arises most frequently in the domestic relations area is the case in which the spouses come together to the attorney's office for a dissolution of marriage, claiming all matters are settled and need only to be put in writing. The Ohio Bar Ethics Committee Formal Opinion No. 30 clarifies this matter.

The lawyer must explain that he can represent only one of the parties. He must give the other spouse full opportunity to evaluate his or her need for legal representation. Furthermore, each spouse must set forth in writing, either in a document attached to the separation agreement or in a paragraph in the separation agreement, his or her understanding that the lawyer represents only one of them and that the other, with full opportunity to obtain counsel, has elected not to, and that both consent to proceeding in that manner.

[Section 34:21]

   [1]D.R. 4-101(D).
   [2]RC 2151.421(A)(2).
   [3]RC 2151.421(A)(2).

§ 34:23 Conflicts of interest—Clause in separation agreement—Form⊚

A sample clause for insertion into a separation agreement when one party is not represented by counsel, and which meets the requirements of Ohio Bar Association Formal Opinion No. 30, follows:

The parties understand that [_____], the attorney who prepared this agreement, represents the wife/husband only, and not the husband/wife. The husband/wife acknowledges that he/she has been given full opportunity to evaluate his/her need for representation, and has decided to proceed without counsel. Both parties consent to proceeding in this fashion.

In addition or in the alternative, the parties may sign a separate waiver.

§ 34:24 Conflicts of interest—Acknowledgment of representation—Form⊚

IN THE COURT OF COMMON PLEAS, [_____], OHIO DIVISION OF DOMESTIC RELATIONS

In the Matter of	:	
NAME OF CLIENT,	:	
and,	:	CASE NUMBER
		JUDGE
NAME OF SPOUSE,	:	
Petitioners.	:	

ACKNOWLEDGMENT OF LEGAL REPRESENTATION FOR DISSOLUTION OF MARRIAGE

I, *[Name of spouse]*, being the spouse of *[Name of client]*, understand that *[name of attorney]*, Attorney at Law, represents only my spouse and does not represent me; that I understand I have the right to retain my own attorney to advise me and represent my interests in said dissolution of marriage; and, that I have been advised to retain my own attorney by *[name of attorney]*.

Dated:[_____]

_____
Name of Spouse

I, *[Name of Client]*, have retained *[name of attorney]*. Attorney at Law, to represent me in all proceedings for a dissolution of my marriage and understand that said attorney does not represent my spouse.

Dated:[_____]

_____
Name of Client

§ 34:25 Conflicts of interest—Consequences of conflicts

In *Longstreet v. Longstreet*,[1] the appellate court based its reversal of the trial court's denial of Civil Rule 60(B) relief upon that court's refusal to conduct an oral hearing in circumstances where the party's motion contained operative facts that could warrant relief. However, it is noteworthy that the opinion recited that both parties were represented by the same lawyer and that one of the assignments of error claimed voidability of the decree based on "dual representation."

A public reprimand was issued to the attorney in *Geauga County Bar Ass'n v. Psenicka*,[2] where he had initially represented a wife in filing for divorce. After the wife obtained new counsel, the attorney entered an appearance on behalf of the husband, despite the wife's vehement objection to the representation. The court adopted the reasoning of the disciplinary panel that the continuing litigation involved confidences of his former client.

Where an attorney represented the husband in a divorce action, and later, when the attorney became an attorney for the Child Support Enforcement Agency, filed a motion in contempt against the husband on behalf of the wife, the court held that there should be a disqualification whenever there is a substantial relationship between the subject matter of the former representation and that of a subsequent representation. The court stated "The primary purpose of disqualification is to protect confidentiality of information, even if the information is only potentially involved in the current action."[3] What is interesting in *Morford* is that attorneys employed by the CSEA specifically do not claim or hold themselves out as attorneys for either party.

The trial court has the inherent authority to supervise members of the bar appearing in actions before it, which includes the power to disqualify counsel. While a trial court has broad discretion, disqualification is a drastic measure. More is required than an ethical violation. Where the husband's present divorce attorney previously represented the wife, three years before the marriage, in an unrelated workers' compensation matter, the court of appeals found no sound reasoning process to support the trial court's grant of a disqualification motion.[4]

The primary question for a court when a party is seeking disqualification on the basis of past representation of one or both parties is whether the attorney acquired confidential information from that party that

---

[Section 34:25]

[1]Longstreet v. Longstreet, 57 Ohio App. 3d 55, 566 N.E.2d 708 (8th Dist. Cuyahoga County 1989).

[2]Geauga Cty. Bar Assn. v. Psenicka, 62 Ohio St. 3d 35, 577 N.E.2d 1074 (1991).

[3]Morford v. Morford, 85 Ohio App. 3d 50, 57, 619 N.E.2d 71 (4th Dist. Lawrence County 1993).

[4]Hollis v. Hollis, 124 Ohio App. 3d 481, 706 N.E.2d 798 (8th Dist. Cuyahoga County 1997); see also Phillips v. Haidet, 119 Ohio App. 3d 322, 695 N.E.2d 292 (3d Dist. Logan County 1997).

would be prejudicial in the present representation.[5]

A lawyer must be careful to avoid influence by persons other than the client. Compensation from one other than a client cannot be accepted except with the client's consent after full disclosure.

It is not necessarily a violation of D.R. 5-102(A) for an attorney, under certain circumstances, to testify as a witness. An attorney does not become incompetent as a witness where he is representing a litigant. D.R. 5-102(A) permits such testimony as listed in D.R. 5-101(B)(1) to D.R. 5-101(B)(4).[6]

§ 34:26   Conflicts of interest—Guardian ad litem

It is fairly common when custody, visitation, or parental rights of minor children are contested for the court to appoint a guardian ad litem for the children.[1] Ordinarily, when an attorney is appointed, it is as attorney and as guardian ad litem.

In *In re Baby Girl Baxter*,[2] the Court stated:

> The duty of a lawyer to his client and the duty of a guardian ad litem to his ward are not always identical and, in fact, may conflict. The role of a guardian ad litem is to investigate the ward's situation, and then to ask the court to do what the guardian feels is in the ward's best interest. The role of the attorney is to zealously represent his client within the bounds of the law. D.R. 7-101; D.R. 7-102.

The Court further held that when an attorney is appointed to represent the person, and also appointed as guardian ad litem, the attorney's first and highest duty is to zealously represent the client and to champion the client's cause. The potential of a conflict when the guardian ad litem recommends something different from the stated desires of the ward was reinforced in *Bawidamann v. Bawidamann*,[3] where the appellate court reversed the trial court's reliance on the guardian ad litem's report, indicating that when the guardian realized that his recommendation was not what the wards wanted, he should have petitioned the court for an order allowing him to withdraw as guardian.

§ 34:27   Competence—In general

D.R. 6-101 provides that a lawyer shall not handle a matter he is not competent to handle without adequate preparation or neglect a matter

---

[5]Hollis v. Hollis, 124 Ohio App. 3d 481, 706 N.E.2d 798 (8th Dist. Cuyahoga County 1997); Verbic v. Verbic, 2000 WL 526107 (Ohio Ct. App. 11th Dist. Portage County 2000).

[6]Miller v. Miller, 1988 WL 36510 (Ohio Ct. App. 8th Dist. Cuyahoga County 1988), citing Mentor Lagoons, Inc. v. Rubin, 31 Ohio St. 3d 256, 510 N.E.2d 379 (1987); In re Skrha, 98 Ohio App. 3d 487, 648 N.E.2d 908 (8th Dist. Cuyahoga County 1994).

[Section 34:26]

[1]Civ. R. 75(B)(2).

[2]In re Baby Girl Baxter, 17 Ohio St. 3d 229, 479 N.E.2d 257 (1985).

[3]Bawidamann v. Bawidamann, 63 Ohio App. 3d 691, 580 N.E.2d 15 (2d Dist. Montgomery County 1989).

entrusted to him. Competence in domestic law requires knowledge of procedure, statutes, current case law, bankruptcy, and tax law, because the transfers of property and spousal and child support payments can have tax ramifications.[1] Surprisingly few lawyers seem to be aware of tax matters and of the many ways in which they affect domestic practice. When in doubt, consult an expert. A lawyer cannot properly advise a client without understanding the field in which the client seeks advice.

§ 34:28   Competence—Neglect of a legal matter

D.R. 6-101 generates a great many complaints arising as a result of dissatisfaction with the outcome of the case and most are without merit. Many complaints are the result of the lawyer not keeping the client informed or simply not returning calls. These types of complaints do not give rise to action under the D.R.s, and they are easily remedied and should be avoided.

An attorney who fails to file an action, after being paid for the service, compounds the problem by repeatedly lying to the client and failing to return the money.[1] Clearly such conduct not only violates D.R. 6-101(A)(3) neglect of a legal matter entrusted to an attorney, but also D.R. 1-102(A)(4) conduct involving fraud, deceit, dishonesty, and misrepresentation and D.R. 7-101(A)(2) failure to carry out a contract of employment.[2]

Where an attorney's conduct demonstrates that he violated D.R. 6-101(A)(3), neglect of a legal matter, and D.R. 6-101(A)(2), handling a legal matter without adequate preparation, as well as being generally undignified, discourteous, and degrading to the tribunal (D.R. 7-106(C)(6)), not only is the attorney subject to sanctions including disbarment,[3] but also where the conduct was egregious, the client who was adversely affected should have been granted a retrial.[4]

The key to avoiding potential claims of neglecting a legal matter is proper record-keeping and preparation and using tools to insure complete follow-through. Indispensable to the domestic practitioner, therefore, is having questionnaires and checklists. The attorney should

---

[Section 34:27]

[1]See Tax Considerations Ch 28.

[Section 34:28]

[1]Lorain Cty. Bar Assn. v. Motsch, 1993 -Ohio- 83, 66 Ohio St. 3d 56, 607 N.E.2d 1069 (1993), reinstatement granted, 76 Ohio St. 3d 1215, 667 N.E.2d 982 (1996) (respondent repeatedly lied to a number of clients that cases were initiated, cases were set for hearing, and matters continued when such was false); Cuyahoga Cty. Bar Assn. v. Jaynes, 1993 -Ohio- 40, 66 Ohio St. 3d 245, 611 N.E.2d 807 (1993) (respondent never filed annulment papers and never returned monies).

[2]Disciplinary Counsel v. Fowerbaugh, 1995 -Ohio- 261, 74 Ohio St. 3d 187, 658 N.E.2d 237 (1995), reinstatement granted, 77 Ohio St. 3d 1221, 672 N.E.2d 1016 (1996); Dayton Bar Assn. v. Overman, 1996 -Ohio- 252, 75 Ohio St. 3d 48, 661 N.E.2d 701 (1996).

[3]Mahoning Cty. Bar Assn. v. Cregan, 1994 -Ohio- 116, 69 Ohio St. 3d 550, 634 N.E.2d 1005 (1994).

[4]Verbanic v. Verbanic, 1994 -Ohio- 297, 70 Ohio St. 3d 41, 635 N.E.2d 1260 (1994).

tailor the checklists according to the nature of the attorney's practice, community, and court. The checklist for documents and checklists for timing will depend upon the court in which the attorney will be filing the action.

While some neglect may or may not violate the disciplinary rules, it may lead to malpractice actions. In addition, legal malpractice actions which have a one year statute of limitations[5] can be extended by the discovery rule. That requires inquiry as to when a "cognizable event" occurred.[6]

An agreement by a party to a divorce settlement does not bar a malpractice case nor preclude recovery against that party's attorney.[7]

§ 34:29 Competence—Client interview questionnaire—Form⊙

Counsel should obtain the information necessary to complete the following checklist. This is a comprehensive checklist. Counsel should select information needed for first interview, as the initial intake form. More detailed, subsequent forms can be used to obtain the additional information needed from the client.

(I) Information regarding parties (obtain this information for *both* husband and wife):

Name [_____]

Address [_____]

Other addresses [_____]

Telephone numbers: home, office or employment, other [_____]

Social security number [_____]

Date of birth [_____]

Maiden name [_____]

Occupation, prior occupation [_____]

Employer, address of employer, length of employment [_____]

Prior employment, length of employment, potential changes or out-of-state transfers, promotion, etc. [_____]

Education [_____]

(II) Information regarding the marriage:

Date of marriage [_____]

Place of marriage [_____]

Antenuptial agreement [_____]

When parties established marital domicile in Ohio [_____]

Are the parties separated Yes [_____] No [_____]

If Yes, date of separation [_____] Party leaving marital home [_____]

---

[5]RC 2305.11(A).

[6]Zimmie v. Calfee, Halter and Griswold, 43 Ohio St. 3d 54, 538 N.E.2d 398 (1989).

[7]Monastra v. D'Amore, 111 Ohio App. 3d 296, 676 N.E.2d 132 (8th Dist. Cuyahoga County 1996); Gibson v. Westfall, 1999 WL 809813 (Ohio Ct. App. 8th Dist. Cuyahoga County 1999).

Prior marital difficulties [_____] Any prior decrees [_____]
Prior attempts at reconciliation [_____]
Present possibility of reconciliation [_____]
Marital difficulties: origin and nature [_____]
[If spouse now living in another state, identify place where parties last lived together as husband and wife.]
(III) Information regarding children of the marriage:
Names [_____]
Date of birth [_____]
Date of adoption if appropriate (court granting final decree, etc.)
[_____]
Age [_____]
Address—living with whom [_____]
Where children lived for past five years (for RC 3109.27 affidavit)
[_____]
Educational possibilities regarding children [_____]
Special educational requirements of child (tutors, etc.) [_____]
Child's health
    Physical [_____]
    Mental and emotional [_____]
Future expenditures expected
    Orthodontics [_____]
    Ophthalmology [_____]
    Allergies [_____]
    Other [_____]
Parent with whom child might choose to live [_____]
Child's understanding of parental difficulties regarding the marriage [_____]
Financial resources of child
    Bank accounts [_____]
    Trust funds [_____]
    Inheritances [_____]
    Other [_____]
Child's interests, activities, expenditures [_____]
Other parties having an interest in the welfare of the child who might desire reasonable companionship or visitation rights [_____]
(IV) Type of action contemplated:
  (a) Dissolution
    Do both parties desire to terminate the marriage [_____]
    Can the parties agree on a separation agreement [_____]
    Provision for minor children: agreed to [_____]
    Ascertain legal representation; explain waiver of representation by one spouse [_____]
  (b) Divorce

Specific grounds:
    1. Another spouse living at time of marriage
    2. Willful absence of spouse for one year
    3. Adultery
    4. Extreme cruelty
    5. Fraudulent contract
    6. Gross neglect of duty
    7. Habitual drunkenness
    8. Imprisonment of adverse party in a state or federal correctional institution at time of filing
    9. Procurement of divorce out of state by adverse party
    10. Living separate and apart for one year without interruption and without cohabitation
    11. Incompatibility (not denied)
(c) Legal separation
Specific grounds:
    1. Another spouse living at time of marriage
    2. Willful absence of adverse party for one year
    3. Adultery
    4. Extreme cruelty
    5. Fraudulent contract
    6. Gross neglect of duty
    7. Habitual drunkenness
    8. Imprisonment of adverse party in a state or federal correctional institution at time of filling
    9. Living separate and apart for one year without interruption and without cohabitation
    10. Incompatibility (not denied)
(V) Resources of the marriage:
Income from employment [_____]
Bank accounts:
    Bank name, address, account number in what name, custodian of bankbook [_____]
Checking accounts:
    Bank name, address, account number in what name, custodian of checkbook [_____]
Insurance (ascertain company name and address, account number, beneficiary)
    Health [_____]
    Disability [_____]
    Life (personal or straight life) [_____]
    Life (group, employment or fraternal policies) [_____]
Stocks/bonds [_____]
Real property:
    Description, how title held, approximate value [_____]
    Amount of mortgage, mortgage holder, equity interest [_____]

Other income:
   Trusts [_____]
   Businesses [_____]
   Expectancies [_____]
      Pensions [_____]
         Heir or remainderman, inheritances, etc. [_____]
      Social security, other government sources [_____]
      Retirement, pensions, 401(K), Keogh, IRA
      Other [_____]
   Automobiles (model, year, and title of automobile, boats, motor-
cycles) [_____]
   Assets that may be considered separate property:
      Assets either party had prior to marriage [_____]
      Gifts to one party during marriage [_____]
      Inheritances [_____]
      Improvements to any of above from labor or efforts of either
   party
(VI) Debts of the marriage:
   Mortgages, real property:
      Amount, mortgage holder, monthly payment [_____]
   Automobile loans:
      Total amount, creditor, amount due per month [_____]
   Charge accounts; bank credit cards:
      List stores, amounts due [_____]
   Medical:
      Amounts due [_____]
   Other:
      Total amount, what purchased, creditor, amount due [_____]
(VII) General information:
   Social and civic activities [_____]
   Marketable skills, experience (if different from employment)
[_____]
   Religious attitudes and observances [_____]
   Prior marriage and reason for termination (death, divorce, dis-
solution) [_____]
   Family background [_____]
   Contribution to marriage
      Financial:
         Property, real and personal [_____]
         Cash or stock, etc. [_____]
         Employment or business interests [_____]
      Aid to education of spouse [_____]
      Degrees acquired during marriage [_____]
      Extraordinary duties, e.g., for wife, entertainment of husband's
   clients or associates [_____]

Physical and mental health, past and present [_____]
Future plans
    Remarriage [_____]
    Employment [_____]
    Geographical changes [_____]
    Capability of self-support with or without rights and responsibilities for children [_____]
    Capability of undergoing job training [_____]
    Capability for further education [_____]
Other dependents or obligations, e.g., spousal, parental or child support [_____]
Reconciliation efforts
    Counselors seen or being seen, joint participation [_____]
(VIII) Witnesses:
    (a) Corroborating witnesses:
    Name [_____]
    Address [_____]
    Telephone [_____]
    Relationship to client [_____]
    Source of information [_____]
    (b) Character witnesses (unnecessary in most counties):
    Name [_____]
    Address [_____]
    Telephone [_____]
    Relationship to client [_____]
    Length of relationship [_____]
(IX) Living expenses:
The party should prepare a detailed list of all living expenses, preferably on a monthly basis. Such figures can be compared to Bureau of Labor statistics for each area based on high, middle or low income to verify client's estimate. Further information should be obtained if gross disparities appear. The preparation of such list of expenses is essential in the event an order for temporary support is required, proves valuable in evaluating the requirements for a future separation agreement, constitutes the basis for presentation of such information to the court in the event of a contested proceeding, and may be of some value in reconciliation discussions.
Expense statement:
    Housing
    Rent or mortgage payment [_____]
    Homeowners or renters insurance
    Utilities
    Electricity [_____]
    Gas [_____]
    Water [_____]

   Telephone [_____]
   Cable [_____]
  Taxes [_____]
  Upkeep and household [_____]
  Equipment and supplies [_____]
Food
  Groceries [_____]
  Dining out, lunches [_____]
Clothing
  Purchase [_____]
  Dry cleaning [_____]
  Laundry [_____]
  Shoe repair [_____]
Personal expenditures
  Haircuts, etc. [_____]
  Dues, memberships [_____]
Entertainment/recreation
  Vacations [_____]
  Entertainment [_____]
Transportation
  Car payments
  Bus, taxi fares [_____]
  Automobile insurance [_____]
  Gas, oil [_____]
  Maintenance [_____]
  Parking [_____]
  License, tags [_____]
Contributions
  Church [_____]
  Charity [_____]
  Civil and social [_____]
Medical expenses
  Health insurance [_____]
  Physician [_____]
  Counseling [_____]
  Dentist [_____]
  Drugs, etc. [_____]
Insurance premiums
  Life insurance [_____]
  Disability insurance [_____]
  Health insurance [_____]
Educational expenses
  Wife/husband [_____]
  Children:
   Tuition, room and board [_____]

　　Books [＿＿＿＿]
　　Expenses, bus, uniforms, fees [＿＿＿＿]
Gifts (including Christmas) [＿＿＿＿]
Debt repayments
　　Charge accounts [＿＿＿＿]
　　Personal loans [＿＿＿＿]
Other expenses [＿＿＿＿]
Total expenses per month [＿＿＿＿]
Income per month:
　　Employment:
　　　　Gross [＿＿＿＿]
　　　　Net [＿＿＿＿]
　　Rents [＿＿＿＿]
　　Interest [＿＿＿＿]
　　Dividends [＿＿＿＿]
　　Royalties [＿＿＿＿]
　　Other [＿＿＿＿]
　　Total income per month [＿＿＿＿]
Taxes
　　Real property [＿＿＿＿]
　　Federal income tax [＿＿＿＿]
　　State income tax [＿＿＿＿]
　　Local income tax [＿＿＿＿]
　　Prior year's taxes [＿＿＿＿]

§ 34:30 Competence—Divorce checklist—Form○®

DIVORCE CHECK LIST

Name: ＿＿＿＿
Date: ＿＿＿＿
　　[＿＿＿＿] Complaint

[＿＿＿＿]　　　　　　　　　　real estate (property description)
Grounds:　　　　　　　　　　[＿＿＿＿] gross neglect of duty
　　　　　　　　　　　　　　[＿＿＿＿] extreme cruelty
　　　　　　　　　　　　　　[＿＿＿＿] one year living separate and
　　　　　　　　　　　　　　apart
　　　　　　　　　　　　　　[＿＿＿＿] incompatibility
　　　　　　　　　　　　　　[＿＿＿＿] other ＿＿＿＿＿＿＿＿＿＿
Demand:　　　　　　　　　　[＿＿＿＿] regular
　　　　　　　　　　　　　　[＿＿＿＿] other ＿＿＿＿＿＿＿＿＿＿

　　[＿＿＿＿] Answer
Admit Paragraphs:　　　　　　＿＿＿＿＿＿＿＿＿＿＿＿＿＿

Deny Paragraphs: _____

[_____] Cross-Complaint (with certificate of service)
[_____] Entry Out of Rule
[_____] Motion/temporary relief/affidavit
[_____] Motion to Vacate
[_____] Restraining Order (Motion/Affidavit/Restraining Order)
  [_____] regular
  [_____] special
[_____] Custody Affidavit
[_____] Assets/Liabilities (if required)
[_____] Written Instructions TO: _____

[_____] Motion for Process Server
[_____] Interrogatories
[_____] Motion/Production Documents
[_____] Medical Insurance Form
[_____] CSEA Application

§ 34:31 Competence—Dissolution checklist—Form⊚

DISSOLUTION CHECK LIST

Name: _____
Date: _____
[_____] Petition
[_____] Separation Agreement
[_____] Custody Affidavit
[_____] Shared Parenting Plan
[_____] Waiver of Attorney
[_____] Assets/Liabilities Form
[_____] Child Support Computation
[_____] Decree
  [_____] Restoration to Maiden/Former _____
  [_____] Notices Paragraph
[_____] Shared Parenting Decree
  [_____] Notices Paragraph
[_____] Medical Insurance Form
[_____] CSEA Application
[_____] Deed (Type _____
)
[_____] Withholding Orders
[_____] Waiver of Service of Withholding Forms
[_____] QDRO

§ 34:32 Zealous representation of clients

Failure to seek the lawful objectives of the client zealously but within the bounds of the law is grounds for complaint against a lawyer, and D.R. 7-101 and D.R. 7-102 should be carefully read and understood. However, under D.R. 7-101(B), a lawyer may refuse to aid or participate in conduct he believes to be unlawful, even though there is some support for argument that the conduct is legal. D.R. 7-102(A)(4) to (8) provide that a lawyer in his representation of a client shall not

(4) Knowingly use perjured testimony or false evidence.

(5) Knowingly make a false statement of law or fact.

(6) Participate in the creation or preservation of evidence when he knows or it is obvious that the evidence is false.

(7) Counsel or assist his client in conduct that the lawyer knows to be illegal or fraudulent.

(8) Knowingly engage in other illegal conduct or conduct contrary to a Disciplinary Rule.

D.R. 7-102(B) provides that a lawyer, informed that during his representation his client has perpetrated a fraud on a person or a tribunal, must call upon the client to rectify the fraud. If the client will not or cannot rectify the fraud, the lawyer shall reveal the fraud to the affected person or tribunal. This requirement appears to conflict with the requirement to preserve confidences and secrets of a client but in fact does not. D.R. 4-101(C)(3) allows the revelation of confidences and secrets when permitted by the D.R.s. Pursuant to D.R. 7-102(B), the duty is mandatory once the fraud is clearly established and the fraud has occurred during the course of representation. An example of the latter would be the concealment of marital assets after representation has begun.

Special problems for the domestic lawyer are found in D.R. 7-104, which requires that a lawyer not communicate or cause another to communicate directly on the subject of the representation with a party known to be represented by another lawyer. The problem can arise in a divorce setting, in which the parties are still living together, and one lawyer will tell the client to work the division of personal effects among themselves. This should not be done without the consent of the other attorney.

D.R. 7-105 states, "A lawyer shall not present, participate in presenting, or threaten to present criminal charges solely to obtain an advantage in a civil matter." This admonition should be considered when discussing the appropriateness of filing criminal charges such as domestic violence, child molestation, or child abuse charges. Care must be exercised to ascertain the validity of the allegations before recommending the filing by a spouse against the other spouse where an action for divorce or custody is pending or anticipated.

It is very tempting to use the threat of revealing the opposing spouse's illegal tax deductions to obtain more favorable settlement terms, but it is unethical to do so in the domestic relations setting. The criminal process, which is designed to protect society as a whole, is undermined when it is used to settle private controversies.[1] An exception to this rule is found in the case of bad checks, but then the threat of prosecution can be used only in an effort to make the check good, not to gain leverage in another civil action.[2]

While the Code of Professional Responsibility requires the family law practitioner to represent the client zealously as an advocate, there are also moral, social, and economic questions which may require referral to other professionals. Such questions dictate that the competent, zealous family law practitioner *at least* recommend the employment of such professionals.[3]

D.R. 7-106 sets forth rules of trial conduct, which are the same for the lawyer appearing before a domestic relations court as they are for the lawyer appearing before any other tribunal.

Pursuant to RC 2323.51 a court may award reasonable attorney fees to any party to an action adversely affected by frivolous conduct arising out of a civil action. The trial court must hold an evidentiary hearing before granting such a motion.[4]

§34:33 Frivolous conduct

The issue of whether a filing is frivolous is not whether the action or motion should have succeeded, but whether its filing was warranted under existing law.[1]

The Eighth District Court of Appeals in *Pisani v. Pisani*[2] reevaluated its prior decisions regarding the necessity for the trial court to conduct a hearing on a motion for attorney fees filed under RC 2323.51(B)(2). In reconsidering its prior holdings and reviewing the other appellate districts, it concluded that the statutory language permitting an award of attorney fees as a sanction for frivolous conduct only after a hearing did not address the converse, and, therefore, a hearing is not required when an award of attorney fees is denied. Thus, no hearing is necessary where the court, having heard the case, and from its own experience, has sufficient knowledge of the circumstances for the denial of the requested relief, and a hearing would be "perfunctory, meaningless, or redundant." A domestic relations court may deny a motion for sanctions

---

[Section 34:32]

[1]E.C. 7-21.

[2]RC 2913.11; Cincinnati Bar Assn. v. Cohen, 1999 -Ohio- 86, 86 Ohio St. 3d 100, 712 N.E.2d 118 (1999) (public reprimand for threatening his former client with criminal action if insufficient funds check not paid).

[3]For a full discussion of D.R. 6-101, see §34:28, Competence—Neglect of a legal matter.

[4]Steiner v. Steiner, 85 Ohio App. 3d 513, 620 N.E.2d 152 (4th Dist. Scioto County 1993).

[Section 34:33]

[1]Mitchell v. Mitchell, 126 Ohio App. 3d 500, 710 N.E.2d 793 (2d Dist. Montgomery County 1998).

[2]Pisani v. Pisani, 101 Ohio App. 3d 83, 654 N.E.2d 1355 (8th Dist. Cuyahoga County 1995).

when the trial court is familiar with the case and the record contains evidence from the proceedings.[3]

Where counsel engages in filing a civil action which is not warranted under existing law and cannot be supported by a good faith argument for the establishment of new law, counsel and the parties who filed the civil action are properly ordered to pay sanctions. The filing of a custody action by grandparents for companionship with their grandchildren when there is no disruptive precipitating event, such as parental death or divorce, and the parents are an intact married couple, is properly found to be frivolous and for the purpose of harassing and/or maliciously injuring the parents of the children.[4]

§ 34:34   Avoiding the appearance of impropriety

Domestic lawyers, as is true of all lawyers, are in the business of selling themselves. They want the client to have faith in them, to trust them, and to believe they are competent. On occasion a lawyer may go so far as to suggest to the client that he has some special influence over the judge or an official. Any statement that implies a lawyer is able to influence improperly any tribunal or public official must be avoided. There is a line between puffery and impropriety.[1]

Another area of impropriety concerns the commingling of client and attorney funds. The matter of trust funds is extremely important. Judging by the number of cases involving the improper use of trust funds, the function of client trust funds apparently is not universally understood.

Funds advanced to the lawyer are to be placed in the lawyer's trust fund. They cannot be removed from there until either the lawyer has earned them or they are to be returned to the client or to be disbursed as directed by the client. The lawyer cannot put any of his own funds into the trust account except those necessary to meet bank charges. Proper accounts must be maintained. The funds in the trust account belong to the client, and in no event can the lawyer use these funds to pay for overhead or office help or for any other purpose than his client's interests until they have been earned and paid to the lawyer.[2]

Commingling of funds has traditionally been dealt with severely by the Ohio Supreme Court. Further, there is strict accountability under this Disciplinary Rule, and attempted defenses of good faith, lack of intent, or ability to restore funds have not exculpated the attorney from charges of wrongdoing.

Attorneys may establish interest-bearing trust accounts for depositing client funds which are nominal in amount or are to be held by the at-

---

[3]Russo v. Russo, 1999 WL 13972 (Ohio Ct. App. 8th Dist. Cuyahoga County 1999).

[4]Matter of Young, 1998 WL 817746 (Ohio Ct. App. 5th Dist. Licking County 1998).

[Section 34:34]
[1]D.R. 9-101(C).
[2]D.R. 9-102.

torney for a short period of time.[3] The determination of whether the amount is nominal or whether the period of time is short rests in the discretion of the attorney. These accounts, known as IOLTA accounts (Interest on Lawyers' Trust Accounts) have been allowed since 1985. The account must be identified as an IOLTA account and the interest earned on these accounts must be transmitted by the financial institution to the treasurer of state for disbursal to the legal aid fund. No part of the interest inures to the benefit of the attorney or the client.

§ 34:35 Communication

Perhaps the one greatest failing of the family law practitioner is client communication. Failure to advise the client of the status of the matter, reasons for delay, or any other activity or nonactivity which affects the client's position often results in not only dissatisfaction, but the initiation of a complaint. Absent adequate communication, a client cannot make informed decisions as to settlement or further litigation.

A simple method for keeping a client informed is to establish routine office procedures which automatically require all written communications regarding a case, whether or not from other counsel or other sources, to be copied and sent to the client. The clients will realize they are not being neglected and that their cases are being handled. It is amazing how many attorneys do not automatically send copies of correspondence to their client. Another method of keeping the client informed as to ongoing service is periodic billing which will also reflect telephone calls. While these suggestions are not mandatory nor in the rules, it may be questioned whether an attorney is acting competently when the attorney is not properly communicating with the client.

A public reprimand was issued to an attorney who failed to advise her client that she had settled a parentage action with a child support enforcement agency.[1] The settlement was without the alleged father's knowledge or consent, and his first notice was from his personnel office regarding the order to withhold the support from his pay.

§ 34:36 Sexual relations with clients

It is generally perceived that divorce clients are especially vulnerable during the proceedings surrounding the breakup of the marriage, feeling rejected, unloved, insecure and unattractive. Ohio does not presently have a Disciplinary Rule expressly prohibiting a sexual relationship with a client. The Ohio Supreme Court has, however, found that engaging in sexual relations with a client in a divorce matter is conduct which adversely reflects upon an attorney's fitness to practice law, in violation

---

[3]RC 4705.09.

[Section 34:35]
[1]Cincinnati Bar Assn. v. Wilson, 65 Ohio St. 3d 296, 603 N.E.2d 985 (1992).

of D.R. 1-102(A)(6).[1] The Court has also found such conduct to be a violation of D.R. 5-101(A) in that an attorney's professional judgment in such a situation would be or might be affected by his own personal and financial interest.[2]

In *Disciplinary Counsel v. Detty*[3] an attorney was sanctioned for attempting both directly and indirectly to communicate with a judge to influence the outcome of a pending action. In *Detty* the attorney was neither the attorney for a party or a party, but was romantically involved with the plaintiff in the pending divorce case.

§ 34:37   Attorney as a party—In general

While most statutes and case law address attorney ethics in the context of representing parties before the court, attorneys themselves appear as parties in domestic relations actions and, as such, are still subject to the Code of Professional Responsibility. D.R. 1-102 prohibits an attorney from engaging in conduct involving dishonesty, fraud, deceit, or misrepresentation. There is no specific prohibition, however, against violating a court order in a domestic action.

In *Disciplinary Counsel v. Donnell*,[1] an attorney, as a party to a post-decree proceeding, persistently contacted his ex-wife, who had her own attorney, while motions he had filed were pending. The Court found that such conduct violated D.R. 7-104(A)(1), which prohibits an attorney from contacting an adverse party who is represented by counsel. That conduct, coupled with other inappropriate behavior, led to a six-month suspension.

It is not an abuse of discretion to hold an attorney party to a higher standard of behavior due to his profession. The trial court in *Evans v. Cole*,[2] found the attorney husband in contempt of a restraining order for his verbal abuse in public of the wife and specifically imposed a higher amount of attorney's fees as a sanction because the court expected the attorney party not to be in contempt since he was an officer of the court.

§ 34:38   Attorney as a party—As support obligor

In 1995, the General Assembly enacted a comprehensive act intended

---

[Section 34:36]

[1]Office of Disciplinary Counsel v. Ressing, 53 Ohio St. 3d 265, 559 N.E.2d 1359 (1990).

[2]Disciplinary Counsel v. Paxton, 1993 -Ohio- 99, 66 Ohio St. 3d 163, 610 N.E.2d 979 (1993).

[3]Disciplinary Counsel v. Detty, 96 Ohio St. 3d 57, 2002-Ohio-2992, 770 N.E.2d 1015 (2002).

[Section 34:37]

[1]Disciplinary Counsel v. Donnell, 79 Ohio St. 3d 501, 684 N.E.2d 36 (1997), reinstatement granted, 1998 -Ohio- 487, 82 Ohio St. 3d 1220, 695 N.E.2d 775 (1998).

[2]Evans v. Cole, 2001 -Ohio- 2486, 2001 WL 688594 (Ohio Ct. App. 4th Dist. Jackson County 2001).

to improve support collection.[1] In numerous statutory sections, the act prohibits the issuance or renewal of, and requires the suspension of, certain professional and occupational licenses,[2] permits, and certificates, including motor vehicle licenses of individuals who are found to be in default of a support order.

Specifically excluded from the statutory requirements are licenses issued by the Supreme Court of Ohio, because only the Supreme Court can determine and regulate who may practice law in the State of Ohio.

The Child Support Enforcement Agency (CSEA) may, under RC 4705.021, send notice of a determination by the court or by a CSEA of a default of a support order by an attorney to the secretary of the Board of Commissioners on Grievances and Discipline of the Ohio Supreme Court and to the disciplinary counsel or to the appropriate personnel of a certified grievance committee.[3]

In response to the request of the legislature, the Ohio Supreme Court enacted Gov. Bar R. V § 5, effective April 21, 1997. It provides for interim license suspension for a felony conviction or for a default under a child support order. A justice, judge, or attorney is subject to an interim suspension upon a final and enforceable determination that such obligor is in default under a child support order. A certified copy of the determination of default, whether issued from the court or the CSEA, is conclusive evidence of the default. A justice, judge, or attorney may be reinstated upon the filing of a certified copy of an entry which reverses the determination of default or upon notice from the court or the CSEA that the obligor is no longer in default or is subject to a withholding or deduction order. As of the middle of 2002, this continues to apply only to a child support order.

While prior to the amendment of Gov. Bar R. V, by the Supreme Court, an attorney could not be deprived of his or her license to practice law simply by virtue of default of a support order, "flaunting the order of a court, being repeatedly held in contempt, and maintaining a considerable arrearage in child support payments must reflect adversely on an applicant who seeks admission to the Bar."[4]

Gov Bar R V Section 5 permits an interim suspension for a felony conviction or default under a child support order. Costs assessed against an attorney for the disciplinary proceedings are not dischargeable in bankruptcy.[5]

§ 34:39   Sales of a Law Practice

Present rules in Ohio do not provide for the sale of a law practice. An

---

[Section 34:38]

[1]1995 H.B. 167, various effective dates.

[2]RC 2301.373(E)(1), eff. 11-15-96.

[3]RC 4705.021, eff. 11-15-96.

[4]Barilatz v. Pailsey, 1995 WL 546931, at *6 n.4 (Ohio Ct. App. 8th Dist. Cuyahoga County 1995).

[5]In re Bertsche, 261 B.R. 436 (Bankr.S.D.Ohio, Dec 13, 2000).

attorney can sell his or her books and equipment, but not good will. This has its most adverse effect on solo practitioners who have not brought in associates to become partners and continue the practice. Proposed rule D.R. 2-111, which was published for comment in 1999, but as of this writing has not been adopted, would permit a sale under specific limiting conditions.

§ 34:40   Judicial conduct

The Code of Judicial Conduct, consisting of seven canons, establishes mandatory standards of conduct for judges and justices.[1]

Judges are precluded from engaging in "ex parte" communications (not including nonsubstantive or procedural matters) concerning a pending proceeding.[2] A trial judge's participation in settlement negotiations without the parties' attorney present has been held not to be an "ex parte" communication and was not found to amount to duress or collusion in *Dutton v. Dutton*.[3] The concurring opinion stated "It is bad practice for a domestic relations trial judge to hold a private settlement conference with the parties for a four-hour period excluding the parties' counsel. This is especially odorous when one of the parties is, in fact, an attorney."[4]

The court in *James v. James*[5] relied on C.J.C. Canon 3C(1)(b) to grant a husband a new trial in his divorce action. The referee hearing the case, prior to being appointed as referee, had been associated in law practice with the wife's attorney at the time the wife's attorney filed pleadings in the case. The appellate court held that referees who perform judicial functions must comply with the Judicial Code of Conduct, and that under C.J.C. Canon 3C(1)(b), must disqualify themselves in such situations. The Code's concern is with the appearance of impropriety, and no actual bias or prejudice must be proven.

C.J.C. Canon 3D provides for the remittal of disqualification by a judge in certain circumstances, which, with written agreement signed by all parties and all lawyers and made part of the record, would allow the judge to participate in the matter. This provision, however, applies only to disqualifications under C.J.C. Canon 3C(1)(c) or 3C(1)(d), and could not be used to avoid disqualification under C.J.C. Canon 3C(1)(b).[6]

An affidavit of disqualification based on the fact that the opposing party/spouse is a practicing attorney who appears before the assigned

---

[Section 34:40]

[1]See Ohio Rev. Code. Ann. Jud. Cond. (Baldwin 1995).

[2]C.J.C. Canon 3 (A)(4).

[3]Dutton v. Dutton, 127 Ohio App. 3d 348, 713 N.E.2d 14 (7th Dist. Mahoning County 1998).

[4]Dutton v. Dutton, 127 Ohio App. 3d 348, 356, 713 N.E.2d 14 (7th Dist. Mahoning County 1998).

[5]James v. James, 101 Ohio App. 3d 668, 656 N.E.2d 399 (2d Dist. Greene County 1995).

[6]James v. James, 101 Ohio App. 3d 668, 656 N.E.2d 399 (2d Dist. Greene County 1995).

judge was dismissed in *In re Disqualification of Panagis*.[7] Chief Justice Moyer repeated a portion of the guidelines for assignment of judges which states: " 'The fact that a local attorney is a litigant should not routinely cause the sitting judge to recuse himself or herself, unless the judge's relationship with that particular lawyer justifies recusal.' "[8]

The pendency of an affidavit of disqualification against the trial court judge in most situations requires the trial court to refrain from proceeding with the case until the affidavit has been ruled upon.[9] Special considerations, such as repeated filings, will permit the court to proceed where it appears that last minute filings are frivolous.[10]

To address the unique standards of professionalism required of a judge or a lawyer acting in a judicial capacity, on July 9, 2001 the Ohio Supreme Court issued a Judicial Creed as an addition to Appendix V to the Rules for the Government of the Bar. The creed is aspirational in form.

---

[7]In re Disqualification of Panagis, 74 Ohio St. 3d 1213, 657 N.E.2d 1328 (1989).

[8]In re Disqualification of Panagis, 74 Ohio St. 3d 1213, 1213, 657 N.E.2d 1328 (1989).

[9]Cuyahoga County Bd. of Mental Retardation v. Association of Cuyahoga County Teachers of Trainable Retarded, 47 Ohio App. 2d 28, 1 Ohio Op. 3d 168, 351 N.E.2d 777 (8th Dist. Cuyahoga County 1975).

[10]Rife v. Morgan, 106 Ohio App. 3d 843, 667 N.E.2d 450 (2d Dist. Clark County 1995) (RC 2701.03 providing procedure for filing affidavit of disqualification is silent as to whether filing divests trial court of jurisdiction to proceed).

Chapter 35

Catholic Declaration of Nullity

By Rev. Gary D. Yanus

> **KeyCite®:** Cases and other legal materials listed in KeyCite Scope can be researched through West Group's KeyCite service on Westlaw®. Use KeyCite to check citations for form, parallel references, prior and later history, and comprehensive citator information, including citations to other decisions and secondary materials.

§ 35:1   Catholics and civil divorce

The Roman Catholic Church is perhaps the strictest defender of the indissolubility of marriage. Based on its understanding of the teachings of Jesus Christ, the church does not recognize a civil divorce action as dissolving a valid marriage. Even though a marriage may be ended in final, irreconcilable separation for whatever cause (culpable or inculpable), the spiritual bond is seen as enduring until the death of one party. The church does not view adultery, in itself, or any action or event subsequent to the consent to marry as breaking a union which was validly contracted. Thus, remarriage is permitted only if a person is not bound to a previous marriage considered valid by the church.

Greater efforts have emerged in Catholic dioceses toward more lengthy preparation and evaluation before a marriage. The church also provides marriage counseling. In addition, the church has an agency for assisting a divorced person who wishes to remarry in the church, known as the diocesan tribunal. The tribunal is an extension of the bishop's ecclesiastical judicial authority and adjudicates marriage cases. Delegated churchpeople judge the validity of marriages according to the norms of canon law, with a jurisprudence formed in the church's vision of a true marriage. The 1983 Code of Canon Law allows not only priests and deacons to be judges but also religious and laypersons. However, if a judge is not a cleric, he or she cannot act as a single judge but must be a member of a three-judge panel.

Canon law is the body of ecclesiastical law by which the Catholic Church governs, teaches, and sanctifies its members. The first general codification was promulgated for the entire Latin church in 1917. The Revised Code of Canon Law was promulgated in 1983 for the Latin Rite. The Code of Canons of the Eastern Churches was promulgated by Pope John Paul II in 1990. The official Latin text, with an English translation under the auspices of the Canon Law Society of America, is available, for both Codes, from the Society.[1] The Canon Law Society of America also commissioned a commentary by various authors.[2] This volume of 1,152 pages provides an extensive interpretation of the entire Revised Code for the Latin Church.[3]

Petitioning the church for a declaration of nullity helps the parties examine the quality of the relationship realistically and in depth. Without attempting to place blame, the inquiry can help both parties gain insight into the real reasons for the failure and hopefully can enable them to enter a new, happy, and lifelong "marriage in the Lord."[4]

A Catholic in the United States may seek a civil separation, divorce, or dissolution, but only for the civil effects, such as custody, alimony, and support. In some dioceses, church permission must be obtained before initiating civil action. A parish priest or other pastoral minister helps a person obtain this permission from the bishop's office. This can be a means for bringing the parties to counseling to determine whether reconciliation is possible and possibly to examine grounds for annulment, more accurately called a "declaration of nullity."

A Catholic who remarries without a declaration of nullity is considered to be in a canonically irregular union and may be excluded from the sacraments (confession and communion). However, such persons are not excommunicated.

Excommunication is a penalty added to the violation of certain laws. The bishops of the United States, in 1884, asked of Pope Leo XIII that this penalty be imposed in their territory for certain Catholics who remarry after civil divorce. They meant the penalty only for those who cause great scandal. However, many divorced Catholics are under the impression that they are excommunicated and feel totally alienated from the church. The penalty was officially removed in 1977 by Pope Paul VI at the request of the American bishops. Although the removal of

---

[Section 35:1]

[1]Office of the Executive Coordinator, Catholic University of America, Washington, DC 20064.

[2]Coriden, Green & Heintschel, eds, *The Code of Canon Law: A Text and Commentary* (Paulist Press, NY 1985).

[3]A sourcebook for the revised marriage legislation is Ladislas M. Orsy, *Marriage in Canon Law* (Michael Glazier, Inc., Wilmington 1986).

[4]See Gaudium et spes, #48, *Vatican Council II: The Conciliar and Port Conciliar Document* (Austin Flannery, O.P., ed., Costello Publ'g Co. 1977).

excommunication as a penalty had little effect in a legal sense, it was significant pastorally, as the church is reaching out to welcome those in irregular unions. Tribunals and compassionate parish priests and other pastoral ministers have reconciled many persons estranged from the church. The establishment of a ministry for divorced and separated Catholics in most dioceses has aided the recovery process.

§ 35:2 Dissolution in the church

Church law views marriage as absolutely indissoluble when it is both sacramental and consummated. If a marriage is not between two baptized Christians (sacramental), or has never been consummated, the church may dissolve it upon certain conditions. This process of a church dissolution is somewhat rare but should be explained briefly.

The Pauline privilege is based on St. Paul's first letter to the Corinthians (7:11). The privilege applies to two nonbaptized persons who divorce, and one becomes a baptized Christian and wishes to marry in the Catholic Church. The bishop of a diocese may now permit this privilege if the proper conditions are fulfilled.

A favor of the faith dispensation is a development of the Pauline privilege in situations where all of the conditions for the privilege are not verified. At least one of the parties is nonbaptized. This can be granted only by the pope, and a number of other conditions must be present.

A marriage which was never consummated can also be dissolved by the pope. Unlike civil law, nonconsummation in itself is not grounds for annulment. In practice, however, nonconsummation usually indicates something seriously and essentially wrong in a marriage. Therefore, most American tribunals will process these cases as formal declarations of nullity rather than seek dissolution by the pope.

§ 35:3 Concepts of nullity of marriage

Marriage is a state that has several definitions, depending on various periods of history and religious and civil requirements. Nullity is similarly ambiguous, depending on the definition of marriage, the purpose of law, etc. In American civil law, annulment is a very restricted concept. Since civil law allows divorce, annulment is reserved for a few very unusual situations.[1]

In canon law, marriage is described as a covenant in which a man and woman establish, between themselves, a communion of their whole lives, by its very nature ordered to the well-being of the spouses, and to the procreation and education of children.[2]

In this respect, there are three basic categories of grounds which render a marriage invalid:

(1) Formalities (Catholics bound by church law to a certain form of marriage);

[Section 35:3]

[1]See Annulment Ch 7.

[2]Revised Code, Canon 1055. Translation from the Latin.

(2) Impediments (church determination of certain obstacles to a valid union); and

(3) Formal grounds, such as essential defects in the consent (discretion, intentions, or capacity for marriage).

Each of these will be examined in the sections which follow.

§ 35:4 Presumption of validity

In canon law, any marriage is presumed valid until proven otherwise by a church tribunal. A common misunderstanding is that only Catholics need a declaration of nullity to remarry in the church. On the contrary, any divorced person is considered by the church to be bound to a previous marriage, if it took place in any recognized form. Recognized forms of marriage include civil or religious ceremonies and in states where it is recognized, such as Ohio, common law marriage.[1] The consequence of this position is that any divorced person who wishes to remarry in the church must present a petition for nullity to a Catholic tribunal. A large percentage of the marriage cases in tribunals are for non-Catholics who wish to marry Catholics. These cases are judged by the same canon law as the marriages of Catholics.

§ 35:5 Catholic form of marriage

Catholics must follow certain formalities to be validly married. Primarily, this means being married in the presence of a delegated priest (or deacon) and two witnesses. This is called the Catholic form of marriage. Permission can be given by a bishop for exceptions if a Catholic marries a non-Catholic, and the law itself makes exceptions for rare situations.

Canon law presently gives a clear criterion for tribunals. If a person is baptized Catholic (whether one ever practiced the faith), the person is bound, for validity, to observe the Catholic form of marriage. A person who marries outside the church without permission and divorces can receive a declaration of nullity in a brief time, with documentary proof, based on a lack of canonical form. The marriage was automatically invalid, no matter how long it lasted.

There is an exception presently in force in the case of a Catholic who marries an Orthodox person, before an Orthodox priest, without permission. The church considers this a valid, although illicit, marriage.

Another exception in the Revised Code, Canon 1117, concerns a Catholic who abandons the faith "by a formal act." This person will no longer be bound by the requirement of the Catholic form for validity, even if the other party is not baptized.

§ 35:6 Impediments

The 1983 Code of Canon Law enumerates the following invalidating

---

[Section 35:4]

[1]Common law marriages which were entered into in Ohio are only valid if they began before October 10, 1991. See RC 3105.12.

(diriment) impediments to marriage: (1) lack of age (sixteen for the man; fourteen for the woman). The United States bishops *could* establish an older age, but not for validity—only to require Chancery permission (they have not, at this time, done so); (2) antecedent and perpetual impotence (not sterility); (3) previous valid bond of marriage; (4) disparity of worship (cult)—if one is Catholic (and has not formally left the church), and the other party is *not baptized*. Dispensation from this impediment is routinely granted if the Catholic promises to do all in one's own power to see that any children are baptized and raised as Catholics; (5) sacred orders (priesthood, diaconate); (6) public perpetual vow of chastity (religious orders); (7) abduction of a woman to induce marriage; (8) murder of a spouse to enter a new marriage; (9) consanguinity (i.e., first cousins or closer); (10) affinity (direct line only, such as mother-in-law or stepdaughter); (11) public propriety (e.g., direct line relatives through concubinage); and (12) legal relationship arising from adoption (e.g., adopted brother and sister).[1]

Tribunal cases based on most of these impediments are extremely rare. These factors are not common. In addition, prior to a Catholic wedding, a priest would investigate whether any of the impediments are present. If the impediment cannot be dispensed by the church, the wedding cannot take place.

The only diriment impediment which occurs more often is that of a previous valid bond. This usually involves a non-Catholic who had been previously, validly married. Based on the presumption of validity of the first marriage, the person would not be considered by the church to be free to contract a second marriage within the lifetime of the first spouse. Even if civil divorce were granted, the church would consider such a second marriage bigamy in canon law.

§ 35:7 Formal process for declaration of nullity

A formal nullity of marriage investigation is the most complicated but also the most common procedure. It concerns those marriages which are presumably valid; that is, proper formalities have been observed, and there are no impediments. The investigations are called "formal" because the presumption of validity must be overturned with sufficient evidence, and the grounds must be proven by a formal trial process prescribed by canon law.

A declaration of nullity is a judgment by a church tribunal that a true, valid marriage never existed. Something which the church considers essential was missing from the very beginning, and these grounds in canon law must be established by proof (testimony of witnesses, etc.). Testimony from one, or even both of the parties, is not, alone, sufficient for this official judgment.

[Section 35:6]

[1]For a further explanation of the impediments, formal grounds of nullity, and the entire section in the Code on marriage, see Doyle, *The Code of Canon Law, A Text and Commentary* 737–833 (Paulist Press, NY 1985); Ladislas M. Orsy, *Marriage in Canon Law* (Michael Glazier, Inc., Wilmington 1986).

A declaration of nullity does not mean there was "nothing." On the contrary, a "marriage" did take place and may have included sincere love, children, good times, etc. But the tribunal is convinced, with "moral certitude," that grounds are proven.

A petition for declaration of nullity must be presented to the tribunal. Any parish priest or other qualified advocate can help a person present a petition to a tribunal. This advocate will give the person a realistic idea of what is involved, especially if the petitioner is not Catholic. The petitioner will be expected to write about the background of the marriage in more than a superficial sense, following a set of questions. This soul-searching analysis is necessary to see if there are any grounds for nullity. It can also be helpful to the petitioner's own personal growth to understand the problems, to learn from them, to aid in the emotional recovery, and to come to forgive the spouse and oneself.

Most tribunals require a preliminary statement and/or a personal interview. A tribunal is interested in the whole course of the courtship and marriage, including family background, and not just in the final events that caused the divorce. This is because a declaration of nullity is a profound judgment that something essential was defective or missing *from the beginning of the marriage*, even if the union lasted for many years. The process can take approximately a year to complete. The time may be somewhat shorter, or much longer, depending on what needs to be proven and what cooperation is received from witnesses, counselors, and other interested persons.

Every diocese in the United States has a tribunal which can judge all formal cases in first instance. A few dioceses delegate a tribunal in another diocese to hear cases. Some countries, like Canada, have a regional system. A court of appeal (second instance) is appointed for every tribunal. Only if the first two decisions are not concordant need a case be appealed for a third instance to the Roman Rota, the Vatican's marriage tribunal. The Vatican (the Apostolic Signatura) has sometimes appointed a court of third instance other than the Rota, such as a third American tribunal.

A tribunal will reject a petition for a declaration of nullity unless there are definite grounds in church law and a reasonable hope of proof. If, by the end of the investigation, the judge cannot reach moral certitude of nullity, he is obliged by the law to render a negative decision, meaning the nullity has not been established.

There is a process of review or appeal for affirmative as well as negative decisions. Mandatory review or appeal is a complicated area. The Revised Code of 1983 requires that every affirmative decision be automatically reviewed by a three-judge panel. The panel can either *ratify* the decision of first instance, or open a new hearing to allow further evidence and issue a second formal decision. If a decision is negative, either party may appeal. A marriage case, since it concerns the important marital status of persons in the church, is never closed and may be reopened under certain conditions, if new significant information is presented.

The expenses actually incurred by a tribunal are high because of the lengthy and elaborate process demanded by canon law. However, most dioceses heavily subsidize their tribunals, so that the fees requested are quite reasonable. At present, fees for a formal case in the Ohio tribunals vary and range up to $450. A case is never refused or treated any differently because of inability to pay all of the suggested amount.

Without going into the procedural law in any depth here, it is important to clarify the usual concerns of the parties. One of the most common fears is that a declaration of nullity renders the children illegitimate, which is not true in church (or civil) law.

Tribunals will usually not accept a case until the civil action is complete. The church first wants to see if reconciliation is possible. Also, a divorce can be contentious and bitter. Petitioning the church for a declaration of nullity is meant to be a healing process in which both parties may benefit; it is not a time for placing blame. In the United States, there are no civil effects resulting from tribunal decisions. They are meant only to clarify their marital status in the church.

The respondent has a right to be heard, that is, to be given an opportunity to testify. If a respondent refuses to cooperate or is not interested, a final decision is still made. If a respondent thinks that a declaration of nullity is unjust, he or she has the right of appeal.

When the final decision is affirmative, i.e., the declaration of nullity is granted, it applies to both parties. However, even when a previous marriage has been declared null, this does not always mean immediate freedom to remarry in the church. A tribunal may place a restriction on parties so that they need special permission of the bishop to remarry. This is to prevent a person from entering into another invalid marriage. It can also protect a party from rushing into marriage with a divorced person, ignorant of the serious problems of the former union that may have formed the basis for the declaration of nullity. In instances of such restrictions on remarriage, a prospective officiant of a new wedding should contact the tribunal to see what the grounds (and problems) were. After learning this information, it is the responsibility of the priest or other pastoral minister to take necessary steps (evaluation, counseling, etc.) and be reasonably assured that there are no significant obstacles to the validity of the new marriage. Often, the officiant must receive permission from the bishop (normally through the Chancery) once the evaluation is complete.

§ 35:8 The assignment of canonical grounds—In general

Once a petition for a declaration of nullity of marriage has been received, the diocesan tribunal studies the allegations in order to determine whether reasons exist to challenge the validity of the marriage under church law. The tribunal is obligated by canon law to cite the respondent with the ground(s) alleged by the petitioner as interpreted by canon lawyers. The respondent's deposition is scrutinized and evaluated in light of the allegations of the petitioner. The testimony of witnesses, which most often include friends and relatives who were privy to the difficulties in the marriage, along with the available reports of professional counselors, psychologists, etc., is evaluated and used to argue the ecclesial status of the marital union under investigation.

The Catholic Church holds that marriage is brought into existence by the lawfully manifested consent of persons who are capable under the law.[1] The question of nullity is based thus on the quality of the consent rendered by the contractants. Canonical grounds for nullity are grouped in categories according to three general defects of consent: (1) non-inclusion of an essential element of marriage, or simulation of consent;[2] (2) incapacity to give consent;[3] and (3) defect of knowledge.[4]

§ 35:9   The assignment of canonical grounds—Simulation of consent

Simulation of consent to marriage can be either total or partial. The ground of total simulation of consent indicates that a marriage is invalid when internal consent of the will does not correspond to the statement of consent during the wedding celebration.[1] Total simulation is identified by an act of the will by which one or both parties exclude from the object of consent marriage as such and all its elements and properties.

Partial simulation of consent signifies invalidity based on the exclusion of an essential element or essential property of marriage as understood in Catholic doctrine.[2] There are four forms of partial simulation: (1) an intention against children when one or both parties exclude children from the marriage;[3] (2) an intention against fidelity in which one or both parties exclude fidelity from the marriage and reserve the right to sexually intimate relationships outside the marital bond;[4] (3) an intention against indissolubility in which one or both parties reserve the right to divorce and remarry;[5] and (4) an intention against the good of the spouses in which one or both parties exclude the intention to establish and maintain marriage as an intimate community of life and conjugal love ordered toward the good of both spouses as well as the procreation and education of children.[6]

§ 35:10   The assignment of canonical grounds—Capacity to consent

The second category involves the capacity of the contractants to

---

[Section 35:8]
[1]See Canon 1057.
[2]Canons 1055–1062.
[3]Canon 1095.
[4]Canons 1096–1100.

[Section 35:9]
[1]Canon 1101, § 2.
[2]Canon 1101, § 2.
[3]Canons 1101, § 2, 1055, § 1.
[4]Canons 1101, § 2, 1056.
[5]Canons 1101, § 2, 1056.
[6]Canons 1101, § 2; 1055, § 1.

exchange marital consent. Canon 1095 distinguishes three types of incapacity: (1) lack of sufficient use of reason;[1] (2) grave lack of discretion of judgment;[2] and (3) incapacity to assume the essential obligations of marriage.[3]

The ground of lack of sufficient use of reason indicates that a marriage is null and void if one or both parties are impaired by a severe psychiatric disorder, severe mental retardation, or intoxication which prohibits the use of reason at the time consent is exchanged.

The ground of grave lack of discretion of judgment indicates invalidity if one or both of the parties suffered a grave lack of discretion of judgment concerning the essential rights and duties of marriage which are to be mutually given and accepted. Individuals giving consent must possess discretion of judgment in proportion to marriage. If marriage is not minimally understood by one or both of the parties in its full scope of rights and responsibilities, or if one or both of the parties does not possess the critical faculty to choose marriage with prudence, the union cannot be said to be a valid marriage under canon law.

Incapacity to assume the essential obligations of marriage is a ground of nullity based on the establishment of the incapacity of one or both of the parties to assume the essential obligations of marriage due to causes of a psychological nature. Besides understanding the rights and responsibilities of marriage, an individual must be capable of assuming the obligations of marriage. If one or both of the parties suffer from a psychological disorder which interferes with the capacity to assume the obligations of a permanent, exclusive, heterosexual partnership, the union cannot be said to be a valid marriage according to church law.

§ 35:11   The assignment of canonical grounds—Lack of knowledge

The third category of canonical grounds invokes situations in which individuals attempted to give marital consent without sufficient knowledge concerning the nature of marriage itself or the person with whom marriage is contracted. Canon law establish six headings for nullity in this category: (1) ignorance;[1] (2) error concerning the person;[2] (3) fraud;[3] (4) error concerning the nature of marriage;[4] (5) condition;[5] and (6) force

---

[Section 35:10]
   [1]Canon 1095, § 1.
   [2]Canon 1095, § 2.
   [3]Canon 1095, § 3.

[Section 35:11]
   [1]Canon 1096, § 1.
   [2]Canon 1097, §§ 1, 2.
   [3]Canon 1098.
   [4]Canon 1099.
   [5]Canon 1102.

and fear.[6]

The ground of ignorance indicates nullity insofar that one or both of the parties at the time of consent were ignorant concerning the essential nature of the matrimonial contract. Catholic doctrine teaches that marriage is a permanent covenant relationship between a man and a woman which is ordered toward the procreation of children by means of sexual cooperation. If one or both parties are ignorant of this fundamental character of marriage, the union cannot be said to be a valid marriage.

Error concerning the person as a ground of nullity of marriage signifies that consent is invalidly placed if one or both of the parties are in error concerning the actual identity of a spouse or are in error concerning a quality directly and principally intended of that spouse. If one or both of the parties are in error as to the actual identity of the other person, the union is invalid. If one or both of the spouses are in error regarding a personal quality upon which the intention to marry is principally based, there is no marriage.

Fraud as a ground for nullity indicates that marital consent was invalidly placed if one or both of the parties were moved to exchange consent due to fraud concerning a quality of one of the persons, which by its very nature could seriously disturb the partnership of conjugal life. Marriage comes into being through the free giving of marital consent to a specific person. If one or both of the parties have been deceived regarding a fundamental quality of the other person which potentially could disrupt the communion of life, the union is said to be invalid.

Condition as a ground of nullity indicates that because marriage is a complete and total commitment to a faithful partnership of the whole of life, if one or both of the parties attach a future condition on the contract of marriage or a condition concerning the past or present, and that condition was not fulfilled, the marriage is invalidly contracted.

The ground of force and fear signifies that marital consent is placed invalidly if one or both parties exchange consent in the presence of external force or grave fear. Marital consent must be given in complete freedom. If one or both of the parties enter marriage because of extreme force or imposed fear, the union is contracted invalidly.

§ 35:12   The attorney's role

At the time of divorce or other civil action terminating a marriage, Catholic clients will often be concerned about status in the church and may wish to initiate a petition for a declaration of nullity. An attorney should direct the parties to a priest, or other pastoral minister, who can give them canonical advice and also the needed pastoral care. Any priest, not just the parties' parish priest, can present a petition for nullity. The attorney should recommend someone who is both competent and compassionate. A good source of recommendations is the Ministry to Divorced and Separated Catholics in the area. The attorney can call any diocese or its tribunal for further information.

---

[6]Canon 1103.

A divorced person, Catholic or not, may not remarry in the Catholic Church unless and until a case is processed by a tribunal. Each and every marriage must be studied. If a previous marriage is presumed to be still binding, a divorced person will not be permitted an official wedding ceremony in any Catholic church. No date for a wedding may be set until a final affirmative decision is given, and there are no restrictions on the decree.

Experts speak of the time needed for healing. Tribunals prefer not to process cases when a person is still engrossed in the emotions of a divorce action, before perspective is gained and insight is reached into one's own contribution to the failure. They also fear a quick and unwise rebound into a second, disastrous marriage.

In some dioceses, a civil attorney is able to participate in the church annulment process. More important is an attorney's willingness to encourage and support the person. The attorney should (1) inform Catholics that they can stay within the good graces of their church community; (2) direct the parties to proper help; and (3) offer to be a witness for them should a church tribunal request the attorney's insights and evaluation.

Chapter 36

Jewish Divorce

*By Rabbi Edward Sukol**

> **KeyCite®:** Cases and other legal materials listed in KeyCite Scope can be researched through West Group's KeyCite service on Westlaw®. Use KeyCite to check citations for form, parallel references, prior and later history, and comprehensive citator information, including citations to other decisions and secondary materials.

§ 36:1 Marriage and divorce under Jewish law

Jewish law, or Halacha, views the relationship of marriage as consisting of a complex intertwining of legal, personal, and religious obligations.[1] The legal obligations imposed upon the husband include providing his wife with sustenance, shelter and clothing, and conjugal rights. The wife owes her husband fidelity and support. Accordingly, the religious ceremony of marriage recognizes both the legal and the religious aspects of the relationship. During the ceremony, in addition to the religious sanctification of marriage, the husband presents the wife with a Ketubah, or marriage contract, detailing his financial obligations to her in the event of divorce or his death. Today, in recognition of new roles for men and women, many Ketubot are egalitarian in nature, outlining both husband's and wife's responsibilities to each other. While an egalitarian Ketubah may not have Halakhic status or validity, it is used by the majority of Jewish couples who are married by non-Orthodox rabbis. The ring, or other article of tangible value presented to the wife during the marriage ceremony, is the "consideration" for her conveyance to the husband of the exclusive right of conjugal access. As with Ketubah, the majority of non-Orthodox wedding ceremonies are double ring ceremonies, in which both groom and bride present the other with a ring as a tangible sign of their commitment. This "transaction" is essentially contractual. For most couples, the aspect of marriage as a transaction has receded into the background. The wedding ceremony,

---

*Based on the 1984 Edition by Harry M. Brown, Esq.

[Section 36:1]

[1]Maurice Lamm, *The Jewish Way in Love and Marriage* (1982).

including the Ketubah, ring, and vows are an expression of commitment, devotion, and love. Nonetheless, marriage within Jewish tradition does retain legal status with rights and responsibilities for both partners. Once having conveyed this right, the wife cannot regain possession of it without a reconveyance by the husband.

Halacha, therefore, requires that the dissolution of a marriage must take cognizance of its dual aspects, the civil and the religious. Originally, the Bet Din, or rabbinical tribunal, fulfilled both functions, determining whether a divorce would be allowed, making all property settlements, and administering the actual divorce. In the United States, rabbinical tribunals no longer have original, exclusive jurisdiction as the arbiters of civil obligations and claims, as they did in other countries. Under general principles of American law, rabbinical tribunals are at best arbitration panels, which obtain their jurisdiction and power solely by agreement of the parties, either in the form of a general contract agreeing to arbitrate all disputes or pursuant to a specific submission agreement.[2] Divorce-related civil matters have been excluded from the jurisdiction of arbitrators, and an agreement to submit divorce issues to arbitration may not be enforceable.[3] Nonetheless, rabbinical tribunals retain the sole jurisdiction to issue a Get, or Jewish law divorce.

The importance of obtaining a Get, in addition to a civilly granted divorce decree, has been noted by commentators.[4] A Jewish woman, civilly divorced but without a Get, remains a married woman under Jewish law, and any subsequent marriage or liaison is considered adulterous. It must be noted that there are internal divisions among people within the Jewish community who view this matter differently. Orthodox Jews attempt to live within a Halakhic (Jewish legal) framework, and therefore the Get is the only valid form of Jewish divorce. Reform Jews, on the other hand, do not require the issuance of a Get. In the Reform Jewish community, a civil divorce is considered adequate for purposes of being divorced and/or remarried. Conservative Judaism, in principle, requires the issuance of a Get. Yet, many, but certainly not all, Conservative rabbis will officiate over a marriage ceremony in which a previously married bride and/or groom does not have a Get.

In addition, within the Reform and Conservative communities, alternatives to the Get have been developed which recognize the egalitarian nature of contemporary society. As with an egalitarian Ketubah, these documents would have no legal standing within a Halakhic framework, but are recognized as valid within the non-Orthodox Jewish world. An observant Jewish man may not marry her, and any children resulting from a subsequent marriage or liaison would be deemed "Mamzerim," which status carries with it serious implications in terms of such children's marriage opportunities as issue of a prohibited

---

[2]*Rabbinical Courts: Modern Day Solomons*, 6 Colum. J.L. & Soc. Probs. 48 (Jan. 1970), reprinted in II Studies of Jewish Jurisprudence (1972).

[3]See Annot., 18 A.L.R. 3d 1264.

[4]Merrill I. Hassenfeld, *A Lawyer's Role in a Jewish Divorce*, 50 Ohio B. 951 (8-8-77).

marriage. Similarly, a Jewish man who has not given a Get may not remarry, although his issue would not be deemed Mamzerim.

The majority of American Jews, and the overwhelming majority of nonobservant Jews, are unfamiliar with the need for a Get, being misinformed as to what a Get is and how it is delivered. The purpose of this article is to clarify some of the misconceptions surrounding this area of law.

§ 36:2   The Get document and its meaning

The Biblical reference to divorce is set forth in *Deuteronomy* as follows:

> When a man takes a wife, and marries her, and it comes to pass, if she finds no favor in his eyes because he has found in her some unseemly thing, that he write her a Bill of Divorcement, and deliver it to her hand, and send her out of his house.[1]

According to Talmudic law, it was possible for a man to divorce his wife against her will. At the beginning of the tenth century, Rabbenu Gershom of Mayence reformed the divorce laws, stipulating among other things that a wife could not be divorced without her consent.

The Bill of Divorcement referred to in verse 1 is called a "Get Peturin" in Aramaic and is written in Aramaic and Hebrew. The word "get" means "instrument" or "document." A "get peturin," therefore, is a "document of release."[2] The text may be translated as follows:

> On the [_____] day of the week, the [_____] day of the month in the year [_____] since creation of the world, according to our accustomed reckoning here, in [_____] the city which is situated on the River [_____] I, [_____], the son of [_____], who stand this day in [_____] the city of [_____] situated upon the River [_____], do hereby grant a Bill of Divorce, to thee, my wife, [_____], daughter of [_____], who have been my wife from time past, and with this I free, release and divorce you, that you may have control and power over yourself, from now and hereafter, to be married to any man whom you may choose, and no man shall hinder you from this day forever more, and you are permitted to any man. And these presents shall be to you from me a Bill of Divorce, a letter of freedom, and a Deed of Release according to the law of Moses and Israel.
>
> [_____], son of [_____], witness
>
> [_____], son of [_____], witness

Clearly, the text of the Get contains no religious formulae, nor does it reference Jewish religious law, save that it is intended to be effective "according to the law of Moses and Israel." The formula of "according to the law of Moses and Israel" hearkens back to antiquity. This phrase is itself recited as part of the marriage ceremony, when the groom says,

---

[Section 36:2]

[1]*Deuteronomy* 24:1-4.

[2]See Machransky v. Machransky, 31 Ohio App. 482, 484, 6 Ohio L. Abs. 315, 166 N.E. 423 (8th Dist. Cuyahoga County 1927) ("The word 'GET' among the Jews signifies a divorce.").

"Be thou sanctified unto me with this ring, according to the law of Moses and Israel."

§ 36:3 Proceedings

The entire process of obtaining a Get takes approximately three hours because the Get must be handwritten by a highly qualified scribe, on parchment or other special medium, and it must be written with requisite intent. Consequently, no preprinted forms may be used. Each Get is specifically written for the man and woman whose relationship will be affected thereby, and the scribe must intend to write it for that couple at that time.

The necessary parties to a Get are the wife or her legally appointed messenger, the husband or his legally appointed messenger, a rabbinical tribunal or Bet Din consisting of three rabbis, a competent scribe, and witnesses who are competent under Jewish law.

When the Bet Din had plenary jurisdiction (as late as the early twentieth century in certain countries), it had the power to determine whether the marriage would be dissolved, and the Bet Din had the discretion to refuse a Get. In modern times, this discretion has been abrogated, and the rabbinical tribunal will invariably assist in the granting of the Get where a civil divorce has been or will be granted, with limited exceptions upon the Halachic status of the original marriage.

Arrangements for the Get proceedings are generally made in advance, and the presiding rabbi will have satisfied himself that a Get is proper and necessary. Preparatory to the proceedings, the presiding rabbi will have obtained all necessary biographical information regarding the identities of the parties, including their Hebrew and English names, and the time, place, and method of solemnization of the marriage.

At the outset of the ceremony, the identity of the parties is established and confirmed through a series of questions and responses, and the presiding rabbi ascertains that no member of the rabbinical tribunal is related to either the husband or the wife and that none of the other participants (i.e., scribe, witnesses, etc.) are related to each other or to the parties. The rabbinical tribunal must then establish that the Halachic requirements of the Get are met, including the following:

(1) That the husband and wife are divorcing of their free will and are subject to no compulsion;

(2) That the husband has appointed the scribe to draft the divorce, and has designated the witnesses to attest to the writing and delivery of the Get, of his own free will;

(3) That the scribe has properly written the Get with the requisite intent;

(4) That the witnesses have been properly designated to witness the Get and its delivery and do so of their free will; and

(5) That the Get has been properly delivered to and accepted by the wife.

The husband designates the scribe to write the Get, appointing him as his agent. The husband then designates and appoints the witnesses to witness the Get and its delivery and acceptance. As part of this formal appointment and designation procedure, the husband publicly declares, in front of the witnesses and the tribunal, that he has not raised and will not raise any questions regarding the validity of the Get, the effect of which would be to jeopardize the wife's status as a divorced woman.

Upon her voluntary acceptance of the Get, the woman signifies her approval by raising it in her hands and redelivering it to the presiding rabbi. The rabbinical tribunal then conducts an inquiry to establish that all of the mandated requirements have been satisfied. The scribe is asked to confirm his proper appointment, as are each of the witnesses, who identify their signatures; the man and woman confirm their voluntary participation.

Upon satisfactory conclusion of the inquiry, the presiding rabbi partially destroys the Get, usually by cutting through the text, so that it may never be used again, and to indicate that it had been properly written, witnessed, delivered, and accepted. The tribunal then announces the completion of the Get proceeding, and that the woman is free to marry any man. The original Get, so defaced, remains in the permanent file of the tribunal; the former spouses are issued a written confirmation of the fact of the proper conduct of the divorce ceremony. Upon completion of the proceedings, the husband is immediately permitted to remarry; the wife must wait at least ninety-one days, to assure that any subsequent pregnancy could not be the result of cohabitation with her former spouse.

The husband and wife need not be present throughout the entire ceremony, although most rabbis desire that they be present or available.

All rabbinical tribunals maintain a permanent record of their proceedings; most rabbis, on remarriage of divorced persons, will request confirmation of the original Get from the tribunal. It is therefore essential that the proceedings be conducted under the aegis of an established tribunal. In Ohio, the premier tribunal is the Orthodox Rabbinical Council of Cleveland.

§ 36:4 Problem of Aguna—Enforcement

Because of the nature of the Get process, voluntary participation by the parties is essential. In fact, the constant inquiry regarding the parties' free will during the procedure is designed to insure that neither party is participating in the Get other than voluntarily. Coercion, intimidation, or bribery is not permitted.

Because of the inability of an observant spouse to remarry without a Get, the withholding of consent and the refusal to participate in the Get have often become negotiating tools. There have been numerous documented cases in which a spouse has refused to participate in the Get process, solely out of spite and in a desire to hurt the other spouse. More often, however, spouses have conditioned their participation in the proceedings on tangible benefits, such as favorable alimony or child support settlements, or as a weapon to extort payments or other financial concessions.

This problem is especially severe as it affects the wife, because she can never remarry without the Get. A woman who has been abandoned by her husband, or whose husband has disappeared, is called an Aguna, or "bound." She is bound by the strictures of Halacha to her first husband, and she cannot remove the bindings without a Get.

When the rabbinical tribunals had plenary authority, a recalcitrant husband could be "convinced" to perform his duty and deliver a Get through various means. The use of such convincing tactics did not constitute impermissible coercion, because they were not deemed to force the husband's participation in the proceeding. Rather, they were deemed to induce his willing participation and overcome his reluctance to cooperate.[1]

As the problem has become more common and because rabbinical tribunals have no enforcement powers, different suggestions have been made to solve this grievous inequity. The most common suggested solution is to include, as part of the negotiations of a separation or property settlement agreement, a specific clause whereby the parties mutually covenant and agree to cooperate in obtaining a Get. If the Get does not become the subject of contention, to be bargained over, the problem can readily be solved.

However, where one of the parties does not desire to participate in the Get proceedings, because of sincere belief, out of spite, or because of a desire for personal gain, there appears to be little that can be done to force such participation through the courts. Many documented cases exist, both in the United States and Israel, in which husbands have refused to grant their wife a Get, thus creating an entire sub-class of women who are Agunot, or "bound women." This problem presents serious challenges within the Orthodox Jewish community. At present, no complete resolution to this problem has been found within a Halakhic framework.

Whether the Get proceeding is religious in nature or inherently secular has been the source of much contention. The difference, of course, relates to the ability of a court to even involve itself in considering the issue, much less compelling participation in a Get proceeding, because of the constitutional safeguard of freedom of religion.

As early as 1954, the New York Supreme Court (a trial court of general jurisdiction) ordered a husband to appear and participate in proceedings before a rabbinical tribunal, by granting specific performance of a clause in a separation agreement which provided for appearance.[2] The court concluded, "Complying with his agreement would not compel the defendant to practice any religion, not even the Jewish faith to which he still admits adherence. . . . Specific performance herein would merely require the defendant to do what he voluntarily agreed to

---

[Section 36:4]
  [1]Moshe Meiselman, *Jewish Woman in Jewish Law* (1978).
  [2]Koeppel v. Koeppel, 138 N.Y.S.2d 366 (Sup 1954).

do."[3]

Subsequent New York cases, however, have seriously clouded the issue. In *Margulies v. Margulies*,[4] the court was faced with the situation of a husband who had agreed (in open court) to appear before the rabbinical tribunal and participate in the Get proceedings. Subsequently, he repeatedly refused to do so. The trial court issued repeated contempt citations, imposed a fine, and ultimately ordered the husband jailed, with the proviso that the husband could purge himself of the contempt by participating in the Get proceedings. On appeal, the appellate division ordered the husband released but allowed the fines to stand. Incarceration was deemed inappropriate because of the court's inability to order a party to "participate in a religious divorce, as such is a matter of one's personal convictions and is not subject to the court's interference."[5] However, the fines were permitted to stand because the defendant, knowing that a Get could only be obtained from a rabbinical tribunal (during the proceedings of which he would have to certify his voluntary participation in such proceedings), had no intention to perform the stipulation. Thus, "he utilized the court for his own ulterior motives" and therefore was fined for the contempt.[6] Thus, enforcement of even a contractual undertaking is not clearly available.

Decisions after *Margulies* have been equally inconsistent. In one celebrated decision, Justice Held ordered a husband to participate in Get proceedings, even in the absence of a separation agreement requiring such participation, on the basis that the Ketubah, or Jewish marriage contract, carries with it a contractual obligation on a husband to participate in Get proceedings.[7]

New York has proposed the only legislative solution to the problem of Aguna. The New York Get statute essentially provides that any party to

---

[3]Koeppel v. Koeppel, 138 N.Y.S.2d 366, 373 (Sup 1954).

[4]Margulies v. Margulies, 42 A.D.2d 517, 344 N.Y.S.2d 482 (1st Dep't 1973).

[5]Margulies v. Margulies, 42 A.D.2d 517, 517, 344 N.Y.S.2d 482 (1st Dep't 1973).

[6]Margulies v. Margulies, 42 A.D.2d 517, 518, 344 N.Y.S.2d 482 (1st Dep't 1973).

[7]Stern v. Stern, (N.Y. Sup., Kings 8-7-79); Avitzur v. Avitzur, 58 N.Y.2d 108, 114, 459 N.Y.S.2d 572, 446 N.E.2d 136, 29 A.L.R.4th 736 (1983) (secular terms of a Ketubah could be enforced independent of their religious nature), citing the "neutral principles of law" approach established by the United States Supreme Court in Jones v. Wolf, 443 U.S. 595, 604, 99 S. Ct. 3020, 61 L. Ed. 2d 775 (1979) (A court may enforce a religious document provided that the court's inquiry does not require it to resolve doctrinal controversies. Where a court's examination of a religious document requires it to decide religious disputes, "the court must defer to the resolution of the doctrinal issue by the authoritative ecclesiastical body."). See also Annot., 29 A.L.R. 4th 746. Several commentators have noted that the *Avitzur* decision may be limited to those marriage contracts which essentially include arbitration clauses similar to antenuptial agreements whereby the parties simply agree to submit their religious disputes to a nonjudicial forum. See J. David Bleich, *Jewish Divorce: Judicial Misconceptions and Possible Means of Civil Enforcement*, 16 Conn. L. Rev. 201 (Winter 1984); Note, *Avitzur v. Avitzur: The Constitutional Implications of Judicially Enforcing Religious Agreements*, 33 Cath. L. Rev. 219 (Fall 1983); Suzanne M. Aiardo, Note, *Avitzur v. Avitzur and New York Domestic Relations Law Section 253: Civil Response to a Religious Dilemma*, 49 Alb. L. Rev. 131 (Fall 1984); Linda S. Kahan, Note, *Jewish Divorce and Secular Courts: The Promise of* Avitzur, 73 Geo. L.J. 193 (Oct. 1984); Lawrence M. Warmflash, *The New*

a marriage who commences an annulment or divorce proceeding must file a sworn complaint that he or she has "taken . . . all steps solely within his or her power to remove any barrier to the defendant's remarriage following the annulment or divorce."[8] The effect of the Get statute is to authorize the court to withhold a civil divorce until, in effect, the party petitioning for divorce removes all barriers to remarriage. This would include the execution of a Get since without it, under Orthodox Jewish law, a spouse would not be entitled to remarry. The New York Get statute has been highly criticized, and in one instance a portion of the law was declared unconstitutional.[9]

Apparently, only one other court (in New Jersey) has reached the same conclusion, holding that the Ketubah itself imposes a legally enforceable, contractual obligation upon the parties to cooperate in obtaining a Get.[10]

As a result, the enforceability of even a specific agreement to participate in Get proceedings is not clear. While the New York cases have been contradictory, for a time, it had appeared that the majority of courts would judicially enforce a separation agreement requiring proceedings before a rabbinical tribunal.[11]

It does not appear that this problem has been faced regularly by Ohio courts. In fact, there are no published opinions which specifically deal with this issue. However, a 1982 unpublished decision of the Eighth District Court of Appeals declared such provisions of separation agreements not to be judicially enforceable.[12]

In *Steinberg v. Steinberg*,[13] the parties had entered into a separation agreement, which provided that they would cooperate in obtaining a Get and had designated the couple's rabbi as the presiding rabbi of the tribunal. The separation agreement was incorporated into the divorce decree, but the wife refused to participate. After a series of hearings, the trial court, while finding that it had no authority to order a party to perform what such party considers a religious act, nevertheless permitted the husband to withhold regular alimony payments until such time as the wife would cooperate with the Get proceedings. On appeal, the court of appeals, relying on the explicit language of Ohio Const. art. I § 7, held:

> Where parties to a separation agreement include therein an obligation relating to a religious practice, said obligation is unenforceable in a court of

---

York Approach to Enforcing Religious Marriage Contracts: From Avitzur *to the Get Statute,* 50 Brook. L. Rev. 229 (Winter 1984).

[8]N.Y. Dom. Rel. L. 253(2)(i).

[9]See Chambers v. Chambers, 122 Misc. 2d 671, 471 N.Y.S.2d 958 (Sup 1983).

[10]Minkin v. Minkin, 180 N.J. Super. 260, 434 A.2d 665 (Ch. Div. 1981).

[11]Waxstein v. Waxstein, 90 Misc. 2d 784, 395 N.Y.S.2d 877 (Sup 1976), judgment aff'd, 57 A.D.2d 863, 394 N.Y.S.2d 253 (2d Dep't 1977).

[12]Seindel v. Steinberg, 1982 WL 2446 (Ohio Ct. App. 8th Dist. Cuyahoga County 1982).

[13]Seindel v. Steinberg, 1982 WL 2446 (Ohio Ct. App. 8th Dist. Cuyahoga County 1982).

law either as a contractual provision or pursuant to the enforcement of a divorce decree which incorporated therein the terms of the separation agreement. Any action by a court to enforce such a provision or to punish a party for contempt for failure to comply with such provision is void. [Citations omitted.]

In its journal entry of November 29, 1979, the trial court attempted to do indirectly what it could not do directly, to wit, induce appellee to perform a religious act. We hold that this order was unconstitutional and void.[14]

Despite the decision of *Steinberg*, the incorporation of a clause which evidences the parties' commitment to a Get is of inestimable value. It may be of great moral value and could support a contempt citation outside of Cuyahoga County. Finally, it could alert the parties and their counsel to the need for immediate action, contemporaneously with the agreement to participate in Get proceedings, without relying on a post-judgment judicial enforcement.

§ 36:5 Conclusion

The Get, or Jewish divorce, is essentially a religiously neutral proceeding involving no ritualistic conduct. It is a legal proceeding, necessary to sever the legal bonds of matrimony and is the only mechanism recognized by Halacha for doing so. It is important for lawyers to counsel their clients as to the need for a Get and to explain to them the nature and particulars of the proceedings. Some parties to a divorce may desire an alternative to a Get, to solemnize the divorce within a Jewish context, even though such alternatives have no Jewish legal validity.

---

[14]Seindel v. Steinberg, 1982 WL 2446, at *3-4 (Ohio Ct. App. 8th Dist. Cuyahoga County 1982).

Chapter 37

Mental Health Experts

By Michael A. Hochwalt, Esq.

> **KeyCite®:** Cases and other legal materials listed in KeyCite Scope can be researched through West Group's KeyCite service on Westlaw®. Use KeyCite to check citations for form, parallel references, prior and later history, and comprehensive citator information, including citations to other decisions and secondary materials.

§ 37:1 Mental health experts in general

Most mental health experts who testify in domestic relations court are either psychologists, social workers, or counselors. Psychologists may have a doctoral degree signified by one of the following abbreviations: Ph.D., Ed.D., or Psy.D. The abbreviation Ph.D. or Ed.D. generally indicates that the therapist has completed approximately three years of study and normally has completed a doctoral dissertation that has taken from one to five years. The Ph.D. or Ed.D. programs usually suggest a strong background in research requirements necessary to complete a doctoral dissertation. The Psy.D. does not have the requirement of the dissertation and may be more heavily oriented in psychological course work and supervision.

Some psychologists in the state of Ohio possess just a master's degree. These psychologists were grandfathered in when the statute was amended to require psychologists to have a doctoral degree. Most master's degrees can be earned in one or two years, compared with the four-plus years that it takes to earn a doctorate degree. Some master's degree programs require a thesis.

§ 37:2 Counselors and social workers

In 1985, the state of Ohio codified the licensure statute for the "licensed professional clinical counselor" (LPCC) and the "licensed professional counselor" (LPC), along with a "licensed independent social worker" (LISW) and the "licensed social worker" (LSW). The LPCC has obtained the board's clinical endorsement to include the unsupervised diagnosis and treatment of mental and emotional disorders within his or her scope of practice,[1] in addition to the privileges of the LPC. The LPC license allows the therapist to offer service involving clinical counseling principles, methods, or procedures to the general public to assist individuals in achieving more effective personal, social, educational, or career development and adjustment.[2] The LISW and LSW apply the specialized knowledge of human development, behavior, socioeconomic, and cultural systems. They directly assist individuals, families, and groups

---

[Section 37:2]
[1]OAC 4757-3-01(O)(1).
[2]RC 4757.01(A).

in a clinical setting to improve or restore their capacity for social functioning, including counseling and the use of psychosocial interventions and social psychotherapy. In addition, the LISW can engage in the private practice of social work as an independent practitioner or as a member of a partnership or group practice, along with all the entitlements granted to the LSW.[3] The LSW may perform for a fee, salary, or other consideration, in a clinical setting, counseling and psychosocial intervention without supervision, and social psychotherapy under the supervision of a LISW, a LPCC, a licensed psychologist, a licensed psychiatrist or other licensed physician, or a registered nurse with a master's degree in psychiatric nursing.[4]

§ 37:3 Ethical obligations—Standards of professions

When dealing with mental health professionals, it is important to understand the various ethical obligations they must observe, which may affect how they respond to a subpoena. The Ohio Counseling and Social Workers Board subscribes to codes of ethics and practice standards for counselors and social workers promulgated by the "American Counseling Association" and the "National Association of Social Workers." These shall be used as aids in resolving ambiguities in the interpretation of the rules of professional ethics and conduct, except that the Board's rules of ethical practice and professional conduct shall prevail whenever any conflict exists between Ohio's rules and the professional associations standards.[1] The state of Ohio adopted the Code of Ethics of the American Association of Counseling and Development, now called as the American Counseling Association (ACA), as the standard for professional and ethical behavior for persons engaged in counseling until they adopted their own laws and rules on July 3, 1997.[2] The Counselor and Social Worker Board adopted six additional provisions specifically designated as standards that must be observed by licensed counselors[3] as follows:

(1) The counselor shall maintain high standards of personal conduct.

(2) The counselor should not practice . . . any form of discrimination.

(3) The counselor should not engage in any action that violates . . . the civil or legal rights of clients.

(4) The counselor should under no circumstances be involved with the sexual exploitation of clients.

(5) The counselor should not claim . . . professional qualifications that differ from his/her actual qualifications.

(6) The counselor should not practice outside the areas of competence listed on his/her professional disclosure statement.

---

[3]RC 4757.09(B)(5).

[4]OAC 4757-15-02(A).

[Section 37:3]

[1]OAC 4757-5-01(A)(4).

[2]OAC 4757-21-01(A).

[3]OAC 4757-21-01(A).

The state of Ohio adopted the Code of Ethics of the National Association of Social Workers as the standard for professional and ethical behavior for persons engaged in social work until they adopted their own laws and rules on July 3, 1997.[4] The Counselor and Social Worker Board adopted seven additional provisions specifically designated as standards that must be observed by licensed social workers[5] as follows:

(1) When the social worker has other relationships, particularly of an administrative, supervisory, and/or evaluative nature with an individual seeking social work services, the social worker must not provide those services. . .. Dual relationships especially must be avoided.

(2) All experimental methods of treatment must be clearly indicated.

(3) The social worker must carefully screen all prospective group participants.

(4) It is unethical for a social worker to use an agency affiliation to recruit clients for a private practice.

(5) The social worker must assume responsibility for the welfare of clients who participate as research subjects.

(6) The social worker neither claims nor implies professional qualifications exceeding those possessed.

(7) The social worker should not practice outside the areas of competence and services provided listed on his/her professional disclosure statement.

On July 3, 1997, Ohio's laws and rules governing the practice of counseling and social work became effective, which can be found in OAC 4757-5-01.

§ 37:4 Ethical obligations—Confidentiality—In general

First and foremost, all counselors have the duty to protect confidential communications. The 1996 U.S. Supreme Court decision in *Jaffee v. Redmond*[1] recognized the importance of protecting confidential communications between a psychotherapist and patient from involuntary disclosure. This decision reaffirmed the position that a privilege between a therapist and patient would serve important private interests. The Supreme Court recognized not only the need for a federal privilege to protect confidential communications between a psychotherapist and the patient, but it also extended that privilege to include confidential communications made to licensed social workers in the course of psychotherapy. The Court was persuaded that the privilege protecting confidential communication "promotes sufficiently important interests to

---

[4]OAC 4757-21-01(B).

[5]OAC 4757-21-01(B).

[Section 37:4]

[1]Jaffee v. Redmond, 518 U.S. 1, 116 S. Ct. 1923, 135 L. Ed. 2d 337, 44 Fed. R. Evid. Serv. 1 (1996).

outweigh the need for probative evidence."[2] The Court noted that, "Effective psychotherapy . . . depends upon an atmosphere of confidence and trust in which the patient is willing to make a frank and complete disclosure of facts, emotions, memories, and fears. Because of the sensitive nature of the problems for which individuals consult psychotherapists, disclosure of confidential communications made during counseling sessions may cause embarrassment or disgrace. For this reason, the mere possibility of disclosure may impede development of the confidential relationship necessary for successful treatment."[3] The Court further noted that, "The mental health of our citizenry, no less than its physical health, is a public good of transcendent importance."[4]

§ 37:5 Ethical obligations—Confidentiality—Counselor

The counselor is under a duty to respect the client's right to privacy and to avoid illegal and unwarranted disclosures of confidential information.[1] The ACA Code notes that the right to privacy may be waived by the client or the client's legally recognized representative. The requirement that counselors keep information confidential does not apply when disclosure is required to prevent clear and imminent danger to the client or to others, or when legal requirements demand that confidential information be revealed.[2] If a counselor receives information that a client has a contagious fatal disease, the counselor is justified in disclosing that information to an identifiable third party, who by his or her relationship with the client, is at a high risk of contracting the disease. Before making disclosure, though, the counselor should ascertain that the client has not already informed the third party about his or her disease, and that the client is not intending to inform the third party in the immediate future.[3]

When the court orders a therapist to release confidential information without a client's permission, the counselor must request the court not to require the disclosure due to the potential harm to the client or the counseling relationship.[4] Therefore, counselors are under an ethical obligation to do everything possible to stop the disclosure of confidential information, which may include filing a motion to quash. Even when ordered to disclose confidential information, the counselor has an ethical obligation to reveal only essential information and, to the extent pos-

---

[2]Jaffee v. Redmond, 518 U.S. 1, 116 S. Ct. 1923, 1928, 135 L. Ed. 2d 337, 44 Fed. R. Evid. Serv. 1 (1996).

[3]Jaffee v. Redmond, 518 U.S. 1, 116 S. Ct. 1923, 1928, 135 L. Ed. 2d 337, 44 Fed. R. Evid. Serv. 1 (1996).

[4]Jaffee v. Redmond, 518 U.S. 1, 116 S. Ct. 1923, 1924, 135 L. Ed. 2d 337, 44 Fed. R. Evid. Serv. 1 (1996).

[Section 37:5]

[1]ACA Code of Ethics and Standards of Practice (hereinafter ACA) § B-1-a.

[2]ACA § B-1-c.

[3]ACA § B-1-d.

[4]ACA § B-1-e.

sible, to inform clients before confidential information is disclosed.[5] Therefore, counselors have the similar duty as psychologists which requires minimal disclosure.

§ 37:6   Ethical obligations—Confidentiality—Social worker

Social workers have the fewest specified requirements regarding confidentiality and privacy. Their Code of Ethics simply states that the social worker should respect the privacy of clients and hold in confidence all information obtained in the course of professional service.[1] "The social worker should share with others confidences revealed by clients without their consent only for compelling professional reasons."[2] Yet, the Code of Ethics does not specify what those compelling professional reasons may be.

§ 37:7   Ethical obligations—Confidentiality—Psychologist

Under the American Psychological Association (APA) Ethical Principles of Psychologists and Code of Conduct, psychologists have a primary obligation to take reasonable precautions to respect the confidentiality rights of those with whom they work or consult.[1] They are under a duty to minimize the intrusions on privacy, and therefore to include in the written and oral reports, consultations, and the like, only information germane to the purpose for which the communication is made.[2] They have the duty not to disclose confidential information without the consent of the individual unless mandated by law, or where permitted by law for a valid purpose, such as to provide needed professional services to the patient, individual, or an organizational client, to obtain appropriate professional consultation, to protect the patient or client or others from harm, to obtain payment for services in which instance disclosure is limited to the minimum that is necessary to achieve the purposes.[3]

Under Section 2.02(B), psychologists must refrain from the misuse of assessment techniques or results and interpretations and take reasonable steps to prevent others from misusing the information these techniques provide. Therefore, psychologists have a duty to refrain from releasing raw test results or raw data to persons other than to patients or clients, as appropriate, who are not qualified to use such information.[4] It should be noted that counselors also have a requirement regarding release of raw data, in that they too are only to release the data to

---

[5]ACA § B-1-f.

[Section 37:6]
[1]National Association of Social Workers Code of Ethics (NASW) § II(H).
[2]NASW § II(H)(1).

[Section 37:7]
[1]APA Ethical Principles of Psychologists and Code of Conduct 1992, § 5.02.
[2]APA Ethical Principles of Psychologists and Code of Conduct 1992, § 5.03(A).
[3]APA Ethical Principles of Psychologists and Code of Conduct 1992, § 5.05(A).
[4]APA Ethical Principles of Psychologists and Code of Conduct 1992, § 2.02(B).

persons recognized by counselors as competent to interpret the data.[5] Therefore, when data is subpoenaed, counselors and psychologists have a duty to give that material only to a therapist, rather than to a person who may misuse the results. Therapists may hinder the discovery process by not disclosing raw data to the attorney, to avoid the possible misuse or misinterpretation of the data. Clearly a court can step in and allow this information to be released to a therapist hired by the defense to review the data. This would allow both the attorney and the therapist to fulfill their ethical requirements.

§ 37:8   Exceptions to confidentiality—Reporting statutes—Child abuse

"No person listed in division (A)(1)(b) of this section [attorney; physician, . . .; person engaged in social work or the practice of professional counseling; or person rendering spiritual treatment through prayer in accordance with the tenets of a well-recognized religion], who is acting in an official or professional capacity and knows or suspects that a child under [18] years of age or a mentally retarded, developmentally disabled, or physically impaired child under twenty-one years of age has suffered or faces a threat of suffering any physical or mental wound, injury, disability, or condition of a nature that reasonably indicates abuse or neglect of the child, shall fail to immediately report that knowledge or suspicion to the public children services agency or a municipal or county peace officer in the county in which the child resides or in which the abuse or neglect is occurring or has occurred."[1] The attorney and physician have statutory exclusions under RC 2151.421(A)(2) for communication that would be privileged under RC 2317.02. The psychologist is given equal treatment, with the physician under the testimonial privileges statute, pursuant to RC 4732.19. Therefore, if the psychologist received the communication from a patient in the patient-psychologist relationship, and it falls within the RC 2317.02(B) testimonial privilege, the psychologist would not be required to make a report. However, the statute provides that the patient is deemed to have waived the privilege if the patient, at the time of the communication, is either a child under 18 years of age or physically or mentally handicapped child under 21 years of age, and the physician knows or suspects as a result of the communication or any observations made during that communication that the patient has suffered or faces a threat of suffering any physical or mental wound, injury, disability, or condition of a nature that reasonably indicates abuse or neglect, and the physician-patient relationship does not arise out of a patient's attempt to have an abortion; then, the psychologist or physician would have a duty to report.

While this requirement appears to be clear cut, in practice it has been very difficult for many therapists. A definition of abuse under RC

---

[5]APA Ethical Principles of Psychologists and Code of Conduct 1992, § 2.02(E)(4)(b).

[Section 37:8]

[1]RC 2151.421(A)(1).

2151.031 includes a victim of sexual activity,[2] an endangered child,[3] a child who exhibits evidence of any physical or mental injury inflicted by other than accidental means, or injury that is at variance with the history given of it,[4] and, because of acts of a parent or custodian, a child who suffers physical or mental injury that harms or threatens to harm the child's health or welfare.[5]

A child is endangered if the child is administered corporal punishment or other physical disciplinary measure, or physically restrained in a cruel manner for a prolonged period, which punishment, discipline, or restraint is excessive under the circumstances and creates a risk of serious physical harm to the child.[6] For the child to be endangered by a parent or custodian, the conduct or endangering must include punishment done in a cruel manner or for prolonged periods in a manner excessive under the circumstances and which creates substantial risk of serious physical harm,[7] or, if the party repeatedly administers unwarranted disciplinary measures to the child, where there is a substantial risk that such conduct, if continued, would seriously impair or retard the child's mental health or development.[8] RC 2151.031(C) specifically states, though, that if a child is receiving corporal punishment by a parent or custodian, the child is not an abused child if it is not prohibited under RC 2919.22.

Courts throughout the United States are having extreme difficulty in determining parental abuse. One court determined that defendant's son's bruised left eyelid, bruises, welts, and lacerations caused by belt whipping on buttocks and lower legs, and swollen hand did not cause the son serious physical harm or threaten substantial risk of physical harm so as to sustain defendant's conviction for child endangering. These injuries did not result in hospitalization, substantial risk of death, permanent incapacity, disfigurement, or substantial pain or suffering, but were rather the result of imposition of corporal punishment by the father, who determined that his son's school conduct and lying about the fact that he was in detention warranted strong physical disciplinary response.[9] This seems to be a "no broken bones or stitches" standard!

During a hearing in one domestic relations court, a children's service bureau social worker, when asked if a particular incident was abuse, stated that he felt abuse had occurred but was not sure that it would be deemed abuse under some of the case law interpretations, such as *State*

---

[2]RC 2151.031(A).

[3]RC 2151.031(B).

[4]RC 2151.031(C).

[5]RC 2151.031(D).

[6]RC 2919.22.

[7]RC 2919.22(B)(1)(c).

[8]RC 2919.22(B)(1).

[9]State v. Ivey, 98 Ohio App. 3d 249, 648 N.E.2d 519 (8th Dist. Cuyahoga County 1994), dismissed, appeal not allowed, 71 Ohio St. 3d 1476, 645 N.E.2d 1257 (1995).

v. Ivey.[10] This difficulty in determining a legal standard of abuse has kept children in violent situations with the fear of greater violence occurring because it was reported to children's services. Another difficulty from a therapeutic standpoint is the fact that many abusers may decide not to receive treatment because of the reporting statutes, when advised that what they say may not be held confidential and that their admissions may be reported to various agencies.

§ 37:9 Exceptions to confidentiality—Reporting statutes—Adult abuse

Any attorney, physician, psychologist, counselor, social worker, clergy member, and any employee of a community mental health facility or any employee of a hospital must report abuse, neglect or exploitation of an adult to the county department of human services.[1] An adult, for purposes of these statutes, is deemed to be any person 60 years of age or older within this state who is handicapped by infirmities of aging or that has a physical or mental impairment that prevents him from providing for his own care or protection and who resides in an independent living arrangement.[2]

§ 37:10 Exceptions to confidentiality—Reporting statutes— Felony

RC 2921.22 states that "No person . . . shall fail to report information to police if they know that a felony happened or is being committed." RC 2921.22(G) does not require this disclosure by an attorney, doctor, licensed psychologist, or religious counselor if the information is privileged by reason of the relationship, or if it is due to a bona fide program of treatment or services for drug dependent persons.[1] Counselors and social workers are not excluded from this duty to report under this statute. This makes it quite difficult for counselors and social workers, as compared to psychologists, because they are more likely to be at the various social service agencies and will see people who are involved in criminal activity. While therapists may be in a position to help, they clearly must give warnings that the information they receive from a client may not be protected and may not be confidential.

The wording of the reporting statute itself is another difficult challenge for therapists. While the statute states that the therapist "shall not fail to immediately report or cause reports to be made of that knowledge or suspicion of child abuse," there is concern among therapists that, by making the report, the child may be further abused because of

---

[10]State v. Ivey, 98 Ohio App. 3d 249, 648 N.E.2d 519 (8th Dist. Cuyahoga County 1994), dismissed, appeal not allowed, 71 Ohio St. 3d 1476, 645 N.E.2d 1257 (1995).

[Section 37:9]
[1]RC 5101.61.
[2]RC 5101.60.

[Section 37:10]
[1]RC 2921.22(G).

the time period between the report being made and action being completed to help the child by the various agencies or a police department. The report may cause a child to be in more danger.

There are also additional potential conflicts that have not been addressed at this time. One such situation may be where a counselor or social worker is providing services under the license of a psychologist and under the psychologist's supervision. If the counselor or social worker is counseling an abuser who is over 18 years of age, some courts may hold that these therapists fall under the same duties as the psychologist. In such a case, the therapist would not have to report the abuse; whereas in the particular role as a social worker or counselor, they clearly would have to report the abuse. A psychologist or physician is only under an obligation to report abuse if: (1) the patient is a child under 18 years of age or a physically or mentally handicapped child under 21; and (2) the physician knows or suspects as a result of communication, or any observations made during the communication, that the patient has suffered or faces the threat of suffering any physical or mental wound, injury, disability, or condition of a nature that reasonably indicates abuse or neglect of the patient; and (3) the physician-patient relationship does not arise out of the patient's attempt to have an abortion.[2] Therefore, it appears that the physician, psychologist, or psychiatrist could treat the abuser without having to report the abuse, but the social worker and the counselor cannot treat without reporting. Again, this creates a great hardship, in that counselors and social workers are more likely to provide services at the various social service agencies where they may be able to deal successfully with the abuser. However, because they are not exempt from reporting by the privilege statute, counselors and social workers must notify the abuser that what they tell them will not be confidential, and therefore they may never be able to deal with those issues.

§ 37:11   Privileged communication—In general

The duty to protect privileged communication is clearly the most difficult area for therapists who are called to testify in a domestic relations action, and has proven to be extremely difficult for attorneys in determining what advice to give therapists. The advice given by an attorney in 1997 may not be good advice in 1998. There have been more than ten amendments to RC 2317.02 since 1987. This area was more critical between 1993, when *Polikoff v. Adam* was decided, and 1998 when RC 2505.02 was amended. In the past, if there was a potential error in a ruling, the attorneys could obtain an immediate appeal of an issue involving privilege. Quite often, the court of appeals would overrule a trial court's decision, allowing the privilege to stand. In *Polikoff*, the Court severely limited what it determined to be a final appealable order. In August 1993, by virtue of the *Polikoff* decision, a ruling on privilege was no longer considered a final appealable order. Prior to *Polikoff*, the

---

[2]RC 2151.421(A)(2).

Court used a balancing approach.[1] After *Polikoff*, a witness had to disclose confidential information or risk being held in contempt of court. Only at the end of the entire trial could the decision to release the allegedly privileged information be appealed under *Polikoff*. During that period, where privileged communication was incorrectly allowed to be discovered, or where it had been incorrectly ordered that a therapist had to testify at a deposition or trial, the critical information would have been disclosed and the damage done, which could not be rectified. It created a situation that could permanently destroy the therapist-client relationship without any remedy until the damage was complete.

In trying to create a special niche in cases like *Polikoff*, the Butler County Court of Appeals held in *Whiteman v. Whiteman*[2] that an order compelling disclosure of treatment in a custody case was a final appealable order and, therefore, the party immediately could appeal the lower court ruling and order to disclose the privileged information. The court held that divorce and custody actions are purely statutory, and therefore are a special statutory proceeding. Thus, the court stated that the order compelling disclosure of the records in *Whiteman* was a final appealable order under RC 2505.02. On many occasions in domestic relations cases, parties have sought discovery not because they needed the information, but simply in an effort to harass or abuse the other side. Parties continue to play control games long after the divorce decree has been filed. The *Whiteman* case allows the court of appeals to act when discovery orders have been deemed to be too broad.

The Supreme Court appears to have put this issue to rest in *Walters v. Enrichment Center of Wishing Well, Inc.*[3] The Court held that, in making the determination that an order is a final appealable order, courts need only look at the underlying action. The type of order being considered is immaterial. The Court recognized the strong policy arguments for the appealability of an order if the issue has to do with privilege, but the Court noted that any changes must be made by the legislature. As of November 1997, House Bill 394, which would allow interlocutory review in situations where the right of privilege applies, had been passed by the Ohio House of Representatives, but was still pending in the Senate Judiciary Committee. On July 22, 1998, RC 2505.02 was amended to include "an order is a final order that may be reviewed, affirmed, modified, or reversed, with or without retrial, when it is one of the following:

An order that grants or denies a provisional remedy and to which both of the following apply:

[Section 37:11]

[1]See Amato v. General Motors Corp., 67 Ohio St. 2d 253, 21 Ohio Op. 3d 158, 423 N.E.2d 452 (1981) (overruled by, Polikoff v. Adam, 67 Ohio St. 3d 100, 616 N.E.2d 213 (1993)).

[2]Whiteman v. Whiteman, 1995 WL 375848 (Ohio Ct. App. 12th Dist. Butler County 1995).

[3]Walters v. Enrichment Center of Wishing Well, Inc., 1997 -Ohio- 232, 78 Ohio St. 3d 118, 676 N.E.2d 890 (1997).

(a) The order in effect determines the action with respect to the provisional remedy and prevents a judgment in the action in favor of the appealing party with respect to the provisional remedy; and

(b) The appealing party would not be afforded a meaningful or effective remedy by an appeal following final judgment as to all proceedings, issues, claims and parties in the action."[4]

§ 37:12 Privileged communication—Criteria for privilege

There are four conditions that must be met to create a privilege:[1]

(1) The communication must originate in confidence that it will not be disclosed;

(2) The element of confidentiality must be essential to the full and satisfactory maintenance of the relationship between the parties;

(3) The relationship must be one which the community believes should be sedulously fostered; and

(4) The injury that would inure to the relationship by the communication's disclosure must be greater than the benefit thereby gained for the correct disposal of litigation.

Communications in all therapy sessions are deemed confidential due to the agreement between the parties and the therapist, given the various exclusions due to the reporting statutes and duties to warn. However, these communications may not, in fact, be privileged.

Wigmore on Evidence[2] has stated that the four conditions that must be met to create a privilege include, first, "that the communication must originate in confidence that it will not be disclosed." The majority of courts have interpreted that a court ordered relationship is not one that has originated in confidence, in that normally court ordered therapy implies that the court will receive some type of report from that counseling. The Supreme Court in *In re Wieland*[3] held that in the absence of a specific statutory waiver or exception, the testimonial privilege established under RC 2317.02(B)(1), RC 4932.19, and RC 2317.02(G) are applicable to communications made by a parent in the course of treatment ordered as part of a reunification plan in an action for dependency and neglect. It would appear that the distinguishing factor is court-ordered *treatment* rather than court-ordered *evaluation* and that certainly treatment implies the need for confidentiality. On April 10, 2001, H.B. 506 became law which included a new exclusion to the privilege statute, namely RC 2317.02(G)(1)(g) which allows an exclusion when the testimony is sought in a civil action and concerns court ordered treatment or services received by a patient as part of a case plan journal-

---

[4]RC 2505.02(B)(4)(a)(b).

[Section 37:12]

[1]8 *Wigmore Evidence*, § 2285 (McNaughton rev. ed. 1961).

[2]8 *Wigmore on Evidence* § 2285 (McNaughton rev. ed. 1961).

[3]In re Wieland, 2000 -Ohio- 233, 89 Ohio St. 3d 535, 733 N.E.2d 1127 (2000).

ized under RC 2151.412 or the court ordered services are necessary or relevant to dependency, neglect or abuse, or temporary or permanent custody proceedings under RC Ch. 2151.

§ 37:13 Privileged communication—Federal law privileges

Rule 501 of the Federal Rules of Evidence governs how the federal courts deal with the issue of privilege. It states that:

> Except as otherwise required by the Constitution of the United States or provided by Act of Congress or in rules prescribed by the Supreme Court pursuant to statutory authority, the privilege of a witness, person, government, State, or political subdivision thereof shall be governed by the principles of the common law as they may be interpreted by the courts of the United States in light of reason and experience. However, in civil actions and proceedings, with respect to an element of a claim or defense as to which State law supplies the rule of decision, the privilege of a witness, person, government, State, or political subdivision thereof shall be determined in accordance with State law.

Therefore, under federal law, there could be as many interpretations of this rule as there are states. That is why the ruling of *Jaffee v. Redmond*[1] is so important. The Supreme Court, through *Jaffee*, gave guidance to courts and therapists nationwide and ended the balancing component of the privilege in federal court.

§ 37:14 Privileged communication—State law privileges

In Ohio, Evidence Rule 501 states that, "The privilege of a witness, person, state, or political subdivision thereof shall be governed by statute enacted by the General Assembly or by principles of common law as interpreted by the courts of this state in the light of reason and experience." The physician-patient and therapist-client privilege is established by RC 2317.02. The statute specifically states that the following persons shall not *testify* under certain conditions: physicians,[1] clergy,[2] licensed counselors and social workers,[3] and psychologists as incorporated by RC 4732.19 giving psychologists the same privilege as the physician under RC 2317.02.

§ 37:15 Privileged communication—State law privileges— Psychologists and physicians

More specifically, as it relates to domestic relations court, a physician or psychologist shall not testify unless the patient is deemed by RC 2151.421 to have waived any testimonial privilege under this section.

[Section 37:13]
    [1]Jaffee v. Redmond, 518 U.S. 1, 116 S. Ct. 1923, 135 L. Ed. 2d 337, 44 Fed. R. Evid. Serv. 1 (1996); See § 37:4, Ethical obligations—Confidentiality—In general.

[Section 37:14]
    [1]RC 2317.02(B)(1).
    [2]RC 2317.02(C).
    [3]RC 2317.02(G).

The physician may then be compelled to testify on the same subject.[1] The physician or psychologist, however, does not have the testimonial privilege and may testify or may be compelled to testify in any civil action in accordance with the discovery provisions of the Rules of Civil Procedure in connection with the civil action if a medical claim or an action for wrongful death or any other type of civil action is filed by the patient.[2] If that exception does apply, however, the physician or psychologist may be compelled to testify or to submit to discovery under the Rules of Civil Procedure only as to communication made to him by the patient in question in that relationship or his advice to the patient in question that related causally or historically to physical and mental injuries that are relevant to issues in the medical claim or civil action.[3] If the exception applies, the psychologist or physician, in lieu of personally testifying as to the results of the test in question, may submit a certified copy of those results and, upon its submission, a certified copy is qualified as authentic evidence and may be admitted as evidence in accordance with the Rules of Evidence.[4] Under RC 2317.02(B)(4)(a), communication is defined broadly as any "acquiring, recording, or transmitting any information, in any manner, concerning any facts, opinions, or statements necessary to enable a physician or dentist, [or a psychologist by incorporation of RC 4732.19,] to diagnose, treat, prescribe or act for a patient." A "communication" may include, but is not limited to, any "medical or dental, office, or hospital communication such as a record, chart, letter, memorandum, laboratory test and results, x-ray, photograph, financial statement, diagnosis, or prognosis." The psychologist may have to testify also if the testimony privilege is waived by way of RC 2151.421 with regard to child abuse, if,

(a) The client or patient, at the time of the communication, is either a child under eighteen years of age or a mentally retarded, developmentally disabled, or physically impaired person under twenty-one years of age.

(b) The attorney or physician knows or suspects, as a result of the communication or any observations made during that communication, that the client or patient has suffered or faces a threat of suffering any physical or mental wound, injury, disability, or condition of a nature that reasonably indicates abuse or neglect of the client or patient.

(c) The attorney-client or physician-patient relationship does not arise out of the client's or patient's attempt to have an abortion without the notification of her parents, guardian, or custodian.[5]

In the domestic relations case, the court should determine on a case-by-case basis, by way of an *in-camera* inspection, whether the particular records are relevant to the issues of custody or visitation.

[Section 37:15]
  [1]RC 2317.02(B)(1).
  [2]RC 2317.02(B)(1)(a)(iii).
  [3]RC 2317.02(B)(3)(a).
  [4]RC 2317.02(B)(3)(b).
  [5]RC 2151.421(A)(2).

§ 37:16 Privileged communication—State law privileges— Clergy

More and more pastoral counselors are being called to testify in domestic relations court. RC 2317.02(C) allows the testimonial privilege to "a member of the clergy, rabbi, priest or regularly ordained, accredited, or licensed minister of an established and legally cognizable church, denomination, or sect, when the cleric, rabbi, priest, or minister remains accountable to the authority of that church, denomination, or sect, concerning a confession made, or any information confidentially communicated, for a religious counseling purpose in professional character; however, the cleric, rabbi, priest, or minister may testify by express consent of the person making the communication, except when the disclosure of the information is in violation of a sacred trust." Therefore, it is critical that the confidential communication was made for a "religious counseling purpose." This creates special problems for the court to determine issues such as whether marital counseling is deemed a religious counseling purpose, or whether a pastoral counselor needs to be licensed in Ohio to provide marital counseling services.

This statute only allows a waiver by express consent of the person making the communication. This seems to imply that if marital counseling is deemed to be a religious counseling purpose, then even if both parties file for custody of the children and both place their mental health at issue, it would appear that the privilege could not be waived without the express written consent of the parties. The Washington Supreme Court, in *State v. Motherwell*,[1] stated that it would not have to distinguish religious counseling from secular counseling. The court held that the definition of social worker applies to religious counselors when they are involved in counseling that directly concerns the welfare of children. "[A] person engages in social work if he provides social services to adults or families, regardless of whether the services are religiously or secularly motivated. . .courts are not called on to distinguish religious and secular activities."[2] Therefore, at least one state supreme court has dealt with this area of law and has come to the conclusion that if a pastoral counselor is actually providing counseling or social work, it would appear she falls under the standards of the counseling profession or social work profession. It also would appear that she would have the same rights and obligations.

In Ohio, the Hamilton County Court of Appeals dealt with a religious counseling issue in *Niemann v. Cooley*.[3] In that case, the Archdiocesan defendants attempted to assert on appeal a clergy privilege in addition to the defendant's therapist-patient privilege. The Archdiocese stated that it felt that Father Cooley's mental health counseling communica-

---

[Section 37:16]

[1]State v. Motherwell, 114 Wash. 2d 353, 367-68, 788 P.2d 1066 (1990).

[2]State v. Motherwell, 114 Wash. 2d 353, 788 P.2d 1066 (1990).

[3]Niemann v. Cooley, 93 Ohio App. 3d 81, 637 N.E.2d 943 (1st Dist. Hamilton County 1994) (disapproved of by, Walters v. Enrichment Center of Wishing Well, Inc., 1997 -Ohio- 232, 78 Ohio St. 3d 118, 676 N.E.2d 890 (1997)).

tions were shared with them in an ongoing pastoral relationship between Cooley, as an ordained Roman Catholic priest, and his spiritual advisors. The court stated that the record did not establish that the communications sought were "confessional" or in the nature of "religious counseling" which is required for the clergy privilege to apply.[4] The court also found in *Niemann* that the clergyman's mental health counselors were assigned by the church for its own use rather than for the purpose of providing treatment, and therefore the therapist-patient privilege did not apply to the records. In *Niemann*, it appears that Father Cooley was evaluated by the church as part of their investigation of the possibility of sexual misconduct and therefore that evaluation was not deemed treatment. It should be noted that the distinction clearly must be made whether the counseling was by a psychologist, a social worker, or a counselor, because the issue was the possibility of sexual abuse of a minor. Treatment of Father Cooley by a psychologist would have been privileged, but his treatment by a social worker or counselor would not be privileged because RC 2317.02(G)(1)(a) expressly affords no privileged communication involving a social worker or counselor where there is a clear and present danger to a client or another person. Clear and present danger includes the definition of present or past child abuse.[5]

§ 37:17   Privileged communication—State law privileges— Counselors and social workers

Licensed counselors and licensed social workers are entitled to a testimonial privilege concerning a confidential communication received from a client or advice given to a client unless a variety of exceptions apply. These exceptions include: (1) clear and present danger to client or others, or child abuse or neglect as it is by definition a clear and present danger; (2) the client gives express consent or the executor gives express consent; (3) if the client is deceased, the surviving spouse, executor or administrator gives express consent; (4) if the client voluntarily testifies, the therapist may be compelled to testify on the same subject; (5) if the court in camera determines that the information communicated by the client is not germane to the counselor-client or social worker-client relationship; or (6) if a court, in an action brought against a school, its administration, or any of its personnel by the client, rules, after an in camera inspection, that the testimony of the school guidance counselor is relevant to that action.[1] This section leaves more questions than answers as written.

The language that applies to physicians and psychologists, i.e., "any

---

[4]Niemann v. Cooley, 93 Ohio App. 3d 81, 89, 637 N.E.2d 943 (1st Dist. Hamilton County 1994) (disapproved of by, Walters v. Enrichment Center of Wishing Well, Inc., 1997 -Ohio- 232, 78 Ohio St. 3d 118, 676 N.E.2d 890 (1997)).

[5]RC 2317.02(G)(1)(a).

[Section 37:17]
[1]RC 2317.02(G)(1)(a).

other type of civil action . . . filed by the patient,"[2] does not appear to apply to the counselor or social worker. Therefore, it does not seem to include the implied waiver that is included for the psychologist. In fact, RC 2317.02(G)(1)(d) states that testimonial privilege applies unless the client voluntarily testifies. Therefore, it would have to be determined if the client was going to testify in a custody dispute before the privilege would be waived. This writer doesn't think this position was intended by the statute. Also, RC 2317.02(G)(1)(e) provides some difficulty in establishing a definition for "germane" as it relates to the counselor-client or social worker-client relationship. There does not appear to be any standard for the court to use to determine in camera what may not be "germane" to that relationship. Because of the importance of confidentiality, the mere fact that anything is discussed in a confidential relationship would suggest that the communication would be germane to that relationship. By disclosing any of the confidential information, the relationship would be damaged. Therefore, one could argue that RC 2317.02(G)(1)(e) would never be an exception.

§ 37:18 Privileged communication—State law privileges— Mediator

The mediator has a testimonial privilege only when acting under a mediation order issued under RC 3109.052(A), in a proceeding for divorce, dissolution, legal separation, annulment, or for the allocation of parental rights and responsibilities for the care of children.[1] The key triggering device with regard to this privilege is an order from the court.

> If a mediation order is issued under division (A) of this section, the mediator shall not be made a party to, and shall not be called as a witness or testify in, any action or proceeding, other than a criminal, delinquency, child abuse, child neglect, or dependent child action or proceeding, that is brought by or against either parent and that pertains to the mediation process, to any information discussed or presented in the mediation process, to the allocation of parental rights and responsibilities for the care of the parents' children, or to the awarding of visitation rights in relation to their children. The mediator shall not be made a party to, or be called as a witness or testify in, such an action or proceeding, even if both parents give their prior consent to the mediator being made a party to, or being called as a witness or to testify in the action or proceeding.[2]

It should be noted that, outside of the allocation of parental rights and responsibilities and visitation issues in domestic relations court, mediation disclosures will be guided in the future by RC 2317.023 which took effect January 27, 1997, and allows disclosure of mediation communication only under certain circumstances.

---

[2]RC 2317.02(B)(1)(a)(iii).

[Section 37:18]
[1]RC 2317.02(H).
[2]RC 3109.052(C).

§ 37:19 Privileged communication—State law privileges— Guardian ad litem

The authority for the guardian ad litem in domestic relations court is found in Civ. R. 75(B)(2) which states that: "When it is essential to protect the interests of a child, the court may join the child of the parties as a party defendant and appoint a guardian ad litem and legal counsel, if necessary, for the child and tax the costs." RC 3109.04(B)(2)(a) also states that the court, in its discretion may, and upon the motion of either parent shall, appoint a guardian ad litem for the child.

In domestic relations court, an attorney acting as guardian ad litem may be placed in one of three different roles. They may have the duty to act as the child's attorney and zealously represent their client's best interests; or, they may act in the child's best interest; or, if there is no conflict they may act as both the child's attorney and in the child's best interest. The same individual, however, cannot act as the child's guardian ad litem and as the child's attorney, if the best interest position is in conflict with the child's wishes.[1] Most courts throughout the United States have ruled that the guardian ad litem has judicial-immunity or some type of quasi-judicial immunity when acting within the scope of their duties in order to allow them to fulfill their roles impartially.[2]

§ 37:20 Privileged communication—Civil Rules

The parties can discover any matter not privileged under Civ. R. 26(B)(1). Civ. R. 35(A) provides that a party must submit to a physical or mental examination when their mental or physical condition is in controversy. Clearly, by statute in a domestic relations case involving children, the parties' mental condition would be at issue, although it may not be in controversy. A court may order the physical or mental examination for good cause shown under Civ. R. 35(A). It would appear that one needs more than mere allegations to meet this good cause standard. In *Colorado v. Turley*,[1] the Colorado court stated that a defendant is not entitled to have a victim undergo a physical examination or discover her mental health records absent compelling need.

In *Gordon v. Gordon*,[2] a father requested that the court evaluate the minor child. The court did not rule in his favor and, on appeal, the appellate court stated that Civ. R. 35 permits, but does not require, physical examinations. The Civil Rules and RC 3109.04 allow some discretion on the part of the court. Civ. R. 35(B), however, states that under some

---

[Section 37:19]

[1]Bawidamann v. Bawidamann, 63 Ohio App. 3d 691, 580 N.E.2d 15 (2d Dist. Montgomery County 1989).

[2]See Brodie v. Summit County Children Services Bd., 51 Ohio St. 3d 112, 554 N.E.2d 1301 (1990). See also Penn v. McMonagle, 60 Ohio App. 3d 149, 573 N.E.2d 1234 (6th Dist. Huron County 1990).

[Section 37:20]

[1]People v. Turley, 870 P.2d 498 (Colo. Ct. App. 1993).

[2]Gordon v. Gordon, 1985 WL 6566 (Ohio Ct. App. 4th Dist. Athens County 1985).

circumstances, the privilege may be waived. Civ. R. 35(B)(1) states that, "A party causing examination shall be entitled upon request to receive from the party against whom the order is made a like report of any examination, previously or thereafter made, of the same condition. After delivery, though, the party causing the examination shall be entitled upon request to receive from the party against whom the order is made a like report of any examination previously or thereafter made of the same condition. . .. " Civ. R. 35(B)(2) provides that, "By requesting or obtaining a report of the examination so ordered, or by taking the deposition of the examiner, the party examined waives any privilege he may have in that action or in any other involving the same controversy, regarding the testimony of every other person who has examined or may thereafter examine him in respect to the same mental or physical condition."

In *Gamble v. Dotson*,[3] one court dealt with this in a different way, stating that an examination of the plaintiff to prepare for a civil lawsuit is not treatment, and therefore, the privilege should not apply automatically. Civil Rule 16 states that the producing by any party of medical reports or hospital records does not constitute a waiver of the privilege granted under RC 2317.02. The Supreme Court of Ohio ruled that a pretrial order providing for discovery of privileged medical information was not improper since it did not purport to rule on the admissibility of such evidence before a waiver of physician-patient privilege.[4] The trial court in a personal injury action ordered that information be disclosed, i.e., that it was discoverable, before determining if the information was privileged.[5] The court maintained that the information may still be privileged and, therefore, no one would be allowed to testify as to that information. *Floyd v. Copas* was determined before various changes to the privilege statute. Today, the plaintiff would be deemed to have waived his medical privilege as soon as he files a lawsuit in which his physical condition is material. Although the waiver shall not be a complete waiver, it will be limited to issues that are relevant.

Under Civ. R. 75(D), in a divorce, annulment, or legal separation proceeding where minor children are involved, or in the filing of a motion for the modification of a decree allocating parental rights and responsibilities for the care of the children, the court may cause an investigation to be made as to the character, family relations, past conduct, earning ability, and financial worth of the parties to the action. The report of the investigation shall be made available to either party or their counsel of record, upon written request, not less than seven days before trial. The report shall be signed by the investigator, and the investigator shall be subject to cross-examination by either party concerning the contents of the report.

---

[3]Gamble v. Dotson, 1991 WL 57229 (Ohio Ct. App. 9th Dist. Lorain County 1991).

[4]State ex rel. Floyd v. Court of Common Pleas of Montgomery County, 55 Ohio St. 2d 27, 9 Ohio Op. 3d 16, 377 N.E.2d 794 (1978).

[5]Floyd v. Copas, 1977 WL 42364, 9 O.O.3d 298 (Ohio Com.Pl., Jun 09, 1977).

§ 37:21   Privileged communication—Allocation of parental rights proceedings

Various courts have dealt with the issue of whether or not a party has placed his or her mental health condition at issue in a variety of different ways. In *Schouw v. Schouw*,[1] the court held that the mere allegation that a parent is unstable is not sufficient to overcome psychotherapist-patient privilege. This was a case where the mother was already the custodial parent. The father filed for a change of custody and was seeking records of the custodial parent, stating that the mother was unstable. The court noted that the mother's mental stability was not placed at issue on the mere allegation of the father. In the Florida decision of *Leonard v. Leonard*,[2] the court held that a patient's seeking of custody or denial of allegations of mental instability does not serve to waive a privilege. The court ordered a psychological examination in *Leonard* rather than breaching the patient-therapist privilege. In *Freshwater v. Freshwater*,[3] the court ruled that a party does not place his or her mental condition at issue merely by seeking custody in marriage dissolution proceedings. The court stated that it was unnecessary to overcome the privilege because a court-appointed therapist could advise the court on the parent's mental condition.

Therefore, after reviewing the decisions of various courts, it is obvious that the courts are split as to whether a contested custody proceeding *always* places the mental condition of the parents in controversy, thereby causing the privilege to be waived. It would appear that if the action is an initial custody proceeding and both parties are requesting custody of the children, they would both be putting their mental condition in controversy in Ohio. If the action is a post-decree custody matter, then possibly only the party who files for the modification of the custody order would be putting his or her mental health issue into controversy. Thus, the non-filing parent or the prior custodial parent may not be putting their mental health issue in controversy. This seems to be logical due to the fact that, in domestic relations court, many control-oriented parties are using the request for discovery as a means to harass or abuse the other party.

In post-decree custody proceedings, when given a choice between conducting an *in-camera* inspection of confidential privileged communications or ordering a Civ. R. 35 mental health investigation, the better choice would be the Civ. R. 35 investigation. The Ohio Supreme Court in the case of *In re Miller*,[4] dealing with a similar issue in an involuntary commitment proceeding, noted that the best procedure to be followed is to have the individual sought to be committed examined by an independent psychiatrist and therefore avoiding the privilege problem

---

[Section 37:21]

[1]Schouw v. Schouw, 593 So. 2d 1200 (Fla. Dist. Ct. App. 2d Dist. 1992).

[2]Leonard v. Leonard, 673 So. 2d 97 (Fla. Dist. Ct. App. 1st Dist. 1996).

[3]Freshwater v. Freshwater, 659 So. 2d 1206 (Fla. Dist. Ct. App. 3d Dist. 1995).

[4]In re Miller, 63 Ohio St. 3d 99, 585 N.E.2d 396 (1992).

altogether. Clearly, the trial court could determine if certain communications are privileged by an *in-camera* inspection, but a better approach may be for the court to use the Civ. R. 35 option and order the parties to submit to a mental examination rather than ordering disclosure of the confidential information.

The Ohio custody statute, now called the "allocation of parental rights and responsibilities for the care of children" and shared parenting, states that in determining the best interest of a child, the court shall consider all relevant factors,[5] including the mental and physical health of all persons involved in the situation.[6] In determining whether to grant companionship or visitation rights to a parent, grandparent, or relative, the court shall consider certain factors, which include the mental and physical health of all parties[7] and any other factor in the best interest of the child.[8] If the court orders a Civ. R. 35 evaluation, the privilege does not apply because the evaluation is not voluntary and, further, it probably would not apply because the evaluation is not for treatment purposes. If the report is court-ordered pursuant to RC 3109.04(A) and Civ. R. 75(D), then the report can be submitted into evidence as direct examination, subject to cross examination.[9]

RC 3109.051(H)(2) is Ohio's equal access to records provision applicable to non-residential parents. Under this provision, the non-residential parent is entitled to access under the same terms and conditions under which access is provided to the residential parent to any record that is related to the child in which the residential parent of the child legally is provided access, unless the court determines it is not in the best interests of the child to grant the parent access, which the court would do by way of a written decision. It is the responsibility of the parent obtaining a restricted order to serve it on the appropriate organization. Therefore, it would appear that unless school officials or employees have received this restrictive order of the court, they should treat the non-residential parent the same way and with the same access to any student records under the same terms and conditions which access is provided to the residential parent of the child. The key phrase here is "access as it is legally permitted."[10]

§ 37:22 Privileged communication—Procedure

The process of discovering privileged information begins with a subpoena issued by an attorney under Civ. R. 45. The subpoena would state that the therapist is commanded to appear before the court, and that failure to appear at the hearing or deposition may result in his or her attachment. The subpoena may state that the witness is commanded

---

[5]RC 3109.04(F)(1).

[6]RC 3109.04(F)(1)(e).

[7]RC 3109.051(D)(9).

[8]RC 3109.051(D)(15).

[9]Roach v. Roach, 79 Ohio App. 3d 194, 607 N.E.2d 35 (2d Dist. Montgomery County 1992).

[10]See also § 37:31, Privileged communication—Waiver—Child's privilege.

to bring with him or her particular documents and that, in lieu of an appearance, he or she can submit these documents to a certain attorney by a certain date. Under RC 2317.21, the court can command the sheriff to arrest a witness who disobeys a subpoena, except for a witness who has demanded but has not been paid his or her traveling expenses and fee for one day's attendance when a subpoena is served on him or her. It is clear under the various mental health therapists' Code of Ethics that they are obliged to assert the privilege if they do not have an express waiver from their client. They can do so by filing a motion to quash under Civ. R. 45(D)(2). This rule requires that the claim of a privilege be supported by a description of the nature of the documents, communications, or things not produced but it must be sufficient to enable the demanding party to contest the claim. What some therapists do not realize is that a notary public subpoena is *not* a court order to turn over various records, but can only be used to compel the therapist to appear and testify at a deposition or court hearing.[1] Therefore, a subpoena can be issued upon the mere request of an attorney, without any determination of the privilege issue. In fact, a psychiatrist who furnished a patient's records to an opposing party in response to a properly served subpoena could be sued for negligence, and also could be held negligent for failing to ensure that only the parts of the medical records that the court found relevant to the proceeding are made public.[2]

A motion to quash triggers Civ. R. 45(C) protection of persons subject to subpoenas. The party serving the subpoena shall not be entitled to production except pursuant to an order of the court by which the subpoena was issued.[3] If the subpoena is objected to, the moving party can move for an order to compel the production. If an order to compel production has been filed, the court, upon timely motion, shall quash or modify the subpoena, or order appearance or production only under specific conditions, if the subpoena requires disclosure of privileged or otherwise protected matter and no exception or waiver applies.[4] The court may, for good cause shown, make an order which justice requires to protect the party or person from annoyance, embarrassment, oppression, or undue burden or expense.[5] Under Civ. R. 26(C)(4), a party may request an *in-camera* review of the documents subpoenaed by the judge or magistrate to limit the disclosure to necessary and relevant information. Again, because of the therapists' Code of Ethics and the sensitive nature of the therapy, the therapist may have to assert that it is in the best interest of the child that disclosure of the information not be granted. If information is granted, therapists should request that the judge or magistrate seal those records and not allow them to be open to

---

[Section 37:22]

[1]Baker v. Quick Stop Oil Change & Tune-Up, 61 Ohio Misc. 2d 526, 580 N.E.2d 528 (C.P. 1990).

[2]Allen v. Smith, 179 W. Va. 360, 368 S.E.2d 924 (1988).

[3]Civ. R. 45(C)(2)(b).

[4]Civ. R. 45(C)(3)(b).

[5]Civ. R. 26(C).

public scrutiny as a way to promote the least amount of damage.

§ 37:23 Privileged communication—Voluntary factor

The relationship between the therapist and the client must be voluntary for the privilege to apply.[1] The court, in the case of *In re Smith*,[2] dealt with this issue, stating that no privilege applied to a situation where the client saw the psychologist per the reunification plan at the request of the children services board. The court stated that because the client was not voluntarily seeking the help from the treating psychologist that the privilege did not apply. In *State v. Blankenship*,[3] the court held, in direct opposition to *In re Smith*, that there is no exception to the psychologist-client privilege created simply by virtue of the fact that the client is required to seek counseling under the terms of the reunification plan approved by the court. The conflict was put to rest with the amendment of RC 2317.02(G)(1)(g), which provides an exception to the privilege statute where the counseling was ordered pursuant to a case plan journalized under RC 2151.412.

The Alaska Supreme Court held that the privilege is waived only for the particular purpose for which an examination is ordered by the court.[4] Therefore, a state or agency could not use the disclosed material in a different hearing two years later without requesting and receiving a separate waiver.

§ 37:24 Privileged communication—Confidential factor—In general

A California court ruled in *California v. Clark*[1] that once a patient's communication to a therapist has lost its confidential status, the privilege no longer existed. This was the situation where a therapist revealed his patient's communications to a third party, believing that the patient may pose a future danger. The court determined that whether or not the patient actually posed a future danger, the privilege ended when the communications were revealed and, therefore, the communications were allowed to be used in a court of law. Prior to 1995, Ohio followed the position established in *State v. Post*[2] that the client's disclosure to a third party of communications made within the attorney-client privilege breached the confidentiality underlying the privilege and constituted a waiver thereof.

[Section 37:23]

[1]In re Winstead, 67 Ohio App. 2d 111, 21 Ohio Op. 3d 422, 425 N.E.2d 943 (9th Dist. Summit County 1980).

[2]In re Smith, 7 Ohio App. 3d 75, 454 N.E.2d 171 (2d Dist. Greene County 1982).

[3]State v. Blankenship, 1993 WL 329962 (Ohio Ct. App. 9th Dist. Summit County 1993).

[4]M.R.S. v. State, 897 P.2d 63 (Alaska 1995).

[Section 37:24]

[1]People v. Clark, 50 Cal. 3d 583, 268 Cal. Rptr. 399, 789 P.2d 127 (1990), as modified on denial of reh'g, (June 7, 1990).

[2]State v. Post, 32 Ohio St. 3d 380, 513 N.E.2d 754 (1987).

In 1995, the Supreme Court of Ohio decided *State v. McDermott*,[3] which held that the Ohio statute on attorney-client privileged communication sets forth the sole criteria for waiving the privilege unless: (1) the client expressly consents, or (2) the client voluntarily testifies on the same subject. The Court also held that prior case law followed in *Post* recognized a "judicially created privilege." The Court then decided how that common law attorney-client privilege could be waived. Therefore, to the extent that *Post* is overbroad and would affect the statutory attorney-client privilege by adding a waiver not within the RC 2317.02(A) exceptions, the *McDermott* decision modified *Post*. The Supreme Court declined to add a "judicially created waiver"[4] to the statutorily created privilege, and held that RC 2317.02(A) provides the exclusive means by which privileged communications directly between an attorney and a client can be waived.[5]

Because the *Post* case has been cited in cases involving counselor-client privileges, the *McDermott* holding is welcomed if the analogy may also be made that RC 2317.02 provides the exclusive means by which other therapist privileged communications can be waived.

§ 37:25 Privileged communication—Confidential factor— Couples therapy

When dealing with couples therapy, most therapists understand that both parties need to agree that the session will be kept confidential and will not be disclosed by the parties unless both parties waive their rights. Still, various courts have ordered the confidential communication in couples therapy to be disclosed because it did not comply with Wigmore's second criterion related to confidentiality,[1] i.e., that the "element of confidentiality must be essential to the full and satisfactory maintenance of the relationship between the parties."

In *Redding v. Virginia Mason Medical Center*,[2] the Washington appellate court stated that the psychologist-patient privilege did not protect statements made by one spouse during a joint counseling session from being disclosed in a later custody dispute between the couple. In 1990, a Connecticut court decision ruled the exact opposite way. The appellate court in *Cabrera v. Cabrera*[3] stated that even if the wife had put her mental health in issue in a marriage dissolution action, that fact alone would not render otherwise privileged testimony admissible from a psychologist who had treated the wife. In *Cabrera*, the therapist had counseled both parties and had treated the wife prior to the divorce. The

---

[3]State v. McDermott, 1995 -Ohio- 80, 72 Ohio St. 3d 570, 651 N.E.2d 985 (1995).

[4]State v. McDermott, 1995 -Ohio- 80, 72 Ohio St. 3d 570, 651 N.E.2d 985 (1995).

[5]State v. McDermott, 1995 -Ohio- 80, 72 Ohio St. 3d 570, 574, 651 N.E.2d 985 (1995).

[Section 37:25]

[1]See § 37:12, Privileged communication—Criteria for privilege.

[2]Redding v. Virginia Mason Medical Center, 75 Wash. App. 424, 878 P.2d 483 (Div. 1 1994).

[3]Cabrera v. Cabrera, 23 Conn. App. 330, 580 A.2d 1227 (1990).

court used a balancing test in this decision to determine if it was more important to the interest of justice that the communication be disclosed than the relationship that needed to be protected. In *Eichenberger v. Eichenberger*,[4] a patient testified about the marital counseling relationship but did not want her records disclosed. The court ruled that the privilege was waived by her testimony.

§ 37:26 Privileged communication—Confidential factor—Group therapy—Family therapy

Clearly, for a therapist to feel protected and for attorneys and therapists to be able to give appropriate advice to their clients, the Ohio legislature should deal with this issue like Maryland has done. The state of Maryland requires the consent of each person involved when records are generated during group or family therapy.[1] In group situations, most courts throughout the United States have ruled that, if abuse of a child is involved, the privilege does not apply. By the very fact the communication was disclosed in a situation where many other people were present, or where there was an awareness that a third party was observing, the privilege does not apply because it wasn't intended to remain confidential. Some therapists request that the information remain confidential within a group, but this clearly is not a position that has been backed by the courts. In fact, some group therapists have their clients sign an acknowledgment of nonconfidentiality when entering a group treatment program. *In re Graves*,[2] the juvenile in custody was receiving treatment at a juvenile rehabilitation center when he admitted to a therapist and a social worker that he had previously committed sexual offenses against a number of juveniles. The court ruled that no privilege was attached to the juvenile's statements because the admissions were made in part of a group setting or with the awareness that a third party was observing.

The court, however, can go to various lengths in protecting group counseling records as it did in *Herald v. Hood*.[3] In this particular case, the group counseling records of sexual victims were held to be privileged. This was a civil trial against Hood for battery and intentional infliction of emotional distress due to memories of sexual abuse that had been repressed. The court required an *in-camera* inspection of the group records with the other group members names concealed. After the inspection, the therapist was ordered to limit her testimony to information obtained as the result of individual sessions with the victim. During cross-examination, when a question arose as to the source of the

---

[4]Eichenberger v. Eichenberger, 82 Ohio App. 3d 809, 613 N.E.2d 678 (10th Dist. Franklin County 1992).

[Section 37:26]

[1]Md. Code Ann., (Health-General), § 4-307(D) (West Supp. 1992).

[2]Matter of Graves, 1995 WL 155367 (Ohio Ct. App. 12th Dist. Clinton County 1995).

[3]Herald v. Hood, 1993 WL 277541 (Ohio Ct. App. 9th Dist. Summit County 1993), appeal dismissed as improvidently allowed, 1994 -Ohio- 150, 70 Ohio St. 3d 1210, 639 N.E.2d 109 (1994).

therapist's testimony, Hood's attorney was able to inspect the group records as amended to conceal the participants' names. This case clearly goes against Wigmore's criteria, that confidentiality be essential to the relationship, which must be met before a privilege can be established.[4]

§ 37:27 Privileged communication—Confidential factor—Confinement

In an involuntary commitment situation, privilege may apply to therapy sessions while confined. In *Pennsylvania v. Fewell*,[1] the patient told her psychiatrist that she had killed her baby. The psychiatrist reported the crime. The patient was then interviewed by an officer and told the officer. The court held that the statement to the psychiatrist was privileged but the statement to the officer was not privileged. Under Ohio law, if that statement was made to a counselor or social worker rather than a psychiatrist or psychologist, the therapist would be under a duty to report the felony crime and the privilege clearly would not apply to them. Again, it is unfortunate that the Ohio legislature has not extended the privilege to licensed counselors and social workers under the same conditions as the physician and psychologist. This is another situation where many of the poor and disadvantaged may receive therapy with a counselor or social worker through community and public programs rather than private therapy. It also appears to be a situation where the Ohio legislature should follow the direction of the U.S. Supreme Court in *Jaffee v. Redmond*,[2] when the Court stated that, "We have no hesitation in concluding in this case that the federal privilege should also extend to confidential communications made to licensed social workers in the course of the psychotherapy. . . .. Today, social workers provide a significant amount of mental health treatment. Their clients often include the poor and those of modest means who could not afford the assistance of a psychiatrist or psychologist, but whose counseling sessions serve the same public goals." In Ohio, licensed social workers and counselors clearly deal with clients of modest means and should have the privilege extended to them as the courts have done with psychologists and physicians with regard to reporting felonies.

§ 37:28 Privileged communication—Waiver—In general

Waivers can be express or implied. If it is an express waiver, there will be a signed release from the client. An implied waiver can arise in either a situation where a client voluntarily testifies on the subject, and thereby puts the issue before the court, or where a client files a civil action and thereby puts their mental or physical condition at issue. If the party files a civil action and thereby brings the issue before the court, or

---

[4]See § 37:12, Privileged communication—Criteria for privilege.

[Section 37:27]

[1]Com. v. Fewell, 439 Pa. Super. 541, 654 A.2d 1109 (1995).

[2]Jaffee v. Redmond, 518 U.S. 1, 116 S. Ct. 1923, 1931, 135 L. Ed. 2d 337, 44 Fed. R. Evid. Serv. 1 (1996) (footnotes omitted).

if he makes a counterclaim that raises a mental health issue as a defense, he will be deemed to have waived his privilege. If a party testifies about a certain condition, he waives any claims of privilege regarding the condition, although merely answering a question on cross-examination at a deposition or at a trial does not generally waive the privilege.[1]

In Ohio, there may be a limited waiver which may apply if a party files a lawsuit where his or her medical condition is material. Generally, the waiver is limited to issues that are relevant. Under RC 2317.02(B)(1)(a)(iii), if the physician or psychologist is compelled to testify, it would be only as to communication or advice which is related causally or historically to physical or mental injuries that are relevant to the civil action. A court may need to hold a pretrial or *in camera* hearing to determine if the material is related and relevant.

The courts are sharply divided when they deal with "judicially created" waivers. Certainly, this is an area that cannot be contemplated when warning the client about the bounds of confidentiality. *Wigmore's* fourth criterion promotes the need for balancing public interest in order to protect society.[2] This condition states that the "injury that would inure to the relationship by the communication's disclosure must be greater than the benefit thereby gained for the correct disposal of litigation."

To balance interests, the court at times has stated that a privilege does not apply even though the statute clearly allows for a privilege, which has been the basis for the sharp division over "judicially created" waivers. Possibly after *Jaffee v. Redmond*,[3] the court can take the direction of the U.S. Supreme Court and reject the balancing test. As noted in *Jaffee*, the Court stated that, "An uncertain privilege or one which purports to be certain but results in widely varying applications by the courts is little better than no privilege at all. If the purpose of the privilege is to be served, the participants in the confidential conversation must be able to predict with some degree of certainty whether particular discussions will be protected." The Ohio Supreme Court, in the case of *In re Miller*,[4] stated that the privilege statute should be strictly construed and privilege applies unless waived. More specifically, the Court stated that, "If the situation does not meet one of the waivers expressly set forth in the statute, the privilege is not waived."[5] The Court determined in *Miller* that the appellant had not expressly waived the privilege. Unfortunately for therapists, though, the Court then stated that, "[T]he facts of this case are not so compelling that a judicially cre-

---

[Section 37:28]

[1]York v. Roberts, 9 Ohio Misc. 2d 21, 460 N.E.2d 327 (C.P. 1983).

[2]See § 37:12, Privileged communication—Criteria for privilege.

[3]Jaffee v. Redmond, 518 U.S. 1, 116 S. Ct. 1923, 1932, 135 L. Ed. 2d 337, 44 Fed. R. Evid. Serv. 1 (1996).

[4]In re Miller, 63 Ohio St. 3d 99, 585 N.E.2d 396 (1992).

[5]In re Miller, 63 Ohio St. 3d 99, 585 N.E.2d 396 (1992).

ated waiver must be invoked."[6]

A strong dissent to judicially created waivers was given by Judge Bryant in *State v. McGriff.*[7] Judge Bryant stated that the majority held that the court, by judicial fiat, is able to abrogate the physician-patient privilege contained in RC 2317.02. Judge Bryant clearly felt that any solution should be crafted by the legislature, or possibly by the Supreme Court. It would appear that the U.S. Supreme Court has resolved this issue by virtue of the *Jaffee* decision as it relates to federal law. It is now up to the various state courts to follow the U.S. Supreme Court lead.

§ 37:29   Privileged communication—Waiver—Custody and visitation

Many attorneys who file a motion to quash regarding a subpoena requesting privileged information in a custody case cite *In re Decker*,[1] which states that the Ohio statute on privileged communications makes no exceptions in custody cases, and therefore the testimony by the therapist should remain privileged. *Decker*, however, was decided before many of the changes to the privileged communications statute. The most specific change is found in RC 2317.02(B)(1)(a)(iii) which provides that the physician-patient privilege is waived when the patient files any type of civil action. This was the position held in *Whiteman v. Whiteman*,[2] when the father sought custody of the minor children but wanted to exclude his medical records regarding his psychiatric treatment. The court ruled that when the father filed the civil action, he waived his privilege.

While this author supports the *Whiteman* decision, it would be better if, in the cases where confidential communication between a physician and patient or therapist and client is at issue, there would be only a limited waiver. A more appropriate position may be for the courts to follow the *Horton v. Addy*[3] decision, which limits the waiver to issues that are relevant to the civil action. In the case of *In re Brown*,[4] a situation where the state was filing an action to remove custody from Brown, the court determined that Brown had not placed her mental health at issue and therefore she had not waived her privilege with regard to her treating psychologist for the period of eight years prior to involvement in the

---

[6]In re Miller, 63 Ohio St. 3d 99, 585 N.E.2d 396 (1992).

[7]State v. McGriff, 109 Ohio App. 3d 668, 672 N.E.2d 1074 (3d Dist. Logan County 1996), dismissed, appeal not allowed, 76 Ohio St. 3d 1473, 669 N.E.2d 856 (1996).

[Section 37:29]

[1]In re Decker, 20 Ohio App. 3d 203, 485 N.E.2d 751 (3d Dist. Van Wert County 1984).

[2]Whiteman v. Whiteman, 1995 WL 375848 (Ohio Ct. App. 12th Dist. Butler County 1995).

[3]Horton v. Addy, 1993 WL 15631 (Ohio Ct. App. 2d Dist. Montgomery County 1993), judgment vacated, appeal dismissed by, 1994 -Ohio- 353, 69 Ohio St. 3d 181, 631 N.E.2d 123 (1994).

[4]In re Brown, 98 Ohio App. 3d 337, 648 N.E.2d 576 (3d Dist. Marion County 1994).

case by children services. The court did allow the testimony with regard to counseling records from the period of time after child services board became involved.

While some courts still believe that all confidential communications should be introduced at trial in custody and visitation matters because the best interests of the children are at stake, this still may not be the best available option. This is especially true in domestic relations courts, where parties continue to use the discovery process to harass, control, or embarrass their prior spouse with no consideration as to what is in the child's best interest. If both parents are requesting custody of their children, then they are both putting their mental condition into controversy such as in an initial custody proceeding. Because RC 3109.04(F)(1)(e) requires that the court investigate the mental and physical health of all persons involved in the situation, and RC 3109.051(D)(9) states that the court shall use as one of the factors the mental health of all parties concerned, it would appear that when both parties are requesting custody, or the individual party is requesting custody, then those parties are putting their mental health at issue and are waiving their privilege. If the action is a post-decree custody matter, however, then possibly only the person who files for the custody modification would be putting his or her mental health issue into controversy. Therefore, the non-filing parent should still have the privilege apply.

Some courts feel that an *in-camera* inspection of the confidential communications is an appropriate option in limiting unnecessary disclosure, but even this may violate the confidentiality principles that are intended to be protected and controlled under the privilege statute. In domestic relations matters, the courts have another option under Civ. R. 35 which allows the court to order the parties to submit to a mental exam rather than ordering the disclosure of confidential information. This option should be used more often than the *in-camera* inspection option when more than "mere allegations" are made with regard to a parent's mental health.

§ 37:30 Privileged communication—Waiver—Grounds for divorce

One New Jersey lower court ruled in *Kinsella v. Kinsella*[1] that when the husband charged the wife with extreme cruelty as a ground for divorce, he put in issue the effect of the alleged cruelty on his state of mind and therefore the wife was granted limited access to the husband's psychotherapy files. The Supreme Court of New Jersey, in overruling the lower court's decision in *Kinsella*, compared the psychotherapist privilege to the attorney-client privilege, and established that it could be overridden if three foundations were met: (1) that the evidence was relevant and material to the issue before the court, (2) that there was a legitimate need for the evidence, and (3) that the party must show that

---

[Section 37:30]

[1]Kinsella v. Kinsella, 287 N.J. Super. 305, 671 A.2d 130 (App. Div. 1996), aff'd in part, rev'd in part, 150 N.J. 276, 696 A.2d 556 (1997).

the information could not be secured from any less intrusive source.[2] While the decision cited the *Jaffee v. Redmond* case, the New Jersey Supreme Court still allowed for a balancing test to determine if there should be a judicial waiver.[3] Clearly, if the *Kinsella* decision is any indication, the U.S. Supreme Court's strong stand in *Jaffee v. Redmond* to do away with the balancing test will be met with resistance by the various state courts.

The court in *In re Marriage of Lombaer* found the opposite result when it stated that the mental condition shall not be deemed to be introduced merely by making or defending a claim under the state's marital dissolution statute.[4] The court noted that the party's mental health would become an issue and be introduced if the witness first testifies concerning their records or their communication with a therapist. In this particular case, the wife did not introduce her mental condition and therefore the privilege was not waived.

§ 37:31 Privileged communication—Waiver—Child's privilege

It has generally been the custom for therapists to give records upon request to parents of very small children with regard to general information about the child's status and progress, unless there is a court order for the therapist not to release those records according to RC 3109.051(H)(1). There is an exception, though, with regard to outpatient mental health services for minors according to RC 5122.04. RC 5122.04 states that:

> Upon the request of a minor fourteen years of age or older, a mental health professional may provide outpatient mental health services, excluding the use of medication, without the consent or knowledge of the minor's parent or guardian. Except as otherwise provided in this section, the minor's parent or guardian shall not be informed of the services without the minor's consent unless the mental health professional treating the minor determines that there is a compelling need for disclosure based on a substantial probability of harm to the minor or to other persons, and if the minor is notified of the mental health professional's intent to inform the minor's parent, or guardian.

The statute further provides that:

> Services provided to a minor pursuant to this section shall be limited to not more than six sessions or thirty days of services whichever occurs sooner. After the sixth session or thirty days of services the mental health professional shall terminate the services or, with the consent of the minor, notify the parent, or guardian, to obtain consent to provide further outpatient services.

Therefore, a child receiving treatment under this statute without a parent's knowledge would be entitled to the same confidentiality and privilege as an adult.

---

[2]Kinsella v. Kinsella, 150 N.J. 276, 696 A.2d 556 (1997).

[3]Kinsella v. Kinsella, 150 N.J. 276, 696 A.2d 556 (1997).

[4]In re Marriage of Lombaer, 200 Ill. App. 3d 712, 146 Ill. Dec. 425, 558 N.E.2d 388 (1st Dist. 1990).

RC 3109.051(H)(1) basically states that both the residential and non-residential parent are on equal footing with regard to records of their children. One Ohio case where this was tested was *Askin v. Askin*,[1] where the father requested the records of the child's psychologist during the custody dispute. The psychologist noted that she was reluctant to release her raw data to the father, because under her professional ethics, she has a duty not to release the raw data to either parent, but she stated that she would release her notes to the father. The father claimed that he was denied access under the equal access clause. The court of appeals reviewed the psychologist's notes and stated that if there was any error it was harmless error. The court, though, did not state whether or not the mother had access to these notes or the raw data. Clearly, under the equal access clause, if one parent is allowed access to that information, then the other parent should be allowed the same access unless there is some detrimental effect to the child. If that is the case, then it should be dealt with by obtaining a restrictive order from the court and the court should enter its written findings of fact and opinion in the journal.[2]

The equal access clause does not give parents unlimited access to records of children. Basically, it states that the same access which is legally provided to one parent shall also be provided to the other upon request.[3] A California court addressed this issue in the case of *In re Daniel C.H.*,[4] when it stated that the equal access clause did not establish a statutory right of access to medical records. It simply stated that a noncustodial parent will not be deprived of existing access to such records or information due to the fact that he or she is not the custodial parent. The court went on to state that, if it is detrimental to the therapeutic relationship and to the child to release the records to either parent, then the law does not provide authority for parental access for either parent.[5]

Several courts have ruled that a parent is not free to waive or to deny a waiver of the child's privilege where the parent's interests are clearly adverse to the child's. In a custody proceeding, there is some uncertainty as to a parent's ability to consider the child's best interests. Therefore, the court in *Bond v. Bond*[6] abused its discretion when it allowed the husband to assert privilege on behalf of his son. Generally, when the parent's interest in suppressing the evidence is obviously adverse to the interest of the child/patient as to an alleged commission of a crime against the child by the parent, that parent does not possess the author-

---

[Section 37:31]

[1]Askin v. Askin, 1995 WL 41600 (Ohio Ct. App. 10th Dist. Franklin County 1995).

[2]RC 3109.051(H)(1).

[3]RC 3109.051(H)(1).

[4]In re Daniel C. H., 220 Cal. App. 3d 814, 269 Cal. Rptr. 624, 630 (6th Dist. 1990).

[5]In re Daniel C. H., 220 Cal. App. 3d 814, 269 Cal. Rptr. 624, 630 (6th Dist. 1990).

[6]Bond v. Bond, 887 S.W.2d 558 (Ky. Ct. App. 1994), reh'g granted, (Dec. 2, 1994).

ity to invoke the privilege.[7] Normally a parent would have the right to claim her child's privilege, but that right exists only when it is in the child's best interests to do so.[8]

§ 37:32   Privileged communication—Child abuse exception

Most state courts agree that child abuse falls into the "exceptions" category with regard to privileges and therefore the privilege does not apply. In *State v. Cartee*,[1] the court ruled that where the mother of a minor releases to a county prosecutor the contents of records made by a social worker during counseling, the counselor-client relationship as to that minor is waived. This was a situation where there was alleged child abuse by the father against the child. The court did not rely on abuse as being an exception but, instead, followed the position of *State v. Post*[2] which held that "a client's disclosure to a third party of communications made pursuant to the attorney-client privilege breaches the confidentiality underlying the privilege, and constitutes a waiver thereof."

Cartee was decided before the various amendments to the privilege statute. In *Cartee*, the court applied the reasoning of *Post* to the counselor-client privilege when it stated that the reason for prohibiting disclosure ceased when the victim's mother released the contents of the records to the various offices and agencies named therein.

State v. McDermott[3] limited the holding in *Post* by stating that RC 2317.02(A) provides the exclusive means by which privileged communications directly between an attorney and a client can be waived. Logically, the *McDermott* reasoning could be extended to imply that, unless the express conditions for a therapist waiver are met according to RC 2317.02, then the privilege would be honored.

Clearly, in abuse cases, for social workers and counselors the privilege does not apply because RC 2151.421, i.e., the reporting of child abuse statute, is specifically listed as an exception under RC 2317.02(G)(2). The psychologist and physician privilege does apply unless their client is the minor and all of the factors in RC 2151.421(A)(2)(a) to (2)(c) apply.

Counselors and social workers may see the abuser far more often than a psychologist or psychiatrist because the abuser may be financially unable to see a psychologist or psychiatrist. Yet, in Ohio, if an individual goes to one type of licensed therapist because he cannot afford the services of the other type of licensed therapist, the abuse must be reported. This generally means treatment stops unless it has been court-ordered. The poor and disadvantaged deserve the same protection as the wealthy. This inequity should be addressed by the legislators. All licensed

---

[7]State v. Hunt, 2 Ariz. App. 6, 406 P.2d 208 (1965).

[8]State v. Evans, 802 S.W.2d 507 (Mo. 1991).

[Section 37:32]

[1]State v. Cartee, 1992 WL 368845 (Ohio Ct. App. 4th Dist. Vinton County 1992).

[2]State v. Post, 32 Ohio St. 3d 380, syl., 513 N.E.2d 754 (1987). See § 37:24, Privileged communication—Confidential factor—In general.

[3]State v. McDermott, 1995 -Ohio- 80, 72 Ohio St. 3d 570, 651 N.E.2d 985 (1995).

therapists should have the same duty to report or not report the abuse so the client would not have to be knowledgeable as to initials and credentials before selecting a therapist.

§ 37:33   Privileged communication—Staff privilege

In 1947, the Ohio Supreme Court in *Weis v. Weis*,[1] held that the privilege statute affords protection only to those relationships which are specifically named. Yet, in 1989, the appellate court in *Johnston v. Miami Valley Hospital*[2] ruled that a hospital's records of nurse's notes are within the statutory definition of "communication" and therefore are protected by the physician-patient privilege. However, *In re Thomas*,[3] a Summit County Court of Appeals decision, held that "the nursing staff communications are not protected within the privilege, nor under an agency theory that the physician directed the overall care." The Summit County Court of Appeals also cited *Weis*, which noted that "because the statute which confers the privilege on communications between certain persons is in derogation of the common law, the statute must be strictly construed and affords protection only to the relationships specifically named within the statute."[4]

§ 37:34   Privileged communication—Drug and alcohol issues

RC 2317.02 provides that the testimonial privilege does not apply in any criminal action concerning any tests or the results of any tests that determine the presence or concentration of alcohol, a drug of abuse, or alcohol and a drug of abuse in the patient's blood, breath, urine, or other bodily substances at any time relevant to the criminal offense in question.[1]

Records or information, other than court journal entries or court docket entries, pertaining to the identity, diagnosis, or treatment of any patient which are maintained in connection with the performance of any drug treatment program licensed by, or certified by, the director of alcohol and drug addiction services under RC 3793.11, shall be kept confidential, may be disclosed only for the purposes and under the circumstances expressly authorized under this section, and may not otherwise be divulged in any civil, criminal, administrative, or legislative proceeding.[2]

The United States Code Annotated provides that "[r]ecords of the

---

[Section 37:33]

[1]Weis v. Weis, 147 Ohio St. 416, 34 Ohio Op. 350, 72 N.E.2d 245, 169 A.L.R. 668 (1947).

[2]Johnston v. Miami Valley Hosp., 61 Ohio App. 3d 81, 572 N.E.2d 169 (2d Dist. Montgomery County 1989).

[3]In re Thomas, 1993 WL 129229 (Ohio Ct. App. 9th Dist. Summit County 1993).

[4]In re Thomas, 1993 WL 129229, at *3 (Ohio Ct. App. 9th Dist. Summit County 1993).

[Section 37:34]

[1]RC 2317.02(B)(1)(b).

[2]RC 3793.11(A).

identity, diagnosis, prognosis, or treatment of any patient which are maintained in connection with the performance of any program or activity relating to substance abuse, education, prevention training, treatment, rehabilitation, or research, which is conducted, regulated, or directly or indirectly assisted by any department or agency of the United States shall, except as provided in subsection (e) of this section, be confidential and be disclosed only for the purposes and under the circumstances expressly authorized under section (b) of this section."[3] This section applies to federally funded drug and alcohol treatment programs which includes most state and county substance abuse programs because most of them receive some type of federal funding. There is still the obligation to report child abuse under 42 U.S.C.A. § 290dd-3(e). Also communications can be disclosed by written consent of the patient or by a court order for good cause shown. In assessing good cause, the court shall weigh the public interest and the need for disclosure against the injury to the patient, to the physician-patient relationship, and to the treatment services. Upon the granting of such order, the court, in determining the extent which any disclosure of all or any part of any record is necessary, shall impose appropriate safeguards against unauthorized disclosure.[4] The Supreme Court of Vermont, in the case of *In re B.S.*,[5] stated that "a finding [of good cause may] be made only upon a finding that alternative means of obtaining the information are not available and that the interest in disclosure outweighs 'the potential injury to the patient, the physician-patient relationship and the treatment services.' " Good cause cannot be demonstrated when production of records is merely cumulative.

§ 37:35 Privileged communication—Federal and state privacy laws

Under the Ohio Privacy Act, RC 1347.08(C), an agency, upon request, shall disclose medical, psychiatric, or psychological information to a person who is the subject of the information, or to his legal guardian, unless a physician, psychiatrist, or psychologist determines for the agency that disclosure of the information is likely to have an adverse effect on the person, in which case the information shall be released to a physician, psychiatrist, or psychologist designated by the person or by his legal guardian. "The purpose of [Ohio's Privacy Act] is to limit public dissemination of personal information collected by a state agency, not to prevent discovery in civil litigation."[1]

With regard to peer review committees, RC 2305.251 makes the proceedings and records of hospitalization review committees immune from discovery or use in civil actions, and bars committee members from

---

[3]42 U.S.C.A. § 290dd-2(a).

[4]42 U.S.C.A. § 290dd-3(2)(C).

[5]In re B.S., 163 Vt. 445, 659 A.2d 1137, 1140 (1995).

[Section 37:35]

[1]Doe v. University of Cincinnati, 42 Ohio App. 3d 227, syl. 4, 538 N.E.2d 419, 53 Ed. Law Rep. 980 (10th Dist. Franklin County 1988).

testifying. The hospital utilization committee provision relates to a not-for-profit health care corporation, and does not apply to the utilization review committee of an HMO which operates for profit.[2]

§ 37:36 Privileged communication—School records

Schools receiving federal funding may not disclose a child's educational records without the parent or guardian's consent under the Family Educational Rights and Privacy Act of 1974.[1] No person shall release or permit access to the names or other personally identifiable information concerning any students attending a public school to any person or group for use in a profit-making plan or activity.[2] Further, no person shall release or permit access to personally identifiable information, other than directory information, concerning any student attending a public school, except with written consent of a parent or guardian, or the student if 18 years of age or older. Note that this prohibits release without parent, guardian, or student consent of any information by the public school officials concerning any illegal drug or alcohol use by students to law enforcement agencies. This also assures access to the child's school records and educational materials by the non-residential parent. Ethical guidelines state that a counselor's records should not be a part of the school's records, yet if the counselor's records are a part of the cumulative file accessible to other school personnel, then they would have to be disclosed.[3] Many times, a school counselor will testify that they make a distinction between the counselor's personal notes versus the school records. That distinction is appropriate for school counselors but it does not appear to be appropriate for therapists in private settings. If a school counselor puts various notes in the school's records, then they would be accessible to anyone.[4] However, if the school counselor maintains the student records as his own personal records and does not include them in the cumulative file, then they would not be permitted to be disclosed.

It should be noted that non-residential parents have the same rights as residential parents to school records, unless access has been prohibited by a court order and that court order has been presented by the residential parent to the keeper of the records. These provisions pertain to records to which the residential parent of the child is "legally" provided access. Again, records may be deemed confidential, and neither parent may be provided access.

---

[2]Lomano v. Cigna Healthplan of Columbus, Inc., 64 Ohio App. 3d 824, 582 N.E.2d 1150 (10th Dist. Franklin County 1990).

[Section 37:36]

[1]Pub. L. 93-380, 88 Stat. 571. See 20 U.S.C.A. § 1221, Historical and Statutory notes; 20 U.S.C.A. § 1232g.

[2]RC 3319.321(A).

[3]RC 3319.321.

[4]When an attorney issues a subpoena, the attorney should request both the school records and the counselor's personal notes.

§ 37:37   Privileged communication—Children's services records

Children's Services records are also confidential, but they are open to inspection by the board or department of human services, the director of the county department of human services, and by other persons, upon the written permission of the executive secretary.[1] The keeper of the records has an obligation to provide reasonable access for inspection by an involved party for good cause. If the executive secretary would conclude that permission should be withheld because of irrelevance, privilege, or sensitivity of the material requested, he or she should so direct and any unresolved conflict should be determined by the court as suggested in RC 1347.10(B). Children's Services generally requests that the court review the records in camera and disclose only the records that are relevant to the particular hearing.

Although Children's Services agency has a duty to keep child abuse records confidential, such confidentiality is not absolute. The records must be made available to the trial court for an in camera inspection to determine the relevancy and necessity of the records and whether their admission outweighs the confidentiality provisions of RC 5153.17.[2]

§ 37:38   Therapist as witness

The therapist as an expert witness is controlled by Rule 702 of the Ohio Rules of Evidence. In Ohio, the law prior to July 1, 1994 stated that, "If scientific, technical, or other specialized knowledge will assist the trier of fact to understand the evidence or to determine a fact in issue, the witness qualified as an expert by knowledge, skill, experience, training, or education, may testify thereto in the form of an opinion or otherwise."

Rule 702 as amended July 1, 1994 states that:

A witness may testify as an expert if all of the following apply:

(A) The witness' testimony either relates to matters beyond the knowledge or experience possessed by lay persons or dispels a misconception common among lay persons;

(B) The witness is qualified as an expert by specialized knowledge, skill, experience, training, or education regarding the subject matter of the testimony;

(C) The witness' testimony is based on reliable scientific, technical or other specialized information.

In addition, Rule 702(C) as amended further provides that:

To the extent that the testimony reports the result of a procedure, test, or experiment, the testimony is reliable only if all of the following apply:

(1) The theory upon which the procedure, test, or experiment is based is objectively verifiable or is validly derived from widely accepted knowledge, facts, or principles;

[Section 37:37]

[1]RC 5153.17.

[2]Johnson v. Johnson, 134 Ohio App. 3d 579, 731 N.E.2d 1144 (3d Dist. Union County 1999).

(2) The design of the procedure, test, or experiment reliably implements the theory;

(3) The particular procedure, test, or experiment was conducted in a way that will yield an accurate result.

The amended Rule was designed to reflect the Ohio Supreme Court's interpretation of the rule's pre-amendment language. There was no intent to change Ohio substantive law regarding the reliability of testimony by experts.[1]

Experts today are being called to perform the difficult task of determining with reliability a person's subjective state several years before the expert's investigation. Today, "experts" are being called to testify on behalf of one party as to the battered woman syndrome,[2] the battered child syndrome,[3] or the proper protocol for interviewing child victims.[4] The very fact that one party is paying for the expert may make the expert biased rather than objective. More biased still are the "experts" who always testify for the defense or always testify for the plaintiff. Their objectivity is clearly suspect, as they quite often testify as to their theory which may have little reliability as it relates to a specific case. Clearly the "court-ordered expert" has a greater chance of maintaining his or her objectivity.

The danger that experts may abuse their power is heightened when an attorney is not sufficiently knowledgeable in the particular area to effectively cross-examine this expert. Indeed, it is difficult to cross-examine an expert where anything a person does is part of the "syndrome," such as a victim who may be happy around the abuser or unhappy around the abuser;[5] or when the victim may have immediately reported the abuse or delayed reporting the abuse, been consistent in their report or inconsistent in their report, or stuck to the story or recanted their initial story;[6] or that the victim may stay in the relationship or leave.[7] Experts' testimony can be useful to rebut the inference that because the victim was happy around the alleged abuser or because the victim stayed in the relationship with the abuser that they must have fabricated their testimony about the abuse. Experts would, however, be more beneficial if they could cite reliable research, such as a study that suggests that certain percentages of abused children appeared happy when around the abuser. Those studies, though, are very difficult to perform and therefore many experts testify as to their particular experience or the testimonials

---

[Section 37:38]

[1]Staff Note to Evid. R. 702, July 1, 1994 amendment.

[2]State v. Koss, 49 Ohio St. 3d 213, 551 N.E.2d 970 (1990).

[3]State v. Nemeth, 1997 WL 39886 (Ohio Ct. App. 7th Dist. Jefferson County 1997), appeal allowed, 78 Ohio St. 3d 1515, 679 N.E.2d 310 (1997) and judgment aff'd and remanded, 1998 -Ohio- 376, 82 Ohio St. 3d 202, 694 N.E.2d 1332 (1998).

[4]State v. Gersin, 1996 -Ohio- 114, 76 Ohio St. 3d 491, 668 N.E.2d 486 (1996).

[5]State v. McMillan, 69 Ohio App. 3d 36, 590 N.E.2d 23 (9th Dist. Lorain County 1990).

[6]State v. Chamberlain, 137 N.H. 414, 628 A.2d 704 (1993).

[7]State v. Koss, 49 Ohio St. 3d 213, 551 N.E.2d 970 (1990).

that they have observed rather than reliable research articles that they have read or studied.

When the expert is testifying as to their perceptions or testimonials and not established research, it is critical that they are cross-examined properly by a person who has an expert understanding of the strengths and weaknesses of testimonials versus scientific research. This understanding is even more critical in domestic relations cases when a party is attempting to obtain custody or halt visitation due to possible sexual abuse of a child by the other parent. Some experts, at times, use legitimacy scales or their own personal tests to determine sexual abuse when there is absolutely no demonstrated reliability with their procedures. It is unfortunate that, too often, attorneys are stymied by the testimony, and allow it to stand as expert testimony when the procedures used by the expert were so flawed that there was absolutely no demonstrated reliability. A party may obtain high test scores on these unproven tests, indicating a strong likelihood that there was sexual abuse. Therefore, the expert may testify as to their own opinion beyond a reasonable degree of psychological certainty that the child was abused by that party. On further questioning, though, it may be determined that none of the expert psychologist's data was derived from the child but only from the opposing party, and only after that party received a complaint for contempt for not allowing visitation. If the psychologist or therapist does not know that the parties are involved in litigation, then the testimony of the therapist would clearly be suspect because the motivation of a party clearly is a factor that must be taken into account by any expert.

Psychology is not an exact science. When an expert testifies as if it is an exact science, he or she is going beyond his or her training and experience. In *State v. Mott*,[8] the expert concluded that the defendant's history of being abused, in conjunction with her limited intelligence, "prohibited" her from being able to decide to take the child to the hospital. The expert could have testified more accurately that the above factors may have "greatly influenced" her ability to make a decision about taking the child to the hospital, but instead testified to an all or nothing statement that these factors "prohibited" her from taking the child to the hospital.[9]

A strong dissent in *State v. Gersin*[10] noted that having two or more experts testify to the proper protocol regarding the method used to evaluate child victims of sexual abuse will only add to the confusion. An article by E.G. Guidry suggests do's and don'ts when interviewing a child who is a suspected victim of sexual abuse, such as do not suggest answers to the child, and do not criticize the child's choice of words. "It does not take specialized knowledge or expertise to identify when an

---

[8]State v. Mott, 187 Ariz. 536, 931 P.2d 1046 (1997).

[9]For an excellent article in evaluating an expert witness, see Rosalyn Schultz, PhD, *Evaluating the Expert Witness; the Mental Health Expert in Sexual Abuse Cases*, 9 Am. J. Fam. L. 1–9 (1995).

[10]State v. Gersin, 1996 -Ohio- 114, 76 Ohio St. 3d 491, 668 N.E.2d 486 (1996).

interview might have been overly suggestive. Protocols detailing the proper forensic examination of the sexually abused child are readily available to medical and legal personnel."[11] If the expert has studied various research procedures, he could demonstrate strengths and weaknesses of various techniques.

The Guidry article also suggests that the interview be conducted in private, and that the interviewer sit at the child's eye level. If those proper protocol techniques were not used, does that mean that the expert's testimony should be disregarded when another expert has testified that they did not comply with the proper protocol? Or, if they complied with every protocol, would it still be important to note that the child had been cross-examined multiple times by a significant number of other people, or that the expert performing the proper protocol was the third or fourth expert to interview the child in the case? This author tends to agree that allowing more experts to testify as to proper protocol just adds to the confusion. It also makes the Rule 702(C) requirement that the testimony be based on reliable information that much more important. Instead of assuming reliability, reliability should be determined, examined, and cross-examined.

§ 37:39 Therapist's liability—Duty to third parties

The Supreme Court held in *Estates of Morgan v. Fairfield Family Counseling Center*,[1] that a psychotherapist, who knows or should have known that his or her patient or outpatient represents a substantial risk of harm to others, is under a duty to exercise professional judgment to prevent such harm. The court gave an in depth analysis of the Restatement of Torts and the different approaches of other state courts concerning professional liability to third parties, separate from the duty of care a therapist or counselor owes to his or her client.

The legislature, in direct response to *Morgan*, enacted RC 2305.51, and amended RC 5122.34[2] to specify what acts would provide immunity for mental health professionals and organizations from civil suits and from disciplinary actions by licensing or regulatory agencies.[3]

---

[11]See E.G. Guidry, *Childhood Sexual Abuse; Role of the Family Physician*, 51 Am. Fam. Physician 407 (Feb. 1, 1995).

[Section 37:39]

[1]Estates of Morgan v. Fairfield Family Counseling Ctr., 1997 -Ohio- 194, 77 Ohio St. 3d 284, 673 N.E.2d 1311 (1997).

[2]Am. H.B. 71, eff. 9-15-99.

[3]See also, Demmit and Russo, Confidentiality or Disclosure?, 12 DRJO 17 (March/April 2000).

APPENDIX

Correlation Table

SUBJECT	EXISTING §	NEW §
Duration of administrative and court child support orders	2151.23(G)(2)	3119.86
Definitions	2301.34	3119.01; 3121.01; 3123.01; 3125.01
CSEA required in each county	2301.35(A)	3125.10
Plan of cooperation with county commissioners	2301.35(B)	3125.12
CSEA operate support enforcement program in county	2301.35(C) first paragraph, first and second sentences	3125.11
CSEA operate under the direction of DHS; DHS ensure compliance with federal law	2301.35(C) first paragraph, second and fifth sentences	3125.24
CSEA does not collect child support; exception	2301.35(C) first paragraph, third sentence	3125.27
Use of social security number only for child support enforcement	2301.35(C) first paragraph, fourth sentence	3125.49
Contracts with vendors to perform CSEA duties	2301.35(C) second paragraph	3125.13
DHS rules governing support enforcement by CSEAs	2301.35(D)(1)	3125.25
Rules governing on-site genetic testing	2301.35(D)(2)	3111.611
Contracts with courts, prosecutors, and law enforcement officials to enforce support	2301.35(E)	3125.14
CSEA records	2301.35(F)(1)	3125.15
Review of CSEA records	2301.35(F)(2)	3125.16
Imposition of administrative charge	2301.35(G)(1) first and third sentence	3119.27

SUBJECT	EXISTING §	NEW §
Payment by obligor of administrative charge; definition of current support payment	2301.35(G)(1) second sentence and (J)(1)	3119.28
Appropriation to CSEAs by county commissioners of funds from state and federal sources	2301.35(G)(2)	3125.19
Federal and state money used for support enforcement	2301.35(G)(3)	3125.21
Waiver of appropriation limitations	2301.35(G)(4)	3125.20
CSEA investment of money	2301.35(G)(5)	3125.22
Collection of support and other amounts prior to conversion to new computer system and prior to authorization	2301.35(H)(1) and (2)--all but last sentence of both divisions	3125.28
Collection of support and other amounts after conversion to new computer system and after authorization	2301.35(H)(4)	3125.29
Amounts collected by collection agents; disposition	2301.35(H)(5)	3125.30
Title IV-D services--application	2301.35(I)	3125.36
Definitions	2301.35(J)(2)	3119.01
CSEA contact consumer reporting agency when obligor in default	2301.353(A)	3123.92
CSEA duty if obligor pays arrearages after consumer reporting agency contact	2301.353(B)	3123.921
CSEA attorneys	2301.354	3125.17
Establishment of county poster programs	2301.355 first paragraph, first sentence	3123.96
Contents of poster	2301.355 first paragraph, second, third, and fourth sentences	3123.961
Selection of obligors for the poster	2301.355 second paragraph	3123.962

SUBJECT	EXISTING §	NEW §
Genetic testing samples	2301.356	3111.61
Contract between DHS and hospitals for paternity establishment	2301.357(B) first sentence of first paragraph and all of last paragraph of (B)	3111.71
Contract requirements	2301.357(B) second sentence of first paragraph and (1) to (10)	3111.72
Report on hospitals that have not entered into contract	2301.357(C)	3111.73
Hospital duty if a man is presumed father	2301.357(D)	3111.74
Administrative officer	2301.358	3111.53
Support payments required to be made to Office of Child Support	2301.36(A) first sentence	3121.44
Payments not made to Office of Child Support shall not be considered support	2301.36(A) second sentence	3121.45
Payments directly to third party	2301.36(B) and (C)	3121.46
Parties must notify CSEA of updates to personal information	2301.36(D)	3121.24
CSEA administration of payments to third party	2301.36(E)	3121.47
Court notification of CSEA of futility of enforcement or failure to enforce support order	2301.37(B)	3123.10
CSEA notification to obligee	2301.37(B)	3123.11
Prohibition against closing a case due to failure to pay	2301.37(C)	3123.12
Rules to implement prohibition	2301.37(C)	3123.121
Withholding of unemployment compensation	2301.371	3121.07
Definitions (applicable to section 3123.41 to 3123.50)	2301.373(A)(2)	3123.41

SUBJECT	EXISTING §	NEW §
Determination of whether an obligor is a professional license holder--after default or after an obligor fails to comply with a warrant or subpoena	2301.373(B)(1) first sentence; (B)(2) first sentence	3123.42
Notice to the obligor and licensing board of obligor's default/failure to comply with a subpoena or warrant	2301.373(B)(1) second and third sentences; (B)(2) second and third sentences	3123.43
Contents of notice to obligor	2301.373(C)	3123.44
Further notice of no default	2301.373(D)(1)	3123.45
Further notice of compliance with warrant or subpoena	2301.373(D)(2)	3123.46
Licensing Board--include social security number on licenses	2301.373(E)(1)	3123.50
Licensing Board duty on receipt of default/failure to comply with subpoena or warrant notice	2301.373(E)(2)	3123.47
Licensing Board maintain a file of notices received	2301.373(E)(3)	3123.471
Licensing Board duty on receipt of no default/no failure to comply with subpoena or warrant notice	2301.373(E)(4)	3123.48
Licensing Board--not to conduct hearing when refusing to issue or renew or when revoking or suspending a license	2301.373(E)(5)	3123.49
Rules to implement all the license removal sections	2301.373(F)	3123.63
Specifying operational date with respect to driver's license removals--prior to that date, sections 3123.53 to 3123.60 are applicable as provided in section 3123.61 to 3123.615	2301.374(A); (B)(1)(a) first sentence	3123.52
License removal provisions of sections 3123.53 to 3123.60 apply only to commercial drivers' licenses and commercial drivers' temporary instruction permits prior to operational date	2301.374(B)	3123.61

SUBJECT	EXISTING §	NEW §
Contents of notice prior to operational date	2301.374(B)(2)(a), (b), and (c)	3123.613
Refusal to issue or renew commercial drivers' licenses and commercial drivers' temporary instruction permits and imposition of disqualification--prior to operational date	2301.374(B)(4)(a)	3123.611
Removal of disqualification and imposition of removal fee--prior to operational date	2301.374(B)(4)(c) first sentence and third sentence	3123.612
Registrar duty on receipt of no default/no failure to comply with subpoena or warrant notice	2301.374(B)(4)(c) and (C)(4)(c)	3123.59
No hearing permitted on whether to impose disqualification--prior to operational date	2301.374(B)(4)(d)	3123.614
Determine if obligor is a driver's license holder--after default or after failure to comply with subpoena or warrant	2301.374(C)(1)(a), first sentence; (C)(1)(b), first sentence	3123.53
Notice to obligor and registrar of default or failure to comply with subpoena or warrant	2301.374(C)(1)(a) second and third sentences; (C)(1)(b) second and third sentences	3123.54
Content of notice to the obligor	2301.374(C)(2)	3123.55
Further notice of no default	2301.374(C)(3)(a)	3123.56
Further notice of subpoena/warrant compliance	2301.374(C)(3)(b)	3123.57
Registrar duty on receipt of default/failure to comply with subpoena or warrant notice	2301.374(C)(4)(a)	3123.58
Registrar maintain list of notices	2301.374(C)(4)(b)	3123.581
No hearing permitted	2301.374(C)(4)(d)	3123.60
Rules to implement all the license removal sections	2301.374(D)	3123.63
Recreational license revocation	2301.375(A) and (B)	3123.62

SUBJECT	EXISTING §	NEW §
Rules to implement all the license removal sections	2301.375(C)	3123.63
Action to collect arrearages on terminated judgment	2301.38(B)	3123.14
Action commenced within 20 days after request	2301.38(C)	3123.15
Special orders administered monthly	2301.39(A)	3123.16
Prohibition against discharging employee because of support related order	2301.39(B)	3123.20
Lien may be asserted against property of obligor in default	2301.43(A)	3123.66
Establishing lien on real and personal property	2301.43(B)(1)	3123.67
Foreign liens	2301.43(B)(2)	3123.68
Liens in effect until discharged by recorder pursuant to discharge request	2301.43(C)	3123.71
Notice requesting discharge--content	2301.43(D)	3123.72
Priority	2301.43(E)	3123.70
Service of copy of lien	2301.44(A)	3123.69
Liability for releasing, selling, or disposing of property subject to lien	2301.44(B)	3123.77
CSEA can cause sale of property	2301.45(A)	3123.73
Procedure for sale	2301.45(B)(1)	3123.74
Court in which complaint for sale may be filed	2301.45(B)(2)	3123.741
Sale of property extinguishes lien	2301.45(C)	3123.75
CSEA may release lien	2301.46(A)	3123.76
Obtaining a lien does not affect other legal remedies	2301.46(B)	3123.78
Penalty for discharging employee because of support enforcement orders/notices	2301.99	3123.99
Duration of administrative and court child support orders	3105.21(D)	3119.86
Duration of administrative and court child support orders	3109.05(E)	3119.86

SUBJECT	EXISTING §	NEW §
Duration of administrative and court child support orders	3111.13(F)(2)	3119.86
Definitions	3111.20(A)	3119.01; 3121.01; 3123.01; 3125.01
Presumed father has duty of support	3111.20(B)	3111.77
Administrative action for support may be taken against presumed father	3111.20(C) second paragraph, first sentence	3111.78
Paternity may be raised in administrative support action	3111.20(C) third paragraph, first sentence	3111.82
Effect of raising paternity in administrative support action	3111.20(C) third paragraph, second sentence	3111.821
Administrative action for child support based on administrative determination of paternity or presumption	3111.20(D) first paragraph	3111.80
Issuance of support order after hearing	3111.20(D)(1) and (2)	3111.81
Notarizing acknowledgment of paternity	3111.21	3111.21
CSEA send notarized acknowledgment to Office of Child Support	3111.21	3111.22
Paternity may be raised in administrative support action	3111.211(A) first sentence, second paragraph	3111.82
Effect of raising paternity in administrative support action	3111.211(A) second to fourth sentences, second paragraph; third paragraph	3111.821
De Novo court action to determine paternity not available; exceptions	3111.22(A)	3111.381
Action for administrative determination of paternity	3111.22(B)	3111.38

SUBJECT	EXISTING §	NEW §
Multiple requests for determination	3111.22(B)	3111.39
Contents of request for administrative determination. of paternity	3111.22(B)(1) to (4)	3111.40
Issuance of administrative order for genetic testing	3111.22(C)(1) first paragraph, first, third, and fourth sentences	3111.41
Conference to sign acknowledgment of paternity affidavit	3111.22(C)(1) first paragraph, second sentence	3111.44
Attachment of notice to testing order	3111.22(C)(1) second paragraph, (a) to (h)	3111.42
Notice and testing order sent under Civil Rules	3111.22(C)(1) second paragraph	3111.421
Genetic tests conducted	3111.22(C)(2) first paragraph, first and second sentences	3111.45
Orders that may be issued on conclusion of tests	3111.22(C)(2)(a) to (c)	3111.46
Orders must contain notice of right to appeal conclusive determination or right to bring paternity action for inconclusive determination	3111.22(C)(2) last paragraph	3111.48
Right to appeal conclusive determination	3111.22(D)	3111.49
Administrative action for child support based on administrative determination of paternity or presumption	3111.22(E)(1)	3111.80
Issuance of support order after hearing	3111.22(E)(1)(a) to (c)	3111.81
Inconclusive determination order issued for willful failure to submit to genetic tests	3111.22(F)	3111.47
Right to bring court paternity action based on inconclusive determination of paternity due to willful failure to submit; lack of evidence	3111.22(F)	3111.50
Personal information contained in paternity order	3111.22(G) first sentence	3111.51

SUBJECT	EXISTING §	NEW §
Change of surname based on paternity determination notification of Department of Health.	3111.22(G) second sentence	3111.52
Effect of prior administrative determination of paternity	3111.22(H)	3111.85
Issuance of new birth record	3111.221 second and third paragraphs	3111.58
Withholding and deduction notices and other orders are required in order to collect support	3111.23(A)	3121.02
Issuing entity (court or CSEA) decide appropriate requirement to enforce support order	3111.23(A)	3121.032
Time period for sending withholding or deduction notice	3111.23(A)	3121.035
General provisions in support order requiring withholding or deduction or other appropriate enforcement order	3111.23(A)	3121.27
Notices and orders are final and enforceable	3111.23(A)	3121.33
Compliance with notice or order issued to enforce support order without need to amend order	3111.23(A)	3121.34
Adoption of standard forms for withholding/deduction notices	3111.23(A)(5)	3121.0311
Withholding and deduction notices and other enforcement orders	3111.23(B)(1)(a); (B)(1)(b) first and second sentences; (B)(2)(a); (B)(2)(b) first and second sentences	3121.03
Contents of withholding or deduction notice	3111.23(B)(1)(b)(i) to (xi) and (B)(2)(b)(i) to (viii)	3121.037
Additional notice attached to the withholding or deduction notice	3111.23(B)(1)(c) and (2)(c)	3121.036

SUBJECT	EXISTING §	NEW §
Appropriate number of notices or orders must be issued to collect	3111.23(C)	3121.033
Priority of multiple withholding or deduction notices	3111.23(D)	3121.034
Service requirements of all withholding and deduction notices and other notices	3111.23(E)(1)	3121.23
Parties must notify CSEA of updates to personal information	3111.23(E)(2)	3121.24
Provision in support orders requiring parties to update personal information	3111.23(E)(3)	3121.29
Termination--Duty to notify	3111.23(E)(4)(a)	3119.87
Termination--Reasons for termination	3111.23(E)(4)(a)	3119.88
Termination--CSEA investigation	3111.23(E)(4)(a)	3119.89
Termination--CSEA duties after investigation	3111.23(E)(4)(a)	3119.90
Termination--Effect of termination on withholding or deduction notice	3111.23(E)(4)(c)	3119.93
Termination--Rules	3111.23(E)(4)(d)	3119.94
Disposition of lump-sum payment made to obligor	3111.23(F)	3121.12
Support order must include obligor DOB and social security number	3111.23(G)(1)	3121.30
Information that may not be included in withholding or deduction notices or other enforcement orders	3111.23(G)(2)	3121.039
Notice in withholding or deduction notices issued for administrative child support orders	3111.23(G)(3)	3121.038
No termination of withholding or deduction notices or other enforcement orders for paying off arrearages	3111.23(H)	3123.13

SUBJECT	EXISTING §	NEW §
Fee that may be charged by payor/financial institution for withholding or deduction	3111.24(A)(2) first paragraph	3121.18
Time period for forwarding amounts withheld or deducted to Office of Child Support	3111.24(A)(2) second paragraph	3121.19
Form in which withheld and deducted amounts may be sent to Office of Child Support	3111.24(B)	3121.20
Support disbursement requirements	3111.24(C)	3121.50
No liability for payors for complying with withholding or deduction notice	3111.24(D)	3121.21
Definitions	3111.241(A)	3119.01
Health insurance provisions must be included in child support orders	3111.241(B)	3119.30
Specific requirements in child support orders concerning health insurance coverage for children	3111.241(C)	3119.31
CSEA notify court when obligor/obligee fails to obtain insurance	3111.241(D) first sentence	3119.40
Court issue health insurance coverage order and send to employer	3111.241(D) second and third sentences	3119.41
CSEA investigation when employment changes	3111.241(E)(1) first sentence	3119.43
CSEA issue notice requiring enrollment of children in health insurance coverage	3111.241(E)(1) second sentence	3119.44
Contents of health insurance notice issued by CSEA	3111.241(E)(2)	3119.45
Orders and notices requiring provisions of health care are binding	3111.241(F)	3119.47
Employer compliance with health insurance requirement/notice is required	3111.241(G)(1) first half of first sentence	3119.48
Release of information to parent/CSEA	3111.241(G)(1) second half of first sentence	3119.49
Limitation on use of information	3111.241(G)(1) second sentence	3119.491

SUBJECT	EXISTING §	NEW §
Employer notify CSEA of change/termination of health coverage	3111.241(G)(2)	3119.50
Insurer required to comply with health insurance notice or order	3111.241(G)(3) first sentence	3119.51
Reimbursement of appropriate parent by insurer	3111.241(G)(3) second sentence	3119.52
Payment of health costs if obligee eligible for medical assistance	3111.241(H)	3119.54
Liability for medical expenses for failure to comply with health insurance order/notice	3111.241(I)	3119.56
Enrollment of child in health insurance plan not required if the child does not meet underwriting standards	3111.241(J)	3119.53
Failure to comply with court child support order or order requiring health insurance is contempt	3111.241(K)	3119.57
Transitional rules	3111.241(L)	3119.301
Contempt for failure to comply with administrative child support orders	3111.242(A)	3121.37
Contempt for failure to submit to genetic testing	3111.242(B)	3111.54
Failure to withhold or deduct--liability for amount not withheld	3111.25(A)(2)	3121.38
Prohibition against disciplining employee because of withholding or deduction notice	3111.25(B)	3121.39
Notice of paternity determination request sent to parties under Civil Rules--contingency if unable to obtain service	3111.26	3111.43
DHS rules governing administrative reviews	3111.27(A)	3119.76
CSEA procedure when preparing to do a review of a child support order	3111.27(B)(1)	3119.60
Failure to provide information pursuant to administrative review of child support orders	3111.27(B)(2)	3119.72

SUBJECT	EXISTING §	NEW §
CSEA procedure when conducting review of administrative child support orders	3111.27(C)(1); (C)(2); and (D)	3119.61
Consideration of health insurance cost required when court or CSEA reviews child support orders	3111.27(C)(3)	3119.73
Failure to provide information pursuant to administrative review of child support orders	3111.28(B)	3119.72
Definitions	3111.30	3111.88
Scope of artificial insemination provisions	3111.31	3111.89
Supervision by physician	3111.32	3111.90
Medical history and examination of donor	3111.33	3111.91
Both spouses must consent	3111.34	3111.92
Contents of consent form, etc.	3111.35	3111.93
Confidentiality and retention of information	3111.36	3111.94
Recipient's husband considered natural father	3111.37	3111.95
Effect of noncompliance	3111.38	3111.96
Penalties	3111.99(C) and (D)	3121.99
Collection of fine amounts considered to be program income	3111.99(E)	3121.59
Duration of administrative and court child support orders	3113.04(C)	3119.86
Collection of prisoner earnings	3113.16(A) and (B)	3121.08
Collection of obligor's prisoner earnings	3113.16(A) and (C)	3123.87
Withholding and deduction notices and other orders are required in order to collect support	3113.21(A)	3121.02
Time period for sending withholding or deduction notice	3113.21(A)	3121.035
General provisions in support order requiring withholding or deduction or other appropriate enforcement order	3113.21(A)	3121.27
Notices and orders are final and enforceable	3113.21(A)	3121.33

SUBJECT	EXISTING §	NEW §
Compliance with notice or order issued to enforce support order without need to amend order	3113.21(A)	3121.34
Issuing entity (court or CSEA) decide appropriate requirement to enforce support order	3113.21(A)	3121.032
Adoption of standard forms for withholding/deduction notices	3113.21(A)(4)	3121.0311
Support withholding initiated when order is in default	3113.21(B)(1)(a)	3123.061
Issuance of court support order to replace certain support orders in default	3113.21(B)(1)(a)	3123.07
General provision requiring withholding or deduction of support for reissued support order	3113.21(B)(1)(a)	3123.071
After a default is identified, investigation initiated	3113.21(B)(1)(a) and (b)	3123.02
Sending advance notice	3113.21(B)(1)(a) and (B)(2)	3123.03
Agency hearing and determination concerning advance notice	3113.21(B)(3)	3123.04
Court hearing and determination concerning advance notice	3113.21(B)(4)	3123.05
Withholding or deduction notices and other appropriate orders issued on exhaustion of rights to contest	3113.21(B)(5)	3123.06
Savings provision in case of failure to send notice	3113.21(B)(5)	3123.062
Adoption of standard forms for advance notices	3113.21(B)(6)	3123.031
Motion to request withholding/deduction notice or other appropriate order to enforce support order	3113.21(C)(1)(a)	3119.80
Issuance of withholding/deduction notice or other appropriate order when child support order is before the court in any proceeding	3113.21(C)(1)(b)	3119.81

SUBJECT	EXISTING §	NEW §
Court issue new child support order including revised amount if obligor or obligee do not request court hearing on CSEA determination	3113.21(C)(1)(c)(i) second sentence	3119.65
Court schedule and conduct hearing if obligor/obligee request review of CSEA revision	3113.21(C)(1)(c)(i) third sentence	3119.66
Court give notice of hearing	3113.21(C)(1)(c)(ii)	3119.67
Obligor/obligee provide financial information	3113.21(C)(1)(c)(ii)	3119.68
Court give notice that failure to provide information is contempt	3113.21(C)(1)(c)(ii)	3119.69
Court determination	3113.21(C)(1)(c)(ii)	3119.70
Consideration of health insurance cost required when court or CSEA reviews child support orders	3113.21(C)(1)(c)(iii)	3119.73
Motion requesting court to order obligor or obligee to provide health insurance coverage	3113.21(C)(1)(d)(i) first sentence	3119.33
CSEA investigate health insurance situation of obligor/obligee	3113.21(C)(1)(d)(i) second and third sentences	3119.34
Court determination	3113.21(C)(1)(d)(i) fourth sentence	3119.35
Motion to modify child support amount because it does not cover health costs	3113.21(C)(1)(d)(ii) first sentence	3119.37
Court determination	3113.21(C)(1)(d)(ii) second sentence	3119.38
Determination of right to claim child as a dependent	3113.21(C)(1)(e)	3119.82
Effective date of modification after CSEA review	3113.21(C)(1)(f)	3119.71
Notice and hearing concerning determination of appropriate withholding, deduction, or other order to enforce the court support order	3113.21(C)(2) first paragraph	3121.031

SUBJECT	EXISTING §	NEW §
Withholding and deduction notices and other enforcement orders	3113.21(D)(1)(a); (D)(1)(b) first and second sentences; (D)(2)(a); (D)(2)(b) first and second sentences; (D)(3) and (4)	3121.03
Contents of withholding or deduction notice	3113.21(D)(1)(b)(i) to (xi) and (D)(2)(b)(i) to (viii)	3121.037
Additional notice attached to the withholding or deduction notice	3113.21(D)(1)(c) and (D)(2)(c)	3121.036
Appropriate number of notices or orders must be issued to collect	3113.21(E)	3121.033
Priority of multiple withholding or deduction notices	3113.21(F)	3121.034
Service requirements of all withholding and deduction notices and other notices	3113.21(G)(1)	3121.23
Parties must notify CSEA of updates to personal information	3113.21(G)(2)	3121.24
Provision in support orders requiring parties to update personal information	3113.21(G)(3)	3121.29
Termination--Duty to notify	3113.21(G)(4)(a)	3119.87
Termination--Reasons for termination	3113.21(G)(4)(a)	3119.88
Termination--CSEA investigation	3113.21(G)(4)(a)	3119.89
Termination--CSEA duties after investigation complete	3113.21(G)(4)(a)	3119.90
Termination--Effect of termination on withholding or deduction notice	3113.21(G)(4)(c)	3119.93
Termination--Rules	3113.21(G)(4)(d)	3119.94
Court notification of CSEA of modification/ enforcement actions regarding a support order	3113.21(G)(5)	3121.25
Notice of lump-sum payment to obligor or default by obligor--action by CSEA	3113.21(G)(6) first paragraph and (b)	3121.11

SUBJECT	EXISTING §	NEW §
Cash bond in cases of noncompliance when assets cannot be reached	3113.21(H)(1)(a)	3121.04
Seek work order--obligor in default has no assets	3113.21(H)(1)(b)	3121.05
Seek work order--pursuant to modification proceeding and obligor has no assets	3113.21(H)(2)	3121.06
Disposition of lump-sum payment made to obligor	3113.21(H)(3)	3121.12
Support order must include obligor DOB and social security number	3113.21(I)(1)	3121.30
Information that may not be included in withholding or deduction notices or other enforcement orders	3113.21(I)(2)	3121.039
No termination of withholding or deduction notices or other enforcement orders for paying off arrearages	3113.21(J)	3123.13
Payment of arrearages to ODHS	3113.21(K) and (N)	3123.19
Court quotas concerning paternity and support cases	3113.21(L)(1)	3125.58
Court issuance of temporary orders in complex cases	3113.21(L)(2)	3125.59
Court appointment of magistrates	3113.21(L)(3)	3125.60
Additional administrative reviews conducted by CSEA	3113.21(L)(4)	3119.74
Termination of support order does not prevent collection of arrearages	3113.21(M)(1)	3121.36
Court authority to enforce court support orders and administrative child support orders	3113.21(M)(2)	3121.35
Prohibition against retroactive modification of delinquent support amount	3113.21(M)(3)	3119.83
Court may modify support amount due after motion to modify filed	3113.21(M)(4)	3119.84
Withholding of unemployment compensation	3113.21(O)	3121.07

SUBJECT	EXISTING §	NEW §
Definitions	3113.21(P)	3119.01; 3123.01; 3125.01
Definitions	3113.21(P) and (Q)	3121.01
Fee that may be charged by payor/financial institution for withholding or deduction	3113.211(A)(2) first paragraph	3121.18
Time period for forwarding amounts withheld or deducted to Office of Child Support	3113.211(A)(2) second paragraph	3121.19
Form in which withheld and deducted amounts may be sent to Office of Child Support	3113.211(B)	3121.20
Support disbursement requirements	3113.211(C)	3121.50
No liability for payors for complying with withholding or deduction notice	3113.211(D)	3121.21
Change in income source or financial account--investigation and issuance of withholding or deduction notice or other order	3113.212(A)	3121.14
Commencement of employment--issuance of withholding notice	3113.212(B)	3121.15
Notice or order sent under 3121.14 or 3121.15 considered sent under 3121.03	3113.212(C)	3121.16
Contempt for failure to comply with order to comply with a withholding or deduction notice	3113.212(D)	3121.371
Failure to send notifications is contempt	3113.213(A)(2)	3121.372
Failure to withhold or deduct--liability for amount not withheld	3113.213(B)	3121.38
Failure to withhold or deduct--fine	3113.213(C)	3121.381
Penalties	3113.213(D) second sentence	3121.99
Prohibition against disciplining employee because of withholding or deduction notice	3113.213(D) first sentence	3121.39
Definition	3113.214(A)	3123.24
Entry of default in case registry if obligor has account in financial institution	3113.214(B)	3123.25

SUBJECT	EXISTING §	NEW §
Imposition of access restriction on account	3113.214(C)	3123.26
CSEA investigation of amount of funds in account	3113.214(D)	3123.27
Issuance of withdrawal directive required if obligor is the only owner of account	3113.214(E)(1) first sentence	3123.28
If obligor is not sole owner of account--CSEA must send notice to other owner	3113.214(E)(1) second sentence	3123.29
Content of notice--notification of issuance of withdrawal directive	3113.214(E)(2)	3123.30
Objection to withdrawal directive--request administrative hearing	3113.214(E)(3) first paragraph	3123.31
Administrative hearing	3113.214(E)(3)(a) first and second paragraph	3123.33
Administrative determination	3113.214(E)(3)(a) third paragraph, first to third sentences	3123.34
Court hearing	3113.214(E)(3)(a) third paragraph, fourth to sixth sentences	3123.35
Court determination	3113.214(E)(3)(a) fourth paragraph	3123.36
Issuance of withdrawal directive if fail to request administrative hearing	3113.214(E)(3)(b)	3123.32
Withdrawal directive	3113.214(F)	3123.37
Immunity for financial institution	3113.214(G)	3123.38
Definitions	3113.215(A)	3119.01
Calculation of child support--requirement to use basic child support schedule and worksheets	3113.215(B)(1) first and second sentence	3119.02
Presumption that amounts calculated using schedule and worksheets are correct	3113.215(B)(1) third sentence up to "due"	3119.03

SUBJECT	EXISTING §	NEW §
Amount calculated for child support must be issued unless deviation is permitted	3113.215(B)(1) third sentence, everything after "due"; (B)(2)(c)	3119.22
Calculation of child support when combined gross income is less than $6,600 or exceeds $180,000	3113.215(B)(2)(a) and (b)	3119.04
Discretionary deviations	3113.215(B)(3)	3119.23
Court modification--10% change requirement	3113.215(B)(4)	3119.79
Factors in computing child support amounts	3113.215(B)(5)	3119.05
Deviation in shared parenting cases; allowed in extraordinary circumstances	3113.215(B)(6)(a) and (b)	3119.24
Minimum support orders	3113.215(B)(7)(a)	3119.06
Determining the obligor	3113.215(C) first paragraph	3119.07
Visitation order must accompany child support order	3113.215(C) second paragraph, first sentence	3119.08
No impoundment/escrowing of child support if noncompliance with visitation	3113.215(C) second paragraph, second sentence	3119.09
Basic child support schedule	3113.215(D)	3119.021
Sole/shared parenting worksheet	3113.215(E)	3119.022
Split parenting worksheet	3113.215(F)	3119.023
Guidelines review	3113.215(G)	3119.024
DHS rules governing administrative reviews	3113.216(B)	3119.76
CSEA procedure when preparing to do a review of a child support order	3113.216(C)(1)	3119.60
Failure to provide information pursuant to administrative review of child support orders	3113.216(C)(2)	3119.72
CSEA procedure when conducting review of court child support orders	3113.216(C)(3)	3119.63

SUBJECT	EXISTING §	NEW §
Consideration of health insurance cost required when court or CSEA reviews child support orders	3113.216(C)(4)	3119.73
Opportunity to request court hearing to review revised amount of child support proposed by CSEA for inclusion in court order	3113.216(D)	3119.64
When CSEA is not required to conduct a review	3113.216(E)	3119.75
Definitions	3113.217(A)	3119.01
Health insurance provisions must be included in child support orders	3113.217(B)	3119.30
Specific requirements in child support orders concerning health insurance coverage for children	3113.217(C)	3119.31
CSEA notify court when obligor/obligee fails to obtain insurance	3113.217(D) first sentence	3119.40
Court issue health insurance coverage order and send to employer	3113.217(D) second and third sentences; (F) second sentence	3119.41
CSEA investigation when employment changes	3113.217(E)(1) first sentence	3119.43
CSEA issue notice requiring enrollment of children in health insurance coverage	3113.217(E)(1) second sentence	3119.44
Contents of health insurance notice issued by CSEA	3113.217(E)(2)	3119.45
Orders and notices requiring provisions of health care are binding	3113.217(F)	3119.47
Employer compliance with health insurance requirement/notice is required	3113.217(G)(1) first half of first sentence	3119.48
Release of information to parent/CSEA	3113.217(G)(1) second half of first sentence	3119.49
Limitation on use of information	3113.217(G)(1) second sentence	3119.491

SUBJECT	EXISTING §	NEW §
Employer notify CSEA of change/termination of health coverage	3113.217(G)(2)	3119.50
Insurer required to comply with health insurance notice or order	3113.217(G)(3) first sentence	3119.51
Reimbursement of appropriate parent by insurer	3113.217(G)(3) second sentence	3119.52
Payment of health costs if obligee eligible for medical assistance	3113.217(H)	3119.54
Liability for medical expenses for failure to comply with health insurance order/notice	3113.217(I)	3119.56
Failure to comply with court child support order or order requiring health insurance is contempt	3113.217(J) first sentence	3119.57
Second time contempt for failure to comply with court child support order or order requiring health insurance coverage--change of circumstances for purposes of child support modification	3113.217(J) second sentence	3119.58
Enrollment of child in health insurance plan not required if the child does not meet underwriting standards	3113.217(K)	3119.53
Transitional rules	3113.217(L)	3119.301
Provision in support order requiring monthly administration	3113.218(B)(1) to (3)	3121.28
Monthly administration of support orders required	3113.218(C) and (F)	3121.51
Orders paid on other than monthly basis-- monthly administration	3113.218(D)	3121.52
Orders paid on other than a monthly basis— monthly administration does not affect method of payment	3113.218(E)	3121.53
New support order--imposition of interest and other costs as part of order	3113.219	3123.17
Obtaining judgment for failure to pay support	3113.2110	3123.18

SUBJECT	EXISTING §	NEW §
Motion for relief from parentage determination or child support order	3113.2111(A)	3119.961
Determination as to whether to grant relief	3113.2111(B) and (C)	3119.962
Genetic tests	3113.2111(D)	3119.963
Proceedings to establish parentage after relief granted	3113.2111(E), all but last sent.	3119.965
Payment of court costs and reasonable attorney's fees	3113.2111(E), last sent., and (H)	3119.966
Effect of granting relief on parenting time rights, visitation rights, and arrearages	3113.2111(F) and (G)	3119.964
Relief available regardless of when parentage determination or child support order was issued	3113.2111(I)	3119.967
Definitions	3113.2111(J)(2)	3119.96
Duration of administrative and court child support orders	3113.31(K)(2)	3119.86
Penalties	3113.99(C) and (D)	3121.99
Collection of fine amounts considered to be program income	3113.99(E)	3121.59
Office of Child Support access to information; definition of cable TV and public utility	5101.31(A) and (G)(1)	3125.41
Creation of the Office of Child Support	5101.31(B) first paragraph, first sentence	3125.02
Establishment and administration of child support enforcement program	5101.31(B) first paragraph, second, third, and fourth sentences	3125.03
Publicize paternity establishment procedure	5101.31(B) second paragraph	3125.04
Title IV-D application fee	5101.31(B) third paragraph	3125.37
Establishment and administration of spousal support enforcement program	5101.31(C)	3125.05

SUBJECT	EXISTING §	NEW §
Agreement with federal government to use parent locator service	5101.31(D)	3125.06
Use of social security number only for child support enforcement	5101.31(E)	3125.49
Prohibition against information disclosure	5101.31(F)(1); (G)(4)(b), second sentence	3125.50
Office of Child Support adopt rules governing access to and disclosure of information in the Office's possession	5101.31(F)(2)	3125.51
Provision of information by persons and entities--general	5101.31(G)(2)	3125.42
Immunity from civil/criminal liability for providing information to Office of Child Support	5101.31(G)(3); (G)(4)(b) first sentence	3125.45
Provision of information by the tax department	5101.31(G)(4)(a) first, second, and fourth sentences	3125.43
Office of Child Support reimburse tax department for providing information	5101.31(G)(4)(a) third sentence	3125.44
Prohibition against failing to provide information (not applicable to tax department)	5101.31(G)(5) first sentence	3125.46
Fine for failing to provide information	5101.31(G)(5) second sentence	3125.47
Court action to collect fine	5101.31(G)(5) third and fourth sentences	3125.48
Consumer reporting agency may contact Office of Child Support to determine if person is an obligor	5101.311(A) first paragraph, first and second sentences	3123.93
Office of Child Support check case registry	5101.311(A) first paragraph, third sentence	3123.931
Provision of information to a consumer reporting agency	5101.311(A) second paragraph	3123.932
Definition of consumer reporting agency	5101.311(B)	3123.91

SUBJECT	EXISTING §	NEW §
Definitions	5101.312(A)	3121.89
New hire reporting requirements	5101.312(B)	3121.891
Content of reports	5101.312(C)	3121.892
Method of making report	5101.312(D)	3121.893
Entry of report data into new hire directory	5101.312(E)(1)	3121.894
Data comparison; notify CSEA of data match	5101.312(E)(2) and first sentence of (E)(3)	3121.895
CSEA duty on receipt of data match notice	5101.312(E)(3) second sentence	3121.896
Furnishing information to national directory of new hires	5101.312(E)(4)	3121.897
Use of reports	5101.312(F) first paragraph, first sentence	3121.898
Rules to implement 3121.89 to 3121.8910	5101.312(F) first paragraph, last sentence	3121.8911
Disclosure of information	5101.312(F) second paragraph	3121.899
Failure to make a report; penalty	5101.312(G)	3121.8910
Putative father registry	5101.313	3111.69
Filing acknowledgment with Office of Child Support	5101.314(A)(1)	3111.23
Office of Child Support examine acknowledgment	5101.314(A)(2)	3111.24
Acknowledgment becomes final--when	5101.314(A)(3)(a) and (b)	3111.25
Effect of final acknowledgment	5101.314 paragraph after (A)(3)(b) and (A)(4)(a), first sentence	3111.26

SUBJECT	EXISTING §	NEW §
Action for child support based on final acknowledgment	5101.314(A)(4)(b)	3111.29
Notification to Health Department of final acknowledgment	5101.314(A)(4)(c)	3111.30
Recision of acknowledgment not yet final	5101.314(B)(1)(a) and (b)	3111.27
Court action to rescind final acknowledgment	5101.314(B)(2)	3111.28
Filing of paternity determinations with Office of Child Support	5101.314(C)	3111.66
Birth registry established	5101.314(D)(1)	3111.64
Birth registry maintained as part of data system	5101.314(D)(2)	3111.65
Rules for registry	5101.314(E)	3111.67
Rules for 3111.20 to .34	5101.314(E)	3111.35
Definitions applicable to paternity sections (3111.20 to 3111.85)	5101.314(F)	3111.20
Agreements by financial institutions to provide account information	5101.315(B)	3121.74
Fee deducted from obligor's account by financial institutions for providing information	5101.315(C)	3121.75
Status of information; prohibition against disclosure	5101.315(D)	3121.76
Immunity	5101.315(E)	3121.77
Rules	5101.315(F)	3121.78
Enforcement of foreign country support orders	5101.316	3121.92
Annual report to Federal government concerning Title IV-D program operation	5101.317(A)	3125.38
Rules for annual report	5101.317(B)	3125.39
Assistance of other states in enforcing support orders	5101.318	3121.91
Creation of case registry	5101.319(B) first sentence	3121.81

SUBJECT	EXISTING §	NEW §
Information to be included in the registry	5101.319(B) second sentence (1) to (6)	3121.82
Maintenance of registry	5101.319(C)	3121.83
Data comparisons and provision of data	5101.319(D) and (E)(3)	3121.84
Entry, maintenance, and monitoring of information in the registry	5101.319(E)(1) and (2)	3121.85
Rules regarding the registry	5101.319(F)	3121.86
Federal tax refund intercept	5101.32	3123.81
State tax refund intercept	5101.321(A)	3123.821
Limitations on state tax refund intercept	5101.321(B)	3123.822
Rules to implement	5101.321(C)	3123.823
Definitions for state tax refund intercept	5101.321(D)	3123.82
Establishment and maintenance of SETS	5101.322(A)	3125.07
Rules regulating use and access to data	5101.322(B)	3125.08
Establishment of statewide poster program of obligors in default	5101.323(A)(1) first sentence	3123.95
Contents of poster	5101.323(A)(1) second, third, and fourth sentences	3123.957
CSEAs may submit names for inclusion on the poster	5101.323(A)(2)	3123.951
Notice to obligors about possible inclusion on the poster	5101.323(A)(3)	3123.956
Office of Child Support review submissions from CSEAs	5101.323(A)(4)	3123.955
Publication and distribution of poster	5101.323(A)(5)	3123.958
Criteria for CSEA in submitting names of obligors	5101.323(B)	3123.952
Submission of photographs	5101.323(C) first sentence	3123.953

SUBJECT	EXISTING §	NEW §
No submission of obligee address or other obligee personal information	5101.323(C) second sentence	3123.954
Rules for poster program	5101.323(D)	3123.9510
Funds to conduct poster program	5101.323(E)	3123.959
Paternity establishment informational pamphlets--creation	5101.324(C) first sentence	3111.32
Distribution of affidavits and pamphlets	5101.324(C) second sentence and (D)(3)	3111.33
Acknowledgment of paternity affidavits--creation	5101.324(D)(1)	3111.31
Rules governing additional evidence to accompany affidavit for new birth record	5101.324(D)(2)	3111.34
Office of Child Support--responsible for collection and distribution of support	5101.325(A)(1)	3121.43
Use of facsimile signatures	5101.325(A)(2)	3121.69
Office of Child Support collects administrative charge	5101.325(B)(1) first sentence	3121.56
Accounting for charge not paid	5101.325(B)(1) second and third sentences	3121.58
Accounting for charge paid	5101.325(B)(1) fourth sentence	3121.57
Administrative charge and fine amounts placed in program income fund	5101.325(B)(2) and (B)(3) first sentence	3121.60
Distribution to counties	5101.325(B)(3) second sentence	3121.64
Administrative charges used only for support enforcement activities	5101.325(B)(3) third sentence	3121.65
Contracts with collection agencies	5101.325(C)	3121.67
Separate accounts for support amounts collected	5101.325(D) first and second sentences	3121.48
Support disbursement requirements	5101.325(D) second sentence	3121.50

SUBJECT	EXISTING §	NEW §
Use of interest from accounts	5101.325(D) fourth sentence	3121.49
Creation of program income fund	5101.325(E)	3121.63
Rules for collection, disbursement, etc.	5101.325(F)	3121.71
Collection of support through federal government offsets	5101.326	3123.85
Collection of obligor's unclaimed funds	5101.327	3123.88
Penalty	5101.99	3125.99
Penalties	5101.99(B)	3121.99
Registration of administrative child support orders	New	3111.83
Creation of registration system	New	3111.831
No fee if file administrative orders	New	3111.832
Appeal of administrative child support determination	New	3111.84
Standard forms for health insurance coverage notices	New	3119.46
Termination--Right to appeal administrative determination concerning termination	New	3119.91
Termination--Appeal to juvenile court	New	3119.92
Withholding and deduction notices and other enforcement orders issued prior to act's effective date	New	3121.0310
Orders commencing on day other than first day of the month	New	3121.54
Collection of at least 20% of arrearages with every current support payment	New	3123.21
Multiple means to collect arrearages amounts	New	3123.22

Table of Laws and Rules

UNITED STATES CONSTITUTION, CODE, AND REGULATIONS

United States Constitution

United States Code Annotated

United States Code Annotated—Continued

United States Code Annotated—Continued

United States Code Annotated—Continued

United States Code Annotated—Continued

Public Laws

Code of Federal Regulations

Code of Federal Regulations—Continued

Federal Rules of Civil Procedure

Federal Rules of Evidence

Revenue Ruling

Treasury Regulations

OHIO CONSTITUTION, CODE, AND REGULATIONS

Ohio Constitution

Ohio Revised Code

Ohio Revised Code—Continued

Ohio Revised Code—Continued

Ohio Revised Code—Continued

Ohio Revised Code—Continued

Ohio Revised Code—Continued

Ohio Revised Code—Continued

Ohio Revised Code—Continued

Ohio Revised Code—Continued

Ohio Revised Code—Continued

Ohio Revised Code—Continued

Ohio Revised Code—Continued

Ohio Revised Code—Continued

Code of Judicial Conduct

Ohio Administrative Code

Ohio Administrative Code—Continued

Ohio Code of Professional Responsibility

Ohio Code of Professional Responsibility—Continued

Ohio Rules of Appellate Procedure

Ohio Rules of Civil Procedure

Ohio Rules of Civil Procedure—Continued

Ohio Rules of Civil Procedure—Continued

Ohio Rules of Civil Procedure—Continued

Ohio Rules of Criminal Procedure

Ohio Rules of Evidence

Ohio Rules of Juvenile Procedure

Rules of Superintendence for the Courts of Ohio

Rules of Superintendence for the Courts of Ohio—Continued

Supreme Court Rules for the Government of the Bar of Ohio

Table of Cases

B

Dziedzic, In re, 9 B.R. 424 (Bankr. S.D. Tex. 1981)—33:8

Dzina v. Dzina, 2002 -Ohio- 2753, 2002 WL 1265585 (Ohio Ct. App. 8th Dist. Cuyahoga County 2002)—24:1

E

Eagleson v. McKee, 19 Ohio Op. 362, 33 Ohio L. Abs. 33, 1 Ohio Supp. 321 (Prob. Ct. 1939)—2:38, 2:57

Earick v. Earick, 1994 WL 66890 (Ohio Ct. App. 5th Dist. Ashland County 1994)—12:10

Eashai, In re, 87 F.3d 1082 (9th Cir. 1996)—33:20

Easterday, State ex rel. v. Zieba, 58 Ohio St. 3d 251, 569 N.E.2d 1028 (1991)—15:3, 15:52, 27:17

East Ohio Gas Co. v. Walker, 59 Ohio App. 2d 216, 13 Ohio Op. 3d 234, 394 N.E.2d 348 (8th Dist. Cuyahoga County 1978)—24:3

E. Cleveland v. Landingham, 97 Ohio App. 3d 385, 646 N.E.2d 897 (8th Dist. Cuyahoga County 1994)—27:26

Economy Fire & Cas. Co. v. Craft General Contractors, Inc., 7 Ohio App. 3d 335, 455 N.E.2d 1037 (10th Dist. Franklin County 1982)—32:38

Eddy v. Eddy, 14 Ohio L. Abs. 277, 1932 WL 2488 (Ct. App. 7th Dist. Monroe County 1932)—11:12, 11:15

Edgar v. Richardson, 33 Ohio St. 581, 1878 WL 29 (1878)—7:23

Edge, In re, 60 B.R. 690 (Bankr. M.D. Tenn. 1986)—33:3

Edgell v. Edgell, 1993 WL 55978 (Ohio Ct. App. 2d Dist. Clark County 1993)—12:7

Edmondson v. Edmondson, 1996 WL 685783 (Ohio Ct. App. 2d Dist. Montgomery County 1996)—14:32

Education of Bath Tp., Board of v. Townsend, 63 Ohio St. 514, 59 N.E. 223 (1900)—9:38

Edwards, In re, 207 B.R. 728 (Bankr. N.D. Fla. 1997)—33:9

Edwards, In re, 263 B.R. 690 (Bankr. D. R.I. 2001)—33:8

Edwards v. Sadusky, 4 Ohio App. 3d 297, 448 N.E.2d 506 (9th Dist. Summit County 1982)—3:37, 20:71

Edwards, In the Matter of v. Edwards, 1994 WL 95253 (Ohio Ct. App. 2d Dist. Montgomery County 1994)—14:5

Egelhoff v. Egelhoff ex rel. Breiner, 532 U.S. 141, 121 S. Ct. 1322, 149 L. Ed. 2d 264 (2001)—30:18

Eggleston v. Eggleston, 156 Ohio St. 422, 46 Ohio Op. 351, 103 N.E.2d 395 (1952)—2:58, 7:4, 11:9, 11:13

Ehret, In re, 238 B.R. 85 (Bankr. D. N.J. 1999)—33:11

Ehritz, In re, 1998 WL 295550 (Ohio Ct. App. 12th Dist. Butler County 1998)—29:12

Eichenberger v. Eichenberger, 82 Ohio App. 3d 809, 613 N.E.2d 678 (10th Dist. Franklin County 1992)—5:8, 37:25

Eickelberger v. Eickelberger, 93 Ohio App. 3d 221, 638 N.E.2d 130 (12th Dist. Butler County 1994)—12:18, 15:50, 29:1, 29:10

Eisenberg v. Peyton, 56 Ohio App. 2d 144, 10 Ohio Op. 3d 158, 381 N.E.2d 1136 (8th Dist. Cuyahoga County 1978)—31:7, 31:13, 31:14

Eisenstadt v. Baird, 405 U.S. 438, 92 S. Ct. 1029, 31 L. Ed. 2d 349 (1972)—2:70

Eisenwein v. Eisenwein, No. 89-C-68 (Ohio Ct. App. 7th Dist. Columbiana County 11-29-90)—12:29

Eisler v. Eisler, 24 Ohio App. 3d 151, 493 N.E.2d 975 (11th Dist. Geauga County 1985)—12:2, 12:27, 32:35

Eitel v. Eitel, 1996 WL 482703 (Ohio Ct. App. 4th Dist. Pickaway County 1996)—11:8

Elder, In re, 12 B.R. 491 (Bankr. M.D. Ga. 1981)—33:3

Elder, In re, 48 B.R. 414 (Bankr. W.D. Ky. 1985)—33:26

Elder v. Elder, 1993 WL 481433 (Ohio Ct. App. 3d Dist. Seneca County 1993)—11:14

Elebrashy, In re, 189 B.R. 922, 105 Ed. Law Rep. 1083 (Bankr. N.D. Ohio 1995)—33:18

Elegant Concepts, Ltd., In re, 61 B.R. 723 (Bankr. E.D. N.Y. 1986)—33:3

Eligado v. Eligado, 1981 WL 4644 (Ohio Ct. App. 8th Dist. Cuyahoga County 1981)—25:36

K

Montague v. Montague, 1997 WL 764829 (Ohio Ct. App. 8th Dist. Cuyahoga County 1997)—13:24

Montano v. Montano, 1993 WL 526940 (Ohio Ct. App. 8th Dist. Cuyahoga County 1993)—24:3

Monteux v. Monteux, 5 Ohio App. 2d 34, 34 Ohio Op. 2d 92, 213 N.E.2d 495 (10th Dist. Franklin County 1966)—3:50

Montisano v. Montisano, 1993 WL 208324 (Ohio Ct. App. 9th Dist. Summit County 1993)—12:19

Moody v. Moody, 1981 WL 6210 (Ohio Ct. App. 5th Dist. Tuscarawas County 1981)—12:2

Moore v. Emmanuel Family Training Center, Inc., 18 Ohio St. 3d 64, 479 N.E.2d 879 (1985)—24:14

Moore v. Moore, 83 Ohio App. 3d 75, 613 N.E.2d 1097 (9th Dist. Summit County 1992)—2:48, 12:10, 12:12, 13:15, 32:33, 32:38

Moore v. Moore, 1984 WL 4965 (Ohio Ct. App. 5th Dist. Stark County 1984)—24:8

Moore v. Moore, 1997 WL 727490 (Ohio Ct. App. 12th Dist. Fayette County 1997)—13:24

Moore v. Moore, 1998 WL 473341 (Ohio Ct. App. 7th Dist. Belmont County 1998)—24:14

Moore v. Moore, 2000 WL 1782328 (Ohio Ct. App. 12th Dist. Brown County 2000)—2:61, 12:4, 12:10

Morford v. Morford, 85 Ohio App. 3d 50, 619 N.E.2d 71 (4th Dist. Lawrence County 1993)—34:25

Morgan v. Atlanta, Ga. Super. Ct. Fulton County, No. E-52854 (12-31-96), 23 Fam. L. Rep. (BNA) 1131—2:67

Morgan v. Morgan, 59 Wash. 2d 639, 369 P.2d 516 (1962)—13:10, 13:17

Morgan v. Morgan, 1993 WL 418495 (Ohio Ct. App. 11th Dist. Portage County 1993)—12:4, 12:10

Morgan v. Morgan, 1994 WL 265899 (Ohio Ct. App. 7th Dist. Columbiana County 1994)—9:48, 10:18, 24:8

Morgan v. North Coast Cable Co., 63 Ohio St. 3d 156, 586 N.E.2d 88 (1992)—3:33

Morgan v. State, 11 Ala. 289, 1847 WL 182 (1847)—7:13

Morgan, Estate of v. Fairfield Family Counseling Ctr., 1997 -Ohio- 194, 77 Ohio St. 3d 284, 673 N.E.2d 1311 (1997)—37:39

Moro v. Moro, 68 Ohio App. 3d 630, 589 N.E.2d 416 (8th Dist. Cuyahoga County 1990)—11:12, 11:14

Morone v. Morone, 50 N.Y.2d 481, 429 N.Y.S.2d 592, 413 N.E.2d 1154 (1980)—2:66, 2:67, 2:72

Moross v. Scott, 1985 WL 7055 (Ohio Ct. App. 6th Dist. Lucas County 1985)—20:23, 21:24

Morris, In re, 193 B.R. 949 (Bankr. S.D. Cal. 1996)—33:30

Morris, In re, 197 B.R. 236 (Bankr. N.D. W. Va. 1996)—33:29

Morris v. Jones, 329 U.S. 545, 67 S. Ct. 451, 91 L. Ed. 488, 168 A.L.R. 656 (1947)—23:8, 23:49

Morris v. Morris, 271 Pa. Super. 19, 412 A.2d 139 (1979)—18:16

Morrison v. Steiner, 32 Ohio St. 2d 86, 61 Ohio Op. 2d 335, 290 N.E.2d 841 (1972)—11:7, 27:1, 27:39, 27:42, 27:48

Morrow v. Family & Community Services of Catholic Charities, Inc., 28 Ohio St. 3d 247, 504 N.E.2d 2 (1986)—31:14

Morton v. Morton, 19 Ohio App. 3d 212, 483 N.E.2d 1192 (8th Dist. Cuyahoga County 1984)—32:16

Moser v. Moser, 5 Ohio App. 3d 193, 450 N.E.2d 741 (9th Dist. Lorain County 1982)—11:11, 12:18, 25:10

Moser v. Moser, 1984 WL 3977 (Ohio Ct. App. 9th Dist. Lorain County 1984)—24:15

Mosier's Estate, In re, 58 Ohio Op. 369, 72 Ohio L. Abs. 268, 133 N.E.2d 202 (Prob. Ct. 1954)—1:4, 1:7, 2:3

Moskovitz v. Mt. Sinai Med. Ctr., 69 Ohio St. 3d 638, 1994 -Ohio- 324, 635 N.E.2d 331, 35 A.L.R.5th 841 (1994)—32:3

Moss v. Moss, 2000 -Ohio- 1802, 2000 WL 1729288 (Ohio Ct. App. 3d Dist. Allen County 2000)—14:37

Mothes v. Mothes, 1991 WL 147412 (Ohio Ct. App. 11th Dist. Lake County 1991)—31:10

O

T

U

W

Index

Cross references to another main heading are in CAPITAL LETTERS.

OHIO NORTHERN
UNIVERSITY

DEC 3 0 2002

TAGGART LAW LIBRARY